T0142155

Lecture Notes in Artificial Intelligence 13369

Subseries of Lecture Notes in Computer Science

Series Editors

Randy Goebel
University of Alberta, Edmonton, Canada

Wolfgang Wahlster
DFKI, Berlin, Germany

Zhi-Hua Zhou
Nanjing University, Nanjing, China

Founding Editor

Jörg Siekmann
DFKI and Saarland University, Saarbrücken, Germany

More information about this subseries at https://link.springer.com/bookseries/1244

Gerard Memmi · Baijian Yang · Linghe Kong ·
Tianwei Zhang · Meikang Qiu (Eds.)

Knowledge Science, Engineering and Management

15th International Conference, KSEM 2022
Singapore, August 6–8, 2022
Proceedings, Part II

Springer

Editors
Gerard Memmi
Télécom Paris
Paris, France

Baijian Yang
Purdue University
West Lafayette, IN, USA

Linghe Kong
Shanghai Jiao Tong University
Shanghai, Shanghai, China

Tianwei Zhang
Nanyang Technological University
Singapore, Singapore

Meikang Qiu ⓘ
Texas A&M University – Commerce
Commerce, TX, USA

ISSN 0302-9743   ISSN 1611-3349 (electronic)
Lecture Notes in Artificial Intelligence
ISBN 978-3-031-10985-0   ISBN 978-3-031-10986-7 (eBook)
https://doi.org/10.1007/978-3-031-10986-7

LNCS Sublibrary: SL7 – Artificial Intelligence

© The Editor(s) (if applicable) and The Author(s), under exclusive license
to Springer Nature Switzerland AG 2022
This work is subject to copyright. All rights are reserved by the Publisher, whether the whole or part of the material is concerned, specifically the rights of translation, reprinting, reuse of illustrations, recitation, broadcasting, reproduction on microfilms or in any other physical way, and transmission or information storage and retrieval, electronic adaptation, computer software, or by similar or dissimilar methodology now known or hereafter developed.
The use of general descriptive names, registered names, trademarks, service marks, etc. in this publication does not imply, even in the absence of a specific statement, that such names are exempt from the relevant protective laws and regulations and therefore free for general use.
The publisher, the authors, and the editors are safe to assume that the advice and information in this book are believed to be true and accurate at the date of publication. Neither the publisher nor the authors or the editors give a warranty, expressed or implied, with respect to the material contained herein or for any errors or omissions that may have been made. The publisher remains neutral with regard to jurisdictional claims in published maps and institutional affiliations.

This Springer imprint is published by the registered company Springer Nature Switzerland AG
The registered company address is: Gewerbestrasse 11, 6330 Cham, Switzerland

Preface

This three-volume set contains the papers presented at the 15th International Conference on Knowledge Science, Engineering, and Management (KSEM 2022), held during August 6–8, 2022, in Singapore.

There were 498 submissions. Each submission was reviewed by at least 3, and on average 3.5, Program Committee members. The committee decided to accept 150 regular papers (30% acceptance rate) and 19 special track papers, giving a total of 169 papers. We have separated the proceedings into three volumes: LNCS 13368, 13369, and 13370.

KSEM 2022 was the fifteenth in this series of conferences which started in 2006. The aim of this interdisciplinary conference is to provide a forum for researchers in the broad areas of knowledge science, knowledge engineering, and knowledge management to exchange ideas and to report state-of-the-art research results. KSEM is in the list of CCF (China Computer Federation) recommended conferences (C series, Artificial Intelligence).

KSEM 2022 was held in Singapore, following the traditions of the 14 previous successful KSEM events in Guilin, China (KSEM 2006); Melbourne, Australia (KSEM 2007); Vienna, Austria (KSEM 2009); Belfast, UK (KSEM 2010); Irvine, USA (KSEM 2011); Dalian, China (KSEM 2013); Sibiu, Romania (KSEM 2014); Chongqing, China (KSEM 2015), Passau, Germany (KSEM 2016), Melbourne, Australia (KSEM 2017), Changchun, China (KSEM 2018); Athens, Greece (KSEM 2019), Hangzhou, China (KSEM 2020), and Tokyo, Japan (KSEM 2021).

The objective of KSEM 2022 was to bring together researchers and practitioners from academia, industry, and government to advance the theories and technologies in knowledge science, engineering, and management. KSEM 2022 focused on three broad areas: Knowledge Science with Learning and AI (KSLA), Knowledge Engineering Research and Applications (KERA), and Knowledge Management with Optimization and Security (KMOS).

We would like to thank the conference sponsors: Springer, Nanyang Technological University, Singapore, and Princeton University, USA. Moreover, we would like to express our gratitude to the honorary chairs and the KSEM Steering Committee chairs, Ruqian Lu (Chinese Academy of Sciences, China) and Dimitris Karagiannis (University of Vienna, Austria), and the members of the Steering Committee, who provided insight and guidance during all the stages of this effort. The KSEM 2022 general co-chairs, Ruby B. Lee (Princeton University, USA), Tianwei Zhang (Nanyang Technological University, Singapore), and Yaxin Bi (Ulster University, Jordanstown, UK), were extremely supportive in the conference organizing, call for papers, and paper review processes, and we thank them for the general success of the conference.

August 2022

Gerard Memmi
Baijian Yang
Linghe Kong
Tianwei Zhang
Meikang Qiu

Organizations

Honorary General Chairs

Ruqian Lu   Chinese Academy of Sciences, China
Dimitris Karagiannis   University of Vienna, Austria

General Co-chairs

Ruby B. Lee   Princeton University, USA
Tianwei Zhang   Nanyang Technological University, Singapore
Yaxin Bi   Ulster University, Jordanstown, UK

Program Chairs

Gerard Memmi   Telecom Paris, France
Baijian Yang   Purdue University, USA
Linghe Kong   Shanghai Jiao Tong University, China

Steering Committee

Ruqian Lu (Honorary Chair)   Chinese Academy of Sciences, China
Dimitris Karagiannis (Chair)   University of Vienna, Austria
Hui Xiong   Rutgers, The State University of New Jersey, USA
Yaxin Bi   Ulster University, Jordanstown, UK
Zhi Jin   Peking University, China
Claudiu Kifor   Sibiu University, Romania
Gang Li   Deakin University, Australia
Yoshiteru Nakamori   Japan Advanced Institute of Science and Technology, Japan
Jorg Siekmann   German Research Centre for Artificial Intelligence, Germany
Martin Wirsing   Ludwig-Maximilians-Universität München, Germany
Bo Yang   Jilin University, China
Chengqi Zhang   University of Technology Sydney, Australia
Zili Zhang   Southwest University, China
Christos Douligeris   University of Piraeus, Greece
Xiaoyang Wang   Zhejiang Gongshang University, China
Meikang Qiu   Texas A&M University–Commerce, USA

Publication Co-chairs

Meikang Qiu   Texas A&M University–Commerce, USA
Cheng Zhang   Waseda University, Japan

Publicity Chair

Shangwei Guo   Chongqing University, China

Technical Committee

Aniello Castiglione   University of Salerno, Italy
Beibei Li   Sichuan University, China
Bo Luo   University of Kansas, USA
Bowen Zhao   Singapore Management University, Singapore
Chaoshun Zuo   Ohio State University, USA
Cheng Huang   Sichuan University, China
Chunxia Zhang   Beijing Institute of Technology, China
Daniel Volovici   ULB Sibiu, Romania
Ding Wang   Peking University, China
Dongxiao Liu   University of Waterloo, Canada
Guangxia Xu   Chongqing University of Posts and
                           Telecommunications, China
Guilin Qi   Southeast University, China
Guowen Xu   Nanyang Technological University, Singapore
Han Qiu   Tsinghua University, China
Hansi Jiang   SAS Institute Inc., USA
Hao Ren   The Hong Kong Polytechnic University, China
Hechang Chen   Jilin University, China
Jiahao Cao   Tsinghua University, China
Jianfei Sun   Nanyang Technological University, Singapore
Jianting Ning   Fujian Normal University, China
Jiaqi Zhu   Chinese Academy of Sciences, China
Jue Wang   SCCAS, China
Jun Zheng   New Mexico Tech, USA
Kewei Sha   University of Houston–Clear Lake, USA
Krzysztof Kluza   AGH University of Science and Technology,
                           Poland
Leilei Sun   Beihang University, China
Man Zhou   Huazhong University of Science and Technology,
                           China
Md Ali   Rider University, USA
Meng Li   Hefei University of Technology, China

Ming Li	Singapore Management University, Singapore
Neetesh Saxena	Bournemouth University, UK
Nhien An Le Khac	University College Dublin, Ireland
Pengfei Wu	National University of Singapore, Singapore
Pietro Ferrara	Università Ca' Foscari di Venezia, Italy
Qiang Gao	Southwestern University of Finance and Economics, China
Richard Hill	University of Huddersfield, UK
Robert Andrei Buchmann	Babeş-Bolyai University of Cluj Napoca, Romania
Salem Benferhat	University d'Artois, France
Serge Autexier	DFKI, Germany
Shangwei Guo	Chongqing University, China
Shaojing Fu	National University of Defense Technology, China
Shengmin Xu	Singapore Management University, Singapore
Shudong Huang	Sichuan University, China
Shuiqiao Yang	University of Technology Sydney, Australia
Songmao Zhang	Chinese Academy of Sciences, China
Ulrich Reimer	University of Applied Sciences St. Gallen, Switzerland
Wei Luo	Deakin University, Australia
Weipeng Cao	Shenzhen University, China
Wenyu Yang	Peking University, China
William de Souza	Royal Holloway, University of London, UK
Xiang Zhao	National University of Defense Technology, China
Xiangyu Wang	Xidian University, China
Xiaokuan Zhang	Georgia Institute of Technology, USA
Ximing Li	Jilin University, China
Xinyi Huang	Fujian Normal University, China
Yangguang Tian	Osaka University, Japan
Yaru Fu	Singapore University of Technology and Design, Singapore
Ye Zhu	Monash University, Australia
Yi Zheng	Virginia Tech, USA
Yiming Li	Tsinghua University, China
Yuan Xu	Nanyang Technological University, Singapore
Yuan Zhang	University of Electronic Science and Technology of China, China
Yueyue Dai	Nanyang Technological University, Singapore
Yunxia Liu	Huazhong University of Science and Technology, China

Zehua Guo   Beijing Institute of Technology, China
Zengpeng Li   Lancaster University, UK
Zheng Wang   Xi'an Jiaotong University, China
Zhisheng Huang   Vrije Universiteit Amsterdam, The Netherlands
Zhiyuan Tan   Edinburgh Napier University, UK
Zongming Fei   University of Kentucky, USA

Contents – Part II

Knowledge Engineering Research and Applications (KERA)

Multi-view Heterogeneous Network Embedding

Ouxia Du[iD], Yujia Zhang[iD], Xinyue Li[iD], Junyi Zhu[iD], Tanghu Zheng[iD], and Ya Li[(✉)][iD]

School of Computer and Information Science,
Southwest University, Chongqing 400715, China
crystal@swu.edu.cn

Abstract. In the real world, the complex and diverse relations among different objects can be described in the form of networks. At the same time, with the emergence and development of network embedding, it has become an effective tool for processing networked data. However, most existing network embedding methods are designed for single-view networks, which have certain limitations in describing and characterizing the network semantics. Therefore, it motivates us to study the problem of multi-view network embedding. In this paper, we propose a Multi-View Embedding method for Heterogeneous Networks, called MVHNE. It mainly focuses on the preservation of the network structure and the semantics, and we do not process them separately, but consider their mutual dependence instead. Specifically, to simplify heterogeneous networks, a semantics-based multi-view generation approach was explored. Then, based on the generated semantic views, our model has two concerns, namely the preservation of single-view semantics and the enhanced view collaboration. With extensive experiments on three real-world datasets, we confirm the validity of considering the interactions between structure and semantics for multi-view network embedding. Experiments further demonstrate that our proposed method outperforms the existing state-of-the-art methods.

Keywords: Heterogeneous network · Multi-view network · Enhanced view collaboration · Network analysis · Network embedding

1 Introduction

Networks are ubiquitous in the real world, such as social networks, academic collaboration networks, citation networks, etc. In recent years, network embedding technology has gradually become an important network analysis tool to study networked data [3,5,11,13,18]. The main idea of network embedding is mapping the network to a low-dimensional latent space to maximize the preservation of

This work is supported by National Natural Science Foundation of China (No. 61603310), the Fundamental Research Funds for the Central Universities (No. XDJK2018B019).

© The Author(s), under exclusive license to Springer Nature Switzerland AG 2022
G. Memmi et al. (Eds.): KSEM 2022, LNAI 13369, pp. 3–15, 2022.
https://doi.org/10.1007/978-3-031-10986-7_1

network topological, as well as node attributes information. The effectiveness of network embedding has been demonstrated in many downstream network learning tasks, such as link prediction [1,3], node classification [21,23], and community detection [6].

Depending on the network topology and semantic features, we can categorize two different types of networks, namely, homogeneous and heterogeneous networks [3]. Usually, there is the only same type of nodes and edges in homogeneous networks, such as academic collaboration networks and citation networks. However, homogeneous networks are difficult to describe objects due to their complex interactions in the real world. Thus, the focus of most current embedding work gradually shifts towards heterogeneous network embeddings. The networks are heterogeneous containing different types of nodes and edges. For example, in E-commerce networks, users are connected via goods and stores. Heterogenous are able to describe richer semantics in nodes and edges than homogeneous networks. In recent years, the research and analysis of heterogeneous networks have become a hot issue in the field of data mining [19]. No matter for homogeneous or heterogeneous networks, most embedding methods are designed for single-view scenarios. The existence of multiple type relations among nodes will be difficult to describe due to the limitations of single network. In addition, the data contained in a single network as a result of sparsity and measurement errors or data access limitations may be noise and incomplete [7]. If the embedding method is applied directly on such data, the final embedding quality will be less ideal. Embedding methods to solve heterogeneous networks from a multi-view perspective have begun to emerge in recent years. The noise or incomplete data contained in one view may be modified or supplemented in another view [14,22]. It overcomes the limitations brought by the single view.

Inspired by [16], we propose a novel Multi-View Embedding model for Heterogeneous Network, called MVHNE. First, to deal with multi-semantic relations in the heterogeneous network, we generate views based on the preset semantics. Usually, meta-path can be used to capture specific semantic of heterogeneous networks. Then, we mainly focus on semantic preservation in single view and collaborative learning across views. In enhanced view collaboration, the interactions between network structure and semantics are explored. After that, the view embeddings are aggregated by a self-attention mechanism. Finally, the global network topological information is used to enhance the final node representation. In summary, our contributions are summarized as follows:

- We propose a novel multi-view network embedding model, which incorporates view semantics with global network topology.
- We propose a novel and flexible enhanced cross-view collaboration, consisting of First collaboration and Second collaboration. The goal of the first collaboration is to align the same nodes in all the views, while the second collaboration is to align the neighbors.
- We conduct extensive experiments with three real-world datasets, and empirically show that our proposed method performs better than the other baselines.

The rest of this paper is organized as follows. Section 2 introduces the work related to our research. Section 3 formalizes the research problem. Then the details of our proposed embedding method are described in Sect. 4. Section 5 summarizes the experimental results. Finally, the conclusion and discussion are made in Sect. 6.

2 Related Work

Network Embedding. Network embedding has emerged as an efficient approach for generating the node representation for real networks or graphs in recent years. In general, network embedding methods can be divided into two categories: homogeneous network embedding and heterogeneous network embedding. In the study of homogeneous network embedding, many works take preserving network topological structural as priority. By applying word embedding to network embedding, DeepWalk [12], Node2vec [4] and LINE [17] take a random walk-based approach to learn the low-dimensional representations of the nodes. GAT [20] embeds network with neighbors' feature using self-attention strategy. The designs of most recent embedding approaches are based on heterogeneous network [15,21]. HERec [15] adopts a meta-path based random walk strategy on heterogeneous information network embedding for recommendation. Heterogeneous network embedding focus on how semantic is extracted from network, and most of these designs are closely related to meta-paths. Although these heterogeneous network embedding methods consider network semantics, the mutual influence among different semantics are not explored deeply.

Multi-view Network Embedding. Due to the complexity of relations in the real world, single-view embedding methods present certain limitations. Therefore, multi-view embedding methods for simplified heterogeneous networks based on split ideas are gaining popularity [7,10,14,16]. Multi-view network embedding aims to capture the multiple relations that exist in the network. [14] studies multi-view network representation learning, which proposes to use attention mechanism to learn the weights of different views to vote for robust node representations. [16] summarizes the two key points of preservation and collaboration in multi-view embedding. [2] applies the multi-view approach on the heterogeneous network and proposes a transformation and inductive model to learn node representation. There are a lot of works involving the topic of multi-view network embeddings, but almost none of them study view collaboration under network structure and semantic interaction.

3 Problem Definition

In this section, for clarity, some important notations are summarized in Table 1. Then we give some definitions relevant to this work as well as the problem to be addressed.

Definition 1 (Heterogeneous network): A heterogeneous network is denoted as $G = (U, E, W)$, consisting of a nodes set U and an edges set E. It is also associated with a node type mapping function $\phi : U \to A$ and an edge type mapping function $\psi : E \to R$. A and R correspond to the set of nodes type and edges type, where $|A| + |R| > 2$. $w_{ij} \in W$ is the weight of the edge $e_{ij} \in E$, indicating the strength of the relation between the nodes u_i and u_j.

Table 1. Notations

Notation	Description
G	Heterogeneous information network
V	Set of all network views
U/A	Set of all nodes/nodes types
E/R	Set of all edges/edges types
W	Weight of the edges
Ω	Set of node pairs generated based on random walk
d	The dimension of common/final embedding
m	The dimension of single view embedding

Definition 2 (Multi-view network): A multi-view network can be defined by the $G' = (U, E, V, U_v, E_v)$, where U and E is nodes set and edges set, respectively. V denotes views set, U_v and E_v respectively indicate the set of nodes and edges in a specific view $v \in V$.

Definition 3 (Multi-view Network embedding): Given a multi-view network G', it goal is learning a mapping function $f : U \to R^{n \times d}$, where $d \ll |U|$ and f can map the original multi-view network G' to a low-dimensional representation space.

4 Methodology

A multi-view embedding model for heterogeneous network (called MVHNE) is presented in this section. MVHNE consists of three major components, including semantics-based view generation, view preservation and collaboration, as well as embedding fusion. the overall framework is shown in Fig. 1.

4.1 Semantics-Based View Generation

For the efficient processing of the heterogeneous networks, we aim at decomposing the complex relations in the original network. To this end, a semantics-based view generation approach is explored. Usually, meta-path is an important concept used to describe patterns of underlying semantic relations among different types of nodes. Here, we extract views corresponding to specific semantics from

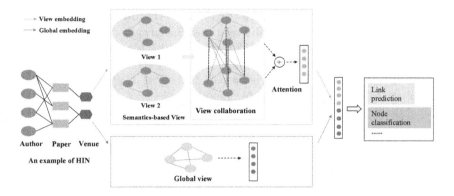

Fig. 1. The framework of our proposed MVHNE model.

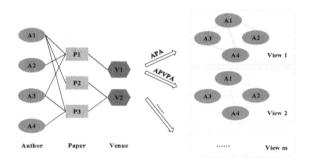

Fig. 2. An illustrative example of the semantics-based view generation in an academic network. Suppose we generate view 1 based on path $P1(A - P - A)$ representing co-author relationships. Under the constraints of the $P1$, we can obtain a sub-network of authors and papers. Then we filtered all paper nodes in this sub-network. Lastly, we treat the remaining part as the final view generated by $P1$.

the original network based on preset meta-paths. And then, we apply constraints and filtering to each view. Constraints and filtering are designed to facilitate processing. Semantic-based view generation is described in detail in a simple example described in Fig. 2.

4.2   View Preservation and Enhanced View Collaboration

Single-View Semantics Preservation. Through the previous section, we know that each view reflects specific network semantics. However, these views are decoupled from each other, so it is necessary to preserve the different relations among nodes separately. Following [2], we define the node u_i's k-th ($0 \leq k \leq K$) level embedding $u_{i,v}^{(k)}$ in view v as the mean aggregation of neighbors' embeddings, i.e., $u_{i,v}^{(k)} = \sigma(\hat{W} \cdot aggregator(u_{i,v}^{(k-1)}, \forall u_j \in N(u_i, v)))$. $N(u_i, v)$ is the neighbors of node u_i in view v, $u_{i,v}^{(0)}$ is a random initialization embedding, the *aggregator* function is a mean aggregator. Then, to preserve the diversity of each view, our main task is to model node pairs relations. Specifically, we generated node sequences using random walk, and skip-gram model is used to update node embeddings. Note that node pairs $\Omega^{(v)}$ are formed by central nodes and context nodes in the sequence. Thus, for node pair $(u_i, u_j) \in \Omega^{(v)}$, MVHNE aim to minimize the following negative log-likelihood:

$$L_S = -\sum_{v \in V} \sum_{(u_i,u_j) \in \Omega^{(v)}} p(u_{j,v}|u_{i,v}) \tag{1}$$

Here, the conditional probability $p(u_{j,v}|u_{i,v})$ is defined by the softmax function, i.e., $p(u_{j,v}|u_{i,v}) = exp(\boldsymbol{\nu}_{i,v} \cdot \tilde{\boldsymbol{\nu}}_{j,v})/\sum_{n \in U} exp(\boldsymbol{\nu}_{i,v} \cdot \tilde{\boldsymbol{\nu}}_{n,v})$, where $\boldsymbol{\nu}_{i,v}$ and $\tilde{\boldsymbol{\nu}}_{i,v}$ are the center embedding and context embedding of node u_i, respectively.

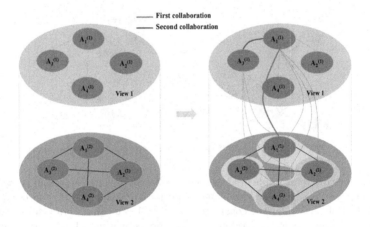

Fig. 3. Enhanced cross-view collaboration.

To improve the training efficiency, Negative sampling [9] is adopted. The objective function can be written as:

$$L_S = -[log\sigma(\boldsymbol{\nu}_{i,v} \cdot \boldsymbol{\nu}_{j,v}) + \sum_{k=1}^{l} E_{u_k \sim P_v(u)} \sigma(\boldsymbol{\nu}_{i,v} \cdot \boldsymbol{\nu}_{k,v'})] \tag{2}$$

where l is the number of negative samples, u_k is negative node sampled from the noise distribution $P_v(u) \sim d_u^{3/4}$, and d_u is the degree of the node u, $\sigma(.)$ denotes an activation function. By optimizing L_S, multiple relations among the nodes are preserved.

Enhanced Cross-View Collaboration. We propose an enhanced cross-view collaboration approach, which achieves a mutual complement of semantics in different views. Enhanced view collaboration consists of the first and second collaboration. Two collaborations among views can be interpreted by Fig. 3.

First Collaboration. To capture self-proximity, first collaboration refers to align the same nodes in each view. Specifically, for the view $v, v' \in V$, node $u_{i,v}$ in view v and node $u_{i,v'}$ in view v' should be aligned, such as $A_1^{(1)}$ and $A_1^{(2)}$ in Fig. 3. The first collaboration loss L_{First} is defined as Eq. (3), where $\boldsymbol{\nu}_{i,v'}$ and $\boldsymbol{\nu}_{i,v}$ are the embedding of the node u_i in views v and v', respectively.

$$
\begin{aligned}
L_{First} &= -\sum_{v \in V} \sum_{u_i \in U} \sum_{v \neq v'} p(u_{i,v'}|u_{i,v}) \\
&= -[log\sigma(\boldsymbol{\nu}_{i,v} \cdot \boldsymbol{\nu}_{i,v'}) + \sum_{k=1}^{L} E_{u_k \sim P_v(u)} \sigma(\boldsymbol{\nu}_{i,v} \cdot \boldsymbol{\nu}_{k,v'})]
\end{aligned}
\tag{3}
$$

Second Collaboration. Inspired by literature of [10], we design the second collaboration with many-to-many ideas. Since the first collaboration does not touch the neighborhood structure of nodes, we design second collaboration for further enhancing the collaboration among views. The main idea of the second collaboration is that for two adjacent nodes in one view, they will also have a similar neighborhood structure in the other. For example, for pair $(A_1^{(1)}, A_3^{(1)})$ in Fig. 3, second collaboration aims to align A_1's neighbors $\{A_2^{(2)}, A_3^{(2)}, A_4^{(2)}\}$ and A_3's neighbors $\{A_1^{(2)}, A_2^{(2)}, A_4^{(2)}\}$.

Formally, for node u_i in view v, we define the neighborhood features $\boldsymbol{\nu}_{i,(v \rightarrow v')}$ via its neighbors $u_k \in N(u_i, v')$ in view v', as shown in Eq. (4). Here, $\boldsymbol{\nu}_{k,v'}$ denotes the embedding of node u_k in view v', W is edge weight.

$$
\boldsymbol{\nu}_{i,(v \rightarrow v')} = \frac{\sum_{u_k \in N(u_i, v')} W_{i,k,v'} \cdot \boldsymbol{\nu}_{k,v'}}{\sum_{u_k \in N(u_i, v')} W_{i,k,v'} + 1}
\tag{4}
$$

Next, for each pair (u_i, u_j) in view v, we measure the proximity $\boldsymbol{\nu}_{i,v}$ and $\boldsymbol{\nu}_{j,v}$ and their corresponding neighborhood feature $\boldsymbol{\nu}_{i,(v \rightarrow v')}$ and $\boldsymbol{\nu}_{j,(v \rightarrow v')}$, respectively. Then we minimize the disagreement between these two proximity as second collaboration loss L_{Second}.

$$
L_{Second} = \sum_{v \in V} \sum_{i,j=1}^{|v|} \sum_{v \neq v'} [\boldsymbol{\nu}_{i,v}(\boldsymbol{\nu}_{j,v})^T - \boldsymbol{\nu}_{i,(v \rightarrow v')}(\boldsymbol{\nu}_{j,(v \rightarrow v')})^T]
\tag{5}
$$

where the superscript T denotes the transposition of the vector, $|v|$ is the number of nodes in view v. To learn enhanced node embedding, we designed the First and Second collaboration between views. The proposed view collaboration also explores the interaction between network structure and semantics while considering the network alignment.

4.3 Embedding Fusion

Semantic Embedding with View Attention. After the above steps, we can obtain the view embedding for each node. However, considering that the diverse connections in the network are of different importance to the nodes. Therefore, we introduce the self-attention mechanism proposed in [8] to model the importance of different views. Specifically, we integrate the obtained view representation $\boldsymbol{\nu}_{i,v}$ with $Concatenate()$ operation by Eq. (6). Further, the view weight coefficient $a_{i,v}$ is calculated by Eq. (7), where $W_v^{(1)}, W_v^{(2)}, b_v^{(1)}, b_v^{(2)}$ are adjustable parameters.

$$\boldsymbol{\nu}_i' = Concatenate(\boldsymbol{\nu}_{i,v}), v \in V \tag{6}$$

$$a_{i,v} = softmax(W_v^{(2)}tanh(W_v^{(1)})\boldsymbol{\nu}_i' + b_v^{(1)}) + b_v^{(2)}) \tag{7}$$

Global Information Fusion. To not lose the global information of the network, we view the final node embedding as consisting of two parts, i.e., view embedding and common embedding. In particular, we add the common embedding $\boldsymbol{\nu}_{i,g}$ for each node u_i, which is shared among different views. The final embedding $\boldsymbol{\nu}_i$ is as follows:

$$\boldsymbol{\nu}_i = \boldsymbol{\nu}_{i,g} + tanh(\sum_{v \in V} a_{i,v}\boldsymbol{\nu}_{i,v}) \tag{8}$$

With the above processes, the finally learned node representation not only contains the semantics relations in multiple views but also grasps the global topological information.

4.4   Optimization Objective

In this section, the overall loss function of MVHNE can be summarized by the loss of semantic preservation in single view, the loss of view collaboration and the loss for specific task. As shown in Eq. (9), the above three losses represented by L_S, L_{First}, L_{task}, respectively. λ, μ, η are adjustable hyper-parameters.

$$L = L_S + \lambda L_{First} + \mu L_{Second} + \eta L_{task} \tag{9}$$

We explore the performance of MVHNE on two tasks, i.e., link prediction and node classification. For the link prediction task, we can view it as a bi-classified task. We define loss $L_{task} = L_{lp} = \frac{1}{|U_t|}\sum_{i,j \in U_t}[-y_{ij}log\tilde{y}_{ij} - (1-y_{ij})log(1-\tilde{y}_{ij})]$, where y_{ij} indicates whether there is a link between the node i and the node j. If there is an edge, $y_{ij} = 1$, otherwise 0. $\tilde{y}_{ij} = f(\boldsymbol{\nu}_i, \boldsymbol{\nu}_j)$ is the result of model prediction, where f is a classification output function, and $U_t \in U$ is a set of nodes for training. Similarly, for the node classification task, we define loss $L_{task} = L_{nc} = \frac{1}{|U_t|}\sum_{i \in U_t}[-y_i log\tilde{y}_i - (1-y_i)log(1-\tilde{y}_i)$, the y_i is the real class of the node i, and the $\tilde{y}_i$ is the result of the model classification prediction. After that, we adopt gradient descent method and the back-propagation method to update and minimize the objective function. When the objective function does not converge, we update the corresponding parameter values in the model by calculating derivative.

Time Complexity. In our method, The time complexity of generating the node view embedding is $O(|E|Sd)$, where $|E| = \sum_{v \in V}|E^{(v)}|$, d is the final node embedding dimension, and S is the number of negative samples. For specific training tasks, such as link prediction, the time complexity is $O(TSd)$, where T is the size of the training dataset. Usually, T is much smaller than E, so the total time complexity of the model is $O(|E|Sd)$.

5   Experiments

5.1   Experimental Setup

Datasets. Three real datasets, ACM, Aminer and DBLP, are used in our experiments. A semantic view of each dataset is generated based on a specific meta-path. More details about the experimental data are shown in Table. 2.

Table 2. Statistics of datasets.

Dataset	# of Nodes	# of Edges	Semantics-based Views
ACM	paper(P):4019 author(A):7167 subject(S):60	17426	PAP PSP
Aminer	paper(P):6564 author(A):13329 reference(R):35890	76838	PAP PRP
DBLP	author(A):4057 paper(P):14328 conference(C):20 term(T):7723	119783	APA APCPA APTPA

Baselines. We compare MVHNE to several state-of-the-art network embedding models for experimental analysis. Note that for the single-view method used for contrast, we first run the model on each view and then report the average performance. DeepWalk [12] adopts a truncated random walk and skip-gram model to generate node embeddings. LINE [17] is a single-view embedding model that preserves the first and second-order similarity of the network. Node2vec [4] exploits a biased random walk and explores the network neighbors through a set of parameters p and q. MNE [22] is a multi-view embedding model. It proposes a high dimensional common embedding and low dimensional additional embedding for each relation type, then learn multiple relations jointly based on a unified embedding model. GATNE [2] is a multiplex heterogeneous network embedding model. Here we only consider the transductive model GATNE-T, because we do not introduce node attribute information. GATNE-T views the overall embedding as consisting of base embedding and edge embedding.

Implementation Details. For all models, we uniformly set the embedding dimension as 32. For DeepWalk and Node2vec, we set walk length as 10, window size as 3, and the number of negative samples as 5. For Node2vec, the high parameter p and q are set as 2 and 0.5. LINE proposes first and second order proximity, in which we set the embedding dimensions of both ways as 16, respectively. The other parameters for baselines are referred from the papers and tuned to be optimal. We chose the parameter $\lambda = 5$, $\mu = 0.5$, and $\eta = 1000$ for MVHNE, and the number of neighbors in view collaboration is fixed to 10.

For the link prediction task, we adopt ROC-AUC, widely used to measure the quality of the model, which can be obtained by summing the area of the parts under the ROC curve. For node classification task, we employ micro-F score to evaluate the accuracy of the model performance.

5.2 Link Prediction

Link prediction is a task commonly used to evaluate the quality of embedding. We evaluated the link prediction performance of MVHNE on the three datasets using ROC-AUC metrics. In experiments, we describe the link prediction task as a binary classification problem, where negative sample are generated by selecting five nodes without relations randomly. Then, the final embeddings are used to further train a logistic regression model using five-fold cross-validation.

The experimental results of three datasets are shown in Table. 3, we can gain the following conclusions. (1) MVHNE achieves the best performance by comparing with all the state-of-the-art approaches on the link prediction task. The results show that the multi-view embedding model has higher prediction accuracy than the single-view model, it demonstrates that the multiple views can capture more comprehensive relations among nodes. (2) Comparison of MVHNE with other multi-view models shows that MVHNE achieves higher AUC. The reason may be that MNE and GATNE only consider the preservation of single-view semantics and ignoring the view collaboration, while MVHNE touches both simultaneously.

Table 3. Performance of different methods on link prediction.

	ACM		DBLP		Aminer	
	ROC-AUC	PR-AUC	ROC-AUC	PR-AUC	ROC-AUC	PR-AUC
Deepwalk	0.7808	0.6962	0.7632	0.7563	0.7334	0.7321
LINE	0.8014	0.7145	0.7956	0.7821	0.7244	0.7169
Node2vec	0.8335	0.7757	0.8133	0.8025	0.7662	0.7654
MNE	0.8359	0.7648	0.8422	0.8201	0.7865	0.7695
GATNE	0.8471	0.7377	0.8281	0.8057	0.7812	0.7649
MVHNE	**0.8509**	**0.7981**	**0.8548**	**0.8492**	**0.8105**	**0.7868**

5.3 Node Classification

We experimentally analyze the effectiveness of the proposed model on the node classification task. Micro-F is used to evaluate the classification performance on different datasets of the proposed model. Figure 4 illustrates MVHNE outperform other comparison models on classification task. Specifically, DeepWalk,

LINE, Node2vec learn the node representations based on the network structure, which only captures one aspect of semantic among the nodes. By contrast, the multi-view embedding models consider the different network semantics while preserving the network structure. In some way, multi-view methods learning more comprehensive information. At the same time, MVHNE shows its superiority when compared to other multi-view models that do not consider view collaboration. Further analysis, MVHNE focused on view collaboration, mining potential relationship between network structure and semantics to generate more robust node representations.

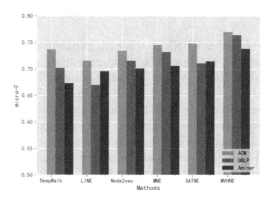

Fig. 4. Performance of different methods on node classification.

5.4   Parameter Sensitivity Analysis

We analyze the sensitivity of λ, μ, η in MVHNE. Since the model has similar performance on each dataset, we take for example the link prediction task on the ACM. λ and μ represent the importance of first collaboration and second collaboration between views, respectively. We take a value of $[0, 0.5, 1, 2, 5, 8]$ for λ and μ, as shown in Fig. 4(a)(b). From the experimental results reflected in Fig. 4(b), the model performs poorly when we do not consider the second collaboration between views (i.e., $\mu = 0$). Combining Figs. 4(a) and 4(b), we can see that the ROC-AUC score rises to the highest when $\lambda = 5$ and $\mu = 0.5$, indicating that the second collaboration between views we considered is very meaningful in enhancing the node representation. In addition, we also analyze the changes of the AUC corresponding to η at $[1,10,100,1000,10000]$. As shown in Fig. 4(c), MVHNE performs best when $\eta = 1000$.

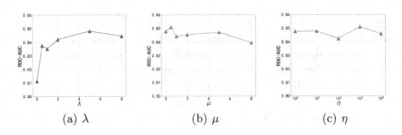

Fig. 5. Influence of the parameter λ, μ, η on ACM dataset.

6   Conclusion

In this paper, we proposed MVHNE to solve the problem of multi-view network embedding. In particular, to obtain the view embedding of node, we proposed First view collaboration and Second view collaboration. The First view collaboration was used to align the same nodes in all views. Furthermore, we have proposed a novel enhanced view collaboration, aiming to align the neighbors of nodes. The interaction between network structure and semantics has been explored through enhanced view collaboration. Extensive experiments were conducted on three real-world datasets, and the empirical results demonstrated that MVHNE outperforms other state-of-art methods on link prediction and node classification tasks. Although the proposed embedding model performs well on different tasks, some node label information needs to be known in advance. In some real-world environments, the acquisition of node label information is very challenging and expensive. Therefore, in future work, we will explore a self-supervised learning method that mines supervised signals from the data itself to learn the representation of nodes on heterogeneous information networks.

References

1. Aziz, F., Gul, H., Muhammad, I., Uddin, I.: Link prediction using node information on local paths. Phys. A: Statist. Mech. Appl. **557**, 124980 (2020)
2. Cen, Y., Zou, X., Zhang, J., Yang, H., Zhou, J., Tang, J.: Representation learning for attributed multiplex heterogeneous network. In: KDD, pp. 1358–1368 (2019)
3. Cui, P., Wang, X., Pei, J., Zhu, W.: A survey on network embedding. IEEE Trans. Knowl. Data Eng. **31**(05), 833–852 (2019)
4. Grover, A., Leskovec, J.: node2vec: scalable feature learning for networks. In: Proceedings of the 22nd ACM SIGKDD International Conference on Knowledge Discovery and Data Mining (KDD 2016), pp. 855–864 (2016)
5. Hao, P., Qing, K., Ceren, B., M., D.R., Yong-Yeol, A.: Neural embeddings of scholarly periodicals reveal complex disciplinary organizations. Sci. Adv. (2021)
6. He, D., et al.: Community-centric graph convolutional network for unsupervised community detection. In: Bessiere, C. (ed.) Proceedings of the Twenty-Ninth International Joint Conference on Artificial Intelligence, pp. 3515–3521 (2020)
7. Kircali, S.A., Yuan, F., Min, W., Jiaqi, S., Keong, C.K., Xiaoli, L.: Multi-view collaborative network embedding. ACM Trans. Knowl. Discov. Data, pp. 1–18 (2021)

8. Lin, Z., et al.: A structured self-attentive sentence embedding. In: ICLR (2017)
9. Mnih, A., Teh, W.Y.: A fast and simple algorithm for training neural probabilistic language models. In: ICML, pp. 419–426 (2012)
10. Ni, J., et al.: Co-regularized deep multi-network embedding. In: WWW '18: The Web Conference 2018, Lyon, April 2018, pp. 469–478 (2018)
11. Niu, J., Gao, Y., Qiu, M., Ming, Z.: Selecting proper wireless network interfaces for user experience enhancement with guaranteed probability. J. Parall. Distrib. Comput. **72**(12), 1565–1575 (2012)
12. Perozzi, B., Al-Rfou, R., Skiena, S.: Deepwalk: online learning of social representations. Proceedings of the 20th ACM SIGKDD International Conference on Knowledge Discovery and Data Mining (KDD 2014), pp. 701–710 (2014)
13. Qiu, M., Liu, J., Li, J., Fei, Z., Ming, Z., Sha, E.H.: A novel energy-aware fault tolerance mechanism for wireless sensor networks. In: 2011 IEEE/ACM International Conference on Green Computing and Communications, pp. 56–61 (2011)
14. Qu, M., Tang, J., Shang, J., Ren, X., Zhang, M., Han, J.: An attention-based collaboration framework for multi-view network representation learning. In: CIKM, pp. 1767–1776 (2017)
15. Shi, C., Hu, B., Zhao, W., Yu, P.S.: Heterogeneous information network embedding for recommendation. IEEE Trans. Knowl. Data Eng. **31**(02), 357–370 (2019)
16. Shi, Y., Han, F., He, X., Yang, C., Luo, J., Han, J.: mvn2vec: preservation and collaboration in multi-view network embedding. arXiv preprint arXiv:1801.06597 (2018)
17. Tang, J., Qu, M., Wang, M., Zhang, M., Yan, J., Mei, Q.: Line: large-scale information network embedding. In: Proceedings of the 24th International Conference on World Wide Web, pp. 1067–1077 (2015)
18. Wang, J., Qiu, M., Guo, B.: Enabling real-time information service on telehealth system over cloud-based big data platform. J. Syst. Archit. **72**, 69–79 (2017). Design Automation for Embedded Ubiquitous Computing Systems
19. Wang, X., Bo, D., Shi, C., Fan, S., Ye, Y., Yu, P.S.: A survey on heterogeneous graph embedding: methods, techniques, applications and sources. arXiv preprint arXiv:2011.14867 (2020)
20. Wang, X., et al.: Heterogeneous graph attention network. The Web Conference on The World Wide Web Conference WWW 2019 (WWW 2019), pp. 2022–2032 (2019)
21. Yu, B., Hu, J., Xie, Y., Zhang, C., Tang, Z.: Rich heterogeneous information preserving network representation learning. Pattern Recogn. **108**, 107564 (2020)
22. Zhang, H., Qiu, L., Yi, L., Song, Y.: Scalable multiplex network embedding. In: IJCAI, pp. 3082–3088 (2018)
23. Zhang, Z., et al.: Anrl: attributed network representation learning via deep neural networks. In: Proceedings of the 27th International Joint Conference on Artificial Intelligence, pp. 3155–3161 (2018)

A Multi-level Attention-Based LSTM Network for Ultra-short-term Solar Power Forecast Using Meteorological Knowledge

Tiechui Yao[1,2] , Jue Wang[1,2(✉)] , Haizhou Cao[1,2], Fang Liu[1],
Xiaoguang Wang[1], Yangang Wang[1,2], and Xuebin Chi[1,2]

[1] Computer Network Information Center, Chinese Academy of Sciences,
Beijing, China
{yaotiechui,caohaizhou,wangxg}@cnic.cn
[2] School of Computer Science and Technology, University of Chinese
Academy of Sciences, Beijing, China
{wangjue,liufang,wangyg,chi}@sccas.cn

Abstract. Deep learning has been widely applied to modeling, prediction, control, and optimization in smart energy systems, especially in solar energy. Accurate forecasting of photovoltaic (PV) power is essential for power system dispatch. However, PV power output is greatly affected by weather conditions. Therefore integrating domain knowledge to improve power prediction accuracy has become a major challenge. To tackle this problem, this paper proposes an effective deep learning model for solar power forecasting based on temporal correlation and meteorological knowledge. The model adopts an encoder-decoder architecture with multi-level attention machines and long short-term memory units. The encoder is designed to dynamically extract the historical features of the in situ measurements of the PV plant, whereas the decoder is used to capture the temporal features of multi-source variables. The domain knowledge (e.g., clearness index, numerical weather prediction, and short-wave radiation) is integrated into the decoder for forecasting solar PV power. A case study is conducted using the dataset collected from real-world PV plants in different weather conditions. The experiment results demonstrate that the forecasting accuracy of the proposed model outperforms three baselines, and the prediction error is reduced by 9.5% on average compared to others.

Keywords: Solar photovoltaic power forecast · Long short-term memory · Attention mechanism · Domain knowledge · Data fusion

1 Introduction

Energy is critical to our society in every aspects, from computer infrastructure [30], healthcare facility [29], to finance industrial [6,21]. With the gradual deterioration of climate change, it has become the mainstream trend in the world

© The Author(s), under exclusive license to Springer Nature Switzerland AG 2022
G. Memmi et al. (Eds.): KSEM 2022, LNAI 13369, pp. 16–28, 2022.
https://doi.org/10.1007/978-3-031-10986-7_2

that new energy sources gradually replace some fossil energy sources for power generation in smart energy [13]. Meanwhile, the COVID-19 pandemic continues to impact global energy demand, with electricity demand trending at the fastest pace in more than a decade. The use of renewable energy is getting more and more attention, thanks to the rapid advances in computer and Internet technologies [28,31]. Solar energy is considered a promising green and sustainable energy and photovoltaic (PV) power plants are a broad way to utilize solar energy. According to the International Energy Agency, solar PV power generation is expected to increase by 145 TWh in 2021, an increase of nearly 18%, and the total power generation is even close to 1,000 TWh [12].

Accurate forecasting of PV power can assist system operators in adjusting the dispatching plan and improve the economy and stability of grid operation [4]. Time series forecasting has always been a fascinating research area, especially using artificial intelligence technology [2,3,47] to solve interdisciplinary application problems such as solar PV power forecasting. Meanwhile, the development of big knowledge engineering [22], multi-source data management [19], and cloud computing in smart cities [32] provides novel insights into smart energy forecasting.

However, PV power generation is difficult to predict due to the influence of the solar radiation cycle, geographical environment, and various meteorological factors [39]. Changeable weather conditions or instantaneous cloud occlusion will reduce the sunlight received by the PV panels and then result in dramatic changes in PV output. The addition of cloud movement information and solar elevation angle is helpful to forecast the fluctuation of PV power. In situ measurement data collected from PV plants is timely and volatile, and most models leverage it as input. Despite that, analyzing the PV power under different weather conditions is necessary [35]. Therefore, there are two main challenges in solar PV power prediction: 1) combining with domain knowledge to hence the input meteorological factors, and 2) modeling the temporal correlations to build an effective power prediction model [8,16].

To address the above challenges, we propose an ultra-short-term PV power forecasting model based on temporal correlation and domain knowledge. Our contributions are summarized as follows:

1. We propose a multi-level *Mechanism of Attention with Fusion module and Long Short-Term Memory* (MAF-LSTM) model in encoder and decoder architecture for solar PV power forecasting. MAF-LSTM can fuse multi-source data and capture the temporal correlation. Combined with meteorological knowledge, this paper is a novel exploration in the field of smart energy using deep learning techniques.

2. We propose a multi-level attention mechanism with a fusion module that integrates domain knowledge such as clearness index, *Numerical Weather Prediction* (NWP), and *ShortWave Radiation* (SWR) data to improve prediction performance.

3. We conduct experiments on real power station datasets and the proposed model achieves better performance than other baselines. Due to the large

installed PV capacity and the unit of power generation being megawatts, grid dispatch can also benefit from a minor improvement in forecast performance.

The rest of this paper is organized as follows. Section 2 discusses the related research on solar PV power prediction. Section 3 presents the details of each module in the MAF-LSTM model. Section 4 introduces the details of the dataset and the results of the experiments. Finally, Sect. 5 presents the conclusions.

2   Related Work

Solar PV power prediction is generally regarded as a nonlinear time series data regression problem. Generally, solar PV power prediction methods can be divided into physical methods and statistical methods in smart energy [1,14].

Physical Methods. The physical methods realized PV power forecast by physical equations, such as PV module operation equations and solar radiation transfer equations [9,10]. Mayer et al. [23] established PV cells basic model and photoelectric conversion efficiency model for PV power forecast. The physical methods do not require extensive historical data to train the model but depend on the accuracy of models for predicted solar irradiance and photoelectric conversion efficiency. The physical equation itself has certain errors and limitations in the migration of various weather conditions, so the accuracy and robustness of the model in real-world scenarios need to be improved.

Statistical Methods. The statistical methods explore a mapping model between historical input data and the output value of the PV power, including classic statistical models, machine learning algorithms [17,26,27], deep learning algorithms [10,41,45].

The commonly used forecasting models include the Markov chain [33], support vector machine (SVM) [46], and artificial neural network [7,38,44]. Huang et al. [11] proposed a PV power forecasting method based on multi-dimensional time sequences. The correlation coefficient was used to analyze historical power sequences at different time scales, and a *Support Vector Regression* (SVR) was adopted to build the forecasting model. However, for drastic weather changes, the forecast accuracy is insufficient, that is, the model is difficult to capture short-term fluctuations in time series. Li et al. [18] proposed a distributed PV power forecasting model based on *AutoRegressive Integrated Moving Average* model (ARIMA) and SVM. This case study considered the use of climatic variables as exogenous inputs (e.g., insolation, daily average temperature, precipitation, humidity, solar irradiation, and wind speed). Although the model has domain knowledge to enhance the prediction performance, the prediction accuracy decreases significantly with the increase of the prediction time step. Mellit et al. [24] applied *Recurrent Neural Network* (RNN) and LSTM model to achieve acceptable accuracy only in the case of cloudy days. Yao et al. [41] integrated the unstructured data processing module and the structured processing module to process satellite cloud images, NWP, and local measurement data respectively. This work utilized the U-Net and encoder-decoder architecture for spatial-temporal modeling to predict future PV power generation. This paper also demonstrated the contribution of domain knowledge to PV power forecasting but did not consider different weather types and the use of the clear sky index as a guide for forecasting.

In still another aspect, the transformer-based model was designed for long sequence time-series forecasting and requires massive data to train, whereas ultra-short-term PV power forecasting is a common but domain-knowledge-requiring time-series forecasting task. Hence, despite the good performance of the transformer-based model (e.g., Informer [48]) in long-term power load forecasting, it is not suitable for ultra-short-term PV power forecasting.

Given that some studies only select in situ measurements or NWP as domain knowledge, and some models are too complex and lack analysis under different weather types, we propose a lightweight but effective time series forecasting model that can integrate multiple knowledge.

3   Architecture

For time series regression problems, the encoder-decoder architecture is usually involved to generate time series. On the other hand, the above architecture also facilitates the incorporation of domain knowledge in the decoder stage. Therefore, as shwon in Fig. 1, the framework of the MAF-LSTM model for PV power prediction adopts an encoder-decoder architecture [20,36]. The encoder of the MAF-LSTM model includes PV plant feature attentions and LSTM units, and aims to encode and extract the historical features of the PV plant. The decoder includes temporal attentions, domain knowledge fusion module, and LSTM units. The domain knowledge fusion module can integrate the clearness index, NWP, and SWR. The temporal attentions and LSTM units are designed to decode the fusion features for forecasting PV power.

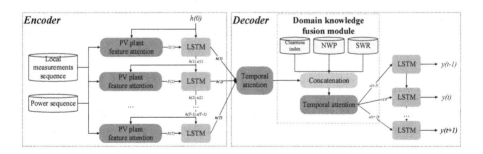

Fig. 1. MAF-LSTM model framework

3.1   Encoder

The local meteorological features of each PV plant have a complex correlation with output power [37]. The meteorological features have different impacts on power according to time and weather condition. PV plant feature attention mechanism is used to assign different weights to input variables for feature extraction. The equation of the feature attention mechanism is expressed as follows.

$$u_{k,t} = p_e^T * tanh(W_e[h_{t-1}; s_{t-1}] + q_e[I_k] + b_e) \tag{1}$$

where $[*; *]$ represents concatenation, $h_{t-1} \in R^a$ is the hidden state, and $s_{t-1} \in R^a$ is the cell state at time $t-1$. I_k is the kth input sequence of the PV plant. $k \in \{irra, scat, temp, pres, y\}$ is the five input features of the PV plant. Furthermore, $I_{irra} \in R^T$ is the total irradiance, $I_{scat} \in R^T$ is the scattered irradiance, $I_{temp} \in R^T$ is the environment temperature, $I_{pres} \in R^T$ is the air pressure, and $I_y \in R^T$ is power. Additionally, T is the length of the input sequences. $p_e \in R^T$, $W_e \in R^{T*2a}$, $q_e \in R^{T*T}$, and $b_e \in R^T$ are learnable parameters, which are determined by back propagation algorithm during model training.

$$U_{k,t} = \frac{\exp(u_{k,t})}{\sum_{j=1}^{5} \exp(u_{j,t})} \tag{2}$$

where $U_{k,t}$ is the attention weight of the k-th sequence at time t. The output vector of the PV plant feature attention mechanism at time t is presented as follows.

$$X_t = (U_{irra,t}I_{irra,t}, U_{scat,t}I_{scat,t}, U_{temp,t}I_{temp,t}, U_{pres,t}I_{pres,t}, U_{y,t}I_{y,t}) \tag{3}$$

The encoder of the MAF-LSTM model includes the PV plant feature attention mechanism and LSTM. The LSTM is used to encode and dynamically capture the correlation between the local features and output power of the PV plant. The input of LSTM is the output vector $X \in R^{T*5}$ of the PV plant attention mechanism. The output of LSTM is the plant feature extraction hidden vector h_t, $t \in [0, T]$.

3.2   Decoder

The decoder of the MAF-LSTM model includes temporal attention mechanism, fusion module, and LSTM. The temporal attention mechanism adaptively extracts the hidden vectors from relevant time intervals. The calculation of the hidden vector attention weight at each historical moment is expressed as follows.

$$v_{t,\tau} = p_d^T * tanh(W_d[h_{\tau-1}'; s_{\tau-1}'] + q_d h_t + b_d) \tag{4}$$

$$V_{t,\tau} = \frac{\exp(v_{t,\tau})}{\sum_{j=1}^{T} \exp(v_{j,\tau})} \tag{5}$$

where $h'_{\tau-1} \in R^b$ and $s'_{\tau-1} \in R^b$ are the hidden state and cell state of LSTM at time $\tau - 1$, respectively. τ is the output time in the future. $p_d \in R^a$, $W_d \in R^{a*2b}$, $q_d \in R^{a*a}$, and $b_d \in R^a$ are learnable parameters. The output vector of the temporal attention mechanism at time τ is expressed as follows.

$$K_\tau = \sum_{t=1}^{T} V_{t,\tau} h_t \tag{6}$$

The meteorological knowledge such as solar radiation, environment temperature, and weather are all affecting PV generation [25]. The fusion module of the MAF-LSTM model integrates seven-dimensional features of the PV plant in the future, namely clearness index, SWR, total irradiance, direct irradiance, environment temperature, relative humidity, wind speed of NWP. Therefore, the fusion module feature vector at time τ is $E_\tau \in R^7$.

The LSTM of the decoder is used to forecast PV power at future time τ. The input of LSTM is a concatenation vector $X' \in R^{a+b+7}$, which is composed of the output vector $K \in R^{*a}$ of the temporal attention mechanism, feature vector $E \in R^7$ of fusion module, and hidden vector $h' \in R^b$ at the previous moment of the decoder.

$$X' = [K; E; h'] \tag{7}$$

The output of LSTM in the decoder is the forecasted power of the PV plant in future time τ.

4   Experiment: Case Study

4.1   Datasets Setting

All the data in this paper are obtained from practical PV plants in Hebei, China. The dataset after preprocessing is divided into the training set, verification set, and test set at 8:1:1 ratio. This dataset contains *Local Measurements Data* (LMD), NWP, and PV power sequences of the PV plant every 15 min from July 1, 2018, to June 13, 2019, and the first release can be found in PVOD [42]. SWR data is a satellite product from a geosynchronous satellite *Himawari-8*, containing cloud movement information and the change of solar elevation angle. The clearness index K_t is used to indicate weather types and is expressed in Eq. 8 [35].

$$K_t = \frac{I_t}{I_0 \cos(\phi_t)} \tag{8}$$

where I_t is the irradiance and the solar constant $I_0 = 1360 \text{ W/m}^2$. ϕ_t the solar zenith angle at time t, which can be calculated by the latitude and longitude of the power station.

The data preprocessing includes missing value processing, outlier detection, removal of no-power-data, and normalization. The missing value processing includes day missing and segment missing. All data is removed for the day missing, while the segment missing value is filled by interpolation. Outliers that are too large or too small are classified as a missing values. The no-power data removal from 19:30 to 05:15 helps reduce the model complexity.

4.2 Experimental Setting

The inputs of the MAF-LSTM model are the measured total irradiance, scattered irradiance, environment temperature, air pressure, and power sequences of the PV plant for one day in the past. Therefore, the length of input historical sequences in the encoder is $T = 58$. We calculated the similarity of variables to power in NWP via the Pearson correlation coefficient (shown in Table 1) and picked salient features as part of domain knowledge. The fusion module inputs the total irradiance, direct irradiance, environment temperature, relative humidity, and wind speed of NWP, clearness index, and SWR as domain knowledge for 15 min in the future. Besides, the length of output future power in the decoder is $\tau = 1$. The output of the MAF-LSTM model is the forecasted power of the PV plant every 15 min in the future.

Table 1. Pearson correlation coefficients of power and variables in numerical weather prediction

	Total irradiance	Direct irradiance	Environment temperature	Relative humidity	Wind speed	PV power
Pearson correlation coefficient	0.88	0.87	0.26	−0.32	0.39	1

Furthermore, we adopt Adam optimizer with a learning rate of 0.001 and train 50 epochs with batch size $= 64$. The hidden layers in Encoder and Decoder are both 128. The drop-out rate is set to 0.3. We further deploy the model using the VenusAI [40] platform.

4.3 Results and Analysis

In this paper, ARIMA, SVR, and GRU models are used for comparative experiments. 1) ARIMA is a time series forecasting model proposed by Box and Jenkins [5]. ARIMA model in this paper is used to approximate future power sequences with features sequences. 2) SVR is a branch of SVM and has become an important tool for forecasting nonlinear time series [15,43]. 3) GRU was proposed to extend RNN memory and address the gradient disappearance in RNN. The input and output of ARIMA, SVR, GRU models are the same as those of the MAF-LSTM model.

According to the weather forecast website [34], three weather types are selected to compare the forecasting results of MAF-LSTM, GRU, SVR, and ARIMA models, namely rainy day on May 26, cloudy day on June 1, and sunny day on May 28. The comparison results are shown in Fig. 2(a), Fig. 2(b), and Fig. 2(c).

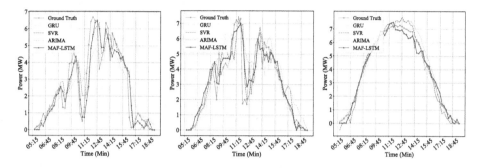

(a) Rainy day on May 26.   (b) Cloudy day on June 1.   (c) Sunny day on May 28.

Fig. 2. Forecasting result under different weather types

The metrics of root mean square error (RMSE) and mean absolute error (MAE) [25] are applied to evaluate the performance of the models.

$$RMSE = \sqrt{\frac{1}{n_{te}} \sum_{i=1}^{n_{te}} (y_i - \hat{y}_i)^2} \tag{9}$$

$$MAE = \frac{1}{n_{te}} \sum_{i=1}^{n_{te}} |y_i - \hat{y}_i| \tag{10}$$

where n_{te} is the number of samples in the test set, y_i is the ground true power, and $\hat{y}_i$ is the forecasted power of the PV plant.

Table.2 and Fig. 2(a) show the comparison results of the MAF-LSTM, GRU, SVR, and ARIMA models in different weather types. The forecasting results of the MAF-LSTM model are better than the other three models. The RMSE and MAE of the MAF-LSTM model are both the lowest in four models for different weather types. The forecasting accuracy of the four models is higher on sunny days because the power curve is smoother on sunny days and easier to forecast. The forecasting accuracy of rainy and cloudy days is lower than that of sunny days. Power fluctuates the most on rainy and cloudy days, and it is

Table 2. Result of four models under different weather types

Date	Model	RMSE	MAE
May 26 (Rainy)	ARIMA	1.081	0.813
	SVR	0.932	0.633
	GRU	0.833	0.639
	MAF-LSTM	**0.799**	**0.538**
June 1 (Cloudy)	ARIMA	1.249	0.881
	SVR	1.118	0.712
	GRU	1.175	0.770
	MAF-LSTM	**0.904**	**0.562**
May 28 (Sunny)	ARIMA	0.469	0.348
	SVR	0.398	0.323
	GRU	0.411	0.363
	MAF-LSTM	**0.325**	**0.265**

difficult for models to dynamically capture the changes in the power curve. The test set includes data from May 20, 2019, to June 13, 2019. The MAF-LSTM, GRU, SVR, and ARIMA models are used to forecast power on the test set. The forecasting results are listed in Table 3.

Table 3. Overall forecasting results of four models

Model	RMSE	MAE
ARIMA	1.073	0.733
SVR	0.701	0.483
GRU	0.687	0.423
MAF-LSTM	**0.640**	**0.390**

The forecasting accuracy of the MAF-LSTM model is better than that of GRU, SVR, and ARIMA models. The MAF-LSTM model performs best in four models and the ARIMA model performs worst. Accordingly, the RMSE of the MAF-LSTM model is reduced by 9.5% on average compared to other models, and MAE is reduced by 23.8%. The proposed model has only approximately 0.64 M parameters and a complexity of 0.72 GFLOPs, which indicates the feasibility and efficiency of the MAF-LSTM model for PV power forecast.

The MAF-LSTM model has the best performance compared to GRU, SVR, and ARIMA models. GRU model only captures the time series of input features in the PV plant. Each feature is given the same weight at each historical moment, and it is hard to efficiently extract the correlation between the input features and forecasted power. The ARIMA model performs almost worst for all weather types. The model can only forecast the general trend of PV power and the forecasting curve is smooth and fluctuates slightly. The SVR model performs slightly worse than the MAF-LSTM model. The kernel function of the SVR model helps to extract the nonlinear relationship between input features and power for ultra-short-term PV power forecast. The MAF-LSTM model adopts a two-layer attention mechanism to attribute different weights to the input features. The two LSTMs in the encoder-decoder can better learn the internal parameters of the model according to the attention mechanisms.

In summary, PV power is affected by various meteorological factors and exhibits severe fluctuation in actual PV generation. The forecasted power of the MAF-LSTM model is more fluctuant. The error between the MAF-LSTM forecasted power and the ground true power is relatively minor compared to other models.

5   Conclusions

This paper proposed an efficient ultra-short-term PV power forecasting model based on temporal attention and meteorological knowledge. The PV power forecasting model used multi-source data and took into account the meteorological characteristics that affect PV power. The PV plant feature attention mechanism assigned different weights to the input variables for extracting the features associated with predicted power. The temporal attention mechanism adaptively captured the temporal correlation of historical meteorological features. A domain knowledge fusion module was integrated into the model to further improve the forecasting accuracy.

Acknowledgement. This work was supported by National Key R&D Program of China (No. 2021ZD0110403) and the Strategic Priority Research Program of the Chinese Academy of Sciences (No. XDA27000000). We would like to thank the MindSpore team for their support.

References

1. Antonanzas, J., Osorio, N., et al.: Review of photovoltaic power forecasting. Solar Energy **136**, 78–111 (2016)
2. Cao, W., Xie, Z., et al.: Bidirectional stochastic configuration network for regression problems. Neural Netw. **140**, 237–246 (2021)
3. Cao, W., Yang, P., et al.: An improved fuzziness based random vector functional link network for liver disease detection. In: IEEE 6th BigDataSecurity/HPSC/IDS, pp. 42–48 (2020)
4. Chunguang, T., Li, T., et al.: Control strategy for tracking the output power of photovoltaic power generation based on hybrid energy storage system. Trans. China Electr. Soc. **31**(14), 75–83 (2016)
5. Das, U.K., Tey, K.S., et al.: Forecasting of photovoltaic power generation and model optimization: a review. Ren. Sustain. Energy Rev. **81**, 912–928 (2018)

6. Gai, K., Du, Z., Qiu, M., Zhao, H.: Efficiency-aware workload optimizations of heterogeneous cloud computing for capacity planning in financial industry. In: 2015 IEEE 2nd International Conference on Cyber Security and Cloud Computing, pp. 1–6. IEEE (2015)

7. He, H., Hu, R., et al.: A power forecasting approach for PV plant based on irradiance index and LSTM. In: 37th Chinese Control Conference (CCC), pp. 9404–9409 (2018)

8. Heo, J., Song, K., et al.: Multi-channel convolutional neural network for integration of meteorological and geographical features in solar power forecasting. Appl. Energy **295**, 117083 (2021)

9. Hu, K., Cao, S., et al.: A new ultra-short-term photovoltaic power prediction model based on ground-based cloud images. J. Clean. Prod. **200**, 731–745 (2018)

10. Hua, C., Zhu, E., et al.: Short-term power prediction of photovoltaic power station based on long short-term memory-back-propagation. Int. J. Dist. Sens. Netw. **15**(10), 1550147719883134 (2019)

11. Huang, L., Shu, J., Jiang, G., Zhang, J.: Photovoltaic generation forecast based on multidimensional time-series and local support vector regression in microgrids. Autom. Electr. Power Syst. **38**(5), 19–24 (2014)

12. IEA. Global energy review 2021 (2021). https://www.iea.org/reports/global-energy-review-2021

13. IEA. World energy outlook 2021 (2021). https://www.iea.org/reports/world-energy-outlook-2021

14. Ineichen, P.: Comparison of eight clear sky broadband models against 16 independent data banks. Solar Energy **80**(4), 468–478 (2006)

15. Lau, K., Wu, Q.: Local prediction of non-linear time series using support vector regression. Pattern Recogn. **41**(5), 1539–1547 (2008)

16. Lei, M., Yang, Z., Wang, Y., Xu, H.: Study on control technology of energy storage station in photovoltaic/storage system. Trans. China Electr. Soc. **31**(23), 87–92 (2016)

17. Li, Y., Song, Y., Jia, L., et al.: Intelligent fault diagnosis by fusing domain adversarial training and maximum mean discrepancy via ensemble learning. IEEE Trans. Indust. Inf. **17**(4), 2833–2841 (2020)

18. Li, Y., Su, Y., Shu, L.: An Armax model for forecasting the power output of a grid connected photovoltaic system. Renew. Energy **66**, 78–89 (2014)

19. Li, Y., Dai, W., et al.: Privacy protection for preventing data over-collection in smart city. IEEE Trans. Comp. **65**(5), 1339–1350 (2015)

20. Liang, Y., Ke, S., et al.: Geoman: multi-level attention networks for geo-sensory time series prediction. In: IJCAI, pp. 3428–3434 (2018)

21. Liu, M., Zhang, S., et al.: H infinite state estimation for discrete-time chaotic systems based on a unified model. IEEE Trans. Syst. Man Cybern. B (2012)

22. Lu, R., Jin, X., et al.: A study on big knowledge and its engineering issues. IEEE TKDE **31**(9), 1630–1644 (2018)

23. Mayer, M.J., Gróf, G.: Extensive comparison of physical models for photovoltaic power forecasting. Appl. Energy **283**, 116239 (2021)

24. Mellit, A., Pavan, A.M., Lughi, V.: Deep learning neural networks for short-term photovoltaic power forecasting. Renew. Energy **172**, 276–288 (2021)

25. Pelland, S., Galanis, G., Kallos, G.: Solar and photovoltaic forecasting through post-processing of the global environmental multiscale numerical weather prediction model. Progr. Photov. Resean. Appl. **21**(3), 284–296 (2013)

26. Qiu, H., Qiu, M., Lu, Z.: Selective encryption on ECG data in body sensor network based on supervised machine learning. Inf. Fusion **55**, 59–67 (2020)

27. Qiu, H., Zheng, Q., Memmi, G., Lu, J., Qiu, M., Thuraisingham, B.: Deep residual learning-based enhanced jpeg compression in the internet of things. IEEE Trans. Indust. Inf. **17**(3), 2124–2133 (2020)
28. Qiu, M., Khisamutdinov, E., et al.: RNA nanotechnology for computer design and in vivo computation. Philos. Trans. R. Soc. A: Math. Phys. Eng. Sci. **371**(2000), 20120310 (2013)
29. Qiu, M., Liu, J., Li, J., et al.: A novel energy-aware fault tolerance mechanism for wireless sensor networks. In: 2011 IEEE/ACM International Conference on Green Computing and Communications, pp. 56–61. IEEE (2011)
30. Qiu, M., Xue, C., et al.: Energy minimization with soft real-time and DVS for uniprocessor and multiprocessor embedded systems. In: IEEE DATE, pp. 1–6 (2007)
31. Qiu, M., et al.: Heterogeneous real-time embedded software optimization considering hardware platform. In: ACM Symposium on Applied Computing, pp. 1637–1641 (2009)
32. Qiu, M., Ming, Z., et al.: Enabling cloud computing in emergency management systems. IEEE Cloud Comp. **1**(4), 60–67 (2014)
33. Song, J., Krishnamurthy, V., et al.: Development of a Markov-chain-based energy storage model for power supply availability assessment of photovoltaic generation plants. IEEE Trans. Sust. Energy **4**(2), 491–500 (2012)
34. Tianqihoubao. Weather forecast (2021). http://www.tianqihoubao.com
35. van der Meer, D., Widén, J., Munkhammar, J.: Review on probabilistic forecasting of photovoltaic power production and electricity consumption. Renew. Sustain. Energy Rev. **81**, 1484–1512 (2018)
36. Vaswani, A., et al.: Attention is all you need. Adv. Neural Inf. Process. Syst. **30** (2017)
37. Xin, W.: Forecast of photovoltaic generated power based on WOA-LSTM. In: 5th IEEE ICMCCE, pp. 1143–1147 (2020)
38. Xue, Y., Wang, L., Zhang, Y., Zhang, N.: An ultra-short-term wind power forecasting model combined with CNN and GRU networks. Renew. Energy **37**(3), 456–462 (2019)
39. Yang, D., Wang, W., Xia, X.: A concise overview on solar resource assessment and forecasting. Adv. Atmosph. Sci. 1–13 (2022)
40. Yao, T., Wang, J., Wan, M., et al.: Venusai: an artificial intelligence platform for scientific discovery on supercomputers. J. Syst. Arch. 102550 (2022)
41. Yao, T., Wang, J., et al.: Intra-hour photovoltaic generation forecasting based on multi-source data and deep learning methods. IEEE Trans. Sustain. Energy **13**(1), 607–618 (2021)
42. Yao, T., Wang, J., et al.: A photovoltaic power output dataset: Multi-source photovoltaic power output dataset with python toolkit. Solar Energy **230**, 122–130 (2021)
43. Yixuan, S., Chunfu, S., Xun, J., Liang, Z.: Urban traffic accident time series prediction model based on combination of Arima and information granulation SVR. J. Tsinghua Uni. **54**(3), 348–353 (2015)
44. Zang, H., Cheng, L., Ding, T., et al.: Day-ahead photovoltaic power forecasting approach based on deep convolutional neural networks and meta learning. Int. J. Electric. Power Energy Syst. **118**, 105790 (2020)
45. Zhang, F., Guo, Z., Sun, X., Xi, J.: Short-term wind power prediction based on EMD-LSTM combined model. IOP Conf. Ser. Earth Environ. Sci. **514**, 042003 (2020)

46. Zhang, Y., Yang, L., Ge, S., Zhou, H.: Short-term photovoltaic power forecasting based on K-means algorithm and support vector machine. Power Syst. Prot. Control **46**(21), 118–125 (2018)
47. Zhao, X., Cao, W., Zhu, H., Ming, Z., Ashfaq, R.A.R.: An initial study on the rank of input matrix for extreme learning machine. Int. J. Mach. Learn. Cybern. **9**(5), 867–879 (2016). https://doi.org/10.1007/s13042-016-0615-y
48. Zhou, H., Zhang, S., et al.: Informer: beyond efficient transformer for long sequence time-series forecasting. In: Proceedings of the AAAI Conference on Artificial Intelligence, vol. 35(12), pp. 11106–11115 (2021)

Unsupervised Person Re-ID
via Loose-Tight Alternate Clustering

Bo Li[1], Tianbao Liang[1], Jianming Lv[1(✉)], Shengjing Chen[2], and Hongjian Xie[2]

[1] South China University of Technology, Guangzhou, China
jmlv@scut.edu.cn
[2] Guangzhou Forsafe Digital Technology Co., Ltd., Guangzhou, China
{shengjing_chen,hongjian_xie}@for-safe.cn

Abstract. Recently developed clustering-guided unsupervised methods have shown their superior performance in the person re-identification (re-ID) problem, which aims to match the surveillance images containing the same person. However, the performance of these methods is usually very sensitive to the change of the hyper-parameters in the clustering methods, such as the maximum distance of the neighbors and the number of clusters, which determine the quality of the clustering results. Tuning these parameters may need a large-scale labeled validation set, which is usually not applicable in unlabeled domain and hard to be generalized to different datasets. To solve this problem, we propose a Loose-Tight Alternate Clustering method without using any sensitive clustering parameter for unsupervised optimization. Specifically, we address the challenge as a multi-domain clustering problem, and propose the Loose and Tight Bounds to alleviate two kinds of clustering errors. Based on these bounds, a novel Loose-Tight alternate clustering strategy is adopted to optimize the visual model iteratively. Furthermore, a quality measurement based learning method is proposed to mitigate the side-effects of the pseudo-label noise by assigning lower weight to those clusters with lower purity. Extensive experiments show that our method can not only outperform state-of-the-art methods without manual exploration of clustering parameters, but also achieve much higher robustness against the dynamic changing of the target domain.

Keywords: Clustering-guided · Person re-identication · Unsupervised optimization · Multi-domain clustering · Loose-Tight Alternate

1 Introduction

Person re-identification (re-ID) aims to match the surveillance images which contain the same person. The recently developed supervised algorithms [15,17,26] have achieved impressive performance based on convolutional neural networks. However, the extremely high cost of labeling the dataset limits the scalability of these methods. How to effectively learn a discriminative model on massive unlabeled data has become a hot research topic in this field.

ⓒ The Author(s), under exclusive license to Springer Nature Switzerland AG 2022
G. Memmi et al. (Eds.): KSEM 2022, LNAI 13369, pp. 29–42, 2022.
https://doi.org/10.1007/978-3-031-10986-7_3

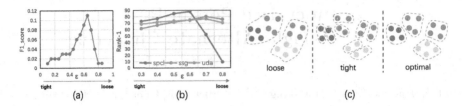

Fig. 1. The influence of the clustering parameter on clustering-guided unsupervised person re-ID tested on Market1501. (a): The F1 score of clustering results under different ϵ of DBSCAN. (b): The Rank-1 score of three methods under different ϵ of DBSCAN. The ϵ corresponds to τ in UDA [14] and d in SPCL [6]. (c): Three types of clustering criteria and the corresponding clustering results. The points in same color means the samples share with the same identity.

Recently, some unsupervised domain adaptive re-ID solutions (UDA) [4,12, 14,24,25,30,31] have been proposed by transferring the prior knowledge learned in labeled source datasets to another unlabeled target dataset. However, these UDA methods still require a large amount of manually annotated source data. In a more extreme configuration, some fully unsupervised methods [10,11,16,23] are proposed to learn a high-performance discriminative model on the unlabeled target dataset without using any labeled source data.

Most of state-of-the-art unsupervised methods [4,6,14,24,25] utilize clustering methods to obtain supervised signals from unlabeled instances. However, according to our observation as shown in Fig. 1, the performance of these methods is usually very sensitive to the change of the clustering parameters, which determine the quality of clustering results. For example, the maximum distance between neighbors, ϵ, is the most important parameter in DBSCAN [2], which affects the clustering results seriously. As shown in Fig. 1(a), the F1 score of the clustering result is very sensitive to the change of ϵ. Figure 1(c) shows the clustering results intuitively. Large ϵ corresponds to a loose clustering criterion which may form large groups of instances, while small ϵ may cause small and tight groups on the other hand. The key of these methods is to find the optimal clustering result closest to the ground truth. Figure 1(b) further shows the performance of the state-of-the-art unsupervised person re-ID methods SPCL [6], SSG [4] and UDA [14], which are all based on DBSCAN [2]. It clearly shows that their performance is very sensitive to ϵ. In particular, the changes of ϵ may lead to the collapse of the SPCL [6], which has much higher peak accuracy than the others. These methods [4,6,14] usually report the best performance using the optimal ϵ, which actually needs large labeled validation set for careful tuning and is difficult to be generalized to different datasets.

To address above problems, we propose a *Loose-Tight Alternate Clustering* (LTAC) framework to learn from noisy pseudo-labels and alleviate the sensitivity of clustering parameters. Distinct from traditional DBSCAN based clustering method, we do not configure the optimized ϵ at first, which is usually hard to tune. We go another way by modeling the challenge as a multi-domain clustering problem and define the loose and tight bounds of the clustering criteria to reduce one kind of clustering errors respectively. Then a novel Loose-Tight Alternate

Clustering strategy is proposed to run the loose and tight clustering alternately to optimize the visual model gradually. Moreover, we propose a *Quality Measurement based Learning* method to further reduce the side-effects of the clustering errors.

Main contributions of this paper are as follows:

- We propose the *Loose and Tight Bounds* of the clustering criteria in the multi-domain clustering problem to reduce two kinds of clustering errors.
- We propose a novel *Loose-Tight Alternate Clustering strategy* (LTAC) for unsupervised person re-ID by generating two types of pseudo-labels alternately based on the Loose and Tight Bounds to optimize the visual model gradually.
- A *Quality Measurement based Learning* method is proposed to reduce the side-effect of the pseudo-label noise by assigning smaller weight to those clusters with lower purity.
- Comprehensive experiments are conducted and show that our method can not only outperform state-of-the-art methods without manually configured sensitive clustering parameters, but also achieve much higher robustness against dynamic change of target domain.

The rest of this paper is organized as follows. In Sect. 2, we discuss some related work. In Sect. 3, we introduce the details of the Loose-Tight Alternate Clustering method for unsupervised person re-ID namely LTAC. After that, we provide the experimental evaluations of the proposed method in Sect. 4. Finally, we conclude our work in Sect. 5.

2   Related Work

2.1   Clustering-Guided Unsupervised Person re-ID

One of the most popular way to tackle unsupervised person re-ID is the clustering-guided framework, which utilizes pseudo-labels based on clustering results. PUL [3] selects samples close to the cluster centroid for training gradually. BUC [10] proposes a bottom-up clustering approach to gradually merge samples into one identity. HCT [23] improves the distance measurement of BUC by using an unweighted pair-group method with arithmetic means. However, the changes of merging steps significantly impact the final performance of BUC and HCT. MMT [5] softly refines the pseudo-labels via mutual mean-teaching, which needs auxiliary models and is sensitive to the k value of K-means. Some methods have verified the effectiveness of DBSCAN [2] in clustering. UDA [14] proposes a vanilla self-training framework with DBSCAN. SSG [4] generates multiple clusters from global body to local parts using DBSCAN. SPCL [6] creates more reliable clusters gradually by tuning the maximum neighbor distance ϵ of DBSCAN to a tight or loose criterion manually to mitigate the effects of noisy pseudo-labels. However, these methods are sensitive to the ϵ. Most of the above clustering-guided methods are somewhat sensitive to the parameters of the clustering algorithms they use. Our method chooses the time-tested clustering algorithm DBSCAN for clustering and tries to alleviate the sensitivity to the ϵ.

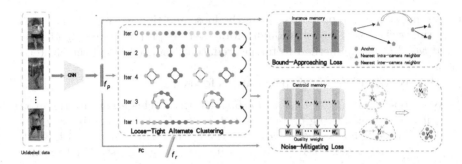

Fig. 2. The overview of the *Loose-Tight Alternate Clustering* method. The *Loose Bound* and *Tight Bound* are applied as clustering criteria alternately. The *Bound-Approaching Loss* narrows the gap between these two bounds, and the *Noise-Mitigating Loss* assigns higher weight to purer clusters during training to reduce the side-effects of clustering errors.

2.2   Camera-Aware Unsupervised Person re-ID

A key challenge in unsupervised person re-ID is the cross-camera scene variation. HHL and ECN [29,30] generate new fake images in the style of each camera for each sample and then enforce the camera-invariance to each person image and its corresponding camera-style transferred images. [12] imposes the neighborhood invariance constraint for inter-camera matching and intra-camera matching separately to improve the vanilla neighborhood invariance. [19] proposes a camera-aware similarity consistency loss which imposes the pairwise similarity distribution invariance upon cross-camera matching and intra-camera matching to alleviate the cross-camera scene variation. These methods play exemplary roles in leveraging the camera information. Our method further explores the integration of camera information with clustering-guided framework.

3   Methodology

3.1   Problem Definition

Under the setting of fully unsupervised person re-ID, a dataset X_t is provided that contains N_t images without any identity annotations. In addition, the number of cameras N_c and the camera-ID of each image (i.e. $C = \{c_i\}_{i=1}^{N_t}, c_i \in [0, N_c))$ is available. The goal is to learn a re-ID model on X_t, which aims to search for the images containing the same person as that in the query image.

As a popularly used unsupervised technique, clustering based pseudo-label methods achieve state-of-the-art performance in unsupervised person re-ID [4,6,14]. Performing a certain clustering mechanism such as DBSCAN on the pedestrian images collected from multiple cameras is the key step in this kind of methods. Due to the visual diversity of different cameras, the distances of inter-camera and intra-camera image pairs vary a lot. The images from the same camera with similar background and lightness tend to have much smaller distance than those from different cameras. The diversity of the distance brings new challenges to the traditional clustering method, which usually cheats each instance equally. We address the challenge of clustering multi-camera pedestrian images as a **Multi-domain Clustering** problem, where each camera can be viewed as a different domain with specific visual style. How to effectively integrate the diversity of domains into the clustering method is one core task addressed in this paper.

3.2   Loose and Tight Clustering Bounds

Most of state-of-the-art unsupervised person re-ID algorithms [4,6,14,24] are based on the DBSCAN [2] clustering algorithm to achieve great performance advances. However, as the most important parameter in DBSCAN, the maximum distance between neighbors (ϵ) affects the clustering results seriously. As shown in Fig. 1(b), the performance of the models are very sensitive to the changing of ϵ.

There are two kinds of errors while conducting DBSCAN: the *Mix Error* and *Split Error* as shown in Fig. 1(c). In particular, applying a large ϵ may yield a loose clustering introducing the *Mix Error*, where the images with large distance from different identities are mixed into one cluster. On the contrary, using a small ϵ may yield a tight clustering causing the *Split Error*, where the images with the same identities may be separated. Most of the DBSCAN based pseudo-label methods need a large labeled validation set for careful tuning of ϵ and are difficult to be generalized to different datasets.

Since the optimal ϵ is not easy to decide according to unlabeled data, we go another way to solve the problem by seeking the proper bounds of clustering criteria. As observed in the research [27], the most similar image pairs in the same camera are very possible from the same person, which are usually sampled from the continuous frames of the camera. On the other hand, while only considering the cross-camera image pairs, the most similar ones also tend to be from the same person who walks across different cameras. Based on these observations, we define two bounds of distance, the **Loose Bound** and **Tight Bound**, for clustering criteria. Specifically, the *Tight Bound* is defined as the average distance of intra-camera nearest neighbors:

$$\epsilon_T = \frac{1}{N_t} \sum_{i=1}^{N_t} \min d_r(x_i, x_{ia}), \forall x_{ia} \in C_i, x_{ia} \neq x_i \qquad (1)$$

C_i is the set of images that are captured from the same camera with x_i and the $d_r(\cdot)$ is the popular and effective jaccard distance computed with k-reciprocal encoding [27]. On the other hand, the *Loose Bound* is defined as the average of the smallest distance between cross-camera images.

$$\epsilon_L = \frac{1}{N_t} \sum_{i=1}^{N_t} \min d_r(x_i, x_{ie}), \forall x_{ie} \notin C_i \qquad (2)$$

While adopted as the hyper-parameter of the maximum neighboring distance in DBSCAN, the *Tight Bound* ϵ_T is small enough to tightly group those positive intra-camera matchings, leading to small *Mix Error* and large *Split Error*. On the other hand, the *Loose Bound* ϵ_L is large enough for DBSCAN [2] to group the instance loosely, which may lead to small *Split Error* and large *Mix Error*. How to balance these two opposite bounds makes up the core task in the following presented Loose-Tight Alternate Clustering model.

3.3   Loose-Tight Alternate Clustering

While performing clustering according to the *Tight Bound* ϵ_T and the *Loose Bound* ϵ_L respectively, two types of pseudo-labels can be achieved based on the tight and loose clustering results. The re-ID model can learn useful knowledge from both types of supervised signals. However, overfitting to any kind of pseudo-labels will limit the final performance of the re-ID model. As shown in Fig. 2, we train the re-ID model with these two types of pseudo-labels alternately to avoid the model being biased towards each kind of pseudo-labels. The detail of the alternate clustering method is shown in Algorithm 1.

Algorithm 1. Loose-Tight Alternate Clustering

Input: unlabeled dataset X_t.

1: Initialize : T : total iterations , I : current number of iterations , Ψ: the visual model needed to optimize, E: learning epochs in each iteration.
2: $I \leftarrow 0$
3: **while** $I < T$ **do**
4:      Compute the *Tight Bound* ϵ_T according to Eq. (1)
5:      Compute the *Loose Bound* ϵ_L according to Eq. (2)
6:      **if** $I\%2 == 0$ **then**
7:          $\overline{M} \leftarrow$ DBSCAN with ϵ_T
8:      **else**
9:          $\overline{M} \leftarrow$ DBSCAN with ϵ_L
10:      **end if**
11:      Train Ψ based on $\overline{M}$ by minimizing L_t (Eq. (6)) for E epochs
12:      $I \leftarrow I + 1$
13: **end while**
14: **return** Ψ

In particular, the clustering result in each iteration of clustering is defined as:

$$\overline{M} = \{\overline{M}_k | 0 \le k < n\} \tag{3}$$

where n is the number of clusters, k is the cluster-ID, and $\overline{M}_k$ is the kth cluster. By assigning the pseudo-label of each sample as its cluster-ID, the re-ID model can be trained with the cross-entropy loss, which is formulated as follows:

$$L_{tc} = -\sum_{k=0}^{n-1} \sum_{x_i \in \overline{M}_k} log(\frac{e^{V_k f_i}}{\sum_{j=0}^{n-1} e^{V_j f_i}}) \tag{4}$$

where V_k is the centroid vector of the kth cluster $\overline{M}_k$ and f_i is the feature vector of the instance x_i. After learning from an instance x_i, the centroid of the kth cluster will be updated by $V_k \leftarrow (V_k + f_i)/2$.

By minimizing the loss L_{tc}, the visual feature of an instance is dragged to the centroid of the cluster it belongs to, and pushed away from other clusters. In this way, while using the *Loose Bound* as the clustering criterion, the feature vectors of the instances, which have lower possibility to come from the same person, are pushed away. Meanwhile, the cross-camera images with relative smaller distance are mixed together, which may help to reduce the cross-domain diversity of visual styles. Furthermore, while using the *Tight Bound*, the feature vectors of intra-camera images with smaller distance are dragged together, which have high possibility to share the same identities. By alternately using these two kinds of bounds, the model can compress the *Split Error* and *Mix Error* alternately.

The *Loose Bound* and the *Tight Bound* are re-calculated in each iteration (Line 4 and 5 of Algorithm 1) and adapt to the visual diversity of different cameras. Larger gap between these two bounds indicates the larger domain diversity of this classic Multi-domain Clustering problem. Thus, reducing the gap may reduce the diversity and help improve the accuracy of the clustering. Motivated by this analysis, we propose a simple *Bound-Approaching Loss* (BAL) to narrow the gap between two bounds by minimizing the difference between the intra-camera nearest neighbor distance and the inter-camera nearest neighbor distance:

$$L_{ba} = \sum_i \max(\min_{x_i \circ x_j} d(x_i, x_j) - \min_{x_i \bullet x_k} d(x_i, x_k), 0) \qquad (5)$$

where $d(\cdot)$ is the simple Euclidean distance. $x_i \circ x_j$ denotes that x_i and x_j are from different cameras, while $x_i \bullet x_k$ denotes that they are from the same camera.

The cross-entropy loss L_{tc} and the *Bound-Approaching Loss* L_{ba} are combined together as follows to optimize the visual model, as used in the Line 11 of Algorithm 1.

$$L_t = L_{tc} + L_{ba} \qquad (6)$$

Furthermore, to facilitate calculating the distance of intra-camera and inter-camera image pairs, we maintain an instance memory bank $\mathcal{I}$ that stores the feature of each sample. During the back-propagation in each iteration, we update the memory bank for the training sample x_i through

$$\mathcal{I}[i] = (\mathcal{I}[i] + f_i)/2 \qquad (7)$$

where $\mathcal{I}[i]$ is the memory of x_i in the i-th slot, f_i is the feature of x_i.

3.4 Quality Measurement Based Learning

During the training in each iteration, the cross-entropy loss L_{tc} of Eq. (4) is used to optimize the visual model based on the pseudo-labels, which are the cluster IDs achieved by the clustering algorithm. The quality of the clustering results determines the correctness of the pseudo-labels. In order to make the model learn more knowledge from more reliable pseudo labels, we further extend this loss to the following *Noise-Mitigating Loss* to consider the quality of each cluster and assign higher weight to the pseudo-labels of purer clusters:

$$L_{nm} = - \sum_{k=0}^{n-1} W_k \sum_{x_i \in \overline{M}_k} log(\frac{e^{V_k f_i}}{\sum_{j=0}^{n-1} e^{V_j f_i}}) \tag{8}$$

where W_k indicates the quality measurement of the kth cluster $\overline{M}_k$. To obtain W_k, we first compute the intra-cluster dissimilarity a_i and the inter-cluster dissimilarity b_i for $\forall x_i \in \overline{M}_k$ by:

$$a_i = \frac{1}{N_k - 1} \sum_{\substack{x_j \in \overline{M}_k \\ j \neq i}} d_r(x_i, x_j) \tag{9}$$

$$b_i = \frac{1}{N_t - N_k} \sum_{x_o \notin \overline{M}_k} d_r(x_i, x_o) \tag{10}$$

where N_k is the size of the cluster $\overline{M}_k$, N_t is the size of the whole dataset, $d_r(\cdot)$ is the jaccard distance computed with k-reciprocal encoding [27]. Then the quality score of $\overline{M}_k$ is then defined as the average silhouette coefficient of the samples within $\overline{M}_k$, which is formulated as follows:

$$Q_k = \frac{1}{N_k} \sum_{x_i \in \overline{M}_k} \frac{b_i - a_i}{\max\{a_i, b_i\}} \tag{11}$$

Furthermore, we normalize the quality score of each cluster via the exp maximum and minimum normalization:

$$W_k = \frac{e^{Q_k} - \min_{j=1..n} (e^{Q_j})}{\max_{j=1..n} (e^{Q_j}) - \min_{j=1..n} (e^{Q_j})} + \alpha \tag{12}$$

where α is the positive constant to prevent the weight of the cluster with the lowest quality score from being set to zero. α is set as 0.01 in all experiments. By using this quality measurement W_k, the clusters that have higher intra cohesion and outer separation from other clusters will be assigned with higher weight when updating the parameters of the visual model. In this way, the negative effects of the noise in pseudo-labels can be further mitigated.

By combining the *Bound-Approaching Loss* L_{ba} with the *Noise-Mitigating Loss* L_{nm}, the complete loss function is defined as follows:

$$L_t' = L_{ba} + L_{nm}, \tag{13}$$

which aims to narrow the gap between the Loose and Tight Bounds and mitigate the pseudo-labels noise. Accordingly, the loss function L_t in Line 11 of Algorithm 1 can be replaced with L_t' here to enhance the performance of the learnt model.

4   Experiments

4.1   Datasets and Evaluation Protocol

Market1501. Market1501 [9] is a large scale person re-ID benchmark that contains 32,688 images of 1501 identities captured by 6 cameras. Specifically, 12,936 images of 751 identities are provided for training and the rest 19,732 images of 750 identities are for testing.

MSMT17. MSMT17 [18] is a newly released benchmark that contains 126,411 images of 4,101 identities collected from 15 non-overlapping camera views. It contains 32,621 images of 1,041 identities for training. The query contains 11,659 images of 3,060 identities and the gallery includes 126,441 images.

Evaluation Protocol. We utilize the Cumulative Matching Characteristic (CMC) curve and the mean average precision (mAP) to evaluate the performance of the proposed method. Furthermore, we report the Rank-1, Rank-5, Rank-10 scores to represent the CMC curve.

4.2   Implementation Details

We adopt the ResNet-50 [7] pre-trained on ImageNet [1] as the backbone of our model. The input image is resized to 256×128. The mini-batch size is 64. Random cropping, flipping, and random erasing [28] are adopted as data augmentation strategies. The SGD optimizer is used with the learning rate as 3.5×10^{-3}. Furthermore, each re-ID model is trained for 60 iterations. During each iteration, 800 epochs are executed.

4.3   Ablation Studies

Effectiveness of Alternate Clustering. To prove the necessity and importance of clustering with the *Loose Bound* ϵ_L and *Tight Bound* ϵ_T, we conduct experiments which only utilize ϵ_L or ϵ_T to cluster. The re-ID model is trained based on the vanilla cross-entropy loss L_{tc} (Eq. (4)). The experimental results are reported in the Table 1. When clustering only with ϵ_L, the clustering criterion is too loose, resulting in a lot of samples being grouped into one cluster. In this case, the *Mix Error* of pseudo-labels is pretty high, leading to the collapse of the re-ID model. When clustering only with ϵ_T, the clustering criterion is tight and the samples in each cluster are possibly fewer. In this case, the clustering accuracy will be higher, and the re-ID model can learn more useful knowledge from these kinds of pseudo-labels. However, the tight clustering criterion may not be able to group those positive inter-camera matchings into the same cluster, limiting the further improvement of the re-ID model. By training with these two types of pseudo-labels alternately (LTAC), the re-ID model is able to learn more useful knowledge and avoids being biased towards either of the two kinds of pseudo-label noise. Furthermore, we illustrate the number of clusters during training

Table 1. Ablation studies of the proposed method on Market-1501 and MSMT17. $LTAC\_L$ means the model only using the Loose Bound, and $LTAC\_T$ means only using the Tight Bound. L_{tc}, L_{ba} and L_{nm} are the three loss functions described in Eqs. 4, 5 and 8 respectively.

Methods	Market-1501				MSMT17			
	mAP	Rank-1	Rank-5	Rank-10	mAP	Rank-1	Rank-5	Rank-10
$LTAC\_L + L_{tc}$	3.1	9.8	21.3	27.7	1.8	6.9	12.3	15.8
$LTAC\_T + L_{tc}$	61.8	81.4	89.7	92.6	15.0	40.1	50.9	55.2
$LTAC + L_{tc}$	69.5	86.6	93.6	95.8	17.7	42.7	53.3	57.9
$LTAC + L_{tc} + L_{ba}$	72.4	88.3	94.8	97.3	18.1	45.6	57.0	62.1
$LTAC + L_{nm}$	70.7	87.9	94.2	95.9	19.4	47.6	58.2	63.3
$LTAC + L_{nm} + L_{ba}$	**73.2**	**89.3**	**95.4**	**97.3**	**21.5**	**51.2**	**61.6**	**67.1**

Table 2. Comparison with state-of-the-arts fully unsupervised person re-ID methods on Market1501 and MSMT17. "None" means using the model pretrained on Imagenet. **Bold** indicates the best and underlined the runner-up. * denotes using the back-bond method Resnet-50 like us.

Methods	Market-1501					MSMT17				
	Source	mAP	Rank-1	Rank-5	Rank-10	Source	mAP	Rank-1	Rank-5	Rank-10
OIM [20]	None	14.0	38.0	58.0	66.3	None	–	–	–	–
BUC [10]	None	38.3	66.2	79.6	84.5	None	–	–	–	–
SSL [11]	None	37.8	71.7	83.8	87.4	None	–	–	–	–
MMCL [16]	None	45.5	80.3	89.4	92.3	None	11.2	35.4	44.8	49.8
HCT [23]	None	56.4	80.0	91.6	95.2	None	–	–	–	–
IICS [21]*	None	67.1	85.5	–	–	None	–	–	–	–
SPCL [6]	None	73.1	88.1	95.1	97.0	None	19.1	42.3	55.6	61.2
Ours	None	**73.2**	**89.3**	**95.4**	**97.3**	None	**21.5**	**51.2**	**62.7**	**67.1**

on Market-1501 in Fig. 3(a). It can be observed that the quantity of clusters is closer to ground-truth identities when training with LTAC using both Loose and Tight Bounds.

Effectiveness of the Bound Approaching Loss. To evaluate the effectiveness of the *Bound-Approaching Loss*, we train the re-ID model in four different settings as reported in the last 4 rows of Table 1. It can be observed that no matter we train the re-ID model with the traditional cross-entropy loss (L_{tc}) or the quality weighted loss (L_{nm}), adding the *Bound-Approaching Loss* L_{ba} can lead to a further improvement on both two large-scale benchmarks. Furthermore, we illustrate the dynamic changes of the gap between the bounds during training on Market-1501 in Fig. 3(b). When we train the re-ID model with L_{ba}, the gap between ϵ_L and ϵ_T decreases to zero gradually. This proves that the *Bound-Approaching Loss* can reduce the visual diversity of different cameras significantly.

Effectiveness of Quality Measurement based Learning. We evaluate the effectiveness of the Noise-Mitigating Loss L_{nm} used in the *Quality Measurement based Learning* as described in Sect. 3.4 on Market-1501 and MSMT17. The experimental results are reported in the Table 1. It can be observed that training the re-ID model with the Noise-Mitigating Loss L_{nm} leads to a higher performance than training the re-ID model with the traditional cross-entropy loss (L_{tc}). Specifically, the mAP improves from 72.4% to 73.2% and 18.1% to 21.5% when training on Market-1501 and MSMT17. The improvement is more obvious on MSMT17, since it is more challenging and the scale of pseudo-labels noise is larger. This proves the effectiveness of the *Quality Measurement based Learning* to mitigate the negative effects of pseudo-label noise.

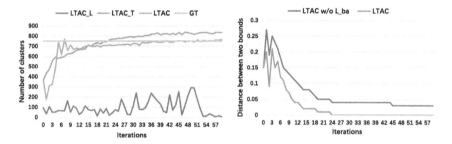

Fig. 3. Result of LTAC on Market-1501. (a): The dynamic changes of cluster numbers. $LTAC\_L$ means only using the Loose Bound ϵ_L and $LTAC\_T$ means only using the Tight Bound ϵ_T. GT indicates the ground-truth cluster number. (b): The distance between ϵ_L and ϵ_T. $LTAC$ w/o L_ba means training without using L_{ba}.

4.4   Comparison with State-of-the-Art Methods

Our method is compared with state-of-the-art fully unsupervised re-ID methods in Table 2, which shows that $LTAC$ can achieve the best performance in all cases. It is interesting to observe that the superiority of our method is more obvious in the larger dataset MSMT17, which verifies the better generalization ability of our method. Furthermore, we also test the performance in the unsupervised domain adaptation (UDA) scenario, where the models are transferred from a labeled source domain to an unlabeled target domain. Table 3 shows the comparison results with state-of-the-art UDA methods. Our method outperforms all UDA methods using DBSCAN (e.g. SSG [4], MMT [5,6] SPCL [6]). More importantly, our method doesn't require any manual tuning of the sensitive clustering parameters, so it is more robust and competitive in real-world applications.

4.5   Robustness Evaluation

To further evaluate the robustness of our method, we design and implement several experiments to simulate the dynamic changing of the target domain. Specifically, we randomly select some different cameras in the dataset and augment

Table 3. Comparison with state-of-the-arts unsupervised domain adaptive person re-ID methods on Market1501 and MSMT17. **Bold** indicates the best and underlined the runner-up.

Methods	Market-1501					MSMT17				
	Source	mAP	Rank-1	Rank-5	Rank-10	Source	mAP	Rank-1	Rank-5	Rank-10
PAUL [22]	MSMT17	40.1	68.5	82.4	87.4	Market	–	–	–	–
ECN++ [31]	MSMT17	–	–	–	–	Market	15.2	40.4	53.1	58.7
SSG* [4]	MSMT17	–	–	–	–	Market	13.2	31.6	-	49.6
DG-Net++ [32]	MSMT17	64.6	83.1	91.5	94.3	Market	22.1	48.4	60.9	66.1
D-MMD [13]	MSMT17	50.8	72.8	88.1	92.3	Market	13.5	29.1	46.3	54.1
MMT-dbscan* [5,6]	MSMT17	75.6	89.3	95.8	97.5	Market	24.0	50.1	63.5	69.3
SPCL [6]	MSMT17	<u>77.5</u>	<u>89.7</u>	<u>96.1</u>	<u>97.6</u>	Market	**26.8**	<u>53.7</u>	<u>65.0</u>	<u>69.8</u>
Ours	MSMT17	**80.4**	**92.8**	**97.2**	**98.0**	Market	<u>26.0</u>	**56.1**	**67.5**	**72.4**

Table 4. Robustness comparison between our method and SPCL. "Supervised" means supervised learning as the upper bound. "Noise/x" indicates the noise is added to x cameras. "Improvement" means the improvement of our method relative to SPCL.

Methods	Market-1501							
	Noise/0		Noise/2		Noise/4		Noise/6	
	mAP	Rank-1	mAP	Rank-1	mAP	Rank-1	mAP	Rank-1
Supervised	82.2	91.8	78.8	90.4	68.8	83.8	65.2	82.3
SPCL [6]	73.1	88.1	**65.9**	82.7	46.9	67.9	41.4	62.7
Ours	**73.2**	**89.3**	65.3	**84.5**	**49.4**	**73.4**	**44.6**	**68.8**
Improvement(%)	0.14↑	1.36↑	0.91↓	2.18↑	5.33↑	8.1↑	7.73↑	9.73↑
Methods	MSMT17							
	Noise/0		Noise/5		Noise/10		Noise/15	
	mAP	Rank-1	mAP	Rank-1	mAP	Rank-1	mAP	Rank-1
Supervised	44.5	70.5	30.3	56.4	21.2	42.6	17.4	39.8
SPCL [6]	19.1	42.3	9.1	21.3	4.8	11.4	4.8	11.8
Ours	**21.5**	**51.2**	**15.9**	**39.6**	**8.4**	**23.3**	**9.2**	**26.7**
Improvement(%)	12.57↑	21.04↑	74.73↑	85.92↑	75.00↑	104.39↑	91.67↑	126.27↑

the images with randomly selected noise generated by the imgaug library [8]. We utilize four types of weather noise including clouds, fog, snow, and rain. Table 4 shows the comparison results with the state-of-the-art unsupervised method SPCL [6] under different experimental settings. As the number of polluted cameras increases, the performance of all methods declines. However, the performance of our method outperforms SPCL [6] with a large margin, especially in the case with the highest ratio of noise. In particular, when we randomly select six cameras of Market1501 for noise augmentation, our method achieves 68.8% Rank-1 precision while SPCL [6] only achieves 62.7% Rank-1 precision. When we randomly select five cameras of MSMT17 for noise augmentation, our method achieves 15.9% mAP and 39.6% Rank-1, which exceeds SPCL [6] by 6.8% and 18.3% respectively. The experimental results in Table 4 illustrate that our method is more robust than SPCL [6]. As we calculate the clustering parameters based on the statistics of unlabeled data without manually setting clustering parameters, our method is more applicable to complex and dynamic realistic scenes.

5   Conclusion

In this paper, we proposed a *Loose-Tight Alternate Clustering* framework which explores the *Loose Bound* and *Tight Bound* in multi-domain clustering, and learns from two types of pseudo-labels alternately. The two bounds were obtained on the basis of the inter-camera nearest neighbor distance and the intra-camera nearest neighbor distance. A *Bound-Approaching Loss* was further proposed to narrow the gap between these two bounds to reduce the domain diversity. Furthermore, a *Quality Measurement based Learning* method was introduced to mitigate the negative effects of the pseudo-label noise. Experiments on two large benchmarks demonstrated the applicability, competitiveness and robustness of our method.

Acknowledgements. This work was supported by the National Natural Science Foundation of China (61876065), the Special Fund Project of Marine Economy Development in Guangdong Province([2021]35), and Guangzhou Science and Technology Program key projects (202007040002).

References

1. Deng, J., Dong, W., Socher, R., Li, L.J., Li, K., Fei-Fei, L.: Imagenet: a large-scale hierarchical image database. In: CVPR (2009)
2. Ester, M., Kriegel, H., Sander, J., Xu, X.: A density-based algorithm for discovering clusters in large spatial databases with noise. In: KDD (1996)
3. Fan, H., Zheng, L., Yan, C., Yang, Y.: Unsupervised person re-identification: clustering and fine-tuning. ACM (TOMM) (2018)
4. Fu, Y., Wei, Y., Wang, G., Zhou, Y., Shi, H., Huang, T.S.: Self-similarity grouping: a simple unsupervised cross domain adaptation approach for person re-identification. In: ICCV (2019)
5. Ge, Y., Chen, D., Li, H.: Mutual mean-teaching: pseudo label refinery for unsupervised domain adaptation on person re-identification. In: ICLR (2020)
6. Ge, Y., Zhu, F., Chen, D., Zhao, R., Li, H.: Self-paced contrastive learning with hybrid memory for domain adaptive object re-ID. In: NeurIPS (2020)
7. He, K., Zhang, X., Ren, S., Sun, J.: Deep residual learning for image recognition. In: CVPR (2016)
8. Jung, A.B., et al.: Imgaug (2020). https://github.com/aleju/imgaug. Accessed 01 Feb 2020
9. Liang, Z., Liyue, S., Lu, T., Shengjin, W., Jingdong, W., Qi, T.: Scalable person re-identification: a benchmark. In: ICCV (2015)
10. Lin, Y., Dong, X., Zheng, L., Yan, Y., Yang, Y.: A bottom-up clustering approach to unsupervised person re-identification. In: AAAI (2019)

11. Lin, Y., Xie, L., Wu, Y., Yan, C., Tian, Q.: Unsupervised person re-identification via softened similarity learning. In: CVPR (2020)
12. Luo, C., Song, C., Zhang, Z.: Generalizing person re-identification by camera-aware invariance learning and cross-domain mixup. In: ECCV (2020)
13. Mekhazni, D., Bhuiyan, A., Ekladious, G.S.E., Granger, E.: Unsupervised domain adaptation in the dissimilarity space for person re-identification. In: ECCV (2020)
14. Song, L., et al.: Unsupervised domain adaptive re-identification: theory and practice. Pattern Recogn. (2020)
15. Sun, Y., Zheng, L., Yang, Y., Tian, Q., Wang, S.: Beyond part models: person retrieval with refined part pooling (and a strong convolutional baseline). In: ECCV (2018)
16. Wang, D., Zhang, S.: Unsupervised person re-identification via multi-label classification. In: CVPR (2020)
17. Wang, G., Yuan, Y., Chen, X., Li, J., Zhou, X.: Learning discriminative features with multiple granularities for person re-identification. In: ACM MM (2018)
18. Wei, L., Zhang, S., Gao, W., Tian, Q.: Person transfer GAN to bridge domain gap for person re-identification. In: CVPR (2018)
19. Wu, A., Zheng, W., Lai, J.: Unsupervised person re-identification by camera-aware similarity consistency learning. In: ICCV (2019)
20. Xiao, T., Li, S., Wang, B., Lin, L., Wang, X.: Joint detection and identification feature learning for person search. In: CVPR (2017)
21. Xuan, S., Zhang, S.: Intra-inter camera similarity for unsupervised person re-identification. In: Proceedings of the IEEE/CVF Conference on Computer Vision and Pattern Recognition, pp. 11926–11935 (2021)
22. Yang, Q., Yu, H., Wu, A., Zheng, W.: Patch-based discriminative feature learning for unsupervised person re-identification. In: CVPR (2019)
23. Zeng, K., Ning, M., Wang, Y., Guo, Y.: Hierarchical clustering with hard-batch triplet loss for person re-identification. In: CVPR (2020)
24. Zhai, Y., et al.: Ad-cluster: augmented discriminative clustering for domain adaptive person re-identification. In: CVPR (2020)
25. Zhang, X., Cao, J., Shen, C., You, M.: Self-training with progressive augmentation for unsupervised cross-domain person re-identification. In: ICCV (2019)
26. Zheng, F., et al.: Pyramidal person re-identification via multi-loss dynamic training. In: CVPR (2019)
27. Zhong, Z., Zheng, L., Cao, D., Li, S.: Re-ranking person re-identification with k-reciprocal encoding. In: CVPR (2017)
28. Zhong, Z., Zheng, L., Kang, G., Li, S., Yang, Y.: Random erasing data augmentation. In: AAAI (2020)
29. Zhong, Z., Zheng, L., Li, S., Yang, Y.: Generalizing a person retrieval model hetero- and homogeneously. In: ECCV (2018)
30. Zhong, Z., Zheng, L., Luo, Z., Li, S., Yang, Y.: Invariance matters: exemplar memory for domain adaptive person re-identification. In: CVPR (2019)
31. Zhun, Z., Liang, Z., Zhiming, L., Shaozi, L., Yi, Y.: Learning to adapt invariance in memory for person re-identification. In: TPAMI (2020)
32. Zou, Y., Yang, X., Yu, Z., Kumar, B.V.K.V., Kautz, J.: Joint disentangling and adaptation for cross-domain person re-identification. In: ECCV (2020)

Sparse Dense Transformer Network for Video Action Recognition

Xiaochun Qu, Zheyuan Zhang, Wei Xiao, Jinye Ran, Guodong Wang, and Zili Zhang[(✉)]

College of Computer and Information Science,
Southwest University, Chongqing 400715, China
zhangzl@swu.edu.cn

Abstract. The action recognition backbone has continued to advance. The two-stream method based on Convolutional Neural Networks (CNNs) usually pays more attention to the video's local features and ignores global information because of the limitation of Convolution kernels. Transformer based on attention mechanism is adopted to capture global information, which is inferior to CNNs in extracting local features. More features can improve video representations. Therefore, a novel two-stream Transformer model is proposed, Sparse Dense Transformer Network(SDTN), which involves (i) a Sparse pathway, operating at low frame rate, to capture spatial semantics and local features; and (ii) a Dense pathway, running at high frame rate, to abstract motion information. A new patch-based cropping approach is presented to make the model focus on the patches in the center of the frame. Furthermore, frame alignment, a method that compares the input frames of the two pathways, reduces the computational cost. Experiments show that SDTN extracts deeper spatiotemporal features through input policy of various temporal resolutions, and reaches 82.4% accuracy on Kinetics-400, outperforming the previous method by more than 1.9% accuracy.

Keywords: Transformer · Action recognition · Two-stream · Frame alignment · Patch crop

1 Introduction

The development of computer technology has been applied in all aspects of life [4–6,16,21,24]. With the diversification of content presentation forms on social platforms, videos have progressively risen to prominence in our lives. Millions of videos are published on YouTube, TikTok, and other platforms on a daily basis. Thus, understanding and analyzing the content of videos play a critical role in video sharing and monitoring fields. Similarly, the explosive growth of video streams has also posed a challenge to today's video field research: how to achieve high-precision video understanding under limited computational cost?

To reduce the computational task, a common practice in action recognition is generally used to sample specific frames from video, feed the sampled

© The Author(s), under exclusive license to Springer Nature Switzerland AG 2022
G. Memmi et al. (Eds.): KSEM 2022, LNAI 13369, pp. 43–56, 2022.
https://doi.org/10.1007/978-3-031-10986-7_4

frame into the designed network, and finally perform action recognition [12]. The original intention of using a specific method to sample frames is to reduce computational cost and redundant frames, making the network more suitable for long-term motion. However, the details of changes between consecutive frames will be inevitably ignored, as with random sampling and sparse sampling. The latest two-stream methods [11,17] used different time resolutions for two pathways, which avoids the problem of missing essential frames and extracts features more efficiently. Therefore, the two-stream method is more extensively utilized in action recognition Convolutional Neural Networks.

The traditional two-stream method [27] feeds optical flow and RGB separately for action recognition. Meanwhile, TSN [33], one of the variants of two-stream, provided a novel idea to process long-term action recognition tasks by segmenting in the temporal dimension. Of course, research on action recognition is not limited to 2D, and even excellent results have been obtained using 3D CNNs [18,20]. 3D CNNs will undoubtedly extract more spatiotemporal features than 2D CNNs [28]. There are two types of cells in the primate visual system, Parvocellular (P-cells) and Magnocellular (M-cells). Among them, M-cells are interested in rapid time changes, and P-cells are sensitive to significant spatial features [31]. SlowFast [11] obtained accurate spatiotemporal information more efficiently by imitating two cells. However, due to the limitation of the size of the convolution kernel, the two-stream network based on CNNs often cannot effectively model the global features, resulting in the lack of feature diversity.

Transformer achieved excellent results in the field of Natural Language Processing (NLP) [32]. In order to apply the Transformer to images, ViT [8] regarded each image as consisting of many 16×16 patches. Video and NLP, as compared to image, have a higher level of similarity, whether sequential or logical [26]. Therefore, the Transformer used in image is also suitable for video and can even achieve better performance in video research. However, when Transformer processes images, it often ignores the intrinsic structure information inside each patch, resulting in the lack of local features [14].

To shed new light on studying the applicability of CNNs architecture on Transformer, a two-stream Transformer architecture is proposed to combine local and global features more effectively. Simultaneously, to achieve precision and speed trade-off, we execute frame alignment operation to ensure that the Sparse pathway's input frames are the same as the Dense pathway's input frames. Thus, the frames feeding the Dense pathway do not need to be processed all at once, reducing the Dense pathway's computation cost. Patch crop, a new cropping method, is also designed to focus on the center of videos.

Our contributions can be summarized as follows:

- A novel architecture, **S**parse **D**ense **T**ransformer Network(SDTN), is proposed to combine two-stream method and Transformer, considerably enhancing action recognition performance.
- A new cropping approach with 16×16 as the basic unit, Patch crop, which allows the network to pay more attention to the patches in the center of videos.

– Experiments demonstrate that SDTN achieves accuracy improvements on Kinetics-400 and presented Light kinetics-400. Additionally, the frame alignment is leveraged as information aggregation method to improve the performance of SDTN.

In the remainder of the paper, we first introduce related work in Sect. 2. In Sect. 3, we illustrate the proposed model. Section 4 and Sect. 5 show the experimental results and analyze based on them. Finally, the conclusion and outlook are presented in Sect. 6.

2   Related Work

2.1   CNNs in Action Recognition

CNNs have long been the standard for the backbone architectures in action recognition. Simonyan and Zisserman proposed two-stream architecture, whose method is to combine RGB and optical flow for action recognition [27]. To some extent, the computational cost of the optical flow is relatively expensive, and researchers continue to do further research on this basis. Subsequently, TSN [33] offered an exciting solution to advance our knowledge of long-term video action recognition tasks: it segments the video into N clips in the time dimension; then, each clip is input into the two-stream network, which is effectively improved the accuracy of the action recognition in long-term videos. ECO [35] provided the ECO-Full network based on TSN, which is also a parallel of two networks.

For 3D CNNs, C3D [28] is a pioneering work that has designed an 11-layer deep network. R3D can be regarded as a combination of two outstanding research of Resnet and C3D [15,30]. I3D [7] extended 2D CNNs to 3D CNNs and showed that 3D CNNs extract features substantially more effectively than 2D CNNs. Because 3D CNNs have a lot of parameters and high computational costs, researchers are trying to lower their computational complexity to that of 2D CNNs. As a result, P3D [25] and R(2+1)D [30] have been trying to replace 3D CNNs with 2D CNNs and have achieved good results on large-scale datasets. V4D [34] achieved accuracy improvements by adding the clip dimension to 3D CNNs. The SlowFast networks [11], inspired by the biological research of retinal ganglion cells in the primate visual system, found that combining multiple time resolutions is helpful for accurate and effective action recognition in experiments.

2.2   Transformer in Action Recognition

Transformer initially achieved excellent performance in NLP, and later it was introduced into computer vision.

Rohit Girdhar et al. [13] used Transformer structure to add the information before and after the video to the final vector for classification and positioning. Then, Vision Transformer (ViT) [8] proposed a brand new idea: can continuous patches represent an image? In other words, ViT decomposes an image into 16×16 patches. Since then, ViT realized the transformation of the backbone of computer vision from CNNs to Transformer. The great success of the image Transformer has also led to the research on the architecture of the action recognition task based on the Transformer. VTN [23] proposed to add a temporal attention encoder to pre-trained ViT, which performed well on action recognition datasets. ViViT [1] was based primarily on ViT and tried to solve the video task completely using the Transformer architecture. ViViT studied four spatial and temporal attention factor designs of the pre-trained ViT model, and recommended a VTN-like architecture. The latest Video Swin Transformer [22] has made the number of tokens less and less through multiple stages, and the receptive field of each token has increased. So the computational cost of the Video Swin Transformer is reduced, while the precision and speed are both improved.

3   Sparse Dense Transformer Network

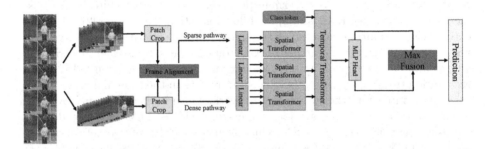

Fig. 1. Sparse Dense Transformer Network processes information with two different time resolutions. The Sparse pathway and the Dense pathway carry out patch crop operation simultaneously. After that, the frames of the two pathways undergo frame alignment and then enter their respective networks. Finally, through max fusion, the video-level prediction results are obtained.

Following the STAM [26], we use the idea of SDTN to simulate the P-cells and M-cells of the biological vision system. As shown in Fig. 1, SDTN can be described as a single stream structure with two different time resolutions as input. The Sparse pathway samples informative frames with lower temporal resolution. The Dense pathway is sampled at high temporal resolution and is sensitive to rapid temporal changes. Meanwhile, we explore how SDTN can benefit from various time resolutions, motivated by Coarse-Fine networks. Moreover, based on the intuition that the action is more concentrated in the center of the video, SDTN adopts a patch-based cropping method to make the pathway focus more on the central patches of the input frame.

In SDTN, we are confronted with two major challenges: (i) how to improve the network's accuracy while reducing the Dense pathway's computational cost; (ii) how to effectively integrate the information of the Sparse pathway and the Dense pathway. First of all, to minimize the Dense pathway's computational cost, we propose frame alignment, which is a method of ensuring that the frames sampled by the Sparse and Dense pathways are consistent, therefore reducing the amount of computing on the Dense pathway. Furthermore, to assure the accuracy of SDTN, we design different degrees of information fusion experiments to contrast the impact of various methods of fusion.

3.1 Frame Alignment

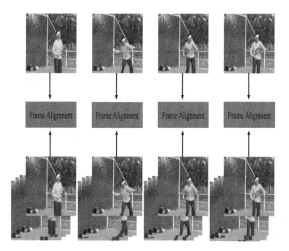

Fig. 2. Frame Alignment compares the sampled frames of the Sparse pathway and the Dense pathway. In this way, the consistency of the processing information of the Sparse pathway and the Dense pathway can be guaranteed. While ensuring the diversity of network input information, it also reduces the computational cost of the Dense pathway.

Specifically, SDTN aims to design a new two-stream Transformer architecture while maintaining the original network features to show a speed-accuracy trade-off. The Sparse and Dense pathways sample various amounts of frames from the whole video. The input to each pathway is $X \in \mathbb{R}^{H \times W \times 3 \times F}$ consists of F RGB frames of size $H \times W$ sampled from the video. During the learning process, each pathway derives the preliminary inference results and finally applies fusion approach to produce the video-level inference.

We expect the Dense pathway to assure excellent accuracy while operating with a minimum computational cost. Therefore, we design frame alignment on the original foundation to ensure the variety of the two networks' input while maintaining the consistency of the features.

As shown in Fig. 2, the Sparse pathway of SDTN samples 16 frames, and the Dense pathway samples 64 frames. Before input, we align the input frames of two networks according to the frame id. The frames of the Dense pathway are compared with the frames of the Sparse pathway before the input to determine whether the two networks' input is consistent. Accordingly, we reduce the input into the Dense pathway following this comparison, reducing the computational cost of SDTN.

3.2 Patch Crop

There should be a subject, a predicate, and an object in a sentence. If the sentence is complicated, then there are attributives and complements. When the Transformer processes a frame, it treats a frame as a complete sentence, with each patch representing a word. To this end, we try to adapt essential human thinking to the computer in this experiment. For example, when processing a sentence, we give greater attention to the subject, predicate, and object. Similarly, we believe that subjects, predicates, and objects in the image are made up of patches. Then, based on the intuition that the behavior mainly occurs in the center of videos, we consider the patches in the center of videos as the subject, predicate, and object of this frame.

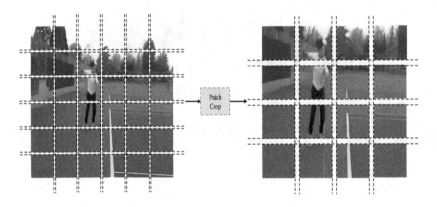

Fig. 3. Patch Crop. Sparse Dense Transformer Network is expected to focus more on the frame's center. To emphasize the significance of the center patches, we offer a novel cropping approach based on the patch as a unit.

The Sparse pathway will pay greater attention to spatial features when we utilize the Sparse pathway to simulate the P-cells in the visual neural network. Based on the intuition that more actions occur in the center of the videos, we hope that the Sparse pathway will focus on the center of the sampled frame for learning. At the same time, the Dense pathway pays some attention to spatial features while extracting temporal features, resulting in improved spatiotemporal information fusion. Therefore, we propose a new crop method called Patch crop, which allows the network to extract patch-based local features more effectively.

We build SDTN on the idea of a frame that can be decomposed into many patches of 16×16 in size. Each frame is scaled to 224×224, which means that each frame will be divided into non-overlapping 196 patches. Then, on this basis, we will first resize the frame $(H \times W)$ to $((H + 2 \times patch\_size) \times (W + 2 \times patch\_size))$. Since the Transformer architecture cannot directly process frames, 2D CNNs are used to process the image into a feature map. The feature map is then split into 256 patches, with the middle 196 patches being sampled, as shown in Fig. 3.

These patches are linearly projected onto an embedding vector after being flattened into vectors:

$$z_{(p,t)}^{(0)} = Ex_{(p,t)} + e_{(p,t)}^{pos} \tag{1}$$

Here $x_{(p,t)} \in \mathbb{R}^{3P \times P}$ is the input vector, and the embedding vector $z_{(p,t)} \in \mathbb{R}^D$ is relevant to a learnable positional embedding vector $e_{(p,t)}^{pos}$, as well as the matrix E. The indices t, and p are the frame and patch index, respectively with $t = 1, \ldots, F$, and $p = 1, \ldots, N$. When using the Transformer model for action classification, we need to add a learnable classification token to the first position of the embedding sequence $z_{(0,0)}^{(0)} \in \mathbb{R}^D$.

$$q_{(p,t)}^{(l,a)} = W_Q^{(l,a)} LN(z_{(p,t)}^{(l-1)}) \in \mathbb{R}^{D_h} \tag{2}$$

$$k_{(p,t)}^{(l,a)} = W_K^{(l,a)} LN(z_{(p,t)}^{(l-1)}) \in \mathbb{R}^{D_h} \tag{3}$$

$$v_{(p,t)}^{(l,a)} = W_V^{(l,a)} LN(z_{(p,t)}^{(l-1)}) \in \mathbb{R}^{D_h} \tag{4}$$

Each pathway consists of L encoding blocks. At each block $\ell \in \{1, \ldots, L\}$, and head $a \in \{1, \ldots, \mathcal{A}\}$, we compute a query, key, and value vector for each patch based on the representation $z_{(p,t)}^{(\ell-1)}$ encoded of the preceding block. Where LN() represents LayerNorm [2]. The dimension of each self-attention head is set to $D_h = D/A$.

$$\alpha_{(p,t)}^{(\ell,a)} = SM \left(\frac{q_{(p,t)}^{(\ell,a)\top}}{\sqrt{D_h}} \cdot \left[k_{(0,t)}^{(\ell,a)} \left\{ k_{(p',t')}^{(\ell,a)} \right\}_{\substack{p'=1,\ldots,N \\ t'=1,\ldots,F}} \right] \right) \tag{5}$$

Self-attention weights $\alpha_{(p,t)}^{(\ell,\alpha)} \in \mathbb{R}^{NF+F}$ are computed by dot-product. Where SM() represents the softmax activation function. Then, according to the research of STAM, global attention is applied to frames to realize action recognition. Finally, we utilize fusion method to combine the two networks' scores to derive the final prediction result. Formally, we employ the method of sampling and feeding twice, and separate it into two network pathways for modeling:

$$SDTN(F_s, F_d) = G(S_p(F_s), D_p(F_d)) \tag{6}$$

Here F_s stands for the Sparse frames sampled from the video, whereas F_d stands for the Dense frames sampled. To generate scores, F_s and F_d use their respective processing methods and then are fed into S_p (the Sparse pathway) and D_p (the Dense pathway). Based on the Sparse pathway and the Dense pathway scores, the fusion function G predicts the probability of each action class in the whole video. For G, we will utilize the commonly used max fusion.

4   Experiments

Implementation Details. SDTN comprises two parts: a Sparse pathway and a Dense pathway. In our experiments, each pathway strictly follows the hierarchical structure of the original STAM consisting of a spatial transformer and a temporal transformer. SDTN is one of the ViT family models and contains 12 Multi-head Self-Attention block layers, each with 12 self-attention heads. Among them, SDTN uses the imagenet-21K pretraining provided by [32]. The temporal transformer we employ only has 6-layers and 8-head self-attention since the time information is extracted at a deep level.

For inference, we use different time resolutions in the entire video to sample the frames twice and resize each frame so that the smaller dimension is 256. Then we random crop all sample frames of the video to a size of 256 × 256; we also apply random flip augmentation and auto-augment with Imagenet policy on all frames. After that, we execute patch crop to sample the central 196 patches. Finally, we use the same method for training and inference.

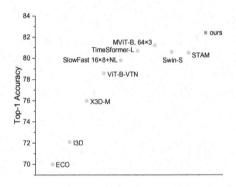

Fig. 4. Top-1 Accuracy on Kinetics-400 for the SDTN(16+64) *vs.* other networks. In terms of accuracy, SDTN is superior to previous architectures based on either CNNs, Transformer, or CNNs+Transformer.

Datasets. Kinetics-400 is a large-scale action recognition dataset, ∼240 k training videos and 20 k validation videos in 400 human action categories [19]. To further assess SDTN's performance on Kinetics-400, we build a Light kinetics-400 dataset based on Kinetics-400, allowing us to finetune our model according to the Kinetics-400 data format. The Light kinetics-400 dataset contains 400 human action categories. Especially, only five videos for each action category has been included to reduce the size of the dataset.

Training. We follow STAM and optimize from this basis. For frame alignment operation, we adjust the sampling rate and batch_size of each network to be the same.

5   Ablation Experiments

In this section, we provide the ablation experiments of SDTN on Kinetics-400 to evaluate the contributions of our two-stream Transformer architecture, frame alignment, and patch crop.

Table 1. Different frames combination

Sparse pathway	Dense pathway	Top-1 acc	Top-5 acc
16 frames	32 frames	81.93	95.52
32 frames	64 frames	81.68	95.34
16 frames	64 frames	**82.45**	**95.66**

The differences between various input frames are presented in Table 1. On the Kinetics-400 dataset, we can observe that our SDTN performs best when the Sparse pathway is 16 frames, and the Dense pathway input is 64 frames. However, when the Sparse pathway is 16 frames, and the Dense pathway is 64 frames, the input strategy is more accurate than when the Sparse path is 32 frames. This is because the Sparse pathway pays more attention to spatial information, and adding additional frames does not result in a significant increase in spatial information. Conversely, redundant frames increase computational cost and result in performance degradation.

On the Kinetics-400 dataset, we compare our approach with others. Table 2 indicates that, even when the number of GPUs is 4, each combination of input frames in SDTN can enhance accuracy and exceed the baseline. In Fig. 4, our model (82.45%) outperforms STAM's previous state-of-the-art by 1.95%.

Although SDTN does not reach SOTA accuracy, it shows promise as an effective Transformer model, that is, one that can explore the potential of a novel backbone based on conventional deep learning frameworks.

We design different patch crop experiments on SDTN(16+64). All Pathway means patch crop on the Dense pathway and the Sparse pathway simultaneously. As shown in Table 3, the effect of patch crop on the Sparse pathway is better than that on the Dense pathway, which is also constant with our intuition. The Sparse pathway pays extra attention to spatial features, making it more suitable for patch crop. Although the patch crop on the Dense pathway can exceed the baseline, the improvement is not significant for comparing with patch crop on the Sparse pathway. All Pathway performs well because in addition to extracting more spatial features, it can also better integrate spatiotemporal information. Actually, patch crop is more like extracting abstracts from a sentence.

Table 2. Comparision with other model on Kinetics-400

Model	Pretrain	Top-1 acc [%]	Top-5 acc [%]	Param [M]
I3D [7]	ImageNet-1K	72.1	90.3	25.0
X3D-M [10]	–	76.0	92.3	3.8
ip-CSN-152 [29]	–	77.8	92.8	32.8
ViT-B-VTN [23]	ImageNet-21K	78.6	93.7	114.0
X3D-XL [10]	–	79.1	93.9	11.0
SlowFast 16×8+NL [11]	–	79.8	93.9	59.9
MViT-B, 32×3 [9]		80.2	94.4	36.6
TimeSformer-L [3]	ImageNet-21K	80.7	94.7	121.4
MViT-B, 64×3 [9]	–	81.2	95.1	36.6
ViViT-L/16x2 320 [1]	ImageNet-21K	81.3	94.7	310.8
Swin-T [22]	ImageNet-1K	78.8	93.6	28.2
Swin-S [22]	ImageNet-1K	80.6	94.5	49.8
STAM(baseline) [26]	ImageNet-21K	80.5	–	96.0
SDTN(16+32)	ImageNet-21K	**81.9**	**95.5**	192.0
SDTN(32+64)	ImageNet-21K	**81.6**	**95.3**	192.0
SDTN(16+64)	ImageNet-21K	**82.4**	**95.6**	192.0

Table 3. Different patch crop pathway

Patch crop pathway	Top-1 acc	Top-5 acc
Dense pathway	82.11	95.50
Sparse pathway	82.31	95.65
All pathway	**82.45**	**95.66**

We compare the complete SDTN(16+64) with SDTN that only uses frame alignment or patch crop in Table 4. As can be seen from the table, both frame alignment and patch crop can enhance the accuracy of the network, surpassing some of the existing Transformer architectures.

Table 4. Frame alignment vs patch crop

Method	Top-1 acc	Top-5 acc
Only frame alignment	82.15	95.48
Only patch crop	81.68	95.54
Full SDTN	**82.45**	**95.66**

In Table 5, we employ several fusion strategies in order to achieve the full potential of SDTN(16+64). Among them, the weight fusion is inspired by Slow-Fast networks [11]. The P-cells and M-cells are interested in spatial and temporal

Table 5. Different fusion methods

Fusion method	Top-1 acc	Top-5 acc
AVG	79.51	94.23
Weight fusion	79.84	94.38
Max	**82.45**	**95.66**

features and account for ~80% and ~15–20% of the visual system, respectively. Consequently, we apply this ratio to SDTN, which combines the Dense pathway score of 20% and the Sparse pathway score of 80%.

The max fusion method is the most effective in experiments. That is because different actions have different requirements for temporal and spatial features. For example, recognizing some actions emphasizes spatial features, while others pay more attention to temporal features. The max fusion will select recognition results with more significant features and higher accuracy.

Table 6. Comparision on Light kinetics-400

Model	Pretrain	Top-1 acc	Top-5 acc
STAM(baseline)	ImageNet-21K	93.93	99.61
SDTN(16+32)	ImageNet-21K	**95.59**	**99.80**
SDTN(32+64)	ImageNet-21K	**95.40**	**99.80**
SDTN(16+64)	ImageNet-21K	**95.69**	**99.80**

Finally, as shown in Table 6, we evaluate the performance of baseline and SDTN on Light kinetics-400. It can be seen that when the size of the dataset decreases, the accuracy of the network rises substantially. On Light kinetics-400, the experimental results are consistent with the performance of SDTN on Kinetic-400, indicating that the dataset and SDTN are competent for the task of action recognition.

6   Conclusion

In this paper, a novel model Sparse Dense Transformer Network, a two-stream Transformer architecture, was proposed for action recognition. Patch crop was a new kind of cropping based on patch, which helps the network pays more attention to the patch in the center of the image. Frame alignment was adopted to assist the Dense pathway in selecting frames for input consistent with the Sparse pathway, improving accuracy while reducing the computational cost. The results of ablation experiments also show that the max fusion is the best fusion method for SDTN. Through extensive experiments in benchmarks, SDTN shows its superiority compared with the previous models, achieving 82.45% accuracy on the Kinetics-400. In the latter research, the extraction of local features for the patch will be considered into two-stream Transformer network for action recognition.

References

1. Arnab, A., Dehghani, M., Heigold, G., Sun, C., Lučić, M., Schmid, C.: ViViT: a video vision transformer. arXiv preprint arXiv:2103.15691 (2021)
2. Ba, J.L., Kiros, J.R., Hinton, G.E.: Layer normalization. arXiv preprint arXiv:1607.06450 (2016)
3. Bertasius, G., Wang, H., Torresani, L.: Is space-time attention all you need for video understanding? arXiv preprint arXiv:2102.05095 (2021)
4. Cao, W.P., et al.: An ensemble fuzziness-based online sequential learning approach and its application. In: International Conference on Knowledge Science, Engineering and Management (KSEM), pp. 255–267 (2021)
5. Cao, W., Xie, Z., Li, J., Xu, Z., Ming, Z., Wang, X.: Bidirectional stochastic configuration network for regression problems. Neural Netw. **140**, 237–246 (2021)
6. Cao, W., Yang, P., Ming, Z., Cai, S., Zhang, J.: An improved fuzziness based random vector functional link network for liver disease detection. In: 2020 IEEE 6th International Conference on Big Data Security on Cloud (BigDataSecurity), IEEE International Conference on High Performance and Smart Computing, (HPSC) and IEEE International Conference on Intelligent Data and Security (IDS), pp. 42–48 (2020)
7. Carreira, J., Zisserman, A.: Quo Vadis, action recognition? A new model and the kinetics dataset. In: Proceedings of the IEEE Conference on Computer Vision and Pattern Recognition (CVPR), pp. 6299–6308 (2017)
8. Dosovitskiy, A., et al.: An image is worth 16 × 16 words: transformers for image recognition at scale. arXiv preprint arXiv:2010.11929 (2020)
9. Fan, H., et al.: Multiscale vision transformers. arXiv preprint arXiv:2104.11227 (2021)
10. Feichtenhofer, C.: X3D: expanding architectures for efficient video recognition. In: Proceedings of the IEEE Conference on Computer Vision and Pattern Recognition (CVPR), pp. 203–213 (2020)
11. Feichtenhofer, C., Fan, H., Malik, J., He, K.: SlowFast networks for video recognition. In: Proceedings of the IEEE International Conference on Computer Vision (ICCV), pp. 6202–6211 (2019)
12. Gao, R., Oh, T.H., Grauman, K., Torresani, L.: Listen to look: action recognition by previewing audio. In: Proceedings of the IEEE Conference on Computer Vision and Pattern Recognition (CVPR), pp. 10457–10467 (2020)
13. Girdhar, R., Carreira, J., Doersch, C., Zisserman, A.: Video action transformer network. In: Proceedings of the IEEE Conference on Computer Vision and Pattern Recognition (CVPR), pp. 244–253 (2019)
14. Han, K., Xiao, A., Wu, E., Guo, J., Xu, C., Wang, Y.: Transformer in transformer. arXiv preprint arXiv:2103.00112 (2021)
15. He, K., Zhang, X., Ren, S., Sun, J.: Deep residual learning for image recognition. In: Proceedings of the IEEE Conference on Computer Vision and Pattern Recognition (CVPR), pp. 770–778 (2016)

16. Hu, F., Lakdawala, S., Hao, Q., Qiu, M.: Low-power, intelligent sensor hardware interface for medical data preprocessing. IEEE Trans. Inf Technol. Biomed. **13**(4), 656–663 (2009)
17. Kahatapitiya, K., Ryoo, M.S.: Coarse-fine networks for temporal activity detection in videos. In: Proceedings of the IEEE Conference on Computer Vision and Pattern Recognition (CVPR), pp. 8385–8394 (2021)
18. Kalfaoglu, M.E., Kalkan, S., Alatan, A.A.: Late temporal modeling in 3D CNN architectures with BERT for action recognition. In: Bartoli, A., Fusiello, A. (eds.) ECCV 2020. LNCS, vol. 12539, pp. 731–747. Springer, Cham (2020). https://doi. org/10.1007/978-3-030-68238-5_48
19. Kay, W., et al.: The kinetics human action video dataset. arXiv preprint arXiv:1705.06950 (2017)
20. Li, J., Liu, X., Zhang, W., Zhang, M., Song, J., Sebe, N.: Spatio-temporal attention networks for action recognition and detection. IEEE Trans. Multimedia **22**(11), 2990–3001 (2020)
21. Li, Y., Song, Y., Jia, L., Gao, S., Li, Q., Qiu, M.: Intelligent fault diagnosis by fusing domain adversarial training and maximum mean discrepancy via ensemble learning. IEEE Trans. Industr. Inf. **17**(4), 2833–2841 (2020)
22. Liu, Z., et al.: Video Swin transformer. arXiv preprint arXiv:2106.13230 (2021)
23. Neimark, D., Bar, O., Zohar, M., Asselmann, D.: Video transformer network. arXiv preprint arXiv:2102.00719 (2021)
24. Qiu, H., Zheng, Q., Msahli, M., Memmi, G., Qiu, M., Lu, J.: Topological graph convolutional network-based urban traffic flow and density prediction. IEEE Trans. Intell. Transp. Syst. **22**(7), 4560–4569 (2020)
25. Qiu, Z., Yao, T., Mei, T.: Learning spatio-temporal representation with pseudo-3d residual networks. In: Proceedings of the IEEE International Conference on Computer Vision (ICCV), pp. 5533–5541 (2017)
26. Sharir, G., Noy, A., Zelnik-Manor, L.: An image is worth 16 × 16 words, what is a video worth? arXiv preprint arXiv:2103.13915 (2021)
27. Simonyan, K., Zisserman, A.: Two-stream convolutional networks for action recognition in videos. arXiv preprint arXiv:1406.2199 (2014)
28. Tran, D., Bourdev, L., Fergus, R., Torresani, L., Paluri, M.: Learning spatiotemporal features with 3d convolutional networks. In: Proceedings of the IEEE International Conference on Computer Vision (ICCV), pp. 4489–4497 (2015)
29. Tran, D., Wang, H., Torresani, L., Feiszli, M.: Video classification with channel-separated convolutional networks. In: Proceedings of the IEEE International Conference on Computer Vision (ICCV), pp. 5552–5561 (2019)
30. Tran, D., Wang, H., Torresani, L., Ray, J., LeCun, Y., Paluri, M.: A closer look at spatiotemporal convolutions for action recognition. In: Proceedings of the IEEE Conference on Computer Vision and Pattern Recognition (CVPR), pp. 6450–6459 (2018)
31. Van Essen, D.C., Gallant, J.L.: Neural mechanisms of form and motion processing in the primate visual system. Neuron **13**(1), 1–10 (1994)
32. Vaswani, A., et al.: Attention is all you need. In: Advances in Neural Information Processing Systems (NIPS), pp. 5998–6008 (2017)
33. Wang, L., et al.: Temporal segment networks: towards good practices for deep action recognition. In: Leibe, B., Matas, J., Sebe, N., Welling, M. (eds.) ECCV 2016. LNCS, vol. 9912, pp. 20–36. Springer, Cham (2016). https://doi.org/10.1007/ 978-3-319-46484-8_2

34. Zhang, S., Guo, S., Huang, W., Scott, M.R., Wang, L.: V4D: 4d convolutional neural networks for video-level representation learning. arXiv preprint arXiv:2002.07442 (2020)
35. Zolfaghari, M., Singh, K., Brox, T.: ECO: efficient convolutional network for online video understanding. In: Ferrari, V., Hebert, M., Sminchisescu, C., Weiss, Y. (eds.) ECCV 2018. LNCS, vol. 11206, pp. 713–730. Springer, Cham (2018). https://doi.org/10.1007/978-3-030-01216-8_43

Deep User Multi-interest Network for Click-Through Rate Prediction

Ming Wu[1], Junqian Xing[2], and Shanxiong Chen[1(✉)]

[1] College of Computer and Information Science, Southwest University, Chongqing, China
csxpml@163.com
[2] Faculty of Engineering, University of Sydney, Sydney, NSW, Australia

Abstract. Click-through rate (CTR) prediction is widely used in recommendation systems. Accurately modeling user interest is the key to improve the performance of CTR prediction task. Existing methods pay attention to model user interest from a single perspective to reflect user preferences, ignoring user different interests in different aspects, thus limiting the expressive ability of user interest. In this paper, we propose a novel Deep User Multi-Interest Network (DUMIN) which designs Self-Interest Extraction Network (SIEN) and User-User Interest Extraction Network (UIEN) to capture user different interests. First, SIEN uses attention mechanism and sequential network to focus on different parts in self-interest. Meanwhile, an auxiliary loss network is used to bring extra supervision for model training. Next, UIEN adopts multi-headed self-attention mechanism to learn a unified interest representation for each user who interacted with the candidate item. Then, attention mechanism is introduced to adaptively aggregate these interest representations to obtain user-user interest, which reflects the collaborative filtering information among users. Extensive experimental results on public real-world datasets show that proposed DUMIN outperforms various state-of-the-art methods.

Keywords: Recommender system · CTR prediction · Multi-interest learning · Multi-headed attention mechanism · Deep learning · Auxiliary loss

1 Introduction

In modern recommendation systems, users behave diversely, including collecting and purchasing, which are subsequent behaviors preceded by the basic behavior: click. In cost per click (CPC) advertising systems, effective cost per mille (eCPM) is calculated by production of advertisement bid price and click-through rate (CTR), which is used to rank advertisements. The CTR requires model prediction, whose performance has direct influence on user experience and corporate profit. Hence, CTR prediction has attracted extensive research in industry and academia [4, 10, 17].

In recommended scene, users have a variety of click interests. For instance, users may click on completely unrelated items such as clothes and electronic devices at a same time in E-commerce. Therefore, aiming at CTR prediction task, accurately capturing user interests in extenso is the key to improve model performance. With the

© The Author(s), under exclusive license to Springer Nature Switzerland AG 2022
G. Memmi et al. (Eds.): KSEM 2022, LNAI 13369, pp. 57–69, 2022.
https://doi.org/10.1007/978-3-031-10986-7_5

development of deep learning, some models based on DNN have been proposed to capture user interest. For instance, DIN [19] believes user behaviors contain a variety of interests, utilizing an attention mechanism to adaptively learn user interest in candidate item. However, it does not address the dependence of interests and lacks the ability of capturing interest transfer with time shift. DIEN [18] utilizes GRU [3] and attention mechanism respectively to model the representation and evolution of interest. While DIEN neglects to capture similarities between users to reflect user preferences. Since the similarity among users can reflect the target user preferences [1], DUMN [8] first learns a unified interest representation for target user and relevant users (**that is, users who have interacted with the candidate item**), and then aggregates these interests according to their similarities. DUMN has further enriched user interest by incorporating relevant information among users. However, it independently learns the interest of each user, and has not established a similar mapping between target user and relevant users, thus failing to fully exploit the collaborative filtering information among users. Most existing models simply put a single perspective into consideration of user interest, while user interests are diverse. Capturing multiple interests in different aspects is of significance to user interest representation.

Based on the observations above, this paper proposes a novel Deep User Multi-Interest Network (DUMIN) that designing Self-Interest Extraction Network (SIEN) and User-User Interest Extraction Network (UIEN) to process multiple different interests to predict CTR. Firstly, in SIEN, Direct Interest Extraction Layer adaptively extracts direct interest by using attention mechanism to measure the correlation between user behavior and the candidate item. Meanwhile, Evolutionary Interest Extraction Layer explicitly extracts the potential interest at each moment from user behavior and regards the last potential interest as evolutionary interest. Next, in UIEN, User Interest Representation Layer uses a multi-head self-attention mechanism to establish a similar interest mapping between target user and relevant users, thus amplifying the collaborative filtering signals among users. User Interest Match Layer adaptly matches interests between target user and each relevant user to aggregate similar interests from User Interest Representation Layer. Finally, a variety of different interests extracted by SIEN and UIEN, candidate item and context are concatenated and fed into Multilayer Perceptron (MLP) to predict CTR. The main contribution of this paper are summarized as follows:

- We point out the importance of multi-interest modeling user interest representation, and propose a novel model called DUMIN that extracts multiple user interests modeling CTR prediction task.
- We utilize a multi-head self-attention mechanism to learn the similar interest between the target user and relevant users in different representation subspaces, amplifying the collaborative filtering singals among users.
- Extensive experiments on public real-world datasets prove that the proposed DUMIN has significant advantages over several state-of-the-art baselines, and our code is publicly available for reproducible[1].

In the following part of this paper, we first review the related work in Sect. 2. Then, we introduce our model in detail in Sect. 3. Next, we conduct extensive experiments to verify the effectiveness of our model in Sect. 4. Finally, the conclusions and future outlooks are presented in Sect. 5.

---

[1] https://github.com/MrnotRight/DUMIN.

2   Related Works

With the widespread application of deep learning [4, 20, 21], deep learning models have been proved to possess great advantages in feature interaction and combination. Traditional linear models, such as LR [12], FM [14], etc., use linear combination and matrix factorization to model CTR prediction task, which pay little attention to capture high-order feature interactions and nonlinear features, and limit the expression ability of model. Wide&Deep [2] combines linear combination and neural network cross features to enhance model expression ability, while the wide part still needs manual designed. DeepFM [5] supersedes the wide part with FM on the basis of Wide&Deep, which avoids feature engineering and improves the ability of capturing second-order features. Limited by combinatorial explosion, FM is difficult to extend to high-order forms. NFM [6] combines FM with DNN to model high-order feature. Besides, PNN [13] introduces outer product and inner product operations to specifically enhance the interaction of different features, making it easier for the model to capture cross-information. However, these methods directly model feature interactions, and rarely pay attention to the abundant interest patterns implied in user's historical behavior data.

In order to dig out the rich information in user's historical behavior data, GRU4REC [7] applies GRU to model the evolution of items in user behavior, while it not pay attention to learn the user interest representation. The attention mechanism is introduced in DIN to learn interest representation from user's historical data, and it's application adequately captures the diversity of user interest. DIEN believes that the user interest migrate with temporal variation. Therefore, DIEN chooses GRU to extract the interests in user behaviors, and adaptively model the evolution of user interest in the candidate item by the attention mechanism. To model user interest representation in multiple subspaces, DMIN [16] introduces a multi-head self-attention mechanism to model the interests in different subspaces. DMR [11] designs user-item network and item-item network to employ different relevances to derive user interests in candidate item. The relevance among users can strengthen the collaborative filtering signals, which are able to learn accurate personalized preferences for users [1]. DUMN employs the correlation between users to improve the accuracy of interest representation learning, thereby improving the performance of the model. Although these methods fully exploit the potential interests of user historical behavior data, they rarely focus on enriching user interest representation modeling from multiple perspectives.

The works mentioned above improve the CTR prediction task through different modeling approaches. However, none of them attempted to learn user multiple interests from different aspects. In a real recommendation scenario, users often have a variety of different interests. Motivated by this, we refer to the interests learned from the user historical behavior data as self-interest, and those from relevant users as user-user interest. Moreover, the self-interest is subdivided into direct interest in the candidate item and evolutionary interest in user behavior. In DUMIN, on the one hand, we extract direct interest and evolutionary interest separately to form self-interest. On the other hand, we use self-interest as query to model the interest similarities between the target user and relevant users in different representation subspaces through the multi-head self-attention mechanism. In this way, we learn a variety of different interests for users, and capture the similarity relationship between self-interest and user-user interest, thereby

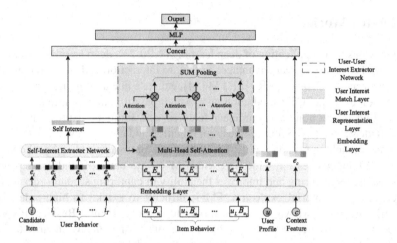

Fig. 1. DUMIN framework. Fed the candidate item and the target user behavior into SIEN to extract self-interest, and then fed self-interest and the candidate item behavior into UIEN to extract user-user interest. These two interests are concatenated to form the user interest representation for subsequent prediction of CTR via MLP.

amplifying the collaborative filtering signals among users, making the user interest representation more abundant and more accurate.

3   The Proposed Model

3.1   Preliminaries

There are five categories of features in DUMIN: *User Profile, Candidate Item, Context, User Behavior* and *Item Behavior*. Among them, *User Profile* contains *user ID*; *Candidate Item* contains *item ID,category ID*, etc.; Features in *Context* are *time, location* and so on. *User Behavior* and *Item Behavior* are defined as follows:

User Behavior. *Given a user u, the user behavior $\mathbf{B}_u$ is a time-sorted list of items that user u has interacted with. Each item has features such as item ID, category ID, etc. $\mathbf{B}_u$ is formalized as $\mathbf{B}_u = [i_1, i_2, ..., i_{T_u}]$, in which i_t is the t-th interacted item, and T_u is the length of $\mathbf{B}_u$.*

Item Behavior. *Given an item i, the item behavior $\mathbf{N}_i$ is a time-sorted list of users who has interacted with item i. Each user contains features such as user ID, user behavior, etc. $\mathbf{N}_i$ is formalized as $\mathbf{N}_i = [(u_1, \mathbf{B}_{u_1}), (u_2, \mathbf{B}_{u_2}), ..., (u_{L_i}, \mathbf{B}_{u_{L_i}})]$, in which u_t is the t-th interacted user, $\mathbf{B}_{u_t}$ is the user behavior of u_t, and L_i is the length of $\mathbf{N}_i$.*

3.2   Embedding

The category features used in DUMIN need to be encoded to low-dimensional dense features that facilitate deep neural network learning. This is widely implemented in

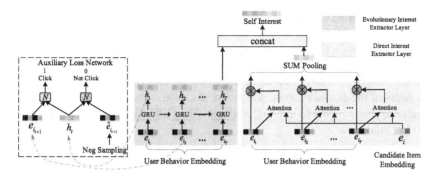

Fig. 2. The architecture of Self-Interest Extractor Network. The green part employs GRU and the auxiliary loss network to extract evolutionary interest from user behavior, and the yellow part employs the attention mechanism to extract user direct interest in candidate item. Concatenate these two interests to form self-interest representation. (Color figure online)

CTR prediction models based on deep learning [11,19]. Target user u, candidate item i, context c, user behavior $\mathbf{B}_u$ and item behavior $\mathbf{N}_i$ go through the embedding layer to obtain embedding vectors $\mathbf{e}_u$, $\mathbf{e}_i$, $\mathbf{e}_c$, $\mathbf{E}_u$ and $\mathbf{X}_i$, where $\mathbf{E}_u = [\mathbf{e}_{i_1}, \mathbf{e}_{i_2}, ..., \mathbf{e}_{i_{T_u}}]$, $\mathbf{X}_i = [(\mathbf{e}_{u_1}, \mathbf{E}_{u_1}), (\mathbf{e}_{u_2}, \mathbf{E}_{u_2}), ..., (\mathbf{e}_{u_{L_i}}, \mathbf{E}_{u_{L_i}})]$.

3.3 Self-Interest Extractor Network

In this subsection, we will introduce the details of SIEN in DUMIN. As shown in Fig. 2, SIEN captures the user self-interest from two different aspects. Direct Interest Extractor Layer extracts interest based on the correlation between user behavior and the candidate item; Evolutionary Interest Extractor Layer only focus on interest evolution in user behavior. Concatenate the two interests to obtain the self-interest for subsequent usage.

Direct Interest Extractor Layer. Direct Interest Extractor Layer measures the correlation between user behavior and the candidate item through the attention mechanism, reflecting the user preference in the candidate item. In this paper, we adopts the interest extraction method that is used in DIN [19], and the formulas are as follows:

$$\hat{\alpha}_t = \mathbf{Z}_d^T \sigma(\mathbf{W}_{d_1} \mathbf{e}_{i_t} + \mathbf{W}_{d_2} \mathbf{e}_i + \mathbf{b}_d) \tag{1}$$

$$\alpha_t = \frac{exp(\hat{\alpha}_t)}{\Sigma_{j=1}^{T_u} exp(\hat{\alpha}_j)}, \quad \mathbf{s}_d = \sum_{j=1}^{T_u} \alpha_j \mathbf{e}_{i_j} \tag{2}$$

where $\mathbf{e}_{i_t}, \mathbf{e}_i \in \mathbb{R}^D$ are the embedding vectors of the t-th interacted item in the target user behavior and the candidate item, respectively. $\mathbf{W}_{d_1}, \mathbf{W}_{d_2} \in \mathbb{R}^{H_d \times D}$, and $\mathbf{Z}_d, \mathbf{b}_d \in \mathbb{R}^{H_d}$ are network learning parameters, α_t is the normalized attention weight for the t-th interacted item, T_u is the length of target user behavior, σ is sigmoid activation function. $\mathbf{s}_d$ is the target user direct interest in the candidate item, formed by sum pooling the embedding vectors of items in user behavior via the attention weight.

Evolution Interest Extractor Layer. It has been proposed in DIEN that user interest evolution over time [18]. Inspired by this, Evolutionary Interest Extractor Layer also utilizes GRU to extract the interest state at each moment in user behavior. Unlike in DIEN, we do not pay attention to the correlation between the interest state and the candidate item. We merely care about capturing an evolutionary interest completely independent of the candidate item, which directly reflects the user preference when the user behavior has evolved to the final moment. The GRU models evolutionary interest can be formulated as:

$$\mathbf{u}_t = \sigma(\mathbf{W}_u \mathbf{e}_{i_t} + \mathbf{V}_u \mathbf{h}_{t-1} + \mathbf{b}_u) \tag{3}$$

$$\mathbf{r}_t = \sigma(\mathbf{W}_r \mathbf{e}_{i_t} + \mathbf{V}_r \mathbf{h}_{t-1} + \mathbf{b}_r) \tag{4}$$

$$\hat{\mathbf{h}}_t = tanh(\mathbf{W}_h \mathbf{e}_{i_t} + \mathbf{r}_t \circ \mathbf{V}_h \mathbf{h}_{t-1} + \mathbf{b}_h) \tag{5}$$

$$\mathbf{h}_t = (1 - \mathbf{u}_t) \circ \mathbf{h}_{t-1} + \mathbf{u}_t \circ \hat{\mathbf{h}}_t \tag{6}$$

where $\circ$ is element-wise product, $\mathbf{W}_u, \mathbf{W}_r, \mathbf{W}_h \in \mathbb{R}^{E \times D}$, $\mathbf{V}_u, \mathbf{V}_r, \mathbf{V}_h \in \mathbb{R}^{E \times E}$, $\mathbf{b}_u, \mathbf{b}_r, \mathbf{b}_h \in \mathbb{R}^E$ are learning parameters in GRU, $\mathbf{h}_t \in \mathbb{R}^E$ is t-th hidden states, E is the hidden dimension. For maximize the correlation between evolutionary interest and item, this paper introduces auxiliary loss network to supervise the learning of them. To construct the auxiliary loss network input samples, for each hidden state in the GRU, use the next clicked item in user behavior as a positive example, and randomly sample one item from all items as a negative example. Auxiliary loss can be formulated as:

$$L_{aux} = -\frac{1}{N}(\sum_{i=1}^{N} \sum_t log\varphi(concat(\mathbf{h}_t, \mathbf{e}_{i_{t+1}}))$$
$$+ log(1 - \varphi(concat(\mathbf{h}_t, \hat{\mathbf{e}}_{i_{t+1}})))) \tag{7}$$

where N is size of the training set, $\hat{\mathbf{e}}_{i_t}$ represents the embedding of t-th unclicked item generated by random negative sampling. φ is the auxiliary loss network whose output layer activation function is sigmoid. Regard the final hidden state in the GRU as the evolutionary interest, and concatenate it with direct interest to form self-interest of the target user. The formulation is listed as follows:

$$\mathbf{s}_u = concat(\mathbf{s}_d, \mathbf{h}_{T_u}) \tag{8}$$

where $\mathbf{s}_d, \mathbf{h}_{T_u}$ and $\mathbf{s}_u$ are the direct interest, evolutionary interest and self-interest of the target user u, respectively.

3.4   User-User Interest Extractor Network

The architecture of User-User Interest Extractor Network (UIEN) is shown in Fig. 1. First, the self-interest extracted from the SIEN is fed into User Interest Representation Layer to learn the unified similar interests between the target user and relevant users. Then, in User Interest Match Layer, all similar interests are aggregated by user-to-user relevance. In the next two subsections, we will introduce UIEN in detail.

User Interest Representation Layer. In User Interest Representation Layer, the objective is to learn a unified interest representation for each relevant user in the candidate item behavior. Existing methods directly measure the item-item correlation between user behavior and the candidate item to extract interest representation, which focus on the correlation of user and item. However, they are not suitable reflections of the correlation among users. In this paper, we utilize a multi-head self-attention mechanism, employing the self-interest as the query to capture the similarities between the target user and each relevant user. Note that the query is only generated by the self-interest. For the relevant user u_m, we can formalize the calculation in the User Interest Representation Layer as follows:

$$\mathbf{H}_{u_m} = concat(\mathbf{s}_u, \mathbf{E}_{u_m}) \tag{9}$$

$$\mathbf{Q} = \mathbf{W}^Q \mathbf{s}_u, \quad \mathbf{K} = \mathbf{W}^K \mathbf{H}_{u_m}, \quad \mathbf{V} = \mathbf{W}^V \mathbf{H}_{u_m} \tag{10}$$

where $\mathbf{E}_{u_m}$ is the user behavior embedding of u_m, $\mathbf{W}^Q$, $\mathbf{W}^K$ and $\mathbf{W}^V$ are projection matrices. $\mathbf{Q}, \mathbf{K}$ and $\mathbf{V}$ are query, key and value, respectively. Self-attention is calculated as:

$$Attention(\mathbf{Q}, \mathbf{K}, \mathbf{V}) = softmax(\frac{\mathbf{Q}\mathbf{K}^T}{\sqrt{d_k}})\mathbf{V} \tag{11}$$

d_k is the dimension of query, key, and value. The similar interest representation in j-th subspaces is calculated as:

$$head_j = Attention(\mathbf{W}_j^Q \mathbf{s}_u, \mathbf{W}_j^K \mathbf{H}_{u_m}, \mathbf{W}_j^V \mathbf{H}_{u_m}) \tag{12}$$

$\mathbf{W}_j^Q \in \mathbb{R}^{d_k \times (E+D)}$, $\mathbf{W}_j^K, \mathbf{W}_j^V \in \mathbb{R}^{d_k \times (E+(T_u+1)*D)}$ are weighting matrices for the j-th head. For capturing the similarities in different representation subspaces [15], we concatenate the multi-head calculation results as a unified interest representation of each relevant user, which is formalized as:

$$\mathbf{r}_{u_m} = concat(\mathbf{e}_{u_m}, head_1, head_2, ..., head_N) \tag{13}$$

$\mathbf{e}_{u_m}$ is the embedding of user u_m, N is the number of heads.

User Interest Match Layer. In User Interest Match Layer, the target is to learn adaptive weights for each similar interest of relevant users, so as to aggregate these similar interests by learned weights to obtain the final user-user interest. Thus, the attention mechanism is implemented to calculate the similarity weights as follows:

$$\hat{\eta}_m = \mathbf{V}_a^T \sigma(\mathbf{W}_{a_1} \mathbf{s}_u + \mathbf{W}_{a_2} \mathbf{r}_{u_m} + \mathbf{b}_a) \tag{14}$$

$$\eta_m = \frac{exp(\hat{\eta}_m)}{\sum_{j=1}^{L_i} exp(\hat{\eta}_j)}, \quad \mathbf{r}_u = \sum_{j=1}^{L_i} \eta_j \mathbf{r}_{u_j} \tag{15}$$

where $\mathbf{W}_{a_1} \in \mathbb{R}^{H \times (E+D)}$, $\mathbf{W}_{a_2} \in \mathbb{R}^{H \times (D+N*d_k)}$, $\mathbf{V}_a, \mathbf{b}_a \in \mathbb{R}^H$ are learning parameters. η_m represents the similarity weight between the target user and relevant user. L_i is item behavior length of the candidate item i. $\mathbf{r}_u$ represents the user-user interest of target user u, which is derived by sum pooling the similarity weight between each relevant user and u.

3.5   Prediction and Optimization Objective

Prediction. The vector representation of self-interest, user-user interest, candidate item, user profile, context are concatenated. Then fed them into MLP for predicting the click probability of target user on candidate item. Formally:

$$\mathbf{input} = concat(\mathbf{s}_u, \mathbf{r}_u, \mathbf{e}_u, \mathbf{e}_i, \mathbf{e}_c) \tag{16}$$

$$p = MLP(\mathbf{input}) \tag{17}$$

The activation function used in the hidden layer of MLP is PReLU, and the output layer of that is sigmoid activation function for normalizing the click probability from 0 to 1.
Optimization Objective. We adopt the most commonly used negative log-likelihood target loss for CTR model training, which is formalized as follows:

$$L_{target} = -\frac{1}{N} \sum_{i=1}^{N} (y_i log(p_i) + (1 - y_i) log(1 - p_i)) \tag{18}$$

where N is the size of the training set, p_i represents the predicted CTR of the i-th sample, $y_i \in \{0, 1\}$ represents the click label. Considering with the auxiliary loss mentioned above, the final optimization objective of our model can be represent as:

$$Loss = L_{target} + \beta \cdot L_{aux} \tag{19}$$

where β is a hyperparameter, which is to balance the weight of the auxiliary loss and the target loss.

4   Experiments

In this section, firstly, we will compare DUMIN with several state-of-the-art methods on public real-world datasets to verify the effectiveness of our model. Then, an ablation study is designed to explore the influence of each part in DUMIN. Finally, the effects of some hyperparameters is analyzed.

Table 1. The statistics of the three datasets

Dataset	#Users	#Items	#Categories	#Reviews	#Samples
Beauty	22363	12101	221	198502	352278
Sports	35598	18357	1073	296337	521478
Grocery	14681	8713	129	151254	273146

Table 2. The bolded result is the best of all methods, and the underlined result is the best result of baselines.

Model	Beauty		Sports		Grocery	
	AUC	Logloss	AUC	Logloss	AUC	Logloss
SVD++	0.6867	0.6831	0.7070	0.6347	0.6385	0.8306
Wide&Deep	0.8064	0.5516	0.7926	0.5488	0.6823	0.6634
PNN	0.8081	0.5509	0.8012	0.5408	0.7033	0.6324
DIN	0.8178	0.5375	0.8074	0.5334	0.7053	0.6284
GRU4Rec	0.8416	0.4923	0.8136	0.5263	0.7949	0.5360
DIEN	0.8530	0.4811	<u>0.8225</u>	<u>0.5167</u>	0.7875	0.5472
DUMN	<u>0.8555</u>	<u>0.4796</u>	0.8173	0.5227	<u>0.8107</u>	<u>0.5159</u>
DUMIN-AN[a]	0.8617	0.4603	0.8244	0.5132	0.8053	0.5216
DUMIN	**0.8721**	**0.4429**	**0.8325**	**0.5041**	**0.8225**	**0.5035**
Improvement	**+1.94%**	**−7.65%**	**+1.22%**	**−2.44%**	**+1.46%**	**−2.40%**

[a] DUMIN without auxiliary loss network.

4.1 Datasets

We conduct experiments on three public real-word subsets of Beauty, Sports, and Grocery in the Amazon dataset[2]. Each dataset contains product reviews and metadata. For the CTR prediction task, we regard all product reviews as positive samples of click. First, sort the product reviews in ascending order according to the timestamp to construct user behaviors and item behaviors. Then, randomly select another item from the unclicked items to replace the item in each review to construct the negative samples. Finally, according to the timestamp, split the former 85% part of the entire dataset as the training set, and the remaining 15% as the testing set. The statistics of datasets are summarized in Table 1.

4.2 Competitors and Parameter Settings

Competitors. We compared DUMIN with the following state-of-the-art methods to evaluate the effectiveness of it:

- **SVD++** [9]. It is a matrix factorization method that combines domain information. In our experiments, we use item behavior as domain information.
- **Wide&Deep** [2]. Wide&Deep combines wide and deep parts for linear combination features and cross features, respectively.
- **PNN** [13]. PNN introduces outer product and inner product in the product layer to learn abundant feature interactions.
- **DIN** [19]. DIN implements the attention mechanism to adaptively learn diverse interest representations in user behavior.

---

[2] http://jmcauley.ucsd.edu/data/amazon/.

- **GRU4Rec** [7]. GRU4Rec utilizes GRU to model user behavior. We develop it to model item behavior as well.
- **DIEN** [18]. DIEN uses a two-layer GRU and attention mechanism to model the extraction and evolution of user interests.
- **DUMN** [8]. DUMN first learns unified representations for users, then measures the user-to-user relevance among users.

The public codes[3] for these baselines are provided in the previous work [8]. What should be noted is that DIEN implemented in it does not use the auxiliary loss network. For fairness, we implement DIEN with the auxiliary loss network.

Parameter Settings. In the experiment, we follow the parameter settings in [8]. We set the embedding vector dimensions of category features as 18. The maximum length of user behavior and item behavior are set as 20 and 25, respectively. Employ Adam optimizer and set the batch size to 128 and the learning rate to 0.001. Furthermore, we set auxiliary loss coefficient and margin to 1, and the number of heads in multi-headed self-attention to 6.

4.3   Experimental Results

Area Under ROC Curve (AUC) and Logloss are utilized as evaluation indicators, which are widely used to evaluate the performance of the CTR prediction models [5,8].

We repeat all experiments 5 times and record the average results. The comparison results on public real-world datasets are shown in Table 2. Compared with the best baseline, the average relative improvement achieved by DUMIN in AUC and Logloss is 1.54% and 4.16% respectively, which is particularly significant in the CTR prediction task. Observing the experimental results, first of all, SVD++ has achieved the worst performance due to its inability to capture nonlinear and high-order features. Secondly, Wide&Deep and PNN introduce a neural network, which is the reason of a huge improvement compared with SVD++, while PNN designs a product layer that enriches the interaction of features and achieved better performance than Wide&Deep. Thirdly, compared to Wide&Deep and PNN, the introduction of the attention mechanism allows DIN to model the CTR prediction task more accurately. Fourthly, GRU4Rec and DIEN are superior to DIN because the former focus on both user behavior and item behavior, while the latter captures the interests evolution in user behavior. The reason for the different outperformances between GRU4Rec and DIEN on the different datasets is that the time-dependent method of DIEN modeling interest representation is more advanced, while GRU4Rec introduces item behavior and captures more useful information. Fifthly, DUMN has achieved the best performance on the Beauty and Grocery datasets compared to other baselines, which reflects that the relevant users interests are particularly effective for CTR prediction. Finally, DUMIN achieves the best performance on all datasets compared with all baselines, which indicates the effectiveness of multi-interest modeling user interests. It is worth mentioning that, compared with DUMN, DUMIN not only extracts self-interest in user behavior, but also adopts

---

[3] https://github.com/hzzai/DUMN.

Table 3. Results of ablation study on the public real-word datasets. The bolded scores are the original model performance. ↓ indicates the most conspicuously declined score in each dataset.

Model	Beauty		Sports		Grocery	
	AUC	Logloss	AUC	Logloss	AUC	Logloss
DUMIN-AN[a]	0.8617	0.4603	0.8244	0.5132	0.8053	0.5216
DUMIN-DI[b]	0.8700	0.4458	0.8269	0.5092	0.8226	0.5046
DUMIN-EI[c]	0.8585	0.4667	0.8204↓	0.5169↓	0.8012	0.5248
DUMIN-UI[d]	0.8557↓	0.4704↓	0.8213	0.5167	0.7592↓	0.5705↓
DUMIN	**0.8721**	**0.4429**	**0.8325**	**0.5041**	**0.8225**	**0.5035**

[a] DUMIN without auxiliary loss network.
[b] DUMIN without direct interest.
[c] DUMIN without evolutionary interest.
[d] DUMIN without user-user interest.

self-interest as a query to establish a similarity mapping between self-interest and user-user interest in item behavior, enhancing collaborative filtering signals between interest representations, which has resulted in huge progress. Moreover, we dropped auxiliary loss network to train DUMIN-AN and got a worse performance compared with DUMIN, which proves the superiority of the auxiliary loss network to enhance correlation between interest and item.

4.4 Ablation Study

In this section, we conducted an ablation study to explore the effectiveness of the various components in DUMIN. The experimental results are shown in Table 3. The following facts can be observed: First of all, DUMIN outperforms DUMIN-AN, which verifies the importance of the auxiliary loss network. Next, the performance of DUMIN-EI is worse than DUMIN-AN because after removing the evolutionary interest, the extra supervision provided by the auxiliary loss network is meaningless. Finally, the performance of DUMIN-DI, DUMIN-EI and DUMIN-UI are all worse than DUMIN, which reflects the effectiveness of our designed different components to capture multiple user interests in different aspects to accurately model the interest representation. Moreover, the significant drop in the performance of DUMIN-UI also verifies the importance of similar interests among users to the CTR prediction task.

4.5 Parameter Analysis

As some hyperparameters in DUMIN have impact on the experimental results, we conducted extensive experiments to explore the effects of these hyperparameters. The experimental results are shown above in Fig. 3, in which we discover: (1) When the maximum length of the item behavior L_{max} is between 25 and 30, the DUMIN performance is the best. When L_{max} increases in the range of 5 to 25, the performance becomes better accordingly. When L_{max} increases in the range of 35 to 50, however, the performance gets worse gradually. It is obvious that when L_{max} is set too low or

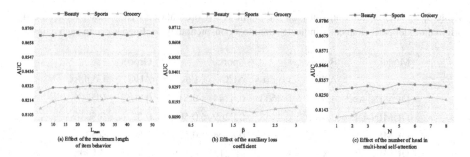

Fig. 3. Parameter analysis. The effect of different hyperparameters in DUMIN on Beauty dataset

too high, the performance will deteriorate, which indicates that a suitable number of relevant users is conducive to learn user-user interest, while too many or few relevant users could affect the learning of accurate representation of user-user interest. (2) When the auxiliary loss coefficient β in the range of 0.5 to 1.0, DUMIN performs best. When β grows bigger, however, the performance gradually decreases. This suggests that it is of positive significance to increase the proportion of the auxiliary loss in Eq.(19), while too high proportion will be detrimental to network parameter optimization. (3) DUMIN achieves the best performance when N is 5 or 6. From an overall point of view, the performance of DUMIN keeps the same trend with N, which indicates that increasing the number of heads in the multi-head self-attention helps to utilize the properties of similar abilities in different subspaces.

5   Conclusions

This paper proposed a novel Deep User Multi-Interest Network (DUMIN) from a multi-interest perspective to accurately model diverse user interest representations. DUMIN not only focuses on different interests in users' historical behavioral data, but also captures the similar interest among users. Moreover, the introduction of the auxiliary loss network enhances the correlation between interest and item, and makes a better interest representation be learned. In the future, we will explore more effective interest extraction methods to improve the accuracy of CTR prediction task.

References

1. Bellogin, A., Castells, P., Cantador, I.: Neighbor selection and weighting in user-based collaborative filtering: a performance prediction approach. ACM Trans. Web **8**(2), 1–30 (2014)
2. Cheng, H.T., et al.: Wide & deep learning for recommender systems. In: Proceedings of the 1st Workshop on Deep Learning for Recommender Systems, pp. 7–10 (2016)
3. Chung, J., Gulcehre, C., Cho, K.H., Bengio, Y.: Empirical evaluation of gated recurrent neural networks on sequence modeling. arXiv preprint arXiv:1412.3555 (2014)
4. Covington, P., Adams, J., Sargin, E.: Deep neural networks for Youtube recommendations. In: Proceedings of the 10th Conference on Recommender Systems, pp. 191–198 (2016)

5. Guo, H., Tang, R., Ye, Y., Li, Z., He, X.: DeepFM: a factorization-machine based neural network for CTR prediction. In: Proceedings of the 26th International Joint Conference on Artificial Intelligence, pp. 1725–1731 (2017)

6. He, X., Chua, T.S.: Neural factorization machines for sparse predictive analytics. In: Proceedings of the 40th International Conference on Research on Development in Information Retrieval, pp. 355–364 (2017)

7. Hidasi, B., Karatzoglou, A., Baltrunas, L., Tikk, D.: Session-based recommendations with recurrent neural networks. In: Proceedings of the 4th International Conference on Learning Representations (2016)

8. Huang, Z., Tao, M., Zhang, B.: Deep user match network for click-through rate prediction. In: Proceedings of the 44th International Conference on Research and Development in Information Retrieval, pp. 1890–1894 (2021)

9. Koren, Y.: Factorization meets the neighborhood: a multifaceted collaborative filtering model. In: Proceedings of the 14th International Conference on Knowledge Discovery and Data Mining, pp. 426–434 (2008)

10. Li, X., Wang, C., Tong, B., Tan, J., Zeng, X., Zhuang, T.: Deep time-aware item evolution network for click-through rate prediction. In: Proceedings of the 29th International Conference on Information and Knowledge Management, pp. 785–794 (2020)

11. Lyu, Z., Dong, Y., Huo, C., Ren, W.: Deep match to rank model for personalized click-through rate prediction. In: Proceedings of the 34th Conference on Artificial Intelligence, pp. 156–163 (2020)

12. McMahan, H.B., et al.: Ad click prediction: a view from the trenches. In: Proceedings of the 19th International Conference on Knowledge Discovery and Data Mining, pp. 1222–1230 (2013)

13. Qu, Y., et al.: Product based neural networks for user response prediction. In: Proceedings of the 16th International Conference on Data Mining, pp. 1149–1154 (2016)

14. Rendle, S.: Factorization machines. In: Proceedings of the 10th International Conference on Data Mining, pp. 995–1000 (2010)

15. Vaswani, A., et al.: Attention is all you need. In: Advances in Neural Information Processing Systems, pp. 5998–6008 (2017)

16. Xiao, Z., Yang, L., Jiang, W., Wei, Y., Hu, Y., Wang, H.: Deep multi-interest network for click-through rate prediction. In: Proceedings of the 29th International Conference on Information and Knowledge Management, pp. 2265–2268 (2020)

17. Xu, Z., et al.: Agile and accurate CTR prediction model training for massive-scale online advertising systems. In: Proceedings of the 2021 International Conference on Management of Data, pp. 2404–2409 (2021)

18. Zhou, G., et al.: Deep interest evolution network for click-through rate prediction. In: Proceedings of the 33th Conference on Artificial Intelligence, pp. 5941–5948 (2019)

19. Zhou, G., et al.: Deep interest network for click-through rate prediction. In: Proceedings of the 24th International Conference on Knowledge Discovery and Data Mining, pp. 1059–1068 (2018)

20. Qiu, H., Zheng, Q., Msahli, M., Memmi, G., Qiu, M., Lu, J.: Topological graph convolutional network-based urban traffic flow and density prediction. IEEE Trans. Intell. Transp. Syst. **22**(7), 4560–4569 (2020)

21. Cao, W., Yang, P., Ming, Z., Cai, S., Zhang, J.: An improved fuzziness based random vector functional link network for liver disease detection. In: Proceedings of the 6th International Conference on Big Data Security on Cloud, pp. 42–48 (2020)

Open Relation Extraction
via Query-Based Span Prediction

Huifan Yang[1] , Da-Wei Li[2], Zekun Li[1], Donglin Yang[1], Jinsheng Qi[1],
and Bin Wu[1(✉)]

[1] Beijing Key Laboratory of Intelligence Telecommunication Software
and Multimedia, Beijing University of Posts and Telecommunications, Beijing, China
{huifunny,lizekun,iceberg,qijs,wubin}@bupt.edu.cn
[2] Bing Multimedia Team, Microsoft Software Technology Center Asia, Beijing, China
daweilee@microsoft.com

Abstract. Open relation extraction (ORE) aims to assign semantic
relationships between arguments, essential to the automatic construction
of knowledge graphs. The previous methods either depend on external
NLP tools (e.g., PoS-taggers) and language-specific relation formations,
or suffer from inherent problems in sequence representations, thus leading to unsatisfactory extraction in diverse languages and domains. To
address the above problems, we propose a **Query-based Open Relation
Extractor (QORE)**. QORE utilizes a Transformers-based language
model to derive a representation of the interaction between arguments
and context, and can process multilingual texts effectively. Extensive
experiments are conducted on seven datasets covering four languages,
showing that QORE models significantly outperform conventional rule-
based systems and the state-of-the-art method LOREM [6]. Regarding
the practical challenges [1] of *Corpus Heterogeneity* and *Automation*,
our evaluations illustrate that QORE models show excellent zero-shot
domain transferability and few-shot learning ability.

Keywords: Open relation extraction · Information extraction ·
Knowledge graph construction · Transfer learning · Few-shot learning

1 Introduction

Relation extraction (RE) from unstructured text is fundamental to a variety of
downstream tasks, such as constructing knowledge graphs (KG) and computing sentence similarity. Conventional closed relation extraction considers only a
predefined set of relation types on small and homogeneous corpora, which is far
less effective when shifting to general-domain text mining that has no limits in
relation types or languages. To alleviate the constraints of closed RE, Banko et
al. [1] introduce a new paradigm: open relation extraction (ORE), predicting
a text span as the semantic connection between arguments from within a context, where a span is a contiguous sub-sequence. This paper proposes a novel
query-based open relation extractor QORE that can process multilingual texts
for facilitating large-scale general-domain KG construction.

© The Author(s), under exclusive license to Springer Nature Switzerland AG 2022
G. Memmi et al. (Eds.): KSEM 2022, LNAI 13369, pp. 70–81, 2022.
https://doi.org/10.1007/978-3-031-10986-7_6

Open relation extraction identifies an arbitrary phrase to specify a semantic relationship between arguments within a context. (An argument is a text span representing an adverbial, adjectival, nominal phrase, and so on, which is not limited to an entity.) Taking a context *"Researchers develop techniques to acquire information automatically from digital texts."* and an argument pair ⟨*Researchers, information*⟩ , an ORE system would extract the span *"acquire"* from the context to denote the semantic connection between *"Researchers"* and *"information"*.

Conventional ORE systems are largely based on syntactic patterns and heuristic rules that depend on external NLP tools (e.g., PoS-taggers) and language-specific relation formations. For example, ClausIE [2] and OpenIE4 [10] for English and CORE [15] for Chinese, leverage external tools to obtain part-of-speech tags or dependency features and generate syntactic patterns to extract relational facts. Faruqui et al. [4] present a cross-lingual ORE system that first translates a sentence to English, performs ruled-based ORE in English, and finally projects the relation back to the original sentence. These pattern-based approaches cannot handle the complexity and diversity of languages well, and the extraction is usually far from satisfactory.

To alleviate the burden of designing manual features, multiple neural ORE models have been proposed, typically adopting the methods of either sequence labeling or span selection. MGD-GNN [9] for Chinese ORE constructs a multi-grained dependency graph and utilizes a span selection model to predict based on character features and word boundary knowledge. Compared with our method, MGD-GNN heavily relies on dependency information and cannot deal with various languages. Ro et al. [12] propose sequence-labeling-based Multi^{2}OIE that performs multilingual open information extraction by combining BERT with multi-head attention blocks, whereas Multi^{2}OIE is constrained to extract the predicate of a sentence as the relation. Jia et al. [7] transform English ORE into a sequence labeling process and present a hybrid neural network NST, nonetheless, a dependency on PoS-taggers may introduce error propagation to NST. Improving NST, the current state-of-the-art ORE method LOREM [6] works as a multilingual-embedded sequence-labeling model based on CNN and BiLSTM. Identical to our model, LOREM does not rely on language-specific knowledge or external NLP tools. However, based on our comparison of architectures in Sect. 4.1, LOREM suffers from inherent problems in learning long-range sequence dependencies [16] that are basic to computing token relevances to gold relations, thus resulting in less satisfactory performances compared with QORE model.

Inspired by the broad applications of machine reading comprehension (MRC) and Transformers-based pre-trained language models (LM) like BERT [3] and SpanBERT [8], we design a query-based open relation extraction framework QORE to solve the ORE task effectively and avoid the inherent problems of previous extractors. Given an argument pair and its context, we first create a query template containing the argument information and derive a contextual representation of query and context via a pre-trained language model, which provides a deep understanding of query and context, and models the information interaction between them. Finally, the span extraction module finds an open relation by predicting the start and end indexes of a sub-sequence in the context.

Besides introducing the ORE paradigm, Banko et al. [1] identified major challenges for ORE systems, including *Corpus Heterogeneity* and *Automation*. Thus, we carry out the evaluation on the two challenges from the aspects of **zero-shot domain transferability** and **few-shot learning ability**, which we interpret in the following. (a) *Corpus Heterogeneity*: Heterogeneous datasets form an obstacle for profound linguistic tools such as syntactic or dependency parsers, since they commonly work well when trained and applied to a specific domain, but are prone to produce incorrect results when used in a different genre of text. As QORE models are intended for domain-independent usage, we do not require using any external NLP tool, and we assess the performances in this challenge via zero-shot domain transferring. (b) *Automation*: The manual labor of creating suitable training data or extraction patterns must be reduced to a minimum by requiring only a small set of hand-tagged seed instances or a few manually defined extraction patterns. The QORE framework does not need predefined extraction patterns but trains on amounts of data. We conduct few-shot learning by shrinking the size of training data for the evaluation of this challenge.

To summarize, the main contributions of this work are:

– We propose a novel query-based open relation extractor QORE that utilizes a Transformers-based language model to derive a representation of the interaction between the arguments and context.
– We carry out extensive experiments on seven datasets covering four languages, showing that QORE models significantly outperform conventional rule-based systems and the state-of-the-art method LOREM.
– Considering the practical challenges of ORE, we investigate the zero-shot domain transferability and the few-shot learning ability of QORE. The experimental results illustrate that our models maintain high precisions when transferring or training on fewer data.

2   Approach

An overview of our QORE framework is visualized in Fig. 1. Given an argument pair and its context, we first create a query from the arguments based on a template and encode the combination of query and context using a Transformers-based language model. Finally, the span extraction module predicts a continuous sub-sequence in the context as an open relation.

2.1   Task Description

Given a context C and an argument pair $A = (A_1, A_2)$ in C, an open relation extractor needs to find the semantic relationship between the pair A. We denote the context as a word token sequence $C = \{x_i^c\}_{i=1}^{l_c}$ and an argument as a text span $A_k = \{x_i^{a_k}\}_{i=1}^{l_{a_k}}$, where l_c is the context length and l_{a_k} is the k-th argument length. Our goal is to predict a span $R = \{x_i^r\}_{i=1}^{l_r}$ in the context as an open relation, where l_r is the length of a relation span.

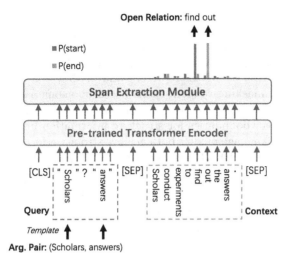

Fig. 1. An overview of QORE framework

2.2 Query Template Creation

Provided an argument pair (A_1, A_2), we adopt a rule-based method to create the query template

$$T = \langle s_1 \rangle \, A_1 \, \langle s_2 \rangle \, A_2 \, \langle s_3 \rangle \qquad (1)$$

having three slots, where $\langle s_i \rangle$ indicates the i-th slot. The tokens filling a slot are separators of the adjacent arguments (e.g., double-quotes, a comma, or words of natural languages) or a placeholder for a relation span (e.g., a question mark or words of natural languages). In this paper, we design two different query templates: (1) the question-mark (QM) style T_{QM}, taking the form of a structured argument-relationship triple, and (2) the language-specific natural-language (NL) style T_{NL}, where each language has a particular template that is close in meaning. (English: *En*, Chinese: *Zh*, French: *Fr*, Russian: *Ru*.)

$$T_{QM} = \text{``}A_1\text{''?``}A_2\text{''} \qquad (2)$$

$$T_{NL^{En}} = \text{What is the relation from ``}A_1\text{'' to ``}A_2\text{''?} \qquad (3)$$

$$T_{NL^{Zh}} = \text{``}A_1\text{''和``}A_2\text{''的关系是?} \qquad (4)$$

$$T_{NL^{Fr}} = \text{Quelle est la relation entre ``}A_1\text{'' et ``}A_2\text{''?} \qquad (5)$$

$$T_{NL^{Ru}} = \text{Какое отношение имеет ``}A_1\text{'' к ``}A_2\text{''?} \qquad (6)$$

2.3   Encoder

BERT [3] is a pre-trained encoder of deep bidirectional transformers [16] for monolingual and multilingual representations. Inspired by BERT, Joshi et al. [8] propose SpanBERT to better represent and predict text spans. SpanBERT extends BERT by masking random spans based on geometric distribution and using span boundary objective (SBO) that requires the model to predict masked spans based on span boundaries for structure information integration into pre-training. The two language models both achieve strong performances on the span extraction task. We use BERT and SpanBERT as the encoders of QORE.

Given a context $C = \{x_i^c\}_{i=1}^{l_c}$ with l_c tokens and a query $Q = \{x_j^q\}_{j=1}^{l_q}$ with l_q tokens, we employ a pre-trained language model as the encoder to learn the contextual representation for each token. First, we concatenate the query Q and the context C to derive the input I of encoder:

$$I = \{[CLS], x_1^q, ..., x_{l_q}^q, [SEP], x_1^c, ..., x_{l_c}^c, [SEP]\} \tag{7}$$

where $[CLS]$ and $[SEP]$ denote the beginning token and the segment token, respectively.

Next, we generate the initial embedding e_i for each token by summing its word embedding e_i^w, position embedding e_i^p, and segment embedding e_i^s. The sequence embedding $E = \{e_1, e_2, ..., e_m\}$ is then fed into the deep Transformer layers to learn a contextual representation with long-range sequence dependencies via the self-attention mechanism [16]. Finally, we obtain the last-layer hidden states $H = \{h_1, h_2, ..., h_m\}$ as the contextual representation for the input sequence I, where $h_i \in \mathbb{R}^{d_h}$ and d_h indicates the dimension of the last hidden layer of encoder. The length of the sequences I, E, H is denoted as m where $m = l_q + l_c + 3$.

2.4   Span Extraction Module

The span extraction module aims to find a continuous sub-sequence in the context as an open relation. We utilize two learnable parameter matrices (feed-forward networks) $f_{start} \in \mathbb{R}^{d_h}$ and $f_{end} \in \mathbb{R}^{d_h}$ followed by the softmax normalization, then take each contextual token representation h_i in H as the input to produce the probability of each token i being selected as the start/end of relation span:

$$p_i^{start} = softmax(f_{start}(h_1), ..., f_{start}(h_m))_i \tag{8}$$

$$p_i^{end} = softmax(f_{end}(h_1), ..., f_{end}(h_m))_i \tag{9}$$

We denote $p^{start} = \{p_i^{start}\}_{i=1}^m$ and $p^{end} = \{p_i^{end}\}_{i=1}^m$.

2.5   Training and Inference

The training objective is defined as minimizing the cross entropy loss for the start and end selections,

$$p_k = p_{y_k^s}^{start} \times p_{y_k^e}^{end} \tag{10}$$

$$\mathbb{L} = -\frac{1}{N} \sum_{k}^{N} \log p_k \tag{11}$$

where y_k^s and y_k^e are respectively ground-truth start and end positions of example k. N is the number of examples.

In the inference process, an open relation is extracted by finding the indices (s, e):

$$(s, e) = \arg\max_{s \leq e}(p_s^{start} \times p_e^{end}) \tag{12}$$

3   Experimental Setup

We propose the following hypotheses and design a set of experiments to examine the performances of QORE models. We arrange the hypotheses based on the considerations as follows: (1) **H$_1$**: By conducting extensive comparisons with the existing ORE systems, we aim to analyze the advantages of QORE framework. (2) **H$_2$** and **H$_3$**: As stated in the Introduction, it is significant to evaluate an open relation extractor on the challenges of *Corpus Heterogeneity* and *Automation*. Thus, we investigate the zero-shot domain transferability and the few-shot learning ability of QORE models.

- **H$_1$**: For extracting open relations in seven datasets of different languages, QORE models can outperform conventional rule-based extractors and the state-of-the-art neural method LOREM.
- **H$_2$**: Considering the zero-shot domain transferability, QORE model is able to perform effectively when transferring to another domain.
- **H$_3$**: When the training data size reduces, QORE model shows an excellent few-shot learning ability and maintains high precision.

3.1   Datasets

We evaluate the performances of our proposed QORE framework on seven public datasets covering four languages, i.e., English, Chinese, French, and Russian (denoted as *En, Zh, Fr,* and *Ru,* respectively). In the data preprocessing, we only retain binary-argument triples whose components are spans of the contexts.

- **OpenIE4[En]** was bootstrapped from extractions of OpenIE4 [10] from Wikipedia.
- **LSOIE-wiki[En]** and **LSOIE-sci[En]** [13] were algorithmically re-purposed from the QA-SRL BANK 2.0 dataset [5], covering the domains of Wikipedia and science, respectively.
- **COER[Zh]** is a high-quality Chinese knowledge base, created by an unsupervised open extractor [15] from heterogeneous web text.
- **SAOKE[Zh]** [14] is a human-annotated large-scale dataset for Chinese open information extraction.

- **WMORC**[Fr] and **WMORC**[Ru] [4] consist of manually annotated open relation data (WMORC$_{human}$) for French and Russian, and automatically tagged (thus less reliable) relation data (WMORC$_{auto}$) for the two languages by a cross-lingual projection approach. The sentences are gathered from Wikipedia. We take WMORC$_{auto}$ for the training and development sets while using WMORC$_{human}$ as the test data.

3.2   Implementations

Encoders. We utilize the *bert-base-cased* or *spanbert-base-cased* language models as the encoders on English datasets (SpanBERT only provides the English version up to now), and *bert-base-chinese* on Chinese datasets. Since there exist few high-quality monolingual LMs for French and Russian, we employ a multilingual LM *bert-base-multilingual-cased* on the datasets of the two languages.

Evaluation Metrics. We keep track of the token-level open relation extraction metrics of F1 score, precision, and recall.

3.3   Baselines

In the experiments, we compare QORE models with a variety of previously proposed methods, some of which were used in the evaluation of the SOTA open relation extractor LOREM [6]. We denote the English (*En*) and Chinese (*Zh*) extractors and the models capable of processing multilingual (*Mul*) texts using the superscripts.

- **OLLIE**[En] [11] is a pattern-based extraction approach with complex relation schemas and context information of attribution and clausal modifiers.
- **ClausIE**[En] [2] exploits linguistic knowledge about English grammar to identify clauses as relations and their arguments.
- **Open IE-4.x**[En] [10] combines a rule-based extraction system and a system analyzing the hierarchical composition between semantic frames to generate relations.
- **MGD-GNN**[Zh] [9] constructs a multi-grained dependency graph and predicts based on character features and word boundary knowledge.
- **LOREM**[Mul] [6] is a multilingual-embedded sequence-labeling method based on CNN and BiLSTM, not relying on language-specific knowledge or external NLP tools.
- **Multi^{2}OIE**[Mul] [12] is a multilingual sequence-labeling-based information extraction system combining BERT with multi-head attention blocks.

4   Experimental Results

4.1   H$_1$: QORE for Multilingual Open Relation Extraction

In **H$_1$**, we evaluate our QORE models on seven datasets of different languages (Tables 1 and 2) to compare with the rule-based and neural baselines. By contrast, QORE models outperform all the baselines on each dataset.

Table 1. Comparison on English datasets. Bolds indicate the best values per dataset. [Query templates: the question-mark (QM) style and the language-specific natural-language (NL) style.]

Model	OpenIE4[En]			LSOIE-wiki[En]			LSOIE-sci[En]		
	P	R	F1	P	R	F1	P	R	F1
OLLIE	–	–	–	18.02	39.77	23.11	21.96	44.46	27.44
ClausIE	–	–	–	28.78	36.24	31.14	37.18	46.58	40.13
Open IE-4.x	–	–	–	32.06	40.79	34.70	37.73	48.07	40.88
LOREM	83.58	81.56	81.50	71.46	70.58	70.87	76.33	75.13	75.53
$QORE_{BERT+QM}$	97.89	97.81	97.75	96.74	97.26	96.82	97.35	97.89	97.50
$QORE_{BERT+NL}$	97.59	97.74	97.51	97.01	97.43	97.11	97.49	98.01	97.63
$QORE_{SpanBERT+QM}$	**98.85**	**99.10**	**98.76**	97.28	97.72	97.37	**97.60**	98.08	**97.71**
$QORE_{SpanBERT+NL}$	98.65	98.71	98.50	**97.38**	**97.96**	**97.51**	97.52	**98.15**	97.70

Table 2. Comparison on Chinese, French and Russian datasets

Model	COER[Zh]			SAOKE[Zh]			WMORC[Fr]			WMORC[Ru]		
	P	R	F1	P	R	F1	P	R	F1	P	R	F1
MGD-GNN	77.84	86.06	81.74	53.38	65.83	58.96	–	–	–	–	–	–
LOREM	41.49	42.40	41.42	46.68	52.92	48.70	83.30	83.88	82.75	82.63	87.86	83.80
$QORE_{BERT+QM}$	**98.11**	98.16	97.88	92.76	**95.00**	92.55	94.94	83.79	85.89	**91.74**	**92.48**	**90.62**
$QORE_{BERT+NL}$	98.10	98.16	**97.89**	**93.19**	94.78	**92.83**	**95.01**	84.85	**86.88**	91.51	92.29	90.24

For OLLIE, ClausIE, Open IE-4.x, and MGD-GNN, their dissatisfactory results are primarily due to the dependence on intricate language-specific relation formations and error propagation by the used external NLP tools (e.g., MGD-GNN utilizes dependency parser for constructing a multi-grained dependency graph.). If we contrast with the SOTA method LOREM, the neural sequence-labeling-based model outperforms the rule-based systems, but still cannot gain comparable outcomes to our QORE models. In the following, we focus on comparing the architectures of QORE and LOREM.

LOREM encodes an input sequence using pre-trained word embeddings and adds argument tag vectors to the word embeddings. The argument tag vectors are simple one-hot encoded vectors indicating if a word is part of an argument. Then LOREM utilizes CNN and BiLSTM layers to form a representation of each word. The CNN is used to capture the local feature information, as LOREM considers that certain parts of the context might have higher chances of containing relation words than others. Meanwhile, the BiLSTM captures the forward and backward context of each word. Next, a CRF layer tags each word using the NST tagging scheme [7]: S (Single-word relation), B (Beginning of a relation), I (Inside a relation), E (Ending of a relation), O (Outside a relation).

Advantages of QORE over LOREM. Our QORE framework generates an initial sequence representation with word, position, and segment embeddings.

Unlike the simple one-hot argument vectors of LOREM, QORE derives the argument information by creating a query template of arguments. We combine the query with the context to form the input of encoder, and the encoder outputs a contextual representation that we utilize to compute the relevance of each token to a gold relation (Eqs. 8 and 9). Moreover, by employing the self-attention mechanism of a Transformers-based encoder, QORE has the benefit of learning long-range dependencies easier and deriving a better representation for computing relevances, which we interpret in the following. Learning long-range dependencies is a key challenge in encoding sequences and solving related tasks [16]. One key factor affecting the ability to learn such dependencies is the length of the paths forward and backward signals have to traverse between any two input and output positions in the network. The shorter these paths between any combination of positions in the input and output sequences, the easier it is to learn long-range dependencies. Vaswani et al. [16] also provide the maximum path length between any two input and output positions in self-attention, recurrent, and convolutional layers, which are $O(1)$, $O(n)$, and $O(\log_k(n))$, respectively. (k is the kernel width of a convolutional layer.) The constant path length of self-attention makes it easier to learn long-range dependencies than CNN and BiLSTM layers. Overall, QORE achieves substantial improvements over LOREM due to the better sequence representations with long-term dependencies, a basis of computing token relevances to gold relations.

In Table 1, if we concentrate on the BERT-encoded and SpanBERT-encoded QORE models, we find that the results from the SpanBERT-encoded models are relatively more significant than the BERT-encoded on all English datasets, which is in line with the advantage of SpanBERT over BERT on the span extraction task [8].

4.2 $\mathbf{H_2}$: Zero-shot Domain Transferability of QORE

A model trained on data from the general domain does not necessarily achieve an equal performance when testing on a specific domain such as biology or literature. In $\mathbf{H_2}$, we evaluate the zero-shot domain transferability of QORE by training models on the general-domain LSOIE-wiki^{En} and testing them on the benchmark of science-domain LSOIE-sci^{En}. We compare our QORE$_{BERT+QM}$ model with BERT Tagger (non-query-based, performed by Multi^{2}OIE). Table 3 illustrates that when transferring from the general to science domain, QORE$_{BERT+QM}$ decreases by F1 score (-0.15%) whereas BERT Tagger reduces by F1 (-14.58%). The slighter decline in QORE's performance shows that our model has superior domain transferability.

Table 3. Results of domain transfer

Model	Train	Test	F1
BERT Tagger	LSOIE-sci^{En}	LSOIE-sci^{En}	74.53
QORE$_{BERT+QM}$	LSOIE-sci^{En}	LSOIE-sci^{En}	97.50
BERT Tagger	LSOIE-wiki^{En}	LSOIE-sci^{En}	59.95 (-14.58)
QORE$_{BERT+QM}$	LSOIE-wiki^{En}	LSOIE-sci^{En}	97.35 (-0.15)

4.3 H$_3$: Few-Shot Learning Ability of QORE

For few-shot learning ability, we carry out a set of experiments with shrinking training data to compare our QORE model with BERT Tagger (non-query-based, performed by Multi^{2}OIE) on LSOIE-wiki^{En}. Figure 2 indicates that by reducing training samples to 50%, BERT Tagger declines by F1 (-2.75%) while QORE$_{BERT+QM}$ achieves an even higher F1 ($+0.26\%$). When reducing the training set to 6.25%, QORE$_{BERT+QM}$ results in a decreased F1 (-1.28%) totally compared with using the whole training set, whereas BERT Tagger reduces by F1 (-7.02%) in total. The comparison results imply that our query-based span extraction framework may bring more enhanced few-shot learning ability to QORE model.

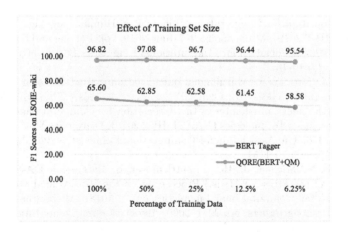

Fig. 2. Results of different training set sizes

5 Conclusion

Our work targets open relation extraction using a novel query-based extraction framework QORE. The evaluation results show that our model achieves significant improvements over the SOTA method LOREM. Regarding some practical challenges, we investigate that QORE models show excellent zero-shot domain transferability and few-shot learning ability. In the future, we will explore further demands of the ORE task (e.g., extracting multi-span open relations and detecting non-existent relationships) and present corresponding solutions.

Acknowledgements. This work is supported by the NSFC-General Technology Basic Research Joint Funds under Grant (U1936220), the National Natural Science Foundation of China under Grant (61972047) and the National Key Research and Development Program of China (2018YFC0831500).

References

1. Banko, M., Cafarella, M.J., Soderland, S., Broadhead, M., Etzioni, O.: Open information extraction from the web. In: Veloso, M.M. (ed.) Proceedings of the 20th International Joint Conference on Artificial Intelligence (IJCAI 2007), Hyderabad, 6–12 January 2007, pp. 2670–2676 (2007). http://ijcai.org/Proceedings/07/Papers/429.pdf
2. Corro, L.D., Gemulla, R.: Clausie: clause-based open information extraction. In: Schwabe, D., Almeida, V.A.F., Glaser, H., Baeza-Yates, R., Moon, S.B. (eds.) 22nd International World Wide Web Conference (WWW 2013), Rio de Janeiro, 13–17 May 2013, pp. 355–366. International World Wide Web Conferences Steering Committee/ACM (2013). https://doi.org/10.1145/2488388.2488420
3. Devlin, J., Chang, M., Lee, K., Toutanova, K.: BERT: pre-training of deep bidirectional transformers for language understanding. In: Burstein, J., Doran, C., Solorio, T. (eds.) Proceedings of the 2019 Conference of the North American Chapter of the Association for Computational Linguistics: Human Language Technologies (NAACL-HLT 2019), Minneapolis, 2–7 June 2019, vol. 1 (Long and Short Papers), pp. 4171–4186. Association for Computational Linguistics (2019). https://doi.org/10.18653/v1/n19-1423
4. Faruqui, M., Kumar, S.: Multilingual open relation extraction using cross-lingual projection. In: Mihalcea, R., Chai, J.Y., Sarkar, A. (eds.) The 2015 Conference of the North American Chapter of the Association for Computational Linguistics: Human Language Technologies (NAACL HLT 2015), Denver, 31 May–5 June 2015, pp. 1351–1356. The Association for Computational Linguistics (2015). https://doi.org/10.3115/v1/n15-1151
5. FitzGerald, N., Michael, J., He, L., Zettlemoyer, L.: Large-scale QA-SRL parsing. In: Gurevych, I., Miyao, Y. (eds.) Proceedings of the 56th Annual Meeting of the Association for Computational Linguistics (ACL 2018), Melbourne, 15–20 July 2018, vol. 1: Long Papers, pp. 2051–2060. Association for Computational Linguistics (2018). https://doi.org/10.18653/v1/P18-1191
6. Harting, T., Mesbah, S., Lofi, C.: LOREM: language-consistent open relation extraction from unstructured text. In: Huang, Y., King, I., Liu, T., van Steen, M. (eds.) The Web Conference 2020 (WWW 2020), Taipei, 20–24 April 2020, pp. 1830–1838. ACM/IW3C2 (2020). https://doi.org/10.1145/3366423.3380252
7. Jia, S., Xiang, Y., Chen, X.: Supervised neural models revitalize the open relation extraction. arXiv preprint arXiv:1809.09408 (2018)
8. Joshi, M., Chen, D., Liu, Y., Weld, D.S., Zettlemoyer, L., Levy, O.: Spanbert: improving pre-training by representing and predicting spans. Trans. Assoc. Comput. Linguist. **8**, 64–77 (2020). https://transacl.org/ojs/index.php/tacl/article/view/1853

9. Lyu, Z., Shi, K., Li, X., Hou, L., Li, J., Song, B.: Multi-grained dependency graph neural network for Chinese open information extraction. In: Karlapalem, K., et al. (eds.) PAKDD 2021. LNCS (LNAI), vol. 12714, pp. 155–167. Springer, Cham (2021). https://doi.org/10.1007/978-3-030-75768-7_13

10. Mausam. Open information extraction systems and downstream applications. In: Kambhampati, S. (ed.) Proceedings of the Twenty-Fifth International Joint Conference on Artificial Intelligence, IJCAI 2016, New York, 9–15 July 2016, pp. 4074–4077. IJCAI/AAAI Press (2016). http://www.ijcai.org/Abstract/16/604

11. Mausam, Schmitz, M., Soderland, S., Bart, R., Etzioni, O.: Open language learning for information extraction. In: Tsujii, J., Henderson, J., Pasca, M. (eds.) Proceedings of the 2012 Joint Conference on Empirical Methods in Natural Language Processing and Computational Natural Language Learning (EMNLP-CoNLL 2012), 12–14 July 2012, Jeju Island, pp. 523–534. ACL (2012). https://aclanthology.org/D12-1048/

12. Ro, Y., Lee, Y., Kang, P.: Multi^{2}oie: Multilingual open information extraction based on multi-head attention with BERT. In: Cohn, T., He, Y., Liu, Y. (eds.) Proceedings of the 2020 Conference on Empirical Methods in Natural Language Processing: Findings, EMNLP 2020, Online Event, 16–20 November 2020. Findings of ACL, vol. EMNLP 2020, pp. 1107–1117. Association for Computational Linguistics (2020). https://doi.org/10.18653/v1/2020.findings-emnlp.99

13. Solawetz, J., Larson, S.: LSOIE: A large-scale dataset for supervised open information extraction. In: Merlo, P., Tiedemann, J., Tsarfaty, R. (eds.) Proceedings of the 16th Conference of the European Chapter of the Association for Computational Linguistics: Main Volume (EACL 2021), Online, 19–23 April 2021, pp. 2595–2600. Association for Computational Linguistics (2021). https://aclanthology.org/2021.eacl-main.222/

14. Sun, M., Li, X., Wang, X., Fan, M., Feng, Y., Li, P.: Logician: a unified end-to-end neural approach for open-domain information extraction. In: Chang, Y., Zhai, C., Liu, Y., Maarek, Y. (eds.) Proceedings of the Eleventh ACM International Conference on Web Search and Data Mining (WSDM 2018), Marina Del Rey, 5–9 February 2018, pp. 556–564. ACM (2018). https://doi.org/10.1145/3159652.3159712

15. Tseng, Y., et al.: Chinese open relation extraction for knowledge acquisition. In: Bouma, G., Parmentier, Y. (eds.) Proceedings of the 14th Conference of the European Chapter of the Association for Computational Linguistics (EACL 2014), 26–30 April 2014, Gothenburg, pp. 12–16. The Association for Computer Linguistics (2014). https://doi.org/10.3115/v1/e14-4003

16. Vaswani, A., et al.: Attention is all you need. In: Guyon, I., et al. (eds.) Advances in Neural Information Processing Systems 30: Annual Conference on Neural Information Processing Systems 2017, 4–9 December 2017, Long Beach, pp. 5998–6008 (2017). https://proceedings.neurips.cc/paper/2017/hash/3f5ee243547dee91fbd053c1c4a845aa-Abstract.html

Relational Triple Extraction with Relation-Attentive Contextual Semantic Representations

Baolin Jia, Shiqun Yin[✉], Ningchao Wang, and Junli Lin

Faculty of Computer and Information Science,
Southwest University, Chongqing, China
qqqq-qiong@163.com

Abstract. As a fundamental task in natural language processing, relation extraction from unstructured text is usually processed with named entity recognition together. These models intend to extract entities and predict relations simultaneously. However, they typically focus on entity pairs representations or relation representations, which ignores the contextual semantic. To tackle these problems, we introduce a three-stage relational triple extraction model with relation-attentive contextual semantic, termed as RARE. As a significant feature, contextual semantic are employed in both subtasks. In relation prediction, we utilize sentence embedding processed by mlp-attention to capture important information in a sentence. In the subject and object extraction, relation-attention mechanism is applied to calculate the relation-aware contextual representations. Extensive experiments on NYT* and WebNLG* show that our model can achieve better performance.

Keywords: Relation extraction · Attention mechanism · Relation attentive contextual semantics

1 Introduction

The goal of information extraction is to extract structured data from large amounts of unstructured or semi-structured natural language text. One of the most important subtasks is relation extraction, which aims to identify entities in the text and extract semantic relation between them. Many natural language processing applications, such as question and answer systems [19], emotion detection [11], and reading comprehension [6], rely heavily on it.

1.1 Challenge of Relation Extraction

Relation extraction results can be represented by triples of SPO structure (Subject, Predication, Object). For example, a sentence "The capital of China is Beijing." can be represented as "China, capital, Beijing". The main workflow of the approach to relation extraction can be described as follows: the relation

© The Author(s), under exclusive license to Springer Nature Switzerland AG 2022
G. Memmi et al. (Eds.): KSEM 2022, LNAI 13369, pp. 82–93, 2022.
https://doi.org/10.1007/978-3-031-10986-7_7

is extracted from the sentences that have been labeled with the target entity pairs, and the triples with entity relations are output as the prediction results. The traditional methods extract relational triples in a pipeline way. The pipeline model ignores the related information between entity and relation and two separate models cause error propagation. To solve these problems, many joint models have been proposed. Joint models [2,4,11] take full advantage of the dependency between entity recognition and relation extraction and turn the two subtasks into a complete model with the joint training, which achieves better result than pipeline models.

As discussed above, Most models limit the task to a single sentence and assumes that every one sentence contains only one entity pair. This assumption is impractical. Complex factual relations, and different relation triples may overlap in a sentence. In fact, 68.2% of the sentences in the WebNLG dataset overlap, which leads to inaccurate model extraction of triples. Considering the shortcomings of these research, researchers classify the overlapping in a sentence into three categories according to the entity overlapping type: NEO (Normal), SEO (Single Entity Overlap) and EPO (Entity Pair Overlap). The typical example is shown in the Table 1. There are three relations between "America" and "New York". We can see there are two or more relation type in a long sentence, and the following problem is that model can not extract all relation and entities in a long sentence. And they typically focus on entity pairs representations, which ignores the relation and sentence information.

Table 1. Examples of overlapping patterns.

Type	Sentence examples	Relational triples
NEO	Mr.Yang was born in China	<Mr.Yang,China,birth_place>
EPO	New York is the capital of America.	<America,New York,Capital>
		<America,New York,Contains>
		<America,New York,Country>
SEO	Dr.Lee who was born in Beijing, studied in Shanghai.	<Dr.Lee,Beijing,birth_plaec>
		<Dr.Lee,Shanghai,live_place>

1.2 Our Contribution

To address these above issues, we propose a relation-attention network for joint relational triple extraction (RARE), which extracts potential relations to realize a better relation extraction. We focus on the task of overlapping entity relation extraction. The contributions of our work are listed as follows:

– We design a joint Relation triples Extraction framework with Relation-Attentive contextual semantic representations, RARE.

- We propose a relation-attention mechanism to get different relation-aware contextual semantic according to different relation, which can help decoder relation type and extract overlapping relational triples.
- Extensive experiments on NYT* and WebNLG* show that our model can achieve better performance in relation extraction. And the results show that our method can solve the problem of entity overlap to a certain extent.

2 Related Work

Most earlier efforts have treated relation extraction as a pipeline task involving two steps: named entity recognition and relation type deduction. For entity recognition, some earlier works treat it as a sequence labeling problem, and various neural networks are adopted to solve these problems, such as CNN [20], GCN [9], RNN [12,14] and Bi-RNN network [8].

Depending on the extraction order, we can divide the joint relation extraction models into two categories: the joint model and the pipeline model. Joint models can extract entity and relation simultaneously. Although the pipeline extraction method is highly flexible by being able to integrate different data source and learning algorithms, these models have some drawbacks, such as error propagation and ignoring the correlation between two subtasks. Recent efforts are paid more to deal with the overlapping problems. [5] obtains the embedding of span by concatenating Elmo word embedding and char embedding, extracting the information from the embedded representation of span generated from Bi-LSTM. In this model, they share the representation in the downstream NER and RE tasks to reduce the loss of information and complexity. Recent researches have investigated end-to-end [1] models. For example, Spert [2] and DyGIE [7] have a promising performance and achieve the state of the art. In the Spert model, the authors encode potential entities through the pre-trained model Bert, and obtain the representations of span by mlp-attention and multi-head attention mechanism. For the sake of better performance, the improved Spert model [4] significantly reduces the training complexity of the model and improves the classification efficiency of the model through a negative sampling mechanism to have higher efficiency.

3 Methodology

Our work mainly consists of two stages, relation prediction and subject and object extraction. The main flowchart of our model is shown in Fig. 1. Rather than classify relations with entity pairs, our model first intends to obtain potential relations in a sentence by contextual semantic embedding. Then, by the correlation between entities and relations, we employ relation embedding and entity embedding with two softmax classifiers to extract subjects and objects separately. Specifically, we introduce a relation-attention mechanism to compute specific embedding of different words in a sentence under a particular relation, improving the effect of relation embedding in entity recognition. At last, a global correspondence matrix is used to determine the correct pairs of subjects and objects.

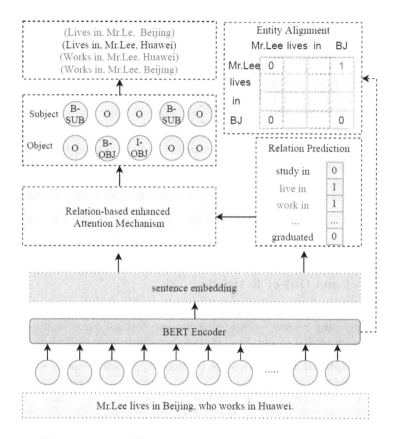

Fig. 1. The overall structure of our proposed RARE model.

3.1 Representations of Token and Relation

In natural language processing, the pre-trained model on a large corpus has also been conducive to the downstream NLP task. To obtain a better embedding, the most widely used Bert model is used to encode the input sentences and get a contextual representation of each word. It can be expanded to other encoders like Elmo, Glove, and Word2Vec. Bert model has shown remarkable results in entity identification and connection extraction.

3.2 Relation Prediction

In relation prediction, we take the output of Bert as the input of Relation Prediction. We employ the mlp-attention [2] to generate contextual semantic representations. In this way, the weight of each word in the sentences can be evaluated.

If a word x_k has an important meaning in the entity recognition and relation classification, it should have a more significant weight. And important information of multiple words can be extracted.

$$\mathcal{V}_k = \mathbf{MLP}_k \left(x_k \right) \quad \text{s.t.} \quad k \in [1, n], \tag{1}$$

$$\alpha_{\mathbf{k}} = \frac{\exp \left(\mathcal{V}_{\mathbf{k}} \right)}{\sum_{m=1}^{n} \exp \left(\mathcal{V}_m \right)}, \tag{2}$$

$$\mathcal{F}_{\mathbf{s}} = \sum_{m=i}^{n} \alpha_m x_m, \tag{3}$$

We denote the $\mathcal{F}_{\mathbf{s}}$ as the sentence semantic representation for relation prediction in a sentence. We take relation classification as a multi-label binary classification, and σ denotes the sigmoid function. The result P_{rel} denotes the possibility of relations in the sentence. We set a threshold to determine whether the sentence contains the relation or not.

$$P_{rel} = \sigma \left(\mathbf{W}_r \mathcal{F}_{\mathbf{s}} + \mathbf{b}_r \right), \tag{4}$$

3.3   Subject and Object Extraction

Different from traditional relation extraction models, we further investigate the effects of generating contextual semantic representations. Specifically, attention mechanism is employed to obtain contextual semantic representations.

Relation-Attention Mechanism. A common approach to entity and relation extraction is first to extract the subject and object. The relation is usually extracted by the concatenation of subject and object. In our model, relation embedding is obtained based on network training. The contextual semantic is inseparable from both entity recognition and relation extraction.

$$a_{ij} = \alpha^T \left[W_1 x_i + b_1; W_2 r_j + b_2 \right], \tag{5}$$

$$\lambda_{ij} = \text{softmax} \left(a_{ij} \right), \tag{6}$$

$$h_s = r_j + \sum_{j=1}^{n} \lambda_{ij} \left(W_3 x_j + b_3 \right), \tag{7}$$

In our model, we utilize relation embedding as an indication to detect the object in order to overcome the problem of relation overlapping. The embedding of subjects and relations is supplied into a deep network model to predict objects based on the association of entities and relations. Specifically, we introduce a relation-attention mechanism to compute the specific representation of different words in a sentence under a particular relation, enhancing the effect of relation embedding on entity classification. For subject and object recognition, we use a relation-attentive contextual semantic to produce different relation-aware sentence representations for relation r_j. We can achieve the contextual semantic representations by dynamically representing the relevance of words in different relations. Finally, the weighted and summed word representations are used to generate sentence semantics.

$$\mathbf{P}_{i,j}^{sub} = \text{Softmax}\left(\mathbf{W}_{sub}\left(x_i + r_j + h_s\right) + \mathbf{b}_{sub}\right), \tag{8}$$

$$\mathbf{P}_{i,j}^{obj} = \text{Softmax}\left(\mathbf{W}_{obj}\left(x_i + r_j + h_s\right) + \mathbf{b}_{obj}\right), \tag{9}$$

The Eqs. (8) and (9) is to judge the object and object probability of the i-th word in the j-th relation.

Subject and Object Alignment. We have assess the object according to the relation and the subject in the extraction. To better model the correlation between subject and object, we remove the correlation between them and determine the probability that the subject and object belong to relation directly. A global correspondence matrix is used to evaluate the confidence of the subject-object pair in a relation.

$$P_{i_{sub},j_{obj}} = \sigma\left(\mathbf{W}_g\left[x_i^{sub}; x_j^{obj}\right] + \mathbf{b}_g\right), \tag{10}$$

The function of the softmax layer is to calculate the probability of each relation label defined in the relation extraction task.

3.4   Training and Inference

We take the cross-entropy loss to calculate the final loss to better train the model. In Eq. (11), $\mathcal{L}_{seq}$ denotes the cross-entropy loss of relation classification. In Eq. (12), $\mathcal{L}_{seq}$ represents the cross-entropy loss of entity pair. In Eq. (13), $\mathcal{L}_{global}$ indicates the cross-entropy loss of the entity alignment, which means the possibility of two tokens in a relation without prior relation information.

$$\mathcal{L}_{rel} = -\frac{1}{n_r}\sum_{i=1}^{n_r}\left(y_i \log P_{rel} + (1 - y_i)\log\left(1 - P_{rel}\right)\right), \tag{11}$$

$$\mathcal{L}_{seq} = -\frac{1}{2 \times n \times n_r^{pot}}\sum_{t\in\{sub,obj\}}\sum_{j=1}^{n_T^{pot}}\sum_{i=1}^{n}\mathbf{y}_{i,j}^t \log \mathbf{P}_{i,j}^t, \tag{12}$$

$$\mathcal{L}_{global} = -\frac{1}{n^2}\sum_{i=1}^{n}\sum_{j=1}^{n}\left(y_{i,j}\log P_{i_{sub},j_{obj}} + (1 - y_{i,j})\left(1 - \log P_{i_{sub},j_{obj}}\right)\right), \tag{13}$$

At the same time, the experiment needs to calculate the probability of the relation between any two words. It takes a lot of time. Then the three parts loss functions are weighted and summed to obtain the total loss.

$$\mathcal{L}_{total} = \alpha\mathcal{L}_{rel} + \beta\mathcal{L}_{seq} + \gamma\mathcal{L}_{global}, \tag{14}$$

4 Experiment and Analysis

In this section, we evaluate the model's overall performance and then test the extraction effect of the model on overlapping triples. In the model training and testing, we simply set $\alpha = \beta = \gamma = 1$.

4.1 Datasets and Settings

We evaluate our model on two public available datasets: NYT* and WebNLG*. NYT* [10] is a dataset published by Google and generated by distant supervision method. It contains 1.18 million sentences with a total of 24 relations. WebNLG* [3] was originally proposed for natural language generation tasks. The dataset contains 246 relations. The two dataset is processed by PRGC [18] for a better usage. The statistics of datasets is listed in Table 2 and 3. In this method, some basic parameters are set as follows. The max sentence length is set to 100 and the training epoch is set to 200. The batch size during training is 8 and the learning rate is 1e-5. The relation recognition threshold of relation is set to 0.1.

Table 2. Statistics of NYT* and Web-NLG* datasets.

Dataset	NYT*	WebNLG*
Relation type	24	171
Train sentence	56195	4999
Test sentence	5000	703
Valid sentence	4999	500

Table 3. Overlapping data in four datasets.

Type	NYT*	WebNLG*
Normal	3266	245
SEO	1297	457
EPO	978	26
SOO	45	84

4.2 Baselines and Evaluation Metrics

We utilize bert-base-uncased for embedding, and we employ Pytorch to implement our model RARE and conduct experiments with 3070 GPU. In this paper, we select some excellent models to compare and analyze with this model. A more rigorous evaluation method is used. Only when the extracted relation and the head and tail of subject and object are entirely correctly extracted triples considered correct. The followings are some related baselines.

RSAN [16] proposes a model that uses the relation-specific attention mechanism to obtain a specific sentence representation for each relation for relation prediction in a sentence, then extracts its corresponding entities. The model uses an attention network to extract entities and relations from a given set of words or phrases.

PRGC [18] In this model, a relation-independent global correspondence matrix is designed to determine the specific subject and object. The model first predicts a subset of possible relations for a given sentence and obtains a global matrix. Then they label the subject and object, respectively. Finally, all entity pairs are enumerated and filtered by the global matrix.

CopyMTL [17] To predict multi-token entities, the model provides a basic but successful combined entity and extraction model. The model also provides a copy method and a non-linear method for extracting entities.

TPLinker [15] proposes a pipeline method for extraction. The model reconstructs the traditional joint entity and relation extraction model, detects the sentence level relation, and then extracts the subject and object. This study primarily develops a new loss function to address the issue of many negative samples and achieves efficient training.

CasREL [13] The authors investigate the overlapping triples from a new perspective. They argue that it is possible to model relation in a sentence as a function that maps head entities to tail entities. In this way, they can find more relational triples.

To make a fair comparison, we use the Precision (P), Recall (R), and F_1 measure (F1) consistent with the baseline method as the evaluation.

4.3   Relation Extraction Results

To verify the effectiveness of the relation extraction model based on the relation-attentive contextual semantic. The experiments are conducted on two datasets. Table 4 shows the precision, recall, and F1 score of the baseline and RARE models on the NYT* and WebNLG* datasets.

Table 4. Main result of our model and baselines on NYT* and WebNLG*.

Model	NYT*			WebNLG*		
	P	R	F1	P	R	F1
CasREL [13]	0.897	0.895	0.896	0.934	0.901	0.918
Copy-MTL [17]	–	–	–	0.447	0.411	0.429
TPLinker [15]	0.913	0.925	0.919	0.918	0.920	0.919
PRGC [18]	0.939	0.919	0.926	0.940	0.921	0.930
RARE (ours)	**0.945**	**0.932**	**0.938**	**0.935**	**0.936**	**0.935**

In Table 4, we can obtain that RARE model has achieved the best performance on the four data sets of NYT * and WebNLG*. Our model is superior to other models. It can be obtained that the RARE model improves in precision, recall and F1 score than other baselines. At the same time, the performance is the best among the results on the NYT* dataset, with the F1 increased by 1.2% than PRGC. The improvement of RARE on WebNLG* is slight, but it still increases by 0.5% over PRGC, reflecting the advantage of our model. Our model adopts a two-stage relation extraction method. It predicts the object with the help of subject embedding and relation embedding through a two-way connection between entity and relation, making the model perform well in terms of precision and F1 score. Compared with the PRGC model, which also utilizes relation filtering, we further consider relation-aware sentence embedding to obtain better contextual semantic information, making the model perform well in terms of precision and F1 score.

There are three main types of overlapping relation extraction, Normal, EPO, and SEO. Extra tests are added to determine whether overlapping triples can be extracted. The overlapping relation extraction results are shown in Table 5. We conduct extensive experiments on NYT* and WebNLG* datasets.

Table 5. F1 score of sentences with different overlapping patterns.

Dataset	Model	Normal	SEO	EPO
NYT*	ETL-Span	0.885	0.876	0.603
	TPLinker	0.901	0.934	0.940
	PRGC	0.910	0.940	0.945
	RARE (ours)	**0.920**	**0.945**	**0.948**
WebNLG*	ETL-Span	0.873	0.915	0.805
	TPLinker	0.879	0.925	0.953
	PRGC	0.904	0.936	0.959
	RARE (ours)	**0.915**	0.949	0.950

As the results shown in Table 5, the RARE model achieved better performance in extracting all three types of sentences in NYT* dataset. The F1 score of our model is higher than other models under the SEO, with 1% increase in F1 score compared to the PRGC model, which proves that this method can alleviate the relation overlapping problem of the SEO type to a certain extent. However, our model improves slightly on WebNLG* dataset. There may be some limit in our model. The RARE model can exploit the association between entities and relation in relation prediction, employing the implicit link between entity and relation as a indication to predict the object, avoiding the overlap challenge. At the same time, contextual semantic information is added to the training process to increase the ability to find entities. As a result, the RARE model can achieve optimal performance even in complex scenarios of EPO and SEO.

In this paper, we also verify the ability of the RARE model to extract relations from sentences with different numbers of triples. The sentences in the dataset can be classified into five categories according to the number of sentences containing different triples, and N denotes the number of relation triples in a sentence. Figure 2 shows the experimental results for each model with different numbers of triples on NYT*.

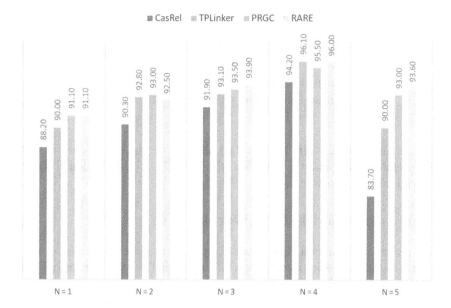

Fig. 2. F1 score (%) of extracting triples from sentences with different number of triples.

The performance of all the baseline models increases as the number of relation triples increases, and the RARE model also increases. Our achieves better performance in the five categories. Compared to the other models, our model is not affected by the length of the input sentences, demonstrating that our model is a considerable improvement on the PRGC model. At the same time, the largest improvements on the NYT* dataset come from the most difficult cases $(N > 5)$, with 0.6% improvement compared to the PRGC model, thus indicating that the model is better adapted to more complex scenarios.

4.4 Ablation Study

Components in our model have different effects in the experiment, so we conduct ablation experiments to evaluate the component' contribution to the experimental performance. In addition, ablation experiments are carried out to examine in detail the contribution of each component of the model to the overall performance. The results of the ablation experiments are shown in Table 6. "–mlp attention" represents the impact of removing the mlp-attention during the relation prediction, and we employ "–relation attention" denotes the impact of the proposed relation-attention and residual structure on the model.

Table 6 shows the ablation test on NYT* dataset. We find that the relation-attention mechanism is helpful to capture relation information in relation classification, and the F1 score drops 1.6% when the sentence information is removed, which demonstrates the importance of relation-attention sentence embedding.

Table 6. Ablation test on NYT* dataset.

Model	P	R	F1
RARE	**0.945**	**0.932**	**0.938**
−mlp-attention	0.929	0.916	0.922
−relation attention	0.932	0.926	0.928

After removing the mlp-attention, we employ the original bert output as the sentence embedding, and the F1 score drops 1.0%. It also demonstrates the contextual information is helpful.

5   Conclusion and Future Works

In this paper, we proposed a relational triples extraction model based on the relational-attention mechanism, in which the implied relation between entities and relations was exploited, and relations were predicted using subject embedding and relational embedding. In contrast, the influence of contextual semantic information on entity relation extraction was considered. The experimental results showed that the model in this paper improved by 1.2% compared to the baseline models, providing a new approach to the relation extraction task. In the future, we plan to study the long-range dependency effect further to enhance the performance of relation extraction.

Acknowledgements. This work is supported by the Science and Technology project (41008114, 41011215, and 41014117).

References

1. Dixit, K., Al-Onaizan, Y.: Span-level model for relation extraction. In: Proceedings of the 57th Annual Meeting of the Association for Computational Linguistics, pp. 5308–5314 (2019)
2. Eberts, M., Ulges, A.: Span-based joint entity and relation extraction with transformer pre-training. In: ECAI 2020, pp. 2006–2013. Spring (2020)
3. Gardent, C., Shimorina, A., Narayan, S., Perez-Beltrachini, L.: Creating training corpora for NLG micro-planners. In: Proceedings of the 55th Annual Meeting of the Association for Computational Linguistics (Volume 1: Long Papers), pp. 179–188 (2017)
4. Ji, B., Yu, J., Li, S., Ma, J., Wu, Q., Tan, Y., Liu, H.: Span-based joint entity and relation extraction with attention-based span-specific and contextual semantic representations. In: Proceedings of the 28th International Conference on Computational Linguistics, pp. 88–99 (2020)
5. Li, F., Lin, Z., Zhang, M., Ji, D.: A span-based model for joint overlapped and discontinuous named entity recognition. arXiv preprint arXiv:2106.14373 (2021)
6. Liu, J., Chen, Y., Liu, K., Bi, W., Liu, X.: Event extraction as machine reading comprehension. In: Proceedings of the 2020 Conference on Empirical Methods in Natural Language Processing (EMNLP), pp. 1641–1651 (2020)

7. Luan, Y., Wadden, D., He, L., Shah, A., Ostendorf, M., Hajishirzi, H.: A general framework for information extraction using dynamic span graphs. In: NAACL-HLT, no. 1 (2019)

8. Luo, L., et al.: An attention-based bilstm-CRF approach to document-level chemical named entity recognition. Bioinformatics **34**, 1381–1388 (2018)

9. Qiu, H., Zheng, Q., Msahli, M., Memmi, G., Qiu, M., Lu, J.: Topological graph convolutional network-based urban traffic flow and density prediction. IEEE Trans. Intell. Transp. Syst. **22**, 4560–4569 (2021)

10. Riedel, S., Yao, L., McCallum, A.: Modeling relations and their mentions without labeled text. In: Balcázar, J.L., Bonchi, F., Gionis, A., Sebag, M. (eds.) ECML PKDD 2010. LNCS (LNAI), vol. 6323, pp. 148–163. Springer, Heidelberg (2010). https://doi.org/10.1007/978-3-642-15939-8_10

11. Tang, H., Ji, D., Zhou, Q.: Joint multi-level attentional model for emotion detection and emotion-cause pair extraction. Neurocomputing **409**, 329–340 (2020)

12. Wang, J., Xu, W., Fu, X., Xu, G., Wu, Y.: Astral: adversarial trained LSTM-CNN for named entity recognition. Knowl. Based Syst. **197**, 105842 (2020)

13. Wei, Z., Su, J., Wang, Y., Tian, Y., Chang, Y.: A novel cascade binary tagging framework for relational triple extraction. arXiv preprint arXiv:1909.03227 (2019)

14. Wu, F., Liu, J., Wu, C., Huang, Y., Xie, X.: Neural Chinese named entity recognition via CNN-LSTM-CRF and joint training with word segmentation. In: The World Wide Web Conference, pp. 3342–3348 (2019)

15. Xie, C., Liang, J., Liu, J., Huang, C., Huang, W., Xiao, Y.: Revisiting the negative data of distantly supervised relation extraction. In: Zong, C., Xia, F., Li, W., Navigli, R. (eds.) Proceedings of the 59th Annual Meeting of the Association for Computational Linguistics and the 11th International Joint Conference on Natural Language Processing, ACL/IJCNLP 2021, (Volume 1: Long Papers), Virtual Event, 1–6 August 2021, pp. 3572–3581. Association for Computational Linguistics (2021)

16. Yuan, Y., Zhou, X., Pan, S., Zhu, Q., Song, Z., Guo, L.: A relation-specific attention network for joint entity and relation extraction. In: IJCAI, pp. 4054–4060 (2020)

17. Zeng, D., Zhang, H., Liu, Q.: Copymtl: copy mechanism for joint extraction of entities and relations with multi-task learning. In: Proceedings of the AAAI Conference on Artificial Intelligence, vol. 34, pp. 9507–9514 (2020)

18. Zheng, H., et al.: PRGC: Potential relation and global correspondence based joint relational triple extraction. In: Proceedings of the 59th Annual Meeting of the Association for Computational Linguistics and the 11th International Joint Conference on Natural Language Processing (Volume 1: Long Papers), pp. 6225–6235 (2021)

19. Zhong, B., He, W., Huang, Z., Love, P.E., Tang, J., Luo, H.: A building regulation question answering system: a deep learning methodology. Adv. Eng. Inf. **46**, 101195 (2020)

20. Zhu, Q., Li, X., Conesa, A., Pereira, C.: Gram-CNN: a deep learning approach with local context for named entity recognition in biomedical text. Bioinformatics **34**(9), 1547–1554 (2018)

Mario Fast Learner: Fast and Efficient Solutions for Super Mario Bros

Chen Lin[(✉)] [iD]

South China University of Technology, Guangzhou 510641, Guangdong, China
201920127742@mail.scut.edu.cn

Abstract. Super Mario Bros (SMB) are popular video games. Reinforcement learning has solved various problems including robot control and the game of Go. This article focuses on reinforcement learning methods for Super Mario Bros (SMB) games. Previous methods could solve all available SMB single player open source levels by using reinforcement learning methods. The article summarizes that previous evaluation metrics include reward function, loss function and the arrival of the endpoint flag but these metrics cannot fully judge the quality of the policies. The article analyzes the difficulties for agents to complete SMB levels and points out the problems that need to be solved. To solve the problems, the article proposes a new judging metric for SMB games called 100 recent accuracy. The article propose a solution to speed up the training procedure and improve the experimental results. According to the experimental results, the new solution has good experimental performance under the new evaluation metrics proposed in this article.

Keywords: Super Mario Bros · Reinforcement learning · Policy optimization · Evaluation indicator · Accelerated training

1 Introduction

This article focuses on Super Mario Bros [1] (SMB), which are popular video games since 1985. Researchers have studied SMB games from multiple perspectives. One article in 2009 [2] uses simple single-neuron model and non-linear approximators and gets more than 60% accuracy. Another paper in 2009 [3] introduces a reinforcement learning method for solving SMB games. The method could solve easy levels but not hard ones. The article in 2012 [4] uses grammatical evolution to evolve levels. An article in 2013 [5] compares methods for generating game controllers and finds that a method based on neuroevolution performs best both in terms of the instrumental similarity measure and in phenomenologic AI evolution by human spectators. For mathematical analysis, one article in 2016 [6] proves that solving SMB games is PSPACE-complete and the problem is weakly NP-hard if the levels can be represented using run-length encoding.

© The Author(s), under exclusive license to Springer Nature Switzerland AG 2022
G. Memmi et al. (Eds.): KSEM 2022, LNAI 13369, pp. 94–103, 2022.
https://doi.org/10.1007/978-3-031-10986-7_8

Reinforcement learning has achieved great application results in various fields and it focuses on solving real-world problems. The most famous reinforcement learning achievement is Alpha Go [7] in the area of the game of Go. The mu-zero method [8] that Deepmind proposed in 2020 could solve atari, go, chess and shogi with superhuman performance. One article in 2019 [9] uses residual reinforcement learning methods for robot control work. Another article in 2022 [10] gives a method for robot hand-eye calibration. For theoretical analysis, there are studies about explainability of Deep Reinforcement Learning [11] and prototypical representations Reinforcement Learning [12].

This article focuses on reinforcement learning methods that can solve SMB games. One article in 2020 [13] use an method based on reinforcement learning and could solve SMB levels with reliable results. Another article in 2021 [14] proposes a method for generating levels and testing levels with the help of reinforcement learning. There is an article in 2021 [15] proposes a new method for reward shaping and uses the method to gain higher reward.

According to the research analysis, researchers have demonstrated that reinforcement learning methods can handle SMB basic problems.
This article poses two problems and tries to solve them:

1. How can different policies be judged when the policy could already bring the agent to the end flag?
2. How to speed up the training process?

Based on the problems this article proposed, the contributions are:

1. The article proposes a new evaluation indicator called 100 recent accuracy. The new indicator represents the accuracy of the policy for getting to the endpoint flag. By observing the accuracy, it is easier to tell the quality of the policy.
2. The article proposes accelerated training techniques to save the training time. The flag factor could indicate if the policy has already brought the agent to the endpoint flag. When flag factor is true, the following training procedure can be accelerated and the accuracy could be higher.
3. The article proposes a new format of the loss function which adds a factor called critic_discount. The new loss function could balance the different components by adjusting parameters. With the flag_factor, a new format of reward function is given.

Section 2 discusses the background. Section 3 presents the details of the proposed method. The fourth section presents the experimental results.

2   Background

2.1   Reinforcement Learning

Reinforcement learning focuses on the interaction between the agent and the environment. It can be assumed that the interactive process fits the framework of Markov Decision Process (MDP). At time t, the agent takes action a_t in state s_t based on policy π and obtains a reward r_t. The cumulative reward is defined as $R_t = \sum_{k=0}^{\infty} \gamma^k r_{t+k}$ where $\gamma \in (0, 1]$ is the discount factor. The goal of reinforcement learning is to find an optimal policy to maximize the cumulative reward. There are value function $V_\pi(s_t) = E(R_t|s_t)$ to calculate the average cumulative reward in state s_t and action value function $Q_\pi(s_t, a_t) = E(R_t|s_t, a_t)$ to calculate the average cumulative reward in state s_t and action a_t. There is advantage function $A_\pi(s_t, a_t) = Q_\pi(s_t, a_t) - V_\pi(s_t)$ for evaluating how good the action is with respect to the average action.

There is gym [16] , an open source reinforcement learning environment on Github designed by OpenAI that is popular for reinforcement learning experimentation.

2.2   Super Mario Bros Games

Super Mario Bros Games [1] originates in 1985 and are popular games in the world. There is a github edition SMB environment [18] based on gym environment [16]. The gym-super-mario-bros environment is written in the Python programming language and can be used on Windows and Linux. The environment includes 32 single player levels.

2.3   Leading Reinforcement Learning Methods

The leading reinforcement learning methods are the methods that based on proximal policy optimization theory. The original method [17] was proposed in 2017. The key concept of PPO is the clipped surrogate objective:

$$L^{clip} = \hat{E}_t[\min(r_t(\theta)\hat{A}_t, \text{clip}(r_t(\theta), 1 - \epsilon, 1 + \epsilon)\hat{A}_t)] \tag{1}$$

where $r_t(\theta) = \frac{\pi_\theta(a_t|s_t)}{\pi_{\theta old}(a_t|s_t)}$ is the probability ratio between the new probability $\pi_\theta(a_t|s_t)$ and the old probability $\pi_{\theta old}(a_t|s_t)$. PPO methods are robust and it is easy to tune PPO parameters in different environments.

2.4   Problems of Previous Methods

Previous work has solved 31 levels of gym-super-mario-bros [18] where the only failed stage 7-4 is incomplete in the original environment. However, there are problems about the previous methods.

First, the agent could get to the endpoint flag but its performance is not easy to measure. Therefore, new evaluation criteria should be given.

Second, parameters need to be tuned in different stages of SMB games. It is hard to find the optimal parameters for different stages. Whatsmore, it is not clear whether parameters need to be added.

Third, it takes a long time to train the policy even with multiprocessing techniques. The main reason is that the sampling process of SMB games takes a long time.

Therefore, it is necessary to propose a new judging indicator for SMB policies. The proposed solutions are shown in the next section.

3   Proposed Methods

To solve the aforementioned SMB problems, there are three parts in the proposed solutions, namely, recent accuracy evaluation, accelerated training skills and target function update.

3.1   Use Accuracy Metrics

The goal of SMB games is to reach the endpoint flag. However, recent studies [13–15] focus on two aspects:

1. Whether the agent could get to the final flag or not.
2. How to make the reward higher.

Based on such considerations, it is necessary to add an accuracy indicator.

The proposed method adds 100 recent accuracy to judge the accuracy of the policy. The formula is:

$$accuracy = length(a)/100 \tag{2}$$

where a is a queue that contains the episodes that the agent could reach the endpoint flag during the last 100 episodes. Formally, the formula is as follows:

$$localflag = \begin{cases} True & \text{reached the flag in the current episode} \\ False & \text{did not reach the flag in the current episode} \end{cases} \tag{3}$$

It is indeed trivial in supervised learning, but novel in SMB games with Reinforcement Learning methods of recent years. For accuracy, the proposed methods use it in two parts: Training goal and reward shaping.

1. Use it as the training goal. The goal is to make the accuracy higher during the training process. And by observing the 100 recent accuracy, it is easier to judge whether the policy is getting better or not. The accuracy indicator is used in the test during the experiments.

2. Add accuracy to reward function. We add the accuracy information to the reward function in specific episodes that the agent could reach the flag. The reward function for that episode is:

$$reward = reward + min(accuracy, int(local\_flag\_get)) \qquad (4)$$

By adding the accuracy component, it could make the agent learn faster for successful episode.

3.2   Accelerated Training Solution

It is obvious that the agent should reach the final flag as fast as possible. In reality, balancing the ability to reach the end with enhanced exploration is the key to successful training procedure. In previous studies, clipping the gradient of the norm is a technique via pytorch to avoid gradient explosion. However, according to the baseline results of 100 recent accuracy, mario can reach the endpoint flag but the following procedure shows that mario may not tend to get to the flag. To achieve the goal, we add a flag check point.

$$flag = \begin{cases} 1 & \text{has reached the flag} \\ 0 & \text{has not reached the flag} \end{cases} \qquad (5)$$

With the flag information, the proposed methods have two points of improvement:

1. Use the flag information to determine the clip grad norm parameter used during training procedure. The flag information is used as clipping parameter to clip grad norm:

$$max\_grad\_norm = 1 + flag * flag\_factor \qquad (6)$$

   where flag_factor is a hyperparameter to be tuned which determines how fast the policy should learn after specific successful episode.
2. Use the flag get information to limit the local steps sampling procedure.

   To balance the exploration and exploitation, the baseline method uses local steps threshold which regulates the multiprocessing procedure. For each episode, the sampling procedure ends when the agent reaches maximum local steps in previous methods. In the proposed methods, the local steps factor decreases after the agent could drive the agent to the endpoint flag. The formula is as follows:

$$local\_steps = num\_local\_steps * (1 - flag * flag\_factor\_steps) \qquad (7)$$

The goal of this formula is to speed up the sampling process. The flag_get_factor could be adaptive and changes in different environments.

The algorithm procedure is shown in Algorithm 1.

Algorithm 1. Fast SMB algorithm

Input: network parameters θ_{old}
Output: new network parameters θ
1: **for** $i \in [0, max\_episodes - 1]$ **do**
2:   local steps changes according to flag_get condition
3:   **for** $i \in [0, local\_steps - 1]$ **do**
4:     Sample from environment
5:   **end for**
6:   **for** $i \in [0, num\_epochs - 1]$ **do**
7:     **for** $j \in [0, batchsize - 1]$ **do**
8:       Optimize loss function wrt θ according to flag_get condition
9:     **end for**
10:   **end for**
11: **end for**

3.3 Target Function Update

The loss function in previous methods [17] is composed of actor loss and critic loss with additional entropy loss:

$$Loss = Loss_{actor} + Loss_{critic} - \beta * Loss_{entropy} \qquad (8)$$

However, it is not a good idea to treat actor loss and critic loss equally due to their difference. Based on this analysis, we use a new loss function format:

$$Loss = Loss_{actor} + \phi * Loss_{critic} - \beta * Loss_{entropy} \qquad (9)$$

In the loss function, L_{actor} means the actor loss, L_{critic} means the critic loss and $L_{entropy}$ the entropy loss respectively. The algorithm adds a new item called critic discount to balance the actor loss and critic loss. There is no need to add another actor discount factor because there is already β in the loss function. The parameters can be better tuned in different environments due to its robustness.

4 Experiments

4.1 Baseline with Accuracy Check

The basic experiment protocol is to use PPO and GAE. There is already an article using PPO and GAE [13] as mentioned before. The article has given clear description of training the agent with PPO methods and is open sourced on Github. The code the experiment uses is based on the paper.

The experiments includes different worlds and different stages. The experimental levels include world 1-1 and 1-2 in World One and 2-1 and 2-2 in World Two. The basic experiment settings are shown in Table 1.

Table 1. Basic experiment settings

Multiprocess	gamma	lr	critic_discount	num_batch
8	0.9	1e−4	1	500

The experimental results of 1-1 and 1-2 with clipping parameter of 1 are shown in Fig. 1. The experimental results of 2-1 and 2-2 in world 2 are shown in Fig. 2.

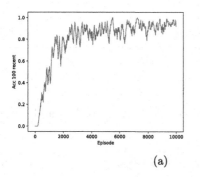
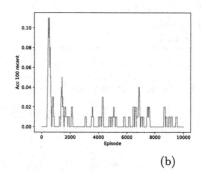

(a)   (b)

Fig. 1. 1-1 and 1-2 original results

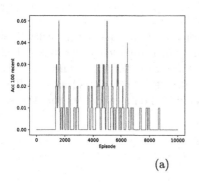
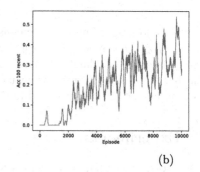

(a)   (b)

Fig. 2. 2-1 and 2-2 clip 1 results

Table 2 shows the differences in settings for different experiments.

Table 2. Experiment settings

Number	World	Stage	Clip grad norm	Other settings
1	1	1	1	Base
2	1	2	1	Base
3	2	1	1	Base
4	2	2	1	Base

The experimental results show that the initial scheme has driven the agent to reach the endpoint flag. But the results are not satisfactory due to the poor accuracy of recent episodes.

4.2 New Method

According to the algorithm, the flag indicator is used in various ways.

For better experimentation, the flag_factor is set to 19 of 1-1 and 1-2 which means that the maximum gradient norm is 20 after the policy could reach the flag. The experiment settings are shown in Table 3. The results are shown in Fig. 3. The results of 4-1 and 5-1 are shown in Fig. 4. The results of 6-1 and 7-1 are shown in Fig. 5. From the experimental results, the new method does not reduce the number of episodes required to reach the endpoint flag for the first time. The method we propose improves the agent's ability to consistently reach the endpoint flag. Based on the accuracy results, the policy works better after it obtains the ability to reach the endpoint flag.

Table 3. New experiment settings

Multiprocess	gamma	lr	critic_discount	num_batch
8	0.9	1e−4	0.5	500

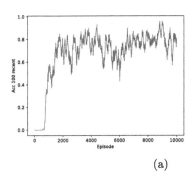
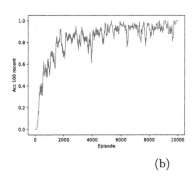

(a)   (b)

Fig. 3. 1-1 and 1-2 clip 20 results

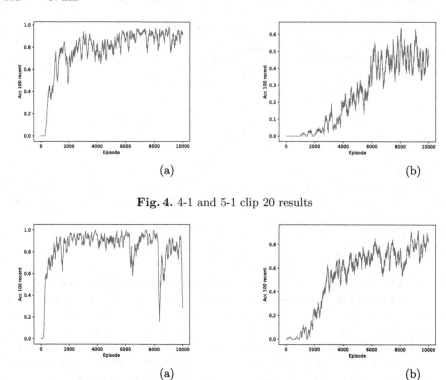

Fig. 4. 4-1 and 5-1 clip 20 results

Fig. 5. 5-1 and 6-1 clip 20 results

On the other hand the parameter $flag\_factor\_steps$ is set to 0.9 in the experiment of the new method. And it could save 10% time during the sampling process after the flag get factor is True.

5   Conclusion

This paper analyzed the problems of the previous SMB solutions. The paper proposed a new evaluation indicator named 100 recent accuracy for SMB games solutions. The new indicator was the key judging metric for the policies. The new indicator was used in neural network parameters update, local steps control and reward function reshaping. The experimental results indicated that the proposed methods could make the agent continue to get to the endpoint flag more frequently and speed up the training process. Future researches are needed to better apply the accuracy information to the training process.

References

1. Bros, S.M.: Nintendo entertainment system. Developed by Nintendo, Nintendo (1985)
2. Pedersen, C., Togelius, J., Yannakakis, G.N.: Modeling player experience in Super Mario Bros. In: 2009 IEEE Symposium on Computational Intelligence and Games, pp. 132–139 (2009). https://doi.org/10.1109/CIG.2009.5286482
3. Togelius, J., Karakovskiy, S., Koutnik, J., Schmidhuber, J.: Super Mario evolution. In: 2009 IEEE Symposium on Computational Intelligence and Games, pp. 156–161 (2009). https://doi.org/10.1109/CIG.2009.5286481
4. Shaker, N., Nicolau, M., Yannakakis, G.N., Togelius, J., O'neill, M.: Evolving levels for Super Mario Bros using grammatical evolution. In: 2012 IEEE Conference on Computational Intelligence and Games (CIG), pp. 304–311. IEEE (2012)
5. Ortega, J., Shaker, N., Togelius, J., Yannakakis, G.N.: Imitating human playing styles in Super Mario Bros. Entertain. Comput. 4(2), 93–104 (2013)
6. Demaine, E.D., Viglietta, G., Williams, A.: Super Mario Bros. Is harder/easier than we thought. In: Demaine, E.D., Grandoni, F. (eds.) 8th International Conference on Fun with Algorithms, FUN 2016. Leibniz International Proceedings in Informatics (LIPIcs), vol. 49, pp. 13:1–13:14. Schloss Dagstuhl-Leibniz-Zentrum fuer Informatik, Dagstuhl, Germany (2016). https://doi.org/10.4230/LIPIcs.FUN. 2016.13. http://drops.dagstuhl.de/opus/volltexte/2016/5880
7. Silver, D., et al.: Mastering the game of go with deep neural networks and tree search. nature 529(7587), 484–489 (2016)
8. Schrittwieser, J., et al.: Mastering Atari, Go, chess and shogi by planning with a learned model. nature 588(7839), 604–609 (2020)
9. Johannink, T., et al.: Residual reinforcement learning for robot control. In: 2019 International Conference on Robotics and Automation (ICRA), pp. 6023–6029. IEEE (2019)
10. Zhang, R., Lv, Q., Li, J., Bao, J., Liu, T., Liu, S.: A reinforcement learning method for human-robot collaboration in assembly tasks. Robot. Comput. Integr. Manuf. 73, 102227 (2022)
11. Heuillet, A., Couthouis, F., Díaz-Rodríguez, N.: Explainability in deep reinforcement learning. Knowl. Based Syst. 214, 106685 (2021)
12. Yarats, D., Fergus, R., Lazaric, A., Pinto, L.: Reinforcement learning with prototypical representations. In: International Conference on Machine Learning, pp. 11920–11931. PMLR (2021)
13. Zhang, N., Song, Z.: Super reinforcement bros: playing Super Mario Bros with reinforcement learning (2020)
14. Shu, T., Liu, J., Yannakakis, G.N.: Experience-driven PCG via reinforcement learning: a Super Mario Bros study. In: 2021 IEEE Conference on Games (CoG), pp. 1–9. IEEE (2021)
15. Bougie, N., Ichise, R.: Fast and slow curiosity for high-level exploration in reinforcement learning. Appl. Intell. 51(2), 1086–1107 (2020). https://doi.org/10.1007/s10489-020-01849-3
16. Brockman, G., et al.: OpenAI Gym (2016)
17. Schulman, J., Wolski, F., Dhariwal, P., Radford, A., Klimov, O.: Proximal policy optimization algorithms. arXiv preprint arXiv:1707.06347 (2017)
18. Kauten, C.: Super Mario Bros for OpenAI Gym. GitHub (2018). https://github. com/Kautenja/gym-super-mario-bros

Few-Shot Learning with Self-supervised Classifier for Complex Knowledge Base Question Answering

Bo Liu, Lei Liu, and Peiyi Wang[✉]

Lenovo Research, Beijing, China
{liubo22,liulei28,wangpy10}@lenovo.com

Abstract. Complex Question Answering (CQA) over Knowledge Base (KB) involves transferring natural language questions to a sequence of actions, which are utilized to fetch entities and relations for final answer. Typically, meta-learning based models regard question types as standards to divide dataset for pseudo-tasks. However, question type, manually labeled in CQA data set, is indispensable as a filter in the support set retrieving phase, which raises two main problems. First, preset question types could mislead the model to be confined to a non-optimal search space for meta-learning. Second, the annotation dependency makes it difficult to migrate to other datasets. This paper introduces a novel architecture to alleviate above issues by using a co-training scheme featured with self-supervised mechanism for model initialization. Our method utilizes a meta-learning classifier instead of pre-labeled tags to find the optimized search space. Experiments in this paper show that our model achieves state-of-the-art performance on CQA dataset without encoding question type.

Keywords: Meta-learning · Few-shot · Reinforcement learning · Question answering · Knowledge graph

1 Introduction

Knowledge-base question-answering (KBQA) task is defined as using facts stored in a knowledge base (KB) [9] to find the answer to a factoid question, which involves mapping natural-language questions to logical forms (annotations) including action sequences and programs that can be directly executed on a KB to retrieve answers [2,17]. Among the subfields of this topic, complex question answering (CQA) [16], different from multi-hop question answering, requires sophisticated operations such as set union and intersection, counting, min/max to be executed to obtain answers. In particular, this paper will focus on a CQA dataset [16], in which questions are classified into seven types. For instance, questions in the 'Simple' category only need 'select' to yield answers, while questions in the 'Quantitative Reasoning' category demand a sequence of 'select', 'union' and 'count' actions to return the answer.

Supported by Lenovo Research.

© The Author(s), under exclusive license to Springer Nature Switzerland AG 2022
G. Memmi et al. (Eds.): KSEM 2022, LNAI 13369, pp. 104–116, 2022.
https://doi.org/10.1007/978-3-031-10986-7_9

Fig. 1. The architecture of MACL

To solve KBQA problem, one-size-fits-all models-e.g., forward neural network, reinforcement learning, etc.-are regular approaches, which fit the training set with single one model and predict on questions of all types [1,2,4,16,21]. However, if questions have great diversity in logics or sentence structures, tacit knowledge may vary across them, leading to bias in predictions for one-size-fits-all model. To address this challenge, a neural program induction (NPI) approach is taken by Complex Imperative Program Induction from Terminal Rewards (CIPITR) [15]. Nevertheless, CIPITR still trains one one-size-fits-all model for seven question types each on CQA dataset instead of equipping the model with the ability to adapt to a certain form when faced with different kinds of questions.

In 2020, a new learning algorithm named MetA Retrieval Learning (MARL) [6] is proposed, in which a retriever and a programmer is jointly trained in two stages. The programmer is optimized in the stage one by meta-learning with retriever parameter fixed. In the second stage, the programmer will not be updated while the difference between support set used and not used can measure the effectiveness of the retriever, thus the retriever can be advanced by the reinforcement learning with the final reward offered by the programmer. In this way the retriever is encouraged to provide more accurate support set that is beneficial to the meta-task, rather than teacher forcing method in S2A, MARL is featured with this weak supervised training process. Besides, S2A employ multiple-round conversation as context, aiming to answer context-dependent questions. By comparison, questions in MARL are all single-round and KB can directly present the answer.

MARL achieves state-of-the-art performance at the time of publication, but this method cannot be well extended to other question answering datasets except CQA. It requires the question set to have accurate category labels which relies on expensive labor cost. This will also cause another problem that the algorithm limits the search space of the support set by filtering it with question type, whereas question with diverse types may also contribute valuable information.

To alleviate the above issues, this paper proposes a new architecture named MetA Classify Learning (MACL) – a model that utilizes a self-learning classifier instead of pre-labeled tags to find the most reasonable search space for support sets. Considering that the classification results could also participate in parameter updating as a part of the overall model adaptation, we extend the structure of MARL from two-stage joint training to three-stage joint training of retriever, programmer and classifier.

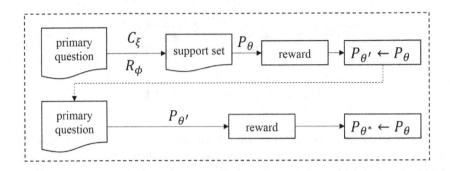

Fig. 2. Answer optimization stage

The classifier is used to predict the label of each question. As mentioned above, in order to reduce the bias introduced by manual labels, we do not use the question type of CQA data set. Instead, we cluster the unlabeled original data to obtain a rough classification as the pseudo-truth. Based on that, we train a classifier as a part of the model, which specifies the search space for meta-learning support set extraction. The parameters of classifier would be updated through reinforcement learning.

The retriever is a question selector that finds similar samples from a group of questions. KB artifacts (i.e., entities, relations, and types) and semantic similarity are used to measure the similarity between main question and support question. In each epoch, the whole data set is split into different groups according to the prediction results of the classifier, then the retriever would search similar samples in the same category for the primary question. The extracted questions together construct the support set for the pseudo task. During the training phase, reinforcement-learning [20] uses rewards from primary question along with pseudo-task to optimize the retriever.

The programmer is an answer generator. In the first step, the programmer encodes the problem into a sequence of actions. In the second step, these sequences are sent to the interpreter and executed to get the final answer in the knowledge base. Finally, the generated answers are evaluated on the ground-truth to produce rewards. Meta-learner trains the programmer to learn fast adaptation to a new primary question that has not been seen before.

The training process is divided into three stages, namely answer optimization stage, search optimization stage and space optimization stage. During these phrases, the programmer, the retriever and the classifier are updated respectively when the parameters of other modules remain fixed. Specially, the programmer is adapted by the meta-learning while the other two are updated by reinforcement-learning.

We evaluated our approach on a large complex QA data set named CQA [16]. MACL does not use manual category labels for dataset, which greatly reduces reliance on human labour. Therefore, this method can now be migrated to other datasets more easily. In terms of performance, our approach is superior to the

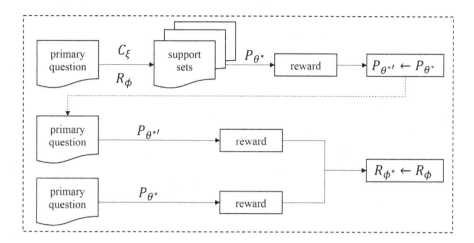

Fig. 3. Search optimization stage

standard imitation learning or RL-based models and achieves state-of-the-art F1 score compared to previous methods on out-of-question-type setting.

2   MACL

The task studied in this paper is Complex Question Answering (CQA) based on Knowledge Base (KB). We see this as a sequence-to-sequence learning task. The question is first transformed into a series of actions, then the triples are extracted from the knowledge base by the actions to obtain the final answer. We tackle this problem with few-shot meta-learning for classifier to decrease the reliance on data annotation and improve the transferability of the model. In this paper, we regard answering a single complex question as a separate task. Our goal is to train a self-learning model that can quickly adapt to new tasks. For this purpose, we leverage a meta-learner to complete each task. Specifically, for each primary question q_{pri}, we first assign a category label to it by classifier. Following that, the most similar N samples with the same category are retrieved to form a support set $S^{q_{pri}}$. Next, Question is decoded by the programmer to obtain the reward signal telling whether the programmer yields the correct answer. In the end, training rewards R_{train} from support set and testing rewards R_{test} from primary question are used to evaluate and update the model. The whole model is iteratively trained in three stages until the global optimal solution is obtained.

2.1   Overview of the Framework

Our architecture for few-shot learning of CQA is illustrated in Fig. 1. Our model adopts a three-stage joint optimization structure. Each stage consists of three working components, classifier, retriever and programmer. In the answer optimization stage, the parameters of BiLSTM-based programmer is updated by

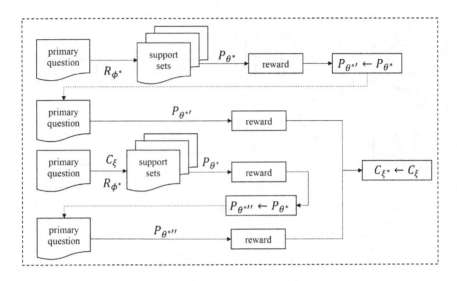

Fig. 4. Space optimization stage

the meta-learning. In the search optimization stage, the retriever based on Deep Structured Semantic Model (DSSM) method [7] is revised by the reinforcement-learning. In the space optimization stage, the parameters of previous modules are fixed and relevant rewards will renew the classifier, which is employed by the LSTM.

2.2 Algorithm

As shown in lines 3 to 9 in Algorithm 1, the programmer is trained by the approach of meta reinforcement learning (meta-RL) in the first stage. Similar to MARL, the gradient-based meta-learning method is employed to solve the meta-RL problem in this procedure. As the meta task is formulated in a RL setting, the vanilla policy gradient (VPG) [18] is performed to retrieve the optimal policy and Monte Carlo integration (MC) [5] strategy is applied for approximation.

For each primary question q_{pri} in training dataset, a support set $S^{q_{pri}}$ consisting of N secondary questions would be obtained after the classifier and the retriever are executed. Next, the primary question q_{pri} and the support set $S^{q_{pri}}$ together are considered as a meta-task. In the meta-training stage, each secondary question will produce K trajectories with probabilities, based on which the expectation of final reward on answering the secondary question can be calculated (Fig. 2). The sum of the rewards is subsequently utilized to adapt θ to θ',

$$L_{S^{q_{pri}}} = \sum_{q_i \in S^{q_{pri}}} E_{\tau \sim \pi(\tau|q_i,\theta)}[R(\tau)] \tag{1}$$

$$\theta' \longleftarrow \theta + \eta_1 \nabla_\theta L_{S^{q_{pri}}} \tag{2}$$

During meta-test stage, another K trajectories of the primary question will be generated by programmer with θ'. The expectation of the reward, regarded as the evaluation of adapted parameter θ', is meant to be maximized. Thus, the base θ is further updated by this objective:

$$L_{q_{pri}} = E_{\tau \sim \pi(\tau | q_{pri}, \theta')}[R(\tau)] \tag{3}$$

$$\theta \longleftarrow \theta + \eta_2 \nabla_\theta \sum_{q_{pri} \in Q_{pri}} L_{q_{pri}} \tag{4}$$

To be more specific, the meta-learned policy is achieved by the Reptile meta-learning algorithm [Nichol and Schulman, 2018].

During the second stage, the retriever is updated by a reinforcement learning approach, represented in lines 10–20. First, each primary question directly yields the answer and corresponding reward through the model optimized in the stage 1. Second, following the probability of each secondary question being selected, M support sets are sampled from Q_s. Based on each support set, θ can be adapted to θ'_m, as the adaptation of θ to θ' in stage 1 (Fig. 3).

$$L_{S_m^{q_{pri}}} = \sum_{q_i \in S_m^{q_{pri}}} E_{\tau \sim \pi(\tau | q_i, \theta)}[R(\tau)] \tag{5}$$

$$\theta'_m \longleftarrow \theta + \eta_1 \nabla_\theta L_{S_m^{q_{pri}}} \tag{6}$$

For each θ'_m, a trajectory corresponding to the primary question can be obtained and then a reward $R(\tau_m^{*\prime})$ can be calculated.

$$\tau_m^{*\prime} \longleftarrow decode(\pi(\tau | q_{pri}, \theta'_m)) \tag{7}$$

After that, the difference between $R(\tau_m^{*\prime})$ and $R(\tau^*)$ can be regarded as the evaluation of the significance of support set, which is exploited to update the retriever.

$$L'_{q_{pri}} = E_{S_m^{q_{pri}} \sim P(S^{q_{pri}} | \phi)}[R(\tau_m^{*\prime}) - R(\tau^*)] \tag{8}$$

$$\phi \longleftarrow \phi + \eta_3 \nabla_\phi \sum_{q_{pri} \in Q_{pri}} L'_{q_{pri}} \tag{9}$$

Following that, space optimization stage will be performed. It is noted that support sets will be retrieved under two different circumstances for each primary question. The first type of support sets will be generated by retriever without the information of question type. In other words, the filter module in the retriever will not work in this condition such that all the questions in support dataset will be input into DSSM module. In contrast, for the retrieval of another kind of support set, the classifier C will first categorize all the questions, based on which DSSM will filter out question that has distinct type from the primary question (Fig. 4).

Algorithm 1. The MACL algorithm

Input: Support dataset Q_s, Training dataset Q_{train}, step size $\eta_1, \eta_2, \eta_3, \eta_4$
Parameter: a classifier C (LSTM) with parameter ξ, a retriever R (DSSM) with parameter ϕ, a programmer P (LSTM) with parameter θ
Output: The parameters ξ^*, ϕ^*, θ^*

1: Initialize $\xi \longleftarrow \xi_0, \phi \longleftarrow \phi_0$, random initialize θ
2: **while** not converged **do**
3:     **for** Q_{pri} sampled from Q_{train} **do**
4:         **for** $q_{pri} \in Q_{pri}$ **do**
5:             Retrieve $S^{q_{pri}}$ from Q_s with ξ and ϕ
6:             $\theta' \longleftarrow \theta + \eta_1 \nabla_\theta \sum_{q_i \in S^{q_{pri}}} E_{\tau \sim \pi(\tau|q_i,\theta)}[R(\tau)]$
7:             $L_{q_{pri}} = E_{\tau \sim \pi(\tau|q_{pri},\theta')}[R(\tau)]$
8:             $\theta \longleftarrow \theta + \eta_2 \nabla_\theta \sum_{q_{pri} \in Q_{pri}} L_{q_{pri}}$
9:     **for** Q_{pri} sampled from Q_{train} **do**
10:         **for** $q_{pri} \in Q_{pri}$ **do**
11:             $\tau^* \longleftarrow decode(\pi(\tau|q_{pri},\theta))$, Compute $R(\tau^*)$
12:             Sample support sets $\mathcal{M}$ with ξ and ϕ
13:             **for** $S_m^{q_{pri}} \in \mathcal{M}$ **do**
14:                 $\theta'_m \longleftarrow \theta + \eta_1 \nabla_\theta \sum_{q_i \in S_m^{q_{pri}}} E_{\tau \sim \pi(\tau|q_i,\theta)}[R(\tau)]$
15:                 $\tau_m^{*\prime} \longleftarrow decode(\pi(\tau|q_{pri},\theta'_m))$, Compute $R(\tau_m^{*\prime})$
16:             $L'_{q_{pri}} = E_{S^{q_{pri}}_m \sim P(S^{q_{pri}}|\phi)}[R(\tau_m^{*\prime}) - R(\tau^*)]$
17:         $\phi \longleftarrow \phi + \eta_3 \nabla_\phi \sum_{q_{pri} \in Q_{pri}} L'_{q_{pri}}$
18:     **for** Q_{pri} sampled from Q_{train} **do**
19:         **for** $q_{pri} \in Q_{pri}$ **do**
20:             Sample support sets $\mathcal{M}_0$ with ϕ
21:             **for** $S_{m_0}^{q_{pri}} \in \mathcal{M}_0$ **do**
22:                 $\theta'_{m_0} \longleftarrow \theta + \eta_1 \nabla_\theta \sum_{q_i \in S_{m_0}^{q_{pri}}} E_{\tau \sim \pi(\tau|q_i,\theta)}[R(\tau)]$
23:                 $\tau_{m_0}^{*\prime} \longleftarrow decode(\pi(\tau|q_{pri},\theta'_{m_0}))$, Compute $R(\tau_{m_0}^{*\prime})$
24:             Sample support sets $\mathcal{M}_1$ with ξ and ϕ
25:             **for** $S_{m_1}^{q_{pri}} \in \mathcal{M}_1$ **do**
26:                 $\theta'_{m_1} \longleftarrow \theta + \eta_1 \nabla_\theta \sum_{q_i \in S_{m_1}^{q_{pri}}} E_{\tau \sim \pi(\tau|q_i,\theta)}[R(\tau)]$
27:                 $\tau_{m_1}^{*\prime} \longleftarrow decode(\pi(\tau|q_{pri},\theta'_{m_1}))$, Compute $R(\tau_{m_1}^{*\prime})$
28:             $R_0 = E_{S_{m_0}^{q_{pri}} \sim P(S^{q_{pri}}|\phi)} R(\tau_{m_0}^{*\prime})$
29:             $L''_{q_{pri}} = E_{S_{m_1}^{q_{pri}} \sim P(S^{q_{pri}}|\xi,\phi)}[R(\tau_{m_1}^{*\prime}) - R_0]$
30:         $\xi \longleftarrow \xi + \eta_4 \nabla_\xi \sum_{q_{pri} \in Q_{pri}} L''_{q_{pri}}$
31: **return** ξ, ϕ, θ

After support sets are produced with these two approaches, θ will adapted to θ'_{m_0} and θ'_{m_1} respectively. The rewards of programmer in these two parameters answering primary question – this is $R(\tau_{m_0}^{*\prime})$ and $R(\tau_{m_1}^{*\prime})$– will have a difference, which represents the effect of classifier.

$$R_0 = E_{S_{m_0}^{q_{pri}} \sim P(S^{q_{pri}}|\phi)} R(\tau_{m_0}^{*\prime}) \tag{10}$$

$$L''_{q_{pri}} = E_{S_{m_1}^{q_{pri}} \sim P(S^{q_{pri}}|\xi,\phi)}[R(\tau_{m_1}^{*\prime}) - R_0] \tag{11}$$

The difference will subsequently be applied to update the parameter of Classifier with reinforcement learning.

$$\xi \longleftarrow \xi + \eta_4 \nabla_\xi \sum\nolimits_{q_{pri} \in Q_{pri}} L''_{q_{pri}} \tag{12}$$

2.3   Objective Function with Reinforcement Learning

Among all procedures, it is worth mentioning that the parameters of DSSM and LSTM for classifier are updated by the final rewards, which are simply values without gradient. Hence, it is vital to design reasonable objective functions to combine rewards and the output of models, in which case the loss can backpropagate and the gradient descent can be operated.

For the DSSM part, the loss function is designed as Eq. (8) such that:

$$
\begin{aligned}
L'_{q_{pri}} &= E_{S_m^{q_{pri}} \sim P(S^{q_{pri}}|\phi)}[R(\tau_m^{*\,'}) - R(\tau^*)] \\
&= \sum_{m=1}^{M} [R(\tau_m^{*\,'}) - R(\tau^*)] \cdot P_\phi(S_m^{q_{pri}}) \\
&= \sum_{m=1}^{M} [R(\tau_m^{*\,'}) - R(\tau^*)] \cdot \prod_{n=1}^{N} P_\phi(q_n)
\end{aligned} \tag{13}
$$

In the above result, $P_\phi(q_n)$ is the output of the DSSM. Compared with the original loss function as the Eq. (14), in our model there are no clearly defined positive and negative samples. Instead, we have rewards representing the contribution of the candidates. Hence, the model is encouraged to choose better support sets by maximizing the objective function (13).

$$L_{DSSM} = -\log \prod_{(Q,D^+)} P(D^+|Q) \tag{14}$$

where D^+ are positive responses

Similar to DSSM, the objective function of LSTM for classification are reasonably adjusted from its original form.

$$
\begin{aligned}
L''_{q_{pri}} &= E_{S_{m_1}^{q_{pri}} \sim P(S^{q_{pri}}|\xi,\phi)}[R(\tau_{m_1}^{*\,'}) - E_{S_{m_0}^{q_{pri}}} R(\tau_{m_0}^{*\,'})] \\
&= \sum_{m_1=1}^{M} [R(\tau_{m_1}^{*\,'}) - \sum_{m_0=1}^{M} R(\tau_{m_0}^{*\,'}) \cdot P_\phi(S_{m_0}^{q_{pri}})] \cdot P_{\phi,\xi}(S_{m_1}^{q_{pri}}) \\
&\overset{\triangle}{=} \sum_{m_1=1}^{M} R^* \cdot \prod_{n=1}^{N} P_\phi(q_n) \cdot P_\xi(q_n)
\end{aligned} \tag{15}
$$

Except for $P_\xi(q_n)$, the rest part, which is approximately regarded as the label value in the common multi-label classification task, decides the direction $P_\xi(q_n)$ is expected to be optimized.

3   Evaluation

In this section, we describe our experimental settings and results on the large-scale CQA dataset [16]. During the experiments, our model is evaluated against with three baselines. In addition, we conduct ablation experiments to investigate the capability of the classifier and the effect of the cluster.

3.1   CQA Dataset

The CQA dataset is generated from the Wikidata KB [19] through a semi-automated process with manual labour. It contains 944K/100K/156K training/validation/test question-answer pairs respectively. There are seven question categories in CQA dataset which are described as follows:

- **Simple Question** can be answered with one hop in the knowledge graph.
- **Logical Reasoning Question** requires several logical deduction over multiple tuples in the knowledge graph.
- **Quantitative Reasoning Question** requires a large amount of quantitative reasoning which includes max, min, at least/at most/approximately/equal to N, etc.
- **Comparative Reasoning Question** requires a comparison between entities based on certain relations which include sort and more/less operations.
- **Verification (Boolean) Question** needs to judge whether the question is correct and return answer of Boolean data type.
- **Quantitative (Count) Question** requires quite a few quantitative reasoning steps which involve standard aggregation count functions.
- **Comparative (Count) Question** requires a comparison between entities based on certain relations and count operations.

For questions whose types are "Verification", "Quantitative (Count)" and "Comparative (Count)", we use "accuracy" as the evaluation metric while "F1 measure" demonstrates the performance of other kinds.

3.2   Comparison Methods

In this paper, several baseline methods on the CQA dataset are applied for comparison, including **HRED+KVmem** [16], **CIPITR** [15] and a variant of MARL [6] named **MARL (no-type)**. MARL proposed a novel meta-learning based algorithm for few-shot CQA task. In MARL, a retrieval model and a programmer model are trained jointly with weak supervision. To evaluate the performance of MARL when the question types are not given, we implemented MARL (no-type) which retrieves similar questions as support data from all question types.

To validate the benefits of each module in MACL, we conducted ablation experiments about the variants of our model. To verify the effect of clustering, we trained a model named **MACL (no-cluster)**. In MACL (no-cluster), each question in CQA dataset is randomly assigned a type rather than being assigned by the clustering result. Similar to MACL, the labeled questions in MACL (no-cluster) are used to pretrain the classifier. Another model **MACL (no-classifier)** is trained for exploring the benefits of the classifier. In this model, question type is annotated based on the clustering result in the beginning and would not be updated in the rest process. Besides, we trained the model named **MACL (random)** to verify the whole effectiveness of cluster and classifier. In MACL (random), we removed the classifier in MACL and randomly initialized the type of questions in CQA dataset. Notably, the number of question types by random initialization is the same as those based on the clustering result.

Table 1. Experimental results on the CQA test dataset. For each category, best result is **bolded** and second-best result is underlined.

Question category	HRED +KVmem	CIPITR	MARL (no-type)	MACL (no-cluster)	MACL (no-classifier)	MACL (random)	MACL
Simple	41.40%	41.62%	85.62%	85.00%	84.94%	85.02%	**85.98%**
Logical reasoning	37.56%	21.31%	79.68%	79.25%	78.57%	78.79%	**80.22%**
Quantitative reasoning	0.89%	5.65%	44.09%	44.97%	44.95%	44.23%	**45.65%**
Verification (Boolean)	27.28%	30.86%	84.99%	85.35%	85.45%	85.32%	**85.84%**
Comparative reasoning	1.63%	1.67%	61.75%	**62.52%**	61.92%	61.61%	61.56%
Quantitative (count)	17.80%	37.23%	62.17%	62.23%	62.21%	62.17%	**62.25%**
Comparative (count)	9.60%	0.36%	39.69%	39.59%	39.71%	39.42%	**40.29%**
Overall macro F1	19.45%	19.82%	65.43%	65.56%	65.39%	65.22%	**65.97%**
Overall micro F1	31.18%	31.52%	76.06%	75.80%	75.66%	75.64%	**76.50%**

3.3 Implementation Details

In MACL, the classifier is pre-trained to speed up the convergence of the full model. To generate the pseudo label for the pre-training of classifier, we adopted K-Means [12] clustering algorithm to cluster questions in CQA dataset. We averaged the embedding representations of each word in a question to obtain the question embeddings and considered it as K-Means input. Specifically, we exploited 50-dimensional GloVe word vectors [14] learned from web crawled data for word embeddings. To determine the value of k in K-means, we calculated the clustering result with SSE, which is defined as the sum of the squared distance between centroid and each member of the cluster. On top of that, elbow method were utilized to select the best k value. Based on the changes in SSE with varying k, we chose $k = 3$ as the number of groups and then annotated the questions into 3 categories.

MACL was implemented in PyTorch. Reptile [13] was employed to simplify the implementation of MAML [3] and avoid the calculation of second-order derivatives which requires magnificent computing expenses. During the stages of retriever and classifier learning, RL-based model optimized the non-differentiable objective by combining the traditional loss function with the rewards, in which the baseline C was imported to reduce the variance and C was set to $1e - 3$. We fixed the step size $\eta_1 = 1e - 4$ in the meta-training stage for all the learning stages. In contrast, different learning rates were set for the meta-test in varying stages. During the answer optimization stage, we let $\eta_2 = 0.1$ for the gradient descent. For search optimization stage, the initial learning rate η_3 was set to $1e-3$ and AdaBound [11] was applied to update the ϕ with the reward derived from programmer. In the space optimization stage, the Adam optimization algorithm [10] optimized ξ and the learning rate was set as $\eta_4 = 1e-3$. Additionally, the number of N for searching the top-N support questions in meta-training stage was set to 5. In the training of MACL, apart from the natural language questions, the entity, entity type and relation in the question were also encoded as the part of input. The batch size was set to 1 and our model converged on the validation set at round 80 epochs.

3.4 Performance Evaluation

In this part, we compare the proposed method with baseline algorithms described in Sect. 3.2 and offer further analysis. Table 1 presents the performance comparison on the CQA dataset. From the results, we can observe that our model MACL outperforms all the baseline models and achieves the state of the art performance. This is thanks to the fact that the classifier in MACL can be dynamically updated and provide the optimal search space for meta-learning. To understand the impact of each part in MACL on performance, we conducted additional experiments on CQA dataset and the results are shown in Table 2. The results demonstrate that the overall micro F1 of MACL (no-cluster) is 0.70% less than that of MACL, which implies the cluster result could pre-train the classifier and make it reach the optimal state sooner. The MACL (no-classifier) achieves 75.66% F1 score, which is 0.84% less than the micro F1 of MACL. It proves that even though the question type is effectively initialized, classifier still needs updating to group the questions better. The MACL (random) performs the worst among the three variants, illustrating that the cluster operation and the classifier updating are all necessary for better performance.

Table 2. Ablation study on the CQA test dataset.

Models	Overall micro F1
MACL	76.50%
- cluster	−0.70%
- classifier	−0.84%
- cluster&classifier	−0.86%

4   Related Work

CQA. For CQA task, HRED+KVmem [16] is proposed together with CQA dataset by Saha et al. In this model, the current sentence and context is first encoded into a vector by a hierarchical encoder-decoder. Then the most relevant memory is retrieved by a key-value memory network. Finally, the model decode the relevant memory and generate the question answer. CIPITR [15] adopts auxiliary rewards to strengthen training signal which can alleviate extreme reward sparsity. Meanwhile, to generate semantically reasonable programs for a certain question, it designs high-level constraints.

Meta-learning. The Meta-learning approaches is proposed for training a base model on a variety of learning task, making new learning task rapidly adapted with only a small number of training instances [3]. In question-answer domain, a method called PseudoTask MAML (PT-MAML) use the top-K relevant examples to build support task for each question in the training dataset [8]. Furthermore, S2A [4] utilizes a retriever to form support sets and update it and the programmer separately. Aiming to update the retriever better, MARL [6] construct a jointly trained structure with reinforcement learning. However, their methodology heavily relies on the information of question type. To make the model more universal, we propose a three-stage loop-learning structure including a classification module which can be jointly adapted in the process.

5   Conclusion

In this paper, we propose a self-classified meta-reinforcement learning method for complex question answering over KB. Our model is capable of effectively adapting to new questions based on the most similar questions retrieved from a reasonable search space. To obtain the optimal search space boundary, the model constructs a semi-supervised classifier to assign each question a label. Thus, our model addresses two essential challenges – the significant distributional biases presented in the dataset, and the high cost associated with manual labelling of question type. When evaluated on the large-scale complex question answering dataset CQA without question types, our model achieves state-of-the-art performance with overall macro and micro F1 score of 65.97% and 76.50%. In the future, we plan to extend the model to other domains that refers to meta-learning.

References

1. Ansari, GA., Saha, A., Kumar, V., Bhambhani, M., Sankaranarayanan, K., Chakrabarti, S.: Neural program induction for KBQA without gold programs or query annotations. In: IJCAI, pp. 4890–4896 (2019)
2. Berant, J., Chou, A., Frostig, R., Liang, P.: Semantic parsing on freebase from question-answer pairs. In: Proceedings of the 2013 Conference on Empirical Methods in Natural Language Processing, pp. 1533–1544 (October 2013). https://aclanthology.org/D13-1160
3. Finn, C., Abbeel, P., Levine, S.: Model-agnostic meta-learning for fast adaptation of deep networks. In: International Conference on Machine Learning, pp. 1126–1135. PMLR (2017)

4. Guo, D., Tang, D., Duan, N., Zhou, M., Yin, J.: Dialog-to-action: conversational question answering over a large-scale knowledge base. In: Advances in Neural Information Processing Systems, pp. 2942–2951 (2018)
5. Guu, K., Pasupat, P., Liu, E.Z., Liang, P.: From language to programs: bridging reinforcement learning and maximum marginal likelihood. arXiv preprint arXiv:1704.07926 (2017)
6. Hua, Y., Li, Y.F., Haffari, G., Qi, G., Wu, W.: Retrieve, program, repeat: complex knowledge base question answering via alternate meta-learning. arXiv preprint arXiv:2010.15875 (2020)
7. Huang, P.S., He, X., Gao, J., Deng, L., Acero, A., Heck, L.: Learning deep structured semantic models for web search using clickthrough data. In: Proceedings of the 22nd ACM international conference on Information & Knowledge Management, pp. 2333–2338 (2013)
8. Huang, P.S., Wang, C., Singh, R., Yih, W., He, X.: Natural language to structured query generation via meta-learning. arXiv preprint arXiv:1803.02400 (2018)
9. Jin, H., Li, C., Zhang, J., Hou, L., Li, J., Zhang, P.: XLORE2: large-scale cross-lingual knowledge graph construction and application. Data Intell. 1(1), 77–98 (2019)
10. Kingma, D.P., Ba, J.: Adam: a method for stochastic optimization. arXiv preprint arXiv:1412.6980 (2014)
11. Luo, L., Xiong, Y., Liu, Y., Sun, X.: Adaptive gradient methods with dynamic bound of learning rate. arXiv preprint arXiv:1902.09843 (2019)
12. Macqueen, J.: Some methods for classification and analysis of multivariate observations. In: 5th Berkeley Symposium on Mathematical Statistics and Probability, pp. 281–297 (1967)
13. Nichol, A., Schulman, J.: Reptile: a scalable metalearning algorithm. arXiv preprint arXiv:1803.02999 2(3), 4 (2018)
14. Pennington, J., Socher, R., Manning, C.D.: GloVe: global vectors for word representation. In: Proceedings of the 2014 Conference on Empirical Methods in Natural Language Processing (EMNLP), pp. 1532–1543 (2014)
15. Saha, A., Ansari, G.A., Laddha, A., Sankaranarayanan, K., Chakrabarti, S.: Complex program induction for querying knowledge bases in the absence of gold programs. Trans. Assoc. Comput. Linguist. 7, 185–200 (2019)
16. Saha, A., Pahuja, V., Khapra, M.M., Sankaranarayanan, K., Chandar, S.: Complex sequential question answering: towards learning to converse over linked question answer pairs with a knowledge graph. In: 32nd AAAI Conference on Artificial Intelligence (2018)
17. Shen, T., et al.: Multi-task learning for conversational question answering over a large-scale knowledge base. arXiv preprint arXiv:1910.05069 (2019)
18. Sutton, R.S., McAllester, D.A., Singh, S.P., Mansour, Y.: Policy gradient methods for reinforcement learning with function approximation. In: Advances in Neural Information Processing Systems, pp. 1057–1063 (2000)
19. Vrandečić, D., Krötzsch, M.: Wikidata: a free collaborative knowledgebase. Commun. ACM 57(10), 78–85 (2014)
20. Williams, R.J.: Simple statistical gradient-following algorithms for connectionist reinforcement learning. Mach. Learn. 8(3), 229–256 (1992)
21. Yih, W., He, X., Meek, C.: Semantic parsing for single-relation question answering. In: Proceedings of the 52nd Annual Meeting of the Association for Computational Linguistics (Volume 2: Short Papers), pp. 643–648 (2014)

Data-Driven Approach for Investigation of Irradiation Hardening Behavior of RAFM Steel

Zongguo Wang[1,2](✉) ⬤, Ziyi Chen[1], Xinfu He[3], Han Cao[3], Yuedong Cui[4], Meng Wan[1], Jue Wang[1,2], and Yangang Wang[1,2]

[1] Computer Network Information Center, Chinese Academy of Sciences, Beijing 100083, China
{wangzg,wanmengdamon}@cnic.cn, {wangjue,wangyg}@sccas.cn
[2] University of Chinese Academy of Sciences, Beijing 100049, China
[3] China Institute of Atomic Energy, Beijing 102413, China
hexinfu@ciae.ac.cn, zcaohan@foxmail.com
[4] University of Wisconsin-Madison, Madison, WI 53706, USA
cui54@wisc.edu

Abstract. Knowledge reasoning plays an important role in applications such as the human relation web and semantic search. However, how to use this method to solve materials problems is still a challenge. Defects and damage induced by neutron irradiation significantly affect the service performance of materials. *Reduced Activation Ferritic/Martensitic* (RAFM) steel is a very promising candidate for application in fusion reactor cladding. Understanding irradiation hardening effects in RAFM steel is one of the critical issues. Some experimental data of RAFM steel under irradiation are collected to construct a data set. The relationship between yield strength variation after irradiation and elements and irradiation conditions is trained by the machine learning method. The influence of irradiation condition and alloy elements on the hardening behavior of RAFM steel was explored, and some optimal alloy elements composition was also recommended. This work will give some direction for RAFM steel research.

Keywords: RAFM steel · Irradiation hardening · Machine learning · Data set

1 Introduction

In recent years, thanks to the rapid development of computer hardware [1–3], network infrastructure [4–6], and new algorithms [7–9], large amounts of data can be processed with fast speed, security [10–12], and good accuracy. For example, machine learning techniques [13, 14] have a widespread application in materials science with increasing research data and theoretical algorithms. How to match this technique with specific materials and bring benefits to the industry has attracted more and more attention. Knowledge reasoning gives a new way to know the relations of materials, which mines the relationship between structure and properties through a data-driven approach [15–17]. *Reduced Activation Ferritic-Martensitic* (RAFM) steel has excellent thermophysical properties

© The Author(s), under exclusive license to Springer Nature Switzerland AG 2022
G. Memmi et al. (Eds.): KSEM 2022, LNAI 13369, pp. 117–127, 2022.
https://doi.org/10.1007/978-3-031-10986-7_10

such as low activation, corrosion resistance, structural stability, high thermal conductivity, low expansion coefficient, and anti-irradiation swelling [18–20], which is considered to be the first choice for the first wall structure material for future fusion demonstration reactors and commercial reactors [21]. After high-energy neutrons irradiate RAFM steel, its physical properties, mechanical properties and service life are affected [22–24]. Under long-term irradiation, radiation defects such as dislocation loops, voids, and segregation will occur [25], and changes in macroscopically mechanical properties [26–28], such as radiation hardening, radiation embrittlement, and other effects will also be observed.

The experimental results of fission neutron irradiation of RAFM steel show that the ductile-brittle transition temperature of typical RAFM steels [29], such as Eurofer97, CLAM steel, etc., rises to about 100 °C when the irradiation temperature is less than 330 °C. The dose is about 15 dpa, which means that the RAFM steel has a risk of brittle fracture [30]. At present, the ideal service temperature range of RAFM steel proposed by international demonstration reactors and commercial reactors is from 250 °C to 650 °C. To improve the radiation resistance of RAFM steel, in-depth research on the radiation hardening/embrittlement mechanism of RAFM steel is required.

Due to the lack of strong current fusion neutron sources, the current neutron irradiation experiments of RAFM steel are carried out in fission reactors and spallation neutron sources, and the primary study is around the effect of irradiation dose, irradiation temperature, and transmutation element content on the properties of RAFM steel. After decades of research, people have a more in-depth understanding of the radiation damage mechanism of RAFM steel. However, due to the many factors that affect the radiation damage and interact with each other, there are still considerable challenges in predicting the radiation properties of RAFM steel under the service conditions and optimizing the composition and preparation process of RAFM steel. With the continuous development of data science and artificial intelligence technology [31–34], materials informatics is also becoming an essential discipline in materials science. Using artificial intelligence technology to perform multi-dimensional analysis and multi-parameter coupling on a large amount of data and mine the relationship between material composition, process and performance [35–37]. Based on the long-term research on the irradiation performance of RAFM steel, this work collected and sorted out a batch of neutron irradiation experimental data of RAFM steel, and used machine learning methods to fit the structure-activity relationship, to quickly predict the hardening behavior of RAFM steel under irradiation conditions. The effect of different material compositions on the radiation hardening behavior of RAFM steel is also further analyzed. The rest part of this paper is organized as follows. In Sect. 2, we have illustrated how to construct the data set of RAFM. Then, in Sect. 3, we have trained the model based on the RAFM dataset, and used the model to predict the optimal composition of RAFM steel. Finally, we have presented our conclusions in Sect. 4.

2   Data Set Construction

In this work, 2047 pieces of neutron irradiation experimental data of RAFM steel and ferritic/martensitic steel published in recent decades have been collected [30, 38]. The collected data include irradiation conditions, including irradiation temperature (T_{irr}), irradiation dose (Dose), transmutation element He produced by irradiation (He), degree of cold working (MAT_CW), alloying elements of RAFM steel, test temperature after irradiation (T_{test}), the variation of yield strength induced by irradiation (YS) and other information. RAFM steel composition information includes a total of 31 alloying elements and impurity elements, namely C, Cr, W, Mo, Ta, V, Si, Mn, N, Al, As, B, Bi, Ce, Co, Cu, Ge, Mg, Nb, Ni, O, P, Pb, S, Sb, Se, Sn, Te, Ti, Zn, Zr, the alloying elements and impurity elements are collectively referred to as RAFM steel components in the next discussion.

3 Model Construction and Application

The hardening behavior induced by irradiation of RAFM steel is characterized by the variation of *yield strength* (YS) in the data set, which is used as the target value of the model, and the rest of the values are used as the feature descriptors to fit the target value. To accurately construct the model, both an appropriate machine learning method and suitable features should be considered.

3.1 Machine Learning Method

CNN-based methods usually have a better prediction accuracy based on a large dataset, but we found that traditional machine learning methods had more accurate results on this RAFM dataset. The main reason we think is the relatively small dataset. Using Support *Vector Machine Regression* (SVR), *Linear Regression* (LR), *Adaptive Boosting* (AB), *K-Nearest Neighbors* (KNN), *Extreme Random Tree* (ET), *Decision Tree* (DT), *Bagging regression* (BR), *Gradient Boosting regression* (GB), *Random Forest* (RF) and other traditional machine learning methods to perform regression analysis on existing data. The data set is divided into a training set and a test set with a split ratio of 9:1. The model's input is 37 features, and the output is the variation of yield strength.

The coefficient of determination R^2 is a statistical measurement that examines how differences in one variable can be explained by the difference in a second variable, when predicting the outcome of a given event. The calculation method for R^2 is shown in Eqs. (1–2).

$$R^2 = \frac{SSR}{SST} = \frac{SST - SSE}{SST} = 1 - \frac{SSE}{SST} \tag{1}$$

$$R^2 = 1 - \frac{\sum (Y - Y_{predict})^2}{\sum (Y - Y_{mean})^2} \tag{2}$$

The value of R^2 is usually from 0 to 1. The closer it is to 1, the better the model fits the data. Nine machine learning methods are used to train the model based on the same dataset, and comparing with other methods, BR, RF and GB are performed more ideal, and the values of R^2 are 0.8386, 0.8404, and 0.8465, respectively.

To select a suitable machine learning method for this dataset, we randomly divide the RAFM data set into the training set and test set with the split ratios of 9:1 and 8:2. The processes of training and test run 10 times for every algorithm with the same model parameters, and the algorithm stability and model accuracy are statistically analyzed.

Standard deviation (SD) is most commonly used in probability statistics as the degree of statistical distribution, and it can also reflect the degree of dispersion of a data set. Among these nine methods, BR, RF and GB regression algorithms have higher R^2 values. For the dataset, the SVR, LR, KNN and GB algorithms also have good stability with a SD value of 0. Based on the model evaluation results and the stability of the algorithm on this data set, the GB algorithm will be selected to be used as the prediction method for model training in the following research of this work.

3.2 Feature Descriptor

The feature is an essential factor affecting the accuracy of the prediction results of material properties. Correlation analysis is carried out for 37 feature descriptors, and the Pearson correlation coefficient is used to characterize whether there is a linear relationship between the features. The calculated Pearson correlation coefficients for this dataset are shown in Fig. 1.

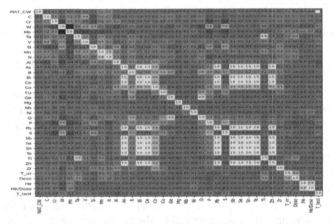

Fig. 1. The Pearson correlation coefficient for 37 feature descriptors.

The Pearson correlation coefficients between all features are between −1 and 1. There is a strong positive correlation between the elements As, Bi, Ce, Pb, Sb, Se, Sn, Te, and Zn, and the Pearson correlation coefficients are 1. We also see that these components are almost fixed values in the dataset. There are also strong positive correlations between the elements Ge and O, elements Ta and Ti, He content and the ratio of He content and irradiation dose, whose Pearson correlation coefficient are all 0.9. There is a nearly linear relation between the data variation for these three pairs. In addition, there is also a strong positive correlation between the elements Mn and N with a correlation coefficient of 0.8. We also found a strong negative correlation between the elements W and Mo with a correlation coefficient of -0.7. Through the analysis of the collected data, the coexistence of these two elements in RAFM steel is relatively rare, even when both elements are contained simultaneously, one of which is much lower than the other. This is determined by the requirement of adding W to limit Mo in the design of RAFM steel composition. There is no apparent linear relationship between other characteristics.

Using the GB algorithm recommended in Sect. 3.1, the importance for target value of 37 feature descriptors was calculated. The effect of numerical changes on the target properties is further analyzed. First, take all 37 features as the input, and use the GB algorithm to train the model. Three ratios of training set and test set of 9:1, 8:2 and 7:3 are considered, their data number are respectively {1842, 205}, {1637, 410}, and {1432, 615}. The values of R^2 for these three cases are 0.8465, 0.8183, and 0.8053, respectively. It can be seen that with the increase of the training set, the reliability of the model increases. Using the first split method to investigate the influence of 37 features on variation of yield strength, we can see that, in additions to the test temperature, irradiation dose, irradiation temperature, RAFM steel composition elements such as the variation of element Mo, C, S, Si, Cr, Ta, W, Al, P, Nb, V, N, Ni, Mn, O, B, Ti, etc. are also the main factors that cause the change of yield strength after irradiation.

3.3 Model Construction

The relationship between the composition, irradiation conditions and variation of yield strength (YS) of RAFM steel was studied by GB regression method, and the effects of composition and process on the hardening behavior of RAFM steel have been respectively considered. Using the above 37 feature descriptors, the data set is divided into the training set and the test set with a split ratio of 9:1. The model prediction effect is shown in Fig. 2(a), and the value of R^2 is 0.8465. In addition, the prediction accuracy of the model is evaluated by relative error (δ), and it is calculated by Eq. (3).

$$\delta = \frac{predicted\ data - experimetal\ data}{experimental\ data} \tag{3}$$

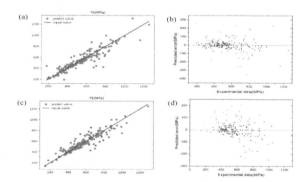

Fig. 2. Data analysis and model evaluation, including model evaluation of machine learning and the predicted error. (a) and (b) are for the case considering 37 features. (c) and (d) are for the case considering 24 features. The predicted errors in (b) and (d) have four types. Black square is denoted that relative error is less than 10%, red circle is from 10% to 20%, blue triangle is from 20% to 30%, green triangle is more than 30%.

In Eq. (3), experimental data is the YS from the collected dataset, the predicted data is that predicted by the model. The smaller of absolute value of δ, the more accuracy of the model. The δ for test set is shown in Fig. 2(b) with different colors.

The test set contains 205 terms of experimental data, 148 of them (more than seventy percent) have a relative error (δ) of prediction results which is less than 10%, of which the maximum absolute error of YS is -61.89 MPa. In addition, 10 terms of data have relative errors greater than 30%, and one experimental data is predicted by the model with a relative error greater than one hundred percent. Comparing the features of this data with those of other two terms of data in the training set which has similar features, and we find that these three data have the same RAFM composition, irradiation temperature (873 K) and test temperature (873 K), the irradiation dose are respectively 37 dpa, 38 dpa, and 39 dpa, and He content are respectively 30, 32, and 36. The difference in features between the test and training data is relatively small. The more considerable difference in variation of yield strength may be caused by sampling at different positions of the RAFM steel. Therefore, the influence of sampling from different parts of the same component is also an essential factor.

3.4 Knowledge Reasoning and Prediction

In order to study whether each component and irradiations have the effect of inhibiting or promoting the generation of irradiation defects, it is necessary to analyze the correlations between feature and feature, and features and YS. In the analysis, we mainly consider the influence of composition (including main alloy elements and some trace elements), heat treatment process, and irradiation conditions on the change of YS. According to the importance calculation in Sect. 3.2, we selected 24 variables, including elements Mo, C, S, Si, Cr, Ta, W, Al, P, Nb, V, N, Ni, Mn, O, B, Ti and irradiation conditions as feature descriptors for training. The training results are shown in Fig. 2(c), and the value of R^2 is 0.8559. Compared with Fig. 2(b), the number of terms of data in Fig. 2(d) with δ less than 10% is increased to 155, and all δ were less than 50%.

We calculated the Pearson correlation coefficient between each element and YS, the results are shown in Fig. 3(a). Between YS and experimental measure temperature (T_{test}) has a moderate negative correlation, it can be simply understood that after irradiation YS generally decreases with the increasing of the measure temperature. Except for T_{test}, there is no obvious linear relationship between YS and other features.

For irradiations and experimental conditions, we considered T_{irr}, Dose, He and T_{test} as the input features to study the relationship between these four features and YS. The GB regression method is used to fit the effect of four features on YS of RAFM steel, and the value of R^2 is 0.7967. According to the fitting coefficient, the importance on the YS is T_{test}, Dose, T_{irr}, and He in turn. Taking the measurement temperature as an example, the influence of the experimental conditions on the irradiation results is shown in Fig. 3(b). The irradiation temperature is 273K, 573K and 732K, respectively. The variation trend of the YS with the measured temperature after irradiation is shown. It can be seen that YS tends to decrease with the increase of the measurement temperature. In addition, from Fig. 3(a), both the correlation coefficients between T_{irr} and YS, and that between dose and YS are less than 0.3, indicating a nonlinear relationship between T_{irr}, Dose and YS.

From the data analysis and Fig. 3(c), it can be concluded that a lower irradiation temperature will induce a more severe hardness after irradiation, and the YS is larger. When the irradiation temperature is lower than about 623 K, a higher irradiation dose will also induce a more severe hardening. YS variation after irradiation increases with the increase of the irradiation dose, but when the irradiation dose reaches 21.1dpa, the irradiation hardening tends to be saturated. When the irradiation temperature is higher than 623 K, the YS shows a decreasing trend with the increasing irradiation dose. In addition, the YS gradually decreases with the increase of irradiation temperature, which is consistent with the experimental conclusion that irradiation hardening varies with temperature.

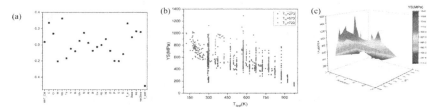

Fig. 3. Relations between YS and its composition and irradiation. (a) is Pearson correlation between YS and 24 feature descriptors. (b) is the influence of measuring temperature on YS at different irradiation temperatures. (c) is the influence of irradiations on YS.

Once the irradiation position in the reactor is determined, the corresponding irradiation temperature, irradiation dose and damage rate are determined. Therefore, the composition becomes the main factor affecting the radiation hardening behavior of RAFM steel. Based on the microscopically experimental data after irradiation, it is speculated that the main factors affecting the radiation hardening are Cr-rich precipitation, Ni-Mn-Si precipitation, and matrix damage. From the microscopic analysis (such as APT, SANS, etc.) and theoretical analysis results after irradiation, the interaction of Cr, Mn, Ni, Si and other elements with irradiation defects is one of the critical factors leading to hardening. Therefore, in addition to the analysis of irradiation conditions, we will focus on the effects of elements such as Cr, Mn, Ni, Si, Ta, and N on the hardening behavior of RAFM steel. From Sect. 3.2, we already know that the changes in the content of elements Cr, Mn, Ni, Si, Ta, and N have significant influences on YS after irradiation. Among these elements, we also found that when the RAFM steel composition does not contain Si, the P is also missing. No such relationship between other elements in the existing data is found.

To study the influences of different elements on the radiation hardening behavior, some representative data fixed components are selected from the collected data set, and the above trained model was used to analyze the influences of the elements on the hardening behavior. Fixing the contents of other elements to study the influences of an element, some values between the minimum and maximum values according to the target element in the collected data are selected. Using the trained model to predict the YS based on this new dataset, we have found that even under different irradiation times, irradiation dose, and measurement temperature, similar results were obtained on the effect of the YS induced by this element. Therefore, the same irradiation conditions are used in the prediction of the following element content relationship.

Element Cr greatly influences the YS of RAFM steel after irradiation. We use the model to predict the Cr content, and the results show that the degree of hardening first increases, then decreases, and finally tends to a saturated state with the increase of Cr (Fig. 4(a)). This agrees with the experimental results that there will be Cr precipitation when the Cr content is high. From our prediction, the Cr content at 7.5% is beneficial to its radiation resistance. Similarly, we use the determined content of Cr at 7.5% and fix other components to respectively predict the optimal content of components Mn, Si, Ta, and trace elements Ni, N. The calculation results are shown in Fig. 4. As can be seen from the Fig. 4, for the element Mn, the degree of hardening increases with the increase of Mn content, and the degree of hardening decreases when the content of Mn is 0.5%, The recommended Mn content is larger than 0.025%. Considering the composition information of RAFM steel, we recommend the content of Mn to be 0.5%. The optimum content of Si is selected as 0.05%. Based on the obtained recommended data, the content of Ta is predicted. The increase of Ta content can form a large number of dispersed carbides, refined grains, and improve the strength of the material. The most suitable content of Ta is 0.14%. Finally, we predict the content of N and Ni elements, the recommended value of N content is 0.014%, and that of Ni is 0.75%. Among them, N and Mn elements have used the same recommended rules.

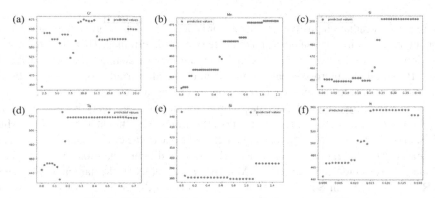

Fig. 4. Relationship between different elements and YS.

Finally, we use the above recommended components as a set of design element, and use three groups of irradiation time and irradiation dose to predict the YS, and the predicted value is smaller than the original experimental value. Besides the main components, other elements and irradiation conditions are the same in the comparing data. The variation of yield strength (YS) collected from the experiment are 570, 717, and 917 MPa, and the predicted value are 444.57, 362.05, and 787.44 MPa, respectively. This test shows that the data-driven method is used to analyze and mine the existing data, which can quickly predict the radiation damage behavior under different components, irradiation conditions, and processes, and the results will provide a reference for material design and experimental preparation.

4 Conclusion

In this study, the experimental data of RAFM steel were collected to construct the RAFM data set, and the relationship model between composition, irradiation, and variation of yield strength of RAFM steel was established by the machine learning method. The coefficient of determination of the training model was 0.8465. The relative error of most sample prediction results was less than ten percent. In this study, the effect of composition and irradiation on the hardening behavior of RAFM steel was further studied, and it was determined that the experimental measure temperature, irradiation temperature, and irradiation dose were the main factors affecting the irradiation hardening behavior and the relationship between them was also studied.

Acknowledgements. This work was supported by the National Natural Science Foundation of China under Grant No. U1867217, Youth Innovation Promotion Association CAS, and Key Research Program of Frontier Sciences, CAS, Grant No. ZDBS-LY-7025.

References

1. Qiu, M., Xue, C., Shao, Z., Sha, E.: Energy minimization with soft real-time and DVS for uniprocessor and multiprocessor embedded systems. In: IEEE DATE Conference, pp. 1–6 (2007)
2. Qiu, M., Guo, M., Liu, M., et al.: Loop scheduling and bank type assignment for heterogeneous multi-bank memory. J. Parallel Distrib. Comput. **69**(6), 546–558 (2009)
3. Qiu, M., Xue, C., Shao, Z., et al.: Efficient algorithm of energy minimization for heterogeneous wireless sensor network. In: IEEE EUC, pp. 25–34 (2006)
4. Lu, Z., Wang, N., Wu, J., Qiu, M.: IoTDeM: an IoT Big Data-oriented MapReduce performance prediction extended model in multiple edge clouds. JPDC **118**, 316–327 (2018)
5. Qiu, M., Liu, J., Li, J., et al.: A novel energy-aware fault tolerance mechanism for wireless sensor networks. In: IEEE/ACM International Conference on GCC (2011)
6. Niu, J., Gao, Y., Qiu, M., Ming, Z.: Selecting proper wireless network interfaces for user experience enhancement with guaranteed probability. JPDC **72**(12), 1565–1575 (2012)
7. Liu, M., Zhang, S., Fan, Z., Qiu, M.: "H state estimation for discrete-time chaotic systems based on a unified model. IEEE Trans. Syst. Man Cybern. (B), **42**(4), 1053–1063 (2012)
8. Qiu, M., Li, H., Sha, E.: Heterogeneous real-time embedded software optimization considering hardware platform. In: ACM Symposium on Applied Computing, pp. 1637–1641 (2009)
9. Qiu, M., Sha, E., Liu, M., et al.: Energy minimization with loop fusion and multi-functional-unit scheduling for multidimensional DSP. JPDC **68**(4), 443–455 (2008)
10. Qiu, H., Qiu, M., Liu, M., Memmi, G.: Secure health data sharing for medical cyber-physical systems for the healthcare 4.0. IEEE J. Biomed. Health Inform. **24**(9), 2499–2505 (2020)
11. Qiu, M., Gai, K., Xiong, Z.: Privacy-preserving wireless communications using bipartite matching in social big data. FGCS **87**, 772–781 (2018)
12. Shao, Z., Xue, C., Zhuge, Q., et al.: Security protection and checking for embedded system integration against buffer overflow attacks via hardware/software. IEEE Trans. Comput. **55**(4), 443–453 (2006)
13. Qiu, H., Qiu, M., Lu, Z.: Selective encryption on ECG data in body sensor network based on supervised machine learning. Inf. Fusion **55**, 59–67 (2020)

14. Qiu, L., Gai, K., Qiu, M.: Optimal big data sharing approach for tele-health in cloud computing. In: IEEE SmartCloud, pp. 184–189 (2016)
15. Wu, G., Zhang, H., Qiu, M., et al.: A decentralized approach for mining event correlations in distributed system monitoring. JPDC **73**(3), 330–340 (2013)
16. Qiu, M., Cao, D., Su, H., Gai, K.: Data transfer minimization for financial derivative pricing using Monte Carlo simulation with GPU in 5G. Int. J. of Comm. Sys. **29**(16), 2364–2374 (2016)
17. Wang, J., Qiu, M., Guo, B.: Enabling real-time information service on telehealth system over cloud-based big data platform. J. Syst. Architect. **72**, 69–79 (2017)
18. Tsuzuki, K., Sato, M., Kawashima, H., et al.: Recent activities on the compatibility of the ferritic steel wall with the plasma in the JFT-2M tokamak. J. Nucl. Mater. **307–311**, 1386–1390 (2002)
19. Salavy, J.-F., Aiello, G., Aubert, P., et al.: Ferritic-martensitic steel test blanket modules: status and future needs for design criteria requirements and fabrication validation. J. Nucl. Mater. **386–388**, 922–926 (2009)
20. Zhan, D.-P., Qiu, G.-X., Li, C.-S., Qi, M., Jiang, Z.-H., Zhang, H.-S.: Effects of yttrium and zirconium additions on inclusions and mechanical properties of a reduced activation ferritic/martensitic steel. J. Iron. Steel Res. Int. **27**(2), 197–207 (2019). https://doi.org/10.1007/s42243-019-00332-9
21. Zinkle, S.J.: Fusion materials science: Overview of challenges and recent progress. Phys. Plasmas **12**, 058101 (2005)
22. Muroga, T., Gasparotto, M., Zinkle, S.J.: Overview of materials research for fusion reactors. Fusion Eng. Des. **61–62**, 13–25 (2002)
23. van der Schaaf, B., Gelles, D.S., et al.: Progress and critical issues of reduced activation ferritic/martensitic steel Development. J. Nucl. Mater. **283–287**, 52–59 (2000)
24. Jitsukawa, S., Tamura, M., et al.: Development of an extensive database of mechanical and physical properties for reduced-activation martensitic steel F82H. J. Nucl. Mater. **307–311**, 179–186 (2002)
25. Qiu, G., Zhan, D., Li, C., Qi, M., Jiang, Z., Zhang, H.: Effect of Y/Zr ratio on inclusions and mechanical properties of 9Cr-RAFM steel fabricated by vacuum melting. J. Mater. Eng. Perform. **28**(2), 1067–1076 (2019). https://doi.org/10.1007/s11665-018-3838-0
26. He Pei, Yao Wei-zhi, YU Jian-ming, Zhang Xiang-dong. "Evaluation of Irradiation Properties for Fusion Structural Materials", Journal of Materials Engineering, **46**(6), 19–26 (2018)
27. Gaganidze, E., Aktaa, J.: Assessment of neutron irradiation effects on RAFM steels. Fusion Eng. Des. **88**, 118–128 (2013)
28. Mansur, L.K., Rowcliffe, A.F., Nanstad, R.K., et al.: Materials needs for fusion, generation IV fission reactors and spallation neutron sources-similarities and differences. J. Nucl. Mater. **329–333**, 166–172 (2004)
29. Cottrell, G.A., Baker, L.J.: Structural materials for fusion and spallation sources. J. Nucl. Mater. **318**, 260–266 (2003)
30. Gaganidze, E., Dafferner, B., et al.: Irradiation programme HFR phase IIb-SPICE. Impact testing on up to 16.3 dpa irradiated RAFM steels. Final report for task TW2-TTMS 001b-D05, 7371, 0947–8620 (2008)
31. Qiu, H., Qiu, M., Lu, Z., Memmi, G.: An efficient key distribution system for data fusion in V2X heterogeneous networks. Inf. Fusion **50**(1), 212–220 (2019)
32. Qiu, H., Zheng, Q., et al.: Topological graph convolutional network-based urban traffic flow and density prediction. IEEE TITS **22**(7), 4560–4569 (2021)
33. Li, Y., Song, Y., et al.: Intelligent fault diagnosis by fusing domain adversarial training and maximum mean discrepancy via ensemble learn. IEEE TII **17**(4), 2833–2841 (2021)
34. Hu, F., Lakdawala, S., et al.: Low-power, intelligent sensor hardware interface for medical data preprocessing. IEEE Trans. Inf. Tech. Biomed. **13**(4), 656–663 (2009)

35. Lu, R., Jin, X., Zhang, S., Qiu, M., Wu, X.: A study on big-knowledge and its engineering issues. IEEE Trans. Knowl. Data Eng. **31**(9), 1630–1644 (2019)
36. Qiu, M., Chen, Z., Ming, Z., Qiu, X., Niu, J.: Energy-aware data allocation with hybrid memory for mobile cloud systems. IEEE Syst. J. **11**(2), 813–822 (2017)
37. Yao, T., Wang, J. Meng Wan, et al.: VenusAI: an artificial intelligence platform for scientific discovery on supercomputers. J. Syst. Archit. **128**, 102550 (2022)
38. Porollo, S.I., Dvoriashin, A.M., et al.: The microstructure and tensile properties of Fe–Cr alloys after neutron irradiation at 400 C to 5.5–7.1 dpa. J. Nucl. Mater., **256**(2–3): 247–253 (1998)

Deep-to-Bottom Weights Decay: A Systemic Knowledge Review Learning Technique for Transformer Layers in Knowledge Distillation

Ankun Wang[1], Feng Liu[1], Zhen Huang[1(✉)], Minghao Hu[2], Dongsheng Li[1], Yifan Chen[1], and Xinjia Xie[1]

[1] National Key Laboratory of Parallel and Distributed Processing, National University of Defense Technology, Changsha, China
{wak,richardlf,huangzhen,dsli,chenyifan,xiexinjia97}@nudt.edu.cn
[2] Information Research Center of Military Science, Beijing, China

Abstract. There are millions of parameters and huge computational power consumption behind the outstanding performance of pre-trained language models in natural language processing tasks. Knowledge distillation is considered as a compression strategy to address this problem. However, previous works have the following shortcomings: (i) distill partial transformer layers of the teacher model, which not only do not make full use of the teacher-side information. But also break the coherence of the information, (ii) neglect the difficulty differences of knowledge from deep to shallow, which corresponds to different level information of teacher model. In this paper, we introduce a deep-to-bottom weights decay review mechanism to knowledge distillation, which could fuse teacher-side information while taking each layer's difficulty level into consideration. To validate our claims, we distill a 12-layer BERT into a 6-layer model and evaluate it on the GLUE dataset. Experimental results show that our review approach is not only able to outperform other existing techniques, but also outperform the original model on partial datasets.

Keywords: Knowledge distillation · Pre-training language model · Model compression

1 Introduction

In recent years, pre-trained language models, such as BERT [4], GPT [15], Switch Transformer [6] have achieved great success in many NLP tasks. However, pre-trained language models suffer from expensive overhead on computation and memory for inference due to the large number of parameters. This makes it impractical to deploy such models on resource-constrained devices. Therefore, it is vital to obtain a lightweight pre-trained language model using the compression method while maintaining performance.

© The Author(s), under exclusive license to Springer Nature Switzerland AG 2022
G. Memmi et al. (Eds.): KSEM 2022, LNAI 13369, pp. 128–139, 2022.
https://doi.org/10.1007/978-3-031-10986-7_11

Knowledge distillation [7] transfers knowledge from "large" teacher model to "small" student model, which can reduce the computation and storage overhead of the model at the same time. So far, several studies [9,12,14,17,20] have used knowledge distillation to compress the pre-trained language model and achieved great success. However, [8] observes an interesting fact that the knowledge learned by each transformer layer of BERT from bottom layer to high layer shows a state from phrase-level information, syntactic-level information, to semantic-level information. Which means the knowledge BERT learned is hierarchical, from shallow to deep, from simple to complex. Thus, the works mentioned above have the following problems from this perspective: (i) just select a subset of the intermediate layers, some important information such as phrase-level information or syntactic-level information may be omitted in the remaining parts. (ii) neglect the difficulty of knowledge in different intermediate layers. The student model does not carry out step-by-step learning, the low layer of it may directly learn the difficult knowledge in the teacher model such as BERT-EMD [12] and ALP-KD [14]. This is not in line with the law of gradual learning.

In this paper, we propose DWD-KD (**D**eep-to-bottom **W**eights **D**ecay: A Systemic Knowledge Review Learning Technique for Transformer Layers in **K**nowledge **D**istillation) to solve these problems from a new perspective, which takes each layer's difficulty level into consideration. The inspiration comes from a familiar phenomenon that human is often taught to review the old knowledge to understand the new knowledge better. [3] has applied knowledge review in computer vision tasks for CNN networks and achieved competitive results. Motivated by these works, DWD-KD can learn new knowledge and review old knowledge at the same time. Our experiments on BERT with GLUE [21] show that DWD-KD outperforms other existing methods, and validate that deep-to-bottom weights decay is an effective review learning technique as compared to others.

Our contributions in this paper can be summarized as follows:

(1) We introduce the review mechanism into the knowledge distillation and propose an effective review strategy.
(2) Extensive experiments on GLUE datasets demonstrate that the proposed DWD-KD not only outperforms existing approaches, but also beyond teacher model on partial datasets.

The rest of the paper is organized as follows. In Sect. 2 we review related works. Section 3 presents the details of our method and Sect. 4 shows the experimental setting. Section 5 shows the experimental results. Finally, we conclude our work in Sect. 6.

2   Related Work

Generally, pre-trained language models can be compressed by low-rank matrix factorization [10], quantization [18,26], knowledge distillation [9,14,17], and pruning [13]. In this paper, our focus is on knowledge distillation. According to the type of student model, it can be divided into non-transformer-based distillation and transformer-based distillation. For the former, the student model is usually a convolutional neural network or recurrent neural network. Previous works like [2] uses a complete CNN as the student model during distillation, [23] distilled BERT into an BiLSTM network via both hard and soft distilling methods.

Our work belongs to the transformer-based distillation, which means the basic structure of student model and teacher model both are transformer architecture. Previous works such as BERT-PKD [20] model to transfer the knowledge from both the final layer and the intermediate layers of the teacher network. TinyBERT [9] performed the Transformer distillation at both pre-training and fine-tuning processes. BERT-EMD [12] borrows the Earth Mover's Distance algorithm of Operations Research for many-to-many layer alignment while distilling the BERT model. ALP-KD [14] gives different weights to the intermediate layer of the teacher model based on the layer-to-layer similarity between the teacher model and student model.

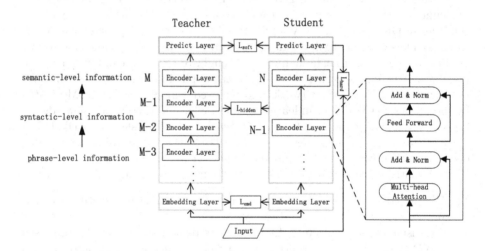

Fig. 1. An overview of the DWD-KD method. Embedding layer and prediction layer of teacher and student model are one-to-one alignment. The intermediate encoder layers are transformer architecture, which use many-to-one alignment by review learning from deep to bottom as Eq. 2 describes.

However, the aforementioned BERT compression approaches struggle to find an optimal layer mapping between the teacher and student networks. Each student layer merely learns from a single teacher layer, which may lose rich linguistic knowledge contained in the teacher network. Different from previous methods. The main difference between our work and previous methods is that they do not discuss the possibility to review knowledge in BERT compression, which is found in our work.

3   Methodology

Suppose that teacher and student models respectively have M and N transformer layers, M is larger than N. We overview DWD-KD method as shown in Fig. 1. It consists of three components: word embedding distillation (3.1), transformer layer distillation with review mechanism (3.2), Prediction layer distillation (3.3).

3.1   Word Embedding Distillation

A good word embedding vector will help to extract text features better, we borrow the idea from [9]. Thus, during the knowledge distillation process, we minimize the mean square error (MSE) between the embedding vector of the teacher model and student model as Eq. 1:

$$L_{emd} = MSE(E^T, E^S) \tag{1}$$

where the matrices E^S and E^T respectively represent the embeddings of student model and teacher model, which have the same shape.

3.2   Transformer Layer Distillation with Review Mechanism

As confirmed by literature [8], from the bottom layer to the high layer, the knowledge goes from easy to difficult. Thus, DWD-KD gives corresponding weight goes from small to large. It's the same as that humans spend more energy learning difficult knowledge. The layer alignment method of DWD-KD is described in Eq. 2, which means n_{th} transform layer of the student model corresponds to first $\lfloor \frac{n*M}{N} \rfloor$ (we use $max(A(n))$ denotes $\lfloor \frac{n*M}{N} \rfloor$ in the rest of the article) transform layers of the teacher model. Then we combine multiple layer's hidden states as Eq. 3 describes. We utilize Eq. 4 to normalize the layer number as weights.

$$A(n) = \{1, \cdots, \lfloor \frac{n*M}{N} \rfloor\} \tag{2}$$

$\forall n \in \{1, \cdots, N\}$, however, we discover that there is no obvious disparity among weights calculated by Eq. 4 during a series of subsequent experiments, which means there is no emphasis between the old knowledge and the new knowledge. The new knowledge represents deeper and more difficult knowledge, the weights of which should be much larger than that of old knowledge.

$$F_{max(A(n))} = \sum_{m=1}^{max(A(n))} w_m \cdot h_m^t \tag{3}$$

$$w_m = m / \sum_{i \in A(n)} i \tag{4}$$

$$w_m = exp(m) / \sum_{i \in A(n)} exp(i) \tag{5}$$

So we also use the softmax function to calculate the weight of each layer as Eq. 5. Then, we take mean square error to calculate loss between $F_{max(A(n))}$ and h_n^t as Eq. 6 and Eq. 7 describe.

$$L_{hidden}^n = MSE(F_{max(A(n))}, h_n^s), \tag{6}$$

$$L_{hidden} = \sum_{n=1}^{N} L_{hidden}^n \tag{7}$$

m, n denotes layer num, h_m^t stands for m_{th} hidden states of teacher model, h_n^s means n_{th} hidden states of student model. w_m represents m_{th} transformer layer's weight of teacher model. $F_{max(A(n))}$ denotes integrated result of first $max(A(n))$ transformer layer's hidden states.

$$L = \{l_{n1}, \cdots, l_{nmax(A(n))}\}$$
$$l_{nk} = MSE(h_n^s, h_k^t) \tag{8}$$
$$k \in A(n)$$

$$w' = exp(l_{nk}) / \sum_{l \in L} exp(l) \tag{9}$$

$$w_{new} = (w' + w_{old})/2 \tag{10}$$

There is still a problem with the weight calculated by Eq. 5. The weights are consistent with the layer assignment scheme. Once the layer assignment scheme is fixed, the weights will not change. However, when the gradient is updated, the knowledge level of the student model will also change. It is supposed to dynamically adjust the above weights. The Eq. 8–Eq. 10 show the way to update weights. We first calculate the loss value of corresponding layers between student model and teacher model after gradient update. The larger the loss value is, the worse the effect of the student model in fitting the distribution of the teacher model is. Therefore, the corresponding weights will be improved in the following training, which is inspired by the fact that humans put more effort into learning what they don't understand. Then we normalize loss value as new weights. The old weights are the ones used in the previous iteration and original old weights are calculated by Eq. 5. Finally, We use the average value of new weight and the old weight as the weight of the next distillation iteration. Algorithm 1 illustrates this process.

3.3   Prediction Distillation

Prediction distillation include soft label loss and hard label loss. Soft label is the probability logits of teacher model. Hard label is one-hot label vector of the

Algorithm 1. weights update

Input: $N, W_{old}(w_{old} \in W_{old}), H^S = \{h_1^s, \cdots, h_N^s\}, H^T = \{h_1^t, \cdots, h_M^t\}$;

Output: W_{new};

1: **for** $n = 1, \cdots, N$ **do**
2:     **for** $k \in A(n)$ **do**
3:         $l_{nk} = MSE(h_n^s, h_k^t)$;
4:     **end for**
5:     **for** $k \in A(n)$ **do**
6:         $w' = exp(l_{nk}) / \sum_{k=1}^{k=max(A(n))} exp(l_{nk})$;
7:     **end for**
8:     **for** $k \in A(n+1)$ **do**
9:         **if** $k < max(A(n))$ **then**
10:             $w_{new} = (w' + w_{old})/2$;
11:             $W_{new} = W_{new} \cup \{w_{new}\}$;
12:         **else**
13:             $W_{new} = W_{new} \cup \{w_{old}\}$;
14:         **end if**
15:     **end for**
16: **end for**
17: **return** W_{new}

sample. Like [7], we utilize KL divergence to calculate soft label loss, and use the Cross Entropy to calculate hard label loss:

$$L_{soft} = KL(Z^T/t, Z^S/t) \tag{11}$$

where Z^T and Z^S respectively represent the probability logits predicted by the teacher and student, t denotes temperature value. V is a one-hot label vector of the sample.

$$L_{hard} = CE(Z^S, V) \tag{12}$$

3.4 Total Loss

Finally, we combine word embedding distillation loss, transformer layer distillation loss, soft label loss, and the hard label loss to form the total loss function as Eq. 13:

$$\begin{aligned} L =\, &\alpha \cdot L_{emd} + \beta \cdot L_{soft} \\ &+ (1 - \beta) \cdot L_{hard} + \gamma \cdot L_{hidden} \end{aligned} \tag{13}$$

α, β and γ are hyper-parameters.

4 Experimental Setup

4.1 Experimental Data

We evaluate our DWD-KD on the General Language Understanding Evaluation (GLUE) [21] benchmark. Following the previous works [12,14,17], we also do not run experiments on WNLI dataset [11], as it is too difficult that both the teacher model and the student model can not perform well.

CoLA. The Corpus of Linguistic Acceptability [22] is a single sentence classification task. The corpus comes from books and journals of language theory. Each sentence is labeled as a word sequence whether it is grammatical or not. This task is a binary classification task. There are two labels, 0 and 1, respectively, where 0 indicates non grammatical and 1 indicates grammatical.

SST-2. The Stanford Sentiment Treebank [19] is a single sentence classification task, which consists of sentences in film reviews and human annotations of their emotions. The goal is to predict whether each review is positive or negative.

MRPC. The Microsoft Research Paraphrase Corpus [5] consists of 3.7k sentence pairs extracted from online news sources, and the goal to predict if each pair of sentences is semantically equivalent.

QQP. The Quora Question Pairs[1] task consists of 393k question pairs from Quora website. The task is to predict whether a pair of questions is semantically equivalent.

STS-B. The Semantic Textual Similarity Benchmark [1] is a collection of sentence pairs extracted from news titles, video titles, image titles and natural language inference data. Each pair is human-annotated with a similarity score from 1 to 5. The task is to predict these similarity scores, which is essentially a regression problem, but it can still be classified into five text classification tasks of sentence pairs.

NLI. The Multi-Genre Natural Language Inference Corpus (**MNLI** [24]), The Questionanswering NLI (**QNLI** [16]) and The Recognizing Textual Entailment (**RTE** [2]) are all natural language inference (NLI) tasks, which consist of 393k/108k/2.5k pairs of premise and hypothesis. The task is to predict whether the premise contains hypothesis (implication), conflicts with hypothesis (contradiction), or neither (neutral). Besides, MNLI test set is further divided into two splits: matched (MNLI-m, in-domain) and mismatched (MNLI-mm, cross-domain).

4.2 Implementation Details

The teacher model is a 12-layer BERT model (BERT-base-uncased), which is fine-tuned for each task to perform knowledge distillation. We initialize the student model with the parameters of the first six layers of the teacher model. We implement DWD-KD using the TextBrewer [25], which is an open-source knowledge distillation library. Specifically, the batch size is 32, the learning rate is tuned from $\{1e-5, 2e-5, 5e-5\}$, the parameter t used in Eq. 11 is tuned from $\{5, 8, 10\}$. the α and γ are tuned from $\{1, 5, 10\}$, β is tuned from $\{0.2, 0.3, 0.5, 0.7\}$.

---

[1] https://data.quora.com/First-Quora-Dataset-Release-Question-Pairs.

[2] It is a collections of several textual entailment challenges.

4.3   Baseline Methods

We not only compare our DWD-KD with fine-tuned 6-layer BERT models (BERT-FT) but also with several BERT compression approaches, including BERT-PKD [20], BERT-EMD, [12], ALP-KD [14], all of them focus on how to distill knowledge from the intermediate layer of the teacher model, We also reproduce the experimental results of the above model through the TextBrewer [25] library. DWD-sum and DWD-softmax respectively mean utilizing the Eq. 4 and Eq. 5 to calculate weights. DWD-adapt denotes that we use Algorithmic 1 to update weights.

Table 1. We evaluate the model on GLUE val sets. The Teacher is a 12-layer BERT model, all other models are 6-layer models and have the same architecture as the teacher. BERT-FT stands for fine-tuning the first 6 layers of the teacher. The data of the last three lines are the results of the strategy comparison experiment. CoLA scores are Matthews Correlation Coefficient. SST-B scores are average value of Pearson correlation coefficient and Spearman correlation coefficient. MPRC scores are F1-Score and the rest are accuracy scores.

Model	MNLI(m/mm)	QQP	QNLI	SST-2	CoLA	STS-B	MRPC	RTE	Average
Teacher	83.82/84.35	90.69	91.32	92.32	59.07	88.13	89.35	66.43	82.83
BERT-FT	80.37/80.64	89.66	86.87	89.68	40.39	87.78	87.62	63.90	78.55
BERT-PKD	83.13/83.03	90.80	89.46	90.83	38.56	87.90	88.89	67.51	80.01
ALP-KD	83.68/83.51	**91.39**	89.36	90.94	46.10	88.82	89.78	66.43	81.11
BERT-EMD	83.44/83.36	91.31	89.09	90.71	44.61	88.82	88.89	66.79	80.78
DWD-sum	83.53/83.96	**91.39**	90.12	91.28	44.12	88.58	89.78	70.04	81.42
DWD-softmax	**84.44/84.39**	91.30	**90.76**	**91.40**	43.27	88.46	**90.29**	69.68	81.55
DWD-adapt	83.46/83.96	91.16	90.11	91.28	45.94	88.28	89.81	**71.00**	**81.67**
DWD-equ	82.74/83.02	91.30	88.49	90.71	44.77	**88.77**	88.74	67.14	80.63
DWD-inc	80.24/79.57	90.66	85.92	88.76	27.19	86.35	85.05	60.65	76.04
DWD-rnd	83.08/83.27	91.23	89.40	**91.40**	**46.19**	88.42	87.66	67.87	80.95

5   Experimental Results

5.1   Main Results

We summarize the experimental results on the GLUE val sets in Table 1. Following previous works [12,14], we also report the average scores. (1) DWD-KD achieves the best average results among all the 6-layer models. DWD-adapt achieves a better result than BERT-FT on all the datasets with an absolute improvement of 3.12% on average score. (2) DWD-softmax performs better than teacher on 5 out of 8 tasks (MNLI, QQP, STS-B, MRPC and RTE) and DWD-adapt achieves a noticeable improvement of 4.57% accuracy on RTE. (3) We observe that all models do not perform well on the CoLA dataset. The CoLA dataset is a corpus of language acceptability, which means the model needs to judge whether a sentence is grammatically correct. The difficulty of grammatical errors between negative samples in CoLA dataset is quite different. The grammatical errors in some negative examples are missing a word or having an extra word in a sentence. Such errors are relatively simple, but other grammatical errors can only be correctly identified with a deeper understanding of linguistic knowledge such as voice and tense. [9] shows pre-trained language models can obtain more linguistic knowledge from more corpus for better results on the CoLA dataset.

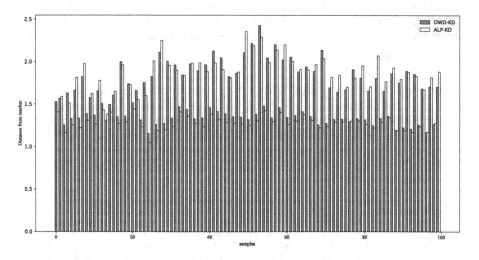

Fig. 2. We visualize the distance of the corresponding layer's outputs between the student model and the original teacher model. The student model are separately compressed by our method and ALP-KD.

To better show the effectiveness of the review mechanism, we select 100 samples from RTE dataset and visualize the Manhattan Distance between the third transformer layer' s output of ALP-KD, DWD-KD and sixth transformer layer' s output of teacher model in Fig. 2. The original output is a 768-dimensional vector, we use PCA to select the first two principal components of it. As we can observe from Fig. 2, The distance between the output of DWD-KD and that of teacher model is slightly larger, which proves that compared with other methods, the performance of our student model can exceed original teacher model.

Moreover, we also compress the 24-layer BERT models with our method. The Table 2 shows that the proposed DWD-KD method can effectively compress 24-layer into a 12-layer BERT model. DWD-KD achieves the best average results among all the 12-layer models, which proves the robustness of our method.

5.2   Strategy Comparison

To prove the effectiveness of the weights decay review mechanism, we also use three other strategies for distillation experiments. The last three lines in Table 1 shows the experiment results. "DWD-equ" denotes the weight of each layer is the same. The weight value is equal to $\lfloor \frac{N}{n*M} \rfloor$. This can also be regarded as an ablation experiment of dynamic review mechanism. "DWD-inc" denotes we reverse the original weights. "DWD-rnd" denotes we randomly shuffle the original weights. Original weights are the same as DWD-softmax. As we can observe from Table 1, student model performs poorly in almost all data sets when we reverse the original weights. The average score is even 2.51% lower than BERT-FT. This is because the old knowledge of the teacher model contains relatively elementary linguistic knowledge, it is insufficient for down-stream tasks. The average score of DWD-rnd is slightly higher than that of DWD-equ. But both are smaller than that of DWD-KD with decreasing weight.

Table 2. We also distill a 24-layer BERT model using our DWD-KD. The student models are 12-layer transformer-based architecture.

Model	MNLI (m/mm)	QQP	QNLI	SST-2	CoLA	STS-B	MRPC	RTE	Average
Teacher	86.69/86.47	91.57	92.31	94.27	62.15	89.66	90.53	71.84	85.05
BERT-PKD	83.09/83.26	91.27	88.14	89.11	21.55	75.94	81.90	57.04	74.59
ALP-KD	84.82/84.38	91.43	91.14	91.06	35.08	87.48	85.53	63.90	79.42
BERT-EMD	81.17/82.10	90.15	89.16	90.14	**43.60**	**89.21**	**85.62**	63.54	79.41
DWD-softmax	**85.54/85.28**	91.45	**91.29**	91.85	35.33	87.46	85.14	64.62	79.77
DWD-adapt	85.64/84.23	**91.55**	90.96	**91.86**	38.99	88.30	85.16	**66.06**	**80.31**

6   Conclusions

In this paper, we have studied knowledge distillation from a new perspective and accordingly proposed the deep-to-bottom weights decay review mechanism applying in BERT compression, which enables the student model systematically learn the knowledge. Moreover, our method can dynamically adjust the corresponding weights according to the training results of the student model. Experimental results on GLUE datasets show that our method achieves competitive results and outperform the original teacher model on 5 out of 8 tasks.

References

1. Cer, D.M., Diab, M.T., Agirre, E., Lopez-Gazpio, I., Specia, L.: SemEval-2017 task 1: semantic textual similarity - multilingual and cross-lingual focused evaluation. CoRR abs/1708.00055 (2017)
2. Chen, D., et al.: AdaBERT: task-adaptive BERT compression with differentiable neural architecture search. In: Proceedings of the 29th International Joint Conference on Artificial Intelligence, IJCAI 2020, pp. 2463–2469 (2020)
3. Chen, P., Liu, S., Zhao, H., Jia, J.: Distilling knowledge via knowledge review. In: IEEE Conference on Computer Vision and Pattern Recognition, CVPR 2021, virtual, 19–25 June 2021, pp. 5008–5017. Computer Vision Foundation/IEEE (2021)
4. Devlin, J., Chang, M., Lee, K., Toutanova, K.: BERT: pre-training of deep bidirectional transformers for language understanding. In: Proceedings of the 2019 Conference of the North American Chapter of the Association for Computational Linguistics: Human Language Technologies, NAACL-HLT 2019, Minneapolis, MN, USA, 2–7 June 2019, Volume 1 (Long and Short Papers), pp. 4171–4186. Association for Computational Linguistics (2019)

5. Dolan, W.B., Brockett, C.: Automatically constructing a corpus of sentential paraphrases. In: Proceedings of the 3rd International Workshop on Paraphrasing, IWP@IJCNLP 2005, Jeju Island, Korea, October 2005 (2005)

6. Fedus, W., Zoph, B., Shazeer, N.: Switch transformers: scaling to trillion parameter models with simple and efficient sparsity. arXiv arXiv:2101.03961 (2021)

7. Hinton, G.E., Vinyals, O., Dean, J.: Distilling the knowledge in a neural network (2015)

8. Jawahar, G., Sagot, B., Seddah, D.: What does BERT learn about the structure of language? In: Proceedings of the 57th Conference of the Association for Computational Linguistics, ACL 2019, Florence, Italy, 28 July–2 August 2019, Volume 1: Long Papers, pp. 3651–3657. Association for Computational Linguistics (2019)

9. Jiao, X., et al.: TinyBERT: distilling BERT for natural language understanding. In: Findings of the Association for Computational Linguistics, EMNLP 2020, Online Event, 16–20 November 2020. Findings of ACL, vol. EMNLP 2020, pp. 4163–4174. Association for Computational Linguistics (2020)

10. Lan, Z., Chen, M., Goodman, S., Gimpel, K., Sharma, P., Soricut, R.: ALBERT: a lite BERT for self-supervised learning of language representations. In: 8th International Conference on Learning Representations, ICLR 2020, Addis Ababa, Ethiopia, 26–30 April 2020 (2020)

11. Levesque, H., Davis, E., Morgenstern, L.: The Winograd schema challenge. In: 13th International Conference on the Principles of Knowledge Representation and Reasoning (2012)

12. Li, J., Liu, X., Zhao, H., Xu, R., Yang, M., Jin, Y.: BERT-EMD: many-to-many layer mapping for BERT compression with earth mover's distance. In: Proceedings of the 2020 Conference on Empirical Methods in Natural Language Processing, EMNLP 2020, Online, 16–20 November 2020, pp. 3009–3018. Association for Computational Linguistics (2020)

13. Michel, P., Levy, O., Neubig, G.: Are sixteen heads really better than one? In: Advances in Neural Information Processing Systems 32: Annual Conference on Neural Information Processing Systems 2019, NeurIPS 2019, 8–14 December 2019, Vancouver, BC, Canada, pp. 14014–14024 (2019)

14. Passban, P., Wu, Y., Rezagholizadeh, M., Liu, Q.: ALP-KD: attention-based layer projection for knowledge distillation. In: 35th AAAI Conference on Artificial Intelligence, AAAI 2021, 33rd Conference on Innovative Applications of Artificial Intelligence, IAAI 2021, The 11th Symposium on Educational Advances in Artificial Intelligence, EAAI 2021, Virtual Event, 2–9 February 2021. pp. 13657–13665. AAAI Press (2021)

15. Radford, A., Narasimhan, K., Salimans, T., Sutskever, I.: Improving language understanding with unsupervised learning (2018)

16. Rajpurkar, P., Zhang, J., Lopyrev, K., Liang, P.: SQuAD: 100,000+ questions for machine comprehension of text. In: Su, J., Carreras, X., Duh, K. (eds.) Proceedings of the 2016 Conference on Empirical Methods in Natural Language Processing, EMNLP 2016, Austin, Texas, USA, 1–4 November 2016, pp. 2383–2392 (2016)

17. Sanh, V., Debut, L., Chaumond, J., Wolf, T.: DistilBERT, a distilled version of BERT: smaller, faster, cheaper and lighter. arXiv arXiv:1910.01108 (2019)

18. Shen, S., et al.: Q-BERT: Hessian based ultra low precision quantization of BERT. In: The 34th AAAI Conference on Artificial Intelligence, AAAI 2020, The 32nd Innovative Applications of Artificial Intelligence Conference, IAAI 2020, The 10th AAAI Symposium on Educational Advances in Artificial Intelligence, EAAI 2020, New York, NY, USA, 7–12 February 2020, pp. 8815–8821 (2020)

19. Socher, R., et al.: Recursive deep models for semantic compositionality over a sentiment treebank. In: Proceedings of the 2013 Conference on Empirical Methods in Natural Language Processing, EMNLP 2013, 18–21 October 2013, Grand Hyatt Seattle, Seattle, Washington, USA, A Meeting of SIGDAT, A Special Interest Group of the ACL, pp. 1631–1642 (2013)

20. Sun, S., Cheng, Y., Gan, Z., Liu, J.: Patient knowledge distillation for BERT model compression. In: Proceedings of the 2019 Conference on Empirical Methods in Natural Language Processing and the 9th International Joint Conference on Natural Language Processing, EMNLP-IJCNLP 2019, Hong Kong, China, 3–7 November 2019, pp. 4322–4331. Association for Computational Linguistics (2019)

21. Wang, A., Singh, A., Michael, J., Hill, F., Levy, O., Bowman, S.R.: GLUE: a multitask benchmark and analysis platform for natural language understanding. In: 7th International Conference on Learning Representations, ICLR 2019, New Orleans, LA, USA, 6–9 May 2019 (2019)

22. Warstadt, A., Singh, A., Bowman, S.R.: Neural network acceptability judgments. Trans. Assoc. Comput. Linguistics **7**, 625–641 (2019)

23. Wasserblat, M., Pereg, O., Izsak, P.: Exploring the boundaries of low-resource BERT distillation. In: Proceedings of SustaiNLP: Workshop on Simple and Efficient Natural Language Processing, pp. 35–40 (2020)

24. Williams, A., Nangia, N., Bowman, S.R.: A broad-coverage challenge corpus for sentence understanding through inference. In: Proceedings of the 2018 Conference of the North American Chapter of the Association for Computational Linguistics: Human Language Technologies, NAACL-HLT 2018, New Orleans, Louisiana, USA, 1–6 June 2018, Volume 1 (Long Papers), pp. 1112–1122 (2018)

25. Yang, Z., et al.: TextBrewer: an open-source knowledge distillation toolkit for natural language processing. In: Proceedings of the 58th Annual Meeting of the Association for Computational Linguistics: System Demonstrations, ACL 2020, Online, 5–10 July 2020, pp. 9–16. Association for Computational Linguistics (2020). https://doi.org/10.18653/v1/2020.acl-demos.2

26. Zafrir, O., Boudoukh, G., Izsak, P., Wasserblat, M.: Q8BERT: quantized 8bit BERT. In: 5th Workshop on Energy Efficient Machine Learning and Cognitive Computing - NeurIPS Edition, EMC2@NeurIPS 2019, Vancouver, Canada, 13 December 2019, pp. 36–39. IEEE (2019)

Topic and Reference Guided Keyphrase Generation from Social Media

Xiubin Yu[1], Xingjun Chen[2] , Zhen Huang[1(✉)], Yong Dou[1], and Biao Hu[1]

[1] National Key Laboratory of Parallel and Distributed Processing, National University of Defense Technology, Changsha, China
{yuxiubin20,huangzhen,yongdou,hubiao}@nudt.edu.cn
[2] Dalian Navy Academy, Dalian, China

Abstract. Automatic keyphrase generation can help human efficiently understand or process critical information from massive social media posts. Seq2Seq-based generation models that can produce both present and absent keyphrases have achieved remarkable performance. However, existing models are limited by the sparseness of posts that are widely exhibited in social media language. Sparseness makes it difficult for models to obtain useful features and generate accurate keyphrases. To address this problem, we propose the Topic and Reference Guided Keyphrase Generation model(TRGKG) for social media posts, which enrich scarce posts features by corpus-level topics and post-level reference knowledge. The proposed model incorporates a contextual neural topic model to exploit topics and a heterogeneous graph to capture reference knowledge from retrieved related posts. To guide the decoding process, we introduce new topic-aware hierarchical attention and copy mechanism, which directly copies appropriate words from both the source post and its references. Experiments on two public datasets demonstrate that TRGKG achieves state-of-the-art performance.

Keywords: Keyphrase generation · Seq2Seq · Neural topic model · Heterogeneous graph

1 Introduction

Social media has become the main way for people to spread and obtain information. Hundreds of millions of social media posts are generated every day. To acquire knowledge from massive social media data, an automated system that can figure out important information is urgently needed. Keyphrase as the smallest unit of semantic expression can accurately describe the central concept or topic of a post. Social media keyphrases are beneficial to a wide range of applications, such as analyzing social behavior [13], constructing knowledge graph for social network [4], summarizing public opinions [9], etc. We denote phrases that do not match any contiguous subsequence of source text as absent keyphrases, and the ones that fully match a part of the text as present keyphrases.

Keyphrase Generation (KG) is a classic and challenging task that aims at predicting a set of keyphrases including present keyphrases as well as

© The Author(s), under exclusive license to Springer Nature Switzerland AG 2022
G. Memmi et al. (Eds.): KSEM 2022, LNAI 13369, pp. 140–154, 2022.
https://doi.org/10.1007/978-3-031-10986-7_12

absent keyphrases for the given text. Exiting generation models will inevitably encounter the data sparsity issue when adapted to social media. It is essentially due to the informal and colloquial nature of social media language, which results in limited features available in the noisy data. To address this, TAKG [17] utilizes topic modeling, where corpus-level latent topics shared with across other documents enable the model to leverage contexts observed in other related posts. Nonetheless, TAKG regards the topic model as a separate component for topic extraction rather than jointly improving KG task and topic modeling in a unified way. Besides, the input of the neural topic model is a BoW (Bag-of-Words) vector, which does not contain the sequence information of the post. [12] shows that the features encoded using a sequence model can help generate more coherent topics. GSEnc [5] argument the title of the post by retrieving absent keywords to enrich the scarce post. These retrieved keywords are regarded as post-level reference knowledge. Reference knowledge can enrich spare training data so that the model can accurately memorize and summarize all candidates. However, the reference knowledge in GSEnc is only from retrieved keywords that lack semantic information, and the potential knowledge in the retrieved posts is ignored.

Thus, we propose a new keyphrase generation model for social media language, named Topic and Reference Guided Keyphrase Generation(TRGKG). TRGKG simultaneously incorporates corpus-level topics and post-level reference knowledge from retrieved posts to enrich scarce posts features. We use the neural topic model to exploit latent topics, using heterogeneous graphs inspired by [19] to obtain explicit knowledge in reference posts that contains semantic information and potential knowledge. Then both post-level reference knowledge and corpus-level latent topics are used to guide the decoding process by introducing a new topic-aware hierarchical attention and copy mechanism, which directly copies appropriate words from both the source post and its references. Besides, we combine Seq2Seq and neural topic model in a joint way so that they can benefit from each other. In detail, the proposed model share the sequence encoder in Seq2Seq with the neural topic model.

Our contributions are as follows: (1). We propose TRGKG, a keyphrase generation model using both corpus-level topics and post-level reference knowledge from retrieved posts as guidance to generate keyphrases. (2). We improve the combination method of neural topic model and Seq2Seq so that they can better promote each other. (3). Extensive experiments on two public datasets demonstrate that TRGKG achieves effective improvements over existing methods, especially on Twitter.

2 Related Work

Predicting keyphrase can be divided into keyphrase extraction and keyphrase generation. The keyphrase extraction requires that the target keyphrase must appear in the source text, and it is impossible to generate absent keyphrase. To generate absent keywords, [8] first propose a Seq2Seq architecture with copy mechanism. [1] proposes a review mechanism to consider the impact of previously generated keywords. Title concisely describes the main focus of the text.

To leverage such structure, [2] uses the title to distinguish the core information in the text. For evaluation, the above model generates multiple keyphrases using beam search decoding with fixed beam size. [21] proposed catSeq with ONE2SEQ paradigm, predicting keyphrases as sequences. However, a predefined order will introduce wrong bias during training. So [20] proposed an ONE2SET paradigm to predict the keyphrases as a set, which eliminates the bias caused by the predefined order in the ONE2SEQ paradigm. Because the ONE2ONE paradigm is known to be better for predicting absent keyphrase [7] and as absent keyphrases are frequently observed in insufficient text social media, our model follows the ONE2ONE paradigm.

For social media keyphrase prediction, target keyphrase appears in neither the target posts nor the given candidate list. [18] proposed a framework of hashtag generation of microblog, which enriches source context with its response post in external data. [5] construct structured posts by augmenting posts with missing keywords as post-level reference knowledge. [17] leverage corpus-level latent topic representations, which can be learned without requiring external data. Because of its fixed and small topic number, it is not able to distinguish different posts with similar topics. [19] retrieves articles not keywords as references because keywords lack semantic information. And it proposed to construct heterogeneous graphs using articles, keywords, reference articles, and use hierarchical attention and copy mechanisms for decoding. Different from the above methods, we use both corpus-level latent topics and post-level reference knowledge to guide keyphrase generation.

3   Methodology

The overall architecture of TRGKG is illustrated in Fig. 1. Given a source post, we firstly retrieve related posts with their keywords from the predefined index(training set) by a retriever. And we regard these related posts as reference posts. Then, source post and reference posts are encoded by sequence encoder. We build a heterogeneous graph using source post and reference posts with keywords to get the enhanced representation of source post which is regarded as the initial hidden state in decoding. Besides, we utilize a contextual neural topic model to exploit latent topics of source posts. Finally, to improve performance, we leverage both corpus-level latent topics and post-level reference knowledge in a topic-reference-aware decoder.

3.1   Retriever

Given a post x, we get related posts from the training corpus by a dense retriever. We represent the source post and all the reference posts as dense vectors. Then we calculate the cosine similarity between the source post and all reference posts to get the most similar B reference posts $X^r = \{x_1^r, x_2^r, \ldots, x_B^r\}$.

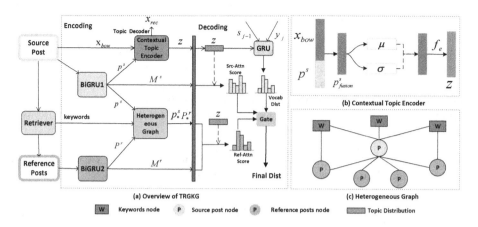

Fig. 1. Graphical illustration of our proposed TRGKG. (a) An overview of our model including encoding and decoding. For the right, we show the structure of contextual topic encoder in topic model (b) and heterogeneous graph in (c).

3.2 Encoder with Heterogeneous Graph

Sequence Encoder. We use two bidirectional gated recurrent unit (Bi-GRU) [3]: one named source sequence encoder for x, another named reference sequence encoder reference posts for $X^r = \{x_1^r, x_2^r, ..., x_B^r\}$. For source post x, firstly, each word gets word embedding vector after looking up table $\mathbf{W}_{emb}$, then using Bi-GRU to get the hidden state representations of each word in the original post $\mathbf{M}^s = \{\mathbf{h}_1^s, \mathbf{h}_2^s, ..., \mathbf{h}_{L_s}^s\}$, L_s is the number of words in source post. And we take $\mathbf{h}_{L_s}$ as the representation of source post $\mathbf{p}^s$. Similarly, using reference sequence encoder encodes B reference posts to get $\mathbf{M}^r = \{\mathbf{M}^{r_1}, \mathbf{M}^{r_2}, ..., \mathbf{M}^{r_B}\}$, here $\mathbf{M}^{r_i} = \{\mathbf{h}_1^{r_i}, \mathbf{h}_2^{r_i}, ..., \mathbf{h}_{L_{r_i}}^{r_i}\}$, and getting the representation of B reference posts $\mathbf{P}^r = \{\mathbf{p}^{r_1}, \mathbf{p}^{r_2}, ..., \mathbf{p}^{r_B}\}$.

Heterogeneous Graph. The heterogeneous graph is used to enhance the feature representation of posts. Below we introduce the heterogeneous graph module through three aspects: constructing the heterogeneous graph, initializing graph, and graph updating.

Muti-post as Heterogeneous Graph. Given a graph, $G = \{V, E\}$, V represents nodes, E represents edges between nodes. Our undirected heterogeneous graph can be formally defined as $V = V_p \cup V_w$, and $E = E_{w2p} \cup E_{p2p}$. Here, $V_p = x \cup X^r$ corresponds to source post node and B reference post nodes. $V_w = \{w_1, .., w_M\}$ means M unique key words retrieved by TF-IDF from source post and reference posts, $E_{p2p} = \{e_1, ..., e_b, ..., e_B\}$, here e_b means edge weight between b-th reference post and source post, $E_{w2p} = \{e_{1,1}, ..., e_{i,j}, ..., e_{M,B+1}\}$, here $e_{i,j}$ means edge weight between i-th keywords and j-th post.

Graph Initializers. For each post node, we apply $\mathbf{p}^s$ and $\mathbf{P}^r$ as the initial feature of node. For the keyword nodes, we apply word embedding as its initial node $\mathbf{w}_i = \mathbf{W}_{emb}(w_i)$. There are two types of edges in heterogeneous graph(i.e. post-to-post edge and word-to-post edge). To include information about the importance of relationships, we infuse cosine similarity between source post and reference posts in the edge weights of E_{p2p}. To include information about the significance of the relationships between keyword and document nodes, we infuse TF-IDF values in the edge weights of E_{w2p}.

Graph Aggregating and Updating. Given a constructed graph G with node features $\mathbf{p}^s$ and $\mathbf{P}^r$ and edge features $\mathbf{E}$, Graph Attention networks(GAT) [16] is used to update the representations of each node in graph. We donate the node hidden state of input node as $\mathbf{l}_i$, $i \in \{1, ..., M+B+1\}$. With the additional edge feature, the graph attention layer is designed as follows:

$$z_{ij} = \text{LeakyReLU}\left(\mathbf{W}_a\left[\mathbf{W}_q\mathbf{l}_i; \mathbf{W}_k\mathbf{l}_j; \mathbf{e}_{ij}\right]\right) \tag{1}$$

$$\alpha_{ij} = \frac{\exp(z_{ij})}{\sum_{l \in \mathcal{N}_i} \exp(z_{il})} \qquad \mathbf{u}_i = \sigma\left(\sum_{j \in \mathcal{N}_i} \alpha_{ij}\mathbf{W}_v\mathbf{l}_j\right) \tag{2}$$

$\mathbf{W}_a, \mathbf{W}_q, \mathbf{W}_k, \mathbf{W}_v$ are the trainable weights, $\mathbf{e}_{ij}$ is the embedding of edge feature and α_{ij} is the attention score between $\mathbf{l}_i$ and $\mathbf{l}_j$. We use muti-head attention is defined as follows, where $\|$ means the operation of concatenation:

$$\mathbf{u}_i = \|_{k=1}^{K} \sigma\left(\sum_{j \in \mathcal{N}_i} \alpha_{ij}^k \mathbf{W}^k \mathbf{l}_j\right) \tag{3}$$

After each attention layer, we introduce a residual connection and position-wise feed-forward (FFN) layer just as Transformer [15]. To transmit the messages between source post node, references nodes, and keywords nodes, after the initialization, we update each type of nodes separately as follows:

$$\begin{aligned}
\mathbf{L}_w^1 &= \text{FFN}\left(\text{GAT}\left(\mathbf{L}_w^0, \mathbf{L}_p^0, \mathbf{L}_p^0, \mathbf{E}_{w2p}\right) + \mathbf{L}_w^0\right) \\
\mathbf{L}_p^1 &= \text{FFN}\left(\text{GAT}\left(\mathbf{L}_p^0, \mathbf{L}_w^1, \mathbf{L}_w^1, \mathbf{E}_{w2p}\right) + \mathbf{L}_p^0\right) \\
\mathbf{L}_p^2 &= \text{FFN}\left(\text{GAT}\left(\mathbf{L}_p^1, \mathbf{L}_p^1, \mathbf{L}_p^1, \mathbf{E}_{p2p}\right) + \mathbf{L}_p^1\right)
\end{aligned} \tag{4}$$

where $\mathbf{L}_w \cup \mathbf{L}_p$ are the node features, $\mathbf{E}_{p2p} \cup \mathbf{E}_{w2p}$ are the edge features. Firstly, we aggregate post-level information to update word nodes, then we aggregate updated word nodes to update the post nodes, finally post nodes updated again by the updated post nodes. Each iteration contains a post-to-word, a word-to-post and a post-to-post update process. The above process is performed I round to get the enhanced post representation $\mathbf{L}_p^I$. We separate $\mathbf{p}_*^s$ and $\mathbf{P}_*^r = \{\mathbf{p}_*^{r_1}, \mathbf{p}_*^{r_2}, ..., \mathbf{p}_*^{r_B}\}$ from $\mathbf{L}_p^I$ as representation of source post and each reference. When the encoder finished, we use $\mathbf{p}_*^s$, $\mathbf{P}_*^r$, $\mathbf{M}^s$ and $\mathbf{M}^r$ to guide keyphrase generation.

3.3   Contextual Neural Topic Model

Neural topic model is based on variational autoencoder [6] framework, discovering latent topics via an encoding-decoding process. Its input is a V-dimensional BoW vector of source post $\mathbf{x}_{bow}$. And we depress it into a K-dimensional latent topic distribution $\mathbf{z}$ by a topic encoder. Then the topic decoder conditioned on $\mathbf{z}$, tries to reconstruct the BoW vector of x and outputs $\mathbf{x}_{rec}$. V is the vocabulary size after removing the stopwords, K is the number of topics. In particular, the decoder simulates the generation process of the topic model.

Topic Encoder. $q_\phi\left(\mathbf{g}|\mathbf{x}_{bow}\right)$, it generates $\mu = f_\mu\left(\mathbf{x}_{bow}\right), \sigma = f_\sigma\left(\mathbf{x}_{bow}\right)$, then obtain $\mathbf{g} = \mu + \sigma \cdot \epsilon$. It learn the latent topic distribution $\mathbf{z} = f_e\left(\mathbf{g}\right)$, where f_μ and f_σ are linear layers with ReLU activation, f_e is a ReLU activation and a Gussian softmax [10].

Topic Decoder. $p_\theta\left(\mathbf{x}_{rec}|\mathbf{g}\right)$, transforms g into predicted probability of each word in vocabulary by using ReLU-activated linear layers f_d:

$$\mathbf{x}_{rec} = \text{softmax}\left(f_d\left(\mathbf{z}\right)\right) \tag{5}$$

The neural topic model above only uses the BoW vector as input. But BoW vector has some limitations, such as ignoring sequence information of the text. Fortunately, the sequence encoder in the encoder can capture post semantics better, so we use the representation of source post $\mathbf{p}^s$ with sequence information as an input of the topic model. Then, the topic model can utilize the BoW vector and contextual representation to exploit latent topics. We call it contextual neural topic model, because it shares the sequence encoder in Seq2Seq.

Contextual Topic Encoder. It can be regarded as a two-step topic encoding process. To keep valuable information in both contextual representation and BoW representation, we first fuse $\mathbf{p}^s$ and $\mathbf{x}_{bow}$ as follows:

$$\mathbf{p}^s_{fusion} = \mathbf{W}_f\left[\mathbf{x}_{bow}; \mathbf{p}^s\right] + \mathbf{b}_f \tag{6}$$

$\mathbf{W}_f$ and $\mathbf{b}_f$ are trainable parameters, $[\mathbf{x}_{bow}; \mathbf{p}^s]$ means the concatenation of $\mathbf{x}_{bow}$ and $\mathbf{p}^s$. $\mathbf{p}^s_{fusion}$ is a V-dimensional vector. And Then we use the same method in topic encoder to get topic distribution $\mathbf{z}$:

$$\mu = f_\mu\left(\mathbf{p}^s_{fusion}\right) \qquad \sigma = f_\sigma\left(\mathbf{p}^s_{fusion}\right) \tag{7}$$

$$\mathbf{g} = \mu + \sigma \cdot \epsilon \tag{8}$$

$$\mathbf{z} = f_e\left(\mathbf{g}\right) \tag{9}$$

For decoder, we use the topic decoder above to reconstruct the BoW vector x_{rec}. In the following, we adapt latent topic distribution $\mathbf{z}$ as the representation of source post and use it to guide generating keyphrases.

3.4   Topic-Reference-Aware Decoder

Sequence Decoder. We use $\mathbf{p}_*^s$ as the initial state of GRU decoder. Besides the general hidden state update, we also take the topic distribution into consideration. $\mathbf{s}_{j-1}$ is the previous step hidden state. The j-th decode process is described as follows:

$$\mathbf{s}_j = \text{GRU}\left([\mathbf{W}_{emb}\left(y_j\right); \mathbf{z}], \mathbf{s}_{j-1}\right) \tag{10}$$

Topic-Aware Hierarchical Attention. To determine important information from source and reference posts, we use new hierarchical attention with latent topics. Because latent topics enable the model to focus on some topic words in source and reference posts. On the other hand, latent topics can correct irrelevant information in reference posts due to retrieval. We generalize topic-aware hierarchical attention with the following formula:

$$\mathbf{c}_j = \text{TAHierAttn}\left(\mathbf{s}_j, \mathbf{M}^s, \mathbf{M}^r, \mathbf{P}_*^r, \mathbf{z}\right) \tag{11}$$

The context vector $\mathbf{c}_j$ is obtained by topic-aware hierarchical attention. $\mathbf{c}_j$ is computed as follows:

$$\mathbf{c}_j^s = \sum_{i=1}^{L_s} \alpha_{ji}^s \mathbf{h}_i^s, \qquad \mathbf{c}_j^r = \sum_{i=1}^{B} \sum_{k=1}^{L_{r_i}} \alpha_{ji}^r \alpha_{jk}^{r_i} \mathbf{h}_k^{r_i} \tag{12}$$

$$\theta = \text{sigmoid}\left(\mathbf{W}_\theta[\mathbf{c}_j^s; \mathbf{c}_j^r] + \mathbf{b}_\theta\right), \qquad \mathbf{c}_j = \theta \cdot \mathbf{c}_j^s + (1 - \theta) \cdot \mathbf{c}_j^r \tag{13}$$

where $\mathbf{c}_j^s$ is context vector from source post and $\mathbf{c}_j^r$ is context vector from reference posts. $\mathbf{W}_\theta$ and $\mathbf{b}_\theta$ are trainable parameters, $\mathbf{h}_i^s \in \mathbf{M}^s$ and $\mathbf{h}_k^{r_i} \in \mathbf{M}^{r_i}$, θ is a gate for two context vectors. α^s is a word-level attention scores over the source post $\mathbf{M}^s$, α^r is a post-level attention scores over the reference posts $\mathbf{P}_*^r$ and α^{r_i} is a word-level attention scores over the i-th reference post $\mathbf{M}^{r_i}$.

We integrate the topic distribution when calculating the attention scores of source post and reference posts. Here's how they are calculated:

$$\alpha_{ji}^s = \frac{\exp\left(f_\alpha\left(\mathbf{h}_i^s, \mathbf{s}_j, \mathbf{z}\right)\right)}{\sum_{i'=1}^{L_x} \exp\left(f_\alpha\left(\mathbf{h}_{i'}^s, \mathbf{s}_j, \mathbf{z}\right)\right)} \tag{14}$$

$$\alpha_{ji}^r = \frac{\exp\left(f_\alpha\left(\mathbf{p}_*^{r_i}, \mathbf{s}_j, \mathbf{z}\right)\right)}{\sum_{i'=1}^{B} \exp\left(f_\alpha\left(\mathbf{p}_*^{r_{i'}}, \mathbf{s}_j, \mathbf{z}\right)\right)} \tag{15}$$

$$\alpha_{jk}^{r_i} = \frac{\exp\left(f_\alpha\left(\mathbf{h}_k^{r_i}, \mathbf{s}_j, \mathbf{z}\right)\right)}{\sum_{i'=1}^{L_{r_i}} \exp\left(f_\alpha\left(\mathbf{h}_{i'}^{r_i}, \mathbf{s}_j, \mathbf{z}\right)\right)} \tag{16}$$

Equation 14 calculates the attention scores of source posts. Equation 15 and Eq. 16 calculate the attention score of reference posts. f_α is defined as follows, $\mathbf{v}_\alpha, \mathbf{W}_\alpha$ and $\mathbf{b}_\alpha$ are trainable parameters:

$$f_\alpha\left(\mathbf{h}_i^s, \mathbf{s}_j, z\right) = \mathbf{v}_\alpha^T \tanh\left(\mathbf{W}_\alpha\left[\mathbf{h}_i^s; \mathbf{s}_j; z\right] + \mathbf{b}_\alpha\right) \tag{17}$$

Final Scores with Copy Mechanism. Firstly the j-th target generation scores on predefined vocabulary p_{gen} are computed by:

$$p_{gen} = \text{softmax}\left(\mathbf{W}_{gen}\left[\mathbf{s}_j; \mathbf{c}_j; \mathbf{z}\right] + \mathbf{b}_{gen}\right) \tag{18}$$

We define the source scores on post's words p_{sou}, the reference scores p_{ref} on reference posts' words. The finial scores p_j is computed as a combination of three scores using soft gate $\lambda \in \mathbb{R}^3$, determining the importance of three scores:

$$\lambda = \text{softmax}\left(\mathbf{W}_\lambda\left[\mathbf{s}_j; \mathbf{c}_t; \mathbf{z}; \mathbf{W}_{emb}(y_{t-1})\right] + \mathbf{b}_\lambda\right) \tag{19}$$

$$p_j = \lambda_1 p_{gen} + \lambda_2 p_{sou} + \lambda_3 p_{ref} \tag{20}$$

where source scores $p_{sou} = \sum_i^{L_s} \alpha_{ji}^s$ are the copy probability from source post, reference scores $p_{ref} = \sum_i^B \sum_k^{L_{r_i}} \alpha_{jk}^{r_i}$ are the copy probability from all the reference posts. We adopt copy mechanism above, which allows keywords to be directly extracted from the source input. We define a post generate its keyphrase y with probability:

$$\Pr(\mathbf{y} \mid \mathbf{x}) = \prod_{j=1}^{|\mathbf{y}|} \Pr\left(y_j \mid \mathbf{y}_{1:j-1}, \mathbf{M}^s, \mathbf{M}^r, \mathbf{P}_*^r, \mathbf{z}\right) \tag{21}$$

where $|\mathbf{y}|$ is the length of the keyphrase, $\Pr\left(y_j \mid \mathbf{y}_{1:j-1}, \mathbf{M}^s, \mathbf{M}^r, \mathbf{P}_*^r, \mathbf{z}\right)$ as a word distribution over vocabulary, denoted $\mathbf{p}_j$, means the how likely a word to fill the j-th slot in target keyphrase.

3.5 Jointly Training

We jointly train our neural network of learning topic modeling and keyphrase generation. The objective function of the topic model is defined as negative of evidence lower bound, as shown as follows:

$$\mathcal{L}_{NTM} = D_{KL}(p_\theta(\mathbf{g}) \mid q_\phi(\mathbf{g} \mid \mathbf{x})) - \mathbf{E}_{q_\phi(\mathbf{g}\mid\mathbf{x})}[p_\theta(\mathbf{x} \mid \mathbf{g})] \tag{22}$$

where the first term D_{KL} is Kullback-Leibler divergence loss, and the second term E reflect the reconstruction loss. $q_\phi(\mathbf{g} \mid \mathbf{x})$ and $p_\theta(\mathbf{x} \mid \mathbf{g})$ means the network of contextual topic encoder and topic decoder.

The loss of keyphrase generation is cross entropy expressed as :

$$\mathcal{L}_{KG} = -\sum_{n=1}^N \log\left(\Pr\left(\mathbf{y}_n \mid \mathbf{x}_n\right)\right) \tag{23}$$

The final loss of the entire network is a linear combination of two loss:

$$\mathcal{L} = \mathcal{L}_{NTM} + \gamma \cdot \mathcal{L}_{KG} \tag{24}$$

γ is a factor to balance two loss. For inference, we use beam search and then use top-ranked keyphrases as final predictions.

4   Experiment Settings

4.1   Datasets

We conduct experiments on two social media English datasets, Twitter and StackExchange [17]. In Twitter including microblog posts, hashtags in the middle of a post were treated as present keyphrases, and hashtags either before or after a post were treated as absent keyphrases and are removed from the post. StackExchange is collected from a Q&A platform. For one text, it is the concatenation of a title and a description, and the hashtags are manually by the user. For model training and evaluation, document-keyphrase pairs are partitioned into train, validation, and test splits consisting of 80%, 10%, and 10% of the entire data respectively. Table 1 gives the details of two datasets.

Table 1. Statistics of datasets. Avg.len: average number of tokens per post. Unq.D and Unq.KP: number of distinct posts and keyphrases. Avg.KP:average number of keyphrases per post. Abs.KP(%): ratio of absent keyphrases. We report average performance with different random seeds of 5 runs.

Datasets	Avg.len	Unq.D	Avg.KP	Unq.KP	Abs.KP(%)
Twitter	19.52	44113	1.13	4347	71.35
StackExchange	87.94	49447	2.43	12114	54.32

4.2   Comparisons and Evaluation

To demonstrate the effectiveness of our method, we compared our method with keyphrase extraction and keyphrase generation models. For keyphrase extraction models, we use TF-IDF scores, TextRank algorithm [11] and keyphrase extraction method based on sequence tagging [22]. For keyphrase generation, we compared the following models: SEQ2SEQ [8] which uses Seq2Seq framework, CopyRNN [8] which based on SEQ2SEQ with copy mechanism, CorrRNN [1] which exploring keyphrases correlations, TAKG [17] using latent topic helping keyphrase generation, CopyRNN-GATER [19] using a heterogeneous graph to capture references knowledge to guide decoding process, TG-NET [2] using the struct of title and descriptions and GSEnc [5] arguments structure using other document and uses a graph to obtain structure-aware representation for the decoding process.

For evaluations, we adopted macro-average F1@K and mean average precision (MAP) as evaluation metrics. We report F1@1/3 for the twitter dataset, F1@3/5 for StackExchange, squaring up the average number of keyphrases in datasets. For two datasets, we report MAP@5 over top-5 predictions.

4.3   Implementation Details

Following the previous work, we train our network in a SEQ2ONE paradigm. We keep the parameter settings used in [17]. For the additional graph module, we set the number of reference posts B among $\{3, 5,10\}$ and the number of keywords M per post among 3, 10, 20. Because of a longer text in StackExchange, B was 3 for StackExchange and 5 for Twitter, M was 10 for StackExchange and 3 for Twitter. We use dense retriever MPNet [14], which is s a pre-training method for language understanding tasks. For a fair comparison, we use the same B, M, and dense retriever in CopyRNN-GATER. In the training process, in order for the contextual neural topic model to utilize the sequence encoder in the SEQ2SEQ model, we pretrain the KG module for 2 epochs. Then since the neural topic model trains slower than the KG module, we also warm up the neural topic model several epochs, specifically, we warm up 50 epochs on Twitter and 20 epochs on StackExchange. We empirically set γ to 1. We set the beam size to 50 for the inferencing process.

Table 2. The performance of keyphrase prediction. The best results are bold. TAKG-CNTM: TAKG with Contextual Neural Topic Model.

Model	Twitter			StackExchange		
	F1@1	F1@3	MAP	F1@3	F1@5	MAP
TF-IDF	1.16	1.14	1.89	13.50	12.74	12.61
TEXTRANK	1.73	1.94	1.89	6.30	8.28	4.76
SEQ-TAG	22.79	12.27	22.44	17.58	12.82	19.03
SEQ2SEQ	34.10	26.01	41.11	22.99	20.65	23.95
CopyRNN	36.60	26.79	43.12	31.53	27.41	33.45
CorrRNN	34.97	26.13	41.64	30.89	26.97	32.87
TG-NET	–	–	–	32.02	27.84	34.05
TAKG	38.49	27.84	45.12	33.41	29.16	35.52
GSEnc	38.80	28.10	45.50	35.20	30.90	37.80
CopyRNN-GATER	41.09	29.69	48.06	37.96	33.33	41.16
TRGKG	**42.20**	**30.68**	**49.69**	**38.66**	**33.76**	**41.75**
TAKG-CNTM	39.24	28.73	46.20	33.80	29.78	36.00

5   Results and Analysis

5.1   Performance of Keyphrase Generation

Table 2 shows the performance of keyphrase predicted by our model and other baselines. Keyphrase extraction models show much worse performance than keyphrase generation models on both datasets. The language style of social media result in a large number of absent keyphrases, which is impossible for to extract from the original post. Among keyphrase generation models, latent topics are useful to prediction, TAKG with latent topics can get better result. However, GSEnc and CopyRNN-GATER achieve the best performance among all baselines. It shows that retrieved posts and keywords are beneficial to prediction of keyphrase. Our model outperform all the state-of-the-art baseline models on both datasets. Because our model incorporates not only latent topics but also reference knowledge. We replace he original topic model in TAKG with the proposed contextual neural topic model marked as TAKG-CNTM. The results show that TAKG-CNTM can achieve better performance than TAKG. This proves the effectiveness of contextual neural topic model.

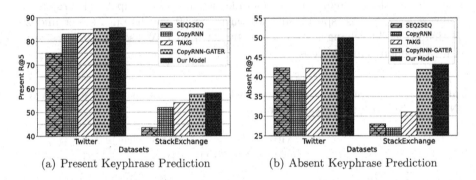

(a) Present Keyphrase Prediction   (b) Absent Keyphrase Prediction

Fig. 2. The prediction results of present and absent keyphrases.

5.2   Prediction of Present and Absent Keyphrase

We further discuss the performance of our model in predicting the present and absent keyphrase. The results are shown in Fig. 2. For the present keyphrase, F1@1 is adopted for evaluating. And we use recall@5 for the absent keyphrases.

An important finding is that reference knowledge from retrieved posts is more helpful than latent topics in generating not only present but also absent keyphrases. Results show that CopyRNN-GATER and our model are better at predicting two types of keyphrases than TAKG. This may be because reference knowledge provides more fine-grained post-level information than corpus-level topics. Especially, reference knowledge enables the model to capture more keywords to copy, which can greatly improve the prediction performance of absent keyphrases. However, the results indicate that our model outperforms all comparison models in predicting two types of keyphrases especially on Twitter. It is attributed to our ability to incorporate post-level reference knowledge and corpus-level topics.

5.3   Ablation Study

Topics Are Useful. To verify the efficiency of topics, we removed topics in two ways: (1). Remove topics when calculating the attention score of source post, in Eq. 14. (2). Remove topics when calculating the attention score of reference posts, in Eqs. 15 and 16. (3). Remove both of the above. The results in Table 3 show that these ablation methods make the model perform worse. This suggests that topics not only facilitate the identification of key information in source post but also the reference posts. One possible explanation is that latent topics of source post can correct irrelevant information in reference posts retrieved.

Table 3. Results of our ablation study. w/o: without, topic-sour: source attention scores with topics, topic-refer: reference attention scores with topics, topic-all: source and reference attention attention scores with topics, joint-train: jointly training.

Model	StackExchange F1@3	Twitter F1@1
Our model (w/o topic-sour)	38.40	41.73
Our model (w/o topic-refer)	38.23	41.87
Our model (w/o topic-all)	38.19	41.70
Our model (w/o joint-train)	38.51	**42.35**
Our full model	**38.66**	42.20

Joint or Pipeline. We train the topic model separately from the rest of the TRGKG as ablation. Surprisingly, this way of training performed almost identically to the joint training method. This is quite different from TAKG, where joint training with TAKG results in a significant improvement in model performance. This may be due to the shared sequence encoder between the neural topic module and Seq2Seq in TRGKG.

5.4   Influence of the Number of Topics

We compare the effect of different topic numbers $k \in [20]$ of keyphrase generation performance, and the results are shown in Fig. 3. On Twitter, the number of topics has little effect on the overall performance, with a maximum difference of about 2%. On the StackExchange, the model performance shows a trend of increasing first and then decreasing when the number of topics is between [20]. Unlike Twitter, the performance of keyword generation starts to drop dramatically when the number of topics is set above 200. This may be due to the different data conditions of the datasets.

5.5   Case Study

We further present a case study, where the top five outputs of some comparison models have displayed in Table 4. As can be seen, only our model successfully generates the golden present keyphrase *'love'* and absent keyphrase *'quote'*. On the contrary, TAKG not only fails to generate the absent keyphrase *'quote'* but also generates irrelevant keyphrases. It is possible that the words *'game'*, *'win'* and *'play'* in the posts are causing the model to identify the wrong topic *'super bowl'*. CopyRNN-GATER fails to generate the present keyphrase *'love'*, missing the understanding of the meaning of the original post. This demonstrates that using both the corpus-level topics and post-level reference knowledge can generate more accurate absent and present keyphrases compared to the baselines.

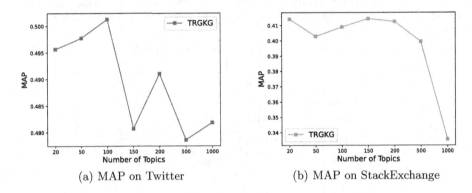

(a) MAP on Twitter   (b) MAP on StackExchange

Fig. 3. Performance for our model with different topic numbers.

Table 4. A keyphrase prediction example of different models. Bolded and italic indicate the golden keyphrases.

Posts	Love is a game that two can play and both win
Golden Keyphrases	*love*, *quote*
TAKG	*love*, super bowl, sb45, packers, steelers
CopyRNN-GATER	oh teen quotes, just saying, *quote*, daily teen, omgsotrue
TRGKG	*love*, real talk, *quote*, fact, omgsotrue

6   Conclusion

We proposed a keyphrase generation model named TRGKG that incorporates both corpus-level latent topics and post-level reference knowledge. We exploited latent topics using a contextual neural topic model and capture knowledge from reference posts based on the heterogeneous graph. And they are fused together by a topic-aware hierarchical attention to guide the decoding process. Experimental results show that our method outperforms all state-of-the-art models on Twitter and StackExchange.

Acknowledgements. This work is supported by the National Key R&D Program of China under Grants (No. 2018YFB0204300).

References

1. Chen, J., Zhang, X., Wu, Y., Yan, Z., Li, Z.: Keyphrase generation with correlation constraints. In: Empirical Methods in Natural Language Processing (2018)
2. Chen, W., Gao, Y., Zhang, J., King, I., Lyu, M.R.: Title-guided encoding for keyphrase generation. In: National Conference on Artificial Intelligence (2019)
3. Cho, K., van Merriënboer, B., Gulcehre, C.: Learning phrase representations using RNN encoder-decoder for statistical machine translation. In: EMNLP (2014)
4. He, Q., Yang, J., Shi, B.: Constructing knowledge graph for social networks in a deep and holistic way. In: Companion Proceedings of the Web Conference (2020)
5. Kim, J., Jeong, M., Choi, S., won Hwang, S.: Structure-augmented keyphrase generation. In: Empirical Methods in Natural Language Processing (2021)
6. Kingma, D.P., Welling, M.: Auto-encoding variational bayes. In: International Conference on Learning Representations (2014)
7. Meng, R., Yuan, X., Wang, T., Zhao, S., Trischler, A., He, D.: An empirical study on neural keyphrase generation. In: NAACL (2021)
8. Meng, R., Zhao, S., Han, S., He, D., Brusilovsky, P., Chi, Y.: Deep keyphrase generation. In: Meeting of the Association for Computational Linguistics (2017)
9. Meng, X., Wei, F., Liu, X., Zhou, M., Li, S., Wang, H.: Entity-centric topic-oriented opinion summarization in twitter. In: Knowledge Discovery and Data Mining (2012)
10. Miao, Y., Grefenstette, E., Blunsom, P.: Discovering discrete latent topics with neural variational inference. Computation and Language. arXiv preprint arXiv:1706.00359 (2017)
11. Mihalcea, R., Tarau, P.: Textrank: Bringing order into text. In: Empirical Methods in Natural Language Processing (2004)
12. Panwar, M., Shailabh, S., Aggarwal, M., Krishnamurthy, B.: Tan-ntm: topic attention networks for neural topic modeling. In: ACL (2021)
13. Ruths, D., Pfeffer, J.: Social media for large studies of behavior. Science 1063–1064 (2014)
14. Song, K., Tan, X., Qin, T., Lu, J., Liu, T.Y.: Mpnet: masked and permuted pre-training for language understanding. Computation and Language. arXiv preprint arXiv:2004.09297 (2020)
15. Vaswani, A., et al.: Attention is all you need. In: Neural Information Processing Systems (2017)
16. Velickovic, P., Cucurull, G., Casanova, A., Romero, A., Lio, P., Bengio, Y.: Graph attention networks. STAT 20 (2017)
17. Wang, Y., Li, J., Chan, H.P., King, I., Lyu, M.R., Shi, S.: Topic-aware neural keyphrase generation for social media language. In: ACL (2019)
18. Wang, Y., Li, J., King, I., Lyu, M.R., Shi, S.: Microblog hashtag generation via encoding conversation contexts. In: North American Chapter of the Association for Computational Linguistics (2019)

19. Ye, J., Cai, R., Gui, T., Zhang, Q.: Heterogeneous graph neural networks for keyphrase generation. Computation and Language. arXiv preprint arXiv:2109.04703 (2021)
20. Ye, J., Gui, T., Luo, Y., Xu, Y., Zhang, Q.: One2set: generating diverse keyphrases as a set. In: Meeting of the Association for Computational Linguistics (2021)
21. Yuan, X., et al.: One size does not fit all: Generating and evaluating variable number of keyphrases. In: Meeting of the Association for Computational Linguistics (2020)
22. Zhang, Q., Wang, Y., Gong, Y., Huang, X.: Keyphrase extraction using deep recurrent neural networks on twitter. In: EMNLP (2016)

DISEL: A Language for Specifying DIS-Based Ontologies

Yijie Wang[1] ⓘ, Yihai Chen[1] ⓘ, Deemah Alomair[2,3] ⓘ, and Ridha Khedri[2(✉)] ⓘ

[1] Shanghai University, Shanghai, China
{wyj981113,yhchen}@shu.edu.cn
[2] McMaster University, Hamilton, ON, Canada
{alomaird,khedri}@mcmaster.ca
[3] Imam Abdulrahman Bin Faisal University, Dammam, Kingdom of Saudi Arabia

Abstract. We present the main syntactical constructs of *DISEL* language, which is designed as a language for specifying DIS-based ontologies. The adoption of this language would enable the creation of shareable ontologies for the development of ontology-based systems. We give the main constructs of the language and we illustrate the specification of the main components of a *DISEL* ontology using a simplified example of a weather ontology. DIS formalism, on which the proposed language is based, enables the modelling of an ontology in a bottom-up approach. The syntax of *DISEL* language is based on XML, which eases the translation of its ontologies to other ontology languages. We also introduce *DISEL Editor* tool, which has several capabilities such as editing and visualising ontologies. It can guide the specifier in providing the essential elements of the ontology, then it automatically produces the full *DISEL* ontology specification.

Keywords: Ontology · Ontology language · Ontology specification · Knowledge engineering · DIS formalism · Ontology visualization

1 Introduction

In the last two decades, we have seen an expansion in the volume and complexity of organized data sets ranging from databases, log files, and transformation of unorganized data to organized data [16,43]. To extract significant knowledge from this data, the use of ontologies allows to connect the dots between information directly inferred from the data to concepts in the domain of the data. Ontology refers to a branch of metaphysics about the study of concepts in a world (i.e., a reality). This world is commonly referred to in information science as domain. The literature abounds with works related to the creation of ontologies, and to the characterisation of the best methods to create representations of reality [20]. Ontologies have been used in several areas of knowledge. For instance, in biological sciences and with the development of the GeneOntology and the creation of the community of the Open Biological and Biomedical Ontology (OBO) Foundry a wide interest rose to use of ontologies in this area [23].

© The Author(s), under exclusive license to Springer Nature Switzerland AG 2022
G. Memmi et al. (Eds.): KSEM 2022, LNAI 13369, pp. 155–171, 2022.
https://doi.org/10.1007/978-3-031-10986-7_13

Another area where ontologies are widely used is that of information sciences. A wide literature has been published related to ontologies and their use in basic reasoning problems (e.g., [46]), learning (ontologies and queries) (e.g., [41]), privacy management (e.g., [40]), interactive query formulation and answering (e.g., [29]), or data cleaning [28]. These are only a few example of the areas of application of ontologies in information sciences.

Ontologies are used to represent and reason about a domain. There are several formalisms with their specific languages that are used to specify domain knowledge, such as graphs (e.g., [22]), mathematical structures (e.g., [49]), and logics (e.g., [17]). We found in [32] that there is no consensus to whether an ontology only includes the concepts and relations of the domain, or if it also includes the instances of concepts. This aspect led researchers to propose several ontology languages based on various formalisms, which only a few of them are widely being used. Two classes of languages are widely used and they are related to the family of logic languages, Common Logic (CL) [3], and Ontology Web Language (OWL) [13,39]. CL is developed from Knowledge Interchange Format (KIF) [21], which is a variant of Lisp, and its dialects [38]. Hence, the main language of CL has a functional programming style. There are indications that CL's main language is becoming a language based on Extensible Markup Language (XML), which is called eXtended Common Logic Markup Language (XCL). On the other hand, OWL has a wider usage and is based on the XML. Several tools, such as Protégé-OWL editor, support the usage OWL.

Starting from a novel data-centered knowledge representation, called Domain Information System (DIS) [31], we propose a high level language for ontology specification. DIS is a formalism that offers a modular structure, which separates the domain knowledge (i.e., the ontology) from the domain data view (i.e., the data or instances of the concepts). It is specific for dealing with Cartesian domains where concepts are formed from atomic concepts through a Cartesian construction. Hence, it is a formalism that takes advantage of a Cartesian perspective on information. The bulk of the data in what is referred to as big data is structured data. It is essentially formed of machine-generated structured data that include databases, sensor data, web log data, security log data, machines logs, point-of-sale data, demographic information, star ratings by customers, location data from smart phones and smart devices, or financial and accounting data. The size of this data is increasing significantly every second. The need for better data analytic techniques that go beyond the capabilities of a Database Management System (DBMS) by connecting the data to concepts that are in the domain but that cannot be defined in a DBMS. In a DIS, the core component of an ontology is a Boolean lattice built from atomic concepts that are imported from the schema of the dataset to be analysed. In [36], we found that DIS enables the integration of several datasets and their respective ontologies for reasoning tasks requiring data-grounded and domain-related answers to user queries. Currently, the language of DIS is a low level language as it is based on a set theory, lattice theory, and graph theory. In this paper, we present a high-level language, called Domain Information System Extended Language (DISEL), that is structured and based on XML. It is built on the top of that of current DIS mathematical language. DISEL uses a mixed structure of directed graphs and trees to precisely capture DIS specifications. It is also based on XML so that it can be easily integrated to many software systems. It aims to make specifying ontologies as easy as possible and without any mathematical complications.

In Sect. 2, we introduce DIS on which DISEL is build. Then, we present the example that is used to illustrate the usage of the constructs of the language. In Sect. 3, we review ontology languages that we found in the literature. In Sect. 4, we introduce the main elements of DISEL and we illustrate their usage using the weather ontology introduced in Sect. 2. In Sect. 5, we give the main design decisions of DISEL. In Sect. 6, we discuss the main features of DISEL, its strengths, and its weaknesses. In Sect. 7, we present our concluding remarks and point to the highlights of our future work.

2   Background

2.1   Domain Information System

DIS is a novel formalism for data-centered knowledge representation that addresses the mapping problem between a set of structured data and its associated ontology [31]. It separates the data structure from the ontology structure and automatically performs the mapping process between the two. A DIS is formed by a domain ontology, a domain data view, and a function that maps the latter to the first. The construction of the domain ontology structure is based on three elements $\mathcal{O} = (\mathcal{C}, \mathcal{L}, \mathcal{G})$, where $\mathcal{C}$ is a concepts structure, $\mathcal{L}$ is a lattice structure, and $\mathcal{G}$ is a set of rooted-graphs. A concept might be atomic/elementary, or composite. A concept that does not divide into sub-concepts is known as atomic concept. In DIS and when for example the data is coming from a database, atomic concepts are the attributes in the database schema. A composite concept is formed by several concepts. The composition of concepts is an operation $\oplus$ defined on C. The set of concepts making the structure $(C, \oplus, c_e)$ is an idempotent communicative monoid, that we denote by $\mathcal{C}$.

The second component of the domain ontology structure is a Boolean lattice $\mathcal{L} = (L, \sqsubseteq_c)$. It is a free lattice generated from the set of atomic concepts. The composition between these concepts make up the remaining concepts of the lattice. The set of concepts of the lattice are either directly obtained from the database schema (i.e., atomic concepts), or obtained through the Cartesian composition of the atomic concepts using the operator $\oplus$. The relationship between a concept and its a composed concept that involves it is the relation partOf denoted by $\sqsubseteq_c$.

The last element of the domain ontology is the set of rooted graphs, where an element $G_{t_i} = (C_i, R_i, t_i)$ is a graph on the set of vertices C_i, having the set of edges R_i, and is rooted at the vertex t_i. Rooted graphs represent the concepts that are somehow related to an atomic or composite concept from the Boolean lattice. In other terms, they introduce the concepts that are not directly generated from the database schemes and are related to an atomic or composite concept of the lattice through a relationship from the domain. In this way, the Boolean lattice might be enriched with multiple rooted-graphs having their roots at different lattice concepts.

Using the previous components, we get the full construction of the domain ontology $O = (\mathcal{C}, \mathcal{L}, \mathcal{G})$. The second component of DIS is the domain data view. Domain data view is abstracted as diagonal-free cylindric algebra $\mathcal{A} = (A, +, *, -, 0_A, 1_A, \{c_k\})_{k \in L}$ [25]. It is a Boolean algebra with cylindrification operators $\{c_k\}$ [31]. The cylindrification operators are indexed over the elements of the carrier set L of the Boolean lattice. The last element of the DIS is the mapping operator τ, which maps the data in $\mathcal{A}$ to its related element in the Boolean lattice of O structure. The mapping τ is a function that takes a datum from the data set and returns its corresponding concept in the lattice. Thus, the complete structure of DIS is $\mathcal{D} = (\mathcal{O}, \mathcal{A}, \tau)$. An illustrative representation of the system is shown in the Fig. 1, where the atoms of the lattice are *Attr1*, *Attr2*, and *Attr3*. We notice two rooted graphs that are attached to two elements of the lattice. The reader can find in [36] a comprehensive case study related to a film and TV domain which illustrates the usage of DIS.

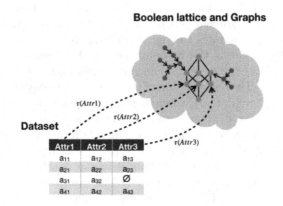

Fig. 1. Abstract view of domain information system.

Hence, the formalism of DIS uses a basic mathematical language which is that of lattices, relations, sets, and graphs. The need for a high level language based on the current mathematical language of DIS would extend its use to users who are not well versed in mathematics.

2.2   Illustrative Example

In this paper, we use an example of a weather ontology. Figure 2a gives the dataset that to considered for the example. Figure 2b gives the Boolean lattice associated with the dataset of Fig. 2a (which is borrowed from [7]). We notice that the first level of the Boolean lattice consists of all attributes of the dataset, which are known as atomic concepts. Then, the upper levels are just compositions between these atomic concepts. The top element of the obtained lattice is called "Weather", which is a composition between all atomic concepts. The lattice alone, while it brings all the concepts obtained from the dataset, is not enough to capture all concepts of the weather domain. For that reason, the need to construct rooted-graphs is essential. More concepts are added to the rooted-graphs, then linked to the Boolean lattice specific concepts by the relation of the graph. For example, the rooted-graph *Seasons* is linked to the top of the lattice *Weather* using *IsAssociated* relation as shown in Fig. 2c.

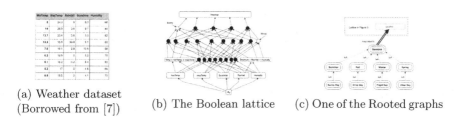

(a) Weather dataset
(Borrowed from [7])   (b) The Boolean lattice   (c) One of the Rooted graphs

Fig. 2. A Dataset, its Boolean lattice, and one example of a rooted graph

3   Literature Review on Languages for Ontologies

The literature (e.g., [35]) reveals that there are two trends in developing ontology languages. The first is based on functional languages. The second is XML-based. For more exhaustive surveys on the ontology languages, we refer the reader to [35]. In the following section, we present a brief review to reflect the latest developments in this area.

3.1   Functional Languages

The main functional languages are KIF and CL. KIF [21] was proposed by Stanford AI Lab in 1992. It can be considered as a Domain-specific Language (DSL) based on Lisp. Although v language is capable of articulating specifications of ontologies, it is designed to interchange the knowledge among different programs. Many organizations designed dialects of KIF or proposed extensions to KIF (e.g., IDEF5 [42] or OBKC [12]) to specify ontologies.

CL [3] is a framework that contains a family of languages, which are called dialects. Currently, CL has three dialects: Common Logic Interchange Format (CLIF), Conceptual Graphs Interchange Format (CGIF), and XCL. The dialect CLIF can be considered a simplified form of KIF 3.0. Therefore, its syntax is very similar to KIF; they have Lisp-like syntax [3]. The dialect CGIF is to describe conceptual graphs. It has two versions: Core CGIF and Extended CGIF. The dialect XCL has an XML-based syntax. Actually, XCL is currently the recommended syntax in CL, and the latter can be converted into XCL directly.

3.2   XML-Based Languages

We explore the two main XML-based languages: DARPA Agent Markup Language + Ontology Interchange Language (DAML+OIL) and OWL. DARPA Agent Markup Language (DAML) [15] was merged with Ontology Interchange Language (OIL), which lead to the name DAML+OIL. The language DAML+OIL is a markup language for web resources and it is based on Resource Description Framework (RDF) and Resource Description Framework Schema (RDFS). It gave a strong base for OWL [39], which is designed by W3C.

OWL is a markup language and it is based on DAML+OIL. That means OWL has a relatively fixed format so that it can be easily reasoned on ontologies written with it. Actually, OWL has become the most used language in ontology modeling. The second version of OWL is called OWL2 [13]. In [13], the reader can find a table comparing the different types of OWL grammars.

OWL2 has two semantics for reasoning. One is the Direct Semantics [24], the other is the RDF-Based Semantics [45]. Using the Direct Semantics, ontologies in OWL2 Description Logic (DL) can be translated to $SROIQ$ which is a particular DL, so that OWL2 could use some DL reasoner. Using the RDF-Based Semantics, ontologies can keep the original meaning. In that way, we can say OWL2 DL is a subset of OWL2 Full. We provide a comparison between all previously mentioned languages in Table 1.

Table 1. Comparison of ontology languages

Language	Original grammar	Based theory	Extension
KIF	Lisp	First-order logic	IDEF5
CL	CFIL, CGIL, XCL	First-order logic	–
DAML+OIL	XML	RDF, RDFS	–
OWL2 DL	RDF/XML, OWL/XML, Turtle, Functional Syntax, Manchester Syntax	Direct Semantics - DL	MOWL, tOWL
OWL2 Full		RDF-based semantics	

3.3   Other Ontology Languages

The area of knowledge representation and reasoning involves an indispensable amount of uncertain, and vague information. However, ontology languages are known to be definite (i.e., a concept or relationship exists or not). By default, no support to uncertainty or vagueness is involved in the existing languages [19]. We started observing the rise in exploring languages for probabilistic or fuzzy ontologies, which are ontology languages that are extended with probabilistic or fuzzy formalisms in order to represent uncertainty and vagueness in the domain knowledge. Several efforts to explore such an extension are ongoing. Existing formalisms to handle uncertainty/vagueness in ontology languages are fuzzy logic [51], Bayesian Network (BN) [19], and Dempster Shafer Theory (DST) [37]. Some of the recent approaches that apply probabilistic ontology using BN framework are: BayesOWL [18] and PR-OWL [14]. BN framework is a well-known model to handle uncertainty. However, it was noticed that extending ontology languages with such structure is not an easy task. Moreover, it produces a complex framework [11]. On the other hand, fuzzy ontology approaches include fuzzyOWL [47], and fuzzyOWL2 [10]. Combining fuzzy logic and BN is another approach to get probabilistic ontologies. An example of DST-based ontology is presented in [9]. Several reviews regarding uncertainty management in ontology modelling are available like (e.g., [34,44]).

3.4   Summary

In [35], we find that the most of the ontology languages have the same source and have been sponsored by Defense Advanced Research Projects Agency (DARPA). This limits the diversity among these languages despite their large number. If not disrupted by new ideas, ontology languages tend to have a relatively predictable direction towards a family of similar languages. There is a trend leading to having a family of languages where its members are simple dialects. This has the risk of limiting the extent of usage of these dialects to a class of ontologies. The diversity of languages based on different formalisms is the way to eventually converge towards the objective of designing more simple and expressive ontology languages. Our efforts to design a new language, DISEL, that is based on DIS formalism is towards reaching this objective.

4   DISEL Syntax and Support Tool

In this section, we present the syntax of DISEL language and the features of DISEL Editor (DISEL) tool, which can be downloaded from [2]. The syntax of DISEL is based on XML language. The main component of DISEL is the part for specifying ontologies. Following the DIS formalism for defining ontologies, DISEL's ontology structure is formed of five elements as indicated in Table 2. We allocate a subsection for the first and second elements and then a subsection is dedicated for each of the three remaining elements of this structure. The complete DISEL specification of the *Weather* ontology of the example given in Subsect. 2.2 is available in [5]. An XML schema of DISEL is given in [6]. We also developed a tool named DISEL Editor. It enables ontology specifiers to use a graphical user interface to enter the necessary elements of an ontology, then the system automatically generates the full specification within DISEL language. The current features of DISEL Editor include visual editing ontology, displaying the Boolean lattice of the ontology and visualizing the rooted graph attached to the concepts of the lattice. In the following subsections, we guide the reader through the specification of the weather ontology to illustrate the usage of DISEL Editor tool to specify the *Weather* ontology.

Table 2. Main constructs of an *ontology*

Element name	Description	Type	Cardinality
include	A language construct for including the needed domain information or ontologies from other files	includeType	$[0, +\infty)$
name	The name of ontology	string	only one
atomDomain	The atoms of the domain	atomDomainType	only one
concept	The definition of the concept	conceptType	$[0, +\infty)$
graph	The relation between concepts	graphType	$[0, +\infty)$

4.1 DISEL Editor Interface Overview

In Subsect. 2.1, we indicated that a DIS ontology is formed by a lattice that is obtained from a given set of atomic concepts. The lattice of concepts is then systematically generated as a free Boolean complete lattice from the given set of atoms. The interface of DISEL Editor, which is shown in Fig. 3, enables users to obtain the lattice of concepts from the set of given atomic concepts. The left dock window of DISEL Editor mainly shows the *Atoms of the domain* and *Concept* information. The right upper tab window shows the Boolean lattice generated from the set of atomic concepts that are provided in the *Atoms of the Domain*. If the user clicks a concept in the shown Boolean lattice, DISEL Editor changes the tab to show the rooted graph attached to (rooted at) this concept. The bottom right text edit shows the definition of the selected concept.

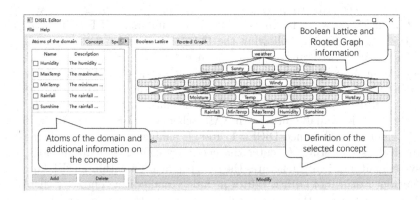

Fig. 3. Interface overview

4.2   Name and Include Constructs

The *name* construct is to be used for giving a unique name to the ontology. As illustrated in [36], DIS allows the integration of several ontologies for a more complex reasoning task than on a single ontology. To allow the usage of concepts and relationships of an external ontology within the specified one, we use the construct *include* to bring the sought external ontology. The *include* construct uses as parameters a *name* attribute and a *filePath* attribute. The *name* element specifies the name of the ontology to be included. The *FilePath* gives the path of included ontology file. Listing 1.1 illustrates the usage of the *include* construct. Sometimes we do not need to include the whole ontology. Sometimes, all what is needed is a vertex (or a set of vertices) that is shared between the constructed ontology and an external ontology. In this case, the usage of that vertex is as illustrated in Listing 1.2, where the vertex *summer* is from an ontology named "OntExample" that has been included using the *include* construct.

Listing 1.1. Code of *include*

```
<include  name="OntExample"  filePath="OntExample.xml"  />
```

Listing 1.2. Code of *include*

```
<edge>
    <from  DIS="OntExample">Summer</from>
    <to>Seasons</to>
</edge>
```

4.3   AtomDomain Construct

AtomDomainType can only be included by an ontology with an alias *atomDomain*. It defines all the atoms of the ontology being specified. An atom is the elementary concept in the sense that it cannot be obtained by the composition of other concepts (for further mathematical details on the notion of atoms, we refer the reader to the theoretical foundation of DIS [31,36]). Several types, such as *concept* or *atomSet*, make use of *atom*. The XML schema of *AtomDomainType* and *AtomDomain* is illustrated in [6]. The main constructs of an *atom* are given in Table 3. Using DISEL Editor, the user can click the "Add" Button (see Fig. 3) to create a new *atom* and show the information. While displaying the details of AtomDomain, DISEL Editor shows the Boolean lattice of the current ontology built by AtomDomain as illustrated in Fig. 3. Hence, the user can have a clear understanding of the structure of the ontology.

4.4   Concept

The construct *concept* is the core element in DISEL language. It is used to specify the concepts that are used in the ontology. The main constructs used in *concept* are given in Table 4. Any concept, other than the atomic ones and the ones generated from them to build the Boolean lattice, is introduced using the construct *concept*. In Listing 1.3, Line 2 introduces the concept *Temp*.

Table 3. Main constructs of an *atom*

Element name	Description	Type	Cardinality
name	The name of the atomic concept	string	only one
description	The description of the *atom* concept	string	at most one

Table 4. Main constructs of a *concept*

Element name	Description	Type	Cardinality
name	The name of ontology	string	only one
latticeOfConcepts	The set of atoms from which the lattice is built	latticeOfConceptsType	only one
fefinition	The formulas used by *concept*	string	at most one
fescription	The description of *concept*	string	at most one

Listing 1.3. Example of latticeOfConcepts

```
<latticeOfConcepts>
    <concept>Temp</concept>
    <atom>minTemp</atom>
    <atom>maxTemp</atom>
</latticeOfConcepts>
```

The construct *LatticeOfConcepts* is a set of atoms from which the lattice of concepts is constructed using a Cartesian product construction. Hence, all the concepts of the lattice are tuples of these atoms. If we have n atoms, then the top element of the lattice is an n-tuple of the atomic concepts. It is possible that under *latticeOfConcepts* we find only the atoms and the concepts obtained from them. Also, not all the concepts obtained from the atom have a meaning in the domain of application. The ones that do have a meaning are given the names used for them in the domain of application. In Listing 1.3, we provide an example of the latticeOfConecpts for the concept *Temp*, which is the name in the weather domain for the tuple formed by atoms *minTemp*, and *maxTemp*. We also provide a syntactic sugar called *atoms* and its usage is illustrated in Listing 1.4. It has been shown that the number of attributes in a well normalized dataset schema rarely exceeds ten [48]. Since each attribute would give an atomic concept, then the number of atomic concepts, associated to a normalized database, rarely exceed ten concepts.

Listing 1.4. Syntactic sugar of *atom* in *LatticeOfConcepts*

```
<latticeOfConcepts>
    <atoms>Rainfall  Humidity</atoms>
</latticeOfConcepts>
```

It is common that in a domain related to a data set we have more concepts than the ones obtained from the atomic concepts. For instance, we might need new concepts related to concepts in the lattice through a rooted graph. In this case, DISEL Editor enables the ontology specifier to add a new concept as shown in Fig. 4.

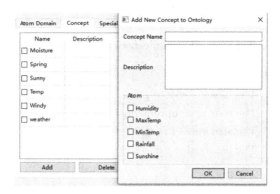

Fig. 4. The concept tab window and dialog

The construct *definition* brings additional information about the concept. For instance, the mathematical definition of the concept can be presented using *definition*. For the convenience of writing, we adopted an Isabelle-like syntax to be used to mathematically define concepts that we omit in this paper for conciseness. At this stage, we can simply say that the type of *definition* is a string. Specific syntactical analytic work is entrusted to a lexer and parser. Operators that contain < and > may cause ambiguity, regarding whether they are part of a markup text or simply part of a textual definition. We recommend to the user to adopt XML CDATA[1] to write the content that goes into *definition*. An example of using CDATA to write the a definition is shown in [6]. The Backus-Naur Form (BNF) of *definition* is shown in [1].

Finally, the construct *description* is to enable the ontology specifier to document the ontology by adding descriptions of the introduced concepts.

4.5   Graph

The part *graph* of the specification of an ontology is to introduce the rooted graphs that bring other concepts than what we have in the lattice of concepts. It also brings relationships among these newly introduced concepts. This part of the specification is for what is called rooted graphs in DIS, which are graphs that must have their roots in the lattice of concepts. The main constructs used to

---

[1] CDATA stands for Character Data and it indicates that the data in between these strings should not be interpreted as XML markup.

introduce rooted graphs are given in Table 5. The constructs *name* and *rootedAt* are self-explanatory. The construct *edge* is to introduce an edge in the specified graph and it uses two sub-constructs, *from* and *to*, to give the endpoints of an edge. The construct *relation* gives the set of edges of the graph. It also uses sub-construct *properties* to introduce the properties of the relations such as symmetry, transitivity, or being an order. The reader can find in [6] the specification of the rooted graph that is presented in Fig. 2c.

Table 5. The main constructs of a *graph*

Element name	Description	Type	Cardinality
name	The name of rooted graph	string	only one
rootedAt	The root node of rooted graph	string	only one
edge	The structure of rooted graph	edgeType	$[0, +\infty)$
relation	The list of edge	relationType	$[0, +\infty)$

5   Design Decisions

In the following, we present the main design decision for DISEL language. The first design decision is related to basing the language on XML. The latter is currently a widely used markup descriptive language. Many tools provide application programming interfaces for XML to store and exchange information. XML has a stable grammar that can be parsed easily. Basing a high level DIS language on XML would increase the usage of DIS-ontologies by a wider community of users. The exchange between the many ontologies languages that are based on XML will be enhanced. We have considered basing DISEL language on functional languages. Most popular languages are imperative languages. These languages focus on how to process the problem. Functional languages recognize function as first-class citizen. In some cases, functional language can regard its code as information and modify its code. Traditional ontology languages, such as KIF, expand Lisp's grammar in this way. But the grammar of functional language is too free and powerful to control. These are the reasons for taking the decision to not base DISEL on functional languages.

6   Discussion

This paper presents the main syntactical constructs of DISEL language, which was designed as a language for specifying DIS-based ontologies. The adoption of this language would enable the creation of shareable ontologies for the development of ontology-based systems such as the ones characterised in [27]. The language DISEL is based on DIS formalism that is conceived for the specification of information system. Therefore, it inherits the strengths and the shortcomings of this formalist. As it is illustrated in [36], the DIS enables the construction of an information system in a bottom-up approach. To model the domain knowledge, which is captured by the ontology element in DIS, we start from the attributes found in the schema of the dataset to form the set of atomic concepts. The latter is then used to form a free Boolean lattice that its elements are constructed from the atomic concepts using a Cartesian product construction. Then, we bring additional concepts to the ontology by adding the rooted graphs. Each of these graphs brings new concepts that are related to the concepts generated from the datasets. Hence, any concept in the ontology is related to the dataset under consideration. That is why the rooted graphs must have roots in the lattice of concepts. As it is indicated in [36], formalisms such as DL [8], Ontology-Based Data Access (OBDA) [50], and Developing Ontology-Grounded Methods and Applications (DOGMA) [26] offer a clear separation of the domain ontology from the data view. Then they need to match the data schema to the concepts in the domain. This activity is called the mapping activity, which introduces non-trivial challenges [50]. To avoid these challenges, the designers of DIS adopted a data-guided approach for the construction of the ontology. The DIS formalism is limited to a Cartesian world: the concepts of the lattice are tuples of concepts. This means that concepts that are composite are formed by the Cartesian product of atomic concepts. This is the case for the realities/domains where data is structured (e.g., relational data bases or log files). DIS puts the data in the data view and the domain knowledge in the ontology. This separation of concern in the design of DIS enables an ease in the evolution and aging of its specification.

As previously indicated, the current language of DIS is formed by basic mathematical languages of lattices, relations, graphs, and relations. We propose DISEL language as a high-level language that eases the specification by guiding the specifier through the specification process and by hiding the above low level mathematical language as much as possible. The DISEL Editor enables the ontology specifier to interactively specify and change the ontology with ease. It constitutes a visualisation system of the specified ontology. We aim at further enhancing this system as we discuss in Sect. 7. The tools that compare to DISEL Editor are Protégé and Eddy [33]. The first supports standard OWL and enables the translation to a family languages. The second, Eddy, has an important feature, which enables the use of Graphol language to graphically handle ontologies.

An ontology specified using DISEL is intended to be compiled into a formal *Isabelle* [4] specification. Then we use the proof assistant *Isabelle/HOL* to automatically generate the DIS theory, as an extension of the HOL-Algebra theories with explicit carrier sets. We explicitly representing the carrier sets of the several algebraic structure used in their corresponding classes and locales. This approach allows us to use a less complex approach for building the free Boolean lattice component, and for reasoning on a DIS [36]. Then, the obtained DIS theory is used to reason on the dataset and to generate fact-grounded knowledge from the given data.

7 Conclusion and Future Work

In this paper, we introduced DISEL and presented its main syntactical constructs. We used an example of a simplified weather ontology to illustrated its usage. We also presented DISEL Editor, which enables us to write, modify, and visualize a DISEL specification. Our future work aims at further enhancing the capabilities of DISEL Editor. First, we plan to add to DISEL Editor capabilities for compiling DISEL specification into a formal *Isabelle* [4] specification. This work is at the publication stage and its software modules are at the testing stage. Second, we aim at enhancing the visualization system of DISEL Editor by adding capabilities related to ontology module visualization. If an ontology is large and there is a need to automatically visualize or extract a module from it, then DISEL Editor should be able to carry the extraction and the visualization of the obtained module. We will consider the modularization techniques presented in [30,32] and that are appropriate for DIS ontologies. Third, we aim at adding to DISEL Editor an API to ease the link between the considered dataset and its ontology.

In [19], we found that there is no support to uncertainty or vagueness is involved in existing ontology languages [19]. We aim at extending the syntax of DISEL to enable the specification of uncertainty in ontologies. This would give DISEL capabilities for data and statistical analysis. In such a way, we would be able to use statistical reasoning on dataset or define probabilistic or fuzzy concepts. We also aim at using ontologies specified using DISEL to tackle data cleaning in continuation of the work given in [28].

References

1. The BNF of DISEL concept definition. https://github.com/YbJerry/DISEL_file/blob/master/BNF.txt. Accessed 15 Mar 2022
2. The GitHub repository of DISEL editor. https://github.com/YbJerry/DISEL_Editor. Accessed 15 Mar 2022
3. Information technology - Common Logic (CL) - a framework for a family of logic-based languages. https://www.iso.org/standard/66249.html. Accessed 15 Mar 2022
4. Isabelle. http://isabelle.in.tum.de/index.html. Accessed 9 Jan 2021
5. A weather example specified using DISEL. https://github.com/YbJerry/DISEL_file/blob/master/dis.xml. Accessed 15 Mar 2022
6. XML schema of DISEL. https://github.com/YbJerry/DISEL_file/blob/master/dis.xsd. Accessed 15 Mar 2022
7. Avagyan, Z.: Weather.csv. www.kaggle.com/zaraavagyan/weathercsv/metadata
8. Baader, F., Calvanese, D., McGuinness, D., Patel-Schneider, P., Nardi, D.: The Description Logic Handbook: Theory, Implementation and Applications. Cambridge University Press, Cambridge (2003)
9. Bellenger, A., Gatepaille, S.: Uncertainty in ontologies: Dempster-Shafer theory for data fusion applications. In: Workshop on Theory of Belief Functions, pp. 1–6. Brest, France, April 2010

10. Bobillo, F., Straccia, U.: An OWL ontology for fuzzy OWL 2. In: Rauch, J., Raś, Z.W., Berka, P., Elomaa, T. (eds.) ISMIS 2009. LNCS (LNAI), vol. 5722, pp. 151–160. Springer, Heidelberg (2009). https://doi.org/10.1007/978-3-642-04125-9_18

11. Carvalho, R.N., dos Santos, L.L., Ladeira, M., da Rocha, H.A., Mendes, G.L.: UMP-ST plug-in: documenting, maintaining and evolving probabilistic ontologies using UnBBayes framework. In: Uncertainty Reasoning for the Semantic Web III. LNCS, vol. 8816. Springer, Cham (2014). https://doi.org/10.1007/978-3-319-13413-0_1

12. Chaudhri, V.K., et al.: OKBC: a programmatic foundation for knowledge base interoperability. In: AAAI/IAAI, pp. 600–607 (1998)

13. Consortium, W.: OWL 2 Web Ontology Language document overview (2012)

14. Costa, P., Laskey, K.: PR-OWL: a framework for probabilistic ontologies. In: Proceedings of the Conference on Formal Ontologies and Information Systems, vol. 150, pp. 237–249, May 2006

15. Dan, C.: DAML+OIL (March 2001) reference description. In: World Wide Web Consortium (2001)

16. De Mauro, A., Greco, M., Grimaldi, M.: A formal definition of Big Data based on its essential features. Libr. Rev. **65**(3), 122–135 (2016). https://doi.org/10.1108/LR-06-2015-0061

17. Del Vescovo, C., Parsia, B., Sattler, U., Schneider, T.: The modular structure of an ontology: atomic decomposition and module count. In: WoMO, pp. 25–39 (2011)

18. Ding, Z., Peng, Y., Pan, R.: A Bayesian approach to uncertainty modelling in OWL ontology. Technical report, Maryland and University Baltimore, Department of Computer Science and Electrical Engineering (2006)

19. Fareh, M.: Modeling incomplete knowledge of semantic web using Bayesian networks. Appl. Artif. Intell. **33**(11), 1022–1034 (2019)

20. Fonseca, F.: The double role of ontologies in information science research. J. Am. Soc. Inf. Sci. Technol. - JASIS **58**, 786–793 (2007)

21. Genesereth, M.R., Fikes, R.E., Brachman, R., Gruber, T., Schubert, L.: Knowledge Interchange Format Version 3.0 Reference Manual. Morgan Kaufmann Publishers, Burlington (1992)

22. Ghafourian, S., Rezaeian, A., Naghibzadeh, M.: Graph-based partitioning of ontology with semantic similarity. In: 2013 3th International eConference on Computer and Knowledge Engineering (ICCKE), pp. 80–85. IEEE (2013)

23. Hoehndorf, R., Schofield, P.N., Gkoutos, G.V.: The role of ontologies in biological and biomedical research: a functional perspective. Brief. Bioinform. **16**(6), 1069–1080 (2015)

24. Horrocks, I., Parsia, B., Sattler, U.: OWL 2 web ontology language direct semantics. In: World Wide Web Consortium, pp. 42–65 (2012)

25. Imielinski, T.W.L., Jr.: The relational model of data and cylindric algebras. J. Comput. Syst. Sci. **28**(1), 80–102 (1984)

26. Jarrar, M., Meersman, R.: Ontology engineering – the DOGMA approach. In: Dillon, T.S., Chang, E., Meersman, R., Sycara, K. (eds.) Advances in Web Semantics I. LNCS, vol. 4891, pp. 7–34. Springer, Heidelberg (2008). https://doi.org/10.1007/978-3-540-89784-2_2

27. Jaskolka, J., Leclair, A., Maccaull, W., Khedri, R.: Architecture for ontology-supported multi-context reasoning systems. Data Knowl. Eng. **140**, 102044:1–14 (2022). ISSN 0169-023X. https://doi.org/10.1016/j.datak.2022.102044, https://www.sciencedirect.com/science/article/pii/S0169023X22000453

28. Khedri, R., Chiang, F., Sabri, K.E.: An algebraic approach for data cleansing. In: the 4th EUSPN, vol. 21, pp. 50–59 (2013). Procedia Computer Science

29. Koopmann, P.: Ontology-based query answering for probabilistic temporal data. In: Proceedings of the AAAI Conference on Artificial Intelligence, vol. 33, no. 01, pp. 2903–2910, July 2019

30. LeClair, A.: A formal approach to ontology modularization and to the assessment of its related knowledge transformation. Ph.D. thesis, Faculty of Engineering, McMaster University, Hamilton, Ontario, Canada, November 2021

31. LeClair, A., Khedri, R., Marinache, A.: Formalizing graphical modularization approaches for ontologies and the knowledge loss. In: Fred, A., Salgado, A., Aveiro, D., Dietz, J., Bernardino, J., Filipe, J. (eds.) IC3K 2019. CCIS, vol. 1297, pp. 388–412. Springer, Cham (2020). https://doi.org/10.1007/978-3-030-66196-0_18

32. LeClair, A., Marinache, A., Ghalayini, H.E., MacCaull, W., Khedri, R.: A review on ontology modularization techniques - a multi-dimensional perspective. IEEE Trans. Knowl. Data Eng., 1–28 (2022). https://doi.org/10.1109/TKDE.2022.3152928

33. Lembo, D., Pantaleone, D., Santarelli, V., Savo, D.F.: Eddy: a graphical editor for OWL 2 ontologies. In: IJCAI (2016)

34. Lukasiewicz, T., Straccia, U.: Managing uncertainty and vagueness in description logics for the semantic web. J. Web Semant. $6(4)$, 291–308 (2008)

35. Maniraj, V., Sivakumar, R.: Ontology languages - a review. Int. J. Comput. Theory Eng. $2(6)$, 887–891 (2010)

36. Marinache, A., Khedri, R., Leclair, A., MacCaull, W.: DIS: a data-centred knowledge representation formalism. In: IEEE RDAAPS21, Hamilton, Ontario, Canada, pp. 1–8. IEEE Computer Society, May 2021

37. Mathon, B.R., Ozbek, M.M., Pinder, G.F.: Dempster-Shafer theory applied to uncertainty surrounding permeability. Math. Geosci. $42(3)$, 293–307 (2010)

38. McCarthy, J.: Recursive functions of symbolic expressions and their computation by machine, part I. Commun. ACM $3(4)$, 184–195 (1960)

39. Mcguinness, D.L., Ed, F.H.: OWL web ontology language: overview (2004)

40. Nuradiansyah, A.: Reasoning in description logic ontologies for privacy management. KI - Künstliche Intelligenz $34(3)$, 411–415 (2020)

41. Ozaki, A.: Learning description logic ontologies: five approaches. Where do they stand? KI - Künstliche Intelligenz (German J. Artif. Intell.) $34(3)$, 317–327 (2020)

42. Peraketh, B., Menzel, C.P., Mayer, R.J., Fillion, F., Futrell, M.T.: Ontology capture method (IDEF5). Technical report, Knowledge Based Systems Inc., College Station, TX (1994)

43. Sabarmathi, G., Chinnaiyan, R.: Investigations on big data features research challenges and applications. In: 2017 International Conference on Intelligent Computing and Control Systems (ICICCS), pp. 782–786, June 2017

44. Samani, Z.R., Shamsfard, M.: The state of the art in developing fuzzy ontologies- a survey, pp. 1–46. arXiv preprint arXiv:1805.02290 (2018)

45. Schneider, M., Carroll, J., Herman, I., Patel-Schneider, P.F.: OWL 2 web ontology language RDF-based semantics. In: W3C Recommendation, December 2012

46. Schneider, T., Simkus, M.: Ontologies and data management: a brief survey. KI - Künstliche Intelligenz (German J. Artif. Intell.) $34(3)$, 329–353 (2020)

47. Stoilos, G., Stamou, G.B., Tzouvaras, V., Pan, J.Z., Horrocks, I.: Fuzzy OWL: uncertainty and the semantic web. In: OWLED, vol. 188, pp. 1–10 (2005)

48. Vassiliadis, P., Zarras, A.V., Skoulis, I.: How is life for a table in an evolving relational schema? Birth, death and everything in between. In: Johannesson, P., Lee, M.L., Liddle, S.W., Opdahl, A.L., López, Ó.P. (eds.) ER 2015. LNCS, vol. 9381, pp. 453–466. Springer, Cham (2015). https://doi.org/10.1007/978-3-319-25264-3_34

49. Wang, L., Liu, X., Cao, J.: A new algebraic structure for formal concept analysis. Inf. Sci. $180(24)$, 4865–4876 (2010)

50. Xiao, G., et al.: Ontology-based data access: a survey. In: Proceedings of the 27th International Joint Conference on Artificial Intelligence, pp. 5511–5519. AAAI Press (2018)
51. Zadeh, L.A.: Fuzzy sets. In: Fuzzy Sets, Fuzzy Logic, and Fuzzy Systems: Selected Papers by Lotfi A Zadeh, pp. 394–432. World Scientific (1996)

MSSA-FL: High-Performance Multi-stage Semi-asynchronous Federated Learning with Non-IID Data

Xiaohui Wei, Mingkai Hou, Chenghao Ren$^{(\boxtimes)}$, Xiang Li$^{(\boxtimes)}$, and Hengshan Yue

College of Computer Science and Technology, Jilin University, Changchun, China
{weixh,lixiang_ccst}@jlu.edu.cn,
{houmk20,rench19,yuehs18}@mails.jlu.edu.cn

Abstract. Federated Learning (FL) is an emerging distributed machine learning framework that allows edge devices to collaborative train a shared global model without transmitting their sensitive data to centralized servers. However, it is extremely challenging to apply FL in practical scenarios because the statistics of the data across edge devices are usually not independent and identically distributed (Non-IID), which will introduce the bias to global model. To solve the above data heterogeneity issue, we propose a novel *Multi-Stage Semi-Asynchronous Federated Learning* (MSSA-FL) framework. MSSA-FL benefits convergence accuracy through making the local model complete multi-stage training within the group guided by combination module. To improve the training efficiency of the framework, MSSA-FL adopts a semi-asynchronous update method. Meanwhile, proposed model assignment strategy and model aggregation method further boost the performance of MSSA-FL. Experiments on several public datasets show that MSSA-FL achieves higher accuracy and faster convergence than the comparison algorithms.

Keywords: Federated learning · Non-IID · Multi-stage · Semi-asynchronous

1 Introduction

Due to the rapid advance and remarkable achievements of artificial intelligence technology [1,2], a growing number of complicated intelligent tasks are pushed to edge devices. How to use private data on edge devices to jointly train a sophisticated machine learning model [3–5] has drawn an unprecedented level of attention. As one of the most recognized approaches to edge training, *Federated Learning* (FL) expects to leverage multiple devices to collaboratively train a shared machine learning model with their local dataset without private data transmission. Through aggregating weight updates from each device, a global model can be efficiently and securely obtained.

This work is supported by the National Natural Science Foundation of China (NSFC) (Grants No. U19A2061), National key research and development program of China under Grants No. 2017YFC1502306.

© The Author(s), under exclusive license to Springer Nature Switzerland AG 2022
G. Memmi et al. (Eds.): KSEM 2022, LNAI 13369, pp. 172–187, 2022.
https://doi.org/10.1007/978-3-031-10986-7_14

A serious problem arises when applying FL to practical training: the data among devices are heterogeneous, i.e., non-independent and identically distributed data (Non-IID) [6,7]. Numerous researches have demonstrated that when training on heterogeneous data, local models based on the same initial model eventually converge to different models, which introduces unpredictable bias to the global model and results the deterioration in accuracy and convergence speed. Previous studies are mainly devoted to addressing the problem of Non-IID data in FL from two main perspectives. In a part of the work, sophisticated federated optimization methods are explored to restrict the weight divergence of local models. For example, FedProx [8] tackled the data heterogeneity by adding a bound term on the locally trained optimization objective. For preventing unstable and slow convergence on Non-IID data, SCAFFOLD [9] used variance reduction to correct the "client-drift" in each client's local updates. Methods in another part of the work such as data extension are used to generate homogeneous data in FL. Zhao et al. proposed to use globally shared data for training to deal with Non-IID. Astrea [10] alleviated the global data imbalance based on Z-score data augmentation and solved the local imbalance by mediator-based multi-device rescheduling.

However, the above researches mainly focus on improving the convergence accuracy, neglecting the training efficiency problems [11–13] that arise when FL is applied to heterogeneous devices. Since it must wait for the straggler devices before aggregating in each round, the server aggregation timing is actually determined by the slowest straggler, which increasing the time per round. Furthermore, fast training devices are idle for a long period of time until aggregation even though they have the capacity to engage in continuous training, leading to low resource utilization.

To solve the above issues, we propose a high-performance *Multi-Stage Semi-Asynchronous FL* (MSSA-FL) framework. Inspired by one of our key insight that unbalanced data can be combined into a large data set approximately balanced, MSSA-FL adopts a group-based multi-stage training method. Especially, combination module aimed at clustering devices with similar data distribution and grouping clusters with complementary data distribution. Through flexible multi-stage training strategy, MSSA-FL obtains approximately IID dataset training effect within group. To achieve the goal of efficiency optimization under the accuracy requirement, our proposed semi-synchronous update method with reasonable aggregation conditions boosts the frequency of model updates and allows more idle devices to participate in the training. To mitigate the impact of model staleness, we propose a heuristic aggregation method by adjusting the model aggregated weights. Considering the impact of different devices on the performance, in our model assignment strategy, we mainly exploring the training order of devices which include the hard-to-train labels and strategically increasing the participation opportunities for capable facilities to obtain the further performance improvement. In summary, the main contributions of our work are as outlined as follows:

- We propose a novel *multi-stage semi-asynchronous federated learning* (MSSA-FL) framework to solve the heterogeneous data issue and improve the training efficiency.
- We design a combination module for MSSA-FL to infer devices data distribution and group devices for the purpose of following multi-stage training. Guided by grouping results, we propose a multi-stage training method to make models trained on an approximate IID dataset combination, achieving the effect of improving the global model accuracy.
- We propose a semi-asynchronous update method to improve the low efficiency of synchronous FL. Furthermore, combining the characteristics of MSSA-FL, a model assignment strategy and an aggregation method for stale models are proposed to further boost the performance of MSSA-FL.
- We conduct extensive experiments to evaluate the effectiveness of the MSSA-FL algorithm on different publicly available datasets. The experimental results show that our approach is effective in both improving model accuracy and accelerating model training.

2   Related Work

The further integration of edge computing [14,15] and artificial intelligence [16,17] has promoted the rapid advancement of federated learning [2]. Federated learning (FL) [18], considered one of the most emerging distributed training techniques, provides a solution for privacy-preserving distributed machine learning. At present, multiple works are devoted to applying FL in real-world scenarios, which are mainly embodied in the following two aspects: (1) achieving higher convergence accuracy of FL with heterogeneous data [19,20,20]. (2) boosting the efficiency of FL.

Convergence Accuracy Improvement. Several efforts had been made to cope with the deterioration in accuracy and convergence speed of FL due to Non-IId data. Li et al. proposed FedProx [8] by adding a heterogeneity bound to tackle heterogeneity. Zhao et al. [7] used the *earth mover's distance* (EMD) to quantify data heterogeneity and proposed to use globally shared data for training to deal with Non-IID. FedMA [21] demonstrated that the result of aggregation can be affected by the permutations of layers and proposed a layer-wise aggregation strategy to improve global model accuracy. Duan et al. proposed Astrea [10] where devices with complementary data are divided into a group every round by mediators and the global model is obtained by synchronously aggregating all mediators' models which are trained sequentially on devices within groups.

Efficiency Improvement. In terms of boosting efficiency of FL, Nishio et al. proposed FedCS [22], in which server selects as many devices as possible to train the model in a limited time interval based on the resource of devices. Xie et al. proposed asynchronous FL [23], where the server performs aggregation as soon as it receives a local model from any device. Wu et al. proposed a new semi-asynchronous federated learning protocol SAFA [24] that classifies devices into latest, stale and tolerable and used discriminative aggregation with caching to solve the problem of inefficient rounds and poor convergence speed of federated learning in extreme cases. In [25], Xu et al. proposed a "soft-training" approach to accelerate the stragglers by compressing the training models of stragglers.

However, there are few efforts to improve the overall performance of FL by considering convergence accuracy and efficiency together. We propose a high-performance *multi-stage semi-asynchronous FL* framework (MSSA-FL), considering the degradation of model accuracy due to Non-IID data and the inefficiency of synchronous updates on heterogeneous devices.

3 MSSA-FL: Multi-stage Semi-asynchronous Federated Learning

3.1 Framework Overview

The overall framework of MSSA-FL is shown in Fig. 1. High-performance multi-stage semi-asynchronous federated learning contains the following components: Multi-Stage Training, Semi-Asynchronous Training, Model Assignment and Model Aggregation. It is worth noting that the combination module in server as the key part of the framework solve the problem of data heterogeneity through clustering and grouping. Devices with similar data distribution are divided into clusters, and multiple clusters with complementary data distribution form a group.

The detail workflow of MSSA-FL can be described as follows. *Step 1:* Server starts one round pre-training and divides the devices into clusters and groups through the combination module. *Step 2:* Selected devices download the global model. *Step 3:* Devices train the received model on local dataset and upload the weight updates to the server after completion. *Step 4:* Server receives the local models and judges whether they have completed the multi-stage training. The completed models are aggregated to update the global model. While the unfinished models are sent to the corresponding devices according to their missing training stages and repeats *Step 2, 3*.

We will introduce our proposed methods in detail in the following subsections.

3.2 Combination Module and Multi-stage Training

Attributing the effect of data heterogeneity to the fact that local models trained on data with different data distributions have different optimization directions and unpredictable biases would be introduced into the global model through model aggregation. Therefore, in this section, we design a combination module to achieve an approximate IID data distribution within the group and accordingly propose a multi-stage training approach to solve the problems caused by data heterogeneity.

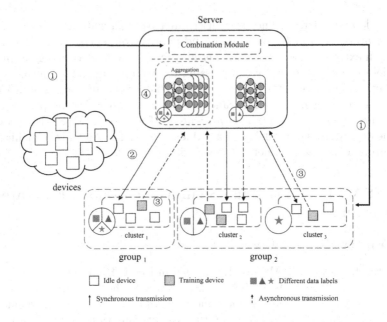

Fig. 1. Overview of MSSA-FL framework.

Combination Module. In order to form a balanced local dataset within a group, the main works of the combination module include: (1) Divide devices with similar data distribution into the same cluster. (2) Divide clusters with complementary data distributions into a group to form a locally balanced dataset.

Device Clustering. Several *cluster federated learning* (CFL) schemes [26–28] have been proposed infer whether customers have similar data distributions from updates of their local models. In this section, we follow the client clustering approach in [26], using the cosine similarity of the clients' weight updates as the proximities of the local optimizations. The cosine similarity between the updates of any two devices i and j is defined as follows:

$$CS(i,j) = \frac{\langle \Delta \omega^{(i)}, \Delta \omega^{(j)} \rangle}{||\Delta \omega^{(i)}|| \, ||\Delta \omega^{(j)}||} \tag{1}$$

In our approach, parameter updates are obtained for the local model of each device through one round pre-training. To reduce the bias of cosine similarity, the mean of absolute differences of pairwise cosine similarity is used as the dissimilarity measure for clustering, as follows:

$$MADC(i,j) = \frac{1}{n-2} \sum_{z \neq i,j} |CS(i,z) - CS(j,z)| \tag{2}$$

With the above clustering method, the server divides all devices into multiple clusters, and the devices in each cluster have similar data distribution. As shown in Fig. 1, there are three clusters and each cluster has multiple devices with similar data distribution.

Cluster Grouping. Although devices are clustered, the data distribution of each cluster is still unknown. So we need to accomplish the following two works, inferring the data distribution of each clusters and determining the group member clusters that may achieve data balance within a group.

We leverage the method proposed in [29], using auxiliary dataset to infer the data composition of each cluster. First, after client clustering, server selects a representative device in each cluster to represents the data distribution of its cluster. Next, establish the (3) to infer the composition of training data by finding the relationship between the data of a specific label and the weight change of the output layer.

$$\Delta\omega_{(p,i)}^p \cdot \widehat{N}_{p,i} + (\sum_{p=1}^{Q} N_p^j - \widehat{N}_{p,i})\frac{\sum_{j=1}^{Q}(\Delta\omega_{(p,i)}^j) - \Delta\omega_{(p,i)}^p}{Q-1} = n_a^p \cdot (\omega_{p,i}^k - \omega_{p,i}^G) \quad (3)$$

where ω^k is the local model of device k after pre-training, ω^G is the initial global model. Q is the number of labels. $\Delta\omega_{(p,i)}^j$ is the i-th weight update of the p-th output node from g_{L_j} and g_{L_j} is the weights update obtained by training the ω^G on the samples of class j in the auxiliary dataset. n_a^p is the sample number of class p in the auxiliary data, $\widehat{N}_p$ is the predicted sample quantity of class p, $\omega_{p,i}^k$ and $\omega_{p,i}^G$ are link weights $\omega_{(p,i)}$ of ω^k and ω^G, respectively. $\sum_{p=1}^{Q} N_p^j$ is the overall number of all samples owned by device k. And we can obtain the final result as the average value of all calculated $\widehat{N}_{p,i}$ (denoted as $\widehat{N}_p$). Finally, cluster's data composition can be obtained after all classes are calculated.

KL divergence is used to measure the similarity of two distributions. The server computes all combinations of clusters and calculates the KL divergence between the data distribution for each combination and the ideal data distribution. Here, the ideal data distribution can be a uniform distribution with balanced labels. The server picks the combination result with the smallest KL divergence until all clusters are included in a certain group. The detail of combination module is described in Algorithm 1.

As illustrated in Fig. 1, since the data distribution of $cluster_1$ is closest to the ideal data distribution, $cluster_1$ forms $group_1$ by itself. Similarly, $cluster_2$ and $cluster_3$ form $group_2$ because their combined data distribution is almost balanced. By combination module, a locally balanced dataset is approximately generated in each group.

Multi-stage Training. A natural motivation to address data heterogeneity in FL is to supplement the imbalanced data in the device so that the local models are trained on IID dataset. Considering the protection of private data, the server transfer the model between multiple devices and perform multiple trainings to solve the local data Non-IID problem in FL.

It is significant to identify the devices that can form a balanced data set. Thus, we present the combination module described above, whose result guide

---

Algorithm 1: Device Grouping Algorithm

Input: the number of clusters $n_{clusters}$, uniform distribution P_u, global initial
model ω_{init}. D_{kl} is Kullback-Leibler divergence.
Output: the grouping result $Group$
Get all devices' weight updates by a round pre-training.
$CS \leftarrow$ Cosine similarity between any two devices according to (1)
$MADC \leftarrow$ Calculate MADC(CS) using (2)
$S_{cluster} \leftarrow$ Hierarchical Clustering($MADC, n_{clusters}$)
$S_{dis} \leftarrow$ Estimates the empirical data distribution of clusters according to (3)
$S_{com} \leftarrow$ COMBINATIONS($S_{cluster}, S_{dis}$)
while $\mid S_{cluster} \mid > 0$ **do**
$\quad$ $g = \arg\min_{k}(D_{kl}(P_k||P_u))$, $k \in S_{com}$
$\quad$ **for** *cluster in g* **do**
$\quad\quad$ $\mid$ $S_{cluster} \leftarrow S_{cluster} - cluster$
$\quad$ **end**
$\quad$ **if** $|S_{cluster}|$ *is changed* **then**
$\quad\quad$ $\mid$ $Group \leftarrow Group + g$
$\quad$ **end**
end
return $Group$

---

the determination of which devices compose the locally IID dataset. In the combination module, devices with similar data distribution generate a cluster, and the data distribution of devices within the cluster can be further inferred. Each cluster appears to be a virtual local device whose data distribution is known. Accordingly, the combination module is capable of grouping clusters with complementary data distributions so that a locally balanced dataset is generated within each group. After completing all stages of training in a group, the local model is equivalent to being trained on the IID dataset, which narrows the gap between local models and reduces the bias introduced to the global model during aggregation in server.

Simultaneously, based on combination module, multiple devices in the same cluster are assigned the same function to provide that stage of training. A device can release training resources after completing local training without waiting for the current model to complete all stages, allowing such devices to immediately provide training for other intra-group models. As a result, the training resources for intra-group models are more flexibly satisfied and the device utilization is improved because of the opportunity for training multiple models.

3.3   Semi-asynchronous Training

Although the multi-stage training strategy can solve the problem of data heterogeneity, it poses a challenge for system efficiency. Compared to single training for each client per round in FedAvg, multi-stage training makes models train multiple times before aggregation, resulting in extended training time per round.

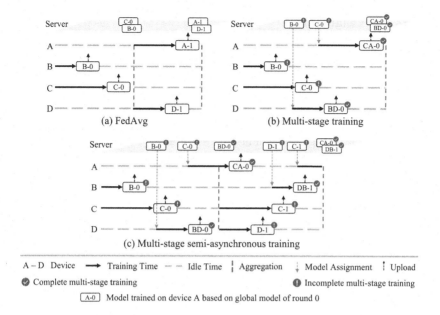

(a) FedAvg   (b) Multi-stage training

(c) Multi-stage semi-asynchronous training

A – D Device ➞ Training Time – – Idle Time ┊ Aggregation ↓ Model Assignment ┊ Upload

✅ Complete multi-stage training   ❗ Incomplete multi-stage training

⬚ A-0 ⬚ Model trained on device A based on global model of round 0

Fig. 2. Illustration of different FL operating principles. Suppose device A and device B are in one cluster, device C and device D are in another cluster. These two clusters form a group.

Furthermore, device heterogeneity may lead longer device idle time when synchronizing updates.

Considering the degradation on efficiency of multi-stage training, we adopt a compromise solution, a semi-asynchronous update approach. In our semi-asynchronous update approach, the server will aggregate the models in the following two cases: (1) A specified number of models complete multi-stage training in the current round. (2) The time limit has been reached in the current round. Consequently, the server only synchronously aggregates models that have completed multi-stage training within the round time. Residual models will keep training asynchronously to participate in aggregation on subsequent rounds.

Figure 2 depicts above synchronous and semi-asynchronous algorithms' operating principles. In FedAvg, only a few devices are selected to train in each round, and the aggregation of models occurs as the slowest device completes its local training. As for multi-stage training, although all devices participate in the training, the round time increases significantly due to the multiple trainings per model (e.g., $B \rightarrow D$, $C \rightarrow A$). With that comes longer wait time for idle devices. In the semi-asynchronous training, because of exceeding the round time limit, the server updates the global model in advance and adds new models in the next round. Thus, semi-asynchronous update increases the frequency of global model updates and makes more models to be trained in a round, providing more devices the opportunity to overtrain.

3.4 Model Assignment

In this section, we propose an assignment strategy for intermediate model which have not completed all stages of training to select the suitable device for next training stage.

Training Sequence Optimization. We observed that the model loses part of the knowledge learned previously when it is trained on a new dataset, so it can be inferred that the last stage of the multi-stage training has the largest contribution to the model. Inspired by the above, we propose a method to determine the order of multi-stage training based on the recognition ability of the global model for different labels.

First, we use recall rate, which can be obtained through the validation of the global model on server, to measure the ability of the model to recognize a certain label samples. Then, we adopt the idea of z-score based outlier detection and consider classes with scores grater than the threshold to be low-accuracy labels and add them to set S_{low}. For a intermediate model, we assume $S_{ls} = [c_1, c_2, ..., c_g]$ as the clusters corresponding to its lacking stages. We add the data proportions of classes in S_{low} to get $[q_1, q_2, ..., q_g]$:

$$q_j = \sum_{l \in S_{low}} Dis_j^l, j \in S_{ls} \tag{4}$$

where Dis_j^l is the proportion of data with label l of cluster j. Clusters with larger q-value usually have more data samples with low-accuracy labels and they are should be trained in the back of the queue, for enhancing the absorption of more difficult knowledge. To maintain stochasticity in the order, we randomly select the next stage of clusters among the $\lceil g/2 \rceil$ clusters with the smallest q.

Device Selection. Device heterogeneity causes a training speed difference among devices. By increasing the probability of being selected for devices with short training time, we expect to involve more high-speed devices in training to get more models aggregated in less time. The probability of a idle device k to be selected is:

$$p_k = \frac{\sum_{j \in IC} \frac{1}{t_j}}{t_k} \tag{5}$$

where IC is the set of idle devices that may be selected for the next stage of the model and t_k is the training time of device k which can be taken from historical performance. To prevent fast devices from being selected frequently and introducing bias, we set a *credit* for all device in each federated round. The *credit* decreases as the device is selected, and the server will not select devices without any *credit*.

3.5 Model Aggregation

Considering the problem that local models accomplished in the same round may originate from different versions of the global model in the asynchronous update method. As shown in Fig. 2(c), the server collects two models with different versions (CA-0 and DB-1) at the end of second round. In this section, we modify the original aggregation method to reduce the influence of staleness models on the global model.

The server maintains a global model version τ_g, which is incremented when completing aggregation. And the version of the model k, τ_k, is defined as the current τ_g when it is first sent to a device. Consequently, the staleness of an aggregated model k is:

$$a_k = \tau_g - \tau_k. \tag{6}$$

Our motivation is to assign larger aggregate weights to models with smaller staleness to support fresher local updates. Thus, we define the aggregated weights of model k as:

$$p_k(t) = \frac{|N_k|\gamma^{a_k(t)}}{\sum_{i \in M(t)} |N_i|\gamma^{a_i(t)}} 1(k \in M(t)) \tag{7}$$

where $|N_k|$ is the data size of model k during training, $a_k(t)$ is the staleness of model k at round t and $M(t)$ is the set of models to be aggregated at round t. Here, γ is a real-valued constant factor less than 1.

Eventually, the global model of MSSA-FL will be updated according to the following equation:

$$\omega^{t+1} = \sum_{k \in M(t)} p_k(t) \times \omega_k^t \tag{8}$$

4   Experiment

4.1   Experimental Setup

We implement our proposed MSSA-FL and verify the effectiveness of our proposed method by comparison and analysis.

Datasets and Models. We adopt two widely used public data sets, MNIST and CIFAR-10, and use convolutional neural networks (CNN) for image classification task. The CNN network for MNIST contains: two 5×5 convolutional layers (the first has 10 channels, the second has 20, each followed with 2×2 max pooling), a fully connected layer with 50 units and ReLu activation, and a final output layer. As for CIFAR-10, the model consists of three 3×3 convolution layer with 128 channels and a fully connected layer with 10 units.

Implementation Details. As for the data heterogeneity between devices, we follow the similar method in [30] and use a Dirichlet distribution $Dir(\alpha)$ to generate data partitions for devices, where α is a hyperparameter that can determine the degree of Non-IID data partition. In order to simulate the heterogeneity of devices, we assume that the performance of the devices follow the Gaussian distribution $\mathcal{N}(a, b)(a = 0.5$ and $b = 0.2)$. Meanwhile, we define the performance of a device as the number of batches it can process per second in training. We ignore the communication latency between devices and the server.

Baseline Algorithms. In order to exhibit the superiority of MSSA-FL, we reimplement other FL schemes for comparison: FedAvg [18], FedProx [8] and FedAsync [23], which are representative synchronous and asynchronous FL protocols. We set μ to 1 for FedProx and keep the maximum staleness of the model at 4 for FedAsync. The settings of other hyperparameters are shown in Table 1.

Table 1. Experimental setup

Parameter	Symbol	MNIST	CIFAR10
Total number of devices	N	100	100
Device selection level	C	0.1	0.1
Local epochs	E	5	5
Mini-batch size	B	50	32
Learning rate	η	0.001	0.005
Maximum time per round (s)	t	400	500
Running time (s)	T	30,000	150,000

4.2   Experimental Results

Accuracy Evaluation. Table 2 and Fig. 3 illustrate the experimental results on convergence accuracy with representative α values. impr. (a) and impr. (b) are the accuracy improvement of MSSA-FL compared with the best and worst baseline FL Algorithm, respectively.

Table 2. Comparison of the best prediction accuracy to baseline approaches.

Dataset	MNIST			CIFAR-10		
	$\alpha = 0.1$	$\alpha = 1$	$\alpha = 10$	$\alpha = 0.1$	$\alpha = 1$	$\alpha = 10$
FedAvg	76.55	91.89	92.28	53.09	68.33	70.42
FedProx	81.02	91.74	92.07	51.36	67.69	70.17
FedAsync	88.13	92.34	92.86	55.19	68.08	68.52
MSSA-FL	90.42	93.71	93.92	59.35	70.93	71.02
Impr. (a)	2.29%	1.37%	1.06%	4.16%	2.60%	0.60%
Impr. (b)	13.87%	1.97%	1.85%	7.99%	3.24%	2.50%

Under all experimental settings, MSSA-FL has the highest model accuracy. It can be seen a greater performance advantage of MSSA-FL as the α decreases. In

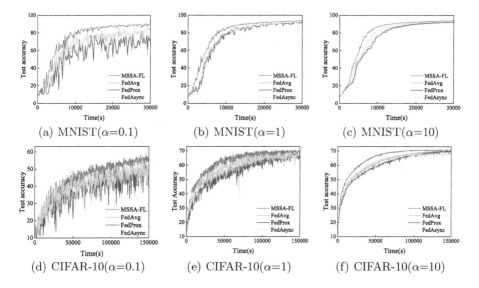

Fig. 3. Performance comparison of different FL algorithms on MNIST and CIFAR-10 with $\alpha = 0.1$, $\alpha = 1$ and $\alpha = 10$.

the MNIST with $\alpha = 0.1$, MSSA-FL outperforms the best baseline FL algorithm, FedAsync, by 2.29%, and the worst baseline algorithm, FedAvg, by 13.87%. In the MNIST with $\alpha = 10$, MSSA-FL outperforms the best baseline FL algorithm, FedAsync, by 1.06%, and the worst baseline algorithm, FedProx, by 1.85%. There is the similar performance result in CIFAR-10. MSSA-FL improves the prediction performance by 6.56%, 2.60%, 0.60% compared to FedAvg with $\alpha = 0.1$, $\alpha = 1$, and $\alpha = 10$. The above results demonstrate that the multi-stage training strategy in MSSA-FL solve the data heterogeneity problem and improves the accuracy of the model. When α is large, MSSA-FL generates more groups with a single cluster (only a single cluster in a group is the best grouping result). Therefore, MSSA-FL would degenerate into a algorithm similar to FedAvg.

Efficiency Evaluation. Table 3 shows the time required to reach the target accuracy when specific α value ($\alpha = 0.1$). In MNIST, MSSA-FL saves 68.56% and 67.98% time over FedAvg and FedProx. As for CIFAR-10, MSSA-FL saves 22.50% and 47.98% time over FedAvg and FedProx. FedAvg and FedProx use the same synchronous update method, so they always take longer to reach the target accuracy. FedAsync outperforms the above synchronous methods in terms of time efficiency. By contrast, MSSA-FL still reduces the training time by 17.06% and 12.37% in MNIST and CIFAR-10.

Figure 4 shows the average idle time per round of devices in different algorithms under homogeneous and heterogeneous device settings. MS-FL is the multi-stage synchronous federated learning described in Sect. 3.3. It can be seen that MSSA-FL has minimal device idle time in heterogeneous setting and also

Table 3. Time(s) to achieve the target accuracy.

Algorithms	MNIST (Acc.= 0.8)	CIFAR-10 (Acc.= 0.5)
FedAvg	27536.14	90590.97
FedProx	27036.13	134954.31
FedAsync	10439.65	80113.95
MSSA-FL	8658.13	70205.36

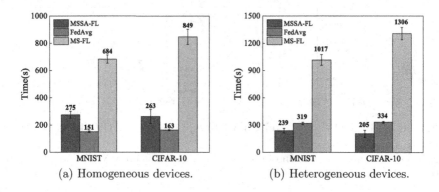

(a) Homogeneous devices.   (b) Heterogeneous devices.

Fig. 4. Average device idle time per round.

good performance in homogeneous setting. MSSA-FL allows faster devices train more frequently, which lessens the time of multi-stage training and lets more devices to train in a round. Though FedAvg achieves the shortest device idle time in homogeneous setting, when devices are heterogeneous, slow devices severely block FedAvg training. Due to the longest round time, MS-FL always has the largest device idle time.

Effectiveness of Combination Module and Model Assignment Strategy. We implement two variants of MSSA-FL, MSSA-RG (MSSA-FL with random groups) and MSSA-NMA (MSSA-FL without model assignment policy). Figure 5 shows the comparison results of MSSA-FL and MSSA-RG, MSSA-NMA in MINST with $\alpha = 1$. In Fig. 5(a), we sample the results every 15 rounds and calculate the accuracy of the model formed in each group at the sampling points (the range of accuracy of different groups' model is marked by error lines). MSSA-FL achieves a faster convergence speed and higher accuracy than MSSA-RG. At the same time, the variance of model accuracy for different groups in MSSA-FL is smaller than MSSA-RG, demonstrating the effectiveness of the combination module. As shown in Fig. 5(b), MSSA-NMA achieves the accuracy as high as MSSA-FL. However, it takes 8835.3 s to reach 80% accuracy, which is 13.46% longer than MSSA-FL (7646.41 s). Consequently, model assignment strategy is able to speed up the convergence of the model.

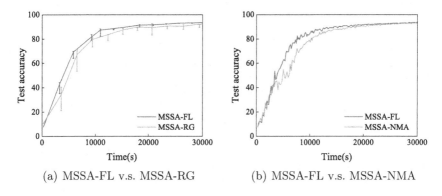

Fig. 5. Efficiency evaluation of proposed methods.

5   Conclusion

In this paper, we have proposed a novel FL framework, MSSA-FL to address the heterogeneous data issues and improve the training efficiency. By combination module, MSSA-FL enables to infer devices data distribution and group devices for the purpose of following multi-stage training. MSSA-FL requires the models trained in multi-stage within the group to achieve approximately IID dataset training effect, reducing the impact of Non-IID data among devices. For boosting training efficiency, MSSA-FL adopts the semi-asynchronous update method. Furthermore, we designed a model scheduling strategy and a heuristic aggregation method to further improve the performance of MSSA-FL. We conducted extensive experimental validation and demonstrated that MSSA-FL has the highest prediction performance and fastest convergence speed compared with advanced synchronous and asynchronous FL algorithms.

References

1. Li, E., Zhou, Z., Chen, X.: Edge intelligence: on-demand deep learning model co-inference with device-edge synergy. In: Workshop on Mobile Edge Communication, pp. 31–36 (2018)
2. Zhou, Z., Chen, X., Li, E., et al.: Edge intelligence: paving the last mile of artificial intelligence with edge computing. Proc. IEEE **107**(8), 1738–1762 (2019)
3. Qiu, H., Zheng, Q., et al.: Topological graph convolutional network-based urban traffic flow and density prediction. IEEE Trans. on Intel. Transpor. Syst. **22**(7), 4560–4569 (2020)
4. Li, Y., Song, Y., et al.: Intelligent fault diagnosis by fusing domain adversarial training and maximum mean discrepancy via ensemble learning. IEEE TII. **17**(4), 2833–2841 (2020)
5. Hu, F., Lakdawala, S., Hao, Q., Qiu, M.: Low-power, intelligent sensor hardware interface for medical data preprocessing. IEEE Trans. Info. Tech. Biomed. **13**(4), 656–663 (2009)

6. Li, X., Huang, K., Yang, W., Wang, S., Zhang, Z.: On the convergence of fedavg on non-iid data (2019). arXiv preprint, arXiv:1907.02189
7. Zhao, Y., Li, M., Lai, L., Suda, N., Civin, D., Chandra, V.: Federated learning with non-iid data (2018). arXiv preprint, arXiv:1806.00582
8. Li, T., Sahu, A.K., Zaheer, M., Sanjabi, M., Talwalkar, A., Smith, V.: Federated optimization in heterogeneous networks. Proc. Mach. Learn. Sys. **2**, 429–450 (2020)
9. Karimireddy, S.P., Kale, S., Mohri, M., Reddi, S., Stich, S., Suresh, A.T.: Scaffold: Stochastic controlled averaging for federated learning. In: International Conference on Machine Learning, pp. 5132–5143 (2020)
10. Duan, M., Liu, D., et al.: Self-balancing federated learning with global imbalanced data in mobile systems. IEEE TPDS **32**(1), 59–71 (2020)
11. Qiu, M., Xue, C., Shao, Z., Sha, E.: Energy minimization with soft real-time and DVS for uniprocessor and multiprocessor embedded systems. In: IEEE DATE, pp. 1–6 (2007)
12. Qiu, M., Liu, J., et al.: A novel energy-aware fault tolerance mechanism for wireless sensor networks. In: IEEE/ACM Conference on GCC (2011)
13. Qiu, M., et al.: Heterogeneous real-time embedded software optimization considering hardware platform. In: ACM Symposium on Applied Computing, pp. 1637–1641 (2009)
14. Lu, Z., et al.: IoTDeM: an IoT Big Data-oriented MapReduce performance prediction extended model in multiple edge clouds. JPDC **118**, 316–327 (2018)
15. Liu, M., Zhang, S., et al.: H infinite state estimation for discrete-time chaotic systems based on a unified model. In: IEEE SMC (B) (2012)
16. Qiu, H., Zheng, Q., et al.: Deep residual learning-based enhanced jpeg compression in the internet of things. IEEE TII **17**(3), 2124–2133 (2020)
17. Qiu, H., Qiu, M., Lu, Z.: Selective encryption on ECG data in body sensor network based on supervised machine learning. Infor. Fusion **55**, 59–67 (2020)
18. McMahan, B., Moore, E., Ramage, D., Hampson, S., y Arcas, B.A.: Communication-efficient learning of deep networks from decentralized data. In: Artificial Intelligence Statistics, pp. 1273–1282 (2017)
19. Wu, G., Zhang, H., et al.: A decentralized approach for mining event correlations in distributed system monitoring. JPDC **73**(3), 330–340 (2013)
20. Qiu, L., et al.: Optimal big data sharing approach for tele-health in cloud computing. In: IEEE SmartCloud, pp. 184–189 (2016)
21. Wang, H., Yurochkin, M., Sun, Y., Papailiopoulos, D., Khazaeni, Y.: Federated learning with matched averaging (2020). arXiv preprint, arXiv:2002.06440
22. Nishio, T., Yonetani, R.: Client selection for federated learning with heterogeneous resources in mobile edge. In: IEEE ICC, pp. 1–7 (2019)
23. Xie, C., Koyejo, S., Gupta, I.: Asynchronous federated optimization (2019). arXiv preprint, arXiv:1903.03934
24. Wu, W., He, L., Lin, W., et al.: Safa: a semi-asynchronous protocol for fast federated learning with low overhead. IEEE Trans. Comput. **70**(5), 655–668 (2020)
25. Xu, Z., Yu, F., Xiong, J., Chen, X.: Helios: heterogeneity-aware federated learning with dynamically balanced collaboration. In: 58th ACM/IEEE DAC, pp. 997–1002 (2021)
26. Duan, M., et al.: Flexible clustered federated learning for client-level data distribution shift. In: IEEE TPDS (2021)
27. Ghosh, A., Chung, J., Yin, D., Ramchandran, K.: An efficient framework for clustered federated learning. Adv. Neural. Inf. Process. Syst. **33**, 19586–19597 (2020)

28. Sattler, F., Müller, K.R., Samek, W.: Clustered federated learning: Model-agnostic distributed multitask optimization under privacy constraints. IEEE Trans. Neural Netw. Learn. Syst. **32**(8), 3710–3722 (2020)
29. Wang, L., Xu, S., Wang, X., Zhu, Q.: Addressing class imbalance in federated learning. In: AAAI Conference, vol. 35, pp. 10165–10173 (2021)
30. Wang, J., Liu, Q., et al.: Tackling the objective inconsistency problem in heterogeneous federated optimization. Adv. Neural Infor. Proc. Syst. **33**, 7611–7623 (2020)

A GAT-Based Chinese Text Classification Model: Using of Redical Guidance and Association Between Characters Across Sentences

Yizhao Wang[1] and Yuncheng Jiang[1,2(✉)]

[1] School of Computer Science, South China Normal University, Guangzhou 510631, Guangdong, China
{wyz0714,jiangyuncheng}@m.scnu.edu.cn
[2] School of Artificial Intelligence, South China Normal University, Foshan 528225, Guangdong, China

Abstract. Cognitive psychology research has shown that humans tend to use objects in the abstract real world as cognition. For the Chinese in particular, the first thing to emerge from the process of writing formation is pictographs. This feature is very useful for Chinese text classification. Fortunately, many basic and extended radical-related systems are also included in all Chinese dictionaries. Moreover, for Chinese texts the graph attention structure can better record the information of features in Chinese texts. To this end, we propose a GAT-based Chinese text classification model considering character, word, sentence position information, character position information and radicals as nodes in Chinese text. The model is based on **R**edical guidance and association between **C**haracters across **S**entences (RCS). In order to better exploit the common features of Chinese characters and sequence features in text, this paper designs a model with context-awareness, which is capable of collecting information at a distance. Finally, we conduct extensive experiments, and the experimental results not only prove the superiority of our model, but also verify the effectiveness of the radical and GAT model in Chinese text classification tasks.

Keywords: GAT · Chinese text classification · Radical

1 Introduction

Text classification is a significant module in text processing with many applications [8], including spam filtering [6], news categorization [11], lexical annotation [1], and so on. Text classification is not much different from classifiers in other domains because the main technique is to first extract the features of the classified data and then select the best match to classify them. Text, on the other hand, has its own peculiarities. The general procedure of text classification is as follows [8]: 1. preprocessing, 2. text representation and feature selection, 3. classifier development and 4. classification. Text classification encompasses a number of steps, including text preparation, word separation, model creation, and classification. Texts and vocabularies have a wide range of

ⓒ The Author(s), under exclusive license to Springer Nature Switzerland AG 2022
G. Memmi et al. (Eds.): KSEM 2022, LNAI 13369, pp. 188–199, 2022.
https://doi.org/10.1007/978-3-031-10986-7_15

properties that are always changing. Text categorization becomes much more difficult as a result of this.

The difference between Chinese and English writing is that there is no discernible distinction between Chinese words, making it more difficult to distinguish Chinese words [10]. When using word separation to handle text, the most frequent tools are direct, using word separation and word separation by developing word separation models using existing dictionaries and algorithms [19]. One of the most distinguishing features of the Chinese writing system is that it is based on pictographs with primordial meanings. That is, radicals are significant bearers of semantics as well as words and letters in expressing certain meanings. This unique trait distinguishes Chinese text classification from English text classification.

Chinese text preprocessing, obtaining Chinese text features, and classification using neural networks are the primary phases in deep neural network-based Chinese text classification [2]. The original Chinese text must be pre-processed as part of the text preprocessing procedure. The text is first separated into Chinese words, then vectorized, and finally the vector Chinese text [3] is used to train and test the neural network. A deep neural network is required to extract the semantic characteristics of the text during the feature extraction step.

Some scholars [7, 12] use individual characters or words for feature extraction and achieve text classification. However, this classification method is more applicable to English text, and for Chinese text these methods extract too few text features to achieve effective text classification. Devlin et al. [4] propose to use BERT for text classification to achieve improved results for Chinese text classification. Tao et al. [13, 14] proposed that using chars, words and radicals together can improve the classification results of Chinese texts. But these optimizations are not complete using all information simultaneously for text classification. These methods do not take into account that information about the position of characters in Chinese text can affect the text classification results, and the position of sentences in the text can also affect the results of Chinese text classification in a positive way.

This paper proposes a GAT-based Chinese text classification model based on redical guidance and association between characters across sentences (RCS-GAT). The method does not only consider characters, words, radicals, character position information and sentence position information. In obtaining location information as well as sentence location information, this paper uses BERT to extract these features. At the same time, this paper uses the above features for composition and uses GAT for Chinese text classification. Specifically, 1) we consider using the association module proposed by Tao and a word association strategy mediated by root words. 2) we use BERT for feature extraction of sentence information in the text, and obtain the sentence position information from the text and the character position information from the sentence, considering both character and word information in the text. 3) We use the text as the core node, the information obtained in 1) and 2) above as the neighbor nodes, set the attention mechanism in the edge information, and use GAT to calculate the classification results of the texts.

2 Methodology

In this part, we present a graph attention-based Chinese text categorization mechanism led by character bias. Because paraphernalia can express the semantics of Chinese characters, it is included in the paraphernalia analysis section. As a result, we employ morphemes to discover characters in the text that include paraphernalia, and then we assess the text's core semantics based on the frequency of the paraphernalia. We employ a BERT model based on absolute position information and adaptive convolution between words for Chinese word separation in the word separation stage. Then, utilizing morphemes as graph nodes, the Chinese text categorization by graph attention method is accomplished. Figure 1 depicts the particular structure.

2.1 Problem Definition

In the case of text classification, all we need to do is to select the label S of the text from a predefined set of labels. Given a Chinese text $T = \{x_1, x_2, \ldots, x_m\}$ without tags and a pre-defined label set S containing K different labels, the goal of our task is to train and obtain a classification function $\mathscr{F}$ with the ability to assign a proper label $l \in S$ for T:

$$\mathscr{F}(T) \to l, \tag{1}$$

where $x_i \in T$ $(0 \le i \le m)$ represents the feature vector of the $i - th$ token in T after text preprocessing.

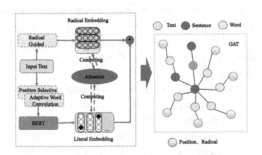

Fig. 1. GAT-based structure of Chinese text classification GCS model

2.2 Technical Details of Classification Model

As shown in Fig. 1, the goal of our research is to develop a complete model RCS of Chinese text utilizing four distinct granularities of characteristics to aid in the categorization of Chinese text. RCS is divided into four sections: the input layer, the embedding layer, the composition expression layer, and the prediction layer. The following are the specifics.

Preliminary: BERT. BERT [4] (Bidirectional Encoder Representations from Transformers) is a pre-trained language model comprising a stack of multi-head self-attention layers and fully connected layers. For each head in the l_{th} multi-head self-attention layers, the output matrix $\mathbf{H}^{\text{out},l} = \left\{ \mathbf{h}_1^{\text{out},l}, \mathbf{h}_2^{\text{out},l}, \ldots, \mathbf{h}_n^{\text{out},l} \right\} \in \mathbb{R}^{n \times d_k}$ satisfies:

$$\mathbf{h}_i^{\text{out},l} = \sum_{j=1}^{n} \left(\frac{\exp \alpha_{ij}^l}{\sum_{j'} \exp \alpha_{ij'}^l} \mathbf{h}_j^{\text{in},l} \mathbf{W}^{v,l} \right)$$

$$\alpha_{ij}^l = \frac{1}{\sqrt{2d_k}} \left(\mathbf{h}_i^{\text{in},l} \mathbf{W}^{q,l} \right) \left(\mathbf{h}_j^{\text{in},l} \mathbf{W}^{k,l} \right)^T,$$

(2)

where $\mathbf{H}^{\text{in},l} = \left\{ \mathbf{h}_1^{\text{in},l}, \mathbf{h}_2^{\text{in},l}, \ldots, \mathbf{h}_n^{\text{in},l} \right\} \in \mathbb{R}^{n \times d_h}$ is the input matrix, and $\mathbf{W}^{q,l}, \mathbf{W}^{\hat{k},l}, \mathbf{W}^{v,l} \in \mathbb{R}^{d_h \times d_k}$ are learnable parameters. n and d_h are sequence length and hidden size respectively, and attention size $d_k = d_h / n_h$, where n_h is the number of attention heads.

The Acquisition of a Feature. We initially presented a feature acquisition procedure to extract the characteristics required by the model, namely characters, radicals, and words, based on the cognitive activity of humans seeing text and collecting features depicted in Fig. 2. There are six sorts of Chinese characters, according to the 11six line script", but only the root of the vocoder semantic compound character carries semantic information [15]. As a result, the focus of this research is on phonograph semantic compound characters and their root forms. Then, with the aid of four Chinese dictionaries, we'll use these roots to find the linked terms.

Masking of Character Types. As illustrated in Fig. 1, given an input Chinese text T having m characters, we first use string arithmetic to divide it into a series of characters $C = \{c_1, c_2, \ldots, c_m\}$, where C represents T's character-level properties. Then, using the Chinese character type dictionary [9], we may assign a type label to each character, enabling the character type masking procedure:

$$\text{Mask}(c_i) = \begin{cases} 1 & c_i = C_p \\ 0 & c_i = \text{Others.} \end{cases}$$

(3)

where C_p denotes the phonograph semantic composite character. Mask $(\cdot)$ denotes the mask function, $c_i (0 \le i \le m)$ is the $i - th$ character in C.

Masking of Sentences Types. As shown in Fig. 3, given an input Chinese text T containing n sentences, we recognize the punctuation marks and classify the sentences into $S = \{s_1, s_2, \ldots, s_m\}$, where S represents T's sentences-level properties.

$$\text{Mask}(s_i) = \begin{cases} 1 & s_i = S_q \\ 0 & s_i = \text{Others.} \end{cases}$$

(4)

where S_q denotes the phonograph semantic composite sentences.

Radical Guiding. After obtaining the mask of each character as well as the word, we performed the following process of radical extraction. That is, in order to extract the radicals (i.e., the roots of the phonograph semantic compound characters) from the text T that have semantic representation and thus help convey the semantics, we will remove some useless characters at the same time. After performing the semantic radical, the problem of having characters containing semantic radicals in the text is addressed using the mask of the sentence. Therefore, we multiply the mask code of each character, the mask code of the sentence and itself to determine which characters can be reserved for querying the root formula in the Chinese dictionary:

$$R = Radical\_Query(C \odot Mask(C) \odot Mask(S)) \tag{5}$$

which $\odot$ is a product operation by element, and the *Radical_Query* operation allows us to map each Chinese character into a root base with the help of the Xinhua dictionary [18].

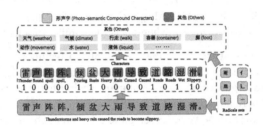

Fig. 2. Chinese visual description of the text feature acquisition process

BERT Feature Selection. As shown in Fig. 3, the distance-lattice consists of spans of different lengths. Given a sentence $s = \{c_1, c_2, \cdots, c_n\}$ as the sequence of characters, each character will be assigned a pre-prepared tag. In order to encode the interaction between spans, this paper propose the absolute position encoding of spans in the sentence. To get two spans x_i and x_j, in the lattice, there are three kinds of relationships among the three of them: intersection, inclusion, and irrelevance, which are determined by their pros and cons. We can't directly encode the three relationships, so we use dense vectors to encode them. This model use their absolute position in the sentence and the absolute position of the sentence in the document to perform continuous transformation. Therefore, this model consider that it not only calculates the relationship between the two position information, but also can express more detailed information, such as the distance between the front character and the back character, and the relative position of the character in the word. Let $distance[i]$ denote the character position of span x_i and denote $sentence[i]$ as the sentence position of span x_i. In summary, these characters can be calculated as:

$$d_{ij}^{(character)} = distance[i] - distance[j], \tag{6}$$

$$d_{ij}^{(sentence)} = sentence[i] - sentence[j], \tag{7}$$

$$d_{ij}^{(s-c)} = character[i]_{sentence[i]} - character[j]_{sentence[j]}, \tag{8}$$

where $d_{ij}^{(character)}$ is the distance among the characters, $d_{ij}^{(sentence)}$ and $d_{ij}^{(s-c)}$ have similar means, where $s-c$ indicates the subtraction of character positions in a sentence.

Ultimately, the conversion is performed by encoding the absolute position information through a simple ReLU activation function of the three distances.

$$R_{ij} = \text{ReLU}\left(W_r\left(\mathbf{P}_{d_{ij}^{(character)}} \oplus \mathbf{P}_{d_{ij}^{(sentence)}} \oplus \mathbf{P}_{d_{ij}^{(s-c)}}\right)\right) \tag{9}$$

where $d_{ij}^{(character)}$, $d_{ij}^{(sentence)}$, $d_{ij}^{(s-c)}$ and k denote the index of dimension of absolute position encoding, W_r is a learnable parameter, $\oplus$ denotes the concatenation operator, and P_d is calculated as in [16]:

$$
\begin{aligned}
\mathbf{p}_d^{(2k)} &= \sin\left(d/10000^{2k/d_{\text{model}}}\right), \\
\mathbf{p}_d^{(2k+1)} &= \cos\left(d/10000^{2k/d_{\text{model}}}\right),
\end{aligned}
\tag{10}
$$

So we define a variant of the self-attention mechanism to combine the span between characters for position encoding, as shown in the following:

$$
\begin{aligned}
\mathbf{A}_{i,j}^* &= \mathbf{W}_q^\top \mathbf{E}_{x_i}^\top \mathbf{E}_{x_j} \mathbf{W}_{k,E} + \mathbf{W}_q^\top \mathbf{E}_{x_i}^\top \mathbf{R}_{ij} \mathbf{W}_{k,R} \\
&\quad + \mathbf{u}^\top \mathbf{E}_{x_j} \mathbf{W}_{k,E} + \mathbf{v}^\top \mathbf{R}_{ij} \mathbf{W}_{k,R}
\end{aligned}
\tag{11}
$$

where $\mathbf{W}_q, \mathbf{W}_{k,R}, \mathbf{W}_{k,E} \in \mathbb{R}^{d_{\text{model}} \times d_{\text{head}}}$ and $\mathbf{u}, \mathbf{v} \in \mathbb{R}^{d_{\text{hepd}}}$ are learnable parameters. We replace A with A^* in Eq. 11.

Radical-Characters-Sentences Association. In contrast to Tao et al.'s[14] study do not employ radicals as supplementary characteristics; instead, we use just radical basic features. It also varies from Tao et al.'s study from 2020 [13], despite the fact that the medium of strong radical word association was evaluated. Word characteristics and extensions were taken into consideration. However, it ignores the presence of numerous contained radicals in a single phrase, which has an impact on the text categorization result. As a result, this research suggests a Radical-Characters-Sentences association strategy. As a result, the corresponding words for the phonetic machine's semantic compound letters are referred to as Words-p (in red). Each distilled radical $r_i \in R = \{r_1, r_2, \ldots, r_n\}$ will correlate to a list of related phrases if you consult the Radical Concept Dictionary. Simultaneously, this article extracts each radical by recording information about the sentence's location during the extraction process:

$$W_i^r = Concept\_Query(r_i) = \left\{w_1^r, w_2^r, \ldots, w_{\rho_i}^r\right\} \odot \left\{w_1^r, w_2^r, \ldots, w_{\sigma_i}^r\right\}. \tag{12}$$

Here, $\rho_i \geq 1$, $\sigma_j \geq 1$ denote the number of associative words and sentences for r_i, which will vary from radical to radical. As a result, all radicals R recovered from the text T may be combined to generate a list of related terms $U = U_c \odot U_s = \{w_1, w_2, \ldots, w_\lambda\} \odot \{w_1, w_2, \ldots, w_\gamma\}$:

$$U = \cup_{i=1}^n W_i^r \odot \cup_{j=1}^n W_j^r, \tag{13}$$

where U is the introduction of character features and sentence-level features representing the exterior of the text T, and $\lambda = \sum_{i=1}^n \rho_i \odot \sum_{j=1}^n \rho_j$ the numbers of all characters and sentences in U is recorded.

GAT (Graph Attention Network). GAT [17], like many deep learning approaches, is made up of numerous blocks that perform the same purpose. One of these blocks is called Graph Attention Layer, and we'll go through its structure first. Eigenvalues of nodes at the input of Graph attention layer: $\overrightarrow{\mathbf{h}} = \left\{ \overrightarrow{h}_1, \overrightarrow{h}_2, \cdots, \overrightarrow{h}_N \right\}$, $\overrightarrow{h}_i \in \mathbb{R}^F$ where N is the number of nodes and F is the dimensionality of the node features. After a Graph Attention Layer, a new feature vector is output. Suppose the dimension of the node features of this feature vector is F', and this feature can be expressed as $\overrightarrow{\mathbf{h}'} = \left\{ \overrightarrow{h'_1}, \overrightarrow{h'_2}, \ldots, \overrightarrow{h'_N} \right\}$, $\overrightarrow{h'}_i \in \mathbb{R}^{F'}$. Here Self-attention is used to improve the expressiveness of $\overrightarrow{\mathbf{h}'}$. In Graph Attention Layer, a weight matrix $\mathbf{W} \in \mathbb{R}^{F' \times F}$ is first applied to each node, and then a self-attention is used for each node to compute an attention coefficient, where the shared self-attention mechanism used is denoted as a:

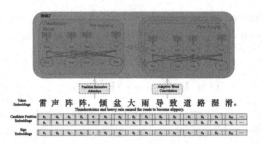

Fig. 3. BERT extracts character and sentence position information

$$e_{ij} = a\left(\mathbf{W}\overrightarrow{h_i}, \mathbf{W}\overrightarrow{h_j}\right) \tag{14}$$

$$\alpha_{ij} = \text{softmax}\, j\,(e_{ij}) = \frac{\exp(e_{ij})}{\sum_{k \in \mathcal{N}_i} \exp(e_{ik})} \tag{15}$$

$$\overrightarrow{h}'_i = \sigma\left(\sum_{j \in \mathcal{N}_i} \alpha_{ij} \overrightarrow{h}_j\right) \tag{16}$$

Information Propagation. This step is to pass all the information h of the tail vector (h, r, t) of the triplet relation e_t headed by $e_{N_h} = \sum_{(h,r,t) \in N_h} \pi(h, r, t) e_t$, $\pi(h, r, t)$ being the weight of the measure message (h, r, t). The implementation of $\pi(h, r, t)$ is done with the attention mechanism.

$$\pi'(h, r, t) = (W_r e_t)^T \tanh(W_r e_h + e_t) \tag{17}$$

$$\pi(h, r, t) = \frac{\exp(\pi'(h, r, t))}{\sum_{(h,r',t') \in N_h} \exp(\pi'(h, r', t'))} \tag{18}$$

where tanh represents the nonlinear activation function. The next step is to do aggregation and update of the delivered messages in three ways.

GCN Aggregator:

$$f_{GCN} = \text{LeakyRelu}\left(W\left(e_h + e_{N_h}\right)\right);$$ (19)

GraphSage Aggregator:

$$f_{GCN} = LeakyRelu\left(W\left(e_h \| e_{N_h}\right)\right);$$ (20)

Bi-interaction Aggregator:

$$f_{GCN} = Leaky\text{ReLu}\left(W_1\left(e_h + e_{N_h}\right)\right) + Leaky\text{ReLu}\left(W_1\left(e_h \odot e_{N_h}\right)\right);$$ (21)

Repeat the three processes of Eqs. 19, 20, 21. The calculation to part l yields the Eq. 22:

$$e_h^{(l)} = f\left(e_h^{(l-1)}, e_{N_h}^{(l-1)}\right), e_h^{(l-1)} = \sum_{(h,r,t) \in N_h} \pi(h,r,t) e_t^{(l-1)}.$$ (22)

Splice all the vectors $e_h^{(l)}$ generated in the process as the embedding of the entity h generated by the RCS iteration. And currently we compute the embedding of u and i, obtain the Eqs. 23, 24:

$$e_u^* = e_u^{(0)} \| \cdots \| e_u^{(L)}, e_i^* = e_i^{(0)} \| \cdots \| e_i^{(L)}$$ (23)

$$\hat{y}(u,i) = (e_u^*)^T e_i^*$$ (24)

The loss function used in this step of the calculation is pairwise BPR loss.

$$g(h,r,t) = \|\mathbf{W}_r \mathbf{e}_h + \mathbf{e}_r - \mathbf{W}_r \mathbf{e}_t\|_2^2$$ (25)

$$L_{CF} = \sum_{(u,i,j) \in O} -\ln \sigma(\hat{y}(u,i) - \hat{y}(u,j))$$ (26)

where $O = \{(u,i,j) \mid (u,i) \in R^+, (u,j) \in R^-\}$.

Model Initialization. Before training, proper initialization facilitates the optimization of our model. The specific settings of the hyperparameters are shown below. Combined with the architecture of RCS, we applied a pre-trained Chinese BERT model with 24 layers, 1024 hides, 16 heads and 330 M parameters. In addition, we obtained a well pre-trained Chinese word embedding model with dimension 256 for representing associated words in U. We set the depth of GAT to three hidden dimensions of 64, 32 and 16, respectively. Finally, we apply the Adagrad optimizer with a learning rate of 0.01. In the implementation, we construct the model using *MXNet* and train it using two Intel (R) Xeon (R) CPUs E5-2630 v3 @ 2.40 GHz with 128 GB and a GTX3090 24 GB*4.

3   Evaluation

3.1   Dataset Description

We use two real-world datasets to assess our model to match the topic explored in this paper: the Chinese News Title Dataset (CNT) [20] and the Fudan Chinese Text Dataset (FCT)[1]. The split ratios of the training and testing sets of these two datasets are consistent with the public datasets to guarantee repeatability.

---

[1] https://www.kesci.com/home/dataset/5d3a9c86cf76a600360edd04.

- **CNT** is a public dataset that includes 32 different types of Chinese news in 32 different categories. It comprises 47,693 texts for coloring and 15,901 texts for testing, which are appropriate for checking the robustness of different approaches after preprocessing and weeding out worthless texts with lengths less than 2.
- **FCT** is Fudan University's official dataset, which comprises 20 categories of rich academic texts for validation. We thoroughly preprocessed this dataset, correcting and eliminating illegible samples, to assure the quality of the implementation. As a result, it comprises 8,220 training texts and 8,115 testing texts.

3.2 Baeline

- **Single Symbol Method.** We choose to compare TextCNN (char/word) [7] and TextRNN (char/word) [12] for Chinese text classification with a single symbol.
- **BERT.** BERT represents [4] the most advanced pre-trained natural language processing model currently in use, which is routinely employed on English content and performs well. As a result, we utilize it as a critical baseline and fine-tune it to ensure that the RCS model design is good and effective.
- **Multi-symbol Method.** C-LSTMs/C-BLSTMs [20] are two specific Chinese text classification models that apply two independent LSTMs to connect word and character features together. Since both characters and words are important features of Chinese texts, they compensate the disadvantage of using one feature unilaterally. C-BLSTM is a bi-directional version of C-LSTM.
- **Symbols + Radical.** RAFG [14] and RAM [13] are two methods that consider all words, characters and radicals for Chinese text classification.

3.3 Experimental Results

Table 1 shows the results of the comparison between the two datasets. The findings are instructive in various ways, including demonstrating that our RCS-GAT model achieves virtually the best performance on both datasets in terms of accuracy, recall, and F1 scores. This demonstrates that RCS-GAT has a better results of Chinese texts, resulting in increased performance.

As shown in Table. 1, we compare two different types of text classification methods: Chinese-specific text classification methods (6–10) and non-Chinese text-specific methods (1–5). In (1–5), we note that when only the characteristics of individual characters or words of text are obtained for classification, good results are not achieved. In the results of (6–7) we can prove that the method of character and word combination has a good effect on the text classification results. In the result (5), BERT shows its excellent ability to extract single character features. In results (8–9), it is demonstrated that introducing radical features can have a positive impact on Chinese text classification. However, reviewing the work in (8–9), although the radical features in the text are considered, it does not effectively combine the sentence and character position features that are still present in the text. Therefore, we consider sentence, character, word and location information, and in this process we completely consider the large amount of hidden information in the text to enhance the effect of text classification. We build a graph with text as the core node and multiple features as the neighbor nodes by framing

Table 1. Experimental results of comparison methods on CNT dataset and FCT dataset.

Methods	CNT				FCT			
	Accuracy	Recall	F1-score	ΔF1 (%)	Accuracy	Recall	F1-score	ΔF1 (%)
(1) TextCNN (char)	0.6123	0.6127	0.6059	−42.47	0.7481	0.4041	0.4095	−118.83
(2) TextCNN (word)	0.7706	0.7707	0.7695	−12.18	0.9012	0.6270	0.6643	−34.89
(3) TextRNN (char)	0.6992	0.6993	0.6995	−23.40	0.8361	0.4925	0.5174	−73.19
(4) TextRNN (word)	0.8023	0.8025	0.8025	−7.56	0.8704	0.5149	0.5372	−66.81
(5) BERT (char, fine-tuned)	0.8124	0.8120	0.8117	−6.34	0.9096	0.7635	0.7910	−13.29
(6) C-LSTM (char+word)	0.8186	0.8187	0.8183	−5.49	0.9204	0.6856	0.7218	−24.15
(7) C-BLSTM (char+word)	0.8230	0.8231	0.8225	−4.95	0.9204	0.6847	0.7216	−24.18
(8) RAFG (char+word+radical)	0.8324	0.8325	0.8325	−3.69	0.9241	0.7140	0.7408	−20.96
(9) RAM (char+word+radical)	0.8464	0.8461	0.8465	−1.97	0.9423	0.8058	0.8383	−6.89
(10) RCS-GAT (char+word+radication+position)	**0.8623**	**0.8641**	**0.8632**	–	**0.9575**	**0.8421**	**0.8961**	–

multiple features. Then the classification of Chinese text is performed by the GAT algorithm, which yields good classification results. At the same time, the excellent results of the method in this paper are reflected in the results (10).

3.4 Ablation Study

As previously mentioned, the RCS is based on the cognitive principle between ideographic text and human associative behavior [5]. To validate the design of the RCS-GAT and to determine how each module affects the final results, we conducted ablation studies by removing each module separately, which is summarized in Table 2. According to the results, we observed a significant decrease in RCS- GAT performance on both datasets, regardless of the removal of radical or character and sentence position information, which indeed validates the necessity of each module. Also, we used a two-layer Convolutional Neural Network (CNN) for feature classification in order to validate the effectiveness of GAT in text classification, and the results are shown as RCS-CNN.

Table 2. Ablation study

Methods	CNT			FCT		
	Accuracy	Recall	F1-score	Accuracy	Recall	F1-score
GCS-GAT-radical	0.8172	0.8247	0.8209	0.9174	0.7905	0.8492
GCS-GAT-position	0.8023	0.8122	0.8072	0.9045	0.6513	0.7573
GCS-CNN	0.7942	0.8011	0.7976	0.9275	0.6432	0.7596
GCS-GAT	0.8623	0.8641	0.8632	0.9575	0.8421	0.8961

4 Conclusion

This paper proposes a GAT-base Chinese text classification model based on Redical guidance and association between Characters across Sentences (RCS-GAT). Characters, words, radicals, character position information, and sentence position information are all taken into account by RCS-GAT. RCS-GAT uses BERT to extract location information as well as sentence location information. RCS-GAT uses the information in the text to frame the text and thus use GAT to classify its core nodes. Through extensive experiments, our study has gone some way towards enhancing our understanding of Chinese and human cognition.

Acknowledgments. The work described in this paper is funded by the National Natural Science Foundation of China under Grant Nos. 61772210 and U1911201, Guangdong Province Universities Pearl River Scholar Funded Scheme (2018) and the Project of Science and Technology in Guangzhou in China under Grant No. 202007040006.

References

1. Bikaun, T., French, T., Hodkiewicz, M., Stewart, M., Liu, W.: Lexiclean: an annotation tool for rapid multi-task lexical normalisation. In: Proceedings of the 2021 Conference on Empirical Methods in Natural Language Processing: System Demonstrations, pp. 212–219 (2021)
2. Chen, W., Xu, B.: Semi-supervised chinese word segmentation based on bilingual information. In: Proceedings of the 2015 Conference on Empirical Methods in Natural Language Processing, pp. 1207–1216 (2015)
3. Chen, X., Qiu, X., Zhu, C., Liu, P., Huang, X.J.: Long short-term memory neural networks for chinese word segmentation. In: Proceedings of the 2015 conference on empirical methods in natural language processing, pp. 1197–1206 (2015)
4. Devlin, J., Chang, M., Lee, K., Toutanova, K.: BERT: pre-training of deep bidirectional transformers for language understanding, pp. 4171–4186. ACL (2019)
5. Ellis, N.C.: Essentials of a theory of language cognition. Mod. Lang. J. **103**, 39–60 (2019)
6. Guzella, T.S., Caminhas, W.M.: A review of machine learning approaches to spam filtering. Expert Syst. Appl. **36**(7), 10206–10222 (2009)
7. Kim, Y.: Convolutional neural networks for sentence classification. In: Moschitti, A., Pang, B., Daelemans, W. (eds.): Proceedings of the 2014 Conference on Empirical Methods in Natural Language Processing, EMNLP 2014, 25–29 October 2014, Doha, Qatar, A meeting of SIGDAT, a Special Interest Group of the ACL, pp. 1746–1751. ACL (2014)
8. Kowsari, K., Jafari Meimandi, K., Heidarysafa, M., Mendu, S., Barnes, L., Brown, D.: Text classification algorithms: a survey. Information **10**(4), 150 (2019)
9. Liu, J., Wu, F., Wu, C., Huang, Y., Xie, X.: Neural Chinese word segmentation with dictionary. Neurocomputing **338**, 46–54 (2019)
10. Lu, S.H., Chiang, D.A., Keh, H.C., Huang, H.H.: Chinese text classification by the naïve bayes classifier and the associative classifier with multiple confidence threshold values. Knowl.-Based Syst. **23**(6), 598–604 (2010)
11. Mallick, P.K., Mishra, S., Chae, G.S.: Digital media news categorization using bernoulli document model for web content convergence. Personal Ubiquit. Comput. 1–16 (2020)
12. Mikolov, T., Kombrink, S., Burget, L., Černocký, J., Khudanpur, S.: Extensions of recurrent neural network language model. In: 2011 IEEE International Conference on Acoustics, Speech and Signal Processing, ICASSP, pp. 5528–5531. IEEE (2011)

13. Tao, H., Tong, S., Zhang, K., Xu, T., Liu, Q., Chen, E., Hou, M.: Ideography leads us to the field of cognition: A radical-guided associative model for Chinese text classification. In: Proceedings of the AAAI Conference on Artificial Intelligence, vol. 35, pp. 13898–13906 (2021)

14. Tao, H., Tong, S., Zhao, H., Xu, T., Jin, B., Liu, Q.: A radical-aware attention-based model for Chinese text classification. In: Proceedings of the AAAI Conference on Artificial Intelligence. vol. 33, pp. 5125–5132 (2019)

15. Tung, T.: The Six Scripts Or the Principles of Chinese Writing by Tai Tung: A Translation by LC Hopkins, with a Memoir of the Translator by W. Cambridge University Press, Perceval Yetts (2012)

16. Vaswani, A., et al.: Attention is all you need. In: NIPS, pp. 5998–6008 (2017)

17. Veličković, P., Cucurull, G., Casanova, A., Romero, A., Lio, P., Bengio, Y.: Graph attention networks (2017). arXiv preprint, arXiv:1710.10903

18. Wei, J.: Xin hua zi dian [xin hua dictionary] (2011)

19. Yu, C., Wang, S., Guo, J.: Learning chinese word segmentation based on bidirectional GRU-CRF and CNN network model. Int. J. Technol. Human Inter. (IJTHI) 15(3), 47–62 (2019)

20. Zhou, Y., Xu, B., Xu, J., Yang, L., Li, C.: Compositional recurrent neural networks for Chinese short text classification. In: 2016 IEEE/WIC/ACM International Conference on Web Intelligence, WI, pp. 137–144. IEEE (2016)

Incorporating Explanations to Balance the Exploration and Exploitation of Deep Reinforcement Learning

Xinzhi Wang$^{(\boxtimes)}$, Yang Liu, Yudong Chang, Chao Jiang, and Qingjie Zhang

School of Computer Engineering and Science, Shanghai University, Shanghai, China
{wxz2017,lliuyang,cydshu,superjiang,ivanzhang}@shu.edu.cn

Abstract. Discovering efficient exploration strategies is a central challenge in reinforcement learning (RL). Deep reinforcement learning (DRL) methods proposed in recent years have mainly focused on improving the generalization of models while ignoring models' explanation. In this study, an embedding explanation for the advantage actor-critic algorithm (EEA2C) is proposed to balance the relationship between exploration and exploitation for DRL models. Specifically, the proposed algorithm explains agent's actions before employing explanation to guide exploration. A fusion strategy is then designed to retain information that is helpful for exploration from experience. Based on the results of the fusion strategy, a variational autoencoder (VAE) is designed to encode the task-related explanation into a probabilistic latent representation. The latent representation of the VAE is finally incorporated into the agent's policy as prior knowledge. Experimental results for six Atari environments show that the proposed method improves the agent's exploratory capabilities with explainable knowledge.

Keywords: Deep reinforcement learning · Explainable AI · Explanation fusion · Variational auto encoder

1 Introduction

Deep reinforcement learning (DRL) has been widely studied and applied in various fields such as gaming, autonomous driving, and robotics [1,14,22]. However, the evaluation-based nature of DRL makes exploitation necessary, and continuous exploration is required to improve decision-making. Therefore, the exploration-exploitation dilemma is a central challenge in DRL [19]. Exploration refers to trying new actions in unknown environments, whereas exploitation refers to acting based on historical experience. The agent must take action based on exploration and exploitation to obtain high cumulative rewards. DRL methods proposed in recent years have mainly focused on improving the generalization of models while ignoring the exploration-exploitation dilemma, and balancing the relationship between exploration and exploitation is difficult.

© The Author(s), under exclusive license to Springer Nature Switzerland AG 2022
G. Memmi et al. (Eds.): KSEM 2022, LNAI 13369, pp. 200–211, 2022.
https://doi.org/10.1007/978-3-031-10986-7_16

Many approaches have been proposed to solve the exploration-exploitation dilemma, such as noise-based exploration strategies [7,16] and intrinsic reward-based exploration methods [2,12,20]. However, the uncertainty caused by existing noise-based exploration strategies is task-independent, which reduces exploration efficiency. The reward function in intrinsic reward-based methods is artificially designed, which does not ensure that it is suitable for complex environments, and the above methods cannot achieve effective exploration.

Moreover, the weak explainability of DRL agents makes it impossible to thoroughly understand and analyze data, models, and applications [5,23]. This causes disparities between the realistic performance of an agent and expectations. One approach to explaining the decision-making of a network is visual explanation, which has been studied in the field of computer vision [9,18]. A visual explanation analyzes the network output factors by generating a heat map, which highlights the critical regions in an input image. Visual explanation methods have also been applied to explain an agent's decision-making process [11,24]. However, these explanatory methods merely analyze how an agent makes decisions and fail to utilize the explained information to optimize the agent.

The agent assesses how well it learns about an environment task based on the uncertainty of network predictions [4,12,15]. The uncertainty of traditional exploration strategies is unrelated to environmental tasks, which leads to inefficient exploration. Recent exploratory approaches suggest that task-related information can guide an agent's exploration, such as discovering bottleneck states [10], learning feature spaces [8], and VARIBAD [25]. The activation maps generated by the visual explanation contain task targets, which can be transformed into task-related uncertainty to guide the agent's exploration.

In this study, an embedding explanation for the advantage actor-critic algorithm (EEA2C) is proposed based on the advantage actor-critic (A2C) architecture. The proposed method provides a novel exploration strategy that employs task-related explanations. EEA2C first uses a gradient-based explanation method to generate activation maps. Meanwhile, a fusion strategy is designed to retain helpful information for exploration from experience. Second, a variational auto-encoder (VAE) is designed to project the fused experience into a probabilistic latent representation, which represents the inherent structure of the task-related environment. Finally, the latent variables are fed to the actor-critic network for training. The agent's policy is conditioned on both the environmental state and latent variables. The contributions of this study are as follows.

- We propose a reinforcement-learning algorithm EEA2C with a novel exploration strategy. The algorithm overcomes the inefficiency of exploration by employing VAE techniques to encode the experience of the fusion explanation.
- The proposed algorithm customizes an explanation module and a fusion strategy, compensating for traditional explanation methods that cannot optimize the agent.
- Experiments are conducted in the ATARI environment to evaluate the performance and advantages of the proposed algorithm. The experimental results prove that the proposed algorithm promotes the agent's policy learning abilities and increases explainability.

2 Preliminaries

This section introduces the concepts of reinforcement learning and variational inference and provides definitions of commonly used symbols.

2.1 Reinforcement Learning

Standard reinforcement learning based on the Markov decision process (MDP) is represented by a five-tuple of $(\mathcal{S}, \mathcal{A}, \mathcal{P}, r, \gamma)$, where $\mathcal{S}$ is a finite set of states, $\mathcal{A}$ is a finite set of actions, and $\mathcal{P}$ is the unknown state-transition probability function. r is the immediate reward associated with taking action $a \in \mathcal{A}$ while transitioning from state $s_t \in \mathcal{S}$ to state $s_{t+1} \in \mathcal{S}$. $\gamma \in [0, 1]$ is the discount factor that represents the trade-off between maximizing immediate and future returns. The goal of the agent is to identify a policy π that maximizes its expected reward, where the cumulative return at each time step is $R_t = \sum_{n=t}^{\infty} \gamma^{n-t} r_n$.

2.2 Variational Inference

The goal of variational inference is to approximate the conditional probabilities of latent variables considering the observed variables. Optimization methods can be used to solve this problem. Suppose $x = x_{1:n}$ denotes a set of observable datasets, and $z = z_{1:m}$ is a set of latent variables. Let $p(z, x)$ denote the joint probability, $p(z|x)$ be the conditional probability, and $p(x)$ be the evidence. The conditional probability, $p(z|x) = \frac{p(z,x)}{p(x)}$, can be solved using Bayesian inference. However, it is difficult to directly compute $p(x)$. Therefore, the probability density function $q(z)$ is determined using variational inference to approximate $p^*(z|x)$. $q*(z) = \arg\min KL(q(z)||p(z|x))$ is optimized to obtain the optimal $q*(z)$, where $q(z) \in Q$ is the approximate distribution and $p(z|x)$ is the required posterior probability distribution. The KL divergence can be expressed as

$$KL(q(z)||p(z|x)) = \mathbb{E}[\log q(z)] - \mathbb{E}[\log p(z, x)] + \log p(x), \tag{1}$$

where $\log p(x)$ is a constant and the KL divergence is greater than zero. The final goal of variational inference is as follows:

$$\begin{aligned} \log p(x) &\geq \log p(z|x) - \log q(z) \\ &= ELBO, \end{aligned} \tag{2}$$

which is called the evidence lower-bound objective (ELBO).

3 Proposed Method

This section describes the architecture of the EEA2C and the workflow of the proposed algorithm.

3.1 Network Architecture

The trained network is shown in Fig. 1. The proposed model includes four main modules: actor, critic, explanation, and inference. The actor and critic share the state encoder and internal network used to train the policy. The explanation module generates a task-related activation map using an activation gradient mapping approach. The activation maps are fused to the original states using a fusion strategy. The inference module extracts the latent structure of the fused information by training a variational autoencoder (VAE). The inference module encodes a fused experience to derive a latent variable distribution. The inferred latent variables are employed to train the actor and critic modules as prior knowledge.

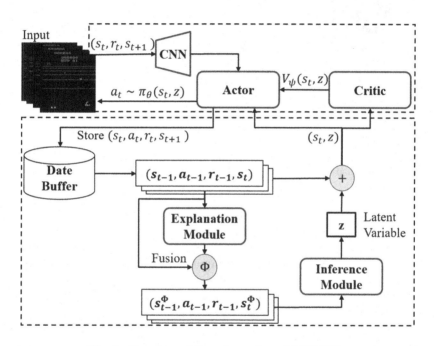

Fig. 1. Overview of the proposed model EEA2C.

Each actor, critic, and inference module is a multilayer neural network. In the inference module, let q_ω denote the encoder with parameters ω. p_ν denotes the decoder with parameter ν. Let z denote the latent variable and $z \sim q_\omega$. Let π_θ denote an actor with parameters θ. Let V_ψ denote the critic with parameter ψ, and let D denote the experience data buffer. The module outputs can either be concatenated or added to obtain the other module's input. This algorithm is introduced in detail in the following sections.

3.2 Explanation of Actions with Activation Maps

During each iteration, the agent employs policy π_θ to interact with the environment and obtain a series of experiences, which are stored in the data buffer D. Then, the experience sample $\tau_{:t}$ is sampled from D and denoted as

$$\tau_{:t} = \{s_0, a_0, r_0, ..., s_m, ..., a_{t-1}, r_{t-1}, s_t\}. \tag{3}$$

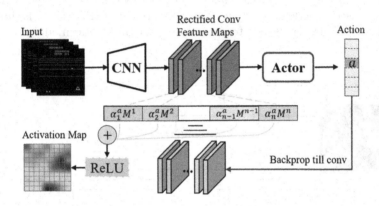

Fig. 2. Explanation module: activation map produced by the explanation module based on the state-action pair.

To obtain the activation map of state s_m in $\tau_{:t}$, an explanation module is designed (see Fig. 2) by modifying the Grad-Cam approach [18]. Each state s_m in $\tau_{:t}$ is convolved and computed by the actor to obtain a_m. Subsequently, the gradient of the score for action a_m is computed with respect to the feature map activations M^k of the last convolutional layer. These gradients flowing back are averaged over the width and height dimensions (indexed by i and j, respectively) to obtain the neuron importance weights $\alpha_k^{a_m}$:

$$\alpha_k^{a_m} = \frac{1}{T} \sum_i \sum_j \frac{\partial \pi^{a_m}}{\partial M_{ij}^k}, \tag{4}$$

where $\alpha_k^{a_m}$ is the weight of action a in the k-th channel. π^{a_m} is the probability that the agent selects action a_m and T denotes the normalization factor used to ensure that the sum of the gradient weights of each channel is 1 (for example, $\sum_k \alpha_k^{a_m} = 1$). The weight $\alpha_k^{a_m}$ represents a partial linearization of the agent downstream from M and captures the importance of feature map k for action a_m. We perform a weighted combination of forward activation maps, followed by a *ReLU*, to obtain the final activation map e_m, which can be denoted as

$$e_m = ReLU(\sum_k \alpha_k^{a_m} M^k), \tag{5}$$

where the $ReLU$ operation is used to retain regions that have a positive effect on action a_m. The activation map e_m takes values in the range of $[0,1]$, indicating the relevance of the region in s_m to a_m. Each state s_m in $\tau_{:t}$ is explained sequentially, and the explanation module outputs the set of activation maps $e_{:t}$:

$$e_{:t} = \{e_0, e_1, ..., e_m, ..., e_t\}. \tag{6}$$

3.3   Fusion Activation Maps and States

Based on the above methods, EEA2C can obtain activation maps $e_{:t}$ of $\tau_{:t}$ from the explanation module. A straightforward method that may be used to focus an agent on the task-related regions is to multiply e_m and s_m. However, when multiplying e_m and s_m, the zero values in the activation maps lead to incomplete state information. This disrupts the agent's training, makes policy learning unstable, and fails to enable the agent to focus on task-related regions. To overcome this problem, we propose a state fusion strategy in which the state in $\tau_{:t}$ is reformulated as the weighted sum of the original state s_m and noisy background image g_m. The original state s_m is replaced with s_m^{Φ} via the fusion operation $\Phi(s_m, e_m)$, which is formulated as follows:

$$s_m^{\Phi} = \Phi(s_m, e_m) = s_m \cdot e_m + g_m \cdot (1 - e_m), \tag{7}$$

where g_m is a blurred image obtained by applying a Gaussian blur filter to the original image s_m [6]. The representation s_m^{Φ} of s_m is located in the natural state-space manifold. This formulation not only creates state s_m^{Φ} that matches the inner feature representation at s_m but also preserves the object localization information in e_m. The weight vector $e_m \in [0,1]$ denotes the significance of each region that contributes to the state representation s_m. The experience sample $\tau_{:t}$ is updated to $\tau_{:t}^{\Phi}$ after fusing the activation map e_m:

$$\tau_{:t}^{\Phi} = \{s_0^{\Phi}, a_0, r_0, ..., s_m^{\Phi}, ..., a_{t-1}, r_{t-1}, s_t^{\Phi}\}. \tag{8}$$

3.4   Encoding the Fused State with Variational Inference

To incorporate the fused experience $\tau_{:t}^{\Phi}$ into the training process of the policy, an additional probabilistic model is constructed to generate prior knowledge of the actor-critic network. The latent variables generated by the probabilistic model serve as task-related uncertainties to motivate exploration. Inferring the latent distribution $p(z|\tau_{:t}^{\Phi})$ is difficult owing to the intractable integrals involved. Inspired by VAEs, an inference module is designed to approximate the posterior distribution with a variational distribution $q(z|\tau_{:t}^{\Phi})$. The inference module consists of an encoder q_{ω} with parameter ω and a decoder p_{ν} with parameter ν. The encoder q_{ω} takes the experience $\tau_{:t}^{\Phi}$ and projects it into latent space Z. This latent space captures the factors of variation within a fused experience. The latent variable z ($z \in Z$) is subject to a normal distribution, and its parameters (μ and σ) are predicted directly by $q_{\omega}(z|\tau_{:t}^{\Phi})$, as shown in Fig. 3.

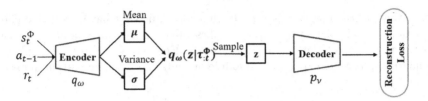

Fig. 3. Inference module: a trajectory of the fused explanation information is processed using an encoder to generate the posterior of the task embedding process. The posterior is trained with a decoder that predicts the past and future states and rewards from the fused state.

The inference module approximates the conditional probability of the latent variables in the posterior sample $\tau_{:t}^{\Phi}$. As with the target function of VAE, the optimization objective of the inference module is to maximize $ELBO$:

$$\mathcal{L}(\omega, \nu) = \mathbb{E}_{z \sim q_\omega(z|\tau_{:t}^{\Phi})}[\log p_\nu(\tau_{:t}^{\Phi}|z)] - KL(q_\omega(z|\tau_{:t}^{\Phi})||p_\nu(z))$$
$$= ELBO(\omega, \nu), \tag{9}$$

where the first term $\log p_\nu(\tau_{:t}^{\Phi}|z)$ denotes the reconstruction loss. The second term $KL(q_\omega(z|\tau_{:t}^{\Phi})||p_\nu(z))$ encourages the approximate posterior q_ω to remain close to the prior over the embedding $p_\nu(z)$. $p_\nu(z)$ is the prior probability of the latent variable z using a standard normal distribution, $p_\nu(z) = N(0, I)$.

Owing to the introduction of the task-related latent variable z, the optimization objective of the actor-critic network becomes

$$\mathcal{L}(\theta) = -log\pi_\theta(a_t|s_t, z)(R_t^n - V_\psi(s_t, z)) - \alpha \mathcal{H}_t(\pi_\theta), \tag{10}$$

$$\mathcal{L}(\psi) = \frac{1}{2}(V_\psi(s_t, z) - R_t^n)^2, \tag{11}$$

where $R_t = \sum_{i=0}^{n-1} \gamma^i r_{t+i} + \gamma^n V_\psi(s_{t+n})$ is the n-step bootstrapped return and α is the weight of the standard entropy regularization loss term. Our overall objective is to minimize

$$\mathcal{L}(\theta, \psi, \omega, \nu) = \mathcal{L}(\theta) + \beta\mathcal{L}(\psi) - \lambda\mathcal{L}(\omega, \nu), \tag{12}$$

where β is the weight for the critic loss and λ is the weight inference module. The actor-critic network and the inference module are trained using different data buffers: the actor-critic network is only trained with the most recent data because we use on-policy algorithms in our experiments; for the inference module, we maintain a separate, larger buffer of observed trajectories.

4 Experiments and Results

4.1 Environment and Experimental Settings

EEA2C was evaluated for six control tasks in OpenAI Gym [3]. In all tasks, the reward for each step of the agent was limited to $[0, 1]$ during training. The algorithm uses 16 parallel actors to collect the agent's experience with a five-step rollout, yielding a minibatch of size 80 for on-policy transitions. The last four observation frames are stacked as inputs, each of which is resized to 84 × 84 and converted to grayscale in [13]. The episode is set as the end of the game instead of losing a life. Each episode is initialized with a random seed of no-ops [14].

The method proposed in this study is based on the A2C framework [13]. The actor and critic networks use the same structure, employing a multi-layer perceptron (MLP) with two implicit layers 64 × 64. The inference module uses a simpler network structure that outputs the mean and variance of the latent variables. The experimental results are obtained by averaging five random seeds, each with 2×10^7 frames.

4.2   Comparisons with Benchmark Algorithms

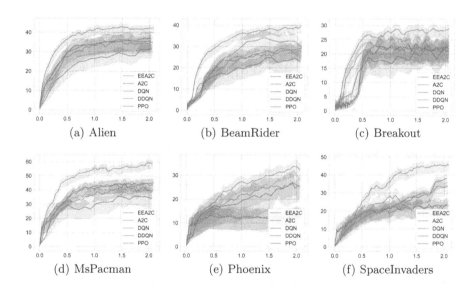

(a) Alien   (b) BeamRider   (c) Breakout

(d) MsPacman   (e) Phoenix   (f) SpaceInvaders

Fig. 4. Learning curves: expected return vs. number of training frames.

The DQN [14], DDQN [21], A2C [13] (with both separate and shared actor-critic networks), and PPO [17] algorithms were employed as benchmark algorithms for comparison. The learning speed of each algorithm was measured over a limited number of game frames. Figure 4 illustrates the learning curves of all algorithms. The learning curves were obtained by averaging the results over five random seeds. The experiments showed that EEA2C outperformed all benchmark algorithms in terms of the learning speed and improved the cumulative score for all exploration tasks.

Figure 4 shows the mean reward for the proposed method and the other benchmark algorithms, and the shaded areas represent the variance of the mean reward for each seed. From the above experimental results, the learning speed and target rewards of the EEA2C algorithm outperformed those of the other algorithms in all control tasks. The rewards that the EEA2C algorithm reaches require 0.2×10^7 time steps, whereas the benchmark algorithms require 1×10^7 time steps to reach these rewards. As the number of training frames increased, superior rewards to the benchmark algorithms were eventually achieved. In each environment, the shaded area of EEA2C is smaller than those of the other algorithms, indicating that EEA2C performs more consistently across multiple seeds.

From Fig. 4, the prior experience sample is shown to be insufficient at the beginning of training, and the target in the activation map is scattered. In this case, the confidence interval of the latent variables is large, which leads to an unstable distribution. Therefore, the agent was more inclined to explore. As more data are collected, the high-value regions in the activation map become concentrated, and the distribution of the latent variables tends to stabilize. Meanwhile, the agent begins to exploit and the cumulative rewards tend to stabilize.

Table 1. Evaluation scores over 50 recent episodes on average. The best scores are in bold.

Environment	Random	DQN	DDQN	PPO	A2C	EEA2C
Alien	240	2391	2041	1970	2091	**3161**
BeamRider	264	3627	3172	2750	3164	**4356**
Breakout	3	518	520	417	435	**624**
MsPacman	150	3180	2960	2350	2880	**4830**
Phoenix	440	10840	12250	20840	22530	**28530**
SpaceInvaders	120	3929	3672	4855	4673	**7673**

Table 1 shows that EEA2C achieves a better performance than the benchmark with a large margin in six tasks. Compared with the best score of the benchmark algorithm, EEA2C achieved a 32.2% improvement on Alien, 20.1% improvement on BeamRider, 20.0% improvement on Breakout, 51.8% improvement on MsPacman, 26.6% improvement on Phoenix, and 58.0% improvement on SpaceInvaders. EEA2C achieved a better average reward than the benchmark when trained with limited frames. Therefore, further performance improvements can be expected when EEA2C uses more training frames or a large-scale distributed computing platform.

4.3 Analysis of Explainability

This section analyzes how the activation maps generated by the explanation module are associated with the action of the agent. The activation map can be overlayed onto the original state to indicate evidence of the agent's action. As shown in Fig. 5, for the action predicted by the agent, a more-intensely red-colored area indicates a more significant contribution, which can be used as the main basis for determining the predicted action. The activation map enables an understanding of the regions that the agent focuses on when taking action, which improves the explainability of the algorithm.

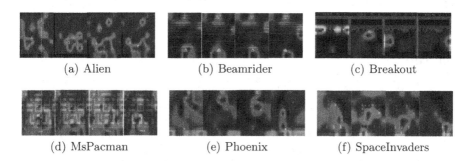

| (a) Alien | (b) Beamrider | (c) Breakout |
| (d) MsPacman | (e) Phoenix | (f) SpaceInvaders |

Fig. 5. Regions related to the agent's decision are shown by adding the activation maps to the image, where red regions correspond to high scores while blue corresponds to low scores. (Color figure online)

The target in the ATARI environment appears periodically at a specific location. Based on Fig. 5, we can conclude that the agent's focus becomes increasingly concentrated. The agent gradually learns to focus on task-related targets and takes corresponding actions rather than reacting irrelevantly to state-specific patterns. For example, in Alien 5(a) and SpaceInvader 5(f), the agent appropriately reacts to the emergence of the enemy. The agent notices the enemy, moves towards it, fires at it, and then turns away. When there are no objects in the image, the agent moves as little as possible to avoid mistakes. The agent learns a path to the target object among the worlds by forwarding planning elements and lattice classes. Figure 5(d) shows an example of MsPacman. The agent scans the route to ensure that there are no enemies or ghosts ahead. When the food appears on the screen, the agent generates a path to this food.

5   Conclusion

This study proposes EEA2C to balance the relationship between exploration and exploitation. Unlike previous research, this algorithm explains the agent's actions and employs the explanation to guide the agent's exploration. Simultaneously, an inference module was designed to encode the explanation into a probabilistic latent representation, which can be incorporated into the policy as task-related uncertainty. Experiments were conducted in the ATARI environment to evaluate the performance and advantages of the proposed algorithm. The experimental results showed that the EEA2C outperformed existing methods in terms of the achieved reward during a single episode. The uncertainty provided by the latent variables promoted policy learning. Furthermore, the activation maps generated by the explanation module augmented the agent's explainability. Task-related uncertainty can be obtained from explanation or provided by external expert experience. In future work, we will consider other ways of capturing task-related uncertainties to guide agents in more efficient exploration.

Acknowledgements. This work is sponsored by Shanghai Sailing Program (NO. 20YF1413800).

References

1. Baker, B., et al.: Emergent tool use from multi-agent autocurricula. In: 8th International Conference on Learning Representations. OpenReview.net (2020)
2. Bellemare, M.G., Srinivasan, S., Ostrovski, G., Schaul, T., Saxton, D., Munos, R.: Unifying count-based exploration and intrinsic motivation. In: Advances in Neural Information Processing Systems, vol. 29, pp. 1471–1479 (2016)
3. Brockman, G., et al.: OpenAI gym. arXiv preprint arXiv:1606.01540 (2021)
4. Burda, Y., Edwards, H., Pathak, D., Storkey, A., Darrell, T., Efros, A.A.: Large-scale study of curiosity-driven learning. arXiv preprint arXiv:1808.04355 (2018)
5. Chakraborty, S., et al.: Interpretability of deep learning models: a survey of results. In: Smartworld, pp. 1–6 (2017)
6. Fong, R.C., Vedaldi, A.: Interpretable explanations of black boxes by meaningful perturbation. In: Proceedings of the IEEE International Conference on Computer Vision, pp. 3429–3437 (2017)
7. Fortunato, M., et al.: Noisy networks for exploration. arXiv preprint arXiv:1706.10295 (2017)
8. François-Lavet, V., Bengio, Y., Precup, D., Pineau, J.: Combined reinforcement learning via abstract representations. In: Proceedings of the AAAI Conference on Artificial Intelligence, pp. 3582–3589 (2019)
9. Fukui, H., Hirakawa, T., Yamashita, T., Fujiyoshi, H.: Attention branch network: learning of attention mechanism for visual explanation. In: Proceedings of the IEEE/CVF Conference on Computer Vision and Pattern Recognition, pp. 10705–10714 (2019)
10. Goyal, A., et al.: InfoBot: transfer and exploration via the information bottleneck. arXiv preprint arXiv:1901.10902 (2019)
11. Greydanus, S., Koul, A., Dodge, J., Fern, A.: Visualizing and understanding Atari agents. In: International Conference on Machine Learning, pp. 1792–1801 (2018)
12. Houthooft, R., Chen, X., Duan, Y., Schulman, J., De Turck, F., Abbeel, P.: VIME: variational information maximizing exploration. In: Advances in Neural Information Processing Systems, vol. 29 (2016)
13. Mnih, V., et al.: Asynchronous methods for deep reinforcement learning. In: International Conference on Machine Learning, pp. 1928–1937. PMLR (2016)
14. Mnih, V., et al.: Human-level control through deep reinforcement learning. Nature **518**(7540), 529–533 (2015)
15. Pathak, D., Agrawal, P., Efros, A.A., Darrell, T.: Curiosity-driven exploration by self-supervised prediction. In: International Conference on Machine Learning, pp. 2778–2787. PMLR (2017)
16. Plappert, M., et al.: Parameter space noise for exploration. arXiv preprint arXiv:1706.01905 (2017)
17. Schulman, J., Wolski, F., Dhariwal, P., Radford, A., Klimov, O.: Proximal policy optimization algorithms. arXiv preprint arXiv:1707.06347 (2017)

18. Selvaraju, R.R., Cogswell, M., Das, A., Vedantam, R., Parikh, D., Batra, D.: Grad-CAM: visual explanations from deep networks via gradient-based localization. In: Proceedings of the IEEE International Conference on Computer Vision, pp. 618–626 (2017)
19. Sutton, R.S., Barto, A.G.: Reinforcement Learning: An Introduction. MIT Press, Cambridge (2018)
20. Tang, H., et al.: Exploration: a study of count-based exploration for deep reinforcement learning. In: Advances in Neural Information Processing Systems, vol. 30, pp. 2753–2762 (2017)
21. Van Hasselt, H., Guez, A., Silver, D.: Deep reinforcement learning with double Q-learning. In: Proceedings of the AAAI Conference on Artificial Intelligence (2016)
22. Vinyals, O., et al.: Grandmaster level in StarCraft II using multi-agent reinforcement learning. Nature **575**(7782), 350–354 (2019)
23. Wang, X., Sugumaran, V., Zhang, H., Xu, Z.: A capability assessment model for emergency management organizations. Inf. Syst. Front. **20**(4), 653–667 (2018). https://doi.org/10.1007/s10796-017-9786-7
24. Wang, X., Yuan, S., Zhang, H., Lewis, M., Sycara, K.P.: Verbal explanations for deep reinforcement learning neural networks with attention on extracted features. In: 28th IEEE International Conference on Robot and Human Interactive Communication, pp. 1–7. IEEE (2019)
25. Zintgraf, L.M., et al.: VariBAD: variational Bayes-adaptive deep RL via meta-learning. J. Mach. Learn. Res. **22**, 289:1–289:39 (2021)

CLINER: Clinical Interrogation Named Entity Recognition

Jing Ren[1], Tianyang Cao[1], Yifan Yang[2], Yunyan Zhang[2], Xi Chen[2],
Tian Feng[1], Baobao Chang[1(✉)], Zhifang Sui[1(✉)], Ruihui Zhao[2],
Yefeng Zheng[2], and Bang Liu[3(✉)]

[1] Key Laboratory of Computational Linguistics,
Peking University, MOE, Beijing, China
{rjj,ctymy,fengtian0808,chbb,szf}@pku.edu.cn
[2] Tencent Techonology Inc., Shenzhen, China
{tobyfyang,yunyanzhang,jasonxchen,zacharyzhao,yefengzheng}@tencent.com
[3] University of Montreal, Montreal, Canada
bang.liu@umontreal.ca

Abstract. The automatic generation of electronic medical record
(EMR) data aims to create EMRs from raw medical text (e.g., doctor-
patient interrogation dialog text) without human efforts. A critical problem is how to accurately locate the medical entities mentioned in the
doctor-patient interrogation text, as well as identify the state of each
clinical entity (e.g., whether a patient genuinely suffers from the mentioned disease). Such precisely extracted medical entities and their states
can facilitate clinicians to trace the whole interrogation process for medical decision-making. In this work, we annotate and release an online
clinical dialog NER dataset that contains 72 types of clinical items and
3 types of states. Existing conventional named entity recognition (NER)
methods only take a candidate entity's surrounding context information
into consideration. However, identifying the state of a clinical entity mentioned in a doctor-patient dialog turn requires the information across the
whole dialog rather than only the current turn. To bridge the gap, we
further propose CLINER, a **CL**inical **I**nterrogation NER model, which
exploits both fine-grained and coarse-grained information for each dialog turn to facilitate the extraction of entities and their corresponding
states. Extensive experiments on the medical dialog information extraction (MIE) task and clinical interrogation named entity recognition task
show that our approach shows significant performance improvement (3.72
on NER F1 and 6.12 on MIE F1) over the state-of-art on both tasks.

Keywords: Clinical named entity recognition · Information
extraction · Coarse-grained and fine-grained context · Historical
pattern memory · BERT

J. Ren and T. Cao—Equal contribution.

© The Author(s), under exclusive license to Springer Nature Switzerland AG 2022
G. Memmi et al. (Eds.): KSEM 2022, LNAI 13369, pp. 212–224, 2022.
https://doi.org/10.1007/978-3-031-10986-7_17

1 Introduction

Electronic medical records (EMR) are widely used in modern health care information systems to store the information concerning individual health histories. While EMRs play a key role in modern health care systems, it is an exhausting and time-consuming task for doctors to write an EMR for a patient. It was reported that the time that doctors spend on administrative work is almost twice as much as the time spent on consultation with patients, and the most time-consuming part is manually creating EMRs [13]. To relieve the heavy burden on doctors, the task of automatically converting doctor-patient dialogs into EMRs has become an emerging field in natural language processing domain in recent years [2,11,14]. To generate high-quality EMRs from doctor-patient dialogs, a core research problem is how to accurately extract the medical entities and their corresponding status from medical dialogs.

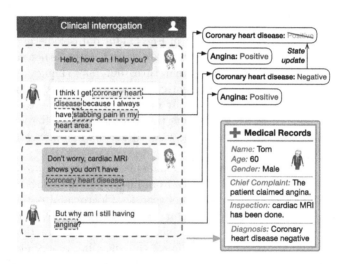

Fig. 1. Clinical interrogation named entity recognition helps medics automatically generate EMRs from the doctor-patient dialogs.

However, existing research focuses on extracting medical information in a turn-level context without considering the global consistency of entities' information. Taking Fig. 1 as an example for illustration, the patient initially thought he had coronary heart disease, but the doctor eventually overturned the hypothesis. In this case, the doctor will write "coronary heart disease: negative" on the EMR, where "coronary heart disease" is a medical named entity, and "negative" is the entity's state. However, existing approaches [2,6,13] only concentrate on extracting the medical items that are expressed in current turns and ignore their states, while the entity state (e.g., presence or absence of a symptom/disease) is critical for automatic generation of EMRs.

To bridge the gap between existing research and real-world scenarios of medical dialog, in this paper, we focus on accurately recognizing medical entities and their states that are expressed according to the entire dialog by considering both turn-level and dialog-level information. Specifically, we define the **state** of a medical item as its genuine condition expressed according to the dialog, including "positive", "negative" and "unknown", among which "positive" indicates that the patient actually suffers from one certain symptom or the doctor's diagnosis confirms one has the disease, while "negative" does the opposite. Specially, "unknown" refers to uncertain condition, i.e., medical report hasn't been prepared or the doctor is explaining some general scientific knowledge of the disease. We then define the state update mechanism. The entity state should comprehensively consider the surrounding dialog turns other than only focus on the current turn. Take the Fig. 1 for illustration, the patient perceives he may get Coronary heart disease, however, the doctor's decision denies his hypothesis, thus the correct state should be "negative".

Based on the above principles, we first annotate and release a dataset for **CL**inical **I**nterrogation **N**amed **E**ntity **R**ecognition (CLINER) considering the state update mechanism as illustrated in Fig. 1. Our dataset distinguishes from the conventional NER datasets since the state of each entity is not simply determined by the context within the current turn, but may change as the dialog proceeds. Besides, one certain named entity can have a massive quantity of variants as the colloquial expressions in our dataset are much more diverse than the formal writing, where it also hinders the conventional NER tools to obtain promising results. For example, in Fig. 1, both *stabbing pain in my heart area* and *angina* refer to a same entity.

To address the two aforementioned challenges, we further propose a novel NER model to recognize named entities from interrogation dialogs. Specifically, we define a window as a dialog turn between the doctor and patient (e.g., we have two dialog windows in Fig. 1). Our model integrates multi-level context information from the dialog, to be specific, label-window interaction and inter-window interaction is combined to enhance the encoding representation of the current window. We then adopt a two-stage prediction manner. Firstly the model classifies whether the window contains a specific type of entity, then it determines the start and end positions of entity spans within the current window.

We evaluate the model on our dataset with two separate tasks: medical dialog information extraction (MIE) and clinical interrogation named entity recognition (CLINER). Experimental results show that the proposed model outperforms the state-of-the-art results by 3.72% and 6.12% F1 score in MIE and NER tasks, respectively.

2 Proposed Method

In this section, we elaborate on the proposed CLINER, an end-to-end clinical interrogation named entity recognition model. The framework of CLINER is presented in Fig. 2, which contains five components: 1) a window encoder that converts the raw input to contextual representation; 2) a fine-grained dialog-aware aggregation module that preserves consistent entity mention semantics in the whole dialog to provide complementary information for each given token; 3) a label-aware fusion module that models the relevance of the label information with the window representation; 4) a coarse-grained global contextual aggregation module that takes the most informative following window into account; and 5) a predictor module that generates the tags for MIE task and NER task, respectively. In addition, we share the model parameters for both MIE and NER tasks, and jointly train them under a multi-task training framework.

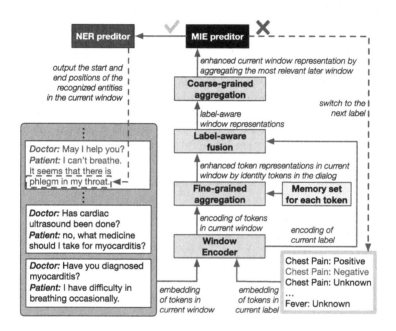

Fig. 2. Overview of the framework of CLINER.

2.1   Model Design

Window Encoder. In our model, we define two consecutive utterances as a window, which is constituted by an utterance from the doctor and an utterance from the patient, respectively. Accordingly, the entire interrogation dialog $\mathcal{D}$ can be divided into multiple windows $\{X_1, X_2, ..., X_N\}$, where N denotes the number of the windows.

For each window X_i, we firstly concatenate the two utterances as a token sequence $X_i = \{x_1, x_2, ..., x_T\}$ and encode them into contextual token representations $H_i = \{h_1, h_2, ..., h_T\}$ as follows:

$$h_t = \text{Encoder}(x_t). \tag{1}$$

Different network architectures can be used for the Encoder, e.g., BiLSTM or BERT. For each candidate label l in the label set $\mathcal{L}$, we also adopt the above method to encode it into contextual semantic vector h^l.

Fine-Grained Dialog-Aware Aggregation. The state of an entity is related to all the identical entities in the entire dialog. Intuitively, we can infer that it is necessary for the model to leverage the holistic information from all other instances into the current entity in order to gain the contextual knowledge. We introduce the dialog-aware representation for each token by leveraging a key-value memory network [9]. Specifically, we define a memory set $\mathcal{M} = \{(k_1, v_1), (k_2, v_2), ..., (k_M, v_M)\}$ for each token to store all the identical tokens within the dialog, where the key k_m represents the positional information of the m-th instance, i.e., its window index amongst the dialog and its token index amongst the window. The value v_m represents the hidden state h_m of the given token. M is the number of instances. The hidden states of tokens are fine-tuned during training and used to update the value part of the memory.

For each token x_t, in order to aggregate the dialog-aware representation, its contextual representation h_t is adopted as attention key to calculate the attention scores amongst the other hidden states h_m in memory set $\mathcal{M}$ as follows:

$$s_{tm} = \frac{h_t \cdot h_m^\top}{\sqrt{d_e}}, \tag{2}$$

where d_e denotes the dimension of token embedding. Accordingly, the dialog-aware representation is computed as:

$$a_{tm} = \frac{\exp(s_{tm})}{\sum_{k=1}^{M} \exp(s_{tk})}, \tag{3}$$

$$h_t^d = \sum_{m=1}^{M} a_{tm} \cdot v_m. \tag{4}$$

Then, we integrate the original hidden state h_t with the dialog-aware representation h_t^d to form a new contextual representation g_t, which will be further fed to the following label-sentence attention module:

$$g_t = \lambda \cdot h_t + (1 - \lambda) \cdot h_t^d, \tag{5}$$

where λ is a hyper-parameter to balance the hidden state h_t and dialog-aware representation h_t^d.

Label-Aware Fusion. The label-sentence attention is devised to incorporate the label information h^l into the current window representation. Formally, we treat label representation h^l as a query in attention mechanism to compute the attention scores towards each contextual token representations g_t within the window. Then we can obtain the label-specific current window representation c^l as follows:

$$s_t^l = \frac{h^l \cdot g_t^\top}{\sqrt{d_e}}, \tag{6}$$

$$a_t^l = \frac{\exp(s_t^l)}{\sum_{k=1}^T \exp(s_k^l)}, \tag{7}$$

$$c^l = \sum_{t=1}^T a_t^l g_t, \tag{8}$$

where T is the sequence length of the current window. In this sense, the model is capable of determining the existence of entities of label l type in the current window, as well as predicting the entity spans.

Coarse-Grained Global Contextual Aggregation. Since the state in the current window is not only determined by the current context, but also the relevant information from the following windows, we need to take the interactions between windows into account. It is unnecessary to consider the windows prior to the current window, as the states only update based on the following interrogation text rather than the previous text.

We employ a dynamic attention mechanism to achieve this. Concretely, we take the current i-th window embedding $c_i^l = c^l$ as attention query $\mathbf{Q}$, the following window embeddings $\{c_{i+1}^l, ..., c_N^l\}$ as key matrix $\mathbf{K}$ and value matrix $\mathbf{V}$. It is so-called "dynamic" as the number of following window embeddings reduces when the dialog proceeds, and the last window does not have any following window embedding.

The following window embedding with the highest attention score c_g^l will be considered as the most informative embedding for the current window, and c_g^l will be adopted as our global contextual embedding and be concatenated to the current window embedding to facilitate predicting the state.

Formally, given the current window embedding c_i^l, we select the most informative following window by:

$$s_{ij}^l = \frac{c_i^l \cdot c_j^{l\top}}{\sqrt{d_e}}, \tag{9}$$

$$a_{ij}^l = \frac{\exp(s_{ij}^l)}{\sum_{k=i+1}^N \exp(s_{ik}^l)}, \tag{10}$$

$$c_g^l = c_{\arg\max_j(a_{ij}^l)}^l, \tag{11}$$

where $i + 1 \le g \le N$. Then the window embedding c_g^l with highest attention score is concatenated to our current window embedding c_i^l to form the global embedding c_G^l:

$$c_{i,G}^l = [c_i^l; c_g^l], \tag{12}$$

where ";" denotes concatenation operation, and c_g^l is set as zero vector if the current window is the last one in the interrogation text.

Predictor

MIE Predictor. The output of the global contextual aggregation module $c_{i,G}^l$ is fed into this module. Specifically, we iterate over each MIE label $l \in \mathcal{L}$ and adopt a binary classifier to predict the MIE label:

$$\tilde{y}_i^l = \mathrm{Sigmoid}(\mathrm{FFN}(c_{i,G}^l)), \tag{13}$$

where $\mathrm{FFN}(\cdot)$ is a feed-forward neural network. A positive result indicates that at least one entity of type l exists in the current i-th window.

NER Predictor. For each window, we first predict the MIE labels, then we align MIE labels to the corresponding spans within the current window as our predicted entities. Given an MIE label l, we adopt a PointerNet [11] to obtain the start and end positions of each entity:

$$\tilde{y}_{i,t,start}^l = \mathrm{Sigmoid}(\mathrm{FFN}([g_{i,t}; h_l])), \tag{14}$$

$$\tilde{y}_{i,t,end}^l = \mathrm{Sigmoid}(\mathrm{FFN}([g_{i,t}; h_l])), \tag{15}$$

where i denotes the i-th window.

Training. In our model, we jointly train the MIE and NER tasks and optimize the cross entropy loss function as the following:

$$\mathcal{L}_{\mathrm{MIE}} = \sum_{l \in \mathcal{L}} \sum_{i=1}^N y_i^l \log \tilde{y}_i^l, \tag{16}$$

$$\mathcal{L}_{\mathrm{NER}} = \sum_{p \in \{s,e\}} \sum_{l \in \mathcal{L}} \sum_{i=1}^N \sum_{t=1}^T y_{i,t,p}^l \log \tilde{y}_{i,t,p}^l, \tag{17}$$

$$\mathcal{L}_{\mathrm{joint}} = \mathcal{L}_{\mathrm{MIE}} + \mathcal{L}_{\mathrm{NER}}, \tag{18}$$

where N is the number of windows in the dialog, and s, e represent the start and end positions, respectively.

3   Experiments

In this section, we carry out experiments on both NER and MIE tasks on the proposed dataset. Dataset & Annotation details are elaborated in our Github.[1]

---

[1] https://github.com/caotianyang/CLINER/tree/master.

3.1 Baselines and Evaluation Metrics

For the NER task, on the one hand, we compare our proposed model with the traditional sequence labeling models, including **BiLSTM-CRF**, **BERT-SOFTMAX**, **BERT-CRF**, **BERT-SPAN**, and **BERT-LSTM-CRF**. On the other hand, we also compare our model with the state-of-the-art NER methods in both the general domain and Chinese medical domain [5,7,9,10,12]. Due to lack of source code and the difficulty of model replication, several Chinese dialog NER models are not selected as our baselines [2,3,6]. We report Precision/Recall/F1 score for evaluation.

For the MIE task, we only use the dialog-level metric, as window-level metric contains massive label redundancy, in which each label may be counted several times for evaluation. Specifically, we merge the results of the windows that belong to the same clinical interrogation, then we evaluate the results of each interrogation text.

3.2 Experimental Settings

For a fair comparison, our setups are basically consistent with MIE [8]. We use 300-dimensional Skip-Gram [5] word embeddings pre-trained on medical dialog corpora from a Chinese online health community. Additionally, we also use Chinese-BERT-wwm [1] as our pre-trained model. The size of the hidden states of both feed-forward network and Bi-LSTM is 400. Adam is adopted for optimization [2], and we use dropout and $L2$ weight regularization to alleviate the overfitting problem and adopt early stopping using the F1 score on the development set. All experiments are run for three times and the averaged score is reported to achieve reliable results.

3.3 Results and Analysis

NER Results. Table 1 shows the precision, recall and F1 score of our model and other baselines on the test set of the NER task. We observe that the BERT-based baselines achieve about 45% F1 score on our dataset. The current state-of-the-art models achieve similar results ranging from 45.42% to 48.13% in F1 score. Furthermore, by fully exploiting the information in the scope of the entire dialog, our proposed CLINER-LSTM outperforms the baseline models and obtained 48.61% F1 score even though we do not utilize pre-trained models. Finally, our CLINER-BERT gains the state-of-the-art result with 52.01% precision, 51.70% recall and 51.85% F1 score, respectively.

We also evaluate our model and baselines on the subset of the test set which only contains samples with updated states. As shown in Table 1, our model outperforms the baseline models and achieves the best performance of 49.06% F1 score. This is because our model involves more useful features from the whole dialog via the designed fine-grained and coarse-grained aggregation models.

Table 1. Experimental results of the NER task.

	Full test set			Test set with updated states only		
	Prec. (%)	Rec. (%)	F1 (%)	Prec. (%)	Rec. (%)	F1 (%)
LSTM-CRF	35.64	41.07	38.16	31.91	42.57	36.48
BERT-CRF	41.19	46.28	43.59	37.44	47.05	41.70
BERT-SOFTMAX	45.75	44.78	45.26	39.62	43.23	41.39
BERT-LSTM-CRF	42.15	<u>49.49</u>	45.53	37.67	<u>49.67</u>	42.85
BERT-SPAN	47.34	44.27	45.75	40.97	42.20	41.58
Qiu et al. [3]	44.90	45.95	45.42	39.49	43.76	41.52
FLAT [1]	44.44	48.24	46.26	41.07	45.61	43.22
Zhang et al. [6]	45.48	49.47	47.39	<u>44.18</u>	46.03	45.08
Sui et al. [4]	48.97	46.67	47.80	43.20	46.61	44.84
Ma et al. [2]	<u>51.33</u>	45.31	48.13	43.93	46.15	45.01
CLINER-LSTM	49.08	48.15	<u>48.61</u>	43.45	48.24	<u>45.72</u>
CLINER-BERT	**52.01**	**51.70**	**51.85**	**46.30**	**52.16**	**49.06**

Table 2. Experimental results of the MIE task with dialog-level evaluation metric [5].

	Category only			Category and state		
	Prec.(%)	Rec. (%)	F1 (%)	Prec. (%)	Rec. (%)	F1 (%)
Plain-classifier	81.75	73.76	77.29	59.98	52.65	56.08
MIE-single	87.02	80.02	83.46	<u>61.15</u>	61.30	61.09
MIE-multi	85.32	80.48	82.83	60.30	60.78	60.54
CLINER-LSTM	<u>88.48</u>	<u>84.10</u>	<u>86.24</u>	59.85	<u>63.60</u>	<u>61.67</u>
CLINER-BERT	**91.02**	**86.97**	**88.95**	**62.31**	**65.72**	**63.97**

MIE Results. The experimental results are shown in Table 2. Both MIE-single and MIE-multi models obtain better results than the Plain-classifier model, which indicates that MIE architecture is more effective than a basic LSTM representation method. Compared to the baseline model in MIE, our model can not only capture the interactions between utterances and labels but also integrate the information from the following windows. Therefore, our proposed CLINER-BERT achieves the state-of-the-art results with 88.95% and 63.97% F1 scores in category level evaluation and category-and-state level, respectively. Even if we utilize the BiLSTM as model encoder as they did in the baselines, our CLINER-LSTM still outperforms all these baselines by 2.78% and 0.58% F1 scores, respectively.

Table 3. The ablation study with different settings.

	Category only			Category and state		
	Prec. (%)	Rec. (%)	F1 (%)	Prec. (%)	Rec. (%)	F1 (%)
CLINER-BERT	**62.31**	**65.72**	**63.97**	**52.01**	**51.70**	**51.85**
Without memory	57.81	67.53	62.29	48.16	51.02	49.55
Without global contextual aggregation	57.01	66.13	61.23	48.49	50.34	49.40
Without label info in NER	56.34	64.40	60.10	46.92	48.54	47.72

Table 4. State-specific evaluation on the NER task, where P., R., F. is abbreviate for Precsion, Recall and F1 score, respectively.

	Positive NER			Negative NER			Unknown NER		
	P. (%)	R. (%)	F1. (%)	P. (%)	R. (%)	F1. (%)	P. (%)	R. (%)	F1. (%)
LSTM+CRF	39.04	56.20	46.07	15.68	7.76	10.39	10.01	13.71	11.56
BERT+CRF	**54.84**	50.19	52.41	41.66	27.78	33.33	31.94	34.67	33.25
CLINER-LSTM	52.32	55.69	53.95	50.01	26.38	34.55	39.46	36.87	38.12
CLINER-BERT	54.42	**57.01**	**55.68**	**52.85**	**30.14**	**38.39**	**41.26**	**38.75**	**39.97**

Ablation Study. In this section, we estimate the effectiveness of the different model components in both NER and MIE tasks. CLINER-BERT represents the full model with all modules that achieves the best performance. The results shown in Table 3 suggest that getting rid of fine-grained dialog-aware representation deteriorates the F1 score with 1.68% and 2.30% drop. We can infer that the model performance is directly related to the information from all instances of the entity, which determines the change of the states in the entity-level. In addition, the model performance decreases by 1.06% and 0.15% without global contextual aggregation, as it incorporates the most informative window embedding in the following text to aid the current window in capturing the change of states. Finally, if we ignore the label information, the model suffers by 1.13% and 1.68% degradation in MIE and NER tasks, respectively. It indicates the label-sentence attention can capture the interaction between the current candidate label and the utterances as the most relevant tokens in the utterances will be highlighted, and NER task is strongly affected by the involvement of label information.

Case Study. We analyze our model by visualizing utterance-level and window-level attention heat maps of our model on a prediction example. Figure 3 presents the visualization of token-level and window-level attention heat maps on a prediction example of our model and baselines. The token-level attention visualization indicates that our model detects the tokens that are semantically related to the given category "myocardial infarction". We can easily find that the label

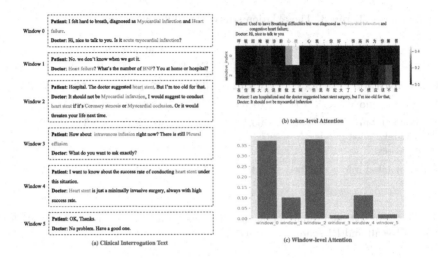

Fig. 3. The token-level and window-level attention visualization of our model on an example from the test set, which is assigned a ground-truth label "myocardial infarction: negative". (a) the clinical interrogation text; (b) token-level attention; and (c) window-level attention.

"myocardial infarction" attends to the text "myocardial infarction" with the highest weight in the current window. To further determine the state, the model computes the attention score between the current window and the following windows. Window 2, which has the highest attention score, is selected as our global information to add to the state prediction. We notice in the heatmap that the token "no" is highlighted and further utilized as a crucial reference to correctly predict the state "negative" for the given label in the current window. On the contrary, conventional NER methods are impossible to predict this label properly without considering the information from window 2, which ultimately leads to the failure of the state prediction in this window.

Performance for State Prediction. In this part, we analyze the effectiveness of the improvement for state prediction by our model. We carry out a quantitative experiment to verify this. Specifically, we split the test set into three groups according to the states and evaluate them separately. The results in Table 4 show that our proposed model outperforms the baselines in NER tasks across all the state types. In particular, our model gains significant improvement over *unknown* by 6.72% and 4.87% in F1 score respectively. As "unknown" is the state that has been updated most frequently, our model can capture these variations and obtain a promising result.

4   Conclusion

In this paper, we built a clinical interrogation NER dataset, and introduced an effective model for the clinical interrogation NER task. Our proposed CLINER model better captures the update of entity states by fully exploiting the relevant context from the following windows of the current window. Experiments in both NER and MIE tasks showed that our model could effectively boost the performance and outperformed the baselines. Our research provides a promising solution for the automatic EMR generation based on clinical interrogation. For future work, we plan to further leverage the internal relations between labels and incorporate medical domain knowledge into our model.

Acknowledgement. This paper is supported by NSFC project U19A2065.

References

1. Cui, Y., et al.: Pre-training with whole word masking for Chinese BERT. arXiv preprint arXiv:1906.08101 (2019)
2. DeLisle, S., et al.: Using the electronic medical record to identify community acquired pneumonia: toward a replicable automated strategy. PLoS ONE **8**(8), e70944 (2013)
3. Du, N., Chen, K., Kannan, A., Tran, L., Chen, Y., Shafran, I.: Extracting symptoms and their status from clinical conversations. arXiv preprint arXiv:1906.02239 (2019)
4. Finley, G., et al.: An automated medical scribe for documenting clinical encounters. In: Proceedings of the 2018 NAACL, pp. 11–15 (2018)
5. Kingma, D.P., Ba, J.: Adam: a method for stochastic optimization, vol. 9. arXiv preprint arXiv:1412.6980 (2018)
6. Li, X., Yan, H., Qiu, X., Huang, X.: FLAT: Chinese NER using flat-lattice transformer. arXiv preprint arXiv:2004.11795 (2020)
7. Lin, X., He, X., Chen, Q., Tou, H., Wei, Z., Chen, T.: Enhancing dialogue symptom diagnosis with global attention and symptom graph. In: Proceedings of the 2019 EMNLP-IJCNLP, pp. 5036–5045 (2019)
8. Ma, R., Peng, M., Zhang, Q., Huang, X.: Simplify the usage of lexicon in Chinese NER. arXiv preprint arXiv:1908.05969 (2019)
9. Mikolov, T., Grave, E., Bojanowski, P., Puhrsch, C., Joulin, A.: Advances in pre-training distributed word representations. arXiv preprint arXiv:1712.09405 (2017)
10. Miller, A., Fisch, A., Dodge, J., Karimi, A.H., Bordes, A., Weston, J.: Key-value memory networks for directly reading documents. arXiv preprint arXiv:1606.03126 (2016)
11. Persell, S.D., Karmali, K.N., et al.: Effect of electronic health record-based medication support and nurse-led medication therapy management on hypertension and medication self-management: a randomized clinical trial. JAMA Internal Med. **178**(8), 1069–1077 (2018)
12. Qiu, J., Zhou, Y., Wang, Q., Ruan, T., Gao, J.: Chinese clinical named entity recognition using residual dilated convolutional neural network with conditional random field. IEEE Trans. Nanobiosci. **18**(3), 306–315 (2019)

13. Sinsky, C., et al.: Allocation of physician time in ambulatory practice: a time and motion study in 4 specialties. Ann. Internal Med. **165**(11), 753–760 (2016)
14. Sui, D., Chen, Y., Liu, K., Zhao, J., Liu, S.: Leverage lexical knowledge for Chinese named entity recognition via collaborative graph network. In: Proceedings of the 2019 EMNLP-IJCNLP, pp. 3821–3831 (2019)

CCDC: A Chinese-Centric Cross Domain Contrastive Learning Framework

Hao Yang[1(✉)], Shimin Tao[1], Minghan Wang[1], Min Zhang[1], Daimeng Wei[1], Shuai Zhao[2], Miaomiao Ma[1], and Ying Qin[1]

[1] 2012 Labs, Huawei Technologies Co., Ltd., Beijing, China
{yanghao30,taoshimin,wangminghan,zhangmin186,weidaimeng,mamiaomiao,
qinying}@huawei.com
[2] Beijing University of Posts and Telecommunications, No. 10 Xitucheng Road,
Haidian District, Beijing, China
zhaoshuaiby@bupt.edu.cn

Abstract. Unsupervised/Supervised SimCSE [5] achieves the SOTA performance of sentence-level semantic representation based on contrastive learning and dropout data augmentation. In particular, supervised SimCSE mines positive pairs and hard-negative pairs through Natural Language Inference (NLI) entailment/contradiction labels, which significantly outperforms other unsupervised/supervised models. As NLI data is scarce, can we construct pseudo-NLI data to improve the semantic representation of multi-domain sentences? This paper proposes a Chinese-centric Cross Domain Contrastive learning framework (CCDC), which provides a "Hard/Soft NLI Data Builder" to annotate entailment/contradiction pairs through Business Rules and Neural Classifiers, especially out-domain but semantic-alike sentences as hard-negative samples. Experiments show that the CCDC framework can achieve both intra-domain and cross-domain enhancement. Moreover, with the Soft NLI Data Builder, the CCDC framework can achieve the best results of all domains with one model, improving 34% and 11% in terms of the Spearman correlation coefficient compared with the baseline (BERT-base) and strong baseline (unsupervised SimCSE). And through empirical analysis, this framework effectively reduces the anisotropy of the pre-trained models and shows semantic clustering over unsupervised SimCSE.

Keywords: Contrastive learning · SimCSE · Cross domain framework

1 Introduction

Learning universal sentence presentation is a fundamental problem in natural language processing and has been extensively studied in [12,16]. Based on Contrastive Learning [1,20], SimCSE [5] provides two simple but strong sentence semantic presentation models: (1) Unsupervised SimCSE, which extracts multi-view features [17] through dropout [15]. A sentence with itself is created as an

© The Author(s), under exclusive license to Springer Nature Switzerland AG 2022
G. Memmi et al. (Eds.): KSEM 2022, LNAI 13369, pp. 225–236, 2022.
https://doi.org/10.1007/978-3-031-10986-7_18

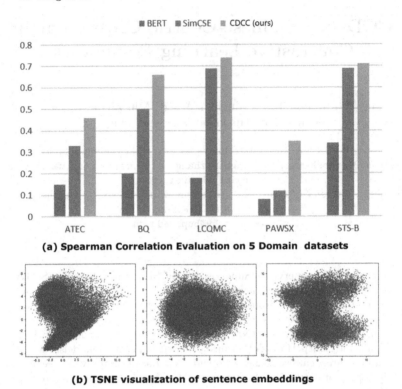

(a) Spearman Correlation Evaluation on 5 Domain datasets

(b) TSNE visualization of sentence embeddings

Fig. 1. Sentence-level representation and visual analysis of anisotropy in multiple domains under SBERT, unsupervised SimCSE and CCDC models

anchor-positive pair, while an anchor-negative pair is formed with other sentences in the batch. InfoNCE [1] loss is used to shorten the positive value and push the negative value away, and model parameters are optimized. Based on the multi-view learning of dropout, unsupervised SimCSE outperforms other unsupervised/supervised models. (2) Supervised SimCSE further improves performance by using NLI data labels as data augmentation. The entailment sentence pair is pictured as the anchor-positive pair, and the contradiction sentence pair as the hard-negative pair. Results show that unsupervised SimCSE exceeded the previous SOTA model IS-BERT [20] by 7.9%, while supervised SimCSE exceeded unsupervised SimCSE by 6.9%. Supervised SimCSE is also 4.6% higher than the previous supervised SOTA models SBERT [14] and BERT-whitening [16].

Extending supervised SimCSE to multi-domain sentence representation scenarios [24] requires solving two problems. One is hard-negative mining for out-domain but semantic-alike samples. Another is how to generate pseudo-NLI data from popular Chinese Sentence corpora, like sentence pairs PAWS-X [25]/BQ [2] or regression sentence pairs STS-B [13], and so on.

To solve these two problems, this paper provides a Chinese-centric Cross Domain Contrastive learning framework (CCDC) that adds two features: (a)

Domain augmentation Constrative Learning and (b) Pseudo NLI Data Generator . Domain augmentation Constrastive Learning uses out-domain but semantic - alike sentences as hard-negatives, improving cross-domain performance. Pseudo-NLI data generators, which help create $\langle anchor, positive, negative \rangle$ triplets from classification/regression sentence pair datasets, include business rule-based Hard NLI Generators and neural classifier-based Soft NLI Generators.

In order to better understand the superiority of CCDC, three model embedding spaces are mapped: the original BERT base model, the unsupervised SimCSE model, and the CCDC model. It finds that the anisotropy properties are optimized by unsupervised SimCSE and CCDC, while the CCDC model shows the domain clustering tendency [22]. Additional singular value experiments are visualized, showing that the domain-enhanced Contrastive Learning objective "flats" the singular value distribution of the sentence embedding space, thereby improving consistency.

2   Related Work

2.1   Contrastive Learning

Contrastive Learning aims to learn effective representation by pulling semantically close neighbors together and pushing apart non-neighbors [7]. It assumes a set of paired examples $D = f\{(x_i, x_i^+)\}_{i=1}^m$, where x_i and x_i^+ are semantically related. Following the contrastive framework in [3], the training object is a cross-entropy loss with in-batch negatives: let h_i and h_i^+ denote the representations of x_i and x_i^+, for a mini-batch with N pairs, the training objective for (x_i, x_i^+) is:

$$l_i = -log\frac{e^{sim(h_i, h_i^+)/\tau}}{\sum_{j=1}^N e^{sim(h_i, h_j^+)/\tau}},\tag{1}$$

where τ is a temperature hyperparameter and $sim(h1, h2)$ is the cosine similarity of $\frac{h_1^T h_2}{||h_1|| \cdot ||h_2||}$.

2.2   Unsupervised SimCSE

The idea of unsupervised SimCSE is extremely simple in a minimal form of data augmentation, where positive pairs are (x_i, x_i) , compared with the traditional (x_i, x_i^+). Unsupervised SimCSE takes exactly the same sentence as the positive pair, and its embeddings only differ in dropout masks.

$$l_i = -log\frac{e^{sim(h_i^{z_i}, h_i^{z_i'})/\tau}}{\sum_{j=1}^N e^{sim(h_i^{z_i}, h_j^{z_j'})/\tau}},\tag{2}$$

where $h_i^{z_i}, h_i^{z_i'}$ are the same sentence x_i with different dropout presentations z_i, z_i'.

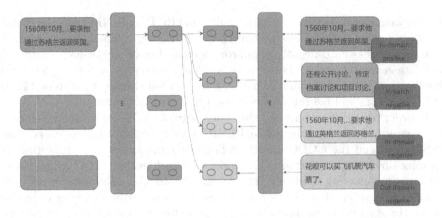

Fig. 2. CCDC framework

2.3 Supervised SimCSE

For supervised SimCSE, an easy hard-negative mining strategy is added that extends (x_i, x_i^+) to (x_i, x_i^+, x_i^-). Prior work [6] has demonstrated that supervised Natural Language Inference (NLI) datasets [21] are effective for learning sentence embeddings, by predicting the relationship between two sentences and dividing it into three categories: entailment, neutral, or contradiction. Contradiction pairs are taken as hard-negative samples and give model significant negative signals.

$$l_i = -log\frac{e^{sim(h_i;h_i^+)/\tau}}{\sum_{j=1}^{N} e^{sim(h_i,h_j^+)/\tau} + e^{sim(h_i,h_j^-)/\tau}}, \tag{3}$$

where h_i, h_j^+ are positive pairs labelled as entailment, while h_i, h_j^- are hard-negative pairs labelled as contradiction.

2.4 Sentence Contrastive Learning with PLMs

The recent success of comparative learning is heavily dependent on the pre-trained language models (PLMs), like BERT [18], Roberta [11], and Albert [9]. Unsupervised/Supervised SimCSE [5], PairSupCon [26], IS-BERT [20], BERT-Position [19], BERT-whitening [16] are based on BERT, Roberta, Albert, and so on, for the pre-training model to improve the training efficiency and result.

3   CCDC Framework

3.1 Cross-Domain Sentences as Hard-Negative Samples

In order to enhance the sentence representation effect of multi-domain contrastive learning [23,24], the CCDC framework is designed as follows based on the supervised SimCSE framework. The pseudo-NLI data format is similar to

Table 1. CCDC samples

	Chinese sentence	Corresponding English sentence
Anchor	1560年10月，...要求他通过苏格兰返回英国。	In October 1560, ... asked him to return to United Kingdom through Scotland.
In-domain-positive	1560年10月，...要求他通过苏格兰返回英国。	In October 1560, ... asked him to return to United Kingdom through Scotland.
In-batch-negative	还有公开讨论，特定档案讨论和项目讨论。	There are also open discussions, file-specific discussions and project discussions.
In-domain-negative	1560年10月，...要求他通过英格兰返回苏格兰。	In October 1560, ... Asked him to return to Scotland through United Kingdom.
Out-domain-negative	花呗可以买飞机票汽车票了	You can buy a plane ticket, a bus ticket.

the SimCSE NLI format in that the former uses (DT:sen0, DT:sen1, DT:sen2) similar to the (anchor, positive, negative) triplet, where DT is short for domain tag. Anchor-negative pairs include negative examples of in-batch, in-domain, and out-domain, as highlighted in yellow, orange, and red in Fig. 2. The in-domain negative example and out-domain negative example can be considered as hard-negative samples, as can be seen in Table 1.

3.2 Hard NLI Data Builder

To construct pseudo-NLI data, the $(x, x+, x-)$ triplet needs to be generated based on three traditional sentence semantic problems, including classification, regression, and NLI. The Hard NLI Data Builder based on domain rules is implemented as follows. If (x_i, x_j) is a positive sample of semantic similarity (classification problem) or the similarity is greater than the average (regression problem), a negative sample of a sentence x_k is randomly selected to form an NLI triplet (x_i, x_j, x_k); if (x_i, x_j) is a negative sample or is less than or equal to the average value, the anchor is repeated to form an NLI triplet (x_i, x_i, x_j). The Hard NLI Data Builder process is as in Fig. 3.

As can be seen, classification/regression data is classified into entailment (positive) and contradiction (negative) categories. The created NLI data can be used to train supervised SimCSE.

3.3 Soft NLI Data Builder

In addition to the rule-based Hard NLI Data Builder, a Soft NLI Data Builder can be built based on a neural network classification model. The Entailment/Contradiction classifier can be encoded like a Siamese network, where two towers of BERT and pooling have shared weights, and output sentence embeddings as a feature. A Softmax Binary Classifier is a simple MLP network based on the feature triplet of $(f(x), f(x'), |f(x) - f(x')|)$, as can be seen in Fig. 3.

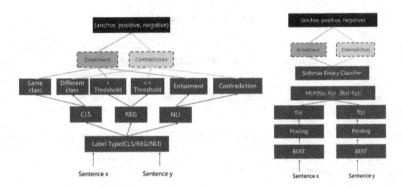

Fig. 3. Diagrams of Hard NLI data builder (left) and Soft NLI data builder (right)

4 Experiment

4.1 Data Preparation

The multi-domain semantic representation of sentences is like a different view enhancement of general semantic representation. Like [16], in order to verify the multi-view enhancement effect of the CCDC framework, the most famous Chinese sentence question pair datasets, Ant Financial Artificial Competition(ATEC) [4], BQ [2], LCQMC [10], PAWS-X from Google [25], and STS-B [2] are used. The detailed datasets are shown in Table 2.

Table 2. Chinese sentence pair datasets in 5 domains

Dataset	Type	Train	Test
ATEC	Semantic identification	62 k	20 k
BQ	Semantic identification	100 k	10 k
LCQMC	Semantic identification	238 k	12 k
PAWS-X	Binary identification	49 k	2 k
STS-B	Semantic similarity	5 k	1.3 k

4.2 Training Details

SBERT [14] is choosen as the training framework, and tiny, small, base, and large pre-trained models are selected for comparison. The training device is NVIDIA-V100, which has a 32G GPU. The batch size is 128 for tiny/small/base PLMs, 96 for huge PLM due to insufficient graphics memory, and the temperature is 0.05 using an Adam [8] optimizer. The learning rate is set as 5e-5 for tiny/small/base models and 1e-5 for large models, and warm-up steps account for 10% of the total training steps. Just like supervised SimCSE, our model is trained with 3 epochs.

4.3   CCDC with One-Domain Training and In-Domain/Out-Domain Testing

Like in [16], BERT-base is chosen as the baseline and unsupervised SimCSE as the strong baseline.

ATEC is used as training/testing data for in-domain experiments. The ATEC Spearman coefficient reached 46%, a performance improvement of 31% over the baseline and of 13% over the strong baseline. The other four in-domain experiments also achieved a 25–56% and 2–21% performance improvement over the baseline and strong baseline respectively, as can be seen in Table 3.

In the In Domain-Enhanced Confusion Matrix, all items are semi-positive, and most of them are positive. In-domain CCDC training can improve cross-domain performance, as can be seen in Table 4.

Table 3. CCDC with one-domain training and in-domain testing

	ATEC	BQ	LCQMC	PAWS-X	STS-B
BERT	0.15	0.2	0.18	0.08	0.34
SimCSE	0.33	0.5	0.69	0.12	0.69
ATEC	0.46 (+0.13)				
BQ		0.65 (+0.15)			
LCQMC			0.74 (+0.05)		
PAWS-X				0.33 (+0.21)	
STS-B					0.71 (+0.02)

Table 4. CCDC results with one-domain training and out-domain testing

	ATEC	BQ	LCQMC	PAWS-X	STS-B	Average
BERT	0.15	0.2	0.18	0.08	0.34	0.19
SimCSE	0.33	0.5	0.69	0.12	0.69	0.46
ATEC	0.46 (+0.31)	0.56 (+0.36)	0.68 (+0.50)	0.09 (+0.01)	0.66 (+0.32)	0.49
BQ	0.38 (+0.23)	0.65 (+0.45)	0.69 (+0.51)	0.10 (+0.02)	0.65 (+0.31)	0.49
LCQMC	0.34 (+0.19)	0.45 (+0.25)	0.74 (+0.56)	0.08 (+0.00)	0.69 (+0.35)	0.46
PAWS-X	0.24 (+0.09)	0.40 (+0.20)	0.55 (+0.37)	0.33 (+0.25)	0.57 (+0.23)	0.42
STS-B	0.23 (+0.08)	0.34 (+0.14)	0.63 (+0.45)	0.09 (+0.01)	0.71 (+0.37)	0.40

Table 5. CCDC results with all-domain training and the Hard/Soft NLI data builder

	ATEC	BQ	LCQMC	PAWS-X	STS-B	Average
BERT	0.15	0.2	0.18	0.08	0.34	0.19
SimCSE	0.33	0.5	0.69	0.12	0.69	0.46
ATEC	0.46	0.56	0.68	0.09	0.66	0.49
BQ	0.38	0.65	0.69	0.10	0.65	0.49
LCQMC	0.34	0.45	0.74	0.08	0.69	0.46
PAWS-X	0.24	0.40	0.55	0.33	0.57	0.42
STS-B	0.23	0.34	0.63	0.09	0.71	0.40
CCDC w/All-Hard-NLI-Builder	**0.46**	**0.66**	**0.74**	0.33	0.67	0.57
CCDC w/All-Soft-NLI-Builder	**0.46**	**0.66**	**0.74**	**0.35**	**0.71**	**0.58**

4.4 CCDC with the Hard/Soft NLI Data Builder

With the Hard NLI Data Builder, a multi-domain CCDC model is trained. Domains ATEC, BQ, LCQMC, and PAWS-X all achieved the best performance of 46%, 66%, 74%, and 33% respectively, with BQ being especially better than in-domain SOTA. Only STS-B falls short by 4%, maybe because the training data volume is insufficient. The average performance achieved 57%.

To eliminate the impact of data imbalances, a multi-domain model is trained with the Soft NLI Data Builder [24]. The CCDC model achieved the best performance in all domains, and even PAWS-X outperformed the in-domain SOTA by 2%. The average performance of all domains achieved 58%, an improvement of 41% and 12% over the baseline and the strong baseline respectively in Table 5.

5 Analysis

Based on the research of [5] on neurolinguistic representation, the baseline of the traditional pre-training model has two problems. (1) Due to the anisotropy of the space, the space will eventually shrink to a narrow cone. (2) The eigenvalues corresponding to the eigenvectors will be attenuated greatly, leading to a huge gap between the head feature and the back feature.

Empirical visual analysis for Anisotropy. visual analysis has been performed on the baseline, strong baseline, and CCDC models. 5000 data entries were extracted from each test set, with a total of 50,000 sentences, and three sentence vectors are visualized. As shown in Fig. 1, the original PLM model has an obvious narrow cone phenomenon, and unsupervised SimCSE shows that all directions are evenly distributed, but there is no multi-domain feature. The CCDC avoids the narrow cone phenomenon and also shows some multi-domain characteristics. It has the most appropriate representation of each domain and has some degree of differentiation between different domains.

Singular Values Decay. In addition, in singular value analysis (Fig. 4), the large gap between the head singular value of the traditional PLM and other singular values is well narrowed in unsupervised SimCSE, while the CCDC model supports sentence representation of multiple domains while still maintaining the uniform characteristics of singular values. In terms of homogeneity of the singular value distribution, the CCDC is comparable to unsupervised SimCSE.

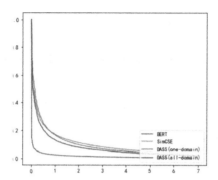

Fig. 4. Singular analysis on BERT, SimCSE, and CCDC (one-domain/all-domain)

6   Conclusion

The paper proposes the CCDC, a multi-domain enhanced contrastive learning sentence embedding framework, which uses a pseudo-NLI data generator to obtain a multi-domain sentence representation model that significantly outperforms the baseline model (BERT) and the strong baseline model (unsupervised SimCSE). Deep analysis shows that the CCDC framework solves the anisotropy and eigenvalue attenuation problems well.

Future research will focus on the knowledge mining in comparative learning. As shown in the preceding analysis, the CCDC performance is less than 50% in PASW-X. It should be able to perform hard-negative mining or multi-view mining based on knowledge graph or terminology knowledge [24] on hard cases such as "Scotland to England" and "England to Scotland" in PASW-X.

7   Appendix

7.1   CCDC with Different PLM and Different Pooling Layer

For comparison of different model architectures, model sizes, and pooling types, [27] is used as a reference, which provides 3 types of ALBERT and 3 types of Roberta based pre-trained models for Chinese. And the pooling type could be mean/cls/max, respectively indicating average pooling, class token pooling, and max pooling. Table 6 lists 19 different PLM + Pooling layer results($6 * 3 + 1 = 19$).

As can be seen, ALBERT is not as good as BERT-base, even with large model ,due to parameter sharing. Roberta large achieved all-domain best performance, and mean pooling achieved most of the best performance in most domains, while ATEC, BQ, and LCQMC offered the best performance with the max pooling layer.

7.2   Case Analysis

The sentence-level similarity of the corresponding three groups of models was calculated, and it was found that: (1) BERT-base, regardless of semantically related or not, similarity score are all over 0.93. (2) For the unsupvised Sim-CSE model, similarity score is 0.90 vs 0.86 for semantic related or not. (3) For the CCDC model, similar score is 0.93 vs 0.81. The CCDC model has better discrimination than BERT and Unsupervised SimCSE, as can be seen in Table 7

Table 6. CCDC results with different PLMs and different pooling layer

	Batch-size	Pooler	ATEC	BQ	LCQMC	PAWSX	STS-B	Average
Bert-base-chinese	128	Mean	0.46	0.66	0.74	0.35	0.71	0.58
Albert-tiny	128	Mean	0.36	0.58	0.64	0.19	0.63	0.48
Albert-tiny	128	cls	0.36	0.58	0.64	0.2	0.63	0.48
Albert-tiny	128	Max	0.34	0.55	0.64	0.15	0.61	0.46
Albert-base	128	Mean	0.4	0.63	0.68	0.19	0.63	0.51
Albert-base	128	cls	0.4	0.62	0.68	0.18	0.63	0.5
Albert-base	128	Max	0.38	0.60	0.68	0.17	0.62	0.49
Albert-large	96	Mean	0.41	0.64	0.68	0.17	0.63	0.51
Albert-large	96	cls	0.40	0.62	0.66	0.17	0.62	0.49
Albert-large	96	Max	0.40	0.63	0.65	0.17	0.62	0.49
Roberta-tiny	128	Mean	0.38	0.58	0.66	0.14	0.62	0.48
Roberta-tiny	128	cls	0.37	0.58	0.64	0.14	0.60	0.47
Roberta-tiny	128	Max	0.36	0.58	0.65	0.14	0.61	0.47
Roberta-base	128	Mean	0.46	0.67	0.75	0.46	0.69	0.61
Roberta-base	128	cls	0.45	0.66	0.74	0.46	0.67	0.60
Roberta-base	128	Max	0.45	0.66	0.74	0.44	0.67	0.59
Roberta-large	96	Mean	0.47	0.67	0.74	**0.48**	**0.72**	0.62
Roberta-large	96	cls	0.47	**0.68**	0.76	0.39	0.7	0.6
Roberta-large	96	Max	**0.48**	**0.68**	**0.77**	0.45	0.7	0.62

Table 7. Case Analysis for BERT-base, Unsup-SimCSE, and CCDC, Label = 1 is semantically identical and vice versa, label = 0

Sentence-a	Sentence-b	Label	BERT	SimCSE	CCDC
1560年10月，他在巴黎秘密会见了英国大使Nicolas Throckmorton，要求他通过苏格兰返回英国。	1560年10月，他在巴黎秘密会见了英国大使尼古拉斯·斯罗克莫顿，并要求他通过英格兰返回苏格兰的护照。	0	0.9789	0.8683	0.8174
(Related Translation)In October 1560, he met secretly in Paris ... to return to England via Scotland.	In October 1560 he met secretly in Paris ... to return to Scotland via England.	–	–	–	–
1975年的NBA赛季 - 76赛季是全美篮球协会的第30个赛季。	1975-76赛季的全国篮球协会是NBA的第30个赛季。	1	0.9697	0.906	0.9335
(Related Translation)The 1975 NBA season-76 was the 30th season of the National Basketball Association.	The 1975-76 season of the National Basketball Association was the NBA's 30th season.	–	–	–	–
还有具体的讨论，公众形象辩论和项目讨论。	还有公开讨论，特定档案讨论和项目讨论。	0	0.9399	0.6389	0.70
(Related Translation)There are also specific discussions, public image debates, and project discussions.	There are also open discussions, file-specific discussions, and project discussions.	–	–	–	–

References

1. Aitchison, L.: Infonce is a variational autoencoder. arXiv preprint arXiv:2107.02495 (2021)
2. Chen, J., Chen, Q., Liu, X., Yang, H., Lu, D., Tang, B.: The BG corpus: a large-scale domain-specific Chinese corpus for sentence semantic equivalence identification. In: Proceedings of the 2018 Conference on Empirical Methods in Natural Language Processing, pp. 4946–4951 (2018)
3. Chen, T., Kornblith, S., Norouzi, M., Hinton, G.: A Simple Framework for Contrastive Learning of Visual Representations, pp. 1597–1607 (2020). http://proceedings.mlr.press/v119/chen20j.html
4. Financial, A.: Ant Financial Artificial Competition (2018)
5. Gao, T., Yao, X., Chen, D.: SimCSE: Simple Contrastive Learning of Sentence Embeddings. arXiv:2104.08821 [cs] (2021). zSCC: 0000087
6. Gillick, D., et al.: Learning dense representations for entity retrieval, pp. 528–537 (2019). https://www.aclweb.org/anthology/K19-1049
7. Hadsell, R., Chopra, S., LeCun, Y.: Dimensionality reduction by learning an invariant mapping. In: 2006 IEEE Computer Society Conference on Computer Vision and Pattern Recognition (CVPR 2006), 17–22 June 2006, New York, pp. 1735–1742. IEEE Computer Society (2006). https://doi.org/10.1109/CVPR.2006.100
8. Kingma, D.P., Ba, J.: Adam: a method for stochastic optimization. arXiv preprint arXiv:1412.6980 (2015)
9. Lan, Z., Chen, M., Goodman, S., Gimpel, K., Sharma, P., Soricut, R.: Albert: a lite bert for self-supervised learning of language representations. arXiv preprint arXiv:1909.11942 (2019)
10. Liu, X., et al.: Lcqmc: a large-scale Chinese question matching corpus. In: Proceedings of the 27th International Conference on Computational Linguistics, pp. 1952–1962 (2018)
11. Liu, Y., et al.: Roberta: a robustly optimized bert pretraining approach. arXiv preprint arXiv:1907.11692 (2019)
12. Meng, Y., et al.: COCO-LM: correcting and contrasting text sequences for language model pretraining. arXiv preprint arXiv:2102.08473 (2021)

13. Reimers, N., Beyer, P., Gurevych, I.: Task-Oriented Intrinsic Evaluation of Semantic Textual Similarity, pp. 87–96 (2016). https://www.aclweb.org/anthology/C16-1009
14. Reimers, N., Gurevych, I.: Sentence-BERT: sentence embeddings using Siamese BERT-networks, pp. 3982–3992 (2019). https://doi.org/10.18653/v1/D19-1410
15. Srivastava, N., Hinton, G., Krizhevsky, A., Sutskever, I., Salakhutdinov, R.: Dropout: a simple way to prevent neural networks from overfitting. J. Mach. Learn. Res. **15**(1), 1929–1958 (2014)
16. Su, J., Cao, J., Liu, W., Ou, Y.: Whitening sentence representations for better semantics and faster retrieval. arXiv preprint arXiv:2103.15316 (2021)
17. Sun, X., Sun, S., Yin, M., Yang, H.: Hybrid neural conditional random fields for multi-view sequence labeling. Knowl. Based Syst. **189**, 105151 (2020)
18. Vaswani, A., et al.: Attention is all you need. arXiv:1706.03762 [cs] (2017). zSCC: 0033821
19. Wang, B., et al.: On position embeddings in Bert. In: International Conference on Learning Representations (2020)
20. Wang, L., Huang, J., Huang, K., Hu, Z., Wang, G., Gu, Q.: Improving neural language generation with spectrum control (2020). https://openreview.net/forum?id=ByxY8CNtvr
21. Williams, A., Nangia, N., Bowman, S.: A broad-coverage challenge corpus for sentence understanding through inference, pp. 1112–1122 (2018). https://doi.org/10.18653/v1/N18-1101
22. Yang, H., Chen, J., Zhang, Y., Meng, X.: Optimized query terms creation based on meta-search and clustering. In: 2008 Fifth International Conference on Fuzzy Systems and Knowledge Discovery, vol. 2, pp. 38–42. IEEE (2008)
23. Yang, H., Deng, Y., Wang, M., Qin, Y., Sun, S.: Humor detection based on paragraph decomposition and BERT fine-tuning. In: AAAI Workshop 2020 (2020)
24. Yang, H., Xie, G., Qin, Y., Peng, S.: Domain specific NMT based on knowledge graph embedding and attention. In: 2019 21st International Conference on Advanced Communication Technology (ICACT), pp. 516–521. IEEE (2019)
25. Yang, Y., Zhang, Y., Tar, C., Baldridge, J.: PAWS-X: a cross-lingual adversarial dataset for paraphrase identification. arXiv preprint arXiv:1908.11828 (2019). zSCC: NoCitationData[s0]
26. Zhang, D., et al.: Pairwise Supervised Contrastive Learning of Sentence Representations, p. 13, zSCC: 0000001
27. Zhang, N., et al.: CBLUE: A Chinese Biomedical Language Understanding Evaluation Benchmark. arXiv preprint arXiv:2106.08087 (2021)

A Multi-objective Optimization Method for Joint Feature Selection and Classifier Parameter Tuning

Yanyun Pang, Aimin Wang, Yuying Lian, Jiahui Li, and Geng Sun[(⊠)]

College of Software and College of Computer Science and Technology,
Jilin University, Changchun 130012, China
{wangam,lianyuying,sungeng}@jlu.edu.cn

Abstract. Feature selection is an efficient method to extract useful information embedded in the data so that improving the performance of machine learning. However, as a direct factor that affects the result of feature selection, classifier performance is not widely considered in feature selection. In this paper, we formulate a multi-objective minimization optimization problem to simultaneously minimize the number of features and minimize the classification error rate by jointly considering the optimization of the selected features and the classifier parameters. Then, we propose an *Improved Multi-Objective Gray Wolf Optimizer* (IMOGWO) to solve the formulated multi-objective optimization problem. First, IMOGWO combines the discrete binary solution and the classifier parameters to form a mixed solution. Second, the algorithm uses the initialization strategy of tent chaotic map, sinusoidal chaotic map and *Opposition-based Learning* (OBL) to improve the quality of the initial solution, and utilizes a local search strategy to search for a new set of solutions near the Pareto front. Finally, a mutation operator is introduced into the update mechanism to increase the diversity of the population. Experiments are conducted on 15 classic datasets, and the results show that the algorithm outperforms other comparison algorithms.

Keywords: Feature selection · Classification · Multi-objective optimization · Grey wolf optimizer

1 Introduction

With the increasing application of computer technology [12,20,21] and artificial intelligence [11,13], different equipment in different industries will generate a large number of high-dimensional datasets [18,19,22]. These high-dimensional datasets promote the application of machine learning in many fields, such as data mining [6], physics [3], medical imaging [1] and finance [5]. However, as the complexity of machine learning models increases, an increasing number of high-dimensional feature space datasets are generated, often containing many

© The Author(s), under exclusive license to Springer Nature Switzerland AG 2022
G. Memmi et al. (Eds.): KSEM 2022, LNAI 13369, pp. 237–248, 2022.
https://doi.org/10.1007/978-3-031-10986-7_19

irrelevant and redundant features. These features will cause the machine learning algorithm to consume too many computing resources when performing classification and other operations and reduce the classification accuracy. Therefore, it is necessary to use the method of feature selection to process the dataset.

The main idea of feature selection is to eliminate irrelevant features from all feature spaces and select the most valuable feature subset [23]. Because irrelevant features are deleted, the number of features specified in the dataset is reduced, so the classification accuracy of machine learning algorithms can be improved and computing resources can be saved. Generally speaking, feature selection methods are divided into three categories, namely, filter-based methods, wrapper-based methods, and embedded methods. Among them, the wrapper-based method trains the selected feature subset with the classifier and uses the training result (accuracy rate) as the evaluation index of the feature subset. Therefore, wrapper-based methods generally perform better than filter-based methods in classification accuracy.

The wrapper-based feature selection methods depend on the performance of the classifier. In general, the feature selection results obtained by using simple classifiers (e.g., KNN and NB) are still applicable in complex classifiers. However, when a complex classifier is used for feature selection, the obtained feature selection results are not applicable since the results are affected by the structure of the classifier. For that matter, the classification parameters also have some influence on the feature selection results. Therefore, the optimization of feature selection can be performed in combination with the classification parameters of the classifier. However, it may increase the complexity of the solution space.

With the continuous increase of the number of features, the search space of feature selection algorithms is getting larger and larger. Therefore, the key factor that affects the feature selection algorithm is the search technology. Traditional subset search techniques, such as *Sequential Forward Selection* (SFS) and *Sequential Backward Selection* (SBS), can find the best feature subset, but this search method is too inefficient and requires a lot of computing time. Compared with traditional search technology, meta-heuristic algorithms such as *dragonfly algorithm* (DA) [14], *particle swarm optimization* (PSO) [7], *whale optimization algorithm* (WOA) [15], *ant colony optimization* (ACO) [9], *genetic algorithm* (GA) [2] has good global search capabilities, and is widely used to solve feature selection problems.

The *grey wolf optimization* (GWO) [16] is a group intelligence optimization algorithm proposed by Mirjalili in 2014. It has the characteristics of strong convergence performance, few parameters, and easy implementation. However, no one algorithm can solve all optimization problems. In addition, the traditional GWO cannot solve the feature selection problem, and there may be some shortcomings, such as easy to fall into local optimality and convergence high speed. Therefore, it is necessary to improve the traditional GWO to make it more suitable for feature selection.

In fact, feature selection is a problem with two goals of minimization: minimizing the classification error rate and minimizing the number of features. Usually these two goals are contradictory, and an optimization algorithm is needed to find their balance. Therefore, this paper proposes to use IMOGWO to solve the feature selection problem.

The main contributions of this research are summarized as follow:

- We consider a multi-objective optimization method for joint feature selection and classifier parameter tuning by formulating a problem with a hybrid solution space.
- We propose an IMOGWO algorithm to solve the formulated problem, in which an initialization strategy using tent chaotic maps, sinusoidal chaotic maps, and OBL to improve the initial solution. Moreover, we propose a local search strategy to search for a new set of solutions near the Pareto front. Furthermore, in the update mechanism, we introduce a mutation operator to improve the diversity of the population.
- Experiments are conducted on 15 classical datasets to evaluate the performance of using IMOGWO for feature selection, and the results are compared with other algorithms to verify the effectiveness of the improvement factor.

The rest of the paper is structured as follows. Section 2 introduces the problem construction for feature selection. Section 3 introduces the conventional MOGWO, followed by the proposed IMOGWO. Section 4 presents the experimental results. Section 5 presents the conclusions and possible future work directions.

2   Problem Formulation

In the problem of feature selection, a dataset includes $N_{row} \times N_{dim}$ specific feature values, where each row represents a sample data, and each column represents the specific values of different sample data about the same feature. The purpose of feature selection is to select the most valuable R features to reduce the data dimension. However, in order to improve the classification performance of the SVM complex classifier, we consider the joint features and the parameters of the classifier, and adjust the parameters of the classifier while selecting the features.

We divide the solution space of feature selection into two parts, the first part is the feature vector N_{dim}, each bit has a value of 1 or 0 (1 and 0 indicate that the feature is selected and not selected, respectively). The second part is the parameter vector N_{parm} of the SVM classifier, which consists of three bits. The first one is the *kernel*, and the value is 1 or 0 (1 and 0 indicate the selection of the Gaussian radial basis kernel function and the hyperbolic tangent kernel function, respectively). The second bit is the parameter c, in the range $[2^{-1}, 2^5]$, and the third bit is the parameter *gamma*, in the range $[2^{-4}, 2^5]$. Therefore, the feature selection situation of the dataset can be represented by a one-dimensional array $X = (x_1, x_2, \cdots, x_{N_{dim}}, x_k, x_c, x_g)$, which is a solution to the feature selection problem.

Since feature selection has two objectives, the feature selection problem is a multi-objective optimization problem (MOP). The first objective to minimize the classification error rate can be expressed as:

$$f_1(X) = 1 - f_{acc}(X),\qquad(1)$$

where $f_{acc}(X)$ represents the classification accuracy of the obtained feature subset. Furthermore, the second goal is to reduce the dimension of feature subsets, which can be expressed as:

$$f_2(X) = \frac{R}{N_{dim}},\qquad(2)$$

where R represents the number of features selected, and N_{dim} represents the total number of features. Accordingly, the feature selection problem can be formulated as follows:

$$\min_{\{X\}} \& F = \{f_1, f_2\},\qquad(3a)$$

$$\text{s.t. } C1: x_i \in \{0,1\}, \quad i = 1, 2, 3, \cdots, N_{dim}\qquad(3b)$$

$$C2: x_k \in \{0,1\},\qquad(3c)$$

$$C3: x_c \in \left[2^{-1}, 2^5\right],\qquad(3d)$$

$$C4: x_g \in \left[2^{-4}, 2^5\right],\qquad(3e)$$

$$C5: 1 < R < N_{dim},\qquad(3f)$$

$$C6: 0 \le f_{acc}(X) \le 1,\qquad(3g)$$

where $C1$ represents the restriction of the value range of each dimension of the feature vector in the solution, $C2$ represents the restriction of the classifier parameter *kernel* in the solution, $C3$ represents the restriction of the classifier parameter c in the solution, and $C4$ represents the constraints of the classifier parameter *gamma* in the solution, $C5$ represents the restriction of the number of selected features, and $C6$ represents the restriction of the classification accuracy.

3   The Proposed Approach

In this section, we introduce traditional MOGWO, then introduce IMOGWO with an improvement factor and use it to solve feature selection problems.

3.1   Traditional MOGWO

Although GWO is relatively new, it is designed to solve single-objective optimization problems. Therefore, it cannot be directly used to solve MOP. [17] proposed MOGWO as a multi-objective variant of GWO. In MOGWO, two new mechanisms are integrated: the first is the archive, which is used to store all non-dominated Pareto optimal solutions obtained so far, and the second is the leader selection strategy, which is responsible for selecting the first leader (α), the second leader (β), and the third leader (δ) from the archive.

Archive: As the algorithm is continuously updated, each iteration will produce a new solution. If there is a solution in the archive that dominates the new solution, it will not be added to the archive. If the new solution dominates one or more solutions in the archive, the new solution replaces the solution dominated by it in the archive. If the new solution and all the solutions in the archive do not dominate each other, the new solution is also added to the archive. However, in such an iterative process, there may be more and more individuals in the archive. Therefore, we will set an upper limit for the archive so that the number of individuals in the archive population does not exceed the upper limit while maintaining population diversity. If the number of individuals in the archive exceeds the set value, use the method in NSGA-II [4] to delete the population.

Leader Selection Strategy: In GWO, the leader (α, β, δ) can be determined by the value of the objective function, but in MOP, the pros and cons of the individual are determined by the dominance relationship and cannot be distinguished by simple function values. To redefine the selection mechanism of α, β and δ wolves. The current optimal solution of the algorithm is stored in the archive. Therefore, the individual is directly selected as the leader from the archive. At the same time, in order to improve the exploration ability of the algorithm, the wolf with a large crowding distance is selected as the leader.

3.2 IMOGWO

MOGWO has some shortcomings in solving optimization problems, such as strong global search ability but weak local search ability. Therefore, we propose IMOGWO, which introduces chaotic mapping and opposition-based learning initialization strategy, local search strategy and mutation operator to improve the performance of MOGWO. The proposed IMOGWO pseudocode is given in Algorithm 1, and the details of introducing the improvement factor are as follows.

Mixed Solution of MOGWO. MOGWO was originally to solve the continuous optimization problem and cannot be directly used to solve the feature selection problem. Therefore, for discrete binary solutions, we introduce a v-shaped transfer function to map the solution from continuous space to discrete space, so that the algorithm is suitable for feature selection problems. The description of the v-shaped transfer function is as follows:

$$P(x) = \left| \frac{x}{\sqrt{x^2 + 1}} \right|, \tag{4}$$

where x represents the position of the gray wolf, and the v-shaped transfer function can frequently change the search variable, which promotes the exploration of the solution space. The method to update the dimensions of the binary solution is as follows:

$$x_{t+1} = \begin{cases} \neg x_t, & N_{rand} < P(x) \\ x_t, & otherwise \end{cases} \tag{5}$$

where x_t is a dimension of a binary solution in iteration t. Through the above binary mechanism, the continuous solution of traditional MOGWO can be effectively transformed into discrete solution, so that the algorithm can be used for feature selection problem.

Algorithm 1: Pseudocode of the Proposed IMOGWO

---

1 Define and initialize the related parameters: population size N_{pop}, solution
   dimension N_{dim} and objective functions, etc.;
2 Use Eqs. (6), (7) and (8) to initialize the population *pop*;
3 The opposition population *Opop* is generated by Eq. (9);
4 Calculate the objective values for each solution;
5 Select N_{pop} fittest ones from $\{pop \cup Opop\}$ as the initial population;
6 Find non-dominated solutions and put them in the Archive;
7 Sort the non-dominated solutions in descending order of crowding distance;
8 **while** $t < T$ **do**
9   Update X_α, X_β, X_δ according to the crowded distance;
10   Update the jth dimension of X_α by using Eqs. (11), (12);
11   **for** $i = 1$ *to* N_{pop} **do**
12 | Update the position of X_i using Algorithm 2;
13   **end**
14   Calculate the objective values of new solutions and update the archive;
15   **if** *the archive is full* **then**
16 | Use methods in NSGA-II to remove partial members in archive;
17   **end**
18   t=t+1;
19 **end**
20 Return archive;

TS-OBL Initialization Strategy. The traditional GWO algorithm uses a random initialization method, which is easy to implement, but this may lead to uneven distribution of wolves and low coverage of the solution space. Therefore, we introduce chaotic map and *Opposition-based Learning* (OBL) strategies to improve the initial solution.

The population initialization strategy of OBL is to find the optimal solution from two directions. It can be combined with other strategies. After using a certain strategy to generate the initial solution, OBL is used to generate its opposite solution, so as to make the distribution of the initial solution more uniform and the diversity of the population higher. Therefore, we combine OBL with chaotic map initialization strategy and propose a TS-OBL initialization strategy. The specific process is as follows:

First, when the number of features is less than 30, half of the individuals in the population adopt the strategy of random initialization, and half of the individuals adopt the strategy of tent chaotic map initialization. When the number of features is greater than or equal to 30, all individuals in the population use the sinusoidal chaotic map initialization strategy. The calculation method of the chaotic map is as follows:

$$tent : y_{i+1} = \begin{cases} \frac{y_i}{0.7}, & y_i < 0.7 \\ \frac{10}{3}(1 - y_i), & y_i \geq 0,7 \end{cases} \quad i = 1, 2, 3, \cdots, T/2 \tag{6}$$

$$Sinusoidal : y_{i+1} = ay_i^2 sin(\pi y_i), \quad a = 2.3 \quad i = 1, 2, 3, \cdots, T \tag{7}$$

where y_i is the ith chaotic variable and T is the maximum number of iterations. The calculation method for mapping the chaotic variable y_i from the interval $[0, 1]$ to the corresponding solution space is as follows:

$$x_i = l_i + (u_i - l_i) y_i, \tag{8}$$

where l_i and u_i are the minimum and maximum values of the variable value range.

Second, OBL is used to generate the opposite solution of the initial solution. The calculation formula of each dimension of the inverse solution is as follows:

$$\tilde{x}_d = l_d + u_d - x_d. \tag{9}$$

Finally, calculate the two objective function values of $2N_{pop}$ initial solutions, use NSGA-II to sort the initial solutions, and select the best N_{pop} solutions as the initial solutions.

Local Search Strategy. Because MOGWO easily falls into the local optimal value in the later stage of the calculation operation. Only a small perturbation of the non-dominated solution set can make the wolf search in a new direction to increase the probability of finding a new optimal value. Therefore, in the later iteration stage, we change the value of the classifier parameter c or $gamma$ of each solution in the non-dominated solution set as the newly generated nearby solution. At the same time, to not increase the computational time complexity, we discard the poorer half of the population and select the better half for updates. The method to find the solutions around the non-dominated solution set is as follows:

$$x^{new} = x + rx, \tag{10}$$

where $r \in [-0.5, 0.5]$, x is the value of the parameter c or $gamma$ in the solution. The main steps of the update mechanism using the local search strategy are shown in Algorithm 2.

Novel Update Mechanism with Mutation Operators. The traditional MOGWO may reduce the diversity of the population. For example, when x_α is far from the optimal solution or falls into the local optimal, the performance of the algorithm may be greatly reduced. Therefore, we set a threshold φ to determine whether a certain feature dimension of α wolf has been mutated. The formula for calculating the threshold φ is as follows:

$$\varphi = 0.5(\frac{t}{T}), \tag{11}$$

where t is the current number of iterations. The mutation method of α is as follows:

$$x_\alpha^j = \begin{cases} 1 - x_\alpha^j, & N_{rand} < \varphi, N_{dim} < 60 \\ x_\alpha^j, & otherwise \end{cases} \tag{12}$$

where x_α^j represents an unselected feature dimension of α wolf.

Algorithm 2: Update Mechanism using Local Search Strategy

---

1 Define and initialize the related parameters;
2 **while** $t < T$ **do**
3   **if** $t < 175$ *or* $N_{dim} >= 60$ **then**
4          $N_{pop} = N_{pop}$;
5   **end**
6   **else**
7          $N_{pop} = N_{pop}/2$;
8   Sort the solutions in the population from good to bad according to NSGA-II;
9   **end**
10   **for** $i = 1$ *to* N_{pop} **do**
11   Updating X_i according to the mathematical model of the grey wolf algorithm;
12   **end**
13   Calculate the objective values of new solutions and update the archive;
14   **if** $t < 175$ *or* $N_{dim} >= 60$ **then**
15   **for** *each non-dominated solution* **do**
16   Update the position of the current non-dominated solution by Eq. (10) to generate a new solution;
17   **end**
18   **end**
19 **end**
20 Return new solutions;

---

4   Experimental Results and Analysis

In this section, we will conduct tests to verify the performance of IMOGWO on the feature selection problem. In addition, we introduce the datasets and setups used in the experiments, and the test results of IMOGWO and several other multi-objective feature selection methods are given and analyzed.

4.1   Datasets and Setups

In order to verify the proposed multi-objective optimization algorithm, we used 15 benchmark datasets collected from UC Irvine Machine Learning Repository. [10] and [8] describe the main information of the used datasets.

In this paper, we use MOPSO, MODA, MOGWO and NSGA-II as comparative experiments. Note that the multi-objective algorithm here is different from the traditional algorithm in that the solutions are all mixed solutions that combine discrete binary solutions and continuous solutions. They are the same as the solution form of IMOGWO. In addition, for the fairness of comparison, each algorithm sets the same population size (20) and iteration (200). In order to avoid the randomness of the experiment, each algorithm runs 10 times on the selected dataset, and 70% of the instances are used for training and 30% for testing.

We used Python 3.8 to conduct the experiment and use SVM to solve the data classification problem.

Table 1. Classification error rate and number of selected features obtained by different algorithms.

Dataset	MOPSO		MODA		MOGWO		NSGA-II		IMOGWO	
	err.	N_{fea}	err.	N_{fea}	err.	N_{fea}	err.	N_{fea}	err.	N_{fea}
Arrhythmia	0.3642	99.13	0.4020	64.67	0.4332	4.33	0.3283	135.09	**0.2962**	**3.15**
Breastcancer	0.0329	**2.20**	0.0296	2.40	0.0379	2.30	0.0288	2.55	**0.0263**	**2.20**
BreastEW	0.0514	5.00	0.0586	3.60	0.0822	3.80	0.0308	9.80	**0.0255**	**2.60**
Dermatology	0.1559	**3.33**	0.1855	4.00	0.1533	6.10	0.1407	14.15	**0.1338**	3.95
Class	0.3144	**2.00**	0.2508	2.40	0.2988	3.00	0.2608	3.33	**0.2411**	2.20
HeartEW	0.1578	2.20	**0.1512**	3.00	0.1650	**2.00**	0.1602	2.75	0.1521	2.10
Hepatitis	0.2908	3.10	0.2900	3.00	0.3305	4.11	0.2655	6.16	**0.2600**	**2.05**
Hillvalley	0.4435	27.00	0.4519	23.25	0.4657	4.00	0.4466	46.00	**0.4238**	**2.21**
Ionosphere	0.1037	4.67	0.1151	6.74	0.1943	4.00	0.0786	10.00	**0.0672**	**2.80**
Krvskp	0.0710	6.00	0.0979	5.20	0.0758	2.80	**0.0645**	9.56	0.0858	**2.60**
Lymphography	0.5519	**2.06**	0.5545	2.43	0.5784	2.60	**0.5385**	3.50	**0.5385**	2.10
Sonar	**0.1778**	14.25	0.2306	8.30	0.2862	**2.67**	0.1844	19.00	0.1815	3.33
WDBC	0.0414	4.60	0.0441	3.33	0.0950	**2.89**	0.0299	9.00	**0.0257**	3.00
Wine	0.0364	3.15	0.0527	2.80	0.0755	**2.66**	0.0347	5.10	**0.0320**	2.70
Zoo	0.1479	**2.30**	**0.1033**	**2.30**	0.1843	2.80	0.1268	2.95	**0.1033**	**2.30**

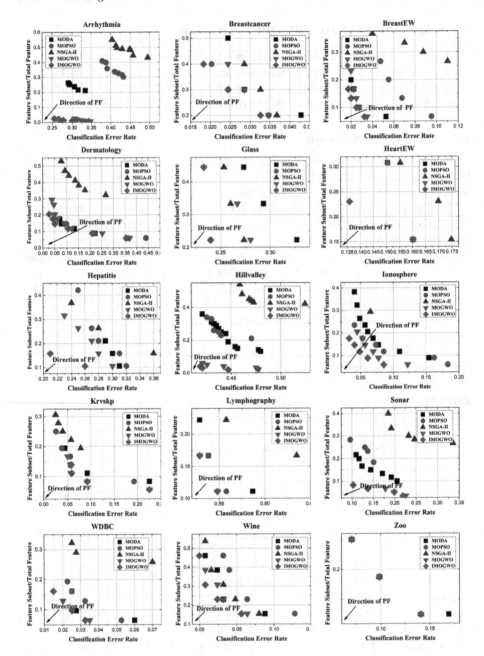

Fig. 1. Solution distribution results obtained by different algorithms on different datasets.

4.2   Feature Selection Results

In this section, the feature selection results obtained by different algorithms are introduced. Figure 1 shows the experimental results of IMOGWO on 15 datasets and compares them with MOPSO, MODA, MOGWO and NSGA-II. Each graph represents a different dataset. The name of the dataset is displayed at the top of the graph, the classification error rate is displayed on the horizontal axis, and the feature subset/total feature is displayed on the vertical axis. It can be seen from Fig. 1 that IMOGWO selected fewer features in most of the datasets and achieved a lower classification error rate. Table 1 shows the average statistics of the classification error rate and the number of selected features for each of the 10 runs based on feature selection for MOPSO, MODA, MOGWO, NSGA-II, and IMOGWO. It is evident from the table that the proposed IMOGWO has better performance on the two objectives of feature selection compared to the other four algorithms. On the whole, compared with other algorithms, IMOGWO has the best performance. Therefore, it is proved that these improvement factors can reasonably improve the performance of traditional MOGWO.

5   Conclusion

This paper studied the problem of feature selection in machine learning and then proposed IMOGWO for jointly selecting features and classifier parameters. In IMOGWO, we proposed an initialization strategy based on a combination of tent chaotic map, sinusoidal chaotic map and opposition-based learning to improve the initial solution. Then, we introduced a local search method to search for solutions near the Pareto front, improving the development capability of the algorithm. Finally, a mutation operator was proposed to enhance the diversity of the population. Experimental results showed that the algorithm has the best performance on 15 datasets, obtaining fewer features and smaller error rates compared to MOPSO, MODA, MOGWO and NSGA-II.

Acknowledgment. This study is supported in part by the National Natural Science Foundation of China (62172186, 62002133, 61872158, 61806083), in part by the Science and Technology Development Plan (International Cooperation) Project of Jilin Province (20190701019GH, 20190701002GH, 20210101183JC, 20210201072GX) and in part by the Young Science and Technology Talent Lift Project of Jilin Province (QT202013). Geng Sun is the corresponding author.

References

1. Alber, M., Buganza Tepole, A., et al.: Integrating machine learning and multiscale modeling-perspectives, challenges, and opportunities in the biological, biomedical, and behavioral sciences. NPJ Digit. Med. **2**(1), 1–11 (2019)
2. Aličković, E., Subasi, A.: Breast cancer diagnosis using GA feature selection and rotation forest. Neural Comput. Appl. **28**(4), 753–763 (2017)

3. Butler, K.T., Davies, D.W., et al.: Machine learning for molecular and materials science. Nature **559**(7715), 547–555 (2018)
4. Deb, K., Pratap, A., et al.: A fast and elitist multiobjective genetic algorithm: NSGA-ii. IEEE Trans. Evol. Comput. **6**(2), 182–197 (2002)
5. Ghoddusi, H., Creamer, G.G., Rafizadeh, N.: Machine learning in energy economics and finance: a review. Energy Econ. **81**, 709–727 (2019)
6. Han, J., Pei, J., Kamber, M.: Data Mining: Concepts and Techniques. Elsevier, Amsterdam (2011)
7. Huda, R.K., Banka, H.: Efficient feature selection and classification algorithm based on PSO and rough sets. Neural Compu. Appl. **31**(8), 4287–4303 (2019)
8. Ji, B., Lu, X., Sun, G., et al.: Bio-inspired feature selection: an improved binary particle swarm optimization approach. IEEE Access **8**, 85989–86002 (2020)
9. Kashef, S., Nezamabadi-pour, H.: An advanced ACO algorithm for feature subset selection. Neurocomputing **147**, 271–279 (2015)
10. Li, J., Kang, H., et al.: IBDA: improved binary dragonfly algorithm with evolutionary population dynamics and adaptive crossover for feature selection. IEEE Access **8**, 108032–108051 (2020)
11. Li, Y., Song, Y., et al.: Intelligent fault diagnosis by fusing domain adversarial training and maximum mean discrepancy via ensemble learning. IEEE TII **17**(4), 2833–2841 (2020)
12. Liu, M., Zhang, S., et al.: H infinite state estimation for discrete-time chaotic systems based on a unified model. IEEE Trans. SMC (B) **42**(4), 1053–1063 (2012)
13. Lu, Z., Wang, N., et al.: IoTDeM: an IoT Big Data-oriented MapReduce performance prediction extended model in multiple edge clouds. JPDC **118**, 316–327 (2018)
14. Mafarja, M., Aljarah, I., et al.: Binary dragonfly optimization for feature selection using time-varying transfer functions. Knowl.-Based Syst. **161**, 185–204 (2018)
15. Mafarja, M., Mirjalili, S.: Whale optimization approaches for wrapper feature selection. Appl. Soft Comput. **62**, 441–453 (2018)
16. Mirjalili, S., Mirjalili, S.M., Lewis, A.: Grey wolf optimizer. Adv. Eng. Softw. **69**, 46–61 (2014)
17. Mirjalili, S., Saremi, S., et al.: Multi-objective Grey Wolf Optimizer: a novel algorithm for multi-criterion optimization. Expert Syst. Appl. **47**, 106–119 (2016)
18. Qiu, L., et al.: Optimal big data sharing approach for tele-health in cloud computing. In: IEEE SmartCloud, pp. 184–189 (2016)
19. Qiu, M., Cao, D., et al.: Data transfer minimization for financial derivative pricing using Monte Carlo simulation with GPU in 5G. Int. J. Commun. Syst. **29**(16), 2364–2374 (2016)
20. Qiu, M., Liu, J., et al.: A novel energy-aware fault tolerance mechanism for wireless sensor networks. In: IEEE/ACM GCC (2011)
21. Qiu, M., Xue, C., et al.: Energy minimization with soft real-time and DVS for uniprocessor and multiprocessor embedded systems. In: IEEE DATE, pp. 1–6 (2007)
22. Wu, G., Zhang, H., et al.: A decentralized approach for mining event correlations in distributed system monitoring. JPDC **73**(3), 330–340 (2013)
23. Yu, L., Liu, H.: Feature selection for high-dimensional data: a fast correlation-based filter solution. In: 20th IEEE Conference on ICML, pp. 856–863 (2003)

Word Sense Disambiguation Based on Memory Enhancement Mechanism

Baoshuo Kan[1], Wenpeng Lu[1(✉)], Xueping Peng[2], Shoujin Wang[3],
Guobiao Zhang[1], Weiyu Zhang[1], and Xinxiao Qiao[1]

[1] School of Computer Science and Technology, Qilu University of Technology
(Shandong Academy of Sciences), Jinan, China
{lwp,zwy,qxxyn}@qlu.edu.cn
[2] Australian Artificial Intelligence Institute, University of Technology Sydney,
Sydney, Australia
xueping.peng@uts.edu.au
[3] School of Computer Science and IT, RMIT University, Melbourne, Australia
shoujin.wang@rmit.edu.au

Abstract. Word sense disambiguation (WSD) is a very critical yet challenging task in natural language processing (NLP), which aims at identifying the most suitable meaning of ambiguous words in the given contexts according to a predefined sense inventory. Existing WSD methods usually focus on learning the semantic interactions between a special ambiguous word and the glosses of its candidate senses and thus ignore complicated relations between the neighboring ambiguous words and their glosses, leading to insufficient learning of the interactions between words in context. As a result, they are difficult to leverage the knowledge from the other ambiguous words which might provide some explicit clues to identify the meaning of current ambiguous word. To mitigate this challenge, this paper proposes a novel neural model based on memory enhancement mechanism for WSD task, which stores the gloss knowledge of previously identified words into a memory, and further utilizes it to assist the disambiguation of the next target word. Extensive experiments, which are conducted on a unified evaluation framework of the WSD task, demonstrate that our model achieves better disambiguation performance than the state-of-the-art approaches (Code: https://github.com/baoshuo/WSD).

Keywords: Word sense disambiguation · Gloss information · Memory mechanism · Memory enhancement

1 Introduction

Word sense disambiguation (WSD) aims at identifying the most suitable sense of an ambiguous word in its given context, which is a classical and challenging task in the natural language processing (NLP) area. Specifically, WSD is an essential and critical component in broad NLP applications, such as text classification [19], machine translation [7] and dialogue tasks [12]. Numerous WSD solutions

© The Author(s), under exclusive license to Springer Nature Switzerland AG 2022
G. Memmi et al. (Eds.): KSEM 2022, LNAI 13369, pp. 249–260, 2022.
https://doi.org/10.1007/978-3-031-10986-7_20

have been introduced, which can be generally categorized into knowledge-based and supervised methods.

Knowledge-Based Methods try to fully utilize the knowledge in lexical knowledge bases such as WordNet and BabelNet [17,24]. They either consider the overlap and similarity between the context and glosses of each ambiguous word's senses, or construct a graph for all candidate senses in the context and employ graph-based algorithms. Although knowledge-based methods are flexible and have achieved successes in WSD task, they usually show inferior performance than their supervised counterpart.

Supervised Methods treat WSD as a classification task, and these methods rely on the semantically-annotated corpus for training the classification models. Recently, the effectiveness of supervised methods have been demonstrated in WSD task [9,21]. Particularly, the methods based on neural models have achieved exceptional successes, and show great potentials for addressing the WSD task [5,11]. To be specific, early neural WSD methods leverage neural sequence models, such as LSTM and Seq2Seq, to disambiguate target words. They focus on learning interactive relations between senses of ambiguous words and their context only [10,22]. Although those neural WSD methods could model the dependencies between the candidate senses and the context, they fail to consider the valuable lexical knowledge employed by the knowledge-based counterpart. Aiming at addressing this deficiency, some works attempt to leverage lexical knowledge to optimize supervised neural methods [5], which incorporate the gloss knowledge together with the context into neural WSD models. Although they break the barriers of supervised methods and knowledge-based ones, they mostly model glosses and context with two independent encoders. These approaches unable to capture the glosses-context interactions to strengthen the representations of each other. Therefore, some works propose to learn sense and context representation interactively by generating sense-level context for WSD task [16,26]. However, these methods only show marginal improvements. The possible reason is that they merely focus on the learning of the glosses of the target ambiguous word and the context, while neglecting the glosses of the other neighboring ambiguous words. In real scenarios, when human identify an ambiguous word, it is natural to utilize the gloss information of the previously identified senses of its neighboring words. However, such practice has not been modeled by existing methods.

As well known, when a person reads a sentence containing multiple ambiguous words, he will memorize the identified senses of ambiguous words, and utilize the sense knowledge to assist the disambiguation of the following words. As shown in Table 1, the context contains three ambiguous words, i.e., *monitor*, *table*, and *mouse*. According to their order in the context, once the senses of *monitor* and *table* are identified, their corresponding glosses, i.e., G^{s_1} for *monitor* and G^{s_2} for *table*, will be memorized and utilized to identify the sense of the following ambiguous word, i.e., *mouse*. With the context and the glosses of identified neighboring ambiguous words, a person can identify the right sense

Table 1. Ambiguous words in context and their sense glosses. The ellipsis "..." indicates the remainder of the gloss.

Context		He looks at the **monitor** on **table** and operate it with a **mouse**
Gloss	Monitor	g1: electronic equipment that is used to check the quality or
		g2: someone who supervises (an examination)
	Table	g1: a set of data arranged in rows and columns
		g2: a piece of furniture having a smooth flat top that is usually ...
	Mouse	g1: any of numerous small rodents
		g2: a hand-operated electronic device

easily, i.e., G^{s_2} for *mouse*. However, existing methods neglect to consider the knowledge from the identified ambiguous words and fail to introduce a suitable mechanism to store them to help the disambiguation of the following words. As a result, the interactions between the glosses of identified ambiguous word's senses and the current ambiguous word are missing, which inevitably hurt the performance on WSD task. To this end, how to enhance the learning on the interactions between identified glosses and current ambiguous word is critical for the further performance improvement.

To overcome these limitations, we propose a novel WSD model based on memory enhancement mechanism. Intuitively, memory mechanism can simulate the human reading behaviors to store and memorize the known information, and infer the unknown information [18]. It provides us with the flexibility and capability to capture interaction enhancement between previously identified glosses and the current ambiguous word in our model. Specifically, we first encode the context of the target word and each candidate gloss of the target word by the context-encoder unit and the gloss-encoder unit, respectively. Next, we propose a memory-enhancement unit to enhance the learning of the current target word by making interactions with the glosses of the identified neighboring words stored in the memory previously. Then, we introduce a prediction unit to score each candidate sense of the target word to select the right sense, which is stored into the memory and is employed to enhance the learning of the following ambiguous words.

We summarize the contributions of this paper as follows:

- We propose a novel model for WSD task, i.e., word sense disambiguation based on memory enhancement mechanism (MEM). As far as we know, this is the first work to leverage memory mechanism to model and enhance the interactions between target ambiguous words and the previously identified ones.
- We propose a memory enhancement mechanism, which stores the gloss knowledge of previously identified words in a memory, and utilizes the memory to enhance the representation of the next ambiguous word.
- Experiments on the real-world dataset demonstrate that the proposed model achieves better performance than the compared state-of-the-art benchmarks.

2   Related Word

2.1   Knowledge-Based WSD

Knowledge-based approaches rely on the lexical knowledge to justify the right sense of ambiguous word, which can be categorized into similarity-based methods and graph-based ones. The similarity-based methods usually consider the similarity between the context and the sense information, such as the gloss of the candidate sense, and adopt the sense with the highest similarity as the right one [2,3]. The graph-based methods usually build a graph based on the context and semantic relations retrieved from a lexical knowledge base, then evaluate the importance of each candidate sense to identify the right one [1,20,24]. Although knowledge-based approaches are flexible and show better performance on the coverage rate, they are hard to achieve satisfied performance on precision as the supervised approaches.

2.2   Supervised WSD

Supervised approaches treat WSD task as a classification problem, which are trained on the sense-annotated corpus. In recent years, the methods based on neural models have shown great potentials to address the classification problem. Unlike knowledge-based approaches, some supervised methods succeed to achieve excellent performance by utilizing sense embedding and contextual embedding, instead of lexical information in knowledge bases [10,14,22]. To explore the ability of lexical knowledge, GAS injects the gloss information into supervised models [16]. Following the work of GAS, more methods attempt to integrate lexical knowledge into supervised models, such as BEM [5] and EWISER [4]. BEM learns the representations of the target words and context in the same embedding space with a context encoder, and models the sense representations with a gloss encoder [5]. In addition to the gloss of the current sense, EWISER further utilizes the external explicit relational information from WordNet to enhance its ability [4]. However, these methods neglect the interactions between context and glosses, which can not enhance each other. To address this limitation, very recent works [15,26] attempt to model the interactions between context and glosses. CAN proposes a mechanism to generate co-dependent representations of glosses and the context [15]. SACE strengthens the learning of sense-level context, which takes into account senses in context with a selective attention layer [26]. However, the methods only achieve limited improvements. The possible reason is that they neglect to utilize the gloss information of previously identified senses to assist the disambiguation of the following target words according to the behavior pattern as human reads ambiguous sentences. In this paper, we strive to design a memory enhancement mechanism to solve the problem for WSD task.

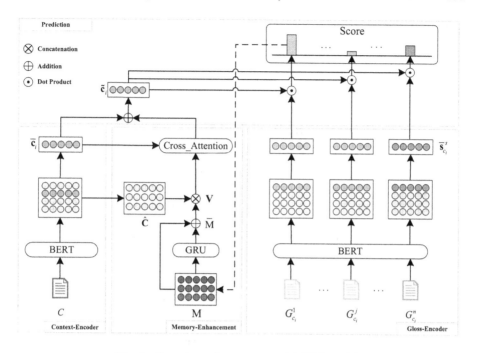

Fig. 1. Overview of our proposed MEM model

3   Methodology

3.1   Task Definition

In the all-words WSD task, the right sense of each ambiguous word in the given context should be identified. Formally, the input of a WSD model is the context $C = \{c_1, c_2, \ldots, c_n\}$ and its output is a sequence of sense predictions $S = \{s^i_{c_1}, s^j_{c_2}, \ldots, s^k_{c_n}\}$, where c_1, c_2, c_n are ambiguous words in the context, and $s^i_{c_1}$, $s^j_{c_2}$ and $s^k_{c_n}$ represent the right senses, i.e., i-th, j-th and n-th sense from the candidate sense sets for c_1, c_2 and c_n. $s \in S_{c_i}$, where S_{c_i} is all candidate senses of the ambiguous word c_i. For each sense s of c_i, we represent its gloss with $G^s_{c_i} = \{g_1, g_2, \ldots, g_n\}$.

3.2   Model Architecture

The overall architecture of our proposed model, called MEM, is shown in Fig. 1. MEM consists of four units, i.e., *the context-encoder unit, the gloss-encoder unit, the memory-enhancement unit* and *the prediction unit.* First, the context-encoder unit and the gloss-encoder unit encode the context and the gloss of each candidate sense of the target ambiguous word, respectively. Then, the memory-enhancement unit enhances the representation of the current target word by learning the its interactions with the glosses of the previously identified neighboring words stored in the memory. Finally, the prediction unit score each candidate sense of the target word to select the right sense for it. Such selected sense is stored into the memory and will be employed to enhance the sense disambiguation of the following ambiguous words.

3.3   Context-Encoder and Gloss-Encoder Units

Inspired by the work of BEM [5], we introduce context-encoder unit and gloss-encoder unit respectively, whose structures are shown in Fig. 1. Both encoders are initialized with BERT to benefit from its powerful ability in capturing interactions between words. The inputs of encoders are padded with BERT-specific start and end symbols, i.e., [CLS] and [SEP]. The context and sense gloss of the target ambiguous word are represented as $C = [\text{CLS}], c_1, c_2, \ldots, c_n, [\text{SEP}]$ and $G_{c_i}^s = [\text{CLS}], g_1, g_2, \ldots, g_n, [\text{SEP}]$, respectively.

The context-encoder unit takes the context C as its input, and encodes it to generate the context representation $\mathbf{C}$ with BERT, described with Eq. (1).

$$\mathbf{C} = \text{BERT}\,(C), \quad \bar{\mathbf{c}}_i = \mathbf{C}[i], \tag{1}$$

where $\bar{\mathbf{c}}_i$ refers to the representation of the i-th word in the context. When the target word is tokenized into multiple subword pieces by BERT tokenizer, its representation is calculated as the average representation of all its subword pieces.

The gloss-encoder unit takes the gloss $G_{c_i}^s$ as its input, and encodes it with BERT. It then selects the output of BERT at the position of [CLS] as the gloss representation.

$$\bar{\mathbf{s}}_{c_i}^s = \text{BERT}^{CLS}(G_{c_i}^s), \tag{2}$$

where $s \in S_{c_i}$ is one of the candidate senses for the target word c_i, $G_{c_i}^s$ is the gloss of s, and $\bar{\mathbf{s}}_{c_i}^s$ is the gloss representation for s.

3.4   Memory-Enhancement Unit

To enhance the representation of the target word, we propose a memory enhancement mechanism. Specifically, we first build a memory to store the representations of the glosses of the previously-identified neighboring words. Then we encourage the interactions between the representation of the target word and gloss representations of those neighboring words stored in the memory. This practice can model human reading behavior, namely, to utilize the previously-identified sense to assist the understanding of the following ambiguous words.

As shown in Fig. 1, one memory component is utilized to store the glosses representations of the previously-identified neighboring words, i.e., $\mathbf{M} = \{\bar{\mathbf{s}}_{c_x}^y\}$. For each representation $\bar{\mathbf{s}}_{c_x}^y$ in the memory, its subscript c_x indicates the c_x-th ambiguous word before the current target word, and its superscript y indicates the identified y-th sense from the candidate sense sets for the c_x-th ambiguous word. For modeling the sequential relations in different glosses, we employ Gated Recurrent Unit (GRU)to reconstruct their representations. Then, the original representation and the reconstructed one are added together to update the memory representation $\bar{\mathbf{M}}$. The above operations are described using Eq. (3).

$$\bar{\mathbf{M}} = [\mathbf{M} \oplus \mathrm{GRU}(\mathbf{M})], \tag{3}$$

where $\oplus$ refers to the addition operation.

Then, in order to utilize the features from neighboring words, we concatenate the context representation $\hat{\mathbf{C}}$ of the neighboring words of the target word and the memory representation $\bar{\mathbf{M}}$ together to generate the auxiliary information representation $\mathbf{V}$ for the current target word:

$$\mathbf{V} = [\hat{\mathbf{C}}; \bar{\mathbf{M}}], \tag{4}$$

where $\hat{\mathbf{C}}$ is obtained by removing the current target word representation from $\mathbf{C}$.

After obtaining the auxiliary information representation $\mathbf{V}$ of the current target word, we employ a cross-attention mechanism [6] to capture the interactions between the representation of the current target word $\bar{\mathbf{c}}_i$ and $\mathbf{V}$ to generate the enhanced representation $\tilde{\mathbf{c}}_i$ of the current target word. The operations are described with Eq. (5).

$$\tilde{\mathbf{c}}_i = f(\bar{\mathbf{c}}_i) + \mathrm{CA}(\mathrm{LN}[f(\bar{\mathbf{c}}_i); \mathbf{V}]), \tag{5}$$

where $f(\cdot)$ is the fully connected function, CA indicates the cross-attention mechanism [6], LN refers to the layer normalization. The detailed operations of cross-attention mechanism is described as Eq. (6).

$$\mathbf{q} = \bar{\mathbf{c}}_i \mathbf{W}_q, \quad \mathbf{k} = \mathbf{V}\mathbf{W}_k, \quad \mathbf{v} = \mathbf{V}\mathbf{W}_v,$$
$$\mathbf{A} = \mathrm{softmax}(\mathbf{q}\mathbf{k}^T/\sqrt{d/h}), \quad \mathrm{CA}(f(\bar{\mathbf{c}}_i); \mathbf{V}) = \mathbf{A}\mathbf{v}, \tag{6}$$

where $\mathbf{W}_q$, $\mathbf{W}_k$ and $\mathbf{W}_v$ are learnable parameters, d and h are the dimension and number of attention heads.

3.5   Prediction Unit

In the prediction unit, we score each candidate sense $s \in S_{c_i}$ for the target word c_i with dot product of $\tilde{\mathbf{c}}_i$ against gloss representation $\bar{\mathbf{s}}_{c_i}^s$ of each sense $s \in S_{c_i}$, described as:

$$score(c_i, s_{c_i}^j) = \tilde{\mathbf{c}}_i \cdot \bar{\mathbf{s}}_{c_i}^j, \tag{7}$$

where $j = 1, \ldots, |S_{c_i}|$ indicates the j-th candidate sense of the target word c_i. According to the scores of all candidate senses, we select the sense $s_{c_i}^h$ with the highest score as the right sense of the target word.

The training object $\mathcal{L}$ is to minimize the focal loss [13]:

$$pt = -\mathrm{CE}(s^r_{c_i}, s^h_{c_i}),$$
$$\mathcal{L}(c_i, s^j_{c_i}) = -\alpha(1 - \exp(pt))^\gamma * pt, \tag{8}$$

where $s^r_{c_i}$ represents the true sense of the target word c_i, CE denotes the cross-entropy function, α and γ are the balance parameter and focusing parameter, respectively.

4   Experiments

4.1   Dataset

Table 2. The details of all datasets

Dataset	Noun	Verb	Adj	Adv	Total
SemCor	87002	88334	31753	18947	226036
SE2	1066	517	445	254	2282
SE3	900	588	350	12	1850
SE07	159	296	0	0	455
SE13	1644	0	0	0	1644
SE15	531	251	160	80	1022

To verify the effectiveness of our proposed model, we employ the publicly available dataset SemCor and a representative open evaluation framework [23] to train and evaluate our model. The framework consists of five evaluation datasets including SensEval-2, SensEval-3, SemEval-07, SemEval-13 and SemEval-15, which are marked with SE2, SE3, SE07, SE13 and SE15, respectively. The details of all datasets are shown in Table 2. SemEval-07 dataset are chosen as our development set, the others are selected as evaluation sets. All sense glosses in our approach are retrieved from the widely-used WordNet 3.0.

4.2   Implementation Details

We utilize the pre-trained BERT to initialize our model, whose number of hidden layer is 768, the number of self-attention heads is 12 and the number of the Transformer blocks is 12. When fine-tuning our model, we use the SE07 as the development set to select the optimal hyperparameters. In the fine-tuned model, the dropout probability of CA is 0.1, the number of CA blocks is 5, the number of CA heads is 8, the balance parameter α and the focusing parameter γ are 0.2

and 0.5, respectively. As the limitation of the hardware condition, the batch size of the context encoder and gloss encoder are 1 and 128, respectively. The initial learning rate is 1e−5.

Table 3. Comparison with state-of-the-art models on F_1-score.

Models	Dev	Test datasets				Concatenation of test datasets				
	SE07	SE2	SE3	SE13	SE15	Noun	Verb	Adj	Adv	ALL
SVC [25]	69.5	77.5	77.4	76.0	78.3	79.6	65.9	79.5	85.5	76.7
EWISE [11]	67.3	73.8	71.1	69.4	74.5	74.0	60.2	78.0	82.1	71.8
LMMS [14]	68.1	76.3	75.6	75.1	77.0	78.0	64.0	80.5	83.5	75.4
GlossBERT [9]	72.5	77.7	75.2	76.1	80.4	79.8	67.1	79.6	**87.4**	77.0
GLU [8]	68.1	75.5	73.6	71.1	76.2	–	–	–	–	74.1
EWISER [4]	71.0	**78.9**	78.4	78.9	79.3	**81.7**	66.3	81.2	85.8	78.3
MEM	**74.9**	78.8	**78.6**	**79.3**	**82.3**	81.4	**69.2**	**83.2**	86.9	**79.1**

4.3 Comparison with the State-of-the-Art Baselines

We compare the performance of our model MEM against seven representative and/or state-of-the-art supervised models. These models include SVC [25], EWISE [11], LMMS [14], GlossBERT [9], GLU [8] and EWISER [4]. SVC exploits the semantic relations between senses to compress the sense vocabulary to reduce the number of sense tags to improve WSD performance. EWISE learns sense representation from a combination of sense-annotated data, gloss definition and lexical knowledge base to perform WSD. LMMS adopts the nearest neighbors algorithm on word representation produced by BERT to select the most suitable sense. GLossBERT utilizes BERT to jointly encode the context and glosses of the target word. GLU employs the pretrained contextualized word representation by BERT to improve WSD accuracy. Based on EWISE, EWISER further incorporates prior knowledge with synset embeddings, i.e., the explicit relational information from WordNet.

Table 3 shows F_1-score of our model and all baselines on dataset SemCor obtained by the public evaluation framework [23]. We observe that although our model is inferior to some baselines on SE2, MEM is still able to achieve the best performance on SE3, SE13, SE15, and ALL datasets. Here, ALL means the concatenation of all datasets. This shows that our model is superior to the baselines. The experimental results demonstrate that our model is effective on WSD task. Such satisfied performance of our model is attributed to its memory enhancement mechanism.

4.4 Ablation Study

Table 4. Comparison of ablation variants.

Ablation variants	Dev F_1-score	Δ
MEM	74.9	–
Del-Memory	73.8	−1.1
Only-Memory	74.1	−0.8
Del-CA	74.4	−0.5
Del-Update	74.5	−0.4

We perform an ablation study by comparing the standard MEM model with its four ablation variants: (a) Del-Memory: removes the memory component described in Eq. (3), the contextual representation will interact with the target word via cross-attention directly; (b) Only-Memory: removes the contextual representation described in Eq. (4), the memory representation $\bar{M}$ will interact with the target word via cross-attention directly; (c) Del-CA: removes the CA mechanism described in Eq. (5); (d) Del-Update: removes the GRU component described in Eq. (3) to stop the update of the gloss representation stored in the memory.

The comparison result of the ablation study is shown in Table 4. According to the table, we have the following observations. First, the performance decrease of Del-Memory and Only-Memory demonstrates that the memory enhancement mechanism is critical for our model. Second, both Del-CA and Del-Update show inferior performance than the standard MEM model, which demonstrates that cross-attention component and memory updating mechanism are effective.

5 Conclusion

This paper proposes a novel model for word sense disambiguation based on memory enhancement mechanism (MEM). To the best of our knowledge, this is the first work to leverage memory mechanism to store the gloss knowledge of previously-identified words to assist the disambiguation of the next target word. Accordingly, we design an effective memory enhancement mechanism to enhance the representation of the target word with the identified glosses. Experimental results on real-world datasets demonstrate that our model outperforms the state-of-the-art models on word sense disambiguation task. This may provide a new perspective for utilizing memory mechanism and gloss knowledge to improve WSD methods.

Acknowledgment. The research work is partly supported by National Nature Science Foundation of China under Grant No. 61502259, and Key Program of Science and Technology of Shandong under Grant No. 2020CXGC 010901 and No. 2019JZZY020124.

References

1. Agirre, E., de Lacalle, O.L., Soroa, A.: Random walks for knowledge-based word sense disambiguation. Comput. Linguist. **40**(1), 57–84 (2014)
2. Banerjee, S., Pedersen, T.: An adapted Lesk algorithm for word sense disambiguation using WordNet. In: International Conference on Intelligent Text Processing and Computational Linguistics, pp. 136–145 (2002)
3. Basile, P., Caputo, A., Semeraro, G.: An enhanced Lesk word sense disambiguation algorithm through a distributional semantic model. In: Proceedings of the 25th International Conference on Computational Linguistics, pp. 1591–1600 (2014)
4. Bevilacqua, M., Navigli, R.: Breaking through the 80% glass ceiling: raising the state of the art in word sense disambiguation by incorporating knowledge graph information. In: Proceedings of the 58th Annual Meeting of the Association for Computational Linguistics, pp. 2854–2864 (2020)
5. Blevins, T., Zettlemoyer, L.: Moving down the long tail of word sense disambiguation with gloss informed bi-encoders. In: Proceedings of the 58th Annual Meeting of the Association for Computational Linguistics, pp. 1006–1017 (2020)
6. Chen, C.F., Fan, Q., Panda, R.: CrossVIT: cross-attention multi-scale vision transformer for image classification. arXiv preprint arXiv:2103.14899 (2021)
7. Emelin, D., Titov, I., Sennrich, R.: Detecting word sense disambiguation biases in machine translation for model-agnostic adversarial attacks. In: The 2020 Conference on Empirical Methods in Natural Language Processing, pp. 7635–7653. Association for Computational Linguistics (2020)
8. Hadiwinoto, C., Ng, H.T., Gan, W.C.: Improved word sense disambiguation using pre-trained contextualized word representations. In: Proceedings of the 2019 Conference on Empirical Methods in Natural Language Processing and the 9th International Joint Conference on Natural Language Processing, pp. 5297–5306 (2019)
9. Huang, L., Sun, C., Qiu, X., Huang, X.J.: GlossBERT: BERT for word sense disambiguation with gloss knowledge. In: Proceedings of the 2019 Conference on Empirical Methods in Natural Language Processing and the 9th International Joint Conference on Natural Language Processing, pp. 3509–3514 (2019)
10. Kågebäck, M., Salomonsson, H.: Word sense disambiguation using a bidirectional LSTM. In: COLING, pp. 51–56 (2016)
11. Kumar, S., Jat, S., Saxena, K., Talukdar, P.: Zero-shot word sense disambiguation using sense definition embeddings. In: Proceedings of the 57th Annual Meeting of the Association for Computational Linguistics, pp. 5670–5681 (2019)
12. Le, H., et al.: FlauBERT: unsupervised language model pre-training for French. In: Proceedings of the 12th Language Resources and Evaluation Conference, pp. 2479–2490 (2020)
13. Lin, T., Goyal, P., Girshick, R., He, K., Dollar, P.: Focal loss for dense object detection. IEEE PAMI **42**(2), 318–327 (2018)
14. Loureiro, D., Jorge, A.: Language modelling makes sense: propagating representations through WordNet for full-coverage word sense disambiguation. In: Proceedings of the 57th Annual Meeting of the Association for Computational Linguistics, pp. 5682–5691 (2019)
15. Luo, F., Liu, T., He, Z., Xia, Q., Sui, Z., Chang, B.: Leveraging gloss knowledge in neural word sense disambiguation by hierarchical co-attention. In: Proceedings of the 2018 Conference on Empirical Methods in Natural Language Processing, pp. 1402–1411 (2018)

16. Luo, F., Liu, T., Xia, Q., Chang, B., Sui, Z.: Incorporating glosses into neural word sense disambiguation. In: Proceedings of the 56th Annual Meeting of the Association for Computational Linguistics, pp. 2473–2482 (2018)

17. Maru, M., Scozzafava, F., Martelli, F., Navigli, R.: SyntagNET: challenging supervised word sense disambiguation with lexical-semantic combinations. In: Proceedings of the 2019 Conference on Empirical Methods in Natural Language Processing and the 9th International Joint Conference on Natural Language Processing, pp. 3534–3540 (2019)

18. Miller, A., Fisch, A., Dodge, J., Karimi, A.H., Bordes, A., Weston, J.: Key-value memory networks for directly reading documents. In: Proceedings of the 2016 Conference on Empirical Methods in Natural Language Processing, pp. 1400–1409 (2016)

19. Moreo, A., Esuli, A., Sebastiani, F.: Word-class embeddings for multiclass text classification. Data Min. Knowl. Disc. 35(3), 911–963 (2021). https://doi.org/10.1007/s10618-020-00735-3

20. Moro, A., Raganato, A., Navigli, R.: Entity linking meets word sense disambiguation: a unified approach. Trans. Assoc. Comput. 2, 231–244 (2014)

21. Pasini, T., Navigli, R.: Train-O-Matic: supervised word sense disambiguation with no (manual) effort. Artif. Intell. 279, 103215 (2020)

22. Raganato, A., Bovi, C.D., Navigli, R.: Neural sequence learning models for word sense disambiguation. In: Proceedings of the 2017 Conference on Empirical Methods in Natural Language Processing, pp. 1156–1167 (2017)

23. Raganato, A., Camacho-Collados, J., Navigli, R.: Word sense disambiguation: a unified evaluation framework and empirical comparison. In: Proceedings of the 15th Conference of the European Chapter of the Association for Computational Linguistics, pp. 99–110 (2017)

24. Tripodi, R., Navigli, R.: Game theory meets embeddings: a unified framework for word sense disambiguation. In: Proceedings of the 2019 Conference on Empirical Methods in Natural Language Processing and the 9th International Joint Conference on Natural Language Processing, pp. 88–99 (2019)

25. Vial, L., Lecouteux, B., Schwab, D.: Sense vocabulary compression through the semantic knowledge of WordNet for neural word sense disambiguation. In: Proceedings of the 10th Global WordNet Conference, pp. 108–117 (2019)

26. Wang, M., Wang, Y.: Word sense disambiguation: Towards interactive context exploitation from both word and sense perspectives. In: Proceedings of the 59th Annual Meeting of the Association for Computational Linguistics and the 11th International Joint Conference on Natural Language Processing, pp. 5218–5229 (2021)

A Spatial Interpolation Using Clustering Adaptive Inverse Distance Weighting Algorithm with Linear Regression

Liang Zhu[✉], Gengchen Hou, Xin Song, Yonggang Wei, and Yu Wang

Hebei University, Baoding 071002, Hebei, China
zhu@hbu.edu.cn

Abstract. The Inverse Distance Weighting (IDW) spatial interpolation algorithm is one of the important methods that are used to estimate the values of specific locations based on an observation dataset of samples. However, it is difficult to obtain highly accurate estimates due to some weaknesses of the IDW algorithm. To address the problems of the IDW algorithm, in this paper, we propose a new spatial interpolation method by integrating the IDW algorithm with the clustering algorithms, adaptive mechanism and weighted linear regression model, namely CAIDWR. (1) By employing the clustering algorithms, the CAIDWR method eliminates abnormal values for cleaning a sample set and clusters the similar attribute values of samples for spatial interpolation. (2) This method adaptively evaluates the distance-decay parameter by calculating the local neighborhood density of a predicted point and using a fuzzy membership function. (3) It adaptively optimizes the interpolation results by using the trend of the cleaned sample set with the weighted linear regression strategy. The CAIDWR method is applied to a system of soil testing and formulated fertilization for intelligent agriculture, we compare our CAIDWR method with the Ordinary Kriging (OK) algorithm and four IDW-like algorithms over a dataset of soil samples, and the results show that our CAIDWR method outperforms the five algorithms significantly.

Keywords: Inverse distance weighting · Spatial clustering · Distance-decay parameter · Weighted linear regression · K nearest neighbor

1 Introduction

Continuous spatial data (e.g., meteorological data, geological data and air pollution data) is the foundation of a variety of scientific model research [9, 11, 16, 21], and accurate spatial data can be obtained by high-density sampling. In many scenarios, however, it is a challenge to obtain highly accurate spatial data due to sampling cost, topographic conditions and other factors. To address this problem, spatial interpolation methods are used to estimate the values of specific locations based on some observation data of samples. Various spatial interpolation methods for this issue are proposed, such as the Inverse Distance Weighting (IDW) [23], Linear Regression (LR) [1], Ordinary Kriging (OK) [13], Support Vector Regression (SVR) [25] and Genetic Programming (GP) [8]

© The Author(s), under exclusive license to Springer Nature Switzerland AG 2022
G. Memmi et al. (Eds.): KSEM 2022, LNAI 13369, pp. 261–272, 2022.
https://doi.org/10.1007/978-3-031-10986-7_21

methods, while each of them has its own advantages and disadvantages, and there is no method that is effective or suitable for different fields [11].

The IDW method has become one of the most commonly used spatial interpolation methods due to its elegant definition, simple implementation, and ease of use. Moreover, the IDW method does not require specific statistical assumptions and models. It can obtain a relatively reasonable result for any sample size; meanwhile, its generalization to an arbitrary number of dimensions arises naturally since the interpolation is defined based on the distance between their points [9]. However, empirical evaluations consistently show that the IDW method has the following weaknesses: (1) Due to the influence of various uncertain factors, the sample data inevitably contain abnormal values, which cannot be eliminated by this method. (2) A single distance-decay parameter is used in the IDW method, in general, which will lead to the inaccuracy of estimated value because of the non-uniform distribution of spatial data. (3) IDW method only considers the influence of the distance between sample points but does not use the trend of the data; moreover, interpolation results of the IDW method are between the maximum and minimum values of sample points.

To address the problems in the IDW method, we discuss a new kind of spatial interpolation algorithm. Our contributions are summarized below: (1) First, we use a clustering mechanism to deal with abnormal sample points for cleaning a set of samples and group the similar attribute values of samples into a cluster. Next, we evaluate the distance-decay parameter based on the local spatial distribution pattern of the neighborhood for a predicted point. Then, we optimize the results of spatial interpolation by using the trend of sample data with the strategy of weighted linear regression. (2) Inspired by the main ideas of the KNN (K Nearest Neighbor, or top-K) query mechanism in [26, 27], we propose a new spatial interpolation method, namely CAIDWR (Clustering Adaptive Inverse Distance Weighting algorithm with weighted linear Regression), which try to overcome the weaknesses of IDW method. (3) Our CAIDWR method is applied to a system of soil testing and formulated fertilization for intelligent agriculture, and we compare this method with the Ordinary Kriging (OK) algorithm and four IDW-like algorithms over a dataset of soil samples.

The rest of this paper is organized as follows. In Sect. 2, we briefly review some related work. Section 3 presents our method CAIDWR. In Sect. 4, we present the experimental results. Finally, we conclude the paper in Sect. 5.

2   Related Work

Many kinds of research on spatial interpolation methods have been proposed. The IDW method is a simple but critical one in many scenarios. There are a variety of IDW-like algorithms being the adaptations or improvements of the IDW method for different applications. Here, we only review some related works involving the IDW-like algorithms.

Chang et al. [5] developed a variable-order distance IDW method based on the generic algorithm to minimize the difference between estimated and measured precipitation data. Lu et al. [19] improved the distance-decay parameter in the IDW method so that the parameter can be automatically adjusted according to the spatial distribution pattern of the sample points in the neighborhood of the predicted point. Shiode and Shiode [24] introduced a network-based IDW method to help predict unknown spatial values more accurately with networks. Greenberg et al. [12] employed the cumulative, raster-based least-cost-distance to define the distance between two locations and found that the method yields more realistic interpolation results. Chen et al. [6] showed that the classic IDW method is essentially a zeroth-order local kernel regression method with an inverse distance weight function and proposed a generalized IDW method with the first- and second orders. Peng et al. [20] proposed a spatial interpolation method based on clustering, and the experimental results showed that IDW interpolation after clustering is better than direct interpolation. Li et al. [18] added a harmonic weight coefficient K to reflect the azimuth of sample points based on the traditional IDW method to reduce or overcome the IDW interpolation defects of uneven distribution of sample points. Ballarin et al. [3] provided an improvement based on a geometric criterion that automatically selects a subset of the original set of control points. Qu et al. [22] studied data normalization, which improves the accuracy of the IDW method. Jeong et al. [14] used a parameter-elevation regression on independent slopes model (PRISM) with the IDW method to improve daily precipitation estimation, which solved the problem of overestimating the precipitation intensity in mountainous regions and overestimating local precipitation areas when using the PRISM (PRISM_ORG) method to estimate daily precipitation. Emmendorfer et al. [9] improved the IDW method based on a distance regression model, and the improved method uses the trend of data, and its interpolation results are not limited to the range of the minimum to maximum values of sample points. Bayat et al. [4] presented a fuzzy IDW (FIDW) method which is used to reduce the complexity of the spatiotemporal procedure of network design by using a fuzzy paradigm.

The above variations of the IDW method improve it by overcoming one of its weaknesses. We will propose a new method, namely CAIDWR, which improves the IDW method from multiple aspects to overcome its three weaknesses.

3   CAIDWR Method

The CAIDWR interpolation method proposed in this paper uses clustering algorithms to clean abnormal sample points and to cluster the cleaned sample points, evaluates the distance-decay parameter based on the KNN mechanism, and finally optimizes the interpolation results by using the trend of the sample data with the strategy of weighted linear regression.

3.1   Cluster of Spatial Data

We deal with abnormal sample points by clustering spatial data. The spatial clustering algorithms used in this paper are based on the main ideas of the Density-Based Spatial Clustering of Applications with Noise (DBSCAN) algorithm [10] and k-means++ [2] algorithm. DBSCAN is a representative density-based clustering algorithm that defines clusters as the largest collection of points connected by density, divides regions with sufficiently high density into clusters, and identifies noise points.

The k-means++ algorithm is an improved algorithm of the classical k-means algorithm. It is based on the principle that the distance between the initial cluster centers should be as far as possible when selecting the initial cluster center. It is used to divide n objects into k clusters so that the objects in the cluster have high similarities while the objects between clusters have low similarities.

Spatial data contains geographical location and attribute characteristics, and the spatial properties are related to both of them. However, the traditional spatial clustering algorithm uses either location distance or attribute distance to calculate distance, leading to some limitations in spatial clustering.

We will discuss the dataset of samples in a metric space. Let $(\Re^n, d(\cdot,\cdot))$ be the n-dimensional real vector space with the distance function $d(\cdot,\cdot)$ that is derived by the ℓ_p norm or the p norm $\|\cdot\|_p$ ($1 \le p \le \infty$). For $x = (x_1, x_2, \cdots, x_n)$ and $y = (y_1, y_2, \cdots, y_n)$ in $\Re^n$, $d_p(x, y)$ is defined as follows

$$d_p(x, y) = \|x - y\|_p = \left(\sum_{i=1}^{n} |x_i - y_i|^p \right)^{1/p} \text{ for } 1 \le p < \infty \tag{1}$$

$$d_\infty(x, y) = \|x - y\|_\infty = \max_{1 \le i \le d} (|x_i - y_i|) \text{ for } p = \infty \tag{2}$$

Moreover, $\|x\|_p \to \|x\|_\infty$ as $p \to \infty$. When $p = 1, 2$, and ∞, $d_p(x, y)$ will be the *Manhattan distance* $d_1(x, y)$, *Euclidean distance* $d_2(x, y)$, and *Maximum distance* $d_\infty(x, y)$ respectively, which are useful in many applications. We define the spatial distance

$$D\big((x_i, a_i), (x_j, a_j)\big) = w d_p(x_i, x_j) + (1 - w) d_p(a_i, a_j) \tag{3}$$

to be the combination of the position distance $d_p(x_i, x_j)$ and the attribute distance $d_p(a_i, a_j)$, where $x_i = (x_{i1}, x_{i2}, \cdots, x_{im})$ is the location coordinate, say, $x_i = (x_{i1}, x_{i2})$ means the latitude and longitude, $a_i = (a_{i1}, a_{i2}, \cdots, a_{in})$ is the n attribute vectors at the position x_i, and w is the weight of the location distance. In our experiments, we use $p = 2$, i.e., Euclidean distance in $D\big((x_i, a_i), (x_j, a_j)\big)$. In order to eliminate the influence of the value units on clusters, the data should be normalized by

$$u_i = (z_i - z_{min})/(z_{max} - z_{min}) \tag{4}$$

where z_{max} and z_{min} are the maximum and minimum values of each dimension value z_i of the sample points.

The process of clustering spatial data is as follows: Firstly, we clean the set of all sample points by using the DBSCAN algorithm to eliminate abnormal sample points. Secondly, the k-means++ algorithm is used to cluster the cleaned data.

3.2 Evaluation of the Distance-Decay Parameter

We determine the distance-decay parameter of predicted points based on the adaptive mechanism [11, 17, 19]. After clustering the cleaned dataset of sample points, for a predicted point, we find its K nearest sample points (i.e., KNN or top-K points) from the cluster where the predicted point is located, and the local neighborhood of the predicted point is a circle containing KNN points. The distance-decay parameter of our CAIDWR method is determined according to the local spatial pattern of the sample points in the neighborhood of the predicted point.

We evaluate the distance-decay parameter of the predicted point according to the density or sparsity of its neighborhood. For dense neighborhoods, the average value of the KNN sample points should be used for the estimated value of the predicted point (i.e., the interpolation), and distance-decay parameters should be smaller because the sample points in a dense neighborhood are likely to have similar characteristics. For sparse neighborhoods, accordingly, distance-decay parameters should be bigger, and then the sample points being closer to the predicted point will have greater weight.

Firstly, we quantify the local spatial pattern of the predicted point neighborhood to obtain the density or sparsity of the neighborhood by using the local nearest neighbor index [7]. The average value of the nearest neighbor distance for the predicted point neighborhood, r_{ave}, is defined as

$$r_{ave} = \left(\sum_{i=1}^{n} d_i\right)\Big/n \tag{5}$$

where n is the number of sample points in the local neighborhood of the predicted point, d_i is Euclidean distance between the predicted point $x = (x_1, x_2, \cdots, x_h)$ and the i-th sample point $y_i = (y_{i1}, y_{i2}, \cdots, y_{ih})$ in the neighborhood ($\subset \Re^h$), which is defined by

$$d_2(x, y) = \|x - y\|_2 = \left(\sum_{j=1}^{h} |x_j - y_{ij}|^2\right)^{1/2} \tag{6}$$

in our experiments $h = 2$. The expected nearest neighbor distance for a random pattern can be derived from

$$r_{exp} = 1\Big/\left(2(N/A)^{1/2}\right) \tag{7}$$

where N is the number of all points in the study area and A is the area of the study region. The nearest neighbor statistic $R(S_0)$ for the predicted point S_0 is defined by the above r_{ave} and r_{exp}

$$R(S_0) = r_{ave}/r_{exp} \tag{8}$$

The smaller $R(S_0)$ value means the denser the local neighborhood for the predicted point S_0, and vice versa. Theoretically, $R(S_0)$ reflects the density or sparsity of sample points in the neighborhood of S_0.

Secondly, we optimize the distance-decay parameter by using a fuzzy membership function [15] to normalize the values of $R(S_0)$, which provides more flexibility than the standard linear normalization. The normalized local nearest neighbor statistic value, μ_R, is defined as follows

$$\mu_R = \begin{cases} 0, & R(S_0) < R_{min} \\ 0.5 + 0.5\sin[(\pi/(R_{max} - R_{min}))(R(S_0) - (R_{max} - R_{min})/2)], & \\ & R_{min} \le R(S_0) \le R_{max} \\ 1, & R_{max} < R(S_0) \end{cases} \tag{9}$$

where, in general, R_{min} and R_{max} are set to the empirical minimum and maximum, respectively, of $R(S_0)$ for all locations of S_0, or other values.

Finally, we utilize the triangular membership function [15] in Fig. 1 to map the normalized local nearest neighbor statistic values to an appropriate distance-decay parameter α. In this triangular membership function, the x-axis is the values of μ_R obtained from normalizing the nearest neighbor statistic values, and the y-axis shows the values of the membership degree. Five levels or categories are used (I, II, III, IV, and V as shown in Fig. 1), and we assign a distance-decay value for each category. Given a value for μ_R, we use the triangular membership function in Fig. 1 to determine an appropriate distance-decay parameter. The determination is based on linear interpolation.

If the $R(S_0)$ is 2.5 for a predicted point S_0, for instance, the corresponding μ_R will be 0.35. According to the triangular membership function in Fig. 1, the μ_R (= 0.35) corresponds to two values 0.25 and 0.75 of the membership degree, i.e., 0.25 for category III with α = c and 0.75 for category II with α = b. Thus, the final α will be 0.75b + 0.25c. Note that the sum of the two membership degrees for any μ_R value is always 1.

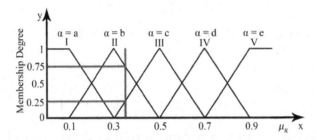

Fig. 1. Triangular membership function [15].

3.3 Inverse Distance Weighted Regression Interpolation

The inverse distance weighted regression interpolation method is derived from a weighted linear regression model [9], being equivalent to the IDW method with an additional term, and is defined below

$$z = z_{idw} + n\left(\sum_{i=1}^{n} z_i - n z_{idw}\right) \Big/ \left(n^2 - \sum_{i=1}^{n} d_i^{-\alpha} \sum_{i=1}^{n} d_i^{\alpha}\right) \qquad (10)$$

where z is the value of the predicted point, and z_{idw} is the value of the predicted point obtained by the classical IDW method, which is calculated by

$$z_{idw} = \sum_{i=1}^{n} w_i z_i \qquad (11)$$

the weight w_i is calculated by

$$w_i = d_i^{-\alpha} \Big/ \sum_{i=1}^{n} d_i^{-\alpha} \qquad (12)$$

z_i is the value of the i-th sample point, n is the number of sample points involved in the interpolation, α is the distance-decay parameter obtained above, and d_i is the Euclidean distance between the predicted point and the i-th sample point.

We provide the algorithm CAIDWR below, which will call the functions GetR($\cdot$) and GetZ($\cdot$), which follow the algorithm CAIDWR.

Algorithm CAIDWR

Input: k, D, C, Y /*$D = \{(x_{i1}, x_{i2}, \cdots, x_{im}); i =1,2, \cdots,s\}$, $C = \{(x_{i1}, x_{i2}, \cdots, x_{ih}); i =1,2, \cdots,t\}$, $Y (\subset D)$ is a small part randomly selected from the dataset D*/

Output: Z // Interpolation result of dataset C

---

1    $D^* = \{(x_{i1}, x_{i2}, \cdots, x_{im}); i =1,2, \cdots,n\} \leftarrow$ A new dataset obtained by performing the DBSCAN algorithm on D to clean abnormal sample points;

2    $A = \{A_1, A_2, \cdots, A_q\} \leftarrow$ Q clusters obtained by the k-means++ algorithm on D^*;
     // Infer the value range of R through a small number of R values

3   **For** each $y_i \in Y$

4   Find A_j in A such that y_i is closest to A_j;

5        $R_i \leftarrow$ Call GetR(A_j, y_i, k);   //Call function

6   **End for**

7   Let $RMax = \max(R_1, R_2, \cdots, R_u)$;   //Empirical maximum value of R

8   Let $RMin = \min(R_1, R_2, \cdots, R_u)$;   //Empirical minimum value of R

9   **For** each $c_i \in C$

10   Find A_j in A such that c_i is closest to A_j;

11       $R_i \leftarrow$ Call GetR(A_j, c_i, k);   //Call function

12   **If** $R_i < RMin$ //Normalized R

13           $\mu_R \leftarrow 0$;

14   **Else if** $R_i > RMax$

15           $\mu_R \leftarrow 1$;

16   **Else**

17           $\mu_R \leftarrow 0.5 + 0.5\sin[(\pi/(RMax - RMin))(R_i - (RMax - RMin)/2)]$;

18   **End if**

19   Get α_i;   //According to the value of μ_R, and using the triangular membership function

20       $z_i \leftarrow$ Call GetZ(A_j, c_i, α_i);   //Call function

21   Add z_i to Z;

22   **End for**

23   **Return** Z

The function GetR($\cdot$) below will be used for each predicted point to find the nearest neighbor statistic R of the predicted point.

Function GetR (D, c, k)   //k is the number of points in local neighborhood

---

1   **For** each $p_i \in D$

2        $d_i \leftarrow$ Euclidean distance between p_i and c;   /*Only longitude and latitude data are considered when calculating distance here*/

3   **End for**

4   sort d_i such that $d_1 < d_2 < \cdots < d_k$;

5    $r_{ave} \leftarrow (\sum_{i=1}^{n} d_i)/k$;   //The average value of the nearest neighbor distance

6    $r_{exp} \leftarrow 1/(2(N/A)^{1/2})$;   //The expected nearest neighbor distance

7    $R \leftarrow r_{ave}/r_{exp}$;   //The nearest neighbor statistic

8   **Return** R

The function GetZ(·) below will be used for each predicted point to find the final interpolation result of the predicted point.

Function GetZ (D, c, α)	
1 $n \leftarrow$ The number of points in D;	
2 **For** each $p_i \in D$	
3 $d_i \leftarrow$ Euclidean distance between p_i and c;	
4 **End for**	
5 **For** each $p_i \in D$	
6 $w_i \leftarrow d_i^{-\alpha}/\sum_{i=1}^{n} d_i^{-\alpha}$;	// Calculate the weight of each point
7 **End for**	
8 $z_{idw} \leftarrow \sum_{i=1}^{n} w_i z_i$;	
9 $z \leftarrow z_{idw} + n(\sum_{i=1}^{n} z_i - n z_{idw})/(n^2 - \sum_{i=1}^{n} d_i^{-\alpha} \sum_{i=1}^{n} d_i^{\alpha})$;	
10 **Return** z	

In our CAIDWR algorithm, C is the dataset of all predicted points, and A is the dataset of all sample points in a cluster. Let $|C|$ (or $|D|$) indicate the number of tuples in dataset C (or D). The time complexity of the CAIDWR algorithm to interpolate all points in C is $O(|C| \cdot |D| \cdot \log|D|)$.

4 Experimental Results

The experiments will be conducted to compare our CAIDWR method with five methods: (1) the classic IDW method, (2) the inverse distance weighted regression (IDWR) method, (3) the density-based adaptive inverse distance weighting (AIDW) method, (4) the cluster-based inverse distance weighting (CIDW) method, and (5) the ordinary Kriging (OK) method, where the CIDW method uses the classic k-means algorithm, while the variogram in the OK method employs the most commonly used spherical model. In order to reduce the influence of the distance-decay parameter on the interpolation results, the most commonly used distance-decay parameters 1, 2, and 3 are used. The number after the method name in the experimental results indicates the value of the distance-decay parameter when this method is used, say, distance-decay parameter $\alpha = 2$ in IDW_2 method.

Cross-validation is adopted for the comparative analyses in our experiments. Randomly selected 80% of all data for the spatial interpolation process and reserved the remaining 20% for validation. The Root Mean Square Error (*RMSE*) will be used to measure the accuracy of each interpolation method, which is given below

$$RMSE = \left((1/n) \sum_{i=1}^{n} \left(z_i - z_i^*\right)^2\right)^{1/2} \tag{13}$$

where n is the number of sample points participated in the validation, z_i is the predicted value of the i-th predicted point, and z_i^* is the actual value of the i-th predicted point.

The experimental data in this paper are from 400 soil nutrient sample points in Luanzhou and Luannan counties in Tangshan City, Hebei Province, China. The data consist of county name, longitude, latitude, organic matter, slowly available potassium, etc. The distribution of sample points is shown in Fig. 2.

Table 1 illustrates the parameters used in the CAIDWR method, including the position distance weight w, the specified radius ε, and the density threshold *minPts* in the DBSCAN algorithm, the number of clusters q in k-means++ algorithm, the number of points k required to determine the local neighborhood, and a, b, c, d, e in the triangular membership function. Figure 3 shows the results of our experiments.

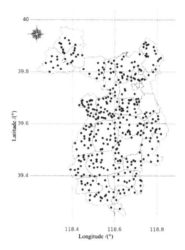

Fig. 2. Distribution map of soil nutrient sample points.

Table 1. Parameter values used in the CAIDWR method for two soil data sets.

	w	ε	minPts	q	k	a, b, c, d, e
Organic matter	0.5	0.11	3	8	15	1, 1.3, 1.6, 1.9, 2.2
Slowly available potassium	0.5	0.1	3	8	15	1.3, 1.6, 1.9, 2.2, 2.5

For "organic matter", it can be seen from Fig. 3(a) that the *RMSE* values of each method from small to large are CAIDWR, CIDW, OK, AIDW, IDWR and IDW; meanwhile, for the IDW, IDWR and CIDW methods with three different distance-decay parameters, the methods with the minimum *RMSE* in the experiments are IDW_1, IDWR_2 and CIDW_1 respectively. For "slowly available potassium", from Fig. 3(b), the *RMSE* values of each method from small to large are CAIDWR, OK, AIDW, IDWR, CIDW and IDW; meanwhile, for the IDW, IDWR and CIDW methods with three different distance-decay parameters, the methods with the minimum *RMSE* in the experiments are IDW_2, IDWR_2 and CIDW_2 respectively.

For both "organic matter" and "slowly available potassium", the interpolation accuracy of our CAIDWR method is significantly better than that of the other five interpolation methods. The interpolation accuracy of the OK, IDWR, AIDW, and CIDW methods is close to or better than that of the IDW method. Moreover, IDW, IDWR, and CIDW methods perform almost identically for the selection of the best α value. The reasons for

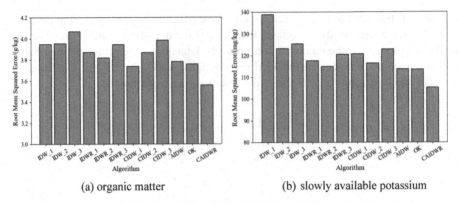

(a) organic matter   (b) slowly available potassium

Fig. 3. The Root Mean Square Error (*RMSE*) of six spatial interpolation methods.

these results are as follows: (1) The AIDW method optimizes the α value according to the local spatial pattern of the predicted point neighborhood. (2) The IDWR method uses the data trend to adjust the interpolation results adaptively. (3) In the CIDW method, the sample points with similar attribute values are grouped in a cluster, and the sample points in the cluster are used to reduce the influence of irrelevant sample points on the interpolation results.

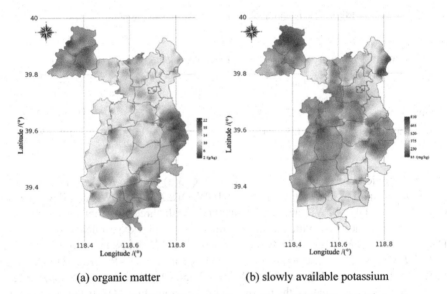

(a) organic matter   (b) slowly available potassium

Fig. 4. Visualization of interpolation results of CAIDWR method.

Our CAIDWR method integrates the advantages of the CIDW, AIDW and IDWR methods and eliminates abnormal points by using the clustering algorithms, then it outperforms the other five methods significantly. Using our CAIDWR method, in addition, the results of interpolation of these 400 soil nutrient sample points are given in Fig. 4.

We have conducted additional experiments to compare the CAIDWR method with the above five methods over the Daily Value Dataset of Climate Data of China Ground International Exchange Station (V3.0), and the accuracy of our CAIDWR is much better than that of the five methods. The results are omitted due to space limitation.

5   Conclusion

To overcome the weaknesses of the IDW algorithm, in this paper, we proposed a new spatial interpolation method, namely CAIDWR, by integrating the IDW algorithm with the clustering algorithms, adaptive mechanism and weighted linear regression model. The CAIDWR method was applied to a system of soil testing and formulated fertilization for intelligent agriculture and compared with the Ordinary Kriging (OK) algorithm and four IDW-like algorithms over a dataset of soil samples. The experimental results demonstrated that our CAIDWR method outperforms the five algorithms significantly and produces more accurate estimates; meanwhile, the estimation accuracy of the OK algorithm, IDWR algorithm, AIDW algorithm, and CIDW algorithm is almost the same as or better than that of the IDW algorithm.

References

1. Anees, M.T., et al.: Spatial estimation of average daily precipitation using multiple linear regression by using topographic and wind speed variables in tropical climate. J. Environ. Eng. Landsc. Manag. **26**(4), 299–316 (2018)
2. Arthur, D., Vassilvitskii, S.: K-means++: the advantages of careful seeding. In: Proceedings of the Eighteenth Annual ACM-SIAM Symposium on Discrete Algorithms, New Orleans. SIAM, pp. 1027–1035 (2007)
3. Ballarin, F., D'amario, A., Perotto, S., Rozza, G.: A POD-selective inverse distance weighting method for fast parametrized shape morphing. Int. J. Numer. Meth. Eng. **117**(8), 860–884 (2018)
4. Bayat, B., Nasseri, M., Delmelle, E.: Uncertainty-based rainfall network design using a fuzzy spatial interpolation method. Appl. Soft Comput. **106**, 107296 (2021)
5. Chang, C.L., Lo, S.L., Yu, S.L.: The parameter optimization in the inverse distance method by genetic algorithm for estimating precipitation. Environ. Monit. Assess. **117**(1), 145–155 (2006)
6. Chen, C., Zhao, N., Yue, T., Guo, J.: A generalization of inverse distance weighting method via kernel regression and its application to surface modeling. Arab. J. Geosci. **8**(9), 6623–6633 (2014)
7. Clark, P.J., Evans, F.C.: Distance to nearest neighbor as a measure of spatial relationships in populations. Ecology **35**(4), 445–453 (1954)
8. Cramer, S., Kampouridis, M., Freitas, A.A.: Decomposition genetic programming: an extensive evaluation on rainfall prediction in the context of weather derivatives. Appl. Soft Comput. **70**, 208–224 (2018)
9. Emmendorfer, L.R., Dimuro, G.P.: A point interpolation algorithm resulting from weighted linear regression. J. Comput. Sci. **50**, 101304 (2021)
10. Ester, M., Kriegel, H., Sander, J., Xu, X.: A density-based algorithm for discovering clusters in large spatial databases with noise. In: KDD, pp. 226–231 (1996)

11. Fan, Z., Li, J., Deng, M.: An adaptive inverse-distance weighting spatial interpolation method with the consideration of multiple factors. Geomat. Inf. Sci. Wuhan Univ. **41**(6), 842–847 (2016)
12. Greenberg, J.A., Rueda, C., Hestir, E.L., Santos, M.J., Ustin, S.L.: Least cost distance analysis for spatial interpolation. Comput. Geosci. **37**(2), 272–276 (2011)
13. Jalili Pirani, F., Modarres, R.: Geostatistical and deterministic methods for rainfall interpolation in the Zayandeh Rud basin. Iran. Hydrol. Sci. J. **65**(16), 2678–2692 (2020)
14. Jeong, H.-G., Ahn, J.-B., Lee, J., Shim, K.-M., Jung, M.-P.: Improvement of daily precipitation estimations using PRISM with inverse-distance weighting. Theoret. Appl. Climatol. **139**(3–4), 923–934 (2014)
15. Kantardzic, M.: Data mining: concepts, models, methods, and algorithms. Technometrics **45**(3), 277 (2002)
16. Li, J., Heap, A.D.: A review of comparative studies of spatial interpolation methods in environmental sciences: performance and impact factors. Ecol. Inform. **6**(3–4), 228–241 (2011)
17. Li, Y., Song, Y., Jia, L., Gao, S., Li, Q., Qiu, M.: Intelligent fault diagnosis by fusing domain adversarial training and maximum mean discrepancy via ensemble learning. IEEE Trans. Industr. Inf. **17**(4), 2833–2841 (2021)
18. Li, Z., Wang, K., Ma, H., Wu, Y.: An adjusted inverse distance weighted spatial interpolation method. In: CIMNS, pp. 128–132 (2018)
19. Lu, G.Y., Wong, D.W.: An adaptive inverse-distance weighting spatial interpolation technique. Comput. Geosci. **34**(9), 1044–1055 (2008)
20. Peng, S.L.: Optimized study on spatial interpolation methods for meteorological element. Geospat. Inf. **15**(07), 86–89 (2017)
21. Qiu, H., Zheng, Q., Msahli, M., Memmi, G., Qiu, M., Lu, J.: Topological graph convolutional network-based urban traffic flow and density prediction. IEEE Trans. Intell. Transp. Syst. **22**(7), 4560–4569 (2021)
22. Qu, R., et al.: Predicting the hormesis and toxicological interaction of mixtures by an improved inverse distance weighted interpolation. Environ. Int. **130**, 104892 (2019)
23. Shepard, D.: A two-dimensional interpolation function for irregularly-spaced data. In: Proceedings of the 1968 23rd ACM National Conference, pp. 517–524 (1968)
24. Shiode, N., Shiode, S.: Street-level spatial interpolation using network-based IDW and ordinary kriging. Trans. GIS **15**(4), 457–477 (2011)
25. Xiang, Y., Gou, L., He, L., Xia, S., Wang, W.: A SVR–ANN combined model based on ensemble EMD for rainfall prediction. Appl. Soft Comput. **73**, 874–883 (2018)
26. Zhu, L., Li, X., Wei, Y., Ma, Q., Meng, W.: Integrating real-time entity resolution with Top-N join query processing. In: Qiu, H., Zhang, C., Fei, Z., Qiu, M., Kung, S.Y. (eds.) Knowledge Science, Engineering and Management. KSEM 2021. Lecture Notes in Computer Science, vol. 12817, pp. 111-123. Springer, Cham (2021). https://doi.org/10.1007/978-3-030-82153-1_10
27. Zhu, L., Meng, W., Yang, W., Liu, C.: Region clustering based evaluation of multiple top-N selection queries. Data Knowl. Eng. **64**(2), 439–461 (2008)

Deep Neural Factorization Machine
for Recommender System

Ronghua Zhang[1,2], Zhenlong Zhu[1], Changzheng Liu[2], Yuhua Li[1(✉)],
and Ruixuan Li[1(✉)]

[1] School of Computer Science and Technology, Huazhong University of Science and
Technology, Wuhan 430074, China
zrh_oea@sina.com, 523064456@qq.com, {idcliyuhua,rxli}@hust.edu.cn
[2] College of Information Science and Technology, Shihezi University, Shihezi 832000, China
liucz@shzu.edu.cn

Abstract. Factorization Machine (FM) and its many deep learning variants are widely used in Recommender Systems. Despite their success in many applications, there still remain inherent challenges. Most existing FM methods are incapable of capturing the similarity of features well and usually suffer from irrelevant features in terms of recommendation tasks. Hence, it is necessary to fully utilize the similarity interaction between different features. In this paper, we propose a Deep Neural Factorization Machine, named DNFM, which contains "wide" and "deep" parts based on Wide&Deep. In the wide part, we elaborately design a Dimension-weighted Factorization Machine (DwFM) to improve the original FM. DwFM assigns different weights vectors to feature interactions from different fields interactions. The "deep" part of DNFM is a neural network, which is used to capture the nonlinear information of the feature interactions. Then we unify both the wide and deep parts to comprehensive learn the feature interactions. Extensive experiments verify that DNFM can significantly outperform state-of-the-art methods on two well-known datasets.

Keywords: Recommender system · Dimension-weighted factorization machine · Deep neural network

1 Introduction

Recommender Systems (RS) are widely used in many online platforms. The main task of RS is to predict the user's preference for the items, which could be expressed as a function that predicts the target of given features. Most features in the recommender systems are discrete and categorical. In order to use these features to build models, a common solution is to convert them to a set of sparse features through one-hot encoding [1, 2]. Therefore, machine learning techniques can learn from the binary features. It has been also proven that learning the effects of feature interaction is helpful to improve the accuracy of prediction. However, feature engineering is an important but high cost work and may suffer from "cold-start" problem. Besides, in the sparse datasets, it is likely

© The Author(s), under exclusive license to Springer Nature Switzerland AG 2022
G. Memmi et al. (Eds.): KSEM 2022, LNAI 13369, pp. 273–286, 2022.
https://doi.org/10.1007/978-3-031-10986-7_22

that the number of data is less than the number of cross features, and only a few cross features can be observed. Most of the parameters are not learned fully which is extremely unfavorable to model learning. In order to solve this problem, FM [3] is proposed, which embeds features as latent vectors and the interaction between features are expressed as the inner product of features' latent vectors. In this way, FM can learn the dependence of the interaction parameters and is also helpful for estimate of the related interactions.

In recent years, many researchers have made great achievements in the recommender system through the strong feature representation ability of deep neural network (DNN). NFM [2] uses DNN to learn the high-order nonlinear information based on feature interaction. Although NFM has achieved better performance, it ignores low-order features. Wide&Deep [1] and DeepFM [4] can jointly learn low-order and high-order features through their hybrid architecture. The architecture consists of a "wide" part and a "deep" part, with the goal of learning both memorization and generalization for recommendation. Their "deep" parts of the input is the connection of the features vectors, which has been shown in NFM to be less useful than directly input the cross-features' vectors.

Despite the successful application of FM and these deep learning methods, there are still three shortcomings. (1) The measurement of feature similarity is not accurate enough. In a sparse scenario, the vector inner product is not a good measure of the correlation between two features. (2) The existing methods usually treat every field interaction fairly; however, different field interactions would be different informativeness. (3) The information of the feature interactions has not been fully utilized. To solve the above problems, we propose a novel model called Deep Neural Factorization Machine (DNFM).

DNFM has both "wide" and "deep" parts, which can handle sparse setting by learning the low-order and high-order features at the same time. The "wide" part of DNFM is our improved FM, named Dimension-weighted Factorization Machine (DwFM). DwFM assigns different weights vectors to feature interactions from different fields interactions, and DwFM can well measure the similarity between two features and reduce the impact of unrelated fields on the results. The "deep" part of DNFM is a neural network, which is used to capture the non-linear information of the feature interactions. The "deep" part increases the generalization capability of the model. Furthermore, we weighted the outputs of "wide" and "deep" parts in terms of different tasks to emphasize different impacts of our model on memorization and generalization.

The main contributions of the paper are as follows. (1) We improve the FM and propose DwFM, which can more accurately calculate the similarity of features in the case of sparse, and reduce the impact of irrelevant features on the results. (2) We propose DNFM method, which consists of "wide" and "deep" parts. The "wide" part is DwFM and the "deep" part is a DNN that capture nonlinear features from feature interactions. DNFM can learn both low-order and high-order features and can balance the weight of both in the task. (3) The experimental results on two well-known datasets show that our method is superior to the state-of-the-art methods.

The rest of the paper is organized as follows: Related work is discussed in Sect. 2; Introduces the proposed approach in Sect. 3; Comparison of experimental results in Sect. 4; Sect. 5 discusses the findings the research.

2 Related Work

FM [3] is a general predictor similar to SVM, which can estimate reliable parameters at very high sparsity. Despite FM's great success, it treats all feature interactions equally, making FM susceptible to noise. Based on this problem, researchers have proposed many solutions. FFM [5] learns multiple vectors for each feature. FwFM [6] tries to solve the problem in a simple way that it gives different weights to different field pairs. AFM [7] adopts the attention mechanism to learn the weight of feature interactions.

Deep neural network has been successfully applied in many fields of artificial intelligence. Many researchers have tried to apply DNN in the field of the recommendation with great success. DeepCross [8] applies the residual network [9] to recommendation system used to efficiently capture feature interactions of bounded degrees. Wide&Deep and DeepFM focus on both low-order and high-order features. Wide&Deep trains wide linear models and deep neural networks at the same time. Since Wide&Deep is a joint training, the "wide" part only needs to complement the weaknesses of the "deep" part with a small number of transformed feature transformations, rather than a full-size wide model. Compared to Wide&Deep requiring feature engineering, DeepFM is an end-to-end method. DeepFM integrates the architecture of FM and deep neural networks to model both low-order and high-order feature interactions.

3 Proposed Approach

Figure 1 illustrates the neural network architecture of our proposed Deep Neural Factorization Machine (DNFM). In this section, we first introduce our improved FM method DwFM. Then, we detail the proposed DNFM. Last, we discuss some methods to prevent overfitting.

3.1 Dimension-Weighted Factorization Machine

We suppose that each instance has m unique features, which can be represented as $x = \{x_1, x_2, \cdots x_m\}$. There are m different fields, each feature belongs to one and only one filed. We define $V \in R^{k*m}$ be the latent matrix, its column vector v_i represent the k dimensional latent vector of feature i. The calculation process of FM is as follows:

$$y_{FM} = w_0 + \sum_{i=1}^{m} w_i x_i + \sum_{i=1}^{m} \sum_{j=i+1}^{m} <v_i, v_j> x_i x_j \tag{1}$$

Compared with the general linear model, FM greatly reduces the number of parameters to be learned, so that FM can work in a sparse environment. However, FM is incapable of fully adapt to the sparse environment. Figure 2 illustrates how the inner product function limit the expression of FM. One possible reason is that the data are sparse, and it is difficult to learn the similarity relationship between the data in the latent space. Increasing the dimensions of latent vectors may solve this problem to some extent, but this increases the complexity of the model and can lead to overfitting.

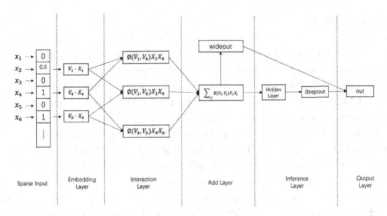

Fig. 1. DNFM model.

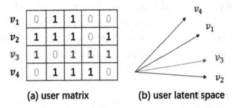

(a) user matrix   (b) user latent space

Fig. 2. From matrix (a), the similarity between v_3 and v_4 is greater than that between v_3 and v_1. However in the latent space (b), placing v_3 closer to v_1 than v_4, incurring a large ranking loss.

In fact, different dimensions of feature vectors would have different importance and should be treated differently. Learning the weights of different dimensions can more accurately learn the correlation between features. Hence, we propose to use Eq. 2 to replace the inner product function, where $\odot$ denotes the element-wise product of two vectors, and h is a vector with the same number of dimensions as v_i and v_j, and the value of h on each dimension represents the importance of this dimension.

$$\Phi_1\left(v_i, v_j\right) = h^T\left(v_i \odot v_j\right) \tag{2}$$

As the importance of the different dimensions of feature interaction may differ, as may the importance of the dimensions of feature interaction between different fields. Therefore, it is nontrivial to learn the importance of the different dimensions of all the feature interactions using one single vector h. In our work, the interactions from different fields have the different parameter h, as shown in Eq. 3.

$$\Phi_2\left(v_i, v_j\right) = h_{ab}^T\left(v_i \odot v_j\right)\left(v_i \subseteq field\ a, v_j \subseteq field\ b\right) \tag{3}$$

We do not limit the norm of parameters. Another benefit of this measure function Φ_2 is that it can learn the importance of different field interactions. It is noted that although FwFM can learn a similar effect, it only focuses on the interaction on field level and ignore the interaction level.

Taking these advantages of Eq. 3 into consideration, DwFM replaces the inner product in FM with Eq. 3, which is shown as follow:

$$y_{DwFM} = w_0 + \sum_{i=1}^m w_i x_i + \sum_{i=1}^m \sum_{j=i+1}^m h_{ij}^T (v_i \odot v_j) x_j \qquad (4)$$

DWFM can calculate feature similarity more accurately in sparse cases and pay more attention to task-related fields.

3.2 Deep Neural Factorization Machine

Similar to Wide&Deep and DeepFM, DNFM has both "wide" and "deep" parts which are used to capture both low-order and high-order features. For a vector $x \in R^n$, DNFM estimates the target as Eq. 5.

$$y_{DNFM} = w_0 + \sum_{i=1}^m w_i x_i + p^T [y_{wide1}, y_{deep}] \qquad (5)$$

The first two terms are the bias of data and the weights of these features. The third term is the combination of second-order and high-order features, where y_{wide1} is the interaction of DwFM, ydeep is the "deep" part of DNFM and p=[p0,p1] that represents the importance of y_{wide1} and y_{deep}. Next we will introduce the details.

Embedding Layer. Embedding layer is a fully connected layer, which is used to transform the input features into latent dense vectors. For a given input data $x = \{x_1, x_2, \cdots x_m\}$, after embedding output vectors $V_x = \{x_1 v_1, x_2 v_2, \ldots x_m v_m\}$ can be obtained. Among them, there are a large number of zero elements in the input data x, and only the features of non-zero elements participate in the calculation.

Interaction Layer. Interaction Layer is used to learn the cross features in the embedding vectors in pairs. For a pair of embedding vectors $v_i x_i$ and $v_j x_j$, we can get interaction vector through Eq. 7.

$$\Phi_3(v_i, v_j) = h_{ab} \odot (v_i \odot v_j)(v_i \subseteq field\ a, v_j \subseteq field\ b) \qquad (6)$$

$$v_{ij_{cross}} = \Phi_3(v_i, v_j) x_i x_j \qquad (7)$$

The difference between Φ_3 and Φ_2 is that Φ_3 operates on a vector, and Φ_2 operates on a scalar, hence we adopt Φ_3 for the rest of the operation due to the feature is a vector.

Add Layer. There are two operations in Add Layer, one is to sum the interaction vectors in Interaction Layer to get vector v_{cross}, and the other is get the ywide1 based on v_{cross}, and these two operations are expressed by Eq. 8 and 9. The $q1$ is the weight vector for v_{cross}.

$$v_{cross} = \sum_{ij} \Phi_3(v_i, v_j) x_i x_j \qquad (8)$$

$$y_{wide1} = q_1^T v_{cross} \qquad (9)$$

The "wide" part of DNFM is y_{wide}, which is expressed by Eq. 10.

$$y_{wide} = w_0 + \sum_{i=1}^m w_i x_i + p0 * y_{wide1} \qquad (10)$$

Inference Layer. Inference Layer includes the hidden layer and the output layer of "deep" part. The hidden layer is a layer of fully connected network used to learn high-order feature from v_{cross}, which can be expressed as follows:

$$z = \sigma(W_1 v_{cross} + b_1) \tag{11}$$

where W_1, b_1 and σ denote the weight matrix, bias vector and activation function for the hidden layer. In our work, we choose Relu as our activation function. The output of "deep" part can be calculated by Eq. 11. The q2 is the weight vector for z.

$$y_{deep} = q_2^T z \tag{12}$$

Output Layer. Finally, Output Layer combines the output of the "wide" and "deep" parts, and contains the first-order, second-order and high-order features of data. Equation 5 can also be written as Eq. 13:

$$y_{DNFM} = y_{wide} + y_{deep} \tag{13}$$

DFNM is memorized and generalized by learning both "wide" and "deep" parts.

Relation to NFM and DeepFM. If the Add Layer removes the "wideout" part, DNFM is similar to NFM. DNFM has the advantages of NFM, both of which take into account the interaction between features. There are two advantages of DNFM over NFM. First, NFM only learns high-order features based on interaction features and does not consider second-order features. This part is the "wideout" of Add Layer in our work. Second, we consider the importance of different dimensions of feature interactions and field interactions, so that DNFM can better learn the similarity between different features.

DNFM is structurally similar to DeepFM, both of which have "wide" and "deep" parts. This structure allows them to learn both low-order and high-order features at the same time. There are two differences between DNFM and DeepFM. First, the "wide" parts of DNFM and DeepFM are DwFM and FM respectively. Compared with FM, DwFM can better learn the relationship between features. Second, the input of "deep" parts of DNFM are interaction-based paradigm while the DeepFM adopts the concatenation of features; hence our method could learn more interaction between features, which has potential to improve the performance of recommendation.

3.3 Learning

DNFM can be applied to a range of prediction tasks such as regression, classification and ranking. In our work, we focus on the regression task. To estimate the parameters of DNFM, we use square loss as objective function:

$$L_{reg} = \sum_{x \in S} (\hat{y}(x) - y(x))^2 \tag{14}$$

where S denotes the training data, $\hat{y}(x)$ and $y(x)$ are the predicted and true values of instance x. During the optimization process, we found that some regularization techniques could effectively prevent overfitting, such as L_1 regularization and dropout [10]. For other tasks, such as classification, you can use hinge loss or log loss [11], pairwise personalized ranking loss are used for ranking [12, 13]. To optimize the objective function, we employ mini-batch Adagrad [14] as the optimizer.

Overfitting Prevention. Overfitting is a common problem in machine learning model training. In the past work, it shows that the traditional FM model is troubled by overfitting [3]. Our DNFM model has more parameters and stronger expressive capacity than FM, which also indicates that DNFM is more likely to encounter fitting problems than FM. In this paper, we use the L_1 regularization and dropout technology to prevent network overfit the training data.

We apply L_1 regularization on the weights of the first-order features to reduce the influence of irrelevant features on the results. In this way, the actual objective function we optimize is Eq. 15.

$$L_{reg} = \sum_{x \in S} \left(\hat{y}(x) - y(x) \right)^2 + \lambda \sum_{i=1}^{m} |w_i| \tag{15}$$

λ is a hyperparameters used to control the weight of regularization in the loss. We do not apply any regularization constraints to the latent matrix V, as we find that applying regularization to the latent matrix V has a negative effect on accuracy.

Neural network has a strong learning ability, but with it, it is easier to overfit. Dropout is an important technology to solve the overfitting of neural network. The key idea of dropout is to randomly discard the unit and its connection with neural network during training. This prevents the units from adapting to each other. In this paper, we use dropout to prevent the possible overfitting problems in DNFM.

4 Experiments

We conduct experiments to answer the following questions:

RQ1 How does DNFM perform as compared to the state-of-the-art methods?

RQ2 Does DwFM learn the relationships between features better than FM?

RQ3 DNFM has only one hidden layer, and whether using more hidden layers makes the result better?

RQ4 How do the key hyper-parameters of DNFM (i.e., dropout and regularization) influence its performance?

4.1 Experimental Settings

In this paper, we follow the same experiment setting as the previous work [2, 7] for a fair comparison of our algorithm.

Datasets. We evaluate our models on two publicly datasets: Frappe[1] [15] and Movie-Lens[2] [16]. Frappe is a context-aware app discovery tool, which has been used for context-aware recommendation and contains 96,203 app usage logs. Each Frappe log contains ten variables, two of which are user ID and app ID, and the remaining eight are context variables, such as weather, city, and so on. MovieLens has been used for personalized tag recommendation, which contains 668,953 tag applications. Each MovieLens tag application contains user ID, movie ID and tag.

Since the original datasets only contains positive samples, and the target value of positive samples is 1, we sampled two negative samples for each user in both datasets, and the target value of negative samples is -1. The Table 1 shows a description of the datasets after processing.

Table 1. Dataset description.

Dataset	Frappe	MoiveLens
Instance	288609	2006859
Feature	5382	90445
User	957	17045
Item	4092	23743

Evaluation Metrics. We randomly split the dataset into training set (70%), validation set (20%), and test set (10%). All the models are trained on the training set, the hyper-parameters are tuned on the validation set, and finally the model effect is checked on the test set. The performance is evaluated by the *root mean square error* (RMSE), where a lower RMSE indicates better the model performed. Because our positive and negative samples have a target value of 1 and -1, we will round the predictions of each model to 1 or -1 if they are out of range.

Baselines. We compare our models with the following methods:

- **libFM** [17]. This is the official c++ implementation[3] of FM released by Rendle. In the experiment, we chose SGD learners since the other methods were optimized by SGD (or its variants).
- **HOFM.** This is the TensorFlow implementation[4] of the high-order FM. In the paper, we set the order size to 3, since the MoiveLens data has only there fields (user, item, and tag).
- **FFM** [5]. Each feature has the same number of vectors as the field, and each latent vector corresponds to a field.

---

[1] http://baltrunas.info/research-menu/frappe.
[2] http://grouplens.org/datasets/movielens/latest.
[3] http://www.libfm.org.
[4] https://github.com/geffy/tffm.

- **Wide&Deep** [1]. This model contains "wide" and "deep" two parts which can learn low-order and high-order at the same time. The "wide" part is the same as the linear regression part of FM, and only the raw features are used for fair comparison with other methods. The "deep" part is a DNN. Because the structure of a DNN is difficult to be tuned, we adopt the same structure as in the paper. The "deep" part is a three-layer MLP with the layer size 1024, 512 and 256.
- **DeepCross** [8]. DeepCross is the first time to apply the residual network in recommender systems. For the same reason as Wide&Deep, we use the network structure in the paper. it stacks 5 residual units (each unit has two layers) with the hidden dimension 512, 512, 256, 128 and 64, respectively.
- **DeepFM** [4]. DeepFM is composed of "wide" and "deep" parts. The "wide" part is FM, and the "deep" part is DNN, which adopts the structure in the paper. DeepFM shares the feature embedding between FM and deep component.
- **NFM** [2]. NFM extracts nonlinear features from second-order features. This is the TensorFlow implementation[5] of the NFM. To be fair, we use the same hyperparameters as in the paper.
- **AFM** [7]. AFM uses the attention mechanism to give each feature an interactive learning coefficient which reduce the impact of irrelevant features on the results. This is the TensorFlow implementation[6] of the AFM. To be fair, we use the same hyper-parameters as in the paper.
- **FwFM** [6]. FwFM learns weights for field pairs, which reduce the impact of irrelevant fields on the results.
- **INN**. INN can learn the weights of both features and fields at the same time. This is the TensorFlow implementation[7] of the AFM. To be fair, we use the same hyper-parameters as in the paper.

Parameter Settings. All models are learned by optimizing the square loss in order to make a fair comparison. All methods except LibFM are learned with small batch Adagrad. The batch size is set to 128 and 4096 for Frappe and MovieLens respectively. The embedding size is set to 256 for all methods. To avoid overfitting, we use L1 regularization and dropout. We apply L1 regularization on the weights of the first-order features and apply dropout on add layer and hidden layer. In addition, we use the early stop strategy on validation set, where we choose to stop training if the RMSE on validation set increased for 4 epochs.

4.2 Model Performance (RQ1)

We compare DNFM with ten state-of-the-art methods, and the experimental results are show in Table 2. It can be seen from the results that our method does not significantly increase the number of parameters, but achieves the best effect on both data sets, which indicates the advancement of our method.

---

[5] https://securityintelligence.com/factorization-machines-a-new-way-of-looking-at-machine-learning.

[6] https://github.com/hexiangnan/attentional-factorization-machine.

[7] https://github.com/cstur4/interaction-aware-factorization-machines.

FFM and FwFM are better than FM, which indicates that traditional FM is not well adapted to the environment with sparse data. FwFM uses far fewer parameters than FFM and achieves better results than it, which indicates that it is more reasonable to consider the weight of field interactions than to give multiple embedding vectors to features.

INN and AFM have achieved good results on all baseline, indicating the validity of considering the importance of different features interaction. Among them, the effect of INN is better than that of AFM, which further proves that different fields interaction have different effects on the results.

HOFM is only slightly better than FM, but much worse than NFM. This is because FM only considers second-order features, which is the limitation of FM performance. HOFM considers third-order features, which is the reason why its effect is better than FM. But it increases the number of parameters and training time, which is not cost-effective in practice. The success of NFM proves the effectiveness of the nonlinear features, and it uses fewer parameters than HOFM but achieves better results.

Table 2. Test error and number of parameters of different methods on embedding size 256. M denotes million.

Method	Frappe		MovieLens	
	Param	RMSE	Param	RMSE
LibFM	1.38M	0.3385	23.24M	0.4735
HOFM	2.76M	0.3331	46.40M	0.4636
FFM	13.8M	0.3304	69.55M	0.4568
Wide&Deep	4.66M	0.3246	24.69M	0.4512
DeepCrossing	8.93M	0.3548	25.42M	0.513
DeepFM	1.64M	0.3308	23.32M	0.4662
NFM	1.45M	0.3095	23.31M	0.4443
AFM	1.45M	0.3102	23.26M	0.4325
FwFM	1.38M	0.324	23.24M	0.423
INN	1.46M	0.3071	23.25M	0.4188
DNFM	**1.46M**	**0.3065**	**23.31M**	**0.4113**

Both Wide&Deep and DeepFM achieve good results, which demonstrated the advantages of wide and deep structured networks. But both of them are worse than NFM and have more parameters than NFM. This illustrates that the nonlinear features based on second-order feature extraction have stronger expression ability.

4.3 Effect of DwFM (RQ2)

DwFM assigns different weights to different dimensions of feature interaction between different fields. Weight vectors play a role in DwFM. To explore the impact, we have done three sets of experiments. The first group is the unit vector with fixed weight, namely the original FM. In the second group, there is only one weight vector, which essentially means that feature interactions from different field interactions have the same importance dimension, which is represented by sDwFM. The third group, DwFM, provides different weight vectors for different field interactions. The result is shown in Table 3.

Table 3. Effect of DwFM.

Method	Frappe	MovieLens
FM	0.3385	0.4735
sDwFM	0.3356	0.4608
DwFM	**0.3369**	**0.4388**

It can be seen from the results that sDwFM has better effect than FM. This proves that the original inner product is not a good measure of the similarity between vectors, and the different dimensions of vectors have different meanings. DwFM achieves the best results, which shows feature interactions from different field interactions have different importance dimensions. DwFM has made great progress in MovieLens, but the progress in Frappe is not so obvious. The reason may be that Frappe has ten fields and contains rich information, and the methods based on linear features cannot be improved greatly.

4.4 Impact of Hidden Layer (RQ3)

The Hidden Layer is used by DNFM to extract nonlinear features, and a good effect is obtained. Here we explore the effect of different hidden layers on the results. In the experiment, we established one, two and three hidden layers, respectively. Relu was used as the activation function for each layer, and the size of each layer was consistent with the embedding size. The models were represented as DNFM-1, DNFM-2 and DNFM-3, respectively. In order to exclude the influence of other factors on the results, dropout and L_1 regularization technologies are not adopted here.

As can be seen from Table 4 that stacking more layers do not improve the performance of the DNFM. The best performance is when we use one hidden layer only. We believe that the reason is similar to NFM [2], the second-order features already contain a lot of information, so the nonlinear information can be well captured by a simple operation and the effect reaches the upper limit of the model.

Table 4. DNFM w.r.t different number of hidden layers.

Method	Frappe	MovieLens
DNFM-1	**0.3075**	**0.42**
DNFM-2	0.3076	0.4203
DNFM-3	0.3076	0.421

4.5   Effect of Hyper-parameters (RQ4)

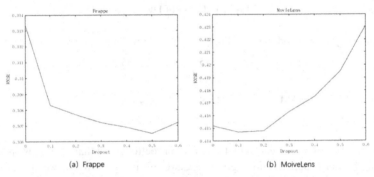

(a) Frappe   (b) MoiveLens

Fig. 3. Different dropout ratios on the Hidden layer.

Dropout. To better show the dropout effect, L_1 regularization is not applied to the model here. We use dropout in the Add layer and Hidden layer, and set 0.5 for Add layer, and then tune value of Hidden layer. The value of dropout indicates what percentage of nodes are dropped. When the value of dropout is zero, all the nodes participate in training. As shown in Fig. 3, we set the keep probability from 0 to 0.6 with increments of 0.1 and it significantly affects the performance of DNFM. When dropout is 0, the model cannot achieve the best effect, and when dropout is too large, the model will be under-fitted. When the dropout value is 0.5 in Frappe and 0.1 in MovieLens, the model can achieve the best effect, which is significantly improved compared with that without dropout.

L_1 **Regularization.** Similarly, we do not use dropout here to better observe the impact of L_1 regularization on the model. We tune the L_1 regularization for DNFM in $\left[0, 1e^{-6}, 5e^{-6}, 1e^{-5}, \cdots, 1e^{-1}\right]$. Figure 4 shows the impact of L_1 regularization on the model. In Frappe, L_1 regularization has little impact on model learning, and the effect is hovering in the attachment of 0.3075. In MovieLens, the best performance is achieved when λ takes $1e^{-6}$, which decreases from 0.42 without constraint to 0.415.

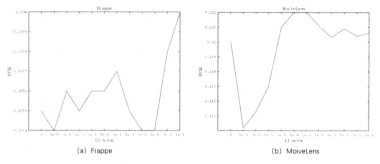

(a) Frappe   (b) MoiveLens

Fig. 4. L1 regularization on weights

5   Conclusion and Future Work

In this paper, we proposed Deep Neural Factorization Machine (DNFM) for Recommender Systems. DNFM has both "wide" and "deep" components to learn both low-order and high-order features. The "wide" part of DNFM is Dimension-weighted Factorization Machine (DwFM) method proposed by us. DwFM has improved the method of measuring the similarity of vectors, considering that the importance of different dimensions of vectors may be different, so it can achieve better results than traditional FM. The "deep" part of DNFM is a neural network like NFM. The Experimental results on two well-known data sets show that the DNFM method is superior to the state-of-the-art methods.

In the future, we will try to apply our approach to the task of migration learning, and use the attention mechanism to learn the characteristics of features, and study the interpretability of weight information related to features.

Acknowledgements. This work is supported by the National Key Research and Development Program of China under grants 2016QY01W0202, National Natural Science Foundation of China under grants U1836204, U1936108 and 62141205, and Major Projects of the National Social Science Foundation under grant 16ZDA092, and the Fund Project of XJPCC under grants 2022CB002-08 and 2019AB001.

References

1. Cheng, H.T., Koc, L., Harmsen, J., et al.: Wide & deep learning for recommender systems, in: Proceedings of the 1st Workshop on Deep Learning for Recommender Systems. ACM. pp. 7–10 (2016)
2. He, X., Chua, T.S.: Neural factorization machines for sparse predictive analytics. In: Proceedings of the 40th International ACM SIGIR Conference on Research and Development in Information Retrieval (SIGIR). ACM. pp. 355–364 (2017)
3. Rendle, S.: Factorization machines. In: 2010 IEEE International Conference on Data Mining (ICDM), pp. 995–1000 (2010)
4. Guo, H., Tang, R., Ye, Y., et al.: Deepfm: a factorization- machine based neural network for ctr prediction. arXiv preprint arXiv:1703.04247 (2017)

5. Juan, Y., Zhuang, Y., Chin, W.S., et al.: Field-aware factorization machines for CTR prediction. In: Proceedings of the 10th ACM Conference on Recommender Systems, pp. 43–50 (2016)

6. Pan, J., Jian, X., Alfonso, L., et al.: Field-weighted factorization machines for click-through rate prediction in display advertising. In: International World Wide Web Conferences, pp. 1349–1357 (2018)

7. Xiao, J., Ye, H., He, X., Zhang, H., Wu, F., Chua, T.S.: Attentional factorization machines: Learning the weight of feature interactions via attention networks. arXiv preprint arXiv:1708.04617 (2017)

8. Shan, Y., Hoens, T.R., et al.: Deep crossing: Webscale modeling without manually crafted combinatorial features. In: Proceedings of the 22nd ACM SIGKDD International Conference on Knowledge Discovery and Data Mining. ACM, pp. 255–262 (2016)

9. He, K., Zhang, X., Ren, S., Sun, J.: Deep residual learning for image recognition. In: Proceedings of the IEEE Conference on Computer Vision and Pattern recognition (CVPR), pp. 770–778 (2016)

10. Srivastava, N., Hinton, G., Krizhevsky, A., Sutskever, I., Salakhutdinov, R.: Dropout: a simple way to prevent neural networks from overfitting. J. Mach. Learn. Res. **15**, 1929–1958 (2014)

11. He, X., Liao, L., Zhang, H., et al.: Neural collaborative filtering. In: Proceedings of the 26th International Conference on World Wide Web (WWW), pp. 173–182 (2017)

12. Rendle, S., Freudenthaler, C., Gantner, Z. et al.: BPR: Bayesian personalized ranking from implicit feedback. In: Conference on Uncertainty in Artificial Intelligence. AUAI Press, pp. 452–461 (2009)

13. Xiang, W., He, X., Nie, L., Chua, T.S.: Item silk road: recommending items from information domains to social users. ACM (2017)

14. Duchi, J., Hazan, E., Singer, Y.: Adaptive subgradient methods for online learning and stochastic optimization. J. Mach. Learn. Res. **12**, 257–269 (2011)

15. Baltrunas, L., Church, K., Karatzoglou, A., Oliver, N.: Frappe: under- standing the usage and perception of mobile app recommendations in-the-wild. arXiv preprint arXiv:1505.03014 (2015)

16. Harper, F.M., Konstan, J.A.: The movielens datasets: history and context. ACM Trans. Interact. Intell. Syst. (TIIS) **5**(4), 1–19 (2015)

17. Rendle, S.: Factorization machines with LIBFM. ACM Trans. Intell. Syst. Technol. **3**, 1–22 (2012)

Adaptive Spatial-Temporal Convolution Network for Traffic Forecasting

Zhao Li[1], Yong Zhang[1,2(✉)], Zhao Zhang[1], Xing Wang[3], and Lin Zhu[3]

[1] School of Electronic Engineering, Beijing University of Posts
and Telecommunications, Beijing 100876, China
yongzhang@bupt.edu.cn
[2] Beijing Key Laboratory of Work Safety Intelligent Monitoring,
Beijing University of Posts and Telecommunications, Beijing 100876, China
[3] China Mobile Research Institute, Beijing 100053, China

Abstract. As a vital part of intelligent transportation system (ITS), traffic forecasting is crucial for traffic management and travel planning. However, accurate traffic forecasting is challenging due to complex spatial-temporal correlations among traffic series and heterogeneities among prediction hirizons. Most existing works focus on extracting spatial features by graph convolution network and ignore the heterogeneities of timestamps in long-term forecasting. Moreover, the fixed spatial-temporal correlations extraction pattern is not sensitive to the changes of traffic environments. In this paper, we propose a general and effective framework called adaptive spatial-temporal convolution network (ASTCN) for traffic flow forecasting. ASTCN can capture inherent spatial-temporal correlations adaptively according to specific prediction task without any prior knowledge, and has strong adaptability to different traffic environments. Moreover, each timestamp over prediction horizon can learn its own unique features aggregation pattern, so as to improve the accuracy of long-term and short-term forecasting concurrently. The experimental results on four public highway datasets show that ASTCN outperforms state-of-the-art baselines and achieves optimal accuracy in all prediction horizons for the first time.

Keywords: Traffic forecasting · Spatial-temporal convolution network · Graph convolution network · Long-term and short-term forecasting

1 Introduction

With the acceleration of urbanization, the growing population and traffic scale introduce severe challenges to traffic management [1]. As a vital part of intelligent transportation system (ITS), traffic forecasting aims to predict future traffic conditions (e.g., traffic flow or speed) according to observed information. It plays a crucial role in travel planning and congestion mitigation [14,19].

© The Author(s), under exclusive license to Springer Nature Switzerland AG 2022
G. Memmi et al. (Eds.): KSEM 2022, LNAI 13369, pp. 287–299, 2022.
https://doi.org/10.1007/978-3-031-10986-7_23

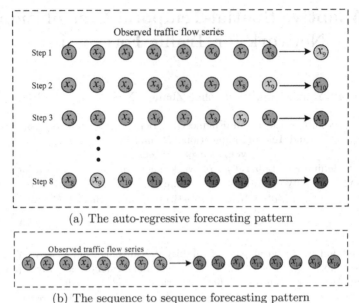

(a) The auto-regressive forecasting pattern

(b) The sequence to sequence forecasting pattern

Fig. 1. The illustration of auto-regressive and seq2seq traffic forecasting pattern.

However, accurate traffic forecasting is challenging due to the complex temporal correlations (intra-dependencies) generated from one traffic series and spatial correlations (inter-dependencies) generated from different sources [2]. Additionally, the timestamps over prediction horizon have unique features update pattern, and the heterogeneities among them are also the key to improve the long-term forecasting accuracy. The existing methods mostly utilize recurrent neural network [2,13] (e.g., Long-Short Term Memory (LSTM) [9] and Gated Recurrent Unit (GRU) [22]) or temporal convolution network (TCN) [17,19] to extract temporal correlations, and capture spatial correlations by graph convolution network (GCN) [7,13,19,23] or its variants [12,15].

Although recent works have made remarkable achievements, they still face the following challenges in long-term forecasting:

1) Error Propagation: As shown in Fig. 1(a), RNN-based methods and TCN follow the auto-regressive pattern for multi-step prediction [23]. The performances of these models have serious defect of short-term dependence, and the prediction error will be gradually amplified with the expansion of prediction horizon. Error propagation has little impact on short-term forecasting, but it is fatal to long-term forecasting.

2) Parameter Sharing: To solve the problem of error propagation, some efforts [2,23] utilize seq2seq pattern to directly output all prediction values (as shown in Fig. 1(b)). However, the parameter sharing principle can not reflect the heterogeneities among timestamps over predicton horizon, that is, they can not learn specific features update pattern. In fact, the patterns between timestamps may be similar when they are close (e.g., timestamp x_9 and x_{10} in Fig. 1(b)), or even opposite when they are farther (e.g., timestamp x_9 and x_{16} in Fig. 1(b)). The uniform parameters among timestamps makes it difficult for the model to take into account the accuracy of long-term and short-term forecasting concurrently.

3) The Poor Adaptability of Model: Existing methods pay more attentions to complex spatial-temporal correlations extraction methods. Additionally, the model can only extract localized spatial-temporal information from fixed neighbors and timestamps, it is not sensitive to the changes of traffic environments. Various deep learning frameworks increase the difficulty of discrimination and the choice without appropriate prior knowledge (e.g., traffic environment or data scale) may be incomplete and biased.

To address the aforementioned challenges, we propose an adaptive spatial-temporal convolution network (ASTCN) for traffic flow forecasting. Instead of designing more complex architectures, we design two concise yet effective deep learning components: adaptive spatial convolution network (ASCN) and adaptive temporal convolution network (ATCN) to capture spatial and temporal correlations respectively. ASTCN can adaptively construct inherent spatial-temporal correlations according to specific prediction tasks, and enhance the adaptability to the traffic environments without any prior knowledge. Moreover, each timestamp over prediction horizon can learn its own unique features aggregation pattern on the basis of sensing all historical information, so as to improve the accuracy both short-term and long-term forecasting concurrently. To our best knowledge, this is the first time to utilize the heterogeneities of parameter among prediction horiozns to improve the long-term forecasting accuracy. In particular, the main contributions of this paper can be summarized as follows:

- We design an adaptive spatial-temporal correlations extraction mechanism. Specifically, the mechanism can automatically construct the temporal and spatial correlations matrix according to specific prediction task without any prior knowledge.
- A general and effective spatial-temporal traffic forecasting framework is constructed. The framework can directly model the correlations between prediction horizons and historical information, and improve the accuracy of short-term and long-term forecasting concurrently.
- Extensive experiments are carried out on four public highway datasets. The results show that the proposed model outperforms state-of-the-art baselines, and obtains the optimal prediction accuracy in each timestamp over the prediction horizon for the first time compared with all baselines.

2   Related Work

2.1   Traffic Forecasting

The purpose of traffic forecasting is to use the observed historical information to predict the traffic conditions in the future. Traffic managers can effectively deal with various emergencies according to the prediction results and improve the efficiency of traffic management. According to the length of prediction, traffic forecasting is generally divided into two categories: short-term forecasting (5~30 mins) and long-term forecasting (over 30 mins) [19].

Traditional traffic prediction models based on statistics strategy, such as Auto-Regressive Integrated Moving Average Model (ARIMA) and Kalman filter algorithm, are based on stationary assumption and can neither mine nonlinear features nor extract spatial correlations among traffic series. Nowadays, deep learning has received more attentions because of its strong ability of features extracting and data fitting. Classical time series processing methods based on deep learning, such as GRU and LSTM, can store experience and improve short-term prediction accuracy. But RNN-based networks generally have the inherent defects of training heavily and complex gated mechanisms [19]. Some studies [17,19] adopt lightweight temporal convolution network (TCN) to process longer traffic sequences. However, these methods all follow auto-regressive strategy for multi-step prediction. In long-term forecasting, the error of the current step will be amplified in further steps. To solve the problem of error propagation, some efforts [2,18,23] try to utilize the seq2seq pattern to directly output total prediction sequences according to historical information. However, the timestamps over prediction horizon still follow the principle of parameter sharing, and has the identical features update and aggregation pattern. When the prediction length is increased, the model cannot meet the demands of features difference between all timestamps and take into account the accuracy of short-term and long-term forecasting concurrently.

2.2 Traffic Forecasting Based on Graph Convolution Network

With the continuous expansion of traffic scale, extracting information from a single traffic series has been difficult to meet the accuracy requirements. In fact, the target node is not only related to its own historical traffic information, but also affected by the traffic conditions of neighborhoods. Accurately grasping the spatial relationships between nodes is of great significance to improve the accuracy of traffic forecasting. To this end, studys [20,21] constrains the road nodes in the standard grid, then they adopt convolution neural network (CNN) to extract the neighborhoods' information of the target node. However, due to the irregularity of traffic network structure, this method is difficult to be generalized to real traffic environments.

With the continuous improvement of graph convolution network [3,5,11], more spatial correlations extraction methods based on graph convolution network and its variants are proposed. STGCN [19] adopts GCN for the first time to realize the aggregation of spatial information according to the predefined spatial adjacency matrix. Later, DCRNN [13] simulates traffic flow through random walk algorithm, which further strengthens the spatial features extraction ability of GCN. Furthermore, ASTGCN [7] and GMAN [23] adopt the attention mechanism [16] to capture the dynamic spatial-temporal correlations. More recently, STSGCN [15] and STFGNN [12] constrain the spatial-temporal relationships in a large matrix and extract the them synchronously. However, most of these methods need appropriate prior knowledge to construct the spatial connection graph, such as the distance or connectivity among nodes [6]. And the model cannot capture the impact of non neighbors on target node. More importantly, the predefined graph structure is not sensitive to the changes of traffic environments, and there is great uncertainty whether it is directly related to the prediction task. In order to enhance the interpretability of spatial graph and deploy it directly to prediction task, Graph WaveNet [17] and AGCRN [2] can adaptively construct global spatial correlations according to specific prediction task without any prior knowledge. Experiments show that the adaptive graph construction method is more effective in extracting spatial information.

3   Problem Definition

The traffic graph can be defined as $G = (V, E, A)$, where $|V| = N$ represents the node set and N represents the number of observation nodes. E represents the edge set. $A \in R^{N \times N}$ is the adjacency matrix, and a_{ij} reflects the spatial correlation between node i and node j in the graph. $X_t \in R^{N \times C}$ represents the traffic values of all nodes at the time t, where C represents the traffic features dimension. $\mathcal{X} = \{X_{t-T_p+1}, \cdots, X_{t-1}, X_t\} \in R^{T_p \times N \times C}$ represents the historical traffic series with time slice length T_p, Our target is to predict the next T_q moments traffic values $Y = \{X_{t+1}, X_{t+2}, \cdots, X_{t+T_q}\} \in R^{T_q \times N \times C}$ according to the observed historical traffic series $\mathcal{X}$. Formally, traffic forecasting based on graph G can be defined as:

$$\{X_{t+1}, X_{t+2}, \cdots, X_{t+q}\} = f(G, \mathcal{X}) \tag{1}$$

4   Model Architecture

Figure 2 illustrates the framework of adaptive spatial-temporal convolution network (ASTCN) proposed in this paper, which mainly includes two deep learning components: adaptive spatial convolution network (ASCN) and adaptive temporal convolution network (ATCN) to capture spatial and temporal correlations respectively. ASCN and ATCN will be introduced in detail next.

4.1   Adaptive Spatial Convolution Network for Spatial Correlations Extraction

The traditional spatial correlations extraction methods depend on the predefined spatial adjacency matrix $A \in R^{N \times N}$, and the GCN-based spatial features update function can be defined as:

$$Z_s = (I_N + D^{-\frac{1}{2}} A D^{-\frac{1}{2}}) X_s W_s + b_s \tag{1}$$

where I_N and D represent the identity matrix and degree matrix respectively. $X_s \in R^{N \times C_i}$ and $Z_s \in R^{N \times C_o}$ are the input and output of GCN-layer,

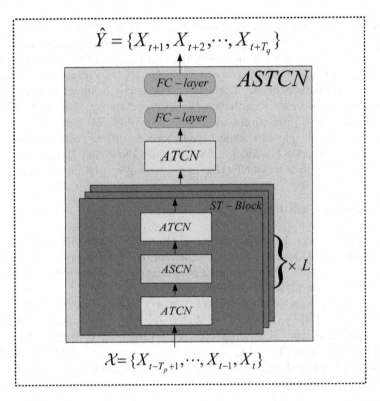

Fig. 2. The framework of adaptive spatial-temporal convolution network (ASTCN), where ATCN represents adaptive temporal convolution network and ASCN represents adaptive spatial convolution network. ASTCN mainly includes L ST-Blocks, one ATCN component and two fully connected layers (FC-layer).

$W_s \in R^{C_i \times C_o}$ and $b_s \in R^{C_o}$ represents the learnable update weights and biases. Even if the GCN-based methods can ensure that the target node extracts information from the neighborhoods, the construction of adjacency matrix needs appropriate prior knowledge, such as node distance or connectivity. Additionally, the predefined neighbors may be biased and incomplete, and there is also great uncertainty whether it is directly related to the prediction task.

In order to extract spatial correlations comprehensively without any prior knowledge and deploy it directly to specific prediction task, inspired by Graph Wavenet [17] and AGCRN [2], we construct the global spatial correlations between nodes through adaptively learning node embedding $\xi \in R^{N \times d}$:

$$\Lambda = I_N + D^{-\frac{1}{2}} A D^{-\frac{1}{2}} = softmax(Relu(\xi \cdot \xi^T)) \tag{2}$$

where $d \ll N$ represents the dimension of the learnable node embedding ξ. $Relu(\cdot)$ and $softmax(\cdot)$ functions are adopted to sparse and normalize the adaptive matrix, respectively. In order to simplify the process, we directly construct the global nodes correlations matrix $\Lambda \in R^{N \times N}$ instead of the adjacency matrix

A or $D^{-\frac{1}{2}}AD^{-\frac{1}{2}}$ [2]. By adaptively constructing the correlations matrix according to specific prediction task, nodes can capture the complete spatial information without any prior knowledge during training, which improves the spatial perception ability and generalization of the model compared with the predefined connection graph. Finally, the adaptive spatial convolution network function can be defined as:

$$Z_s = \Lambda X_s W_s + b_s \tag{3}$$

4.2 Adaptive Temporal Convolution Network for Temporal Correlations Extraction

The auto-regressive prediction methods based on iterative mechanism have the problem of error propagation. And the parameter sharing principle followed in seq2seq pattern is difficult to take into account the accuracy of short-term and long-term forecasting concurrently. In fact, there may be strong heterogeneities among timestamps over prediction horizon, and it is critical to get a timestamp-specific information aggregating pattern in long-term forecasting.

To address the challenge, we extract temporal correlations by adaptive temporal convolution network (ATCN). Assuming that the input and output time lengths of ATCN-layer are T_i and T_o. The adaptive temporal correlations extraction function can be expressed as:

$$Z_t = \Gamma X_t W_t + b_t \tag{4}$$

where $Z_t \in R^{T_o \times C_o}$ and $X_t \in R^{T_i \times C_i}$ represents the input and output of ATCN-layer. $W_t \in R^{C_i \times C_o}$ and $b_t \in R^{C_o}$ are the learnable update weights and biases. And $\Gamma \in R^{T_o \times T_i}$ is the learnable temporal correlations matrix, which represents the relationships among timestamps. Different from the construction of adaptive spatial correlations matrix, we directly construct the temporal matrix Γ rather than time embedding. We believe that the length of time series T_i or T_o is much smaller than the node number N in the field of traffic forecasting, and neural network has the ability to directly learn the optimal parameters in the temporal correlations matrix Γ. In addition, we abandon the $Relu(\cdot)$ activation and $Softmax(\cdot)$ normalization functions used in adaptive spatial matrix Λ. We argue that the interactions among timestamps are not always positive, and the learning of negative contributions is necessary to improve the prediction accuracy when the matrix dimension is low.

Through the construction of temporal correlations matrix, the timestamps of ATCN-layer can capture all input information comprehensively. Furthermore, each timestamp can learn its own unique temporal features aggregation pattern, which is directly related to forecasting tasks. The independence among timestamps can realize the optimal strategy to improve the prediction accuracy both long-term and short-term concurrently.

4.3   The Framework of Adaptive Spatial-Temporal Convolution Network

Figure 2 shows the framework of ASTCN, which includes L spatial-temporal correlations extraction blocks (ST-Block), one ATCN component and two fully connected layers (FC-layer). In ST-Block, one ASCN bridges two ATCN to form a sandwich structure. In our opinion, temporal correlations extraction is the major part of traffic forecastiing, and this structure can realize the rapid aggregation of spatial-temporal information. In addition, residual network [8] and batch normalization [10] are utilized to accelerate training speed and avoid overfitting.

The input values $X \in R^{T_p \times N \times C}$ and output values $Y \in R^{T_q \times N \times C}$ of the ASTCN are all 3-D tensors. Firstly, the input $X \in R^{T_p \times N \times C}$ is transformed into spatial-temporal features extraction result $H_l \in R^{T_p \times N \times C_l}$ through L ST-Blocks. Then, H_l converts the time length into T_q and outputs $H_{l+1} \in R^{T_q \times N \times C_l}$ through an ATCN component. Finally, H_{l+1} generates the prediction result $Y \in R^{T_q \times N \times C}$ after passing through the two-layer fully connected networks.

The *mean absolute error* (MAE) between predict values Y and ground truth values $\hat{Y}$ is adopted as the loss function to train the parameters of ASTCN model:

$$Loss = \frac{1}{T_q} \sum_{t=1}^{T_q} \left| Y - \hat{Y} \right| \tag{5}$$

Table 1. The attributes of PEMS03, PEMS04, PEMS07, PEMS08 datasets.

Attributes	Dataset			
	PEMS03	PEMS04	PEMS07	PEMS08
Nodes	358	307	883	170
Edges	547	340	886	295
TimePoints	26208	16992	28224	17856
MissingRatio	0.672%	3.182%	0.452%	0.696%

5   Experiments

5.1   Datasets

We evaluate the performance of the ASTCN proposed in this paper based on four public highway datasets namely PeMS03, PeMS04, PeMS07 and PeMS08 from Caltrans performance measurement system (PEMS) [4]. The attributes of each dataset are shown in Table 1 [15].

Data Processing: The values in the datasets are aggregated every 5 min, resulting in 288 time stamps per day. All missing values are processed by linear interpolation. The historical time length T_p and prediction time length T_q are both

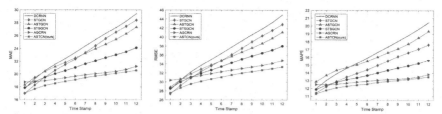

(a) The performance over 12 forecasting horions of different models in PeMS04 dataset

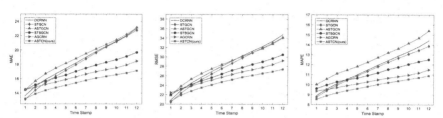

(b) The performance over 12 forecasting horions of different models in PeMS08 dataset

Fig. 3. Performance changes over 12 forecasting horizons of different models in PEMS04 and PEMS08 datasets

12, i.e., we use one-hour historical traffic values to predict the next hour traffic conditions. All datasets are divided into training set, verification set and test set according to the ratio of 6:2:2. In addition, z-score data normalization method is adopted to ensure the stability of training.

5.2 Experimental Setting

The parameters are trained with RMSprop strategy after global initialization. We train the model over 100 epochs with batch size 50, and the initial learning rate is set to 0.001 with a decay rate of 0.8 after every 5 epochs. The node embedding dimension d is 5 and the number of ST-block L is 2. All the code is written in Python and implemented on Tensorflow platform. All experiments are repeated 10 times, the mean of results are taken as the final output.

5.3 Baselines and Metrics

- LSTM [9]: Long Short Term Memory network, a special RNN model.
- STGCN [19]: Spatio-Temporal Graph Convolutional Networks, which utilize GCN and temporal convolution to extract spatial-temporal features.
- DCRNN [13]: Diffusion Convolutional Recurrent Neural Network, which use diffusion process to further enhance the ability of spatial correlations extraction.

Table 2. The overall performances of different methods over 12 forecasting horizons in PeMS03, PeMS04, PeMS07 and PeMS08 datasets. "*" indicates the experiment results from references, and "_" indicates the optimal baseline results.

Datasets	Metrics	LSTM	DCRNN	STGCN	ASTGCN	STSGCN	STFGNN	AGCRN	ASTCN
PeMS03	MAE	21.33	17.55	17.49	18.25	*17.48	*16.77	15.93	15.03
	RMSE	35.11	29.74	29.80	30.17	*29.21	*28.34	28.06	26.64
	MAPE (%)	23.33	16.96	17.23	18.8	*16.78	*16.30	15.17	14.65
PeMS04	MAE	27.14	23.80	22.89	22.86	*21.19	*19.83	19.76	19.27
	RMSE	41.59	36.95	35.43	35.34	*33.65	*31.88	32.43	31.13
	MAPE (%)	18.20	16.30	14.69	15.95	*13.90	*13.02	13.00	12.71
PeMS07	MAE	29.98	24.61	25.18	26.69	*24.26	*22.07	21.65	20.71
	RMSE	45.94	37.74	38.10	40.69	*39.03	*35.80	34.94	33.72
	MAPE (%)	13.25	10.70	10.91	12.16	*10.21	*9.21	9.17	8.81
PeMS08	MAE	22.20	18.52	18.26	19.03	*17.13	*16.64	16.24	15.40
	RMSE	34.06	28.31	27.84	28.74	*26.80	*26.22	25.78	24.46
	MAPE (%)	14.20	11.70	11.48	12.58	*10.96	*10.60	10.29	9.85

- ASTGCN(r) [7]: Attention Based Spatial-Temporal Graph Convolutional Networks, which utilize attention mechanism to dynamically extract spatial-temporal features. ASTGCN utilizes three components of trend, daily and weekly to extract the period features of traffic data. In order to ensure the fairness, we only use the trend component for comparison.
- STSGCN [15]: Spatial-Temporal Synchronous Graph Convolutional Networks, which captures spatial-temporal correlations by stacking multiple localized GCN layers with adjacent matrix over the time axis.
- AGCRN [2]: Adaptive Graph Convolutional Recurrent Network, which adaptively extracts spatial correlations by node embedding and temporal correlations by GRU.
- STFGNN [12]: Spatial-Temporal Fusion Graph Neural Networks for Traffic Flow Forecasting, which utilizes data-driven method to generate spatial-temporal fusion graph for traffic forecasting.

In order to effectively evaluate the performanceof different models, *mean absolute errors* (MAE), *mean absolute percentage errors* (MAPE), and *root mean squared errors* (RMSE) are recommended as the evaluation metrics.

5.4   Experiment Results

Table 2 shows the average forecasting performance of MAE, MAPE and RMSE metrics over 12 time horizons for each models. We can see from the table that: 1) GCN-based methods have obvious advantages in traffic network prediction by extracting spatial information. 2) Compared with complex spatial-temporal features extraction mechanisms, such as attention mechanism in ASTGCN and spatial-temporal synchronous convolution in STSGCN, the adaptive graph construction method can obtain higher prediction accuracy with simple structure.

Table 3. Comparison of parameters and training time of different methods in PeMS04 dataset

Model	Metrics	
	Parameters	Training time (s/epoch)
STGCN	211596	7.23
ASTGCN	450031	37.66
STSGCN	2872686	47.72
AGCRN (dim = 10)	748810	17.53
ASTCN	635727	30.34

3) ASTCN achieves significant profit in all datasets and brings about 4% performance improvement compared with the optimal baseline. The method of building spatial-temporal correlations adaptively according to specific prediction task can make the model have stronger adaptability to traffic environments.

Figure 3 further shows the accuracy over 12 prediction horizons in PeMS04 and PeMS08 datasets. We can see that ASTCN achieves the optimal performance in all timestamps for the first time. Compared with the auto-regressive pattern (e.g., STGCN and ASTGCN), ASTCN can significantly reduce the error propagation problem in long-term forecasting. More importantly, ASTCN can independently model the relationship between prediction horizons and historical information. And it also has strong competitiveness in short-term forecasting compared with the current seq2seq methods (e.g., AGCRN).

In short, ASTCN can accurately capture spatial-temporal correlations according to specific prediction task without any prior knowledge, and improve long-term and short-term prediction accuracy concurrently.

5.5   Computational Complexity Analysis

In order to further evaluate the computational complexity between ASTCN and baseline models, we compare the parameters, training time with STGCN, AST-GCN, STSGCN, and AGCRN models (as shown in Table 3). STGCN has the least computation cost due to its simple spatial-temporal extraction structure. ASTGCN and STSGCN have longer training time and massive parameters due to the complex spatio-temporal correlations extraction mechanism. AGCRN improves the node embedding dimension to get higher forecasting accuracy, resulting in a significant increase in the number of model parameters. However, AGCRN has a shorter training time, because it directly outputs all forecasting sequences rather than iteratively. By contrast, ASTCN completely relies on neural network to extract spatial-temporal correlations and learn timestamp-specific features update pattern, so it needs more training time. Considering the computational cost and performance improvement, the computational complexity of ASTCN is reasonable.

6   Conclusion and Future Work

In this paper, we propose a general and effective seq2seq traffic forecasting framework called adaptive spatial-temporal convolution network (ASTCN), which mainly includes two deep learning components: adaptive spatial convolution network (ASCN) and adaptive temporal convolution network (ATCN). ASTCN can adaptively model the spatial-temporal correlations according to specific prediction task, and enhance the adaptability to the traffic environments. More importantly, we first utilize the parameter allocation difference to reflect the heterogeneities of each timestamp over prediction horizon. The timestamps possess a unique features aggregation pattern, which can improve the long-term forecasting ability and ensure the accuracy of short-term forecasting concurrently. The experimental results in four public highway datasets show that the ASTCN model can outperform the optimal baseline under appropriate parameters, and achieve the optimal accuracy in each timestamp over the prediction horizon for the first time. In the future work, we will further optimize the model and apply adaptive spatial-temporal convolution network to other spatial-temporal forecasting fields.

Acknowledgment. This work is supported by the National Natural Science Foundation of China under Grant No. 61971057 and MoE-CMCC "Artifical Intelligence" under Project No. MCM20190701.

References

1. Bai, L., Yao, L., Kanhere, S.S., Wang, X., Sheng, Q.Z.: Stg2seq: spatial-temporal graph to sequence model for multi-step passenger demand forecasting. In: Proceedings of the AAAI Conference on Artificial Intelligence, pp. 1981–1987 (2019)
2. Bai, L., Yao, L., Li, C., Wang, X., Wang, C.: Adaptive graph convolutional recurrent network for traffic forecasting. In: Advances in Neural Information Processing Systems 33: Annual Conference on Neural Information Processing Systems 2020, NeurIPS 2020, 6–12 December 2020, Virtual (2020)
3. Bruna, J., Zaremba, W., Szlam, A., LeCun, Y.: Spectral networks and locally connected networks on graphs. In: Bengio, Y., LeCun, Y. (eds.) Conference Track Proceedings 2nd International Conference on Learning Representations, ICLR 2014, Banff, AB, Canada, 14–16 April 2014 (2014)
4. Chen, C., Petty, K., Skabardonis, A., Varaiya, P., Jia, Z.: Freeway performance measurement system: mining loop detector data. Transp. Res. Record **1748**(1), 96–102 (2001)
5. Defferrard, M., Bresson, X., Vandergheynst, P.: Convolutional neural networks on graphs with fast localized spectral filtering. In: Advances in Neural Information Processing Systems 29: Annual Conference on Neural Information Processing Systems, pp. 3837–3845 (2016)
6. Geng, X., et al.: Spatiotemporal multi-graph convolution network for ride-hailing demand forecasting. In: The Thirty-Third AAAI Conference on Artificial Intelligence, pp. 3656–3663 (2019)

7. Guo, S., Lin, Y., Feng, N., Song, C., Wan, H.: Attention based spatial-temporal graph convolutional networks for traffic flow forecasting. In: Proceedings of the AAAI Conference on Artificial Intelligence, vol. 33, pp. 922–929 (2019)
8. He, K., Zhang, X., Ren, S., Sun, J.: Deep residual learning for image recognition. In: Proceedings of the IEEE Conference on Computer Vision and Pattern Recognition (CVPR) (2016)
9. Hochreiter, S., Schmidhuber, J.: Long short-term memory. Neural Comput. 9(8), 1735–1780 (1997)
10. Ioffe, S., Szegedy, C.: Batch normalization: accelerating deep network training by reducing internal covariate shift. In: Proceedings of the 32nd International Conference on Machine Learning, vol. 37, pp. 448–456 (2015)
11. Kipf, T.N., Welling, M.: Semi-supervised classification with graph convolutional networks. In: 5th International Conference on Learning Representations (2017)
12. Li, M., Zhu, Z.: Spatial-temporal fusion graph neural networks for traffic flow forecasting. In: Thirty-Fifth AAAI Conference on Artificial Intelligence, AAAI 2021, pp. 4189–4196 (2021)
13. Li, Y., Yu, R., Shahabi, C., Liu, Y.: Diffusion convolutional recurrent neural network: data-driven traffic forecasting. In: 6th International Conference on Learning Representations (2018)
14. Lv, Z., Xu, J., Zheng, K., Yin, H., Zhao, P., Zhou, X.: LC-RNN: a deep learning model for traffic speed prediction. In: Proceedings of the Twenty-Seventh International Joint Conference on Artificial Intelligence, pp. 3470–3476 (2018)
15. Song, C., Lin, Y., Guo, S., Wan, H.: Spatial-temporal synchronous graph convolutional networks: a new framework for spatial-temporal network data forecasting. In: Proceedings of the AAAI Conference on Artificial Intelligence, vol. 34, pp. 914–921 (2020)
16. Vaswani, A., et al.: Attention is all you need. In: Advances in Neural Information Processing Systems 30: Annual Conference on Neural Information Processing Systems, pp. 5998–6008 (2017)
17. Wu, Z., Pan, S., Long, G., Jiang, J., Zhang, C.: Graph wavenet for deep spatial-temporal graph modeling. In: Proceedings of the Twenty-Eighth International Joint Conference on Artificial Intelligence, pp. 1907–1913 (2019)
18. Xu, M., et al.: Spatial-temporal transformer networks for traffic flow forecasting. arXiv preprint arXiv:2001.02908 (2020)
19. Yu, B., Yin, H., Zhu, Z.: Spatio-temporal graph convolutional networks: a deep learning framework for traffic forecasting. In: Proceedings of the Twenty-Seventh International Joint Conference on Artificial Intelligence, pp. 3634–3640 (2018)
20. Zhang, J., Zheng, Y., Qi, D.: Deep spatio-temporal residual networks for citywide crowd flows prediction. In: Proceedings of the AAAI Conference on Artificial Intelligence, vol. 31 (2017)
21. Zhang, J., Zheng, Y., Qi, D., Li, R., Yi, X.: DNN-based prediction model for spatio-temporal data. In: Proceedings of the 24th ACM SIGSPATIAL International Conference on Advances in Geographic Information Systems, pp. 92:1–92:4 (2016)
22. Zhao, L., Song, Y., Zhang, C., Liu, Y., Li, H.: T-GCN: a temporal graph convolutional network for traffic prediction. IEEE Trans. Intell. Transp. Syst. 99, 1–11 (2019)
23. Zheng, C., Fan, X., Wang, C., Qi, J.: Gman: a graph multi-attention network for traffic prediction. In: Proceedings of the AAAI Conference on Artificial Intelligence, vol. 34, pp. 1234–1241 (2020)

Structural and Temporal Learning for Dropout Prediction in MOOCs

Tianxing Han, Pengyi Hao$^{(\boxtimes)}$, and Cong Bai

Zhejiang University of Technology, Hangzhou, China
{txhan,haopy,congbai}@zjut.edu.cn

Abstract. In recent years, Massive Online Open Courses (MOOCs) have gained widespread attention. However, the high dropout rate has become an important factor limiting the development of MOOCs. Existing approaches typically utilize time-consuming and laborious feature engineering to select features, which ignore the complex correlation relationships among entities. For solving this issue, in this paper, we propose an approach named structural and temporal learning (STL) for dropout prediction in MOOCs. The multiple entities and the complex correlation relationships among entities are modeled as a heterogeneous information network (HIN). To take full advantage of the rich structural information in the HIN, we present a hierarchical neural network, in which a series of calculations are used to guide and learn the importance of intra-correlation and inter-correlation. Besides, we fully exploit the temporal features of user activities based on activity sequences. Finally, structural and temporal features are fused to predict dropout. The experiments on the MOOCCube dataset demonstrate the effectiveness of STL.

Keywords: Dropout prediction · Heterogeneous information network · Hierarchical neural network · Bi-LSTM · MOOCs

1 Introduction

In recent years, MOOCs have received widespread attention because they break through the constraints of time and space [1]. However, some studies point out that less than 10% of users can complete the courses they take and receive the corresponding certificates [9], which has become a major obstacle to the development of MOOCs. Therefore, it is extremely crucial to accurately identify users who have a tendency to drop out early in their learning process, so that timely and appropriate measures can be taken to keep them learning.

Most of the researchers viewed the dropout prediction as a binary problem based on machine learning. They predicted whether a user would drop out by modeling the user's behaviors. For example, Chen et al. [2] combined decision trees and extreme learning to make prediction. Jin et al. [10] calculated and optimized the weights of training samples based on the definition of the max neighborhood. Nitta et al. [13] extracted the relationship among users' actions

© The Author(s), under exclusive license to Springer Nature Switzerland AG 2022
G. Memmi et al. (Eds.): KSEM 2022, LNAI 13369, pp. 300–311, 2022.
https://doi.org/10.1007/978-3-031-10986-7_24

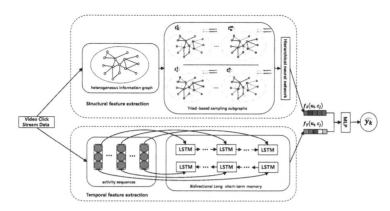

Fig. 1. The architecture of the proposed approach

by tensor decomposition and transformer. Zhang et al. [19] analyzed users' learning behavior and pointed out that introductory learning resources are beneficial in guiding users and preventing them from dropping out. Feng et al. [5] proposed a model that uses CNN to smooth the context and integrates the attribute information of users and courses with an attention mechanism. However, such researches use only user- or course-based statistics as contextual information. They ignored the deep correlation relationships among entities, such as classmate relationships between users who have taken the same course, correlations between courses taken by the same user, etc. These correlation relationships are complex and diverse. If they can be explored to describe the features of users and courses, the prediction of dropout will be more in line with the users' reality.

Meta-path [20], a composite path connecting a pair of entities, through which we can not only capture the rich and diverse structural and semantic information in the network, but also introduce the prior knowledge. Therefore, it has been widely applied to data mining related tasks such as node classification [16], link prediction [3] and recommendation [4,7], but there is no research to employ meta-path for dropout prediction as far as we know. The scenario in which user learns in MOOCs typically contains three types of entities (i.e., user, course, video) and rich semantic relations among entities (e.g., the elective relation between the user and the course, the subordinate relation between the video and the course, the watching relation between the user and the video). Inspired by meta-paths, we design multiple entity triads to explore the correlation relationships among entities, such as <user,course,user> and <course,video,user>. <user,course,user> implies that two users have taken the same course, while <course,video,user> indicates that a course is equipped with some videos, and these videos have been watched by some users recently.

Based on such entity triads, we propose an approach named structural and temporal learning (STL) for dropout prediction in MOOCs in this paper. On the one hand, hierarchical neural network is proposed to extract the structural information among users and courses according to the entity triples designed for

Table 1. Explanations of the main notations used in this paper.

Notation	Explanation
t_u, t_c	Triad sets for users and courses
$<U, X, Y>, <C, X, Y>$	A triad set for users and a triad set for courses
$N_\eta^1(u_i)$	Sampled first-order neighbors of u_i based on triad η
$N_\eta^2(u_i)$	Sampled second-order neighbors of u_i based on triad η
$R(u_i^{l_2}, u_i|\eta)$	Non-normalized relevance score of $u_i^{l_2}$ to u_i
$R'(u_i^{l_2}, u_i|\eta)$	Normalized relevance score of $u_i^{l_2}$ to u_i
$f(u_i^{l_2})$	Relevance-guided embedding of $u_i^{l_2}$
$f_\eta(u_i)$	Correlation-specific representation of u_i based on triad η
$\widetilde{f_{t_u}}, \widetilde{f_{t_c}}$	Structural features of u_i and c_j
$f_S(u_i, c_j)$	Structural feature of user u_i on course c_j
$A(u_i, c_j)$	Activity sequence of user u_i on course c_j
$f_T(u_i, c_j)$	Temporal feature of user u_i on course c_j

them. In this network, we use relevance calculation to assist in generating initial representations of nodes, and then enable the network to automatically focus on important neighbor nodes and correlations by intra-correlation calculation and inter-correlation calculation. On the other hand, the activity information is processed by Bidirectional Long Short-Term Memory (Bi-LSTM) [8] to extract time-influenced temporal features. Finally, the structural features and temporal features are fused to predict dropout. The proposed STL is evaluated on a public real-world dataset called MOOCCube [18] and compared with several state-of-the-art methods. The evaluations demonstrate the effectiveness of STL.

2   The Proposed Method

2.1   Problem Description

Given the video click stream data, we extract the set of users U, the set of courses C and the set of videos V. If a user $u_i \in U$ takes a course $c_j \in C$, the purpose of our study is to predict whether u_i will dropout from c_j or not in the future. Figure 1 illustrates the overall framework of the proposed model, which includes structural feature extraction based on hierarchical neural network shown in Fig. 2, and the temporal activity feature extraction based on Bidirectional Long Short-Term Memory. The main notations used in this paper and their explanations are presented in Table 1.

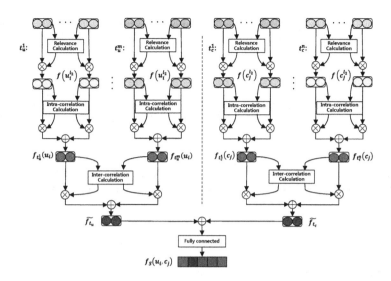

Fig. 2. The framework of hierarchical neural network

2.2 Hierarchical Neural Network

Since the complex correlation relationships among entities in MOOCs may affect dropouts, a heterogeneous information graph G is constructed to model the MOOCs scenario, and hierarchical neural network as shown in Fig. 2 is proposed to extract the structural features among entities. The graph G contains a series of user, course and video nodes based on the sets U, C and V, and the edges between different types of nodes represent different meanings, e.g., user-course edge represents the elective relationship, user-video edge represents the watching relationship and course-video edge represents the subordinate relationship. Then based on prior knowledge, a triad set $t_u = [t_u^1, \ldots, t_u^m]$ with m triads for users and a triad set $t_c = [t_c^1, \ldots, t_c^n]$ with n triads for courses are designed. Each triad $\eta \in t_u$ can be denoted as $<U, X, Y>$, where $X = [x_1, \ldots, x_{n_x}]$, $Y = [y_1, \ldots, y_{n_y}]$ represent subsets of entities, n_x and n_y represent the number of elements in X and Y, respectively. Similarly, each triad $\xi \in t_c$ can be denoted as $<C, X, Y>$.

We now present how to extract structural features by hierarchical neural network. By taking a triad $\eta \in t_u$ as an example. First, we form a first-order neighbor set $N_\eta^1(u_i)$ for the target node u_i by randomly sampling n_1 nodes from neighbor set $X(u_i)$. Let $u_i^{l_1}$ be a node of $N_\eta^1(u_i)$. For $\forall u_i^{l_1} \in N_\eta^1(u_i)$, a subset of the second-order neighbor set of $u_i : N_\eta^1(u_i^{l_1})$ is obtained by randomly sampling n_2 nodes from the neighbor set $Y(u_i^{l_1})$. By the above operation, we obtain the sampled second-order neighbor set of u_i: $N_\eta^2(u_i) = \left\{ N_\eta^1(u_i^{l_1}), \forall u_i^{l_1} \in N_\eta^1(u_i) \right\}$. Let $u_i^{l_2}$ be a node of $N_\eta^2(u_i)$.

- Relevance Calculation. To make a good input to hierarchical neural network, we use HeteSim [14] to calculate the relevance score between $u_i^{l_2}$ and u_i:

$$R(u_i^{l_2}, u_i | \eta) = \frac{|TI_{u_i^{l_2} \sim u_i}|}{|O(u_i^{l_2})||I(u_i)|}, \tag{1}$$

where $TI_{u_i^{l_2} \sim u_i}$ denotes the triad instances between $u_i^{l_2}$ and u_i following the triad η, $O(u_i^{l_2})$ denotes the out-degree of $u_i^{l_2}$, and $I(u_i)$ denotes the in-degree of u_i. Note that it is unreasonable for $R(u_i^{l_2}, u_i | \eta) \neq 1$ if $u_i^{l_2}$ is equal to u_i. In order to solve it, we normalize the equation using the cosine of the probability distribution that $u_i^{l_2}$ and u_i arrive at the node x_j of the set X.

$$R'(u_i^{l_2}, u_i | \eta) = \frac{R(u_i^{l_2}, u_i | \eta)}{\sqrt{\sum_{j=1}^{n_x} P^2 \left(u_i^{l_2}, x_j\right)} \cdot \sqrt{\sum_{j=1}^{n_x} P^2 \left(x_j, u_i\right)}}, \tag{2}$$

where $P\left(u_i^{l_2}, x_j\right)$ and $P\left(x_j, u_i\right)$ denote the probability of starting from $u_i^{l_2}$ to x_j and the probability of starting from x_j to u_i under the triad η, respectively. Then the relevance-guided embedding $f(u_i^{l_2}) \in \mathbb{R}^{1 \times d_I}$ can be obtained as

$$f(u_i^{l_2}) = Xavier(u_i^{l_2}) * R'(u_i^{l_2}, u_i | \eta). \tag{3}$$

where $Xavier(u_i^{l_2}) \in \mathbb{R}^{1 \times d_I}$ is a trainable parameter vector with dimensions d_I by the Xavier [6] initializer.

- Intra-correlation Calculation. Based on second-order neighbor set $N_\eta^2(u_i)$ and relevance-guided embedding $f(u_i^{l_2})$, the weight α_η between u_i and its sampled neighbor $u_i^{l_2}$ can be obtained by $\alpha_\eta = softmax(v \cdot tanh(f(u_i^{l_2}) \cdot w_1 + b_1))$, where v, w_1 and b_1 are trainable parameters. Then the correlation-specific feature $f_\eta(u_i) \in \mathbb{R}^{1 \times d_I}$ can be calculated as:

$$f_\eta(u_i) = \sum_{u_i^{l_2} \in N_\eta^2(u_i)} (\alpha_\eta * f(u_i^{l_2})) \tag{4}$$

- Inter-correlation Calculation. After iterating over the triad sets t_u and t_c, respectively, we obtain the correlation features $f_{t_u}(u_i) = f_{t_u^1}(u_i) \oplus \cdots \oplus f_{t_u^m}(u_i)$ and $f_{t_c}(c_j) = f_{t_c^1}(c_j) \oplus \cdots \oplus f_{t_c^n}(c_j)$ for user-course pair(u_i, c_j), where $f_{t_u}(u_i) \in \mathbb{R}^{m \times d_I}$, $f_{t_c}(c_j) \in \mathbb{R}^{n \times d_I}$ (abbreviated as f_{t_u} and f_{t_c}) and $\oplus$ denotes the concatenation operation. In order to incorporate multiple types of correlations, we adopt self-attention [15] to calculate the attention value between each two correlations. Firstly, Q_u is calculated by $Q_u = \sigma(f_{t_u} \cdot w_q + b_q)$, E_u is calculated by $E_u = \sigma(f_{t_u} \cdot w_e + b_e)$, Z_u is calculated by $Z_u = \sigma(f_{t_u} \cdot w_z + b_z)$, where Q_u, E_u and $Z_u \in \mathbb{R}^{m \times d_a}$, $d_I < d_a$, $\sigma(\cdot)$ is the sigmoid function with an output between 0 and 1, $w_q, w_e, w_z, b_q, b_e, b_z$ are trainable parameters. Then the converged structural feature $\widetilde{f_{t_u}} \in \mathbb{R}^{m \times d_a}$ for user u_i is calculated as

$$\widetilde{f_{t_u}} = \text{softmax}\left(\frac{Q_u E_u^T}{\sqrt{d_a}}\right) * Z_u \tag{5}$$

where E_u^T denotes the transpose of E_u. Similarly, the converged structural feature $\widetilde{f_{t_c}} \in \mathbb{R}^{n \times d_a}$ for course c_j is calculated as

$$\widetilde{f_{t_c}} = \text{softmax}\left(\frac{Q_c E_c^T}{\sqrt{d_a}}\right) * Z_c \tag{6}$$

where Q_c, E_c and $Z_c \in \mathbb{R}^{m \times d_a}$ are obtained by feeding f_{t_c} into three linear layers, respectively and E_c^T denotes the transpose of E_c. Additionally, in order to further fuse the converged features, the final structural features $f_S(u_i, c_j) \in \mathbb{R}^{1 \times d_s}$ with dimensions d_s can be obtained by:

$$f_S(u_i, c_j) = \sigma(\delta(\widetilde{f_{t_u}} \oplus \widetilde{f_{t_c}}) \cdot w_2 + b_2), \tag{7}$$

where w_2 and b_2 are trainable parameters, $\delta(\widetilde{f_{t_u}} \oplus \widetilde{f_{t_c}})$ flattens matrix $(\widetilde{f_{t_u}} \oplus \widetilde{f_{t_c}}) \in \mathbb{R}^{(m+n) \times d_a}$ to a row vector with dimension $\mathbb{R}^{1 \times (m+n)d_a}$. The overall flow of the hierarchical neural network is given in Algorithm 1.

Algorithm 1: Hierarchical neural network

Input: Graph G; the triad sets t_u and t_c; sampling number n_1, n_2;
Output: structural feature $f_S(u_i, c_j)$

1 **for** *each* $\eta \in t_u$ **do**
2    $N_\eta^1(u_i) \leftarrow$ sample n_1 nodes
3   from $X(u_i)$
4    $N_\eta^2(u_i) = \{\}$
5   **for** *each* $u^{l_1} \in N_\eta^1(u_i)$ **do**
6      $N_\eta^1(u_i^{l_1}) \leftarrow$ sample n_2 nodes
7   from $Y(u_i^{l_1})$
8   add $N_\eta^1(u_i^{l_1})$ to $N_\eta^2(u_i)$
9   **end**
10   **for** *each* $u_i^{l_2} \in N_\eta^2(u_i)$ **do**
11   Calculate $f(u_i^{l_2})$ by Eq. (1, 2, 3)
12   **end**
13   Generate $f_\eta(u_i)$ by Eq. (4)
14 **end**
15 $f_{t_u} \leftarrow f_\eta(u_i), \forall \eta \in t_u$
16 Generate $\widetilde{f_{t_u}}$ by Eq. (5)
17 **for** *each* $\xi \in t_c$ **do**
18    $N_\xi^1(c_j) \leftarrow$ sample n_1 nodes
19   from $X(c_j)$
20    $N_\xi^2(c_j) = \{\}$
21   **for** *each* $c_j^{l_1} \in N_\xi^1(c_j)$ **do**
22      $N_\xi^1(c_j^{l_1}) \leftarrow$ sample n_2
23   nodes from $Y(c_j^{l_1})$
24   add $N_\xi^1(c_j^{l_1})$ to $N_\xi^2(c_j)$
25   **end**
26   **for** *each* $c_j^{l_2} \in N_\xi^2(c_j)$ **do**
27   Calculate $f(c_j^{l_2})$ by
28   Eq. (1, 2, 3)
29   **end**
30   Generate $f_\xi(c_j)$ by Eq. (4)
31 **end**
32 $f_{t_c} \leftarrow f_\xi(c_j), \forall \xi \in t_c$
33 Generate $\widetilde{f_{t_c}}$ by Eq. (6)
34 Generate $f_S(u_i, c_j)$ by Eq. (7)
35 return $f_S(u_i, c_j)$

2.3   Temporal Activity Feature Extraction

Dropouts may exhibit dramatically different learning behaviors over time, especially in the early stage of his/her learning. Therefore, modeling users' learning behaviors based on temporal relationships is crucial to the dropout prediction. In order to cope with it, a recurrent network, Bidirectional Long Short Term Memory (Bi-LSTM) [8] is applied in our model to extract the temporal activity feature $f_T(u_i, c_j) \in \mathbb{R}^{1 \times d_t}$ for user-course pair (u_i, c_j).

From the video click stream data, some statistical data can be extracted, such as the number of times the user watches the video, the number of days the user is active on the platform, and so on. In order to express the user's activity information, an activity sequence $A(u_i, c_j) = [a_1, \cdots, a_e, \cdots, a_d]$ is established based on the data of first d days after u_i started learning on c_j, where a_e is a row vector containing a fixed number of types of activities.

In Bi-LSTM model, there is a forward LSTM network and a reverse LSTM network that jointly capture the past and future contextual information. We take the generation of activity feature h_e on e-th day as an example. For the memory cell at the e-th day time step, the forget gate f_e, the input gate i_e and the output gate o_e are used to control the information flowing into and out of the current memory cell. f_e, i_e, o_e are calculated by the following equations,

$$
\begin{cases}
f_e = \sigma \left(w_f \cdot a_e + w'_f \cdot h_{e-1} + b_f \right) \\
i_e = \sigma \left(w_i \cdot a_e + w'_i \cdot h_{e-1} + b_i \right) \\
o_e = \sigma \left(w_o \cdot a_e + w'_o \cdot h_{e-1} + b_o \right)
\end{cases}
\tag{8}
$$

where $w_f, w'_f, w_i, w'_i, w_o, w'_o, b_f, b_i, b_o$ are trainable parameters, h_{e-1} represents the value of previous hidden layer. Then the value of the current memory unit C_e can be obtained by selectively forgetting the previous information and adding the current information appropriately as $C_e = f_e * C_{e-1} + i_e * \tilde{C}_e$. Here $\tilde{C}_e = \tanh \left(w_c \cdot a_e + w'_c \cdot h_{e-1} + b_c \right)$ denotes alternate information for the current time step, w_c, w'_c, b_c are trainable parameters. Once the current memory cell C_e is updated, the activity feature h_e for the e-th time step can be obtained as

$$
h_e = o_e * \tanh \left(C_e \right).
\tag{9}
$$

Similarly we can obtain the activity feature for each time step on the forward and reverse LSTM networks: $\overrightarrow{h} = [\overrightarrow{h_1}, \cdots, \overrightarrow{h_e}, \cdots, \overrightarrow{h_d}]$ and $\overleftarrow{h} = [\overleftarrow{h_1}, \cdots, \overleftarrow{h_e}, \cdots, \overleftarrow{h_d}]$. In addition, to further represent the temporal relationship of user activities, the final temporal activity feature $f_T(u_i, c_j)$ is obtained by adding the forward and reverse activity features and mapping them to a higher dimension,

$$
f_T(u_i, c_j) = tanh(w_3(\overrightarrow{h} + \overleftarrow{h}) + b_3).
\tag{10}
$$

In the above equation, $f_T(u_i, c_j) \in \mathbb{R}^{1 \times d_t}$, d_t is the same as d_s, w_3 and b_3 are trainable parameters.

2.4   Model Learning

Based on the set of users U and the set of courses C, if there exist K user-course selective pairs, then the prediction score $\hat{y}_k \in (0,1)$ for whether a user u_i dropout from a course c_j can be obtained by

$$\hat{y}_k = sigmoid(MLP(f_S(u_i, c_j) \oplus f_T(u_i, c_j))), \qquad (11)$$

where the $MLP(\cdot)$ is the Multi-Layer Perceptron layer, $sigmoid(\cdot)$ is the sigmoid layer with an output between 0 and 1. All the parameters in our model can be trained by minimizing the following objective function:

$$\text{Loss}(\Theta) = \sum_{k \in [1,K]} [y_k \log(\hat{y}_k) + (1 - y_k) \log(1 - \hat{y}_k)] + \lambda ||\Theta||_2^2, \qquad (12)$$

where Θ is the parameter set of proposed model, y_k denotes the corresponding ground truth of user u_i in course c_j and λ is the regularizer parameter.

3   Experiments

3.1   Dataset and the Definition of Dropout

The dataset used in this paper is from MOOCCube [18], a large-scale data repository, which stores more than 700 courses, 38k videos and 200k students. The user log file in MOOCCube records 4,873,530 video watch logs of 48,639 learners enrolled in 685 courses from 26 June 2015 to 16 April 2020.

It is difficult to define dropout, because the user can be inactive for a period of time without dropping out of the course and continuing to learn later. Inspired by [12], we introduce the concept of inactive period, i.e., the maximum of the period between interactions and the inactivity period to the end of data collection. According to the statistics for MOOCCube, over 95% of users who are inactive for 365 days actually give up studying, 365 days is chosen as an inactive period to consider dropping out. In addition, unlike assignments and exams, videos as a core resource of MOOCs are widely available in different courses, so we give a novel definition of dropout by combining inactive period and the percentage of watched videos. Specifically, if a user u_i has been inactive for more than 365 days and has not watched 80% of the videos in a course c_j, then this enrollment record will be marked as "dropout".

Based on the above definition, we obtained a dataset containing 232,864 enrollment records generated by 47,074 users in 556 courses. There are 220,045 enrollment records for dropouts. We divided the dataset into training and test sets in the ratio of 7:3, with the same proportion of positive and negative samples. In the following experiments, we use the user's seven-day activity log to predict whether the user will drop out in the future.

3.2   Evaluation Metrics and Implementation Details

Considering the highly unbalanced proportion of positive and negative samples in the dataset, we use Area Under the ROC Curve (abbreviated as AUC) to depict the ability of the model to distinguish between positive and negative samples under different thresholds. AUC calculates a score for each sample based on how close the model's predicted probability value is to the true label, and the closer the predicted value is to the true label, the higher the AUC is and the better the model's predictive power is.

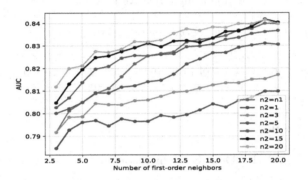

Fig. 3. The effect of different sampling numbers

We implement the STL based on tensorflow. For our model, we design three triads for users, including t_u^1:<user,course,user>, t_u^2:<user,video,course> and t_u^3:<user,video,user> and two triads for courses, including t_c^1:<course,user, course> and t_c^2:<course,video,user>. We randomly initialize the parameters with the Xavier [6] initializer. Adam [11] optimizer with an initial learning rate of 1×10^{-3} is chosen to learn the parameters. Dropout rate is set to be 0.5 and regularization parameter λ is set to be 1×10^{-4} to avoid overfitting.

3.3   Parameters in Hierarchical Neural Network

In this subsection, we explore the effect of some parameters in hierarchical neural network. For unobtrusive comparison, we only use hierarchical neural network to extract structural features. Figure 3 illustrates the model performance with different number of aggregated neighbors, where the horizontal axis represents the number of first-order neighbors n_1 and the different colored dashes represent the different number of second-order neighbors n_2. In general, the performance of the model steadily improves as the number of aggregated neighbors increases, which indicates that the neighbor information is beneficial to enhance the embedding representation of the target nodes, and the richer neighbor information helps to characterize the nodes. However, it can be clearly observed that the growth momentum of red line slows down significantly when $n_1 = 13$, and the growth almost stops when $n_1 = 19$. This suggests that as the number of neighbors increases, the neighbor information gradually tends to saturate and may introduce some noise information. Similar conclusions can be drawn on second-order neighbors by comparing different folds. In order to keep a balance between accuracy and complexity, $n_1 = 19$, $n_2 = 15$ are chosen in the next experiments.

Table 2. Evaluation on several commonly used feature processing methods.

AUC(%) triad node	Concat	MaxPool	Soft-Attention	Self-Attention
MaxPool	83.35	80.53	81.92	83.98
Mean	83.18	82.5	82.88	83.96
Soft-Attention	83.26	82.54	82.95	**84.61**

In hierarchical neural networks, we enrich and enhance the node representations of users and courses by aggregating intra-correlation information from different neighbor nodes and aggregating inter-correlation information from different triads. To explore the effectiveness of different feature processing methods, we evaluate MaxPool, Mean and Soft-Attention [17] for intra-correlation calculation among nodes, and evaluate Concat, MaxPool, Soft-Attention and Self-Attention for the inter-correlation calculation among triads. As can be seen in Table 2, the combination of Soft-Attention and Self-Attention boosts the AUC from 0.63% to 4.08% compared to other combinations. This suggests that Soft-Attention can capture the importance of triad-based neighbors and aggregate meaningful neighbor information, and on the other hand, the degree of dependency between different triads can be captured by Self-Attention and thus give us the enhanced representation of users and courses.

3.4   Comparison with Other Methods

To verify the validity of our method, we consider three versions of STL. They are STL without structural feature, STL without temporal feature and STL which uses both structural feature and temporal feature. They are compared with machine learning based methods such as LR (Logistic Regression), RF (Random Forest), GBDT (Gradient Boosting Decision Tree) and a deep learning-based method named CFIN [5] that uses CNN to learn the representation of each activity by leveraging its statistics, and uses soft-attention to learn the importance of different activities by combining attribute information. For LR, RF, GBDT and STL without structural feature, we use the activity sequence $A(u, c)$ extracted from the video click stream data as input. For CFIN, we extract the activity matrix, statistics of activity matrix and the information of users and courses from the video click stream data as input. For STL without temporal feature, we obtain the relevance-guided embedding as input. To make a fair comparison, the most suitable parameters are chosen for them. For RF, the

Table 3. Comparison with other methods.

Method	AUC (%)
Logistic Regression	86.32
Random Forest	90.29
Gradient Boosting Decision Tree	91.34
CFIN [5]	90.43
STL without structural feature	90.62
STL without temporal feature	84.61
STL	**92.04**

number of trees in the forest is set to 500. For GBDT, the number of weak learners is set to 200 and the maximum depth is set to 7, with a learning rate of 0.1. For CFIN, it is trained by the Adam optimizer with a learning rate of 1×10^{-4} and an L2 regularization strength of 1×10^{-5}.

The results are given in Table 3. STL without structural feature achieves an AUC of 90.62%, second only to GBDT, while after adding structural features, STL obtains an AUC of 92.04%, which increases by 0.7% to 5.72% compared with LR, RF, GBDT and CFIN. Although STL is only 0.7% higher than GBDT in terms of AUC, STL greatly outperforms GBDT in terms of time overhead. Not only because GBDT is difficult to parallel the processing due to the dependencies among weak learners, but also because GBDT requires the use of grid search to find the optimal parameters. Meanwhile, STL is 1.61% higher compared with CFIN. The reasons are that, STL enriches the representations of users and courses by deep correlation relationships among entities, and extracts temporal features from the activity sequence. Overall, our proposed STL obtains optimal performance and has good generalizability.

4   Conclusion

In this paper, a general approach named structural and temporal learning (STL) was proposed to improve dropout prediction on MOOCs. The multiple entities and the complex correlation relationships among entities were modeled as a heterogeneous information network (HIN). To take full advantage of the rich structural information in the HIN, we designed multiple triples to represent the correlation relationships between different entities and proposed a hierarchical neural network in which relevance calculation, intra-correlation calculation and inter-correlation calculation were jointly used to bootstrap and learn the importance of neighbor nodes and triads. Besides, we used Bi-LSTM to fully exploit the temporal features of user activities based on activity sequences. Finally, structural and temporal features were fused to predict dropout. The experiments on the MOOCCube dataset demonstrated the effectiveness of our proposed method. In the future, we will deploy STL to the MOOCs platform and establish a complete intervention mechanism for users.

Acknowledgements. This work is supported by Natural Science Foundation of Zhejiang Province of China under grants No. LR21F020002, and the First class undergraduate course construction project in Zhejiang Province of China.

References

1. Blum-Smith, S., Yurkofsky, M.M., et al.: Stepping back and stepping in: facilitating learner-centered experiences in MOOCs. Comput. Educ. **160**, 104042 (2021)
2. Chen, J., Feng, J., Sun, X., Wu, N., Yang, Z., Chen, S.: MOOC dropout prediction using a hybrid algorithm based on decision tree and extreme learning machine. Math. Prob. Eng. **2019**, 1–11 (2019)
3. Fan, H., Zhang, F., et al.: Heterogeneous hypergraph variational autoencoder for link prediction. IEEE Trans. Pattern Anal. Mach. Intell. (2021). https://doi.org/10.1109/TPAMI.2021.3059313
4. Fan, S., Zhu, J., et al.: Metapath-guided heterogeneous graph neural network for intent recommendation. In: KDD, pp. 2478–2486 (2019)
5. Feng, W., Tang, J., et al.: Understanding dropouts in MOOCs. In: Proceedings of the AAAI, vol. 33, pp. 517–524 (2019)
6. Glorot, X., Bengio, Y.: Understanding the difficulty of training deep feedforward neural networks. In: AISTATS, pp. 249–256 (2010)
7. Gong, J., Wang, S., et al.: Attentional graph convolutional networks for knowledge concept recommendation in MOOCs in a heterogeneous view. In: ACM SIGIR, pp. 79–88 (2020)
8. Graves, A., Schmidhuber, J.: Framewise phoneme classification with bidirectional LSTM and other neural network architectures. Neural Netw. **18**(5–6), 602–610 (2005)
9. He, J., Bailey, J., et al.: Identifying at-risk students in massive open online courses. In: Proceedings of the AAAI, vol. 29 (2015)
10. Jin, C.: Dropout prediction model in MOOC based on clickstream data and student sample weight. Soft. Comput. **25**(14), 8971–8988 (2021)
11. Kingma, D.P., Ba, J.: Adam: a method for stochastic optimization. In: ICLR (2015)
12. Moreno-Marcos, P.M., Munoz-Merino, P.J., et al.: Temporal analysis for dropout prediction using self-regulated learning strategies in self-paced MOOCs. Comput. Educ. **145**, 103728 (2020)
13. Nitta, I., Ishizaki, R., et al.: Graph-based massive open online course (MOOC) dropout prediction using clickstream data in virtual learning environment. In: ICCSE, pp. 48–52 (2021)
14. Shi, C., Kong, X., et al.: HeteSim: a general framework for relevance measure in heterogeneous networks. IEEE Trans. Knowl. Data Eng. **26**(10), 2479–2492 (2014)
15. Vaswani, A., Shazeer, N., et al.: Attention is all you need. In: NeurIPS (2017)
16. Wang, X., Ji, H., et al.: Heterogeneous graph attention network. In: World Wide Web, pp. 2022–2032 (2019)
17. Xu, K., Ba, J., et al.: Show, attend and tell: neural image caption generation with visual attention. In: ICML, pp. 2048–2057 (2015)
18. Yu, J., Luo, G., et al.: MOOCCube: a large-scale data repository for NLP applications in MOOCs. In: ACL (2020)
19. Zhang, J., Gao, M., Zhang, J.: The learning behaviours of dropouts in MOOCs: a collective attention network perspective. Comput. Educ. **167**, 104189 (2021)
20. Zhao, J., Wang, X., et al.: Heterogeneous graph structure learning for graph neural networks. In: Proceedings of the AAAI (2021)

Document-Level Multi-event Extraction via Event Ontology Guiding

Xingsheng Zhang[1,2], Yue Hu[1,2(✉)], Yajing Sun[1,2], Luxi Xing[1,2],
Yuqiang Xie[1,2], Yunpeng Li[1,2], and Wei Peng[1,2]

[1] Institute of Information Engineering, Chinese Academy of Sciences, Beijing, China
{zhangxingsheng,huyue,sunyajing,xingluxi,xieyuqiang,
liyunpeng,pengwei}@iie.ac.cn
[2] School of Cyber Security, University of Chinese Academy of Sciences,
Beijing, China

Abstract. Document-level Event Extraction (DEE) aims to extract event information from a whole document, in which extracting multiple events is a fundamental challenge. Previous works struggle to handle the Document-level Multi-Event Extraction (DMEE) due to facing two main issues: (a) the argument in one event can correspond to diverse roles in different events; (b) arguments from multiple events appear in the document in an unorganized way. Event ontology is a schema for describing events that contains types, corresponding roles, and their structural relations, which can provide hints to solve the above issues. In this paper, we propose a document-level Event Ontology Guiding multi-event extraction model (EOG), which utilizes the structural and semantic information of event ontology as role-oriented guidance to distinguish multiple events properties, thus can improve the performance of document-level multi-event extraction. Specifically, EOG constructs Event Ontology Embedding layer to capture the structural and semantic information of event ontology. A transformer-based Guiding Interact Module is then designed to model the structural information cross-events and cross-roles under the guidance of event ontology. Experimental results on the DMEE dataset demonstrate that the proposed EOG can achieve better performance on extracting multiple events from the document over baseline models.

Keywords: Event extraction · Document-level · Multi-event · Event ontology · Transformer

1 Introduction

Document-level Event Extraction (DEE) aims to extract structural event information from a unstructured document according to the predefined event ontology, which is an essential task in Natural Language Processing (NLP). DEE can provide valuable structural information to facilitate various NLP tasks, such as language understanding, knowledge base construction, question answering, etc.

© The Author(s), under exclusive license to Springer Nature Switzerland AG 2022
G. Memmi et al. (Eds.): KSEM 2022, LNAI 13369, pp. 312–324, 2022.
https://doi.org/10.1007/978-3-031-10986-7_25

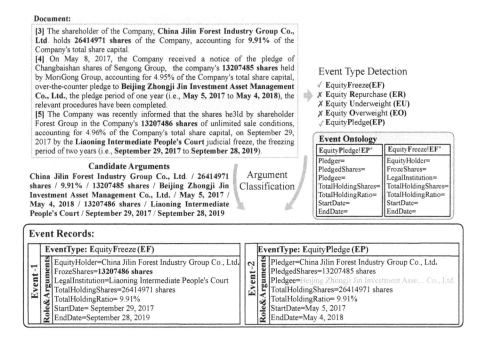

Fig. 1. An example of Document-level Multi-Event Extraction (DMEE). Words in colored are arguments that scatter across multiple sentences.

Existing DEE research [1,2,6,8,10,11] mainly focuses on extracting single event record from a document, but ignores the fact that multiple events appear in one document, which becomes a common issue in the document-level events extraction. As shown in Fig. 1, there are two events *Event-1* and *Event-2* appearing in the document simultaneously. However, existing models have poor ability to extract multiple events from document because the dependency relationships among different events and arguments are hard to capture. Therefore, multi-event is one crucial problem towards completing the DEE task.

In contrast to extracting single event from document, DMEE faces two critical challenges. The first challenge indicates that one event argument corresponds to different roles in different events. Figure 1 illustrates an example that the argument '*China Jilin Forest Industry Group Co., Ltd.*' plays *EquityHolder* role in *Event-1* with type *EquityFreeze*, and plays *Pledger* role in *Event-2* with event type is *EquityPledge* meanwhile. In order to distinguish different event records and different roles, model should have a global understanding of the entire document. Furthermore, it will be more difficult to extract events when a document coupled with the second challenge, in which arguments of multiple events appear disorderly in a document. As shown in Fig. 1, the arguments of *Event-1* appear in sentence [3] and [5], and the arguments of *Event-2* appear in sentence [3] and [4], indicate these events interlacing each other in the document. This issue requires model to recognize the dependency between these arguments among multiple events. As a result of these challenges and requirements, the DMEE model calls for a global guidance to integrate effectively multiple events information from the document.

Ontology is the generalization of people's understanding of concrete entities, which reflects the relationship between the concepts beyond the concrete entities. In the event extraction task, event ontology depicts the relationships between the events and roles. Such structural schema provides the global guidance for distinguishing different events information and roles information. Specifically, event ontology contains event type, corresponding roles and the structural relationships between them. Previous works neglect the structural and semantic information of event ontology, and have difficulty in solving the **multi-roles** and **disorderly appearing** challenges, leading to poor performance in document-level multi-event extraction task.

Motivated by this, we attempt to incorporate event ontology as guidance to improve the performance of model in DMEE. In this paper, we propose a document-level **E**vent **O**ntology **G**uiding multi-event extraction model (EOG), which utilizes the structural and semantic information of event ontology as a role-orientated guidance to capture the multiple dependency relationships (i.e., event-event, role-role, event-role) Specifically, EOG constructing event ontology embedding layer to model the structural and semantic information of event ontology. To implement the guiding by event ontology, we design a transformer-based Guiding Interact Module (GIM) to model the interaction between document context and event ontology. GIM could capture the difference between the different events through interaction of sentences embeddings and event types embedding, and the dependency relationship between arguments and different roles through interaction of arguments embeddings and event roles embeddings. In this way, EOG constructs structural information cross-events and cross-roles under the guidance of event ontology. Then, we leverage a event ontology-aware decoder module for generating the event records (i.e., the predefined type with several event arguments corresponding to roles). At the stage of event type detection in the decoder, event type embedding is used to enhance the type-aware document embedding to improve the accuracy of event type detection. At the stage of argument classification in the decoder, event role embedding is used to enhance the role-aware arguments embedding to improve the accuracy of argument classification. Thus, EOG is encouraged to incorporate the inter-dependency and intra-dependency of event records under the guidance of event ontology to improve the ability to extract multiple events.

In summary, our contributions are as follows:

- We propose a **E**vent **O**ntology **G**uiding extraction model (EOG) for document-level multi-event extraction. EOG adopts a event ontology embedding layer, a transformer-based Guiding Interact Module (GIM) and a event ontology-aware decoder extract multiple events from document under the guidance of event ontology.
- We design a transformer-based guiding interact module (GIM) in EOG. GIM capture the dependency of different events and different roles by modeling the interaction between document context and event ontology.

– We conduct extensive experiments on the document-level multi-event extraction dataset, which is split from a widely used DEE dataset. Experiment results illustrate the superiority of EOG over state-of-the-art methods and verify the effectiveness of the guidance of event ontology in DMEE.

2   Related Work

Document-level EE has received widespread attention in recent years. [9] extract key-event from sentence and find other arguments from surrounding sentences to achieve document-level event extraction. [1] try to encode arguments in multi-granularity way for a larger context information. [11] design a two step approach to reduce the number of candidate arguments. [5] proposes an end-to-end neural event argument extraction model by conditional text generation. [2] leverage a structured prediction algorithm with deep value networks (DVN). However, these works mainly focus on solving the problem arguments scattering and ignored the challenge of multi-event.

To address the multi-event issue in document-level extraction, [12] reformulate DMEE as a table filling task, and propose an entity-based directed acyclic graph to fulfill event table. [10] design a multi-granularity decoder to extract events in parallel. [8] construct a heterogeneous graph to model the correlation among sentences and arguments. However, these methods model capture dependency between arguments and sentences only on document itself, and it is insufficient for document-level multi-event extraction.

3   Task Formulation

Before introducing our proposed model, we describe the formalization of the Document-level Multi Event Extraction (DMEE) task. Formally, we first clarify the following key notions: (a) **Entity Mention** is a text span that refers to an entity object, such as '*26414971 shares*' in *Document* in Fig. 1. (b) **Event Argument** stands for the entity's participant property in one event. Generally, an entity object plays a specific event role, such as '*13207486 shares*' plays the role *FrozeShares* in Fig. 1, thus the '*13207486 shares*' is the argument in this event. (c) **Event Role** provides the structural relations and semantic information between event type and its arguments. A type of event contains a set of corresponding roles which the arguments will play, such as *Pledger, Pledgee* corresponding to *EF* in Fig. 1. (d) **Candidate Argument** refers to the entity which can be identified as a specific argument in events, such as *Candidate Arguments* in Fig. 1. (f) **Event Ontology** is the predefined schema for event extraction containing n^T event types and corresponding event roles, such as *Event Ontology* in Fig. 1. It is notated as $\mathcal{O} = \{\mathcal{T}, \mathcal{R}\}$, where $\mathcal{T}$ is a set of event types, and $\mathcal{R}$ stands for the total event roles of all event types. Specifically, $\mathcal{T} = \{t_i\}_{i=1}^{n^T}$, and n^T is the number of event types, each event type t_i corresponding to event roles $\{r_1^{t_i}, r_2^{t_i}, ...\}$, and $\mathcal{R} = \{r_i\}_{i=1}^{n^R}$, and n^R is the number of total event roles.

(e) **Event Record** refers to an entry of a specific event type t_i containing arguments $\{a_1, a_2, ...\}$ corresponding to particular roles$\{r_1^{t_i}, r_2^{t_i}, ...\}$, such as *Event-1* record with type *EF*, *Role* and *Arguments* in Fig. 1;

For the DMEE task, given an input document comprised of n_s sentences $\mathcal{D} = \{s_i\}_{i=1}^{n_s}$, and each sentence s_i is a sequence of tokens $s_i = \{w_j^{s_i}\}_{j=1}^{n_w}$, where n_w is the number of tokens. The DMEE task aims to extract n_e structured event records $\mathcal{E} = \{e_i\}_{i=1}^{n_e}$.

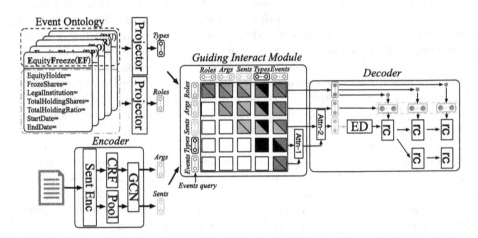

Fig. 2. The overall framework of EOG. Firstly, EOG encodes each sentences of document separately and recognize candidate arguments. Then a multi-layer GCN is used to get the document-level contextual representation. Meanwhile, EOG get representation of event ontology through two projectors. Next, a guiding interact module is designed to capture the dependency among different events and candidate arguments based on interaction between document context and event ontology representations. Finally, EOG generate the event records through event ontology-aware decoder.

4   Methodology

As shown in the Fig. 2, the proposed document-level Event Ontology Guiding multi-event extraction model (EOG) is composed of the following three modules: Encoder, Guiding Interact Module and Decoder. Specifically, (1) Encoder (Sect. 4.1) extracts candidate arguments from document and get contextualized embedding of candidate arguments and sentences. (2) Guiding Interact Module (GIM, Sect. 4.2) models the interaction between document context and event ontology, and enhance the embeddings of candidate arguments and document with the guidance of event ontology. (3) Decoder (Sect. 4.3) generates event records with the type-aware document embedding for detecting event type and the role-aware candidate arguments embedding for role classification.

4.1 Encoder

Given a document $\mathcal{D}$ contains n_s sentences, and each sentence contains n_w words. Encoder aims to get contextualized representation of candidate arguments and sentences. Encoder module is composed of four parts: (1) Sentence-level Encoder layer calculates the semantic representations based on transformer architecture. (2) Conditional Random Field (CRF) layer extracts the candidate arguments from each sentence. (3) Pooling layer gets representation of sentences and entity mentions. (4) Graph Convolution Network (GCN) layer enhances the representation of sentences and entity mentions by capturing the contextual information at document-level.

EOG adopts n_{se} layers Multi-head Self-Attention as the sentence-level encoder to obtain the sentence-level contextualized representation, each sentence s_i is embedded as follow:

$$\left(h_1^i, \ldots, h_{N_w}^i\right) = \text{Sent-Encoder}\left(w_1^i, \ldots, w_{N_w}^i\right) \tag{1}$$

where $h_j^i \in \mathbb{R}^d$ is the representation of jth token in i^{th} sentence. And the representation of ith sentence is obtained by max-pooling on all tokens representation in sentence s_i. Next, EOG employs a CRF layer to extract the entity mentions from each sentence through the BIO(Begin, Inside, Other) labels, and collects entity mentions extracted from all sentences of the input document. The task of extract entity mentions is optimized by the following loss:

$$\mathcal{L}_{er} = -\sum_{i=1}^{n_s} \log p\left(y_i^s \mid s_i\right) \tag{2}$$

where y_i^s is golden label sequence of s_i. An entity mention usually contains multiple tokens, EOG leverage max-pooling operation on multiple tokens representations of each entity mention to get the entity mention representation $S_{em} \in \mathbb{R}^{d \times n_{em}}$, n_{em} is the number of collected entity mentions of the document.

EOG introduces a document-level graph G to capture the dependency relationship between entity mentions at document-level. Specifically, there are two types nodes (sentences nodes and entity mentions nodes) and four types of edges (sentence-sentence edge, sentence-mention edge, Intra-Mention-Mention edge and Inter-Mention-Mention edge) in G. EOG applys Graph Convolution Network (GCN)[4] to model the contextual information at document-level. Specifically, the l-th layer graph convolution representation for node v in graph G is computed as:

$$h_v^{(l+1)} = \sigma \left(\sum_{u \in \mathcal{N}(v) \cup \{v\}} p_{uv} \left(W_{K(u,v)}^{(l)} h_u^{(l)} \right) \right) \tag{3}$$

where σ is the activation function(ReLU); $K(u, v)$ indicates the type of edge between node u and v, $W_{K(u,v)}^{(l)} \in \mathbb{R}^{d \times d}$ is the weight matrix; $p_{(uv)}$ is the normalization constant of the neighbor node u when updating node v; $\mathcal{N}(v)$ denotes the neighbors for node v.

And then the global information of one entity can be obtained by gathering its multiple entity mentions' feature through computing the average of its mention node representation. We regard these entity objects gathered from entity mentions as candidate arguments. In this way, we obtain the contextual representation of sentences $\mathcal{S} \in \mathbb{R}^{d \times n_s}$ and candidate arguments $\mathcal{A} \in \mathbb{R}^{d \times n_a}$, where n_a is the number of candidate arguments.

Besides, event ontology embedding layer contains two projectors are proposed to project each event type to a learnable embedding and each role to a learnable embedding respectively.

$$\mathbf{E}_{\text{types}} = \left(h_1^T, \ldots, h_{n^T}^T\right) = \text{Projector}_{Type}\left(t_1, \ldots, t_{n^T}\right) \qquad (4)$$

$$\mathbf{E}_{\text{roles}} = \left(h_1^R, \ldots, h_{n^R}^R\right) = \text{Projector}_{Role}\left(r_1, \ldots, r_{n^R}\right) \qquad (5)$$

Event types representation and event roles representation are denoted as $\mathbf{E}_{\text{types}} \in \mathbb{R}^{d \times n^T}$ and $\mathbf{E}_{\text{roles}} \in \mathbb{R}^{d \times n^R}$. These event ontology representations to represent the structure and semantic information of event ontology.

4.2   Guiding Interact Module

The encoder module only captures the contextual information of document, it is insufficient for model to distinguish the properties of different events. Thus, EOG apply a transformer-based[7] Guiding Interact Module (GIM) to introduce the structural and semantic information of event ontology as guidance to capture the dependency among different events and candidate arguments. In order to construct the relation among different records, EOG use n^Q learnable embeddings to denoted as event records $\mathbf{E}_{\text{events}} \in \mathbb{R}^{d \times n^Q}$. Then, the document-level representations (sentences representation $\mathcal{S}$ and candidate arguments representation $\mathcal{A}$), the event ontology representations (event types representation $\mathbf{E}_{\text{types}}$ and $\mathbf{E}_{\text{roles}}$), and the event records representations $\mathbf{E}_{\text{events}}$ are interacted with each other in GIM to facilitate the information exchange among these representations:

$$\left[\mathcal{A}^{pro}; \mathcal{S}^{pro}; \mathbf{E}_{\text{types}}^{pro}; \mathbf{E}_{\text{roles}}^{pro}; \mathbf{E}_{\text{events}}^{pro}\right] = \text{GIM}\left(\mathcal{A}; \mathcal{S}; \mathbf{E}_{\text{types}}; \mathbf{E}_{\text{roles}}; \mathbf{E}_{\text{events}}\right) \qquad (6)$$

With the guidance of event ontology, the candidate arguments $\mathcal{A}^{pro}$ representation aggregate more information related to the various roles of different event records and various dependency relationship between arguments and event roles after interaction. And the sentences representations $\mathcal{S}^{pro}$ aggregate more structural and semantic information related to different events included in the document. Meanwhile, the event type representations $\mathbf{E}_{\text{types}}^{pro}$ and roles representations $\mathbf{E}_{\text{roles}}^{pro}$ are enhanced by infusing contextual information of current document.

To further model the co-existing relationships between event types and events, EOG utilize contextualized event types representation $\mathbf{E}_{\text{types}}^{pro}$ as query and the enhanced event records representation $\mathbf{E}_{\text{events}}^{pro}$ as key and value to enhance the event types representation through the attention weights:

$$\mathbf{E}_{\text{types}}^{plus} = \text{Attn}_1\left(\mathbf{E}_{\text{types}}^{pro}, \mathbf{E}_{\text{events}}^{pro}, \mathbf{E}_{\text{events}}^{pro}\right)$$

$$= \text{softmax}\left(\frac{\mathbf{E}_{\text{types}}^{pro}(\mathbf{E}_{\text{events}}^{pro})^T}{\sqrt{d}}\right)\mathbf{E}_{\text{events}}^{pro} \tag{7}$$

Formally, after this module, we obtain the enhanced candidate argument representations $\mathcal{A}^{pro}$ with the guidance of event ontology, the contextualized event roles representations $\mathbf{E}_{\text{roles}}^{pro}$, and the further enhanced event types representations $\mathbf{E}_{\text{types}}^{plus}$. These aggregated representation serve the next module to generate event records.

4.3   Decoder

The decoder is responsible for generating the event records, which contains event detection and argument classification. Because of the multi-roles and disorderly appearing challenge for multi-event records, it's difficult to extract the accurate and meaningful information from the comprehensive representation for each event record. Therefore, EOG adopts event ontology representation as type-oriented and role-oriented guidance to generate each event record.

At the first stage of decoding, EOG leverage contextualized event types representations $\mathbf{E}_{\text{types}}^{plus}$ as query, and enhanced sentences representations $\mathcal{S}^{pro}$ to obtain the event type aware document representation $\mathbf{E}_{\text{doc}}$:

$$\mathbf{E}_{\text{doc}} = \text{Attn}_2\left(\mathbf{E}_{\text{types}}^{plus}, \mathcal{S}^{pro}, \mathcal{S}^{pro}\right)$$

$$= \text{softmax}\left(\frac{\mathbf{E}_{\text{types}}^{plus}(\mathcal{S}^{pro})^T}{\sqrt{d}}\right)\mathcal{S}^{pro} \tag{8}$$

And then formulate the event detection subtask as a multi-label classification. EOG devises a classifier, which is marked as ED in Fig. 2, to judge whether each event type is triggered based on the type-aware document semantic representation $\mathbf{E}_{\text{doc}}$. The event type detection task adopt the following loss:

$$\mathcal{L}_{td} = -\sum_{i=1}^{n^T}\log p\left(y_i^t \mid \mathbf{E}_{\text{doc}}\right) \tag{9}$$

If the i-th event type is triggered in the document, then $y_i^t = 1$, otherwise $y_i^t = 0$.

Next, in the argument classification stage, EOG classifies the roles of each triggered event type according to the roles' predefined order. For each triggered event type, we formulate the argument classification subtask as task of expanding a tree orderly as previous methods[8,12]. We first define a event role order, and view each event record as a linked list of arguments following this order, where each argument node is either an entity or a special empty node. Classification starts from a root node, and expands by predicting arguments in a sequential order. For each node, we will judge whether candidate arguments playing the current role (role classification), and it will expand several branches by linking the arguments assigned to the current role. The role classification is formulated as multi-label classification task. In this way, each path from the root node to the leaf node is identified as a unique event record.

EOG concat the candidate arguments embedding with the current role representation to obtain role-aware candidate argument representation $\mathcal{A}^{plus}$:

$$\mathcal{A}^{plus} = \mathbf{e}_i^R + \mathcal{A}^{pro} \tag{10}$$

And then EOG concatenate four representations for role classification: (1) role-aware candidate arguments representation $\mathcal{A}^{plus}$; (2) sentence representation $\mathcal{S}^{pro}$; (3) path memory [12], which is initialized by a memory tensor with the sentence representation at the beginning and updates when expanding the path by appending either the associated argument, to track the arguments already contained by the path; (4) global path memory [8], which encodes the argument representation sequence into to vector with an Long Short Term Memory networks (LSTM), to track the argument information of all paths.

EOG formulate the role classification as a multi-label classification. EOG devises a role classifier for each role, which is marked as rc in Fig. 2, to judge whether candidate arguments playing the current role based on the concatenated representation. Therefore, we drive the argument classification loss $\mathcal{L}_{ac}$:

$$\mathcal{L}_{ac} = -\sum_{i=1}^{n_r} \sum_{j=1}^{n_a} \log p \left(y_{ij}^r \mid a_{ij}^{plus} \right) \tag{11}$$

where n_r is the number of all role classification nodes in event records trees; $a_{ij}^{plus} \in \mathcal{A}^{plus}$ denotes the j-th candidate argument representation for i-th role classification node. For i-th role classification node, if the j-th candidate argument plays the current role, then $y_{ij}^r = 1$, otherwise $y_{ij}^r = 0$.

During training, we sum the losses coming from three tasks together as the final loss: $\mathcal{L}_{all} = \lambda_1 \mathcal{L}_{er} + \lambda_2 \mathcal{L}_{td} + \lambda_3 \mathcal{L}_{ac}$ where $\lambda_1, \lambda_2, \lambda_3$ are hyper-parameters.

5   Experiments

5.1   Experimental Settings

Dataset. We evaluate our model on a Chinese financial DEE dataset proposed by [12]. It contains five event types: Equity Freeze (EF), Equity Repurchase (ER), Equity Underweight (EU), Equity Overweight (EO) and Equity Pledge (EP), with 35 different kinds of argument roles in total. This dataset contains 32,040 documents in total, but only 29% documents of it express multiple events. In order to evaluate the effectiveness of the model for multi-event extraction, we split the multi-event version dataset (i.e., $Train_m$, Dev_m, $Test_m$) from the original version dataset (i.e., $Train_o$, Dev_o, $Test_o$) according to the number of events contained in a document. The proposed EOG model is trained on $Train_m$, evaluated on $Test_m$ and $Test_o$. The Dev_m and Dev_o are used to select the parameters for the proposed EOG model respectively.

Metrics. We adopt the standard evaluation metrics, i.e., Precision (P), Recall (R), and F1 score (F1), as originally used in Doc2EDAG [12]. The following results are reported with micro-averaged role-level scores as the final event-level metric.

Implementation Details. The event ontology contains 5 event types and 35 roles in total. The dimensions of event ontology embedding and the representation of candidate arguments and sentences are 768. The max sentences length is 128. The max sentences number in one document is 64. The number of GCN layers is 3. The number of Transformer-blocks in the Global Interact Module is 2. The number of learnable embeddings for generated event records is 4. During training, we employ Adam [3] optimizer with 1e-4 learning rate for 100 epochs. The training batch size is 64 and the steps of gradient accumulation is 16. We se t $\lambda_1 = 0.05$, $\lambda_2 = \lambda_3 = 1$ for the loss function. We run all models on the 11G GeForce GTX 1080 Ti GPU.

Table 1. Overall event-level Precision (P.), Recall (R.) and F1 on the multi-event version test set (Test_m).

Models	EF			ER			EU			EO			EP			Overall		
	P	R	F1	P	R	F1	P	R	F1	P	R	F1	P	R	F1	P	R	F1
DCFEE-M	42.9	43.9	43.4	38.8	54.4	45.3	39.1	38.3	38.7	44.7	42.6	43.6	51.0	53.5	52.2	48.6	51.3	49.9
Doc2EDAG	72.6	49.1	58.6	72.8	60.7	66.2	72.8	56.1	63.4	73.9	60.8	66.7	78.9	66.5	72.1	77.5	64.0	70.1
GIT	**76.7**	48.5	59.4	73.9	**68.1**	70.9	72.5	**58.7**	**64.9**	72.2	**66.0**	69.0	73.4	**70.5**	71.9	73.4	**67.9**	70.6
Ours EOG	67.3	**61.8**	**64.4**	**76.7**	67.7	**71.9**	**75.7**	56.7	64.8	**77.2**	63.2	**69.5**	**79.6**	67.7	**73.1**	**78.1**	66.4	**71.8**

Table 2. F1 scores of each event type on the original dataset (Test_o) and the average F1 scores (Avg.) on respective single-event split and multi-event split.

Models	EF		ER		EU		EO		EP		Avg.		
	S.	M.	S.	M.	S.	M.	S.	M.	S.	M.	S.	M.	S.&M.
DCFEE-O	49.6	41.7	70.0	50.8	51.3	38.8	45.8	46.8	61.2	53.1	55.6	46.2	52.3
DCFEE-M	42.6	41.4	57.9	44.2	47.3	41.1	41.5	41.6	56.7	52.3	49.2	44.1	47.6
GreedyDec	70.4	37.9	74.1	49.0	57.6	31.3	62.0	29.6	77.0	36.9	68.2	36.9	55.4
Dco2EDAG	67.9	57.5	74.7	66.9	68.5	61.2	**69.5**	66.4	**79.2**	71.7	72.0	64.8	68.9
GIT	72.5	59.7	71.1	67.1	**70.4**	61.6	66.7	67.9	75.3	71.0	71.6	65.5	69.0
Ours EOG	**73.1**	60.8	**76.2**	**68.6**	70.1	**65.7**	68.2	**69.1**	77.6	**73.0**	**73.1**	**67.4**	**70.7**

5.2 Baselines

We compare the proposed EOG model with the following baseline methods: (1) **DCFEE** [9] processes a sentence-level extraction model based on a sequence tagging model and expanded the arguments from the surrounding sentences as the result of document-level extraction. The model has two variants which are **DCFEE-O** that only produces one event record and **DCFEE-M** that can produce multiple event records from a document. (2) **Doc2EDAG** [12] uses transformer encoder to obtain sentence and entity embeddings and regards multiple event records generation as path expanding based entity. (3) **GreedyDec** [12] is a simple varient of Doc2EDAG, which generate one event record greedily. (4) **GIT** [8] proposes a heterogeneous graph to get the interactions between sentences and entity mentions, and utilizes a tracker-based RNN to memory the information of multiple events for multiple event records generation.

5.3   Main Results

Overall Performance. In multi-event version split dataset (i.e., $Train_m$, Dev_m and $Test_m$), as shown in Table 1, the proposed EOG achieves significant improvements overall baselines, thanks to the guidance of event ontology. Specifically, EOG improves 1.2 micro F1 compared with the previous state-of-the-art, GIT, especially EOG gains 5.0 improvement in Equity Freeze (EF) event type. Compared to other event types, the number of documents that contain EF events is the least, which leads to the low performance for general models. However, the improved performance indicates that the correlation between different event types is also helpful for current event extraction. With the learnable embedding of event ontology, EOG could improve the extraction performance of EP event records with the knowledge learned from other event types of documents. Furthermore, the vast improvement of EF events extraction also proves the effectiveness of event ontology guidance in event extraction.

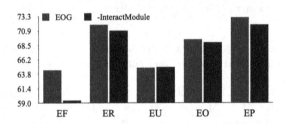

Fig. 3. F1 score of ablation studies on EOG for each event type.

Single-event vs. Multi-event. Multi-Event documents are more complex, as they owns longer text and more entities, than single-event documents. We assume that the model trained on a Multi-Event dataset can also work out the Single-Event extraction. To evaluate the effectiveness of our model in the actual scenario with a mixture of documents comprising Single-Event and Multi-Event, We train EOG model on multi-event train dataset ($Train_m$ and evaluate on original dataset (Dev_o/$Test_o$). Table 2 shows the F1 score on single-event and multi-event sets for each event type and the averaged (Avg.) under the experiment setting ($Train_m$/Dev_o/$Test_o$). We can observe that EOG surpasses the SOTA baseline by 1.1 and 1.9 on single-record and multi-record sets, respectively. The above result demonstrates that event ontology guidance is effective in multi-event extraction and single-event scenario.

5.4 Ablation Studies

To verify the essential designs of EOG, we conduct ablation tests by removing the interact module. The results are shown in Fig. 3, we can observe that: 1)the micro F1 decreases 1.5 on average demonstrates the effectiveness of event ontology guidance for event extraction; 2)significant drop on Equity Freeze(EF) type has been discussed in 5.3. 3)event ontology guidance contributes less on Equity Repurchase(ER) type mainly because ER documents are much longer than other documents, the encoder could not work effectively for arguments scattering.

6 Conclusion

We propose a multi-event extraction model via event ontology guiding (EOG) to tackle multi-roles and disorderly appearing challenges in Document-level Multi-Event Extraction (DMEE). EOG introduces event ontology in the form of learnable embedding to provide structural and semantic information of event. And EOG designs a Guiding Interact Module to model and enhance features of events through the cross-event and cross-roles interaction under the guidance of the event ontology. Then, EOG employs a decoder to generate the event records with the event ontology aware event features. Experimental results show that EOG can significantly outperform previous methods in the multi-event scenario. Further analysis verifies the effectiveness of event ontology guidance for multi-event extraction.

Acknowledgement. We thank all anonymous reviewers for their constructive comments and we have made some modifications. This work is supported by the National Natural Science Foundation of China (No. U21B2009).

References

1. Du, X., Cardie, C.: Document-level event role filler extraction using multi-granularity contextualized encoding. In: Proceedings of the ACL, pp. 8010–8020 (2020)
2. Huang, K.H., Peng, N.: Document-level event extraction with efficient end-to-end learning of cross-event dependencies. In: Proceedings of the Third Workshop on Narrative Understanding, pp. 36–47 (2021)
3. Kingma, D.P., Ba, J.: Adam: a method for stochastic optimization. In: Bengio, Y., LeCun, Y. (eds.) 3rd International Conference on Learning Representations, ICLR 2015, San Diego, 7–9 May 2015, Conference Track Proceedings (2015)
4. Kipf, T., Welling, M.: Semi-supervised classification with graph convolutional networks. arXiv preprint arXiv:1609.02907 (2017)
5. Li, S., Ji, H., Han, J.: Document-level event argument extraction by conditional generation. In: Proceedings of the NAACL, pp. 894–908 (2021)
6. Lou, D., Liao, Z., Deng, S., Zhang, N., Chen, H.: MLBiNet: a cross-sentence collective event detection network. In: Proceedings of the ACL, pp. 4829–4839 (2021)
7. Vaswani, A., et al.: Attention is all you need. arXiv preprint arXiv:1706.03762 (2017)

8. Xu, R., Liu, T., Li, L., Chang, B.: Document-level event extraction via heterogeneous graph-based interaction model with a tracker. In: Proceedings of the ACL, pp. 3533–3546 (2021)
9. Yang, H., Chen, Y., Liu, K., Xiao, Y., Zhao, J.: DCFEE: a document-level Chinese financial event extraction system based on automatically labeled training data. In: Proceedings of ACL 2018, System Demonstrations, pp. 50–55 (2018)
10. Yang, H., Sui, D., Chen, Y., Liu, K., Zhao, J., Wang, T.: Document-level event extraction via parallel prediction networks. In: Proceedings of the ACL, pp. 6298–6308 (2021)
11. Zhang, Z., Kong, X., Liu, Z., Ma, X., Hovy, E.: A two-step approach for implicit event argument detection. In: Proceedings of the ACL, pp. 7479–7485 (2020)
12. Zheng, S., Cao, W., Xu, W., Bian, J.: Doc2EDAG: an end-to-end document-level framework for Chinese financial event extraction. In: Proceedings of the EMNLP-IJCNLP, pp. 337–346 (2019)

Integrating Global Features into Neural Collaborative Filtering

Langzhou He[1], Songxin Wang[2], Jiaxin Wang[3], Chao Gao[4(✉)], and Li Tao[1(✉)]

[1] College of Computer and Information Science, Southwest University,
Chongqing 400715, China
tli@swu.edu.cn
[2] School of Information Management and Engineering,
Shanghai University of Finance and Economics, Shanghai 200433, China
sxwang@mail.shufe.edu.cn
[3] State Grid Information & Telecommunication Group Co., Ltd., Beijing, China
wangjiaxin1@sgitg.sgcc.com.cn
[4] School of Artificial Intelligence, Optics and Electronics (iOPEN),
Northwestern Polytechnical University, Xi'an 710072, China
cgao@nwpu.edu.cn

Abstract. Recently, deep learning has been widely applied in the field of recommender systems and achieved great success, among which the most representative one is the Collaborative Filtering based Deep Neural Network. However, the input of such a model is usually a very sparse one-hot coding vector of users and items. This makes it difficult for the model to effectively capture the global features interaction between users and items. What is more, it also increases the training difficulty, making the model easily fall into a local optimum. Therefore, this paper proposes a two-stage Integrating Global Features into Neural Collaborative Filtering (GFNCF) model. To begin with, the AutoEncoder model with sparse constraint parameters is used to accurately extract the global features of users and items. Following that, the global features extracted in the previous step are integrated into the neural collaborative filtering framework as auxiliary information. It alleviates the sparse input problem and integrates more auxiliary features to improve the learning process of the model. Extensive experiments on several publicly available datasets demonstrate the effectiveness of the proposed GFNCF model.

Keywords: Deep learning · Recommender system · Collaborative filtering · AutoEncoder · Feature extraction

1 Introduction

Living in an "information society", recommender systems greatly solve the problem of information overload [5]. The task of the personalized recommender systems is to recommend users potential interest items according to their preferences, and the system has been widely applied in many fields such as news

© The Author(s), under exclusive license to Springer Nature Switzerland AG 2022
G. Memmi et al. (Eds.): KSEM 2022, LNAI 13369, pp. 325–336, 2022.
https://doi.org/10.1007/978-3-031-10986-7_26

[3,6] and music [2,16]. Rating prediction is a main task in the personalized recommender systems. The key to the prediction is to model the characteristics of users and items according to the rating interaction between them, and realize the rating prediction of items (such as 1–5 stars) [19]. For recommender services, predicting users' preference for pushed items through rating predictions can improve users satisfaction effectively, and provide support for corporate decision-making and bring huge economic benefits to the company.

In recent years, Collaborative Filtering, acts as one of the effective means of rating prediction, has made big progress. Researchers applied all kinds of deep learning technology to the Collaborative Filtering and made it successfully [11]. Deep Neural Network has been widely used to extract High-level features in user-item interactive information [7,18]. The quality of these high-level interactive features decides the performance of the model directly most of the time. Although DNN has massive advantages in high-level features extraction and parameters learning, the input feature vector of this type of model is often extremely sparse due to the sparseness of the data in the recommender systems. In this case, the optimization result of the model is easy to fall into a local optimum, which affects the performance of the model.

Global features, known as the overall properties of the user image, are always difficult to be captured effectively since most Collaborative Filtering models based neural network ofter take the one-hot representation of users and items as input for feature learning. Studies have shown some global features of users and items can effectively improve the prediction accuracy of the model [13]. Therefore, some recent methods use neighborhood information or global information of users and items to replace one-hot representation to input into the neural network model for feature extraction [1,4,17]. Although this type of model uses neighborhood information or its own global information to enhance the interaction capabilities of the model to a certain extent, it also weakens the ability of user-project single interaction modeling.

Based on the considerations above, we find that alleviating the sparse input feature problem and making full use of user item interaction information can further improve the performance of the CF method. Therefore, this paper incorporates them into the proposed Integrating Global Features into Neural Collaborative Filtering (GFNCF) model. First, for the sparse input feature problem, we use an improved feature extraction method to extract the dense global feature vector of users and items accurately, and then we use the extracted global feature vector as an additional input to fuse neural collaborative filtering [8] in the framework, thus alleviating the training difficulty learning from sparse features of the model. Moreover, the different features in the fused model are crossed and combined through joint training, thereby effectively improving the accuracy of the final rating prediction. The main contributions of our work are as follows :

– This paper introduces the sparsity constraint parameters into the AutoEncoder-based collaborative filtering model to make the model more adaptable to the sparsity characteristics of the data in the recommender systems, and to accurately extract the global features of users and items.

- This paper integrates the global characteristics of users and items as auxiliary information in the neural collaborative filtering framework, which effectively expands the framework and further improves the performance of the method.
- This paper conducts extensive experiments on five real-world data sets to prove the effectiveness of the proposed method.

2   Integrated Global Features Neural Collaborative Filtering

The main process of our proposed method is shown in Fig. 1. It consists of two parts, namely the extraction of global features and the integration of global features. The extraction of global features part inputs the rating matrix of users and items into the AutoEncoder to extract the global features of each entity (user or item). These global features will be used for the global feature interaction modeling. The integration of global features part integrates extracted global features into the neural collaborative filtering model which makes the model capture the interaction between users and items more accurately.

In general, our proposed GFNCF model is a model-based method, which assumes that the rating data is generated by the model. To estimate the parameters in the model, existing methods generally adopt the method of optimizing the loss function in machine learning. In this paper, we use point-wise loss as the optimization loss function, that is, the parameters in the GFNCF model are estimated by minimizing the square loss between predicted value and true value.

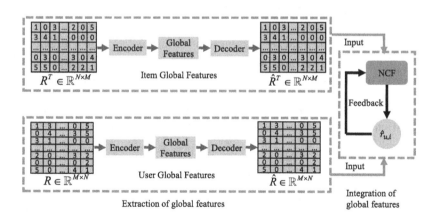

Fig. 1. The proposed method is divided into two parts.

2.1   Extraction of Global Features

Let M and N respectively represent the total number of users and items in the recommender systems, then the users set and items set can be expressed as $U = \{U_1, U_2, ..., U_M\}$ and $V = \{V_1, V_2, ..., V_N\}$. Construct a user-item rating matrix $R \in R^{M \times N}$ based on the explicit ratings feedback of users on items

$$R_{u,i} = \begin{cases} r_{u,i}, & if \ user \ u \ has \ rated \ item \ i \\ 0, & otherwise \end{cases} \tag{1}$$

where $r_{u,i}$ represents the rating of user u on item i, $u \in \{1, 2, ..., M\}$ and $i \in \{1, 2, ..., N\}$. $R_{u,i}$ equals to 0 does not mean that user u has rated item i as 0. It may because user u has not rated item i.

AutoEncoder is an unsupervised learning algorithm, mainly used for data dimensionality reduction or feature extraction [10]. In order to extract the global features of the item, the rating information of each item i is expressed as:

$$r^{(i)} = (R_{1,i}, R_{2,i}, ..., R_{M,i}) \tag{2}$$

Taking the use of a deep autoencoder to extract the global features of item i as an example, the feature extraction process of this model can be defined as:

$$g_f = g_l \left(W_l^T z_{l-1} + b_l \right) \tag{3}$$

where $g_l(\cdot)$, W_l, b_l represent the activation function, parameter matrix, and bias vector of the l-th neural network, respectively, g_f represents the extracted global features of item i.

The process of reconstructing rating information through the global features of item i can be defined as:

$$\hat{r}^{(i)} = g_{2l-1} \left(W_{2l-1}^T z_{2l-2} + b_{2l-1} \right) \tag{4}$$

where $\hat{r}^{(i)}$ represents the rating information reconstructed from the global features of item i. Then we input the items rating vector $\{r^{(i)}\}_{i=1}^N$ set into deep autoencoder model to obtain the reconstructed rating vector set. In order to make the reconstructed rating vector as close as possible to the original rating vector in observed rating part, the following loss function is used as the optimization target of the autoencoder model [7]:

$$\min_{\theta} \sum_{i=1}^N \left\| r^{(i)} - h(r^{(i)}; \theta) \right\|_O^2 + \lambda \|\theta\|_F^2 \tag{5}$$

where $h(r^{(i)}; \theta)$ represents the rating information of item i reconstructed by the autoencoder, θ represents the parameters of the deep autoencoder model, and the λ parameter is used to control the complexity of the model and prevent over-fitting together. $\| \cdot \|_O^2$ means that only the errors of the ratings observed in the training set are considered.

It is widely acknowledged that the overall item rating quantity information in the recommender system presents a long tail distribution [15]. For items with sparse ratings, the integration of global features will provide effective additional features for the model to fit these items and improve the learning process of the model. Therefore, we introduce a sparsity constraint parameter into the AutoEncoder model for extracting global features, which can help the model fit sparse items as much as possible, and provide effective auxiliary features for sparsely rated items. We introduce the sparsity constraint parameter to obtain the following loss function:

$$Loss = \sum_{i=1}^{N} \frac{\alpha}{\sum_{j=1}^{M} I\left(r_j^{(i)} \neq 0\right)} ||r^{(i)} - \hat{r}^{(i)}||_o^2 + \lambda||\theta||_F^2 \qquad (6)$$

where $I(X)$ is the indicator function. If x is true, then $I(x)$ is 1, otherwise $I(x)$ is 0. It can be noticed that when the rating information of an item is sparse, the model prediction is not accurate. The greater the error, the greater the penalty for the model. α is a constraint factor, and the value is generally greater than 1. By adjusting the value of α, we can control the degree to which the model tends to fit sparse data well. λ is a regularisation parameter used to control model complexity and prevent overfitting of the model.

2.2 Integration of Global Features

After extracting the global features of users and items, the global features are transformed by Multi-Layer Perceptron (MLP) to obtain the final features that are concatenated into the neural collaborative filtering model for joint training. The additional input information not only alleviates the problem of sparse input features but also increases the ability of the neural collaborative filtering model to capture global feature interactions. The overall GFNCF model is shown in Fig. 2, which shows deep matrix decomposition model can be used to learn a more accurate representation for both user and item using a deep neural network. Therefore, similar to the network architecture in DeepCF, this paper uses a deep matrix decomposition architecture for user and item representation learning in GFNCF.

Figure 2 plots the three parts of the overall GFNCF model, namely the deep matrix decomposition representation learning part, the MLP matching function learning part, and the global feature integration part.

Representation Learning. In order to model a single user-item interaction feature, we input users and items into deep matrix factorization through one-hot encoding for representation learning. For the sake of generality, assume that the input user is u and the item is i, which are encoded as x_u and x_i by one-hot later. Let the latent vector of user u be denoted as p_u, and the latent vector of item i as q_i. Since the neural network is used in the deep matrix factorization to replace the linear embedding operation in the traditional matrix factorization, the low-dimensional representation learning process of the user u is:

$$p_u = a_K = g\left(W_K^T a_{K-1} + b_K\right) \qquad (7)$$

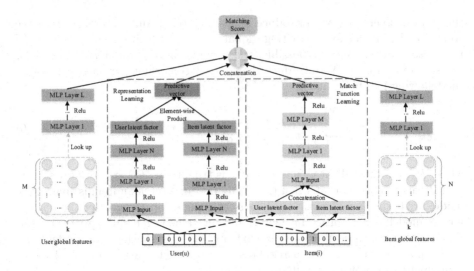

Fig. 2. The architecture of our proposed model.

where W_l, b_l and a_l represent the weight matrix, bias vector and output value of the l-th layer perceptron, respectively. $g(\cdot)$ is the activation function, this paper uses the *relu* activation function.

In the same way, the low-dimensional representation learning process of item i is:

$$q_i = a_K = g\left(W_K^T a_{K-1} + b_K\right) \tag{8}$$

We use the element-wise product of the low-dimensional representation vectors of users and items to calculate the feature vectors representing the learning part:

$$\phi_{MF} = p_u \odot q_i \tag{9}$$

where $\odot$ represents element-wise product.

Matching Function Learning. CF methods based on matching function learning usually use a linear embedding layer to learn low-dimensional latent representations of users and items, and then use dense low-dimensional latent representations to learn matching functions between users and items. We utilize MLP to learn the matching function in the user-item feature interaction. We assume P and Q respectively represent linear embedding layer parameter matrices that map x_u and x_i to low-dimensional dense representations. Therefore, the one-hot encoding of users and items in the embedding layer is converted into low-dimensional dense representation. The part can be described as:

$$p_u = P^T x_u \tag{10}$$

$$q_i = Q^T x_i \tag{11}$$

In order to fully cross the features and enhance the model's ability to model user-item interaction characteristics, in this paper, the obtained low-dimensional representation vectors of users and items are connected together and then sent to MLP for matching function learning.

$$\phi_{MLP} = a_M = g\left(W_H^T a_{H-1} + b_H\right) \tag{12}$$

Global Features Learning. Let $p_{g_f}^u$ and $q_{g_f}^i$ respectively represent the global feature vector of user u and item i. In order to make the global features have better expressive ability in the GFNCF model, the GFNCF model sends the extracted global features into the MLP for feature transformation to transform them into a global feature representation that is more suitable for the model. The user's global feature embedding part of the model is as follows:

$$p_u^{GF} = a_E = g\left(W_L^T a_{L-1} + b_L\right) \tag{13}$$

The embedded part of the project's global features is as follows:

$$q_i^{GF} = a_L = g\left(W_L^T a_{L-1} + b_L\right) \tag{14}$$

Finally, the global characteristics of users and items are connected into a vector representation:

$$\phi_{GF} = \begin{bmatrix} p_u^{GF} \\ q_i^{GF} \end{bmatrix} \tag{15}$$

Fusion of Feature Vectors. The above three feature vectors express different forms of feature representation. In order to obtain a more accurate joint representation of user items, we need a strategy to fuse them so that they can enhance as well as interacting with each other, thereby enhancing the expressive ability of the model. The most common fusion strategy is to connect the obtained multiple feature vector representations to obtain a joint representation, and then input them into a fully connected layer for joint training. The fully connected layer can assign different weights to each feature contained in the joint representation. This adaptive combination of weight features makes the ultimate calculated matching scores of users and items more accurate, so the final output of the model in this paper is:

$$\hat{r}_{u,i} = W_{\text{out}}^T \begin{bmatrix} \phi_{MF} \\ \phi_{MLP} \\ \phi_{GF} \end{bmatrix} + b \tag{16}$$

where W_{out} represents the weight parameter of the output layer of the model.

During the training process of the model, this paper uses the mean square error of the predicted rating $\hat{r}_{u,i}$ and the true rating $r_{u,i}$ as the loss function to calculate the back propagation as well as optimizing the network parameters.

3   Experiments

3.1   Experimental Setup

Datasets. We evaluate our proposed models on five public datasets, i.e., movie-Lens (ml-la, ml-1m, ml-10m), filmtrust and ciaodvd in Table 1. To verify the effectiveness of the proposed model, this paper selects five publicly available datasets in the real world.

Table 1. The statistics of datasets. #User represents the number of users, #Items represents the number of items, #Ratings represents the number of ratings, #Sparsity represents the sparsity of datasets.

Dataset	#Users	#Items	#Ratings	#Sparsity
ml-la	610	9724	100836	98.30%
ml-1m	6040	3706	1000209	95.53%
ml-10m	69878	10677	10000054	99.69%
ciaodvd	17615	16121	72665	99.97%
filmtrust	1508	2071	35497	98.86%

The statistical indicators of each dataset are given in Table 1. It is easy to see from the statistical indicators that there are differences in the scale of each dataset, therefore we can verify the universality of the model. In this paper, each dataset is divided randomly at a ratio of 4:1 into training set and test set for the following experiments.

Evaluation Metrics and Baselines. We compared the performance of our proposed GFNCF model with following six algorithms, namely, UserCF [9], PMF [14], DeepCF [8], NeuMF [4], DMF [18], BPAM [17].

Table 2. Comparison results on the public datasets evaluated by RMSE and MAE, where the best result is in bold.

Dataset	Measure	UserCF	PMF	DeepCF	NeuMF	DMF	BPAM	GFNCF
ml-la	RMSE	1.1072	0.9976	0.8727	0.8511	0.9004	0.8942	**0.8409**
	MAE	0.8329	0.7746	0.6791	0.6602	0.6974	0.6891	**0.6527**
ml-1m	RMSE	1.1777	0.9319	0.8837	0.8743	0.8816	0.9583	**0.8647**
	MAE	0.8687	0.7345	0.6885	0.6864	0.6875	0.7479	**0.6693**
ml-10m	RMSE	1.3105	0.9162	NA	0.8577	0.8684	0.9237	**0.8327**
	MAE	0.9218	0.7207	NA	0.6576	0.6817	0.7259	**0.6431**
ciaodvd	RMSE	1.3084	1.1947	1.0225	0.9507	1.0489	1.0241	**0.9307**
	MAE	0.9158	0.8663	0.8374	0.7393	0.8104	0.7932	**0.7255**
filmtrust	RMSE	1.0907	0.9724	0.8371	0.8002	0.87009	0.8212	**0.7845**
	MAE	0.8164	0.7453	0.6487	0.6284	0.6887	0.6457	**0.6074**

Parameter Settings. For the sake of fairness, we use the parameter settings from the original model in the neural collaborative filtering part of the GFNCF model whenever possible to assess the effectiveness of the proposed method. Therefore, this paper utilizes Gaussian distribution (mean value is 0, standard deviation is 0.01) to randomly initialize the model parameters, and uses mini-batch gradient descent and Adam [12] algorithm to optimize the model. Set the learning rate to 0.001 and the batch size to 1024 (set the batch size to 4096 on the ml-10m large dataset to speed up training). In addition, this paper sets the feature dimension size of users and items extracted from the neural collaborative filtering model to 32. Silimar to latent factor model, we defaults that the global features dimension of users and items is same. We set up different number of layers in neural networks to transform global features and 2–3 layers in the neural network can achieve great results.

3.2   Overall Comparison

This article uses root mean square error (RMSE) and mean absolute error (MAE) to evaluate the performance of the prediction results. The smaller the values of RMSE and MAE are, the better the performance is. The RMSE and MAE are defined as follows:

$$RMSE = \sqrt{\frac{7}{N} \sum_{(u,i)\in R^+} \left(r_{u,i} - r_{u,i}\right)^2}$$

$$MAE = \frac{1}{N} \sum_{(u,i)\in R^+} \left|r_{u,i} - r_{u,i}\right|$$

(17)

First, we can find that our proposed GFNCF method achieved an average improvement of 1.8% compared with the sub-optimal method (NeuMF). Note that NeuMF is a specific implementation under the neural collaborative filtering. These experimental results proved that integrates global features to neural collaborative filtering can effectively improve the performance of the model. Compared with DMF, the GFNCF model achieved a huge average improvement of 7.1% on all datasets. The main reason is that the GFNCF model adds auxiliary information of global features and matching function learning part to enhance the ability of model to capture the non-linear features of user-item interaction. In addition, compared with the DeepCF method, the GFNCF method models the user-item interaction information by combining the global features interactions with user-item interactions, while DeepCF only utilizes global information for modeling, ignoring the single interaction relationship between users and items. As a result, GFNCF achieved an average improvement of 3.7% compared with DeepCF. What's more, the results on MovieLens datasets (ml-1a, ml-1m and ml-10m) in Table 2 illustrates that as the data size and data sparsity increase, the improvement effect achieved by the GFNCF method gradually increases from 1.2% to about 3%. It shows that taking the global features as extra input alleviates the problem of sparsity input and effectively improve the performance of the model. In general, GFNCF alleviates the sparse input feature problem after fusing the global features and provides more feature information for model training, which improves the model performance to a certain extent.

3.3　Detailed Model Analysis

Model Ablation Analysis. In the design of GFNCF, we integrate the global features of users and items learned from the rating matrix into the existing framework to train the network jointly. In order to verify the effectiveness of users and items global features embedded in the model, we compared the model with the following three model variants: GFNCF-UF (without users global features in GFNCF), GFNCF-IF (without items global features GFNCF), NCF (GFNCF without users and items global features). As shown in Table 3, we have the following observation results: (1) The addition of items global features and users global features in the five datasets has improved the effect of the algorithm to a certain extent. (2) As the dataset changes, the optimizing degree on the model slightly differentiates. (3) When the global features of users and items are added at the same time, we have the best performance of the model. The reason for above results is that the more the global features of the user and the item are crossed and combined in the neural network, the better the learning process of the model, which leads to the best performance of the proposed method.

Table 3. The comparison results of different variants of GFNCF model evaluated by RMSE and MAE, and the best results are shown in bold.

Dataset	Measure	NCF	GFNCF-UF	GFNCF-IF	GFNCF
ml-la	RMSE	0.8521	0.8491	0.8445	**0.8409**
	MAE	0.6602	0.6506	0.6511	**0.6527**
ml-1m	RMSE	0.8743	0.8671	0.8705	**0.8647**
	MAE	0.6864	0.6729	0.6788	**0.6693**
ml-10m	RMSE	0.8577	0.8512	0.8453	**0.8327**
	MAE	0.6576	0.6537	0.6489	**0.6431**
ciaodvd	RMSE	0.9517	0.9438	0.9487	**0.9307**
	MAE	0.7403	0.7332	0.7368	**0.7255**
filmtrust	RMSE	0.8002	0.7973	0.7904	**0.7845**
	MAE	0.6284	0.6184	0.6105	**0.6074**

Influence of Sparsity Constraint Parameters. We utilize the loss function shown in Eq. 6 to extract the global features of users and items. The most important parameter in this loss function is sparsity constraint parameters. By setting different values of α, the degree to which the model tends to fit sparse data can be controlled. We integrate the global features extracted from different values of α into the model for comparative experiments. As shown in Fig. 3, except for the filmtrust dataset, all other datasets have the best RMSE performance in the range of user α and item α between 4–6. On filmtrust dataset, the best performance can be obtained when user α and item α are within the range of 2–4. Comparing the experimental results on the ml-1m and ml-10m datasets, it can be seen that when the sparsity and the size of the dataset increases, the proper enhancement of the sparsity constraint parameters of the AutoEncoder can improve the model performance.

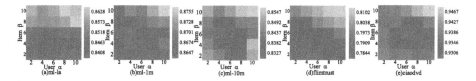

Fig. 3. RMSE index of the model after integrating global features extracted from different α

4 Conclusion

This paper proposed an integrated global features neural collaborative filtering model which captured both user-item and user-item global feature interaction information and alleviated the sparseness problem of inputting feature vectors, avoiding the model training fall into a local optimum. Meanwhile, the paper utilized a kind of auxiliary information to develop another model with high performance. It is worth mentioning that the method used to extract auxiliary information should be as simple and effective as possible, so as to avoid adding too much additional load to the integrated model. Experimental results showed that the method in this paper has achieved certain advantages over traditional methods on datasets of different scales. Moreover, with the increase of data sparsity and data size, the advantages of this method become more apparent. In the future, we will use more auxiliary information, such as user portraits, comments, images and social information, as well as adding more data sources to explore better feature extraction methods for further research.

Acknowledgement. This work was supported by the National Key R&D Program of China (No. 2019YFB2102300), National Natural Science Foundation of China (No. 61976181, 11931015), Fundamental Research Funds for the Central Universities (No. D5000210738).

References

1. Bai, T., Wen, J.R., Zhang, J., Zhao, W.X.: A neural collaborative filtering model with interaction-based neighborhood. In: Proceedings of the 2017 ACM on Conference on Information and Knowledge Management, pp. 1979–1982 (2017)

2. Chen, H.C., Chen, A.L.: A music recommendation system based on music data grouping and user interests. In: Proceedings of the 10th International Conference on Information and Knowledge Management, pp. 231–238 (2001)
3. Chen, X., Li, S., Li, H., Jiang, S., Qi, Y., Song, L.: Generative adversarial user model for reinforcement learning based recommendation system. In: International Conference on Machine Learning, pp. 1052–1061 (2019)
4. Deng, Z.H., Huang, L., Wang, C.D., Lai, J.H., Philip, S.Y.: Deepcf: a unified framework of representation learning and matching function learning in recommender system. In: Proceedings of the AAAI Conference on Artificial Intelligence, pp. 61–68, no. 01 (2019)
5. Edmunds, A., Morris, A.: The problem of information overload in business organisations: a review of the literature. Int. J. Inf. Manag. **20**(1), 17–28 (2000)
6. Gao, C., Liu, J.: Network-based modeling for characterizing human collective behaviors during extreme events. IEEE Trans. Syst. Man Cybern. Syst. **47**(1), 171–183 (2016)
7. Gupta, U., et al.: The architectural implications of facebook's DNN-based personalized recommendation. In: IEEE International Symposium on High Performance Computer Architecture (HPCA), pp. 488–501 (2020)
8. He, X., Liao, L., Zhang, H., Nie, L., Hu, X., Chua, T.S.: Neural collaborative filtering. In: Proceedings of the 26th International Conference on World Wide Web, pp. 173–182 (2017)
9. Herlocker, J.L., Konstan, J.A., Borchers, A., Riedl, J.: An algorithmic framework for performing collaborative filtering. In: Proceedings of the 22nd Annual International ACM SIGIR Conference on Research and Development in Information Retrieval, pp. 230–237 (1999)
10. Hinton, G.E., Salakhutdinov, R.R.: Reducing the dimensionality of data with neural networks. Science **313**(5786), 504–507 (2006)
11. Huang, L., Jiang, B.L.S., et al.: Survey on deep learning based recommender systems. Chin. J. Comp. **41**(7), 1619–1647 (2018)
12. Kingma, D.P., Ba, J.: Adam: a method for stochastic optimization. arXiv preprint arXiv:1412.6980 (2014)
13. Koren, Y., Bell, R., Volinsky, C.: Matrix factorization techniques for recommender systems. Computer **42**(8), 30–37 (2009)
14. Mnih, A., Salakhutdinov, R.R.: Probabilistic matrix factorization. In: Advances in Neural Information Processing Systems, pp. 1257–1264 (2008)
15. Park, Y.J., Tuzhilin, A.: The long tail of recommender systems and how to leverage it. In: Proceedings of the 2008 ACM Conference on Recommender Systems, pp. 11–18 (2008)
16. Pereira, B.L., Ueda, A., Penha, G., Santos, R.L., Ziviani, N.: Online learning to rank for sequential music recommendation. In: Proceedings of the 13th ACM Conference on Recommender Systems, pp. 237–245 (2019)
17. Xi, W.D., Huang, L., Wang, C.D., Zheng, Y.Y., Lai, J.: BPAM: Recommendation based on BP neural network with attention mechanism. In: International Joint Conference on Artificial Intelligence, pp. 3905–3911 (2019)
18. Xue, H.J., Dai, X., Zhang, J., Huang, S., Chen, J.: Deep matrix factorization models for recommender systems. In: International Joint Conference on Artificial Intelligence, pp. 3203–3209 (2017)
19. Zhang, S., Yao, L., Sun, A., Wang, S., Long, G., Dong, M.: Neurec: on nonlinear transformation for personalized ranking. arXiv preprint arXiv:1805.03002 (2018)

A Link Prediction Method Based on Graph Neural Network Using Node Importance

Luomin Du📷, Yan Tang$^{(\boxtimes)}$📷, and Yuan Yuan📷

College of Computer and Information Science,
Southwest University, Chongqing 400715, China
{duluomin5686,y947136085}@email.swu.edu.cn, ytang@swu.edu.cn

Abstract. Link prediction is a challenging task in complex networks and data mining. Its primary purpose is to predict the possibility of links in the future. Link prediction has many application scenarios, such as product recommendations on e-commerce platforms, friend mining on social platforms, etc. Existing link prediction methods focus on utilizing neighbor and path information, ignoring the contribution of link formation of different node importance. For this reason, we propose a novel link prediction method based on node importance. The importance of node is calculated by using the topology structure of the directed network and the path information between nodes, and a graph convolutional network model suitable for directed graphs is designed. The importance of nodes is used to control the model to aggregate the neighbor information, thereby generating the vector representation of the node and obtaining the prediction score through the multi-layer perceptron (MLP). We investigate the proposed method and conduct extensive experiments on 6 real-world networks from various domains. The experiments results illustrate that the proposed method outperforms existing state-of-the-art methods.

Keywords: Link prediction · Graph convolutional networks · Data mining

1 Introduction

Link prediction aims to predict the possibility of a connection between two nodes that have not yet generated edges through the existing information of the network, including but not limited to network structure, node attributes, edge attributes, etc. Link prediction has many practical application scenarios, such as product recommendations on e-commerce platforms [13] and friend relationship mining on social platforms [1].

The existing link prediction methods can be roughly divided into two categories [7]: heuristic-based methods and learning-based methods. Heuristic methods often use a limited variety of network features to predict, for example, the common neighbor (CN) index, which argues that the more shared neighbors

© The Author(s), under exclusive license to Springer Nature Switzerland AG 2022
G. Memmi et al. (Eds.): KSEM 2022, LNAI 13369, pp. 337–348, 2022.
https://doi.org/10.1007/978-3-031-10986-7_27

between two nodes, the more likely it is to generate link. Therefore, it is based on the shared information between nodes as a feature. Based on this idea, several other similar indicators are derived, including the Salton index [9], Jaccard [16], etc. These methods are still very popular in link prediction due to their advantages of low computational complexity and strong interpretability. However, because these methods usually only consider a limited number of specific network characteristics, they lack universality for networks of various types. For example, the common neighbor index has good performance in social networks. However, it performs poorly in biological networks [23].

With the rapid development of machine learning [12,18,20], more and more scholars consider utilizing the deep learning for link prediction. The methods of deep learning do not specify characteristics of the network but use the strong fitting ability to learn the characteristics of the network automatically. Theoretically, they can adapt to networks of various types, not limited to a specific type of network. Zhang et al. [33] combine link prediction with the graph classification task of deep learning. Graph convolutional networks (GCNs) [5,11,17,28,37] are specially used to deal with graph-related tasks [15,22]. Zhang et al. [34,35] proposed a novel graph convolutional network and used it to replace multi-layer perceptron for link prediction, which achieved better results. Cai et al. [6] went further by converting the subgraph to be predicted into a line graph. In this way, the link will be converted into a node, and the graph classification task will be converted into a node classification task, further reducing the computational overhead.

However, most methods ignored the difference in the contribution of the links formed by nodes of different importance. For example, in social networks, opinion leaders can influence the attitudes of ordinary users more, resulting in more links. Therefore, it can be considered that the important information of the node has a significant influence on link formation.

In order to use the importance information of nodes to improve the accuracy of link prediction, we propose a link prediction method based on the node importance (LPNI) in this paper. We examine the network from two different perspectives, defining the global and local importance of nodes. The global importance represents the node's importance for the entire network, while the local importance represents the node's importance for different nodes in the local curtain scope. The local importance of nodes constitutes the local importance matrix. We use it to construct a Laplacian matrix which is suitable for directed graphs and further design a graph convolutional network model suitable for directed graphs. After the graph convolutional network, the node vector representation containing the importance information is obtained, and we utilize the MLP to calculate the prediction result. We investigate the proposed method and conduct extensive experiments on 6 real-world networks from various domains. The experiments results illustrate that the proposed method outperforms existing state-of-the-art methods.

The rest of the paper is organised as follows. In Sect. 2, we state some relevant prerequisites for link prediction tasks. In Sect. 3, we detail the proposed method.

In Sect. 4, we present our experiments and analyze the experimental results. Finally Sect. 5 gives some concluding remarks with possible future directions.

2   Preliminaries

Given a network $G(V, E)$, $V = \{v_1, v_2, \cdots v_N\}$ denotes the set of nodes of the network, where N represents the number of nodes, and $E = \{e_1, e_2, \cdots e_M\}$ denotes the set of edges of the network, where M represents the number of edges. A pair of nodes can also represent the edges of the network, that is, $e = \{v_x, v_y\}$ represents the edge between node v_x and v_y. We focus on the simple directed networks, which satisfy the following four conditions:

(1) There are no self-loop edges. That is, there will be no edges such as $e = \{v_x, v_x\}$ in the network.
(2) There are at most two edges in different directions between nodes. That is, for any two edges, there will be no situation where $e_i = e_j = \{v_x, v_y\}$.
(3) There is a directionality between the edges, that is, $\{v_x, v_y\} \neq \{v_y, v_x\}$.
(4) There can be weights on the connected edges. If there is an unweighted network, the weight of all existing connected edges is 1.

The task of link prediction is to give a network G, the predict method f assigns a score for certain unconnected nodes. The highest probability of node pair is connected.

3   Method

3.1   Global and Local Node Importance

The symbol $I_G(v_x)$ is used to represent the global importance of node v_x, that is, the importance of the node v_x to the entire network. $I_G \in \mathbb{R}^N$ represents the vector of the global importance of all nodes.

In some cases, the global importance of a node cannot well reflect the individual importance of different nodes. For example, in a scientist cooperation network, the data mining network includes a sub-network for link prediction. Experts of the link prediction sub-network usually have a more substantial influence in the field and do not necessarily significantly influence the whole data mining field. Therefore, The local importance of a node represents the importance of a node in a specific local range of the network. Since mining subnets is cumbersome, in order to simplify the representation of this information, the symbol $I_L(v_x, v_y)$ is used to represent the importance of node v_y in the directed graph to the node v_x, that is, the local importance of the node. Therefore, in this paper, the local importance of a node refers to the relative importance between two nodes. Our study is based on directed networks, therefore, $I_L(v_x, v_y) \neq I_L(v_y, v_x)$. And the $I_L \in \mathbb{R}^{N \times N}$ represents the local importance matrix formed by all node pairs.

The research of Zareie et al. [32] shows that the influence of a node is related to the positions of the node and the neighbor nodes in the network. Therefore, we use the k-shell decomposition algorithm [8] to divide the network into different sub-networks. The nodes in each sub-network have their corresponding ks values. The larger the value, the closer the distance to the network core. By examining the ks value of the node itself, calculate the node's global importance with the ks value of the neighbor node. Use the notation $ks(v_x)$ to denote the ks value of node v_x.

It is considered that the neighbor nodes also represent the important information of the node to a certain extent. Therefore, we further examine the ks value of neighbor nodes. The Shannon entropy of the distribution of ks values of neighbor nodes is calculated as representing the diversity of neighbor nodes. The calculation formula of neighbor diversity of node v_x is as follows

$$diversity(v_x) = -\sum_k p(k) \cdot \log p(k) \tag{1}$$

the above formula means to traverse all possible k values, where $p(k)$ represents the probability that the ks value of the neighbor node is k.

Consider a situation where two nodes v_x and v_y, have three neighbor nodes with different ks values. For example, the neighbor ks values of node v_x are 1, 2, 3, and the neighbor ks values of node v_y are 4, 5, 6, and Eq. 1 calculates that the neighbor diversity values of nodes v_x and v_y are the same. Therefore, it is not only necessary to consider the diversity of neighbor nodes, but also to measure the ks value of neighbor nodes. Consider using the mean ks value of neighbor nodes to construct the global importance of node. The formula for calculating the mean ks value of neighbors of node v_x is as follows:

$$mean\_ks(v_x) = \frac{\sum_{v_y \in \Gamma(v_x)} ks(v_y)}{d(v_x)} \tag{2}$$

where $d(v_x)$ represents the degree of node v_x. $\Gamma(v_x)$ represents the set of neighbor node.

The global importance calculation formula of node v_x is as follows:

$$\boldsymbol{I}_G(v_x) = ks(v_x) \cdot diversity(v_x) \cdot mean\_ks(v_x) \tag{3}$$

Note that in the process of calculating the global importance of nodes, we deliberately ignore the direction of the link for simplicity.

The theory of small-world networks [3] argues that some people who do not know each other in social networks can be linked together through a very short chain of acquaintances. It can be considered that the shorter the chain of acquaintances, the greater the probability that two people know each other, so we consider computing the local importance by computing the shortest path between two nodes. Define a specific path between nodes v_x and v_y as

$$path_{v_x,v_y} = \{v_1, e_1, v_2, e_2, \cdots, e_{l-1}, v_l\} \tag{4}$$

where $e_i = \{v_i, v_{i+1}\}$.

In a directed graph, the path is also directed. That is $path_{v_x, v_y} \neq path_{v_y, v_x}$. The definition symbol $|path|$ represents the length of the path, that is, the number of nodes on the path, and the distance between two nodes is defined as the length of the shortest path. The normalized global importance of all nodes on the shortest path are multiplied together as the local importance of nodes:

$$I_L(v_x, v_y) = \prod_{v_z \in path_{v_x, v_y}} I_{G-norm}(v_z) \tag{5}$$

where $I_{G-norm}(v_z) = I_G(v_z) / \max\{I_G(v)\}$. If there are multiple shortest paths, choose the one with the largest local importance.

Therefore, it can be seen that all node pairs constitute a local importance matrix $I_L \in \mathbb{R}^{N \times N}$, where N represents the count of node.

3.2 GCN with Local Node Importance

Considering the excellent performance of graph convolutional networks on graph-related tasks, we combine node importance information with graph convolutional networks (GCN). Existing graph convolutional network models usually have two combination forms for this kind of data structure. The first is to use each row of the nodes' local importance matrix as the attribute vector of the node, and the second is to use the nodes' local importance matrix as a special adjacency matrix that controls the calculation process of the information aggregation stage. Adopting the second form brings the following advantages:

1. Decouple the attribute information of the node from the scale of the network. That is, the dimension of the attribute vector of the node will not change with the scale of the network.
2. The graph convolutional network model can learn the information of neighbor nodes farther away, which alleviates the over-smoothing problem [19] to a certain extent and reduces the training parameters.

Inspired by the literature [21], we regard matrix I_L as the adjacency matrix of the network to construct the Laplacian matrix of the graph convolutional network. First, insert the auxiliary node v_ξ into the adjacency matrix, and let all nodes generate reciprocal links with it, so that the network is transformed into a strongly connected network, the weight from other nodes to the auxiliary node v_ξ is α, and the weight from the auxiliary node to other nodes is $1/N$. The weight of other links is reduced by $(1 - \alpha)$ times. Use the symbol $\tilde{I}_L \in \mathbb{R}^{(N+1) \times (N+1)}$ to denote the local importance matrix after inserting auxiliary node. The calculation formula is as follows:

$$\tilde{I}_L = \begin{pmatrix} (1-\alpha)I_L & \alpha\mathbf{1} \\ \frac{1}{N}\mathbf{1} & 0 \end{pmatrix} \tag{6}$$

This operation makes the local node importance matrix of the network aperiodic and irreducible, achieving Perron's theorem's precondition [14]. Using Perron's theorem, the left eigenvector $\tilde{\pi} \in \mathbb{R}^{N+1}$ that owns all positive entries can be obtained. We can decompose the $\tilde{\pi}$ vector into two parts, namely $\tilde{\pi} = \{\pi_L, \pi_\xi\}$, $\pi_L \in \mathbb{R}^N$ represents the approximation of the Perron vector composed of N nodes in the original network, and $\pi_\xi \in \mathbb{R}^1$ represents the Perron vector part of the auxiliary node. Diagonalize the π_L vector to get $\Pi_L \in \mathbb{R}^{N \times N}$. And use Π_L to construct a Laplacian matrix suitable for directed graphs:

$$\mathcal{L} = E - \frac{1}{2}(\Pi_L^{\frac{1}{2}} \cdot I_L \cdot \Pi_L^{-\frac{1}{2}} + \Pi_L^{-\frac{1}{2}} \cdot I_L^T \cdot \Pi_L^{\frac{1}{2}}) \tag{7}$$

The definition symbol $\hat{A}$ is expressed as:

$$\hat{A} = \frac{1}{2}(\Pi_L^{\frac{1}{2}} \cdot I_L \cdot \Pi_L^{-\frac{1}{2}} + \Pi_L^{-\frac{1}{2}} \cdot I_L^T \cdot \Pi_L^{\frac{1}{2}}) \tag{8}$$

We define our graph convolutional network model as two convolutional layers:

$$Z = f(X, I) = Softmax(\hat{A} ReLU(\hat{A} X W^0) W^1) \tag{9}$$

where $Z \in \mathbb{R}^{N \times d}$ is the vector representation matrix of nodes. $X \in \mathbb{R}^{N \times 3}$ represents the matrix formed by the attribute vector of the node. We use the three-dimensional vector formed by the out-degree $d_{out}(v_x)$ and in-degree $d_{in}(v_x)$ and the global importance $I_G(v_x)$ as the attribute vector of the node v_x. $W^0 \in \mathbb{R}^{3 \times h}$ and $W^1 \in \mathbb{R}^{h \times d}$ represent trainable parameters, respectively. The details of process of the graph convolutional network are shown in Fig. 1.

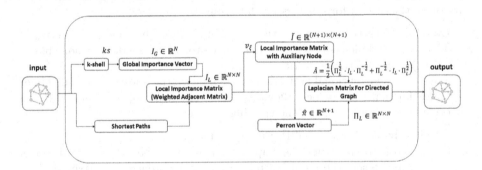

Fig. 1. Details of process of the graph convolutional network.

3.3   Make Prediction

The traditional method of the dot product of the node vectors in the undirected graph is not applicable because of the link direction. Consider using a multi-layer perceptron to splice the vectors of the two nodes so that the splicing result $[z_{v_x} || z_{v_y}] \neq [z_{v_y} || z_{v_x}]$, so the direction information is preserved. Our method computes the prediction score using a multi-layer perceptron of the form:

$$\hat{y} = Softmax([\boldsymbol{z}_{v_x} || \boldsymbol{z}_{v_y}] \boldsymbol{W}) \tag{10}$$

where $\hat{y}$ is the prediction result vector, the first element represents the existing possibility of a link, and the other element represents the non-existing possibility of a link. $\boldsymbol{W} \in \mathbb{R}^{d \times 2}$ is a trainable parameter. And we utilize the cross entropy as our loss function.

$$loss = \sum_n \sum_i -y_i \log \hat{y}_i + \frac{\mu}{2n}(\boldsymbol{W} + \boldsymbol{W}^0 + \boldsymbol{W}^1) \tag{11}$$

where n is the sample size, y_i represents the ith element of the label vector $\boldsymbol{y} \in \mathbb{R}^2$, μ is index of weight decay to alleviate overfitting.

4   Experiments

4.1   Evaluation Indicators

The evaluation indicators used in the experiments are listed below.
(1) AUC. Each time an edge is randomly selected from the test set and then randomly selected another edge from the non-existent test set. After n times independent comparisons in this way, if there are n' times, the score value in the test set is greater than the non-existing edge score. There are n'' times the two scores are equal, and then the AUC calculation formula is:

$$AUC = \frac{n' + 0.5n''}{n} \tag{12}$$

(2) ACC (Accuracy). The accuracy is the proportion of correct predictions (both true positives and true negatives) among the total number of cases examined. The formula is

$$ACC = \frac{TP + TN}{TP + TN + FP + FN} \tag{13}$$

where TP = True positive; FP = False positive; TN = True negative; FN = False negative.

4.2   Baseline Methods

To verify the model's effectiveness, we use the following baseline methods to compare with our proposed method in experiments. To thoroughly verify the performance of the proposed method, these baselines are also divided into two categories, namely graph convolutional methods, and heuristic methods.

(1) DCN [36]: Directed version of CN index.
(2) DAA [36]: Directed version of AA index.
(3) DRA [36]: Directed version of RA index.

(4) Cheb [11]: A spectral-based graph convolutional network proposed by Defferrard et al. This model uses Chebyshev polynomials to achieve fast localization and low complexity, hence the name Chebyshev network.

(5) GCN [17]: A spectral-based graph convolutional network proposed by Kipf and Maxwell. This model is further simplified on the basis of Chebyshev network to form a classic graph convolutional network.

(6) GAT [28]: A spatial-based graph convolutional network proposed by Veličković et al. The model combines the attention mechanism [27] with the graph convolutional network to extract more critical information.

(7) GIN [31]: A spatial-based graph convolutional network proposed Xu et al. From the perspective of Weisfeiler-Lehman test, Xu et al. considered the expressive ability of graph neural network, and proposed this model with the same powerful ability as Weisferler-Lehman test in theory.

(8) DiGCN [26]: A spectral-based graph convolutional network for directed graphs proposed by Tong et al. This model utilizes the idea of Inception [25] and is the latest graph convolutional network for link prediction.

4.3   Datasets

Comparative experiments are carried out on 6 real datasets of different scales in various fields, namely:

(1) High-school (HIG) [10]: A social network from a high school

(2) C.elegans (C-ele) [29]: A neural network of the nematode C.elegans, node representation in the network Neurons, edges represent information transmission between neurons.

(3) SmallW (SMW) [24]: A social network within a company, the nodes in the network are represented by users, edges represent the message passing between nodes.

(4) SmaGri (SMG) [4]: A citation network in which nodes represent papers and edges represent citations.

(5) Political blogs (PB) [2]: An American political blog network, where nodes in the network represent Blog page, the edge represents the hyperlink jump relationship existing between blogs.

(6) Air traffic control (ATC) [24]: An aviation network from the US Flight Control Center. The nodes in the network represent airports or service centers, and the edges represent recommended routes (Table 1).

4.4   Experiment Settings

We divide the edge set of the network into the training set and test set, and the division ratio is 10%. That is, the number of test edges accounts for 10% of the total number of edges. All existing edges have positive labels. Then randomly sample the same number of negative edges from the non-exiting edge of network, and their labels are negative.

Table 1. Statistical properties of the datasets. $|V|$ represents the number of nodes, $|E|$ represents the number of edges, ρ represents the density of the network, $\langle k \rangle_{out}$ represents the average out degree, and cc represents the clustering coefficient of the network.

Name	$|V|$	$|E|$	$\langle k \rangle_{out}$	ρ	cc	Type
HIG	70	366	5.228	0.0758	0.3624	Social network
C-ele	131	764	5.832	0.0449	0.1495	Neural network
SMW	181	756	4.176	0.0232	0.3426	Social network
SMG	1024	4919	4.803	0.0047	0.154	Citation network
PB	1224	19025	15.543	0.0127	0.2184	Hyperlink network
ATC	1226	2615	2.133	0.0017	0.0404	Aviation network

The number of layers of all the above graph convolutional networks is set to 2, the vector representation dimension of nodes is 16, the dropout rate during training is set to 0.5.

The dimension of the representation vector is 16, and the feature of the node is a 2-dimension vector composed of the in-degree and out-degree of the node. We set $\alpha = 0.05$ and the hidden layer dimension $h = 32$ and $d = 16$ in experiments.

4.5   Results and Analysis

All results are the average of 10 independent experiments. The experiment results are shown in Table 2 and Table 3, the proposed method represented by "LPNI." The highest value is shown in bold characters.

Table 2. The AUC results of experiments.

Method	HIG	C-ele	SMW	SMG	PB	ATC
DCN	0.5123	0.7212	0.8714	0.6865	0.8836	0.5455
DAA	0.5185	0.7188	0.8734	0.6845	0.8815	0.5452
DRA	0.5185	0.7173	0.8716	0.6835	0.8771	0.5472
Cheb	0.5790	0.7291	0.8778	0.7799	0.8640	0.6318
GCN	0.6420	0.7444	0.8323	0.7541	0.8949	0.6393
GAT	0.6788	0.7086	0.8296	0.6722	0.8139	0.6361
GIN	0.6508	0.6905	0.6987	0.7068	0.8507	0.5677
DiGCN	0.7129	0.7812	0.9118	0.8847	0.8942	0.6278
LPNI	**0.7411**	**0.8147**	**0.9143**	**0.8909**	**0.8986**	**0.6518**

Heuristic methods include DCN, DAA, and DRA, which only have ranking results and cannot define a threshold for calculating the ACC value. Therefore, their ACC results are not available in Table 3.

Table 3. The ACC results of experiments.

Method	HIG	C-ele	SMW	SMG	PB	ATC
Cheb	0.5778	0.6932	0.8043	0.6962	0.7661	0.5471
GCN	0.6587	0.7292	0.7776	0.6792	0.8191	0.6363
GAT	0.6841	0.6786	0.7651	0.6265	0.7561	0.6259
GIN	0.6207	0.6734	0.6603	0.6601	0.7612	0.5761
DiGCN	0.7127	0.7448	0.8428	0.8079	0.8103	0.6388
LPNI	**0.7241**	**0.7622**	**0.8603**	**0.8179**	**0.8274**	**0.6495**

As can be seen from Table 2 and Table 3, our proposed method outperforms other baseline methods in two evaluation metrics and in all datasets, proving that considering the information of node importance in link prediction can improve the prediction accuracy.

As can be seen from Table 2, comparing the graph convolutional network-based methods (such as LPNI, DiGCN [26], and Cheb [11]) with traditional heuristic methods (such as DCN [36], DAA [36], and DRA [36]), it can be found that the graph convolutional network-based prediction methods show higher accuracy in various types of networks, indicating that methods based on graph convolutional networks can capture the characteristics of different types of networks and are suitable for different types of networks.

As shown from Table 2 and Table 3, DiGCN [26] has the highest prediction accuracy compared with all baseline methods. DiGCN also uses the PageRank algorithm to calculate the personalized PR value of nodes, which can be regarded as a node importance value, which indicates that considering the importance information of nodes can improve the link prediction accuracy. However, its accuracy is lower than that of the LPNI method, indicating our node importance information is more effective.

5 Conclusion

This paper proposed a novel link prediction method that utilizes the node importance information. We conducted many experiments on 6 real networks from various fields and compared them with other baseline methods. The results suggested that our method can work directly on the directed graph in the link prediction tasks. Our method outperforms all baseline methods, including the traditional heuristic methods and graph convolutional network based methods.

In our experiments, the datasets we used are static. That is, the time when the link is generated is ignored. The research work of Xia et al. [30] shows that considering the time when the link appears has a positive impact on the prediction accuracy, so we consider utilize the time information in future work to improve the link prediction accuracy further. In addition, Zhang et al.'s [33] research uses subgraph sampling for link prediction, which significantly reduces the computational complexity. Therefore, our further work will also consider using subgraph sampling technology to reduce the model under the premise of complete node importance information to reduce the computational cost of training.

References

1. Adamic, Lada A., Adar, Eytan: Friends and neighbors on the Web. Soc. Netw. **25**(3), 211–230 (2003)
2. Adamic, L.A., Glance, N.: The political blogosphere and the 2004 U.S. election: Divided they blog. In: Proceedings of the 3rd International Workshop on Link Discovery, LinkKDD 2005, pp. 36–43. Association for Computing Machinery, New York, NY, USA (2005)
3. Barabási, A.L., Albert, R.: Emergence of scaling in random networks. Science **286**(5439), 509–512 (1999)
4. Batagelj, V., Mrvar, A.: Pajek-program for large network analysis. Connections **21**(2), 47–57 (1998)
5. Bruna, J., Zaremba, W., Szlam, A., LeCun, Y.: Spectral networks and locally connected networks on graphs. arXiv preprint arXiv:1312.6203 (2013)
6. Cai, L., Ji, S.: A multi-scale approach for graph link prediction. In: Proceedings of the AAAI Conference on Artificial Intelligence, vol. 34, pp. 3308–3315 (2020)
7. Cai, L., Li, J., Wang, J., Ji, S.: Line graph neural networks for link prediction. IEEE Trans. Pattern Anal. Mach. Intell. (2021)
8. Carmi, S., Havlin, S., Kirkpatrick, S., Shavitt, Y., Shir, E.: A model of internet topology using k-shell decomposition. Proc. Natl. Acad. Sci. **104**(27), 11150–11154 (2007)
9. Chowdhury, G.G.: Introduction to Modern Information Retrieval. Facet Publishing (2010)
10. Coleman, J.S., et al.: Introduction to Mathematical Sociology (1964)
11. Defferrard, M., Bresson, X., Vandergheynst, P.: Convolutional neural networks on graphs with fast localized spectral filtering. In: Lee, D., Sugiyama, M., Luxburg, U., Guyon, I., Garnett, R. (eds.) Advances in Neural Information Processing Systems, vol. 29. Curran Associates, Inc. (2016)
12. Goodfellow, I., Bengio, Y., Courville, A.: Deep Learning. MIT Press (2016)
13. He, X., Deng, K., Wang, X., Li, Y., Zhang, Y., Wang, M.: LightGCN: simplifying and powering graph convolution network for recommendation. In: Proceedings of the 43rd International ACM SIGIR Conference on Research and Development in Information Retrieval, pp. 639–648 (2020)
14. Horn, R.A., Johnson, C.R.: Matrix Analysis. Cambridge University Press (2012)
15. Hu, F., Lakdawala, S., Hao, Q., Qiu, M.: Low-power, intelligent sensor hardware interface for medical data preprocessing. IEEE Trans. Inf. Technol. Biomed. **13**(4), 656–663 (2009)
16. Jaccard, P.: Étude comparative de la distribution florale dans une portion des alpes et des jura. Bull. Soc. Vaudoise Sci. Nat. **37**, 547–579 (1901)
17. Kipf, T.N., Welling, M.: Semi-supervised classification with graph convolutional networks. arXiv preprint arXiv:1609.02907 (2016)
18. LeCun, Y., Bengio, Y., Hinton, G.: Deep learning. nature **521**(7553), 436–444 (2015)

19. Li, Q., Han, Z., Wu, X.M.: Deeper insights into graph convolutional networks for semi-supervised learning. In: 32nd AAAI Conference on Artificial Intelligence (2018)
20. Li, Y., Song, Y., Jia, L., Gao, S., Li, Q., Qiu, M.: Intelligent fault diagnosis by fusing domain adversarial training and maximum mean discrepancy via ensemble learning. IEEE Trans. Industr. Inf. **17**(4), 2833–2841 (2021)
21. Ma, Y., Hao, J., Yang, Y., Li, H., Jin, J., Chen, G.: Spectral-based graph convolutional network for directed graphs. arXiv preprint arXiv:1907.08990 (2019)
22. Qiu, H., Zheng, Q., Msahli, M., Memmi, G., Qiu, M., Lu, J.: Topological graph convolutional network-based urban traffic flow and density prediction. IEEE Trans. Intell. Transp. Syst. **22**(7), 4560–4569 (2021)
23. Ravasz, E., Somera, A.L., Mongru, D.A., Oltvai, Z.N., Barabási, A.L.: Hierarchical organization of modularity in metabolic networks. Science **297**(5586), 1551–1555 (2002)
24. Rossi, R., Ahmed, N.: The network data repository with interactive graph analytics and visualization. In: 29th AAAI Conference on Artificial Intelligence (2015)
25. Szegedy, C., et al.: Going deeper with convolutions. In: Proceedings of the IEEE Conference on Computer Vision and Pattern Recognition (CVPR) (June 2015)
26. Tong, Z., Liang, Y., Sun, C., Li, X., Rosenblum, D., Lim, A.: Digraph inception convolutional networks. In: Larochelle, H., Ranzato, M., Hadsell, R., Balcan, M.F., Lin, H. (eds.) Advances in Neural Information Processing Systems, vol. 33, pp. 17907–17918. Curran Associates, Inc. (2020)
27. Vaswani, A., et al.: Attention is all you need. In: Guyon, I., et al. (eds.) Advances in Neural Information Processing Systems, vol. 30. Curran Associates, Inc. (2017)
28. Veličković, P., Cucurull, G., Casanova, A., Romero, A., Lio, P., Bengio, Y.: Graph attention networks. arXiv preprint arXiv:1710.10903 (2017)
29. Watts, D.J., Strogatz, S.H.: Collective dynamics of 'small-world' networks. nature **393**(6684), 440–442 (1998)
30. Xia, L., et al.: Knowledge-enhanced hierarchical graph transformer network for multi-behavior recommendation. In: Proceedings of the AAAI Conference on Artificial Intelligence, vol. 35, pp. 4486–4493 (2021)
31. Xu, K., Hu, W., Leskovec, J., Jegelka, S.: How powerful are graph neural networks? arXiv preprint arXiv:1810.00826 (2018)
32. Zareie, A., Sheikhahmadi, A., Jalili, M.: Influential node ranking in social networks based on neighborhood diversity. Fut. Gener. Comput. Syst. **94**, 120–129 (2019)
33. Zhang, M., Chen, Y.: Weisfeiler-Lehman neural machine for link prediction. In: Proceedings of the 23rd ACM SIGKDD International Conference on Knowledge Discovery and Data Mining, pp. 575–583 (2017)
34. Zhang, M., Chen, Y.: Link prediction based on graph neural networks. Adv. Neural. Inf. Process. Syst. **31**, 5165–5175 (2018)
35. Zhang, M., Cui, Z., Neumann, M., Chen, Y.: An end-to-end deep learning architecture for graph classification. In: 32nd AAAI Conference on Artificial Intelligence (2018)
36. Zhang, X., Zhao, C., Wang, X., Yi, D.: Identifying missing and spurious interactions in directed networks. Int. J. Distrib. Sens. Netw. **11**(9), 507386 (2015)
37. Zhang, Z., Cui, P., Zhu, W.: Deep learning on graphs: a survey. IEEE Trans. Knowl. Data Eng. **34**(1), 249–270 (2022)

Proposal of a Method for Creating a BPMN Model Based on the Data Extracted from a DMN Model

Krzysztof Kluza[1]([✉]) [ID], Piotr Wiśniewski[1] [ID], Mateusz Zaremba[1] [ID],
Weronika T. Adrian[1] [ID], Anna Suchenia[2] [ID], Leszek Szała[3] [ID],
and Antoni Ligęza[1] [ID]

[1] AGH University of Science and Technology,
al. A. Mickiewicza 30, 30-059 Krakow, Poland
{kluza,wpiotr,mzaremba,wta,ligeza}@agh.edu.pl
[2] Cracow University of Technology, ul. Warszawska 24,
31-155 Kraków, Poland
asuchenia@pk.edu.pl
[3] Department of Mathematics, Faculty of Chemical Engineering, University of
Chemistry and Technology Prague, Technicka 5, 166 28 Prague 6, Czech Republic
leszek.szala@vscht.cz

Abstract. Operational processes are usually modeled using the standardized Business Process Model and Notation (BPMN). Processes may include the decisions, however, best practices include modeling operational decisions using the Decision Model and Notation (DMN) standard. This paper presents a proposal for creating BPMN models based on the data extracted from the DMN models. Although there is no one to one correspondence between the diagrams modeled in BPMN and DMN, we show that it is possible to construct prototype process models based on the data from the decision model. As there are several possibilities for the translation, a user may choose how to translate particular elements or fragments of the model, which can be later manually refined and extended. Such a process model is directly related to the source DMN model, so in this case, the DMN model specifies the decision logic, the integrated BPMN and DMN models are executable.

1 Introduction

Both Business Process Model and Notation (BPMN) [22] and Decision Model and Notation (DMN) [23] constitute established standards for modeling and managing process and decision knowledge of organizations.

As DMN filled the gap in the market of decision modeling, it became a standardized solution for modeling decision and is often used with BPMN. The notation provides decision logic representation, as well as other decision elements, and requirements specification. It can be used for implementing decision-making, automated or not.

© The Author(s), under exclusive license to Springer Nature Switzerland AG 2022
G. Memmi et al. (Eds.): KSEM 2022, LNAI 13369, pp. 349–358, 2022.
https://doi.org/10.1007/978-3-031-10986-7_28

These two complementary techniques enact particular types of knowledge, namely procedural knowledge and data-centric organizational knowledge (decision logic). An integrated model of processes and rules may bring numerous benefits to the knowledge management systems. This is why more and more methods that facilitate mining, extracting, constructing or prototyping integrated models are of great importance.

DMN models are no longer just an add-on to BPMN, but are also used with other notations or just as a stand-alone decision support technique used in business analysis [25] and can be seen as a part of the knowledge management process [10].

Process mining techniques [1,2,11] constitute popular methods for process acquisition. In the case of decision models, there exist several methods for deriving or extracting decision models from other models, event logs (decision mining), or execution data [4,6–9,13–15,17,20,21]. Among them, there is a method of extracting DMN models from the BPMN process models [8].

This paper aims to discuss the possibility of automatic or semi-automatic creation of prototype business process models in BPMN based on the data from business decision models in DMN. As the mapping between these two notations is not straightforward, and there might be several possibilities for the translation, in the case of doubts about the choice of mapping, the system might use the most popular one or allow the user to decide how to translate a particular element or fragment of the model. As the resulting model is a prototype model, it should be later manually examined and refined.

The paper is structured as follows. Section 2 presents the related works in the area of BPMN and DMN mapping. In Sect. 3, we present a simple yet illustrative motivating example. Section 5 discusses the possible mappings from DMN fragments to their corresponding BPMN structures. The proposed mapping was applied to the motivating example in Sect. 6. We conclude the paper with the summary and future works description in Sect. 7.

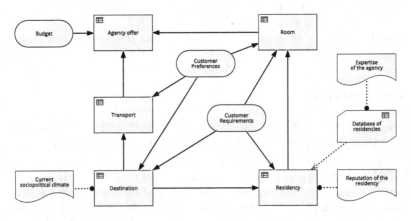

Fig. 1. The motivating example for the presented method (based on [18])

2 Related Works

Process and decision models are closely interrelated. Although DMN is perceived as a notation that complements BPMN [16], there have been research works that aimed to derive decisions from BPMN process diagrams [7] which, at the later stage, led to extracting decision requirements diagram from process models [4,9]. In a recent study, a set of mapping rules from BPMN to DMN was proposed [8].

Integrated BPMN and DMN models can be generated based on Attribute Relationship Diagrams [20], but such an approach requires the ARD specification. In addition to the well-established research area of process mining, there exists also decision mining that is based on extracting decision models from event-based logs containing extensive instance data [6,13] or, in more general terms, using process execution data to discover decision models [14]. Decision diagrams may also come as a result of extracting knowledge from existing natural language text documents [15].

Fig. 2. The types of DMN elements

Decision Model and Notation can be used to augment process information by providing an integrated model [17] or to enhance declarative process models [21].

3 Motivating Example

Let us present a motivating example (see Fig. 1) that uses the DMN model and shows a decision process for the agency. We adopted the DMN model from [18].

DMN standard provides the graphical notation for decision modeling, in which the decisions can be clearly presented in an understandable manner [26]. Other DMN purposes include modeling human decision-making, the requirements for automated decision-making, and implementing automated decision-making [23]. DMN decisions determine the result (or selects some option) based on input data. The decision models use four types of elements: *Decision, Business Knowledge Model, Input Data*, and *Knowledge Source* (see Fig. 2).

Decisions are used to determine an output from a number of inputs using some decision logic. *Business Knowledge Models* encapsulates business knowledge, such as decision tables, business rules or analytic models. *Input Data* elements specify the input of a Decision or Business Knowledge Model. *Knowledge Sources* model authoritative knowledge sources in a decision model. These elements can be connected using different requirement connectors, such as *Information, Knowledge*, and *Authority*.

A higher level decision model can be represented as Decision Requirements Graph (DRG), which may be split into one or more Decision Requirements Diagrams (DRD), presenting a particular view of the model [23]. For the lower level of decision modeling, i.e., rules, DMN provides a dedicated language – Friendly Enough Expression Language (FEEL). Such rules can be evaluated using some dedicated FEEL environment or transformed into a more specific executable representation.

4 Procedural-Related Data in Decision Models

Annex A "Relation to BPMN" of the DMN specification [23] defines that a BPMN Business Rule Task is the most natural way to express the DMN Decision functionality; it also specifies that a Decision can be associated with any BPMN Task type. This allows for the interpretation depending on the semantics of the decisions as well as flexibility in implementation.

For the purpose of the description of the creating BPMN models we adapted the formalization of BPMN and DMN from [20]:

Definition 1. A BPMN process model is a tuple $\mathcal{PM} = (\mathcal{O}, \mathcal{A}, \mathcal{F}, \mathcal{C})$, where:

- $\mathcal{O}$ is the set of flow objects, $o_1, o_2, o_3, \ldots \in \mathcal{O}$,
- $\mathcal{A}$ is the set of other process artifacts such as data objects, data stores, and annotations.
- $\mathcal{F}$ is the set of sequence flows, such as $\mathcal{F} \subset \mathcal{O} \times \mathcal{O}$,
- $\mathcal{C}$ is the set of connecting elements (associations), such as $\mathcal{C} \subset \mathcal{A} \times \mathcal{O} \cup \mathcal{A}$.

The set $\mathcal{O}$ of flow objects is divided into three distinct sets $\mathcal{O} = \mathcal{T} \cup \mathcal{S} \cup \mathcal{E} \cup \mathcal{G}$:

- $\mathcal{T}$ is the set of tasks $(\tau_1, \tau_2, \tau_3, \ldots \in \mathcal{T})$
  and $\mathcal{S}$ is the set of sub-processes,
- $\mathcal{E}$ is the set of events, $e_1, e_2, e_3, \ldots \in \mathcal{E}$,
- $\mathcal{G}$ is the set of gateways, $g_1, g_2, g_3, \ldots \in \mathcal{G}$.

Definition 2. A DMN decision requirement diagram is a tuple $\mathcal{DM} = (\mathcal{D}, \mathcal{I}, \mathcal{R}_\mathcal{I}, T_\mathcal{D})$, where:

- $\mathcal{D}$ is the set of decision nodes,
- $\mathcal{I}$ is the set of input data nodes,
- $\mathcal{B}$ is the set of business knowledge model nodes,
- $\mathcal{K}$ is the set of knowledge source nodes,
- $\mathcal{R}_\mathcal{I} \subseteq \mathcal{D} \cup \mathcal{I} \times \mathcal{D}$ is the set of information requirements,
- $\mathcal{R}_\mathcal{K} \subseteq \mathcal{D} \cup \mathcal{I} \times \mathcal{D}$ is the set of knowledge requirements,
- $\mathcal{R}_\mathcal{A} \subseteq \mathcal{B} \times \mathcal{D} \cup \mathcal{B}$ is the set of authority requirements,
- $T_\mathcal{D}$ is a set of the decision tables related to decision nodes (usually a single decision table for a specific decision node).

Definition 3. Business process model integrated with the decision model is a tuple: $\mathcal{M} = (\mathcal{PM}, \mathcal{DM}, map)$, where:

- $\mathcal{PM}$ is a BPMN 2.0 process model,
- $\mathcal{DM}$ is a decision model,
- map is a mapping function between the Business Rule tasks and the decisions from the $\mathcal{DM}$ decision model, i.e., $map: \mathcal{T}_{Business\,Rule} \to \mathcal{D}$.

This simple notation presented above will be used in the next section for the description of the algorithm.

5 Mapping from DMN to BPMN

The method proposed in this paper uses the refined DMN model and follows a mapping algorithm from DMN to BPMN. During the mapping, certain keywords in the model might be a suggestion of the potential names for the tasks [27].

The sets of potential verbs for generating task names, the sets of selected keywords for detecting data stores and objects, and the set of keywords for detecting start events in the destination BPMN diagram are based on [27], e.g.:

- $Verb(decide) = \{approve, choose, decide, determine, evaluate, review\}$,
- $Verb(calculate) = \{calculate, compute, derive, estimate, price, solve\}$,
- $Keywords(data\ stores) = \{DB, archive, backup, base, repository, store\}$,
- $Keywords(data\ objects) = \{contract, data, document, file, note, object\}$,
- $Keywords(start\ event) = \{booking, call, claim, inquiry, order, request\}$.

5.1 Refining Information Requirements

Assuming that some of the input data elements are mapped into BPMN tasks, in the final BPMN model, we can omit connections that lead to consecutive decisions. In other words, if there exists a succession relation [21] between two decisions and both of them need the same input, then for the purpose of this work, we can temporarily remove the connection between the data input and the decision that occurs later. A formalized concept of information requirements is explained in Definition 4.

Definition 4. Let $\mathcal{DM}$ be a decision requirement diagram as described in Definition 2. An information requirement $r \in \mathcal{R}_\mathcal{J}$ is redundant in the final process model if and only if:

1. There is an information requirement r_0 connecting input data node i with decision node d_1: $r_0 = \{i, d_1\} : i \in \mathcal{J}, d_1 \in \mathcal{D}$.
2. Information requirement r connects the same input data node with another decision node $r = \{i, d_2\} : d_2 \in \mathcal{D} \land d_2 \neq d_1$.
3. There is a succession relation between decision nodes d_1 and d_2.

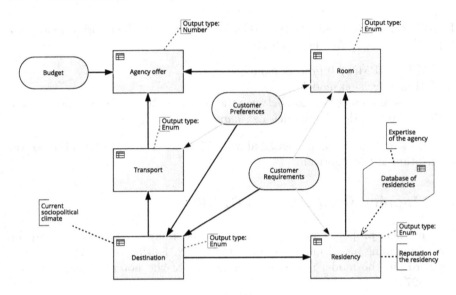

Fig. 3. The temporary refined DMN model

Refining the model consists in removing all the information requirements $r \in \mathcal{R}_j$ that satisfy conditions formulated in Definition 4.

Figure 3 shows the result of the temporary model refinement. The removed Information Requirements are presented in gray, while the optional information about the decision output type is presented in red. Additionally, the Knowledge Sources were removed and replaced by annotations.

5.2   Algorithm for Creating Process Model

Input for the algorithm:

a) a temporary refined DMN decision model with the removed unnecessary information requirements,

b) optionally, the corresponding DMN logic model (decision tables),

c) optionally, the guidelines from the user, concerning translation method (otherwise: default translation will be chosen).

Output of the algorithm:

– a business process model integrated with the decision model $\mathcal{M}$.

Goal: Automatically (input: a, b) or semi-automatically (input: a, b, c) generate a BPMN business process model integrated with the DMN decision model based on the refined decision model.

Algorithm draft:

1. Create a process model integrated with decision model $\mathcal{M}$ = $(\mathcal{PM}, \mathcal{DM}, map)$.

2. In the temporary refined decision model, find the set of start decision elements $\mathcal{D}_{start} \subseteq \mathcal{D}$ (the decisions which does not use as input any other decision i.e. there is no information requirement pointing to this decision from other decision), and construct the subset $\mathcal{I}_{start} \subseteq \mathcal{I}$ of input data used by these start decisions.

3. For each input data $i \in \mathcal{I}_{start}$:
   (a) if i contains any keyword from the set $Keywords(start\ event)$, create a message start event $e_{start} \in \mathcal{E}$ with the name:
   $name(e_{start}) = "name(i) + received"$,
   (b) otherwise, create a user task $\tau_{User} \in \mathcal{T}$ named:
   $name(\tau_{User}) = "Provide + name(i)"$.

4. For each decision $d \in \mathcal{D}_{start}$ create a corresponding Business Rule task $\tau_{BR} \in \mathcal{T}$ with the name created in the following way:
   (a) if the output type of the decision table $t_d \in T_{\mathcal{D}}$ is *number*, choose the most popular collocation $name(\tau_{BR}) = "Verb(Calculate)_i + name(d)"$,
   (b) if the output type of the decision table $t_d \in T_{\mathcal{D}}$ *boolean*, *string* or *enum*, choose the most popular collocation $name(\tau_{BR}) = "Verb(Decide)_i + name(d)"$,
   (c) otherwise (the output type not known) choose the most popular collocation $name(\tau_{BR}) = "Verb(Decide \cup Calculate)_i + name(d)"$.
   Create also a relation to the DMN decision $map(\tau_{BR}) = d$.

5. For each business knowledge model $b \in \mathcal{B}$ connected to the decisions from $\mathcal{D}_{start}$, create a corresponding data store or data object depending on the keywords from $Keywords(data\ stores)$ or $Keywords(data\ objects)$:
   (a) if $name(b)$ contains a keyword of data store, create a data store,
   (b) if $name(b)$ contains a keyword of data object, create a data object,
   (c) otherwise, create a corresponding annotation.

6. For each knowledge source $k \in \mathcal{K}$ connected to the decisions from $\mathcal{D}_{start}$, create an annotation $a \in \mathcal{A}$ connected to the corresponding task τ_{BR}.

7. For each knowledge source $k \in \mathcal{K}$ connected to the business knowledge model from $\mathcal{B}_{start}$, create an annotation $a \in \mathcal{A}$ connected to the corresponding data object.

8. Connect the message start events (created in 3.) with user tasks using sequence flow (in the case of many events or tasks use a parallel gateway). Then, connect the user tasks or message start events with the Business Rule task (created in 4.).

9. Find all decisions that use as input the decision from $\mathcal{D}_{start}$, replace the set $\mathcal{D}_{start}$ with them, construct the subset $\mathcal{I}_{start} \subseteq \mathcal{I}$ of input data used by these decisions, and go to the point 3.

10. If the start event was a receive message event, create a sent message end event $e_{end} \in \mathcal{E}$ with the name: $name(e_{end}) = "name(d) + sent"$, where d is the last decision.

6   Application of the Proposed Method

We applied the algorithm into the model from the motivating example presented in Fig. 1. The result of the proposed approach along with the corresponding source DMN model is shown in Fig. 4. As the result process model is associated with the source DMN model, so if the DMN model also specified the decision logic, such integrated BPMN and DMN model may be executed in the system supporting both standards.

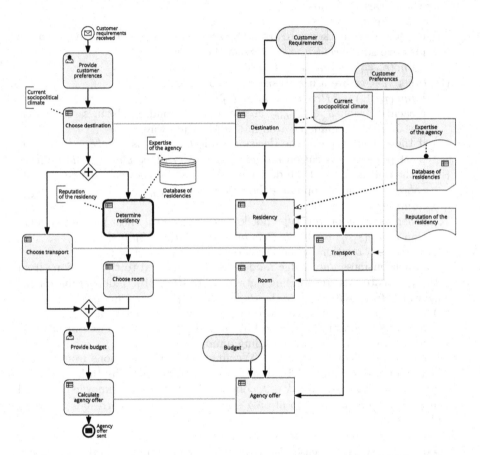

Fig. 4. The obtained BPMN model along with the corresponding DMN model

The obtained model might be also manually examined or validated [3], formally verified [5,12], analyzed [16,18] extended with other elements or perspectives [19], refined [7], or integrated with other methods where the DMN constitutes a part responsible for modeling decisions [24].

7 Conclusions and Future Works

To the best of our knowledge, we introduced a novel method that automatically or semi-automatically creates a prototype of a BPMN model integrated with the DMN model based on the refined decision model. Our mapping takes into account different semantics of data artifacts specified in the decision model. During the extraction of the data from the DMN model, it is possible to use default settings for automatic processing. The result of the proposed method is a prototype BPMN model consistent with the source DMN model, which might be further processed. Such a model can be useful both for rapid prototyping and simulation. The integrated models can also be quickly refined with more information needed for complete execution (e.g., rules) and executed in any run-time environment supporting BPMN and DMN. Our future works will be focused on enhancing the process models created using the proposed method with additional BPMN elements. We also plan to exploit dedicated domain ontologies and knowledge graphs to support creating more specific elements.

References

1. van der Aalst, W.: Process Mining: Data Science in Action. Springer, Berlin (2016). https://doi.org/10.1007/978-3-662-49851-4
2. Augusto, A., et al.: Automated discovery of process models from event logs: review and benchmark. IEEE Trans. Knowl. Data Eng. **31**(4), 686–705 (2018)
3. Batoulis, K., Baumgraß, A., Herzberg, N., Weske, M.: Enabling dynamic decision making in business processes with DMN. In: Reichert, M., Reijers, H.A. (eds.) BPM 2015. LNBIP, vol. 256, pp. 418–431. Springer, Cham (2016). https://doi.org/10.1007/978-3-319-42887-1_34
4. Batoulis, K., Meyer, A., Bazhenova, E., Decker, G., Weske, M.: Extracting decision logic from process models. In: Zdravkovic, J., Kirikova, M., Johannesson, P. (eds.) CAiSE 2015. LNCS, vol. 9097, pp. 349–366. Springer, Cham (2015). https://doi.org/10.1007/978-3-319-19069-3_22
5. Batoulis, K., Weske, M.: Soundness of decision-aware business processes. In: Carmona, J., Engels, G., Kumar, A. (eds.) BPM 2017. LNBIP, vol. 297, pp. 106–124. Springer, Cham (2017). https://doi.org/10.1007/978-3-319-65015-9_7
6. Bazhenova, E., Buelow, S., Weske, M.: Discovering decision models from event logs. In: Abramowicz, W., Alt, R., Franczyk, B. (eds.) BIS 2016. LNBIP, vol. 255, pp. 237–251. Springer, Cham (2016). https://doi.org/10.1007/978-3-319-39426-8_19
7. Bazhenova, E., Weske, M.: Deriving decision models from process models by enhanced decision mining. In: Reichert, M., Reijers, H.A. (eds.) BPM 2015. LNBIP, vol. 256, pp. 444–457. Springer, Cham (2016). https://doi.org/10.1007/978-3-319-42887-1_36
8. Bazhenova, E., Zerbato, F., Oliboni, B., Weske, M.: From BPMN process models to DMN decision models. Inf. Syst. **83**, 69–88 (2019)
9. Bazhenova, E., Zerbato, F., Weske, M.: Data-centric extraction of DMN decision models from BPMN process models. In: Teniente, E., Weidlich, M. (eds.) BPM 2017. LNBIP, vol. 308, pp. 542–555. Springer, Cham (2018). https://doi.org/10.1007/978-3-319-74030-0_43
10. Bitkowska, A., et al.: The relationship between business process management and knowledge management-selected aspects from a study of companies in poland. J. Entrepreneu. Manag. Innov. **16**(1), 169–193 (2020)
11. Brzychczy, E.: Process modelling based on event logs. Multi. Aspects Prod. Eng. **1**(1), 385–392 (2018)

12. Calvanese, D., Dumas, M., Laurson, Ü., Maggi, F.M., Montali, M., Teinemaa, I.: Semantics, analysis and simplification of DMN decision tables. Inf. Syst. **78**, 112–125 (2018)

13. De Smedt, J., vanden Broucke, S.K.L.M., Obregon, J., Kim, A., Jung, J.-Y., Vanthienen, J.: Decision mining in a broader context: an overview of the current landscape and future directions. In: Dumas, M., Fantinato, M. (eds.) BPM 2016. LNBIP, vol. 281, pp. 197–207. Springer, Cham (2017). https://doi.org/10.1007/978-3-319-58457-7_15

14. De Smedt, J., Hasić, F., vanden Broucke, S.K., Vanthienen, J.: Holistic discovery of decision models from process execution data. Knowl. Based Syst. **183**, 104866 (2019)

15. Etikala, V., Van Veldhoven, Z., Vanthienen, J.: Text2Dec: extracting decision dependencies from natural language text for automated DMN decision modelling. In: Del Río Ortega, A., Leopold, H., Santoro, F.M. (eds.) BPM 2020. LNBIP, vol. 397, pp. 367–379. Springer, Cham (2020). https://doi.org/10.1007/978-3-030-66498-5_27

16. Figl, K., Mendling, J., Tokdemir, G., Vanthienen, J.: What we know and what we do not know about DMN. Enterp. Model. Inf. Syst. Architectures **13**, 1–2 (2018)

17. Hasić, F., De Smedt, J., Vanthienen, J.: Augmenting processes with decision intelligence: principles for integrated modelling. Decis. Support Syst. **107**, 1–12 (2018)

18. Hasić, F., Vanthienen, J.: Complexity metrics for DMN decision models. Comput. Stan. Interfaces **65**, 15–37 (2019)

19. Horita, F.E., de Albuquerque, J.P., Marchezini, V., Mendiondo, E.M.: Bridging the gap between decision-making and emerging big data sources: an application of a model-based framework to disaster management in brazil. Decis. Support Syst. **97**, 12–22 (2017)

20. Kluza, K., Wiśniewski, P., Adrian, W.T., Ligęza, A.: From attribute relationship diagrams to process (BPMN) and decision (DMN) models. In: Douligeris, C., Karagiannis, D., Apostolou, D. (eds.) KSEM 2019. LNCS (LNAI), vol. 11775, pp. 615–627. Springer, Cham (2019). https://doi.org/10.1007/978-3-030-29551-6_55

21. Mertens, S., Gailly, F., Poels, G.: Enhancing declarative process models with DMN decision logic. In: Gaaloul, K., Schmidt, R., Nurcan, S., Guerreiro, S., Ma, Q. (eds.) CAISE 2015. LNBIP, vol. 214, pp. 151–165. Springer, Cham (2015). https://doi.org/10.1007/978-3-319-19237-6_10

22. OMG: Business Process Model and Notation (BPMN): Version 2.0 specification. Tech. Rep. formal/2011-01-03, Object Management Group (January 2011)

23. OMG: Decision Model and Notation (DMN). Version 1.1. Tech. Rep. formal/16-06-01, Object Management Group (2016)

24. Ortner, E., Mevius, M., Wiedmann, P., Kurz, F.: Design of interactional decision support applications for e-participation in smart cities. Int. J. Electr. Govern. Res. (IJEGR) **12**(2), 18–38 (2016)

25. Pankowska, M.: Business models in CMNN, DMN and archimate language. Proc. Comput. Sci. **164**, 11–18 (2019)

26. Taylor, J., Fish, A., Vanthienen, J., Vincent, P.: iBPMS: intelligent BPM systems: intelligent BPM systems: impact and opportunity. In: Emerging standards in decision modeling - An introduction to Decision Model & Notation, pp. 133–146. BPM and Workflow Handbook Series, Future Strategies, Inc. (2013)

27. Thorpe, M., Holm, J., van den Boer, G., et al.: Discovering the decisions within your business processes using IBM blueworks live. In: IBM Redbooks (2014)

PartKG2Vec: Embedding of Partitioned Knowledge Graphs

Amitabh Priyadarshi and Krzysztof J. Kochut[✉]

Department of Computer Science, University of Georgia, Athens, GA 30602, USA
{amitabh.priyadarshi,kkochut}@uga.edu

Abstract. Large-scale knowledge graphs with billions of nodes and edges are increasingly common in many domains. Such graphs often exceed the capacity of the systems storing the graphs in a centralized data store, not to mention the limits of today's graph embedding systems. Unsupervised machine learning methods can be used for graph embedding, which can then be used for various machine learning tasks. State-of the art embedding techniques are often unable to achieve scalability without losing accuracy and efficiency. To overcome this, large knowledge graphs are frequently partitioned into multiple sub-graphs and placed in nodes of a distributed computing cluster. Graph embedding algorithms convert a graph into a vector space where the structure and the inherent property of the graph is preserved. Running such algorithms against these fragmented sub-graphs poses new challenges, such as maximizing the likelihood of preserving network neighborhood of nodes. Also, the learned embeddings of the individual graph partitions need to be merged into one overall embedding to maximize the likelihood of preserving network neighborhood of nodes. This paper introduces a novel method for embedding of partitioned knowledge graphs. It partitions the knowledge graph and executes learning algorithm in parallel on the partitions and merge their outputs to produce an overall embedding. Our evaluation demonstrates that the runtime performance is improved after partitioning of knowledge graph against complete knowledge graph and the quality of the embedding is like that of an embedding produced on the complete, unpartitioned graph.

Keywords: Knowledge graphs · Graph partitioning · Feature learning · Node embedding · Graph representation learning

1 Introduction

Recently, large-scale knowledge graphs, have been used for representation of transportation networks, e-commerce and shopper preference networks, social and communication networks, and many other real-world systems. Such graphs often hold hundreds of millions, or even billions of vertices and edges. Many data processing methods rely on large-scale graph analytics, which are often based on nodes and graph embedding and node feature extraction, which can further be used in a various machine learning tasks. However, state-of the art techniques are not scalable to large graphs without losing accuracy and/or efficiency. A knowledge graph often needs to be partitioned into multiple

© The Author(s), under exclusive license to Springer Nature Switzerland AG 2022

G. Memmi et al. (Eds.): KSEM 2022, LNAI 13369, pp. 359–370, 2022.
https://doi.org/10.1007/978-3-031-10986-7_29

sub-graphs, called shards, and stored at multiple computing nodes, which then requires distributed or parallel graph processing.

Graph embedding, also known as network embedding, is a frequently used technique for learning low-dimensional representations of a graph's vertices, attempting to capture and retain the graph's structure, as well as its inherent properties. Many tasks on graphs, such as link prediction, node classification, and visualization, greatly benefit by embedding a very large, web-scale graph into a low-dimensional vector space. More specifically, we might be interested in estimating the most likely labels for nodes in a network, or predicting user interests in a social network, or we might be interested in predicting functional labels of proteins in a protein-protein interaction network [1]. Similarly, in a link prediction task [2], we might want to know if a pair of nodes in a graph should be connected by an edge. Link prediction is beneficial numerous fields. For example, in bioinformatics, it aids in the discovery of novel protein interactions [3], and it can recognize "real-world buddies" on social networks [4].

A knowledge graph (KG) is a directed graph G (V, E) whose nodes $v_i \in V$ are entities and edges $e_i \in E$ are relations connecting entities. Knowledge graphs are often represented as RDF [5] datasets, where triples (v_i, e_i, v_j) represent some type of semantic dependency between the connected entities and nodes/entities are identified by URI's. Target nodes in triples are either URIs or literals, and edge/relationships have types represented by URIs, as well. RDFS [6] is used to define a schema for an RDF knowledge graph. KGs are closely related to Heterogeneous Information Networks (HIN) [21].

Various approaches to graph embedding have been presented in the machine learning literature, e.g., [7–9]. They function well on smaller networks, but real-world knowledge graphs, which often have millions of nodes and billions of edges, present a far more difficult situation. For example, a decade ago, the Twitter's followee-follower network had 175 million active users and approximately twenty billion edges [10]. Most of the existing graph embedding algorithms do not scale up to networks of this magnitude.

Knowledge graphs can be partitioned into smaller subgraphs, with a hope that many tasks can take advantage of distributed and/or parallel processing. Given a graph G = (V, E), where V is a set of vertices and E is a set of edges and a number $k > 1$, a graph partitioning of G is a subdivision of vertices of G into subsets of vertices $V_1,\ldots, V_k$ that partitions the set V. A balance constraint requires that all partitioned subgraphs be equal, or close, in size. In addition, a common objective is to minimize the total number of cut edges (min-cut), i.e., edges crossing (cutting) partition boundaries.

In this paper we propose PartKG2Vec, an algorithm for scalable feature learning in partitioned knowledge graphs. Our approach creates embeddings based on random walks in partitioned knowledge graphs and offers significant runtime improvements due to performing the walks in parallel. This is important in random walk-based methods, especially in semantics based, such as metapath2vec [29], due to the high cost of selecting the next node at each step during a random walk.

The rest of the paper is structured as follows. In Sect. 2, we briefly discuss related work. We present the technical details for PartKG2Vec in Sect. 3. In Sect. 4, we briefly explain the implementation of PartKG2Vec. In Sect. 5, we empirically evaluate PartKG2Vec. We conclude with a discussion of the PartKG2Vec framework and highlight some interesting directions for future work in Sect. 6.

2   Related Work

Recently, graph representation learning has attracted a lot of attention. In general, there are two types of graph representation learning methods: unsupervised and supervised. The goal of unsupervised approaches is to learn low-dimensional representation that preserves the structure of a given graph. The supervised methods work in the same way as the unsupervised methods, but for a specific prediction task, such as node or graph classification. Only unsupervised approaches are discussed in this paper.

Unsupervised *embedding methods* map a graph's nodes and edges, into a continuous vector space. Several of the graph embedding techniques have been motivated by the Word2Vec algorithm [12], which originated in natural language processing. One type of this algorithm relies on the *skip-gram embedding models*, where a word's embedding is optimized to predict its context or adjacent words. A random walk in a graph is akin a sequence of words in a sentence, where the nodes visited in the walk can be thought of words in a sentence.

Deepwalk [13] is one of the first approaches to embedding of graph-structured data. Deepwalk relies on the parallels between graph nodes and words and its neural networks are trained to maximize the likelihood of predicting the context nodes for each target vertex in a graph, in terms of vertex proximity.

node2vec [14], is a popular unsupervised graph embedding algorithm, which extends Deepwalk's sampling strategy. It utilizes random walks. Also, node2vec utilizes breadth-first and depth-first to capture both local and global community structures, resulting in more informative embeddings.

LINE [15], which is an acronym of Large-scale Information Network Embedding, produces embeddings ensuring first- and second-order proximity. For first order, LINE minimizes the graph regularization loss, and for second order, decodes embeddings into context conditional distributions for each node, which is computationally expensive. Negative sampling is used by LINE to sample negative edges based on a noisy distribution over edges. Finally, LINE combines first and second order embedding with concatenation.

HARP [16], or Hierarchical representation learning for networks lowers the number of nodes in the graph by coarsening the graph in a hierarchical manner. Iteratively grouping nodes into super nodes, it creates a graph with similar properties to the original network, resulting in graphs of reduced size. Existing approaches, such as LINE or Deepwalk, are then used to learn node embedding for each coarsened graph. The random walk technique on G_{t-1} uses the embedding learned for G_t as initialized embedding at time-step t. This technique is repeated until each node in the original graph is embedded.

2.1   Embedding of Partitioned Graphs

PyTorch-BigGraph [17], also known as PBG, is a multi-relation embedding system that can scale to graphs with billions of nodes and trillions of edges by incorporating various improvements to existing multi-relation embedding systems. PBG can train very large embedding using a distributed cluster using graph partitioning. The adjacency matrix is decomposed into N buckets, with each bucket training on the edges individually. PBG then performs distributed execution across multiple machines or swaps embedding from each partition to disk to reduce memory use.

MILE [18], or Multi-Level Embedding, is a graph embedding framework that can scale to large graphs. It uses a hybrid matching technique to repeatedly coarsen the graph into smaller ones while maintaining its structure. It then uses known embedding methods on the coarsest graph and uses a graph convolution neural network to refine the embedding to the original graph. It is independent of the underlying graph embedding techniques and may be applied to a wide range of existing graph embedding methods without requiring them to be modified. It has been demonstrated that, MILE dramatically improves graph embedding time (by an order of magnitude).

Accurate, Efficient and Scalable Graph Embedding [19] relies on the GCN [20] model and its variants are strong graph embedding tools for enabling graph classification and clustering. A unique graph sampling based GCN parallelization strategy that achieves excellent scalable performance on very large graphs without sacrificing accuracy. To scale, it uses parallelism within and across many sampling instances for the graph sampling step and devises an efficient data structure for concurrent accesses. Data partitioning improves cache utilization within the sampled graph. On several large datasets, its parallel graph embedding exceeds state-of-the-art approaches in terms of scalability, efficiency, and accuracy.

PartKG2Vec, presented in this paper, is a parallel processing of partitioned knowledge graph to generate the random walk for the embedding. PartKG2Vec is a graph embedding system capable of handling big graphs. A parallelization approach, that achieves good scalability on very large graphs while maintaining accuracy. PartKG2Vec can be used with any random walk generator algorithm with minor adjustments.

The nodes in the knowledge graph are partitioned into the sub-graphs using METIS [11]. First, random walks of the subgraphs in a partitioned graph generate partial random walks. These partial walks are then combined to form complete walks. This way, the likelihood of preserving network neighborhoods of nodes in a d-dimensional feature space is maximized. The random walks are performed independently, starting with the initial nodes within each partition. Some of these walks will be incomplete (shorter than a desired length), as they reach a partition boundary. These walks are then completed with fragments of random walks in the neighboring partitions. A full set of complete walks is then used for representational learning to generate knowledge graph embedding.

PBG and PartKG2Vec use partitioning to support Knowledge Graph which is too large for a single machine and helps in distributed training of the model. PBG creates buckets from the cross edges (p_i, p_j), These buckets are loaded and subdivided among the CPU threads for training. PartKG2Vec is different, as we create the metadata of cut edges for each partition and complete or partial random walks are generated separately in each partition. Before the representation learning, the partial random walks are completed by concatenation with other walk fragments (from neighboring partitions). MILES repeatedly coarsening the graph into smaller graph, where multiple nodes in graph are collapsed to form super nodes and edges between them are the union of edges. Whereas in PartKG2Vec, we partition the knowledge graph to reduce the size of graph while maintaining the structure.

3   Partitioned Knowledge Graph Embedding

Our method, PartKG2Vec, (1) partitions a knowledge graph into k partitions, (2) distributes the resulting shards to k computing nodes, (3) in each shard, *complete* and/or *partial random walks* are created; a walk is partial, if a cut edge on a walk is encountered, before a desired walk length is reached, (4) a complete set of random walks is obtained from already existing complete walks in individual shards and by concatenating partial walks with sub-walks in neighboring partitions; a sub-walk is a fragment of a walk beginning with the target node in a cut edge terminating the corresponding partial walk, and (5) using the complete walks for graph embedding. Further downstream, graph embedding can be used to solve other problems, including link prediction, node classification, and many other tasks.

Knowledge graphs used in the method presented in this paper are represented as RDF datasets. However, others graph representations can be easily adapted and used in PartKG2Vec. This method has a time complexity bounded by O(|V | log |V |).

3.1   Graph Indexing and Partitioning and Segregator

To speed up the process of learning embedding for the knowledge graph, we created indices, using Apache Lucene [22], on all triples in the knowledge graph, based on their subjects, predicates, and objects. Using these indexes, the graphs triples of the form (S, P, O) can be efficiently searched, similarly as we have done in our prior works WawPart [27] and in AWAPart [28]. This indexing helps the system to convert the knowledge graph into a representation suitable for graph partitioning, as the URIs used in triples are also converted to numeric identifiers. This new graph representation is then partitioned into several sub-graphs using METIS [11]. We have experimented with other ways to partition the knowledge graph, including bisection methods, community detection methods, and others, but found METIS to produce the best partitions with a low number of cut edges in acceptable runtime.

The partitioning outputs the node list and their partition identifiers. Our system compares this list with the complete graph to produce the list of cut edges. Consequently, along with its edges, each partition stores information about the cut edges. The cut edges are replicated across the shards which share the cut edges. That is, a cut edge {u, v} is stored with both partitions, to which the nodes u and v belong.

3.2   Random Walk Generation

The created knowledge graph partitions (sub-graphs) are stored as shards at computing nodes for the processing and random walk generation. Figure 1(a) shows an example of two partitions *P1* and *P2* with vertices {a, b, c, d, u, v} and {m, n, o, p, q, v, u}, respectively. The partitions are connected with a cut edge {u, v}. A modified node2vec algorithm attempts to generate random walks of *walk_length* length, within each partition. However, if a walk in partition P1 encounters a cut edge {u, v} transitioning to partition P2, the random walk is terminated and recorded it as a *partial_walk*. The node

v is recorded as the *exit node* of P1 and an *entry node* of P2. Figure 1(b) shows a partial random walk, interrupted because it attempted to cross to *P2* using the cut edge $\{u, v\}$. Node v is an exit node for partition p1 and an entry node for partition p2. The *exit* and *entry nodes* and the current walk length is stored with the partial walk. This data is later used to complete the partial walk, as described below.

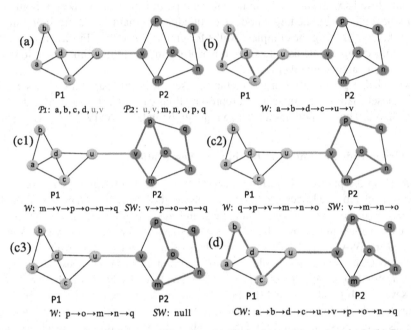

Fig. 1. Completion of walk from partial walks. (a) Nodes in partition p1 and p2. (b) Random walk on partition p1 is interrupted because of the exit node $\{v\}$. (c) Random walks W and sub walks SW passing through the entry node $\{v\}$ on p2. (d) Formation of a complete walk CW from a partial walk in P1 and a sub-walk in P2.

A random walk in a partition may traverse a node v which is also a node in a cut edge. However, even though the node is in a cut edge, the walk does not terminate at v (as a partial walk) and continues within the same partition. A *sub-walk* is a sub-sequence of nodes in a random walk, beginning at a node v of a cut edge, but not crossing to the other partition. The modified node2vec algorithm also records and indexes all *sub-walks* within each partition. Figures 1(c1) and 1(c2) show random walks and sub-walks in P2. In Fig. 1(c3), a sub-walk does not exist, because the walk in the figure does not traverse node v, which is in the cut edge.

3.3   Accumulator and Graph Embeddings

The Random Walk Accumulator collects all the partial and complete random walks collected within all partitions. Complete walks do not need any further work, as they already have the desired walk length. However, any partial walks must be extended to the required walk length. For each partial walk, a sub-walk with the same starting node as the partial walk's exit node is randomly selected and concatenated to the partial walk to make a complete random walk. As shown in Fig. 1(d), a complete random walk *a, b, d, c, u, v, p, o, n, q* is created using the sub-walk from Fig. 1(c1) and the partial walk from Fig. 1(b). Once the full set of complete random walks is created, it can be used by the representation learning module.

PartKG2Vec pipeline	
Input	Knowledge Graph **KG**
1:	Indexing the Knowledge graph $\mathbf{KG_{index}}$
2:	Numerical Representation of **KG** into $\mathbf{KG_N}$
3:	Partitioning $\mathbf{KG_N}$ into k parts using Metis
4:	Segregate the Graph $\mathbf{KG_N}$ into P_1 to P_k
5:	Distributes P_1 to P_k for partial random walk generation $\mathbf{PRW_{P1\dots Pk}}$
6:	Aggregates all partial walk $\mathbf{PRW_{P1\dots Pk}}$ into complete walk **CRW**
7:	Learn Embedding $\mathbf{EMB_N}$ on CRW
8:	Search in graph index $\mathbf{KG_{index}}$ to construct embedding, $\mathbf{EMB_N}$ into $\mathbf{EMB_{KG}}$.
Output	Output $\mathbf{EMB_{KG}}$

Fig. 2. PartKG2Vec pipeline

4   Implementation

Figure 2 shows the processing pipeline used in PartKG2Vec, while Fig. 3 shows the architecture of the system. A knowledge graph is given as input and its embedding is produced as the output. KG2Index Converter indexes the knowledge graph using Lucene [22] and converts it to a format suitable for partitioning. The graph is partitioned using METIS [11] into *k* partitions by the Partition Engine. The partition data (the edge lists) are sent to the Graph Partition Segregator, which creates the final partitions and identifies cut edges to be included with each partition.

The *k* partitioned sub-graphs (shards) are then sent to the *k* processing nodes to produce random walks. All partial (PRW) and complete walks (CRW) are transferred from the processing nodes to the master node. The master-node runs an Accumulator, which gathers all the walks (partial/sub-walks and complete walks) and other critical information. Already complete walks are simply retained, but the Accumulator uses partial walks and matching sub-walks to create complete walks (of the desired length). At the end of accumulation process, a corpus of complete random walks is finalized. This set of random walks is then used for representation learning. Finally, the Lucene index is applied to restore the original node identifiers (URIs) in the knowledge graph embedding.

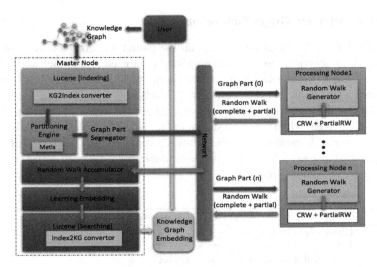

Fig. 3. PartKG2Vec architecture

5   Evaluation

Two popular datasets, Yago39K [23] and NELL [24], were used for the evaluation of PartKG2Vec. Yago39K contains a subset of the Yago knowledge base [25], which includes data extracted from Wikipedia, WordNet and GeoNames. Yago39K contains 123,182 unique entities (nodes) and 1,084,040 edges, using 37 different relation types. NELL is a knowledge graph mined from Web documents and contains 49,869 unique nodes, 296,013 edges, using 827 relation types. The evaluation experiments discussed here were conducted on an Intel i7-based cluster.

Two experiments were used to evaluate the performance of PartKG2Vec. The first experiment was designed to evaluate the runtime of producing the embedding on the complete vs. partitioned graph. The second experiment intended to compare the graph embedding produced by PartKG2Vec (based on the modified node2vec and DeepWalk algorithms) with the embedding produced by the original algorithms on un-partitioned graphs. In the two experiments, both knowledge graphs (Yago39K and NELL) were partitioned into $N = 10$ partitions. We set all walk parameters to their default values, namely the number of walks to 10, walk length to 80, number of workers to 8, and the window size to 10, and the walk parameters of p and q both sets to 1.

5.1   Experiment 1: Runtime Improvement

This experiment demonstrates the improvement in the runtime of the random walk generation on the partitioned graph as compared to the random walks produced on the complete graph by the original algorithms. In Fig. 4, the runtime of node2vec and PartKG2Vec (with modified node2vec) on Yago39K and NELL is shown, while in Fig. 5, the runtime of Deepwalk and PartKG2Vec (with modified Deepwalk) on Yago39K and NELL is shown. Graph preprocessing and the 10 iterations of random walk generation are shown.

Node2vec did not require all the steps before graph preprocessing and accumulation of random walks. All these extra steps were required for PartKG2Vec, but it did not require considerable time. Consequently, we can consider these steps as insignificant. Figure 4 indicates that the time required by PartKG2Vec for graph preprocessing took 32% of the time required by node2vec (695 vs 2175 s). Ten iterations of random walk generation were used in both algorithms, but PartKG2Vec runs in parallel, so it took only 17.75% of the time required by the original node2vec (480 vs. 2702 s) on the complete knowledge graph.

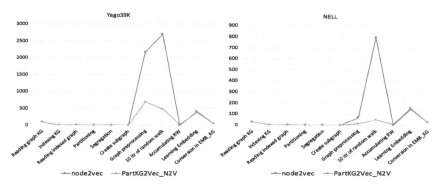

Fig. 4. PartKG2Vec (node2vec) runtime comparison with node2vec on Yago39K and NELL

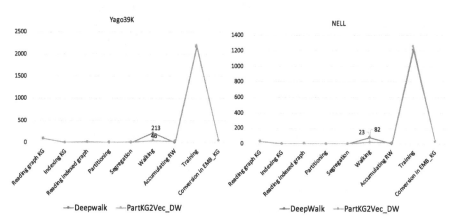

Fig. 5. PartKG2Vec (Deepwalk) runtime compared to Deepwalk on Yago39K and NELL

Similarly, Fig. 4, shows that the time required by PartKG2Vec for graph preprocessing was only 20.5% of the time required by node2vec (13.5 vs. 66 s), on the NELL dataset. Ten iterations of random walk generation were used in both algorithms, but PartKG2Vec_N2V runs in parallel, so it took only 6.5% of time (51 vs. 794 s) of the time taken by node2vec on the complete graph. Learning the graph embedding takes the same time for node2vec and PartKG2Vec, because at this point both algorithms work on the similar random walk pool.

Figure 5, with the results for the YAGO dataset, shows that the time required for the generation of random walks by PartKG2Vec is only 21.6% of the time used by Deepwalk (46 vs. 213 s), and for NELL dataset, the time required for the random walk generation by PartKG2Vec is only 28% of the time used by Deepwalk (23 vs. 82 s).

5.2 Experiment 2: Embedding Quality

This experiment demonstrates the embedding quality based on the random walks generated by PartKG2Vec vs. node2vec and Deepwalk. Again, the experiment used the same two knowledge graphs (NELL and Yago39K) and produce their embeddings by PartKG2Vec vs. node2vec and Deepwalk, with varied dimensions $d \in \{128, 64, 32, 16\}$. The algorithms were executed 25 times, for each dimension. To compare the produced embeddings, the average divergence scores [26] $S_{A,d}$ were computed. Broadly speaking, a divergence score is the result of comparing a graph with the edges re-created from an embedding produced for a graph and the original graph. When comparing embeddings, a lower divergence score indicates a better embedding and, conversely, a higher divergence score means that a given embedding is not as good.

Figure 6 shows divergence scores of the embeddings of the Yago39K dataset produced by node2vec and PartKG2Vec_N2V (modified node2vec) and embeddings produced by Deepwalk and PartKG2Vec_DW (a PartKG2Vec implementation on Deepwalk). The embeddings have very similar divergence scores at every dimension. Incidentally, node2vec (and PartKG2Vec_N2V) produce better embeddings than those produced by Deepwalk and PartKG2Vec_DW. Comparing the embeddings produced for the NELL dataset leads to similar conclusions, as the divergence scores for node2vec and PartKG2Vec_N2V and for Deepwalk and PartKG2Vec_DW are very similar.

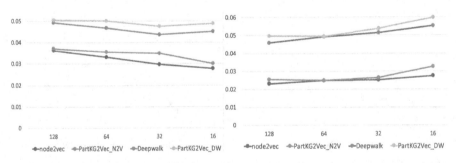

Fig. 6. Average divergence scores of embeddings on Yago39K and NELL produced by node2vec and Deepwalk and their corresponding PartKG2Vec_N2V and PartKG2Vec_DW methods.

This demonstrates that the embeddings generated from node2vec on the original graph are very similar to those generated by PartKG2Vec_N2V and the embeddings generated from Deepwalk are similar to those from PartKG2Vec_DW.

6 Conclusions and Future Work

We propose a system, PartKG2Vec, to create embeddings of partitioned knowledge graphs. The method uses modified node2vec and Deepwalk random walk algorithms to take advantage of the partitioning and perform in parallel. Our experiments showed that the embeddings produced on the original knowledge graphs are very similar to those produced by our method on the partitioned graphs. Importantly, PartKG2Vec offers significant performance improvements over the embedding algorithms on the unpartitioned (original) knowledge graphs, which would improve the runtime of embedding very large graphs.

In the future, we intend to study other embedding algorithms utilizing different types of random walks, especially incorporating the semantics in knowledge graphs, such as metapath2vec [29] and RegPattern2Vec [30].

References

1. Radivojac, P., et al.: A large-scale evaluation of computational protein function prediction. Nat. Methods **10**(3), 221–227 (2013)
2. Liben-Nowell, D., Kleinberg, J.: The link-prediction problem for social networks. J. Am. Soc. Inform. Sci. Technol. **58**(7), 1019–1031 (2007)
3. Vazquez, A., Flammini, A., Maritan, A., Vespignani, A.: Global protein function prediction from protein-protein interaction networks. Nat. Biotechnol. **21**(6), 697–700 (2003)
4. Backstrom, L., Leskovec, J.: Supervised random walks: predicting and recommending links in social networks. In: Proceedings of the Fourth ACM International Conference on Web Search and Data Mining, pp. 635–644 (2011)
5. RDF Working Group: Rdf - semantic web standards. https://www.w3.org/RDF/. Accessed 1 July 2021
6. World Wide Web Consortium: Rdfs - semantic web standards. https://www.w3.org/2001/sw/wiki/RDFS. Accessed 1 July 2021
7. Cox, M., Cox, T.: Multidimensional scaling. In: Chen, C., Härdle, W., Unwin, A.: Handbook of Data Visualization. Springer Handbooks Comp.Statistics, pp. 315–347. Springer, Heidelberg (2008). https://doi.org/10.1007/978-3-540-33037-0_14
8. Tenenbaum, J.B., De Silva, V., Langford, J.C.: A global geometric framework for nonlinear dimensionality reduction. Science **290**(5500), 2319–2323 (2000)
9. Belkin, M., Niyogi, P.: Laplacian eigenmaps and spectral techniques for embedding and clustering. In: Nips, vol. 14, no. 14, pp. 585–591 (2001)
10. Myers, S.A., Sharma, A., Gupta, P., Lin, J.: Information network or social network? The structure of the Twitter follow graph. In: Proceedings of the 23rd International Conference on World Wide Web, pp. 493–498 (2014)
11. Karypis, G., Kumar, V.: METIS--unstructured graph partitioning and sparse matrix ordering system, version 2.0 (1995)
12. Mikolov, T., Sutskever, I., Chen, K., Corrado, G.S., Dean, J.: Distributed representations of words and phrases and their compositionality. In: Advances in Neural Information Processing Systems, pp. 3111–3119 (2013)
13. Perozzi, B., Al-Rfou, R., Skiena, S.: DeepWalk: online learning of social representations. In: Proceedings of the 20th ACM SIGKDD International Conference on Knowledge Discovery and Data Mining, pp. 701–710 (2014)

14. Grover, A., Leskovec, J.: node2vec: scalable feature learning for networks. In: Proceedings of the 22nd ACM SIGKDD International Conference on Knowledge Discovery and Data Mining, pp. 855–864 (2016)

15. Tang, J., Qu, M., Wang, M., Zhang, M., Yan, J., Mei, Q.: Line: large-scale information network embedding. In: Proceedings of the 24th International Conference on World Wide Web, pp. 1067–1077 (2015)

16. Chen, H., Perozzi, B., Hu, Y., Skiena, S.: Harp: hierarchical representation learning for networks. In: Proceedings of the AAAI Conference on Artificial Intelligence, vol. 32, no. 1 (2018)

17. Lerer, A., et al.: Pytorch-biggraph: a large scale graph embedding system. In: Proceedings of Machine Learning and Systems, vol. 1, pp. 120–131 (2019)

18. Liang, J., Gurukar, S., Parthasarathy, S.: Mile: a multi-level framework for scalable graph embedding. arXiv preprint arXiv:1802.09612 (2018)

19. Zeng, H., Zhou, H., Srivastava, A., Kannan, R., Prasanna, V.: Accurate, efficient and scalable graph embedding. In: 2019 IEEE International Parallel and Distributed Processing Symposium (IPDPS). IEEE, pp. 462–471 (2019)

20. Kipf, T.N., Welling, M.: Semi-supervised classification with graph convolutional networks. arXiv preprint arXiv:1609.02907 (2016)

21. Sun, Y., Han, J.: Mining heterogeneous information networks: a structural analysis approach. ACM SIGKDD Explor. Newslett. **14**, 20–28 (2013)

22. Białecki, A., Muir, R., Ingersoll, G., Imagination, L.: Apache lucene 4. In: SIGIR 2012 Workshop on Open Source Information Retrieval, p. 17 (2012)

23. Lv, X., Hou, L., Li, J., Liu, Z.: Differentiating concepts and instances for knowledge graph embedding," arXiv preprint arXiv:1811.04588 (2018)

24. Wan, G., Du, B., Pan, S., Haffari, G.: Reinforcement learning based meta-path discovery in large-scale heterogeneous information networks. In: Proceedings of the AAAI Conference on Artificial Intelligence, vol. 34, no. 04, pp. 6094–6101 (2020)

25. Suchanek, F.M., Kasneci, G., Weikum, G.: YAGO: a large ontology from wikipedia and wordnet. J. Web Semant. **6**(3), 203–217 (2008)

26. Dehghan-Kooshkghazi, A., Kamiński, B., Kraiński, Ł., Prałat, P., Théberge, F.: Evaluating Node embeddings of complex networks. arXiv preprint arXiv:2102.08275 (2021)

27. Priyadarshi, A., Kochut, K.J.: WawPart: workload-aware partitioning of knowledge graphs. In: Fujita, H., Selamat, A., Lin, J.CW., Ali, M. (eds.) Advances and Trends in Artificial Intelligence. Artificial Intelligence Practices. IEA/AIE 2021. Lecture Notes in Computer Science, vol. 12798, pp. 383–395. Springer, Cham (2021). https://doi.org/10.1007/978-3-030-79457-6_33

28. Priyadarshi, A., Kochut, K.J.: AWAPart: adaptive workload-aware partitioning knowledge graphs. In: SEMAPRO 2021, The Fifteenth International Conference on Advances in Semantic Processing, Barcelona, Spain. Thinkmind Digital Library, pp. 12–17 (2021)

29. Dong, Y., Chawla, N.V., Swami, A.: metapath2vec: scalable representation learning for heterogeneous networks. In: Proceedings of the 23rd ACM SIGKDD International Conference on Knowledge Discovery and Data Mining, pp. 135–144 (2017)

30. Keshavarzi, A., Kannan, N., Kochut, K.: RegPattern2Vec: link prediction in knowledge graphs. In: 2021 IEEE International IOT, Electronics and Mechatronics Conference (IEMTRONICS). IEEE, pp. 1–7 (2021)

SPBERTQA: A Two-Stage Question Answering System Based on Sentence Transformers for Medical Texts

Nhung Thi-Hong Nguyen[1,2], Phuong Phan-Dieu Ha[1,2],
Luan Thanh Nguyen[1,2(✉)], Kiet Van Nguyen[1,2],
and Ngan Luu-Thuy Nguyen[1,2]

[1] University of Information Technology, Ho Chi Minh City, Vietnam
{18521218,18521268}@gm.uit.edu.vn, {luannt,kietnv,ngannlt}@uit.edu.vn
[2] Vietnam National University, Ho Chi Minh City, Vietnam

Abstract. Question answering (QA) systems have gained explosive attention in recent years. However, QA tasks in Vietnamese do not have many datasets. Significantly, there is mostly no dataset in the medical domain. Therefore, we built a **Vi**etnamese **Health**care **Q**uestion **A**nswering dataset (ViHealthQA), including 10,015 question-answer passage pairs for this task, in which questions from health-interested users were asked on prestigious health websites and answers from highly qualified experts. This paper proposes a two-stage QA system based on Sentence-BERT (SBERT) using multiple negatives ranking (MNR) loss combined with BM25. Then, we conduct diverse experiments with many bag-of-words models to assess our system's performance. With the obtained results, this system achieves better performance than traditional methods.

Keywords: Information retrieval · Sentence transformer · SBERT · Question answering

1 Introduction

Today, many websites have QA forums, where users can post their questions and answer other users' questions. However, they usually take time to wait for responses. Moreover, data for question answering has become enormous, which means new questions inevitably have duplicate meanings from the questions in the database. In order to reduce latency and effort, QA systems based on information retrieval (IR) retrieving a good answer from the answer collection is essential. QA relies on open domain datasets such as texts on the web or closed domain datasets such as collections of medical papers like PubMed [8] to find relevant passages. Moreover, in the COVID-19 pandemic, people care more about their health, and the number of questions posted on health forums has increased rapidly. Therefore, QA in the medical domain plays an important role. Lexical gaps between queries and relevant documents that occur when

© The Author(s), under exclusive license to Springer Nature Switzerland AG 2022
G. Memmi et al. (Eds.): KSEM 2022, LNAI 13369, pp. 371–382, 2022.
https://doi.org/10.1007/978-3-031-10986-7_30

both use different words to describe similar contents have been a significant issue. Table 1 shows a typical example of this issue in our dataset. Previous studies applied word embeddings to estimate semantic similarity between texts to solve [26]. Various research studies approached deep neural networks and BERT to extract semantically meaningful texts [11]. Primarily, SBERT has recently achieved state-of-the-art performance on several tasks, including retrieval tasks [7]. This paper focuses on exploring fine-tuned SBERT models with MNR.

We contribute: (1) Introduce a ViHealthQA dataset containing 10,015 pairs in the medical domain. (2) Propose two-stage QA system based on SBERT with MNR loss. (3) Perform multiple experiments, including traditional models such as BM25, TF-IDF cosine similarity, and Language Model to compare our system.

Table 1. A typical example of Lexical gaps in ViHealthQA dataset.

ID	392
Question	Tôi bị dị ứng thuốc kháng sinh và dị ứng khi ăn thịt cua đồng. Trường hợp của tôi có được tiêm vaccine phòng Covid-19 không? (*I am allergic to antibiotics and eating crab meat. Can my case be vaccinated against Covid-19?*)
Answer passage	Trường hợp của anh theo hướng dẫn của Bộ Y tế là thuộc đối tượng cần cẩn trọng khi tiêm vaccine Covid-19 và tiêm tại bệnh viện hoặc cơ sở y tế có đầy đủ năng lực cấp cứu ban đầu. (*According to the guidance of the Ministry of Health, your case is one of the subjects that need to be careful when injecting the Covid-19 vaccine and injecting it at a hospital or medical facility with total initial first aid capacity.*)

2   Related Work

In early-stage works of QA retrieval, several studies [3] presented sparse vector models. Using unigram word counts, these models map queries and documents to vectors having many 0 values and rank the similarity values to extract potential documents. In 2008, Manning et al. [14] did many experiments to gain a deeper understanding of the role of vectors, including how to compare queries with documents. Moreover, many researchers [4,19] pay attention to BM25 methods in IR tasks.

IR methods with sparse vectors have a significant drawback: lexical gap challenges. The solution to this problem is using dense embedding to represent queries and documents. This idea was proposed early with the LSI approach [2]. However, the most well-known model is BERT. BERT applied encoders to compute embeddings for the queries and the documents. Liu et al. [13] installed the final mean pooling layer and then calculated similarity values between outputs. Instead, Karpukhin et al. [9] used the initial CLS token. Many studies [10,12] applied BERT and reached significant results. Significantly, SBERT [18] uses Siamese and triplet network structures to represent semantically meaning-ful sentence embeddings. Multiple research approaches have approached SBERT for Semantic Textual Similarity (STS) and Natural Language Inference (NLI) benchmarks. In 2021, Ha et al. [5] utilized SBERT to find similar questions in community question answering. They did several experiments on SBERT with multiple losses, including MNR loss.

Because of our task in the medical domain, we reviewed some related corpus. For example, CliCR [22] comprises around 100,000 gap-filling queries based on clinical case reports, and MedQA [28] includes answers for real-world multiple-choice questions. In Vietnam, Nguyen et al. 2021 [24] published ViNewsQA, including 22,057 human-generated question-answer pairs. This dataset supports machine reading comprehension tasks.

3   Task Description

There are n question-answer passage pairs in the database. We have a col-lection of questions $Q = \{q_1, q_2, ..., q_n\}$ and a collection of answer passages $A = \{a_1, a_2, ..., a_n\}$. Our task is creating models with question i (q_i) belongs to collection Q $(q_i \in Q)$ can retrieve precise answer passage a_i $(a_i \in A)$.

4   Dataset

4.1   Dataset Characteristics

We release ViHealthQA, a novel Vietnamese dataset for question answering and information retrieval, including 10,015 question-answer passage pairs. We col-lect data from Vinmec[1] and VnExpress[2] websites by using the BeautifulSoup[3] library. These ones are forums where users ask health-related questions answered by qualified doctors. The dataset consists of 4 features: index, question, answer passage, and link.

4.2   Overall Statistics

After the collecting data phase, we divide our dataset into train, dev, and test sets. In particular, there are 7,009 pairs in Train, 993 pairs in Dev, and 2,013 pairs in Test (Table 2).

According to Table 3, most of the answer passages are in the range of 101–300 words (34.1%), the second ratio is the number of answer passages with 301–500 words (31.13%), followed by 501–700 words (15.88%), and 701–1000 words (9.98%). Longer answer passages (over 1000 words) comprise a small proportion (above 7.58%).

---

[1] https://www.vinmec.com/.
[2] https://vnexpress.net/.
[3] https://pypi.org/project/beautifulsoup4/.

Table 2. Statistics of ViHealthQA dataset.

ViHealthQA	Value
Train	7,009
Dev	993
Test	2,013
Average length answer	495.33
Average length question	103.87
Vocabulary (word)	18,271
Average number of sentences	3.95

Table 3. Distribution of the answer passage length (%).

Length	Answer passage			
	Train	Val.	Test	All
<100	1.24	1.31	1.64	1.33
101–300	34.46	34.34	32.89	34.1
301–500	31.13	30.72	31.25	31.13
501–700	15.99	16.31	15.2	15.88
701–1000	9.8	8.66	11.23	9.98
>1000	7.38	8.66	7.8	7.58

4.3 Vocabulary-Based Analysis

To understand the medical domain, we use the WordClouds tool[4] to display visual word frequency that appears commonly in the dataset (Fig. 1). Table 4 shows the top 10 words with the most frequency. These words are related to the medical domain. Besides, users ask many questions about Coronavirus (COVID-19), children, inflammatory diseases, and allergies.

Table 4. Top 10 common words in the ViHealthQA dataset.

No.	Word	Freq.	English
1	bác sĩ	7790	doctor
2	bé	3409	baby
3	xét nghiệm	3316	test
4	trẻ	3012	children
5	triệu chứng	2858	symptom
6	dị ứng	2628	allergic
7	mũi	2479	nose
8	da	1979	skin
9	tiêm chủng	1912	vaccination
10	gan	1856	liver

Fig. 1. Word distribution of ViHealthQA.

5   SPBERTQA: A Two-Stage Question Answering System Based on Sentence Transformers

In this paper, we propose a two-stage question answering system called SPBERTQA (Fig. 2), including BM25-based sentence retriever and SBERT using

---

[4] https://www.wordclouds.com/.

PhoBERT fine-tuning with MNR loss. After training, the inputs (the question and the document collection) feed into BM25-SPhoBERT. Then, we rank the top K cosine similarity scores between sentence-embedding outputs to extract top K candidate documents.

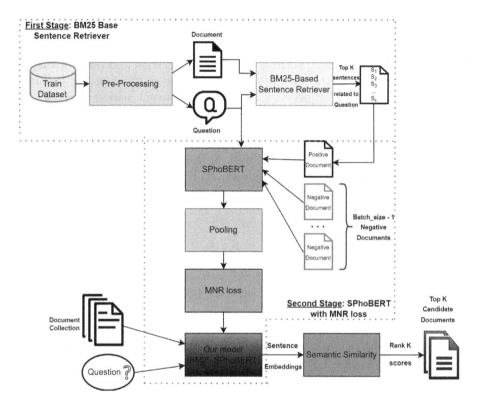

Fig. 2. Overview of our system.

5.1 BM25 Based Sentence Retriever

We aim to train the model by focusing on the meaningful knowledge of our dataset. Thus, we propose the sentence retriever stage that extracts the K sentences in every answer passage the most relevant to the corresponding question. Moreover, this stage helps solve the obstacle of the maximum length sequence of every pre-trained BERT model is 512 tokens (max_seq_length of PhoBERT = 256 tokens), while the number of answer passages over 300 tokens in Train accounts for above 65.47%.

We use BM25 for the first stage because BM25 mostly brings good results in IR systems [20]. Besides, most answer passages have below four sentences (Average number of sentences in every answer passage = 3.95 in Table 2), so we choose $K = 5$.

5.2   SBERT Using PhoBERT and Fine-Tuning with MNR Loss

Multiple Negatives Ranking (MNR) Loss: MNR loss works great for IR, and semantic search [7]. The loss function is given by Equation (1).

$$L = -\frac{1}{N} \cdot \frac{1}{K} \cdot \sum_{i=1}^{K} \left[S(x_i, y_i) - \log \sum_{j=1}^{K} e^{S(x_i, y_j)} \right] \tag{1}$$

In every batch, there are K positive pairs (x_i, y_i: question and positive answer passage), and each positive pair has $K - 1$ random negative answer passages ($y_j, i \neq j$). The similarity between question and answer passage ($S(x, y)$) is cosine similarity. Moreover, N is the Train size.

In the second stage, we use the pre-trained PhoBERT model. PhoBERT [15] is the first public large-scale monolingual language model for Vietnamese. PhoBERT pre-training approach is based on RoBERTa, which optimizes more robust performance. Then, we fine-tune PhoBERT with MNR loss.

6   Experiments

6.1   Comparative Methods

We compare our system with traditional methods such as BM25, TFIDF-Cos, and LM; pre-trained PhoBERT; and fine-tuned SBERT such as BM25-SXMLR and BM25-SmBERT.

BM25. BM25 is an optimized version of TF-IDF. Equation (2) portrays the BM25 score of document D given a query q. d_{avg} is the length of the average document. Moreover, BM25 adds two parameters: k helps balance the value between term frequency and IDF, and b adjusts the importance of document length normalization. In 2008, Manning et al. [14] suggested reasonable values are $k = [1.2, 2.0]$ and $b = 0.75$.

$$BM25(D, q) = \underbrace{\frac{f(q, D) * (k + 1)}{f(t, D) + k * \left(1 - b + b * \frac{D}{d_{avg}}\right)}}_{TF} * \underbrace{\log\left(\frac{N - N(q) + 0.5}{N(q) + 0.5} + 1\right)}_{IDF} \tag{2}$$

TF-IDF Cosine Similarity (TFIDF-Cos). Cosine similarity is one of the most popular similarity measures applied to information retrieval applications and is superior to the other measures such as the Jaccard measure and Euclidean measure [21]. Given a and b as the respective TF-IDF bag-of-words of question and answer passage. The similarity between a and b is calculated by Equation (3) [16].

$$Cos(\boldsymbol{a}, \boldsymbol{b}) = \frac{\boldsymbol{a} \cdot \boldsymbol{b}}{\|\boldsymbol{a}\| \|\boldsymbol{b}\|} = \frac{\sum_1^n a_i b_i}{\sqrt{\sum_1^n a_i^2} \sqrt{\sum_1^n b_i^2}} \tag{3}$$

Language Model (LM). LM is a probabilistic model of text [23]. Questions and answers are modeled based on a probability distribution over sequences of words. The original and basic method for using LM is unigram query likelihood (Equation (4)).

$$P(q_i \mid D) = (1 - \alpha_D) * P(q_i \mid D) + \alpha_D * P(q_i \mid C) \tag{4}$$

$P(q|D)$ is the probability of the query q under the language model derived from D. $P(q|C)$ denotes a background corpus to compute unigram probabilities to avoid 0 scores [27]. Besides, various smoothing based on how to handle α_D and $\alpha_D \in [0, 1]$.

PhoBERT. We directly use PhoBERT to encode question and answer passages. Then, we rank the top K answer passages having the highest cosine similarity scores with the corresponding question.

BM25-SXLMR. Similar to our model, but in the second stage, we use XLM-RoBERTa instead of PhoBERT. XLM-RoBERTa [1] was pre-trained on 2.5TB of filtered CommonCrawl data containing 100 languages (including Vietnamese).

BM25-SmBERT. Similar to our model, but in the second stage, we use BERT multilingual. BERT multilingual was introduced by [17]. This model is a transformers model pre-trained on the enormous Wikipedia corpus with 104 languages (including Vietnamese) using a masked language modeling (MLM) objective.

6.2 Data Preprocessing

We pre-process data such as lowercase, removing uninterpretable characters (e.g., new-line and extra whitespace). In order to tokenize data, we employ the RDRSegmenter of VnCoreNLP [25]. Moreover, stop-words can become noisy factors for traditional methods working well on pairs with high word matching between query and answer. Therefore, we conduct the removing stop-words phase. Firstly, we use TF-IDF to extract stop-words, and then we remove these words from the data.

6.3 Experimental Settings

We choose *xlm-roberta-base*[5], *bert-base-multilingual-cased*[6], and *vinai/phobert-base*[7]. Then, we fine-tune SBERT with 15 epochs, batch size of 32, learning rate

---

[5] https://huggingface.co/xlm-roberta-base.
[6] https://huggingface.co/bert-base-multilingual-cased.
[7] https://huggingface.co/vinai/phobert-base.

of $2e^{-5}$, and maximum length of 256. Our experiments are performed on a single NVIDIA Tesla P100 GPU on the Google Collaboratory server[8].

6.4   Evaluation Metric

$P@K$ (Equation (5)) is the percentage of questions for which the exact answer passage appears in one of the K retrieved passages [24].

$$P@K = \frac{1}{|Q|} \sum_{1}^{n} \begin{cases} 1 & a_q \in A_K(q) \\ 0 & Otherwise \end{cases} \tag{5}$$

where, $Q = q_1, q_2, ..., q_n$: collection of questions and $q \in Q$. $A = a_1, a_2, ..., a_n$: collection of answer passages. a_q is exact answer-passage of question q. $A_K(q) \subseteq A$ is the K most relevant passages extracted for question q.

Besides, mean average precision (mAP) is used to evaluate the performance of models.

7   Experiments

7.1   Results and Discussion

With the results shown in Tables 5 and 6, our system achieves the best performance with 62.25% mAP score, 50,92% $P@1$ score, and 83.76% $P@10$ score on the Test. BM25-SXLMR and BM25-SmBERT utilizing multilingual BERT do not work better than our system using monolingual PhoBERT. Compared to the PhoBERT model without fine-tuning with MNR loss, models fine-tuned with MNR (BM25-SXLMR, BM25-SmBERT, and our system) have good results, which proves that using MNR loss to fine-tune models for this task is suitable.

Table 5. Results on Dev and Test with $P@K$ score (%).

Model	$P@1$		$P@10$	
	Dev	Test	Dev	Test
BM25	51.86	44.96	75.93	70.09
LM	52.27	47.19	78.15	72.38
TFIDF-Cos	47.63	39.54	75.13	70.39
PhoBERT	8.36	6.95	31.72	23.10
BM25 - SXLMR	53.58	46.05	85.90	79.04
BM25 - SmBERT	49.85	44.91	81.97	75.71
Our system	**69.52**	**50.92**	**89.12**	**83.76**

Table 6. Results on Dev and Test with mAP score (%).

Model	Dev	Test
BM25	64.62	56.93
LM	56.01	56.00
TFIDF-Cos	57.12	50.31
PhoBERT	16.08	12.45
BM25-SXLMR	59.96	53.85
BM25-SmBERT	60.77	55.52
Our system	**69.52**	**62.25**

---

[8] https://colab.research.google.com/.

7.2   Analysis

To understand deeply about our system is more robust than traditional methods, and traditional methods have disadvantages in lexical gap issues, we run models on pairs having lexical overlap (the number of duplicate words between question and answer passage - X) from 0 to 10. As results are shown in Fig. 3, with $X < 4$, bag-of-words methods cannot extract the precise answer. Especially with $X = 0$, these models mostly do not work. While, with $X = 0$, fine-tuned models have results with an upper 50% $P@1$ score. From $K = 3$, these models have good scores with an upper 80% $P@1$ score. Moreover, we provide typical examples of Dev predicted by BM25, LM, and our system (Table 7). ID 169 has word matching between question and answer passage. The models that can retrieve precise answers are BM25, LM, and our system. In contrast, in ID 776, no words of question appear in the answer passage. Hence, the models must understand the semantic backgrounds instead of capturing high lexical overlap information to retrieve the precise answer. BERT models capture context and meaning better than bag-of-words methods [6]. In particular, SBERT can derive semantically meaningful sentence embeddings [18]. Therefore, our system based on sentence transformers can find the exact answer passage for the question with ID 776.

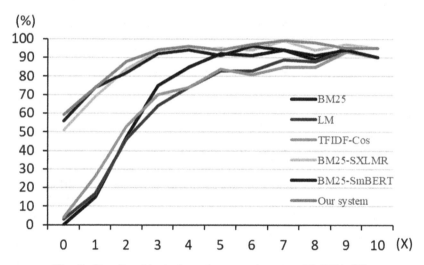

Fig. 3. Results of lexical overlap experiments with P@1 (%).

Table 7. Examples in Dev predicted by traditional methods and our system.

ID	Question	Answer passage	Models
776	Tai biến, chân tay tê bì điều trị như thế nào? (*How is the stroke and tingling in hands and feet treated?*)	Nếu vấn đề chính là rối loạn điện giải, nhiễm trùng huyết và gan thận, bạn nên đưa bố đến khám chuyên khoa Nội tiết hoặc Nội tổng quát. Về thần kinh, bác sĩ khám cần xem lại phim CT/MRI não để đánh giá lại tổn thương não mới có thể có được kế hoạch phòng ngừa đột quy tái phát, điều trị giảm đau thần kinh và phục hồi chức năng tối ưu. (*If the main problem is electrolyte disturbances, sepsis, and hepatobiliary disease, you should take him to see an Endocrinologist or General Internal Medicine. Neurologically, the examining doctor needs to review the brain CT/MRI film to re-evaluate the brain damage so that he can have a plan to prevent recurrent stroke, treat neuropathic pain, and restore optimal function.*)	Our system
169	**Bệnh suy tủy xương vô căn** có nguy hiểm không và **điều trị** thế nào? (*Is **bone marrow failure syndromes** dangerous and how is **treatment**?*)	Suy tủy xương vô căn tùy thuộc vào từng giai đoạn thì cách **điều trị** khác nhau. Nếu số lượng máu quá thấp thì phải điều trị ức chế miễn dịch hoặc ghép tủy. Có những bệnh nhân không đáp ứng với **điều trị**, tuy nhiên cũng có nhiều bệnh nhân chữa khỏi. (***Bone marrow failure syndromes** depends on the stage, the **treatment** is different. If the blood count is too low, then immunosuppressive therapy or bone marrow transplant is required. Some patients do not respond to **treatment**, but many patients are cured.*)	BM25, LM, and our system

8   Conclusion and Future Work

In this paper, we created the ViHealthQA dataset that comprises 10,015 question-answer passage pairs in the medical domain. Every answer passage is a doctor's reply to the corresponding user's question, so the ViHealthQA dataset is suitable for real search engines. Secondly, we propose the SPBERTQA, a two-stage question answering system based on sentence transformers on our dataset. Our proposed system performs best over bag-of-word-based models and fine-tuned multilingual pre-trained language models. This system solves the problem of linguistic gaps.

In future, we plan to employ the machine reading comprehension (MRC) module. This module helps extract answer spans from answer passages so that users can comprehend the meaning of the answer faster.

Acknowledgement. Luan Thanh Nguyen was funded by Vingroup JSC and supported by the Master Scholarship Programme of Vingroup Innovation Foundation (VINIF), Vingroup Big Data Institute (VinBigData), VINIF.2021.ThS.41.

References

1. Conneau, A., et al.: Unsupervised Cross-Lingual Representation Learning at Scale, pp. 8440–8451 (2020)
2. Deerwester, S., Dumais, S.T., Furnas, G.W., Landauer, T.K., Harshman, R.: Indexing by latent semantic analysis. J. Am. Soc. Inf. Sci. **41**(6), 391–407 (1990)
3. Dierk, S.F.: The smart retrieval system: experiments in automatic document processing - Gerard Salton, ed. (Englewood Cliffs, NJ.: Prentice-Hall, 1971, 556 pp., $15.00). IEEE Trans. Profess. Commun. **PC-15**(1), 17 (1972)
4. Géry, M., Largeron, C.: Bm25t: a bm25 extension for focused information retrieval. Knowl. Inf. Syst. **32**, 1–25 (2011)
5. Ha, T.-T., Nguyen, V.-N., Nguyen, K.-H., Nguyen, K.-A., Than, Q.-K.: Utilizing Sbert for finding similar questions in community question answering. In: 2021 13th International Conference on Knowledge and Systems Engineering (KSE), pp. 1–6 (2021)
6. Han, S., Wang, X., Bendersky, M., Najork, M.: Learning-to-rank with bert in TF-ranking. arXiv preprint arXiv:2004.08476 (2020)
7. Henderson, M., et al.: Efficient natural language response suggestion for smart reply. arXiv preprint arXiv:1705.00652 (2017)
8. Jin, Q., Dhingra, B., Liu, Z., Cohen, W.W., Lu, X.: A dataset for biomedical research question answering. In: EMNLP, Pubmedqa (2019)
9. Karpukhin, V., et al.: Dense passage retrieval for open-domain question answering. arXiv preprint arXiv:2004.04906 (2020)
10. Laskar, Md.T. Rahman, Huang, J.X., Hoque, E.: Contextualized embeddings based transformer encoder for sentence similarity modeling in answer selection task. In: Proceedings of the 12th Language Resources and Evaluation Conference, Marseille, May 2020, pp. 5505–5514. European Language Resources Association (2020)
11. Rahman, Md.T., Laskar, X.H., Hoque, E.: Contextualized embeddings based transformer encoder for sentence similarity modeling in answer selection task. In: Proceedings of the 12th Language Resources and Evaluation Conference, pp. 5505–5514 (2020)
12. Lee, K., Chang, M.-W., Toutanova, K.: Latent retrieval for weakly supervised open domain question answering, pp. 6086–6096 (2019)
13. Liu, C.-W., Lowe, R., Serban, I., Noseworthy, M., Charlin, L., Pineau, J.: How NOT to evaluate your dialogue system: an empirical study of unsupervised evaluation metrics for dialogue response generation. In: Proceedings of the 2016 Conference on Empirical Methods in Natural Language Processing, Austin, Texas, November 2016, pp. 2122–2132. Association for Computational Linguistics (2016)
14. Manning, C., Raghavan, P., Schütze, H.: An Introduction to Information Retrieval DRAFT, vol. 1 (2008)
15. Nguyen, D.Q., Nguyen, A.T.: PhoBERT: pre-trained language models for Vietnamese. In: Findings of the Association for Computational Linguistics: EMNLP 2020, November 2020, pp. 1037–1042. Association for Computational Linguistics (2020)
16. Pathak, B., Lal, N.: Information retrieval from heterogeneous data sets using moderated IDF-cosine similarity in vector space model. In: 2017 International Conference on Energy, Communication, Data Analytics and Soft Computing (ICECDS), pp. 3793–379 (2017)
17. Pires, T., Schlinger, E., Garrette, D.: How multilingual is multilingual bert? arXiv preprint arXiv:1906.01502 (2019)

18. Reimers, N., Gurevych, I.: Sentence-bert: sentence embeddings using Siamese bert-networks, pp. 3973–3983 (2019)
19. Robertson, S., Zaragoza, H., Taylor, M.: Simple bm25 extension to multiple weighted fields, pp. 42–49 (2004)
20. Robertson, S., Zaragoza, H., Taylor, M.: Simple bm25 extension to multiple weighted fields. In: Proceedings of the Thirteenth ACM International Conference on Information and Knowledge Management, pp. 42–49 (2004)
21. Subhashini, R., Jawahar Senthil Kumar, V.: Evaluating the performance of similarity measures used in document clustering and information retrieval. In: 2010 First International Conference on Integrated Intelligent Computing, pp. 27–31 (2010)
22. Šuster, S., Daelemans, W.: CliCR: a dataset of clinical case reports for machine reading comprehension. In: Proceedings of the 2018 Conference of the North American Chapter of the Association for Computational Linguistics: Human Language Technologies, vol. 1 (Long Papers), New Orleans, Louisiana, June 2018, pp. 1551–1563. Association for Computational Linguistics (2018)
23. Tan, B., Shen, X., Zhai, C.: Mining long-term search history to improve search accuracy. In: Proceedings of the 12th ACM SIGKDD International Conference on Knowledge Discovery and Data Mining (KDD 2006), New York, pp. 718–723. Association for Computing Machinery (2006)
24. Van Nguyen, K., Van Huynh, T., Nguyen, D.-V., Nguyen, A.G.-T., Nguyen, N.L.-T.: New Vietnamese corpus for machine reading comprehension of health news articles. arXiv preprint arXiv:2006.11138 (2020)
25. Vu, T., Nguyen, D.Q., Nguyen, D.Q., Dras, M., Johnson, M.: VnCoreNLP: a Vietnamese natural language processing toolkit. In: Proceedings of the 2018 Conference of the North American Chapter of the Association for Computational Linguistics: Demonstrations, New Orleans, Louisiana, June 2018, pp. 56–60. Association for Computational Linguistics (2018)
26. Ye, X., Shen, H., Ma, X., Bunescu, R., Liu, C.: From word embeddings to document similarities for improved information retrieval in software engineering. In: 2016 IEEE/ACM 38th International Conference on Software Engineering (ICSE), pp. 404–415 (2016)
27. Zhai, C., Lafferty, J.: A study of smoothing methods for language models applied to information retrieval. ACM Trans. Inf. Syst. $22(2)$, 179–214 (2004)
28. Zhang, X., Wu, J., He, Z., Liu, X., Su, Y.: Medical exam question answering with large-scale reading comprehension. In: Proceedings of the Thirty-Second AAAI Conference on Artificial Intelligence and Thirtieth Innovative Applications of Artificial Intelligence Conference and Eighth AAAI Symposium on Educational Advances in Artificial Intelligence, AAAI'18/IAAI'18/EAAI'18. AAAI Press (2018)

Tree Edit Distance Based Ontology Merging Evaluation Framework

Zied Bouraoui, Sébastien Konieczny, Thanh Ma[✉], and Ivan Varzinczak

CRIL, Artois University & CNRS, Lens, France
{bouraoui,konieczny,ma,varzinczak}@cril.fr

Abstract. Merging structured knowledge has been widely investigated to build common resources in recent years. Indeed, many merging operators have been proposed and developed. However, the majority of them lack comparison and evaluation. Finding ontology sources for evaluation is not an effortless task. To this end, we propose a framework for evaluating the quality of ontology merging operators. The primary strategy starts with an original ontology as a gold standard to create noisy ontologies as datasets and use them to evaluate the merging operators. We generate the noisy ontologies using some perturbations of the tree structure of the original ontology based on tree edit operations. Then, we use tree edit distance to measure the existing merging operators with these noisy sources. We provide the details to assess the merging operators' efficiency in the computation time and their ability to cover (or be close to) the original ontology.

Keywords: Evaluation · Noisy ontology · Belief merging · Tree edit distance

1 Introduction

Structured knowledge relating to concepts and properties is widely employed in a variety of domains, including natural language processing (NLP) [17], information retrieval (IR) [9], and semantic web [12]. They are generally encoded beneath the backbone of tree structures or knowledge graphs (i.e., a hierarchy of ontology). The main difference is that knowledge graphs are less expressive than ontologies [13]. As such, it might be considered as a simplified variant of ontologies[1].

In the context of ontologies (structured knowledge), researchers and practitioners have to contend with the difficulties of various fresh information emerging from multiple sources. Since these knowledge sources are given by different agents (i.e., ontologies), merging many diverse sources might result in inconsistencies and conflicts. From this point, ontology merging has been widely studied in the last years aimed at obtaining the common consistent source. Ontology merging and alignment have attracted much attention in the literature [3,8,20]. Ontology merging aims to combine two (or more) ontologies having *the same terminology* when handling conflict. In contrast, ontology alignment (or matching) is the process of determining correspondences between terminologies of ontologies. Otherwise, the problem of ontology (or DL) merging is close to the problem of belief merging in a propositional setting [2,21] and several concrete

---

[1] In this paper, we use ontologies to refer to knowledge graphs.

© The Author(s), under exclusive license to Springer Nature Switzerland AG 2022
G. Memmi et al. (Eds.): KSEM 2022, LNAI 13369, pp. 383–395, 2022.
https://doi.org/10.1007/978-3-031-10986-7_31

merging operators have been proposed [14,15]. For instance, Benferhat et al. [3] studied merging assertional bases in *DL-Lite* fragment. They have determined the minimal subsets of assertions to resolve conflicts based on the inconsistency minimization principle. Wang et al. [21] provided an ontology merging operator. Their operators based on a new semantic characterisation. Namely, the minimality of changes is realised via a model (semantic) distance.

In general, numerous merging operators have been proposed and developed in the last years. The postulates are actually used to evaluate the behaviours of operators. However, to the best of our knowledge, there is no evaluation framework to assess and compare the quality of different merging operators. For evaluating operators, this work is motivated by two primary reasons: (1) *evaluating the merging models for inputs from multiple fields (open-domain) is a difficult challenge.* Namely, even-though the open-domain concept names are same, their meanings differ. i.e., *Rock is-a Stone* while *Rock is-a Music* (in the music domain). Naturally, when merging these sources, there will be no meaningful relationship between *Stone* and *Music*. (2) *Another challenge is to evaluate the merging models that require the same terminologies (signatures).* In fact, ontologies are naturally constructed based on the differing views of their builder. Therefore, even if they are the same field, the concept names are also different. i.e., *Vacation* and *Holiday*. At these points, *finding ontology sources for the model evaluation is not an effortless task.* To solve them, noisy sources generated from an initial source are a potential solution for measuring the efficacy of ontology merging operators. In this perspective, we take inspiration Tree Edit Distance (TED)[2] [18,22,23] to create noise trees and measure a distance between these attributed trees (or graphs). Here, the distance has defined as the minimum amount of edit operations *(deletion, insertion, and substitution of nodes and edges)* needed to transform a tree into another. We generate noisy ontologes (NoiOn(s)) via the edit operation.

Taking account of the foregoing, we propose an ontology merging evaluation framework to assess the quality of the ontology merging operators. The idea is to start with an ontology (gold standard), then build some NoiOn(s) (a merging profile), apply the merging operators to them, and compare the results to the gold standard. Particularly, we build the NoiOn(s) generation with "local" perturbation to make sense because neighboring concepts can be related to each other. Hence, we implement the modification of the substructure with a node's parent, child, and siblings to obtain the NoiOn. To this end, we provide an algorithm. Then, we use the existing merging procedures to obtain the merged ontologies. We compare the merged result and the original one to evaluate the operators. Considering the ability of noise reduction after merging will be a key to assess the operators. Note that the ontology is represented as a tree (graph). The generation of NoiOn(s) and the merging of ontologies are two independent processes.

2   Background

Our approach implements on two foundations: (1) we rely on a lightweight Description Logic (DL) framework to encode terminological Boxes of ontologies, (2) we use edit operations and TED for creating NoiOn(s).

---

[2] http://tree-edit-distance.dbresearch.uni-salzburg.at.

2.1 Description Logics

$\mathcal{EL}$ is a family of lightweight DLs, which underlies the Ontology Web Language profile OWL2-EL, that is considered as one of the main representation formalisms to express terminological knowledge [1].

The main ingredients of DLs are individuals, concepts, and role. More formally, let N_C, N_R, N_I be three pairwise disjoint sets where N_C, N_R, N_I denote a set of atomic concepts, atomic relations (roles), and individuals, respectively. In this paper, we consider $\mathcal{EL}_\perp$ concept expressions [11] which are built according to the grammar: $C ::= \top \mid \perp \mid N_C \mid C \sqcap C \mid \exists r.C$ where $r \in N_R$. Let $C, D \in N_C$, $a, b \in N_I$, and $r \in N_R$. An $\mathcal{EL}$ ontology $\mathcal{O} = \langle \mathcal{T}, \mathcal{A} \rangle$ (a.k.a. knowledge base) comprises two components, the TBox (Terminological Box denoted by $\mathcal{T}$) and ABox (denoted by $\mathcal{A}$). The TBox consists of a set of General Concept Inclusion (GCI) axioms of the form $C \sqsubseteq D$, meaning that C is more specific than D or simply C is subsumed by D, and axioms of the form $C \sqcap D \sqsubseteq \perp$, meaning that C and D are disjoint concepts. The ABox is a finite set of assertions on individual objects of the form $C(a)$ or $r(a, b)$.

The semantics is given in terms of interpretations $\mathcal{I} = (\Delta^{\mathcal{I}}, \cdot^{\mathcal{I}})$, which consist of a non-empty interpretation domain $\Delta^{\mathcal{I}}$ and an interpretation function $\cdot^{\mathcal{I}}$ that maps each individual $a \in N_I$ into an element $a^{\mathcal{I}} \in \Delta^{\mathcal{I}}$, each concept $A \in N_C$ into a subset $A^{\mathcal{I}} \subseteq \Delta^{\mathcal{I}}$, and each role $r \in N_R$ into a subset $r^{\mathcal{I}} \subseteq \Delta^{\mathcal{I}} \times \Delta^{\mathcal{I}}$, each axiom $C \sqsubseteq D$ into $C^{\mathcal{I}} \subseteq D^{\mathcal{I}}$, each $C \sqcap D$ into a subset $C^{\mathcal{I}} \cap D^{\mathcal{I}} \in \Delta^{\mathcal{I}}$, a top concept $\top$ into $\Delta^{\mathcal{I}}$, and the bottom concept $\perp$ into the empty set $\emptyset$. An interpretation $\mathcal{I}$ is said to be a model of (or satisfies) an axiom Φ, denoted by $\mathcal{I} \models \Phi$. For instance, $\mathcal{I} \models C \sqsubseteq D$ if and only if $C^{\mathcal{I}} \subseteq D^{\mathcal{I}}$. Similarly, $\mathcal{I}$ satisfies a concept (resp. role) assertion, denoted by $\mathcal{I} \models C(a)$ (resp. $\mathcal{I} \models r(a, b)$), if $a^{\mathcal{I}} \in C^{\mathcal{I}}$ (resp. $(a^{\mathcal{I}}, b^{\mathcal{I}}) \in r^{\mathcal{I}}$). In this paper, we assume that the input ontologies are provided in a specific normal form, which we apply completion rules (see [1] for more details) for classification. Note that the classification process works before the merging operation such that all axioms are in the normal form. We denote a set of ontologies is a profile. This profile is able to use for ontology merging.

2.2 Edit Operation and Tree Edit Distance

We here provide several formal definitions related to the TED to use in the sequels. A rooted tree, denoted by $\mathcal{T}$, is a connected graph with nodes $V(\mathcal{T})$ and edges $E(\mathcal{T}) \subseteq V(\mathcal{T}) \times V(\mathcal{T})$. The root of $\mathcal{T}$ is denoted by $\Re(\mathcal{T})$. Here, we write $\mathcal{T}$ to represent the set of nodes of $\mathcal{T}$ (replacing $\mathcal{T}$ by $V(\mathcal{T})$). For two nodes $v_1, v_2 \in \mathcal{T}$, a parent of v_1, denoted by $p(v_1)$, is the closest ancestor of A. We denote ϑ as a finite alphabet and $lb_{\mathcal{T}} : \mathcal{T} \to \vartheta$ as a labelling function.

The tree edit distance [18,22,23] between two trees $\mathcal{T}_1$ and $\mathcal{T}_2$ is defined as the minimum cost of edit operations to transform a tree to another. In order to implement edit operations, we denote ϵ as a blank symbol and $\vartheta_\epsilon = \vartheta \cup \{\epsilon\}$ to represent the edit operations. Here, we denote each of the edit operations by **a pair** denoted as $\vartheta_\epsilon \times \vartheta_\epsilon \setminus \{(\epsilon, \epsilon)\}$. We now define edit operations.

Definition 1 (Edit operations). *Let $\mathcal{T}$ be a tree and $v_1, v_2 \in \mathcal{T}$. Edit operations on $\mathcal{T}$ include: Replacing a node labeled v_1 by other node labeled v_2 in $\mathcal{T}$ is denoted by*

$Rep(v_1, v_2, \mathcal{T})$; Deleting a node labeled v_1 in T such that the children of v_1 will be the children of $p(v_1)$ is denoted by $Del(v_1, \epsilon, \mathcal{T})$; Inserting a node labeled v_1 into $\mathcal{T}$ such that v_1 is a child of v_2 is denoted by $Ins(\epsilon, v_1, v_2, \mathcal{T})$.

Now, let us denote a cost function on edit operations by $dist : \vartheta \times \vartheta \setminus \{(\epsilon, \epsilon)\} \to \mathbb{R}^+$. Notice that we simply write $dist(v_1, v_2)$ to represent $dist(lb(v_1), lb_2(v_2))$, where lb_1 and lb_2 are labelling functions on two trees $\mathcal{T}_1$ and $\mathcal{T}_2$. *Normally, the edit operation cost of each operation is 1, i.e., $dist(v_1, v_2) = 1$ or $dist(v_1, \epsilon) = 1$.* However, we may also re-define this cost (see [4] for more details). Notice that we will use the cost of each operation equals to 1 for this whole work. Moreover, an edit mapping is a description of how a sequence of edit operations transforms from $\mathcal{T}_1$ into $\mathcal{T}_2$. Now, we present a mapping between two trees for computing the distance between them. An edit mapping between $\mathcal{T}_1$ and $\mathcal{T}_2$, denoted by $M_{\mathcal{T}_2}^{\mathcal{T}_1}$, is a subset of $\mathcal{T}_1 \times \mathcal{T}_2$ (a.k.a. $M_{\mathcal{T}_2}^{\mathcal{T}_1} \subseteq V(\mathcal{T}_1) \times V(\mathcal{T}_2)$). A pair $(v_1, v_2) \in M_{\mathcal{T}_2}^{\mathcal{T}_1}$ is called a node alignment between $v_1 \in \mathcal{T}_1$ and $v_2 \in \mathcal{T}_2$. The set of all mappings between $\mathcal{T}_1$ and $\mathcal{T}_2$ is denoted by $\mathcal{M}(\mathcal{T}_1, \mathcal{T}_2)$. The cost of computing a mapping between the two trees is defined as:

Definition 2. *Let $\mathcal{T}_1$ and $\mathcal{T}_2$ be two trees, $M_{\mathcal{T}_2}^{\mathcal{T}_1}$ be a mapping between them, and $(v_1, v_2) \in M_{\mathcal{T}_2}^{\mathcal{T}_1}$. The cost of a mapping between $\mathcal{T}_1$ and $\mathcal{T}_2$ is defined as follows:*

$$dist(M_{\mathcal{T}_2}^{\mathcal{T}_1}) = \sum_{(v_1, v_2) \in M_{\mathcal{T}_2}^{\mathcal{T}_1}} dist(v_1, v_2) + \sum_{v_1 \in \mathcal{T}_1} dist(v_1, \epsilon) + \sum_{v_2 \in \mathcal{T}_2} dist(\epsilon, v_2).$$

Intuitively, the cost of mapping is a total of the cost of all edit operations with a mapping $M_{\mathcal{T}_2}^{\mathcal{T}_1}$ to transform $\mathcal{T}_1$ into $\mathcal{T}_2$. Now, we present how to compute the edit tree distance between two trees referring to [19,22] as follows:

Definition 3 (Tree Edit Distance). *Let $\mathcal{T}_1$ and $\mathcal{T}_2$ be two trees. The edit distance between $\mathcal{T}_1$ and $\mathcal{T}_2$ is defined as: $dist(\mathcal{T}_1, \mathcal{T}_2) = \min\{dist(M_{\mathcal{T}_2}^{\mathcal{T}_1}) \mid M_{\mathcal{T}_2}^{\mathcal{T}_1} \in \mathcal{M}(\mathcal{T}_1, \mathcal{T}_2)\}$.*

3   Ontology Merging Evaluation Framework

We propose an evaluation framework to assess the quality of the existing ontology merging operators including generating and merging NoiOn(s). We first establish a profile with many different NoiOn(s) from a single ontology source, then merge them using the merging operator. A noisy ontology builds on the local perturbations. Namely, our framework includes six steps S_i.

S_1 - Given an input ontology, we randomly collect the concepts' number ($rP\%$). These selected concepts are the signatures to build NoiOn(s). S_2 - For each selected concept (from S_1), we filter the local relatives *including Children, Fathers, Siblings*. This process is the collection of concept's nearest neighbors. We focus on the surrounding neighbourhoods of concepts since the close concepts can be interconnected. S_3 - After collecting the concepts and their neighbors, we use the edit operations [23] to create NoiOn(s). Note that we do not generate NoiOn(s) from all nodes that only concentrate on the ($rP\%$) random nodes with their relatives. Here, we call *a local perturbation*. In particular, we re-structure the hierarchy of ontology by two methods: (1) [DI] Delete a node (or a concept) and insert it into an arbitrary position in the ontology hierarchy;

Algorithm 1: Generating Noisy Ontologies

---

input: rP: A Random Percentage of Concepts, n: Number of Noisy Trees, t: Threshold, $\mathcal{O}$: An OriOn
output: $\mathcal{P}$: A Set of Noisy Ontologies

1 **begin**
2     $\mathscr{T} \longleftarrow \mathbb{H}(\mathcal{O}), \mathcal{P} \longleftarrow \emptyset$
3   **while** $|\mathcal{P}| \leq n$ **do**
       //   Randomly collect r% concepts from ontologies
4        $\alpha \longleftarrow \Re_C(\mathcal{O}, rP)$
       //   Collect the neighbourhood concepts of the concepts in α
5        $V \longleftarrow \boxplus_{Neighbours}(\mathcal{O}, \alpha)$
       //   Extract the hierarchical structure of ontology
6        $\mathscr{T}^N \longleftarrow \mathbb{H}(\mathcal{O})$
7   **foreach** $(v_C, v_D) \in V \times V$ **do**
         //   Randomly select one edit operation for a pair
         //   True: use $[DI]$ method, False: use $[Sw]$ method
8   **if** $\Re_M()$ *is True* **then**
9             $\mathscr{T}' \longleftarrow Del(v_C, \epsilon, \mathscr{T}^N)$
10            $\mathscr{T}^N \longleftarrow Ins(\epsilon, v_C, v_D, \mathscr{T}')$
11   **else**
12            $\mathscr{T}^N \longleftarrow Rep(v_C, v_D, \mathscr{T}^N)$
13   **if** $0 < dist(\mathscr{T}^N, \mathscr{T}) \leq t$ *and* $\mathscr{T}^N \notin \mathcal{P}$ **then**
14          $\mathcal{P} \longleftarrow \mathcal{P} \cup \mathscr{T}^N$
15   **return** $\mathcal{P}$

---

(2) $[Sw]$ Swap between two nodes in the ontology hierarchy. S_4 - We here select n-top NoiOn(s) close to the original one (based on the TED) to create a profile for merging. To this end, we compute the distances between an OriOn and NoiOn(s). Moreover, we use a threshold t to detect the close NoiOn(s) and n to limit the number of NoiOn(s). S_5 - We take advantage of the existing ontology merging method for the framework. Noteworthy, if we only merge the NoiOn(s), the merging result can lose some axioms of the OriOn. Hence, we add m input ontologies into the profile to guarantee that the merging outcome cover fully the original one. Then, a profile includes m OriOn(s) and k NoiOn(s) called *a hybrid profile*. S_6 - After the merged result obtains, we compute the distance between the merged result and the OriOn to measure the quality of merging operators. For this work, we evaluate the two above operators ([6] and [7]).

In the sequel, we explicitly present how to collect NoiOn(s) based on the edit operations to create a profile for merging.

4 Building Ontology Profile

To begin, an ontology structure (tree) is denoted by $\mathscr{T}$. Here, the input of this process is an ontology, and the output is a set of NoiOn(s). Before collecting NoiOn(s), we define $\mathscr{T} \overset{\text{def}}{=} \mathbb{H}(\mathcal{O})$, where $\mathcal{O}$ is an ontology and $\mathbb{H}(\mathcal{O}) = \{A \sqsubseteq B \in \mathcal{O} \mid \forall A, B \in N_C\}$ is a function to structure a hierarchical tree. We here take an account of axioms of the form $A \sqsubseteq B$ since one of the most common forms to build the ontology's hierarchy [5,16]. If concepts do not have a father, the "Thing" concept ($\top$) will be assigned as their father.

Collection of Noisy Ontologies. We now provide how to collect NoiOn(s) from an input ontology. The idea is to select some concept pairs and edit them. Formally, we represent how to collect the NoiOn(s) by Algorithm 1.

We call Algorithm 1 as $\mathbb{G}(rP, n, t, \mathcal{O})$. The algorithm works as follows: we randomly collect concepts $(rP\%)$ from OriOn(s) (line 4). e.g., $rP = 5$ and $n = 80$, then we have $5\% \times 80 \; concepts = 4 \; concepts$. We here define $\alpha = \Re_C(\mathcal{O}, rP) \stackrel{\text{def}}{=} \{C \in \sigma \mid \sigma \subseteq N_C, |\sigma| < nr\}$ where $nr = \frac{rP \times |N_C|}{100}$. Next, we collect the relative nodes in α (Children, Father, Sibling) at line 5. Given $A \in \alpha$, the concepts related to A denote as A's neighbors. We define $\boxplus_{Neighbours}(\mathcal{O}, \alpha) = \{g(\mathcal{O}, A) \mid A \in \alpha\}$ where $g = \{NC, NF, FC, NS\}$. Therein, $NC(\mathcal{O}, A) = \{(A, B) \mid B \in \mathcal{O}, B$ is a Child of $A\}$, $NF(\mathcal{O}, A) = \{(B, A) \mid B \in \mathcal{O}, B$ is a Father of $A\}$, $FC(\mathcal{O}, A) = \{(B, A) \mid B \in \mathcal{O}, B$ is a close ancestor of $A\}$, $NS(\mathcal{O}, A) = \{(A, B) \mid B \in \mathcal{O}, B$ is a sibling of $A\}$. From each node pair in $\boxplus_{Neighbours}$, we select randomly one method to modify the ontology, including the Deletion-Insertion operation ($[DI]$) (using $Del(v_C, \epsilon, \mathcal{T}^N)$ and $Ins(\epsilon, v_C, v_D, \mathcal{T}')$ (from line 9 to 10)) and the swap operation ($[Sw]$) (using replacement operation $Rep(v_C, v_D, \mathcal{T}^N)$ (at line 12)). Here, we define $\Re_M()$ is *a binary random function* (return True or False) to select either $[DI]$ or $[Sw]$. We denote $\mathcal{P}$ as a set of NoiOn(s) or a profile. After the NoiOn obtains, we compute the distance between the NoiOn $\mathcal{T}^N$ and the OriOn $\mathcal{T}$ to measure their closeness. A NoiOn is collected into $\mathcal{P}$ ($\mathcal{P} \longleftarrow \mathcal{P} \cup \mathcal{T}^N$) if the distance is less than or equal to a threshold t ($dist(\mathcal{T}^N, \mathcal{T}) \leq t$) at line 13 and 14. We choose the acceptable threshold based on the number of concepts. The goal of threshold is to find a NoiOn close to the original one. Finally, the number of NoiOn(s) depends on the parameter n at line 3 with the condition $|\mathcal{P}| \leq n$. This "*while*" loop works until the number of NoiOn(s) is fully collected. Note that the collection process of NoiOn(s) from line 3 to 14 runs in parallel to improve the computation time. Formally, a set of NoiOn(s) is defined as $\mathcal{P} \stackrel{\text{def}}{=} \mathbb{G}(rP, n, t, \mathcal{O})$. Here, Algorithm 1 runs in a time that is polynomial on the number n of NoiOn(s), given access to an NP oracle in one step (line 3). Indeed, (i) the size of $\mathcal{P}$ depends on threshold t (line 13), (ii), the function $Del, Ins, Rep,$ and $\Re$ are computed in $O(1)$. (iii) the iteration's number from line 7 is in $O(|V \times V|)$. The algorithm complexity is in FP^{NP}.

Collecting a Merging Profile. After collecting the n NoiOn(s), we use the TED to filter the k NoiOn(s) that are closest to the OriOn. To this end, we say $\preceq_\mathcal{P}$ is a pre-order[3] on $\mathcal{P}$ such that $\forall \mathcal{T}_1^N, \mathcal{T}_2^N \in \mathcal{P} : \mathcal{T}_1^N \preceq_\mathcal{P} \mathcal{T}_2^N$ iff $dist(\mathcal{T}_1^N, \mathcal{T}) \leq dist(\mathcal{T}_2^N, \mathcal{T})$ where $\mathcal{T}$ is a hierarchical structure of the OriOn $\mathcal{O}$. Note that, the noisy trees in $\mathcal{P}$ are always distinct since the condition $\mathcal{T}^N \notin \mathcal{P}$ at line 13 (Algorithm 1) is implemented.

Definition 4. *Let $\mathcal{T}$ be an ontology tree and $\preceq_\mathcal{P} = \{\mathcal{T}_1^N, \ldots, \mathcal{T}_n^N\}$ be a pre-ordered set of all noisy ontology trees. The set of "top-k" NoiOn trees close to the OriOn is defined as follows: $\mathcal{P}_{Top}^k \stackrel{\text{def}}{=} \{\mathcal{T}_i^N \in \preceq_\mathcal{P} \mid 1 \leq i \leq k < n\}$.*

Here, $\mathcal{P}_{Top}^k$ is a profile with k NoiOn(s). e.g., a profile with three noisy trees is $\mathcal{P}_{Top}^3$. As explained in S_5, because noisy trees are generated using randomization, in the worst-case scenario, an axiom of the original tree is not existing in all noisy trees. Therefore, it leads to no source stating that constraint. As a result, they may lose some of the axioms in OriOn. This is why we add some original trees to the profile to ensure that the merged result covers the OriOn. Formally, an extended profile is defined as:

---

[3] A preorder is a reflexive and transitive relation.

Definition 5. *Let* $\mathcal{P}^k_{Top}$ *be a set of "k" NoiOn trees and* $\mathcal{T}$ *be an OriOn tree. A "hybrid" profile extended by adding "m" original trees is defined as follows:* $\mathcal{P}^{k,m} \stackrel{\text{def}}{=} \mathcal{P}^k_{Top} \cup \{\mathcal{T}_i = \mathcal{T} \mid 1 \leq i \leq m\}.$

Note that we denote $\mathcal{P}^{k,m} = \{\mathcal{T}_i\}$ corresponding to $\mathcal{P}^{k,m} = \{\mathcal{O}_i\}$, where $\mathcal{T}_i$ are hierarchical structures of $\mathcal{O}_i$. Now we apply the merging methods to the profile created.

5   Ontology Merging Operators

This section provides some existing merging operators designed for the $\mathcal{EL}$ intending to evaluate them. Namely, two merging operators investigate in this paper, including (1) the model-based ontology merging framework of [6] and (2) the ontology merging method via merging the *Qualitative Constraint Network (QCN)* of [7]. Now, a brief description of the merging frameworks is as follows:

For the (1) merging method, this approach implements with DL $\mathcal{EL}$ to encode the knowledge. Regarding this setting, There are no logical contradictions in ontology because *negative (or bottom) notions* do not exist in them. This method crucially focuses on handling the semantic conflicts and objects to model-based merging. Here, we denote $\mathbb{M}_{MBM}$ *as a "model-based merging" function* [6]. Regarding the (2) merging method, Bouraoui et al. has proposed an ontology merging method via merging the QCNs. Their merging procedure focuses on the DL $\mathcal{EL}_\perp$. Their approach allows us to benefit from the expressivity and the flexibility of RCC5 while dealing with conflicting knowledge in a principled way. From this approach, we investigate the subsumption ($A \sqsubseteq B$) and disjoints ($A \sqcap B \sqsubseteq \perp$) for our NoiOn(s) merging work. Formally, we denote $\mathbb{M}_{QM}$ *as a "QCN merging" function* [7].

Let us denote $\mathcal{O}^M$ as the NoiOn merged result (using $\mathbb{M}_{MBM}$ and $\mathbb{M}_{QM}$). Note that the merging profiles are always different since the NoiOn(s) generated are different. Note that, let us denote $dist(\mathcal{O}^M, \mathcal{O})$ as $dist(\mathcal{T}^M, \mathcal{T})$, where $\mathcal{T}^M = \mathbb{H}(\mathcal{O}^M)$. An merged result using the existing merging operators is defined as follows:

Definition 6. *Let* $\mathcal{P}^{k,m}$ *be a "hybrid" profile of NoiOn(s). An ontology merged result is defined as:* $\mathcal{O}^M \stackrel{\text{def}}{=} y(\mathcal{P}^{k,m})$ *where* $y = \{\mathbb{M}_{MBM}, \mathbb{M}_{QM}\}.$

6   Experimental Evaluation

In this section, we describe our implementation and interpret the experimental results.

6.1   Description of Implementation

We implement the framework[4] to assess the operators with 09 practical ontologies[5], including *conference, cmt-2, ekaw, sigkdd, swo, Cree-hydro, pto, human, and mouse*. The information of ontologies is showed in Table 1a. Here, we select these sources since we investigate how the operators reacts as the number of concepts and axioms increases. Recall that the process of merging and generating NoiOn(s) is discrete.

---

[4] https://github.com/ontologymerging/NoisyOntologyMerging.
[5] https://oaei.ontologymatching.org/2021/.

Table 1. Information and quantitative results.

Ontology name	Nbr of concepts	Nbr of *is-a* relations	Nbr of axioms
conference	57	55	397
cmt-2	30	38	318
ekaw	74	85	341
sigkdd	50	49	193
swo	86	144	349
cree-hydro	80	183	6,252
pto	1,541	1,747	16,148
human	3,304	5,423	30,364
mouse	2,744	4,493	11,043

(a) Number of concepts and axioms in ontologies

Ontology name	n	k, m	rP	t	TG	TM	
						$\mathbb{M}_{MBM}$	$\mathbb{M}_{QM}$
conference	400	20,5	15%	40	281.96	77.21	61.47
cmt-2	400	20,5	15%	40	129.86	58.68	42.54
ekaw	300	20,5	15%	40	212.47	91.49	85.27
sigkdd	300	15,3	15%	50	244.39	74.52	59.46
swo	200	15,5	10%	50	301.26	439.67	171.23
cree-hydro	200	15,5	10%	80	255.62	682.26	235.43
pto	100	10,5	3%	150	637.18	3,162.98	1,586.68
human	80	10,5	3%	400	1,765.21	7,158.19	3,758.22
mouse	80	10,5	3%	400	1,177.16	6,024.52	2,981.21

(b) Parameters and the computation time

For generating NoiOn(s), we implement the whole framework on pure python (python 3.8). Moreover, we use an Owlready2 library[6] to extract all information of ontology. We take account of the ontology hierarchy as a tree structure. We here use the python library named "networkx"[7] to optimize the paths (transitive relations) in the tree structure. The transitive axioms will be represented explicitly by this library. Note that the pre-processing step carries out to normalize the OriOn's axioms into the $\mathcal{EL}$ normal form [1] before generating and merging the NoiOn(s). In addition, we use the "zss" python library[8] to compute the distance (i.e., TED) between two trees *(using simple_distance())*. We implement the multi-processing procedure to improve the running time for generating noisy ontologies.

For implementing merging operations, instead of taking account of all axioms into merging process, we filter the set of the same axioms, a.k.a. agreements statements and the set of distinguishable axioms, a.k.a. disagreement statements. Here, the disagreement statements will be taken into the merging procedures. This process reduces the number of axioms and improves the running time. Now, we present how to implement merging frameworks: (1) For the $\mathbb{M}_{MBM}$ approach [6], since the process of generating all possible interpretations is huge; therefore, a timeout variable is implemented to seek out the acceptable result. Otherwise, if the number of disagreement statements is large *(i.e., greater than 80 axioms for the human ontology)*, we cluster the axioms independently in order to collect local sub-trees, which we subsequently merge. A local sub-tree corresponds to a sub-hierarchy within a general ontology structure. If a sub-tree remains enormous (i.e., more than 40 axioms per sub-tree), we split those sub-trees into smaller ones. This step resolves the data enumeration explosion problem. (2) For the $\mathbb{M}_{QN}$ approach [7], along with the subsumption relation, the author investigates the disjoint in this research (i.e., $A \sqcap B \sqsubseteq \bot$). We here use a "PyRCC8" python library[9] to check the consistency of the QCN. As we know, the number of concepts (regions) increases, the enumeration of all possible QCNs will be huge. Therefore, we solve the

---

[6] https://owlready2.readthedocs.io/en/v0.36/.

[7] https://networkx.org/.

[8] https://pythonhosted.org/zss/.

[9] https://pypi.org/project/PyRCC8/.

problem of generating all possible QCNs by the P-MAXSAT [10]. First, we translate the merged QCN into the CNF format using the FCTE encoding. Next, we build a CNF file underlying a DMACS format based on this encoding. Then, we use a MAXSAT solver[10] (using RC2) to enumerate the possible consistent QCNs. After collecting the consistent solutions from the solver, we translate back the CNF models into the QCNs. Leveraging the power of the MAXSAT solver is a suitable selection to improve the processing time in the enumeration process because consistent solutions are always able to be found (with tolerable confidence) that do not need to enumerate all possible cases.

6.2 Quantitative Results

We evaluate the computation time of the two main parts for each dataset, including the time of generating NoiOn(s) denoted as TG and the time of merging them denoted as TM. Therein, we test our proposal with several parameters, including (1) the number of noisy trees generated n, (2) the number of noisy trees selected into a profile k (3) combined with m OriOn(s), (4) the percentage of nodes to generate the NoiOn(s) rP, (5) the threshold t of selecting close NoiOn(s), and (6) finally the merged ontology's number q. These parameters and the computation time are shown in Table 1(b). We investigate our framework on two merging methods, including $\mathbb{M}_{MBM}$ [6], and $\mathbb{M}_{QM}$ [7] (see Sect. 5).

From the result obtained, the merging time of $\mathbb{M}_{QM}$ is faster than $\mathbb{M}_{MBM}$ (see Table 2). A reason is that the effective existing support tools of $\mathbb{M}_{QM}$ improve the computation time. Regarding the large ontology, such as *human* and *mouse*, $\mathbb{M}_{QM}$'s merging time is acceptable and effective in practice with about 50–70 min i.e., 3,758.22 s for *human* ontology. At the same time, $\mathbb{M}_{MBM}$ can spend about two hours for around 100 concepts ($3\% \times 3,304 = 99.12$). i.e., 7158.19 s for human ontology. In general, the merging time of $\mathbb{M}_{MBM}$ increases rapidly in proportion to the number of ontology (subsumption) axioms, while the number of concepts influences the merging time of $\mathbb{M}_{QM}$. Otherwise, regarding TG, the computation time is also suitable in practice with around 20 min for a large ontology (i.e., 1,765.21 for human ontology). Although the number of noisy ontologies collected is high (400 NoiOn(s)), the TG is still around 6–7 min (i.e., it is 377.60 s for the "conference" ontology). The threshold t has a direct impact on TG because NoiOn(s) collected depend on this threshold. Moreover, TG also depends on the number of CPUs since we implement this procedure with multiprocessing.

6.3 Qualitative Results

First of all, we provide a distance measurement table (see Table 2). It includes the distance between the OriOn and the NoiOn(s) (column 3–5) denoted by $[ON]$ and the distance between the OriOn and merged results denoted by $[OM]$ (column 6–7). Here, the TED is a measurable tool of an operator's noise-canceling ability. From these distances, we can compare and evaluate the quality of the operator. Otherwise, we also shows how the merging operators work with noisy ontologies. In general, the $\mathbb{M}_{MBM}$

---

[10] https://pysathq.github.io/.

Table 2. A measurement of the distance (TED) to evaluate merging operators.

Ontology name	Times	Distance ($[ON]$) (OriOn and NoiOn)			Distance ($[OM]$) (OriOn and merged result)	
		Avg	Min	Max	$\mathbb{M}_{MBM}$	$\mathbb{M}_{QM}$
conference	50	12.70	3	27	4.46	5.82
cmt-2	50	11.48	2	25	4.12	5.37
ekaw	50	12.78	2	28	6.78	7.86
sigkdd	50	15.85	3	32	5.83	7.03
swo	40	21.78	6	33	10.18	12.79
cree-hydro	40	33.86	9	67	14.25	16.76
pto	20	43.62	14	107	22.78	25.40
human	20	187.57	62	376	127.68	134.52
mouse	20	143.70	42	307	86.47	91.88

seems to be better than $\mathbb{M}_{QM}$ (*compare between column 6 and 7 in Table* 2). However, both $\mathbb{M}_{MBM}$ and $\mathbb{M}_{QM}$ are effective because the $[OM]$ is always smaller than the average distance of $[ON]$. The TEDs have shown that the merge operator reduces the noise of the sources. Intuitively, the difference in the quality of the two operators is not much since the variance of distance between them is small (i.e., regarding *conference* ontology, 4.46 of $\mathbb{M}_{MBM}$ and 5.82 $\mathbb{M}_{QM}$; the difference is $5.82 - 4.46 = 1.36$). Recall that, the distance of each edit operation is 1, for *human* ontology, we have 127.68 of $\mathbb{M}_{MBM}$ (or 134.52 of $\mathbb{M}_{QM}$) is corresponding to 127.68 (or 134.52) modifications. Hence, if we compare 127.68 modifications with 30, 364 of input axioms, these changes are quite minimal (implying that the merged ontology is close to the OriOn).

In the following example, we provide the input sub-tree and the result of merging to illustrate that the merging outcome fully covers the original one.

Example 1. Let us take account of a *ExtremityPart* sub-tree of the "human" conference in (*i-ii*) of Fig. 1. Several new constraints using the $\mathbb{M}_{MBM}$ are as follows: $Toe \sqsubseteq Foot$, $Forearm \sqsubseteq Arm$, $Finger \sqsubseteq Hand$, $Hand \sqsubseteq Arm$, $Foot \sqsubseteq Leg$, others. In this case, the merging result is plausible and acceptable. Since we add $m = 5$ OriOn(s), the main structure holds.

Example 2. Let us have a sub-hierarchy of "Conference" as (*iii-v*) in Fig. 1. Several new constraints using the $\mathbb{M}_{QM}$ are as follows: $InvSpe \sqsubseteq RegAut$, $ActConPar \sqsubseteq RegAut$, $InvSpe \sqsubseteq ConPar$, $ConCon \sqcap PassConPar \sqsubseteq \perp$, $InvSpe \sqcap PassConPar \sqsubseteq \perp$, $RegAut \sqcap PassConPar \sqsubseteq \perp$ showed in the (b) of (ii) of Fig. 1. There are some disjoints in these cases, including $Con1ThAut \sqcap ConCoAuth \sqsubseteq \perp$, $EarPaiApp \sqcap LatPaiApp \sqsubseteq \perp$, $ActConPar \sqcap PasConPar \sqsubseteq \perp$.

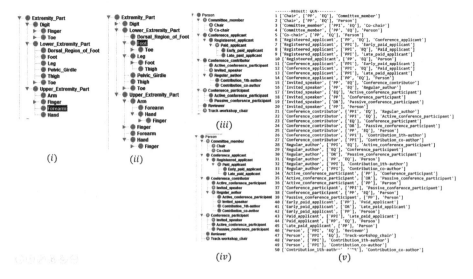

Fig. 1. Results of ontology merging. (i–ii) Structure of $ExtremityPart$ in the "Human" ontology including (i) is an original hierarchy, (ii) is the merged result using $\mathbb{M}_{MBM}$; (iii–iv) Structure of $Person$ in the "Conference" ontology including (iii) is an original hierarchy, (iv) is the merged result using $\mathbb{M}_{QM}$, (v) is the merged QCN result.

7 Conclusion

In this paper, we introduced a framework to assess ontology merging operators. Therein, we also provided an algorithm to create noisy ontologies by modifying the structure of a source. Moreover, this framework evaluates ontology merging models on computation time and distance measurement. Finally, an experimental result using the practical ontologies was provided and discussed. Intuitively, most merged outcomes are acceptable and sensible since they cover the OriOn and are constantly cross-checked against the original one (using TED). Otherwise, generating the NoiOn(s) is separate from the ontology merging process. Therefore, the evaluation of the operators is unaffected by any other external factors. Additionally, using TED to evaluate the quality of operators makes sense because we can quantify their capacity to eliminate noise. In the future, we will enhance the process of re-structuring noisy ontologies by taking account of the semantics of concept names rather than randomly selecting them. Additionally, leveraging machine learning is also our next direction to predict the potential axioms for editing ontology structures.

Acknowledgments. This work has benefited from the support of the AI Chair BE4musIA of the French National Research Agency (ANR-20-CHIA-0028) and FEI INS2I 2022-EMILIE.

References

1. Baader, F., Brandt, S., Lutz, C.: Pushing the $\mathcal{EL}$ envelope. In: Proceedings of the 19th International Joint Conferences on Artificial Intelligence, IJCAI 2005, pp. 364–369 (2005)
2. Benferhat, S., Bouraoui, Z., Lagrue, S., Rossit, J.: Min-based assertional merging approach for prioritized DL-Lite knowledge bases. In: Proceedings of the 8th International Conference on Scalable Uncertainty Management, SUM 2014, pp. 8–21 (2014)
3. Benferhat, S., Bouraoui, Z., Papini, O., Würbel, E.: Assertional removed sets merging of DL-Lite knowledge bases. In: Proceedings of the 13th International Conference of Scalable Uncertainty Management, SUM 2019, pp. 207–220 (2019)
4. Bernard, M., Boyer, L., Habrard, A., Sebban, M.: Learning probabilistic models of tree edit distance. Pattern Recogn. **41**, 2611–2629 (2008)
5. Bobillo, F., Bobed, C., Mena, E.: On the generalization of the discovery of subsumption relationships to the fuzzy case. In: Proceedings of the 26th IEEE International Conference on Fuzzy Systems, FUZZ-IEEE 2017, pp. 1–6 (2017)
6. Bouraoui, Z., Konieczny, S., Ma, T.T., Varzinczak, I.: Model-based merging of open-domain ontologies. In: Proceedings of the 33rd IEEE International Conference on Tools with Artificial Intelligence, ICTAI 2020, pp. 29–34 (2020)
7. Bouraoui, Z., Konieczny, S., Ma, T., Schwind, N., Varzinczak, I.: Region-based merging of open-domain terminological knowledge. In: Proceedings of the 19th International Conference on Principles of Knowledge Representation and Reasoning, KR 2022 (2022)
8. Chang, F., Chen, G., Zhang, S.: FCAMap-KG results for OAEI 2019. In: Proceedings of the 18th International Semantic Web Conference, OM@ISWC 2019, pp. 138–145 (2019)
9. Zheng, C., Sun, Y., Wan, S., Yu, D.: RLTM: an efficient neural IR framework for long documents. In: Proceedings of the 28th International Joint Conference on Artificial Intelligence, IJCAI 2019, pp. 5457–5463 (2019)
10. Condotta, J.F., Nouaouri, I., Sioutis, M.: A SAT approach for maximizing satisfiability in qualitative spatial and temporal constraint networks. In: Proceedings of the 15th International Conference on Principles of Knowledge Representation and Reasoning, KR 2016, pp. 342–442 (2016)
11. Francesco, K.: Most specific consequences in the description logic $\mathcal{EL}$. Discrete Appl. Math. **273**, 172–204 (2020)
12. Hahmann, T., Powell II, R.W.: Automatically extracting OWL versions of FOL ontologies. In: Proceedings of the 20th International Semantic Web Conference, ISWC 2021 (2021)
13. Hogan, A., et al.: Knowledge graphs. ACM Comput. Surv. **54**(4), 1–37 (2022)
14. Konieczny, S., Pérez, R.P.: Merging information under constraints: a logical framework. J. Log. Comput. **12**(5), 773–808 (2002)
15. Lin, J., Mendelzon, A.O.: Knowledge base merging by majority. In: Pareschi, R., Fronhöfer, B. (eds.) Dynamic Worlds, pp. 195–218. Springer, Dordrecht (1999). https://doi.org/10.1007/978-94-017-1317-7_6
16. Movshovitz-Attias, D., Whang, S.E., Noy, N., Halevy, A.: Discovering subsumption relationships for web-based ontologies. In: Proceedings of the 18th International Workshop on Web and Databases, WebDB 2015, pp. 62–69 (2015)
17. Navigli, R.: Natural language understanding: instructions for (present and future) use. In: Proceedings of the 27th International Joint Conference on Artificial Intelligence, IJCAI 2018, pp. 5697–5702 (July 2018)
18. Schwarz, S., Pawlik, M., Augsten, N.: A new perspective on the tree edit distance. In: Similarity Search and Applications, pp. 156–170 (2017)
19. Tai, K.C.: The tree-to-tree correction problem. J. ACM **26**(3), 422–433 (1979)

20. Thiéblin, É., Haemmerlé, O., Trojahn, C.: CANARD complex matching system. In: Proceedings of the 17th International Semantic Web Conference, OM@ISWC 2018, pp. 138–143 (2018)
21. Wang, Z., Wang, K., Jin, Y., Qi, G.: OntoMerge: a system for merging DL-Lite ontologies. CEUR Workshop Proceedings, vol. 969, pp. 16–27 (01 2012)
22. Zhang, K., Shasha, D.: Simple fast algorithms for the editing distance between trees and related problems. SIAM J. Comput. **18**(6), 1245–1262 (1989)
23. Zhang, K., Statman, R., Shasha, D.: On the editing distance between unordered labeled trees. Inf. Process. Lett. **42**(3), 133–139 (1992)

Designing a Model of Driving Scenarios for Autonomous Vehicles

Haythem Chniti[1(✉)] and Mariem Mahfoudh[2]

[1] Institute of Computer Science and Management, University of Kairouan,
Avenue Khemais El Alouini, 3100 Kairouan, Tunisia
haythemchniti1@gmail.com
[2] MIRACL Laboratory, University of Sfax, Route de Tunis Km 10,
B.P. 242, 3021 Sfax, Tunisia

Abstract. Advanced Driver Assistance Systems (ADAS) must undergo
an extensive testing before they are put into production. But, testing
on real vehicles is long, expensive, difficult to replicate and risky. In the
future, it will always be necessary to use real vehicles for testing. But,
this is not enough to meet all the requirements of reliability and safety.
The self-driving will continue to make driving easier and safer. Nevertheless, the final question remains: what is the best evaluation method
that will be able to verify the expected behavior and performance of the
on-board systems in smart and autonomous cars? To do this, this article proposes several solutions, distributed in three parts. The first part
"object detection architecture" depicts an approach for object detection
based on YOLO with a good accuracy. The second "Lane detection architecture" is dedicated to detailed detection approach guidelines based on
OpenCV. The last and third part "Traffic sign architecture" is dedicated
to a detailed ConvNet approach to detection of signs based on CNN
formed at OpenCV using the reverse propagation method. We achieved
remarkable results, a real-time detection accuracy of 99.98%.

Keywords: ADAS · Convolutional Neural Network (CNN) · Self
driving car · YOLO · ConvNet · OpenCV

1 Introduction

Every year more than 1.25 million people are victim of traffic accidents and more
than 20 to 50 million are injured, many of them become disabled [1]. Reducing
the number of accidents is therefore mandatory. According to the road safety
association, human factors are responsible for more than 90% of accidents [2].
Thus, when a car becomes able of making an important part of the decisions
then this would greatly reduce the risk of accidents.

To do this, cars must take advantage of the latest technological advances, such
as artificial intelligence, which will also be a key component of future autono-
mus vehicles. With deep learning, self-driving cars will be able to concoct vast

International Conference on Knowledge Science, Engineering and Management (KSEM
2022).

© The Author(s), under exclusive license to Springer Nature Switzerland AG 2022
G. Memmi et al. (Eds.): KSEM 2022, LNAI 13369, pp. 396–405, 2022.
https://doi.org/10.1007/978-3-031-10986-7_32

amounts of data to determine what types of situations typically lead to accidents and act accordingly when similar situations arise.

The development of intelligent transport systems is mainly based on the exploitation of information and communication technologies, collection, processing and dissemination. In an integrated system, information is exchanged automatically between transport infrastructures and vehicles equipped with appropriate telecommunications devices.

The main objective of the article is to propose a new approach to the evaluation of advanced driver assistance systems in an intelligent or highly automated vehicle driven by an external entity during the deployment phase, who has limited access to the information in the driver assistance system to be tested. We have concentrated on the three main models of a car's range: Object detection, line of conduct and traffic sign, and achieved remarkable results in real time.

The paper is structured as follows: in Sect. 2, we discussed about some related works of object detection techniques, traffic signs and guideline detection. Section 3 is about a detailed study of our proposed approach. Section 4 dedicated to detail the results obtained from each approach. Section 5 draws the conclusion.

2   Related Work

Detecting objects from images and videos has always been the active research point for applications of computer vision and artificial intelligence robotics, autonomous cars, automated video surveillance, etc.

Shetty et al. [3] detailed two types of region-based object detection models applied in both live video and image streams (SSD Single-Shot Detector, Faster R-CNN Faster Regional Convolutional Neural Network).

Gene Lewis [4] proposed SimpleNet as a deep object detection approach that makes bounding box predictions for an image without the need for costly preprocessing or expensive deep evaluations. Simple-Net is capable of making predictions at a rate of about 11 frames per second, and achieves an mAP accuracy of about 12.83% on the KITTI Object Detection Benchmark set.

Redmon et al. [5] proposed YOLO as a unified model for object detection that is formed on a loss function that directly corresponds to the detection performance and the whole model is formed jointly. This model processes images in real time at 45 frames per second.

Another approach proposed by Ross Girshick [6] a region-based convolutional network method (Fast R-CNN) which is the extended version of R-CNN to improve the speed of the training and testing phase and to improve the detection accuracy. Fast R-CNN forms a deep network VGG16 9 faster than R-CNN, is 213 faster at test time.

Alex et al. [7] proposed an approach is known as DetectorNet in which the last layer of the AlexNet architecture is replaced by the regression layer in order to locate objects using DNN-based object mask regression.

Lane recognition is an important part of environmental perception. Many efforts have been made in recent decades. However, developing efficient detectors under infinite conditions is still difficult. Because there are too many variables such as fog, rain, light changes, partial occlusion, etc.

And for this, Chen et al. [8] proposed a DeepLab V3+ network-based model where the weight matrix generated by the attention structure module was merged into the characteristics map to obtain the final characteristics maps with the weight characteristics.

Long et al. [9] and Pizzati et al. [10] proposed a model based on CNN network have divided the task of segmentation of lane lines into two stages. In the first step, the efficient residual factored ConvNet network (ERFNet) is used as the basic model to semantically segment the input image, and the segmentation result will be obtained in the last step.

Neven et al. [11] proposed a model based on encoder-decoder encoder; the encoder-decoder is an end-to-end model. The model can directly display the segmentation result through the data entry. The LaneNet line detection network which is based on the improvement of SegNet, which has two decoder structures.

The detection algorithm is the essential part of sign recognition systems. Generally, detection algorithms are used in automotive assistance systems, which is why it is extremely important to achieve the highest possible real-time detection speed with the highest achievable accuracy.

Lin et al. [12] proposed an Inception-v3 detection model based on transfer learning. First, use data preprocessing technology to improve the Belgian database of road signs, including data improvement and histogram equalization. Subsequently, the visualization analysis toolbox shows the representation of data characteristics, in which the layer-by-layer representation of convolutive characteristics is analyzed.

Lee and Kim [13] proposed a model based on the deep neural network with focal regression loss. Deep neural network (DNN) to detect small traffic lights (TL) in images captured by cameras mounted in vehicles. The proposed TL detector has a DNN encoder-decoder architecture with focal regression loss; this loss function reduces the loss of simple, well-regressive examples.

Zuo et al. [3] proposed an advanced method called Faster R-CNN to detect road signs. This new method represents the highest level of object recognition, no need to manually extract the image function, and it allows to segment the image to automatically obtain the proposed candidate area.

Meng et al. [14] proposed a method for detecting small objects from large images. In particular, due to the limited memory available on the current GPU, it is difficult for CNN to process large images, such as 2048 * 2048, and it is even more difficult to detect small objects from large images. Thus, using the VGG-16 network as a base network to generate patch-level object detection results.

3   Proposed Methodology

In this part, we have detailed each proposed approach (detection of objects, detection of guidelines and detection of signs).

3.1 Object Detection Architecture

We use Convolutional Neural Networks (CNN) as the framework for YOLO since CNNs have recently been shown to achieve very significant results in computer vision tasks.

The choice of which functions to create recursively varies widely. But it typically involves a convolution operation, followed by a non-linear activation, followed in turn by a max-pooling operation; we collectively refer to the combination of these three functions as a "layer".

In our YOLO architecture, we choose to have n layers, followed by a final convolution/non-linearity and a dense fully-connected layer that outputs a prediction matrix. We trained a 3-layer and 5-layer model to examine the effects of network depth on predictions. More details are given in the Experiments section.

Hidden Unit. For each Convolution Layer, we use a filter size of 3×3 in order to train each neuron to respond to a more local area and get the maximum number of activations as a result. Each Convolution Layer also had 3 neurons; this choice was made to keep the volume size similar to the input volume, keep the number of parameters relatively small.

Non-linear Activation Function. For our non-linear activation we used the Rectified Linear Unit (ReLU) activations, which take the form of:

$$ReLU(x) = maxf(0; x) \tag{1}$$

ReLU's are standard activations used in the computer vision literature that allow for large gradients while suppressing negative activations.

Dataset. For detection and classification, we have used the ImageNet classification dataset and the COCO detection dataset. This dataset consists of 328K images. Each image is accompanied by a list of detections, where each detection indicates the detection's classification, image bounding box coordinates, the detection's latitude, longitude, and altitude (in meters), and the detection's 3D position and orientation in world coordinates.

3.2 Lane Detection Architecture

As shown in Fig. 1, our detection algorithm consists of 5 steps. First, we corrected the distortion of our input image and converted it from RGB (Red, Green, Blue) to grayscale for tricky edge detection. After, Gaussian filter was applied to remove noise from the image using a Gaussian smoothing function. Subsequently, for the edge detection we used the Canny filter because the contrast between the track and the surface of the surrounding road provides us with useful information on the detection of the track lines. For the next step, extracting the region of

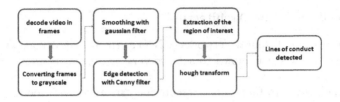

Fig. 1. The flow chart of the lane detection.

interest, we can filter out foreign pixels by creating an area of polygon of interest and deleting all other pixels that are not in the polygon.

The final step of our architecture, the transformation of Hough. It converts a line "x against y" to a point in the space gradient against interception. The points in the image will correspond to lines in the hollow space. An intersection of lines in the hollow space will therefore correspond to a line in the cartesian space.

3.3   Traffic Sign Architecture

In this section, ConvNet architecture and its key components are presented in the model that is used for traffic sign recognition. This is a process of, first, locating, then automatic recognition of road signs, including speed limit signs, etc. to help and protect drivers.

This process starts at the beginning with the reception of the data by the acquisition unit which consists of a Raspberry Pi card linked to a pi camera module.

Once the data is ready to be sent to the model, we need to define the model architecture and compile it with the necessary adaptations. The architecture adopted here is 2 convolution layers followed by a pooling layer, a fully connected layer and a flattening layer respectively. After the maxpool and fully connected layer are introduced as regularization in our model. The neural network is formed at OpenCV by using the reverse propagation method.

The model is trained using the above dataset and the loss is reported at each training step. The model was trained using TensorFlow on an NVIDIA GEFORCE 940M GPU.

Dataset. We will use a Collection of images (43 classes) was performed using a 16-megapixel camera that supports an image resolution of 800 × 600 pixels. A total of 131k photos were taken during the day. The pre-processing of these selective frames is done by resizing them to a size of 32 × 32 pixels which are then used for labelling. Figure 2 shows these labelled images used as dataset for training and testing of the model.

Fig. 2. Examples of labelled images according to dataset.

4   Experimental Results

4.1   Result Object Detection

On the ImageNet and COCO test set, YOLO is 99.78% to 100% accurate in real time (See Fig. 3) YOLO models the size and shape of objects, as well as relationships between objects and where objects often appear.

Fig. 3. Object detection.

The resulting system is interactive and engaging. While YOLO processes one image at a time, when connected to a webcam, it works like a tracking system, detecting objects as they move and change their appearance.

4.2   Result Lane Detection

The experiments are run in the OpenCV environment. The identification process is shown in Fig. 1. The application first reads in color video frames. It converts the color image of each frame to a grayscale image, as shown in Fig. 4 (left image). Only the pixels in the ROI are extracted from the edge image.

The ROI is about 1/3 of a frame. Computational effort can only be reduced in ROI. Local differences of adjacent pixels are used to search for edges. This is an image gradient processing method. It pinpoints edges and applies image segmentation to obvious edges. Figure 4 (right image) shows the edge line image in the ROI. A modified Hough transform algorithm is applied to the parameter space settings.

Fig. 4. After edge detection Canny process in ROI.

Extraction of the Region of Interest: The region of interest for the car camera is only two lanes immediately in its field of view and nothing extraordinary. We can filter out foreign pixels by creating a polygon area of interest and removing all other pixels that are not in the polygon. We know that the tracks will be located in the lower half of the image (see Fig. 5).

Fig. 5. Extraction of the ROI.

Subsequently, an identification of the track lines with Hough was realized.

Once the perspective is transformed, a sliding window can then be executed on the line to calculate the polynomial fit line for the track line curve (as shown in Fig. 6). If a lane line moved away from the side of the image, the original sliding window would continue vertically to the top of the image.

The experiment detected 2620 frames. The accuracy rate reached 97.8%.

4.3   Result Traffic Sign

When we run our python script here, an epoch is a hyper parameter that means a forward and a backward pass of all learning samples (Fig. 7).

Fig. 6. Road lane line prediction.

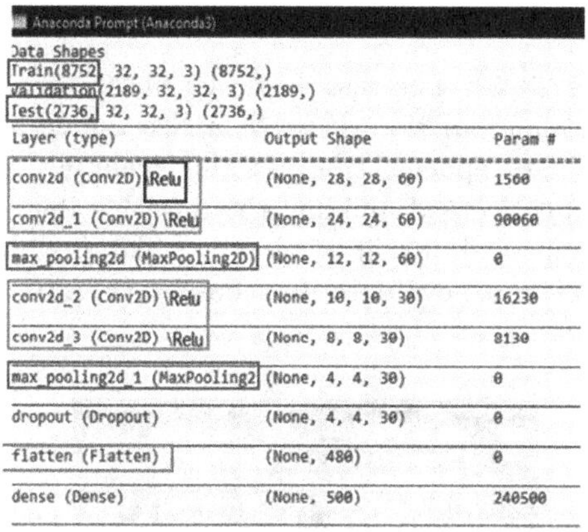

```
Anaconda Prompt (Anaconda3)
Data Shapes
Train(8752, 32, 32, 3) (8752,)
Validation(2189, 32, 32, 3) (2189,)
Test(2736, 32, 32, 3) (2736,)
Layer (type)                    Output Shape             Param #
=================================================================
conv2d (Conv2D) Relu            (None, 28, 28, 60)        1560

conv2d_1 (Conv2D) \Relu         (None, 24, 24, 60)        90060

max_pooling2d (MaxPooling2D)    (None, 12, 12, 60)        0

conv2d_2 (Conv2D) \Relu         (None, 10, 10, 30)        16230

conv2d_3 (Conv2D) \Relu         (None, 8, 8, 30)          8130

max_pooling2d_1 (MaxPooling2    (None, 4, 4, 30)          0

dropout (Dropout)               (None, 4, 4, 30)          0

flatten (Flatten)               (None, 480)               0

dense (Dense)                   (None, 500)               240500
```

Fig. 7. Basic structure.

The more we increase the number of epochs, the more we give the network a chance to see the previous data to readjust and improve the model parameters so that it is more efficient. The result of the training (see Fig. 8):

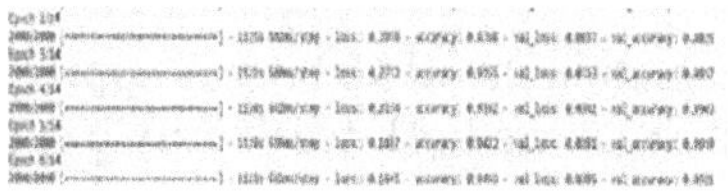

Fig. 8. Result of the training.

Now, the formed model must be serialized. The architecture or structure of the model will be stored in an hdf5 file format. The model formed must be evaluated in terms of performance as follows (Fig. 9):

The result above shows that for the training data, our driven algorithm achieves an accuracy of 96 (ACC: 0.9686) and the loss function decreases with each gradient back-propagation phenomenon and reaches 0.101 at the last weight and bias adjustment while during the first back-propagation, the loss function

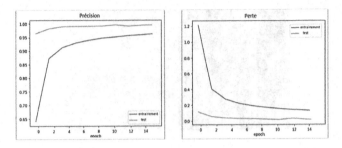

Fig. 9. Accuracy, loss curve.

has a value of (loss: 1,2023). The test accuracy of 99% which implies that the model is well trained for prediction. If we visualize the entire training log, then with a greater number of epochs, the loss and accuracy of the model on the training and test data converged, making the model stable.

Once the model is formed, it will be able to make predictions about the new panel data that it is given to evaluate its accuracy (Fig. 10).

Fig. 10. Example of real-time sign detection.

5   Conclusion

In this work, we have discussed in detail about our approach based on convolutive neural networks (CNN) that allows both to identify a set of worst-case scenarios for an ADAS application (detection of objects through the YOLO algorithm, line of conduct detection and road signs with OpenCV which is the best in terms of real-time accuracy). Since the proposed evaluation approach combines the three evaluation approaches mentioned above, the results obtained show that there is high accuracy in real time.

We consider the following perspectives of our work:

Adapt, improve efficiency and apply the proposed approach on different ADAS systems such as: Adaptive Cruise Control ACC, Automatic Emergency Braking AEB, etc.

Improved sampling strategy despite the computational power we have today, CNN algorithms remain very expensive in terms of real-time calculations.

References

1. https://www.who.int/fr/news-room/fact-sheets/detail/road-traffic-injuries , June 2021
2. Association Prévention Routière. Récupéré sur. https://www.preventionroutiere. asso.fr/
3. Zuo, Z., Yu, K., Zhou, Q., Wang, X., Li, T.: Traffic signs detection based on faster R-CNN. In: 2017 IEEE 37th International Conference on Distributed Computing Systems Workshops (ICDCSW), pp. 286–288. IEEE (2017)
4. Pandey, R., Malik, A.: Object detection and movement prediction for autonomous vehicle: a review. In: 2021 2nd International Conference on Secure Cyber Computing and Communications (ICSCCC), pp. 60–65 (2021)
5. Redmon, J., Farhadi, A.: Yolo9000: better, faster, stronger. In: Proceedings of the IEEE Conference on Computer Vision and Pattern Recognition, pp. 7263–7271 (2017)
6. Girshick, R.: Fast R-CNN. In: Proceedings of the IEEE International Conference on Computer Vision, pp. 1440–1448 (2015)
7. Tung, C.-L., Wang, C.-H., Su, Y.L.: Real-time face mask-wearing detection and temperature measurement based on a deep learning model. J. Imaging Sci. Technol. **66**, 10 (2021)
8. Chen, W., Wang, W., Wang, K., Li, Z., Li, H., Liu, S.: Lane departure warning systems and lane line detection methods based on image processing and semantic segmentation-a review. J. Traffic Transp. Eng. (Engl. Ed.) **7**, 748–774 (2020)
9. Long, J., Shelhamer, E., Darrell, T.: Fully convolutional networks for semantic segmentation. In: Proceedings of the IEEE Conference on Computer Vision and Pattern Recognition, pp. 3431–3440 (2015)
10. Pizzati, F., Allodi, M., Barrera, A., Garcia, F.: Lane detection and classification using cascaded CNNs. arXiv preprint arXiv:1907.01294 (2019)
11. Neven, D., De Brabandere, B., Georgoulis, S., Proesmans, M., Van Gool, L.: Towards end-to-end lane detection: an instance segmentation approach. In: 2018 IEEE Intelligent Vehicles Symposium (IV), pp. 286–291. IEEE (2018)
12. Lin, C., Li, L., Luo, W., Wang, K.C., Guo, J.: Transfer learning based traffic sign recognition using inception-v3 model. Periodica Polytechnica Transp. Eng. **47**(3), 242–250 (2019)
13. Lee, E., Kim, D.: Accurate traffic light detection using deep neural network with focal regression loss. Image Vis. Comput. **87**, 24–36 (2019)
14. Meng, Z., Fan, X., Chen, X., Chen, M., Tong, Y.: Detecting small signs from large images. In: 2017 IEEE International Conference on Information Reuse and Integration (IRI), pp. 217–224. IEEE (2017)

Ride-Hailing Order Matching and Vehicle Repositioning Based on Vehicle Value Function

Shun Li[1], Zeheng Zhong[1], and Bing Shi[1,2(✉)]

[1] School of Computer Science and Artificial Intelligence,
Wuhan University of Technology, Wuhan 430070, China
{shunli,bingshi}@whut.edu.cn
[2] Shenzhen Research Institute, Wuhan University of Technology,
Shenzhen 518000, China

Abstract. Online ride-hailing platforms, such as Uber, DiDi and Lyft, have significantly revolutionized the way of travelling and improved traffic efficiency. How to match orders with feasible vehicles and how to dispatch idle vehicles to the area with potential riding demands are two key issues for the ride-hailing platforms. However, existing works usually deal with only one of them and ignore the fact that the current matching and repositioning results may affect the supply and demand in the future since they will affect the future vehicle distributions in different zones. In this paper, we use the vehicle value function to characterize the spatio-temporal value of vehicles. At each decision-making round, we first match orders with vehicles by using bipartite graph maximum weight matching with the vehicle value function. Then we will provide idle vehicles with repositioning suggestions, where we predict the riding demand in each zone in the future, and then use a greedy strategy combined with vehicle value function to maximize social welfare. Extensive experiments based on real-world data as well the analytic synthetic data demonstrate that our method can outperform benchmark approaches in terms of the long-term social welfare and service ratio.

Keywords: Ride-hailing · Order matching · Vehicle repositioning · Value function · Demand forecasting

1 Introduction

Online ride-hailing service has played an important role in today's urban traffic system. Online ride-hailing platforms, e.g., Uber and Didi Chuxing, have greatly benefited our daily lives by allowing passengers to book a trip in advance and matching available vehicles with riding demands in real time. Order matching and vehicle repositioning are two key issues for the ride-hailing platforms, where order matching determines the matching between idle drivers (vehicles) with the riding orders, and vehicle repositioning is a strategy that can deploy idle vehicles to specific locations that are expected to generate demand in the future.

© The Author(s), under exclusive license to Springer Nature Switzerland AG 2022
G. Memmi et al. (Eds.): KSEM 2022, LNAI 13369, pp. 406–416, 2022.
https://doi.org/10.1007/978-3-031-10986-7_33

In this paper, we intend to address the problems of order matching and vehicle repositioning on a ride-hailing platform. Our objective is to maximize the long-term social welfare and improve the service ratio. In order to achieve these objectives, firstly, we design a vehicle value function to characterize the spatio-temporal value of vehicles. Then we transform the order matching problem into a bipartite graph maximum weight matching problem based on the vehicle value function, which is solved by using Kuhn-Munkres algorithm. Furthermore, we need to reposition idle vehicles to specific areas in order to fill the supply-demand gap in the future. We design a demand predicting method to forecast the number of orders in each area in the future. Based on the information of vehicles in the "matched" state and the "serving" state, we can know in which area these vehicle will become idle in the future. With such a demand information, we use a greedy strategy combined with the vehicle value function to maximize social welfare. The experimental results show that our approach can outperform benchmark approaches in terms of the long-term social welfare and service ratio.

The structure of this paper is as follows. In Sect. 2, we introduce the related work. In Sect. 3, we describe the basic settings of the problem. In Sect. 4, we describe the proposed algorithm in detail, and in Sect. 5, we experimentally evaluate our proposed approach. Finally, we conclude the paper in Sect. 6.

2   Related Work

For order matching/dispatching on ride-hailing platforms, extensive literature has been proposed on, such as dynamic matching [10], network flow optimization with rolling horizon [1], neural ADP for carpooling [7], and (deep) reinforcement learning [8]. For vehicle repositioning, a number of works are under the setting of grid world, and RL related methods have been proposed for this problem, e.g., DQN [2], multi-agent RL [4] and hierarchical RL [3].

To the best of our knowledge, existing works usually analyzed the order matching and repositioning problems separately, and did not consider the impacts of current decision of order matching and idle vehicle repositioning on the future matching. Therefore, in this paper we take the spatio-temporal value of vehicles and the demand information in each area into account, and consider the order matching and idle vehicle repositioning problem as a whole to maximize the long-term social welfare.

3   Problem Formulation

In this section, we first introduce how the online ride-hailing system works, and then describe the basic settings of orders and vehicles.

We assume that vehicles belong to the online ride-hailing platform, which means that vehicles are a part of the platform and the platform can determine the behavior of vehicles. Then in the ride-hailing system, there are two main roles, passengers and the platform. For the workflow of ride-hailing system, firstly, passengers submit orders to the platform according to their own demands, in which the order information includes the maximum price they would like to pay. The platform collects the submitted order requests and then matches orders with available vehicles. After finishing order matching, the platform computes the payment of the matched orders. If there are idle vehicles left, the platform needs to provide them with repositioning suggestions to satisfy the future riding demands. The entire time is split into a set of discrete time steps $\tau = \{1, 2, ..., T\}$ with time step length Δt. In each time step, the platform will finish order matching and provide idle vehicles repositioning suggestions for this round. In the below, we give the definition of some key elements in the ride-hailing system.

Definition 1 (Order). *Order $o \in \mathcal{O}$ is defined as a tuple $(l_o^p, l_o^d, t_o^r, t_o^w)$, where l_o^p, l_o^d is the pick-up and drop-off locations of order o respectively, t_o^r means the time when the order o is raised, t_o^w is the maximum time that a passenger of order o is willing to wait for the service.*

In this paper, we assume that when the order o is not matched by the driver within t_o^w time, the order o will be automatically cancelled and the passenger is not willing to wait.

Definition 2 (Vehicle). *Vehicle $v \in \mathcal{V}$ is defined as a tuple (l_v, c_v), where l_v is the current position and c_v is the unit driving cost of vehicle v.*

Definition 3 (Social Welfare). *The long-term social welfare is the sum of the profits of the platform and passengers over the whole time step.*

$$SW = \sum_{t=1}^{T} \sum_{o \in \mathcal{O}_t^w} (val_o - C_{\Theta_t(o)}^o) \tag{1}$$

where val_o is the highest price passengers willing to pay to the platform for accessing travel service, which can be regarded as the value of this order for the passenger, $\mathcal{O}_t^w$ is the set of matched orders in round t, Θ_t is the matching result in round t, and $\Theta_t(o) = v$ denotes the matching of order o and vehicle v. $C_{\Theta_t(o)}^o$ is the cost for vehicle $\Theta_t(o)$ to complete order o.

4   Method

We design a vehicle state value function, which implies the ability of vehicles to make social welfare in different spatio-temporal states. Then, based on the vehicle value function, we design the order matching and idle vehicle repositioning algorithm.

4.1   Vehicle Value Function Design

The vehicle value function shows the potential social welfare that the vehicle can make in the future in the current spatial-temporal state. It is defined as $V(t, g, c)$, where $t \in T$ is the time step, $g \in G$ is the zone index where the vehicle is located, and c is the vehicle unit travel cost.

In a multi-round matching and repositioning process, we can capture how the current vehicle state can affect the future social welfare, i.e. the vehicle value function. This process can be considered as a sequential decision process, and thus Markov decision process(MDP) can be used to model the real-time order matching and idle vehicle repositioning process.

In the following, we define the attributes in the MDP $M = \langle S, A, P, r, \gamma \rangle$ in detail and describe the state transfer involved.

State: The state of each vehicle is defined as a tuple $s = (t, g, c) \in S$, which is the vehicle value function.

Action: The action is $a \in A = \{a_1, a_2, a_3\}$, where a_1 is to match an order with a vehicle. a_2 means that the vehicle will be stationary in a zone for a certain time, and a_3 is to reposition an idle vehicle to an adjacent zone.

Reward: The reward r is the profit of the passenger and the platform when the action is taken. The reward value r is calculated as follows:

$$r = p_o - C_{\Theta(o)} \tag{2}$$

where p_0 is the payment for an order o and $C_{\Theta(o)}$ is the cost required for the vehicle $\Theta(o)$ to complete the order o. The cumulative reward R_γ is calculated as follows:

$$R_\gamma = \sum_{t=0}^{T-1} \gamma^t \frac{r}{T} \tag{3}$$

where γ is a discount factor that decreases the impacts of the past rewards.

We obtain the vehicle value function by using value iteration. When the action performed by the agent is to match an order, the agent receives an immediate reward R_γ and performs a state transfer, and the TD update rule is:

$$V(s) \leftarrow V(s) + \alpha \left[R_\gamma + \gamma V(s') - V(s) \right] \tag{4}$$

where $s = (t, g, c)$ is the state of the vehicle at the current time step, $s' = (t + \Delta t_1, g_{l_d}, c)$ is the state of the vehicle after completing the matched order, g_{l_d} is the destination of the order, and Δt_1 is the time required to depart from the time step t to pick up the passenger and deliver the passenger to destination g_{l_d}. When the agent acts as stationary, the immediate reward of the agent is 0. The TD update rule is as follows:

$$V(s) \leftarrow V(s) + \alpha \left[0 + \gamma V(s'') - V(s) \right] \tag{5}$$

Since the agent performs a stationary action, the position of the agent does not change, i.e., $s'' = (t + 1, g, c)$. When the action performed by the agent is idle vehicle repositioning, we construct a virtual order where the payment is 0, the origin of the order is g, and the destination of the order is one of the neighboring zones of g. The TD update rule is as follows:

$$V(s) \leftarrow V(s) + \alpha \left[R_\gamma' + \gamma V(s''') - V(s) \right] \tag{6}$$

where R_γ' is calculated by Eq. 3, and the payment for the corresponding order is 0. $s''' = (t + \Delta t_2, g', c)$ is the state of the vehicle after the repositioning is completed. and $g' \in g_{near}$ is a neighboring zone of g.

The platform first collects historical state transfer data, and then uses a dynamic programming based value iteration algorithm to backward recursively calculate the value $V(s_i)$ in each state to obtain the vehicle value function $V(s)$. The details of the algorithm are shown in Algorithm 1.

Algorithm 1: Dynamic Programming based Value Iteration Algorithm (DPVI)

Data: History state transfer tuple $D = \{(s_i, a_i, r_i, s_i')\}$, where each state $s_i = (t_i, g_i, c)$ consists of the vehicle's time step, geographic location index and cost

Result: Vehicle value function V

1 **for** $t = T - 1$ **to** 0 **do**
2       $D_t \leftarrow \{(s_i, a_i, r_i, s_i') | \forall s_i = (t_i, g_i, c), t_i = t\}$;
3   **foreach** $(s_i, a_I, r_i, s_i') \in D_t$ **do**
4           $N(s_i) \leftarrow N(s_i) + 1$;
5           $V(s_i) \leftarrow V(s_i) + \frac{1}{N(s_i)} \left(\gamma^{\Delta t(a_i)} V(s_i') + R_\gamma(a_i) - V(s_i) \right)$;
6   **end**
7 **end**
8 **return** V

4.2   Order Matching and Vehicle Repositioning Algorithm

In this section we introduce the Value Function and Demand based Order Matching and Vehicle Repositioning algorithm (VFDOMVR). Overall speaking, we first complete the order matching, and then perform the demand forecasting. We then complete vehicle repositioning according to the vehicle value function and the results of demand forecasting. This algorithm is described in Algorithm 2.

Order Matching: Given the known order information and vehicle information, this problem can be transformed into a maximum weight bipartite graph matching problem (lines 2–4). Note that only edges with weight greater than 0 are added to the bipartite graph (lines 7–9). We use Kuhn-Munkres (KM) [6] algorithm to get the result of order matching (line 11).

Demand Forecasting: If we only use the value function to reposition the idle vehicles, it is likely that an excessive number of idle vehicles will be repositioned to a higher value area. Therefore, we use the SARIMAX model to predict how many vehicles will be needed in a certain area at a certain time (line 12). Through demand forecasting, we can provide guidance for future idle vehicle repositioning.

Vehicle Repositioning: We first iterate through all the vehicles in the "matched" and "serving" states to know which area these vehicles will become idle again in the future. The number of vehicles dispatched in the area should be reduced accordingly (lines 13–17). Next, we iterate through all idle vehicles, and during the iteration we try to give repositioning suggestions for each idle vehicle (lines 18–29). We judge whether the demand for the area to be dispatched will be exceeded if this repositioning option is executed (lines 21–23). If it does not exceed, it is determined to reposition the vehicle to the area with the greatest gains, and the demand for idle vehicles at the corresponding time of the area is reduced by 1 (lines 24–28). Finally, we update the related system information (line 30).

Algorithm 2: Value Function and Demand based Order Matching Vehicle Repositioning Algorithm (VFDOMVR)

Data: The set $\mathcal{O}$ of orders, the set of $\mathcal{V}$ of vehicles, and the vehicle state value function V

Result: The set of matched orders $\mathcal{O}^w$, matching result Θ, repositioning result $\mathcal{R}$, and the social welfare results SW

1   **for** $t = 0$ **to** T **do**
2     $\mathcal{O}_t \leftarrow \{o \in \mathcal{O}|t_o^r + t_o^w \leq t + \Delta t\}$;
3     $\mathcal{V}_t \leftarrow select\_empty\_vehicles(\mathcal{V}, t)$;
4   Initialize the bipartite graph $G = (\mathcal{O}_t, \mathcal{V}_t, E)$;
5   **foreach** $\langle o, v \rangle \in \mathcal{O}_t \times \mathcal{V}_t$ **do**
6   calculate the vehicle state value difference ΔV corresponding to $\langle o, v \rangle$;
7   **if** $\Delta V > 0$ **then**
8   assign the weights of edges $\langle o, v \rangle$ to ΔV and insert into the bipartite graph;
9   **end**
10   **end**
11    $\mathcal{O}_t, \Theta_t \leftarrow KM(G)$;
12    $\mathcal{D}_t \leftarrow Demand\_Forecasting(\mathcal{O}, \mathcal{V}, t)$;
13    $\mathcal{V}' \leftarrow select\_matched\_and\_servicing\_state\_vehicles(\mathcal{V}, t, \Theta_t)$;
14   **foreach** $v \in \mathcal{V}'$ **do**
15       $t', l' \leftarrow become\_idle\_again(v)$;
16       $\mathcal{D}_t(t', l') \leftarrow \mathcal{D}_t(t', l') - 1$;
17   **end**
18   **foreach** $v \in \mathcal{V}_t$ and $v \notin \mathcal{V}'$ **do**
19   **foreach** $g \in g_{near}$ **do**
20   calculate the time t' of the vehicle reaching the neighboring zone g;
21   **if** $\mathcal{D}_t(t', g) \leq 0$ **then**
22   Continue;
23   **end**
24   calculate the difference $\Delta V'$ of the state value of the vehicle v from the current position to the neighboring zone g;
25   insert $t', g, \Delta V'$ into an Array A;
26   **end**
27       $t'', g', \mathcal{R}_t(v) \leftarrow \arg\max A$;
28       $\mathcal{D}_t(t'', g') \leftarrow \mathcal{D}_t(t'', g') - 1$;
29   **end**
30   update $SW_t, SW, \mathcal{O}^w, \Theta_t, \Theta, \mathcal{R}$;
31 **end**
32 **return** $\mathcal{O}^w, \Theta, \mathcal{R}, SW$

---

5 Experiment

In this section, we run experiments to evaluate the proposed algorithm based on the data from New York City Taxi and Limousine Comission (TLC)[1]. We use Manhattan taxi zone map provided by TLC as the map data, and collect the order data from 19:00 to 21:00 in the weekday within this area. Because we cannot find the fuel consumption of New York taxies, so we collect the related information from China Automobile Fuel Consumption Query System[2] instead. And finally we remove some unreasonable orders (e.g. orders with invalid fares, orders in isolated zones and zero trip milage).

For the experimental parameters, the length of each time step is set as 60 s. The maximum waiting time for passengers is chosen randomly from {3 min, 4 min, 5 min, 6 min, 7 min, 8 min}. The average vehicle travel speed V_{avg} is set to 7.2 mph, and for each vehicle, the unit travel cost is randomly selected from {6, 8, 10} × 2.5/6.8/1.6\$/km. The initial location of the vehicle is randomly selected in Manhattan taxi zone map. In the experiments, we try different numbers of vehicles, which are {1500, 2000, 2500, 3000, 3500}. For each experiment, we repeat it for 10 times and then compute the average result.

5.1 Evaluation of Vehicle Value Function

The vehicle value function is the basis for the order matching and repositioning algorithm, and therefore we first analyze the effectiveness of this value function, which is shown in Fig. 1.

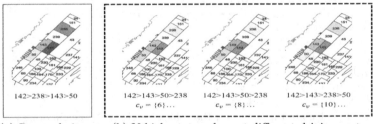

(a) Demand situation

(b) Vehicle state values at different driving costs

Fig. 1. Effectiveness analysis of vehicle value function

The number in each block is the index of zones, where zone 142, 143 and 50 are adjacent to each other on the road network. In Fig. 1(a), the darker the color means that there are more orders in the current zone. Figure 1(b) shows the vehicle value under the vehicle travel cost $c_v = \{6, 8, 10\} \times 2.5/6.8/1.6$ respectively. The

---

[1] https://www1.nyc.gov/site/tlc/about/tlc-trip-record-data.page.

[2] https://yhgscx.miit.gov.cn/fuel-consumption-web/mainPage.

darker the color indicates the higher the value of the vehicle in the current zone. Comparing Fig. 1(a) with Fig. 1(b), we can find that the riding demand situation of the zone is consistent with the vehicle value, i.e., when there are more riding orders in that zone, vehicle value in that zone is also higher.

Furthermore, we also find that although zone 238 has greater riding orders than zone 50 and 143, vehicles in zone 50 and 143 can travel to neighboring zone 142 to pick up orders, and therefore the vehicle value is higher in zone 50 and 143. We also find that as the vehicle travel cost increases, the vehicle value of zone 50 decreases. Especially when the vehicle travel cost is $c_v = 10 \times 2.5/6.8/1.6$, the vehicle value of zone 50 is lower than that of zone 238. This is because when the unit travel cost increases, the additional cost of travelling to the neighboring zone increases, which results in the loss of social welfare. This may imply that vehicles with high cost should try to serve nearby orders.

In summary, from the above analysis we can conclude that the vehicle value function can reflect the zone demand situation to a certain extent, and can reflect the ability of vehicles with different driving costs to obtain social welfare in different zones, and thus can be used in the order matching and idle vehicle repositioning to increase the social welfare.

5.2   Evaluation of Order Matching and Vehicle Repositioning Algorithm

In this section, we evaluate the proposed algorithm against **mdp** [9], **mT-share** [5], **Greedy&Gpri** [11] and **Nearest-Matching** in terms of social welfare and service ratio (the ratio of the number of matched orders to the total number of orders submitted by passengers).

The experimental results are shown in Fig. 2. From Fig. 2(a), we find that as the number of vehicles increases, the social welfare increases since more orders are served. We also find that **VFDOMVR** algorithm achieves the highest social welfare.

We also look into the service ratio in Fig. 2(b). We find that the **VFDOMVR** algorithm achieves the maximum service ratio. This means the **VFDOMVR** algorithm can help the platform serve more orders.

In summary, it can be found that our **VFDOMVR** algorithm can make the highest social welfare through the above experiments. What's more, it also provides higher service ratio. Therefore, we believe that the **VFDOMVR** algorithm can help the online ride-hailing platform to make more social welfare and serve more orders.

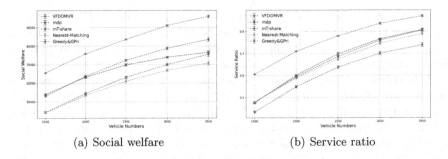

(a) Social welfare   (b) Service ratio

Fig. 2. Results of order matching and vehicle repositioning

5.3   Vehicle Repositioning Analysis

In this section, we further analyze the effectiveness of the idle vehicle repositioning algorithm. In order to evaluate the performance of the idle vehicle repositioning, we combine different benchmark repositioning algorithms such as **Empty**, **Random** and **Nearest** with the order matching of **VFDOMVR** to generate the benchmark algorithms. And the metrics are social welfare, service ratio and idle vehicle ratio (the ratio of the number of idle vehicles to the total number of vehicles).

The experimental results are shown in Fig. 3. From Fig. 3(a), we find that **VFDOMVR** algorithm achieves the largest social welfare. As the number of vehicles increases, the social welfare obtained by all algorithms increases.

From Fig. 3(b), we find that **VFDOMVR** algorithm achieves the maximum service ratio. This means that after using the proposed repositioning algorithm, the platform can serve more orders, and thus can achieve the maximum social welfare.

From Fig. 3(c), we can find that the **Nearest** dispatching algorithm achieves the minimum idle vehicle ratio, followed by **VFDOMVR** algorithm, **Random** dispatching algorithm and **Empty** dispatching algorithm. Among them, the results of **Nearest** dispatching algorithm, **VFDOMVR** algorithm and **Random** dispatching algorithm are close, while the results of **Empty** dispatching algorithm are obviously much higher. It indicates that our repositioning algorithm can effectively improve the utilization of idle vehicles.

In summary, we find that the repositioning of idle vehicles in the **VFDOMVR** algorithm can utilize idle vehicles and satisfy more order requests, thus improving social welfare. This is mainly because the repositioning of idle vehicles in the **VFDOMVR** algorithm takes the spatio-temporal value of vehicles into account and dispatches vehicles to zones where more vehicles are needed, and thus can increase service ratio and the social welfare.

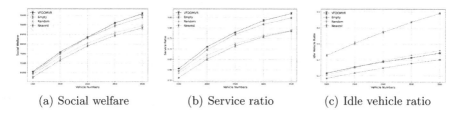

|(a) Social welfare|(b) Service ratio|(c) Idle vehicle ratio|

Fig. 3. Results of vehicle repositioning

6   Conclusion

In this paper, we focus on the problem of real-time order matching and idle vehicle repositioning to maximize the long-term social welfare. We need to consider the impacts of current decision on the future rounds. In more detail, we consider the spatio-temporal value of vehicle, and use the vehicle value function to transform order matching into a maximum weight bipartite graph matching problem. For idle vehicle repositioning, we use vehicle value function to learn which area is more profitable to move to, and use demand forecasting to avoid too many vehicles being moved to the same area. In order to verify the effectiveness of the proposed algorithm, we further carry out experimental analysis based on the taxi data in Manhattan, and evaluate the **VFDOMVR** algorithm against some typical benchmark algorithms. The results show that the **VFDOMVR** algorithm can help online ride-hailing platforms to dispatch idle vehicles efficiently, improve the utilization of idle vehicles, and increase the service ratio and social welfare.

Acknowledgement. This paper was funded by the Shenzhen Fundamental Research Program (Grant No. JCYJ20190809175613332), the Humanity and Social Science Youth Research Foundation of Ministry of Education (Grant No. 19YJC790111), the Philosophy and Social Science Post-Foundation of Ministry of Education (Grant No.18JHQ0 60) and the Fundamental Research Funds for the Central Universities (WUT: 202 2IVB004).

References

1. Bertsimas, D., Jaillet, P., Martin, S.: Online vehicle routing: the edge of optimization in large-scale applications. Oper. Res. **67**(1), 143–162 (2019)
2. Holler, J., et al.: Deep reinforcement learning for multi-driver vehicle dispatching and repositioning problem. In: 2019 IEEE International Conference on Data Mining (ICDM), pp. 1090–1095. IEEE (2019)
3. Jin, J., et al.: CoRide: joint order dispatching and fleet management for multi-scale ride-hailing platforms. In: Proceedings of the 28th ACM International Conference on Information and Knowledge Management, pp. 1983–1992 (2019)
4. Lin, K., Zhao, R., Xu, Z., Zhou, J.: Efficient large-scale fleet management via multi-agent deep reinforcement learning. In: Proceedings of the 24th ACM SIGKDD International Conference on Knowledge Discovery & Data Mining, pp. 1774–1783 (2018)

5. Liu, Z., Gong, Z., Li, J., Wu, K.: Mobility-aware dynamic taxi ridesharing. In: 2020 IEEE 36th International Conference on Data Engineering (ICDE), pp. 961–972. IEEE (2020)

6. Munkres, J.: Algorithms for the assignment and transportation problems. J. Soc. Ind. Appl. Math. 5(1), 32–38 (1957)

7. Shah, S., Lowalekar, M., Varakantham, P.: Neural approximate dynamic programming for on-demand ride-pooling. In: Proceedings of the AAAI Conference on Artificial Intelligence, vol. 34, pp. 507–515 (2020)

8. Tang, X., et al.: A deep value-network based approach for multi-driver order dispatching. In: Proceedings of the 25th ACM SIGKDD International Conference on Knowledge Discovery & Data Mining, pp. 1780–1790 (2019)

9. Xu, Z., et al.: Large-scale order dispatch in on-demand ride-hailing platforms: a learning and planning approach. In: Proceedings of the 24th ACM SIGKDD International Conference on Knowledge Discovery & Data Mining, pp. 905–913 (2018)

10. Yan, C., Zhu, H., Korolko, N., Woodard, D.: Dynamic pricing and matching in ride-hailing platforms. Nav. Res. Logist. (NRL) **67**(8), 705–724 (2020)

11. Zheng, L., Cheng, P., Chen, L.: Auction-based order dispatch and pricing in ridesharing. In: 2019 IEEE 35th International Conference on Data Engineering (ICDE), pp. 1034–1045. IEEE (2019)

District-Coupled Epidemic Control via Deep Reinforcement Learning

Xinqi Du[1,2], Tianyi Liu[1,2(✉)], Songwei Zhao[1,2], Jiuman Song[1,2],
and Hechang Chen[1,2(✉)]

[1] School of Artificial Intelligence, Jilin University, Changchun, China
{duxq18,tianyi21}@mails.jlu.edu.cn, chenhc@jlu.edu.cn
[2] Key Laboratory of Symbolic Computation and Knowledge Engineering of Ministry
of Education, Changchun, China

Abstract. The rapid spread of the Coronavirus (COVID-19) poses an unprecedented threat to the public health system and social economy, with approximately 500 million confirmed cases worldwide. Policymakers confront with high-stakes to make a decision on interventions to prevent the pandemic from further spreading, which is a dilemma between public health and a steady economy. However, the epidemic control problem has vast solution space and its internal dynamic is driven by population mobility, which makes it difficult for policymakers to find the optimal intervention strategy based on rules-of-thumb. In this paper, we propose a <u>D</u>eep <u>R</u>einforcement <u>L</u>earning enabled <u>E</u>pidemic <u>C</u>ontrol framework (DRL-EC) to make a decision on intervention to effectively alleviate the impacts of the epidemic outbreaks. Specifically, it is driven by reinforcement learning to learn the intervention policy autonomously for the policymaker, which can be adaptive to the various epidemic situation. Furthermore, District-Coupled Susceptible-Exposed-Infected-Recovered (DC-SEIR) model is hired to simulate the pandemic transmission between inter-district, which characterize the spatial and temporal nature of infectious disease transmission simultaneously. Extensive experimental results on a real-world dataset, the Omicron local outbreaks in China, demonstrate the superiority of the DRL-EC compared with the strategy based on rules-of-thumb.

Keywords: COVID-19 · Epidemic control · Intervention strategy · Deep reinforcement learning · Epidemiological model

1 Introduction

Outbreaks of infectious diseases tremendously threaten human health and economic development [3], for example, the Spanish flu has caused around 20 million people death tolls [7]. The current Coronavirus Disease 2019 (COVID-19)

This work is supported in part by the National Natural Science Foundation of China (No. 61902145), the National Key R&D Program of China (2021ZD0112501, 2021ZD0112502), and the Philosophy and Social Sciences Intelligent Library Foundation of Jilin Province (No. 2021JLSKZKZB080).

© The Author(s), under exclusive license to Springer Nature Switzerland AG 2022
G. Memmi et al. (Eds.): KSEM 2022, LNAI 13369, pp. 417–428, 2022.
https://doi.org/10.1007/978-3-031-10986-7_34

[8,22] sweeps worldwide and leads to an unprecedented crisis, where have been about 500 million confirmed cases of COVID-19. Epidemics are mainly caused by infectious viruses that transmit through close person-to-person contact. Various public health interventions are used to control the spread of infectious diseases, such as vaccination [2], mask-wearing [10], social distancing [18], school closures [11], and so forth [1], which often involving the lose of economic. How and when to enact the interventions involves a trade-off between public health and steady economics. Therefore, it is vital for the policymaker to layout effective interventions to control the spread of infectious diseases and thus alleviate the impact of the infectious disease outbreaks.

The problem of epidemic control has long time been studied, which mainly relies on the epidemiological models that portray and predict the process of the pandemic. There are two main types of models, i.e., compartmental model [6] and agent-based model [13], which model the pandemic on macro-level and micro-level, respectively. The most widely used model is the Susceptible-Exposed-Infected-Recovered (SEIR) model, and its extension [20]. The origin intervention strategies were largely based on the human experience and rules-of-thumb, which were inflexible to the pandemic situation. Recently, researchers have employed machine learning techniques to control the pandemic [5], which are beneficial to fitting the infectious disease features. Deep reinforcement learning (DRL) [12,14,16], as a promising artificial intelligent method, is also used for epidemic control by allowing the agent to interact with the epidemiological model [9,17,21].

Despite the success that existing studies have achieved in epidemic control, there are two significant challenges remain unsettled. *Challenge I:* How to integrate spatial mobility patterns into the epidemic model? Population mobility is the main force to drive the spread of infectious disease, which is conducive to estimating the spread risk. However, most existing studies only consider transmission features of the time series [4], or use agent-based epidemiological models [13], which involve complexity and privacy concerns. *Challenge II:* How to provide optimal control policies during the outbreak of epidemic? The way of executing the interventions has a significant impact on the tendency of infectious disease development. An effective intervention can minimize the infected cases without destroying the economy. However, the epidemic control problem is dynamic and has a vast solution space, which is hard for the policymaker to empirically identify the optimal intervention strategy.

In view of this, we propose a Deep Reinforcement Learning enabled Epidemic Control framework (DRL-EC), which can autonomously learn the policy for intervention decision. Specifically, this framework employs the DRL method to make a decision on interventions for epidemic control, which is adaptive to the rapidly changing epidemiological situation. Meanwhile, District-Coupled SEIR (DC-SEIR) model is devised to take the inter-district infectious disease transmission risk into consideration, which models the dynamic transmission of infectious diseases in a fine-grained way. Furthermore, we conduct extensive experiments with the real-world dataset and make visualizations to demonstrate the superiority of the proposed DRL-EC. Our contributions of this paper are in three-folds:

- An effective and adaptive framework called DRL-EC is proposed to select intervention strategies for epidemic control. Under this framework, the policymakers can successfully learn optimal policies for epidemic control.
- The DRL-EC is driven by the DRL method to autonomously learn the epidemic control policy. Besides, we devise a novel epidemiological model called DC-SEIR, which integrates the inter-district information to capture the spatial feature of infectious disease transmission.
- We conduct extensive simulation experiments and compared them with actual data collected on Omicron local outbreaks in China. Substantial results demonstrate that DRL-EC is more competitive than the strategies based on rules-of-thumb.

2   Preliminaries

In this section, we detail the notation and review the classic epidemiological model, i.e., Susceptible-Exposed-Infected-Recovered (SEIR) compartmental model to provide the theoretical support for our method.

2.1   Notations

We model the epidemic control problem as a Markov decision process (MDP) [19], which is a sequential decision making model. It can be represented by a tuple $G = \langle \mathcal{S}, \mathcal{A}, T, R, \gamma \rangle$, where $\mathcal{S}$ is the state set and $\mathcal{A}$ is the action set. During interaction, agent uses a stochastic policy to choose an action, i.e., $\pi_\phi : s_t \mapsto a_t, a_t \in A$, which induces a transition to the next state according to state transition function: $T := \mathcal{S} \times \mathcal{A} \times \mathcal{S} \mapsto [0,1]$. The agent can observe the next state of environment s_{t+1} and obtain the reward $r_{t+1} := \mathcal{S} \times \mathcal{A} \mapsto \mathbb{R}$. Replay buffer is employed to restore history transitions $H = \langle s_t, a_t, s_{t+1}, r_{t+1}, done \rangle$ for training. The objective for the agent is to maximize its accumulated reward:

$$J(\pi_\phi) = \mathbb{E}[R_T] = \mathbb{E}_{a \sim \pi_\phi(\cdot|s)} \left[\sum_{t=0}^{T} \gamma^t r_{t+1}(s, a) \right], \tag{1}$$

where γ is discount factor to balance immediate reward and long-term gain.

2.2   SEIR Epidemiological Model

Various epidemiology models are being proposed to assist the governments assessing the current situation of infectious diseases and implementing intervention to prevent the epidemic spread. The Susceptible-Exposed-Infectious-Recovered (SEIR) model, a compartmental model, is one of the most widely used to projects the dynamic spread of infectious disease. It divides the populations into four groups: the susceptible (S), the exposed (E), the infected (I) and the recovered (R). At each time step t, the susceptible may contact with the infected and transfer to the exposed state. The infected entities get a chance to pass the infection along to each of the exposed entities, with a probability equal to the transmission rate. Meanwhile, they can transit to the recovered state, indicating that they're no longer capable of being infected again themselves. This process can be generated using ordinary differential equations (ODE) as follows:

$$
\begin{aligned}
\frac{\mathrm{d}S(t)}{\mathrm{d}t} &= -\beta S(t)\frac{I(t)}{N}; \\
\frac{\mathrm{d}E(t)}{\mathrm{d}t} &= \beta S(t)\frac{I(t)}{N} - \alpha E(t); \\
\frac{\mathrm{d}I(t)}{\mathrm{d}t} &= \alpha E(t) - \lambda I(t); \\
\frac{\mathrm{d}R(t)}{\mathrm{d}t} &= \lambda I(t),
\end{aligned}
\tag{2}
$$

where β controls the contact frequency between susceptible population and infected population. α is the transferred rate from the exposed state to the infective state. λ indicates the recover rate.

3   Methodology

In this section, we elaborate an autonomous learning framework called Deep Reinforcement Learning enabled Epidemic Control (DRL-EC), that is DRL-driven and enables adaptive decision-making for infectious disease interventions. The district-coupled epidemiological compartmental model is employed to describe the dynamic transmission process of the epidemic, and is also integrated into the deep reinforcement learning framework as the environment. At each time step t, the DRL agent acquires a state from the environment, and then selects the infectious disease intervention action to be executed at the next timestep according to its control policy. The overall architecture is illustrated in Fig. 1, which is consists of 1) the district-coupled epidemiological model and 2) the DRL-enabled dynamic intervention decision framework.

3.1   District-Coupled Epidemiological Compartmental Model

SEIR, a traditional epidemiological compartmental model, portrays the time-series characteristics of the transmission of infectious diseases between different groups. However, population mobility becomes a significant force in driving the transmission of infectious diseases in reality. Most existing epidemiological compartmental models do not take population mobility into account, which would fail to characterize the spatial transmission of infectious diseases. In view of this, we propose a novel compartmental model called District-Coupled Susceptible-Exposed-Infectious-Recovered (DC-SEIR), which is an extension of the SEIR

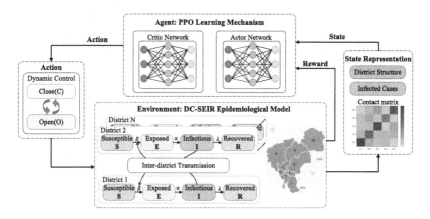

Fig. 1. The overall architecture of DRL-EC. It relies on a feedback loop where the DRL agent obtains the observation from the epidemic environment and chooses an intervention action according to its policy. The epidemic will transmit to the next state dynamically. Besides, the DC-SEIR epidemiological compartmental model, incorporating the population mobility information, portrays the spatiotemporal characteristics of the spread of infectious diseases.

model and naturally incorporates inter-district connectivity. DC-SEIR can characterize the spatial and temporal nature of infectious disease transmission simultaneously.

Specifically, we will fine-grained the cities with outbreaks of COVID-19 according to China's administrative division[1] rules, where $\mathcal{D}$ denotes the set of districts D_i obtained after division. The inter-district population mobility is approximately modeled, which is conducive to capturing the spatial feature of COVID-19 transmission. Formally, we define a contacts matrix $\mathcal{M}$ to depict the interactions between districts as follows:

$$
\mathcal{M} = \begin{bmatrix} m_{11} & \cdots & m_{1|\mathcal{D}|} \\ \vdots & \ddots & \vdots \\ m_{|\mathcal{D}|1} & \cdots & m_{|\mathcal{D}||\mathcal{D}|} \end{bmatrix}, \mathcal{M} \in \mathbf{R}^{|\mathcal{D}| \times |\mathcal{D}|},
\tag{3}
$$

where m_{ij} denotes the degree of contact between district i and j. It is determined by demography[2] and territorial statistics. Note that $\mathcal{M}$ is a $|\mathcal{D}| \times |\mathcal{D}|$ matrix, and $|\mathcal{D}|$ is the number of the districts in the city with COVID-19 outbreak. The incorporation of the matrix $\mathcal{M}$ will affect the propagation pattern of COVID-19 between districts, which we describe in detail subsequently.

For any district D_i, we develop the SEIR model to capture the transmission of COVID-19 within D_i. The SEIR model defines four populations, i.e., four states: the susceptible (S), the exposed (E, those in the latent phase), the infected (I), and the recovered (R). People in the incubation period belong to state E, which

[1] http://www.gov.cn/index.htm.
[2] http://www.stats.gov.cn/.

gives a good representation of the latent transmission of COVID-19. In addition, we ignore the effect of birth rate and death rate on the spread of COVID-19 due to the short time period in our study. In other words, we assume that the sum of these four groups of populations among all districts is always equal to the total population size N:

$$N = \sum_{i=1}^{|\mathcal{D}|} N_i = \sum_{i=1}^{|\mathcal{D}|} S_i + E_i + I_i + R_i, \tag{4}$$

where N_i is the total population for district i. In general, we use the following set of equations to describe our model:

$$
\begin{aligned}
\frac{dS_i}{dt} &= -\sum_{j \in \mathcal{D}} \frac{\beta m_{ij}(\epsilon E_j + \delta I_j)}{N_j} S_i; \\
\frac{dE_i}{dt} &= \sum_{j \in \mathcal{D}} \frac{\beta m_{ij}(\epsilon E_j + \delta I_j)}{N_j} S_i - \alpha E_i; \\
\frac{dI_i}{dt} &= \alpha E_i - \lambda I_i; \\
\frac{dR_i}{dt} &= \lambda I_i,
\end{aligned}
\tag{5}
$$

where β denotes the contact rate between susceptible and infectious disease carriers, including most of I, and a small part of E (because the incubation period of COVID-19 is also infectious). α denotes the probability of moving from a latent state E to an infected state I. λ is the probability of recovery of an infected person.

It is worth noting that, unlike the traditional SEIR model, the transmission probability of state S to state E is redefined as the following equation $p_i(t)$:

$$p_i(t) = \sum_{j \in \mathcal{D}} \frac{\beta m_{ij}(\epsilon E_j + \delta I_j)}{N_j}, \tag{6}$$

where m_{ij} denotes the movement frequency between districts. Given that COVID-19 is also infectious during the exposed period, a transmission factor ϵ is used to simulate this phenomenon. Besides, the Chinese government has a zero-tolerance attitude towards COVID-19, and therefore part of the infected individuals will be quarantined, which is about $(1 - \delta)$. Thus, we use $(\epsilon E_j + \delta I_j)/N_j$ represents the proportion of infectious cases in the districts j. The $p_i(t)$ means that the current state transmission within a district i is jointly influenced by the contact and proportion of infections in all other districts.

3.2 DRL-enabled Dynamic Intervention Decision Framework

Epidemic control problems are dynamic, stochastic, and with large solution space, making it difficult to effectively control the development of infectious diseases with empirical knowledge. To this end, we design an intervention decision framework for infectious disease, which is driven by deep reinforcement learning. Based on the infectious disease control context, we reformulate the reinforcement learning essential components, i.e., environment, agent, state, action, reward, and transition function, as follows:

- **Environment and agent:** We employ the proposed DC-SEIR epidemiological model as the environment for DRL agent. The agent, playing the role of a government, uses the policy $\pi_\phi(\cdot|s)$, a learned function, to make appropriate intervention depending on the state of the environment.
- **State:** We simulate the spread of COVID-19 on a scale of days and take the number of populations in four states as the state observed by the agent. For the sake of realism, the economic damage caused by the closure of the city can also be observed.
- **Action:** The action in this scenarios is defined as whether to closure a district which influencing the quota for each inter-district's contact matrix. The agent's goal is to maximize its reward over the horizon of the pandemic by choosing action from the action set $\mathcal{A} = \{Unlockdown, Lockdown\}$.
- **Reward:** We define the reward to reflect the change of infected cases, which encourages agent to minimized the number of infected cases. Meanwhile, the economy constrain is imposed to keep stable socio-economic development. To this end, we use a reward that is a weighted sum of two objectives:

$$r(s,a) = (1 - \omega)(\Delta S(s)) + \omega r_e, \tag{7}$$

where $\Delta S(s)$ denotes the difference between the cumulative number of susceptible population at adjacent moments. r_e indicates the economic loss due to the lockdown of the city. ω is a parameter to trade-off relation between epidemic control and economic loss.
- **Transition function:** The infectious disease dynamics, i.e., Eq. (5), drives the transition of states. On this basis, we add noise to reflect the uncertainty existing in reality, which makes the model more realistic.

We deploy the Proximal Policy Optimization (PPO) [15] agent, an on-policy method, to learning a epidemic control policy autonomously. It is an actor-critic method with the critic and policy networks, respectively. The critic network is used to estimate the action value, which can guide the policy to choose an optimal action and further maximize the cumulative reward. Algorithm 1 summarizes the whole epidemic control process in pseudo-code.

In general, DRL-EC is an autonomous learning framework that is driven by the DRL method to make a decision on infectious disease interventions. Secondly, the DC-SEIR compartmental model is proposed to capture epidemic transmission of inter-district, which is conducive to characterizing the spatial and temporal nature of infectious disease transmission simultaneously. In a nutshell, DRL-EC is an effective and adaptive approach that is more competitive than the strategies based on rules-of-thumb.

Algorithm 1: District-Coupled Epidemic Control via DRL

Input: The number of the populations in each district N_i, and the epidemiological parameters.

Output: Parameters for policy π_ϕ.

1 Initialize the DC-SEIR with epidemiological parameters;
2 Initialize the contact matrix $\mathcal{M}$;   ▷ Initialization
3 Initialize the policy network π_ϕ and critic network V_θ;
4 **for** $i \in \{1, 2, \cdots, L_{epi}\}$ **do**
5   **for** $t \in \{1, 2, \cdots, T\}$ **do**
6   Select actions $a \sim \pi_i(\cdot|s)$;
7   Execute action a and update the contact matrix $\mathcal{M}$;   ▷ Simulation
8   Calculate the difference in each group:$\varDelta S, \varDelta E, \varDelta I, \varDelta R$;
9   Update the state s, and obtain reward r;
10   Update π_ϕ with simulation data;
11   Use PPO [15] to train and update the policy and critic;   ▷ Training

Return: The policy network parameter ϕ.

---

4 Experiments

In this section, we first describe the datasets, and then we conduct extensive experiments to evaluate the effectiveness and practicability of the proposed DRL-EC model. Overall, we will investigate the following three questions.

- **Q1:** Is the proposed model effective, i.e., whether the strategy can be learned?
- **Q2:** What strategy does DRL-EC adopt to reduce the number of infections?
- **Q3:** How does critical parameters affect the performance of the model?

4.1 Experimental Setup

Datasets. Changchun is major city in China with COVID-19 outbreaks in 2022. So we collect recent epidemic data[3] in Changchun, and use the latest 2021 census data from this city made available by the National Bureau of Statistics of China. The epidemic datasets are the infected cases number of COVID-19 in this city: Changchun from March 04 to April 03. We combine census data with epidemic data to evaluate the proposed DRL-EC model.

Baselines. At present, there is no suitable epidemic control method based on reinforcement learning, so two manual methods are selected to demonstrate the superiority of our proposed method, which are detailed as follows:

- Random-policy: When training the model, it randomly executes the intervention policy at any stage of the epidemic transmission process.
- Non-intervention: When training the model, it stays open continuously and does not execute the intervention policy.

---

[3] http://www.nhc.gov.cn/.

4.2   Results and Analysis

Validation of Model Effectiveness (Q1): To verify the effectiveness of the DRL-EC model in the infectious disease control tasks, we selected the epidemic data of Changchun to train this model. Figure 2(a) presents the episode reward curve of our method, and it is evident that the reward value converges steadily to −0.4 at about 40 thousand episodes. Other manual methods have no obvious convergence process, especially the non-intervention method, and its reward value is −3 at the end of each training episode. In contrast, we can infer that the DRL-EC model has obviously learned effective policy for epidemic control in the training process. The episode reward maintains the upward trend in continuous iteration, and the convergence of the final curves demonstrates the ability of the DRL-EC model to find suitable solutions to control the epidemic, which verifies the effectiveness of the DRL-EC model.

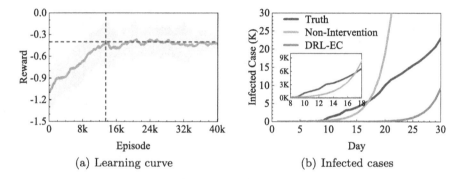

(a) Learning curve	(b) Infected cases

Fig. 2. (a) The overall results on Changchun dataset. The X-axis denotes the episode number and Y-axis denotes the per-step average reward. (b) The number of cumulative cases of infection under different interventions. The partial magnifications are set up to present the differences.

Validation of Model Feasibility (Q2): After training, we test the feasibility of the DRL-EC model to answer question 2. As shown in Fig. 2(b), the epidemic curve obtained from the DRL-EC model consistently maintains a lower infection situation compared to the actual curve and the no-intervention policy. We further analyzed the curves and found an overlap between the actual curve and the non-intervention curve from day 10 to day 15. It seems unreasonable, but there is a covert state in the early stages of the epidemic transmission, and it will take some time for the epidemic control policy to take effect. Therefore, there is an overlap phenomenon caused by shift on time scale and policy delay on the two curves. Combined with the analysis of the three curves, the epidemic situation under the DRL-EC policy is the best, which reflects the feasibility and superiority of the proposed method.

Figure 3 shows the specific policy adopted by the DRL-EC model, represented by the frequency of actions performed. DRL-EC method implements a low-intensity closure policy when the number of previous infections is small. When the infection cases reach a certain threshold, i.e., in the middle of the epidemic transmission, the DRL-EC method begins to maintain a high-intensity closure policy. As a result, the lockdown action frequency of the DRL-EC in this period is significantly higher than that in the previous period. During the final period, the DRL-EC method gradually reduces the intensity of the closure.

In summary, we can draw the following general conclusions: 1) the DRL-EC model can significantly reduce the number of infections (Fig. 2(b)); 2) the DRL-EC policy is to perform lockdown action in succession in the early stages and to perform a high-intensity closure policy on the 10th day (Fig. 3).

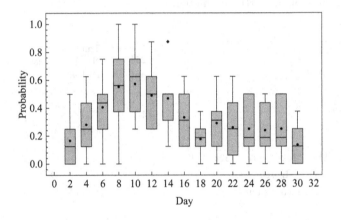

Fig. 3. The frequency of interventions changes over time of outbreaks.

4.3   Parameter Sensitivity (Q3)

In this subsection, we mainly study the influence of economy loss weight ω and basic reproductive number R_0 on the proposed model. The experiment results on ω are shown in Fig. 4(a), the red and orange curves perform better, and these ω settings can better balance the relationship between epidemic control and the economy. The higher ω pays more attention to reducing the economic loss caused by the closure, and the blue curve indicates that the model converges to around -1.2. It is only slightly higher than the score of the non-intervention method, and the high infection situation caused by the higher ω is unacceptable. Compared with the red and orange curves, the orange curve has a lower ω, indicating that it is more concerned about epidemic control. The economic constraints are minimal in this situation, and the closure strategy is strictly enforced. Although the number of infections decreases, the economic loss is more significant. We finally choose $\omega = 0.01$, which has a higher overall reward than the stricter control policy, i.e., converges to around -0.4, and can pay balanced attention to economic factors while maintaining epidemic control. R_0 is used to indicate the intensity of infectious diseases transmission, and We set the test range of R_0 from 3.5 to 4.5. Figure 4(b) shows that the curves can converge effectively. For the outbreak of Omicron in China, we use $R_0 = 4.0$.

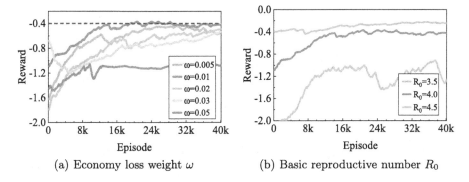

(a) Economy loss weight ω (b) Basic reproductive number R_0

Fig. 4. Effect of loss weight and basic reproductive number to performance.

5   Conclusion

In this paper, we study the problem of intervention decisions in epidemic control. We propose a deep reinforcement learning-enabled intervention decision framework, which can autonomously learn the epidemic control policy to adapt to the current pandemic, e.g., COVID-19. Meanwhile, DC-SEIR, an extension of the SEIR model, is devised to take the inter-district mobility into consideration, which portrays the spatiotemporal feature of epidemic transmission. Finally, we conduct extensive experiments and analyses in the context of Omicron outbreaking in China, which demonstrates that the DRL-EC achieves better performance when compared to the strategies based on rules-of-thumb. For further work, we will explore making a decision on multiple intervention strategies simultaneously and apply it to more cities.

References

1. Bastani, H., et al.: Efficient and targeted COVID-19 border testing via reinforcement learning. Nature **599**(7883), 108–113 (2021)
2. Beigi, A., Yousefpour, A., Yasami, A., Gómez-Aguilar, J., Bekiros, S., Jahanshahi, H.: Application of reinforcement learning for effective vaccination strategies of coronavirus disease 2019 (COVID-19). Eur. Phys. J. Plus **136**(5), 1–22 (2021)

3. Chen, H., Yang, B., Liu, J.: Partially observable reinforcement learning for sustainable active surveillance. In: Liu, W., Giunchiglia, F., Yang, B. (eds.) KSEM 2018. LNCS (LNAI), vol. 11062, pp. 425–437. Springer, Cham (2018). https://doi.org/10.1007/978-3-319-99247-1_38

4. Colas, C., et al.: EpidemiOptim: a toolbox for the optimization of control policies in epidemiological models. J. Artif. Intell. Res. **71**, 479–519 (2021)

5. Hao, Q., Chen, L., Xu, F., Li, Y.: Understanding the urban pandemic spreading of COVID-19 with real world mobility data. In: Proceedings of the 26th ACM SIGKDD International Conference on Knowledge Discovery & Data Mining, pp. 3485–3492 (2020)

6. Hao, Q., Xu, F., Chen, L., Hui, P., Li, Y.: Hierarchical reinforcement learning for scarce medical resource allocation with imperfect information. In: Proceedings of the 27th ACM SIGKDD Conference on Knowledge Discovery & Data Mining, pp. 2955–2963 (2021)

7. Hopkin, M.: Mice unlock mystery of Spanish flu. Nature (2004). https://doi.org/10.1038/041010-12

8. Iketani, S., et al.: Antibody evasion properties of SARS-CoV-2 Omicron sublineages. Nature (2022). https://doi.org/10.1038/s41586-022-04594-4

9. Kompella, V., et al.: Reinforcement learning for optimization of COVID-19 mitigation policies. arXiv preprint arXiv:2010.10560 (2020)

10. Liao, M., et al.: A technical review of face mask wearing in preventing respiratory COVID-19 transmission. Curr. Opin. Colloid Interface Sci. **52**, 101417 (2021)

11. Libin, P.J.K., et al.: Deep reinforcement learning for large-scale epidemic control. In: Dong, Y., Ifrim, G., Mladenić, D., Saunders, C., Van Hoecke, S. (eds.) ECML PKDD 2020. LNCS (LNAI), vol. 12461, pp. 155–170. Springer, Cham (2021). https://doi.org/10.1007/978-3-030-67670-4_10

12. Lillicrap, T., et al.: Continuous control with deep reinforcement learning. In: Proceedings of the 33rd International Conference on Machine Learning, pp. 1501–1506 (2016)

13. Lima, L., Atman, A.: Impact of mobility restriction in COVID-19 superspreading events using agent-based model. PLoS ONE **16**(3), e0248708 (2021)

14. Mnih, V., et al.: Human-level control through deep reinforcement learning. Nature **518**(7540), 529–533 (2015)

15. Schulman, J., Wolski, F., Dhariwal, P., Radford, A., Klimov, O.: Proximal policy optimization algorithms. arXiv preprint arXiv:1707.06347 (2017)

16. Silver, D., Schrittwieser, J., et al.: Mastering the game of go without human knowledge. Nature **550**(7676), 354–359 (2017)

17. Song, S., Zong, Z., Li, Y., Liu, X., Yu, Y.: Reinforced epidemic control: saving both lives and economy. arXiv preprint arXiv:2008.01257 (2020)

18. Sun, C., Zhai, Z.: The efficacy of social distance and ventilation effectiveness in preventing COVID-19 transmission. Sustain. Urban Areas **62**, 102390 (2020)

19. Sutton, R.S., Barto, A.G.: Reinforcement Learning: An Introduction. MIT Press (2018)

20. Vasiliauskaite, V., Antulov-Fantulin, N., Helbing, D.: On some fundamental challenges in monitoring epidemics. Phil. Trans. R. Soc. A **380**(2214), 20210117 (2022)

21. Wan, R., Zhang, X., Song, R.: Multi-objective model-based reinforcement learning for infectious disease control. In: Proceedings of the 27th ACM SIGKDD Conference on Knowledge Discovery & Data Mining, pp. 1634–1644 (2021)

22. World Health Organization: World health organization coronavirus (COVID-19) dashboard (2021). https://covid19.who.int/. Accessed 2 Apr 2022

Multi-modal Face Anti-spoofing Using Channel Cross Fusion Network and Global Depth-Wise Convolution

Qian Zhou[1], Ming Yang[1(✉)], Shidong Chen[2], Mengfan Tang[1], and Xingbin Wang[1]

[1] College of Computer and Information Science, Southwest University, Chongqing, China
{andreaszhou,tangmengfan,w718096321}@email.swu.edu.cn,
yangming@swu.edu.cn
[2] Chongqing Scivatar Intelligent Technology Co. Ltd, Chongqing, China
ljchen@scivatar.com

Abstract. The rapid deployment of facial biometric system has raised attention about their vulnerability to presentation attacks (PAs). Currently, due to the feature extraction capability of convolution neural network (CNN), it has achieved excellent results in most multi-modal face anti-spoofing (FAS) algorithms. Similarly, we proposed multi-modal FAS using Channel Cross Fusion Network (CCFN) and Depth-wise Convolution (GDConv), FaceBagNets for short. The CCFN is utilized to cross-fuse multi-modal feature by using the pairwise cross approach before fusing multi-modal feature in the channel direction, and the GDConv replaces the global average pooling (GAP) to raise the performance. We also utilized the patch-based strategy to obtain richer feature, the random model feature erasing (RMFE) strategy to prevent the over-fitting and the squeeze-and-excitation network (SE-NET) to focus on key feature. Finally, we conducted extensive experiments on two multi-modal datasets, then verified the effectiveness of the CCFN and the GDConv. Much advanced results were acquired and outperformed most state-of-the-art methods.

Keywords: Face anti-spoofing · Multi-modal · Channel Cross Fusion Network · Depth-wise convolution · Convolution neural network · Attention network

1 Introduction

With the boom in deep learning, CNN has permeated various domains. Biometric face recognition in one of these domains has a large number of risks need to be considered in automated border control, etc. The topic of how to develop a FAS system that is resistant to various PAs has attracted extensive attention in academia and industry. FAS is used to determine whether a face image captured in real time is living or not, and thus to determine whether biometric information is obtained. The corresponding common PAs in face models include printed photo, video playback, stereo 3D mask, etc. In essence, these PAs fool the biometric face models to gain erroneous results. Corresponding to the widely used methods include voice verification, color texture analysis, user

© The Author(s), under exclusive license to Springer Nature Switzerland AG 2022
G. Memmi et al. (Eds.): KSEM 2022, LNAI 13369, pp. 429–441, 2022.
https://doi.org/10.1007/978-3-031-10986-7_35

cooperation action detection, etc. In addition, researchers utilize many auxiliary devices such as infrared camera to avoid losses. Currently, hardware-based FAS methods require abundant high-quality and high-precision sensors, which can't cater to meet daily life. However, the software-based FAS methods don't have this fatal problem, which can be divided generally into two directions: (1) FAS based on machine learning, and (2) FAS based on deep learning. For the former methods, the artificially designed features are extracted from the face image, and then the FAS is transformed into a classification task, mainly using LBP [7, 8], SURF [1], etc. For the later methods, network models such as ResNet [2] and DenseNet [3] are published and attention mechanism networks such as SE-NET [4] are proposed, the neural network model can efficiently and intensively extract rich feature for various tasks. Sometimes, CNN methods for FAS of generalization performance isn't very high. With the emergence of datasets such as CASIA-SURF [5] and CASIA-SURF CeFA [6], multi-modal FAS methods are one of the principal methods for PAs.

The main works and contributions are as follows: (1) We proposed the CCFN to fuse the feature of each layer by the pairwise cross approach to obtain 99.8052% (TPR@FPR-= 10e–4). (2) We utilized the GDConv to replace the GAP, the patch-based to extract feature, the RMFE to avoid over-fitting and the SE-NET to obtain significant feature. (3) Firstly, we trained, validated and tested on the CASIA-SURF dataset, then gained the score of 100.000% (TPR@FPR = 10e–4) on the validation set and the score of 99.8912% (TPR@FPR = 10e–4) on the test set. Next, we verified the effectiveness of the CCFN and the GDConv. Finally, we analyzed models through visual. (4) We also trained and validated on the CASIA-SURF CeFA dataset, then obtained the 0.0000% (ACER) on the validation dataset.

The rest of this article is organized as follows. In Sect. 2, we discuss related works. In Sect. 3, we describe the proposed method and module. In Sect. 4, we elaborate the experimental details, procedure and results. Finally, we conclude our work in Sect. 5.

2 Related Work

Previous works utilize the artificially designed features for FAS. Chingovska et al. [7] used LBP to extract discriminant feature from grayscale images, and then processed the classification task through three classifiers. Maatta et al. [8] proposed a feature extraction method based on multiple LBP. Kose and Dugelay et al. [9] proposed a method to analyze the reflection characteristics of mask and living for face mask detection. Wen et al. [10] proposed face living detection based on image distortion and analyzed distorted images. Zhang et al. [11] used multi-DoG filter to remove noise and low-frequency information. Pereira et al. [12] used spatial and temporal descriptors to encode and obtain richer information. Li et al. [13] proposed remote biometrics and remote heart rate, extracted feature through a cascaded texture LBP extractor. Boulkenafet et al. [14] detected whether the image is a real face through color texture analysis, and classified the joint color texture feature in different brightness and chroma channels. However, due to the illumination and posture, these methods can't capture the distinguishing feature well, resulting in poor performance.

Researchers turn their attention to deep learning, Atoum et al. [15] first considered using CNNs to extract local face color image features and depth image feature and took the depth image feature as difference feature. Lucena et al. [16] and Chen et al. [17] fine-tuned pre-training the network model for FAS. Deb and Jain [18] proposed using full convolution network to learn local discrimination cues. Heusch et al. [19] considered the lightweight mobilenetv2 network to achieve efficient FAS. Ma et al. [20] proposed multi-region CNN for local binary classification of local blocks. Hao [21] et al. and Almeida et al. [22] introduced contrast loss and triplet loss to enhance the discrimination ability of deep embedded features. Chen et al. [23] used the binary focal loss to guide the model to distinguish hard samples well. With the completion and promotion of multi-modal datasets, Parkin and Grinchuk [24] proposed multi-level feature aggregation module and used other datasets to pretrain the model. Shen et al. [25] proposed the random modal feature erasing to prevent over-fitting and multi-stream fusion strategy to obtain multi-modal fusion feature. Zhang et al. [26] proposed lightweight neural network model and streaming model to improve the performance. Meanwhile, researchers proposed various methods, including generalized learning [27, 28] and cross-modal translation [29], etc. But the calculation and the security need to be considered.

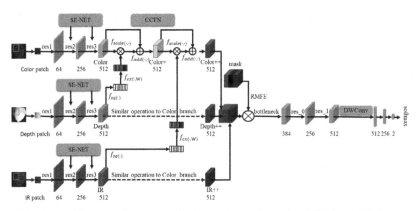

Fig. 1. Architecture of multi-modal face anti-spoofing using CCFN and GDConv.

3   Methods

In this work, we proposed the multi-modal method is shown in Fig. 1. The model is trained with end-to-end strategy. RGB patch, Depth patch and IR patch are input simultaneously into the model. From the method proposed by Shen et al. [25], we also adopted the patch-based to extract rich feature, the multi-stream fusion to aggregate multi-modal feature in channel direction and the RMFE to prevent over-fitting. In addition to, we introduced the deep feature extraction module, GDConv and CCFN. The main modules and strategies are introduced in detail below.

3.1   Deep Feature Extraction Module

Multi-modal model has three branches is shown in Fig. 1. For each branch, there is a corresponding patch image exacted randomly from original modal image as input. Then by using deep feature extraction module to obtain rich feature from each patch. As shown in Table 1, the output feature and specific parameter are recorded in detail. In Fig. 1, for each convolution of res2 and res3, we add SE-NET attention network combined with the residual blocks during training phase to focus on useful feature.

Table 1. FaceBagNets network structure ($3 \times 48 \times 48$ for an example)

Layer	Output feature	Specific parameters
res1	$64 \times 12 \times 12$	$\begin{bmatrix} \text{conv } 7 \times 7, \text{ stride } 2 \\ \text{Maxpool } 3 \times 3, \text{ stride } 2 \end{bmatrix}$
res2	$256 \times 12 \times 12$	$\begin{bmatrix} \text{conv } 1 \times 1 \\ \text{conv } 3 \times 3, \text{ group } 32, \text{ stride } 2 \\ \text{conv } 1 \times 1 \end{bmatrix} \times 2$
res3	$512 \times 6 \times 6$	$\begin{bmatrix} \text{conv } 1 \times 1 \\ \text{conv } 3 \times 3, \text{ group } 32, \text{ stride } 2 \\ \text{conv } 1 \times 1 \end{bmatrix} \times 2$
bottleneck	$384 \times 6 \times 6$	$[\text{conv } 1 \times 1, \text{ stride } 1]$
res_0	$256 \times 3 \times 3$	$\begin{bmatrix} \text{conv } 3 \times 3, \text{ stride } 2 \\ \text{conv } 3 \times 3, \text{ stride } 2 \end{bmatrix} \times 2$
res_1	$512 \times 2 \times 2$	$\begin{bmatrix} \text{conv } 3 \times 3, \text{ stride } 2 \\ \text{conv } 3 \times 3, \text{ stride } 2 \end{bmatrix} \times 2$
GDConv	$512 \times 1 \times 1$	$[\text{conv } 2 \times 2, \text{ group } 512, \text{ stride } 1]$

3.2   Channel Cross Fusion Network

In Fig. 1, we introduced the CCFN to gain fusion feature by the pairwise cross method (Taking the color layer as an example). Let C_c define the Color feature, D_c define the Depth feature, I_c define the IR feature, C_c^+ define the Color+ feature, and C_c^{++} define the Color++ feature. Z_c, S_c, Z_c^+, S_c^+ are variables, the process is as follows,

1. The Depth feature is compressed along the spatial dimension, the number of input channel matches output channel, as in (1), where H is the height, W is the width.

$$Z_c = f_{sq}(D_c) = \frac{1}{H \times W} \sum_{i=1}^{H} \sum_{j=1}^{W} D_c(i,j) \tag{1}$$

2. According to the correlation between channels, a weight value is generated to represent the importance of each channel, as in (2), where $W_1 \in R^{\frac{C}{r} \times C}$, $W_2 \in R^{C \times \frac{C}{r}}$.

$$S_c = f_{ex}(Z_c, W) = \sigma(g(Z_c, W)) = \sigma(W_2 ReLU(W_1 Z_c)) \tag{2}$$

3. The weight value of each channel number is weighted to the Color feature channel by channel through multiplication, and then the weighted result is added with the original Color feature to obtain the Color+ feature, as in (3).

$$C_c^+ = f_{add}(f_{scale}(C_c, S_c), C_c) = C_c \cdot S_c + C_c \tag{3}$$

4. The IR feature is processed similarly in step 1, as in (4),

$$Z_c^+ = f_{sq}(I_c) = \frac{1}{H \times W} \sum_{i=1}^{H} \sum_{j=1}^{W} I_c(i, j) \tag{4}$$

5. After the processing in step 4, Z_c^+ is processed similarly in step 2, as in (5),

$$S_c^+ = f_{ex}(Z_c^+, W) = \sigma(W_2 ReLU(W_1 Z_c^+)) W_1 \in R^{\frac{C}{r} \times C}, W_2 \in R^{C \times \frac{C}{r}} \tag{5}$$

6. The weight value is weighted to the Color+ feature channel by channel through multiplication, and then the weighted result is added with the original Color+ feature to obtain the Color++ feature, as in (6).

$$C_c^{++} = f_{add}(f_{scale}(C_c^+, S_c^+), C_c^+) = C_c^+ \cdot S_c^+ + C_c^+ \tag{6}$$

3.3 GDConv

The specific operation steps as in (7), C is channel, H is height and W is width. $X_{i,j}$ is the one-dimension feature, F is a $C \times H \times W$ feature, K is the depth-wise convolution kernel, the stride size is 1, the group is C, the padding is 0 and (i, j) is spatial position.

$$X_{i,j} = \sum_{c=0}^{C-1} \sum_{m=0}^{H-1} \sum_{n=0}^{W-1} K_{c,m,n} F_{c,i+m,j+n} \tag{7}$$

4 Experiments

4.1 Implementation Details

The complete images are resized to 112×112, and the dataset is enhanced by random flipping, rotation, cropping and affine, etc. The image patches are 16×16, 32×32, 48×48 and 96×96, respectively, which are randomly extracted from the 112×112 face images. All models are trained using NVIDIA TITAN RTX 24G GPU with a batch size of 128 and 500 epochs. Color patch, Depth patch and IR patch are input simultaneously in the multi-layer network and are fused after CCFN, and the values of weigh decay and momentum are set to 0.0005 and 0.9, respectively. Meanwhile, we use the PyTorch as deep learning framework, stochastic gradient descent optimizer with a cyclic cosine annealing learning rate schedule and cross entropy loss function. During the validation and test, the experiment data are recorded and compared.

4.2   Model Evaluation Results Analysis

In the experiments, firstly, we used the FaceBagNets to compare with other teams on the CASIA-SURF test set. As shown in Table 2, we gained the score of 99.8912%, which is superior to the VisionLabs by 0.0173%, superior to the ReadSensor by 0.0860%, superior to the Feather by 1.7471%, superior to the Hahahaha by 6.7362%, and superior to the MAC-adv-group by 10.3333%. Then, we used the FaceBagNets to compare with other FAS methods on CASIA-SURF test set. As shown in Table 3, FaceBagNets takes the lead in other methods on the NPCER(%), the ACER(%), the TPR(%)@FPR $= 10e-2$, the TPR(%)@FPR $= 10e-3$ and the TPR(%)@FPR $= 10e-4$. Meanwhile, our method only used a one-stage and end-to-end training strategy. Consequently, we confirmed the superiority of ours. We also compared with other teams on CASIA-SURF CeFA validation set. As shown in Table 4, we obtained the score of 0.0000% (ACER) to achieve ranked first.

Table 2. Test results comparison between ours and the CVPR@2019 face anti-spoofing attack detection challenge teams (%) (The best result is bold, the second result is underlined)

Team name	FP	FN	APCER	NPCER	ACER	TPR(%)@FPR		
						$=10e-2$	$=10e-3$	$=10e-4$
VisionLabs	3	27	**0.0074%**	0.1546%	**0.0810%**	99.9885	99.9541	99.8739
ReadSensor	77	1	0.1912%	**0.0057%**	0.0985%	**100.000**	99.9472	99.8052
Feather	48	53	0.1192%	0.1392%	0.1292%	99.9541	99.8396	98.1441
Hahahaha	55	214	0.1366%	1.2257%	0.6812%	99.6849	98.5909	93.1550
MAC-adv	825	30	2.0495%	0.1718%	1.1107%	99.5131	97.2505	89.5579
Ours	109	4	0.2708%	0.0229%	0.1469%	**100.000**	**99.9828**	**99.8912**

Table 3. Test results comparison between ours and other face anti-spoof algorithms (%)

Method	APCER	NPCER	ACER	TPR(%)@FPR		
				$=10e-2$	$=10e-3$	$=10e-4$
NHF fusion [30]	5.6%	3.8%	4.7%	89.1	33.6	17.8
Single-scale SE fusion [30]	3.8%	1.0%	2.4%	96.7	81.8	56.8
Multi-scale SE fusion [5]	1.6%	0.08%	0.8%	99.8	98.4	95.2
Shi.et al. [31]	–	–	3.0%	93.0	75.9	45.3
Li.et al. [32]	**0.05%**	1.79%	0.92%	99.9	–	–
Kuang.et al. [33]	1.3%	1.0%	1.1%	98.7	91.1	76.1
Wang.et al. [34]	0.2%	0.3%	0.2%	99.9	99.1	97.6
PSMM-Net [6]	0.7%	0.06%	0.4%	99.9	99.3	96.2
PSMM-Net(CeFA)[6]	0.5%	**0.02%**	0.2%	99.9	99.7	97.6
Ours	0.27%	**0.02%**	**0.15%**	**100.0**	**100.0**	**99.9**

Table 4. The validation results comparison between ours and multi-modal cross-ethnicity FAS recognition challenge@CVPR2020 (%)

User	APCER	BPCER	ACER/Rank
harvest	**0.0000%**	**0.0000%**	**0.0000%/(1)**
ccq195	**0.0000%**	**0.0000%**	**0.0000%/(1)**
ZhangTT	**0.0000%**	**0.0000%**	**0.0000%/(1)**
itrushkin	0.6667%	0.6667%	0.6667%/(2)
TOP	5.6667%	5.6667%	5.6667%/(3)
gesture_challenge	12.0000%	13.0000%	12.5000%/(4)
ours	**0.0000%**	**0.0000%**	**0.0000%/(1)**

4.3 Ablation Experiment

Effectiveness of CCFN. In the experiments, we explored the effectiveness of CCFN.

Validation Results Analyses. As shown in Table 5. For the 16×16, 32×32 and 48×48 patches, the FaceBagNet (CCFN) is superior to the FaceBagNet on the TPR(%)@FP-R $= 10e{-}4$. On the 96×96 patch, compared with the FaceBagNet, the performance is poor. But we obtain the scores of 100.000% on the 32×32 and the 48×48 patches. So CCFN can effectively raise the ability of model on the validation set. The ACER (%) values are relatively close, so CCFN hasn't negative impact on the model.

Table 5. Validation results comparison between FaceBagNet and FaceBagNet (CCFN) (%)

Patch size	Network	ACER	TPR(%)@FPR $= 10e{-}4$
16×16	FaceBagNet	1.1467%	92.5518
	FaceBagNet (CCFN)	0.9810%	**95.4242**
32×32	FaceBagNet	0.0803%	99.8998
	FaceBagNet (CCFN)	0.1058%	**100.000**
48×48	FaceBagNet	0.0302%	**100.000**
	FaceBagNet (CCFN)	0.0454%	**100.000**
96×96	FaceBagNet	0.8542%	**99.8998**
	FaceBagNet (CCFN)	1.0253%	97.5952

Test Results Analyses. As shown in Table 6. For the TPR(%)@FPR $= 10e{-}4$, the Face-BagNet (CCFN) achieves the score of 99.8052% and exceeds the FaceBagNet on the 32×32 and the 48×48 patches. On the 16×16 and the 96×96 patches, the performances are lower than FaceBagNet, but the highest score is obtained by adding the CCFN on the

32×32 patch, and is higher than many advanced methods. So the patch is proper and the CCFN is added, the performance surpasses many methods. In Fig. 2, FaceBagNet (CCFN) achieves the best result on the 32×32 patch and gets the largest area.

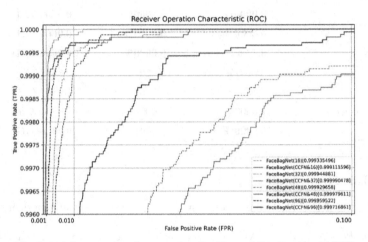

Fig. 2. ROC comparison between FaceBagNet and FaceBagNet (CCFN)

Effectiveness of GDConv. In the experiments, we verified the effectiveness of the GDConv. FaceBagNets are equivalent to FaceBagNet (CCFN) plus GDConv.

Table 6. Test results comparison between FaceBagNet and FaceBagNet (CCFN) (%)

Network	Patch size	APCER	NPCER	ACER	TPR(%)@FPR		
					=10e–2	=10e–3	=10e–4
FaceBagNet	16×16	1.0236%	1.5294%	1.2765%	99.9198	98.4420	**94.2605**
	32×32	0.3677%	0.2520%	0.3099%	100.000	99.9542	98.9747
	48×48	0.3925%	0.3666%	0.3796%	100.000	99.9141	98.8888
	96×96	2.2906%	0.0115%	1.1510%	100.000	99.9714	**99.4558**
FaceBagNet (CCFN)	16×16	1.5950%	1.3223%	1.4591%	99.9026	97.9952	92.7712
	32×32	0.4348%	0.0229%	0.2288%	100.000	99.9885	**99.8052**
	48×48	0.1764%	0.1317%	0.1541%	100.000	99.9656	**99.7652**
	96×96	2.4371%	0.2119%	1.3245%	99.9943	99.5303	95.9789

Effectiveness of GDConv. In the experiments, we verified the effectiveness of the GDConv. FaceBagNets are equivalent to FaceBagNet (CCFN) plus GDConv.

Validation Results Analyses. As shown in Table 7. For the 32×32, 48×48 and 96×96 patches, the FaceBagNets is superior to the FaceBagNet (CCFN) on the TPR(%)@F-PR = 10e–4. On the 16×16 patch, the performance is poor, but the overall performance is improved and the GDConv is added on the 32×32 and 48×48, which achieves scores of 100.000%, while maintaining a lower error rate. Therefore, GDConv effectively enhances the detection ability on the validation set.

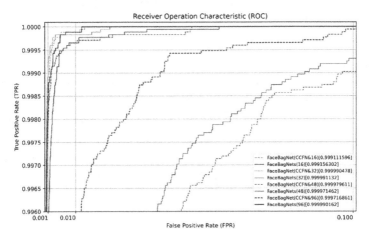

Fig. 3. ROC comparison between FaceBagNet (CCFN) and FaceBagNets.

Test Results Analyses. The test set results are shown in Table 8. By comparing the TP-R(%)@FPR = 10e–4, FaceBagNets achieves the score of 99.8912%, which is 0.0860% superior to the best result of the FaceBagNet (CCFN). The FaceBagNets is ahead of the FaceBagNet (CCFN) on the 32×32 and 96×96 patches. On the 16×16 and 48×48 patches, the performances are lower than the FaceBagNet (CCFN), but adding the GDConv achieves two better results, which are superior to the highest score of the

Table 7. Validation results comparison between FaceBagNets and FaceBagNet (CCFN) (%)

Patch size	Network	ACER	TPR(%)@FPR = 10e–4
16×16	FaceBagNet (CCFN)	0.9810%	**95.4242**
	FaceBagNets	1.0720%	92.8524
32×32	FaceBagNet (CCFN)	0.1058%	**100.000**
	FaceBagNets	0.0302%	**100.000**
48×48	FaceBagNet (CCFN)	0.0454%	**100.000**
	FaceBagNets	0.0302%	**100.000**
96×96	FaceBagNet (CCFN)	1.0253%	97.5952
	FaceBagNets	0.9903%	**99.6994**

FaceBagNet (CCFN) and achieve scores over most advanced methods. So the patch size is proper, the CCFN and the GDConv are added, the model can achieve the best results. In Fig. 3, FaceBagNets achieves the best result and obtains the largest area.

Table 8. Test results comparison between FaceBagNets and FaceBagNet (CCFN) (%)

Network	Patch size	APCER	NPCER	ACER	TPR(%)@FPR		
					=10e−2	=10e−3	=10e−4
FaceBagNet (CCFN)	16 × 16	1.5950%	1.3223%	1.4591%	99.9026	97.9952	**92.7712**
	32 × 32	0.4348%	0.0229%	0.2288%	100.000	99.9885	99.8052
	48 × 48	0.1764%	0.1317%	0.1541%	100.000	99.9656	**99.7652**
	96 × 96	2.4371%	0.2119%	1.3245%	99.9943	99.5303	95.9789
FaceBagNets	16 × 16	1.5055%	1.3976%	1.4516%	99.9313	97.9837	92.3015
	32 × 32	0.2708%	0.0229%	0.1469%	100.000	99.9828	**99.8912**
	48 × 48	0.1689%	0.2921%	0.2305%	100.000	99.9656	99.4673
	96 × 96	1.7689%	0.0000%	0.8844%	100.000	99.9885	**99.8511**

4.4 Visual Analysis

Table 9. Hard samples visual results

No.	Type	Color	Depth	IR	FaceBagNet	Ours
1	Attack				0.5402759	**0.32479393**
2	Attack				0.5540096	**0.19917136**
3	Attack				0.52794313	**0.20145279**
4	Live				0.5626166	**0.98602587**
5	Live				0.51954865	**0.98302966**
6	Attack				0.47713676	**0.29086655**
7	Attack				0.49889222	**0.13500738**
8	Attack				0.47621176	**0.07708357**
9	Live				0.47990653	**0.78681415**
10	Live				0.4292608	**0.9588385**

We selected ten difficult classification samples to visually compare our method with the benchmark network. As shown in Table. 9, the scores of FaceBagNets are lower than benchmark network in the first three lines. Meanwhile, the scores of FaceBagNet are greater than 0.5, but the actual samples are labeled as attack, so the discriminant result is wrong. In the fourth and fifth lines, the scores are higher than the FaceBagNet.

In the sixth, seventh and eighth lines, the scores of the FaceBagNets is lower than FaceBagNet. In the ninth and tenth lines, the scores are higher than FaceBagNet, and the scores of FaceBagNet are less than 0.5, but the actual samples are labeled as living, so the classification result is wrong. So the FaceBagNets can detect effectively living and non-living on the hard face simples and reduce discrimination and classification error rate.

5 Conclusions

In this paper, we proposed multi-modal face anti-spoofing using channel cross fusion network and global depth-wise convolution based on multi-stream convolution neural network and attention network, FaceBagNets for short, which exceeds most excellent face anti-spoofing methods and detects effectively living and non-living on the hard simples by visual analysis. We also utilized two multi-modal datasets to train and compare the different results, respectively, which can confirm the effectiveness of the FaceBag-Nets. For all results, we gained the result of 99.8912% (TPR@FPR = 10e–4) on the CASIA-SURF test set and 0.0000% (ACER) CASIA-SURF CeFA validation set. Due to generalize poorly on unseen conditions and unknown attack types, it is crucial to enhance the generalization ability of the deep face anti-spoofing models in academic and industrial fields, which is my future direction.

Acknowledgment. Science and Technology to Boost the Economy 2020 Key Project (SQ2020YFF0410766), Scientific Research Foundation of Southwest University (SWU2008045) and Chongqing Technology Innovation and Application Development Project (cstc2020jscx-msxmX0147).

References

1. Boulkenafet, Z., Komulainen, J., Hadid, A.: Face antispoofing using speeded-up robust features and fisher vector encoding. IEEE Signal Process. Lett. **24**(2), 141–145 (2017)
2. He, K., Zhang, X., Ren, S., Sun, J.: Deep residual learning for image recognition. In: Proceedings of the Conference on Computer Vision and Pattern Recognition (CVPR), pp. 770–778 (2016)
3. Huang, G., Liu, Z., Laurens, V., Weinberger, K. Q.: Densely connected convolutional networks. In: Proceedings of the Conference on Computer Vision and Pattern Recognition (CVPR), pp. 2261–2269 (2017)
4. Hu, J., Shen, L., Albanie, S., Sun, G., Wu, E.: Squeeze-and-excitation networks. IEEE Trans. Pattern Anal. Mach. Intell. **42**(8), 2011–2023 (2020)
5. Zhang, S., et al.: CASIA-SURF: A large-scale multi-modal benchmark for face anti-spoofing. IEEE Trans. Biometrics, Behav. Identity Sci. **2**(2), 182–193 (2020). https://doi.org/10.1109/TBIOM.2020.2973001
6. Liu, A., Tan, Z., Wan, J., Escalera, S., Guo, G., Li, S.Z.: CASIA-SURF CeFA: A benchmark for multi-modal cross-ethnicity face anti-spoofing. In: Proceedings of the Winter Conference on Applications of Computer Vision (WACV), pp. 1178–1186 (2021)
7. Chingovska, I., Anjos, A., Marcel, S.: On the effectiveness of local binary patterns in face anti-spoofing. In: Proceedings of the International Conference of the Biometrics Special Interest Group (BIOSIG), pp. 1–7 (2012)

8. Maatta, J., Hadid, A., Pietikainen, M.: Face spoofing detection from single images using micro-texture analysis. In: Proceedings of the International Joint Conference on Biometrics (IJCB), pp. 1–7 (2011)
9. Kose, N., Dugelay, J.L.: Reflectance analysis based countermeasure technique to detect face mask attacks. In: Proceedings of the International Conference on Digital Signal Processing (DSP), pp. 1–6 (2013)
10. Wen, D., Han, H., Jain, A.K.: Face spoof detection with image distortion analysis. IEEE Trans. Inf. Forensics Secur. **10**(4), 746–761 (2015). https://doi.org/10.1109/TIFS.2015.2400395
11. Zhang, Z., Yan, J., Liu, S., Lei, Z., Yi, D., Li, S.Z.: A face antispoofing database with diverse attacks. In: Proceedings of the 2012 5th IAPR International Conference on Biometrics (ICB), pp.26–31. IEEE (2012)
12. de Freitas Pereira, T., Anjos, A., De Martino, J.M., Marcel, S.: LBP − TOP based counter-measure against face spoofing attacks. In: Proceedings of the Computer Vision Workshops-ACCV 2012, pp. 121–132 (2012)
13. Li, X., Komulainen, J., Zhao, G., Yuen, P., Pietikainen, M.: Generalized face anti-spoofing by detecting pulse from face videos. In: Proceedings of the 23rd International Conference on Pattern Recognition (ICPR), pp.4244–4249 (2016)
14. Boulkenafet, Z., Komulainen, J., Hadid, A.: Face spoofing detection using colour texture analysis. IEEE Trans. Inf. Forensics Secur. **11**(8), 1818–1830 (2016). https://doi.org/10.1109/TIFS.2016.2555286
15. Atoum, Y., Liu, Y., Jourabloo, A., Liu, X.: Face anti-spoofing using patch and depth-based CNNs. In: Proceedings of the International Joint Conference on Biometrics (IJCB), pp.319–328 (2017)
16. Lucena, O., Junior, A., Moia, V., Souza, R., Valle, E., Lotufo, R.: Transfer learning using convolutional neural networks for face anti-spoofing. In: Proceedings of the International Conference Image Analysis and Recognition, pp. 27–34 (2017)
17. Chen, H., Hu, G., Lei, Z., Chen, Y., Robertson, N.M., Li, S.Z.: Attention-based two-stream convolutional networks for face spoofing detection. IEEE Trans. Inf. Forensics Secur. **15**, 578–593 (2020). https://doi.org/10.1109/TIFS.2019.29-22241
18. Deb, D., Jain, A.K.: Look locally infer globally: A generalizable face anti-spoofing approach. IEEE Trans. Inf. Forensics Secur. **16**, 1143–1157 (2021). https://doi.org/10.1109/TIFS.2020.3029879
19. Heusch, G., George, A., Geissbuhler, D., Mostaani, Z., Marcel, S.: Deep models and short-wave infrared information to detect face presentation attacks. IEEE Trans. Biometrics Behav. Identity Sci. **2**(4), 399–409 (2020). https://doi.org/10.1109/TBIOM.2020.3010312
20. Ma, Y., Wu, L., Li, Z., Liu, F.: A novel face presentation attack detection scheme based on multi-regional convolutional neural networks. Pattern Recogn. Lett. **131**, 261–267 (2020). https://doi.org/10.1016/j.patrec.2020.01.002
21. Hao, H., Pei, M., Zhao, M.: Face liveness detection based on client identity using siamese network. In: Lin, Z., Wang, L., Yang, J., Shi, G., Tan, T., Zheng, N., Chen, X., Zhang, Y. (eds.) PRCV 2019. LNCS, vol. 11857, pp. 172–180. Springer, Cham (2019). https://doi.org/10.1007/978-3-030-31654-9_15
22. Almeida, W.R., et al.: Detecting face presentation attacks in mobile devices with a patch-based CNN and a sensor-aware loss function. PLoS ONE **15**(9), e0238058–e0238058 (2020). https://doi.org/10.1371/journal.pone.0238058
23. Chen, B., Yang, W., Li, H., Wang, S., Kwong, S.: Camera invariant feature learning for generalized face anti-spoofing. IEEE Trans. Inf. Forensics Secur. **16**, 2477–2492 (2021). https://doi.org/10.1109/TIFS.2021.3055018
24. Parkin, A., Grinchuk, O.: Recognizing multi-modal face spoofing with face recognition networks. In: Proceedings of the IEEE Conference on Computer Vision and Pattern Recognition Workshops (CVPRW), pp. 1617–1623 (2019)

25. Shen, T., Huang, Y., Tong, Z.: FaceBagNet: Bag-of-local-features model for multi-modal face anti-spoofing. In: Proceedings of the IEEE Conference on Computer Vision and Pattern Recognition Workshops (CVPRW), pp. 1611–1616 (2019)
26. Zhang, P., et al.: FeatherNets: Convolutional neural networks as light as feather for face anti-spoofing. In: Proceedings of the IEEE Conference on Computer Vision and Pattern Recognition Workshops (CVPRW), pp. 1574–1583 (2019)
27. Li, H., Li, W., Cao, H., Wang, S., Huang, F., Kot, A.C.: Unsupervised domain adaptation for face anti-spoofing. IEEE Trans. Inf. Forensics Secur. **13**(7), 1794–1809 (2018). https://doi.org/10.1109/TIFS.2018.2801312
28. Sanghvi, N., Singh, S.K., Agarwal, A., Vatsa, M., Singh, R.: MixNet for generalized face presentation attack detection. In: Proceedings of the 25th International Conference on Pattern Recognition (ICPR), pp. 5511–5518 (2021)
29. Liu, A., et al.: Face anti-spoofing via adversarial cross-modality translation. IEEE Trans. Inf. Forensics Secur. **16**, 2759–2772 (2021). https://doi.org/10.1109/TIFS.2021.3065495
30. Zhang, S., et al.: A dataset and benchmark for large-scale multi-modal face anti-spoofing. In: Proceedings of the IEEE Conference on Computer Vision and Pattern Recognition (CVPR), pp. 919–928 (2019)
31. Shi, L., Zhou, Z., Guo, Z.: Face anti-spoofing using spatial pyramid pooling. In: Proceedings of the International Conference on Pattern Recognition (ICPR), pp. 2126–2133 (2021)
32. Li, Z., Li, H., Luo, X., Hu, Y., Lam, K., Kot, A.C.: Asymmetric modality translation for face presentation attack detection. IEEE Trans. Multimedia, 1–1 (2021). https-://doi.org/https://doi.org/10.1109/TMM.2021.3121140
33. Kuang, H., Ji, R., Liu, H., Zhang, S., Zhang, B.: Multi-modal multi-layer fusion network with average binary center loss for face anti-spoofing. In: Proceedings of the 27th ACM International Conference on Multimedia, pp. 48–56 (2019)
34. Wang, G., Lan, C., Han, H., Shan, S., Chen, X.: Multi-modal face presentation attack detection via spatial and channel attentions. In: Proceedings of the IEEE Conference on Computer Vision and Pattern Recognition Workshops (CVPRW), pp. 1584–1590 (2019)

A Survey of Pretrained Language Models

Kaili Sun[1], Xudong Luo[1(✉)], and Michael Y. Luo[2]

[1] Guangxi Key Lab of Multi-Source Information Mining and Security,
School of Computer Science and Engineering,
Guangxi Normal University, Guilin 541001, China
`luoxd@mailbox.gxnu.edu.cn`
[2] Emmanuel College, Cambridge University, Cambridge CB2 3AP, UK

Abstract. With the emergence of Pretrained Language Models (PLMs) and the success of large-scale PLMs such as BERT and GPT, the field of Natural Language Processing (NLP) has achieved tremendous development. Therefore, nowadays, PLMs have become an indispensable technique for solving problems in NLP. In this paper, we survey PLMs to help researchers quickly understand various PLMs and determine the appropriate ones for their specific NLP projects. Specifically, first, we brief on the main machine learning methods used by PLMs. Second, we explore early PLMs and discuss the main state-of-art PLMs. Third, we review several Chinese PLMs. Fourth, we compare the performance of some mainstream PLMs. Fifth, we outline the applications of PLMs. Finally, we give an outlook on the future development of PLMs.

Keywords: Machine learning · Natural Language Processing · Pretrained Language Models · BERT · GTP

1 Introduction

Pretrained Language Models (PLMs) are a new paradigm in Natural Language Processing (NLP) [22]. As shown in Fig. 1, a PLM is a large neural network. It is pre-trained on a large-scale text corpus through self-supervised learning (which is used to learn common sense from a large corpus with nothing to do with a specific downstream task). Pre-training can be regarded as regularisation to prevent the model from overfitting small data [16]. After being pre-trained, a PLM needs to be fine-tuned for a specific downstream task.

In early NLP tasks, low-dimensional and dense vectors are often used to represent language's syntactic or semantic features through various deep neural networks [32]. However, since deep neural networks usually have many parameters and the dataset used for training is limited, it may often lead to the phenomenon of overfitting. Transfer learning can apply the knowledge learnt in the source domain to the learning task in the target domain [40], alleviating the pressure caused by limited manual annotation data. However, unlabelled data is much larger than labelled data, so it is necessary to learn how to extract useful information from unlabelled data. The emergence of self-supervised learning

© The Author(s), under exclusive license to Springer Nature Switzerland AG 2022
G. Memmi et al. (Eds.): KSEM 2022, LNAI 13369, pp. 442–456, 2022.
https://doi.org/10.1007/978-3-031-10986-7_36

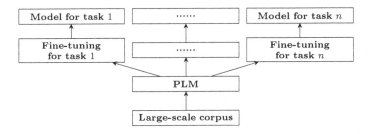

Fig. 1. The training process of a language model

and unsupervised learning solves this problem. Transformer [41] (a deep learning model) is proposed to solve the problem of slow training and low efficiency of Recurrent Neural Networks (RNNs) [36], and integrated with the self-attention mechanism to achieve fast parallel effects. Since then, PLMs have entered a boom phase. Large-scale PLMs such as BERT [11] and GPT [33] succeed greatly, and various improvements to them have been made to solve various NLP tasks.

Although PLMs are crucial to NLP tasks, there are not many surveys for helping researchers to quickly understand various PLMs from different viewpoints and determine the appropriate ones for their specific NLP projects. To amend this, in this paper, we provide a survey of PLMs. We found only two surveys on PLM through Google scholar, although ours in this paper is unique from them. The first one is provided by Li *et al.* [22], concerning the general task definition, the mainstream architectures of PLMs for text generation, the usage of existing PLMs to model different input data and satisfy unique properties in the generated text, and several critical fine-tuning strategies for text generation. However, they did not discuss the mainstream PLMs one by one as we do in this paper. The second survey we found was provided by Qiu *et al.* [32] in 2020. They comprehensively review PLMs, and, in particular, they systematically categorise various PLMs. However, the survey was published in March 2020, so it does not cover PLMs published afterwards, particularly Chinese PLMs in 2020 and 2021. So, instead, we cover the recent two years, especially the Chinese ones.

The rest of this paper is organised as follows. Section 2 briefs three main machine learning methods for training PLMs. Section 3 recalls early PLMs that focus on word vectors. Section 4 reviews the second generation of PLMs, including ELMo, BERT, GPT, and their derivatives. Section 5 briefs several Chinese PLMs and compares them with several typical English PLMs. Section 6 lists the main NLP tasks for which PLMs can be used and gives an application example for each task. Finally, Sect. 7 summarises this paper with the future work.

2   Basic Machine Learning Methods for PLMs

This section will brief machine learning methods for PLMs: Long-Short Term Memory (LSTM) [19], Attention Mechanism (AM) [6], and Transformer [41].

2.1 Long-Short Term Memory

RNNs are often used to process sequence data such as machine translation and sentiment analysis, but they are short-term memory networks. When faced with a long enough data sequence, it is difficult to transmit the earlier information to them later because RNNs may meet gradient disappearance in the reverse transmission. LSTM is an improved RNN model. Based on RNN, an input gate, a forgetting gate and an output gate are added to control and retain information, which overcomes the limitation of short-term memory. The forget gate controls how much of the unit status at the last moment can be retained to the current moment. The input gate determines how much of the immediate status can be input into the unit status. Finally, the output gate is responsible for controlling how much of the unit status can be used as the current output value of the LSTM. However, in both RNN and LSTM, much of the information carried by the input word vector may be lost in the face of long sequences.

2.2 Attention Mechanism

AM sets a weight for all hidden states in the encoder and inputs the information of the hidden states after the weighted summation to the decoder layer. AM pays more attention to inputs relevant to the current task. The AM acts between the encoder and the decoder. When RNNs are integrated with the attention mechanism, they can predict a particular part of the output sequence and focus their attention on a specific part of the input sequence to generate a higher quality output. Thus, Yu *et al.* [49] integrated LSTM with an AM and two-way LSTM for the Chinese question answering system, which solves the difficulties caused by Chinese grammar, semantics and lexical limitations in the Chinese question answering dataset. The AM+LSTM model retains the intermediate outputs of the LSTM encoder on the input sequences and then trains the model to selectively learn these inputs and associate the output sequences with the model outputs.

Later on, a self-AM was proposed [41]. The self-AM acts on the encoder or the decoder, and can connect longer-distance words in the same sentence. General embedding methods, such as Word2Vec, need to be integrated with context to clarify the semantics, and the sequence information of the sentence is lost. Self-AM can effectively solve these problems. Moreover, self-AM replaces the most commonly used loop layer in the encoder-decoder architecture with multi-headed self-attention. Multi-headed attention focuses on information from different representation subspaces in different positions, leading to a dramatic improvement in training speed [24, 27].

2.3 Transformer

Transformer [41] uses multiple encoders and decoders. The encoder contains a self-attention layer and a feed-forward neural network in addition to the self-attention layer and the feed-forward neural network. The advantage of the Transformer model is that it can solve the problems of slow training and low efficiency

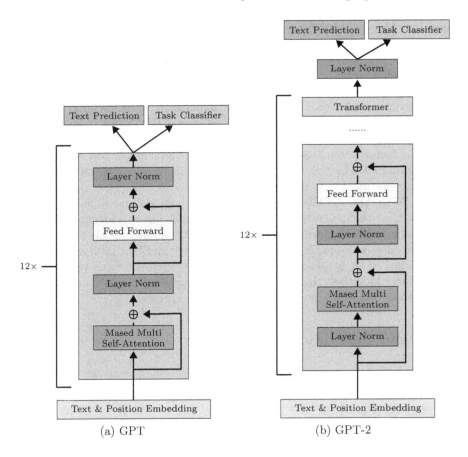

Fig. 2. Transformer architecture used by GPT and GPT-2

of the RNN model and use self-attention to achieve fast parallel effects. Moreover, it can deeply mine the characteristics of a Deep Neural Network (DNN) to improve the efficiency and performance of the model. After the Transformer model was proposed, PLMs entered a boom phase. Figure 2 shows the Transformer architectures used by GPT [33] and GPT-2 [34].

3 Early PLMs

From 2013 to 2021, PLMs have upgraded year by year. As early as 2013, Mikolov *et al.* [28] proposed the first PLM, called Word2Vec, which generates word vectors. According to the corpus, the optimised model trained expresses a word as a vector quickly and effectively. After Word2Vec trains the word vector, each independent word has a fixed dimension vector corresponding to its semantics. The Word2Vec model is also a widely used word embedding model in sentiment analysis with excellent analysis performance [1]. The Word2Vec model uses two algorithms for generating word vectors, Skip-Gram (SG) and Continuous Bag of Words (CBoW). SG has a good performance on small training data, but CBoW is also very efficient in big training data, and its accuracy rate for frequent words is also higher than SG.

Later on, Pennington, Socher, and Manning [30] proposed GloVe to overcome the shortcomings of Word2Vec: its vector dimensionality is low, and it cannot completely cover the data in the corpus. Moreover, GloVe can be more generalised than Word2Vec in the process of word embedding. However, GloVe uses the matrix factorisation method and the method based on shallow windows. So, it can contain local or global information of specific words in the corpus, which is necessary for improving its performance.

Both Word2Vec and GloVe map the input to a fixed-dimensional vector representation, so the generated word vectors are all context-independent. Thus, they cannot handle linguistic phenomena like polysemous words. For example, "open" has different meanings in "the door is open" and "the farm is in the open countryside". So, it is unreasonable that its word vectors for the two sentences are the same. Moreover, these models are no longer needed in downstream tasks because their computational efficiency usually is low.

4   Second Generation of PLMs

This section will review representative PLMs of second generation.

4.1   ELMo Model

To solve the problem of polysemy and understand complex context, in 2018, Peters *et al.* [31] proposed ELMo (Embedding from Language Models). It learns word vectors via the internal state of a deep bidirectional language model. It extracts embeddings from a bi-directional LSTM pre-trained on a sizeable unsupervised corpus. The resulting embeddings are derived from a weighted combination of internal layers that can be easily applied to existing models. When doing the downstream task, ELMo extracts word embeddings from a pre-trained network corresponding to words from each layer of the network as new embeddings to be added to the downstream task. It is a typical PLM residing in feature fusion. In many NLP tasks in different domains, ELMo performs very well [3, 15, 47].

4.2   BERT Family

ELMo is a one-way language model, and its ability to model semantic information is limited. To remove these limitations, Google AI launched pre-training language model BERT (Bidirectional Encoder Representations from Transformers) at the end of 2018 [11], which uses Masked Language Model (MLM) and Next Sentence Prediction (NSP) for deep two-way joint training. The task of

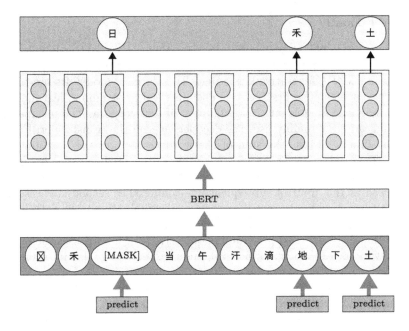

Fig. 3. Masked LM

MLM is to randomly erase one or several words in a given sentence and predict the erased words according to the remaining words. For the erased words, MASK can replace 80% of cases; for any word, it can replace 10% of cases; and for unchanged words, it can do 10% of cases. This is more conducive to the model to grasp the context information. Figure 3 shows the MLM process. Moreover, BERT uses NSP to capture the relationship between sentences [11]. Its performance, ease of use and versatility surpass many models. The difference between BERT's pre-training and downstream specific task training is only the top-level output layer, and it can be used in many tasks. BERT has achieved significant improvements in 11 basic tasks in NLP.

The emergence of BERT has extensively promoted the development of the NLP field. Since its emergence, researchers have proposed many improved models based on BERT. RoBERTa [23] uses a more extensive dataset, changes the static mask to the dynamic mask, and cancels the NSP task. AlBERT [21] can share parameters cross-layer, which significantly reduces parameters. It factors Embedding into two smaller embedding matrices and changes the NSP task in BERT to SOP (sentence-order prediction). XLNet [48] uses Permutation Language Modeling (PLM), which can capture contextual information in the language model and has apparent advantages over BERT in text generating tasks with long document input. ELECTRA [7] replaces the MLM in BERT with RTD (Replaced Token Detection), which solves the inconsistency between the pre-training phase and the fine-tuning phase of MASK. ELECTRA is better than BERT under the same computing power, data, and model parameters. It is also better than RoBERTa and XLNet under the same amount of calculation.

4.3   GPT Family

Although the unlabelled text corpus is rich, there is very little labelled data for learning for specific tasks. To address the issue, in 2018, Radford *et al.* [33] proposed the GPT (Generative Pre-trained Transformer) model. Its pre-training includes two stages. The first stage is unsupervised pre-training, learning high-capacity language models on a large number of text corpora. The unsupervised pre-training in GPT mainly uses the decoder layer in the transformer; Fig. 2(a) shows the process. First, the sum of the word vector and the position vector is input. Then, after 12 layers of transformers, the predicted vector and the vector of the last word are obtained. Finally, the word vector of the last word will be used as the input of subsequent fine-tuning. The second stage is supervised fine-tuning, which adapts the model to discriminative tasks with labelled data. GPT is the first model that integrates the modern Transformer architecture and the self-supervised pre-training objective [45]. It surpasses the previous model in various assessments of natural language reasoning, classification, question answering, and comparative similarity.

In 2019, Radford *et al.* [34] proposed GPT-2 to predict the next word in a sentence. GTP-2 can answer questions, summarise texts, and translate texts without training in a specific field. However, GPT-2 still uses the one-way transformer mode of GPT with simple adjustments. Figure 2(b) shows the minimum model of GPT-2. It puts layer normalisation before each sub-block and adds a layer normalisation after the last self-attention. The training data of GPT-2 has been greatly improved in quantity, quality, and breadth. However, the network parameters have also increased, and the network parameters of the largest GPT-2 has reached 48 layers. As a result, both Zero-Shot (especially the tiny dataset Zero-Shot) and long text (long-distance dependence) perform well.

In 2020, Brown *et al.* [5] proposed GPT-3, which has 175 billion parameters. GPT-3 has excellent performance on many NLP datasets, including translation, question answering, and text filling. It is highly efficient, especially in text generation, and it is almost indistinguishable from a human-generated text. Although GPT-3 has made significant progress, it does not follow the real intentions of users very well, and it often produces unreal, harmful or unresponsive emotional outputs. To remove this flaw, Open AI uses reinforcement learning from human feedback to fine-tune GPT-3 - the resulting fine-tuned model is called Instruct-GPT [29]. The three main steps of its training process are: 1) perform supervised learning with a manually written demo dataset, 2) train the reward model RM on this dataset, and 3) use RM as the reward function for reinforcement learning. After over a year of testing, the experiments show that although InstructGPT still has simple errors, compared with GPT-3, it reduces harmful output and significantly improves its ability to follow user intentions.

5   Chinese PLM

This section will discuss important Chinese PLMs.

5.1   PLMs from IFLYTEK and Harbin Institute of Technology

In 2019, Cui *et al.* [9] of IFLYTEK and Harbin Institute of Technology released the Chinese PLM BERT-wwm based on the whole word mask. For Chinese, if part of a complete word is masked, other parts of the same word also are masked. Their experiments show that BERT-wwm outperforms BERT in various Chinese NLP tasks. They also increase the training data level and the training steps to upgrade BERT-wwm to BERT-wwm-ext. In addition, they also proposed a series of Chinese PLMs based on BERT, such as RoBERTa [26], in the same year, which achieved good experimental results. In 2020, Cui *et al.* [8] trained the Chinese PLM XLNet-mid based on the XLNet open source code using large-scale Chinese corpus. As a result, it surpassed the effects of BERT-wwm and BERT-wwm-ext on most NLP tasks and achieved significant performance improvements in machine reading comprehension tasks.

5.2   ERNIE Family from Baidu

In 2019, Zhang *et al.* [51] in Baidu released the Chinese PLM ERNIE, which has a greatly enhanced general semantic representation ability by uniformly modelling the grammatical structure, lexical structure, and semantic information in its training data. Moreover, they use a higher quality Chinese corpus, making ERNIE more effective on Chinese NLP tasks. Their experiments show that on 5 Chinese NLP tasks, ERNIE surpassed BERT. In December 2019, ERNIE topped the list in the authoritative dataset GLUE (General Language Understanding Evaluation) in the field of NLP.[1] In 2020, Sun *et al.* [39] released ERNIE 2.0. This model extracts more valuable information from the training corpus through continuous multi-task learning. Their experiments show that ERNIE 2.0 outperforms BERT and XLNet on 16 tasks, including the English task on the GLUE benchmark and several similar tasks in Chinese. In 2021, Sun *et al.* [38] released ERNIE 3.0 by integrating autoregressive and autoencoder networks with general semantic layers and task-related layers. Once the pre-training of the generic semantic layer is completed, it is not updated anymore. Only task-dependent layers are fine-tuned when performing downstream tasks, significantly improving efficiency. Their experiments show that the model outperforms state-of-the-art models on 54 Chinese NLP tasks.

5.3   TinyBERT from Huawei

Large-scale PLMs such as BERT have huge parameters and complex computing processes, making it challenging to apply them on edge devices with limited computing power and memory. To this end, many model compression techniques have been proposed, mainly including quantisation [17], weights pruning [18], and knowledge distillation [35]. In 2019, Huawei proposed TinyBERT [20], which uses a new knowledge distillation method to perform transformer distillation

---

[1] https://gluebenchmark.com/.

Table 1. Comparison of the characteristics of some pre-trained models

PLMs	Characteristic			
	Learning method	Language model	Language type	Params
Elmo [7]	LSTM	BiLM	English	96M
GPT [33]	Transformer Dec	LM	English	117M
BERT [11]	Transformer Enc	MLM	English	110M
RoBERTa [26]	Transformer Enc	MLM+ RTD	English	355M
ELECTRA [7]	Transformer Enc	MLM	English	335M
BERT-wwm-ext [9]	Transformer Enc	PLM	Chinese	108M
XLNet-mid [46]	Transformer Enc	MLM+ DEA	Chinese	209M
ERNIE [51]	Transformer Enc	95.06	Chinese	114M

in pre-training and task-specific learning stages. This two-stage learning framework enables TinyBERT to acquire a general knowledge of "teacher" BERT and task-specific knowledge. The research results show that although the size of TinyBERT is only 13.3% of BERT, its computing speed is 9.4 times that of BERT, and the testing effect on the GLUE benchmark is comparable to BERT.

5.4 WuDao Family from BAAI

In March 2021, the Beijing Academy of Artificial Intelligence (BAAI) released large-scale Chinese PLM WuDao 1.0, called WenHui.[2] It replaces the Transformer model in GPT with Transformer-XL [10], generating human-based text and better maintaining content consistency. It can also learn concepts between different modalities, overcoming the limitation of large-scale self-supervised PLMs that do not possess such cognitive capabilities. Two months later, BAAI released WuDao 2.0 with a parameter volume of 1.75 trillion.[3] China's first trillion-level PLM with ten times the number of parameters than GPT-3. Wudao 2.0 can be applied not only to a single text field but also to the visual field. It can generate pictures according to text, and it can also retrieve text according to pictures. WuDao 2.0 achieved first place in 9 benchmarks in terms of precision.[4]

5.5 PLUG from Alibaba Dharma Academy

In April 2021, Alibaba Dharma Academy released the world's largest Chinese text PLM, PLUG (Pre-training for Language Understanding and Generation).[5] According to the strengths of their NLU (Natural Language Understanding)

---

[2] https://mp.weixin.qq.com/s/BUQWZ5EdR19i40GuFofpBg.

[3] https://mp.weixin.qq.com/s/NJYINRt_uoKAIgxjNyu4Bw.

[4] https://wudaoai.cn/home.

[5] https://m.thepaper.cn/baijiahao_12274410.

Table 2. Performance comparison of some pretrained models

PLMs	Dataset			Results		
	GLUE dev set	SST-2	CMRC	F1-score	Accuracy	GLUE
Elmo [7]	✓			N/A	N/A	71.2
GPT [33]		✓		N/A	91.3	72.8
BERT [11]		✓		N/A	94.9	82.1
RoBERTa [26]		✓		N/A	96.7	88.1
ELECTRA [7]		✓		N/A	97.1	89.4
BERT-wwm-ext [9]			✓	73.23	N/A	N/A
XLNet-mid [46]			✓	66.51	N/A	N/A
ERNIE [51]		✓		N/A	97.8	91.1

language model StructBERT [44] and NLG (Natural Language Generation) language model PALM [33], they jointly train NLU & NLG of PLUD. The joint training makes PLUG understand an input text better and generate more relevant content accordingly. It also uses more than 1TB of high-quality Chinese training datasets, setting a new record for Chinese GLUE with a score of 80.614 on language understanding tasks. PLUD performs excellently in long text generation such as novel creation, poetry generation, and intelligent question answering. Its goal is to surpass humans in various tasks of Chinese NLP.

5.6   Comparison of Some Chinese and English PLMs

Table 1 and Table 2 compares some Chinese and English PLMs on datasets GLUE/CLUE, MRPC, and SST-2. GLUE is a benchmark dataset for evaluating and analysing the performances of various models in various existing NLU tasks [42], and CLUE is a Chinese NLU evaluation benchmark [46]. The SST-2 (Stanford Sentiment Treebank v2) dataset consists of 215,154 phrases with fine-grained sentiment labels from movie reviews [37]. MRPC (Microsoft Research Paraphrase Corpus), introduced by Dolan et al. [13], is a corpus of 5,801 sentence pairs collected from newswire articles.

6   Practical Applications of Pretrained Models

This section will briefly review the main NLP tasks that PLMs can be applied.

6.1   Sentiment Analysis

During the COVID-19 pandemic, it is critical to identify negative public sentiment characteristics and adopt scientific guidance to alleviate the public's concerns. To more accurately analyse the sentiment of online reviews, Wang et al. [43] first uses unsupervised BERT to classify the sentiment of the collected text and then uses the TF-IDF algorithm to extract text topics. The accuracy of this method outperforms all baseline NLP algorithms.

6.2   Named Entity Recognition

To solve the accuracy of biomedical nomenclature recognition in low-resource languages and improve the efficiency of text reading, Boudjellal *et al.* [4] proposed a model named ABioNER based on BERT. They first pre-trained AraBERT on a general-domain Arabic corpus and a corpus of biomedical Arabic literature and then fine-tuned AraBERT using a single NVIDIA GPU. Their test result values demonstrate that building a monolingual BERT model on small-scale biomedical data can improve understanding of data in the biomedical domain.

6.3   Summarisation

Liu, Wu, and Luo [25] proposed a method for summarising legal case documents. First, they extract five key components of a legal case document. Thus, the text summarisation problem becomes five text compression and integration problems for sentences of five different categories. Then they fine-tune five models of PLM GPT-2 for each key component. Next, they use the five fine-tuned models to conduct text compression and integration for summarising each key component. Finally, they put all the summaries of five key components together to obtain the summary of the entire legal case document. They did lots of experiments to confirm the effectiveness of their approach.

6.4   Question Answering

The current BERT-based question answering systems suffer several problems. For example, a system of this kind may return wrong answers or nothing, cannot aggregate questions, and only consider text contents but ignore the relationship between entities in the corpus. As a result, the system may not be able to validate its answer to a question. To address these issues, Do and Phan [12] developed a question answering system based BERT and knowledge graph. They used BERT to build two classifiers: (1) BERT-based text classification for content information and (2) BERT-based triple classification for link information. Their experiments show that their method significantly outperformed the state-of-the-art methods in terms of accuracy and executive time.

6.5   Machine Translation

Zhang *et al.* [50] proposed a BERT-based method for machine translation, called BERT-JAM. The proposed method has the following features. First, BERT-JAM fuses BERT's multi-layer representations into an overall representation that the neural machine translation model can use. Second, BERT-JAM can dynamically integrate the BERT representation with the encoder/decoder representations.

Third, they fine-tune BERT-JAM using a three-phase optimisation strategy. The strategy can gradually ablate different components to beat catastrophic forgetting during fine-tuning. Their experiments show that the performance of BERT-JAM on multiple translation tasks is state-of-the-art.

7   Conclusions

Before being fine-tuned, PLMs already perform very well. After fine-tuning, their performances are even better, and the fine-tuned models are well-converged. Therefore, PLMs have been used for many NLP tasks [2,11,14,48]. Thus, this paper provides a survey on PLMs to help researchers quickly understand various PLMs and determine which ones are appropriate for their specific NLP projects. Specifically, we brief the main machine learning methods used by PLMs and review early PLMs, main state-of-art PLMs, and several well-known Chinese PLMs. Moreover, we compare the performance of some mainstream PLMs. In addition, we list the main NLP tasks for which PLMs have been used and review some state-of-art work for each task of them.

Although the emergence and application of PLMs have promoted the rapid development of many NLP tasks, due to the complexity of natural language, PLM technology still faces many challenges. First of all, the performance of PLMs is far from reaching its upper limit. Longer training steps and larger datasets could potentially improve its performance. Secondly, fine-tuning is required when applying PLM to downstream tasks, but the fine-tuning is specific, which may result in low efficiency. When applying PLMs in specialised fields such as biomedical science and law, PLMs may be susceptible to learning and amplifying biases in datasets due to the specificity of datasets in specialised fields. For example, a PLM may generate biases against age groups and gender. Finally, there are many different languages, and many ways to express their linguistic information. So, a single pre-trained language model cannot meet people's needs fully. Hence, multi-lingual PLMs and multi-modal PLMs have become a particular focus of attention as it is vital to improve their performance to meet various needs now and in the future.

Acknowledgment. This work was supported by the National Natural Science Foundation of China (No. 61762016) and the Graduate Student Innovation Project of School of Computer Science and Engineering, Guangxi Normal University (JXXYYJSCXXM-2021-001).

References

1. Alnawas, A., Arici, N.: Effect of word embedding variable parameters on Arabic sentiment analysis performance. arXiv preprint arXiv:2101.02906 (2021)
2. Bao, H., et al.: UniLMv2: pseudo-masked language models for unified language model pre-training. In: Proceedings of the 37th International Conference on Machine Learning, pp. 642–652 (2020)

3. Barlas, G., Stamatatos, E.: Cross-domain authorship attribution using pre-trained language models. In: Maglogiannis, I., Iliadis, L., Pimenidis, E. (eds.) AIAI 2020. IAICT, vol. 583, pp. 255–266. Springer, Cham (2020). https://doi.org/10.1007/978-3-030-49161-1_22

4. Boudjellal, N., et al.: ABioNER: a BERT-based model for Arabic biomedical named-entity recognition. Complexity **2021**, 1–6 (2021)

5. Brown, T., et al.: Language models are few-shot learners. In: Advances in Neural Information Processing Systems, vol. 33, pp. 1877–1901 (2020)

6. Chaudhari, S., Mithal, V., Polatkan, G., Ramanath, R.: An attentive survey of attention models. ACM Trans. Intell. Syst. Technol. **12**(5), 1–32 (2021)

7. Clark, K., Luong, M.T., Le, Q.V., Manning, C.D.: ELECTRA: pre-training text encoders as discriminators rather than generators. arXiv preprint arXiv:2003.10555 (2020)

8. Cui, Y., Che, W., Liu, T., Qin, B., Wang, S., Hu, G.: Revisiting pre-trained models for Chinese natural language processing. In: Findings of the Association for Computational Linguistics, EMNLP 2020, pp. 657–668 (2020)

9. Cui, Y., Che, W., Liu, T., Qin, B., Yang, Z.: Pre-training with whole word masking for Chinese BERT. IEEE/ACM Trans. Audio Speech Lang. Process. **29**, 3504–3514 (2021)

10. Dai, Z., Yang, Z., Yang, Y., Carbonell, J., Le, Q.V., Salakhutdinov, R.: Transformer-XL: attentive language models beyond a fixed-length context. arXiv preprint arXiv:1901.02860 (2019)

11. Devlin, J., Chang, M.W., Lee, K., Toutanova, K.: BERT: pre-training of deep bidirectional transformers for language understanding. In: Proceedings of the 2019 Conference of the North American Chapter of the Association for Computational Linguistics: Human Language Technologies, pp. 4171–4186 (2019)

12. Do, P., Phan, T.H.V.: Developing a BERT based triple classification model using knowledge graph embedding for question answering system. Appl. Intell. **52**(1), 636–651 (2021). https://doi.org/10.1007/s10489-021-02460-w

13. Dolan, B., Brockett, C.: Automatically constructing a corpus of sentential paraphrases. In: Proceedings of the 3rd International Workshop on Paraphrasing, pp. 9–16 (2005)

14. Dong, L., et al.: Unified language model pre-training for natural language understanding and generation. In: Proceedings of the 33rd International Conference on Neural Information Processing Systems, pp. 13063–13075 (2019)

15. El Boukkouri, H., Ferret, O., Lavergne, T., Noji, H., Zweigenbaum, P., Tsujii, J.: CharacterBERT: reconciling ELMo and BERT for word-level open-vocabulary representations from characters. In: Proceedings of the 18th International Conference on Computational Linguistics, pp. 6903–6915 (2020)

16. Erhan, D., Courville, A., Bengio, Y., Vincent, P.: Why does unsupervised pre-training help deep learning? In: Proceedings of the 13th International Conference on Artificial Intelligence and Statistics, pp. 201–208 (2010)

17. Gong, Y., Liu, L., Yang, M., Bourdev, L.: Compressing deep convolutional networks using vector quantization. arXiv preprint arXiv:1412.6115 (2014)

18. Han, S., Pool, J., Tran, J., Dally, W.: Learning both weights and connections for efficient neural network. In: Advances in Neural Information Processing Systems 28 (2015)

19. Hochreiter, S., Schmidhuber, J.: Long short-term memory. Neural Comput. **9**(8), 1735–1780 (1997)

20. Jiao, X., et al.: TinyBERT: distilling BERT for natural language understanding. arXiv preprint arXiv:1909.10351 (2019)

21. Lan, Z., Chen, M., Goodman, S., Gimpel, K., Sharma, P., Soricut, R.: ALBERT: a lite BERT for self-supervised learning of language representations. arXiv preprint arXiv:1909.11942 (2019)

22. Li, J., Tang, T., Zhao, W., Wen, J.: Pretrained language models for text generation: a survey. In: Proceedings of the 30th International Joint Conference on Artificial Intelligence, pp. 4492–4497 (2021)

23. Li, L.H., Yatskar, M., Yin, D., Hsieh, C.J., Chang, K.W.: VisualBERT: a simple and performant baseline for vision and language. arXiv preprint arXiv:1908.03557 (2019)

24. Lin, Y., Wang, C., Song, H., Li, Y.: Multi-head self-attention transformation networks for aspect-based sentiment analysis. IEEE Access **9**, 8762–8770 (2021)

25. Liu, J., Wu, J., Luo, X.: Chinese judicial summarising based on short sentence extraction and GPT-2. In: Qiu, H., Zhang, C., Fei, Z., Qiu, M., Kung, S.-Y. (eds.) KSEM 2021. LNCS (LNAI), vol. 12816, pp. 376–393. Springer, Cham (2021). https://doi.org/10.1007/978-3-030-82147-0_31

26. Liu, Y., et al.: RoBERTa: a robustly optimized BERT pretraining approach. arXiv preprint arXiv:1907.11692 (2019)

27. Meng, Z., Tian, S., Yu, L., Lv, Y.: Joint extraction of entities and relations based on character graph convolutional network and multi-head self-attention mechanism. J. Exp. Theoret. Artif. Intell. **33**(2), 349–362 (2021)

28. Mikolov, T., Chen, K., Corrado, G., Dean, J.: Efficient estimation of word representations in vector space. arXiv preprint arXiv:1301.3781 (2013)

29. Ouyang, L., et al.: Training language models to follow instructions with human feedback. arXiv preprint arXiv:2203.02155 (2022)

30. Pennington, J., Socher, R., Manning, C.: GloVe: global vectors for word representation. In: Proceedings of the 2014 Conference on Empirical Methods in Natural Language Processing, pp. 1532–1543 (2014)

31. Peters, M., et al.: Deep contextualized word representations. In: Proceedings of the 2018 Conference of the North American Chapter of the Association for Computational Linguistics: Human Language Technologies, pp. 2227–2237 (2018)

32. Qiu, X.P., Sun, T.X., Xu, Y.G., Shao, Y.F., Dai, N., Huang, X.J.: Pre-trained models for natural language processing: a survey. Sci. Chin. Technol. Sci. **63**(10), 1872–1897 (2020). https://doi.org/10.1007/s11431-020-1647-3

33. Radford, A., Narasimhan, K., Salimans, T., Sutskever, I.: Improving language understanding by generative pre-training (2018). https://www.cs.ubc.ca/~amuham01/LING530/papers/radford2018improving.pdf

34. Radford, A., Wu, J., Child, R., Luan, D., Amodei, D., Sutskever, I., et al.: Language models are unsupervised multitask learners. OpenAI Blog **1**(8), 9 (2019)

35. Romero, A., Ballas, N., Kahou, S.E., Chassang, A., Gatta, C., Bengio, Y.: FitNets: hints for thin deep nets. arXiv preprint arXiv:1412.6550 (2014)

36. Sherstinsky, A.: Fundamentals of recurrent neural network (RNN) and long short-term memory (LSTM) network. Physica D **404**, 132306 (2020)

37. Socher, R., et al.: Recursive deep models for semantic compositionality over a sentiment treebank. In: Proceedings of the 2013 Conference on Empirical Methods in Natural Language Processing, pp. 1631–1642 (2013)

38. Sun, Y., et al.: ERNIE 3.0: large-scale knowledge enhanced pre-training for language understanding and generation. arXiv preprint arXiv:2107.02137 (2021)

39. Sun, Y., et al.: ERNIE 2.0: a continual pre-training framework for language understanding. In: Proceedings of the AAAI Conference on Artificial Intelligence, vol. 34, pp. 8968–8975 (2020)

40. Torrey, L., Shavlik, J.: Transfer learning. In: Handbook of Research on Machine Learning Applications and Trends: Algorithms, Methods, and Techniques, pp. 242–264. IGI Global (2010)
41. Vaswani, A., et al.: Attention is all you need. In: Proceedings of the 31st International Conference on Neural Information Processing Systems, pp. 6000–6010 (2017)
42. Wang, A., Singh, A., Michael, J., Hill, F., Levy, O., Bowman, S.R.: GLUE: a multi-task benchmark and analysis platform for natural language understanding. arXiv preprint arXiv:1804.07461 (2018)
43. Wang, T., Lu, K., Chow, K.P., Zhu, Q.: COVID-19 sensing: negative sentiment analysis on social media in China via BERT model. IEEE Access 8, 138162–138169 (2020)
44. Wang, W., et al.: StructBERT: incorporating language structures into pre-training for deep language understanding. arXiv preprint arXiv:1908.04577 (2019)
45. Xu, H., et al.: Pre-trained models: past, present and future. arXiv preprint arXiv:2106.07139 (2021)
46. Xu, L., et al.: CLUE: a Chinese language understanding evaluation benchmark. In: Proceedings of the 28th International Conference on Computational Linguistics, pp. 4762–4772 (2020)
47. Yang, M., Xu, J., Luo, K., Zhang, Y.: Sentiment analysis of Chinese text based on Elmo-RNN model. J. Phys: Conf. Ser. **1748**(2), 022033 (2021)
48. Yang, Z., Dai, Z., Yang, Y., Carbonell, J., Salakhutdinov, R.R., Le, Q.V.: XLNet: generalized autoregressive pretraining for language understanding. Adv. Neural. Inf. Process. Syst. **32**, 5753–5763 (2019)
49. Yu, X., Feng, W., Wang, H., Chu, Q., Chen, Q.: An attention mechanism and multi-granularity-based Bi-LSTM model for Chinese Q&A system. Soft. Comput. **24**(8), 5831–5845 (2019). https://doi.org/10.1007/s00500-019-04367-8
50. Zhang, Z., Wu, S., Jiang, D., Chen, G.: BERT-JAM: maximizing the utilization of BERT for neural machine translation. Neurocomputing **460**, 84–94 (2021)
51. Zhang, Z., Han, X., Liu, Z., Jiang, X., Sun, M., Liu, Q.: ERNIE: enhanced language representation with informative entities. In: Proceedings of the 57th Annual Meeting of the Association for Computational Linguistics, pp. 1441–1451 (2019)

Intervention-Aware Epidemic Prediction by Enhanced Whale Optimization

Songwei Zhao[1,2], Jiuman Song[1,2], Xinqi Du[1,2], Tianyi Liu[1,2],
Huiling Chen[3(✉)], and Hechang Chen[1,2(✉)]

[1] School of Artificial Intelligence, Jilin University, Changchun, China
{duxq18,tianyi21}@mails.jlu.edu.cn, chenhc@jlu.edu.cn
[2] Key Laboratory of Symbolic Computation and Knowledge Engineering of Ministry
of Education, Changchun, China
[3] College of Computer Science and Artificial Intelligence, Wenzhou University,
Zhejiang, China
chenhuiling.jlu@gmail.com

Abstract. In recent decades, new epidemics have seriously endangered people's lives and are now the leading cause of death in the world. The prevention of pandemic diseases has therefore become a top priority today. However, effective prevention remains a difficult challenge due to factors such as transmission mechanisms, lack of documentation of clinical outcomes, and population control. To this end, this paper proposes a susceptible-exposed-infected-quarantined (hospital or home)-recovered (SEIQHR) model based on human intervention strategies to simulate and predict recent outbreak transmission trends and peaks in Changchun, China. In this study, we introduce *Levy* operator and random mutation mechanism to reduce the possibility of the algorithm falling into a local optimum. The algorithm is then used to identify the parameters of the model optimally. The validity and adaptability of the proposed model are verified by fitting experiments to the number of infections in cities in China that had COVID-19 outbreaks in previous periods (Nanjing, Wuhan, and Xi'an), where the peaks and trends obtained from the experiments largely match the actual situation. Finally, the model is used to predict the direction of the disease in Changchun, China, for the coming period. The results indicated that the number of COVID-19 infections in Changchun would peak around April 3 and continue to decrease until the end of the outbreak. These predictions can help the government plan countermeasures to reduce the expansion of the epidemic.

Keywords: Epidemic prediction · Intervention strategy · SEIQHR model · Whale optimization algorithm

S. Zhao and J. Song—The authors contribute equally.
We truly thank the reviewers for their great effort and pertinent comments on our submission. This work is supported in part by the National Natural Science Foundation of China (No. 61902145), the National Key R&D Program of China (2021ZD0112501, 2021ZD0112502), and the Philosophy and Social Sciences Intelligent Library Foundation of Jilin Province (No. 2021JLSKZKZB080).

© The Author(s), under exclusive license to Springer Nature Switzerland AG 2022
G. Memmi et al. (Eds.): KSEM 2022, LNAI 13369, pp. 457–468, 2022.
https://doi.org/10.1007/978-3-031-10986-7_37

1 Introduction

Predicting the outbreak of epidemics is a fundamental task for subsequent prevention and control. It dominates the intervention strategies of policymakers and daily behaviors of individuals, e.g., schools closure [5,10,15] and quarantine [8,23]. Existing mechanical models are widely used for epidemic prediction, e.g., SIS (susceptible-infected-susceptible) [21], SIR (susceptible-infected -recovered) [4], and SEIR (susceptible-exposed-infected-recovered) [7]. Nevertheless, the assumptions of these models are too idealistic, e.g., without considering intervention strategies, disabling their application for new emerging epidemics in the real world. Therefore, considering more realistic factors will be helpful to improve the predictive ability of the model.

Researchers have proposed and improved various models for epidemic prediction studies. The earliest was in 1927, when Kermack and McKendrick [12] proposed the SIR model. The SIR model has since been refined by numerous scientists as epidemics have changed [3,11,27]. The exposed phase (E) was later added to the SIR model to fit the epidemiological characteristics better [22,25]. Multiple models with different status populations have been further developed and improved as vaccinations are administered to susceptible individuals [14,16,28]. In 2020, Fanelli and Piazza [6] proposed the SIRD model in a study of coronavirus outbreaks in countries (Italy, France, and China), considering the state of death based on SIR. The model learned that the recovery rates were similar across countries. In contrast, there were significant differences in infection and mortality rates. In 2021, Mohammad et al. [1] proposed optimizing the parameters in the susceptible-exposed-infected-quarantined-recovered-dead (SEIQRD) model using the particle swarm algorithm, allowing the model to predict the trend in the number of people infected with the novel coronavirus in Italy.

Despite the success that existing studies have achieved in epidemic prediction [29], two significant challenges remain unsettled. *Challenge I:* How to integrate intervention strategies into the epidemic model? Traditional model construction is idealistic and does not consider control strategies. Still, control strategies play a decisive role in actual epidemic outbreaks, e.g., government closures of public places, residents wearing masks outside the home, and quarantine at home. *Challenge II:* How to explore optimal solutions for the epidemic model? Conventional model-solving methods do not meet the requirements of accuracy and adaptability of predictive models. Therefore, there is the urgent need for an optimized parameter identification method to help the model find suitable parameters for different regions quickly and accurately.

In view of this, we propose an adaptive SEIQHR model for COVID-19 prediction based on human interventions and an enhanced swarm intelligence algorithm for parameter optimization. Specifically, we first improve the predictive ability of the mechanical SEIQHR model by considering the infectiousness of exposed individuals, the preventive measures of the local government, and the public's self-awareness. Then, to make the whale optimization algorithm (WOA) [19] more accurate in identifying the model's parameters, we proposed an enhanced WOA called LMWOA by introducing the *Levy* stochastic operator and the random mutation mechanism. Finally, to verify the effectiveness of the proposed model, it is applied to fit trends in cities that have already experienced outbreaks and to predict outbreak trends over time in areas with ongoing outbreaks, e.g., Changchun, China. The contributions of this study are as follows:

- An improved epidemiological model is proposed that takes into account the characteristics of COVID-19 and human intervention strategies to make the model more compatible with new epidemics.
- An enhanced WOA based on *Levy* operator and random mutation mechanism is proposed for the shortcomings of WOA in terms of low convergence accuracy to optimize parameter identification of the epidemic model.
- The validity and adaptability of the model are verified by fitting the data to three cities where outbreaks have occurred. Subsequently, the trend in the direction of the epidemic in Changchun, China, is predicted.

2 Methodology

This section introduces infectious disease transmission to forecast the spread of COVID-19 risk. First, a model of infectious disease transmission based on human intervention strategies is proposed. Then the LMWOA is described. Finally, the method for solving the transmission model using LMWOA-based parameter optimization is presented.

2.1 The SEIQHR Model Formulation

Numerous studies show that the source of COVID-19 infection consists mainly of asymptomatic and symptomatic infected persons [13]. The main weakness in controlling the COVID-19 epidemic is the asymptomatic infected, as they cannot be detected in a timely matter. Based on the complexity of COVID-19 and current government measures, this study proposes a SEIR model based on human intervention strategies. The model is based on the SIR model that was designed by Kermack and Mckendrick. The proposed model effectively solves the problem of over-prediction based on SIR and SEIR models, as it takes into account hospitalization and quarantine. The inclusion of human intervention strategies can simulate the measures taken by the government during the outbreak.

The model is based on certain assumptions. Firstly, the total population of the location is held constant over the study period, namely, without regard to the local natural mortality and birth rates. Secondly, individuals who have recovered are immune to the virus, which means that they do not rejoin the susceptible population. Finally, there are no jumps in the state of the individual; that is, the individual proceeds from one state to the next in a gradual manner.

The proposed model is shown in Fig. 1, where *S, E, I, Q, H* and *R* refer to susceptible, exposed (asymptomatic infected individuals), infected, quarantined (hospital quarantine of infected individuals), Home-quarantined of susceptible persons and recovered, respectively. Since the model takes into account intervention strategies, the total number of people for *S* will be intervened depending

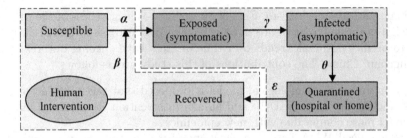

Fig. 1. The SEIQHR model based on human intervention strategies.

on the outbreak. While the total population of the entire region is constant: $N(t) = S(t) + E(t) + I(t) + Q(t) + H(t) + R(t)$. According to the properties of COVID-19, E asymptomatic infected persons are potentially infectious to others [2, 26]. The model is expressed through the following suite of ordinary differential equations.

$$\frac{dS(t)}{dt} = -\alpha \cdot (I(t) + E(t)) \cdot \frac{S(t)}{N} - c \cdot \beta S(t) \qquad (1)$$

$$\frac{dE(t)}{dt} = \alpha \cdot (I(t) + E(t)) \cdot \frac{S(t)}{N} - \gamma \cdot E(t) \qquad (2)$$

$$\frac{dI(t)}{dt} = \gamma \cdot E(t) - \theta \cdot I(t) \qquad (3)$$

$$\frac{dQ(t)}{dt} = \theta \cdot I(t) - \varepsilon \cdot Q(t) \qquad (4)$$

$$\frac{dH(t)}{dt} = c \cdot \beta S(t) \qquad (5)$$

$$\frac{dR(t)}{dt} = \varepsilon \cdot Q(t) \qquad (6)$$

where α is the infection rate, $c \cdot \beta$ is the corresponding intensity, indicating the intensity of government intervention, γ is the latent rate, θ is the inpatient quarantine rate, and then ε is the cure rate.

The proposed model does not take into account factors such as the vaccination status of susceptible individuals and asymptomatic Self-quarantine. Still, these have been implicitly included in the choice of parameters. In addition, the model does not take into account mortality status, as there is now a strong government effort to control the disease, and mortality has been largely absent in several recent outbreaks in China.

2.2   Enhanced WOA

WOA is a recently proposed swarm intelligence algorithm inspired by the foraging behavior of whales [20]. The model is divided into three stages: encircling prey, spiral bubble-net foraging, and search for prey. The enhanced whale optimization algorithm (LMWOA) is proposed to address the shortcomings of WOA, which is prone to local optimum and unsatisfactory convergence accuracy. Firstly, the spiral bubble net foraging is improved by using the *Levy* stochastic operator to enhance the exploration capability of search agents and increase the probability of the algorithm finding the most promising solution. Then the random mutation mechanism is introduced to improve the exploitation ability of the population and avoid falling into local optima.

Encircling Prey. Since the location of the search space is unknown, it is assumed that the best candidate solution for the WOA is currently the target prey or close to the optimal solution. The best candidate solution has a guiding role, and other candidate solutions will continuously try to get closer to the best candidate solution and update the position. The modeling of this behavior is calculated in the following expression:

$$\vec{D} = \left| \vec{C} \cdot \vec{X^*}(t) - \vec{X}(t) \right| \tag{7}$$

$$\vec{X}(t+1) = \vec{X^*}(t) - \vec{A} \cdot \vec{D} \tag{8}$$

where t is the current number of iterations, $\vec{C}$ and $\vec{A}$ both refer to the vector of coefficients that can be adjusted to reach all positions around the best candidate solution to achieve the behavior that simulates encircling prey, $\vec{X^*}(t)$ denotes the best search agent, who is updated during each iteration, and $\vec{X}(t)$ refers to the current position of the agent.

Spiral Bubble-Net Foraging. Two methods are devised to better simulate humpback whale bubble-net prey attack behavior.

Shrinking encircling mechanism: This behavior is accomplished mainly by reducing the fluctuating range of $\vec{A}$. The content of A is set at $[-1, 1]$ so that the search agent chooses to update the position between the best candidate solution and the original position.

Levy-spiral updating position: This behavioral simulation first requires the calculation of the Euclidean distance between the current status of the search agent and the best search agent. The spiral equation is then established to simulate the spiral movement of the humpback whale. The *Levy* stochastic operator is subject to the *Levy* distribution, which is similar to the Pareto principle, namely that most of the property in the world is concentrated in the hands of a few people. The *Levy* operator is a short-step search, but there are occasional long steps, which increase the likelihood that the agent will jump out of the local optimum [30]. The operator is calculated as follows:

$$\text{Levy}(\delta) \sim \frac{\varphi \times \mu}{|v|^{1/\delta}} \tag{9}$$

$$\varphi = \left[\frac{\Gamma(1+\delta) \times \sin(\pi \times \delta/2)}{\Gamma\left(\left(\frac{\delta+1}{2}\right) \times \delta \times 2^{(\delta-1)/2}\right)} \right]^{1/\delta} \tag{10}$$

where μ and v both refer to random numbers that follow a standard normal distribution and δ as a constant. Γ denotes a standard gamma function.

The radius of the spiral is constantly contracting as the humpback whale moves in a circle to hunt its prey. So in order to allow both behaviors to take place simultaneously, it is assumed here that there is a probability of 50% that either the Shrinking encircling mechanism or the levy-spiral updating position will be chosen to take place as a way of updating the location of the agent. Therefore the mathematical model for this stage is expressed as follows:

$$\vec{X}(t+1) = \begin{cases} \vec{X^*}(t) - \vec{A} \cdot \vec{D}, & \text{if } p < 0.5 \\ \text{Levy} \cdot \vec{\text{Dis}} \cdot e^{b \cdot l} \cdot \cos(2\pi l) + \vec{X^*}(t), & \text{if } p \geq 0.5 \end{cases} \tag{11}$$

where $\vec{\text{Dis}}$ is the distance between the current search agent position and the optimal solution currently obtained, b as a constant in the spiral function, and l is a random number between $[-1, 1]$.

Search for Prey. Variation based on the vector $\vec{A}$ can also be used to search for prey. Hence the use of random values $|A| > 1$ forces the search agent away from the best solution. Unlike the exploitation phase, the location of the current search agent is updated using a randomly selected agent during the exploration phase rather than the best solution. This stage focuses mainly on the global exploration of the population, and the mathematical model is expressed as follows:

$$\vec{D} = \left| \vec{C} \cdot \vec{X_{\text{rand}}} - \vec{X}(t) \right| \tag{12}$$

$$\vec{X}(t+1) = \vec{X_{\text{and}}} - \vec{A} \cdot \vec{D} \tag{13}$$

where $\vec{X_{\text{rand}}}$ is a randomly selected individual from the population of whales.

Random Mutation Mechanism. This mechanism is based on the greedy algorithm, which randomly selects a characteristic of the optimal solution obtained so far and then performed a random mutation. By calculating its fitness value, the mutation solution is then replaced with the optimal solution at the moment, whenever its fitness value is better than the optimal solution obtained so far, based on a greedy mechanism. The mutability of the optimal solution is enhanced, thus preventing the algorithm from falling into local optima.

2.3   LMWOA-Based SEIQHR Prediction Model

A set of parameter values within the size range of the SEIQHR model parameter values is chosen to minimize the fitness value of the proposed model. Our study decides on the proposed LMWOA to solve this optimization problem. The dimension of the population of individuals in the algorithm is determined by the size of the optimization problem, so the extent of the LMWOA is set to 5 to solve the optimization of the parameters in the prediction model. The study evaluates the discrepancy between the model data generated by LMWOA and the original data as an error value. Therefore, the sum of the absolute error values of the partially infected and recovered data is used as the fitness value.

$$f = \sum_{n}^{N} (|I_{real} - I_{model}| + |R_{real} - R_{model}|) \tag{14}$$

- Initial stage: Set the parameters of the LMWOA, such as the population size, the maximum number of iterations, and dimension. Afterward, the whale population is randomly initialized.
- Location update: The LMWOA location update has similarities to the original WOA. The population is updated in three main phases, where *Levy* enhancement is applied to the second phase, after the addition of the random variation phase.
- Parameter optimization: The optimal individual is selected by evaluating the fitness values of all search agents. The location coordinates of the optimal individual are the values of the parameters in the requested SEIQHR model.
- Model predictions: The obtained optimal parameters are fitted to the epidemic to predict the future course of the epidemic, e.g., the peak.

3   Experiments

In this section, we first introduce the datasets and the parameter setting of the experiments. Then, we evaluate the LMWOA-based SEIQHR's effectiveness in predicting the outbreak trend of emerging infectious diseases. Overall, we seek to answer the following questions:

- **Q1:** What are the advantages of the proposed model over the SEIQHR model based on other swarm intelligence algorithms?
- **Q2:** Can the LMWOA-based SEIQHR model accurately fit the existing outbreak trend of emerging infectious diseases?
- **Q3:** Is the model able to predict regional outbreak trends of emerging infectious diseases based on changes in human intervention strategies?

3.1   Experiment Setting

Datasets. The datasets used in the experiment is the number of existing infections of COVID-19 in three different cities of China with different periods, which are Nanjing from July 21 to August 31, 2021, Wuhan from February 2 to March 1, 2020, and Xi'an from December 13, 2021, to January 11, 2022.

Table 1. The parameter setting of the optimization algorithms

Algorithm	Related parameter setting
LMWOA	$\delta = 1.5; b = 1; r_1 \in [0,1]; r_2 \in [0,1]; p \in [0,1]; l \in [-1,1]$
MFO	$b = 1; t \in [-2,1]$
WOA	$b = 1; r_1 \in [0,1]; r_2 \in [0,1]; p \in [0,1]; l \in [-1,1]$
PSO	$v_{max} = 6; C_1 = 2; C_2 = 2; \omega_{max} = 0.9; \omega_{min} = 0.2; r_1 \in [0,1]; r_2 \in [0,1]$
SCA	$a = 2; r_2 \in [0,2\pi]; r_3 \in [0,2]; r_4 \in [0,1]$
SSA	$c_2 \in [0,1]; c_3 \in [0,1]$

Parameters Setting. To ensure the fairness of the comparison experiment, there are three parameters whose settings need to be consistent in each prediction model. The population scale is 80, the total number of iterations is 10000, and the number of parallel runs is 10. The prediction models involved in the comparative experiment are based on other five swarm intelligent optimization algorithms, including the original WOA inspired by the bubble-net attack strategy used by humpback whales for predation, the earliest and most popular particle swarm optimization (PSO) [24], the moth-flame optimization (MFO) [17] that inspired by the lateral positioning of the navigation mechanism adopted by moths flying at night, the sine and cosine algorithm (SCA) [9] which obtained by simulating the mathematical properties of the sine and cosine functions, and the salp swarm algorithm (SSA) [18] that inspired by the predation mechanism of the salp chain in the ocean. The exclusively related parameters and the corresponding values of LMWOA and the other optimization algorithms are shown in Table 1. The parameter settings of these optimization algorithms are derived from their respective original papers.

3.2   Validation of Model Effectiveness (Q1 and Q2)

To address the first and second questions (Q1 and Q2), taking the COVID-19 that has recently ravaged the world as an example, we conduct the comparative experiment to fit outbreak trends in three cities with different periods. The models involved in the comparative experiment are the LMWOA-based SEIQHR prediction model and the SEIQHR model based on another five swarm intelligent optimization algorithms, which are MFO, WOA, PSO, SCA, and SSA. The experiment results are shown in Table 2. For a fair comparison, we present the minimum (*Max*) and maximum (*Min*) values of the evaluation indicator obtained by each model among ten fitting results. By comparing the six groups of the results, the minimum value of the *Min* is expressed in bold. In the COVID-19 outbreak trends fitting experiment of three cities, LMWOA can obtain the minimum evaluation indicator. This is because the LMWOA has better performance in searching for the global optimal solution than the other five swarm intelligence algorithms. Therefore, LMWOA can find the parameters of the SEIQHR model that minimize the fitting error.

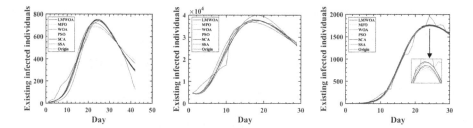

Fig. 2. Model simulations of COVID-19 outbreak trends for different cities. (Color figure online)

Table 2. The fitness values obtained for the different algorithms.

City		LMWOA	MFO	WOA	PSO	SCA	SSA
Nanjing	Max	4.34E+02	4.39E+02	4.44E+02	4.14E+02	4.51E+02	5.27E+02
	Min	**3.12E+02**	4.04E+02	3.79E+02	3.99E+02	3.23E+02	3.87E+02
Wuhan	Max	1.02E+03	6.21E+03	6.65E+03	7.94E+02	2.88E+03	1.08E+04
	Min	**7.21E+01**	2.35E+03	3.45E+03	2.21E+02	2.44E+03	3.83E+03
Xi'an	Max	1.35E+02	1.46E+02	1.64E+02	9.36E+01	1.56E+02	8.80E+02
	Min	**1.35E+01**	2.49E+01	6.96E+01	1.37E+01	5.92E+01	3.19E+01

Figure 2 shows the fitting curve of the COVID-19 outbreak trend for three cities: Nanjing, Wuhan, and Xi'an (from left to right), using the SEIQHR model based on six different swarm intelligent optimization algorithms. The horizontal axis is the cumulative number of days calculated from the outbreak of the epidemic, the vertical axis is the number of existing infected individuals on that day, and the red curve is the actual outbreak trend. The blue curve is the fitting curve of the outbreak trend by the LMWOA-based SEIQHR model, which has a better fitting capability no matter during the rising phase, peak area, or falling phase of the outbreak trend curve. Therefore, it can be concluded that the LMWOA-based SEIQHR model has the ability to capture the diffusion process with human intervention strategies for COVID-19 infectious diseases more accurately.

In summary, this experiment verifies that the LMWOA has better optimization performance and can adaptively find suitable parameter values for the SEIQHR model so that the model can fit the outbreak trends of emerging infectious diseases with the smallest error.

3.3   Validation of Predictive Ability (Q3)

To address the third question (Q3), the LMWOA-based SEIQHR prediction model is used to predict the COVID-19 outbreak for Changchun, China, where the outbreak has occurred. The total experiment period is 40 days, from March

4 to April 12, 2022. The prediction experiment is divided into three groups. The first eight days, the first eighteen days, and the first twenty-eight days are used as known data to predict the future regional outbreak trend, respectively. The model prediction results are shown in Fig. 3. The iterative convergence curves show that the LMWOA-based SEIQHR model can obtain a relatively minimum evaluation indicator, enabling the model to fit the known dataset better and obtain a more accurate prediction ability. Changchun carried out enclosed management on March 11, and the degree of the government control measures was upgraded on March 20. Therefore, in the three groups of the prediction experiment, the human interventions, which are the degree of the government control measures and public awareness, gradually increased (from left to right in Fig. 3). The prediction result of the first group shows that without control measures, the number of infected people will reach one-third of Changchun's resident population by the end of March. The prediction result of the second group shows that after a certain degree of enclosed management is implemented, the regional epidemic outbreak trend will peak around the 36th day. The prediction result of the last group shows that, with the enhancement of the government control strength and public awareness, the COVID-19 outbreak trend in Changchun will peak around April 3, when the existing number of confirmed cases will be less than 15,000. After that, this number will continue to decline.

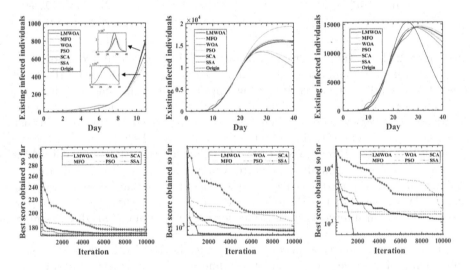

Fig. 3. Model predictions for three time periods of the COVID-19 outbreak.

In summary, the LMWOA-based SEIQHR model has the following three advantages: 1) It can adaptively predict the outbreak trend of emerging infectious diseases with human intervention factors; 2) The model can predict the outbreak peak according to the spread actuality of the infectious disease so as to feedback on whether the current control measures can effectively control the further outbreak of the infectious disease; 3) The model can predict the downward trend of the number of confirmed cases so as to guide decision-makers to formulate strategies in advance and prevent the one size fits all policy from damaging citizens' lives and economic development.

4 Conclusion

In this paper, we proposed an improved SEIQHR model based on the identification of LMWOA parameters, which simulates human risk avoidance behavior to make the model a better match for novel epidemics. We first refine the SEIQHR model by considering the disturbance that asymptomatic infected individuals can infect susceptible populations, followed by fitting human intervention strategies by using a segmentation function, with the specific different approaches implicitly concentrated in the parameters. The model parameters are then optimally identified by introducing the *Levy* operator and random mutation mechanism in combination with WOA to find the optimal parametric model. Experimental results demonstrate the validity and applicability of said proposed model when fitting predictions to cities that have had outbreaks and are in the process of epidemics. Other optimization methods and artificial intelligence techniques may be involved in future work, and crossover among regions and critical care will also be considered to make the model more complete.

References

1. Abdallah, M.A., Nafea, M.: PSO-based SEIQRD modeling and forecasting of COVID-19 spread in Italy. In: 2021 IEEE Symposium on Computer Applications and Industrial Electronics, pp. 71–76 (2021)
2. Ali, Z., Rabiei, F., Rashidi, M.M., Khodadadi, T.: A fractional-order mathematical model for COVID-19 outbreak with the effect of symptomatic and asymptomatic transmissions. Eur. Phys. J. Plus **137**(3), 395 (2022)
3. Anderson, R.M., May, R.M.: Population biology of infectious diseases: Part i. Nature **280**, 361–367 (1979)
4. Bagal, D.K., Rath, A., Barua, A., Patnaik, D.: Estimating the parameters of susceptible-infected-recovered model of COVID-19 cases in India during lockdown periods. Chaos, Solitons Fract. **140**, 110154 (2020)
5. Cauchemez, S., Valleron, A.J., Boelle, P.Y., Flahault, A., Ferguson, N.M.: Estimating the impact of school closure on influenza transmission from sentinel data. Nature **452**(7188), 750–754 (2008)
6. Fanelli, D., Piazza, F.: Analysis and forecast of COVID-19 spreading in China, Italy and France. Chaos, Solitons Fract. **134**, 109761 (2020)
7. Greenhalgh, D.: Some results for an SEIR epidemic model with density dependence in the death rate. Math. Med. Biol. J. IMA **9**(2), 67–106 (1992)
8. Górski, M., Garbicz, J., Buczkowska, M., Marsik, G., Polaniak, R.: Depressive disorders among long-term care residents in the face of isolation due to COVID-19 pandemic. Psychiatria Polska **56**(1), 101–114 (2020)
9. Hafez, A.I., Zawbaa, H.M., Emary, E., Hassanien, A.E.: Sine cosine optimization algorithm for feature selection. In: 2016 International Symposium on INnovations in Intelligent SysTems and Applications, pp. 1–5 (2016)

10. Haug, N., Geyrhofer, L., Londei, A., Dervic, E., Klimek, P.: Ranking the effectiveness of worldwide COVID-19 government interventions. Nat. Hum. Behav. **4**(12), 1303–1312 (2020)
11. Hethcote, H.W.: Qualitative analyses of communicable disease models. Math. Biosci. **28**(3), 335–356 (1976)
12. Kermack, W.O., McKendrick, A.G., Walker, G.T.: A contribution to the mathematical theory of epidemics. Proc. R. Soc. London Ser. A Containing Papers Math. Phys. Charact. **115**(772), 700–721 (1927)
13. Koo, J.R., et al.: Interventions to mitigate early spread of SARS-CoV-2 in Singapore: a modelling study. Lancet Infect. Dis. **20**(6), 678–688 (2020)
14. Li, M.Y., Graef, J.R., Wang, L., Karsai, J.: Global dynamics of a SEIR model with varying total population size. Math. Biosci. **160**(2), 191–213 (1999)
15. Liu, Q.H., Zhang, J., Peng, C., Litvinova, M., Ajelli, M.: Model-based evaluation of alternative reactive class closure strategies against COVID-19. Nat. Commun. **13**(1), 322 (2022)
16. Martcheva, M., Castillo-Chavez, C.: Diseases with chronic stage in a population with varying size. Math. Biosci. **182**(1), 1–25 (2003)
17. Mirjalili, S.: Moth-flame optimization algorithm: a novel nature-inspired heuristic paradigm. Knowl.-Based Syst. **89**, 228–249 (2015)
18. Mirjalili, S., Gandomi, A.H., Mirjalili, S.Z., Saremi, S., Faris, H., Mirjalili, S.M.: SALP swarm algorithm: a bio-inspired optimizer for engineering design problems. Adv. Eng. Softw. **114**, 163–191 (2017)
19. Mirjalili, S., Lewis, A.: The whale optimization algorithm. Adv. Eng. Softw. **95**, 51–67 (2016)
20. Mohammed, H.M., Umar, S.U., Rashid, T.A.: A systematic and meta-analysis survey of whale optimization algorithm. Comput. Intell. Neurosci. **2019**(1), 25 (2019)
21. Momani, S., Ibrahim, R.W., Hadid, S.B.: Susceptible-infected-susceptible epidemic discrete dynamic system based on Tsallis entropy. Entropy **22**(7), 769 (2020)
22. Newton, E., Reiter, P.: A model of the transmission of dengue fever with an evaluation of the impact of ultra-low volume insecticide applications on dengue epidemics. Am. J. Trop. Med. Hyg. **47**(6), 709 (1992)
23. Niu, Y., Xu, F.: Deciphering the power of isolation in controlling COVID-19 outbreaks. Lancet Glob. Health **8**(4), 452–453 (2020)
24. Poli, R., Kennedy, J., Blackwell, T.: Particle swarm optimization. Swarm Intell. **1**(1), 33–57 (2007)
25. Schwartz, I.B., Smith, H.L.: Infinite subharmonic bifurcation in an SEIR epidemic model. J. Math. Biol. **18**(3), 233–253 (1983)
26. Seres, G., et al.: Face masks increase compliance with physical distancing recommendations during the COVID-19 pandemic. J. Econ. Sci. Assoc. **7**(2), 139–158 (2021). https://doi.org/10.1007/s40881-021-00108-6
27. Hiorns, R.W.: Time lags in biological models. J. R. Stat. Soc. Ser. A (Gen.) **145**(1), 140–141 (1982)
28. Sun, C., Hsieh, Y.H.: Global analysis of an SEIR model with varying population size and vaccination. Appl. Math. Model. **34**(10), 2685–2697 (2010)
29. Tomchin, D.A., Fradkov, A.L.: Prediction of the Covid-19 spread in Russia based on SIR and SEIR models of epidemics. IFAC-PapersOnLine **53**(5), 833–838 (2020)
30. Zhao, S., Wang, P., Heidari, A.A., Chen, H., He, W., Xu, S.: Performance optimization of SALP swarm algorithm for multi-threshold image segmentation: comprehensive study of breast cancer microscopy. Comput. Biol. Med. **139**, 105015 (2021)

Scientific Item Recommendation
Using a Citation Network

Xu Wang[1,2(✉)], Frank van Harmelen[1,2], Michael Cochez[1,2],
and Zhisheng Huang[1]

[1] Vrije Universiteit Amsterdam, De Boelelaan 1105, 1081 HV Amsterdam,
The Netherlands
{xu.wang,frank.van.harmelen,m.cochez,z.huang}@vu.nl
[2] Discovery Lab, Elsevier, Amsterdam, The Netherlands

Abstract. Scientific items (such as papers or datasets) discovery and
reuse is crucial to support and improve scientific research. However, the
process is often tortuous, and researchers end up using less than ideal
datasets. Search engines tailored to this task are useful, but current systems only support keyword searches. This hinders the process, because the
user needs to imagine what kind of keywords would give useful datasets. In
this paper, we investigate a new technique to recommend scientific items
(paper or datasets). This technique uses a graph consisting of scientific
papers, the corresponding citation network, and datasets used in these
works as background information for its recommendation. Specifically, a
link-predictor is trained which is then used to infer useful datasets for the
paper the researcher is working on. As an input, it uses the co-author information, citation information, and the already used datasets. To compare
different scientific items recommendation approaches fairly and to prove
their efficiency, we created a new benchmark. This benchmark includes
more than three million scientific items to evaluate the performance of recommendation approaches. We experiment with a variety of methods and
find that an ensemble technique which uses link prediction on the citation
network yields a precision of nearly 70%.

Keywords: Data discovery · Data reuse · Scientific items
recommendation · Recommendation benchmark · Link prediction

1 Introduction

Data discovery and reuse play an essential role in helping scientific research by supporting to find data [4, 19]. Researchers typically reuse datasets from colleagues or
collaborators, and the credibility of such datasets is critical to the scientific process [11, 25]. Datasets sourced from a network of personal relationships (colleagues
or collaborators) can carry limitations as they tend only to recommend datasets
that they themselves find helpful [2]. However, due to the research variability, one
person's noisy data may be another person's valuable data. Also, datasets retrieved
from relational networks can be limited to certain research areas.

© The Author(s), under exclusive license to Springer Nature Switzerland AG 2022
G. Memmi et al. (Eds.): KSEM 2022, LNAI 13369, pp. 469–484, 2022.
https://doi.org/10.1007/978-3-031-10986-7_38

As an emerging dataset discovery tool, a dataset search engine can help researchers to find datasets of interest from open data repositories. Moreover, due to the increasing number of open data repositories, many dataset search engines, such as Google Dataset Search [3] and Mendeley Data[1], cover more than ten million datasets. While dataset search engines bring convenience to researchers, they also have certain limitations. Similar to general search engines, such dataset search engines require the researcher to provide keywords to drive the search; filtering, ranking, and returning all datasets based on the given keywords. In order to use a dataset search engine, researchers need to summarize the datasets they are looking for into these keywords, with the risk that they do not cover all the desired properties, and that unexpected but relevant datasets will be missed. Thus, the standard pathway "scientific items → keywords → scientific items sets"[2] used by existing dataset search engines has inherent limitations.

This paper proposes a recommendation method based on entity vectors trained on citation networks. This approach is a solution for data discovery following the more direct "scientific items → scientific items" pathway. Because our approach does not require converting scientific items (papers and datasets) into keywords, we can avoid the earlier drawbacks. Furthermore, we combine this new recommendation method with existing recommendation methods into an integrated ensemble recommendation method. This paper also provides a benchmark corpus for scientific item recommendation and a benchmark evaluation test. By performing benchmark tests on randomly selected scientific items from this benchmark corpus, we conclude that our integrated recommendation method using citation network entity embedding can obtain a precision rate of about 70%.

Specifically, in this paper, we study three research questions:

- Will a citation network help in scientific item discovery?
- Can we do dataset discovery purely by link prediction on a citation network?
- Will the addition of citation-network-link-prediction help for scientific item discovery?

The main contributions of this paper are: 1) we propose a method for recommending scientific items based on entity embedding in an academic citation graph, 2) we propose a benchmark corpus and evaluation test for scientific items recommendation methods, 3) we identify an ensemble method that has high precision for scientific items recommendation, and 4) we provide the pre-trained entity embeddings for our large-scale academic citation network as an open resource for re-use by others.

2   Related Work

Data reuse aims to facilitate replication of scientific research, make scientific assets available to the public, leverage research investment, and advance research

---

[1] https://data.mendeley.com/.

[2] We use the term "scientific items" to refer to both papers and datasets.

and innovation [19]. Many current works focus on supporting and bringing convenience to data reuse. Wilkinson et. al. provided FAIR guiding principles to support scientific data reuse [28]. Pierce et. al. provided data reuse metrics for scientific data so that researchers can track how the scientific data is used or reused [22]. Duke and Porter provided a framework for developing ethical principles for data reuse [10]. Faniel et. al. provided a model to examine the relationship between data quality and user satisfaction [12].

Dataset recommendation is also a popular research trend in recent years. Farber and Leisinger recommended suitable dataset for given research problem description [14]. Patra et. al. provided an Information retrieval (IR) paradigm for scientific dataset recommendation [20]. Altaf et. al. recommended scientific dataset based on user's research interests [1]. Chen et. al. proposed a three-layered network (composed of authors, papers and datasets) for scientific dataset recommendation [5].

3 Link Prediction with Graph Embedding on a Citation Network

The link prediction training method we use is KGlove [7]. KGlove finds statistics of co-occurrences of nodes in random walks, using personalized page rank. Then Glove [21] is used to generate entity embeddings from the co-occurrence matrix. In this paper, we apply KGlove on 638,360,451 triples of the Microsoft Academic Knowledge Graph (MAKG) [13] citation network (containing 481,674,701 nodes) to generate a co-occurrence matrix of the scientific items. Then we use the Glove method on this co-occurence matrix to obtain the scientific entity (item) embeddings. The trained embeddings are made available for future work[3]. After training the entity embedding based on the MAKG citation network, we perform link predictions between scientific items (papers and/or datasets) by a similarity metric in the embedding space. We use cosine similarity, which is the most commonly used similarity for such embeddings.

Definition 1 (Link Prediction for scientific items with Entity Embedding). *Let $E = \{e_1, e_2, ...\}$ be a set of scientific entities (also known as scientific items). Let* emb *be an embedding function for entities such that* emb(e) *is the embedding of entity $e \in E$, and* emb(e) *is a one-dimensional vector of a given length.*

Let $\cos : (a, b) \rightarrow [0, 1]$ *be a function such that* $\cos(a, b) = \frac{\text{emb}(a) \cdot \text{emb}(b)}{||\,\text{emb}(a)||\cdot|| \text{emb}(b)||}$ *where $a, b \in E$.*

Given a threshold t, we define Link *prediction with Entity Embedding in E as a function* $LP_E : E \rightarrow 2^E$ *where* $LP_E(e_s) = \{r_1, r_2, ..., r_n | \forall i = 1 ... n, \cos(e_s, r_i) < t\}$.

---

[3] https://zenodo.org/record/6324341.

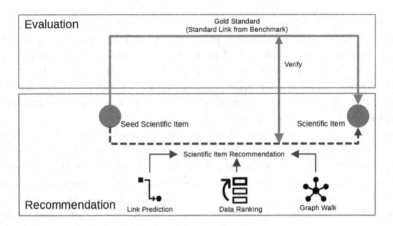

Fig. 1. Pipeline of Scientificset Data Recommendation and Evaluation Benchmark.

4   Dataset Recommendation Methods

In this section we use the previous definition of link prediction to introduce two new dataset recommendation methods, as well as three methods from our previous work. We also propose an open-access scientific items recommendation evaluation benchmark, including corpus and evaluation pipeline (Fig. 1).

4.1   Dataset Recommendation Methods

The dataset recommendation methods in this section use a combination of link-prediction and ranking approaches to recommend a recommended scientific item based on given scientific items.

Data Recommendation with Link Prediction Using a Citation Network. This scientific entity (item) recommendation method is based on Definition 1, where a set of entities is returned such that the cosine distance between these entities and the given entity is smaller than a threshold t. Based on the list of scientific items returned by the link prediction algorithm, the recommendation method considers only the TOP-n results of that list, with the value of n to be chosen as a parameter of the method. Formally, this is defined as follows:

Definition 2 (Top-n scientific entity (items) Recommendation with Link Prediction). *Let $E = \{e_1, e_2, ...\}$ be a set of scientific entities (also known as scientific items). Let LP_E be a link prediction function using embeddings in E (see Definition 1). Top-n Scientific entity recommendation with link prediction using embedding is a function $DRLP_E^n$, which maps an entity e_s to $(r_1, \ldots r_m)$ which is the longest ordered list of $m <= n$ pairwise distinct elements of $LP_E(e_s)$ where $\forall i = 1 \ldots m - 1, \cos(e_s, r_i) <= \cos(e_s, r_{i+1})$.*

In words, this function maps an entity (scientific item) to a list of at most n other entities (scientific items) which are closest to it in the embedded space, ordered by the distance.

We can now combine this general definition with a specific embedding function emb to create a specific link-prediction-based recommendation method. In particular, we use KGloVe embeddings from the MAKG citation network to create a recommendation method based on link prediction from a citation network.

Scientific Items Recommendation with BERT-based Link Prediction. The method from the previous subsection used the embeddings computed on the citation graph to determine similarity between data items. This is a plausible choice, since we can expect the MAKG citation graph to give us a reasonable signal for similarity in the scientific domain: it captures the scientific relationships between items in the science domain. In contrast to this, we also experimented with using other models to compute the similarity between items. In particular, we used the pretrained BERT model [9,23] as an example of a cross-domain model to see if such a generic pretrained model would also suffice to compute the similarity metric that is the basis for our link-prediction-based recommendation algorithm. The pretrained BERT model used in this paper is the *all-mpnet-base-v2* model from the SentenceTransformers Python library[4]. Such BERT-based link prediction for scientific items is obtained by applying the pretrained BERT model to the descriptive metadata of the scientific items to obtain the BERT embedding of scientific items. Such metadata consists of the title of the dataset and a short text that accompanies the dataset. Then, we apply the BERT embedding of the scientific items to Definition 2 to do scientific items recommendations.

Scientific Items Recommendation with BM25-based Data Ranking. BM25-based Data Ranking is the recommendation approach provided in our previous paper [27]. Given a seed scientific item, we rank the list of candidate recommended scientific items using the popular BM25 method from information retrieval according to the descriptive metadata of the scientific items (consisting of title and textual description), where a higher ranking position means a better recommendation [24].

Scientific Items Recommendation with Graph Walk. The co-author network-based graph walk method is also a scientific items recommendation method that we have previously proposed in [26]. Such a graph walk on a co-author network performs the recommendation task according to the "scientific items → author → co-author network → author → scientific items" pathway. In order to reduce the number of candidate recommendations we only consider items connected to authors within an n-hop distance to the author of the seed data item in the co-author network.

---

[4] https://www.sbert.net/docs/pretrained_models.html.

Table 1. Statistics of benchmark corpus

	Number of items	Number of links
All	3,227,206	15,979,748
Paper-Paper	2,909,755	14,391,413
Dataset-Dataset	1,544	2,335

Dataset Recommendation with Pre-trained Author Embedding. Similar to the method based on citation-based embeddings, we have proposed in earlier work [26] a recommendation method for scientific items based on pre-trained co-authorship embeddings. This approach is similar to our proposed method using embeddings from the MAKG citation network (Definition 1), but uses embeddings computed from the MAKG co-author network instead.

5   Scientific Items Recommendation Benchmark

To evaluate the performance scientific items recommendation methods, we propose here an open-source generalized benchmark corpus and process for scientific items recommendation. scientific items in general can be publications, datasets, graphs, tables, geographic data, etc.

5.1   Benchmark Corpus

The benchmark corpus is an HDT/RDF graph [15,18] stored as triples of the form "[scientific item] [link] [scientific item]." The scientific items are the intersection of scientific items in ScholeXplorer[5] and MAKG (Microsoft Academic Knowledge Graph). This intersection is computed by matching the DOI of scientific items (datasets and/or papers) between ScholeXplorer and MAKG. We have chosen to represent all the scientific items by the identificatier used in the Microsoft Academic Graph (MAG). With help of these MAG identifiers, the information (such as title, providers, publishers, or creators) of scientific items is easily accessible in MAKG. The bi-directional links between these items are from ScholeXplorer and all the links are provided by data sources managed by publishers, data centers, or other organizations.

In Table 1, we show the statistics of our benchmark corpus. There are more than 3 million items and more than 15 million bi-directional links between them. We provide the data subset with only bi-directional links between scientific *papers*, consisting of 2.9 million scientific papers and 14.3 million links between them. We also provide the data subset of only the bi-directional links between scientific *datasets*, with 1,544 scientific items and 2,335 million links between them. We have made this corpus available at https://zenodo.org/record/6386897.

---

[5] https://scholexplorer.openaire.eu/.

Table 2. Statistics of experiments

	Number of seeds	Number of candidates
Exp1	12	115
Exp2	109	27,242
Exp3	181	28,960

5.2 Benchmark Evaluation

The goal of our benchmark is to evaluate the performance of scientific item recommendation methods on all datasets in the benchmark corpus, with the option to only use a randomly selected subset. We use the F1-measure method [6] to evaluate the performance of recommendation methods on reconstruction of bidirectional links between scientific items. The F1-measure method consists of three evaluation metrics: recall, precision and F1-score. Recall is the percentage of recommendations (i.e. links as given in the dataset that start from the seed data) that the recommendation method can recommend. Precision is the percentage of scientific items recommended by the recommendation method that is correct (i.e., present in the standard). Finally, the F1-score is the harmonic mean of recall and precision.

6 Experiments and Results

This section will present the setup and results of our experiments on the proposed recommendation methods from Sect. 4 using the evaluation benchmark from Sect. 5. The implementation of recommendation methods and the code of all experiments could be found at https://github.com/XuWangVU/datarecommend.

6.1 Experimental Setup

We set up three evaluation experiments using three sets of data randomly selected from the benchmark corpus. The statistics of the selected data are shown in Table 2. For each seed scientific item, we look for recommendations among all the candidate scientific items and return a sorted subset of these candidates.

The recommendation methods evaluated in the experiments comprise the five methods described in Sect. 4. Beyond these single methods, we also tested ensemble methods by combining multiple methods to make recommendations. All methods (including the ensemble methods) fall into two types of pathway-based categories: pathways with author and pathway without authors. All the methods (including the ensemble methods) used in our experiments can be found in Table 3.

We use thresholds for two methods: a distance threshold for graph walks and a threshold for similarity between author embeddings. The distance threshold

Table 3. Scientific items recommendation methods used for experiments.

Approach name	Link prediction (Citation)	Data ranking (BM25)	Link prediction (BERT)	Graph walk	Author embedding
Citation	X				
BERT			X		
BM25		X			
Citation + BM25	X	X			
Citation + BERT	X		X		
BERT + BM25		X	X		
Citation + BM25 + BERT	X	X	X		
Pure walk				X	
Hop(n) + Embed(T)				X	X
Hop(n) + Embed(T) + Citation	X			X	X
Hop(n) + Embed(T) + BM25		X		X	X
Hop(n) + Embed(T) + BERT			X	X	X
Hop(n) + Embed(T) + BERT + BM25		X	X	X	X
Hop(n) + Embed(T) + BM25 + Citation	X	X		X	X
Hop(n) + Embed(T) + BERT + Citation	X		X	X	X
Hop(n) + Embed(T) + All	X	X	X	X	X

for graph walks is the maximum number of hops that make up a graph walk. For example, hop1 means that only authors with a distance of 1 from the given author are considered. The author embedding similarity threshold means that only authors with an embedding similarity greater than or equal to the threshold with the given author are considered.

Each recommendation method is assigned a parameter. For the graph walk method, we use the parameter of hop1, hop2, or hop3, to represent the distance threshold used for graph walk. For the similarity method between pretrained MAKG author embeddings, we use similarity threshold parameters ranging from 0.3 to 0.7, increasing in steps of 0.1. For the BM25-based ranking method, we use the parameter $p_{bm25} = 2 * outdegree(seed)$, where $outdegree(seed)$ is the number of scientific items linked from the seed in the benchmark corpus. In other words, we will only consider the top p_{bm25} results in the list returned by the ranking method. For both link prediction methods using citation network embeddings and BERT-based link prediction methods, we use a parameter of 0.8, which means we only consider the top 80% of the sorted lists returned by both methods.

6.2   Experimental Results

Table 4 show the results of the scientific items recommendation methods which do not consider authors in the pathway, while Tables 5, 6 and 7 show the results of methods considering authors. We use color-coding of the cells to indicate different ranges of values: Red means relative poor performance in comparison with related settings; green code means outstanding performance in comparison; and yellow means average performance.

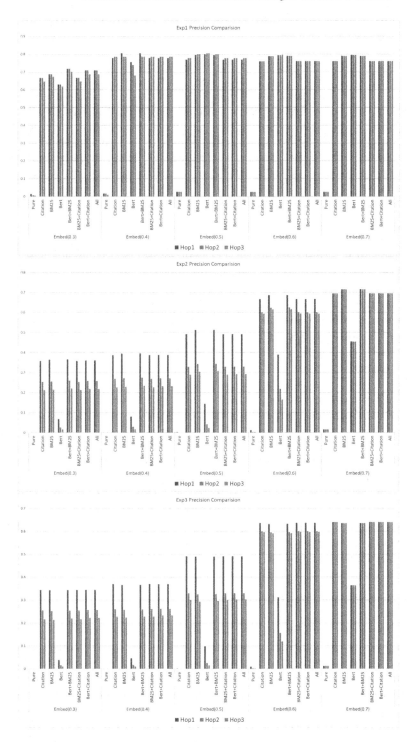

Fig. 2. Precision comparison in Experiment 1, Experiment 2, and Experiment 3.

Table 4. Results of Experiment(EXP) 1, 2 & 3 without graph walk and author embedding.

	EXP1			EXP2			EXP3		
	R	P	F1	R	P	F1	R	P	F1
Citation	0,12458	0,22561	0,16052	0,28681	0,17941	0,22074	0,2986	0,1869	0,2299
Bert	0,15825	0,19583	0,17505	0,96881	0,0127	0,02507	0,9700	0,0076	0,0151
BM25	0,15488	0,2201	0,18182	0,35851	0,17925	0,239	0,3720	0,1860	0,2480
Citation+BM25	0,12458	0,22561	0,16052	0,28681	0,17941	0,22074	0,2986	0,1869	0,2299
Citation+Bert	0,12458	0,27007	0,17051	0,28681	0,18736	0,22665	0,2986	0,1937	0,2350
Bert+BM25	0,15488	0,27381	0,19785	0,35851	0,18738	0,24612	0,3720	0,1930	0,2542
Citation+BM25+Bert	0,12458	0,27007	0,17051	0,28681	0,18736	0,22665	0,2986	0,1937	0,2350

In the experiments which do not consider authors, we found that recall, precision, and F1-score were usually not high, except for the method which only uses BERT, where we could obtain a recall of over 0.95. However, this situation does not achieve sufficiently high precision rates.

When the author network is taken into consideration, the precision rate improves considerably, and in some integrated methods, we achieve precision results of 0.7 or even 0.8. Unfortunately, these high precision rates come with a decreased recall rate, which means that the methods return few, but often correct recommendations.

This behavior, i.e., high precision rates at relative low recall, is typical and sufficient for recommendation engines. Hence, we explore these results in more detail. A comparison of the precision rates of the different methods can be found in Fig. 2. For experiment 1, we observe little variability, likely due to the small data size. For experiments 2 and 3, however, the precision rate increases with a higher distance threshold for the graph walk or with a higher threshold for the author embedding similarity.

Based on the comparison of the results of the different methods in Tables 5, 6 and 7 and Fig. 2, we can conclude that all recommendation methods that use data ranking (BM25) or link prediction (Citation Embedding) have a high precision on our scientific items recommendation benchmark experiments when using graph walking and author embedding similarity methods in an ensemble of methods.

7   Conclusion and Discussion

In this paper, we have investigated the use of a large scale citation network for the purposes of recommending scientific items, on the basis of a given scientific item by the user, according to the well-known paradigm "if you like this dataset, you might also like these other datasets". The method uses low-dimensional vector space embeddings computed from the citation graph in order to compute the cosine similarity between datasets as the basis for its recommendations. By itself, this method performed unsatisfactorily on our benchmark under a variety of experimental settings.

We therefore also studied the behaviour of this method in an ensemble with a number of other methods: recommendations based on n-hops walks in a co-author graph ($n = 1, 2, 3$), recommendations based on embeddings computed over this co-author graph, recommendations based on the BERT large language model, and the BM25 method from information retrieval. We studied a large variety of the most promising combinations of methods under different experimental settings. In our largest experimental setting, the ensemble methods that used the embeddings from the citation network outperformed those that didn't, with a precision of 0.64 under a variety of settings. This acceptable precision in a recommendation setting comes at the price of a low recall, a behaviour that is typical in recommendation engines.

This allows us to succinctly answer the research questions we formulated in the introduction of this paper:

- Will a citation network help in dataset discovery? Answer: yes
- Can we do dataset discovery purely by link prediction on a citation network? Answer: no
- Will the addition of citation-network-link-prediction help for dataset discovery? Answer: yes

We performed our experiments on a newly constructed benchmark set, using the KGlove method for training scientific entity (item) embeddings from the Microsoft Academic Knowledge Graph, containing a citation network of 100 million edges. We have made this benchmark corpus available online.

The methods that we designed and evaluated in this paper are clearly not the final word on how to recommend scientific items. Likely, the results can be improved not only by using tuning parameters to specific datasets, but also by adding other existing applicable methods. Also, the dataset could be expended. We have used both citation and co-author networks as signals for academic similarity, but also other academic networks exist. Including those is subject of future work.

The link prediction mentioned in this paper uses pre-trained embedding models. One drawback of this type of models is that this requires an embedding for each entity in the graph, and hence many existing models do not scale well enough. In the future several approaches could be investigated to overcome, one option is to use a model which can work in an inductive setting, based on the description, or even the content of the datasets. An example of such a method is BLP [8]. To reduce the number of embeddings, we could also use a model which only keeps embeddings for some entities in the graph, like NodePiece [16]. Another direction could be to attempt scaling models using summarization, as was done in [17].

Acknowledgments. This work was funded in part by Elsevier's Discovery Lab (https://discoverylab.ai/). This work was also funded by the Netherlands Science Foundation NWO grant nr. 652.001.002 which is also partially funded by Elsevier. The first author is funded by the China Scholarship Council (CSC) under grant nr. 201807730060. Part of this work was inspired by discussions with other members of the discovery lab, like Daniel Daza and Dimitrios Alivanistos.

A   Detailed Results of the Different Experiments

Table 5. Results of Experiment 1 with graph walk and author embedding.

Exp1	Hop1			Hop2			Hop3		
	R	P	F1	R	P	F1	R	P	F1
Pure walk	0.2189	0.0139	0.0261	0.2189	0.0048	0.0095	0.2189	0.0047	0.0092
Embed(0.3)	0.2189	0.0139	0.0262	0.2189	0.0071	0.0138	0.2189	0.0052	0.0101
Embed(0.3)+Citation	0.0741	0.6667	0.1333	0.0741	0.6667	0.1333	0.0741	0.6471	0.1329
Embed(0.3)+BM25	0.1111	0.6875	0.1913	0.1111	0.6875	0.1913	0.1111	0.6735	0.1908
Embed(0.3)+BERT	0.1145	0.6296	0.1937	0.1145	0.6296	0.1937	0.1145	0.6182	0.1932
Embed(0.3)+BERT+BM25	0.1111	0.7174	0.1924	0.1111	0.7174	0.1924	0.1111	0.7021	0.1919
Embed(0.3)+BM25+Citation	0.0741	0.6667	0.1333	0.0741	0.6667	0.1333	0.0741	0.6471	0.1329
Embed(0.3)+BERT+Citation	0.0741	0.7097	0.1342	0.0741	0.7097	0.1342	0.0741	0.6875	0.1337
Embed(0.3)+All	0.0741	0.7097	0.1342	0.0741	0.7097	0.1342	0.0741	0.6875	0.1337
Embed(0.4)	0.2189	0.0166	0.0308	0.2189	0.0162	0.0301	0.2189	0.0096	0.0184
Embed(0.4)+Citation	0.0707	0.7778	0.1296	0.0741	0.7857	0.1354	0.0741	0.7857	0.1354
Embed(0.4)+BM25	0.1111	0.8049	0.1953	0.1111	0.7857	0.1947	0.1111	0.7857	0.1947
Embed(0.4)+BERT	0.1145	0.7556	0.1988	0.1145	0.7391	0.1983	0.1145	0.6800	0.1960
Embed(0.4)+BERT+BM25	0.1111	0.8049	0.1953	0.1111	0.7857	0.1947	0.1111	0.7857	0.1947
Embed(0.4)+BM25+Citation	0.0707	0.7778	0.1296	0.0741	0.7857	0.1354	0.0741	0.7857	0.1354
Embed(0.4)+BERT+Citation	0.0707	0.7778	0.1296	0.0741	0.7857	0.1354	0.0741	0.7857	0.1354
Embed(0.4)+All	0.0707	0.7778	0.1296	0.0741	0.7857	0.1354	0.0741	0.7857	0.1354
Embed(0.5)	0.2121	0.0260	0.0463	0.2155	0.0261	0.0465	0.2155	0.0261	0.0465
Embed(0.5)+Citation	0.0673	0.7692	0.1238	0.0707	0.7778	0.1296	0.0707	0.7778	0.1296
Embed(0.5)+BM25	0.1044	0.7949	0.1845	0.1077	0.8000	0.1899	0.1077	0.8000	0.1899
Embed(0.5)+BERT	0.1077	0.8000	0.1899	0.1111	0.8049	0.1953	0.1111	0.8049	0.1953
Embed(0.5)+BERT+BM25	0.1044	0.7949	0.1845	0.1077	0.8000	0.1899	0.1077	0.8000	0.1899
Embed(0.5)+BM25+Citation	0.0673	0.7692	0.1238	0.0707	0.7778	0.1296	0.0707	0.7778	0.1296
Embed(0.5)+BERT+Citation	0.0673	0.7692	0.1238	0.0707	0.7778	0.1296	0.0707	0.7778	0.1296
Embed(0.5)+All	0.0673	0.7692	0.1238	0.0707	0.7778	0.1296	0.0707	0.7778	0.1296
Embed(0.6)	0.2088	0.0270	0.0478	0.2088	0.0270	0.0478	0.2088	0.0270	0.0478
Embed(0.6)+Citation	0.0640	0.7600	0.1180	0.0640	0.7600	0.1180	0.0640	0.7600	0.1180
Embed(0.6)+BM25	0.1010	0.7895	0.1791	0.1010	0.7895	0.1791	0.1010	0.7895	0.1791
Embed(0.6)+BERT	0.1044	0.7949	0.1845	0.1044	0.7949	0.1845	0.1044	0.7949	0.1845
Embed(0.6)+BERT+BM25	0.1010	0.7895	0.1791	0.1010	0.7895	0.1791	0.1010	0.7895	0.1791
Embed(0.6)+BM25+Citation	0.0640	0.7600	0.1180	0.0640	0.7600	0.1180	0.0640	0.7600	0.1180
Embed(0.6)+BERT+Citation	0.0640	0.7600	0.1180	0.0640	0.7600	0.1180	0.0640	0.7600	0.1180
Embed(0.6)+All	0.0640	0.7600	0.1180	0.0640	0.7600	0.1180	0.0640	0.7600	0.1180
Embed(0.7)	0.2088	0.0270	0.0478	0.2088	0.0270	0.0478	0.2088	0.0270	0.0478
Embed(0.7)+Citation	0.0640	0.7600	0.1180	0.0640	0.7600	0.1180	0.0640	0.7600	0.1180
Embed(0.7)+BM25	0.1010	0.7895	0.1791	0.1010	0.7895	0.1791	0.1010	0.7895	0.1791
Embed(0.7)+BERT	0.1044	0.7949	0.1845	0.1044	0.7949	0.1845	0.1044	0.7949	0.1845
Embed(0.7)+BERT+BM25	0.1010	0.7895	0.1791	0.1010	0.7895	0.1791	0.1010	0.7895	0.1791
Embed(0.7)+BM25+Citation	0.0640	0.7600	0.1180	0.0640	0.7600	0.1180	0.0640	0.7600	0.1180
Embed(0.7)+BERT+Citation	0.0640	0.7600	0.1180	0.0640	0.7600	0.1180	0.0640	0.7600	0.1180
Embed(0.7)+All	0.0640	0.7600	0.1180	0.0640	0.7600	0.1180	0.0640	0.7600	0.1180

Table 6. Results of Experiment 2 with graph walk and author embedding.

Exp2	Hop1			Hop2			Hop3		
	R	P	F1	R	P	F1	R	P	F1
Pure walk	0.2230	0.0005	0.0009	0.4425	0.0001	0.0003	0.6225	0.0001	0.0002
Embed(0.3)	0.1903	0.0006	0.0011	0.3838	0.0002	0.0003	0.5330	0.0001	0.0002
Embed(0.3)+Citation	0.0635	0.3581	0.1079	0.1230	0.2521	0.1654	0.1665	0.2115	0.1863
Embed(0.3)+BM25	0.0813	0.3639	0.1329	0.1554	0.2540	0.1928	0.2099	0.2129	0.2114
Embed(0.3)+BERT	0.1886	0.0680	0.0999	0.3804	0.0258	0.0483	0.5283	0.0158	0.0307
Embed(0.3)+BERT+BM25	0.0813	0.3658	0.1330	0.1554	0.2588	0.1942	0.2099	0.2193	0.2145
Embed(0.3)+BM25+Citation	0.0635	0.3581	0.1079	0.1230	0.2521	0.1654	0.1665	0.2115	0.1863
Embed(0.3)+BERT+Citation	0.0635	0.3602	0.1080	0.1230	0.2569	0.1664	0.1665	0.2178	0.1887
Embed(0.3)+All	0.0635	0.3602	0.1080	0.1230	0.2569	0.1664	0.1665	0.2178	0.1887
Embed(0.4)	0.1258	0.0008	0.0016	0.2525	0.0002	0.0004	0.3279	0.0001	0.0002
Embed(0.4)+Citation	0.0424	0.3868	0.0765	0.0821	0.2680	0.1257	0.1056	0.2258	0.1439
Embed(0.4)+BM25	0.0547	0.3942	0.0961	0.1042	0.2710	0.1505	0.1337	0.2279	0.1685
Embed(0.4)+BERT	0.1246	0.0804	0.0977	0.2506	0.0288	0.0517	0.3255	0.0163	0.0310
Embed(0.4)+BERT+BM25	0.0547	0.3952	0.0962	0.1042	0.2744	0.1511	0.1337	0.2335	0.1700
Embed(0.4)+BM25+Citation	0.0424	0.3868	0.0765	0.0821	0.2680	0.1257	0.1056	0.2258	0.1439
Embed(0.4)+BERT+Citation	0.0424	0.3878	0.0765	0.0821	0.2715	0.1261	0.1056	0.2313	0.1450
Embed(0.4)+All	0.0424	0.3878	0.0765	0.0821	0.2715	0.1261	0.1056	0.2313	0.1450
Embed(0.5)	0.0645	0.0021	0.0040	0.0996	0.0004	0.0008	0.1092	0.0002	0.0004
Embed(0.5)+Citation	0.0225	0.4909	0.0430	0.0331	0.3279	0.0602	0.0358	0.2892	0.0637
Embed(0.5)+BM25	0.0302	0.5123	0.0571	0.0438	0.3422	0.0777	0.0475	0.3034	0.0822
Embed(0.5)+BERT	0.0639	0.1437	0.0884	0.0988	0.0420	0.0589	0.1083	0.0227	0.0375
Embed(0.5)+BERT+BM25	0.0302	0.5125	0.0571	0.0438	0.3435	0.0777	0.0475	0.3070	0.0823
Embed(0.5)+BM25+Citation	0.0225	0.4909	0.0430	0.0331	0.3279	0.0602	0.0358	0.2892	0.0637
Embed(0.5)+BERT+Citation	0.0225	0.4912	0.0430	0.0331	0.3292	0.0602	0.0358	0.2927	0.0638
Embed(0.5)+All	0.0225	0.4912	0.0430	0.0331	0.3292	0.0602	0.0358	0.2927	0.0638
Embed(0.6)	0.0462	0.0113	0.0182	0.0478	0.0039	0.0072	0.0480	0.0022	0.0043
Embed(0.6)+Citation	0.0178	0.6667	0.0347	0.0179	0.6007	0.0348	0.0180	0.5941	0.0349
Embed(0.6)+BM25	0.0242	0.6861	0.0467	0.0245	0.6241	0.0471	0.0245	0.6155	0.0471
Embed(0.6)+BERT	0.0457	0.3905	0.0818	0.0473	0.2188	0.0778	0.0475	0.1642	0.0737
Embed(0.6)+BERT+BM25	0.0242	0.6861	0.0467	0.0245	0.6241	0.0471	0.0245	0.6155	0.0471
Embed(0.6)+BM25+Citation	0.0178	0.6667	0.0347	0.0179	0.6007	0.0348	0.0180	0.5941	0.0349
Embed(0.6)+BERT+Citation	0.0178	0.6667	0.0347	0.0179	0.6007	0.0348	0.0180	0.5941	0.0349
Embed(0.6)+All	0.0178	0.6667	0.0347	0.0179	0.6007	0.0348	0.0180	0.5941	0.0349
Embed(0.7)	0.0452	0.0145	0.0219	0.0452	0.0144	0.0219	0.0452	0.0144	0.0219
Embed(0.7)+Citation	0.0176	0.6950	0.0343	0.0176	0.6950	0.0343	0.0176	0.6950	0.0343
Embed(0.7)+BM25	0.0239	0.7157	0.0463	0.0239	0.7157	0.0463	0.0239	0.7157	0.0463
Embed(0.7)+BERT	0.0447	0.4549	0.0814	0.0447	0.4543	0.0814	0.0447	0.4543	0.0814
Embed(0.7)+BERT+BM25	0.0239	0.7157	0.0463	0.0239	0.7157	0.0463	0.0239	0.7157	0.0463
Embed(0.7)+BM25+Citation	0.0176	0.6950	0.0343	0.0176	0.6950	0.0343	0.0176	0.6950	0.0343
Embed(0.7)+BERT+Citation	0.0176	0.6950	0.0343	0.0176	0.6950	0.0343	0.0176	0.6950	0.0343
Embed(0.7)+All	0.0176	0.6950	0.0343	0.0176	0.6950	0.0343	0.0176	0.6950	0.0343

Table 7. Results of Experiment 3 with graph walk and author embedding.

Exp3	Hop1			Hop2			Hop3		
	R	P	F1	R	P	F1	R	P	F1
Pure walk	0.2582	0.0003	0.0007	0.4450	0.0001	0.0002	0.5955	0.0001	0.0001
Embed(0.3)	0.2235	0.0004	0.0007	0.3973	0.0001	0.0002	0.5276	0.0001	0.0001
Embed(0.3)+Citation	0.0827	0.3440	0.1334	0.1331	0.2548	0.1748	0.1706	0.2165	0.1908
Embed(0.3)+BM25	0.1041	0.3431	0.1597	0.1650	0.2518	0.1994	0.2104	0.2130	0.2117
Embed(0.3)+BERT	0.2215	0.0385	0.0657	0.3941	0.0155	0.0298	0.5234	0.0097	0.0191
Embed(0.3)+BERT+BM25	0.1041	0.3434	0.1597	0.1650	0.2541	0.2001	0.2104	0.2193	0.2147
Embed(0.3)+BM25+Citation	0.0827	0.3440	0.1334	0.1331	0.2548	0.1748	0.1706	0.2165	0.1908
Embed(0.3)+BERT+Citation	0.0827	0.3442	0.1334	0.1331	0.2569	0.1753	0.1706	0.2227	0.1932
Embed(0.3)+All	0.0827	0.3442	0.1334	0.1331	0.2569	0.1753	0.1706	0.2227	0.1932
Embed(0.4)	0.1577	0.0005	0.0010	0.2826	0.0001	0.0003	0.3485	0.0001	0.0001
Embed(0.4)+Citation	0.0600	0.3702	0.1032	0.0951	0.2610	0.1394	0.1150	0.2281	0.1529
Embed(0.4)+BM25	0.0751	0.3663	0.1246	0.1181	0.2578	0.1620	0.1414	0.2235	0.1732
Embed(0.4)+BERT	0.1563	0.0457	0.0708	0.2804	0.0170	0.0320	0.3459	0.0101	0.0197
Embed(0.4)+BERT+BM25	0.0751	0.3664	0.1246	0.1181	0.2594	0.1623	0.1414	0.2286	0.1748
Embed(0.4)+BM25+Citation	0.0600	0.3702	0.1032	0.0951	0.2610	0.1394	0.1150	0.2281	0.1529
Embed(0.4)+BERT+Citation	0.0600	0.3702	0.1032	0.0951	0.2626	0.1397	0.1150	0.2334	0.1541
Embed(0.4)+All	0.0600	0.3702	0.1032	0.0951	0.2626	0.1397	0.1150	0.2334	0.1541
Embed(0.5)	0.0921	0.0016	0.0031	0.1311	0.0003	0.0006	0.1418	0.0001	0.0003
Embed(0.5)+Citation	0.0380	0.4917	0.0706	0.0485	0.3297	0.0845	0.0519	0.3005	0.0885
Embed(0.5)+BM25	0.0486	0.4902	0.0884	0.0606	0.3252	0.1021	0.0642	0.2938	0.1054
Embed(0.5)+BERT	0.0913	0.0978	0.0944	0.1301	0.0253	0.0424	0.1408	0.0149	0.0270
Embed(0.5)+BERT+BM25	0.0486	0.4902	0.0884	0.0606	0.3256	0.1021	0.0642	0.2961	0.1055
Embed(0.5)+BM25+Citation	0.0380	0.4917	0.0706	0.0485	0.3297	0.0845	0.0519	0.3005	0.0885
Embed(0.5)+BERT+Citation	0.0380	0.4917	0.0706	0.0485	0.3303	0.0845	0.0519	0.3029	0.0886
Embed(0.5)+All	0.0380	0.4917	0.0706	0.0485	0.3303	0.0845	0.0519	0.3029	0.0886
Embed(0.6)	0.0681	0.0096	0.0169	0.0700	0.0033	0.0064	0.0704	0.0020	0.0039
Embed(0.6)+Citation	0.0319	0.6364	0.0607	0.0324	0.6009	0.0615	0.0325	0.5969	0.0616
Embed(0.6)+BM25	0.0411	0.6323	0.0772	0.0416	0.5961	0.0778	0.0417	0.5919	0.0780
Embed(0.6)+BERT	0.0675	0.3122	0.1110	0.0694	0.1573	0.0963	0.0698	0.1192	0.0880
Embed(0.6)+BERT+BM25	0.0411	0.6323	0.0772	0.0416	0.5961	0.0778	0.0417	0.5919	0.0780
Embed(0.6)+BM25+Citation	0.0319	0.6364	0.0607	0.0324	0.6009	0.0615	0.0325	0.5969	0.0616
Embed(0.6)+BERT+Citation	0.0319	0.6364	0.0607	0.0324	0.6009	0.0615	0.0325	0.5969	0.0616
Embed(0.6)+All	0.0319	0.6364	0.0607	0.0324	0.6009	0.0615	0.0325	0.5969	0.0616
Embed(0.7)	0.0668	0.0122	0.0206	0.0668	0.0121	0.0205	0.0668	0.0121	0.0205
Embed(0.7)+Citation	0.0315	0.6404	0.0600	0.0315	0.6404	0.0600	0.0315	0.6404	0.0600
Embed(0.7)+BM25	0.0405	0.6355	0.0762	0.0405	0.6355	0.0762	0.0405	0.6355	0.0762
Embed(0.7)+BERT	0.0663	0.3640	0.1122	0.0663	0.3637	0.1121	0.0663	0.3637	0.1121
Embed(0.7)+BERT+BM25	0.0405	0.6355	0.0762	0.0405	0.6355	0.0762	0.0405	0.6355	0.0762
Embed(0.7)+BM25+Citation	0.0315	0.6404	0.0600	0.0315	0.6404	0.0600	0.0315	0.6404	0.0600
Embed(0.7)+BERT+Citation	0.0315	0.6404	0.0600	0.0315	0.6404	0.0600	0.0315	0.6404	0.0600
Embed(0.7)+All	0.0315	0.6404	0.0600	0.0315	0.6404	0.0600	0.0315	0.6404	0.0600

References

1. Altaf, B., Akujuobi, U., Yu, L., Zhang, X.: Dataset recommendation via variational graph autoencoder. In: IEEE International Conference on Data Mining (ICDM), pp. 11–20 (2019)
2. Borgman, C.: One scientist's data as another's noise. Nature **520**(7546), 157 (2015)
3. Brickley, D., Burgess, M., Noy, N.: Google dataset search: building a search engine for datasets in an open web ecosystem. In: WWW Conference, WWW 2019, pp. 1365–1375. ACM (2019). https://doi.org/10.1145/3308558.3313685
4. Chapman, A., et al.: Dataset search: a survey. VLDB J. **29**, 251–272 (2019). https://doi.org/10.1007/s00778-019-00564-x
5. Chen, Y., Wang, Y., Zhang, Y., Pu, J., Zhang, X.: Amender: an attentive and aggregate multi-layered network for dataset recommendation. In: IEEE International Conference on Data Mining (ICDM), pp. 988–993. IEEE (2019)
6. Chinchor, N.: MUC-4 evaluation metrics. In: Proceedings of the 4th Conference on Message Understanding, MUC4 1992, pp. 22–29. ACL (1992). https://doi.org/10.3115/1072064.1072067
7. Cochez, M., Ristoski, P., Ponzetto, S.P., Paulheim, H.: Global RDF vector space embeddings. In: d'Amato, C., et al. (eds.) ISWC 2017. LNCS, vol. 10587, pp. 190–207. Springer, Cham (2017). https://doi.org/10.1007/978-3-319-68288-4_12
8. Daza, D., Cochez, M., Groth, P.: Inductive entity representations from text via link prediction. In: Proceedings of The Web Conference (2021). https://doi.org/10.1145/3442381.3450141
9. Devlin, J., Chang, M.W., Lee, K., Toutanova, K.: BERT: pre-training of deep bidirectional transformers for language understanding. In: Proceedings of NAACL-HLT, vol. 1, pp. 4171–4186. ACL, June 2019. https://doi.org/10.18653/v1/N19-1423
10. Duke, C.S., Porter, J.H.: The ethics of data sharing and reuse in biology. BioScience **63**(6), 483–489 (2013)
11. Faniel, I.M., Jacobsen, T.E.: Reusing scientific data: how earthquake engineering researchers assess the reusability of colleagues' data. Comput. Supported Coop. Work **19**(3–4), 355–375 (2010). https://doi.org/10.1007/s10606-010-9117-8
12. Faniel, I.M., Kriesberg, A., Yakel, E.: Social scientists' satisfaction with data reuse. J. Assoc. Inf. Sci. Technol. **67**(6), 1404–1416 (2016)
13. Färber, M.: The microsoft academic knowledge graph: a linked data source with 8 billion triples of scholarly data. In: Ghidini, C., et al. (eds.) ISWC 2019. LNCS, vol. 11779, pp. 113–129. Springer, Cham (2019). https://doi.org/10.1007/978-3-030-30796-7_8
14. Färber, M., Leisinger, A.K.: Recommending datasets for scientific problem descriptions. In: International Conference on Information & Knowledge Management, p. 3014 (2021)
15. Fernández, J.D., Martínez-Prieto, M.A., Gutiérrez, C., Polleres, A., Arias, M.: Binary RDF representation for publication and exchange (HDT). Web Semant. Sci. Serv. Agents World Wide Web **19**, 22–41 (2013). http://www.websemanticsjournal.org/index.php/ps/article/view/328
16. Galkin, M., Wu, J., Denis, E., Hamilton, W.L.: NodePiece: compositional and parameter-efficient representations of large knowledge graphs. arXiv preprint arXiv:2106.12144 (2021)
17. Generale, A., Blume, T., Cochez, M.: Scaling R-GCN training with graph summarization (2022). https://doi.org/10.1145/3487553.3524719

18. Martínez-Prieto, M.A., Arias Gallego, M., Fernández, J.D.: Exchange and consumption of huge RDF data. In: Simperl, E., Cimiano, P., Polleres, A., Corcho, O., Presutti, V. (eds.) ESWC 2012. LNCS, vol. 7295, pp. 437–452. Springer, Heidelberg (2012). https://doi.org/10.1007/978-3-642-30284-8_36

19. Pasquetto, I.V., Randles, B.M., Borgman, C.L.: On the reuse of scientific data. Data Sci. J. **16**, 8 (2017)

20. Patra, B.G., Roberts, K., Wu, H.: A content-based dataset recommendation system for researchers-a case study on gene expression omnibus (geo) repository. Database **2020**, 1 (2020)

21. Pennington, J., Socher, R., Manning, C.: GloVe: global vectors for word representation. In: Empirical Methods in Natural Language Processing (EMNLP), pp. 1532–1543. ACL (2014). https://doi.org/10.3115/v1/D14-1162

22. Pierce, H.H., Dev, A., Statham, E., Bierer, B.E.: Credit data generators for data reuse (2019)

23. Reimers, N., Gurevych, I.: Sentence-BERT: sentence embeddings using Siamese BERT-networks. In: Conference on Empirical Methods in Natural Language Processing and International Joint Conference on Natural Language Processing (EMNLP-IJCNLP), pp. 3982–3992. ACL (2019). https://doi.org/10.18653/v1/D19-1410

24. Robertson, S., Walker, S., Jones, S., Hancock-Beaulieu, M.M., Gatford, M.: Okapi at TREC-3. In: Overview of the 3rd Text REtrieval Conference (TREC-3), pp. 109–126 (1995). https://www.microsoft.com/en-us/research/publication/okapi-at-trec-3/

25. Tenopir, C., et al.: Changes in data sharing and data reuse practices and perceptions among scientists worldwide. PLOS ONE **10**(8), 1–24 (2015). https://doi.org/10.1371/journal.pone.0134826

26. Wang, X., van Harmelen, F., Huang, Z.: Recommending scientific datasets using author networks in ensemble methods (2022). https://datasciencehub.net/paper/recommending-scienti%EF%AC%81c-datasets-using-author-networks-ensemble-methods

27. Wang, X., van Harmelen, F., Huang, Z.: Biomedical dataset recommendation. In: International Conference on Data Science, Technology and Applications - DATA, pp. 192–199 (2021). https://doi.org/10.5220/0010521801920199

28. Wilkinson, M.D., et al.: The FAIR guiding principles for scientific data management and stewardship. Sci. Data **3**(1), 1–9 (2016)

LAM: Lightweight Attention Module

Qiwei Ji[1,3], Bo Yu[1,3(✉)], Zhiwei Yang[2,3(✉)], and Hechang Chen[1,3(✉)]

[1] School of Artificial Intelligence, Jilin University, Changchun, China
{jiqw20,byu20}@mails.jlu.edu.cn, chenhc@jlu.edu.cn
[2] College of Computer Science and Technology, Jilin University, Changchun, China
yangzw18@mails.jlu.edu.cn
[3] Key Laboratory of Symbolic Computation and Knowledge Engineering of Ministry of Education, Changchun, China

Abstract. The attention mechanisms have been widely used in existing methods due to their effectiveness. In the field of computer vision, these mechanisms can be grouped as 1) channel attention mechanisms, which highlight the important channels for images, and 2) spatial attention mechanisms, which focus on the location features for all channels of images. These two groups of mechanisms, which have various strategies for capturing features, actually play complementary roles in image classification. Existing lightweight models based on one group of attention mechanisms have fewer parameters than convolutional networks. However, few works consider their integration and maintain their merits for lightweight neural networks. In this paper, we propose a new Lightweight Attention Module (LAM) for lightweight convolutional neural networks to efficiently integrate these attention mechanisms. Specifically, we use element-wise addition and smaller convolutional kernels in the spatial module, avoiding the vanishing gradient problem. Besides, we replace the multi-layer perceptron (MLP) layer with squeeze-and-excitation layers in the channel module, alleviating the problem of channel dependencies. Finally, we adopt a parallel mechanism to coordinate these two attention modules with low computational complexity. Experimental results on benchmark datasets demonstrate the effectiveness of LAM in terms of image classification tasks, ablation study and robustness analysis.

Keywords: Attention mechanism · Lightweight model · Convolutional neural networks

1 Introduction

The attention mechanisms [1] can well improve models' accuracy by capturing key information of pictures, e.g., find 'where' and 'what' to focus on. As an effective component of neural networks [2], attention modules have shown good

We truly thank the reviewers for their great effort and pertinent comments on our submission. This work is supported in part by the National Natural Science Foundation of China (No. 61902145), the National Key R&D Program of China (2021ZD0112501, 2021ZD0112502).

© The Author(s), under exclusive license to Springer Nature Switzerland AG 2022
G. Memmi et al. (Eds.): KSEM 2022, LNAI 13369, pp. 485–497, 2022.
https://doi.org/10.1007/978-3-031-10986-7_39

performances in various visual tasks, including image classification [3], object detection [4], semantic segmentation [5] and object tracking [6].

Existing studies introduce two kinds of fundamental attention modules widely used in computer vision: channel and spatial attention modules [7]. These two modules strengthen the representations by combining the feature maps from all the positions with different strategies. There have been many useful implemental architectures for these years. For channel attention modules, Jie Hu et al. [8] automatically recalibrate channel-wise feature reflections by explicitly modeling interdependencies between channels. Xiang Li et al. [9] employ a dynamic selection mechanism that enables every cell to automatically adjust its receptive field size on the basis of multiple scales of input representations. For spatial attention modules, Jun Fu et al. [10] encode a wider range of contextual information into local features, which improves their representative capability. Moreover, researchers try to aggregate both of the attention mechanisms, Sanghyun et al. [7] sequentially infer attention maps along the channel and spatial dimensions, then the attention maps are multiplied to the input feature maps for adaptive feature refinement. All these methods introduce attention modules for the neural networks to learn feature representations of images.

However, the above attention modules are designed mainly for normal networks. When adapted to lightweight models [11], they usually have various kinds of problems. First, the neural networks with single spatial or channel attention modules, like SENet [8], may ignore the other dimensions' information. They don't make full use of other dimensions' representations of images, and the lightweight models with rare parameters can't absorb the information well, which leads to poor performances. Second, the complex mixed architecture like CBAM [7] violates the principle of lightweight models, which will result in poor efficiency. Specifically, it concats mean and max spatial feature maps. After convolution operations with a large kernel, the concated feature maps will return to the original size, and multiply with the initial feature map. The complex concat and convolution functions respond to the vanishing gradient problem. Therefore, it will be beneficial to visual tasks by incorporating the information of the two dimensions in a simple and effective architecture.

In view of this, we propose a novel attention module called Lightweight Attention Module (LAM). For the spatial part, we use element-wise addition to process the average and max pooled feature maps, and use a smaller convolutional kernel to extract features. For the channel part, we also add the max-pooling and average-pooling feature maps first, then use the squeeze-and-excitation layers [8] to extract features. At last, we add the two output feature maps in a parallel arrangement. Overall, our model simplifies extensive convolution operations, which may cause vanishing gradient problems in previous modules. Meanwhile, we use the parallel instead of the traditional sequential arrangement [7]. As a result, our model efficiently helps the information flow into the next layer within the lightweight neural networks by learning which points to emphasize.

The key contributions can be summarized as follows:

– A novel lightweight attention module called LAM is proposed, which is capable of capturing information by incorporating the features of the channel and spatial dimensions with a parallel arrangement.
– The superiority of the LAM is demonstrated compared with the previous methods using image classification datasets, and in-depth analysis gives the rationality and robustness of the proposed method.

2 Related Work

In this section, we introduce the related works in the area of lightweight neural networks and attention mechanisms separately.

2.1 Lightweight Model

Since AlexNet [12] had excellent performances on the ImageNet competition in 2012 [13], deep neural networks started to explode researchers' interest again. The 2014 ImageNet champion GoogleNet [14] got 74.8 top-1 accuracy. Afterwards, In The 2017 ImageNet match, SENet [8] won the game with 82.7 top-1 accuracy. However, these models are too big to be applied in our real life. These models have reached the hardware limitations. So experts started to reduce the size of model by gaining efficiency in place of accuracy. Since smart phones get popular, there comes various efficient lightweight models like ShuffleNet [15,16], MobileNet [17–19], and EfficientNet [20]. Later, neural architecture search (NAS) [21] cut a striking figure in designing lightweight models. They perform better than the hand-crafted neural networks by adapting the models' width, channels, kernels and sizes. While most of the neural network designing ways focus on the aspects of depth, width and cardinality, we care about the other influence factor, 'attention', which draws lessons from human visual system.

2.2 Attention Module

Attention is one of the most important concepts in the deep learning field [22, 23], inspired by human visual system that cannot manipulate all the information of the same image immediately [24]. As a replacement, people use a series of partial scans and conditionally pay attention to the obvious part for more information.

Recently, there have been many experts trying to combine the channel and spatial attention modules with models for real-world tasks. RAN (Residual Attention Network) [25] makes use of an encoder and decoder to make up attention module. Through purifying the feature maps, the model gets high accuracy even faced up with noisy datasets. Instead of processing the whole 3D attention feature maps, we resolve the procedure that comprehends channel and spatial representations respectively. The single attention-generating part for 3D feature maps has fewer parameters, and the end-to-end design enables it to be a plug-and-play module, which is very suitable for existing lightweight deep neural networks.

Close to our work, CBAM illustrates a channel and spatial mixed module to find the inner relationships of various feature maps. In CBAM's channel part, it uses MLP layers to get global average features for channel-wise attention. But we find that the linear layers for inferring attention maps may affect the feature extraction process in the lightweight models, so we replace them and use squeeze-and-excitation module, which has better performances both in speed and feature capturing ability. Similar to the channel part, we also delete the 7×7 convolutional kernel, which multiplies with the concat map, and that may cause vanishing gradient problems. Instead, we use a smaller kernel to multiply with the overlying map. In our LAM, we employ both channel and spatial attention in a simplified way intended for lightweight networks. The experiments verify that LAM not only improves the accuracy but also considers the handiness.

3   Methodology

In this section, we propose an attention module intended for lightweight neural networks called LAM. To understand the module, we first introduce the overall framework of the algorithm, then the channel attention module, the spatial attention module and the arrangement of attention modules part, respectively.

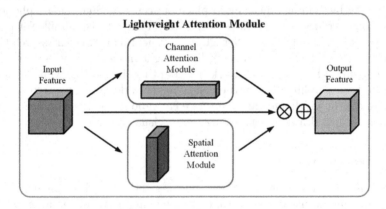

Fig. 1. Overview of LAM. The module has two parallel parts: channel and spatial. The feature map is refined by our module at every convolutional step of neural networks.

3.1   Attention Module

LAM is built on a transformation, which separately uses a one dimension channel attention map $\mathbf{M}_c \in \mathbf{R}^{C \times 1 \times 1}$ and a two dimension spatial attention map $\mathbf{M}_s \in \mathbf{R}^{1 \times H \times W}$ to map an input $\mathbf{X} \in \mathbf{R}^{C \times H \times W}$ to feature maps $\mathbf{U} \in \mathbf{R}^{C \times H \times W}$ as shown in Fig. 1. The computational procedure can be written as:

$$\mathbf{X}_1 = \mathbf{M}_c(\mathbf{X}) \otimes \mathbf{X} \tag{1}$$

$$\mathbf{X}_2 = \mathbf{M}_s(\mathbf{X}) \otimes \mathbf{X} \tag{2}$$

$$\mathbf{U} = \mathbf{X}_1 \oplus \mathbf{X}_2 \tag{3}$$

where $\otimes$ means element-wise multiplication, $\oplus$ means element-wise addition. In the computational process, the attention maps are dispersed to all the dimensions: spatial attention maps are broadcasted along the channel dimension, and vice versa. $\mathbf{U}$ is the final output result. The following part will detailedly talk about the core of each attention module and computation process.

3.2 Channel Attention Module

In the LAM module, we use a channel attention computational unit to dig the inner channel information of feature representations. Because every channel is seen as a detector, channel attention pays attention to what is the important part of the images. To get the channel attention maps efficiently, we use the squeeze-and-excitation part to process the input feature representations. In the squeeze-and-excitation block, they use global squeeze information in a channel descriptor [26] to solve the problem of channel dependencies. And the squeeze part uses average-pooling in their module to get spatial statistics. To obtain the feature representations in the squeeze part, they use a second operation for fully capturing channel-wise dependencies. They employ a simple gating mechanism [27], which consists of a dimensionality reduction and increasing layer returning to the channel dimension of the transformation, with sigmoid activation.

In CBAM, they propose that max-pooling can help collect another key clue about obvious objects to obtain better channel-wise attention. So they use both average and max pooling to process feature maps simultaneously, which highly improves the effectiveness of models.

Different from these works, we argue that although the two pooling ways do improve the ability to capture key features, the linear layers in MLP deeply affect the simple architecture of lightweight neural networks and bring extra computation. So we remove the linear and activation layer and use the convolutional layers to multiply with feature maps. We describe the detailed operation below (Fig. 2).

We first aggregate spatial features by using both max and average pooling to generate two kinds of spatial descriptors: $\mathbf{X}^c_{avg}$ and $\mathbf{X}^c_{max}$, which represent max and average features along the spatial dimensions. These two descriptors are then forwarded by a squeeze-and-excitation module to generate the final attention map $\mathbf{M}_c \in \mathbf{R}^{C \times 1 \times 1}$. The squeeze-and-excitation module consist of a dimensionality reduction and increasing convolutional layer to decrease parameters overhead. After the squeeze-and-excitation layer is applied to both descriptors, we add the output vectors with element-wise addition. The channel attention module can be summarized as follows:

$$\begin{aligned} \mathbf{M}_c(\mathbf{X}) &= \sigma(SE(AvgPool(\mathbf{X})) + SE(MaxPool(\mathbf{X}))) \\ &= \sigma(\mathbf{W}_1(\mathbf{W}_0(\mathbf{X}^c_{avg})) + \mathbf{W}_1(\mathbf{W}_0(\mathbf{X}^c_{max}))) \end{aligned} \tag{4}$$

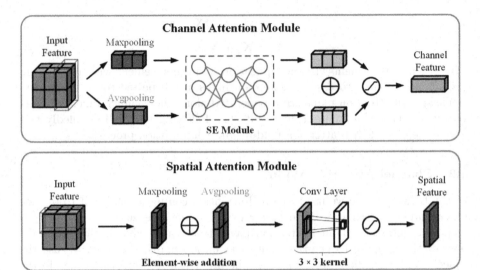

Fig. 2. Diagram of each attention sub-module. The figure shows that the channel sub-module emphasizes both max-pooling outputs and average-pooling outputs with a squeeze-and-excitation architecture. The spatial sub-module emphasizes the channel and spatial output features that are pooled along the channel axis and forward them to a convolutional layer.

where σ means the sigmoid function, $\mathbf{W}_0 \in \mathbf{R}^{C/r \times C}$, $\mathbf{W}_1 \in \mathbf{R}^{C \times C/r}$. And the squeeze-and-excitation weight $\mathbf{W}_1$ and $\mathbf{W}_1$ are shared for both input feature maps. Pay attention that the ReLU activation function is followed by $\mathbf{W}_0$.

3.3   Spatial Attention Module

In the LAM module, we get a spatial attention map by exploiting the inner spatial relationships of feature vectors. Unlike the channel attention module, the spatial attention module pays more attention to the location of images, which is seen as an important part complementary to the channel attention module. We also use average-pooling and max-pooling computational operations across the channel axis. And then sum them to get an efficient feature descriptor. On the summed feature descriptor, we feed it into a convolutional layer to get a spatial attention map $\mathbf{M}_s(\mathbf{F}) \in \mathbf{R}^{H \times W}$, which contains the information where to emphasize. We describe the detailed operation below.

We first aggregate channel features by using both max-pooling and average-pooling to generate two kinds of 2D feature maps: $\mathbf{M}_{avg}^s(\mathbf{X}) \in \mathbf{R}^{1 \times H \times W}$ and $\mathbf{M}_{max}^s(\mathbf{X}) \in \mathbf{R}^{1 \times H \times W}$, which represent average and max features across the channel dimensions respectively. The vectors are then added with element-wise addition and convolved by a standard convolutional layer to get the final 2D feature maps. The spatial attention module can be summarized as follows:

$$\mathbf{M}_c(\mathbf{X}) = \sigma(f^{3\times3}(AvgPool(\mathbf{X})) + MaxPool(\mathbf{X}))$$
$$= \sigma(f^{3\times3}(\mathbf{X}_{avg}^c)) + (\mathbf{X}_{max}^c))) \tag{5}$$

where σ means the sigmoid function. $f^{3\times3}$ means a convolutional layer with the kernel size of 3×3.

3.4 Arrangement of Attention Modules

The two attention modules pay attention to the channel and spatial dimension separately with complementary computing attention. Unlike CBAM, we adopt a parallel arrangement. The sequential arrangement will affect the lightweight in a bad way, whether it is channel-first order or spatial first-order. We will discuss experimental results in the next section (Fig. 3).

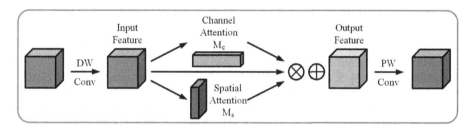

Fig. 3. LAM is integrated with a Basicblock in lightweight models. This figure shows the exact position of our module when integrated within a depthwise separable block [17]. We apply LAM to the convolution outputs in each block.

4 Experiment

In this section, we first introduce the experiment settings, including datasets, baselines and evaluation methods. Then we evaluate the effectiveness of the LAM in image classification tasks and ablation studies. In general, we seek to answer the following questions:

- **Q1:** Does the LAM have better performances than other attention modules when adapted to lightweight neural networks?
- **Q2:** Is the current arrangement most suitable for the LAM?
- **Q3:** Is the proposed LAM model sensitive to the main parameters, e.g., the learning ratio and kernel size?

4.1 Datasets and Experimental Setting

We conduct experiments on two standard image classification datasets [28]: Cifar10 and Cifar100 [29]. Both of the two standard datasets comprise a collection of 50k training and 10k test 32×32 pixel RGB real-world images, labelled with 10 and 100 classes respectively.

Besides, experiments use the same data augmentations [30,31] and parameter settings. The input images are randomly horizontally flipped and zero-padded on each side with 4 pixels before taking a random 32×32 cropping operation. We also adopt mean and standard deviation normalization. We use the Top-1 accuracy to compare our model with other baselines for image classification tasks. We use the authors' released code for baseline models.

Baselines and Metrics Here we present some existing lightweight neural networks as baselines, which proves that the LAM fits into lightweight models well.

- MobileNetV1 [17]: This model uses depthwise separable convolutions to decrease computational complexity.
- MobileNetV2 [18]: It builds inverted residuals and linear bottlenecks to filter features as a source of non-linearity.
- MobileNetV3 [19]: It uses a combination of complementary search techniques as well as a novel architecture ang.
- ShuffleNetV1 [15]: It utilizes pointwise group convolution and channel shuffle operations to greatly reduce computation cost.
- ShuffleNetV2 [16]: It uses an additional convolutional layer right before global averaged pooling to mix up features.
- EfficientNet [20]: It uses neural architecture search to design a new baseline network and scale it up.

Here we present some attention modules as baselines, which can prove that the LAM has better performances than other attention modules when applied to the lightweight models.

- Squeeze-and-excitation module [8]: It adaptively recalibrates channel-wise feature responses by explicitly modelling interdependencies between channels.
- Convolutional block attention module [7]: It emphasizes meaningful features along those two principal dimensions: channel and spatial axes.

4.2 Results and Analysis (Q1)

To address the first question (Q1), we conduct experiments to measure the LAM's quality and compare it with other baseline methods. We train the models on the training dataset and test them on the validation dataset. PyTorch and Adam optimizer are used in our model (Learning Rate = 0.05, Weight Decay = 0.0001, Batch Size = 64). We report the average results of Top-1 accuracy by

Table 1. Accuracy of image classification in lightweight neural networks

Architecture	Params	MFlops	Cifar10 Top-1 acc	Cifar100 Top-1 acc
MobileNetV1	13.12	356.16	88.33	66.48
MobileNetV1 + CBAM	15.56	359.42	$-^a$	–
MobileNetV1 + SE	18.49	360.05	89.12	67.30
MobileNetV1 + LAM	18.18	360.23	**89.37**	**68.09**
MobileNetV2	2.91	32.14	90.54	64.15
MobileNetV2 + CBAM	3.09	33.34	90.69	64.61
MobileNetV2 + SE	3.20	32.54	90.17	62.38
MobileNetV2 + LAM	3.17	32.63	**91.08**	**64.97**
MobileNetV3small	4.98	35.55	78.01	66.64
MobileNetV3small + CBAM	4.90	35.78	–	–
MobileNetV3small + LAM	4.95	35.55	**79.46**	**67.75**
MobileNetV3large	10.69	158.85	84.22	64.23
MobileNetV3large + CBAM	10.52	158.98	–	–
MobileNetV3large + LAM	10.67	158.85	**84.66**	**64.35**
ShuffleNetV1G3	4.07	91.79	85.12	**68.91**
ShuffleNetV1G3 + CBAM	4.16	92.33	–	–
ShuffleNetV1G3 + SE	4.40	92.09	83.06	65.83
ShuffleNetV1G3 + LAM	4.34	92.01	**85.24**	68.89
ShuffleNetV2	5.50	90.46	83.28	65.32
ShuffleNetV2 + CBAM	5.61	92.03	–	–
ShuffleNetV2 + SE	5.99	91.84	83.26	64.53
ShuffleNetV2 + LAM	5.62	90.83	**83.87**	**66.07**
EfficientNetB0	20.95	20.16	88.51	72.48
EfficientNetB0 + CBAM	21.38	22.03	79.32	62.53
EfficientNetB0 + LAM	21.54	21.54	**88.75**	**72.79**

^{a}The empty result means vanishing problem happens in the models.

running the model 100 epochs [32]. The learning rate drops at the 40_{th}, 60_{th} and 80_{th} epoch by a factor of 10.

Table 1 summarizes the experimental results. The networks with LAM outperform all the baselines significantly, showing that the LAM can generalize well on lightweight models in the image classification datasets. Moreover, the models with LAM improve the accuracy compared to other attention modules. Firstly, although the CBAM improves the accuracy when applied in the MobileNetV2, it results in vanishing gradient problems in other models due to the complicated convolutional layers. So we use both channel and spatial attention modules but simplify convolutional parts. Secondly, the MobileNetV3 and EfficientNet use the squeeze-and-excitation layer to extract features, which provides a significant improvement. But it's not robust to other models, specifically, improvements on the MobileNetV1, deteriorations on the MobileNetV2, ShuffleNetV1 and ShuffleNetV2. Although it may help models find channel features, it pays too much attention to the channel dimension and ignores spatial information, thus being sensitive when faced with different tasks.

Finally, our LAM absorbs the strengths of these two modules to pay attention to both channel and spatial dimensions. In addition, we use a parallel arrangement to process the output feature maps, which operation gives them equal weights. The experiment results imply that our proposed module is powerful, showing the efficacy of a new method that generates a richer descriptor that complements the two attention effectively. The LAM also obeys the rule of lightweight, which means small amounts of parameters and fast forward speed.

4.3   Ablation Study (Q2)

To answer the second question (Q2), we will verify whether the current arrangement are the most beneficial to the effectiveness of the model. In the experiment, we design three variants of the proposed model:

- **LAM(I):** using the LAM before depthwise convolution;
- **LAM(II):** using the LAM after pointwise convolution;
- **LAM(III):** using sequential arrangement.

We measure the accuracy of these three variants. As shown in Table 2, our model performs the best when all latent variables are introduced. The performances of the LAM(I) and LAM(II) are worse than the current module. This shows that the current arrangement, which places the module after the depthwise filters, helps the attention to be applied to the largest representations. The results of LAM(III) show that vanishing gradient problems happen in MobileNetV1, and the sequential arrangement has more parameters and lower speed than the parallel arrangement.

Table 2. Ablation study of the LAM

Architecture	Params	MFlops	Cifar10 Top-1 acc	Cifar100 Top-1 acc
MobileNetV1 + LAM	18.18	360.23	**89.37**	**68.09**
MobileNetV1 + LAM(I)	18.18	360.63	88.64	67.53
MobileNetV1 + LAM(II)	20.22	361.59	89.02	67.92
MobileNetV1 + LAM(III)	18.18	360.23	–	–
MobileNetV2 + LAM	3.17	32.63	**91.08**	**64.97**
MobileNetV2 + LAM(I)	3.17	33.15	89.96	64.10
MobileNetV2 + LAM(II)	3.59	34.82	90.07	64.58
MobileNetV2 + LAM(III)	3.17	32.63	85.31	60.19

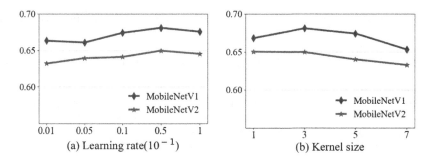

Fig. 4. Parameter sensitivity analysis on Cifar100 dataset.

4.4 Sensitivity Analysis (Q3)

In this subsection, we test the robustness of the model and verify whether the settings of super parameters have an impact on the model. We conduct two groups of experiments, i.e., the learning rates (0.001, 0.005, 0.01, 0.05, 0.1) and the kernel sizes of convolutional layers in the spatial attention part (1, 3, 5, 7). As shown in Fig. 4, our model still keeps a high accuracy between a small range under the change of learning rates and kernel sizes. It implies that the proposed LAM model is not sensitive to these main parameters, and thus has good robustness.

5   Conclusion

In this paper, we propose a novel attention module called LAM for lightweight neural networks, which uses two attention mechanisms but simplifies the components effectively. Specifically, in the spatial attention module, we use element-wise addition and smaller convolutional kernels to avoid the previous vanishing gradient problem. In the channel module, we use the squeeze-and-excitation layers in place of the MLP layers. At last, we take a parallel architecture to integrate the two parts efficiently. The experimental results on the two image classification datasets verify the effectiveness of the proposed attention module for lightweight models. The LAM is ready to be applied to other tasks related to lightweight neural networks, e.g., object tracking in the field of computer vision.

References

1. Bahdanau, D., Cho, K., Bengio, Y.: Neural machine translation by jointly learning to align and translate. Computer Science, pp. 1–15 (2014)
2. Li, Z., Liu, F., Yang, W., Peng, S., Zhou, J.: A survey of convolutional neural networks: analysis, applications, and prospects. IEEE Trans. Neural Netw. Learn. Syst., 1–13 (2021)

3. Machado, G.R., Silva, E., Goldschmidt, R.R.: Adversarial machine learning in image classification: a survey toward the defender's perspective. ACM Comput. Surv. (CSUR) **55**(1), 1–38 (2021)
4. Liu, Y., Sun, P., Wergeles, N., Shang, Y.: A survey and performance evaluation of deep learning methods for small object detection. Exp. Syst. Appl. **172**, 114602 (2021)
5. Yuan, X., Shi, J., Gu, L.: A review of deep learning methods for semantic segmentation of remote sensing imagery. Exp. Syst. Appl. **169**, 114417 (2021)
6. Luo, W., Xing, J., Milan, A., Zhang, X., Liu, W., Kim, T.K.: Multiple object tracking: a literature review. Artif. Intell. **293**, 103448 (2021)
7. Woo, S., Park, J., Lee, J.-Y., Kweon, I.S.: CBAM: convolutional block attention module. In: Ferrari, V., Hebert, M., Sminchisescu, C., Weiss, Y. (eds.) ECCV 2018. LNCS, vol. 11211, pp. 3–19. Springer, Cham (2018). https://doi.org/10.1007/978-3-030-01234-2_1
8. Hu, J., Shen, L., Sun, G.: Squeeze-and-excitation networks. In: Proceedings of the IEEE Conference on Computer Vision and Pattern Recognition, pp. 7132–7141 (2018)
9. Li, X., Wang, W., Hu, X., Yang, J.: Selective kernel networks. In: Proceedings of the IEEE Conference on Computer Vision and Pattern Recognition, pp. 510–519 (2019)
10. Fu, J., et al.: Dual attention network for scene segmentation. In: Proceedings of the IEEE Conference on Computer Vision and Pattern Recognition, pp. 3146–3154 (2019)
11. Roesch, M.: Snort: lightweight intrusion detection for networks. In: LISA, pp. 229–238 (1999)
12. Krizhevsky, A., Sutskever, I., Hinton, G.E.: ImageNet classification with deep convolutional neural networks. Commun. ACM **60**, 84–90 (2012)
13. Deng, J., Dong, W., Socher, R., Li, L.J., Li, K., Fei-Fei, L.: ImageNet: a large-scale hierarchical image database. In: Proceedings of the IEEE Conference on Computer Vision and Pattern Recognition, pp. 248–255 (2009)
14. Szegedy, C., et al.: Going deeper with convolutions. In: Proceedings of the IEEE Conference on Computer Vision and Pattern Recognition, pp. 1–9 (2015)
15. Zhang, X., Zhou, X., Lin, M., Sun, J.: ShuffleNet: an extremely efficient convolutional neural network for mobile devices. In: Proceedings of the IEEE Conference on Computer Vision and Pattern Recognition, pp. 6848–6856 (2018)
16. Ma, N., Zhang, X., Zheng, H.-T., Sun, J.: ShuffleNet V2: practical guidelines for efficient CNN architecture design. In: Ferrari, V., Hebert, M., Sminchisescu, C., Weiss, Y. (eds.) Computer Vision – ECCV 2018. LNCS, vol. 11218, pp. 122–138. Springer, Cham (2018). https://doi.org/10.1007/978-3-030-01264-9_8
17. Howard, A.G., et al.: MobileNets: efficient convolutional neural networks for mobile vision applications. In: Proceedings of the IEEE Conference on Computer Vision and Pattern Recognition, pp. 1–9 (2017)
18. Sandler, M., Howard, A., Zhu, M., Zhmoginov, A., Chen, L.C.: MobileNet V2: inverted residuals and linear bottlenecks. In: Proceedings of the IEEE Conference on Computer Vision and Pattern Recognition, pp. 4510–4520 (2018)
19. Howard, A., et al.: Searching for MobileNetV3. In: Proceedings of the IEEE Conference on Computer Vision and Pattern Recognition, pp. 1314–1324 (2019)
20. Tan, M., Le, Q.: EfficientNet: rethinking model scaling for convolutional neural networks. In: International Conference on Machine Learning, pp. 6105–6114 (2019)
21. Zoph, B., Le, Q.V.: Neural architecture search with reinforcement learning. In: International Conference on Learning Representations, pp. 1–16 (2016)

22. Marvasti-Zadeh, S.M., Cheng, L., Ghanei-Yakhdan, H., Kasaei, S.: Deep learning for visual tracking: a comprehensive survey. IEEE Trans. Intell. Transp. Syst. **23**, 3943–3968 (2021)
23. Yang, Z., Ma, J., Chen, H., Zhang, Y., Chang, Y.: HiTRANS: a hierarchical transformer network for nested named entity recognition. In: Findings of the Association for Computational Linguistics, EMNLP 2021, pp. 124–132 (2021)
24. Salin, P.A., Bullier, J.: Corticocortical connections in the visual system: structure and function. Physiol. Rev. **75**(1), 107–154 (1995)
25. Wang, F., et al.: Residual attention network for image classification. In: Proceedings of the IEEE Conference on Computer Vision and Pattern Recognition, pp. 3156–3164 (2017)
26. Qian, K., Wu, C., Yang, Z., Liu, Y., Zhou, Z.: PADS: passive detection of moving targets with dynamic speed using PHY layer information. In: 2014 20th IEEE International Conference on Parallel and Distributed Systems (ICPADS), pp. 1–8 (2014)
27. Miyazawa, A., Fujiyoshi, Y., Unwin, N.: Structure and gating mechanism of the acetylcholine receptor pore. nature **423**(6943), 949–955 (2003)
28. Brigato, L., Barz, B., Iocchi, L., Denzler, J.: Image classification with small datasets: overview and benchmark. IEEE Access **10**, 49233–49250 (2022)
29. Krizhevsky, A., Hinton, G., et al.: Learning Multiple Layers of Features from Tiny Images, pp. 1–60 (2009)
30. Lin, M., Chen, Q., Yan, S.: Network in network. In: International Conference on Learning Representations, pp. 1–10 (2013)
31. Huang, G., Sun, Yu., Liu, Z., Sedra, D., Weinberger, K.Q.: Deep networks with stochastic depth. In: Leibe, B., Matas, J., Sebe, N., Welling, M. (eds.) ECCV 2016. LNCS, vol. 9908, pp. 646–661. Springer, Cham (2016). https://doi.org/10.1007/978-3-319-46493-0_39
32. Shen, L., Lin, Z., Huang, Q.: Relay backpropagation for effective learning of deep convolutional neural networks. In: Leibe, B., Matas, J., Sebe, N., Welling, M. (eds.) ECCV 2016. LNCS, vol. 9911, pp. 467–482. Springer, Cham (2016). https://doi.org/10.1007/978-3-319-46478-7_29

Sentiment Analysis Based on Deep Learning in E-Commerce

Ameni Chamekh[1]([✉]), Mariem Mahfoudh[1,2], and Germain Forestier[3]

[1] ISIGK, University of Kairouan, 3100 Kairouan, Tunisia
amenichamekh959@gmail.com
[2] MIRACL Laboratory, University of Sfax, 3021 Sfax, Tunisia
[3] University of Hautes Alsace, 68093 MULHOUSE Cedex, France
germain.forestier@uha.fr

Abstract. Social media allow businesses to find out what customers are thinking about their products and to participate in the conversation. Companies, therefore, have an interest in using them to market their products, identify new opportunities and improve their reputation. The main objective of our study was to recognize feelings expressed in opinions, ratings, recommendations about a product using a construction based on a corpus of sentiment lexicon with different deep learning algorithms. In this work, we will then analyze an e-commerce platform in order to know the feelings of customers towards the products. This study is conducted based on a static dataset of 41,778 smartphone product reviews in french collected on Amazon.com. For the classification of reviews, we applied the Long short-term memory network (LSTM). The results showed that the LSTM deep learning algorithm yielded a good performance with an accuracy of 95%.

Keywords: Sentiment analysis · The e-commerce platform (Amazon) · Long short-term memory network (LSTM)

1 Introduction

Sentiment analysis has attracted a lot of attention in recent years. It is known as opinion mining and it is used by companies to identify what impression people have of their services and products through user reviews, tweets and comments on social media platforms [Jahanzeb Jabbar, 2019]. These masses of data become essential and effective information to predict the consumer preferences and consumption trends of sentiment expressed in reviews, which benefits companies to improve their marketing strategies and products [Mohammad Erfan Mowlaei, 2020]. The fundamental purpose of sentiment analysis is to process human emotions, expressed in a text. Users freely express their opinions regarding the products they have already purchased. These reviews tend to become powerful tools that help customers analyze them for further reuse in their product purchases on e-commerce sites [Sergey Smetanin, 2019]. Sentiment analysis,

© The Author(s), under exclusive license to Springer Nature Switzerland AG 2022
G. Memmi et al. (Eds.): KSEM 2022, LNAI 13369, pp. 498–507, 2022.
https://doi.org/10.1007/978-3-031-10986-7_40

is present in many areas such as politics, finance, and education. In this article, we address the field of e-commerce. The number of online purchases has been particularly increased in recent years. Therefore, e-commerce sites generate a lot of data every day in the form of customer reviews of products they have already purchased. User opinions form a kind of discussion with which they can interact in order to have recommendations and advice on products or services. As well as, analyzing these opinions will help online retailers understand customer expectations, provide a better shopping experience and increase sales. The objective of our work is to automatically analyze the textual data extracted from the most popular e-commerce platform amazon in order to detect customer sentiment towards particular smartphone products. This, using a construction based on a corpus of feelings lexicon with the deep learning algorithm. In this study, we first extracted a corpus of static data from amazon, then we applied different natural language processing techniques such as tokenization, stopword removal and stemming, then we evaluated the performance and efficiency of the classification algorithm: Long short-term memory (LSTM). The performance result shows that LSTM performed with an accuracy of 95%. The advantage of our work over other works is that we extracted a massive amount of data from the amazon e-commerce site on smartphone products specifically using a scraping process and this helped us in our classification of reviews with LSTM since deep learning algorithms usually require a lot of data to train properly. Moreover, we opted for LSTM algorithm in our classification model, and we also achieved a very high accuracy rate compared to other previous works that used LSTM model. The rest of this paper is organized as follows: Sect. 2 discusses related work. Section 3 describes in detail the proposed method. We report in Sect. 4 our experimental results and give our conclusion on this work in Sect. 5.

2   Related Work

[Li Yang, 2020] proposed a new sentiment analysis model SLCABG to improve the accuracy of sentiment analysis of product reviews. They combined the advantages of sentiment lexicon, CNN model, GRU and the attention mechanism for building the SLCABG model. The authors used the dataset consisting of book review data collected from Dangdang.com, it is a famous Chinese e-commerce website. After manually filtering product reviews by star rating, the authors had a data set of 100,000 reviews. To evaluate the performance of SLCABG model, [Li Yang, 2020] explored the impact of several factors such as: the length of the input text sentence, the size of the lexicon, the number of iterations of the model, the value dropout and the weighted word vector. The experimental results show that all these factors influenced the model. Thus, [Li Yang, 2020] compared the sentiment analysis effects of the SLCABG model with common sentiment analysis models (NB, SVM, CNN and BiGRU) on the dataset. The comparison results show that the classification performance of the proposed SLCABG model is effectively improved over the commonly used deep learning model. [Shervin Minaee, 2019] presented a model based on a set of models; bi-directional LSTMs

(Bi-LSTM), and convolutional neural network (CNN), one to capture temporal information from data, and the other to extract local structure to perform sentiment analysis. They used popular databases such as IMDB review and SST2 dataset to test the proposed model. The experimental results showed that this model can outperform the two individual models hence [Shervin Minaee, 2019] observed some performance gain with 90% compared to the individual LSTM and CNN models. [Fangyu Wu, 2020] introduced a new model, SenBERT-CNN for analyzing customer reviews. The SenBERT-CNN model combines a pre-trained bidirectional encoder representation network from transformers (BERT) with a convolutional neural network (CNN) to capture more sentiment information in sentences. So SenBERT-CNN is a pre-trained language representation model for the e-commerce review domain. Specifically, [Fangyu Wu, 2020] used the BERT structure to better express the semantics of the sentence as a text vector, and then they extracted the deep features of the sentence through a convolutional neural network. The authors collected reviews on the JD.com commerce platform for smartphones. [Fangyu Wu, 2020] compared their model with 4 basic models such as TextCNN, BiGRU-Attention, Bert and LSTM. Therefore, the experimental results indicate that the proposed hybrid model outperforms individual BERT and CNN. SenBERT-CNN also significantly outperforms other models, including BiGRU-Attention and LSTM. Then the proposed SenBERT-CNN model is significantly better with 95% compared to other methods. [Junchao Dong, 2020] proposed a BERT-CNN based sentiment analysis model for commodity product reviews. This BERT-CNN sentiment analysis model is therefore a proposal to improve the original BERT model to improve the accuracy of commodity sentiment analysis. They based the experiment on the dataset of real cell phone reviews on the JD Mall e-commerce platform. The authors then compared the BERT-CNN model to the original CNN model and to the BERT model. In order to ensure the accuracy and objectivity of the experimental results, [Junchao Dong, 2020] ran the three models 10 times on the same training set and the same test set. The final results revealed that the values F1 of the BERT-CNN model and the BERT model are higher than those of the CNN model in the training set and the test set. Therefore, the BERT-CNN model has a favorable capacity in general. The following Table 1 summarizes the researches in the field of sentiment analysis by indicating their objectives, the classification techniques and the Corpus of data used in their work.

3   Methodology

Our work aims to analyze the data extracted from the most popular e-commerce site in the field; Amazon to detect customer sentiment towards products. The main steps of the proposed approach are illustrated in Fig. 1. It is based on five fundamental steps. In the following, we will describe this procedure for detecting the sentiment polarity of Amazon customers :

1. **Data Collection.** This step consits to collect reviews from amazon customers.

2. **Data preprocessing.** This is the step of normalizing raw data using different preprocessing techniques.
3. **Feature Extraction.** This the step of the Word embedding representation method aimed at representing the words of a text in the form of numerical vectors [ThomasB, 2020].
4. **Sentiment Classification.** This step include the classification using the deep learning algorithm; Long Short Term Memory (LSTM).
5. **Evaluation.** In order to evaluate the performance of the model, we used accuracy and recall metrics as evaluation measures.

Table 1. Comparison table between research works

Article	Objective	Dataset	Tools
[Li Yang, 2020]	Construction of a new sentiment analysis model SLCABG whose goal is to improve classification performance	dangdang.com website	Dictionary of Sentiment, BERT Model, CNN Model, BiGRU Model and Attention Mechanism
[Shervin Minaee, 2019]	Creation of a model based on the set of models; bi-directional LSTMs (Bi-LSTM), and convolutional neural network (CNN), to perform sentiment analysis	The IMDB Review dataset and the SST2 dataset.	Bidirectional LSTM (Bi-LSTM) and Convolutional Neural Network (CNN)
[Fangyu Wu, 2020]	Creating a hybrid SenBERT-CNN model helps to accurately identify sentiment from product reviews and analysis	Reviews of the JD.com commerce platform for smartphones	The BERT model and the convolutional neural network (CNN)
[Junchao Dong, 2020]	Building a Sentiment Analysis Model Based on BERT-CNN for Product Reviews	Reviews of mobile phones in the JD Mall e-commerce platform	The convolutional neural network (CNN) and the BERT model

3.1 Data Collection

Many platforms have become important sources of information such as Twitter, Facebook, Instagram and Youtube. They are powerful communication tools that allow to analyze the state of public opinion on a given subject in just a few clicks and reading comments. However, as a general rule e-commerce datasets are proprietary and therefore difficult to find among publicly available data. The extraction of data from E-commerce sites then differs from that of social networks. Hence, a process called Scraping is required. The data set consists of 41577 customer reviews of smartphones, published in the "Amazon" site.

3.2 Data Preprocessing

To perform the analysis of textual data, a preprocessing step is necessary to normalize the unstructured data. Thereafter, we will detail the different preprocessing techniques used to ensure efficient sentiment classification.

Tokenization. This process involves breaking down the sequence of characters in a text by marking word boundaries, the points where one word ends and another begins [Ong Jun Ying, 2020]. The result of this segmentation is a series of elements called Tokens separated by spaces (*e.g.*, Super mobile...Samsung est très facile A manipuler. ⟹ ['super', 'mobile', 'samsung', 'est', 'très', 'facile', 'manipuler']).

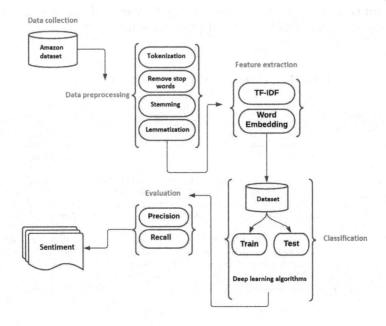

Fig. 1. Overview framework of our proposed approach.

Remove Stop Words. Stop words are too frequent words do not bring meaning to the text. they are useless to use in classification. In French for example, the stop words could be: the logical connectors (*e.g.*, Super mobile...Samsung est très facile A manipuler. ⟹ ['super', 'mobile', 'samsung', 'facile', 'manipuler']). we notice that the stop words that are going to be removed after the result are: est, très and A.

Stemming. It is the process of reducing a word to its root form [Jahanzeb Jabbar, 2019]. This transformation aims to truncate the word of any chord by removing its prefixes and suffixes. Stemming therefore leads to forms that are not words since it consists of deleting the end of words (*e.g.*, Super mobile...Samsung est très facile A manipuler. ⟹ ['super', 'mobil', 'samsung', 'facil', 'manipul']).

Lemmatization. This technique aims to obtain the lemma of a word by reducing it to a normalized form. Lemmatization then consists in reducing a term, whatever its agreements, to its simplest form [Mayuri Mhatre, 2017]. For example for French, obtaining its infinitive form for a verb and its masculine singular form for a noun, adjective ... (*e.g.*, Super mobile...Samsung est très facile A manipuler. $\implies$ ['super', 'mobile', 'samsung', 'facile', 'manipuler']).

3.3   Feature Extraction

To ensure that we obtain a better result for our classification model, a step of transforming textual data into numerical data is necessary in order to transfer this data to the learning algorithms so that they can analyze it. We have used the Glove Embedding model [Ghannay, 2018].

3.4   Sentiment Classification

Sentiment classification is a method where algorithms are trained to learn and extract insights from data. Data is collected, pre-trained and made available for analysis. Since LSTMs showed good performance for sentiment classification, we decided to use the long-term memory network (LSTM) for our work. An LSTM network which stands for Long Short-Term Memory is a variant of a recurrent neural network (RNN). Generally, the architecture of an LSTM is composed of a memory cell, typically a layer of neurons, as well as three gates: an entry gate, an exit gate and a forgetting gate. These three gates will make it possible to manipulate the flow of information at the input, at the output and to be memorized in an analog way to a sigmoid type activation function.
The architecture of the model used is detailed as follows:

1. Embedding layer. used to generate an embedding vector for each input sequence.
2. Conv1D layer. which is used to convolve the data into smaller feature vectors.
3. LSTM. which has a memory state cell for learning the context of words that are further in the text whose purpose is to take on contextual meaning instead of neighboring words as in the case of RNN.
4. Dense. These are fully connected layers intended for classification.

The data breakdown is an optimization step that should not be left out, otherwise we risk over-evaluating our model (over-fitting) or quite simply the opposite (under-fitting). It is essential to have at least two data sets: one for training the model and the other will allow it to be tested for validation. For our work, it is up to us to define the distribution proportion of the dataset. We randomly split the dataset in two: 20% (8316 opinions) for the test data set aside and the rest 80% (33262 opinions) for training using the library of *scikit-learn* "*train_test_split*" which takes the desired proportion as a parameter. Since the training set must be representative of all the data to train the classifier in order to learn and provide results that is why generally the "Training set" takes the majority of the data. However, the "Testing set" is used to provide an unbiased assessment of a final fit of the model to the "training set" data set. Finally, we predicted the feelings of amazon customers on smartphone products through the LSTM classifier, and it showed us a high performance with an accuracy of 95% on the test set.

4 Experiment

Our data set is composed of **41577** customer reviews on smartphones, published in the "Amazon" site. The step of collecting reviews was done using a process called **Scraping** allowing the recovery of the content of a website in an automated way. So, we used scraping to extract data from the Amazon e-commerce site. Positive reviews represent roughly 90% (37242 positive reviews) of the collected data set, while negative reviews represent only 10% (4290 negative reviews) of the data set. In Fig. 2, we will show examples of positive reviews in frensh. While Fig. 3 shows examples of negative reviews. In the experiment, the preprocessing step is necessary to normalize unstructured data using different preprocessing techniques to ensure efficient sentiment classification. The result is shown in the Table 2. Then, We have explained our LSTM model in detail as follows:

	review_verified	review_content	polarity	subjectivity	sentiment
1	Achat vérifié	super mobile...samsung facile manipuler	0.333333	0.666667	Positive
2	Achat vérifié	téléphone niquel -1 étoile colis	0.000000	0.000000	Positive
3	Achat vérifié	bon entrée gamme.un écran top visionner videos	0.500000	0.500000	Positive
4	Achat vérifié	l'instant bon téléphone	0.000000	0.666667	Positive
5	Achat vérifié	corresponds descriptif attentes	0.000000	0.000000	Positive

Fig. 2. Examples of positive reviews

	review_verified	review_content	polarity	subjectivity	sentiment
0	Achat vérifié	dommage manque écouteurs j'ai regardé commenta...	0.100000	0.4	Négative
16	Version: FranceCouleur: NoirTaille: 32 GoAchat...	téléphone lent u démarrage	0.000000	0.0	Négative
35	Achat vérifié	vois écouteurs.c scandaleux qu vendus principe...	0.000000	0.0	Négative
41	Version: FranceCouleur: NoirTaille: 32 GoAchat..	j'ai acheté téléphone problème : grisaillement.	0.000000	0.0	Négative
44	Achat vérifié	impossible paramétrer mms vraiment déçu	-0.666667	1.0	Négative

Fig. 3. Examples of negative reviews

1. An input layer for variable-length integer sequences.
2. The model uses an embedding layer which is used to generate an embedding vector for each input sequence. Knowing that, the entries have a maximum number of words 30, and the dimension of the vector representation equals 300. Then, the embedding layer will associate each word of a sentence with a feature vector of 300 dimensions.

Table 2. Examples of normalized review

Id	Original review	Normalized review
0	Dommage il manque les écouteurs j'ai regardé les commentaires précédent apparemment ça arrive souvent	['dommage', 'manqu', 'écouteur', 'commentaire', 'précédent', 'apparemment', 'arrive']
1	Super mobile...Samsung est très facile A manipuler	['super', 'mobile', 'samsung', 'facile', 'manipuler']
3	Très bon entrée de gamme. Un écran au top pour visionner les videos	['bon', 'entrée', 'écran', 'visionner']

3. The number of embedding parameters is equal to 7879800.
4. The output of this layer is then passed to a convolution layer with 64 different filters, in order to capture the local information needed to classify sentiment.
5. Next, a Bidirectional LSTM layer takes the output from the convolutional layer and it will run the memory state cell to learn the context of words that are further in the text to convey contextual meaning.
6. After passing through the Bidirectional LSTM layer, the fully connected layer with 512 hidden neurons connects all input and output neurons. A vector that passes through this layer forms an output that is classified as positive or negative by applying the activation function Relu.

The model configuration is shown in the Fig. 4 below. The LSTM network is a variant of recurrent neural network (RNN) allowing to capture the long-term dependence between words thanks to their door systems. The sentiment of each review can then be effectively categorized as positive or negative. We used the LSTM for sentiment classification and it showed great performance with 95% accuracy.

```
Model: "model_2"

Layer (type)                    Output Shape           Param #
=================================================================
input_3 (InputLayer)            [(None, 30)]           0

embedding_1 (Embedding)         (None, 30, 300)        7879800

spatial_dropout1d_2 (Spatial    (None, 30, 300)        0

conv1d_2 (Conv1D)               (None, 26, 64)         96064

bidirectional_2 (Bidirection    (None, 128)            66048

dense_6 (Dense)                 (None, 512)            66048

dropout_2 (Dropout)             (None, 512)            0

dense_7 (Dense)                 (None, 512)            262656

dense_8 (Dense)                 (None, 1)              513
=================================================================
Total params: 8,371,129
Trainable params: 491,329
Non-trainable params: 7,879,800

None
```

Fig. 4. The LSTM model configuration.

5   Evaluation and Discussion

The performance results table shows that the deep learning algorithm LSTM obtained a high accuracy: 95%. We believe this is primarily because the LSTM has the ability to learn the context of words that are later in the text for the purpose of taking on contextual meaning. Moreover, by comparing our results with those of other works which have worked on Amazon product reviews as well, we notice that we obtained better results. For example in [Santhosh Kumar K L, 2016], the authors have worked on Amazon product reviews and they have obtained the following precision values: 55%, 64% and 65% with three different algorithms.

6   Conclusion

Nowadays, online business and shopping has become more popular. Therefore analysis of huge user feedback becomes essential to judge what people think about the product, which benefits companies to improve the products. In this study, we applied sentiment analysis with the amazon dataset. In order to achieve our goal, we spent a lot of time reading and reviewing publications and articles to see and understand the concepts and how to apply a deep learning model to our problem. Then, a data collection step is performed by automatically extracting 41,577 customer reviews in french on smartphones, published on the "Amazon" site using the process called scraping. Then, to perform an analysis of textual data, we performed a preprocessing step to normalize unstructured data to structured data. After the normalization, a step of transforming the textual data into numerical data is necessary to transfer this data to the learning algorithms so that they can analyze them in order to ensure the obtaining of a better result for our classification model. We have applied the GLOVE model. Finally, the data is collected, pre-trained and made available for classification. As a result, LSTM classifier shows good performance with 95% accuracy. The advantage of our work over other works is that we extracted massive amount of data from amazon e-commerce site on smartphone products specifically using a scraping process and this helped us in our classification of reviews with LSTM since deep learning algorithms generally require a lot of data to train properly. Moreover, the choice of the LSTM algorithm in our classification model allows us to achieve a very high accuracy. So, these results show that our model is efficient. For future preferences, we think to go a little further in the analysis with the following ideas: in the beginning, we will test our model on other data sets: we can pull data from other e-commerce platforms and do the comparison. In addition, we can collect a larger amount of data sets and with other categories of products not only smartphones. Moreover, it is not enough to use notices in French only. But, it is necessary to test the classification with other different languages. This allows us to study the influence of the challenges of various languages on the classification.

References

Wu, F., Shi, Z., Dong, Z., Pang, C., Zhang, N.: Sentiment analysis of online product reviews based on SenBERT-CNN. In: The International Conference on Machine Learning and Cybernetics, ICMLC, vol. (12) (2020)

Ghannay, S.: Etude sur les representations continues de mots appliquees à la detection automatique des erreurs de reconnaissance de la parole. Number 29. Mémoire présenté en vue de l'obtention du grade de Docteur de Le Mans Université sous le sceau de l'Université Bretagne Loire (2018)

Jabbar, J., Urooj, I., Wu, J., Azeem, N.: Real-time Sentiment Analysis On E-Commerce Application. IEEE xplore (2019)

Dong, J., He, F., Guo, Y., Zhang, H.: A Commodity Review Sentiment Analysis Based on BERT-CNN Model. In: International Conference on Computer and Communication Systems, vol. (14) (2020)

Li, Y., Li, Y., Wang, J., Simon Sherratt, R.: Sentiment Analysis for E-Commerce Product Reviews in Chinese Based on Sentiment Lexicon and Deep Learning, vol. (8). IEEE Xplore (2020)

Mhatre, M., Phondekar, D., Kadam, P., Chawathe, A., Ghag, K.: Dimensionality Reduction for Sentiment Analysis using Pre-processing Techniques. In: International Conference on Computing Methodologies and Communication, ICCMC, vol. (28) (2017)

Erfan Mowlaei, M., Mohammad Saniee Abadeh, H.K.: Aspect-based sentiment analysis using adaptive aspect-based lexicons, vol. (21). Elsevier (2020)

Ying, O., Ahmad Zabidi, M.M., Ramli, N., Sheikh, U.U.: Sentiment analysis of informal Malay tweets with deep learning. IAES Int. J. Artifi. Intelli. (IJ-AI) (23), 212 (2020)

Santhosh Kumar, K.L, Jayanti Desai, J.M.: Opinion Mining and Sentiment Analysis on Online Customer Review, vol. (10). IEEE Xplore (2016)

Sergey Smetanin, M.K. Sentiment Analysis of Product Reviews in Russian using Convolutional Neural Networks. In: IEEE 21st Conference on Business Informatics, CBI, vol. (19) (2019)

Minaee, S., Elham Azimi, A.A.: Deep-Sentiment: Sentiment Analysis Using Ensemble of CNN and Bi-LSTM Models, vol. (11) (2019). arXiv.org

ThomasB Word2vec : NLP & Word Embedding. Number 16. DataScientes (2020)

An Interpretability Algorithm of Neural Network Based on Neural Support Decision Tree

Li Xu[1], Wohuan Jia[1], Jiacheng Jiang[1], and Yuntao Yu[2(✉)]

[1] College of Computer Science and Technology, Harbin Engineering University, Harbin 150001, China
[2] China Electronics Standardization Institute, Beijing 100007, China
yuyt@cesi.cn

Abstract. In view of the poor interpretability of the current neural network models, the neural support decision tree model is used to enhance its interpretability. The model combines the characteristics of high recognition accuracy of neural network and strong interpretation of decision tree. We employ the ResNet18 model to solve the gradient disappearance problem with the increase of network depth. By constructing induction hierarchy and establishing hierarchy in weight space, a higher accuracy is obtained. The hierarchical structure derived from the model parameters is adopted to avoid over fitting. And the trained network weights are utilized to construct a tree structure to complete the tree monitoring loss training, and the classification network is retrained or finetuned with additional hierarchy-based loss items. We exploit the neural network backbone to characterize each sample, and establish a decision tree in the weight space is run to enhance the interpretability of the model. At the same time, the optimization of the model is completed. Compared with the original model, the traditional hard decision tree reasoning rules are abandoned and the soft decision tree reasoning rules are adopted to complete the soft tree supervision loss to improve the classification accuracy and generalization ability of the model, which not only ensures high accuracy, but also completes the explicit display of recognition and classification process.

Keywords: Deep learning · Artificial intelligence · Neural networks · Interpretability · Neural support decision trees

1 Introduction

In recent years, deep learning aims to learn the intrinsic laws and hierarchical representation of target data so that machines can have the same ability to recognize that type of data as a human. The most advanced classification models are usually considered black boxes because their decision process is implicit to humans. For this challenge, humans try to explain the entire process of the model in making decisions in some interpretable way, thus improving the model so that it can be used confidently in various domains. The need for interpretability arises from the incompleteness of the problem formalization, which means that for some problems or tasks, obtaining the prediction alone does not

© The Author(s), under exclusive license to Springer Nature Switzerland AG 2022
G. Memmi et al. (Eds.): KSEM 2022, LNAI 13369, pp. 508–519, 2022.
https://doi.org/10.1007/978-3-031-10986-7_41

satisfy the need; the model must also explain how it obtained the prediction, since the correct prediction only partially solves the original problem [1].

Deep learning, as a black box model, is often unable to point out the basis for the system to get decisions for the output results. The research on interpretability analysis of deep learning models can be divided into interpretability research based on visualization, interpretability research based on robustness perturbation testing, and interpretability research based on sensitivity analysis.

(1) Visualization-based interpretability studies.Google researchers explores and analyzes the interpretability of deep learning by combining human visual perception capabilities and the computational power of deep learning algorithms in its work on visual analysis of deep models based on TensorFlow [2].Krizhevsky et al. in 2012 used a large convolutional network model on tests on the ImageNet benchmark dataset demonstrated impressive classification performance [3]. However, there is no more reasonable way to explain why the model performs well or to show the basis for making judgments. Therefore, Zeiler et al. [4] proposed a novel CNN implicit visualization technique in 2014, starting from the information availability aspect, by visualizing the features and viewing the accuracy variation to know what kind of features the CNN learns.

(2) Interpretability study based on robustness perturbation test. The methods based on robustness perturbation are mainly based on adding perturbation elements to the input data [5]. For example, by fitting simpler models locally around the test points [6] or by perturbing the test points to understand the changes in model predictions [7–9]. One of the more representative works is the one proposed by Koh et al. [10] in 2017 to understand the predictive effect of deep learning black box models through influence functions. The training points responsible for a given prediction are identified by learning algorithms that track the predictions of the model [11] and return its training data [12].

Researchers have conducted exploratory studies on the theory of deep learning interpretability.Lipton [13] first analyzed the connotation of interpretability in deep learning models in 2018 in terms of four aspects: trustworthiness, causal correlation, transfer learnability, and information availability, and pointed out that decisions made by interpretable deep learning models tend to gain higher trust, even when the results given by the trained models are different from When the results given by the trained models disagree with the actual situation, people can still maintain trust in them.

The application areas of image recognition are extremely broad. For example, image recognition is applied in medicine to perform intelligent medical image recognition [14]. Image recognition is applied in animal husbandry to identify pigs and determine whether they are in heat or not; image recognition is applied in the military to perform military infrared target identification and tracking [15]; image recognition can also be applied in commodity recognition classification to perform recognition of fruits, clothing, and other commodities.

This paper is divided into five parts, the contents are as follows: The first part is an introduction, which mainly introduces the research background of the subject and discusses the research status at home and abroad, and at the same time explains the work content and organizational structure of the whole article. The second part is related work, which mainly introduces the related research work of neural support decision tree, residual neural network and interpretable model used in the article. The third part is appprocah. A decision tree-supported approach is proposed to enhance deep learning interpretability, and optimization of neural-supported decision tree network models is performed. The fourth part is the experiment. The neural support decision tree is extensively evaluated on the constructed data set. After building the optimized neural support decision tree model, the same data set is trained and tested, and the identification and classification results are compared. The final results are displayed, and the results are analyzed to draw conclusions. The fifth part summarizes the full text.

2 Related Work

2.1 Neural Support Decision Trees

The neural support decision tree [16] model is a model proposed in a paper by UC Berkeley and Poston University in April 2020 with the acronym NBDT, and the datasets on which the model is trained as well as tested are in CIFAR10, CIFAR100, and ImageNet200 [17] formats. The neural support decision tree is able to obtain higher accuracy than arbitrary tree models, present an explanatory display of the model's step-by-step prediction results, and tell you how it performs the recognition step by step. Inspired by NBDT [18], this paper uses a neural support decision tree model to enhance its explanatory power. To address the problem of insufficient explanatory power of modern network models for commodity recognition and classification, the neural support decision tree model is applied in a commodity recognition and classification system. We use Pytorch to annotate images in a two-label format, construct the corresponding dataset, complete the training of the model on the images, and display the visualization results in the web page at the same time to realize a commodity recognition classification model with high accuracy and strong explanatory power to solve the problem of difficult classification of commodity recognition.

2.2 Residual Neural Network

Residual neural networks. In the model training and prediction of image recognition, a single hidden layer of convolutional neural network can get good prediction results, so it is natural to have the idea of increasing the layers to get higher accuracy. Residual neural network is an important concept of deep learning and a kind of convolutional neural network, whose main feature is to improve the accuracy of model prediction by increasing the depth and can successfully solve the problem of network degradation and gradient disappearance caused by increasing the depth [19].

2.3 Explainable Models

Explainable models: Before the success of deep learning, decision trees were the state-of-the-art in a wide variety of learning tasks and the gold standard for explainability. Research on the intersection of neural networks and decision trees dates back 30 years, when neural networks were given the weight of decision trees, which were created from queries of neural networks. This research has performed poorly in modern simulation evaluations satisfying feature-sparse, sample-sparse mechanisms such as UCI datasets or MNIST when applied to standard image classification tasks.

3 Methods

The construction of neural support decision trees is used to enhance deep learning interpretability. The optimization of the neural support decision tree network model is also performed.

3.1 Construction Method of Neural Support Decision Tree

Neural support decision trees are trained in two phases: 1) loading the weights of the last fully connected layer of the neural network to construct the tree structure; 2) training or fine-tuning the model using a tree-supervised loss function. And inference also occurs in two stages: 1) using the backbone or all layers to provide features for the examples before the final fully connected layer; 2) running the decision rules embedded in the fully connected layer.

For simplicity, consider a skewed decision tree, each with non-axial hyperplane bifurcation decisions: each node in the decision tree is associated with a representative vector. During inference, before reaching a leaf node, each example iteratively traverses the child nodes that have more similarity. A more general hierarchical classifier simply extends it to branching factors greater than 2, but the decision rule is the same: take the sample and the inner product between each, then select the child node with the highest inner product.

Hierarchies are built on the weight space to obtain interpretable models with higher accuracy. This is in contrast to existing decision tree-based approaches that use existing hierarchies such as WordNet or hierarchies built in feature space with data-dependent heuristics such as information gain.

This paper also faces a major problem faced by all previously proposed decision trees: while the original neural network is encouraged to separate representative vectors for each class, it is not trained to separate representative vectors for each internal node. To solve this problem, a loss term can be added. The soft-tree supervised loss is defined as the cross-entropy loss on this distribution, represented by the neural network separating the internal nodes, with 2 different cross-entropy loss terms - the original cross-entropy loss term and the soft-tree supervised loss term with weighted hyperparameters. The specific formula for the cross-entropy loss is shown below.

$$L = \mathrm{C_{ROSS}E_{NTROPY}}\left(D_{pred}, D_{label}\right) + \omega \mathrm{C_{ROSS}E_{NTROPY}}\left(D_{nbdt}, D_{label}\right) \qquad (1)$$

The first half of the equation is expressed as the original cross-entropy loss term, and the second half is the soft tree supervision loss term.

3.2 Interpretable Implementations

The interpretability of the decision tree is perfect, and the final prediction can be decomposed into a series of decisions that can be evaluated independently. In this section, the hypothetical meaning of each intermediate node is analyzed qualitatively and quantitatively. To more directly represent the interpretability of node visualization, the model NBDT will be cited in this paper, along with inter-model comparisons.

Since the induced hierarchy is constructed using model weights, intermediate nodes are not forced to split on foreground objects. While hierarchies like WordNet provide assumptions about the meaning of nodes, the tree may split based on unexpected contextual semantics and visual mathematical properties. To diagnose the visual meaning of nodes, the following 4-step test is performed.

(1) Assume the meaning of the node. This hypothesis can be computed automatically based on the given classification or can be derived by manually examining the leaves of each child.
(2) Collect a dataset with a new, invisible class for testing the meaning of the hypothesis in step (1). The samples in this dataset are called nondistributed samples, and they are drawn from an independent labeled dataset.
(3) The samples from this dataset are passed through the nodes. For each example, the selected sub-nodes are checked for consistency with the hypothesis.
(4) The accuracy of the hypothesis is the percentage of samples passed to the correct sub-node. If the accuracy is low, repeat with a different hypothesis.

3.3 Neural Support Decision Tree Optimization

The most important feature of neural support decision tree is that any neural network applied in the field of image classification can be converted into NBDT by fine-tuning and customizing the loss, which provides an idea of whether model optimization can be performed at the point of customizing the loss, which goes back to the process of model construction to verify the idea.

The induced hierarchy is first built, then a tree-supervised loss adjustment model is used, and finally the neural network backbone is used to characterize the samples as well as to run decision rules embedded in the fully connected layers. The characterization of the samples by the neural network backbone is completed while inference is performed using the embedded decision rules. After that, at each node, the inner product between the characterized sample and the representative vector of each child node is taken. Finally, the inner product is used to make a hard or soft decision.

In general, the classification accuracy of soft decision trees is higher than that of traditional decision trees, and it is more suitable for classification of targets. nbdt chooses a combination of hard decision tree inference as well as soft decision tree inference for the inference rules, and uses the corresponding trees for different inference rules in the subsequent tree supervised loss for training. For hard decision trees, the hard tree supervised loss is used because each node is a probability distribution, so each node is counted once for cross entropy. And for soft decision trees, use soft trees to supervise the loss, because the whole obeys a probability distribution, so the cross entropy is counted only once on the leaves. So NBDT takes a compromise approach and combines the two. And this paper compares the inference rules and supervised loss training effects of hard decision tree and soft decision tree, and considers the amount of data set for model optimization in the selection of decision tree.

In this paper, we choose to use only soft decision trees for training and testing of the model. The soft decision tree, as a class of fuzzy decision trees, is structured by combining tree growth and pruning to determine the structure of the soft decision tree, and the tree is modified to improve its generalization ability. The decision criterion of a soft decision tree is a range interval rather than a specific value. Compared with the standard decision tree, the classification result of the soft decision tree is more accurate. However, one of the disadvantages of soft decision trees is the gradient descent problem, which can easily fall into local minima in the process of finding the best value. However, at this time, the residual neural network can solve the problem well, so we try to complete the grafting and reorganization of ResNet18 model and soft decision tree. Different from the comparison model construction process, this paper only uses soft decision tree inference rules and soft tree supervised loss, and adds cross entropy loss.

4   Experiments

In this section, neural support decision trees are extensively evaluated on the constructed dataset. After constructing the optimized neural support decision tree model, the same dataset was trained as well as tested and compared with ResNet18. Differential results generated during model training were also analyzed. Due to the difference in the amount of fruit and clothing datasets, the control variables method can also be used to summarize the difference in the training results of the two models when training different amounts of data.

In this paper, we use Pytorch to construct and train the dataset, which is divided into two major categories, with three sub-categories in each major category. The two major categories are clothing and fruit, where the clothing category contains longsleeve, hoddy and shirt; the fruit category contains apple, banana and pineapple. In the process of constructing the dataset, a two-label format is used. The first label is the recognition category: fruit, clothing; the second label is the classification category: apple, banana, pineapple, hoddy, longsleeve, shirt. 1000 images are trained for each small category of clothing, and 500 images are trained for each small category of fruit.

4.1   Training Model Results

After the overall network model is built and trained, the visualization results of the training are presented in the front-end.

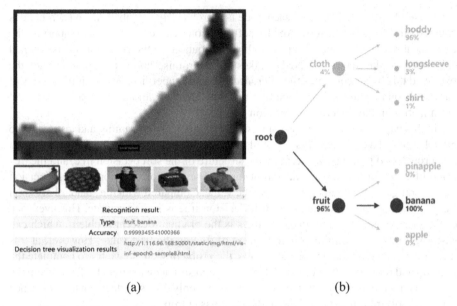

(a)   (b)

Fig. 1. (a) Example for fruit recognition; (b) The decision tree recognition process

Figure 1 shows the recognition results of the model for the banana subclass and the whole process of the decision tree to make this decision. It can be seen that the model first identifies the images as fruit class with 96% probability, and then later as banana with nearly 100% probability.

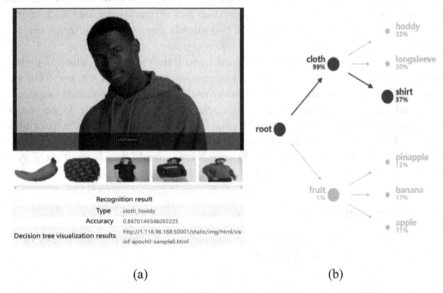

(a)   (b)

Fig. 2. (a) Example for clothes recognition; (b) The decision tree recognition process

Figure 2 (left) shows the recognition results of the model for the hoddy subclass, which is much less accurate than the recognition accuracy of banana in the fruit class, as seen from the figure, which has a great relationship with the constructed dataset. The fruit dataset has obvious feature values for all kinds of pictures, both in terms of color and shape, and has a high degree of differentiation. For example, the difference between shirt and hoddy is very small, so the recognition result is not so satisfactory.

Figure 2 (right) shows the recognition process of the neural support decision tree for the shirt subcategory. It can be seen that although the recognition rate of the clothing category is as high as 99%, the difference between the three subcategories in the clothing category is small: the model identifies this image as hoddy with 33% probability, as longsleeve with 30% probability, and as shirt with 37% The maximum differentiation of the three subclasses does not exceed 7%, and its classification results are not satisfactory. It can be seen that the model has high requirements on the dataset, and there is great room for improvement in both the selection of the dataset and the training of the model.

The results shown in Fig. 2 deviate slightly from the expected results, for which some analysis is made in this paper. The accuracy of image recognition is closely related to the constructed dataset, and the result of fruit class recognition is much better than that of clothing class recognition. Because the features of the fruit class are relatively obvious and easy to extract, while the features of the clothing class are difficult to distinguish. the composition of the dataset of the fruit class is similar to that of the clothing class, both of which have the characteristics of close sample number, uniform distribution, high differentiation of different samples, each having obvious features, and easy processing in the double-label format. the clothing class and the fruit class Both the clothing and fruit datasets were constructed using pytorch in a two-label format, and the training volume of the clothing class was twice that of the fruit class. 3000 images were trained for the clothing class, while only 1500 images were trained for the fruit class. However, compared to the fruit class dataset, the sample features of theothing class dataset are not obvious enough, so the generated results will be different from the recognition results of the fruit class.

4.2   Comparison of Results

First, the accuracy of the training test using the optimized model and the traditional convolutional neural network is compared, and the specific comparison results are shown in Fig. 3.

Figure 3(a) shows the training results using the optimized neural support decision tree model and Fig. 3(b) shows the training results using the basic ResNet18 model. Comparing the results of the two models, it is easy to find that the recognition accuracy of the neural support decision tree model is only 1%–2% lower than that of the ResNet18 model, and its recognition accuracy is better. The model accomplishes the implementation of model interpretation at the expense of less accuracy, and can explicitly show the decision process as well as the classification results, which the ResNet18 model cannot do.

Figure 3(c) shows the changes in the training recognition accuracy of both models as the training batches increase, and it can be seen that the difference in accuracy between the two models is small during the overall training process. After the training batches reached 50, the recognition accuracy of both models improved less, and finally the accuracy of the ResNet18 model was around 87% and the accuracy of the neural support decision tree model was around 85%.

```
==> Preparing data..
Training with dataset MyData3 and 6 classes
Testing with dataset MyData3 and 6 classes
==> Building model..
==> Checkpoints will be saved to: ./checkpoint/ckpt-MyData3-ResNet18-lr0.01.pth
==> Resuming from checkpoint..

Best accuracy: 85.69864548972431 // checkpoint name: ckpt-MyData3-ResNet18-Ir0.01
```

(a)

```
==> Preparing data..
Training with dataset MyData3 and 6 classes
Testing with dataset MyData3 and 6 classes
==> Building model..
==> Checkpoints will be saved to: ./checkpoint/ckpt-MyData3-ResNet18-lr0.01.pth
==> Resuming from checkpoint..

Best accuracy: 87.21991701244814 // checkpoint name: ckpt-MyData3-ResNet18-Ir0.01
```

(b)

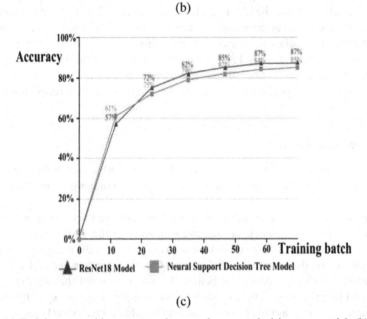

(c)

Fig. 3. (a) Training recognition accuracy by neural support decision tree model; (b) Training recognition accuracy by ResNet18 model; (c) Comparison of two models on accuracy

After the comparison between the neural support decision tree model and the ResNet18 model was completed, the neural support decision tree model was compared for the before and after optimization. Firstly, the two models were trained separately for the fruit class and the same image was predicted to compare the decision tree results, which are shown in Fig. 4(a) and Fig. 4(b) below, where Fig. 4(a) shows the prediction results of the unimproved model and Fig. 4(b) shows the prediction results of the improved model.

Comparing Fig. 4(a) and Fig. 4(b), it is easy to find that the recognition accuracy of the improved model is higher, and both models are very good in small class differentiation, which of course has a great relationship with the data set.

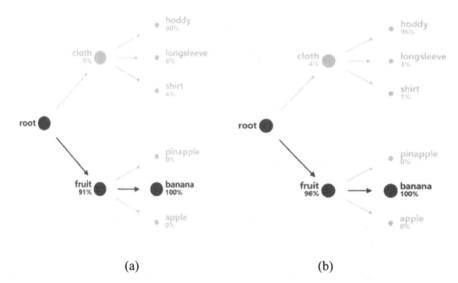

(a)   (b)

Fig. 4. (a) Unimproved model banana decision tree results show; (b) Improved model banana decision tree results show

In order to make the improved model more convincing, the clothing class dataset will be selected to continue the training as well as prediction on both models. The following images are selected for prediction that do not work well on the original model to see if they can be optimized.

Comparing Fig. 5(a) with Fig. 5(b), it is easy to find that the improved model has improved the accuracy of product recognition, but has limited improvement in the confidence of classification. the differentiation of the clothing class is lower than that of the fruit class, which has much to do with the data set. banana, apple and pineapple are easier to differentiate, while shirt, hoddy, and longsleeve are more difficult to distinguish.

On the whole, the soft decision tree has a small effect on the accuracy of the model, and combined with the ResNet18 model can effectively avoid the network degradation and other problems when it is traversed in depth.

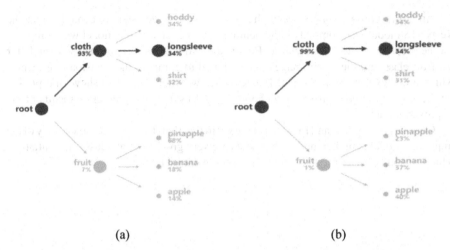

(a)   (b)

Fig. 5. (a) Unimproved model longsleeve decision tree results show; (b) Improved model longsleeve decision tree results show

5   Conclusion(Future)

In this paper, a neural support decision tree was proposed to solve the problem of poorly interpreted neural networks. Firstly, the basic network model was constructed based on convolutional neural network, the training algorithm of neural decision tree and embedded inference function was implemented, and the collection of neural decision tree and neural network as well as inference function was completed at the same time to enhance the interpretability of the model. And the performance of the model was verified using the constructed dataset CIFAR10, and a comparison was made with the ResNet18 model, and it was concluded that the recognition accuracy of this model is higher than that of the baseline model.

Neural support decision trees blazed a new path with the advantage of linking accuracy and interpretability to build a model with high accuracy and strong explanatory power at the same time, which provided more diverse options for the development of computer vision. The model still has room for improvement, with its high dataset requirements and a very large overall dataset construction effort. The model still needs to be improved. It has high requirements on the dataset, and the overall dataset construction workload is very large. On the whole, the neural support decision tree algorithm not only ensures a high accuracy rate, but also can explicitly display the recognition results and processes, and explain them step by step. The algorithm has great potential in practical applications, and has a very broad development space in e-commerce, medicine, finance and other fields.

Funding. This research was funded in part by the National Natural Science Foundation of China, grant number 62172122, and the Scientific and Technological Innovation 2030 - Major Project of "Brain Science and Brain-Like Intelligence Technology Research", grant number 2021ZD0200406.

References

1. Ji, S.L., Li, J.F., Du, T.Y., Li, B.: Review on interpretability methods, applications and security of machine learning models. Comput. Res. Dev. **56**(10), 2071–2096 (2019)
2. Wu, F., Liao, B.B., Han, Y.H.: Interpretability of deep learning. Aviation Weapon **26**(1), 39–46 (2019)
3. Krizhevsky, A., Sutskever, I., Hinton, G.E.: ImageNet classification with deep convolutional neural networks. Neural Inf. Process. Syst. **141**(5), 1097–1105 (2012)
4. Zeiler, M.D., Fergus, R.: Visualizing and understanding convolutional networks. In: Fleet, D., Pajdla, T., Schiele, B., Tuytelaars, T. (eds.) ECCV 2014. LNCS, vol. 8689, pp. 818–833. Springer, Cham (2014). https://doi.org/10.1007/978-3-319-10590-1_53
5. Donahue, J., Jia, Y., Hoffman, J., Darrell, T.: Decaf: A deep convolutional activation feature for generic visual recognition. Proc. Int. Conf. Mach. Learn. **32**, 647–655 (2014)
6. Xin, Y.: Evolving artificial neural networks. Proc. IEEE **87**(9), 1423–1447 (1999)
7. Bertsimas, D., Sim, M.: Robust discrete optimization and network flows. Math. Program. **98**(1/2/3), 49–71 (2003)
8. Eitel, A., Springenberg, J.T., Spinello, L., Riedmiller, M.: Multimodal deep learning for robust RGB-D object recognition. IEEE/RSJ Int. Conf. Intell. Robots Syst. (IROS), 681–687 (2015)
9. Milanese, M., Tempo, R.: Optimal algorithms theory for robust estimation and prediction. IEEE Trans. Autom. Control **30**(8), 730–738 (1985)
10. Koh, P.W., Liang, P.: Understanding black-box predictions via influence functions. Int. Conf. Mach. Learn. **70**, 1885–1894 (2017)
11. Reitmayr, G., Drummond, T.: Going out: Robust model-based tracking for outdoor augmented reality. IEEE/ACM Int. Symp. Mixed Augmented Reality, 109–118 (2006)
12. Shrikumar, A., Greenside, P., Kundaje, A.: Learning important features through propagating activation differences. Int. Conf. Mach. Learn. **70**, 3145–3153 (2017)
13. Lipton, Z.C.: The mythos of model interpretability. Commun. ACM **61**(10), 31–57 (2016)
14. Zhou, T., Huo, B.Q., Lu, H.L., Ren, H.L.: Residual neural network and its application in medical image processing. J. Electron. **48**, 1436–1447 (2020)
15. Huang, R.R.: Application of deep learning in military aircraft recognition and detection. Lanzhou University (2020)
16. Wan, A., Dunlap, L., Ho, D., Yin, J.: NBDT: Neural-backed decision trees. arXiv:2004.00221 (2020)
17. Russakovsky, O., et al.: ImageNet large scale visual recognition challenge. Int. J. Comput. Vision **115**(3), 211–252 (2015). https://doi.org/10.1007/s11263-015-0816-y
18. Cheng, K.Y., Wang, N., Shi, W.X.: Research progress on interpretability of deep learning. Comput. Res. Dev. **6**, 1208–1217 (2020)
19. Gao, L., Fan, B.B., Huang, S.: Improved convolution neural network image classification algorithm based on residual. Comput. Syst. Appl., 139–144(2019)

Towards Better Personalization: A Meta-Learning Approach for Federated Recommender Systems

Zhengyang Ai[1,2], Guangjun Wu[1(✉)], Xin Wan[3], Zisen Qi[1], and Yong Wang[1]

[1] Institute of Information Engineering, Chinese Academy of Sciences, Beijing, China
{aizhengyang,wuguangjun,qizisen,wangyong}@iie.ac.cn
[2] School of Cyber Security, University of Chinese Academy of Sciences, Beijing, China
[3] National Computer Network Emergency Response Technical Team/Coordination Center of China, Beijing, China
wanxin@cert.org.cn

Abstract. Recommender systems (RSs) seek to suggest items that may be of interest to users by primarily modeling their historical interactions. In today's context, due to privacy and security constraints, it is becoming increasingly attractive to implement RSs based on federated learning frameworks, in which users' private data need not be uploaded to a central server. However, two major limitations remain unaddressed by existing works about federated RSs. First, canonical federated learning only develops a common output for all users and does not adapt the model to each user. This is an important missing feature, especially given the heterogeneity of the distribution of historical interaction data across users. Second, many current advanced recommendation algorithms, such as self-attention-based methods, have not been applied to federated RSs due to mobile devices' limited storage and computing power. To address these issues, we propose a personalized variant of the well-known Federated Averaging algorithm, where the Model-Agnostic Meta-Learning (MAML) framework is applied to provide a more personalized recommendation model for each user. Meanwhile, we investigate a sparse attention mechanism for sequential recommendation that significantly reduces the time complexity and memory usage when computing attention scores. Extensive experiments on six benchmark datasets reveal that our method consistently outperforms other federated RSs.

Keywords: Recommender system · Sequential recommendation · Attention mechanism · Federated learning · Meta-learning

© The Author(s), under exclusive license to Springer Nature Switzerland AG 2022
G. Memmi et al. (Eds.): KSEM 2022, LNAI 13369, pp. 520–533, 2022.
https://doi.org/10.1007/978-3-031-10986-7_42

1 Introduction

Recommender systems (RSs) help users efficiently discover the most useful information or service in the case of information overload by learning their tastes and preferences. Existing deep learning-based recommendation methods usually necessitate centralized storage of all user-item interaction data to learn deep neural networks and the representations of users and items, which means that users' private data need to be uploaded and aggregated. However, user-item interaction data is highly privacy-sensitive, and transmitting it can lead to privacy concerns and data leakage [15]. Moreover, under the pressure of strict data protection regulations such as GDPR[1], user behavior data is no longer allowed to be arbitrarily used without the user's explicit permission. Therefore, these kinds of centrally trained recommendation models may not be applicable in the future.

Federated learning (FL) is a machine learning technique that learns intelligent models collectively based on decentralized user data [7,11]. Unlike existing machine learning approaches based on centralized storage of user data, in FL, user data is kept locally on user devices to preserve privacy maximally [18]. Given this property of FL, many works combine it with RSs to achieve privacy-preserving recommendations [1,3,12]. Federated RSs train a global recommendation model in a decentralized manner and distribute it to users' devices for personalized recommendations. However, there are still two unresolved issues in these methods. First, the historical interaction data of users is highly heterogeneous, which can be reflected in the following two aspects: (i) The user's interaction with the items depends heavily on the user's own interests and preferences. The interests of different users vary greatly, and this leads to a wide variation in the types of items that different users interact with. (ii) The number of interaction items also shows great variability across users. In this case, a common recommendation model cannot meet the personalized recommendation needs of different users. Second, as self-attention mechanism [17] has been proven effective in capturing long-term dependencies, many research works of RSs have adopted it to model the dynamic preferences of users [6,8]. Nevertheless, the atom operation of self-attention, namely canonical dot-product, causes large time complexity and memory usage, which hinders the deployment of self-attention-based models on resource-constrained user devices.

To tackle these above limitations, we herein propose FMLRec, a recommendation framework based on federated meta-learning. For the first issue, we introduce Model-Agnostic Meta-Learning (MAML) [4] into the FL framework to improve the personalization of the recommendation model. Specifically, we treat each user's local training process as a *training task*, and each training task consists of a *support set* and a *query set* that are disjoint from each other. The recommendation model is trained on the support set and then its loss on the query set is calculated. Afterwards, the gradient of this loss is uploaded to the central server, where the global model is updated accordingly. The updated

---

[1] https://gdpr-info.eu.

global model is then distributed to user devices for a new round of training and updating. Our goal is to find an *initial shared model* that new users can easily adapt to their local dataset by performing one or several gradient descent steps on their own data. This way, while the initial model is derived in a distributed manner across all users, the final model implemented by each user has a high degree of personalization based on his or her own data. For the second issue, inspired by the research works on sparse self-attention mechanisms aiming to reduce computational effort [2,9,19], we propose a sparse self-attention mechanism oriented to the deep interests of users. In particular, we present a measurement to adaptively measure the correlation between interactions and users' deep interests. With this measurement, we can discard the computation of interactions that are irrelevant to users' interests without compromising the recommendation performance of the model. We conduct massive experiments on six widely used benchmark datasets for recommendation, and the results demonstrate that our method consistently outperforms existing centralized deep learning-based methods as well as FL-based methods, while effectively protecting user privacy. The main contributions of this work are summarized as follows:

- We propose a personalized variant of federated learning for recommendation based on MAML, which can find a model initialization shared between all users that performs well after each user updates it with respect to its own loss function, potentially by performing a few steps of a gradient-based method.
- We propose a novel sparse self-attention mechanism to significantly reduce the time complexity and memory usage when computing attention scores, in which a measurement is designed to adaptively measure the relevancy between items and users' real interests.
- We conduct extensive experiments and analysis on six benchmark datasets, and the results show that our method consistently outperforms existing recommendation methods and meanwhile protect user privacy.

2   Proposed Method

2.1   Problem Formulation

Let $\mathcal{U}$ and $\mathcal{I}$ represent the user and item set respectively. For user $m \in \mathcal{U}$, his interaction sequence is denoted by $\mathcal{L}^m = (s_1^m, s_2^m, \ldots, s_{|\mathcal{L}^m|}^m)$, where $s_t^m \in \mathcal{I}$ is the item that m has interacted with at time step t. We manually divide the sequence of user interactions into multiple sessions according to a specific time idle threshold. As such, for user m, the interaction sequence $\mathcal{L}^m$ is divided into k interaction sessions as $\mathcal{L}^m = \{\mathcal{S}_1^m, \mathcal{S}_2^m, \ldots, \mathcal{S}_k^m\}$, and these sessions are viewed as the basic units of model training. For session $\mathcal{S}_1^m = (s_1^m, s_2^m, \ldots, s_{|\mathcal{S}_1^m|}^m)$, the model's input is $(s_1^m, s_2^m, \ldots, s_{|\mathcal{S}_1^m|-1}^m)$ and its expected output as a shifted' version of the same sequence: $(s_2^m, s_3^m, \ldots, s_{|\mathcal{S}_1^m|}^m)$. Note that in Fig. 1 we have simplified the process in order to show the overall framework more clearly.

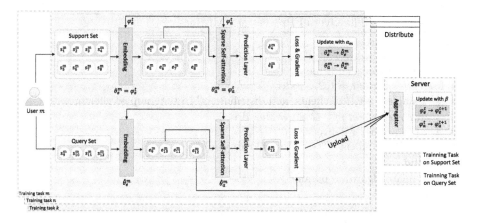

Fig. 1. The overview framework of the proposed FMLRec.

2.2 FMLRec Framework

We now introduce the framework of our FMLRec method for privacy-preserving recommendation. Overall, it consists of an external framework based on federated learning and a training and parameter updating approach based on MAML, as shown in Fig. 1. Following the FedAvg algorithm in [11], FMLRec also contains a central server and a large number of user clients. At each iteration, the central server selects a subset of user clients $\overline{\mathcal{U}} \in \mathcal{U}$ to participate in training. Each client trains a recommendation model in the training manner of MAML using its local dataset. Then the central server aggregates the gradients of all local models to update the global model, which is distributed to clients on the next iteration. In the following, we introduce how they work in detail.

The goal of FMLRec is to *meta-train* an algorithm $\mathcal{A}$ that can quickly train a well-performing recommendation model after deployment to a new user client. The algorithm $\mathcal{A}_\varphi$ is in general parameterized, where its parameter φ is updated during the meta-training process using a collection of *training tasks*. The training process for each user client is considered a training task, *e.g.*, user m training a model using its local data is the training task m. As described in Sect. 2.1, the interaction sequence of user m is sliced into k interaction sessions. Further, these sessions are divided into two parts: a *support set* $\mathcal{D}_S^m = \{(x_i, y_i)\}_{i=1}^{|\mathcal{D}_S^m|}$ and a *query set* $\mathcal{D}_Q^m = \{(x_i', y_i')\}_{i=1}^{|\mathcal{D}_Q^m|}$. User m trains a model f and output the parameter $\hat{\theta}^m$ based on the support set $\mathcal{D}_S^m$, which we call *inner update*. The model $f_{\hat{\theta}^m}$ is then evaluated on the query set $\mathcal{D}_Q^m$, and test loss $\mathcal{L}_{\mathcal{D}_Q^m}(\hat{\theta}^m)$ is computed to reflect the training ability of $\mathcal{A}_\varphi$. Finally, $\mathcal{A}_\varphi$ is updated to minimize the test loss, which we call *outer update*. Note that the support and query sets are disjoint to maximize the generalization ability of $\mathcal{A}_\varphi$. Hence, the optimization objective of algorithm $\mathcal{A}_\varphi$ is as follows:

$$\min_\varphi \mathbb{E}_{m\sim\overline{\mathcal{U}}} \left[\mathcal{L}_{\mathcal{D}_Q^m} \left(\hat{\theta}^m \right) \right] = \min_\varphi \mathbb{E}_{m\sim\overline{\mathcal{U}}} \left[\mathcal{L}_{\mathcal{D}_Q^m} \left(\mathcal{A}_\varphi \left(\mathcal{D}_S^m \right) \right) \right]. \tag{1}$$

Algorithm 1: The Overall Process of FMLRec

// Run on the server
1 **AlgorithmUpdate:**
2 Initialize φ^0 for algorithm;
3 **for** *each episode* $t = 1, 2, \ldots$ **do**
4   Sample a set $\overline{\mathcal{U}}$ of clients, and distribute φ^0 to the sampled clients;
5   **for** *each client* $m \in \overline{\mathcal{U}}$ *in parallel* **do**
6   Parameter delivery as $\theta^m \leftarrow \varphi^t$;
7   Get gradient $g^m \leftarrow$ **ModelTraining**(θ^m);
8   **end**
9   Update algorithm parameters $\varphi^{t+1} \leftarrow \varphi^t - \frac{\beta}{|\overline{\mathcal{U}}|} \sum_{m \in \overline{\mathcal{U}}} g^m$;
10 **end**
// Run on the client m
11 **ModelTraining**(θ^m):
12 Sample support set $\mathcal{D}_S^m$ and query set $\mathcal{D}_Q^m$;
13 $\mathcal{L}_{\mathcal{D}_S^m}(\theta^m) \leftarrow \frac{1}{|\mathcal{D}_S^m|} \sum_{(x,y) \in \mathcal{D}_S^m} \ell(f_{\theta^m}(x), y)$;
14 $\hat{\theta}^m \leftarrow \theta^m - \alpha \nabla \mathcal{L}_{\mathcal{D}_S^m}(\theta^m)$;
15 $\mathcal{L}_{\mathcal{D}_Q^m}(\hat{\theta}^m) \leftarrow \frac{1}{|\mathcal{D}_Q^m|} \sum_{(x',y') \in \mathcal{D}_Q^m} \ell(f_{\hat{\theta}^m}(x'), y')$;
16 $g^m \leftarrow \nabla \mathcal{L}_{\mathcal{D}_Q^m}(\hat{\theta}^m)$;
17 Return g^m to server;

Following MAML algorithm [4], our algorithm trains the model with gradient update steps. The algorithm $\mathcal{A}$ is simply used to provide the initialization of the model on each user client. Specifically, the parameter φ^t of algorithm $\mathcal{A}_\varphi$ in episode t is distributed to user client m as the initial value of the parameter of model f: $\theta^m = \varphi^t$. Then f_{θ^m} is trained on support set $\mathcal{D}_S^m$ and θ^m is updated to $\hat{\theta}^m$ using one or more gradient descent steps with training loss $\mathcal{L}_{\mathcal{D}_S^m}(\theta^m) :=$ $\frac{1}{|\mathcal{D}_S^m|} \sum_{(x,y) \in \mathcal{D}_S^m} \ell(f_{\theta^m}(x), y)$, where ℓ is the loss function. Next, $f_{\hat{\theta}^m}$ is tested on the query set $\mathcal{D}_Q^m$ and the test loss $\mathcal{L}_{\mathcal{D}_Q^m}(\hat{\theta}^m) := \frac{1}{|\mathcal{D}_Q^m|} \sum_{(x',y') \in \mathcal{D}_Q^m} \ell(f_{\hat{\theta}^m}(x'), y')$ is calculated. The optimization objective in Eq. (1) is instantiated as follows:

$$\min_{\theta^m} \mathbb{E}_{m \sim \overline{\mathcal{U}}} \left[\mathcal{L}_{\mathcal{D}_Q^m} \left(\theta^m - \alpha \nabla \mathcal{L}_{\mathcal{D}_S^m}(\theta^m) \right) \right], \tag{2}$$

where α is the learning rate for the inner gradient update. Finally, the gradient g^m of $\mathcal{L}_{\mathcal{D}_Q^m}(\hat{\theta}^m)$ is calculated and uploaded to the central server, where the parameter φ^t is updated accordingly as $\varphi^t \rightarrow \varphi^{t+1}$ with learning rate β. The pseudo-code of the whole process is given in Algorithm 1.

2.3 Sparse Self-Attention for Recommendation

In this section, we detail our proposed *IntSparse* self-attention mechanism and show how it effectively reduces the computation of attention scores in RSs. As illustrated in Fig. 1, the parameters distributed from the central server to the user clients can be divided into the parameters of the embedding layer φ_e and the parameters of the attention layer φ_a. They, in turn, contain several different parameters as $\varphi_e = \{\mathbf{M}^I, \mathbf{P}\}$ and $\varphi_a = \{\mathbf{W}^Q, \mathbf{W}^K, \mathbf{W}^V, \mathbf{W}^{(1)}, \mathbf{W}^{(2)}, b^{(1)}, b^{(2)}\}$. In the following, we will describe how these parameters work.

Embedding Layer: For the training session $(s_1^m, s_2^m, \ldots, s_{|\mathcal{S}^m|-1}^m)$, we first transform it into a fixed-length sequence $(s_1, s_2, \ldots, s_l)$. Then we retrieve the input embedding matrix $\mathbf{I} \in \mathbb{R}^{l \times d}$ through the item embedding matrix $\mathbf{M}^I \in \mathbb{R}^{|\mathcal{T}| \times d}$, where d is the latent dimensionality. Because there are no recurrence or convolution modules in the self-attention model, it is unaware of the actual placements of items in a sequence. Like [6], we inject the learnable position embedding $\mathbf{P} \in \mathbb{R}^{l \times d}$ into the input embedding: $\mathbf{E} = \mathbf{I} + \mathbf{P}$, where $\mathbf{E} \in \mathbb{R}^{l \times d}$.

The Canonical Self-attention: The scaled dot-product attention in [17] is defined as:

$$A(\mathbf{Q}, \mathbf{K}, \mathbf{V}) = \text{softmax}\left(\frac{\mathbf{Q}\mathbf{K}^\top}{\sqrt{d}}\right)\mathbf{V}, \tag{3}$$

where $\mathbf{Q} \in \mathbb{R}^{L_Q \times d}$, $\mathbf{K} \in \mathbb{R}^{L_K \times d}$, $\mathbf{V} \in \mathbb{R}^{L_V \times d}$ represent queries, keys, and values respectively, and are converted from the input embedding $\mathbf{E}$ through linear projections with $\mathbf{W}^Q$, $\mathbf{W}^K$, $\mathbf{W}^V$. Following [16], we performed Eq. (3) as a kernel smoother in a probability form:

$$A(\mathbf{q}_i, \mathbf{K}, \mathbf{V}) = \sum_j \frac{k(\mathbf{q}_i, \mathbf{k}_j)}{\sum_l k(\mathbf{q}_i, \mathbf{k}_l)} \mathbf{v}_j = \mathbb{E}_{p(\mathbf{k}_j|\mathbf{q}_i)}[\mathbf{v}_j], \tag{4}$$

where $\mathbf{q}_i$, $\mathbf{k}_i$, $\mathbf{v}_i$ stand for the i-th row in $\mathbf{Q}$, $\mathbf{K}$, $\mathbf{V}$ respectively, $p(\mathbf{k}_j|\mathbf{q}_i) = k(\mathbf{q}_i, \mathbf{k}_j)/\sum_l k(\mathbf{q}_i, \mathbf{k}_l)$ and $k(\mathbf{q}_i, \mathbf{k}_j)$ selects the asymmetric exponential kernel $\exp(\mathbf{q}_i \mathbf{k}_j^\top/\sqrt{d})$. The self-attention calculates the probability $p(\mathbf{k}_j|\mathbf{q}_i)$ for each $\mathbf{q}_i$ in $\mathbf{Q}$, depending on which the values are combined for the final outputs. Our motivation is to reduce the computational effort by calculating the probability only for those important $\mathbf{q}_i$ and ignoring the rest. We consider the queries corresponding to those items that truly represent the user's interests to be important. So, the next question is how to distinguish them?

Query Sparsity Measurement: The interests of different users vary considerably. Therefore, if an item accurately reflects a user's genuine interests, the probability distribution p of the query corresponding to it should be substantially different from that of other users. In other words, suppose we define a globally fixed distribution as $q(\mathbf{k}_j|\mathbf{q}_i)$, if a query's attention distribution differs little from distribution q, then the item it corresponds to is likely to be of little relevance to the user's interests. We set this default distribution as a scaled exponential function as $q(\mathbf{k}_j|\mathbf{q}_i) = e^j/\sum_{j=1}^{L_k} e^j$. Naturally, the "similarity" between distributions p and q can be used to distinguish "important" queries. We measure the "similarity" by Kullback-Leibler divergence:

$$KL(q \,||\, p) = \log \sum_{j=1}^{L_k} e^{\frac{\mathbf{q}_i \mathbf{k}_j^\top}{\sqrt{d}}} - \sum_{j=1}^{L_k} \log q(\mathbf{k}_j|\mathbf{q}_i) \frac{\mathbf{q}_i \mathbf{k}_j^\top}{\sqrt{d}} + \sum_{j=1}^{L_k} q(\mathbf{k}_j|\mathbf{q}_i) \log q(\mathbf{k}_j|\mathbf{q}_i).$$

$$(5)$$

To simplify the calculation, we obtain a subset $\overline{\mathbf{K}}$ by randomly sampling $\mathbf{K}$ according to a sampling factor $\rho \in (0,1]$, and replace $p(\mathbf{k}_j|\mathbf{q}_i)$ with its unbiased distribution $p(\overline{\mathbf{k}}_j|\mathbf{q}_i)$, where $\overline{\mathbf{k}}_j$ stand for the i-th row in $\overline{\mathbf{K}}$. Dropping the constant term in Eq. (5), we define the i-th query's sparsity measurement as:

$$M\left(\mathbf{q}_i, \overline{\mathbf{K}}\right) = \log \sum_{j=1}^{L_{\overline{K}}} e^{\frac{\mathbf{q}_i \overline{\mathbf{k}}_j^\top}{\sqrt{d}}} - \sum_{j=1}^{L_{\overline{K}}} \frac{e^j \frac{\mathbf{q}_i \overline{\mathbf{k}}_j^\top}{\sqrt{d}}}{\sum_{L_{\overline{K}}} e^j}.$$

$$(6)$$

User's genuine interests in the item encourage the corresponding query's attention probability distribution away from the fixed distribution.

Multi-head IntSparse Self-Attention: Based on $M(\mathbf{q}_i, \overline{\mathbf{K}})$ in Eq. (6), we have the *IntSparse* self-attention by allowing each key to focus on only n interest-relevant queries:

$$\mathbf{S} = \overline{\mathrm{A}}(\mathbf{Q}, \mathbf{K}, \mathbf{V}) = \mathrm{Softmax}\left(\frac{\overline{\mathbf{Q}}\mathbf{K}^\top}{\sqrt{d}}\right)\mathbf{V},$$

$$(7)$$

where $\overline{\mathbf{Q}}$ is a sparse matrix of $\mathbf{Q}$ that only contains the Top-n queries under $M(\mathbf{q}_i, \overline{\mathbf{K}})$. We set $n = \lceil \rho \cdot L_Q \rceil$, where ρ is the same sampling factor as when sampling $\mathbf{K}$. Under the multi-head perspective, this attention extracts different sparse query-key pairs for each head, avoiding severe information loss. We ignore the computation of attention scores for the remaining $(L_Q - n)$ queries and instead assign values directly using the default distribution $q(\mathbf{k}_j|\mathbf{q}_i)$.

Point-Wise Feed-Forward Network: After attention layer, we employ a two-layer feed-forward network with ReLU activation in between, which could endow the model with the nonlinearity and consider interactions between different latent dimensions:

$$\mathrm{FFN}(\mathbf{S}) = \mathrm{ReLU}(\mathbf{S}\mathbf{W}^{(1)} + \mathbf{b}^{(1)})\mathbf{W}^{(2)} + \mathbf{b}^{(2)},$$

$$(8)$$

where $\mathbf{W}^{(1)}, \mathbf{W}^{(2)} \in \mathbb{R}^{d \times d}$ and $\mathbf{b}^{(1)}, \mathbf{b}^{(2)} \in \mathbb{R}^d$. To make the whole network more robust, we utilize layer normalization, residual connections and dropout:

$$\mathbf{S} = \mathbf{S} + \mathrm{Dropout}(\mathrm{FFN}(\mathrm{LayerNorm}(\mathbf{S}))).$$

$$(9)$$

2.4   Prediction Layer

After attention layer, we obtain the user interests representation adaptively and hierarchically extracted from the previous items. We utilize a latent factor model to generate users' preference score for item i in order to forecast the following item, as illustrated below:

$$R_{i,t} = \mathbf{S}_t \mathbf{I}_i^{\mathcal{I}}, \tag{10}$$

where $\mathbf{I}_i^{\mathcal{I}} \in \mathbb{R}^d$ is the embedding vector of item i and $\mathbf{S}_t$ is the user interests representation generated after the previous t items (i.e., $s_1, s_2, \ldots, s_t$) are given.

3 Experiments

In this section, we present our experimental setup and conduct experiments on six real-world datasets for recommendations to evaluate our proposed method.

3.1 Datasets

We study the effectiveness of our proposed method on six datasets from two real-world platforms, which are very different in domains, size and sparsity:

- **Amazon**[2]: This is a series of product review datasets, composed of product reviews and metadata crawled from Amazon.com by McAuley et al. [10]. Top-level product categories on Amazon are treated as separate subsets. We adopt four subsets, 'Movies and TV', 'CDs and Vinyl', 'Video Games' and 'Beauty'.
- **MovieLens**[3]: This is a popular movie rating data used to evaluate recommendation algorithms. In this work, we adopt two versions, ML-1m and ML-10m, which includes 1 million and 10 million user ratings, respectively.

Follow the preprocessing procedure in [6,13], we transform the presence of a review or rating to implicit feedback (i.e., the user interacted with the item) for all datasets. To ensure the quality of the dataset, we discard users and items with fewer than 5 related actions. In all experiments, we randomly select 80% of the clients as training clients, 10% as validation clients, and the rest as test clients, since we consider the ability to generalize to new clients as a key property of federated learning. For each client, its local data is divided into support set and query set in the ratio of 8:2.

3.2 Evaluation Protocols

Now we describe how to evaluate our method using test clients. After training with training clients and selecting hyperparameters with validation clients, we obtain an algorithm $\mathcal{A}_\varphi$. For each test client u, we first update $\mathcal{A}_\varphi$ to $\mathcal{A}_{\hat{\varphi}}^u$ with one step of stochastic gradient descent using its support set $\mathcal{D}_S^u$, and then evaluate the recommendation performance of $\mathcal{A}_{\hat{\varphi}}^u$ with its query set $\mathcal{D}_Q^u$.

For performance evaluation, we employ two widely adopted Top-N metrics including Hit@10 and NDCG@10. Hit@10 intuitively measures whether ground-truth items appear in the top 10 list, and NDCG@10 indicates where the hits are

---

[2] http://jmcauley.ucsd.edu/data/amazon/.
[3] https://grouplens.org/datasets/movielens/.

by assigning higher scores to the top-ranked hits. Since it is too time-consuming to rank all items for every client during evaluation, we follow the strategy in [6] that randomly samples 100 items that are not interacted with by the client, ranking the test item among those items. We calculate both metrics for each test client and report the average score.

3.3   Baselines

We compare the performance of our proposed FMLRec solution with several recommendation baselines based on centralized storage of user data as well as several privacy-preserving ones based on federated learning, including:

- **BPR** [14]: A typical method for general item recommendation that optimizes matrix factorization using a pairwise ranking loss.
- **FPMC** [13]: A classic hybrid model combing matrix factorization with first-order Markov chains to captures users' general preferences.
- **GRU4Rec** [5]: A seminal method that uses RNNs to model user action sequences for session-based recommendation.
- **SASRec** [6]: A representative work of applying self-attention to sequential recommendation, which adaptively considers interacted items for prediction.
- **FCF** [1]: A privacy-preserving recommendation method based on federated collaborative filtering.
- **FedMF** [3]: A privacy-preserving recommendation method based on secure matrix factorization.
- **FedFast** [12]: A method that demonstrably improve the convergence speed required to train a federated recommendation model.

3.4   Overall Performance Comparison

Table 1 summarizes the recommendation performance of all the methods on the six datasets, and we have the following observations.

Among the four centralized training baselines, the only non-sequential method BPR performs the worst overall, proving that considering the sequential information in historical interactions helps improve the recommendation performance. SASRec consistently outperforms other methods by a large margin, illustrating the superiority of self-attention mechanism in modeling sequential information.

The performance of the three federated learning-based baselines is not very different, and the top-performing method FedFast achieves competitive results with the centralized method BPR. This indicates that federated learning can protect user privacy without compromising recommendation performance. However, there is a significant performance gap compared to SASRec, which uses a more advanced model, suggesting that it is meaningful to explore the application of self-attention mechanism in federated learning framework.

According to the results, it is evident that FMLRec performs best among all methods on six datasets in terms of two evaluation metrics. It gains **3.34%**

HR@10, **5.81%** NDCG@10 improvements (on average) against the strongest centralized baseline, and **50.58%** HR@10, **72.01%** NDCG@10 improvements (on average) against the strongest federated learning-based baseline.

Table 1. Performance of different methods for recommendation task. Bold scores are the best in each row, while underlined scores are the second best.

Dataset	Metric	BPR	FPMC	GRU4Rec	SASRec	FCF	FedMF	FedFast	FMLRec
ML-1m	NDCG	0.3249	0.5135	0.5346	<u>0.5751</u>	0.3041	0.3261	0.3354	**0.6043**
	Hit	0.5813	0.6898	0.7138	<u>0.8093</u>	0.5513	0.5789	0.5849	**0.8178**
ML-10m	NDCG	0.3297	0.5013	0.5312	<u>0.6031</u>	0.3067	0.3227	0.3617	**0.6342**
	Hit	0.5901	0.6891	0.7142	<u>0.8186</u>	0.5683	0.5890	0.6165	**0.8312**
Movies&TV	NDCG	0.3419	0.3871	0.3971	<u>0.4780</u>	0.3129	0.3407	0.3580	**0.5111**
	Hit	0.5514	0.5791	0.5897	<u>0.6998</u>	0.5294	0.5520	0.5712	**0.7307**
CDs&Vinyl	NDCG	0.3613	0.3471	0.3301	<u>0.4930</u>	0.3315	0.3593	0.3643	**0.5055**
	Hit	0.5513	0.4989	0.4814	<u>0.7098</u>	0.5224	0.5494	0.5509	**0.7241**
Games	NDCG	0.2819	0.3451	0.3609	<u>0.4922</u>	0.2616	0.2801	0.3101	**0.5201**
	Hit	0.4316	0.4518	0.4434	<u>0.7110</u>	0.3906	0.4301	0.4468	**0.7314**
Beauty	NDCG	0.1453	0.1591	0.1817	<u>0.3143</u>	0.1381	0.1534	0.1514	**0.3441**
	Hit	0.2412	0.2595	0.2911	<u>0.4826</u>	0.2312	0.2513	0.2536	**0.5219**

3.5 Effectiveness of Framework and Model

Our proposed FMLRec contains a federated meta-learning framework (denoted by **FML**) as well as a recommendation model based on *IntSparse* self-attention (denoted by **ISSA**). To validate the effectiveness of each component, we conduct several experiments on Beauty and ML-1m datasets to analyze the contribution of each component.

As for the overall framework, we consider the standard federated learning framework **FedAvg** proposed in [11]. Given our motivation to conduct a more in-depth framework analysis study, we also consider a meta-learning variant of FedAvg, denoted by **FedAvg(Meta)**. Prior to testing, FedAvg(Meta) updates the model initialization received from the server with one step of stochastic gradient descent using the support set of the test clients, which reflects the essence of meta-learning - "learning to fine-tune". Both FedAvg and FedAvg(Meta) use all the data on the training clients during the training process.

As for the recommendation model, we first consider the traditional matrix factorization-based model **BPR** [14]. Second, to illustrate the strength of our proposed *IntSparse* self-attention mechanism in terms of recommendation performance, we compare it with the canonical self-attention mechanism (denoted by **SA**) proposed in [17].

The results are shown in Fig. 2. As can be seen, the overall recommendation performance is only slightly improved after adding the fine-tuning of the support set on top of FedAvg, especially when the recommendation model is based on

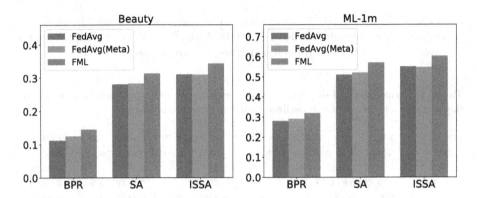

Fig. 2. Performance (NDCG@10) comparison of different frameworks and recommendation models on Beauty and ML-1m.

the self-attention mechanism. In contrast, our proposed federated meta-learning framework achieves a significant improvement over FedAvg, which indicates that applying the MAML approach to the federated recommender system can effectively improve the model's adaptability to the user's local data. In terms of recommendation models, our proposed ISSA-based model is consistently optimal. This is an encouraging phenomenon, demonstrating that computing only the dot-product of those important queries can effectively reduce the negative impact of interest-irrelevant interactions on user interest representations.

3.6   Sensitivity of FMLRec to Sampling Factor

This experiment demonstrates the sensitivity of FMLRec to the sampling factor ($\rho \in (0, 1]$) hyperparameter, which is presented in Sect. 2.3 and is used to control the proportion of dot-product pairs to be calculated. We illustrate the impact of ρ on FMLRec in terms of both recommendation quality and computational complexity.

Figure 3 shows the recommendation performance on four datasets with varying ρ from 0.2 to 1.0. First, it is immediately apparent that as ρ increases, the performance curves present a similar trend regardless of the dataset, i.e., they first rise to the highest point and then start to fall. The noticeable difference is the value of ρ when the highest point is reached. Second, the performance of FMLRec on the three Amazon datasets is more sensitive to ρ changes than the performance on Ml-1m. This proves that the Amazon dataset contains more noise interactions irrelevant to user interests.

Next, we illustrate the effect of ρ on the time complexity and memory usage of FMLRec. Suppose l represents the length of the input session, under the control of ρ, only a fraction of the dot-product pairs are computed when calculating the attention scores, which changes the time complexity and memory usage from $\mathcal{O}(l^2)$ to $\mathcal{O}(\rho l^2)$. Recall that before computing the attention scores we also need to compute the query sparsity measure M. This part of the computation also results in $\mathcal{O}(\rho l^2)$ time complexity and memory usage. So the final consumption is the sum of the two parts as $\mathcal{O}(2\rho l^2)$, which means that when ρ is less than 0.5, our *IntSparse* self-attention mechanism brings a smaller computational and storage cost than the canonical self-attention mechanism. For example, from the figure, on CDs&Vinyl dataset, our model requires only 40% ($\rho = 0.2$) of the time complexity and memory usage to achieve better recommendation performance.

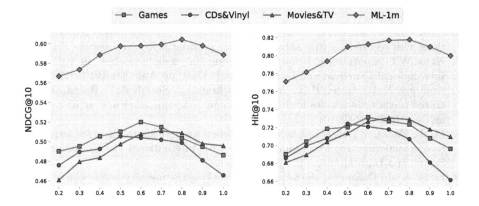

Fig. 3. Performance with different sampling factor ρ.

The tuning of ρ allows FMLRec to seek a balance between recommendation quality and computational complexity, which grants it sufficient flexibility to adapt to different application scenarios.

4   Conclusion

In this paper, we propose a federated meta-learning framework to address the problem that federated recommendation models do not adapt well to users' local data. In addition, we explore a novel sparse self-attention mechanism that can effectively reduce the time complexity and memory usage when computing attention scores without compromising the recommendation accuracy. We evaluate our technique against standard centralized and federated learning baselines using six real-world datasets. The experimental results show that our method is consistently optimal, and the proposed components play essential roles, respectively.

Acknowledgements. This work is supported by the National Key Research and Development Program of China under Grant 2021YFB3101502; by the National Natural Science Foundation of China under Grant 61931019.

References

1. Ammad-Ud-Din, M., et al.: Federated collaborative filtering for privacy-preserving personalized recommendation system. arXiv preprint arXiv:1901.09888 (2019)
2. Beltagy, I., Peters, M.E., Cohan, A.: Longformer: the long-document transformer. arXiv preprint arXiv:2004.05150 (2020)
3. Chai, D., Wang, L., Chen, K., Yang, Q.: Secure federated matrix factorization. IEEE Intell. Syst. **36**(5), 11–20 (2020)
4. Finn, C., Abbeel, P., Levine, S.: Model-agnostic meta-learning for fast adaptation of deep networks. In: International Conference on Machine Learning, pp. 1126–1135 (2017)
5. Hidasi, B., Karatzoglou, A., Baltrunas, L., Tikk, D.: Session-based recommendations with recurrent neural networks. arXiv preprint arXiv:1511.06939 (2015)
6. Kang, W.C., McAuley, J.: Self-attentive sequential recommendation. In: 2018 IEEE International Conference on Data Mining (ICDM), pp. 197–206. IEEE (2018)
7. Konečný, J., McMahan, H.B., Yu, F.X., Richtárik, P., Suresh, A.T., Bacon, D.: Federated learning: strategies for improving communication efficiency. arXiv preprint arXiv:1610.05492 (2016)
8. Li, J., Wang, Y., McAuley, J.: Time interval aware self-attention for sequential recommendation. In: Proceedings of the 13th International Conference on Web Search and Data Mining, pp. 322–330 (2020)
9. Li, S., et al.: Enhancing the locality and breaking the memory bottleneck of transformer on time series forecasting. Adv. Neural. Inf. Process. Syst. **32**, 5243–5253 (2019)
10. McAuley, J., Targett, C., Shi, Q., Van Den Hengel, A.: Image-based recommendations on styles and substitutes. In: Proceedings of the 38th International ACM SIGIR Conference on Research and Development in Information Retrieval, pp. 43–52 (2015)
11. McMahan, B., Moore, E., Ramage, D., Hampson, S., Arcas, B.A.: Communication-efficient learning of deep networks from decentralized data. In: Artificial Intelligence and Statistics, pp. 1273–1282 (2017)
12. Muhammad, K., et al.: FedFast: going beyond average for faster training of federated recommender systems. In: Proceedings of the 26th ACM SIGKDD International Conference on Knowledge Discovery & Data Mining, pp. 1234–1242 (2020)
13. Rendle, S., Freudenthaler, C., Schmidt-Thieme, L.: Factorizing personalized Markov chains for next-basket recommendation. In: Proceedings of the 19th International Conference on World Wide Web, WWW 2010, Raleigh, North Carolina, USA, 26–30 April 2010
14. Rendle, S., Freudenthaler, C., Gantner, Z., Schmidt-Thieme, L.: BPR: Bayesian personalized ranking from implicit feedback. arXiv preprint arXiv:1205.2618 (2012)
15. Shin, H., Kim, S., Shin, J., Xiao, X.: Privacy enhanced matrix factorization for recommendation with local differential privacy. IEEE Trans. Knowl. Data Eng. **30**(9), 1770–1782 (2018)
16. Tsai, Y.H.H., Bai, S., Yamada, M., Morency, L.P., Salakhutdinov, R.: Transformer dissection: a unified understanding of transformer's attention via the lens of kernel. arXiv preprint arXiv:1908.11775 (2019)

17. Vaswani, A., et al.: Attention is all you need. In: Advances in Neural Information Processing Systems, pp. 5998–6008 (2017)
18. Yang, Q., Liu, Y., Chen, T., Tong, Y.: Federated machine learning: concept and applications. ACM Trans. Intell. Syst. Technol. (TIST) **10**(2), 1–19 (2019)
19. Zhou, H., et al.: Informer: beyond efficient transformer for long sequence time-series forecasting. In: Proceedings of the AAAI Conference on Artificial Intelligence (2021)

A BERT-Based Two-Stage Ranking Method for Legal Case Retrieval

Junlin Zhu, Xudong Luo$^{(\boxtimes)}$, and Jiaye Wu

Guangxi Key Lab of Multi-Source Information Mining and Security,
School of Computer Science and Engineering, Guangxi Normal University,
Guilin 541004, China
`luoxd@mailbox.gxnu.edu.cn`

Abstract. Legal case retrieval is crucial for the adjudication of similar cases. However, the existing methods (*e.g.*, keyword matching) cannot understand a legal case well at a semantic level. To this end, this paper proposes a BERT-based method for Chinese legal case retrieval. Specifically, our method first uses the well-known BM25 ranking function to quickly retrieve top n case candidates from the candidate pool. Then it uses the pre-training model BERT to accurately sort the recalled case candidates. In particular, we fine-tune the BERT model by combining the pointwise method with auxiliary learning to learn a model that can understand the deep semantics of a legal judgement text. Then we further train a model suitable for the accurate ranking of case candidates based on the fine-tuned Bert model in conjunction with the pairwise method. Finally, we do experiments to confirm that the proposed method outperforms several state-of-art baseline methods in legal case retrieval. Moreover, we applied our method in the Challenge of AI in Law competition in 2021 (CAIL 2021) and won a runner-up in the track of similar legal case retrieval.

Keywords: Legal case retrieval · Auxiliary learning · Ranking network · BM25 · BERT

1 Introduction

Legal case retrieval is an indispensable part of the judicial judgment process because it is essential for ensuring the similar judgment of similar cases to guarantee fairness and justice. A similar legal case retrieval system can significantly improve legal professionals' efficiency, providing them with solid support for realising similar judgments for similar cases, and further promoting the research and development of intelligent legal systems.

Some legal case retrieval systems employ the method of word-to-word matching. For example, Zhong *et al.* [20] proposed a word-to-word match model for similar legal case retrieval. They define the most similar case as the one that can match as many keywords as possible and exhibiting as few redundant keywords as possible. Their model is based a logic argumentation theory and so can

© The Author(s), under exclusive license to Springer Nature Switzerland AG 2022
G. Memmi et al. (Eds.): KSEM 2022, LNAI 13369, pp. 534–546, 2022.
https://doi.org/10.1007/978-3-031-10986-7_43

explain the most case it retrieves. However, the methods of this kind may not be able to find the case which does not have the searching words but which context meaning is exactly what the searcher wants.

Therefore, many researchers study how to use semantics in similar legal case retrieval. For example, Ranera *et al.* [14] used document embedding techniques to calculate the semantic similarity between cases. Hong *et al.* [7] proposed the semantic text matching model for similar case retrieval. It uses pre-training language model BERT [4] as the encoding layer to capture long-range dependencies in a case document.

Dhanani, Mehta, and Rana [5] proposed a graph clustering based model for similar legal case retrieval. It first forms clusters of referentially similar case judgments and then find semantically similar cases within the clusters. However, few of them consider the semantics of the entire court judgment of a case in similar case retrieval.

To the end, in this paper, we propose a BERT-based method for legal case retrieval. Specifically, we first use BERT as an encoder to extract the semantics of the judgment document of a case. We fine-tune BERT using Legal Case Retrieval Dataset (LeCaRD) from the Challenge of AI in Law competition in 2021 (CAIL 2021) [11]. Each piece of data we use consists of two parts: query and 100 case candidates. A query contains the description features of a case query and the corresponding accusation. Normally BERT is for bi-classification. However, we add an extra task of learning four-classification during fine-tuning BERT so that we can capture more semantics of a judgment document.

Next, we train a case rank model. Before the training, we use BM25 method [15] to choose the top 30 cases from each piece of data we utilise in the LeCaRD dataset. Then we pair any two of the top 30 cases corresponding to the same query (*i.e.*, a pair of the cases means that one case is more similar to the case description of the same case than the other). Sequentially, we input each pair to the fine-tuned BERT and then output it to a multi-layer neural network to train a case rank model.

The main contributions of this paper are as follows:

1. We propose a joint learning approach by integrating pointwise with an auxiliary learning approach to learn a classification model that can utilise the semantic information of legal texts to rank the case candidates for a query.
2. We analyse the LeCaRD dataset and construct inputs to BERT using different features targeted according to the characteristics of the legal text in the LeCaRD dataset. Our experiments show that using different features to construct inputs to BERT can improve the effectiveness of our entire model.
3. We propose a cascade architecture of recall and ranking the case candidates of a query. The architecture is an integration of the BM25 information retrieval method with BERT and a multi-layer neural network. Our experiments show that such architecture can significantly improve the efficiency of legal case retrieval.

4. We applied our method in the Challenge of AI in Law competition in 2021 (CAIL 2021) and won a runner-up in the track of similar legal case retrieval.[1]

The rest of the paper is organised as follows. Section 2 briefs related work. Section 3 presents the definition of our problem and the overall architecture of our model. Section 4 discusses fine-tuning BERT for our purpose. Section 5 explains our ranking model. Section 6 details the joint-learning part of our model. Section 7 experimentally evaluate our model against several state-of-art baseline methods. Finally, Sect. 8 concludes this paper with future work.

2   Related Work

Information Retrieval (IR) is a fundamentally important research area in this era of information overload. Therefore, researchers proposed many models for IR in various domains, such as justice, e-commerce, healthcare, and finance. Recently, similar case retrieval in the judicial domain has received increasing attention from researchers.

There are mainly two categories of IR models. 1) *Traditional IR models.* They include vector space models (*e.g.*, VSM [16]), probabilistic retrieval models (*e.g.*, BM25 [15]), and statistical language-based models (*e.g.*, LMIR [18]). However, these models ignore the semantic information of the text, so their performance is limited. 2) *Advanced models for IR.* They mainly include machine learning-based models [9], deep learning [17], and pre-training-based models [21].

The machine learning-based IR models mainly Learn To Rank (LTR) candidates to a query, including pointwise, pairwise and listwise [9]. The pointwise method transforms the ranking task into multiple classifications or regression problems. The pairwise method turns the task into a document pair classification problem. The listwise method reconstructs a query and its answer candidate set to a list of feature vectors.

With the rapid development of deep learning, researchers have developed many deep learning IR models. For example, Pathak, Pakray, and Das [13] propose an LSTM neural network [6] based model for math IR. LSTM [6] to model text sequences to capture the text's global semantic information. However, most deep learning models can only model short documents. In other words, it is hard for them to capture the global semantic information of a long document and are more suitable for IR concerning short documents. It is hard to use them for legal case retrieval tasks because judicial decisions are often long (over 3,000 words).

Currently, pre-training models have attracted significant attention in the whole field of Natural Language Process (NLP). For example, BERT [4] achieves state-of-the-art results in 11 NLP tasks. However, in legal case retrieval, few studies use pre-trained models to model relationships between long texts of judicial cases, especially for Chinese legal case retrieval. Therefore, legal case retrieval is a crucial and worthwhile research topic. The task of legal case retrieval involves

---

[1] https://weibo.com/ttarticle/x/m/show/id/2309404708913139548514?
_wb_client_=1.

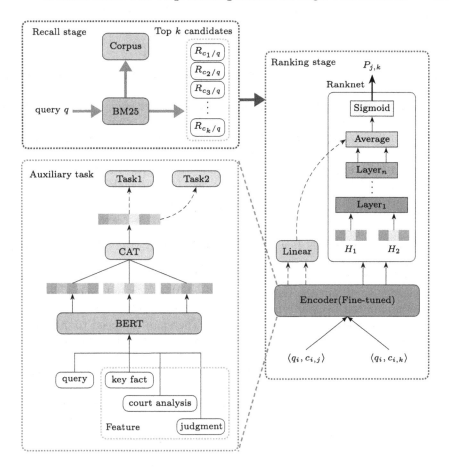

Fig. 1. The architecture of the two-stage ranking

a lot of expertise, such as the logical method of case description, professional terminology. Therefore, it is incredibly challenging to obtain global semantic information about long text cases and model their relationships. That is what we make a great effort to do in this paper.

3   Overview

This section will presents the definition of similar case retrieval problem and the overall architecture of our model for similar case retrieval.

In general, legal case retrieval filters the case candidates similar to a given query from a pool of case candidates and ranks them according to similarity to the case description of the query. Formally, given a case query q and a case candidate set $C = \{c_i \mid i = 1, \cdots, n\}$ then similar case retrieval is to retrieve the most similar case from C by ranking them. That is, for query q, let the ranking of case candidate $c_i \in C$ be $R_{c_i/q}$, the most similar case is

$$c_{*/q} = \arg\max\{R_{c_i/q} \mid c_i \in C\}. \tag{1}$$

Figure 1 shows the architecture of our model. We first use a multi-task learning method to fine-tune the Bert model (*i.e.*, the auxiliary task in Fig. 1). We then use the BM25 method to filter out top k similar cases (*i.e.*, the recall stage in Fig. 1) and build pairwise pair $\langle q, c_i, c_j \rangle$, using BERT as an encoder to obtain a deep semantic representation of $\langle q, c_i, c_j \rangle$. Compared with deep learning networks, the conventional BM25 method has the advantages of stability, efficiency and high recall rate. So, we use the method to increase the recall rate in the recall stage. Finally, we train a ranking model (*i.e.*, the ranking stage in Fig. 1).

4   Fine-Tuning BERT

This section will discuss how to fine-tuning the pre-trained language model BERT for our purpose.

To make our case ranking model more stable and accurate, we need a reliable encoder to obtain the semantic representation of a judgement document. After studying the LeCaRD dataset, we find that a query and its similar case candidates are diverse in case descriptions. Therefore, we need to measure the similarity between them by their semantics. Thus, our model needs to learn the deep semantic representation of a judgement document and use the semantic information to calculate the similarity. Unfortunately, traditional models such as BM25 that need to match words cannot compute their similarity accurately. In contrast, the BERT model, pre-trained with a large amount of text, can act as a reliable encoder. So, to obtain the semantic representation of the text in judicial cases, we use the LeCaRD dataset to fine-tune BERT.

Specifically, we input BERT the case description paragraphs from each query case and the key information of each case candidate (such as the basic case situation, the analysis process of the decision and the verdict result from the candidate case). Formally, the input can be defined as

$$\langle Q, C^{jk} \rangle = \{(q_i, \{(c_{i,j}^1, c_{i,j}^2, c_{i,j}^3) \mid 1 \le j \le m\}) \mid 1 \le i \le n\}, \tag{2}$$

where n is the total number of query cases in the dataset and m is the total number of case candidates corresponding to each query.

The output of BERT is the deep semantic vector representations. Formally, we have

$$(H^{(1)}, H^{(2)}, H^{(3)}) = \text{BERT}(\langle Q, C^{jk} \rangle), \tag{3}$$

where the vector representations $H^k \in \mathbb{R}^{n \times d}$ ($1 \le k \le 3$).

Then we concatenate the three vector representations and input them into two fully connected layers for auxiliary task learning of bi-classification and multi-classification. Formally, the predicted value of bi-classification or multi-classification is given by

$$\hat{y} = \text{Softmax}(W_h^T \cdot CAT(H^{(1)}, H^{(2)}, H^{(3)}) + b_h), \tag{4}$$

where $W_h \in \mathbb{R}^{3 \times H^k}$ and b_h is the bias term.

Meanwhile, we use focal loss [8] as the objective function (which reflects cross-entropy loss) to solve the class imbalance problem between samples. Formally, it is defined as follows:

$$\mathcal{L}(\widehat{y}) = -\alpha(1 - \widehat{y})^\gamma \cdot \ln \widehat{y}, \tag{5}$$

where α and γ are two weighted hyper parameters. For the multi-classification task, we set

$$\alpha_x = \frac{1}{\ln(1.10 + class(x))}, \tag{6}$$

where x is a certain class and $class(x)$ denotes the proportion of the number of samples of class x to the total number of samples.

5   Case Candidate Ranking

The previous section's BERT model that we fine-tuned does not compare which case candidate is more similar to the query case. So we need a ranking model for this task. This section will explain the model.

Inspired by Burges *et al.* [1], we design a multi-layer neural network as a ranking model called Ranknet. Formally, for an query q_i in the query set $Q = \{q_1, \cdots, q_n\}$, let its case candidate set be $C_i = \{c_{i,1}, \cdots, c_{i,m}\}$. For $c_{i,j}, c_{i,k} \in C_i$ ($1 \le i \le n$, $1 \le j, k \le m$, and $j \ne k$), we define

$$c_{i,j} \succeq c_{i,k} \tag{7}$$

if and only if $c_{i,j}$ is more similar to q_i than $c_{i,k}$. Let the vector representation of $c_{i,j}$ as $H_{i,j} \in \mathbb{R}^d$.

When training the ranking model, we input $H_{i,j}$ into the neural network to learn the ranked distribution representation. The neural network layers are as follows:

$$L^{(1)} = \rho(W_0^T \cdot H_{i,j} + b_0), \tag{8}$$

where $L^{(1)}$ denotes the vector representation after learning by the neural network, ρ is an activation function that we use LeakyReLu to implement, $W_0 \in \mathbb{R}^d$ is a weight matrix, and b_0 is the bias term. We can further learn the ranking distribution by stacking multiple neural network layers as follows:

$$L^{(k'+1)} = \rho(W_{k'}^T \cdot L^{k'} + b_{k'}), \tag{9}$$

where k' is the number of neural network layers and $L^{(0)} = H_{i,j}$. Finally, we use a fully connected layer to obtain the similarity score.

The loss function of the ranked network is defined as the cross-entropy loss to fit the true and predicted probability distributions:

$$\mathcal{L} = -\bar{P}_{j,k} \ln P_{j,k} - (1 - \bar{P}_{j,k}) \ln(1 - P_{j,k}), \tag{10}$$

where $P_{j,k} = P(c_{i,j} \succeq c_{i,k})$ denotes the predicted probability of relevance (*i.e.*, the probability that $c_{i,j}$ is more similar to q_i than $c_{i,k}$), and $\bar{P}_{j,k}$ is given by

$$\bar{P}_{j,k} = \begin{cases} 1 & \text{if } s_j > s_k, \\ 0.75 & \text{if } s_j = s_k, \\ 0.5 & \text{otherwise,} \end{cases} \tag{11}$$

where s_j and s_k denote the true correlation scores of $c_{i,j}$ and $c_{i,k}$, respectively.

6   Joint Training

This section will detail the joint-learning part of our model.

The fine-tuned BERT is trained jointly with ranking network, and each pair of case candidates is input, as a sample, into the BERT model to obtain a deep semantic vector representation as follows:

$$H_j, H_k = \text{Encoder}(\langle q_i, c_{i,j}, c_{i,k} \rangle). \tag{12}$$

For H_j and H_k, we first input them to the fully connected layer and the softmax layer to obtain the initial scores $I_j^{(l)}$ and $I_k^{(l)}$.

Then we input them into our ranking model Ranknet and get the score that $c_{i,j}$ is similar to q_i and the score that $c_{i,k}$ is similar to q_i as follows:

$$S_j^{(l)}, S_k^{(l)} = \text{Softmax}(\text{Ranknet}(H_j, H_k)), \tag{13}$$

where $l \in \{0, 1\}$. That is, $S_j^{(0)}$ is the score that $c_{i,j}$ is dissimilar to q_i and $S_j^{(1)}$ is the score that $c_{i,j}$ is similar to q_i. Similarly, we can understand $S_k^{(0)}$ and $S_k^{(1)}$.

Finally, the model predicts the probability that $c_{i,j}$ is more similar to q_i than $c_{i,k}$ as follows:

$$P_{j,k} = P(c_{i,j} \succeq c_{i,k}) = \frac{1}{1 + e^{-\theta(A_j^* - A_k^*)}}, \tag{14}$$

where θ represents the parameter to be learned and

$$A_j^* = \frac{1}{2}\left(I_j^{(1)} + S_j^{(1)}\right) - \frac{1}{2}\left(I_j^{(0)} + S_j^{(0)}\right), \tag{15}$$

$$A_k^* = \frac{1}{2}\left(I_k^{(1)} + S_k^{(1)}\right) - \frac{1}{2}\left(I_k^{(0)} + S_k^{(0)}\right). \tag{16}$$

7   Experiments

This section will focus on the evaluation experiments of the model, involving the dataset used, the evaluation criteria and the experimental details. The task of our system is to find cases similar to a query case from the candidate pool.

Table 1. Dataset statistics of LeCaRD. Avglen is the abbreviation of average length. Pair* denotes the number of $\langle q_i, c_{i,j}, c_{i,k} \rangle$.

Query number	Case number	Query Avglen	Case Avglen	Pair*
107	10,718	445	6,319	30,885

7.1 Datasets

The dataset we use in our evaluation experiments is LeCaRD [11]. It contains 107 query cases divided into two types: 77 common ones and 30 controversial ones. Each query case corresponds to a pool of 100 case candidates. The degree of similarity between a query and a case candidate takes the value in $\{0, 1, 2, 3\}$ (the more similar, the higher the value). Table 1 shows the dataset statistics of LeCaRD.

Notably, in the experiments, we first use the BM25 model to recall the top 30 cases from the 100 case candidates of each query case, then use the recalled case to construct 30,885 tuples of $\langle q_i, c_{i,j}, c_{i,k} \rangle$.

7.2 Baseline Methods

To evaluate the performance and stability of our models, we compare our model with the following state-of-art models:

- BM25 [15] and LMIR [18]: They are classical information retrieval models based on bag-of-words and widely used in information retrieval.
- BERT-wwm-ext [2]: It is a Chinese pre-training model based on the original BERT structure and trained with a larger corpus and Whole Word Masking (WWM) generation strategy, which can capture word-level and sentence-level representations.
- OpenCLaP [19]: It is a multi-domain Chinese pre-training model developed by the Institute of Artificial Intelligence of Tsinghua University. Its advantage is that it uses 6.63 million criminal law documents for pre-training based on BERT-base [4], which is very effective in criminal law.
- RoBERTa [3]: We use the Chinese RoBERTa-wwm-ext version, which removes the Next Sentence Prediction (NSP) task and pre-trains with a whole word masking strategy compared to the original BERT. So, it significant outperforms BERT in several natural language processing tasks.
- Legal-RoBERTa [10]: It is a pre-trained model specifically applied to the Chinese judicial domain, with the main feature of using a Chinese legal corpus to continue pre-training the model on RoBERTa-wwm-ext checkpoints.

7.3 Experimental Detail

By studying dataset LeCaRD, we find that if the similarity between a query and its case candidate is high, the case description of the query is highly similar to

Table 2. The performance of multiple retrieval models on the test set

Model	P@5	P@10	MAP	NDCG@10	NDCG@20	NDCG@30
BM25	45.00	47.50	54.61	76.01	79.85	89.21
LMIR	53.00	49.00	55.96	77.88	81.52	90.48
BERT-wwm$_{ext}$	47.00	48.00	61.03	82.64	83.21	86.93
OpenCLaP	41.00	41.00	53.35	79.31	81.93	84.56
RoBERTa	43.00	40.50	54.61	73.35	76.79	80.27
Legal-RoBERTa	45.00	45.00	54.96	74.94	76.82	81.23
BM25+BERT-wwm$_{ext}$	47.00	47.90	60.12	84.50	87.38	93.51
BM25+OpenCLaP	41.00	41.00	52.16	81.12	86.22	92.17
BM25+RoBERTa	43.00	40.00	55.31	80.14	85.81	92.09
BM25+Legal-RoBERTa	45.00	45.00	56.04	82.74	86.50	92.44
Our model	**61.00**	**56.50**	**66.23**	**90.35**	**92.16**	**95.83**

that of the candidate. Therefore, in the recall stage, we input the case description of the query into the BM25 model to calculate the similarity degree between the query case and a case candidate, as shown in Fig. 1 (Recall stage). The legal case retrieval task requires us to accurately find the top N candidates, and we set $N = 30$ (the top 30 candidates for each query). In the recall stage, the recall rates of the training set and test set are 0.9804 and 0.985, respectively, which indicates that the BM25 model is well suitable for the recall task.

We use the PyTorch framework [12] to implement our model in the ranking stage. The first step is to fine-tune BERT as an encoder. The BERT used here is the BERT-large version [2], which is a variant of BERT (*i.e.*, its architecture is same as that of BERT, but it is pre-trained on the Chinese Wikipedia using the Whole Word Mask (WWM) strategy).

The maximum input length of BERT-large is 512 tokens, while the description text of a query or a case candidate is very long (their average lengths are 445 and 6,319, respectively). So we cannot input the entire content of the description text of a query or a case candidate into BERT-large for fine-tuning. Therefore, we set the maximum lengths of the case description of a query and that of its case candidate to 100 and 409, respectively; the maximum lengths of the criminal charge of a query and the court analysis of its case candidate case to 20 and 489, respectively; and the maximum length of the court judgement of a case candidate to 130, as shown in Fig. 1 (Auxiliary learning).

Specifically, first we use a single GPU (Tesla V100) for fine-tuning BERT-large. When fine-tuning, we use the BERTAdam optimiser and set the learning rate to $1e^{-5}$, the batch size to 16, gradient accumulation to 2, and epoch to 60. To prevent the model from overfitting, we stop training early if the F1 value on the validation set cannot be improved. Next, we use fine-tuned BERT as an encoder to train our ranking model Ranknet, a neural network with 17 layers in Linear, Dropout, and LeakyReLU. When training the network, we set the learning rate to $5e^{-4}$, batch size to 64, dropout to 0.2, and epoch to 60. We also

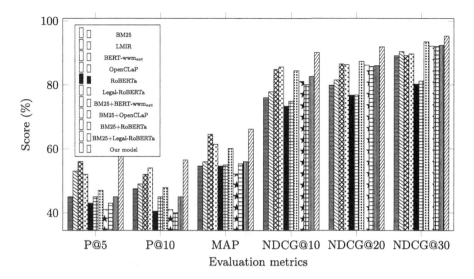

Fig. 2. The performance comparison of different retrieval models on the test set.

stop training earlier if we cannot the F1 value improved. In addition, to compare our model with the baselines fairly, we set the baseline models to the default parameters in the original paper or implementation and use the same training set and validation set to conduct experiments on the same GPU environment.

7.4   Evaluation Result

We benchmark our model against the baselines on the same LeCaRD test set according to the criteria of *precision* (*i.e.*, P@5, P@10, and MAP) and *ranking* (*i.e.*, NDCG@10, NDCG@20, and NDCG@30). Table 2 and Fig. 2 show the evaluation results. From the table and figure, we can see that our model significantly outperforms all the baseline models with a notable improvement. Besides, we also integrate BM25 with the pre-trained baseline model in the cascade architecture and benchmark with our model. The results of the experiments still show that our approach outperforms all the baseline models integrated with BM25.

We argue that our model outperforms the baselines for our model can recapture the semantics of case texts. The legal case retrieval task requires the model to predict the similarity of a query case and a case candidate. Therefore, the model needs to learn the semantic information of a case document at a more fine-grained and complete level. However, traditional models such as BM25 and LMIR cannot understand the semantic information of the text. Moreover, the pre-trained baseline models cannot read the full-text information due to the limitation of input tokens. So they can only obtain part of the information through truncation and summarisation, and so do not perform well on the test set.

Table 3. Ablation tests on the test set

Model	P@5	P@10	MAP	NDCG@10	NDCG@20	NDCG@30
Full model	**61.00**	**56.50**	**66.23**	**90.35**	**92.16**	**95.83**
-Feature+Auxiliary+Ranknet	49.00	43.00	59.62	82.70	87.42	93.41
+Feature-Auxiliary+Ranknet	56.00	52.00	63.36	88.35	91.04	95.07
+Feature+Auxiliary-Ranknet	60.00	52.50	63.07	88.80	91.43	95.23

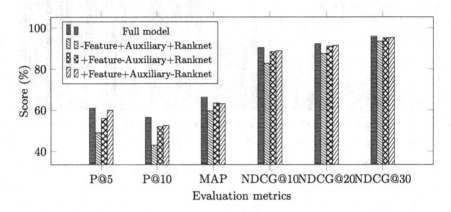

Fig. 3. Ablation test on the test set

7.5   Ablation Experiment

We also investigate the effects of different components of our model on similar case retrieval through a series of ablation experiments. We use the same parameter settings and the same experimental environment based on BERT-large in all these experiments. Table 3 and Fig. 3 show the experimental results From there, we can see: 1) for the model without component Feature (*i.e.*, case features), its evaluation results of various criteria drop a lot; 2) for the model without component Auxiliary (*i.e.*, the use of auxiliary learning to fine-tune BERT), its results drop by about 1%; and 3) for the model without Ranknet (*i.e.*, case candidate ranking network), the model dropped by about 0.6%. In conclusion, the experiment shows that each component of our method is necessary in similar case retrieval and significantly improves its performance.

8   Conclusions

Similar case retrieval is essential for legal practice. This paper presented a BERT-based approach for Chinese legal case retrieval. Specifically, we first used the well-known BM25 ranking function to narrow the search range. Then we fine-tuned a BERT model to get semantic information of case texts. Finally, we trained a multi-layer neural network to rank case candidates for a query. We conducted extensive experiments on a public dataset called LeCaRD dataset and showed that our approach outperforms two classical methods and four pre-trained methods. In addition, we applied our method to the Challenge of AI in Law competition in 2021 (CAIL 2021) and won a runner-up in the track of similar legal case retrieval (just slightly worse than the champion). In the future, it is worth adopting a more efficient approach to extract the complete information of long legal texts and improve the accuracy of the ranking of case candidates.

Acknowledgment. This work was supported by the National Natural Science Foundation of China (No. 61762016) and the Graduate Student Innovation Project of School of Computer Science and Engineering, Guangxi Normal University (JXXYYJSCXXM-2021-001).

References

1. Burges, C., et al.: Learning to rank using gradient descent. In: Proceedings of the 22nd International Conference on Machine Learning, pp. 89–96 (2005)
2. Cui, Y., Che, W., Liu, T., Qin, B., Wang, S., Hu, G.: Revisiting pre-trained models for Chinese natural language processing. In: Proceedings of the 2020 Conference on Empirical Methods in Natural Language Processing, pp. 657–668 (2020)
3. Cui, Y., Che, W., Liu, T., Qin, B., Yang, Z.: Pre-training with whole word masking for Chinese BERT. IEEE/ACM Trans. Audio Speech Lang. Process. **29**, 3504–3514 (2021)
4. Devlin, J., Chang, M.W., Lee, K., Toutanova, K.: BERT: Pre-training of deep bidirectional transformers for language understanding. In: Proceedings of the 17th Annual Conference of the North American Chapter of the Association for Computational Linguistics: Human Language Technologies, vol. 1, pp. 4171–4186 (2019)
5. Dhanani, J., Mehta, R., Rana, D.: Legal document recommendation system: a cluster based pairwise similarity computation. J. Intell. Fuzzy Syst. **41**(5), 5497–5509 (2021)
6. Hochreiter, S., Schmidhuber, J.: Long short-term memory. Neural Comput. **9**(8), 1735–1780 (1997)
7. Hong, Z., Zhou, Q., Zhang, R., Li, W., Mo, T.: Legal feature enhanced semantic matching network for similar case matching. In: Proceedings of 2020 International Joint Conference on Neural Networks, pp. 1–8 (2020)
8. Lin, T.Y., Goyal, P., Girshick, R., He, K., Dollár, P.: Focal loss for dense object detection. In: Proceedings of the IEEE International Conference on Computer Vision, pp. 2980–2988 (2017)
9. Liu, T.Y.: Learning to rank for information retrieval. Found. Trends® Inf. Retriev. **3**(3), 225–331 (2009)
10. Liu, Y., et al.: RoBERTa: a robustly optimized BERT pretraining approach. arXiv preprint arXiv:1907.11692 (2019)
11. Ma, Y., et al.: LeCaRD: a legal case retrieval dataset for Chinese law system. Inf. Retrieval **2**, 22 (2021)
12. Paszke, A., et al.: Pytorch: an imperative style, high-performance deep learning library. Adv. Neural. Inf. Process. Syst. **32**, 8026–8037 (2019)
13. Pathak, A., Pakray, P., Das, R.: LSTM neural network based math information retrieval. In: Proceedings of the Second International Conference on Advanced Computational and Communication Paradigms, pp. 1–6 (2019)

14. Ranera, L.T.B., Solano, G.A., Oco, N.: Retrieval of semantically similar Philippine supreme court case decisions using Doc2Vec. In: Proceedings of 2019 International Symposium on Multimedia and Communication Technology, pp. 1–6 (2019)

15. Robertson, S.E., Walker, S.: Some simple effective approximations to the 2-Poisson model for probabilistic weighted retrieval. In: Proceedings of the 17th Annual International ACM SIGIR Conference on Research and Development in Information Retrieval, pp. 232–241 (1994)

16. Salton, G., Buckley, C.: Term-weighting approaches in automatic text retrieval. Inf. Process. Manag. **24**(5), 513–523 (1988)

17. Soni, S., Roberts, K.: An evaluation of two commercial deep learning-based information retrieval systems for COVID-19 literature. J. Am. Med. Inform. Assoc. **28**(1), 132–137 (2021)

18. Zhai, C., Lafferty, J.: A study of smoothing methods for language models applied to ad hoc information retrieval. ACM Spec. Interest Group Inf. Retriev. **51**(2), 268–276 (2017)

19. Zhong, H., Zhang, Z., Liu, Z., Sun, M.: Open Chinese language pre-trained model zoo. Technical report, Tsinghua University (2019). https://github.com/thunlp/openclap

20. Zhong, Q., Fan, X., Luo, X., Toni, F.: An explainable multi-attribute decision model based on argumentation. Expert Syst. Appl. **117**, 42–61 (2019)

21. Zou, L., et al.: Pre-trained language model based ranking in Baidu search. In: Proceedings of the 27th ACM SIGKDD Conference on Knowledge Discovery & Data Mining, pp. 4014–4022 (2021)

Towards Explainable Reinforcement Learning Using Scoring Mechanism Augmented Agents

Yang Liu, Xinzhi Wang$^{(\boxtimes)}$, Yudong Chang, and Chao Jiang

School of Computer Engineering and Science, Shanghai University, Shanghai, China
{lliuyang,wxz2017,cydshu,superjiang}@shu.edu.cn

Abstract. Deep reinforcement learning (DRL) is increasingly used in application areas such as medicine and finance. However, the direct mapping from state to action in DRL makes it challenging to explain why decisions are made. Existing algorithms for explaining DRL policy are posteriori, explaining to an agent after it has been trained. As a common limitation, these posteriori methods fail to improve training with the deduced knowledge. Face with that, an end-to-end trainable explanation method is proposed, in which an Adaptive Region Scoring Mechanism (ARS) is embedded into DRL system. The ARS explains the agent's action by evaluating the features of the input state that are most relevant action before DRL re-learn from task-related regions. The proposed method is validated on Atari games. Experiments demonstrate that agent using the explainable proposed mechanism outperforms the original models.

Keywords: Deep reinforcement learning · Explainable AI · Adaptive region scoring mechanism

1 Introduction

In recent years, deep reinforcement learning (DRL) has achieved unprecedented success in many practical applications [5]. DRL models train agents that process continuous input information from the environment to learn and implement a policy that maximizes the expected returns. This structure has proven to be very effective. Unfortunately, both deep learning and reinforcement learning are poorly explainable. It is not easy to understand how decisions are made, what information is used, and why mistakes are made, all of which are necessary for many real-world application fields, such as finance, medical care, and robotics. This motivates the design of explainable DRL agents and modifying existing architectures for easier explanation.

Conventional DRL algorithms have low explainability and process state features uniformly at the beginning of training, which prevents the agent from focusing on valuable features quickly. Researchers have noticed that the human

© The Author(s), under exclusive license to Springer Nature Switzerland AG 2022
G. Memmi et al. (Eds.): KSEM 2022, LNAI 13369, pp. 547–558, 2022.
https://doi.org/10.1007/978-3-031-10986-7_44

visual system cannot perceive and process all visual information presented at once. Instead, we selectively focus on different parts of the visual input to collect relevant information sequentially and attempt to combine each step of information over time to construct an abstract representation of the entire input [11]. The emergence of a saliency map [8,10] proves that the deep learning model will focus particular attention on a specific area when making decisions rather than treating all input information equally. Part of the interpretive approach shifts from trying to explain models that have been trained toward building models that are self-explanatory [10]. First, self-explanatory methods can be embedded in DRL models to generate saliency maps that relate to decisions generated during the decision-making process without additional supervision. Second, since the explanation is generated within the model, the agent can optimize the DRL agent according to the explanation information it has generated during the training process.

When faced with large-scale or high-dimensional state-space tasks, DRL agents can use a convolutional neural network (CNN) to extract the features of the image state and then train the model on the extracted information through reinforcement learning. However, the knowledge acquired by the agent consists of all the features of the whole original image. The model cannot focus on valuable feature information, and some critical information is lost in the forward propagation process [9]. The same weight is applied to calculating each feature image, but some features play a vital role in the image description, and the traditional CNN algorithm cannot fully use key features at the beginning of training. This paper proposes an evaluation mechanism to explain an agent's decision and help the agent focus on features with high policy value. This mechanism enables the agent to learn the optimal policy accurately and quickly.

Inspired by the popularity of saliency map, a method called *Adaptive Region Scoring* (ARS) is proposed to improve both the explainability and performance of the DRL agent. The ARS method changes the architecture of the feature extractor by incorporating a scoring module between each convolution layer. The ARS generates the score maps by evaluating the task-related regions in the state. The score maps can then be integrated to reveal how an agent makes decisions. In addition, ARS merges the score maps with the original state representations to optimize the training process.

The main contributions of this paper are highlighted as follows:

- A method is proposed to explain the actual rationale used in inference for decision-making by generating score maps. We can understand how the agent solves the task by analyzing the resulting score maps.
- The score maps are incorporated with the original unweighted representation of states, forcing the agent to focus on task-related information, which can effectively improve policy learning of the agent system.
- Experiments are conducted on the Atari platform. The experimental results show that the ARS module can effectively improve policy learning. In contrast, previous posterior explanation approaches do not improve performance.

2 Preliminaries

The standard DRL setting, where an agent learns to solve a sequential decision problem, is modeled as a Markov decision process (MDP), which can be denoted as $(\mathcal{S}, \mathcal{A}, \mathcal{P}(s, s'), r_a(s, s'), \gamma)$. Here, $\mathcal{S}$ is a finite set of states, $\mathcal{A}$ is a finite set of actions, $\mathcal{P}$ is the unknown state-transition probability function, $r_a(s, s')$ is the immediate reward associated with taking action $a \in \mathcal{A}$ while transitioning from state $s \in \mathcal{S}$ to $s' \in \mathcal{S}$, and $\gamma \in [0, 1]$ is the discount factor that represents a tradeoff between maximizing immediate returns versus future returns. The goal of the agent is to identify a policy π to maximize its expected reward, where the cumulative return at each time step is:

$$R_t = \sum_{\tau=t}^{\infty} \gamma^{\tau-t} r_\tau \tag{1}$$

The purpose of policy gradient algorithms is to maximize the cumulative expected rewards $L = \mathbb{E}[\sum_t r(s_t, a_t)]$. The most commonly used gradient of objective function L with baseline can be written in the following form:

$$\nabla_\theta L = \int_S \mu(s) \int_A \nabla_\theta \pi_\theta(a|s) A(s, a) \tag{2}$$

where $\mathcal{S}$ denotes the set of all states and $\mathcal{A}$ denotes the set of all actions. $\mu(s)$ is an on-policy distribution over states. π is a stochastic policy that maps state $s \in \mathcal{S}$ to action $a \in \mathcal{A}$, and A is an advantage function.

Gradient-based actor-critic methods split the agent into two components: an actor that interacts with the environment using policy $\pi_\theta(a|s)$ and a critic that assigns values to these actions using value function $V_\theta(s)$. Both the policy and the value function are directly parameterized by θ. The policy and value function is updated through gradient descent:

$$\theta_{t+1} = \theta_t + \nabla_{\theta_t}(a_t|s_t) A_t(a_t|s_t) \tag{3}$$

The advantage function represents how good a state-action pair is compared with the average value of the current state, $A(a|s) = Q(a|s) - V(s)$. The most commonly used technique for computing the advantage function is generalized advantage estimation (GAE) [6]. One very common style that can be easily applied to A2C or any policy-gradient-like algorithm is:

$$A_t(a_t|s_t) = r_t + \gamma r_{t+1} + \dots + \gamma^{T-t+1} r_{t+1} + \gamma r^{T-t} V_{s_T} - V(s_t) \tag{4}$$

where T denotes the maximum length of a trajectory but not the terminal time step of a complete task, and γ is a discounted factor. If the episode terminates, we only need to set $V(s_t)$ to zero, without bootstrapping, which becomes $A_t = R_t - V(s_t)$. To ensure exploration early, the entropy regularization term H is introduced into the policy gradient:

$$\theta_{t+1} = \theta_t + \nabla_{\theta_t} log \pi_{\theta_t}(a_t|s_t) A_t + \beta \nabla_{\theta_t} H(\pi_{\theta_t}(s_t)) \tag{5}$$

where β is a hyperparameter that discounts the entropy regularization.

3   Proposed Method

This section proposes and provides a comprehensive description of our novel ARS algorithm. Traditional DRL agents rely on convolution and fully connected components to process input information step by step. This structure does not help people understand how the agents make decisions, what information they use, and why they make mistakes, nor can it enable agents to make a timely modification of their decisions based on the explanation information. First, the ARS evaluates the action of agents and output explanation that humans understand easily. Second, the agents utilize the evaluation results to modify their actions to focus on task-related information.

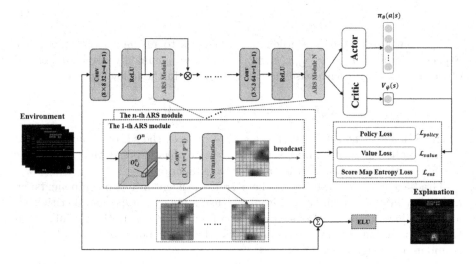

Fig. 1. Overview of the proposed method.

3.1   Model Overview

The complete architecture is illustrated in Fig. 1. Our image encoder Ψ_θ is a three-layer CNN interleaved with ReLU activation functions. The inputs to the channel are the images where the preprocessing procedure follows [1] and hence consists of a sequence of 4 frames stacked together, where each frame is 84×84 in grayscale. We use 4 frames because a single image state in an Atari game is non-Markovian. For example, the direction of an object's movement is ambiguous if we only see a single frame. As a built-in module, ARS calculates importance scores for state sub-regions based on the results of each convolutional layer. The results can be incorporated to generate saliency maps. Each score map is combined with the original state representation, forcing the agent to focus on task-relevant sub-regions during strategy learning.

The policy network π_θ and value network V_θ are encoded by multi-layer perceptron (MLP) with parameter θ. The policy network is a 3-layer MLP with a size of 64 for both hidden layers and a ReLU activation function. The output layer of the policy network has 16 units, producing the mean and the standard deviation for each action dimension. Before executing an action in the environment, a Tanh activation function is applied to enforce action bounds in the range of $[-1, 1]$. The value network is represented as a 2-layer MLP that outputs a scalar value specifying the corresponding value of a state. The value network uses a hidden layer size of 128 units with a ReLU activation function.

3.2   Adaptive Region Scoring Mechanism

At each time step t, an observation $s_t \in \mathbb{R}^{H \times W \times C}$ (here a sequence frames stacked together of height H and width W) is passed through the image encoder Ψ_θ with parameters θ. The visual frame s_t is fed into the model and aims to predict the action a ($a \in \mathcal{A}$) taken by the agent. Our motivation is that the agent should focus on the most relevant part of the observation, which is controllable by the agent, to be able to classify the actions.

We determine whether each region in a $H \times W$ grid is useful for predicting the agent's action. The feature map $O^n = \psi_\theta^n(O^{n-1}) \in \mathbb{R}^{h^n \times w^n \times c^n}$ is computed based on the observation s_t ($O^0 = s_t$), where ψ_θ^n is the n-th convolutional layer of Ψ_θ, $n \in N$ represents the serial number of the ARS module, $O^n \in \mathbb{R}^{h^n \times w^n \times c^n}$ is the n-th feature map, c^n denotes the size of the channel dimension and h^n, w^n denotes the height and width dimensions. We estimate a set of feature vectors, denoted $O_{i,j}^n \in \mathbb{R}^{c^n}$, for action classification from each grid cell (i, j) of the convolutional feature map. The feature map are converted to $h^n \times w^n$ vectors in which each vector has c^n dimension as follows:

$$O^n = [O_{1,1}^n, O_{1,2}^n, ..., O_{i,j}^n, ..., O_{h^n,w^n}^n], O_{i,j}^n \in \mathbb{R}^{c^n} \qquad (6)$$

where $O_{i,j}^n$ corresponds to the features extracted by ψ_θ^n at different image regions. Then, tensor O^n is fed to the n-th ARS model to compute a score map that describes the importance of the state feature vector at the corresponding location. In other words, the input frame is divided into $h^n \times w^n$ regions, and the ARS mechanism attempts to score their relevance.

The ARS module takes the n-th convolution features O^n as input to derive the score maps $m^n \in \mathbb{R}^{h^n \times w^n}$ as:

$$\begin{aligned} m^n &= Q_\rho^n(O^n | W_\rho^n, B_\rho^n) \\ &= [m_{1,1}^n, m_{1,2}^n, ..., m_{i,j}^n, ..., m_{h^n,w^n}^n], m_{i,j}^n \in \mathbb{R} \end{aligned} \qquad (7)$$

where W_ρ^n and B_ρ^n are parameters for the calculation, and function Q_ρ^n includes one convolution calculation with an 1×1 kernel whose stride is set to be 1. Each element in m^n corresponds to a spatial position on O^n and describes the importance of the image feature vector at that position. The score maps m^n are then passed to the normalization layer to generate a meaningful probability distribution over $h^n \times w^n$ regions. In the experiment, the softmax function is used to implement the normalization layer. Let p^n be denoted as the final probability distributions after normalizing m^n, which can be considered as the amount of the importance of the corresponding vector $m_{i,j}^n$ among of $h^n \times w^n$ vectors in the input image:

$$p^n = \frac{exp(m_{i,j}^n)}{\sum_{i',j'} exp(m_{i',j'}^n)},$$

$$= [p_{1,1}^n, p_{1,2}^n, ..., p_{i,j}^n, ..., p_{h^n,w^n}^n], p_{i,j}^n \in [0,1] \tag{8}$$

where $p^n \in \mathbb{R}^{h^n \times w^n}$ is the counterpart of the learned probability distributions. The ARS module attempts to identify which regions of $O_{i,j}^n$ are important for the agent in taking action. The degree of correlation between regions and decisions is described by an probability of importance score $p_{i,j}^n$, where $p_{i,j}^n \in [0,1]$ denotes the correlation of regions (i,j) of $O_{i,j}^n$ for the agent taking action. A higher value indicates that regions (i,j) of O^n is more important for the agent when taking action.

The score map p^n is used to visualize the decision-making basis of the agent. The probability p^n should be high only on regions (i,j) that are predictive of the agent's actions. The resulting score map p^n can be bilinearly extrapolated to the size of the input state s_t to obtain $\hat{p}^n$, which can then be overlaid on top of the state to produce a high-quality heatmap that indicates regions that motivate the agent to take action. Let s_{ARS}^a be denoted as the final heatmap that indicates relevant regions that indicate regions that motivate the agent to take action a, $\hat{p}^n$ be the converted score map for state s_t in module n. The state is then weighted by the score map and passes through an Exponential Linear Unit (ELU) activation function to produce a high-quality heatmap, which can be denoted as:

$$s_{ARS}^a = \frac{1}{N} ELU(\sum_{n=1}^{N} \hat{p}^n \cdot s_t) \tag{9}$$

where $\hat{p}^n$ has values in the range $[0,1]$ with higher weights corresponding to a stronger response to the input state. The ELU function has been chosen in favour of the ReLU due to the dying ReLU effect. A visual representation of this process is depicted in Fig. 3.

The score map p^n can evaluate which positions in the current state representation are important. The representation $O_{i,j}^n$ are linearly combined using the score probabilities $p_{i,j}^n$, each score map p^n is broadcast along the channel dimension of tensor O^n and point-wise multiplied to produce the next result tensor $\hat{O}^n \in \mathbb{R}^{h^n \times w^n \times c^n}$, which can be described as:

$$\hat{O}^n = p^n \cdot O^n \tag{10}$$

The agent can learn to emphasize the high-scoring part of the input frame based on the given state. Note that the ARS model is fully differentiable, which allows training the system in an end-to-end manner. After the score map linearly weights the feature map vector set, the new vector set replaces the original vector set. At this time, the agent will focus on the information of value from the feature map to strengthen the influence of important features on the subsequent training. This operation forces the agent system to locate the object of interest, and then the final convolution features O^N for consecutive frames are fed into different multi-layer perceptron (MLP) to derive $V_\theta(s_t)$ and $\pi_\theta(a_t|s_t)$:

$$V_\theta = MLP_{value}(O^N) \in \mathbb{R} \tag{11}$$

$$\pi_\theta = softmax(MLP_{policy}(O^N) \in \mathbb{R}^{|\mathcal{A}|}. \tag{12}$$

3.3   Training

The model is optimized with the standard cross-entropy loss $\mathcal{L}_{action} = \mathbb{E}[\mathcal{L}_{policy} + \mathcal{L}_{value}]$ with respect to the ground-truth action $a^* \in \mathcal{A}$ that the agent actually has taken. The cost function $\mathcal{L}_{action}$ is based on:

$$\mathcal{L}_{policy} = -log\pi_\theta(a_t|s_t)(R_t^n - V_\theta(s_t)) - \alpha\mathcal{H}_t(\pi_\theta) \tag{13}$$

$$\mathcal{L}_{value} = \frac{1}{2}(V_\theta(s_t) - R_t^n)^2 \tag{14}$$

$$\mathcal{H}_t(\pi_\theta) = -\sum_a \pi_\theta(a|s_t)log\pi_\theta(a|s_t) \tag{15}$$

where $R_t = \sum_{-=0}^{n-1}\gamma^i r_{t+i} + \gamma^n V_\theta(s_{t+n})$ is the n-step bootstrapped return and α is a weight for the standard entropy regularization loss term $\mathcal{H}(\pi_\theta)$. According to this formulation, the score map P^n should be high only on regions (i, j) that are predictive of the agent's actions. Our formulation enables learning to localize related regions in a self-supervised manner without any additional supervisory signal.

Here, we adopt a few additional objective functions. We encourage the score map to attain a high entropy by including a score entropy regularization loss, $\mathcal{L}_{ent} = -\sum_n^N \mathcal{H}(P^n)$. This term penalizes overconfident score maps, making the scores closer to uniform whenever actions cannot be predicted, and allows the model to learn from unseen observations even when the score fails to perform well at first. The entire training objective becomes:

$$\mathcal{L}_{all} = \mathcal{L}_{action} + \lambda_{ent}\mathcal{L}_{ent} \tag{16}$$

where λ_{ent} is a mixing hyperparameter.

4   Experiments and Results

In this section, we conduct experiments to evaluate the explanations and performance of the proposed method. We trained the agent system with an A2C algorithm on the Atari platform. The following subsections will cover details about the environment and results.

Table 1. Hyperparameters of the experiments.

Hyperparameter	Value	Hyperparameter	Value
Activation function	ReLU	Number of parallel environments	16
Roll-out Steps	5	Max grad norm	0.5
Optimizer	RMSprop	Value loss coefficient	0.5
Entropy coefficient	0.01	GAE coefficient	0.95
Seeds	[10,100]	Total frames	20000000

4.1 Settings

The proposed algorithm was tested on environments provided by the OpenAI Gym library [12], specifically their NoFrameskip-V4 versions, which are very challenging for reinforcement learning and provide a wide range of interesting games that are useful as a standard test for evaluating the proposed algorithms. The agent uses the game coding interface provided by the Gym platform to obtain the dynamic pictures and scores to self-learn the game. To evaluate the performance and verify that our algorithm can easily explain the agents, we conducted experiments on 6 Atari games: Phoenix, Alien, Breakout, Seaquest, Beamrider, Frostbite, MsPacman, and SpaceInvaders. All baseline agents were trained using the publicly available code for A2C with the same hyperparameters and model details. Details on the hyperparameter settings are shown in Table 1.

To extract convolutional features, we used three stacks of convolutions plus ReLU activation layers with filters 32 8×8, 64 4×4, and 64 3×3 and strides 4, 2, and 1. For the preprocessing step, we followed[4], in which each frame is converted from RGB format into single-channel grayscale and downsampled from a resolution of 210×160 to 84×84 via bilinear interpolation. In this way, to prevent causing loss of information, the computational resources and duration of the network training were reduced. At each time step, four consecutive preprocessed frames were stacked along the channel dimension as input. During the training, rewards were clipped in the range of $[-1, 1]$. To ensure stable learning, gradients were clipped to a value of 0.5, the discount factor was set to $\gamma = 0.99$, and the networks were trained for 2 million frames. All network weights were updated by the RMSProp optimizer with a decay factor of 0.95 and momentum of 0.1. The learning rate was 0.0002. Advantage actor-critic used entropy regularization with weight 0.01. Training and testing for all the games were performed with the same network architecture and hyperparameters.

4.2 Performance

For each environment, the agent was trained with different random seeds. We recorded a smoothed curve for the agent's episode rewards during training. The reward curves in Fig. 2 show the mean score at every timestep. Experience was collected in 16 threads that were executed 5 steps at a time under default hyperparameters, for a total of 80 environment frames between agent updates. We reported the average score across 100 test episodes for the final performance evaluation.

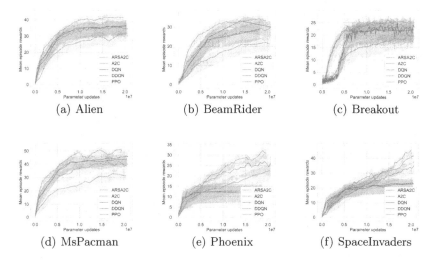

Fig. 2. Reward curves during training. Cumulative reward comparison on 6 Atari tasks.

Figure 2 shows the reward curves obtained during training. From these plots, it can be seen that our ARS-A2C architecture, which is the baseline model with an extra scoring module, performs well, while the A2C architecture achieves worse rewards. Experimental results show that the ARS scoring module improves the performance of the A2C algorithm. As the figure shows, the ARS-A2C algorithm has a better learning effect than the A2C algorithm at the early stage of training. The ARS-A2C agent can quickly obtain high scores, and its learning performance tends to be stable and improves in later training. There is little difference between the ARS-A2C algorithm and the A2C algorithm in the early stage of training. However, as the training stage increases, the average reward value of the ARS-A2C algorithm gradually exceeds that of the A2C algorithm, which proves that the ARS-A2C algorithm still has better learning performance than the A2C algorithm. We conclude that the ARS module helps the agent focus on the important regions of the input image by scoring the regions, which avoids incurring a higher calculation cost to process parts with low policy value. Therefore, in the subsequent training process, there will be no significant variance. The change in the shaded area of the curve shows that ARS-A2C is better than A2C in learning performance and obtains a more minor variance when converging, which alleviates the volatility problem of the A2C algorithm to a certain extent.

For comparisons, we use DQN [5], DDQN [3], A2C [4] (both with separate and shared actor-critic networks), and PPO [7] algorithms. Table 2 shows that ARS-A2C achieves better performances than other algorithms for all 6 games. Compared with the best score of other algorithms, ARS-A2C achieves 7.0% point improvement on Alien, 9.5% point improvement on Beamrider, 4.2% point improvement on Breakout, 32.5% point improvement on MsPacman, and 3.5% point improvement on Phoenix, 9.5% point improvement on SpaceInvaders.

Table 2. Performance comparison on 6 Atari tasks.

Environment	Random	DQN	DDQN	PPO	A2C	ARS-A2C
Alien	240	2391	2041	1970	2091	**2560**
BeamRider	264	3627	3172	2750	3164	**3975**
Breakout	3	518	520	417	435	**542**
MsPacman	150	3180	2960	2350	2880	**4215**
Phoenix	440	10840	12250	20840	22530	**23340**
SpaceInvaders	120	3929	3672	4855	4673	**5320**

The ARS explains the agent through the scoring mechanism and stabilizes the training process to some extent. The learning performance of the agent with ARS is better than the other algorithms, which proves that ARS can help the agent process the game state information more accurately so that the agent can make the optimal decision more quickly and efficiently.

4.3 Explanations

Although score maps may not explain the entire decision-making process, they reveal some of the strategies used by the agent. To visualize the score map, we displayed the original input frame and overlaid the score map, producing bright areas indicating high scores and darker areas indicating low scores. Furthermore, the range of score values indicated that as the training process proceeded, the weight of the score graph for areas unrelated to the reward goal became very close to zero, meaning that little information was "mixed" in these areas during the summation process in Formula 10. The general pattern we observed is that agents learned to focus on task-related regions in the scene. This usually means that the agent received higher value rewards from the relevant region, which is essential in calculating the value function.

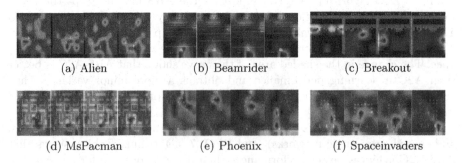

(a) Alien   (b) Beamrider   (c) Breakout

(d) MsPacman   (e) Phoenix   (f) Spaceinvaders

Fig. 3. Game explanations. Areas related to the agent for decision making are shown by adding the information from the scores map to the image, red regions corresponds to high score while blue corresponds to low. (Color figure online)

The score maps reflect the agent's degree of attention to each area when making decisions, including strengthening the tracking of targets and focusing on multiple targets, which can help the agent better understand the spatial information from the state input. Agents that have received ARS feedback also show a higher level of ability in a multi-target environment. As shown in Fig. 3(f) and Fig. 3(b), the agent determines whether the shield is protecting it by focusing on the area above the spacecraft and firing at the enemy. Figure 3(e) shows the ability of an agent trained using ARS to focus on multiple enemies in the environment; the agent is concerned about the enemy plane and making life and death decisions in the environment. Figure 3(d) and Fig. 3(a) show the ARS-A2C agent's score for its nearby environment. Figure 3(c) shows the agent repeatedly orienting the ball to part of the brick wall in order to pass through it through the tunnel.

The proposed method focuses on improving the ability of the agent to process the input information. The ARS module scores the state, which is then combined with the original input to produce a more meaningful state embedding so that the agent can better understand the current input. This ability to better understand input states allows the agents to make more informed decisions, which is essential for any reinforcement learning task.

5 Conclusion

This paper explains the DRL model from the perspective of a built-in explainer and explores how to use the explanation to improve the model's performance. An end-to-end trainable explanation method based on the A2C algorithm is proposed, in which an Adaptive Region Scoring mechanism is embedded into the agent. The proposed ARS approach embeds explainability into the agent system, achieving clear information visualization and excellent performance. Experimental results show that the model with the ARS outperformed the baseline model in various environments. In addition, the agent with ARS is proven to be capable of easily generating explanations, providing value for real-world applications. In future work, we plan to use a post-hoc explanation method to optimize the agents, and it will be interesting to integrate our ARS module with other DRL models, such as SAC [2] and Proximal Policy Optimization [7].

Acknowledgement. This work is sponsored by Shanghai Sailing Program (NO. 20YF1413800).

References

1. Brockman, G., et al.: OpenAI gym. arXiv preprint arXiv:1606.01540 (2016)
2. Haarnoja, T., Zhou, A., Abbeel, P., Levine, S.: Soft actor-critic: off-policy maximum entropy deep reinforcement learning with a stochastic actor. In: International Conference on Machine Learning, pp. 1861–1870 (2018)

3. van Hasselt, H., Guez, A., Silver, D.: Deep reinforcement learning with double Q-learning. In: Proceedings of the Thirtieth AAAI Conference on Artificial Intelligence, pp. 2094–2100 (2016)
4. Mnih, V., et al.: Asynchronous methods for deep reinforcement learning. In: International Conference on Machine Learning, pp. 1928–1937 (2016)
5. Mnih, V., et al.: Human-level control through deep reinforcement learning. Nature **518**(7540), 529–533 (2015)
6. Schulman, J., Moritz, P., Levine, S., Jordan, M.I., Abbeel, P.: High-dimensional continuous control using generalized advantage estimation. In: 4th International Conference on Learning Representations (2016)
7. Schulman, J., Wolski, F., Dhariwal, P., Radford, A., Klimov, O.: Proximal policy optimization algorithms. arXiv preprint arXiv:1707.06347 (2017)
8. Simonyan, K., Vedaldi, A., Zisserman, A.: Deep inside convolutional networks: visualising image classification models and saliency maps. arXiv preprint arXiv:1312.6034 (2013)
9. Wang, X., Sugumaran, V., Zhang, H., Xu, Z.: A capability assessment model for emergency management organizations. Inf. Syst. Front. **20**(4), 653–667 (2018)
10. Wang, X., Yuan, S., Zhang, H., Lewis, M., Sycara, K.P.: Verbal explanations for deep reinforcement learning neural networks with attention on extracted features. In: 28th IEEE International Conference on Robot and Human Interactive Communication, pp. 1–7 (2019)
11. Wang, X., Lian, L., Yu, S.X.: Unsupervised visual attention and invariance for reinforcement learning. In: IEEE Conference on Computer Vision and Pattern Recognition, pp. 6677–6687 (2021)
12. Wang, Z., Schaul, T., Hessel, M., Hasselt, H., Lanctot, M., Freitas, N.: Dueling network architectures for deep reinforcement learning. In: International Conference on Machine Learning, pp. 1995–2003 (2016)

ACRM: Integrating Adaptive Convolution with Recalibration Mechanism for Link Prediction

Thanh Le[1,2(✉)] , Anh-Hao Phan[1,2] , and Bac Le[1,2]

[1] Faculty of Information Technology, University of Science,
Ho Chi Minh City, Vietnam
{lnthanh,lhbac}@fit.hcmus.edu.vn
[2] Vietnam National University, Ho Chi Minh City, Vietnam

Abstract. Link prediction is one of the important tasks of knowledge graphs. Recently, some convolutional models inherited from computer vision have shown many advantages over other methods. The convolution-based method is capable of exploiting the full interactions between entities and relations. However, the feature maps between channels generated from the convolution step are independent, and each channel operating on the local receptacle cannot use context information outside the local receptacle. Therefore, we propose a combined ACRM model based on adaptive convolution and recalibration mechanism. This idea is inherited from ConvR model. We evaluated our proposed model on standard benchmark datasets and achieved improved results compared to baseline models for the link prediction task. Especially those datasets with no inverse relation test leakage. The experimental results show that the recalibration mechanism has improved the limitation of feature maps in convolutional neural models. In addition, we also show the convergence of the loss value during training and demonstrate the model's ability to predict the head and tail entities on common evaluation metrics.

Keywords: Knowledge graph embedding · Link prediction · Representation learning · Convolutional neural network · Recalibration mechanism

1 Introduction

Knowledge graphs (KGs) have become the primary resource for building artificial intelligence applications including natural language understanding, recommender systems, question answering. Recently, some knowledge bases, such as Freebase [1], YAGO [2], and DBpedia [3], have been built on the events that happen in life. However, these datasets still face some problems such as a lack of information about vertices, and lack of link information. As a result, the use of these KGs encountered some challenges and affected the performance of the models. Therefore, among these problems, we are interested in the task of predicting missing links in KGs.

© The Author(s), under exclusive license to Springer Nature Switzerland AG 2022
G. Memmi et al. (Eds.): KSEM 2022, LNAI 13369, pp. 559–570, 2022.
https://doi.org/10.1007/978-3-031-10986-7_45

A typical knowledge graph is a multi-relational graph consisting of nodes linked together through edges. Nodes represent entities and edges represent relations. From a different perspective, they are represented as triples (subject, relation, object) denoted as (s, r, o), e.g., *(Leonardo_da_Vinci, author_of, Mona_Lisa)*. Since there are millions of such triplets in KGs, we have to deal with their completeness and need to add new knowledge to the real world.

Link prediction is a phrase introduced to overcome these problems. Its goal is to predict the existence of relations between entities. In order for models to learn data from the knowledge graph, they replace the relation of each triple with all possible relations to obtain the samples in the KGs. Then, they determine whether the new triple is valid via the scoring function. Most of the current research to solve the link prediction are based on the knowledge graph embedding (KGE). KGE is the process of embedding KG components (including entities and relations) into a continuous low-dimensional vector space to simplify operations while preserving the inherent structure of KGs.

The approaches in the KGE for the link prediction include translation-distance-based, semantic information-based, and neural network-based models. Translation-distance-based and semantic information-based methods are simple, easy to train, and get good results. However, the efficiency is not high compared to the neural network-based method. Recently, convolutional neural networks (CNNs) have been proposed to capture the expressive features with parameter efficient operators. Hence, automatically learning through neural networks offers many important advantages. However, these CNN-based models have some limitations as follows: (i) the interaction between input entities and relations has not been exploited sufficiently. (ii) Processing of feature maps is limited. (iii) Convolutional layers are not diverse. Therefore, in this paper, we proposed an improvement that uses the relation as a filter instead of a global filter and operates the recalibration mechanism to solve the interdependence problem between channels.

In summary, the main contributions are as follows:

- We propose ACRM model inspired by the recalibration mechanism applied in ConvR. The experiments on the standard benchmark datasets show that the proposed model improved compared to the ConvR model.
- The recalibration mechanism effectively improves feature maps between channels that cannot utilize the context information outside the local receptive field.
- The further evaluation indicated that the size of the filters has little effect on the model's performance.

The rest of the paper consists of four sections. Section 1 summarizes related work in link prediction. The next section describes our proposed model in detail. Experiments and performance comparisons with baseline models are mentioned in the Sect. 3. Finally, we conclude and give future research directions.

2   Related Work

KGE models to solve the link prediction are described in this section. We list well-known models in each branch and point out their strengths and weaknesses.

Typical models such as TransE [4] and its variants (e.g. TransD [5], STransE [6], TransF [7]) have been proposed to solve the link prediction. These models usually use distance-based functions to define the scoring function. The advantages of these models are that they are easy to train, contain a small number of parameters, and can scale up to large graphs. However, it has many limitations on the imbalance between the types of relations and also does not accurately generalize the actual knowledge. Another approach is the semantic information-based method. These methods use similarity-based functions to define scoring functions for traditional semantic matching models, e.g. Distmult [9], ComplEx [10], HolE [11]. The benefit is the ability to continuously mine deeper semantic information, including path information, entity type, and context information. Nevertheless, this exploitation makes the model more complex, and the effect is not really significant.

With the strong development of neural networks in many fields, they are recently applied in the link prediction on KGs. In general, the neural network-based models achieve good results. ConvE [12] is the first model in this branch that uses 2D convolutional layers. Experimental analysis has shown that 2D convolution outperforms 1D convolution in terms of extracting interactions between entities and relations. By using multiple layers of non-linear features, ConvE has demonstrated expression and extensibility in large KGs. However, it can not capture the global relational features, and the model loses translational properties when reshaping embedding entities and relations. HypER [13] is suggested to avoid specifically implying any fixed 2D structure during the embedding. It utilizes a specific 1D relational filter to handle object embedding, which helps the model simplify interactions between entities and relations. The disadvantage of HypER is that it does not maximize these interactions.

Recently, ConvR [14] was proposed to solve the problem of full interaction. Instead of using global filters like ConvE, ConvR uses relations into filters of the same size, and the vector representation of the subject entity is provided as input to the convolution layer. Through this adaptive convolution, all generated features can capture entity-relation interactions. However, the problem of neural network-based models is that feature maps between the channels are independent, and each of them operates on the local receptive field which cannot utilize the context information outside the local receptive field [8]. Hence, it affects the performance of the model. For this reason, in this work, we propose to operate the recalibration mechanism to ConvR model to tackle these problems.

3   Proposed Model

Before going into detail, we restate the problem with fundamental concepts. Given a knowledge graph $G = (s, r, o) \subseteq E \times R \times E$ denotes a collection of triples, where E is the set of entities and R is the set of relations. Each triple has s as the subject entity, o as the object entity, and a relation r linking between the two entities s and o. The main idea of the model consists of two parts: the adaptive convolution and the recalibration mechanism. Figure 1 provides the illustration of this architecture.

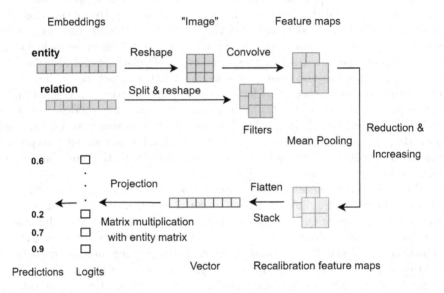

Fig. 1. The architecture of the ACRM model.

In our proposed model named ACRM, the subject entity embedding is reshaped into a 2D matrix. The relation embedding is split and reshaped into filters in the first step. In the next step, the 2D matrix is used as the input for the convolutional layers to obtain feature maps. In the third step, the feature maps through the recalibration mechanism obtain the same size recalibration feature maps. Then, the recalibration feature map is vectorized and projected into a k-dimensional space. Finally, the result matches all candidate object embeddings.

3.1 The Adaptive Convolution

Instead of global filters, the adaptive convolution step uses relations as filters. This process maximizes the interactions between entities and relations. Given the input triplet (s, r, o), the embedding vectors $\mathbf{e_s}, \mathbf{e_o} \in \mathbb{R}^{d_e}$ and $\mathbf{r} \in \mathbb{R}^{d_r}$ are generated through mapping two entities s, o and the relation r, where d_e and d_r are the embedding sizes of entities and relations. The embedding vector $\mathbf{e_s}$ is then reshaped into a 2D matrix $\mathbf{S} \in \mathbb{R}^{d_e^h \times d_e^w}$, where $d_e = d_e^h d_e^w$. The embedding vector $\mathbf{r}$ is splitted into c matrices of equal size $d_r^h \times d_r^w$, where $d_r = c d_r^h d_r^w$, which is used as a 2D convolution filter $\mathbf{R}^{(i)} \in \mathbb{R}^{d_r^h \times d_r^w}$. Specifically, c is the number of filters, i is the index of filter, d_r^h and d_r^w are the height and width of the filter. In the next step, the matrix $\mathbf{S}$ is put into the convolutional layers $\mathbf{R}$. The convolution process is illustrated in Fig. 2.

After convolution of 2D matrices, each filter $\mathbf{R}^{(i)}$ is applied to create a corresponding feature map $\mathbf{C}^{(i)} \in \mathbb{R}^{(d_e^h - d_r^h + 1) \times (d_e^w - d_r^w + 1)}$, and calculated as follows:

$$c_{m,n}^{(i)} = f \left(\sum_{j,k} s_{m+j-1,n+k-1} \times r_{j,k}^{(i)} \right) \tag{1}$$

where m,n-th entry is the index of the 2D feature map, and $f\,(.)$ is a non-linear function ReLU [15].

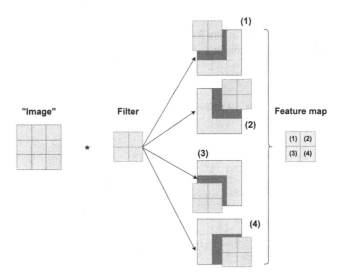

Fig. 2. The illustration of the convolution process.

3.2   The Recalibration Mechanism

With the recalibration mechanism, feature maps between channels can utilize the context information outside the local receptive field. Given the feature maps $\mathbf{C}$ obtained from the convolution, they are compressed through an aggregation operation that computes the averages for the patches, known as mean pooling. A set of channel descriptions of feature maps $\mathbf{Z} = [z_1, z_2, ..., z_n]$ is calculated as follows:

$$z_i = \frac{1}{h' \times w'} \sum_{a=1}^{h'} \sum_{b=1}^{w'} c_{a,b}^{(i)} \tag{2}$$

where z_i represents the global average information of the feature map c_i, h' and w' are the size of the feature maps. This information is then simply controlled through the reduction and increasing operation. Feature weights are given by:

$$\mathbf{U} = \sigma(\mathbf{W_b}g(\mathbf{W_a Z})) \tag{3}$$

where $\mathbf{W_a}$ is a fully-connected reduction transformation matrix to merge feature maps information through channel descriptors $\mathbf{Z}$, $\mathbf{W_b}$ is a fully-connected increasing transformation matrix returning to the channel dimension of $\mathbf{C}$, $g(.)$ is a non-linear function ReLU, and $\sigma(.)$ is the sigmoid function used to learn weights from feature weights $\mathbf{U}$. As a result, the recalibration feature map is calculated by multiplying the original feature map by the feature weight:

$$\mathbf{V} = \mathbf{CU} = c_i \times u_i \tag{4}$$

where $\mathbf{V}$ represents recalibration feature maps, c_i is the feature map and u_i is the corresponding feature weights. The recalibration mechanism is illustrated in Fig. 3.

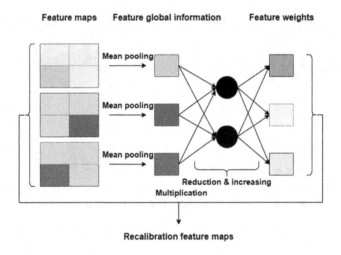

Fig. 3. The illustration for the recalibration mechanism.

3.3   The Integration for Link Prediction

The feature maps obtained from the adaptive convolution process as input to the recalibration mechanism to obtain the recalibration feature maps. For computing the triplet score $\psi(s, r, o)$, we flatten the recalibration feature maps $\mathbf{V}$ and stack them into a vector $\mathbf{y}$, which is then projected into $\mathbb{R}^{d_e}$ by a fully-connected layer, and matched with the object vector $\mathbf{e_o}$ with an inner product:

$$\psi(s,r,o) = f(\mathbf{Wy} + b)^{\top}\mathbf{e_o} \tag{5}$$

where $\mathbf{W} \in \mathbb{R}^{d_e \times c(d_e^h - h + 1)(d_e^w - w + 1)}$ and $b \in \mathbb{R}^{d_e}$ are parameters of the fully-connected layer, and $f(.)$ is a ReLU function. The 1-to-many scoring is involved to speed up training and evaluation for learning model parameters. Specifically, (s, r) is taken as input and scored against all objects $o \in E$ simultaneously. The sigmoid function $\sigma(.)$ is applied to calculate the score, which is $p_o^{s,r} = \sigma(\psi(s, r, o))$, and the cross-entropy loss function is given by:

$$\mathcal{L}(s,r) = -\frac{1}{|\varepsilon|} \sum_{o \in \varepsilon} q_o^{s,r} \log(p_o^{s,r}) + (1 - q_o^{s,r}) \log(1 - p_o^{s,r}) \tag{6}$$

where $q_o^{s,r}$ is a binary label. If (s, r, o) is a valid triple then $q_o^{s,r} = 1$, otherwise $q_o^{s,r} = 0$. During the training process, we use dropout to prevent overfitting. Batch normalization is applied to stabilize, normalize, and speed up the convergence of the model. We also use Adam [16] as the optimizer and label smoothing [17].

4 Experiments

4.1 Datasets and Baselines

To evaluate the performance of ACRM model in link prediction, four standard datasets including FB15k [4], WN18 [4], FB15k-237 [18], and WN18RR [12] are placed in the experiment.

FB15k is the subset of the Freebase dataset for generic facts. It has a total of 592,213 triplets with 14,951 entities and 1,345 relations. Similarly, FB15k-237 is also a subset of Freebase but inverse relations are removed to avoid test leakage. FB15k-237 includes 14,541 entities, 237 relations and a total of 310,116 triples.

WN18 is the subset of the WordNet dataset for lexical relations between words. It has a total of 151,442 triplets with 40,943 entities and 18 relations. Similarly, WN18RR is also a subset of Freebase but inverse relations are removed. WN18RR includes 40,943 entities, 11 relations and a total of 93,003 triples.

The baseline models employed for comparison include:

- Translation-distance-based methods: TransE [4], TransD [5], STransE [6].
- Semantic information-based methods: DistMult [9], ComplEx [10], HolE [11], CrossE [19].
- Neural network-based methods: R-GCN [20], ConvE [12], ConvR [14].

4.2 Experimental Setup

ACRM model is trained on an Intel i7-10700K (16) @ 5,100 GHz, Ubuntu 18.04.5 LTS operating system, and 8 GB NVIDIA GeForce RTX 3070 GPU. The source code is programmed based on Python language and PyTorch 3.7 library.

Parameter Settings. The details of the hyperparameters in our experiments are as follows: entity embedding size is taken at values $\{100, 200\}$; relation embedding size is based on number of filters $\{100, 150, 200\}$; size of filters $\{2 \times 2, 3 \times 3, 4 \times 4, 5 \times 5\}$; embedding dropout $\{0.0, 0.1, 0.2, 0.3\}$; feature map dropout and projection dropout $\{0.1, 0.2, 0.3, 0.5\}$. For each experiment, we train in 1000 epochs to find the best hyperparameter for each dataset. The batch sizes are $\{128, 256\}$, label smoothing coefficient and learning rate are both 0.1.

Based on the results obtained from the experiments, we give the optimal configuration for ACRM model by grid search method on each dataset, as shown in Table 1.

Table 1. The optimal configuration for ACRM model on four datasets, where d_e is the entity embedding size, c is the number of filters, $h \times w$ is the size of the filter, and p_1, p_2, p_3 are the input dropout, feature maps dropout, and hidden dropout respectively

Dataset	d_e	c	$h \times w$	p_1	p_2	p_3
FB15k	200	100	3×3	0.2	0.3	0.3
WN18	200	100	3×3	0.3	0.2	0.3
FB15k-237	100	100	5×5	0.3	0.2	0.3
WN18RR	200	200	3×3	0.2	0.2	0.5

Evaluation Protocal. We apply "filtered" setting to triples, in which the corrupted triples are removed from training, validation and test set. Common metrics including Mean Reciprocal Rank (MRR), Hits@k with k = 1, 3, 10 are used to evaluate models. MRR takes the average of the reciprocal rank assigned to the true triple and Hits@k calculates the percentage of triple cases that actually appear in the top k highest-ranked triples. The performance is better when these two measures are higher.

4.3   Results and Analysis

Experimental results on FB15k and WN18 datasets are shown in Table 2. Table 3 reports the results of FB15k-237 and WN18RR datasets. The results of the baseline models are taken from original studies. The ConvR model is reprogrammed and retrained because the entity-relation interaction of this model is better than that of its branch models, and the evaluation performance is good on standard datasets. The results in bold represent the best model in our comparison tables.

In Table 2, ACRM model archives a good performance compared to the baseline models on the FB15k and WN18. On FB15k dataset, ACRM achieved the best result on Hits@3 and Hits@10, and the second-best result on MRR and Hits@1 compared to the baseline models. For FB15k-237 and WN18RR in Table 3, results of our model have the best performance on all metrics. It proves that the interaction between the entity and the relation is maximized when we use adaptive convolution. The recalibration mechanism applied after the convolution step solves the problem that the feature maps between channels cannot use context information outside the local receptacle. In other words, the steps performed in the recalibration mechanism help the model to extract low-level features from neighborhoods. This mechanism also responds to the specificity of the channel dimension by modeling interdependencies across channels and improves the expressiveness of the network. Moreover, the overfitting is prevented during the training.

Table 2. Link prediction results on FB15k and WN18

Models	FB15k				WN18			
	MRR	Hits@1	Hits@3	Hits@10	MRR	Hits@1	Hits@3	Hits@10
TransE	0.380	0.231	0.472	0.641	0.454	0.089	0.823	0.934
TransD	–	–	–	0.773	–	–	–	0.922
STransE	0.543	–	–	0.797	0.657	–	–	0.934
DistMult	0.654	0.546	0.733	0.824	0.822	0.728	0.914	0.936
ComplEx	0.692	0.599	0.759	0.840	0.941	0.936	0.936	0.947
HolE	0.524	0.402	0.613	0.739	0.938	0.930	0.945	0.949
CrossE	0.728	0.634	0.802	–	0.830	0.741	0.931	–
ConvR	**0.770**	**0.706**	0.814	0.880	0.950	0.945	0.953	0.958
R-GCN	0.696	0.601	0.760	0.842	0.814	0.686	0.928	0.955
ConvE	0.657	0.558	0.723	0.831	0.943	0.935	0.946	0.956
ACRM (ours)	0.767	0.700	**0.816**	**0.883**	**0.950**	**0.946**	**0.954**	**0.958**

In addition to comparing the proposed model's performance, we also experiment with loss and Hits@10 values on standard datasets. The results are shown in Fig. 4. In Fig. 4a, the loss values converge early around the 100th epoch on four datasets. These values decrease over epochs, which proves the model is efficient. The Hits@10 values in Fig. 4b converges quite early at about the 100th epoch.

To compare the performance based on the efficiency of the filter size, we experiment on two datasets, FB15k-237 and WN18RR. The results in Table 4 indicate that when increasing the filter size, the performance of ACRM model increases but not much on the FB15k-237 dataset. For WN18RR dataset, the best performance is shown in the filter size 3 × 3. Consequently, increasing or decreasing the filter size does not affect the model's performance much, but it helps the model to avoid the overfitting.

In Table 5, the training results show that the head entity prediction on the datasets has high performance. However, the tail entity prediction results have not achieved good results compared to the head entity prediction. The reason is that the interaction between the relations and the entities is not optimal.

Table 3. Link prediction results on FB15k-237 and WN18RR

Models	FB15k-237				WN18RR			
	MRR	Hits@1	Hits@3	Hits@10	MRR	Hits@1	Hits@3	Hits@10
TransE	0.257	0.174	0.284	0.420	0.182	0.027	0.295	0.444
TransD	–	–	–	–	–	–	–	–
STransE	–	–	–	–	–	–	–	–
DistMult	0.241	0.155	0.263	0.419	0.430	0.390	0.440	0.490
ComplEx	0.247	0.158	0.275	0.428	0.440	0.410	0.460	0.510
HolE	–	–	–	–	–	–	–	–
CrossE	0.299	0.211	0.331	0.474	–	–	–	–
ConvR	0.348	0.258	0.382	0.528	0.474	0.442	0.489	0.534
R-GCN	0.249	0.151	0.263	0.417	–	–	–	–
ConvE	0.325	0.237	0.356	0.501	0.430	0.400	0.440	0.520
ACRM (ours)	**0.35**	**0.26**	**0.382**	**0.535**	**0.475**	**0.444**	**0.490**	**0.539**

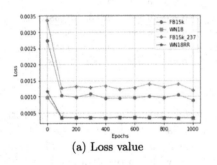

(a) Loss value

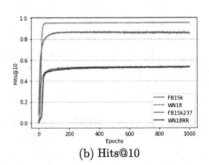

(b) Hits@10

Fig. 4. Loss value and Hits@10 after some epochs

Table 4. The influence of filter sizes on the performance on FB15k-237 and WN18RR datasets

Filter size	FB15k-237		WN18RR	
	MRR	Hits@10	MRR	Hits@10
2×2	0.347	0.529	0.468	0.533
3×3	0.349	0.530	0.475	0.539
4×4	0.348	0.534	0.473	0.535
5×5	0.350	0.535	0.474	0.534

Table 5. The head and tail entity prediction on datasets

Datasets	MRR		Hits@1		Hits@3		Hits@10	
	Head	Tail	Head	Tail	Head	Tail	Head	Tail
FB15k	0.791	0.742	0.726	0.674	0.842	0.79	0.907	0.859
WN18	0.95	0.949	0.946	0.945	0.953	0.954	0.958	0.958
FB15k-237	0.451	0.249	0.357	0.163	0.493	0.271	0.64	0.429
WN18RR	0.499	0.451	0.468	0.42	0.515	0.465	0.556	0.522

5   Conclusion

Deriving from advantages of the adaptive convolution and the recalibration mechanism, we proposed ACRM model to improve the performance in the link prediction on KGs. We aim to enhance the feature maps of CNN-based models because they could not use context information outside of the local receptive field. To tackle this issue, we integrate the recalibration mechanism into this architecture. Experiments on benchmark datasets achieve good results compared to baseline models shows that the recalibration mechanism works effectively. We also analyses the coverage and the influence of difference parameters. We recognized that ACRM model converges quite early and size of the filters has litter effect. Therefore, it can scale up to large KGs. However, the object representation in ACRM model can only interact with one hidden vector. It causes the model not to extract the information from other hidden vectors. In future work, we intend to create a more complex recalibration mechanism to mining the interaction between relations and entities better.

Acknowledgments. This research is funded by the University of Science, VNU-HCM, Vietnam under grant number CNTT 2022-2 and Advanced Program in Computer Science.

References

1. Bollacker, K.D., Evans, C., Paritosh, P.K., Sturge, T., Taylor, J.: Freebase: a collaboratively created graph database for structuring human knowledge. In: SIGMOD Conference (2008)
2. Suchanek, F.M., Kasneci, G., Weikum, G.: YAGO: a core of semantic knowledge. In: Proceedings of the 16th International Conference on World Wide Web, pp. 697–706, May 2007
3. Lehmann, J., et al.: DBpedia-a large-scale, multilingual knowledge base extracted from Wikipedia. Semant. Web **6**(2), 167–195 (2015)
4. Bordes, A., Usunier, N., Garcia-Duran, A., Weston, J., Yakhnenko, O.: Translating embeddings for modeling multi-relational data. In: Advances in Neural Information Processing Systems, vol. 26 (2013)

5. Ji, G., He, S., Xu, L., Liu, K., Zhao, J.: Knowledge graph embedding via dynamic mapping matrix. In: Proceedings of the 53rd Annual Meeting of the Association for Computational Linguistics and the 7th International Joint Conference on Natural Language Processing (Volume 1: Long Papers), pp. 687–696, July 2015
6. Nguyen, D.Q., Sirts, K., Qu, L., Johnson, M.: STransE: a novel embedding model of entities and relationships in knowledge bases. arXiv preprint arXiv:1606.08140 (2016)
7. Do, K., Tran, T., Venkatesh, S.: Knowledge graph embedding with multiple relation projections. In: 2018 24th International Conference on Pattern Recognition (ICPR), pp. 332–337. IEEE, August 2018
8. Li, Z., Liu, H., Zhang, Z., Liu, T., Shu, J.: Recalibration convolutional networks for learning interaction knowledge graph embedding. Neurocomputing **427**, 118–130 (2021)
9. Yang, B., Yih, W.T., He, X., Gao, J., Deng, L.: Embedding entities and relations for learning and inference in knowledge bases. arXiv preprint arXiv:1412.6575 (2014)
10. Trouillon, T., Welbl, J., Riedel, S., Gaussier, É., Bouchard, G.: Complex embeddings for simple link prediction. In: International Conference on Machine Learning, pp. 2071–2080. PMLR, June 2016
11. Nickel, M., Rosasco, L., Poggio, T.: Holographic embeddings of knowledge graphs. In: Proceedings of the AAAI Conference on Artificial Intelligence, vol. 30, no. 1, March 2016
12. Dettmers, T., Minervini, P., Stenetorp, P., Riedel, S.: Convolutional 2D knowledge graph embeddings. In: Proceedings of the AAAI Conference on Artificial Intelligence, vol. 32, no. 1, April 2018
13. Balažević, I., Allen, C., Hospedales, T.M.: Hypernetwork knowledge graph embeddings. In: Tetko, I.V., Kůrková, V., Karpov, P., Theis, F. (eds.) ICANN 2019. LNCS, vol. 11731, pp. 553–565. Springer, Cham (2019). https://doi.org/10.1007/978-3-030-30493-5_52
14. Jiang, X., Wang, Q., Wang, B.: Adaptive convolution for multi-relational learning. In: Proceedings of the 2019 Conference of the North American Chapter of the Association for Computational Linguistics: Human Language Technologies, Volume 1 (Long and Short Papers), pp. 978–987, June 2019
15. Krizhevsky, A., Sutskever, I., Hinton, G.E.: ImageNet classification with deep convolutional neural networks. In: Advances in Neural Information Processing Systems, vol. 25 (2012)
16. Kingma, D.P., Ba, J.: Adam: a method for stochastic optimization. arXiv preprint arXiv:1412.6980 (2014)
17. Szegedy, C., Vanhoucke, V., Ioffe, S., Shlens, J., Wojna, Z.: Rethinking the inception architecture for computer vision. In: Proceedings of the IEEE Conference on Computer Vision and Pattern Recognition, pp. 2818–2826 (2016)
18. Toutanova, K., Chen, D.: Observed versus latent features for knowledge base and text inference. In: Proceedings of the 3rd Workshop on Continuous Vector Space Models and Their Compositionality, pp. 57–66, July 2015
19. Zhang, W., Paudel, B., Zhang, W., Bernstein, A., Chen, H.: Interaction embeddings for prediction and explanation in knowledge graphs. In: Proceedings of the Twelfth ACM International Conference on Web Search and Data Mining, pp. 96–104, January 2019
20. Schlichtkrull, M., Kipf, T.N., Bloem, P., van den Berg, R., Titov, I., Welling, M.: Modeling relational data with graph convolutional networks. In: Gangemi, A., et al. (eds.) ESWC 2018. LNCS, vol. 10843, pp. 593–607. Springer, Cham (2018). https://doi.org/10.1007/978-3-319-93417-4_38

Bridging Signals and Human Intelligence
Log Mining-Driven and Meta Model-Guided Ontology Population in Large-Scale IoT

David Graf[1,2(✉)], Werner Retschitzegger[1], Wieland Schwinger[1], Elisabeth Kapsammer[1], and Norbert Baumgartner[2]

[1] Johannes Kepler University, Linz, Austria
{werner.retschitzegger,wieland.schwinger,elisabeth.kapsammer}@jku.at
[2] team Technology Management GmbH, Vienna, Austria
{david.graf,norbert.baumgartner}@te-am.net

Abstract. Large-scale Internet-of-Things (IoT) environments such as Intelligent Transportation Systems are facing tremendous challenges wrt. monitoring their operational technology (OT) not least due to its inherent heterogeneous and evolutionary nature. This situation is often aggravated by the lack of machine-interpretable information about the interdependencies between OT objects in terms of "semantic relationships", thus considerably impeding the detection of root causes of cross-system errors or interrelated impacts. Therefore, we propose a novel hybrid approach for identifying semantic relationships based on both, mined functional correlations between OT objects based on log files and domain knowledge in terms of an IoT meta model. For this, we firstly contribute a systematic discussion of associated challenges faced in large-scale IoT environments, secondly, we put forward an IoT meta model based on both, industry standards and academic proposals, and finally, we employ this meta model as guidance and target template for the automatic population of semantic relationships into an OT ontology.

Keywords: IoT · Operational Technology Monitoring · Hybrid Approach · OT Ontology Population · Intelligent Transportation Systems

1 Introduction

Operational Technology Monitoring. Large-scale *Internet-of-Things (IoT)* environments such as *Intelligent Transportation Systems (ITS)* are characterized by massive heterogeneities [11,21] of the underlying IoT-based Operational Technology (OT), due to different manufacturers, evolving standards, diverse capabilities and partly legacy components. Consequently, the monitoring of OT objects (e.g., video camera, traffic sensor), aka. *Operational Technology Monitoring (OTM)*,

This work is supported by: the Austrian Research Promotion Agency (FFG) under grant FFG Forschungspartnerschaften 874490 and by Erasmus+ under grant agreement No 2021-1-SI01-KA220-HED-000032218, project ID KA220-HED-15/21.

© The Author(s), under exclusive license to Springer Nature Switzerland AG 2022
G. Memmi et al. (Eds.): KSEM 2022, LNAI 13369, pp. 571–585, 2022.
https://doi.org/10.1007/978-3-031-10986-7_46

across different subsystems of an ITS (e.g., video system, tunnel control systems) is challenging. This is aggravated by the fact that the majority of historically grown and therefore rather isolated subsystems lack machine-interpretable information about the semantic of interdependencies between OT objects. This is, however, an indispensable prerequisite for efficient OTM allowing to automatically identify *root causes* of cross-system errors (e.g., communication hub failure leads to unreachable devices) or *interrelated impacts* (e.g., CO_2 sensor warning goes along with ventilation system start up) as well as for effective, e.g., predictive, maintenance strategies.

Hybrid Approach for OT Ontology Population. Defining all the semantic interdependencies on instance-level *manually*, is, however, not feasible for such large-scale systems due to the *sheer amount* of objects and its *omnipresent evolution* since objects and interdependencies are added, removed, and changed on a daily basis. Therefore, in our previous work [12,13] as a first step towards identifying these interdependencies, we proposed an automatic mining method focusing on identifying time-based functional correlations between pairs of OT objects (e.g., a sensor object is *functionally correlated* with a controller object) from log data comprising message streams of OT objects. Building on this work, we now put forward a dedicated approach for automatically instantiating semantic relationships (e.g., *isSensorFor* relationship between a sensor object and a controller object) based on mined functional correlations between OT objects by populating a corresponding OT ontology. Thereby, we adhere to a hybrid approach as also proposed in other domains like process mining [23], synergistically combining *"signal intelligence"* concealed in OT object's log data and *"human intelligence"* in terms of domain experts' apriori ontological knowledge about the environment under control.

Contribution and Paper Structure. paginationThe contribution of our paper is three-fold: Firstly, after elaborating on related work in Sect. 2, we discuss the complexity of real-world IoT environments and identify thereupon prevalent *challenges* throughout the process of mining interdependencies and the population of an OT ontology in Sect. 3. Secondly, in order to tackle these challenges, we elaborate a *meta model*, based on commonly used industry standards (*OPC-UA* [2]) and academic proposals (*IoT-O* [24]), comprising generic concepts for the IoT domain while at the same time allowing to plug-in further domain specific concepts in a framework-like manner in Sect. 4. Thirdly, we propose an *approach* exploiting the proposed meta model for the *automatic population of an OT ontology*, by instantiating semantic relationships between OT objects based on mined interdependencies and demonstrate the approach's applicability by means of *canonical semantic relationship patterns* prevalent in large-scale IoT systems in Sect. 5. Finally, we present evaluation details in Sect. 6 before discussing future work in Sect. 7.

2   Related Work

Addressing our primary goal namely populating an ontology with OT objects and their semantic relationships, closely related work can be found in the areas of (i) *IoT event log mining*, (ii) *organizational process mining*, (iii) *complex event (stream) processing*, as well as of course (iv) *ontology population* in various domains, which will be discussed in the following.

IoT Event Log Mining. Putting emphasize on the data characteristics of our work, [6] apply data mining techniques in order to enrich event log data, whereas [26] aim to mine patterns from semi-structured event logs. Both, however, focus on the enrichment of the log itself, rather than using logs for ontology population and further failure reasoning. Hromic et al. [15] transform air quality sensor data to a semantic representation, focusing in contrast to our approach, however, on the event data itself, rather than on the underlying resources, i.e., the individual sensors. Based on the correlation mined between events of a log, [25] determine dependencies between events among sensor data, whereas we focus on semantic relationships between OT objects.

Organizational Process Mining. Aiming to extract knowledge about underlying resources from event logs, promising mining approaches are reviewed by [19]. While most of them are widely similar to our approach, [8] discovers unknown dependencies in the medical domain, but in contrast to us, enriches the event logs themselves instead of populating a dedicated ontology.

Complex Event Processing. Regarding the streaming aspect in our application domain, the event-stream-based pattern matching approach [18] based on Allens interval-algebra [5] identifies temporal patterns rather than addressing the semantics of relationships. Endler et al. [9] transfer real-time sensor event data to a semantic model in terms of RDF triples, but, in contrast to our work, focus on context information of events, rather than deriving knowledge of underlying resources (OT objects and their semantic relationships).

Ontology Population in Various Domains. Regarding ontology population in various domains, [22] aims at populating a web service ontology using data-driven techniques such as clustering, however, primarily based on unstructured text documents rather than on semi-structured streaming data originating from event logs. This also applies to the work of [17] using semi-supervised classification to populate the content of text documents into an ontology. The approach of [7] populates an event ontology for monitoring vineyards grounded on a IoT sensor network aiming to mine causality relationships between events, instead of semantic relationships between IoT objects.

3   Ontology Population Challenges in Real-World IoT

This section systematically discusses ontology population challenges in real-world IoT from two different angles, firstly from the viewpoint of IoT data characteristics and - secondly - based on a brief summary of our functional correlation mining approach [12,13], from the perspective of deriving semantic relationships out of these rather basic functional correlations.

Challenges Arising from IoT Data Characteristics. The IoT-based ITS environment focused by our work, a national highway network, comprises *more than 1.000.000 OT objects* of more than 200 different objectTypes, ranging from simple sensors (e.g. CO_2-sensor) and actuators (e.g., traffic light) to more complex systems (e.g., a video system) consisting of many objects of various types, being geographically distributed over 2.220 highway kilometers and 165 tunnels. Information about the object's *states* (e.g., warnings & failures) and *services* (e.g., traffic jam detections) is provided in terms of several logs, recording a stream of ten thousands messages per hour, the amount being strongly dependent on the kind of object - some reporting regularly, some seldom, some never at all in the considered period of time. Thus, *available information in log files about certain objects is limited*, especially considering a rather short period of time. Another crucial challenge are potentially different OT objects reporting with different messages (often having different message texts) about the same event *redundantly* being the result of partly isolated sub-systems where OT objects themselves report about their states or getting reported about by monitoring agents. In addition challenging are potentially *unreliable timestamps* exhibiting different semantics and expressing a partial order, only, due to differences in recording time or transmission delays. Last but not least, OT objects repeatedly report via *duplicate* messages about the same event or even report *irrelevant messages*, which is due to their intended usage regarding (i) *which kind of* information is recorded about objects and underlying events since often model- or vendor-dependent, and (ii) *how* often such information is recorded.

Mining Functional Correlations at a Glance. In order to address these challenges, in our previous work [12,13], we put forward a message-driven approach for mining interdependencies in terms of so-called *functional correlations*, between OT objects based on log files as a first step towards automatically populating an OT ontology. Thereby, a functional correlation arises when (i) an OT object's proper functioning is impeded by the (failure) *state* of another OT object (e.g., network failure) or (ii) an OT object realizes together with another OT object a certain *service* (e.g., traffic monitoring). Functional correlations, in a nutshell, are calculated based on the so-called *z-score* [20] representing the statistical dependence of two objects within a certain period of time. This dependence results from the temporal co-occurrence of messages (based on a configurable time lag) reported about these two objects (e.g., a videoServer object failure will occur nearly simultaneously with a failure reported by a camera object connected thereto). Random co-occurrences are explicitly considered by the z-score allowing to quantify the likelihood of OT objects being functionally correlated (values between 0.0 and 1.0). Those functional correlations with a likelihood below a certain (use-case specific and configurable) threshold (e.g., likelihood threshold of 0.5) are excluded for further processing. Which crucial challenges arise from these functional correlations between objects, when being used to derive meaningful semantic relationships, is outlined in detail in the following.

Challenges Arising from Functional Correlations. paginationDue to their nature of solely being calculated on mere temporal co-incidence, functional correlations lack any further semantics. Thus, the challenges for a proper "semantification" of functional correlations are manifold, comprising the determination of the *underlying semantic relationshipType* (e.g., isSensorFor), a *possible direction* (e.g., isEnergyDependentOn from sensor to energySupplyObject) and whether there is just a *single* semantic relationship underlying a functional correlation or even *multiple ones* (e.g., isSensorFor and plausibilizes). Another crucial challenge is that *knowledge conflicts* have to be dealt with in case that certain mined functional correlations do not correspond to domain knowledge, representing either *false positives* or indicating unexpected system behavior, thus being non-conform to domain knowledge. Finally, since functional correlations consider pairs of OT objects, only, handling more coarse-grained relationship-patterns like, e.g., *transitivity* of semantic relationships (e.g., transitive relationship between sensor, actuator and controller in-between) also quite relevant in practice, is challenging.

Since objects are able to play different roles when interacting with other objects (e.g., an object's role naturally differs between providing sensor values and notifying about its energySupply status), a vital challenge is to correctly interpret the object's role within co-occurring events by determining the events' type. Thereby, the type of an event can be exploited indicating which specific semantic relationshipType is represented by a certain functional correlation.

As already mentioned, the information about interdependencies between OT objects which can be mined from log files is limited due to several reasons, ranging from the infrequent reporting nature of certain OTs (i.e., sparsity of messages) to a lack of integration of individual parts of OT (i.e., unmonitored areas). Thus, although there are functional correlations in real-world, they are not mineable from log files. Thus, the challenge is to deal with such "blind spots" by properly exploiting available domain knowledge in order to establish appropriate semantic relationships without having inductive knowledge about functional correlations.

Last but not least, two further challenges arise with respect to providing for trustworthiness in terms of traceability of functional correlations and their derived semantic relationships. Firstly, it is challenging to estimate the *quality of functional correlations* in the sense of trustworthiness of the instantiation of a certain semantic relationship. By its very nature that, the more often a certain functional correlation between two dedicated objects can be mined in a log stream, the higher is its quality and the resulting trustworthiness of the established semantic relationship, in contrast to a functional correlation being based on rare and divergent minings. Secondly, omnipresent evolution of (i) the real-world, i.e., underlying OT is changed on a daily basis, and of (ii) the virtual-world, i.e., learning progress about underlying OT objects and relationships while more data is processed, is challenging.

4   A Meta Model for OT Ontology Population

As a *central prerequisite* in order to address these challenges in terms of our
OT ontology population approach (cf. Sect. 5), we put forward an IoT meta
model (cf. Fig. 1) allowing the incorporation of domain knowledge in the entire
ontology population process. In other words, this meta model enables to bridge
the gap between *"signal intelligence"*, i.e., knowledge gained from data in terms
of functional correlations and *"human intelligence"*, i.e., knowledge gained from
domain experts in terms of T-Box information. In particular, it describes core
IoT concepts and their interdependencies in a generic way on both, instance-level
and type-level, using UML class diagrams as basic formalism.

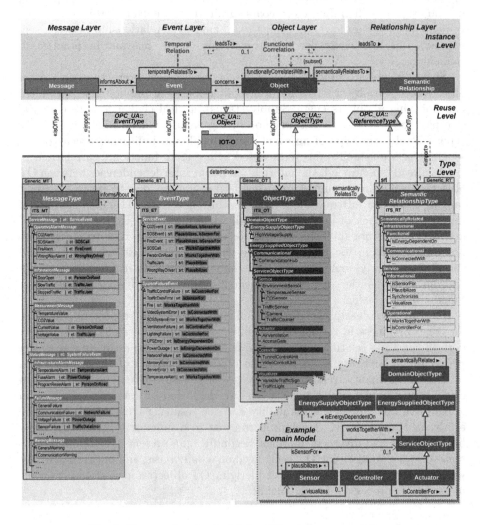

Fig. 1. Proposed meta model for OT ontology population

It serves as the central backbone of our ontology population approach and is used for the following purposes: Firstly, the instance-level concepts are, in terms of an ontology's A-Box, used as the target of our log-mining driven population approach as already mentioned in Sect. 3. Secondly, the type-level concepts are, in terms of an ontology's T-Box, used as a kind of template, further guiding the population approach by providing not only an extensive *generic type system*, but also packages of *domain-specific types* plugged in as subclasses. Based on the concepts of our meta model, a simple running example has been build up covering four IoT objectTypes as well as their basic semantic relationshipTypes (cf. bottom right of Fig. 1). The rationale behind the concepts contained in this meta model are manifold:

(1) The core *instance- and type-level* concepts covering *Message(Types)*, *Event(Types)*, *Object(Types)*, and *Relationship(Types)* are derived via subclassing from the *Open Platform Communications Unified Architecture (OPC UA)* [2], a widely used service-oriented, manufacturer and platform independent standard for industrial IoT applications, thus providing a solid basis for broad applicability in different domains (cf. Fig. 1 reuse-level).

(2) The *generic type system* represented as subclasses of the core concepts builds upon one of the most promising IoT ontologies (*IoT-O* [24]), as factored out in our previous survey on the 'IoT ontology jungle" [10], being a modular core-domain IoT ontology to represent connected devices reusing several other prominent ontologies like the *W3C SSN standard* [14]. It has to be noted that Fig. 1 just exemplary illustrates some of the available generic types, whereby the reuse of IoT-O has been denoted by package import dependencies.

(3) The *domain-specific types* are derived from the *DATEX-standard* [1] commonly used in the domain of ITS, again showing only a small fraction of several hundred objectTypes fully representing our application domain.

(4) The distinction between *Message(Types)* and *Event(Types)* was motivated by the need to bridge the gap between low-level log entries in terms of messages and high-level events representing occurrences of interest for the ITS operator, as also proposed in other domains like process mining [3,16]. This allows to aggregate messages sent by eventually different objects about the same real-world occurrence to a dedicated event. In Fig. 1, this aggregation is denoted by the corresponding "et" attribute within messageType subclasses being used in favor of explicit associations specializations for the sake of readability.

(5) The explicit representation and thus *"reification" of semantic relationship-Types* in terms of a *class hierarchy* provides the benefit of type reusability between arbitrary subclasses of the eventType-hierarchy, depending on the requirements of the application domain. Analogous to message aggregations described before, the determination of these semantic relationshipTypes is denoted by an attribute "srt" within the eventType subclasses.

(6) The explicit representation of *TemporalRelation* and *FunctionalCorrelation* in terms of *UML association classes* represents the basis for recording *provenance information*, thereby providing the rationale for the population of certain semantic relationshipTypes (cf. Sect. 5).

5   OT Ontology Population Approach

By applying the proposed meta model, we aim to incorporate domain knowledge along the entire ontology population process, from the early message-level, via the mining of functional correlations, to the instantiation of semantic relationships thereof. Overall, we stick to the "closed-world-assumption", more precisely, each functional correlation between a pair of objects being mined from the log data, is aligned with domain knowledge provided by the meta model in form of explicated relationshipTypes and their properties (e.g., multiplicities) to derive semantic relationships. In case the domain knowledge is not sufficient to unambiguously interpret the functional correlation, additional *heuristic guidelines* (e.g., how to deal with optional relationships) are used for populating an appropriate semantic relationship into the ontology. Based on that overall rationale, our ontology population approach can be characterized along our challenges described in Sect. 3 leading to the following main cases, namely (1) *semantification of functional correlations*, (2) *semantic differentiation of relationships based on eventTypes*, (3) *instantiation of silent objects and silent relationships*, and (4) *allocation of provenance information*.

Canonical Relationship Constellations. In order to illustrate the details of these cases as well as to get a grip on the complexity of coarse-grained real-world relationships between numerous OT objects while preserving, at the same time, the general applicability of our approach, we *focus on canonical constellations of relationships* between a minimal number of necessary OT objects as a baseline. The rational behind these canonical constellations is mainly derived from the expressiveness of our T-Box formalism provided by the meta model, covering relationship properties like name, direction, multiplicity, multi-dependencies, transitivity, inheritance, single/multiple relationships, and relationship roles. By focusing on these relationship properties, Figs. 2, 3, 4, 5 and 6 visualize the instantiation of semantic relationships between OT objects derived from functional correlations thereby basing on the exemplary domain model shown in Fig. 1.

(1) *Semantification of Functional Correlations.* In its most basic case, semantification of a functional correlation entails the instantiation of a relationshipType between the functionally correlated objects. Thereby, fundamentals like a meaningful name and a navigation direction are manifested (see Fig. 2(a))[1]. However, the instantiation is naturally constrained by the relationship's corresponding objectTypes' multiplicity, thereby expressing mandatory and optional semantic relationships (see Fig. 2 (b) and (c)).

Furthermore, supposedly mined functional correlations can be simply discarded if no relatonshipType counterpart can be found in the T-Box. This is specifically relevant wrt. real-world relationships involving numerous objects, i.e., forming a "functional correlation cluster" where each object is functionally

---

[1] Please note that the notation sticks to UML class and object diagrams, whereas the red lines between objects represent a functional correlation and yellow arrows represent the impact one object has on another object in real-world.

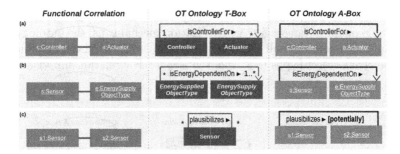

Fig. 2. Providing a meaningful name and direction (a) as well as considering mandatory (b) and optional (c) multiplicity constraints

correlated with all other objects. However, not necessarily each object has a direct relationship to each other object (i.e., false-positives), thus not all functional correlations lead to an instantiation of a semantic relationship (cf. (a) and (b) in Fig. 3). This goes along with real-world transitive relationships being not expressed by pairwise functional correlations. Thus, T-Box information of semantic relationshipTypes between intermediate objectTypes allows to put functional correlation between pairs of objects and the semantic relationships in-between "in the correct order" (see sensor - controller - actuator constellation of Fig. 3 (c)). Finally, if semantic relationshipTypes between objectTypes are not foreseen in the T-Box, this also allows to eliminate functional correlations being irrelevant (i.e., again false-positives).

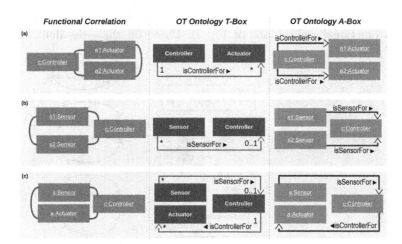

Fig. 3. Discarding false-positive functional correlations resulting from complex real-world relationship Constellation

Since domain knowledge might be expressed at more general levels, i.e., exploiting modeling "languages" generalization mechanisms, the ontology population approach considers all relationshipTypes along the inheritance hierarchy of the involved objectTypes (e.g., like the isSensorFor relationship visualized in Fig. 4).

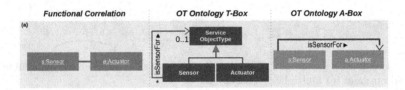

Fig. 4. Exploiting modeling "languages" generalization mechanisms

(2) *Semantic Differentiation of Relationships Based on EventTypes.* Multiple semantic relationshipTypes between two objectTypes might not necessarily all hold between two specific objects of those objectTypes simultaneously. This is because objects might relate in different roles to individual objects at different times. For example, while sensors and controllers may be in an *isSensorFor* and in a *visualizes* relationship, a sensor's controller might not necessarily visualize the sensor, thus the sensor and the controller might not always play a role in both relationships at the same time. To address this challenge, we extended our mining approach (discussed in Sect. 3) in order to exploit also eventTypes. For this, we calculate functional correlations between pairs of eventTypes about distinct objects rather than between pairs of objects, only (see colored circles next to functional correlations of Fig. 5). Based on that, the domain model

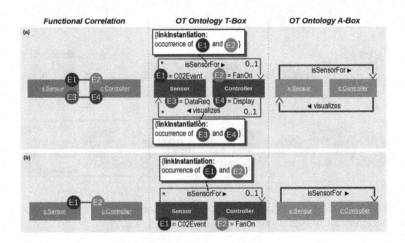

Fig. 5. Semantic differentiation of relationships based on event types

defines which specific semantic relationship shall be instantiated in the light of an eventType-specific functional correlation (see Fig. 1 association between eventType and semantic relationshipType).

Capitalizing on that, it also allows, even for a single possible semantic relationship, a more fine-grained differentiation in which cases, based on the event-Type, a specific semantic relationship is instantiated.

(3) *Instantiation of Silent Objects and Silent Relationships.* The "prescriptive nature" of the domain knowledge can be utilized to address semantic relationships to certain objects which are required, although underlying functional correlations are not yet mineable from event log data, representing "blind spots". Concretely, we exploit domain knowledge in terms of semantic relationshipType multiplicity constraints (specifying that certain objects need to be in a relationship with another object) to populate those semantic relationships to not (yet) perceived objects as *"silent"* ones into the ontology (see Fig. 6). In contrast to the previous population cases, which are data-driven by functional correlations, the instantiation of silent objects and silent relationships is driven by domain knowledge. In the light of OTM, this mechanism is beneficial, since it enables identifying objects being the potential cause of or being affected by a failure of an object not (yet) recorded in the log. On the downside, this, however, comes at the costs that, as mining continues, already existing silent objects and relationships eventually have to be replaced by objects now perceived in the log (cf. Sect. 7). Thus, the existence of a particular silent object and its silent relationships in the A-Box might be temporary, only.

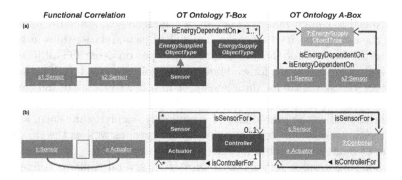

Fig. 6. Silent objects and silent relationships

(4) *Allocation of Provenance Information.* In order to improve trustworthiness and support traceability as well as to trace evolution aspects, our ontology population approach enables adding further semantics in terms of provenance information of functional correlations directly in the OT ontology's A-Box. Currently, provenance information manifested includes (i) a history of the probability values of functional correlations to trace their evolution over time, (ii) meta-information

about underlying number of messages over time, functional correlation values and their underlying z-score values, thus being an indicator for the trustworthiness of functional correlations, and (iii) the concrete eventTypes underlying functional correlations, since those may give an indication about previously not explicated semantic relationships of the real-world, thus pointing the way for a (semi-)automatic evolving T-Box (cf. Sect. 7).

6   Scenario-Based Evaluation

Evaluation Based on Simulated Domain-Derived Scenarios. As a first step towards evaluating the appropriateness of our approach in the light of constellations of relationships prevalent in large-scale IoT systems (cf. example domain model in Fig. 1), our evaluation is based on a set of domain-derived scenarios. Thereby, scenarios comprise *abnormal operation cases* (the improper function of OT objects is impeded by other OT objects), as well as *normal operation cases* (inter-operating objects in the light of certain services). Since ground-truth data (gold standard A-Box) needed for evaluating those scenarios and accompanying relationship information is not readily available, we resort to simulated data based on real-world datasets. Thereby, characteristics of simulated data, such as the distribution of messages, the frequency of failures of certain OT types, correspond to the characteristics of real-world data.

Synthetic Log Data Generation Framework. In order to generate the simulated data, i.e., synthetic log data used for evaluation, we developed a log data generation framework able to simulate the message behavior of real-world OT objects in an artificial IoT environment. Thereby, we define a gold standard A-Box considering the domain-derived scenarios, i.e., OT objects, relationships in-between as well as the impacts of their corresponding types on other OT objects being finally used as ground-truth for evaluation. The gold standard itself is then used as input for the synthetic log data generator in order to simulate the contained OT objects and outputs a synthetic log file. Parameterization of the (i) message rate, which specifies the probability of a randomly occurring message, allows to control the message behavior of certain objectTypes, as well as the (ii) amount and time of manually injected messages allow to control the domain scenarios (e.g., simulating a video server failure impacting several cameras connected to that video server).

Scenario-Specific Experiments Evaluating Performance and Robustness. Based on the synthetic log data of six different domain scenarios, we applied our hybrid approach and systematically evaluated two dimensions, namely (1) *performance* of our approach in terms of (i) *accuracy*, (ii) *efficiency*, and (iii) *effectivity*, as well as (2) *robustness* of our approach regarding (a) *amount of data* by varying the temporal extent of simulated log data, (b) *parameterization* by varying functional correlation mining configurations, and (c) *number of objects* by varying simultaneity of co-occurring scenario instances. As a benchmark for our evaluation, we use performance and robustness results of experiments realized without exploiting domain knowledge provided by the meta model of Fig. 1.

Lessons Learned. To briefly sum up our lessons learned of 54 experiments (combinations of two evaluation dimensions, i.e., performance and robustness, for each of the 6 domain-derived scenarios), first of all, regarding *accuracy*, we are able to achieve noticeable improvements in terms of precision compared to the benchmark, which is due to the employed semantic type-model (message-, event-, object-, and relationshipTypes), whereas at the same time, there is no degradation with respect to runtime recognizable. Regarding *efficiency*, we are able to achieve noticeable improvements in runtime while accuracy remained stable, which is due to applying objectType-specific configurations (considering their message behavior) when mining functional correlations. Finally, analyzing *effectivity*, semantic relationships are recognized faster, which is due to considering the sparsity of certain message- and eventTypes.

7 Future Work

One major issue for future work results from the fact that our ontology population approach does not yet sufficiently address the evolution aspect being omnipresent in real-world large-scale ITS. We therefore intend to provide mechanisms for identifying different kinds of *real-world evolution* meaning that objects and their corresponding semantic relationships are added, removed, and changed on a daily basis and based on that, to seamlessly co-evolve the *virtual-world* in terms of learning/unlearning real-world objects and semantic relationships thereby resembling the digital shadow paradigm [4]. This especially includes mechanisms of merging silent objects and relationships with real ones, identified at a later time. Furthermore, our approach relies on the existence and the quality of incorporated domain knowledge, which might lead to improper results in case of insufficient domain knowledge expressed by the T-Box. Regarding evaluation, we have to mention that, because of the canonical character of our domain-derived scenarios, completeness of possible cases was favored instead of covering real-world complexity. Therefore, for providing a more in-depth evaluation, a thorough and systematic combination of our canonical relationship constellations would be a crucial prerequisite, complemented by a chart-based visualization using rapid prototyping environments like Oracle APEX.[2]

References

1. DATEX II. https://www.datex2.eu
2. Open Platform Communications Unified Architecture (OPC UA). https://opcfoundation.org

---

[2] https://apex.oracle.com/.

3. Pecchia, A., Weber, I., Cinque, M., Ma, Y.: Discovering process models for the analysis of application failures under uncertainty of event logs. Knowl.-Based Syst. **189**, 105054 (2020)
4. Brauner, P., et al.: A computer science perspective on digital transformation in production. ACM Trans. Internet Things **3**(2), 1–32 (2022)
5. Allen, J.F.: Maintaining knowledge about temporal intervals. Commun. ACM **26**(11), 832–843 (1983)
6. Amato, F., et al.: Detect and correlate information system events through verbose logging messages analysis. Computing **101**(7), 819–830 (2019)
7. Belkaroui, R., et al.: Towards events ontology based on data sensors network for viticulture domain. In: Proceedings of the 8th International Conference on the Internet of Things, pp. 1–7. ACM (2018)
8. Detro, S., et al.: Enhancing semantic interoperability in healthcare using semantic process mining. In: Proceedings of International Conference on Information Society and Technology, pp. 80–85 (2016)
9. Endler, M., et al.: Towards stream-based reasoning and machine learning for IoT applications. In: Intelligent System Conference, pp. 202–209. IEEE (2017)
10. Graf, D., et al.: Cutting a path through the IoT ontology jungle - a meta survey. In: International Conference on Internet of Things and Intelligence Systems. IEEE (2019)
11. Graf, D., Schwinger, W., Retschitzegger, W., Kapsammer, E., Baumgartner, N.: Event-driven ontology population - from research to practice in critical infrastructure systems. In: Rocha, Á., Adeli, H., Dzemyda, G., Moreira, F., Ramalho Correia, A.M. (eds.) WorldCIST 2021. AISC, vol. 1366, pp. 405–415. Springer, Cham (2021). https://doi.org/10.1007/978-3-030-72651-5_39
12. Graf, D., et al.: Dependency mining in IoT - from research to practice in intelligent transportation systems. In: Rocha, A., Adeli, H., Dzemyda, G., Moreira, F. (eds.) Information Systems and Technologies. WorldCIST 2022. LNCS, vol. 469. Springer, Cham (2022). https://doi.org/10.1007/978-3-031-04819-7_26
13. Graf, D., et al.: Semantic-driven mining of functional dependencies in large-scale systems-of-systems. In: Rocha, Á., Ferrás, C., Méndez Porras, A., Jimenez Delgado, E. (eds.) Information Technology and Systems. ICITS 2022. LNCS, vol. 414. Springer, Cham (2022). https://doi.org/10.1007/978-3-030-96293-7_31
14. Haller, A., et al.: The SOSA/SSN ontology: a joint WEC and OGC standard specifying the semantics of sensors observations actuation and sampling. In: Semantic Web, vol. 1, pp. 1–19. IOS Press (2018)
15. Hromic, H., et al.: Real time analysis of sensor data for the IoT by means of clustering and event processing. In: Proceedings of International Conference on Communications, pp. 685–691. IEEE (2015)
16. Janiesch, C., el al.: The Internet of Things meets business process management: a manifesto. IEEE Syst. Man Cybern. Mag. **6**(4), 34–44 (2020)
17. Jayawardana, V., et al.: Semi-supervised instance population of an ontology using word vector embeddings. In: Proceedings of International Conference on Advances in ICT for Emerging Regions, pp. 217–223. IEEE (2017)
18. Körber, M., Glombiewski, N., Morgen, A., Seeger, B.: TPStream: low-latency and high-throughput temporal pattern matching on event streams. Distrib. Parallel Databases **39**(2), 361–412 (2019)
19. Matzner, M., Scholta, H.: Process mining approaches to detect organizational properties in CPS. In: European Conference on Information Systems (2014)
20. Messager, A., et al.: Inferring functional connectivity from time-series of events in large scale network deployments. Trans. Netw. Serv. Manag. **16**(3), 857–870 (2019)

21. Noura, M., Atiquzzaman, M., Gaedke, M.: Interoperability in Internet of Things infrastructure: classification, challenges, and future work. In: Lin, Y.-B., Deng, D.-J., You, I., Lin, C.-C. (eds.) IoTaaS 2017. LNICST, vol. 246, pp. 11–18. Springer, Cham (2018). https://doi.org/10.1007/978-3-030-00410-1_2

22. Reyes-Ortiz, J., et al.: Web services ontology population through text classification. In: Proceedings of Conference on Computer Science and Information Systems, pp. 491–495. IEEE (2016)

23. Schuster, D., et al.: Utilizing domain knowledge in data-driven process discovery: a literature review. Comput. Ind. **137**, 103612 (2022)

24. Seydoux, N., Drira, K., Hernandez, N., Monteil, T.: IoT-O, a core-domain IoT ontology to represent connected devices networks. In: Blomqvist, E., Ciancarini, P., Poggi, F., Vitali, F. (eds.) EKAW 2016. LNCS (LNAI), vol. 10024, pp. 561–576. Springer, Cham (2016). https://doi.org/10.1007/978-3-319-49004-5_36

25. Zhu, M., et al.: Service hyperlink: modeling and reusing partial process knowledge by mining event dependencies among sensor data services. In: Proceedings of International Conference on Web Services, pp. 902–905. IEEE (2017)

26. Zhuge, C., Vaarandi, R.: Efficient event log mining with LogClusterC. In: Proceedings of International Conference on Big Data Security on Cloud, pp. 261–266. IEEE (2017)

Deep Learning-Based Sentiment Analysis for Predicting Financial Movements

Hadhami Mejbri[1]([✉]), Mariem Mahfoudh[1,2], and Germain Forestier[3]

[1] Kairouan University, ISIGK, Avenue Khemais El Alouini, 3100 Kairouan, Tunisia
hadhamimejbriinfo@gmail.com
[2] MIRACL Laboratory, University of Sfax, Route de Tunis Km 10 B.P. 242,
3021 Sfax, Tunisia
[3] IRIMAS, University of Haute-Alsace, 12 rue des Frères Lumière,
68093 Mulhouse Cedex, France
germain.forestier@uha.fr

Abstract. Sentiment analysis is a computational study of opinions, feelings, emotions, ratings and attitudes towards entities such as products, services, organizations, individuals, issues, events, subjects and their attributes. Our research is used to predict stock market movements, aims to improve the accuracy of polarity of comments, in order to accurately predict financial movements. This by creating a dictionary of emojis that contains the emoji as keys and its meanings as values. We used the dictionary at the preprocessing level to keep the meanings of emojis because they carry a lot of emotions that help us to clearly specify the polarity of the comments. We have also created a list of stopwords related to the financial field to properly clean our database. Time series and linking sequences of data is very important to properly predict stock market movements. We have therefore chosen to work with the Long short-term memory (LSTM) model. Next, we came up with two models: the first model to predict stock market movements using investor sentiment analysis of Amazon stock which gives us 93% accuracy. The second model is used to predict financial movements through historical Amazon prices. We extracted the database we used for the sentiment analysis from Twitter as the Twitter comments are up to date. As for the historical prices of Amazon stock we extracted from the most famous trading platform YahooFinance.

Keywords: Sentiment analysis · Stock movement prediction · Opinion mining · Automatic Natural Language Processing (NLP) · Deep learning · Machine learning · Time series

1 Introduction

Sentiment analysis have been used in diverse fields such as health, finance, sports, politics, hospitality, and consumer behavior. We are interested in our work to the financial field, more specifically in online trading platforms.

© The Author(s), under exclusive license to Springer Nature Switzerland AG 2022
G. Memmi et al. (Eds.): KSEM 2022, LNAI 13369, pp. 586–596, 2022.
https://doi.org/10.1007/978-3-031-10986-7_47

Online trading is simply buying and selling financial securities through onLine trading platforms or mobile trading apps, to make money between buying and reselling, and vice versa. Intervening on the financial markets represents risks that can lead to financial losses. For example, market risk due to price instability linked to general economic and market fluctuations, liquidity risk and the difficulty of finding a counterparty (to sell a financial instrument at a reasonable price at a given time), etc. [9], so to minimize the risk of loss, we help through our proposed model to create a computer system that helps investors make the right decision in order to have a good trading experience in the financial markets. There are several areas of trading like commodity trading, currency trading and stock trading. Statistic shows that 90% of traders do not make money when trading the stocks [8], so we chose stock trading in the research and particularly we chose to predict the financial movements of Amazon.

Our research is divided into three main parts: the first part consists of analyzing investor sentiment towards Amazon. The reviews are taken from the official twitter page of Amazon. The second part is to predict the financial movement of Amazon stocks using sentiment analysis. Finally, the third part focuses on the use of historical prices extracted from the most famous trading site: YahooFinance.

Our article is composed of three parts. The first part is the related works in which we presented some works related to sentiment analysis in the financial field whereas in the second part, we presented our proposed approach and in the third part we discussed the results of our research.

2   Related Work

Kordonis et al. [3] predicted how the market would subsequently behave via sentiment analysis on a set of tweets over the past few days, so they developed a system that collects past tweets, drafts, and examines the usefulness of various machine learning techniques such as Naive Bayes Bernoulli classification and Support Vector Machine (SVM), to provide positive or negative sentiment on the tweet corpus. The results still show that changes in public sentiment can affect the stock market.

Kalyani et al. [2] predicted market trends, and for this they used a polarity detection algorithm to label news articles. For this algorithm, a dictionary-based approach was used. Positive and negative word dictionaries are created using general and finance-specific sentiment words. They created a dictionary for stop-word removal that also includes finance-specific stopwords. Based on this data, they implemented three classification models which they tested in different test scenarios. Then, after comparing their results, Random Forest performed very well for all test cases ranging from 88% to 92% accuracy. The accuracy tracked by SVM is also considerable around 86%. The performance of the Naive Bayes algorithm is around 83%.

There are some work on Deep Learning architecture for sentiment analysis. Nti et al. [6] investigated the application of the attention-based deep neural network LSTM in predicting future stock market movements. They also built an aggregate stock dataset, and an individual dataset, including stock history data, financial tweets sentiment, and technical indicators on the US stock market. The experiment investigates the temporal sensitivity of financial tweet sentiment and methods for calculating collective sentiment. The researchers also experimented with conventional LSTM and attention-based LSTM for performance comparison. The results prove that financial tweets published from the close to the open of the market have more predictive power on the movement of stocks the next day.

Liu et al. [7] proposed a model named RCNK (Recurrent Convolutional Neural Kernel) for the prediction of stock price movement. In order to improve the prediction accuracy of the model and the cumulative returns of the trading simulation, the RCNK model has been optimized in three aspects: data collection, textual data processing, and the model classifier.

Researchers have proposed several models that improve the results of predicting financial movements with several techniques.

There is researchers who analyze the temporal system (when are the periods of time which represent well the prices of stocks, and give better predictions), on the other hand there is researchers who have worked well to improve the results of sentiment analysis towards stocks. In our approach we tried to improve on both, we used "Open" and "High" respectively, as the training dataset, The "Open" column, which represents the stock's opening price each day and the "High" column, which represents the highest stock price reached each day. Furthermore, we created a dictionary of emojis and a list of financial stopwords to improve the stock sentiment analysis result (in our research we analyzed amazon stocks).

3   Proposed Approach

To improve the trading experience, it is important to know the opinion of the investors on the share price as well as on the stocks. The objective of our work is to identify the courses of action that will be descending and those that will be ascending. That's why we offer sentiment analysis of tweets to help investors choose when and which stock to buy or sell in order to increase their earnings. In the other hand we predict the stock market movements using the historical prices extracted from the most famous trading site "Yahoo finance". The purpose of these two methods is to improve the prediction through comparing the results of the sentiment analysis and the historical prices methods.

Figure 1 illustrates the steps and techniques of our proposed sentiment analysis approach which includes seven main components:

1. *Data collection.* Collection of tweets from the Amazon page and the date of each. Extract the historical prices of Amazon stocks from the Yahoo finance trading site and the date of each.
2. *Data pre-processing.* it consists to clean the data and extract the relevant information in order to have an accurate classification of the sentiments.

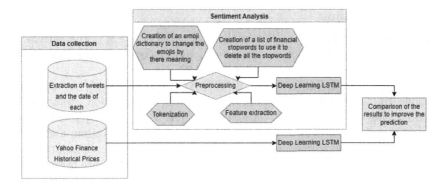

Fig. 1. Summary of our proposed approach

3. *Feature extraction.* use word integration (count vectorization, tf-idf transformation, BOW) to convert tweets into digital representations.
4. *Sentiment classification.* use the LSTM long short-term memory numeric representation of tweets.
5. *Prediction of financial movements using tweets.* Representation of sentiment classification results in a curve that represents the polarity of tweets over time.
6. *Prediction of financial movements using historical stock prices.* Creation of an LSTM model to predict stock prices over time and compare the results with actual stock prices.
7. *Evaluation.* Once the model is built on the training data, we use it to predict the evaluation of the test data. To assess performance, we calculated accuracy.

3.1 Data Collection

We created a *Developer* twitter account to have an API that allows us to extract tweets from the official Amazon page and the date of each one. In our experiment, we used tweets which were posted from 2021-02-12 to 2021-08-17.

We examined the tweets to see if there is any relation between the future stock price and users sentiment. In other words, we want to see if we can predict a future stock price based on the current sentiment of many users in order to improve the prediction using the historical prices of the stock, so we have loaded AMAZON's past stock price data. From the most famous trading site YahooFinance, we have selected the values of the first and second columns ("Open" and "High" respectively) as training dataset. The "Open" column represents the stock's opening price each day and the "High" column represents the highest stock price reached each day.

We used historical stock prices from Amazon from 2018/08/01 to 2021/07/29 to train our lstm model, and prices from August 2021 to test our model. We used Textblob library to label our tweets.

3.2 Pre-processing

1. *Date standardization.* Transfer the dates of each comment to the date format necessary for the prediction of financial movements over time *(2021-02-12T17:22:53Z to 2021-02-12 17:22:53)*.

2. *Cleaning emojis.* Before starting the known natural language processing techniques (punctuation removal, stopword removal, tokenization, stemming and TfIdf), We noticed that our database contains a lot of emojis with a lot of feelings and which must be removed if we removes punctuation, and for this reason we decided to create a dictionary of emojis. We have chosen to extract the twitter emojis with their meanings from the French website fr.piliapp.com in order to have a dictionary that contains all the emojis with their meanings (1665 emojis) in this form 'emoji':'meaning' (the emoji as keys and the meaning as value) the dictionary we created is in French and since the tweets in our database are in English, we used the translate library to translate it into English. After creating our data dictionary, we created a function clean_text_round1 which uses the re library and the string library to replace emojis with its meaning and remove punctuations in order to apply known NLP techniques to our data.

3. *Tokenization.* Tokenization is a method of dividing a piece of text into smaller units called tokens. Here the tokens can be words, characters or sub-words. Therefore, tokenization can be roughly divided into 3 types: word, character, and subword (n-gram characters) tokenization. In our research we need the sentiments of the words so we applicated word tokenization.

4. *Remove stop words.* Stop words are words that don't add much meaning to a sentence and don't convey any emotion so they don't indicate any valuable information about the sentiment of a sentence. They can be safely ignored without sacrificing the meaning of the sentence. For example, words like the, he, have etc. We used the nltk library to import English stopwords to remove unnecessary words from our database. And like our research done in financial databases, we created a new Word stop list related to the financial domain (new_stopword), and removed all the financial stop words in our list from our database. And to be sure that our database is well cleaned, we used wordcloud to display the words, repeat the most and add the superfluous words to our list of stopwords.

5. *Feature extraction.* Machines cannot understand characters and words. So when it comes to textual data, we need to represent it in numbers for it to be understood by the machine. A simple text could be converted into features with various techniques such as Bag of Words (BOW), tf-idf wish is very often used for text features, there is also another class called TfidfVectorizer that combines all the options of CountVectorizer and TfidfTransformer in a single model, so in our research we used the TfidfVectorizer technique.

3.3 Sentiment Analysis and Prediction

In our research, we used time series and linking data sequences which are very important to predict stock market movements well. So we have chosen to work with the LSTM model which uses a technique allowing it to process information over extended time intervals.

The LSTM technique learns to store information over extended time intervals via recurrent back-propagation is time consuming mainly due to insufficient and decreasing error feedback [1].

4   Results and Discussion

In this section, we will explain our results curves. At first, we have presented the result of our expected stock price using historical prices and actual stock prices in the Fig. 2. Then, we have presented the opinions of Internet users over time as shown in the Fig. 3, 4, 5, 6 (sentiments on the vertical axis and time on the horizontal axis polarities). Although the exact prices of the predicted prices are not always close to the actual price, our model always indicates general trends, such as upwards or downwards. This research tells us that LSTMs can be effective in time series forecasting.

Fig. 2. Prediction of financial movements with the LSTM model using historical prices

This prediction can be improved by merging the two prediction methods used in our research: sentiment analysis of tweets and historical prices.

We evaluated our model to improve it based on what we learn to evaluate it, and whether our model is useful, whether we need to train our model on more data to improve its performance, and whether we should we include more features? The three main parameters used to evaluate a classification model are: accuracy, precision and recall. The best result we got using LSTM model is 93% accuracy. Using sentiment analysis, we found that tweets with date 2021/08/03 are positive tweets, which affects stock prices which therefore increased, which is the case as shown in Fig. 2 of actual stock prices.

On the day of 2021/08/04 the comments are increasingly negative throughout the day, which clearly affects the prices of stocks which will therefore go down.

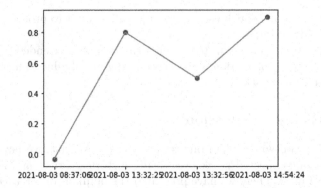

Fig. 3. Prediction of financial movements with the LSTM model using sentiment analysis on August 3, 2021.

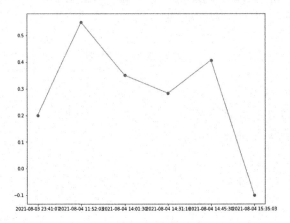

Fig. 4. Prediction of financial movements with the LSTM model using sentiment analysis on August 4, 2021.

But as Fig. 5 shows at the end of the day 2021/08/04 and the beginning of the day 2021/08/05, the feedback becomes positive, which will affect the stock prices, and what is coming rise, as indicated by the curve of actual stock prices from the Fig. 2.

And since August 6, 2021 until 16 august 2021, the comments are increasingly negative, and at the same time, we find that the prices of actual Amazon stocks are decreasing considerably.

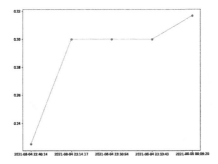

Fig. 5. Prediction of financial movements with the LSTM model using sentiment analysis on August 4 and 5, 2021.

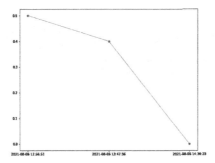

Fig. 6. Prediction of financial movements with the LSTM model using sentiment analysis on August 6, 2021.

Our research is inspired by the works [2,3] and [6]. Such as the work [3] the researchers created a dictionary of emojis which indicates the polarity of the emojis which carries a feeling. Which makes us think about creating a dictionary of emojis which carries the meaning of the emojis and we have put all the emojis without exception. In order to attract all the feelings of our twitters and find out if there is any sarcasm. We also adopted the idea of [2] to create a list of financial stopwords wish improve sentiment analysis results. And finally, the work [3] that analyzes the aspect of time on the prediction results, that guided us to try different stock prices on the same day and choose to use the Open and High columns as our training data set. The Open column represents the stock's opening price each day and the High column represents the highest stock price reached each day. As the Table 1 indicate our model give the best accuracy (Fig. 7).

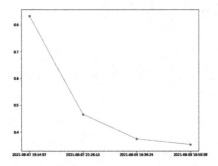

Fig. 7. Prediction of financial movements with the LSTM model using sentiment analysis on August 7 and 8, 2021.

Table 1. Comparison of our work with previous works

Works	Database	The technique used	Algorithm	Accuracy
[3]	Yahoo-Finance, Twitter	They have created a dictionary of emojis that indicates the polarity of emojis that carry sentiment	Naive Bayes	80%
[2]	Yahoo-Finance, Reuters	They have created a dictionary for stopword removal which also includes finance-specific stopwords	Random Forest	92%
[6]	Yahoo-Finance, Twitter	The experiment investigates the time sensitivity of financial tweet sentiment and methods for calculating collective sentiment	LSTM	62%
[7]	Guba eastmoney	The different from previous studies is that The researchers treated the text data as sequential data and they used the RCNK model to train sentiment embeddings with the temporal features	Recurrent convolutional neural kernel	66.62%
Our work	Yahoo-Finance, Twitter	We created a dictionary of emojis that contains the emoji as keys and its meanings as values, this dictionary we used at the preprocessing level to keep the meanings of emojis, we have also created a list of stopwords related to the financial field to properly clean our database	LSTM	93%

5   Conclusion

The stock market is often volatile and changes abruptly due to economic conditions, the political situation and major events for the country. To improve the trading experience: it is important to know the opinion of investors on the share price as well as on stocks, and thanks to social networks now, we can know the opinions of Internet users. In our research, we used Amazon page tweets to do Amazon customer sentiments analysis to identify which courses of action are going to be bottom-up. Our task consists in two main steps: in the first step, we cleaned our database by creating a dictionary of emojis that replaces emojis with their meanings, and we created a list of stopwords related to the financial field, then we applied the TF/IDF, to represent the words numerically. Time series and linking data sequences are very important for predicting stock market movements well. And for that we then chose to use several models of the "LSTM" classifier and a model of the "decision tree" classifier. After a comparison between these models, the results of our proposed approach, the LSTM classifier that demonstrates the best reliability demonstrates a performance of 93%. The second part of our proposed approach is to use our investor sentiment analysis to predict market movements of Amazon stocks. As for the other method, we used to predict the stock market movement, the method using historical prices extracted from the most famous trading site Yahoo Finance for this prediction we used LSTM which gives us good results as showing Fig. 2. The perspectives of our work consist in changing our database to make it dynamic in real time, and in uniting the results of the sentiment analysis with the results of historical prices, in order to develop and exploit a computer system allowing to invest in the financial markets automatically (without human intervention). We also aim to solve the problem of ironic sentences using our dictionary of emojis because an opposition between the emotion of the emoji and the emotion of the text usually constitutes sarcasm.

References

1. Hochreiter, S., Schmidhuber, J.: Long short-term memory. Neural Comput. J. **9**, 1735–1780 (1997)
2. Kalyani, J., Bharathi, P., Jyothi, P.: Stock trend prediction using news sentiment analysis. Int. J. Comput. Sci. Inf. Technol. (IJCSIT) (2016)
3. Kordonis, J., Symeonidis, S., Arampatzis, A.: Stock price forecasting via sentiment analysis on Twitter. In: Proceedings of the 20th Pan-Hellenic Conference on Informatics, November 2016
4. Zhang, K., Li, L., Li, P., Teng, W.: Stock trend forecasting method based on sentiment analysis and system similarity model. In: Proceedings of 2011 6th International Forum on Strategic Technology, vol. 2, pp. 890–894 (2011)
5. Bhat, A., Kamath, S.: Automated stock price prediction and trading framework for Nifty intraday trading. In: 2013 Fourth International Conference on Computing, Communications and Networking Technologies, pp. 1–6 (2013)
6. Xu, Y., Keselj, V.: Stock prediction using deep learning and sentiment analysis. In: 2019 IEEE International Conference on Big Data (Big Data) (2019)

7. Liu, S., Zhang, X., Wang, Y., Feng, G.: Recurrent convolutional neural kernel model for stock price movement prediction. PLoS ONE **15**, e0234206 (2020)
8. Gillham, D.: Trading the Stock Market - Why Most Traders Fail (2021). https://www.wealthwithin.com.au/learning-centre/share-trading-tips/trading-the-stock-market
9. Hugo, T.: What are the different types of financial risks (2020). https://study.com/academy/lesson/financial-risk-types-examples-management-methods.html

Student Behavior Analysis and Performance Prediction Based on Blended Learning Data

Juan Chen[1,2,3] (iD), Fengrui Fan[2], Haiyang Jia[1,2,3(✉)] (iD), Yuanteng Xu[2],
Hanchen Dong[2], Xiaopai Huang[2], Jianyu Li[2], and Zhongrui Zhang[2]

[1] College of Computer Science and Technology, Jilin University, Changchun 130012, China
{chenjuan,jiahy}@jlu.edu.cn
[2] College of Software, Jilin University, Changchun 130012, China
{fanfr5519,xuyt5519,donghc5520,huangxp,lijy,
zhangzr5519}@mails.jlu.edu.cn
[3] Key Laboratory of Symbolic Computation and Knowledge Engineering of Ministry
of Education, Jilin University, Changchun 130012, China

Abstract. Blended teaching has the characteristics of small scale, strong controllability, definite learning tasks and consideration of both online and offline teaching. The quantitative evaluation indicators of learners' blended learning behavior enthusiasm and stability are proposed, and then used for learning behavior analysis and performance prediction. It analyzes the distribution, correlation, consistency and effectiveness of online and offline learning behavior indicators, and it is found that there is a high correlation between learning behavior indicators and the final grade. The prediction is carried on the data set composed of learning behavior indicators, students' basic information, online and offline learning data. The improved forest optimization algorithm is applied to select features. The naive Bayes, decision tree and random forest classifier are used to predict the final performance. The experiments show that the learning behavior indicators can effectively reduce the scale of feature set and improve the performance prediction effect.

Keywords: Learning behavior analysis · Performance prediction · Blended teaching · Data mining · Information entropy · Feature engineering

1 Introduction

Since the wave of MOOC (*Massive Open Online Course*) swept the world in 2012, MOOC platform has become the main source of big educational data. The 2016 global MOOC statistical report released by Class Central, an online course aggregation platform, shows that MOOC has no longer pursued the scope of courses and the huge number of learners, but turned to serving the regular teaching of colleges and universities [1]. The separation of COVID-19 has accelerated the transformation of teaching mode in most colleges and universities. The combination of online courses and traditional offline teaching is becoming the trend of global university teaching [2]. Based on MOOC data, many scholars have carried out a lot of meaningful works about student portraits

© The Author(s), under exclusive license to Springer Nature Switzerland AG 2022
G. Memmi et al. (Eds.): KSEM 2022, LNAI 13369, pp. 597–609, 2022.
https://doi.org/10.1007/978-3-031-10986-7_48

[3, 4], learning behavior analysis and predictions [5–7], learning recommendations and platform improvements [8, 9]. Compared with MOOC, blended teaching has its own characteristics: online learning records are rich, but most of them are task-based learning, *i.e.*, learning tasks must be completed. It is difficult to effectively reflect the whole picture of students' learning process simply by online learning. Offline learning data is not as rich as online but has high discrimination. Teachers can give better guidance, and the data authenticity is higher. Few works are carried on the analysis and mining of blended teaching data. It needs more studies.

The outline of this paper is as follows: Section 2 introduces the related work of learning behavior analysis and performance prediction. Section 3 gives the definition and analysis of the two indicators of learners' blended learning behavior in detail. Section 4 describes the performance predication through experiments. Section 5 summarizes the work of this paper and discusses future works.

2 Related Work

Learning behavior analysis and performance prediction based on online data has become the hot topic in the field of educational data mining, thanks to the rapid development of computer facility [10, 11], network infrastructure [12, 13], and new algorithms [14, 15]. How to extract behavioral features from raw data [16] and how to select prediction algorithms are the key concerns [17].

XIE *etc.* [6] established learner profile labels based on online data from psychological and pedagogical dimension, and analyzed the impact of different learning behavior features on performance. Gardner *etc.* [18] classified online data into five categories of indicators: click-through rate, assignment completion, course metadata, discussion content, and demographic information. Mubarak *etc.* [19] focused on video watching data and extracted video click streams, including pause, play, and fast forward, as indicators. Sunar *etc.* [20] used online discussion data as the basis for classifying learner types.

Besides the common machine learning classification algorithms, such as K-nearest neighbor classification, decision tree, gradient boosting decision tree, and plain Bayes are. Xu *etc.* [21] used correlation coefficient analysis to build a linear model. Chan *etc.* [22] designed a multi-classification algorithm, which combines the feature selection method based on genetic algorithms and error-correcting output code, to train the prediction model. The study applying transfer learning to performance prediction [23] appears with the development of neural network.

A few works have been conducted for blended learning. Lu *etc.* [24] analyzed the correlation between learning behavior feature and final grades based on blended data, eliminated low correlation features such as the days of video watching per week, the number of video watching per week, *etc.*, and conducted a comparative experiment on the prediction performance of different datasets. Dimic *etc.* [25] conducted the performance prediction which used a correlation-based feature selection algorithm to reduce data dimension, and obtained the best feature subset of online and offline learning features.

To sum up, the study of learning behavior analysis and performance prediction mostly focuses on MOOC data, and lacks the method of extracting behavioral features from raw data. The analysis of blended learning data mining is less, and it is necessary to carry out the research in this area.

3 Analysis of Learning Behavior in Blended Study

Online learning is characterized by scattered learning time and place, strong learners' autonomy and diverse learning strategies. Offline learning is relatively concentrated in time and place with clearer and more consistent learning tasks and progress, in addition, the real-time interactions between teachers and students. In blended teaching, the motivation of students is basically the same, students' mental development and knowledge level are roughly same, and the learning tasks are mostly prescriptive, so it is difficult to characterize learning behaviors through aggregate information (e.g., total number of completed exercises, total time spent in watching videos). The temporal features in learning behavior can better describe the learning process and contribute to the depth analysis [26]. Therefore, based on the temporal characteristics of learning behavior, two learning behavior indicators are defined: learning enthusiasm and stability; and then the distribution, correlation, consistency, and effectiveness of the indicators are analyzed based on actual data.

3.1 Learning Enthusiasm and Stability

Regardless of online or offline learning, the learning process can be abstracted as learners completing the corresponding learning tasks within a specified period of time, and the concatenation of these periods is called a semester. The time points at which learner complete tasks are scattered throughout the semester. Early or late completions can portray students' learning enthusiasm. The stability of a learner's learning can be portrayed by whether the learner is able to consistently complete each task in a stable state. Learning tasks have many forms. Online quizzes and video watching are as examples to illustrate the quantitative analysis of enthusiasm and stability.

Enthusiasm. Assume that the kth Learner are asked to complete n quizzes in a semester, and the learner can schedule his/her own completion time $T_{i,k}$ for the ith task. The absolute enthusiasm of this learner, LE_k, can be quantified as:

$$LE_k = \frac{1}{n} \sum_{i=1}^{n} \frac{Time\_Diff\left(T_{i,k}, T_{i,last}\right)}{Time\_Diff\left(T_{i,first}, T_{i,last}\right)} \tag{1}$$

where $T_{i,first}$, $T_{i,last}$ are the earliest and latest completion time of all students in the ith quiz, and the function $Time\_Diff$ calculates the temporal interval.

The standardized relative enthusiasm of the learner is defined as follows, where $LE_{sample-max}$ is the maximum value of the sample.

$$Score_{LE,k} = \frac{LE_k}{LE_{sample-max}} \tag{2}$$

Stability. In blended study, learners are often required to watch instructional videos online to acquire the corresponding knowledge [27]. Assume that students' completion time of watching m videos is abstracted as $T = (t_1, t_2 \ldots t_m)$ where $t_i < t_{i+1}$ then the intervals can be defined as $D = (d_1, d_2 \ldots d_{m-1})$, $d_i = Time\_Diff(t_i, t_{i+1})$. For brevity, student's number k is omitted.

D can be normalized to a set of random variables P. And the information entropy of P can quantify the stability of student video learning LS.

$$p_i = \frac{d_i}{\sum_i d_i} \tag{3}$$

$$LS = -\sum_{i=1}^{m-1} p_i \log_a p_i \tag{4}$$

The stability score of students' learning stability is obtained after normalization, where $LS_{sample-max}$ is the maximum value of the sample.

$$Score_{LS} = \frac{LS}{LS_{sample-max}} \tag{5}$$

3.2   Case Analysis

The actual data is from the desensitized data of the blended course 2020 "Programming fundamentals" of Jilin University in China, including 872 students. The online activities include: video watching, chapter quizzes and online jobs. The offline activities are mainly reflected in the five phase programming exams.

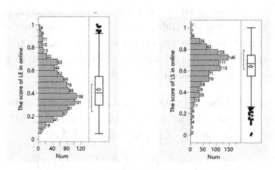

Fig. 1. Distribution of enthusiasm and stability of online learning behavior, where LE represents level of enthusiasm, LS represents level of stability.

Online Learning Behavior Analysis. Based on the enthusiasm and stability proposed in the previous section, the comprehensive enthusiasm and stability of online learning behaviors are calculated as follows:

$$Score_{LE-online} = k_1 \times Score_{LE-video} + k_2 \times Score_{LE-Job} + k_3 \times Score_{LE-quiz} \tag{6}$$

k_1, k_2, k_3 are normalized weight coefficients ($k_1 + k_2 + k_3 = 1$), and determined by the Pearson correlation coefficient corresponding to enthusiasms and final score, student discrimination and expert knowledge. Similarly, stability is defined as:

$$Score_{LS-online} = k_1 \times Score_{LS-video} + k_2 \times Score_{LS-Job} + k_3 \times Score_{LS-quiz} \tag{7}$$

The analysis of online and offline learning behaviors yields the following analysis results. The distribution of enthusiasm and stability of online learning is shown in Fig. 1. The vertical axis of the bar chart is the enthusiasm and stability values. The horizontal axis is the cumulative number of students within the certain value intervals. The square brackets outside the box identifies the shortest half-set, which is the densest 50% of the observations, and the scatters are the outliers. It can be seen that the enthusiasm is positively skewed and the stability is negatively skewed. It indicates that the online learning enthusiasm is generally low while the stability is high.

Among the multiple online activities, video watching has the highest mean enthusiasm, online job is in the middle, and chapter quiz is the lowest, as shown in Fig. 2. The enthusiasms of above activities have a strong correlation. And the correlation coefficients and joint distribution are shown in Fig. 3.

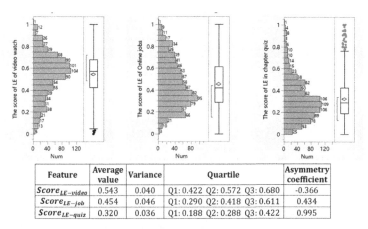

Feature	Average value	Variance	Quartile	Asymmetry coefficient
$Score_{LE-video}$	0.543	0.040	Q1: 0.422 Q2: 0.572 Q3: 0.680	-0.366
$Score_{LE-job}$	0.454	0.046	Q1: 0.290 Q2: 0.418 Q3: 0.611	0.434
$Score_{LE-quiz}$	0.320	0.036	Q1: 0.188 Q2: 0.288 Q3: 0.422	0.995

Fig. 2. Distribution of three kinds of online learning enthusiasms

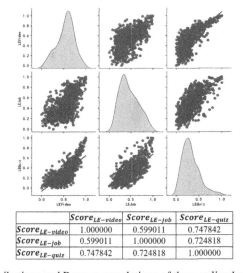

	$Score_{LE-video}$	$Score_{LE-job}$	$Score_{LE-quiz}$
$Score_{LE-video}$	1.000000	0.599011	0.747842
$Score_{LE-job}$	0.599011	1.000000	0.724818
$Score_{LE-quiz}$	0.747842	0.724818	1.000000

Fig. 3. Joint distributions and Pearson correlations of three online learning enthusiasms

Offline Learning Behavior Analysis. The offline learning activities include four stage exams and one final exam where students complete a number of OJ (Online Judge) programming questions in the same location and within the same time period. Offline learning enthusiasm is defined by the point when students make their first submission of each question, and offline learning stability is defined by the students' response time of each question.

The distributions of enthusiasm and stability of offline learning are shown in Fig. 4, where enthusiasm and stability are approximate normal distribution, and the skewness of both is small.

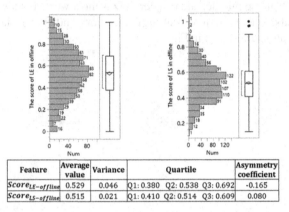

Feature	Average value	Variance	Quartile	Asymmetry coefficient
$Score_{LE-offline}$	0.529	0.046	Q1: 0.380 Q2: 0.538 Q3: 0.692	-0.165
$Score_{LS-offline}$	0.515	0.021	Q1: 0.410 Q2: 0.514 Q3: 0.609	0.080

Fig. 4. The distribution of enthusiasm and stability of offline learning behavior

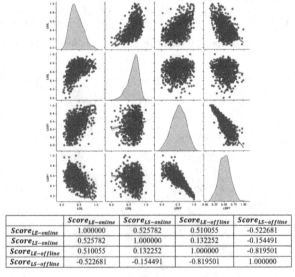

	$Score_{LE-online}$	$Score_{LS-online}$	$Score_{LE-offline}$	$Score_{LS-offline}$
$Score_{LE-online}$	1.000000	0.525782	0.510055	-0.522681
$Score_{LS-online}$	0.525782	1.000000	0.132252	-0.154491
$Score_{LE-offline}$	0.510055	0.132252	1.000000	-0.819501
$Score_{LS-offline}$	-0.522681	-0.154491	-0.819501	1.000000

Fig. 5. Joint distribution and correlations of online and offline learning initiative and stability, where OL represents Online and OFF is Offline

Consistency Analysis of Learning Behavior. In blended learning, do students' online and offline learning behaviors show consistent patterns? The distribution analysis of their distribution difference as above. The joint distribution of the two learning behavior indicators in both online and offline environments.

As shown in Fig. 5, different behavior indicators in the same teaching environment are strongly correlated, comprehensive online stability is weakly correlated with all offline indicators, comprehensive online enthusiasm is strongly correlated with all offline indicators. Among all strongly correlated pairs, the pairs including offline stability show negative correlation, while others are positively correlated.

In order to analyze the differences of online and offline behaviors, the offline are subtracted from the online. The distribution of the differences is shown in Fig. 6. It indicates that the online enthusiasm is slightly lower than the offline, the online stability is slightly higher than the offline, and the two differences are not related.

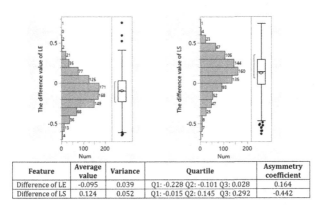

Feature	Average value	Variance	Quartile	Asymmetry coefficient
Difference of LE	-0.095	0.039	Q1: -0.228 Q2: -0.101 Q3: 0.028	0.164
Difference of LS	0.124	0.052	Q1: -0.015 Q2: 0.145 Q3: 0.292	-0.442

Fig. 6. Distribution of the difference between learning enthusiasm and stability

Analysis of the Effectiveness of Learning Behavior. The offline final exam reflects the comprehensive learning effect. The final exam grade s, $0 \leq s \leq 1$, adopts the standard score in the form of ranking percentage, 0 is the best score and 1 is the worst. if $s \leq 0.8$, of the students are qualified, others are unqualified. The correlations between the learning behavior indicators and the final grade s are evaluated to describes the effectiveness of learning behavior.

The grouping histogram of the correlation between online and offline indicators with final grade are shown in Fig. 7. It can be seen that final grade is significantly negatively correlated with online and offline enthusiasm (correlation coefficients are -0.48 and -0.62) and has a significant positive correlation with offline stability (correlation coefficient is 0.58), while has a weak negative correlation with online stability (correlation coefficient is -0.21).

The correlation between the joint distribution of learning behavior indicators and the final grade is shown in Fig. 8. The values in each region on the heat map correspond to the average grade of students in the region spanning that indicator. Green refers to a good learning effect with high ranks, while red with low ranks. Under the same teaching environment, the online indicators have a strong positive correlation with the learning effect. Interestingly in offline teaching, it shows that students with low stability and high enthusiasm would get a better learning effect.

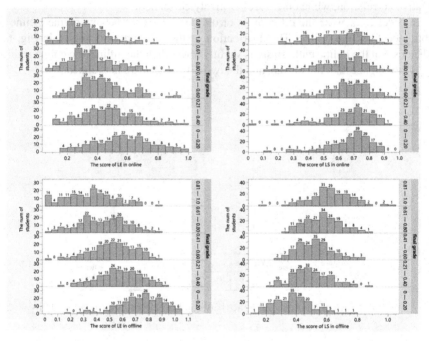

Fig. 7. Correlations between learning enthusiasm, stability and final grade

The correlation between the difference of online and offline indicators with final rank is shown in Fig. 9. The enthusiasm difference has a positive correlation with the rank (correlation coefficient is 0.23), and the stability difference is strongly negatively correlated with the rank (correlation coefficient is -0.51).

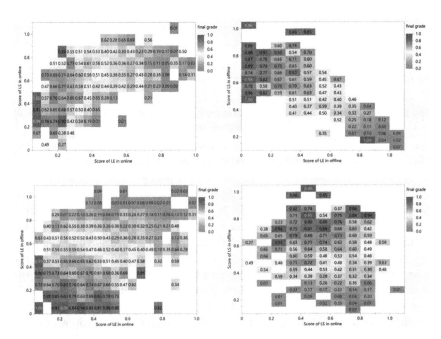

Fig. 8. Heat map of correlations between final rank with enthusiasm and stability

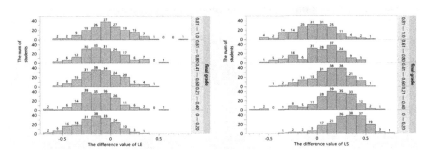

Fig. 9. The correlations of difference between online and offline indicators

4 Performance Prediction

The prediction problem in this section is to predict whether a student would pass the final exam. According to the data source, the data features can be divided into learner base information, online learning data and offline learning data, as shown in Table 1.

Table 1. Feature set description

Feature dimension	Feature description
Basic Information (BI)	4 features include learners' physiological characteristics and existing knowledge level
Online Information (ONI)	12 features include online learning completions, online task scores and online stability and enthusiasm proposed in this paper
Offline Information (OFFI)	17 features include the scores of 4 offline exams, answer quality, the offline enthusiasm and stability proposed in this paper

Naive Bayes classifier (NB), *Decision Tree classifier* (DT) and *Random Forest classifier* (RF) are used. The data set is divided into the training and the test set in a 7:3 ratio and four feature set are selected, *i.e.*, BI + ONI, OFFI, BI + ONI + OFFI and *reduced feature set* (RFS). RFS is selected with forest optimization feature selection algorithm [28] on BI + ONI + OFFI. Experiments shows that the average reduction rate of the feature set of basic information and online data is 37.5%, while 52.9% of the offline feature set. In each iteration, 3 or 4 of the proposed learning behavior indicators are retained. The results of each classifier with different feature sets are shown in Table 2 and Fig. 10, where the underlined bold values are the best results.

Table 2. Prediction results of the experiment

Feature set	Classifier	Accuracy	Precision	Recall	F-score
BI + ONI	NB	77.9	65.9	67.7	47.3
	DT	80.5	59.3	53.0	13.6
	RF	77.5	58.4	54.8	23.4
OFFI	NB	79.0	72.5	83.2	62.6
	DT	84.0	77.5	64.0	43.2
	RF	85.9	78.6	72.6	58.4
BI + ONI + OFFI	NB	79.0	73.1	84.7	63.6
	DT	85.5	77.3	73.9	59.6
	RF	84.0	74.5	71.5	55.3
RFS	NB	81.5	77.9	**89.3**	71.5
	DT	86.3	77.9	81.8	67.9
	RF	**90.1**	**85.7**	81.2	**72.3**

Through the above experiments, it is found that (1) The classifier can get an acceptable prediction about 80% accuracy based on the BI + ONI. (2) A better prediction can be obtained only by OFFI with 85% accuracy; (3) the prediction using all features is as good as that only using OFFI; (4) the best prediction is on the RFS with 90% accuracy.

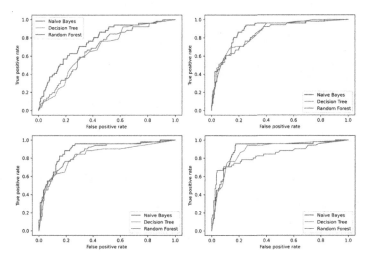

Fig. 10. ROC curves for different feature sets. The feature sets from top to bottom and from left to right are BI + ONI, OFFI, BI + ONI + OFFI and RFS respectively.

To sum up, the offline features contribute more to the prediction, offline teaching activities are necessary and reflect the learning effect better in blended teaching. The proposed learning behavior indicators effectively compress the feature set and obtain better prediction results, which prove that the indicators are of great importance.

5   Conclusion and Future Work

Different from MOOC, most learning tasks in blended teaching are mandatory, and the completion is basically at the same level. Aggregated data cannot correctly describe the learning process and state. This paper focused on the temporal factor in the learning process, defines learning behavior indicators: enthusiasm and stability; then analyzed the distribution, correlation, consistency and effectiveness of online and offline indicators; finally based on the basic learners' information, online and offline learning data, the learning effect is predicted. The conclusions are: (1) There is a strong correlation between different behavior indicators in the same teaching environment, and the same behavior indicator in different teaching environments has a strong correlation too. (2) All the learning behavior indicators are strongly correlated with the final rank. (3) Compared the online indicators with offline indicators of the same student, the offline enthusiasm is higher and the stability is lower. The stability difference is related to the final learning grade. (4) Learning enthusiasm and stability can help classifier get better predictions.

In summary, the learning behavior indicator based on temporal factor can better describe the process and state of blended learning and give a better performance prediction. Further enrich offline teacher-student interaction, classroom practice, quizzes and other data, joint analyze multiple blended teaching courses and then establish a general blended learner model, all of these are the future research directions.

Acknowledgments. This paper is supported by National Natural Science Foundation of China under Grant Nos. 61502198, 61472161, 61402195, 61103091, U19A2061;the Science and Technology Development Plan of Jilin Province under Grant No. 20210101414JC, 20160520099JH, 20190302117GX, 20180101334JC, 2019C053–3; Research Topic of Higher Education Teaching Reform in Jilin Province under Grant No. 20213F2QZ6100FV; Jilin University Undergraduate Teaching Reform Research Project under Grant No. 2021XYB125.

References

1. Shah, D.: Monetization over massiveness: A review of MOOC stats and trends in. Class Central (2016)
2. Yang, Y., Zhang, H., Chai, H., Xu, W.. Design and application of intelligent teaching space for blended teaching. Interactive Learning Environments, 1–18 (2022)
3. Hu, J., Peng, Y., Chen, X., Yu, H.: Differentiating the learning styles of college students in different disciplines in a college English blended learning setting. PLoS ONE **16**(5), e0251545 (2021)
4. Baneres, D., Rodríguez-Gonzalez, M.E., Serra, M.: An early feedback prediction system for learners at-risk within a first-year higher education course. IEEE Trans. Learn. Technol. **12**(2), 249–263 (2019)
5. Xie, S.-T., Chen, Q., Liu, K.H., Kong, Q.Z., Coa, X.J.: Learning behavior analysis using clustering and evolutionary error correcting output code algorithms in small private online courses. Sci. Program. (2021)
6. Xie, S.-T., H,e Z.-B., Chen, Q., etc. Predicting learning behavior using log data in blended teaching. Sci. Program. 2021
7. Luo, Y., Chen, N., Han, X.: Students' online behavior patterns impact on final grades prediction in blended courses. In: Proceedings of the 9th IEEE Conference of Educational Innovation through Technology (EITT) (2020)
8. Luan, H., Tsai, C.-C.: A review of using machine learning approaches for precision education. Educ. Technol Soc. **24**(1), 250–266 (2021)
9. Lin, Y., Feng, S., Lin, F., Zeng, W., Liu, Y., Wu, P.: Adaptive course recommendation in MOOCs. Knowl.-Based Syst. **224**, 107085 (2021)
10. Qiu, M., Xue, C., Shao, Z.. Sha, E.: Energy minimization with soft real-time and DVS for uniprocessor and multiprocessor embedded systems. In: Proceedings of the IEEE Conference and Exhibition on Design, Automation & Test in Europe (DATE), pp. 1–6 (2007)
11. Qiu, M., Liu, J., Li, J., et al.: A novel energy-aware fault tolerance mechanism for wireless sensor networks. In: Proceedings of the IEEE/ACM International Conference on GCC (2011)
12. Lu, Z., Wang, N., et al.: IoTDeM: An IoT Big Data-oriented MapReduce performance prediction extended model in multiple edge clouds. JPDC **118**, 316–327 (2018)
13. Qiu, L., Gai, K., et al.: Optimal big data sharing approach for tele-health in cloud computing. In: Proceedings of the IEEE SmartCloud, pp. 184–189 (2016)
14. Liu, M., Zhang, S., et al.: H infinite state estimation for discrete-time chaotic systems based on a unified model. IEEE Trans. on Syst. Man Cybern. (B) (2012)
15. Qiu, M., Li, H., Sha, E.: Heterogeneous real-time embedded software optimization considering hardware platform. ACM Sym. Applied Comp., 1637–1641 (2009)
16. Wu, G., Zhang, H., et al.: A decentralized approach for mining event correlations in distributed system monitoring. JPDC **73**(3), 330–340 (2013)
17. Li, Y., Song, Y., et al.: Intelligent fault diagnosis by fusing domain adversarial training and maximum mean discrepancy via ensemble learning. IEEE TII **17**(4), 2833–2841 (2020)

18. Gardner, J., Brooks, C.: Student success prediction in MOOCs. User Model. User-Adap. Inter. **28**(2), 127–203 (2018)
19. Mubarak, A.A., Cao, H., Ahmed, S.A.: Predictive learning analytics using deep learning model in MOOCs' courses videos. Educ. Info. Tech. **26**(1), 371–392 (2021)
20. Sunar, A.S., Abbasi, R.A., Davis, H.C.: Modelling MOOC learners' social behaviours. Comput. Human Behav. **107**, 105835 (2020)
21. Xu, Z., Yuan, H., Liu, Q.: Student performance prediction based on blended learning. IEEE Trans. Educ. **64**(1), 66–73 (2020)
22. Chan, K.T.: Embedding formative assessment in blended learning environment: The case of secondary Chinese language teaching in Singapore. Edu. Sci. **11**(7), 360 (2021)
23. Tsiakmaki, M., Kostopoulos, G., Kotsiantis, S., Ragos, O.: Transfer learning from deep neural networks for predicting student performance. Appl. Sci.-Basel **10**(6), 2145 (2020)
24. Lu, H., Huang, Y.: Applying learning analytics for the early prediction of students' academic performance in blended learning. J. Educ. Tech. Soc. **21**(2), 220–232 (2018)
25. Dimic, G., Rancic, D., Macek, N., Spalevic, P., Drasute, V.: Improving the prediction accuracy in blended learning environment using synthetic minority oversampling technique. Info. Disc. Delivery **47**, 76–83 (2019)
26. Knight, S., Wise, A.F., Chen, B.: Time for change: Why learning analytics needs temporal analysis. J. Learn. Anal. **4**(3), 7–17 (2017)
27. Guo, P.J., Kim, J., Rubin, R.: How video production affects student engagement: An empirical study of MOOC videos. In: Proceedings of the 1st ACM Conference on Learning@ Scale Conference (2014)
28. Chu, B., Li, Z.S., Zhang, M.L., Yu, H.H.: Research on improvements of feature selection using forest optimization algorithm. J. Softw. **29**(9), 2547–2558 (2018). (in Chinese)

Multi-objective Beetle Swarmoptimization for Portfolio Selection

Tan Yan[✉]

College of Computer Science, Sichuan University, Chengdu, China
tany@stu.scu.edu.cn

Abstract. The multi-objective portfolio optimization is regarded as an multi-objective optimization problem which is complicated and hard to find a satisfactory solution in a limited time. It is more complex and difficult to use the conventional method to solve this problem. In this paper, we first establish a mean-CVaR-entropy model with transaction costs and investment weight restrictions, and then propose a Multi-objective Optimization Algorithm for BeetleSearch(MOBSO), a meta-heuristic optimization algorithm, and a variant of Beetle Antennae Search (BAS) algorithm, which is applied into portfolio optimization to solve this constraint multi-objective optimization problem. Finally, we use the 20 stocksfrom January 2017 to December 2021 in the US stock market to do case studyand compare the results with other meta-heuristic optimization algorithms. It shows that the MOBSO outperforms swarm algorithms such as the particle swarm optimization (PSO) and the genetic algorithm(GA).

Keywords: Multi-objective portfolio optimization · Beetle Antennae Search (BAS) · Particle Swarm Optimization (PSO) · Meta-heuristic optimization · Finance problem

1 Introduction

With the increase in household income and the improvement of the financial system, investment has become the main solution to maintain and add the value of assets for more and more people. However, Financial markets are complicated and uncertain which makes it difficult for people to determine a proper investment solution. How realize the effective allocation of capital is essential for both investment institutions and individual investors [29–30]. To maximize the expected mean return and minimize the risk, the investment portfolio theory is introduced [31].

Modern Portfolio Theory (MPT) [1] is proposed by Markowitz in 1952. The idea of MPT is to take the mathematical expectation of asset returns as the portfolio return and take the mathematical covariance of the asset as portfolio risk. However, It has some limitations [2]: First, the decision-making results excessively depend on the expected level of return on assets [3], since the assumptions of MPT derived from the mean-variance model and its framework are relatively strict. Second, the optimal allocation is often concentrated on a single asset or security, which is not satisfied in terms of risk

© The Author(s), under exclusive license to Springer Nature Switzerland AG 2022
G. Memmi et al. (Eds.): KSEM 2022, LNAI 13369, pp. 610–620, 2022.
https://doi.org/10.1007/978-3-031-10986-7_49

diversification [4]. Third, the model is too sensitive to the input parameters [5].Slight changes in parameters may lead to drastic changes in the allocation results. To solve these limitations, researchers take efforts via different criteria portfolio models.

To consider the complicated financial market environment, Rockafellaretal [7] proposed CVaR (Conditional Value-at-Risk) model, which not only satisfies sub-additivity but also adequately measures the risk profile in extreme situations. The diversification of investment risk has attracted much attention from researchers. The concept of entropy is introduced to judge the correlation degree between various assets [8]. The entropy value canbe used to measure the dispersion degree of the portfolio [9]. Based on this, a mean-CVaR-entropy model is established. The model uses CVaR and entropy as objective functions [10].

Since the portfolio selection is regarded as amulti-objective optimization problem [27], meta-heuristic approaches become very popular to solve it, because of their powerful performance on the optimization problem. Some outstanding work has been done using meta-heuristic algorithms, which include particle swarm optimization (PSO) [11–15], and genetic algorithm (GA) [15, 16]. Some hybrid techniques, which include quadratic programming and local minima search are also employed [17, 18]. The obtained results show that novel methods outsmart the prior techniques in efficiency and accuracy. In recent years, a new algorithm called the beetle antennae search (BAS) algorithm [19–25] is widely studied. The BAS algorithm is inspired via the searching behavior of longhorn beetles, which imitates the function of antennae and the random walking mechanism of beetles in nature, and then two main steps of detecting and searching are implemented. In this paper, we design an improved multi-objective PSO based on the BAS algorithm (BSO) to solve the multi-objective optimization problem under the mean-CVaR-entropy model. Compared with the optimization algorithms, such as PSO and GA, it is neither computationally expensive nor time-consuming nor complex as it involves a single particle to search through space and reaches the optimal solution. To test the algorithm efficiency, we use stock data from Nasdaq and apply BSO on different stacks of stocks and then compared its performance with PSO and GA.

The rest of the paper is organized as follows. Section 2 discusses how to establish a mean-CVaR-entropy model, considering the real-world investment transaction scenario. Section 3 describes the PSO based on the BAS algorithm in detail, and then MOBSO is proposed and discussed step by step. Section 4 is case study, via solving the portfolio selection problem with several stocks from Nasdaq, and then MOBSO performance is compared with PSO, GA. In the end, conclusions and future works are given in Sect. 5.

2 Portfolio Selection Model

Consider an investor has the total amount of investment as T, who wants to choose some assets out of n kinds of assets available. Each asset expects to gain some anticipated mean return, and also some risks are attached to it. The investor has to decide which assets to invest in and how much for it. This is a portfolio selection problem. The investor wants to maximize his profit while minimizing the risk involved, which is seen as a multi-objective optimization problem. To compute the portfolio, it is a trade-off between maximizing profit and minimizing the risk to attain its optimal global value.

2.1 Mean-CVaR-Entropy Model Under Transaction Cost Consideration

Assume the proportion of each investment asset to the total investment is, prefers to the expected return of the portfolio, CVaR refers to the average loss suffered by the portfolio, $x_i lnx_i$ is the information entropy, which represents the average uncertainty of information transmission. λ is the proportion of information entropy, set to 0.2. The objective function of the mean-CVaR-entropy model can be expressed.

$$minM = (1 - \lambda)r_{CVaR} + \lambda \sum_{i=1}^{20} x_i lnx_i$$

$$maxr_p$$

Considering that the sum of the investment ratio of each asset is equal to 1, and the securities market prohibits short-selling and short-selling, the investment amount can only be used to invest in n stocks or risk-free assets.

$$\sum_{thei=1}^{20} x_i = 1$$

$$x_i \geq 0(i = 1, 2, \ldots, n)$$

The expected return of the portfolio is the weighted sum of the expected returns of each stock, minus the transaction costs incurred in the transaction (including taxes and various transaction fees) [26].

Transaction costs include the following fees:

(1) Stamp duty. It will be charged to the seller at 1‰ of the transaction amount, and it will be withheld by the brokerage and paid by the stock exchange.
(2) Commission fee. 5 dollars each time.
(3) Commission. After the transaction is completed, the investor pays the brokerage a fee of 3‰ of the transaction amount, starting from a minimum of 5 dollars.

Then all transaction costs for risky securities are:

$$C_i(n_i) = k_0 + k_1(n_i)$$

which includes,

$$k_0 = 5$$

$$k_1(n_i) = max\{5, 100\mu_1 n_i p_i\}$$

Among them, $C_i(n_i)$ represents the transaction cost when investing in the i-th stock and the trading lot is n_i. k_0 is the commission fee, $k_1(n_i)$ is the commission when the i-th stock trading lot is n, and μ_1 is the cost coefficient of the commission. The expected rate of return can be expressed as:

$$r_p = \sum_{i=1}^{20} r_i x_i - C_i(n_i)$$

The portfolio model and its constraints are expressed as follows:

$$minM = (1 - \lambda) r_{CVaR} + \lambda \sum_{i=1}^{20} x_i ln x_i$$

$$maxr_p$$

subject to:

$$\begin{cases} \sum_{i=1}^{20} x_i = 1 \\ x_i \geq 0 (i = 1, 2, \ldots, 20) \\ r_p = \sum_{i=1}^{20} r_i x_i - C_i(n_i) \\ C_i(n_i) = k_0 + k_1(n_i) \end{cases}$$

3   Particle Swarm Optimization Algorithm Based on Beetle Search

3.1   Beetle AntennaeSearch Algorithm

The beetle antennae search (BAS) algorithm is for multi-objective function optimization based on the foraging principle of the beetle proposed in 2017 [12]. Its biological principle is: when the beetle is foraging, It does not know where the food is, but instead forages according to the strength of the food's smell. The beetle has two long antennae. If the smell intensity received by the left antenna is stronger than that of the right, the beetle will fly to the left in the next step, otherwise, it will fly to the right. According to this simple principle, the beetle can effectively find food. Like genetic algorithm, particle swarm algorithm, etc., BAS can automatically realize the optimization process without knowing the specific form and gradient information of the function, and its individual is only one, and the optimization speed is significantly improved. The modeling steps are as follows:

(1)   Create a random vector of the direction of the beard of the beetle and normalize:

$$\overrightarrow{b} = \frac{rands(k, 1)}{\|rands(k, 1)\|}$$

where:$rands()$ is a random function; k is the spatial dimension.

(2) Create the spatial coordinates of the left and right whiskers of the beetle

$$\begin{cases} x_{rt} = x^t + d_0 * \overrightarrow{b}/2 \\ x_{lt} = x^t - d_0 * \overrightarrow{b}/2 \end{cases} (t = 0, 1, 2, \ldots, n)$$

In the formula: x_{rt} represents the position coordinates of the right whiskers of the beetles at the t-th iteration; x_{lt} represents the position coordinates of the left beards of the beetles at the t-th iteration; x_t represents the centroid coordinates of the beetles at the t-the iteration; d_0 Indicates the distance between the two whiskers.

(3) Judging the odor intensity of the left and right whiskers according to the fitness function, that is, the intensity of $f(x_l)$ and $f(x_r)$, and the $f()$ is the fitness function.

(4) Iteratively update the position of the beetle

$$x^{t+1} = x^t - \delta^t * \overrightarrow{b} * sign(f(x_{rt}) - f(x_{lt}))$$

In the formula: x^t represents the centroid coordinate in the t-th iteration of the beetle, x_{lt} represents the left antenna coordinate in the t-th iteration, x_{rt} represents the right-side antenna coordinate in the t-th iteration. δ_t represents the Step factor at iteration t; $sign()$ is the sign function.

3.2 Multi-objective Particle Swarm Algorithm Based on BAS

The BAS algorithm is only for individuals and does not consider the connections between groups. PSO focuses on the influence of groups on individual particles, ignoring the particle's own judgment in the search process. Therefore, this paper integrates the BAS and PSO models and proposes a Multi-Objective Optimization Algorithm for Beard Search (MOBSO) [13]. Each particle in the PSO is described as a beetle and searched, and the process of the initial position and velocity of the beetle is the same as that of the standard PSO. Individuals in MOBSO will compare their left and right fitness function values during each iteration, and compare the better value of the two, which can be used to update the position of the beetle herd. The MOBSO constructed by this method can well overcome the problems of poor stability caused by the PSO algorithm and tend to be local optimum. The modeling steps are as follows (Fig. 1):

(1) Initialize the algorithm parameters, set the size of the PSO as N, the learning factors as c_1, c_2, c_3, the inertia weight as W, and the distance between the two antennas of each beetle as d_0.

(2) Randomly initialize the position x and velocity v, calculate the fitness of each position, use the current position as the individual optimal solution P_{best}, and finally obtain the current global optimal value G_{best} through comparison.

(3) Iteration:

a) Randomize the beetle heads. Calculate each beetle's left distance X_{left} and fitness f_{left}, and right distance X_{right} and fitness f_{right} for each beetle based on the beetle's position. By comparing the two, the obtained is generated by the left and right fitness of each beetle in the colony The speed update rule of

$$vb_i = -\delta^t * \overrightarrow{b} * sign(f(x_{rt}) - f(x_{lt}))$$

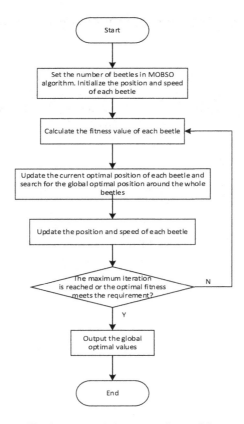

Fig. 1. The modeling steps of MOBSO.

b) By comparing the fitness sum of the current position of each beetle, the individual optimal solution P_{best} and the global optimal solution G_{best} are obtained.

c) Current update rules for the antenna speed of each beetle:

$$v_i^{k+1} = v_i^k + c_1 * rand * \left(Pb_i^k - x_i^k \right) + c_2 * rand * \left(Pg_i^k - x_i^k \right) + c_3 * rand * vb_1$$

Location update rules:

$$x_i^{k+1} = x_i^k + v_i^{k+1}$$

d) The updated learning factors and inertia weights are c_1, c_2, c_3, w, respectively, the updated individual optimal solution P_{best} and the global optimal solution G_{best}.

e) After the iteration is completed, the global optimal solution G_{best} and the corresponding optimal solution position $f(G_{best})$ can be obtained.

4 Particle Swarm Optimization Algorithm Based on Beetle Search

4.1 Data Description

Select daily index data from January 2017 to December 2021 in the US stock market. Select 20 assets, including AAPL, ADBE, AMD, AMZN, CSCO, CTXS, EA, EBAY, FB, GOOGL, HP, IBM, INTC, JNPR, MSFT, NFLX, NTAP, NVDA, QCOM.. The descriptive statistics of the sample data are shown in Table 1. It can be seen from Table 1 that the relative returns of AMD, AMZN, FB, NFLX, and NVDA stock indexes are relatively high, and correspondingly, the returns of these indexes are also more volatile [26].

Table 1. Descriptive statistics of sample

Stock	Annualized rate of return	Return standard deviation	Stock	Annualized rate of return	Return standard deviation
AAPL	7.86%	14.59%	GOOGL	8.79%	13.87%
ADBE	13.82%	15.32%	HP	2.96%	22.79%
AMD	18.80%	37.77%	IBM	1.44%	11.87%
AMZN	15.06%	18.23%	INTC	7.06%	13.94%
CSCO	6.00%	13.25%	JNPR	2.84%	18.03%
CTXS	3.06%	17.70%	MSFT	10.38%	14.20%
DE	5.25%	13.14%	NFLX	22.15%	27.34%
EA	17.52%	20.05%	NTAP	5.21%	16.94%
EBAY	1.17%	22.83%	NVDA	25.61%	22.34%
FB	16.59%	20.09%	QCOM	1.10%	16.16%

As mentioned above, in the construction of the portfolio model, it is necessary to meet the requirement that the sum of the risk contributions of all assets in the portfolio is equal to the overall risk of the portfolio, and in this process, the correlation between asset returns must be considered. Therefore, The income correlation of each asset in the analysis sample is as follows. Due to space limitations, only some asset income correlations are shown, as shown in Table 2.

Table 2. Relationship among the asset

	AAPL	ADBE	AMD	AMZN	CSCO	CTXS	EA	EBAY	FB	GOOGL
AAPL	100.00%	10.41%	3.78%	12.36%	12.09%	3.22%	9.45%	2.59%	13.07%	20.55%
ADBE	11.68%	100.00%	5.22%	23.88%	19.21%	19.32%	15.57%	8.59%	18.94%	33.85%
AMD	34.40%	40.97%	100.00%	23.13%	28.34%	11.09%	22.77%	12.61%	18.27%	7.88%
AMZN	18.42%	34.17%	4.13%	100.00%	12.01%	13.92%	19.41%	6.01%	31.38%	64.93%
CSCO	12.03%	15.42%	2.54%	8.65%	100.00%	12.60%	7.18%	4.70%	4.75%	14.81%
CTXS	9.24%	30.43%	2.22%	16.64%	27.92%	100.00%	12.86%	9.37%	11.85%	27.88%
EA	17.25%	27.03%	5.20%	24.02%	12.49%	13.08%	100.00%	5.13%	13.41%	28.80%
EBAY	7.61%	21.90%	3.99%	11.72%	14.22%	14.55%	8.34%	100.00%	6.46%	32.13%
FB	27.11%	35.23%	4.26%	39.89%	8.31%	13.00%	14.35%	4.44%	100.00%	57.97%
GOOGL	14.90%	24.06%	0.00%	33.67%	8.90%	11.17%	11.87%	8.89%	23.37%	100.00%

4.2   Case Study

This paper also uses U.S. stocks to verify the data with numerical examples. The comparison results show that from the perspective of yield, Sharpe ratio, volatility, and other metrics, the overall performance of the bas optimization algorithm is better than that of pso, ga, and other algorithms.

4.2.1   Return on Equity

Return on Equity (ROE) equals net profit divided by net assets, and is a measure of how efficiently a company uses its capital. The higher the value of this indicator, the higher the returns brought by the investment, and it is an important indicator to measure the profitability of the investment portfolio. The higher the ROE, the stronger the profitability. In a market economy, every investor will pursue the goal of maximizing profit, so the return on the investment portfolio is very important [28].

Return rate comparison between MOBSO and PSO, GA is shown as Fig. 2. At the beginning of iteration, MOBSO, PSO and GA selected initial points randomly. After that (5 iterations later), MOBSO outperforms the other two algorithm. In Fig. 2, the return rate of MOBSO is much higher than PSO and GA after 20 times of iteration. When iteration number gets to 100, It is shown that PSO falls into the local optimal solution while GA does not fall into the local optimal solution temporarily. The iteration efficiency of PSO and GA is much slower than MOBSO.

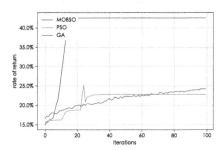

Fig. 2. Return on Equity by three optimization algorithms.

4.2.2   Sharpe Ratio

To evaluate the performance of the portfolio selection, sharperatio [28] is used from the perspective of risk-adjusted return. Sharpe ratio not only focuses on the return of assets, but also the risk of assets [32]. It measures the return of assets adjusted for risk and is the price display of unit risk. Because Sharpe ratio comprehensively reflects the risk-return characteristics of the capital market, it has been widely used to evaluate the performance of asset portfolio, evaluate the operating efficiency of the capital market, construct effective asset portfolio, and guide investment decisions [33].

Figure 3 shows the sharpe ratio comparison between MOBSO and PSO, GA. The sharpe ratio of MOBSO is lower than GA at the beginning, since MOBSO select initialization points randomly. Over 20 times of iteration, PSO is prone to fall into local optimum. MOBSO outperforms PSO and GA. The convergence speed of MOBSO is much higher than PSO and GA. That means MOBSO has much better risk-adjusted return than PSO and GA.

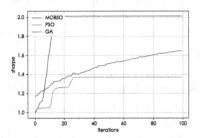

Fig. 3. Sharpe ratio by three optimization algorithms.

Overall, BSO has the best performance in terms of yield, volatility, and Sharpe ratio, far outperforming PSO and GA.

In Table 3, we summarize earnings performance between MOBSO, PSO and GA. MOBSO outperforms PSO and GA, in terms of yield, volatility, and Sharpe ratio.The iteration time of BSO is the same as that of GA, both about 55 s, but the convergence effect of BSO is significantly better than that of GA at the same time. Meanwhile, BSO not only consumes less time than PSO, but also has better convergence effect.

Table 3. Comparisions on earings performance of several strategies

Evaluation factors	BSO	PSO	GA
Optimal Portfolio Mean Return	42.55%	22.78%	24.22%
Optimal Portfolio Risk	12.81%	15.50%	14.40%
Maximized Sharpe-Ratio	2.01	1.37	1.64
The iteration time	55s	60s	55s

5   Conclusion

Under the premise of considering realistic constraints, this paper established a mean-CVaR-entropy model with transaction costs and investment weight restrictions and proposed a multi-objective particle swarm optimization algorithm based on Beetle Antenna Search (BAS). In the iterative process, the update rule of each particle was derived from the BAS, and the method of updating the particle swarm position no longer only depends on the historical optimal solution and the current global optimal solution of the individual particle but adds particles in each iteration. Self-judgment of environmental space.

From case study, it showed that the convergence speed of MOBSO is much faster than that of PSO and GA algorithms, and MOBSO can avoid the dilemma of PSO, GA. MOBSO has stronger global searchability, and it is more stable and effective to find the global optimal solution when solving multidimensional constrained problems.

In this paper, we selected portfolio optimization as a research sample to verify the practical application of the MOBSO algorithm. How to expand the application field of the MOBSO algorithm and apply the proposed algorithm to more optimization problems in different fields needs further exploration and research. Portfolio optimization is based on the principle of risk diversification, which distributes money into different investments. It is widely used in low-frequency trading of modern financial industry.

References

1. Markowitz, H.M.: Portfolio Selection. Journal of Finance, **7**(1), 77–91 (1952)
2. Ross, S.: The Arbitrage Theory of Capital Asset Pricing. Journal of Economic Theory **13**, 341–360 (1976)
3. Mao, J.C.T.: Models of capital budgeting, E-V versus E-S. Journal of Financial and Quantitative Analysis **4**(05), 657–675 (1970)
4. Bawa, V.S., Brown, S.J., Klein, R.W.: Estimation risk and optimal choice. North-Holland (1979)
5. Black, F., Litterman, R.: Asset allocation: combining investors views with market equilibrium. Golden Sachs Fixed income Research, NewYork (1990)
6. Meucci, A.: Beyond Black-Litterman:views on non-normal markets. Available at SSRN 848407 (2005)
7. Gaivoronski, G.A., Pflug, G.: Finding optimal portfolios with constraints on value at risk. Proceedings of the III Stockholm Seminar on Risk Behavior and Risk Management, stockholm 1 (1999)
8. Rockafellar, R.T., Uryasev, S.: Optimization of conditional value-at-risk. J. Risk **3**(2), 21–41 (2000)
9. Mccauley: Thermodynamic analogies in economics and finance: on stability of markets. Physica. A **329,** 199–212 (2003)
10. huangxiaoxia Transactions on Mean-entropy models for fuzzyportfolio selection,IEEE Fuzzy Systems,2008,16:1096–1101. Mccauley. Thermodynamic analogies in economics and finance: on stability of markets. Physica. A **329**, 199–212 (2003)
11. Kamali, S.: Portfolio optimization using particle swarm optimization and genetic algorithm. J. Mathemtics Computer Sci. **10**, 85–90 (2014)
12. Shi Y., Eberhart R.C.: A modified particle swarm otimizer. In: Proceeding of IEEE International Conference on Evolutionary Computation. IEEE Press, Piscataway, NJ pp. 68–73 (1998)
13. Shi, Y., Eberhart, R.C.: Empirical study of particle swarm optimization. In: Proceedings of the World Multi Conference on Systemics. Cybernetics and Informatics, Orlando, FL, pp. 1945–1950 (1999)
14. Clerc, M.: The swarm and the queen: towards a deterministic and adaptive particle swarm optimization. In: Proc. CEC 1999. pp. 1951–1957 (1999)
15. Clerc, M.: Initialisations for Particle Swarm Optimization (2008). http://clerc.maurice.free.fr/PSO/
16. Zhu, H.: Particle swarm optimization (PSO) for the constrained portfolio optimization problem. Expert System with Appl. **38**, 10161–10169 (2011)

17. Rockafellar, R.T., Uryasev, S.: Optimization of conditional value-at-risk. Journal of Risk **2**, 21-24 (2008)
18. Curat: Particle swarm optimization approach to port-folio optimization. Nonlinear Analysis : Real World Applications, **10**, 2396–2406 (2009)
19. Kennedy, J., Eberhart, R.C.A.: New optimizer using particle swarm optimizer. In: Proceedings Congress on Evolutionary Computation. IEEE Press, Piscataway, NJ, pp. 281–286 (1995)
20. Zhu, Z.Y., Zhang, Z.Y., Man. W.S., et al.: A new beetle antennae search algorithm for multi-objective energymanagement in microgrid. In: 2018 13th IEEE Conference on Industrial Electronics and Applications (ICIEA). Wuhan, China. pp. 1599–1603 (2018)
21. Eberhart, R., Kennedy, J.: A new optimizer using particle swarm theory. In: Proceedings of the Sixth International Symposium on Micro Machine and Human Science. Nagoya, Japan, Japan, pp. 39–43 (1995)
22. Wang, J.Y., Chen, H.X.: BSAS: Beetle Swarm Antennae Search Algorithm for Optimization Problems (2018). arXiv:1807.10470
23. Jiang, X.Y., Li, S.: BAS: Beetle Antennae Search Algorithm for Optimization Problems (2017). arXiv: 1710.10724
24. Chen, T.: Beetle swarm optimization for solving investment portfolio problems. Journal of Eng. (2018). https://doi.org/10.1049/joe.2018.8287
25. Wang, D.S.,Tan, D.P.,Liu, L.: Particle swarm optimization algorithm:an overview. Soft Computing **22**(2), 387–408 (2018)
26. https://finance.yahoo.com
27. Akay, K.D.: Artificial bee colony algorithm for large-scale problems and engineering design optimization. Journal of Intelligent Mannufacturing (2012)
28. Jack, F.: Inequality, stock market participation, and the equity premium. Journal of Financial Economics (2012)
29. H infinite State Estimation for Discrete-Time Chaotic Systems Based on a Unified Model, IEEE Trans. on Systems, Man, and Cybernetics (B) (2012)
30. IoTDeM: An IoT Big Data-oriented MapReduce performance prediction extended model in multiple edge clouds, Journal of Parallel and Distributed Computin, **118**, 316–327 (2018)
31. A study on big knowledge and its engineering issues, IEEE Transactions on Knowledge and Data Engineering **31**(9), 1630–1644 (2018)
32. Efficient portfolios when housing needs change over the life cycle. LorianaPelizzon,Guglielmo Weber. Journal of Banking and Finance **11** (2009)
33. Portfolio Choice in the Presence of Background Risk .JohnHeaton,DeborahLucas. The Economic Journal 460 (2001)

A New K-Multiple-Means Clustering Method

Jingyuan Zhang[✉]

School of Computer Science, China University of Geosciences (Wuhan),
Wuhan, China
jyz.cug@foxmail.com

Abstract. In the field of clustering, non-spherical data clustering is a relatively complex case. To satisfy the practical application, the solution should be able to capture non-convex patterns in data sets with high performance. At present, the multi-prototype method can meet the former requirement, but the time cost is still high. This paper proposes a new multi-prototype extension of the K-multiple-means type algorithm, which aims to further reduce the computation time in processing non-spherical data sets with a concise principle while maintaining close performance. Compared with other methods, the method still adopts the idea of multiple prototypes and uses agglomerative strategies in the phase of class cluster connection. However, to reduce the amount of data involved in the computation and the interference of incorrect partition, the subclass data of the first partition is filtered. In addition, the agglomeration is divided into two stages: the agglomeration between prototypes and the agglomeration between clusters, and two agglomeration modes are provided to deal with different clustering tasks. Before updating the means, the filtered data needs a quadratic partition. Experimental results show that compared with the state-of-the-art approaches, the proposed method is still effective with lower time complexity in both synthetic and real-world data sets.

Keywords: Unsupervised learning · K-multiple-means · Clustering · Agglomerative strategies · Quadratic partition

1 Introduction

Clustering is one of the basic problems in data mining and unsupervised learning. Under the assumption of data similarity, unlabeled data with high similarity are grouped into the same class with the metrics selected by users. So far, all kinds of clustering algorithms [1–7] emerge one after another, partition-based algorithm [8–15] is an important role. Among them, K-means [16] as a hard partition algorithm has become one of the most popular algorithms. In contrast, Fuzzy C-means [17], as a variant of K-means, is representative of the soft partition class algorithm. The latter has higher robustness because it takes into account the overlap between subclasses and transforms category membership into a degree of category membership.

© The Author(s), under exclusive license to Springer Nature Switzerland AG 2022
G. Memmi et al. (Eds.): KSEM 2022, LNAI 13369, pp. 621–632, 2022.
https://doi.org/10.1007/978-3-031-10986-7_50

Although the K-means method performs well in spherical cluster data, lacks applicability for non-spherical data sets. There are two main research ideas: nonlinear clustering [26–30] and multi-prototype clustering [19–24,31,32]. The fundamental principle of nonlinear clustering is to map the original data by nonlinear technique and use the algorithms for clustering. For example, in kernel clustering and spectral clustering, the former uses a kernel function to map data into a certain feature space for a linear partition, and the latter uses low-dimensional embedding of similarity matrix generated by original data to obtain embedding vector for clustering. However, it is difficult to design suitable kernel functions or construction data graphs for each clustering problem. Another way is the multi-prototype method, which considers that each cluster can be represented by multiple prototypes, to better adapt to non-spherical data sets. Each prototype represents a subclass, which is still linear clustering. To achieve a specified number of clusters, it is necessary to merge subclasses, and the merging process is nonlinear clustering. At present, most methods adopt the aggregation strategy, but the selection of an appropriate combination point is not easy, which has a direct impact on the clustering effect. To merge multiple prototypes optimally on the global, a graph-based multi-prototype clustering algorithm was proposed. However, this method inevitably needs matrix calculation. When the data scale is large, matrix decomposition, spectral analysis and other operations can be very time expensive, so it needs further improvement. Aiming at the above defects, this paper presents a new K-multi-means extension method. The main contributions of this paper can be summarized as follows:

- To reduce the time cost of the algorithm and augment the feature of each subclass, part of the data is screened according to the distance relationship between the prototype and the data, so that the reserved data has better representativeness.
- The method in this paper divides the agglomerative strategy into two stages for decreasing the difficulty of the agglomeration: the merging between prototypes and the merging between clusters. In addition, to enhance the robustness of the algorithm, the proposed method provides two merging modes.
- The filtered data are likely to be partitioned incorrectly, so these data need a quadratic partition to improve the clustering effect of the algorithm.
- Experimental results show that the proposed method has similar performance to the state-of-the-art approaches with a lower time cost.

The remainder of this paper is organized as follows: Sect. 2 introduces the related work in this field. In Sect. 3, this paper describes the principle of the new k-multi-means extension and its computational complexity analysis. In Sect. 4, the experimental results and analysis are reported. Finally, the paper is summarized in Sect. 5.

2   Related Work

The multi-prototype method is an extension of traditional K-means to capture the non-convex pattern of data sets. As shown in Fig. 1, the data in the figure

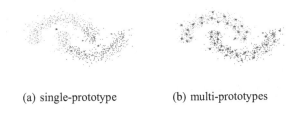

(a) single-prototype   (b) multi-prototypes

Fig. 1. The difference between single-prototype representation (a) and multi-prototypes representation (b). The blue pentagrams are prototypes. (Color figure online)

should be divided into two classes. The traditional K-means method only initializes the corresponding number of prototypes. As the features of the data cannot be captured, the data is incorrectly partitioned. The multi-prototype method initializes multiple prototypes and distributes them in the data. The data is divided into multiple independent subclasses, which can fully adapt to the shape and distribution of the data and discover non-convex patterns in the data.

Tao [19] generates multiple prototypes based on hierarchical subtractive clustering and then merges them according to the relationship between region density and subclass density of two subclasses. Liu et al. [20] proposed a simple multi-prototype clustering algorithm, which used squared-error clustering for splitting and then merged according to the density of overlapping regions of subclasses. Luo et al. [21] divided the data based on the minimum spanning tree and then merged the data according to the threshold value set by the user and the data distribution of the two subclasses. Ben et al. [22] proposed a multi-prototype method based on Fuzzy clustering. In the splitting stage, Fuzzy C-means and intra-cluster nonconsistency values were used to perform iterative dichotomy for subclasses, and then they were merged iteratively according to the overlap degree between clusters. Liang et al. [23] proposed a multi-prototype algorithm to deal with unbalanced distributed data. Reliable prototypes were obtained by Fast Global Fuzzy K-means, and the best-M Plot method was used to divide data. Finally, the grouping multi-center (GMC) algorithm is used to complete the merging. Nie et al. [24] proposed the multi-prototype algorithm based on the bipartite graph. Firstly, the distance relationship between the prototype and the data were used to construct the bipartite graph to obtain its Laplace matrix, and the clusters with a specified number were obtained by restricting the rank of the Laplace matrix [25]. This method transforms the clustering problem into an optimization problem, which is the state-of-the-art multi-prototype algorithm at present because of its superior clustering effect and relatively low time complexity.

The clustering effect of the agglomerative method heavily depends on the subclass merging, if there is any error merging, all the subclasses of subsequent merging will be wrong, so the selection of connection points is a challenging problem. And the graph-based method can model the prototype and data globally, and delete part of the cut edges according to the feature matrix of the graph, which belongs to the split strategy. In the next section, this paper will describes a clustering method using the aggregation strategy, which is close to the state-of-the-art method and has a lower time overhead.

3   The Proposed Clustering Algorithm

3.1   The New K-Multiple-Means

The method in this paper also includes two stages of splitting and merging. In the splitting stage, squared-error clustering is still used.

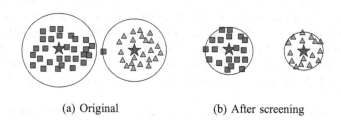

(a) Original   (b) After screening

Fig. 2. Data filtering. The blue pentagram in the figure is the prototype, the red square and green triangle are two classes of data, and the circle represents the data division area. Figure (a) shows the original partition of the data, in which a red square is incorrectly partitioned to the prototype on the right. Figure (b) shows the division after screening, and the wrongly divided data has been eliminated. (Color figure online)

Due to the use of squared error clustering for division, the subclasses divided may have two types of data in one subclass. If the merging is performed directly, the accuracy will be greatly affected. Therefore, we have added a subclass data screening link. For each subclass, only those data with small absolute distance and large relative distance are retained, so that the retained data has a strong membership property to the prototype. See Fig. 2. The absolute distance is the distance between the data and the nearest prototype, and the relative distance is the difference between the distance between the data and the closest prototype and the distance between the next closest prototype. Denote a_i as the i-th data point, C_{ij} is the j-th nearest prototype to the data point a_i, $d(a_i, C_{ij})$ represents the distance between a_i and C_{ij}, then the membership degree $S(a_i)$ of the data point a_i is defined in the Eq. (1)

$$S(a_i) = \frac{d(a_i, C_{i2}) - d(a_i, C_{i1})}{d(a_i, C_{i1})} \tag{1}$$

After that, the median of all data points in the subclass is calculated, and only data points whose membership degree is not lower than the median are allowed to participate in the subsequent calculation.

In the merging stage, a certain number of prototypes that are as dispersed as possible are randomly selected as control points, and the remaining prototypes are merged. The control points can cover most of the prototypes of the class and naturally grow and expand according to the distance relationship between the data points and the prototypes, thus forming several clusters. The remaining prototypes require two rounds of voting to finally calculate which prototype should belong. The first round of voting is to obtain the most likely connected prototype of each data in the subclass, and calculate the connection probability p_{ij} of the data point a_i and its k nearest neighbors C_{ij} (see Eq. (2)), if there is a connection between the neighbors, that is, there are multiple neighbors that belong to the same cluster, the probability is accumulated.

$$p_{ij} = \frac{d(a_i, C_{ik+1}) - d(a_i, C_{ij})}{k * d(a_i, C_{ik+1}) - \sum_{j=1}^{k} d(a_i, C_{ij})} \tag{2}$$

Then, the connection probability of each data point is counted, and the probability of belonging to the same cluster is accumulated. The ratio of the sum of the connection probability of each cluster to the sum of the probability is the probability that the non-control prototypes match the corresponding prototype. See Eq. (3), $P(\alpha, \beta)$ is the probability that the unmatched prototype α merges with the prototype β, $p_{i,\beta}$ is the probability that the data point a_i in the unmatched prototype α is connected to the prototype β. The prototype with the highest connection probability is selected for merging to complete the second round of voting.

$$P(\alpha, \beta) = \frac{\sum_{i=1}^{l} p_{i\beta}}{\sum_{i=1}^{L} p_{ij}} \tag{3}$$

If the non-control prototype matches the control point, it will be merged directly. If it matches the non-control prototype, the two will be merged, and they will be used as the new control point, and then continue to merge. Therefore, in the process of merging non-control prototypes, the number of control prototypes will increase. This operation is to avoid prototypes that do not completely cover all clusters due to improper selection of control points. In addition, there may be some control points that are not merged with the prototypes, and do not play the role of control points. Therefore, when all non-control prototypes are completely merged, the isolated control points that have not been merged are merged with other control points, and the merging method is still using the second round of voting above.

When the non-control points are completely matched, several larger subclusters will be formed, usually, the number of clusters is greater than K. Therefore, further merging is needed to make the number of clusters reach K. At this time, the subclass cluster has formed a large scale, which contains rich cluster correlation information, and the method in this paper uses this information to merge. Referring to the relative inter-connectivity (Eq. (4)) and relative closeness (Eq. (5)) in the Chameleon algorithm [18] as the merging indicators, select the cluster with the largest value of Eq. (6) to merge until K clusters. In the

626   J. Zhang

following equations, all connecting edges are included in the connecting edges between each data point and its k nearest neighbors. $|EC_{\{C_i,C_j\}}|$, $\bar{S}_{EC_{\{C_i,C_j\}}}$ is the sum and expectation of the probability of all cutting edges of the cluster C_i and the cluster C_j, $|EC_{C_i}|$, $\bar{S}_{EC_{C_i}}$ are the sum and expectation of all cutting edge probabilities inside the cluster C_i. $|C_i|$ is the number of data points in C_i.

$$RI\,(C_i, C_j) = \frac{2 * |EC_{\{C_i,C_j\}}|}{|EC_{C_i}| + |EC_{C_j}|} \tag{4}$$

$$RC\,(C_i, C_j) = \frac{(|C_i| + |C_j|) * \bar{S}_{EC_{\{C_i,C_j\}}}}{|C_i|\,\bar{S}_{EC_{C_i}} + |C_j|\,\bar{S}_{EC_{C_j}}} \tag{5}$$

$$f\,(C_i, C_j) = RI\,(C_i, C_j) * RC\,(C_i, C_j)^\alpha \tag{6}$$

Generally speaking, the above merging methods can achieve good results, especially when the distribution of the dataset is unbalanced, it is easy to find scarce classes with small sample sizes. However, when the data distribution is relatively balanced, but there are outliers in a certain category, the above-mentioned merging method will cause a wide range of wrong connections, and individual outliers may be classified into one category. To enhance the robustness of the algorithm, our method provides an additional merging mode. First, merge small-scale clusters according to the above indicators to form new clusters, until the current number of clusters $K' = K$, if $K' > K$, continue to merge clusters according to the indicators and don't care about cluster size anymore. Also, merges between new clusters are not allowed in merges. If $K' > K$, use the original merging method to merge larger clusters or new clusters. The user can choose the merging method according to the characteristics of the dataset. If there is a lack of understanding of the characteristics of the data set, a relatively stable merging method with a better clustering effect can be selected through multiple experiments. Hereinafter, the first merging mode is referred to as mode 1, and the latter is referred to as mode 2.

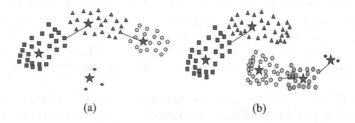

(a)   (b)

Fig. 3. The illustration of two merging modes. The graph meaning in the figure is the same as that in Fig. 2, where the connecting line represents the merging of two subclasses. In (a), merge only according to metrics, and small class clusters can be found. In (b), there is an extreme case in which there are only two samples of subclasses, so the subclasses with small scale are merged first to prevent the clusters combination of different classes from leading to a large-scale wrong partition.

After the cluster merging is completed, the data eliminated in the data screening stage needs to quadratic partition, and the wrongly divided data points are corrected. Using the above-mentioned first-round voting method, since there are only K clusters, the probabilities of the k nearest neighbors belonging to the same category are superimposed, and divided according to the accumulated probabilities, as shown in Eq. (7).

$$f\left(a_i\right) = \underset{C_j}{argmin} \left\{ dis \left(a_i, \underset{C}{argmax} \left\{ \sum_{j=1}^{\tilde{l}} \bar{p}_{ij} \right\} \right) \right\}, 0 < \tilde{l} \leq k \qquad (7)$$

In Eq. (7), $\bar{p}_{ij}$ is the connection probability between data a_i and a prototype C_j, C is a set of prototypes of a certain class, $\tilde{l}$ is the number of prototypes of the a certain cluster. After the quadratic partition is over, the prototypes are updated according to $C_j = \frac{1}{\tilde{l}} * \sum_{i=1}^{l} a_{ij}$, where a_{ij} represents the data a_i divided into C_j, after which the next iteration is performed until the algorithm converges. See Algorithm 1 for a summary of the algorithm.

Algorithm 1 :The New K-Multiple-Means

Input: Data matrix $A \in R^{n*d}$, cluster number K, prototype number m, merging mode
Output: K clusters
 1: Initialize multiple-means C_j.
 2: Picking some prototypes as the control points at random.
 3: **while** *not converge* **do**
 4:     Partition all data by Squared-error clustering;
 5:     For each j, screen data of C_j with Eq. (1);
 6:     Merging the non-control points and outlying control points with Eqs. (2–3);
 7:     **while** *the number of clusters is greater than K* **do**
 8:         Merging the clusters with Eqs.(4–6) and selected merging mode;
 9:     **end while**
10:     Quadratic partition for the filtered data with Eq. (7);
11:     For each j,update C_j;
12: **end while**

3.2   Computational Complexity

In this subsection, we will analyze the computational complexity of Algorithm 1. The time overhead of the initial partition of data is $O(nmd)$, n is the number of data, and d is the feature dimension of the data. The time complexity of the data filtering is $O(nm+\tilde{n}^2m)$, and $\tilde{n}$ is the number of samples in the subclass. In addition, the time cost of selecting prototypes as the control points is $O(\tilde{m}md)$, and $\tilde{m}$ is the number of control points. The time overhead of the merging stage includes non-control points merging and clusters merging, which is accumulated to $O(m\tilde{n}k^2 + nm^2 + nmk)$, where k is the number of neighbors. Quadratic partition requires $O(nmk^2)$ time cost. In summary, the total time complexity of the method in this paper is $O(n(m^2 + mk + mk^2)t + \tilde{n}^2 mt + nmdt)$, and t is the number of algorithm iterations.

When merging clusters, based on the k nearest neighbors distance relationships, only the nearest three clusters are selected for each cluster to calculate their weights respectively, and then they are merged according to the selected merging mode. Therefore, the method not only learns useful information but also eliminates the interference of errors, which further speeds up the running speed while ensuring the effect.

4 Experiments

In this section, we show the performance of the new K-Multiple-Means method on synthetic data and real benchmark datasets. For the convenience of description, the method in this paper is hereinafter referred to as nKMM. All the experiments are implemented in MATLAB R2020a, and run on a Windows 10 machine with 2.30 GHz i5-6300HQ CPU, 24 GB main memory.

4.1 Experiments on Synthetic Data

Performance Comparison. This subsection mainly shows that the nKMM algorithm can process non-convex data sets, and its comparison method is KMM[1] There are two types of synthetic datasets used. The multi-prototype approach can be fully adapted to non-spherical data, capturing non-convex patterns. As shown in Fig. 4, the nKMM method can correctly partition the data and has the same performance as KMM. Both methods initialize the same number of prototypes, i.e., $m = \sqrt{n * K}$. The number of neighbors of nKMM is 5, and the number of neighbors of KMM is appropriately adjusted according to the data set. In addition, nKMM uses mode 1 for merging.

In the dataset Twomoons, the KMM algorithm incorrectly partitions the data at the intersection of the two classes of data, and these data are outliers for the subclass, and the KMM algorithm does not capture these subtle features. The nKMM algorithm improves this situation by partitioning the peripheral data twice.

Computation Time. Table 1 shows the specific information of the two datasets, as well as the performance of the KMM and nKMM algorithms on the two datasets. Since the number of iterations for each running of the algorithm is different, there will be a large error in calculating the total running time, so the average time of each iteration is calculated. In Table 1, the average time of each iteration of the algorithm is calculated, and nKMM has less time overhead than KMM.

---

[1] https://github.com/CHLWR/KDD2019_K-Multiple-Means.

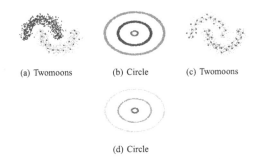

(a) Twomoons   (b) Circle   (c) Twomoons

(d) Circle

Fig. 4. KMM:(a)(b), nKMM:(c)(d). In (a) and (c), the red points and blue pentagrams are prototypes. (Color figure online)

Table 1. Statistics of synthetic datasets and run time of clustering algorithms (s).

Datasets	Sample	Features	Clusters	KMM	nKMM
Twomoons	1000	2	2	0.146	0.11
Circle	3000	2	3	0.34	0.29

4.2 Experiments on Real Benchmark Datasets

Performance Comparison. To reflect the effectiveness of the method in this paper, the same real data set and evaluation index [24] are directly used, and other comparison algorithms are also the same.

Table 2. Statistics of real benchmark datasets and run time of multi-means clustering algorithms (s).

Datasets	Sample	Features	Clusters	KMM	nKMM
Wine	178	13	3	0.026	0.018
Ecoli	336	7	8	0.044	0.039
BinAlpha	1854	256	10	0.386	0.233
Palm	2000	256	100	0.819	0.430
Abalone	4177	8	28	1.237	0.718
HTRU2	17898	8	2	5.188	2.333

The experimental data includes Wine, Ecoli, Abalone, HTRU2, Palm, BinAlpha. The specific information of the data set is shown in Table 2. In addition to KMM, the comparison algorithms also include traditional K-means, SSC (Spectral Clustering), KKmeans (Kernel-based Clustering), RSFKC (Fuzzy Clustering), CLR (Graph-based Clustering), MEAP and K-MEAP (Exemplar-based Clustering). Evaluation indicators used Accuracy (ACC), Normalized Mutual Information

(NMI) and Purity. For different datasets, nKMM uses different merging methods and records stable experimental results. KMM and nKMM set the same number of prototypes and neighbors, $m = \sqrt{n * K}$, $k = 5$, the number of control prototypes in nKMM is $\tilde{m} = \sqrt{m * K}$. In addition, mode 1 is used in Ecoli and Abalone, and mode 2 is used for the other data sets. Since the K-means algorithm is more sensitive to initialization, to reflect the effect of the method, it is randomly initialized 100 times, and the average value of the evaluation index is recorded. The specific experimental data are shown in Table 3. The results of the CLR, MEAP and K-MEAP algorithms on HTRU2 are missing because the complexity of these three algorithms on large-scale datasets is too high. As can be seen from the table, nKMM achieves more than 90% of the performance of KMM with lower time complexity and is better than other algorithms.

Table 3. Clustering performance comparison on real-world datasets (%).

	Metric	K-means	SSC	KKmeans	RSFKC	CLR	MEAP	K-MEAP	KMM	nKMM	Percentage
Wine	ACC	94.94 (±0.51)	66.85	96.06 (±0.32)	95.50 (±3.72)	93.25	94.94	48.31	97.19 (±1.41)	93.95 (±2.75)	96.67
	NMI	83.23 (±1.53)	40.32	85.81 (±0.16)	84.88 (±4.57)	77.29	83.18	5.22	86.13 (±3.86)	81.21 (±5.03)	94.29
	Purity	94.94 (±0.51)	66.85	96.06 (±0.32)	95.50 (±1.71)	93.25	94.94	48.31	95.76 (±1.41)	93.94 (±2.75)	98.10
Ecoli	ACC	62.79 (±6.21)	59.82	34.52 (±1.16)	58.03 (±9.76)	52.38	42.55	74.10	78.85 (±4.46)	76.49 (±6.02)	97.01
	NMI	53.44 (±3.10)	54.80	25.92 (±1.85)	51.64 (±16.65)	53.08	44.12	58.77	69.48 (±4.86)	67.11 (±4.87)	96.59
	Purity	79.76 (±3.06)	82.33	61.30 (±3.00)	79.46 (±11.45)	79.76	42.55	80.41	82.37 (±3.95)	81.97 (±3.54)	99.51
BinAlpha	ACC	64.88 (±3.34)	66.82	28.26 (±0.74)	59.11 (±9.87)	67.40	40.99	62.94	68.87 (±7.00)	70.78 (±7.14)	102.77
	NMI	62.81 (±1.87)	70.01	20.99 (±0.38)	61.95 (±13.25)	71.05	41.03	60.96	72.94 (±7.05)	72.58 (±3.35)	99.51
	Purity	72.33 (±2.82)	76.00	35.54 (±0.50)	71.19 (±11.96)	78.00	45.41	69.84	76.59 (±6.37)	76.18 (±4.83)	99.46
Palm	ACC	63.65 (±3.45)	59.78	68.70 (±0.83)	71.13 (±6.80)	68.65	71.55	40.20	76.40 (±2.21)	84.65 (±1.70)	110.80
	NMI	87.55 (±1.08)	79.98	89.06 (±0.68)	89.82 (±8.51)	90.27	90.60	71.23	92.30 (±0.94)	95.63 (±0.39)	103.61
	Purity	71.80 (±2.81)	62.90	74.60 (±0.46)	76.11 (±7.44)	79.45	77.80	45.70	81.75 (±1.66)	87.46 (±1.23)	106.98
Abalone	ACC	14.62 (±0.88)	13.96	14.79 (±0.26) 26.43 (±0.34)	19.12 (±1.88)	14.96	19.70	16.51	20.20 (±1.02)	19.01 (±1.43)	94.11
	NMI	15.09 (±0.29)	14.37	14.76 (±0.14)	6.52 (±3.32)	15.07	7.53	15.52	16.03 (±1.75)	16.14 (±1.19)	100.69
	Purity	27.36 (±0.63)	27.68	26.43 (±0.34)	19.89 (±2.08)	27.67	19.70	27.31	25.2 (±1.33)	25.02 (±1.13)	99.29
HTRU2	ACC	91.85 (±2.10)	92.22	59.29 (±1.20)	92.17 (±2.55)	–	–	–	95.49 (±2.21)	92.79 (±3.71)	97.17
	NMI	30.30 (±1.01)	34.90	7.97 (±0.56)	27.02 (±2.26)	–	–	–	40.12 (±1.55)	35.80 (±22.20)	89.23
	Purity	91.89 (±1.32)	93.35	90.84 (±0.78)	92.17 (±3.58)	–	–	–	95.49 (±1.92)	93.66 (±2.42)	98.08

Computation Time. The computation time comparison between nKMM and KMM is shown in Table 2. Synthetic datasets are inferior to real benchmark datasets in terms of feature dimension and number of samples, it fails to fully reflect the efficiency of the algorithm. In Table 2. The nKMM algorithm achieves a similar performance to the KMM algorithm with relatively lower time complexity and is even better than the KMM algorithm on Palm, which reflects that nKMM is effective and efficient.

5   Conclusion

This paper proposes a new multi-prototype extension with agglomerative strategies. The method filters the data after the first partition, only uses the data with obvious subclass features for calculation, and then partitions the filtered data twice. In addition, the method refines the previous agglomerative strategy, innovatively divides the merging into two stages: prototype merging and cluster merging, and provides two different merging modes for different datasets. The experimental results show that the nKMM can achieve similar performance to the KMM with lower time complexity, and even achieve better results with half the time overhead on individual data sets, demonstrating the method is effective and efficient in this paper.

References

1. Dhillon, I.S.: Co-clustering documents and words using bipartite spectral graph partitioning. In: ACM SIGKDD (2001)
2. Jain, A.K., Narasimha Murty, M., Flynn, P.J.: Data clustering: a review. ACM Comput. Surv. **31**(3), 264–323 (1999)
3. Nie, F., Tian, L., Li, X.: Multiview clustering via adaptively weighted procrustes. In: ACM SIGKDD(2018)
4. Nie, F., Wang, X., Huang, H.: Clustering and projected clustering with adaptive neighbors. In: ACM SIGKDD (2014)
5. Von Luxburg, U.: A tutorial on spectral clustering. Statist. Comput. **17**(4), 395–416 (2007)
6. Von Luxburg, U.: Clustering stability: an overview. Found. Trends Mach. Learn. **2**(3) (2010)
7. Ben-Hur, A., Elisseeff, A., Guyon, I.: A stability based method for discovering structure in clustered data. Pac. Symp. Biocomput. 6–17 (2002)
8. Arthur, D., Vassilvitskii, S.: k-means++: the advantages of careful seeding. In: 18th Annual ACM-SIAM Symposium on Discrete Algorithms, pp. 1027–1035. Society for Industrial and Applied Mathematics (2007)
9. Banerjee, A., Merugu, S., Dhillon, I.S., Ghosh, J.: Clustering with Bregman divergences. J. Mach. Learn. Res. **6**, 1705–1749 (2005)
10. Bezdek, J.C., Ehrlich, R., Full, W.: FCM: the fuzzy C-means clustering algorithm. Comput. Geosci. **2**(3), 191–203 (1984)
11. Cannon, R.L., Dave, J.V., Bezdek, J.C.: Efficient implementation of the fuzzy C-means clustering algorithms. IEEE Trans. Pattern Anal. Mach. Intell. **2**, 248–255 (1986)
12. Ding, C., He, X.: K-means clustering via principal component analysis. In: Twenty-First International Conference on Machine Learning, vol. 29. ACM (2004)
13. Hamerly, G., Elkan, C.: Learning the K in k-means. Adv. Neural Inf. Process. Syst. 281–288 (2004)
14. Pal, N.R., Bezdek, J.C.: On cluster validity for the fuzzy C-means model. IEEE Trans. Fuzzy Syst. **3**(3), 370–379 (1995)
15. Wagstaff, K., Cardie, C., Rogers, S., Schrödl, S., et. al.: Constrained k-means clustering with background knowledge. In: ICML, vol. 1, pp. 577–584 (2001)
16. MacQueen, J., et. al.: Some methods for classification and analysis of multivariate observations. In: Fifth Berkeley Symposium on Mathematical Statistics and Probability, Oakland, vol. 1, pp. 281–297 (1967)
17. Ruspini, E.H.: A new approach to clustering. Inf. Control **15**(1), 22–32 (1969)
18. Karypis, G., Han, E.-H., Kumar, V.: Chameleon: a hierarchical clustering using dynamic modeling. Computer **32**(8), 68–75 (1999). https://doi.org/10.1109/2.781637
19. Tao, C.-W.: Unsupervised fuzzy clustering with multi-center clusters. Fuzzy Sets Syst. **128**(3), 305–322 (2002)

20. Liu, M., Jiang, X., Kot, A.C.: A multi-prototype clustering algorithm. Pattern Recogn. **42**(5), 689–698 (2009)
21. Luo, T., Zhong, C., Li, H., Sun, X.: A multi-prototype clustering algorithm based on minimum spanning tree. In: Fuzzy Systems and Knowledge Discovery (FSKD), 2010 Seventh International Conference on, vol. 4, pp. 1602–1607. IEEE (2010)
22. Ben, S., Jin, Z., Yang, J.: Guided fuzzy clustering with multi-prototypes. In: IJCNN (2011)
23. Liang, J., Bai, L., Dang, C., Cao, F.: The K-means-type algorithms versus imbalanced data distributions. IEEE Trans. Fuzzy Syst. **20**(4), 728–745 (2012)
24. Nie, F., Wang, C.-L., Li, X.: K-multiple-means: a multiple-means clustering method with specified K clusters. In: ACM SIGKDD (2019)
25. Nie, F., Wang, X., Jordan, M.I., Huang, H.: The constrained Laplacian rank algorithm for graph-based clustering. In: AAAI (2016)
26. Dhillon, I.S., Guan, Y., Kulis, B.: Kernel k-means: spectral clustering and normalized cuts. In: ACM SIGKDD (2004)
27. Ng, A.Y., Jordan, M.I., Weiss, Y.: On spectral clustering: analysis and an algorithm. In: NIPS (2001)
28. Zha, H., He, X., Ding, C., Gu, M., Simon, H.D.: Spectral relaxation for k-means clustering. Adv. Neural Inf. Process. Syst. 1057–1064 (2002)
29. Bai, L., Liang, J.: A three-level optimization model for nonlinearly separable clustering. In: AAAI(2020)
30. Wang, C.D., Lai, J.H., Zhu, J.Y.: Graph-based multiprototype competitive learning and its applications. IEEE Trans. Syst. Man Cybern. C Appl. **42**(6), 934–946 (2012)
31. Wang, C.-D., Lai, J.-H., Suen, C.Y., Zhu, J.-Y.: Multi-exemplar affinity propagation. IEEE Trans. Pattern Anal. Mach. Intell. **35**(9), 2223–2237 (2013)
32. Wang, Y., Chen, L.: K-MEAP: multiple exemplars affinity propagation with specified K clusters. IEEE Trans. Neural Netw. Learn. Syst. **27**(12), 2670–2682 (2016)

Cross Transformer Network for Scale-Arbitrary Image Super-Resolution

Dehong He, Song Wu, Jinpeng Liu, and Guoqiang Xiao[(✉)]

College of Computer and Information Science,
Southwest University, ChongQing, China
{swu20201514,jinpengliu}@email.swu.edu.cn, {songwuswu,gqxiao}@swu.edu.cn

Abstract. Since implicit neural representation methods can be utilized for continuous image representation learning, pixel values can be successfully inferred from a neural network model over a continuous spatial domain. The recent approaches focus on performing super-resolution tasks at arbitrary scales. However, their magnified images are often distorted and their results are inferior compared to single-scale super-resolution methods. This work proposes a novel CrossSR consisting of a base Cross Transformer structure. Benefiting from the global interactions between contexts through a self-attention mechanism of the Cross Transformer, the CrossSR could efficiently exploit cross-scale features. A dynamic position-coding module and a dense MLP operation are employed for continuous image representation to further improve the results. Extensive experimental and ablation studies show that our CrossSR obtained competitive performance compared to state-of-the-art methods, both for lightweight and classical image super-resolution.

Keywords: Super-resolution · Transformer · Arbitrary scale · Computer vision · Deep learning

1 Introduction

With the rapid development of deep learning and computer vision [7,13,20], image super-resolution has shown a wide range of real-world applications, driving further development in this direction. Image super-resolution is a classical computer vision task, which aims to restore high-resolution images from low-resolution images. Generally, according to the manner of feature extractions, image super-resolution methods can be roughly divided into two categories, i.e., traditional interpolation methods, such as bilinear, bicubic, and deep convolutional neural network-based methods, such as SRCNN [6], DRCN [11], CARN [2], etc. Image super-resolution methods based on CNNs have achieved progressive performance. However, these methods cannot solve the problem of continuous image representation, and additional training is required for each super-resolution scale, which greatly limits the application of CNN-based image super-resolution methods.

© The Author(s), under exclusive license to Springer Nature Switzerland AG 2022
G. Memmi et al. (Eds.): KSEM 2022, LNAI 13369, pp. 633–644, 2022.
https://doi.org/10.1007/978-3-031-10986-7_51

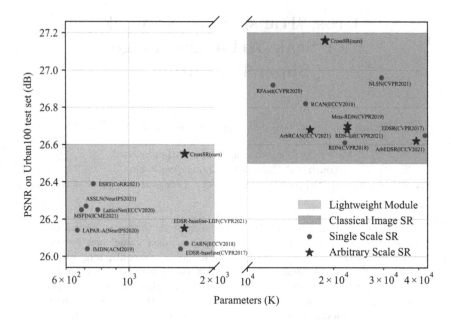

Fig. 1. PSNR results v.s the total number of parameters of different methods for image SR (×4) on Urban100 [9]. Best viewed in color and by zooming in. (Color figure online)

The LIIF [5] was proposed using implicit image representation for arbitrary scale super-resolution, aiming to solve the continuous image representation in super-resolution. However, the implicit function representation of MLP-based LIIF [5] cannot fully utilize the spatial information of the original image, and the EDSR feature encoding module used in LIIF lacks the ability to mine the cross-scale information and long-range dependence of features, so although LIIF has achieved excellent performance in arbitrary-scale super-resolution methods, there is a certain gap compared with the current state-of-the-art single-scale methods.

The currently proposed transformer [21] has attracted a lot of buzz through remarkable performance in multiple visual tasks. The transformer is mainly based on a multi-head self-attention mechanism, which could capture long-range and global interaction among image contexts. The representative methods employing transformers for single-scale image super-resolution are SwinIR [14] and ESRT [17], which obtained superior performance than traditional deep neural networks-based methods.

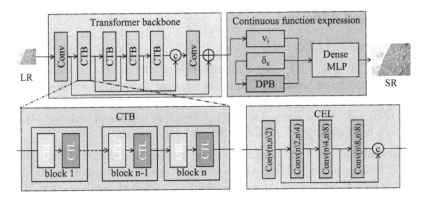

Fig. 2. The architecture of CrossSR is in the top, it consists of two modules: a transformer backbone for feature encoding and an continuous image implicit function representation module. CTB is the inner structure of Cross Transformer Blocks, CEL is the structure of Cross-scale Embedding Layer we proposed, the n and n/2 in Conv(n,n/2) are the number of channels for input and output features.

This paper employs a novel framework of Cross Transformer for effective and efficient arbitrary-scale image super-resolution (CrossSR). Specifically, CrossSR consists of a Cross Transformer-based backbone for feature encoding and an image implicit function representation module. The feature encoding module is mainly based on the framework of Cross Transformer [23] with residual aggregation [16]. The Cross Transformer consists of four stages, and each stage contains multiple cross-scale feature embedding layers and multiple Cross Transformer layers. The image implicit function representation module is based on a modification of LIIF [5]. Specifically, it includes a dynamic position encoding module and a dense MLP module. Extensive experiments on several benchmark datasets and comparisons with several state-of-the-art methods on image super-resolution show that our proposed CrossSR achieves competitive performance with less computing complex. The main contributions of our proposed method include the following three aspects:

- Firstly, a novel image super-resolution network backbone is designed based on a Cross Transformer block [23] combined with a residual feature aggregation [16], and a new cross-scale embedding layer (CEL) is also proposed to reduce the parameters while preserving the performance.
- A series of new network structures are designed for continuous image representation, including dynamic position coding, and dense MLP, which could significantly increase the performance of super-resolution.
- The experiments evaluated on several benchmark datasets show the effectiveness and efficiency of our proposed CrossSR, and it obtained competitive performance compared with state-of-the-art methods on image super-resolution.

2 Proposed Method

2.1 Network Architecture

As shown in Fig. 2, our proposed CrossSR framework consists of two modules: a transformer backbone based on Cross Transformer for feature extraction and a continuous function expression module which utilize a dynamic position encoding block (DPB) [23] and a dense multi-layer perception machine (dense MLP) to reconstruct high quality (HQ) images at arbitrary scales.

Transformer Backbone: Convolutional layers operated at early visual processing could lead to more stable optimization and better performance [25]. Given an input image x, we can obtained the shallow feature through a convolutional layer:

$$F_0 = L_{shallow}(x) \tag{1}$$

where $L_{shallow}$ is the convolutional layer, F_0 is the obtained shallow feature maps.

After that, the deep features F_{LR} are extracted through some Transformer blocks and a convolutional layer. More specifically, the extraction process of the intermediate features and the final deep features can be represented as follows:

$$F_i = L_{CTB_i}(F_{i-1}), i = 1, 2, ,, k \tag{2}$$

$$F_{LR} = L_{Conv}(Concat(F_1, F_2, ,, F_k)) + F_0 \tag{3}$$

where L_{CTB_i} denotes the i-th Cross Transformer block (CTB) of total k CTBs, L_{Conv} is the last convolutional layer, $Concat(\cdot, \cdot)$ indicates cascading them on the channel direction. Residual Feature Aggregation structure is designed by cascading the output of the transformer block of each layer and passing through a convolutional layer, thus, the residual features of each layer can be fully utilized [16].

Continuous Function Expression: In the continuous function expression module, a continuous image representation function f_θ is parameterized by a dense MLP. The formulation of continuous function expression is as follow:

$$F_{SR} = f_\theta(v_i, \delta_x, dpb(\delta_x)) \tag{4}$$

where F_{SR} is the high-resolution result that to be predicted, v_i is the feature vector for reference, and δ_x is the pixel coordinate information of the F_{SR}, $dpb(\cdot)$ means the dynamic position encoding block [23]. The reference feature vector v_i is extracted from the LR feature map $F_{LR} \in R^{C \times H \times W}$ in its spacial location $\delta_{vi} \in R^{H \times W}$ which is close to δ_x. f_θ is the implicit image function simulated by the dense multi-layer perception machine.

Loss Function: For image super-resolution, the L_1 loss is used to optimize the CrossSR as previous work [5,14,17,19] done,

$$L = |F_{SR} - HR|_1 \tag{5}$$

where F_{SR} is obtained by taking low resolution image as the input of CrossSR, and HR is the corresponding high-quality image of ground-truth.

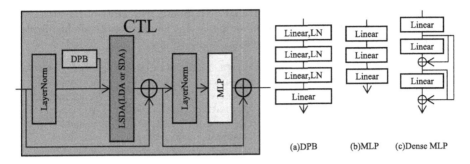

Fig. 3. The architecture of Cross Transformer Layer (CTL) is on the left, SDA and LDA are used alternately in each block. The a diagram on the right shows the architecture of DPB. The middle figure b is the structure of the original MLP, and the rightmost figure c is a schematic of part of the structure of the dense MLP. These three structures contain a ReLU activation layer after each linear layer, which is omitted in the figure.

2.2 Cross Transformer Block

As shown in Fig. 2, CTB is a network structure consisting of multiple groups of small blocks, each of which contains a Cross-scale Embedding Layer (CEL) and a Cross Transformer Layer (CTL). Given the input feature $F_{i,0}$ of the $i-th$ CTB, the intermediate features $F_{i,1}, F_{i,2},,, F_{i,n}$ can be extracted by n small blocks as:

$$F_{i,j} = L_{CTL_{i,j}}(L_{CEL_{i,j}}(F_{i,j-1})), j = 1, 2, , , , n \qquad (6)$$

where $L_{CEL_{i,j}}(\cdot)$ is the j-th Cross-scale Embedding Layer in the i-th CTB, $L_{CTL_{i,j}}(\cdot)$ is the j-th Cross Transformer Layer in the i-th CTB.

Cross-scale Embedding Layer(CEL): Although Cross Transformer [23] elaborates a Cross-scale Embedding Layer (CEL), it is still too large to be directly applied in image super-resolution. In order to further reduce the number of parameters and the complex operations, a new CEL is designed based on four convolutional layers with different convolutional kernel sizes. Benefiting from each convolution operation with different kernel size is based on the result of the previous convolution, the subsequent convolutions can obtain a substantial perceptual field with only one small convolution kernel, instead of using a 32×32 kernel as large as in Cross Transformer [23]. Moreover, to further reduce the number of complex operations, the dimension of the projection is reduced as the convolution kernel increases. This design could significantly reduce computational effort while achieving excellent image super-resolution results. The output feature of Cross-scale Embedding Layer (CEL) $F_{cel_{i,j}}$ is formulated as:

$$F_{i,j,l} = L_{Conv_l}(F_{i,j,l-1}), l = 1, 2, 3, 4 \qquad (7)$$

$$F_{cel_{i,j}} = Concat(F_{i,j,1}, F_{i,j,2}, F_{i,j,3}, F_{i,j,4}) \qquad (8)$$

Cross Transformer Layer (CTL): Cross Transformer Layer (CTL) [23] is based on the standard multi-head self-attention of the original Transformer

Table 1. Quantitative comparison (average PSNR/SSIM) with state-of-the-art methods for lightweight image SR on benchmark datasets. The best results are highlighted in red color and the second best is in blue.

Scale	Method	Params	Set5 PSNR/SSIM	Set14 PSNR/SSIM	BSD100 PSNR/SSIM	Urban100 PSNR/SSIM
×2	CARN [2]	1,592 K	37.76/0.9590	33.52/0.9166	32.09/0.8978	31.92/0.9256
	LAPAR-A [12]	548 K	38.01/0.9605	33.62/0.9183	32.19/0.8999	32.10/0.9283
	IMDN [10]	694 K	38.00/0.9605	33.63/0.9177	32.19/0.8996	32.17/0.9283
	LatticeNet [18]	756 K	38.15/0.9610	33.78/0.9193	32.25/0.9005	32.43/0.9302
	ESRT [17]	677 K	38.03/0.9600	33.75/0.9184	32.25/0.9001	32.58/0.9318
	EDSR-baseline [15]	1,370 K	37.99/0.9604	33.57/0.9175	32.16/0.8994	31.98/0.9272
	EDSR-baseline-liif [5]	1,567 K	37.99/0.9602	33.66/0.9182	32.17/0.8990	32.15/0.9285
	CrossSR (ours)	1,574 K	38.13/0.9607	33.99/0.9218	32.27/0.9000	32.63/0.9325
X3	CARN [2]	1,592 K	34.29/0.9255	30.29/0.8407	29.06/0.8034	28.06/0.8493
	LAPAR-A [12]	544K	34.36/0.9267	30.34/0.8421	29.11/0.8054	28.15/0.8523
	IMDN [10]	703 K	34.36/0.9270	30.32/0.8417	29.09/0.8046	28.17/0.8519
	LatticeNet [18]	765 K	34.53/0.9281	30.39/0.8424	29.15/0.8059	28.33/0.8538
	ESRT [17]	770 K	34.42/0.9268	30.43/0.8433	29.15/0.8063	28.46/0.8574
	EDSR-baseline [15]	1,555 K	34.37/0.9270	30.28/0.8417	29.09/0.8052	28.15/0.8527
	EDSR-baseline-liif [5]	1,567 K	34.40/0.9269	30.37/0.8426	29.12/0.8056	28.22/0.8539
	CrossSR (ours)	1,574 K	34.53/0.9283	30.53/0.8460	29.21/0.8082	28.64/0.8616
×4	CARN [2]	1,592 K	32.13/0.8937	28.60/0.7806	27.58/0.7349	26.07/0.7837
	LAPAR-A [12]	659 K	32.15/0.8944	28.61/0.7818	27.61/0.7366	26.14/0.7871
	IMDN [10]	715 K	32.21/0.8948	28.58/0.7811	27.56/0.7353	26.04/0.7838
	MSFIN [24]	682 K	32.28/0.8957	28.66/0.7829	27.61/0.7370	26.25/0.7892
	LatticeNet [18]	777 K	32.30/0.8962	28.68/0.7830	27.62/0.7367	26.25/0.7873
	ESRT [17]	751 K	32.29/0.8964	28.69/0.7844	27.66/0.7384	26.27/0.7907
	ASSLN [28]	708 K	32.19/0.8947	28.69/0.7833	27.69/0.7379	26.39/0.7962
	EDSR-baseline [15]	1,518 K	32.09/0.8938	28.58/0.7813	27.57/0.7357	26.04/0.7849
	EDSR-baseline-liif [5]	1,567 K	32.24/0.8952	28.62/0.7823	27.60/0.7366	26.15/0.7879
	CrossSR (ours)	1,574 K	32.46/0.8975	28.79/0.7856	27.70/0.7405	26.55/0.7995

layer. The main differences lie in short-distance attention (SDA), long-distance attention (LDA), and dynamic position encoding block (DPB). The structure of Cross Transformer is shown in the Fig. 3. For the input image, the embedded features are firstly cropped into small patches to reduce the amount of operations. For short-distance attention, each $G \times G$-adjacent pixel point is cropped into a group. For long-distance attention, pixel points with fixed distance I are grouped together, and then these different grouping features X are used as input for long and short distance attention, respectively. The specific attentions are defined as follows:

$$Attention(Q, K, V) = Softmax(\frac{QK^T}{\sqrt{d}} + B)V \qquad (9)$$

where $Q, K, V \in R^{G^2 \times D}$ represent query, key, value in the self-attention module, respectively. And $\sqrt{d}$ is a constant normalizer. $B \in R^{G^2 \times G^2}$ is the position bis matrix. Q, K, V are computed as

$$Q, K, V = X(P_Q, P_K, P_V) \qquad (10)$$

where X is the different grouping features for LDA and SDA, P_Q, P_K, P_V are projection matrices implemented through different linear layers.

Next, a multi-layer perception (MLP) is used for further feature transformations. The LayerNorm (LN) layer is added before the LSDA (LDA or SDA) and the MLP, and both modules are connected using residuals. The whole process is formulated as:

$$X = LSDA(LN(X)) + X \tag{11}$$

$$X = MLP(LN(X)) + X \tag{12}$$

2.3   DPB and Dense MLP

Dynamic Position encoding Block (DPB): Image super-resolution aims to recover the high-frequency details of an image. And a well-designed spatial coding operation allows the network to effectively recover the details in visual scenes [26]. With the four linear layers of DPB, we expand the two-dimensional linear spatial input into a 48-dimensional spatial encoding that can more fully exploit the spatial location information, and such design could effectively reduce structural distortions and artifacts in images. The network structure of DPB is shown in Fig. 3.a, and the location information followed the DPB encoding operation is represented as:

$$dpb(\delta_x) = L_4(L_3(L_2(L_1(\delta_x)))) \tag{13}$$

where L_1, L_2, L_3 all consist of three layers: linear layer, layer normalisation, and ReLU. L_4 only consists of one linear layer. Then, the DPB encoded spatial information $dpb(\delta_x)$ and the original location information δ_x are cascaded and input into the dense MLP to predict the high-resolution image as shown in Eq. 4.

Dense MLP: Considering that dense networks have achieved good results in image super-resolution and the fascinating advantages of densenets: they reduce the problem of gradient disappearance, enhance feature propagation, encourage function reuse, and greatly reduce the number of parameters. We design a dense MLP network structure, which connects each layer to each other in a feedforward manner. As shown in Fig. 3.c, for each layer of Dnese MLP, all feature maps of its previous layer are used as input, and its own feature map is used as input of all its subsequent layers.

3   Experiment

3.1   Dataset and Metric

The main dataset we use to train and evaluate our CrossSR is the DIV2K [1] dataset from NTIRE 2017 Challenge. DIV2K consists of 1000 2 K high-resolution images together with the bicubic down-sampled low-resolution images under scale ×2, ×3, and ×4. We maintain its original train validation split, in which we use the 800 images from the train set in training and the 100 images from the

Table 2. Quantitative comparison (average PSNR/SSIM) with state-of-the-art methods for classical image SR on benchmark datasets. NLSA [19] and SWIR [14] train different models for different upsampling scales. The rest methods train one model for all the upsampling scales. The best results are highlighted in red color and the second best is in blue.

Dataset	Method	×2	×	×	×6	×8	×12
Set5	NLSA [19]	38.34/0.9618	34.85/0.9306	32.59/0.9000	–	–	–
	SWIR [14]	38.35/0.9620	34.89/0.9312	32.72/0.9021	–	–	–
	Meta-RDN [8]	38.23/0.9609	34.69/0.9292	32.46/0.8978	28.97/0.8288	26.95/0.7671	24.60/0.6812
	RDN-LIIF [5]	38.17/0.9608	34.68/0.9289	32.50/0.8984	29.15/0.8355	27.14/0.7803	24.86/0.7062
	CrossSR (ours)	38.32/0.9615	34.84/0.9305	32.73/0.9006	29.31/0.8396	27.37/0.7873	24.89/0.7090
Set14	NLSA [19]	34.08/0.9231	30.70/0.8485	28.87/0.7891	–	–	–
	SWIR [14]	34.14/0.9227	30.77/0.8503	28.94/0.7914	–	–	–
	Meta-RDN [8]	33.95/0.9209	30.56/0.8469	28.79/0.7869	26.52/0.6986	25.00/0.6383	23.16/0.5658
	RDN-LIIF [5]	33.97/0.9207	30.53/0.8466	28.80/0.7869	26.64/0.7021	25.15/0.6457	23.24/0.5771
	CrossSR (ours)	34.29/0.9240	30.76/0.8501	28.97/0.7914	26.77/0.7062	25.22/0.6498	23.36/0.5812
BSD100	NLSA [19]	32.43/0.9027	29.34/0.8117	27.78/0.7444	–	–	–
	SWIR [14]	32.44/0.9030	29.37/0.8124	27.83/0.7459	–	–	–
	Meta-RDN [8]	32.34/0.9012	29.26/0.8092	27.72/0.7410	25.91/0.6506	24.83/0.5952	23.47/0.5365
	RDN-LIIF [5]	32.32/0.9007	29.26/0.8094	27.74/0.7414	25.98/0.6540	24.91/0.6010	23.57/0.5445
	CrossSR(ours)	32.41/0.9022	29.37/0.8127	27.84/0.7465	26.06/0.6596	25.00/0.6062	23.62/0.5481
Urban100	NLSA [19]	33.43/0.9394	29.25/0.8726	26.96/0.8109	–	–	–
	SWIR [14]	33.40/0.9393	29.29/0.8744	27.07/0.8164	–	–	–
	Meta-RDN [8]	32.93/0.9356	28.85/0.8662	26.70/0.8017	23.99/0.6927	22.60/0.6182	20.99/0.5281
	RDN-LIIF [5]	32.87/0.9348	28.82/0.8659	26.68/0.8036	24.20/0.7024	22.79/0.6334	21.15/0.5482
	CrossSR (ours)	33.39/0.9393	29.31/0.8745	27.16/0.8164	24.59/0.7191	23.11/0.6496	21.37/0.5604

validation set for testing. Follows many prior works, we also report our model performance on 4 benchmark datasets: Set5 [4], Set14 [27], B100 [3], Urban100 [9]. The SR results are evaluated by PSNR and SSIM metrics on the Y channel of transformed YCbCr space.

3.2   Implementation Details

As with LIIF, we set the input patch size to 48 × 48. We set the number of channels for the lightweight network and the classic image super-resolution task to 72 and 288, respectively. Our models were trained by ADAM optimizer using $\beta 1 = 0.9$, $\beta 2 = 0.99$ and $\epsilon = 10^{-8}$. The model of the lightweight network was trained for 10^6 iterations with a batch size of 16, and the learning rate was initialized to 1×10^{-4} and then reduced to half at 2×10^5 iterations. In contrast, the classical network has a batch size of 8 and an initial learning rate of 5×10^{-5}. We implemented our models using the PyTorch framework with an RTX3060 GPU.

Table 3. Comparison of PSNR (dB) of non-integer scales of different arbitrary scale super-resolution methods

	Params	Set5			Set14		
		×1.6	×2.4	×3.1	x×1.5	×2.8	×3.2
Bicubic	–	36.10	32.41	29.89	32.87	27.84	26.91
Meta-RDN [8]	21.4M	40.66	36.55	34.42	37.52	30.97	28.90
ArbRCAN [22]	16.6M	40.69	36.59	34.50	37.53	31.01	28.93
ArbRDN [22]	22.6M	40.67	36.55	34.43	37.53	30.98	28.90
RDN-LIIF [5]	21.8M	40.62	36.48	34.49	37.54	31.09	29.97
CrossSR(ours)	18.3M	**40.73**	**36.62**	**34.70**	**37.54**	**31.28**	**30.18**

3.3   Results and Comparison

Table 1 compares the performances of our CrossSR with 8 state-of-the-art light weight SR models. Compared to all given methods, our CrossSR performs best on the four standard benchmark datasets: Set5 [4], Set14 [27], B100 [3], Urban100 [9]. We can find a significant improvement in the results on Urban100. Specifically, a gain of 0.4 dB over EDSR-LIIF [5] on super-resolution for the Urban100 dataset is achieved. This is because Urban100 contains challenging urban scenes that often have cross-scale similarities, as shown in the Fig. 4, and our network can effectively exploit these cross-scale similarities to recover a more realistic image. On other datasets, the gain in PSNR is not as large as the improvement on the Urban100 dataset, but there is still a lot of improvement, all of which is greater than 0.1 dB.

We also compared our method with the state-of-the-art classical image super-resolution methods in Table 2. As can be seen from the data in the table, the results of some current arbitrary-scale methods [5,8] are somewhat worse than those of single-scale super-resolution [14,19]. Our CrossSR is an arbitrary-scale method that simultaneously achieves results competitive with state-of-the-art single-scale methods on different data sets in multiple scenarios, demonstrating the effectiveness of our method.

In Table 3, we also compared the performance of some arbitrary-scale image super-resolution models [8,22] with our CrossSR at different non-integer scales. It can be found that the PSNR results of our model are consistently higher than those of MetaSR and ArbRDN at all scales.

3.4   Ablation Studies

To verify the effectiveness of modified Transformer, DPB and Dense MLP, we conducted ablation experiments in Table 4. Our experiments were performed on the Set5 dataset for x2 lightweight super-resolution.

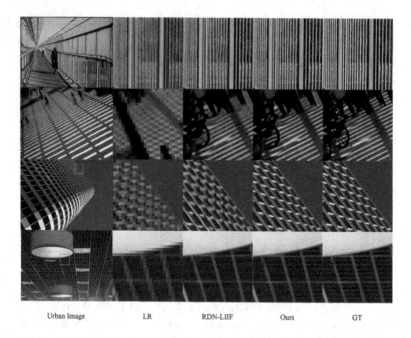

Fig. 4. Visualization comparison with liif on dataset Urban at ×4 SR.

Table 4. Quantitative ablation study. Evaluated on the Set5 validation set for ×2 (PSNR (dB)) after 300 epochs.

Modified transformer	DPB	Dense MLP	PSNR(dB)
×	×	×	37.92
✓	×	×	37.97
×	✓	×	37.93
×	×	✓	37.96
✓	✓	✓	38.01

As can be seen from the data in Table 4, the addition of the modified Transformer improved the test set by 0.05 dB compared to the baseline method, and the addition of DPB and Dense MLP improved it by 0.01 dB and 0.04 dB respectively. This demonstrates the effectiveness of the Transformer backbone, DPB and Dense MLP.

4   Conclusions

In this paper, a novel CrossSR framework has been proposed for image restoration models of arbitrary scale on the basis of Cross Transformer. The model consists of two components: feature extraction and continuous function representation. In particular, a Cross Transformer-based backbone is used for feature extraction, a dynamic position-coding operation is used to incorporate spatial information in continuous image representation fully, and finally, a dense MLP for continuous image fitting. Extensive experiments have shown that CrossSR achieves advanced performance in lightweight and classical image SR tasks, which demonstrated the effectiveness of the proposed CrossSR.

References

1. Agustsson, E., Timofte, R.: NTIRE 2017 challenge on single image super-resolution: dataset and study. In: 2017 IEEE Conference on Computer Vision and Pattern Recognition Workshops, CVPR Workshops 2017, Honolulu, HI, USA, 21–26 July 2017, pp. 1122–1131. IEEE Computer Society (2017)
2. Ahn, N., Kang, B., Sohn, K.-A.: Fast, accurate, and lightweight super-resolution with cascading residual network. In: Ferrari, V., Hebert, M., Sminchisescu, C., Weiss, Y. (eds.) ECCV 2018. LNCS, vol. 11214, pp. 256–272. Springer, Cham (2018). https://doi.org/10.1007/978-3-030-01249-6_16
3. Arbelaez, P., Maire, M., Fowlkes, C., Malik, J.: Contour detection and hierarchical image segmentation. IEEE Trans. Pattern Anal. Mach. Intell. **33**(5), 898–916 (2010)
4. Bevilacqua, M., Roumy, A., Guillemot, C., Alberi-Morel, M.: Low-complexity single-image super-resolution based on nonnegative neighbor embedding. In: Bowden, R., Collomosse, J.P., Mikolajczyk, K. (eds.) British Machine Vision Conference, BMVC 2012, Surrey, UK, 3–7 September 2012, pp. 1–10. BMVA Press (2012)
5. Chen, Y., Liu, S., Wang, X.: Learning continuous image representation with local implicit image function. In: CVPR, Computer Vision Foundation/IEEE, pp. 8628–8638 (2021)
6. Dong, C., Loy, C.C., He, K., Tang, X.: Image super-resolution using deep convolutional networks. IEEE Trans. Pattern Anal. Mach. Intell. **38**(2), 295–307 (2015)
7. Hu, F., Lakdawala, S., Hao, Q., Qiu, M.: Low-power, intelligent sensor hardware interface for medical data preprocessing. IEEE Trans. Inf Technol. Biomed. **13**(4), 656–663 (2009)
8. Hu, X., Mu, H., Zhang, X., Wang, Z., Tan, T., Sun, J.: Meta-sr: a magnification-arbitrary network for super-resolution. In: CVPR, Computer Vision Foundation/IEEE, pp. 1575–1584 (2019)
9. Huang, J., Singh, A., Ahuja, N.: Single image super-resolution from transformed self-exemplars. In: IEEE Conference on Computer Vision and Pattern Recognition, CVPR 2015, Boston, MA, USA, 7–12 June 2015, pp. 5197–5206. IEEE Computer Society (2015)
10. Hui, Z., Gao, X., Yang, Y., Wang, X.: Lightweight image super-resolution with information multi-distillation network. In: Amsaleg, L., et al., (eds.) Proceedings of the 27th ACM International Conference on Multimedia, MM 2019, Nice, France, 21–25 October 2019, pp. 2024–2032. ACM (2019)
11. Kim, J., Lee, J.K., Lee, K.M.: Deeply-recursive convolutional network for image super-resolution. In: 2016 IEEE Conference on Computer Vision and Pattern Recognition, CVPR 2016, Las Vegas, NV, USA, 27–30 June 2016, pp. 1637–1645. IEEE Computer Society (2016)
12. Li, W., Zhou, K., Qi, L., Jiang, N., Lu, J., Jia, J.: LAPAR: linearly-assembled pixel-adaptive regression network for single image super-resolution and beyond (2021). CoRR abs/2105.10422

13. Li, Y., Song, Y., Jia, L., Gao, S., Li, Q., Qiu, M.: Intelligent fault diagnosis by fusing domain adversarial training and maximum mean discrepancy via ensemble learning. IEEE Trans. Ind. Informatics **17**(4), 2833–2841 (2021)
14. Liang, J., Cao, J., Sun, G., Zhang, K., Gool, L.V., Timofte, R.: Swinir: image restoration using swin transformer. In: IEEE/CVF International Conference on Computer Vision Workshops, ICCVW 2021, Montreal, BC, Canada, 11–17 October 2021, pp. 1833–1844. IEEE (2021)
15. Lim, B., Son, S., Kim, H., Nah, S., Lee, K.M.: Enhanced deep residual networks for single image super-resolution. In: 2017 IEEE Conference on Computer Vision and Pattern Recognition Workshops, CVPR Workshops 2017, Honolulu, HI, USA, 21–26 July 2017, pp. 1132–1140. IEEE Computer Society (2017)
16. Liu, J., Zhang, W., Tang, Y., Tang, J., Wu, G.: Residual feature aggregation network for image super-resolution. In: CVPR, Computer Vision Foundation/IEEE, pp. 2356–2365 (2020)
17. Lu, Z., Liu, H., Li, J., Zhang, L.: Efficient transformer for single image super-resolution (2021). CoRR abs/2108.11084
18. Luo, X., Xie, Y., Zhang, Y., Qu, Y., Li, C., Fu, Y.: LatticeNet: towards lightweight image super-resolution with lattice block. In: Vedaldi, A., Bischof, H., Brox, T., Frahm, J.-M. (eds.) ECCV 2020. LNCS, vol. 12367, pp. 272–289. Springer, Cham (2020). https://doi.org/10.1007/978-3-030-58542-6_17
19. Mei, Y., Fan, Y., Zhou, Y.: Image super-resolution with non-local sparse attention. In: CVPR, Computer Vision Foundation/IEEE, pp. 3517–3526 (2021)
20. Qiu, H., Zheng, Q., Msahli, M., Memmi, G., Qiu, M., Lu, J.: Topological graph convolutional network-based urban traffic flow and density prediction. IEEE Trans. Intell. Transp. Syst. **22**(7), 4560–4569 (2021)
21. Vaswani, A., et al.: Attention is all you need. In: NIPS, pp. 5998–6008 (2017)
22. Wang, L., Wang, Y., Lin, Z., Yang, J., An, W., Guo, Y.: Learning A single network for scale-arbitrary super-resolution. In: ICCV, pp. 4781–4790. IEEE (2021)
23. Wang, W., Yao, L., Chen, L., Cai, D., He, X., Liu, W.: Crossformer: a versatile vision transformer based on cross-scale attention (2021). CoRR abs/2108.00154
24. Wang, Z., Gao, G., Li, J., Yu, Y., Lu, H.: Lightweight image super-resolution with multi-scale feature interaction network. In: 2021 IEEE International Conference on Multimedia and Expo, ICME 2021, Shenzhen, China, 5–9 July 2021, pp. 1–6. IEEE (2021)
25. Xiao, T., Singh, M., Mintun, E., Darrell, T., Dollár, P., Girshick, R.B.: Early convolutions help transformers see better (2021). CoRR abs/2106.14881
26. Xu, X., Wang, Z., Shi, H.: Ultrasr: spatial encoding is a missing key for implicit image function-based arbitrary-scale super-resolution (2021). arXiv preprint arXiv:2103.12716
27. Zeyde, R., Elad, M., Protter, M.: On single image scale-up using sparse-representations. In: Boissonnat, D., et al. (eds.) Curves and Surfaces 2010. LNCS, vol. 6920, pp. 711–730. Springer, Heidelberg (2012). https://doi.org/10.1007/978-3-642-27413-8_47
28. Zhang, Y., Wang, H., Qin, C., Fu, Y.: Aligned structured sparsity learning for efficient image super-resolution. In: Advances in Neural Information Processing Systems, vol. 34 (2021)

EEG Emotion Classification Using 2D-3DCNN

Yingdong Wang⬤, Qingfeng Wu$^{(\boxtimes)}$⬤, and Qunsheng Ruan⬤

Xiamen University, No. 422, Siming South Road, Siming District, Xiamen, China
{yingdongwang,qsruan}@stu.xmu.edu.cn, qfwu@xmu.edu.cn

Abstract. Automatic emotion recognition is important in human-computer interaction (HCI). Although extensive electroencephalography (EEG)-based emotion recognition research has been conducted in recent years, effectively identifying the correlation between EEG signals and emotions remains a challenge. In this study, a new method that combines a novel pre-processing technique with a 3D convolutional neural network (3DCNN)-based classifier is proposed. After the data undergo preprocessing, 3DCNN is used to extract temporal and spatial features from the 2D-map EEG feature sequences. The features are then fed to a fully connected network to obtain binary or multi-category results. Extensive experiments are conducted on the DEAP dataset, and results show that the proposed method surpasses other state-of-the-art methods. The process of selecting the hyper-parameters of 3DCNN is also investigated by comparing three models. Source codes used in this study are available on https://github.com/heibaipei/V-3DCNN.

Keywords: EEG · Emotion recognition · Emotion classification

1 Introduction

Emotion recognition has emerged as a new direction in research, attracting considerable attention in many different fields. For example, in human-computer interaction (HCI), identifying user emotions can be used as a form of feedback to provide better content and enhance a user's experience in e-learning, computer games, and information retrieval [3,12]. Recently, Kim and Kang [6] applied electroencephalography (EEG) signals to investigate the emotional characteristics of mentally healthy groups and the addiction levels of smartphone users. To achieve a positive communication experience, emotion recognition has become an important part of the human-machine interface [1,8]. The rapid development of portable computer interface devices has made signal processing easier, and

This work was supported by the Key Project of National Key R&D Project (No. 2017YFC1703303); Natural Science Foundation of Fujian Province of China (No. 2019J01846, No. 2018J01555, No. 2017J01773); External Cooperation Project of Fujian Province, China (No. 2019I0001); Science and Technology Guiding Project of Fujian Province, China (2019Y0046).

© The Author(s), under exclusive license to Springer Nature Switzerland AG 2022
G. Memmi et al. (Eds.): KSEM 2022, LNAI 13369, pp. 645–654, 2022.
https://doi.org/10.1007/978-3-031-10986-7_52

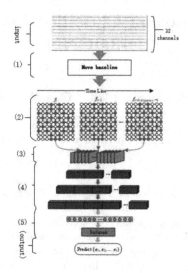

Fig. 1. Five-step flow of the algorithm.

more EEG emotion recognition algorithms based on machine learning have been proposed. In summary, emotion classification can be divided into three stages: preprocessing, feature extraction, and classification [16].

Preprocessing. Preprocessing includes many procedures, such as removing the baseline, filtering, and reducing noise via independent component analysis. For baselines, there is no uniform method for selecting the baseline period.

Feature Extraction. The EEG characteristics of emotion classification can be roughly classified into four, namely, frequency-spatial [2], spatial [13], temporal-frequency [4], and nonlinear characteristics [5].

Classification. Researchers usually compare their methods with support vector machine (SVM), decision tree, and naive Bayesian (NB) methods, which are regarded as baseline classifiers suitable for small datasets. EEG datasets are an example of small datasets. However, these three methods cannot be used to choose key features automatically. Deep learning (DL) methods [11] can choose features automatically, but the model will overfit the small dataset.

To solve these problems, we propose a novel method 2D-3DCNN. The main flow of the algorithm is shown in Fig. 1. (1) Remove the baseline. The principle is to use a signal that does not receive any stimulus as a representation of the basic emotional state. Instead, the difference between the stimulus signal and the basic emotional state is used to represent the emotional state of a certain period. (2) Convert the preprocessed data into a 2D sequence. Here, 1D data at one sample are converted into 2D grid data. (3) Feed the 2D sequences into the CNN to obtain a sequence of spatial features. (4) Cut the spatial feature sequence into small cubes and feed the cubes into the 3DCNN to obtain the spatiotemporal features. To reduce training time and create additional data, a sliding window on the spatial sequence is used, the spatial feature sequence is divided into small patches, and then the cubes are fed into 3DCNN layers to extract the spatial and temporal features. (5) Use FC and Softmax to predict the labels. A 2DCNN model and a 3DCNN model are compared in detail to explain the proposed method. The two models accurately identify human emotional states by learning the temporal and spatial representations of the preprocessed 2D EEG sequence effectively. Extensive research results on the DEAP[1] dataset have shown that two of the three models can achieve accuracies of 95.37% and 92.88% for binary classification and multi-category classification, respectively. In summary, the main contributions of this study are as follows:

– In the model, recurrent neural network (RNN) is replaced with CNN to learn the temporal features, and 3DCNN is applied to mine the time dependence of these 2D frames. In this process, EEG temporal and spatial features are extracted without any basic physiological knowledge and EEG signal processing skills.
– With our preprocessing methods, 2D-3DCNN significantly outperforms current state-of-the-art approaches.

The rest of the research is structured as follows. Section 2 briefly reviews the related work. Section 3 introduces the EEG database and how labels and data are handled. Next, the details of the pre- processing method and classifier are given. Section 4 shows the performance and accuracy and provides useful discussions about current algorithms. Section 5 presents the contribution of our research.

2   Methods and Dataset

2.1   Method

The algorithm includes three aspects. (1) Remove baselines. (2) Construct 2D frame sequences. (3) Classify with different DL models.

Remove Baseline. To extract the salient EEG-based emotion features, we applied the deviation between observed signal and baseline signals to represent the emotional state. A 3 s EEG signal with no stimulus is used as the baseline. Figure 2(a) details the process of calculating the average of the multi-channel baseline signal. T-second multi-channel baseline signals refer to a $c \times t$ matrix, where c denotes the number of channels, and t ($T \times frequency$) denotes the sampling number in the T-second period. Then, a sliding window with size S is used to segment the baseline signals into m $[c \times S]$ matrices, and the matrix refers to mat_i. HCI products require timely feedback from the human emotional

---

[1] http://www.eecs.qmul.ac.uk/mmv/datasets/deap/.

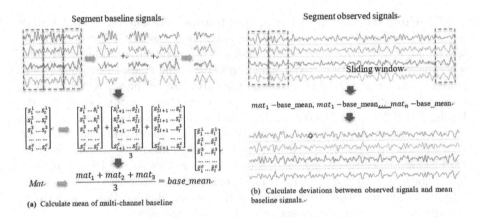

Fig. 2. Main flow of baseline removal.

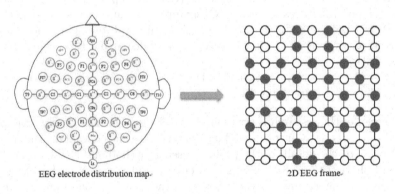

Fig. 3. EEG electrode map of headset and the corresponding 2D EEG frame (9×9).

state. Thus, the test time is set to 1 s in this study. The parameter m is 3; and thus the baseline can be divided into three without overlap. Finally, the average baseline signal can be calculated as follows:

$$mat_{avg} = \frac{\sum_1^m mat_i}{m} \tag{1}$$

After acquiring the average baseline matrix, we must obtain the deviation between observed signals and mean baseline in Fig. 2(b). A sliding window with the same size is used to divide the observed signals into n ($c \times l$) matrices; the matrix refers to mat_j, The deviation is calculated as follows:

$$d_j = mat_j - mat_{avg} \tag{2}$$

After these steps, each deviation matrix is used to represent the human emotional state of the S-second period.

Construct 2D EEG Frame Sequences. Human-computer interaction (HCI) systems use headsets with multiple electrodes to capture the EEG signals. These multiple electrodes follow the standards of the International 10–20 System, an internationally recognized method of describing the locations of scalp electrodes and underlying areas of the cerebral cortex. Figure 3 shows a view of the International 10–20 System, which depicts the placement of electrodes. The location of the red circles are the test points used in the DEAP dataset. From the EEG electrode diagram, we see that each electrode has a few neighbor electrodes. EEG is the result of a group of brain cells discharging. Therefore obtaining features from areas signal is meaningful. Thus, to make full use of this spatial information, multi-channel EEG signals are converted to 2D EEG frames ($h \times w$) according to the electrode distribution maps, where h is the maximum number of vertical electrodes, and w is the maximum number of horizontal electrodes. In our experiment, h and w are set to 9.

After transformation, the EEG segment $d\epsilon R^{c \times t}$ is converted to 2D EEG frame sequences $D\epsilon R^{h \times w \times t}$. Finally, the 2D EEG frames segment G_j is denoted as follows:

$$G_j = [f_t, f_{t+1}, ..., f_{t+(S \times frequency)-1}] \tag{3}$$

where $G_j \epsilon R^{h \times w \times (S \times frequency)}$, S is the window size, and subscript j is used to identify the different segments during the observation period. The goal of this study is to develop an effective model to recognize a set of human emotions $E = \{e_1, e_2, ...e_k\}$ from each segment S_j. After these steps, each deviation matrix is used to represent the human emotional state of the S-second period.

The classifier includes two parts: 2DCNN and 3DCNN. First, there are four continuous 2D convolution layers. The first three layers have the same kernels with 4×4 for spatial feature extraction, and the fourth convolution layer has a 1×1 kernel for dimension reduction. Emotion is a psychological state of a period, and the observed EEG signal is a time series data. Therefore, their time dependence must be mined based on their spatial features. However, according to the previous description, each 2D EEG frame is resolved to 32 feature maps after three continuous convolution operations. This finding means that the input segment is $S_j \epsilon R^{h \times w \times (S \times frequency)}$, the combined feature map cube is $FMC_j \epsilon R^{h \times w \times 32 \times (S \times frequency)}$. The FMC_j has a very large size, which will be time-consuming in the training stage and requires a lot of memory. To address this problem, a 1×1 convolution kernel is applied in the fourth layer to compress the 32 $h \times w$ feature maps into one $h \times w$ feature map. These maps are then stacked together for further temporal dependence mining. The 1×1 filter is widely used for dimension reduction and integration of information across feature maps [9,14].

As shown in Fig. 1, the stacked feature map cube FMC_j can be denoted as follows:

$$FMC_j = [fm_t, fm_{t+1}, ...fm_{t+(S \times frequency)-1}] \tag{4}$$

where fm_t is a compressed feature map at time stamp t. For sliding window size S, there are ($S \times frequency$) h by w feature maps. After stack operation, three continuous 3D convolution layers are adapted to extract temporal dependence among the feature maps. At the first 3D convolution layer, a $1 \times 1 \times (S \times frequency)$ $(width \times height \times depth)$ kernel is applied to mine the information along the timeline. To extract temporal features from all these feature maps, the depth of the kernel is set to $(S \times frequency)$. The second and third layers have the same kernel size of $4 \times 4 \times 4$ for further temporal feature extraction. Similar to the previous 2D convolution part, the three 3D convolution layers each have 8, 16, and 32 feature maps, respectively.

After the cascade 2D and 3DCNN, a fully connected layer is added to map the blended spatiotemporal features into a vector $v_j \epsilon R^{1024}$. A softmax layer receives v_j to yield final probability prediction of each target class for segment S_j:

$$P_j = Softmax(v_j), P_j \epsilon R^k \tag{5}$$

where the superscript k denotes the number of target categories. To avoid overfitting, we apply dropout operation after a fully connected layer. An L2 regularization term is also added to cross entropy the loss function and improve the generalization ability of the model.

$$Loss = cross\_entropy(Pre, y) + \alpha * L2 \tag{6}$$

In summary, 2D-3DCNN takes segment as input, and the segments are classified into k categories. Each segment S_j contains $S \times frequency$ 2D EEG frames. Three continuous 2DCNN are applied to each 2D EEG frame to extract spatial features. A 1×1 convolution operation is adopted to compress the 32 feature maps into a single feature map. Then, the feature maps from each frame are stacked into a feature map cube FMC_j. Three 3D convolution layers are followed to extract temporal features from the FMC_j. A fully connected layer is added to map the blended spatiotemporal features into a vector. A Softmax layer finally calculates the classification probabilities over k emotional states for this segment S_j.

2.2   Dataset

The DEAP [7] dataset has been widely employed in emotion recognition, which consists of 32 participants. EEG signals and other peripheral physiological signals were recorded while 32 subjects watched 40 music videos individually. Each piece of music video was 1 min long. Before EEG signals were recorded, every subject's eyes were closed for 3 s. Thus, each EEG data were 40×60 s long and had a 3 s baseline. The public data contained EEG signals and peripheral physiological signals. The peripheral physiological signals have 8 channels, while the EEG signals have 32 channels that were down-sampled 128 Hz after the EOG was removed. A bandpass frequency filter ranging from 4.0 Hz to 45.0 Hz was applied. For the labels, participants rated the levels of arousal, valence, liking, and dominance for each trial. Rating values ranged from 1 to 9.

To improve the classification of granularity, we focused on a 2D emotion model in which emotional states could be determined by the position in the

2D plane. The data can be classified into four items: (1) high valence and high arousal (HVHA); (2) high valence and low arousal (HVLA); (3) low valence and low arousal (LVLA); and (4) low valence and high arousal (LVHA). The items balanced among different emotions, ensure the balance of the neural network classification training. And the emotion test time is set to 1 s in this study.

3   Results

We validated the proposed model on the public DEAP dataset and compared it with other models previously reported. 10-fold cross-validation applied to evaluate the proposed approach. The mean score of the 10-fold results was taken as the final experiment result. The models were implemented with Tensorflow and trained on an NVIDIA Titan Xp pascal GPU. The Adam optimizer is adopted to minimize the cross-entropy loss function, and the learning rate is 10^{-4}. The parameter of dropout operation was set to 0.5. The penalty strength of L2 was 0.5. Both fully connected layers have the same size of 1024.

Compare with Other Models. In this experiment, we compared our model with six algorithms. The first three of which are based on the public DEAP dataset for two binary classifications of arousal and valence. Liu et al. [10] used a bi-modal deep auto-encoder (BDAE) network to extract features from EEG signals, eye signals, and a linear SVM classifier for final classification. Li et al. [17] proposed a hybrid DL model that integrates CNN and RNN to extract inter-channel correlation information from a constructed data frame and learn contextual information from sequences. Tang et al. [15] focused on emotion recognition based on EEG signals and eye signals and developed a bimodal-LSTM model, which can use both temporal and frequency-domain information of features for final prediction. In [19], LSTM is used to extract the temporal feature, it greatly improves the recognition accuracy of EEG. To prove the effect of temporal features, we also compared 2DCNN model and 3DCNN model. The 2DCNN model extracts spatial and temporal features over a time series. We combine all spatial features extracted by three 2DCNN layers from each frame. Then, a fully connected layer with softmax receives the blended spatio-temporal features for sentiment recognition. All parameters are the same as in the 2D-3DCNN model. The 3DCNN model extracts the spatial and temporal features simultaneously, the input 3DCNN model is still a segment of the 2D EEG frames S_j, and the model directly stacks these frames into a frame cube FC_j. Then three continuous 3D convolution layers are used to extract spatio-temporal features from FC_j. The proposed method obtains the highest accuracy (Fig. 4).

3.1   Discussion

About the Baseline. The results of the three models tested with baseline are shown in Table 1. PRCNN [18] used the method of [19] tested on the DEAP dataset. Case 1 indicates that the 3 s baseline signal is not considered, and Case

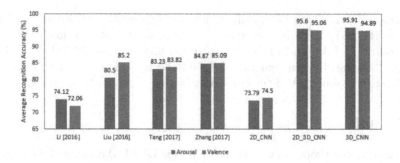

Fig. 4. Mean accuracy comparison between relevant approaches.

Table 1. The accuracy of different models. Case 1 represents models without moving baseline. Case 2 represents models with the baseline removed.

	Case	Arousal	Valence
2D-CNN	1	0.699 ± 0.101	0.639 ± 0.073
	2	0.737 ± 0.0089	0.745 ± 0.0926
2D-3D-CNN	1	0.6334 ± 0.123	0.564 ± 0.087
	2	0.956 ± 0.034	0.950 ± 0.0031
3D-CNN	1	0.608 ± 0.119	0.569 ± 0.067
	2	0.959 ± 0.030	0.948 ± 0.043
PRCNN [18]	1	0.61 ± 0.096	0.5705 ± 7.01
	2	0.908 ± 0.038	0.9103 ± 0.0299

2 indicates the proposed preprocessing method. The accuracy of sentiment classification is found to be greatly improved when baseline signals are considered. The principle of the preprocessing method is to use a signal that does not receive any stimulus as a representation of the basic emotional state, using the difference between stimulus signal and the basic emotional state to represent the emotional state of a certain period. Experimental results show that the proposed preprocessing method is effective.

Among the three methods proposed in this study, the 2D-3DCNN and 3DCNN methods have higher accuracy than the 2DCNN does, and the accuracy of the two methods differ a little, but the performance is quite different. The detailed training processes of 2D-3DCNN and 3DCNN are shown in Fig. 5. Unlike the previous classification methods, these models were tested on the multi-category label. In the first 60 epochs, the accuracies of the 2D-3DCNN and 3DCNN methods trained on Subject 1 have many commonalities. They all have high CRR, but the 3DCNN model converges faster and is more stable. The difference between the two models is that the 3DCNN model extracts spatial and temporal features simultaneously, but the 2D-3DCNN spatial features and temporal features are separate and the temporal feature delays after the spatial

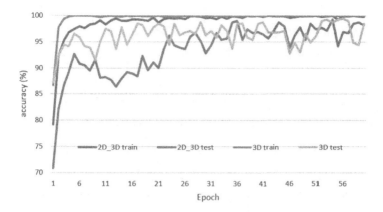

Fig. 5. Visualization of training accuracy and test accuracy on subject 1 (multi-classification).

features. Hence, more iterations are needed for time features, and spatial features can be better integrated. In terms of the number of parameters, 3DCNN has 169,887,885 parameters, while 2D-3DCNN has 169,892,896.

4   Conclusion

In this research, the baseline signals were taken into account and used to propose an effective preprocessing method to improve EEG-based emotion recognition accuracy. A novel method was used to transform multi-channel EEG signals to 2D EEG frame sequences, which could preserve the spatial information of channels. We focused on subject-independent emotion recognition. In other words, models with data that came from the same subject were trained and tested, while cross-subject emotion recognition was more meaningful and can be more highly beneficial in HCI application. Therefore, in the future, our work will focus on transfer learning (training on one set of subjects and testing on another).

References

1. Alarcao, F.: Emotions recognition using EEG signals: a survey. IEEE Trans. Affect. Comput. **10**(3), 374–393 (2017)
2. Ang, K., Yang Chin, Z., Zhang, H., Guan, C.: Filter bank common spatial pattern (FBCSP) in brain-computer interface. In: Proceedings of the International Joint Conference on Neural Networks, pp. 2390–2397 (2008). https://doi.org/10.1109/IJCNN.2008.4634130
3. Chanel, G., Rebetez, C., Betrancourt, M., Pun, T.: Emotion assessment from physiological signals for adaptation of game difficulty. Syst. Man Cybern. **41**(6), 1052–1063 (2011)
4. Ieracitano, C., Mammone, N., Bramanti, A., Hussain, A., Morabito, F.C.: A convolutional neural network approach for classification of dementia stages based on 2D-spectral representation of EEG recordings. Neurocomputing **323**, 96–107 (2019)

5. Jie, X., Cao, R., Li, L.: Emotion recognition based on the sample entropy of EEG. Bio-Med. Mater. Eng. **24**(1), 1185 (2014)
6. Kim, S., Kang, H.: An analysis of smartphone overuse recognition in terms of emotions using brainwaves and deep learning. Neurocomputing **275**, 1393–1406 (2018)
7. Koelstra, S., et al.: DEAP: a database for emotion analysis; using physiological signals. IEEE Trans. Affect. Comput. **3**(1), 18–31 (2012)
8. Lee, Y.Y., Hsieh, S.: Classifying different emotional states by means of EEG-based functional connectivity patterns. PLoS ONE **9**(4), e95415 (2014)
9. Lin, M., Chen, Q., Yan, S.: Network in network. In: International Conference on Learning Representations (2014)
10. Liu, W., Zheng, W.-L., Lu, B.-L.: Emotion recognition using multimodal deep learning. In: Hirose, A., Ozawa, S., Doya, K., Ikeda, K., Lee, M., Liu, D. (eds.) ICONIP 2016. LNCS, vol. 9948, pp. 521–529. Springer, Cham (2016). https://doi.org/10.1007/978-3-319-46672-9_58
11. Luo, T.J., Zhou, C.L., Chao, F.: Exploring spatial-frequency-sequential relationships for motor imagery classification with recurrent neural network. BMC Bioinform. **19**(1), 344 (2018). https://doi.org/10.1186/s12859-018-2365-1
12. Mao, X., Li, Z.: Implementing emotion-based user-aware e-learning. In: Human Factors in Computing Systems, pp. 3787–3792 (2009)
13. Schirrmeister, R.T., et al.: Deep learning with convolutional neural networks for EEG decoding and visualization. Hum. Brain Mapp. **38**(11), 5391–5420 (2017). https://doi.org/10.1002/hbm.23730, https://onlinelibrary.wiley.com/doi/abs/10.1002/hbm.23730
14. Szegedy, C., et al.: Going deeper with convolutions. In: Computer Vision and Pattern Recognition, pp. 1–9 (2015)
15. Tang, H., Liu, W., Zheng, W.L., Lu, B.L.: Multimodal emotion recognition using deep neural networks. In: Liu, D., Xie, S., Li, Y., Zhao, D., El-Alfy, E.S.M. (eds.) Neural Information Processing, pp. 811–819. Springer, Cham (2017). https://doi.org/10.1007/978-3-319-70093-9_86
16. Wagh, K.P., Vasanth, K.: Electroencephalograph (EEG) based emotion recognition system: a review. In: Saini, H.S., Singh, R.K., Patel, V.M., Santhi, K., Ranganayakulu, S.V. (eds.) Innovations in Electronics and Communication Engineering. LNNS, vol. 33, pp. 37–59. Springer, Singapore (2019). https://doi.org/10.1007/978-981-10-8204-7_5
17. Li, X., Song, D., Zhang, P., Yu, G., Hou, Y., Hu, B.: Emotion recognition from multi-channel EEG data through convolutional recurrent neural network. In: 2016 IEEE International Conference on Bioinformatics and Biomedicine (BIBM), vol. 1, pp. 352–359, December 2016. https://doi.org/10.1109/BIBM.2016.7822545
18. Yang, Y., Wu, Q., Qiu, M., Wang, Y., Chen, X.: Emotion recognition from multi-channel EEG through parallel convolutional recurrent neural network. In: 2018 International Joint Conference on Neural Networks (IJCNN), vol. 1, pp. 1–7, July 2018. https://doi.org/10.1109/IJCNN.2018.8489331
19. Zhang, D., Yao, L., Zhang, X., Wang, S., Chen, W., Boots, R.: EEG-based intention recognition from spatio-temporal representations via cascade and parallel convolutional recurrent neural networks, p. 1. Arxiv (2017)

BLSHF: Broad Learning System with Hybrid Features

Weipeng Cao[1,2] , Dachuan Li[3], Xingjian Zhang[1], Meikang Qiu[4] ,
and Ye Liu[2(✉)]

[1] CAAC Key Laboratory of Civil Aviation Wide Surveillance and Safety Operation
Management and Control Technology, Civil Aviation University of China,
Tianjin, China
caoweipeng@szu.edu.cn
[2] College of Computer Science and Software Engineering, Shenzhen University,
Shenzhen, China
ly@szu.edu.cn
[3] Department of Computer Science and Engineering, Southern University of Science
and Technology, Shenzhen, China
lidc3@mail.sustech.edu.cn
[4] Department of Computer Science, Texas A&M University-Commerce,
Commerce, TX, USA

Abstract. Broad Learning System (BLS), a type of neural network with
a non-iterative training mechanism and adaptive network structure, has
attracted much attention in recent years. In BLS, since the mapped features are obtained by mapping the training data based on a set of random
weights, their quality is unstable, which in turn leads to the instability
of the generalization ability of the model. To improve the diversity and
stability of mapped features in BLS, we propose the BLS with Hybrid
Features (BLSHF) algorithm in this study. Unlike original BLS, which
uses a single uniform distribution to assign random values for the input
weights of mapped feature nodes, BLSHF uses different distributions
to initialize the mapped feature nodes in each group, thereby increasing the diversity of mapped features. This method enables BLSHF to
extract high-level features from the original data better than the original BLS and further improves the feature extraction effect of the subsequent enhancement layer. Diverse features are beneficial to algorithms
that use non-iterative training mechanisms, so BLSHF can achieve better
generalization ability than BLS. We apply BLSHF to solve the problem
of air quality evaluation, and the relevant experimental results empirically prove the effectiveness of this method. The learning mechanism of
BLSHF can be easily applied to BLS and its variants to improve their
generalization ability, which makes it have good application value.

Keywords: Broad Learning System · Air quality prediction · Neural
networks

© The Author(s), under exclusive license to Springer Nature Switzerland AG 2022
G. Memmi et al. (Eds.): KSEM 2022, LNAI 13369, pp. 655–666, 2022.
https://doi.org/10.1007/978-3-031-10986-7_53

1 Introduction

In recent years, deep learning technology has made breakthroughs in many fields [7,19]. Here we mainly focus on deep neural networks in deep learning. The complex connection between neurons and hidden layers enables the related model to extract multi-levels of feature information from the original data. Based on the extracted feature information, the model can construct the relationship between the feature description of training samples and their labels for predicting the labels of new samples. Traditional neural networks generally use the iterative training mechanism. Specifically, they first calculate the prediction error of the model based on the initialization parameters and training samples and then use the error back-propagation method to iteratively fine-tune all the weights in the neural network to make the prediction error of the model reach an acceptable threshold. This process is time-consuming, and the demand for hardware computing resources is huge. For example, GPU is often necessary for deep model training. This makes it difficult to train and deploy related models on-site in many scenarios with limited computing power.

To alleviate the defects of traditional neural networks, neural networks using non-iterative training mechanisms have attracted more and more attention in recent years [2,17]. This kind of neural network has one thing in common, that is, some parameters in the neural network remain unchanged in the subsequent model training process after initialization, and the parameters to be calculated only need to be solved at one time. Compared with traditional neural networks, this training method undoubtedly greatly improves the learning efficiency of the model. Relevant representative algorithms include Random Vector Functional Link network (RVFL) [16], Pseudo-Inverse Learning (PIL) [8], Extreme Learning Machine (ELM) [9], Stochastic Configuration Network (SCN) [14], and Broad Learning System (BLS) [3]. This study mainly focuses on BLS.

BLS is an upgraded version of RVFL proposed by Chen et al. in 2017 [3] which has two obvious characteristics. First, BLS uses a non-iterative training mechanism, which makes it very efficient in training. Second, the network structure of BLS has flexible scalability. Specifically, the number of its mapped feature nodes and enhancement nodes can be dynamically increased or pruned according to different tasks. After two feature mappings of the mapped feature layer and the enhancement layer, the different classes of the original data can be linearly separable in a high-dimensional space, and then the parameters of the model can be solved based on the ridge region theory. The universal approximation capability of BLS has been proved in [4]. Thanks to the excellent performance of BLS in multiple scenarios and a relatively complete theoretical foundation, it quickly attracted the attention of researchers. Improved BLS-based algorithms and applications are constantly being proposed. Related representative works include fuzzy BLS [6], recurrent BLS [15], weighted BLS [5], BLS with Proportional-Integral-Differential Gradient Descent [21], dense BLS [20], multi-view BLS [13], semi-supervised BLS [18], etc.

Although the above-mentioned BLS and its variants have shown great potential in many scenarios, their model performance is still expected to be further improved. Because we found that their input parameters are randomly generated based on a uniform distribution. BLS grouped the mapped feature nodes at the beginning of the design, but few studies use different distributions to initialize different groups of mapped feature nodes. In the early research of Cao et al., they found that for RVFL, using different distribution functions to initialize the input weights will have different effects on the performance of the model [1]. Moreover, using uniform distribution to initialize the input weights cannot always guarantee that the model has good generalization ability. Later, they further studied and found that in ensemble learning scenarios, using multiple distributions to initialize the sub-models can effectively improve the generalization ability of the final model [12].

Inspired by the above work, in this study, we propose to use multiple distribution functions to initialize different groups of mapped feature nodes, thereby enhancing the diversity of mapped features. We call this method: BLS with Hybrid Features (BLSHF). For many machine learning algorithms, the more diverse the features, the better the generalization ability of the model. BLSHF uses multiple distributions to initialize input weights in the mapped feature layer, which can obtain multi-level feature abstractions from the original data, and indirectly improves the diversity of enhancement features. Abundant features help the model to better mine the mapping relationship between the original feature description of the training samples and their labels, thereby improving the generalization ability of the model.

The contributions of this study can be summarized as follows.

- A novel BLS algorithm with hybrid features (i.e., BLSHF) was proposed in this study, which can greatly improve the diversity of the mapped features and enhancement features.
- The idea of BLSHF can be easily transferred to other BLS algorithms to further improve the performance of related models.
- To verify the effectiveness of BLSHF, we applied it to build an air quality prediction model. Extensive experimental results on two public air quality evaluation data sets show that BLSHF can achieve better generalization ability than BLS. The air quality prediction model based on BLSHF also provides a feasible solution for real-world related scenarios.

The remainder of this study is organized as follows: Sect. 2 briefly reviews the learning mechanism of BLS and related work. Details of the proposed BLSHF are presented in Sect. 3, followed by experimental results and analysis in Sect. 4. We conclude this study in Sect. 5.

2   Related Work

In this section, we review the training mechanism of BLS and the existing literature related to this study. As mentioned in Sect. 1, BLS is a feedforward neural network that uses a non-iterative training mechanism, and its basic network structure is shown in Fig. 1. Note that here we use the version that does not directly connect the input and output layers.

It can be observed from Fig. 1 that BLS is a four-layer neural network: input layer, mapped feature layer, enhancement layer, and output layer. In this study, we denote the input weights between the input layer and the mapped feature layer as W_input, the weights between the mapped feature layer and the enhancement layer as $W\_enhance$, and the output weights between the mapped feature layer and the enhancement layer and the output layer as W_output.

The mapped feature layer performs the first feature mapping on the original data transmitted from the input layer by groups and then concatenates the features extracted from all groups as input and transmits them to the enhancement layer for the second feature mapping. Then, the mapped feature and enhancement feature are connected to obtain the final feature matrix, which will be used to calculate the output weights (i.e., W_output) based on the ridge regression theory. Different from traditional neural networks, the training process of BLS is completed at one time, so it is called a neural network with a non-iterative training mechanism.

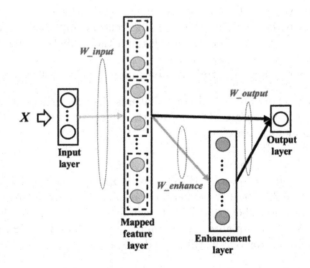

Fig. 1. Network structure of BLS.

In the above model training process, the input weights between the input layer and the mapped feature layer (i.e., W_input) are randomly generated according to a uniform distribution, and these parameters will remain unchanged in the subsequent model training process.

According to [1], using different distribution functions to initialize input weights will have different effects on the performance of non-iterative neural networks. BLS groups different mapped feature nodes in the mapped feature layer but does not use diversified strategies to initialize different groups of mapped feature nodes. Therefore, the original BLS model may still face the problem of failing to achieve optimal performance in some specific scenarios.

Liu et al. found that if multiple distributions are used to initialize the sub-models separately, and then the ensemble learning mechanism is used to integrate their prediction results, the prediction ability of the final model can be effectively improved [12].

Inspired by this idea, we try to use different distributions to initialize different groups of mapped feature nodes in BLS to get a model with better generalization ability.

3 The Proposed Method

The core idea of the method proposed in this study is to initialize different groups of mapped feature nodes in the BLS with different distributions to obtain multi-levels of feature extraction. Diversified feature expression and fusion can allow the model to better mine the relationship between the original features of training samples and their label, and then obtain a model with better generalization ability. We call the proposed method: BLS with Hybrid Features (BLSHF).

The network structure of BLSHF is shown in Fig. 2. Except that the initialization of mapped feature nodes is different from the original BLS, other parts are the same. Note that for the consideration of control variables, we do not group enhancement nodes here. In other words, in the enhancement layer, we use a uniform distribution to generate random parameters for enhancement nodes in accordance with BLS. According to Fig. 2, we can easily implement the BLSHF algorithm. Its pseudo-code is shown in Algorithm 1.

It can be observed from Algorithm 1 that the difference between our proposed BLSHF algorithm and BLS is that we use different distribution functions to initialize mapped feature nodes to obtain more diverse features.

Universal Approximation Property of BLSHF: As mentioned above, if we reduce the number of the distribution function that initializes random parameters to 1 (i.e., the Uniform distribution), BLSHF will degenerate into BLS. In other words, BLSHF only improves the generalization ability of the model by increasing the diversity of mapped features and enhancement features, and does not significantly modify the network architecture or non-iterative training mechanism of the original BLS. The universal approximation property of BLS has been proven in [4]. Therefore, one can infer that the proposed BLSHF also has the same approximation property.

In the next section, we will empirically prove the effectiveness of this approach through experiments on air quality assessment.

4 Experimental Settings and Results

In this section, we evaluate the performance of the proposed BLSHF algorithm on two real-world air quality index prediction problems.

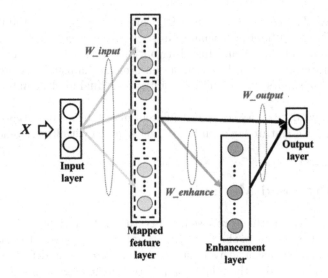

Fig. 2. Network structure of BLSHF.

These two data sets describe the urban air pollution in Beijing and Oslo in a specific period, respectively. As shown in Table 1, the Beijing PM 2.5 data set contains 41,757 samples, and each sample has 11 attributes, which depict the values of related indicators that may lead to a specific PM 2.5 value. Similarly, the Oslo PM 10 data set contains 500 samples, and each sample has 7 attributes, which depict the values of related indicators that may lead to a specific PM 10 value. Information about the specific meaning of each attribute of the sample can be viewed from the data source: Beijing PM 2.5 [11] and Oslo PM 10[1]. This study focuses on the modeling and performance evaluation of the proposed method on these two data sets.

In our experiment, we set the number of mapped feature nodes to 6, and the number of feature window to 3, which corresponds to three different distribution functions, namely: Uniform distribution, Gaussian distribution, and Gamma distribution. The number of enhancement nodes is set to 41. The activation functions of BLS and BLSHF are uniformly selected as the *Sigmoid* function.

For each data set, we split it into a training set and a testing set according to 7:3. Root Mean Square Error ($RMSE$) and Normalized Mean Absolute Error ($NMAE$) are chosen as the indicator to evaluate the performance of the model. The smaller these two indicators are, the better the model performance is. They can be calculated according to the following equations.

$$RMSE = \sqrt{\sum_{i=1}^{N} \frac{(y_i^* - y_i)^2}{N}} \tag{1}$$

---

[1] http://lib.stat.cmu.edu/datasets/.

Algorithm 1: BLSHF Algorithm

Input: Training data X, activation functions $\phi1(.)$ and $\phi2(.)$ for the mapped feature layer and the enhancement layer, respectively.

Output: All parameters of the BLSHF model.

Randomly assign the values of W_input_i for the i-th group of mapped feature nodes under the i-th distribution.

Use $\phi1(.)$ to project and get the mapped feature of the i-th group of mapped feature nodes Z_i. Specifically, $Z\_i = \phi1(X * W\_input + \beta\_input)$, where β_input is the thresholds of mapped feature nodes.

Concatenate the mapped features of all groups: $Z = [Z\_1, \ldots, Z\_k]$, where k is the number of the groups.

Randomly assign the values of $W\_enhance$ for the enhancement nodes under the uniform distribution.

Use $\phi2(.)$ to enhance the mapped feature by the enhancement layer: $H = \phi2(Z * W_enhance + \beta\_enhance)$, where $\beta\_enhance$ is the thresholds of enhancement nodes.

Calculate the output weights $W\_output = [Z|H]^+Y$, where Y is the real label matrix of the training samples.

Return: Input weights of mapped feature nodes in each group (i.e., W_input), input weights of enhancement feature nodes (i.e., $W\_enhance$), and the output weights W_output.

Table 1. Details of experimental datasets

Dataset	Number of attributes	Number of samples
Beijing PM 2.5	11	41757
Oslo PM 10	7	500

$$NMAE = \frac{MAE(y_i^*, y_i)}{\frac{1}{N}\sum_{i=1}^{N}|y_i|} \qquad (2)$$

where y_i^* is the predicted label of the model for the i-th sample, y_i is the real label of the i-th sample, and N is the number of samples. $MAE(.)$ means the mean absolute error.

The experimental results of BLS and BLSHF on two air quality prediction data sets are shown in Table 2. For ease of comparison, we have bolded better metrics.

It can be observed from Table 2 that the BLSHF model can achieve lower prediction errors on all data sets than the BLS model, which implies that the proposed BLSHF model has better generalization ability than the original BLS model. This experimental phenomenon verifies a consensus in the field of machine learning: the diversification of data features helps the model to better learn the implicit patterns in the data.

In addition, we can also observe an interesting experimental phenomenon, that is, the training time of the BLSHF model is shorter than that of the BLS. This phenomenon may be because the sampling efficiency of the partial distribution function is higher than that of the Uniform distribution, thus improving the training efficiency of the overall model. However, this is only a speculation, and we will analyze this in more depth from a mathematical point of view in the future.

To show our experimental results more clearly, we visualized them separately, namely: Figs. 3–8. From these visualized figures, it can be intuitively found that our proposed BLSHF algorithm can not only achieve lower prediction errors than BLS, but also have faster training efficiency.

For the above experimental phenomenon, a speculative explanation is given here: using different distribution functions to initialize mapped feature nodes can allow the model to extract more diverse features, which is beneficial to improve the generalization ability of the model. Therefore, the prediction error of the BLSHF model is lower than that of the BLS.

Table 2. Details of experimental results

Dataset	Performance	BLS	The proposed BLSHF
Beijing PM 2.5	Training RMSE	0.0731	**0.0716**
	Testing RMSE	0.0741	**0.0726**
	Training NMAE	0.5349	**0.5275**
	Testing NMAE	0.5378	**0.5286**
	Training time	0.0669	**0.0434**
Oslo PM 10	Training RMSE	0.1506	**0.1471**
	Testing RMSE	0.1768	**0.1585**
	Training NMAE	0.2173	**0.2127**
	Testing NMAE	0.2408	**0.2252**
	Training Time	0.0493	**0.0401**

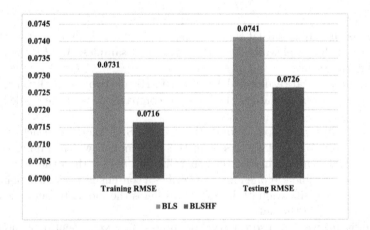

Fig. 3. RMSE of BLS and BLSHF models on Beijing PM 2.5 dataset.

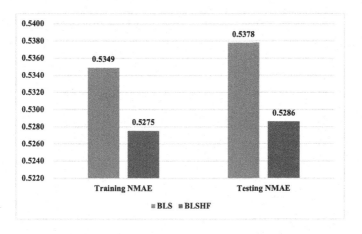

Fig. 4. NMAE of BLS and BLSHF models on Beijing PM 2.5 dataset.

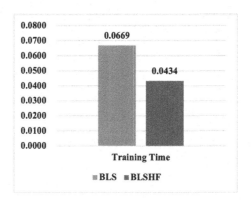

Fig. 5. Training time of BLS and BLSHF models on Beijing PM 2.5 dataset.

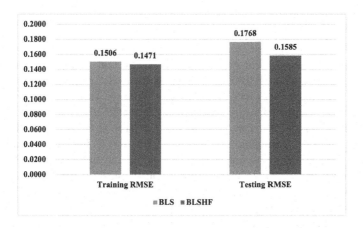

Fig. 6. RMSE of BLS and BLSHF models on Oslo PM 10 dataset.

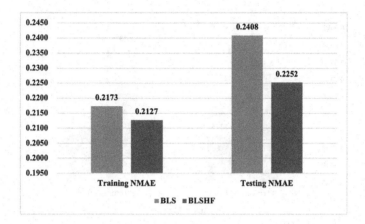

Fig. 7. NMAE of BLS and BLSHF models on Oslo PM 10 dataset.

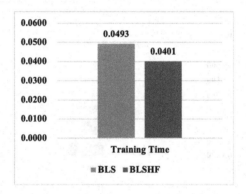

Fig. 8. Training time of BLS and BLSHF models on Oslo PM 10 dataset.

5   Conclusions

To improve the feature extraction capability of BLS, we innovatively design an improved BLS algorithm called BLSHF. Different from the original BLS, BLSHF uses multiple initialization strategies for each group of mapped feature nodes, which enables them to provide more diverse features for model learning. The diversity of mapped features further improves the diversity of enhancement features. The diversity of features helps the algorithm to better mine the internal patterns of the data, resulting in a model with better generalization ability.

BLSHF also inherits the non-iterative training mechanism of BLS, so it has the advantages of extremely fast training speed and low hardware computing power requirements. We apply BLSHF to model two real-world air pollution assessment problems, and the experimental results show that it can achieve better generalization ability than the BLS model. The air pollution perception model based on BLSHF also provides a new idea for real-world air quality monitoring research.

However, the current version of the BLSHF algorithm is still a shallow feedforward neural network. Even if we have improved the feature extraction capability of the original BLS, the existing solution may still be stretched in the face of complex datasets such as ImageNet [10]. In the future, we will consider using BLSHF as a stacking unit to build a more complex neural network to solve the modeling problem of complex scenarios.

Acknowledgment. This work was supported by National Natural Science Foundation of China (Grant No. 62106150), CAAC Key Laboratory of Civil Aviation Wide Surveillance and Safety Operation Management and Control Technology (Grant No. 202102), and CCF-NSFOCUS (Grant No. 2021001).

References

1. Cao, W., Patwary, M.J., Yang, P., Wang, X., Ming, Z.: An initial study on the relationship between meta features of dataset and the initialization of nnrw. In: 2019 International Joint Conference on Neural Networks, IJCNN, pp. 1–8. IEEE (2019)
2. Cao, W., Wang, X., Ming, Z., Gao, J.: A review on neural networks with random weights. Neurocomputing **275**, 278–287 (2018)
3. Chen, C.P., Liu, Z.: Broad learning system: An effective and efficient incremental learning system without the need for deep architecture. IEEE Trans. Neural Netw. Learn. Syst. **29**(1), 10–24 (2017)
4. Chen, C.P., Liu, Z., Feng, S.: Universal approximation capability of broad learning system and its structural variations. IEEE Trans. Neural Net. Learn. Syst. **30**(4), 1191–1204 (2018)
5. Chu, F., Liang, T., Chen, C.P., Wang, X., Ma, X.: Weighted broad learning system and its application in nonlinear industrial process modeling. IEEE Trans. Neural Netw. Learn. Syst. **31**(8), 3017–3031 (2019)
6. Feng, S., Chen, C.P.: Fuzzy broad learning system: a novel neuro-fuzzy model for regression and classification. IEEE Trans. Cybern. **50**(2), 414–424 (2018)
7. Goodfellow, I., Bengio, Y., Courville, A.: Deep learning. MIT Press (2016)
8. Guo, P., Chen, C.P., Sun, Y.: An exact supervised learning for a three-layer supervised neural network. In: 1995 International Conference on Neural Information Processing, ICNIP, pp. 1041–1044 (1995)
9. Huang, G.-B., Zhu, Q.-Y., Siew, C.-K.: Extreme learning machine: a new learning scheme of feedforward neural networks. In: 2004 IEEE International Joint Conference on Neural Networks, IJCNN, vol. 2, pp. 985–990. IEEE (2004)
10. Krizhevsky, A., Sutskever, I., Hinton, G.E.: Imagenet classification with deep convolutional neural networks. Commun. ACM **60**(6), 84–90 (2017)
11. Liang, X., et al.: Assessing beijing's pm2. 5 pollution: severity, weather impact, apec and winter heating. Proc. Royal Soc. A Math. Phys. Eng. Sci. **471**(2182), 20150257 (2015)
12. Liu, Y., Cao, W., Ming, Z., Wang, Q., Zhang, J., Xu, Z.: Ensemble neural networks with random weights for classification problems. In: 2020 3rd International Conference on Algorithms, Computing and Artificial Intelligence, ACAI, pp. 1–5 (2020)

13. Shi, Z., Chen, X., Zhao, C., He, H., Stuphorn, V., Wu, D.: Multi-view broad learning system for primate oculomotor decision decoding. IEEE Trans. Neural Syst. Rehabil. Eng. **28**(9), 1908–1920 (2020)
14. Wang, D., Li, M.: Stochastic configuration networks: fundamentals and algorithms. IEEE Trans. Cybern. **47**(10), 3466–3479 (2017)
15. Xu, M., Han, M., Chen, C.P., Qiu, T.: Recurrent broad learning systems for time series prediction. IEEE Trans. Cybern. **50**(4), 1405–1417 (2018)
16. Zhang, L., Suganthan, P.N.: A comprehensive evaluation of random vector functional link networks. Inf. Sci. **367**, 1094–1105 (2016)
17. Zhang, L., Suganthan, P.N.: A survey of randomized algorithms for training neural networks. Inf. Sci. **364**, 146–155 (2016)
18. Zhao, H., Zheng, J., Deng, W., Song, Y.: Semi-supervised broad learning system based on manifold regularization and broad network. IEEE Trans. Circuits Syst. I Regul. Pap. **67**(3), 983–994 (2020)
19. Zhao, Z.-Q., Zheng, P., Xu, S.-T., Wu, X.: Object detection with deep learning: a review. IEEE Trans. Neural Netw. Learn. Syst. **30**(11), 3212–3232 (2019)
20. Zou, W., Xia, Y., Cao, W.: Dense broad learning system based on conjugate gradient. In: 2020 International Joint Conference on Neural Networks, IJCNN, pp. 1–6. IEEE (2020)
21. Zou, W., Xia, Y., Cao, W., Ming, Z.: Broad learning system with proportional-integral-differential gradient descent. In: Qiu, M. (ed.) ICA3PP 2020. LNCS, vol. 12452, pp. 219–231. Springer, Cham (2020). https://doi.org/10.1007/978-3-030-60245-1_15

Multi-Attention Relation Network for Figure Question Answering

Ying Li⑩, Qingfeng Wu$^{(\boxtimes)}$, and Bin Chen

School of Informatics, Xiamen University, Xiamen 361005, China
2432019115254 2@stu.xmu.edu.cn, qfwu@xmu.edu.cn

Abstract. Figure question answering (FQA) is proposed as a new multimodal task for visual question answering (VQA). Given a scientific-style figure and a related question, the machine needs to answer the question based on reasoning. The Relation Network (RN) is the proposed approach for the baseline of FQA, which computes a representation of relations between objects within images to get the answer result. We improve the RN model by using a variety of attention mechanism methods. Here, we propose a novel algorithm called Multi-attention Relation Network (MARN), which consists of a CBAM module, an LSTM module, and an attention relation module. The CBAM module first performs an attention mechanism during the feature extraction of the image to make the feature map more effective. Then in the attention relation module, each object pair contributes differently to reasoning. The experiments show that MARN greatly outperforms the RN model and other state-of-the-art methods on the FigureQA and DVQA datasets.

Keywords: Attention mechanism · Figure question answering · Relation network · Deep Learning

1 Introduction

Charts, such as line plots, bar graphs, pie charts, and so on, are effective and commonly used methods for presenting complex data. They exist in various text files such as academic papers and business reports and are widely used in various fields. After the machine understands the characteristics of the chart, it can help people extract relevant information from a large number of documents. Therefore, the use of computer vision to analyze chart information has high practical significance and application value. This task has only been proposed in recent years, and there are still many challenges.

Figure question answering (FQA) is an independent task of visual question answering (VQA) [1]. VQA is usually regarded as a classification problem about natural images, while FQA is to make inferences and predictions for a given chart and a related question to get the answer. Different from VQA, FQA will completely change the information of the chart even if only minor modifications are made to the image, resulting in different results [2]. In recent years, there have been many good results on FQA tasks. On the FigureQA [3] and DVQA [2] datasets, the model relational network (RN) [4]

© The Author(s), under exclusive license to Springer Nature Switzerland AG 2022
G. Memmi et al. (Eds.): KSEM 2022, LNAI 13369, pp. 667–680, 2022.
https://doi.org/10.1007/978-3-031-10986-7_54

performs well, but the RN model still has some shortcomings, such as the limita-tion of the information extracted from images. Figure 1 is an example of a graph type with questions and answers pairs on the FigureQA dataset.

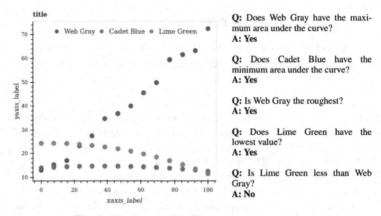

Fig. 1. Dot-line graph with question answer pairs.

In this paper, we present a novel algorithm called Multi-attention Relation Network (MARN) to improve the performance of the FQA task. In the image encoder, we use Convolutional Block Attention (CBAM) module [5] to calculate the attention map of the feature map from channel and space dimensions and then multiply the attention map with the feature map to carry out adaptive feature learning. And we propose an attention-driven relation module to filter useful object pairs. The experimental results show that our proposed method achieves better performance than the RN model and other state-of-the-art methods.

The key contributions of this paper are:

1. We propose a novel method called MARN to improve the performance of the FQA task. MARN surpasses the RN model and most existing methods on the FigureQA and DVQA datasets.
2. To obtain more useful image features, we use the CBAM to calculate the attention map of the feature map obtained by CNN. In this way, the feature map can be more effective to represent the features of the image information.
3. To make the relation features more concise, we propose a novel attention-driven relation module to give each object pair a different weight. A larger weight indicates a larger impact on reasoning.

2 Related Work

In recent years, many VQA datasets [1, 6, 7] and VQA methods [8, 9] have been proposed. Due to the difference between FQA and VQA, the algorithm proposed for VQA is not

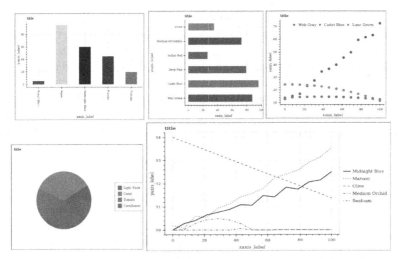

Fig. 2. The example of five types of charts in FigureQA database: vertical and horizontal bar graphs, line plots, dot-line plots, and pie charts.

suitable for figure question answering. For example, a small change in a natural image usually only affects a local area, and because the chart information is concise, even a small change will change the entire image information.

2.1 FQA Dataset

Many datasets have been proposed to study FQA tasks, such as FigureQA, DVQA, PlotQA [10], and LEAF-QA [11]. Because only the data of FigureQA and DVQA datasets is open source, we verify the performance of our model on these two datasets.

Table 1. The detailed information on FigureQA dataset.

Dataset split	# Images	# Questions	Has answers & annotations?	Color scheme
Train	100,000	1,327,368	Yes	Scheme 1
Validation 1	20,000	265,106	Yes	Scheme 1
Validation 2	20,000	265,798	Yes	Scheme 2
Test1	20,000	265,024	No	Scheme 1
Test2	20,000	265,402	No	Scheme 2

The FigureQA dataset is a synthetic corpus, which contains more than one million questions and answer pairs of more than 100,000 images for visual reasoning. It contains 5 forms of charts: line plots, dot-line plots, vertical and horizontal bar graphs, and pie charts, as shown in Fig. 2. The drawing elements of FigureQA are color-coded, with 100 unique colors. These colors are divided into the two-colored scheme: scheme 1 and scheme 2. Each scheme has 50 colors and does not overlap with each other. The dataset is divided into five separate packages, including one training set, two validation sets, and two testing sets. These packages differ by train/validation/test split and the color-to-figure assignment scheme that is used. Each drawing type in the data set has the corresponding question and answer pairs and some bounding boxes. The detailed information on the training set and two validation sets is shown in Table 1.

The DVQA dataset is a large open-source statistical graph question and answer data set proposed by Kushal Kafle and others in cooperation with the Adobe Research Laboratory. It contains a training set and two test sets (Test-Familiar and Test-Novel). The training set consists of 200,000 images and 2325316 questions, the Test-Familiar test set consists of 50,000 images and 580557 questions, and the Test-Novel test set consists of 50,000 images and 581321 questions. There are three types of questions in the DVQA data set: the first type is Structure Understanding, which is about the understanding of the overall structure of an image, the second type is Data Retrieval, and the third is reasoning. The reasoning is a type of reasoning problem about the relationship between elements in the image.

2.2 Existing FQA Algorithms

At present, four types of basic algorithms are proposed based on the FigureQA dataset. They are Text-only baseline, CNN+LSTM, CNN+LSTM on VGG-16 features, and Relation Network (RN), of which RN has the best effect. The Text-only baseline is a text-only model, which is trained with batch size 64. CNN+LSTM uses the MLP classifier to connect the received LSTM to generate the problem code and the learned visual representation of the CNN with five convolutional layers. And CNN+LSTM on VGG-16 features extracts features from the fifth-layer pool of the ImageNet pre-trained VGG-16 network [12]. RN is currently the best baseline method, a simple and powerful neural module for relational reasoning. RN is proven to have the most advanced performance on a challenging data set called CLEVR [13].

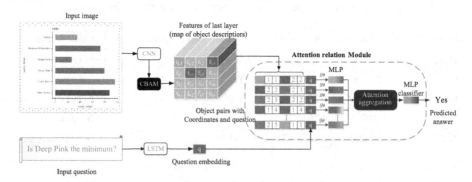

Fig. 3. The framework of our proposed Multi-attention Relation Network (MARN).

Recently, many novel methods have been proposed for FQA tasks. The FigureNet [14] model proposes a multi-module algorithm framework to solve the question and answer of statistical graphs. The LEAF-Net [11] model uses several open-source pre-training models. First, the character information in the image is recognized through OCR, and then it is located in the problem for embedding. At the same time, the image feature map is obtained through the pre-trained ResNet-152. The ARN [15] model is a relation network framework algorithm. It first recognizes the elements, characters, structure, and other information of the image through multiple recognition modules, then constructs it into the form of a table through the obtained information, and finally passes a form question and answer model to get the answer.

2.3 Attention Mechanism

It is well known that attention plays an important role in human perception [16, 17]. An important feature of the human visual system is that people don't try to process the whole scene at the same time. On the contrary, to better capture the visual structure, humans use a series of partial glimpses and selectively focus on the salient [18].

Lately, several attempts incorporate attention processing to improve the performance of CNNs in large-scale classification tasks. Wang et al. [19] propose a Residual Attention Network that uses an encoder-decoder style attention module. Hu et al. [20] introduce a compact module to exploit the inter-channel relationship.

3 Methods

In this section, we give a detailed introduction to the proposed method, namely, Multi-attention Relation Network (MARN), as shown in Fig. 3. In the image representation, we employ a Convolutional Block Attention (CBAM) module on the feature map obtained by CNN to capture the more effective information. The final feature map is denoted as F. In the question representation, we apply an LSTM module to convert the text content into a low-dimension embedding. We regard the hidden state as the question representation, denoted as q. At last, F and q feed into the attention relation module to get the result.

3.1 Image Representation

In the image decoder, the feature map firstly comes to form a CNN with five convolutional layers, each with 64 kernels of size 3×3, stride 2, zero-padding of 1 on each side, and batch normalization [21]:

$$F_i = ConvBlock(F_{i-1}), F_0 = I \tag{1}$$

where F_0 is the original image I and $F_i\{1 \leq i \leq 5\}$ denote the feature map after the ith convolutional layer. After the CNN module, the feature map $F_5 \in R^{H*W*C}$, $H = 8$, $W = 8$, $C = 64$ is obtained. H is the height of the feature map, W is the width, and C denotes the number of channels.

To make the feature map more effectively show the information of image I, we apply the CBAM to the feature map F_5 after CNN. The framework of the CBAM module is shown in Fig. 4. It can be seen that the CBAM module is divided into two steps: the channel attention module and the spatial attention module.

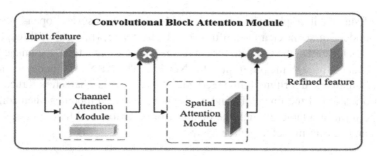

Fig. 4. CBAM module.

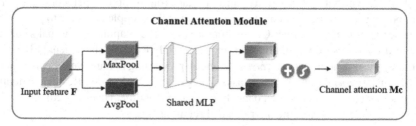

Fig. 5. Channel attention module.

The channel attention module focuses on which channels in the feature map F_5 are more useful. Figure 5 shows the structure of the channel attention module. We use max pooling and average pooling to compress the feature map in the spatial dimension and get two different spatial background description vectors F_{max}^c and $F_{avg}^c \in R^{1*1*C}$:

$$F_{max}^c = MaxPool(F_5) \qquad (2)$$

$$F_{avg}^c = AvgPool(F_5) \qquad (3)$$

Then for F_{max}^c and F_{avg}^c, shard MLP is used to calculate the channel attention map $M_c \in R^{1*1*C}$:

$$M_c = \sigma\left(W_1\left(W_0\left(F_{max}^c\right)\right) + W_1\left(W_0\left(F_{avg}^c\right)\right)\right) \qquad (4)$$

where σ is the sigmoid function, and $W_0 \in R^{\frac{C}{r}*C}$, $W_1 \in R^{C*\frac{C}{r}}$, r is the reduction ratio. Then, F_5 is multiplied by M_c to get F':

$$F' = F_5 * M_c \qquad (5)$$

where * denotes the element-wise multiplication.

The spatial attention module focuses on location information (where). Figure 6 shows the structure of the channel attention module. This time, we use max pooling and average pooling to compress the feature map in the channel dimension and get two vectors: F^s_{max} and $F^s_{avg} \in R^{H*W*1}$:

$$F^s_{max} = MaxPool\left(F^{'}\right) \tag{6}$$

$$F^s_{avg} = AvgPool\left(F^{'}\right) \tag{7}$$

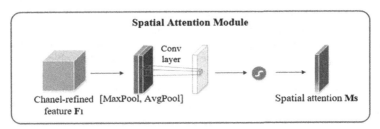

Fig. 6. Spatial attention module.

The two vectors are merged by concatenation and use the convolutional layer to generate the spatial attention map $M_s \in R^{H*w*1}$:

$$M_s = \sigma(ConvBlock2([F^s_{max}; F^s_{avg}])) \tag{8}$$

where ConvBlock2 represents the 7×7 convolutional layer. The final feature map $F \in R^{H*W*C}$ after the image decoder is obtained by:

$$F = F^{'} * M_s \tag{9}$$

3.2 Question Representation

Like the RN model, we first combine all the existing words into a dictionary. Then each question can be expressed as $Q = [x_1, \ldots, x_T]$, where x_t represents the vector after the one-hot encoding in the dictionary, and T is the length of the question. We apply the simple unidirectional LSTM with 512 hidden units to obtain the hidden state:

$$h_t = LSTM(x_t), 1 \le t \le T \tag{10}$$

We regard the hidden state in the last step as the question representation, i.e., $q = h_T \in R^{512}$.

3.3 Attention Relation Module

The core idea of RN is to regard the feature map F of the image as a set of objects and combine two objects into a pair and then connect the question representation vector q after each pair.

For a feature map of size n × n, the object set can be denoted as $F = \{f_{i,j} | 1 \le i, j \le n\} \in R^{64*64}$, where $f_{i,j} \in R^{64}$ denotes the ith row and jth column of the feature map F, and n = H = W = 8. Then the set of all object pairs is represented as:

$$P = \{p_{(i,j),(u,v)} | 1 \le i, j, u, v \le n\} \tag{11}$$

where $p_{(i,j),(u,v)}$ is the concatenation of the corresponding object vectors, their location information, and the question vector q, i.e., $p_{(i,j),(u,v)} = [f_{i,j}, i, j, f_{u,v}, u, v, q] \in R^{644}$. Each object is paired with all objects including itself, i.e., $p_{(1,1),(1,1)}, p_{(1,1),(1,2)}, \cdots, p_{(n,n),(n,n)}$. Then $P \in R^{4096*644}$ is the matrix containing 4096 object pairs representations.

Then, every object pairs are separately processed by MLPs to produce a feature representation $o_{(i,j),(u,v)}$ of the relation between the corresponding objects:

$$O = \{o_{(i,j),(u,v)} = g_\theta(p_{(i,j),(u,v)}) | 1 \le i, j, u, v \le n\} \tag{12}$$

where g_θ is implemented as MLPs.

Then the RN model is to average all feature O to get the final result. But we think that the contribution of the generated feature $o_{(i,j),(u,v)}$ of each object pairs to the final result is different, so we propose a new aggregation method, namely, attention aggregation. The structure of attention aggregation is shown in Fig. 7.

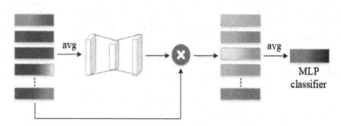

Fig. 7. Attention aggregation.

As shown in Fig. 7, we average each feature $o_{(i,j),(u,v)}$ and splice it into a vector $A \in R^{4096}$. Then, through two layers of MLP, we get an attention map M_a to represent the contribution of each object pair feature to the final result. At last, O is multiplied by M_a to get the attention-based object pair features O_a. This process can be formulated as:

$$M_a = \sigma(W_1'(W_0'(O))) \tag{13}$$

$$O_a = O * M_a \tag{14}$$

where W_0' and W_1' are the weight matrixes of two MLPs.

At last, the sum over all relational features O_a is then processed by MLP, yielding the predicted outputs:

$$Label = f_\varphi(\frac{1}{N^2} \sum_{i,j,u,v} o_{a(i,j),(u,v)}) \tag{15}$$

where f_φ is implemented as MLP, and N = 64 is the number of all objects. The classifier f_φ has two hidden layers with 256 ReLU units and the second layer applies the dropout with a rate of 50%.

4 Experiments

4.1 Experimental Setting

We evaluate our proposed MARN model on the FigureQA and DVQA datasets. For FigureQA, we use the train data as the training set and the validation2 data as the validation set. Then we verify the effectiveness of our model on validation1 and validation2 data because test sets are non-publicly available. For DVQA, we use two versions to verify our model: the method without a dynamic dictionary (No OCR) and the method with Oracle Version (Oracle).

The accuracy is adopted as the evaluation metric. The images in the dataset are resized into a size of 256 × 256. For data augmentation, each image is padded to 264 × 264 and then is randomly cropped back to 256 × 256. And at each training step, we compute the accuracy of one randomly selected batch from the validation set and keep an exponential moving average with a decay of 0.9. Starting from the 100th update, we perform early-stopping using this moving average. The train batch size is 160, and the validation batch size is 64. We trained our model in 350000 steps. Our model is trained using the Adam optimizer with a learning rate of 1.25e-4.

4.2 Experimental Results

In this section, we show the comparison of our model with other methods both on FigureQA and DVQA datasets. Table 2 shows our results and comparison with other methods on the FigureQA dataset, such as QUES [5] (Text only), IMG+QUES [5] (CNN+LSTM), RN [5], FigureNet [14], LEAF-Net [11] and ARN [15]. It should be noted that FigureNet carries out the experiments only on three types of charts, i.e., vBar, hBar, and Pie, in the Validation1 data of the FigureQA dataset. Then Table 3 shows the performance of our model compared with other methods on two versions, such as SANDY (No OCR+ Oracle) [2], ARN (No OCR+Oracle) [15], and LEAF-Net (Oracle) [11].

In FigureQA, our approach significantly outperforms the RN baseline model both on two validation sets. Specifically, our method obtains an accuracy promotion of approximately 8.04%, 10.78%,4.37%, 10.92%, and 11.58% in the five types of charts of validation1 data and 14.06%, 13.49%, 8.47%, 9.45%, and 13.23% in the five types of charts of validation2 data, respectively. Overall, the accuracy of our model is improved by 9.40% on validation1 data and 11.24% on validation2 data compared with the RN model. Then compared with FigureNet, MARN obtains a promotion of approximately 6.39%, 10.78%, and 3.80% in the vBar, hBar, and pie charts of validation1 data. LEAF-Net reaches an accuracy of about 81.15% on validation2 data, while our approach performs slightly better, about 83.78%. At last, we also improve the accuracy by 0.31% and 0.83% on both validation sets compared with ARN. In addition, we also found that the accuracy

Table 2. Results comparisons with other methods on FigureQA dataset.

	Validation 1 -same colors						Validation 2 -alternated colors					
	vBar	hBar	Pie	Line	Dot-line	Overall	vBar	hBar	Pie	Line	Dot-line	Overall
QUES	–	–	–	–	–	–	–	–	–	–	–	50.01
IMG+QUES	61.98	62.44	59.63	57.07	57.35	59.41	58.60	58.05	55.97	56.37	56.97	57.14
RN	85.71	80.60	82.56	69.53	68.51	76.39	77.35	77.00	74.16	67.90	69.40	72.54
FigureNet	87.36	81.57	83.13	–	–	–	–	–	–	–	–	–
LEAF-Net	–	–	–	–	–	–	–	–	–	–	–	81.15
ARN	92.49	91.20	84.25	**81.31**	**81.03**	85.48	90.46	89.56	80.29	**77.60**	78.28	82.95
MARN(Ours)	**93.75**	91.38	**86.93**	80.45	80.09	**85.79**	91.41	90.49	82.63	77.35	**82.63**	83.78

Table 3. Results comparisons with other methods on DVQA dataset.

	Test-familiar	Test-novel
IMG+QUES	32.01	32.01
SANDY (No OCR)	36.02	36.14
ARN (No OCR)	44.50	44.51
MARN (ours)	**45.10**	**44.97**
SANDY (Oracle)	56.48	56.62
LEAF-Net (Oracle)	72.72	72.89
ARN (Oracle)	79.43	79.58
MARN (Oracle)	**79.96**	**80.23**

of our model in the bar and pie charts is significantly higher than that in the line charts. After analysis, this may be because line charts often contain more complex information and the questions are quite more difficult to answer, so the accuracy of line charts is relatively low.

On DVQA, first, compare the performance of the No OCR version, it can find that our method achieves the best results, which achieves higher accuracy of 13.09% and 12.86% than the IMG+QUES baseline and 0.6% and 0.46% higher than ARN in the two verification sets, respectively. In the Oracle version, we also achieve the best performance compared with these three methods on both two test sets.

In general, our method greatly improves the performance of the original Relation Network (RN) model and proves the effectiveness of introducing the attention mechanism into the RN model both on FigureQA and DVQA datasets.

4.3 Ablation Study on Modules of Our Approach

We conduct an ablation study on the FigureQA dataset to explore the importance of each module in MARN. The detailed results are shown in Table 4, where RN+CBAM indicates that the RN model adds the CBAM module in the image encoding module, and RN+attention aggregation indicates we use the attention aggregation module in the RN model.

Table 4. Results for ablation studies on our method.

Ablation model	Val 1	Val 2
RN+CBAM	81.45	79.65
RN+attention aggregation	80.34	79.89
MARN (Full model)	85.79	83.78

Table 5. Accuracy comparison per question type on the validation1 and validation2.

Template	Validation 1	Validation 2
Is X the minimum?	92.45	89.38
Is X the maximum?	96.71	94.41
Is X less than Y? (bar,pie)	97.92	95.46
Is X greater than Y? (bar,pie)	97.99	95.53
Is X the low median?	78.42	7573
Is X the high median?	80.99	78.88
Does X have the minimum area under the curve?	86.86	86.00
Does X have the maximum area under the curve?	91.65	90.29
Is X the smoothest?	65.01	64.60
Is X the roughest?	6472	63.63
Does X have the lowest value?	83.38	81.19
Does X have the highest value?	88.24	86.73
Is X less than Y? (line)	81.40	79.43
Is X greater than Y? (line)	81.18	79.67
Does X intersect Y?	80.78	78.79

As shown in Table 4, the model using one of the attention modules alone performs better than the original RN model. And the relation network using multi attention (MARN) can achieve the best performance.

4.4 Comparison Per Question Type

Tables 5 show the performances of the MARN on each question type of the FigureQA dataset. There are 15 question types in the FigureQA dataset.

From Table 5, we can see that the prediction accuracy of different problem types is different. For instance, 'Is X the minimum?', 'Is X the maximum?', 'Is X less than Y? (bar, pie)', 'Is X greater than Y? (bar, pie)', and 'Does X have the maximum area under the curve?' these five question types all achieves more than 90% accuracy, while 'Is X the smoothest?', and 'Is X the roughest?' these two question types have an accuracy rate of only over 60%. After analysis, we conclude that this type of question like 'Is X the smoothest?' is more complex, and even human beings are difficult to answer.

In addition, we can find that even for the same problem, the accuracy of the model is different due to different chart types. For example, 'Is X less than Y?' this type of question can reach the accuracy of 97.92% on bar and pie chart, but only 81.40% in a line chart on the validation1 data. This also proves that the line charts are more difficult to answer than the bar and pie charts because they contain more complex picture information.

4.5 Comparison with Human Annotates

Table 6 shows the accuracy of the overall validation set and shows a comparison with the results of human annotations. We can find that although the accuracy of our MARN model is 11.33% higher than that of the previous RN model, there is still a certain gap compared with the accuracy of human annotation. There are still many big challenges for figure question answering to improve the performance.

Table 6. Performance of our method, other method and human annotates on full validation set.

Model	Accuracy
IMG+QUES	58.27
RN	74.46
MARN (ours)	**85.79**
Human	91.21

5 Conclusion

In this paper, we proposed a multi-attention relation network (MARN) to improve the performance of the original relation network. Our model uses the CBAM module in the image representation to make the feature map more effective. And we propose a novel attention relation module to give the different weights to the object pairs features, which can help the model to find more useful information. Our proposed MARN performs significantly better than the original relation network baseline and most state-of-the-art methods. In future work, we intend to improve the performance of these low-accuracy figure types and question types. And we will try to change the structure of the model and use more complex image and text models to improve the accuracy.

References

1. Zhou, B., Tian, Y., Sukhbaatar, S., Szlam, A., Fergus, R.: VQA: Visual question answering. In: Proceedings of the IEEE International Conference on Computer Vision, pp. 2425–2433 (2015)
2. Kafle, K., Price, B., Cohen, S., Kanan, C.: Dvqa: Understanding data visualizations via question answering. In: Proceedings of the 2018 IEEE/ CVF Conference on Computer Vision and Pattern Recognition, pp. 5648–5656. IEEE (2018)
3. Kahou, S.E., Michalski, V., Atkinson, A., Kadar, A., Trischler, A., Bengio, Y.: Figureqa: An annotated figure dataset for visual reasoning (2017). arXiv preprint arXiv:1710.07300
4. Santoro, A., Raposo, D., Barrett, D.G., Malinowski, M., Pascanu, R.: A simple neural network module for relational reasoning (2017). arXiv preprint arXiv:1706.01427
5. Woo, S., Park, J., Lee, J.-Y., Kweon, I.S.: CBAM: Convolutional block attention module. In: Ferrari, V., Hebert, M., Sminchisescu, C., Weiss, Y. (eds.) ECCV 2018. LNCS, vol. 11211, pp. 3–19. Springer, Cham (2018). https://doi.org/10.1007/978-3-030-01234-2_1
6. Goyal, Y., Khot, T., Summers-Stay, D., Batra, D., Parikh, D.: Making the V in VQA matter: Elevating the role of image understanding in visual question answering. In: Proceedings of the 2017 IEEE Conference on Computer Vision and Pattern Recognition (CVPR), pp. 6325–6334 (2017). doi: https://doi.org/10.1109/CVPR.2017.670
7. Krishna, R., Zhu, Y., Groth, O., Johnson, J., Hata, K.: Visual genome: connecting language and vision using crowdsourced dense image annotations. Int. J. Comput. Vis. 123(1), 32–73 (2017)
8. Kafle, K., Kanan, C.: Answer-type prediction for visual question answering. In: Proceedings of the 2016 IEEE Conference on Computer Vision and Pattern Recognition (CVPR), pp. 4976–4984 (2016)
9. Andreas, J., Rohrbach, M., Darrell, T., Klein, D.: Deep compositional question answering with neural module networks. Comput. Sci. 27 (2015)
10. Methani, N., Ganguly, P., Khapra M., Kumar, P.: PlotQA: Reasoning over scientific plots. In: Proceedings of the 2020 IEEE Winter Conference on Applications of Computer Vision (WACV), pp. 1516–1525 (2020)
11. Ritwick, C., Sumit, S., Utkarsh, G., Pranav, M., Prann, B., Ajay, J.: Leaf-qa: Locate, encode and attend for figure question answering. In: Proceedings of the 2020 IEEE Winter Conference on Applications of Computer Vision (WACV), pp. 3501–3510 (2020)
12. Simonyan, K., Zisserman, A.: Very deep convolutional networks for large-scale image recognition. In: Proceedings of the International Conference on Learning Representations (2015)
13. Johnson, J., Hariharan, B., Maten, L. Fei-Fei, L.: CLEVR: A diagnostic dataset for compositional language and elementary visual reasoning. In: Proceedings of the 2017 IEEE Conference on Computer Vision and Pattern Recognition (CVPR), pp. 1988–1997 (2017)
14. Reddy, R., Ramesh, R.: Figurenet: A deep learning model for question-answering on scientific plots. In: Proceedings of the 2019 International Joint Conference on Neural Networks (IJCNN), pp. 1–8 (2019)
15. Jialong, Z., Guoli, W., Taofeng, X., Qingfeng, W.: An affinity-driven relation network for figure question answering. In: Proceedings of the 2020 IEEE International Conference on Multimedia and Expo (ICME), pp. 1–6 (2020)
16. Itti, L., Koch, C., Niebur, E.: A model of saliency-based visual attention for rapid scene analysis. IEEE Trans. Pattern Anal. Mach. Intell. (TPAMI) 20, 1254–1259 (1998)
17. Rensink, R.A.: The dynamic representation of scenes. Vis. Cogn. 7, 17–42 (2000)
18. Larochelle, H., Hinton, G.E.: Learning to combine foveal glimpses with a thirdorder Boltzmann machine. Neural Inf. Process. Syst. (NIPS) (2010)

19. Wang, F., et al.: Residual attention network for image classification. In: Proceedings of the 2017 IEEE Conference on Computer Vision and Pattern Recognition (CVPR), arXiv preprint arXiv:1704.06904 (2017)
20. Hu, J., Shen, L., Sun, G.: Squeeze-and-excitation networks. IEEE Trans. Pattern Anal. Mach. Intell. arXiv preprint arXiv:1709.01507 (2017)
21. Ioffe, S., Szegedy, C.: Batch normalization: Accelerating deep network training by reducing internal covariate shift. In: Proceedings of the International Conference on Machine Learning (2015)

Multi-layer LSTM Parallel Optimization Based on Hardware and Software Cooperation

Qingfeng Chen, Jing Wu$^{(\boxtimes)}$, Feihu Huang, Yu Han, and Qiming Zhao

School of Computer Science and Technology, Wuhan University of Science and Technology, Wuhan 430065, China
{chqhong,wujingecs,huangfeihu,kenlig}@wust.edu.cn

Abstract. LSTM's special gate structure and memory unit make it suitable for solving problems that are related to time series. It has excellent performance in the fields of machine translation and reasoning. However, LSTM also has some shortcomings, such as low parallelism, which leads to insufficient computing speed. Some existing optimization ideas only focus on one of the software and hardware. The former mostly focuses on model accuracy, and CPU accelerated LSTM doesn't dynamically adjust to network characteristics; While the latter can be based on the LSTM model structure. Customized accelerators are often limited by the structure of LSTM and cannot fully utilize the advantages of the hardware. This paper proposed a multi-layer LSTM optimization scheme based on the idea of software and hardware collaboration. We used the pruning by row scheme to greatly reduce the number of parameters while ensuring accuracy, making it adapt to the parallel structure of the hardware. From the perspective of software, the multi-layer LSTM module was analyzed. It was concluded that some neurons in different layers could be calculated in parallel. Therefore, this paper redesigned the computational order of the multilayer LSTM so that the model guaranteed its own timing properly and it was hardware friendly at the same time. Experiments showed that our throughput increased by 10x compared with the CPU implementation. Compared with other hardware accelerators, the throughput increased by 1.2x-1.4x, and the latency and resource utilization had also been improved.

Keywords: LSTM · Software and hardware cooperation · Parallelism · RNN · NLP

1 Introduction

With the fast advances in Information technologies [1–3] and big data algorithms [4–6], NLP *(natural language processing)* is a fast growing area with the powerful *recurrent neural network* (RNN) [7] that is more sensitive to temporal tasks. However, the problem of gradient explosion or gradient disappearance occurs

© The Author(s), under exclusive license to Springer Nature Switzerland AG 2022
G. Memmi et al. (Eds.): KSEM 2022, LNAI 13369, pp. 681–693, 2022.
https://doi.org/10.1007/978-3-031-10986-7_55

when the neural network is too deep or has too much temporal order. So, RNN can learn only short-term dependencies. To learn long-term dependencies, the long short-term memory network LSTM [8] emerged based on RNNs. LSTM uses unique gate structure to avoid RNN-like problems by forgetting some information. LSTM has a wide range of applications in NLP, especially in the field of machine translation, where it is much more effective than RNN. Although the special "gate" of LSTM solves the problem that RNN cannot learn long-term dependencies, it also strengthens the data dependency between modules, leading to its high requirement for temporality. It causes LSTM's low parallelism.

Many optimizations for LSTMs have also emerged. Some optimization models [9–11] tended to optimize for model accuracy, and most of them ignored model training speed and model size. There were also some optimizations to accelerate the inference speed of the model by hardware accelerators [12–14]. FPGA became the primary choice for hardware-accelerated LSTMs due to their excellent performance in accelerating CNNs. [15] accelerated the LSTM model characteristics by designing custom accelerators. By analyzing the LSTM model, implementing each module in hardware, and designing custom hardware structure to complete the acceleration according to the model characteristics.

Based on the idea of hardware-software collaborative optimization, this paper presents a modular analysis and collaborative design of LSTM. By implementing pruning, quantization, and improved data flow, the network optimization is carried out in collaboration with hardware and software to maximize parallelization while ensuring normal timing and no data dependencies. The contributions of this article are:

1) The pruning method in this paper uses pruning by row, by which the final pruning result can ensure the same number of elements in each row and prepare for the parallelism design of the hardware. 2) In this paper, we propose a method for optimizing neural networks based on collaborative ideas of hardware and software, and a specific design on a multilayer LSTM model. 3) The modularity analysis of LSTM from a software perspective concludes that it is possible to compute some cells in different layers in parallel. Based on this, the computational order of the multilayer LSTM is redesigned in this paper so that the model is hardware-friendly while properly ensuring its timing.

The rest of the paper is organised as follows: Sect. 2 describes the related work; Sect. 3 introduces the idea of software and hardware co-optimization of the LSTM and the implementation details in software; Sect. 4 describes the design of the corresponding hardware structure based on the optimization effect on the software; The results and analysis of the experiments are presented in Sect. 5. Section 6 concludes this paper.

2   Related Work

Machine learning [16,17] have been widely applied in various areas and applications, such as finance [18,19], transportation [20], and tele-health industries [21]. The optimization problem [22,23] of neural networks is top-rated, and it is divided into two main directions including, optimizing network models and designing hardware accelerators.

The design of hardware accelerators can be divided into two main categories. One category is for data transmission. Three types of accelerators were designed by [14] for different data communication methods. The first one was to stream all data from off-chip memory to the coprocessor. This had high performance but was limited by the off-chip memory bandwidth. The second one used on-chip memory to store all the necessary data internally. This scheme achieved a low off-chip memory bandwidth, but it is limited by the available on-chip memory. The third one balanced the former two options to achieve high performance and scalability.

The other category focused on computational processes. Paper [24] proposed a hardware architecture for LSTM neural networks that aimed to outperform software implementations by exploiting their inherent parallelism. Networks of different sizes and platforms were synthesized. The final synthesized network ran on an i7-3770k desktop computer and outperformed the custom software network by a factor of 251. Paper [25] proposed an fpga-based LSTM-RNN accelerator that flattened the computation inside the gates of each LSTM, and the input vectors and weight matrices were flattened together accordingly. Execution was pipelined between LSTM cell blocks to maximize throughput. A linear approximation was used to fit the activation function at a cost of 0.63% error rate, significantly reducing the hardware resource consumption.

Optimizing network models and designing hardware accelerators could have the effect of optimizing the network, but they only considered one optimization direction. The former only considered the optimization of the network and ignores the reconfigurable design of hardware. The latter focuseed on hardware design without considering the characteristics of the network itself, and there was no synergistic design between software and hardware.

3   LSTM Software and Hardware Co-optimization

Our design is based on both of the software dimension and the hardware dimension, considering how to design to make it hardware friendly when optimizing the algorithm. And when designing the hardware architecture, consider how to adapt the hardware architecture to better support the software algorithm. In this paper, we propose the idea of software and hardware co-optimization. It is a spiral optimization method that considers the software optimization method while adjusting the software optimization and hardware structure with feedback according to the characteristics of the target hardware structure. The software optimization is combined with the hardware design to design the hardware structure supporting the above model from the hardware perspective while the structure of the neural network model and the number of parameters are reasonably designed.

3.1   Approach

In this paper, we discuss on that neural network algorithms and hardware architectures interact with each other in the computational process with a considerable degree of collaboration. Therefore, software optimization needs to combine with hardware optimization. Often, the number of model parameters is too large for the hardware, and it is necessary to determine whether direct deployment to the hardware is feasible before performing the analysis. If the model parameters put too much pressure on the computational resources of the hardware, the number of model parameters can be reduced using pruning. There are various pruning methods, and while reducing the number of parameters, it is necessary to choose a pruning method that is more compatible with hardware storage and computation. If the transfer pressure of data in each computing module is too high, the data can be quantized to relieve the transfer pressure.

After compressing the model, we need to analyze the model as a whole. From a software perspective, the algorithms and data flow between different modules are analyzed. The relationship between the modules also needs to be sorted. From the hardware perspective, the data dependencies of each module of the model are analyzed, and which parts can be optimized by parallelization, data flow design, and pipeline design are considered. It is worth noting that these two tasks are carried out at the same time. While considering algorithm optimization and tuning the model structure, one needs to consider how to tune it to make it hardware-friendly. While considering hardware optimization, one needs to consider how to tune the algorithm and structure to make it decoupled and design hardware structures with higher parallelism and lower latency. Finally, the model structure and hardware architecture have good adaptability through the collaborative design of hardware and software.

3.2   Model Compression

With the development of neural networks, the accuracy of model is no longer the only metric to evaluate a model, and researchers are increasingly focusing on other metrics of the model in the application domain, such as model size, model consumption of resources, etc. [26]. While pruning and quantization as the common methods for model compression, their algorithms are being optimized as the demand expands. [27] proposed a deep compression by designing a three-stage pipeline: pruning, trained quantization and Huffman coding. Combining multiple compression methods onto a neural network, it was finally demonstrated experimentally that the requirements of the model were reduced by a factor of $35\times$ to $49\times$ without the accuracy loss.

Pruning: Network pruning is one of the commonly used model compression algorithms. In the pruning process, we can construct redundant weights and keep important weights according to certain criteria to maintain maximum accuracy. There are many pruning methods, and they each have their focus. Since the computation process of LSTM contains a large number of matrix vector multiplication operations, this paper focuses on the pruning operation of the weight matrix of LSTM. The pruning method in this paper is the less common pruning by row, which differs from the general pruning by threshold method in that the selection of pruning range by row is changed. It takes a row of the weight matrix as a whole and selects a threshold for pruning according to the percentage of a row, and by this way, the final pruning result can ensure a consistent number of elements in each row. In the hardware implementation of matrix operations for high parallelism in computation, we expand the matrix by rows and compute it in parallel from row to row. The idea of hardware-software collaboration is fully reflected here. The accuracy of the model was degraded after pruning, so retraining was performed after pruning as a way to improve the accuracy. It is worth noting that the pruned parameters can easily be added with an offset value, which will cause the pruning effect to be lost without doing something during the retraining process. Therefore, we add a mask matrix during retraining to ensure that the 0 elements of the weight matrix are not involved in training before the weight matrix is involved during retraining. The shape of the mask matrix is the same as that of the weight matrix. When the element value of the weight matrix is 0, the element value of the mask matrix for the position is also 0.

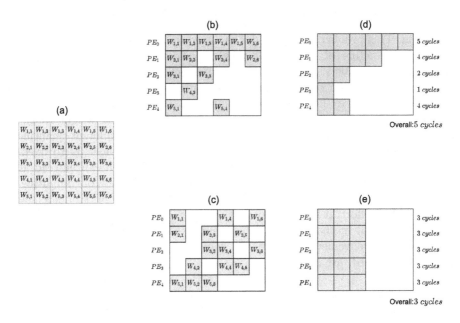

Fig. 1. Pruning by row and its benefit for parallel processing.

Figure 1(a) shows the matrix of memory gate O_i's weights in a certain neuron. Figure 1(b) shows the result map O_i^a after unbalanced pruning while Fig. 1(c) is the result map O_i^b after pruning by row. After pruning the weight matrix, we assign each row of the matrix to different PEs for parallel computation. Figure 1(d) and Fig. 1(e) are the running times of several PEs after the two pruning, respectively, and we can see that the unbalanced pruning Fig. 1(d) will result in a different amount of data per row, which leads to a large difference in the elapsed time between the parallel PEs.

The total elapsed time will be determined by the computation time of the most loaded PEs, while the other PEs will have different degrees of waiting, which leads to a decrease in running efficiency. The total time is five clocks. While pruning by row makes each row have the same amount of data, parallel PEs do not experience waiting, making the overall operation efficiency guaranteed to be high. With the guarantee that all rows require the same clock cycle, the total time is only three clock cycles.

Quantification: Quantification is another universal approach to model compression. In general, when a well-trained model infers, the model can deal with some input noise. It means that the model can ignore all non-essential differences between the inference and training samples. To some extent, low precision can be considered as a source of noise that provides non-essential differences. Therefore, theoretically, the neural network can give accurate results even if the data precision is low. At the same time, neural networks may occupy a large amount of storage space. This means that the network requires not only a large amount of memory but also a large number of computational resources during operation. This problem also provides the need for quantification.

The parameters of the LSTM weight matrix are 32-bit single-precision floating-point numbers. The memory requirement is very large when the network size is large, and the computation of floating-point numbers requires a lot of hardware resources. [28] used a linear quantification strategy for both weights and activation functions. The authors analyzed the dynamic weight range of all matrices in each LSTM layer and explore the effect of different quantification bits on the LSTM model. In this paper, we quantify float-32 to fixed-8. Although a certain amount of accuracy is lost, multiple data can be read at a time for processing, which substantially improves the efficiency of computing.

By compressing the model, we greatly reduce the number of parameters and computational effort. It is worth noting that when choosing the pruning method, we abandoned the method with a higher compression rate and chose row pruning which is more convenient for hardware computation, which paves the way for the following hardware design.

4   Hardware Design

There are many hardware designs for LSTM, but most of them did not consider the characteristics of the hardware structure afterward in the process of software optimization. Therefore, the final design of the hardware structure was often limited by the characteristics of the model and data. In this paper, we take into account the design characteristics of the hardware structure in the process of model compression and choose a compression method that is more compatible with our hardware design to ensure hardware friendliness to the maximum extent.

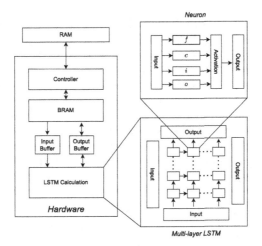

Fig. 2. Overall architecture diagram

4.1 Overall Structure

The overall architecture of the hardware is shown in Fig. 2. The entire hardware architecture consists of the controller, the input and output buffers, BRAM, and LSTM computation blocks. The ARM core controls the overall flow of the model by transmitting instructions to the hardware's controller. In addition, the parameters and input data required for the operation are pre-processed by model compression and stored in BRAM. The controller accepts instructions from the ARM core and then coordinates and calls other areas according to the instructions. The input and output buffer temporarily stores the data in the BRAM to reduce the data transfer latency of the LSTM computation block. The LSTM computational block implements the computational logic of multi-layer LSTM. Each neuron in this unit corresponds to and implements the computational flow of a single neuron in the LSTM algorithm, while the LSTM neurons are densely connected by input and output ports to implement the data path between neurons.

4.2 Compute Optimization

The main computations of LSTM cells are four matrix multiplications, activation functions, dot-product, and addition. Our optimization scheme focuses on matrix multiplication, which accounts for a large part of the overall compute. We block the matrix by rows and perform the input in parallel. In matrix computation, the internal loop is unrolled when the elements of multiple rows are simultaneously assigned to different PE. Since the pruning by row in model compression allows the same number of elements in each row of the weight matrix, it ensures that the data assigned to different PEs in different rows have the same computation time. After computing finishes, PE can proceed directly to the next cycle without waiting for other PEs. Given the limited resources on the hardware, the number of parallel PEs can be fine-tuned according to the application scenario. If PE resources are sufficient, we reduce the time complexity to O(N) in an ideal case.

The computation process of an LSTM cell is shown in Fig. 3. On the left is the processed weight matrix. We divide it into rows and assign them to different PEs. And on the top is the input vector x and the previous neuron input h_{t-1}. After the input parameters(h_{t-1}, x_t, c_{t-1}) enter LSTM cell, h_{t-1}, x_t first carry out matrix multiplication and addition operations with the four weight matrices(W_f, W_i, W_c,W_o) and then obtain the intermediate results(i_t, f_t, g_t,o_t) after σ and tanh activation functions. The compute process of LSTM includes cell state c_t and hidden state h_t. The cell state c_t is obtained from the dot product of i_t and g_t plus the dot product of f_t and another input parameter c_{t-1}, while the hidden state h_t is the result of c_t after tanh and then dot product with o_t. The computation of input parameters and weight matrix is the most time-consuming portion of the entire procedure. Since the four matrix calculations are independent, this paper replicates the input parameters so that the four matrix operations are no longer limited by the transmission delay of the input parameters and are computed simultaneously, which reduces the overall computation time.

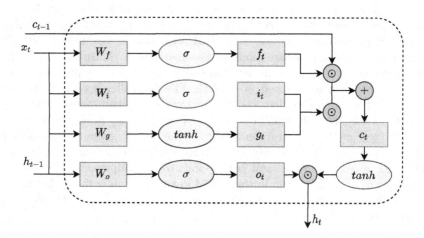

Fig. 3. Computational process of a single LSTM neuron.

4.3   Data Flow Optimization

We analyze the data flow between each neuron in the layer dimension and time dimension of the LSTM. The LSTM of the same layer is executed sequentially in 2 dimensions on the CPU, which leads to low parallelism of the model. In the hardware implementation, the strong timing of the LSTM results in a parallel strategy that can only be carried out in two separate dimensions including, between different layers of the same sequence, such as Layer1_1, Layer2_1 and Layer3_1; And between different times of the same layer, such as Layer1_1, Layer1_2 and Layer1_3.

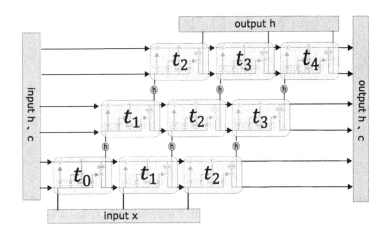

Fig. 4. Multi-layer LSTM data stream (take 3 layers as an example).

The distinction between hardware and software implementations inspires us. Hardware LSTMs often choose to implement each cell computation in turn and spread it out to match the rich hardware resources, while software calls the same cell module in turn. This difference in implementation brings a new perspective on the data flow. As shown in Fig. 4, when the first time step of the first layer LSTM is computed at t_0 moment, the output h_0 at the moment t_0 is passed to the second time step of the first layer and the first time step of the second layer LSTM after completion of the computation. After that, at t_1 moment, the first time step of the second layer LSTM and the second time step of the first layer LSTM can compute simultaneously, and so on. Thus some cells of LSTM can compute in parallel to achieve acceleration, which is similar to the acceleration idea of the pulsating array [29]. After optimizing the computational order, we can observe that the overall model is more parallelized. As a result, we can adjust the timing of the cells that satisfy the computational prerequisites at the same moment in the hardware implementation. Figure 5(a) shows the timing diagram before the adjustment, where the whole computation process took nine clock cycles, while in Fig. 5(b), the computation process took only five clock cycles after the adjustment. For this stepwise computation order, Layer1_3, Layer2_2, and Layer3_1, which are in different layers, start running at the same time because they satisfy the computation prerequisites at the same time, thus satisfying the two parallel strategies at the same time.

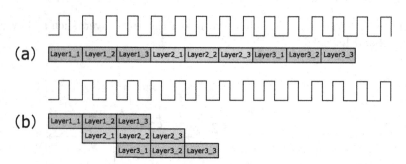

Fig. 5. Pipeline structure of multi-layer LSTM.

5   Experimental Results and Analysis

We implemented the LSTM neural network on the MNIST [30] dataset using the pytorch framework. The LSTM neural network was trained on the MNIST dataset, which consists of four main components: the training set, the test set, the validation set images and the label information. There are 55,000 images in the training set, each with a size of 784 (28*28); 55,000 labels in the training set, each label being a one-dimensional array of length 10; 10,000 images in the test set and 5,000 images in the validation set.

The experimental results showed that the accuracy before pruning reached 95.75%. After pruning the weight matrix, the compression rate reached 21.99×, but as we were pruning uniformly by row, this inevitably led to the loss of valid parameters and the accuracy dropped to 68%, such a reduction in accuracy is unacceptable. We therefore retrained after the pruning was completed, and the final accuracy was 96%. Finally, we had completed the effective compression of our model.

We implemented the LSTM computation process on Vivado High-Level Synthesis V2020.2 and the results are shown in Table 1. The device we chose was the XC7Z020, and in order to make the best use of hardware resources, we explored the relationship between the size of the weight matrix and the consumption of hardware resources and its percentage of the total amount of each resource. It is clear from Table 1 that when the size of the weight matrix is 32×18, the percentage of BRAM_18 K, DSP and FF usage is small, but the LUT usage reaches 27132, accounting for 51% of the total resources.

As the size of the weight matrix increases, all the hardware resources increase with it, except for FF, whose percentage did not change much. Among them, BRAM_18 K increases the most, directly from the initial 34% to 103%. As the scale increases to 64×256, the resources required for BRAM_18 K exceed the total resources available from the hardware. When the model size is 50×200, the proportion of each resource is more reasonable.

Table 1. Hardware resource usage for different model sizes

Matrix size	BRAM_18K	DSP	FF	LUT
32 × 18	48 (34%)	26 (12%)	12768 (12%)	27132 (51%)
50 × 200	66 (47%)	99 (45%)	28728 (27%)	30324 (57%)
64 × 256	144 (103%)	130 (59%)	24472 (23%)	37242 (70%)

We compared the hardware resource consumption before and after optimization and computed the percentage of total resources on the hardware accounted for by LUT, FF, DSP, and BRAM_18 K. Before optimization, LUT and BRAM_18 K account for a large proportion of the hardware resource consumption, accounting for 52% and 34% of the total number of resources, respectively. Due to the use of various hardware optimization schemes, the latency is reduced while the consumption of various resources is significantly increased. Since LSTM compute contains many matrix multiplications, our optimized DSP has the largest increase in consumption with 40%, accounting for 70% of the total DSP resources.

6   Conclusion

In this paper, we proposed the method of optimizing neural networks based on the idea of hardware-software collaboration for multilayer LSTM. The selection of the pruning scheme and the corresponding hardware design in this paper fully reflected the idea of hardware-software collaboration. After analyzing the data flow and data dependency of the LSTM, we redesigned the computational order of the multilayer LSTM to parallelize the serial computation of some neurons. The final experiment proved that our solution had 10× the throughput of CPU and improved in terms of throughput, latency, and resource utilization compared to other hardware accelerators.

References

1. Qiu, M., Xue, C., et al.: Energy minimization with soft real-time and DVS for uniprocessor and multiprocessor embedded systems. In: IEEE DATE, pp. 1–6 (2007)
2. Qiu, M., Xue, C., et al.: Efficient algorithm of energy minimization for heterogeneous wireless sensor network. In: IEEE EUC, pp. 25–34 (2006)
3. Qiu, M., Liu, J., et al.: A novel energy-aware fault tolerance mechanism for wireless sensor networks. In: IEEE/ACM Conference on GCC (2011)
4. Wu, G., Zhang, H., et al.: A decentralized approach for mining event correlations in distributed system monitoring. JPDC **73**(3), 330–340 (2013)
5. Lu, Z., et al.: IoTDeM: an IoT big data-oriented MapReduce performance prediction extended model in multiple edge clouds. JPDC **118**, 316–327 (2018)

6. Qiu, L., Gai, K., Qiu, M.: Optimal big data sharing approach for tele-health in cloud computing. In: IEEE SmartCloud, pp. 184–189 (2016)
7. Zaremba, W., Sutskever, I., Vinyals, O.: Recurrent neural network regularization (2014). arXiv preprint, arXiv:1409.2329
8. Hochreiter, S., Schmidhuber, J.: Long short-term memory. Neural Comput. 9(8), 1735–1780 (1997)
9. Graves, A., Schmidhuber, J.: Framewise phoneme classification with bidirectional LSTM and other neural network architectures. Neural Netw. 18, 602–610 (2005)
10. Gers, F.A., Schmidhuber, J., Cummins, F.: Learning to forget: Continual prediction with LSTM. Neural Comput. 12(10), 2451–2471 (2000)
11. Donahue, J., Anne Hendricks, L., et al.: Long-term recurrent convolutional networks for visual recognition and description. In: IEEE CVPR, pp. 2625–2634 (2015)
12. Bank-Tavakoli, E., Ghasemzadeh, S.A., et al.: POLAR: a pipelined/overlapped FPGA-based LSTM accelerator. IEEE TVLSI 28(3), 838–842 (2020)
13. Liao, Y., Li, H., Wang, Z.: FPGA based real-time processing architecture for recurrent neural network. In: Xhafa, F., Patnaik, S., Zomaya, A.Y. (eds.) IISA 2017. AISC, vol. 686, pp. 705–709. Springer, Cham (2018). https://doi.org/10.1007/978-3-319-69096-4_99
14. Chang, X.M., Culurciello, E.: Hardware accelerators for recurrent neural networks on fpga. In: IEEE Conference on ISCAS, pp. 1–4 (2017)
15. Li, S., Wu, C., et al.: Fpga acceleration of recurrent neural network based language model. In: IEEE Symposium on Field-Programmable Custom Computing Machine, pp. 111–118 (2015)
16. Li, Y., et al.: Intelligent fault diagnosis by fusing domain adversarial training and maximum mean discrepancy via ensemble learning. IEEE TII 17(4), 2833–2841 (2020)
17. Qiu, H., Zheng, Q., et al.: Deep residual learning-based enhanced jpeg compression in the internet of things. IEEE TII 17(3), 2124–2133 (2020)
18. Gai, K., et al.: Efficiency-aware workload optimizations of heterogeneous cloud computing for capacity planning in financial industry. In: IEEE CSCloud (2015)
19. Qiu, M., et al.: Data transfer minimization for financial derivative pricing using monte carlo simulation with GPU in 5G. JCS 29(16), 2364–2374 (2016)
20. Qiu, H., et al.: Topological graph convolutional network-based urban traffic flow and density prediction. IEEE TITS 22, 4560–4569 (2020)
21. Qiu, H., et al.: Secure health data sharing for medical cyber-physical systems for the healthcare 4.0. IEEE JBHI 24, 2499–2505 (2020)
22. Qiu, M., Zhang, L., et al.: Security-aware optimization for ubiquitous computing systems with seat graph approach. JCSS 79(5), 518–529 (2013)
23. Qiu, M., Li, H., Sha, E.: Heterogeneous real-time embedded software optimization considering hardware platform. In: ACM SAC, pp. 1637–1641 (2009)
24. Ferreira, J.C., Fonseca, J.: An FPGA implementation of a long short-term memory neural network. In: IEEE Conference on ReConFigurable, pp. 1–8 (2016)
25. Guan, Y., Yuan, Z., Sun, G., Cong, J.: Fpga-based accelerator for long short-term memory recurrent neural networks (2017)
26. Ledwon, M., Cockburn, B.F., Han, J.: High-throughput FPGA-based hardware accelerators for deflate compression and decompression using high-level synthesis. IEEE Access 8, 62207–62217 (2020)
27. Han, S., Mao, H., Dally, W.J.: Deep compression: compressing deep neural networks with pruning, trained quantization and huffman coding (2015). arXiv preprint, arXiv:1510.00149

28. Han, S., Kang, J., et al.: ESE: Efficient speech recognition engine with sparse LSTM on FPGA. In: ACM/SIGDA FPGA, pp. 75–84 (2017)
29. Jouppi, N.P., Young, C., et al.: In-datacenter performance analysis of a tensor processing unit. In: 44th IEEE ISCA, pp. 1–12 (2017)
30. Yadav, C., Bottou, L.: Cold case: The lost mnist digits (2019)

Author Index

Printed in the United States
by Baker & Taylor Publisher Services